Parkers' ASTROLOGY

Parkers' ASTROLOGY

The Essential Guide to Using Astrology in Your Daily Life

JULIA & DEREK PARKER

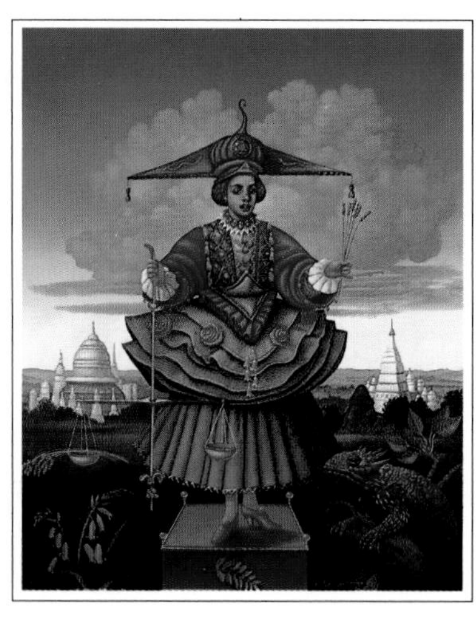

For Barbara Gainsford Brackley, with love

A DORLING KINDERSLEY BOOK

Project Editor	Josephine Buchanan
Consultant Editor	Jane Struthers
Managing Editor	Carolyn King
Managing Art Editor	Nick Harris

This book designed for Dorling Kindersley by Peter Luff

First published in Canada in 1994 by élan press,
an imprint of General Publishing Co. Limited,
30 Lesmill Road, Toronto, Canada, M3B 2T6

ISBN 1-55144-060-1
Canadian cataloguing-in-publication data available
upon request from the National Library of Canada

Reproduced by Colourscan, Singapore
Printed and bound in Italy by New Interlitho Spa

Contents

·3· ASTROLOGY IN ACTION 128

·4· THE PLANETS AT WORK 208

·5·
Astrological Tables 348

Foreword

When you picked up this book, you probably turned immediately to the pages describing your Sun sign characteristics. Few people with the slightest interest in the subject can resist reading these. But it was only in 1930 that a British astrologer, R.H. Naylor, started the fashion that has laid a greater emphasis on the Sun sign than the classical astrologers would ever have tolerated. In fact, as you begin to appreciate the full range of the absorbing subject of astrology, you may well feel that the Sun signs are only the tip of the astrological iceberg.

For the Sun signs are just a beginning. Anyone who goes on to read a more advanced book on the subject will soon realize that the more you learn about astrology, the more fascinating it becomes. This book offers you an opportunity to come to grips with a discipline that has absorbed the minds of men and women for well over four millennia.

And the fascination continues, for as with all sciences, almost every year sees new discoveries, new theories, and new speculations. The twentieth century, through the invention of the computer and the development of the study of human psychology, has seen elaborate testing of the astrological theory – not only its use by Jungian analysts in exploring human psychology but also the collation of statistics bearing on traditional astrological theories, which have opened out interesting new areas for discussion.

The craft of astrology

Parkers' Astrology is the product of over 20 years' study of astrology. In the centuries-long span of the history of the subject, 20 years is a brief time; nor, in a single book can a full study of the subject be more than roughly mapped. What we offer is a stepping stone from simple Sun sign astrology to a point from which the depths of the subject can be glimpsed, and the reader can begin to swim confidently towards deeper waters.

Growing confidence in the craft and technique of the subject may well lead to your wanting to become another cog in the great wheel – a practicing astrologer ready, perhaps, in your turn to pass your experiences and knowledge on to a younger generation.

No "gifts" are needed to become an astrologer, with one rather special exception: that one is interested in other people. Astrology has no concern with the supernatural – and astrologers need hold no particular religious faith. Go to an astrolgical conference and you will find Christian – Catholic and Protestant – Buddhist, Jewish, Hindu and Muslim astrologers, as well as those who hold no particular faith.

The skills of the astrologer

The question of intuition will also arise. Yes, we do need intuition – but the kind of intuition a doctor uses when reaching conclusions about a diagnosis, when deciding which group of symptoms is the most important in recognizing a condition. Astrology is emphatically not a matter of calculating a chart, gazing at it, then drifting off into a trance and making statements off the top of your head. It involves hard work – but work that is ever-fascinating and revealing.

Learning and practicing astrology is not easy – nothing worthwhile ever is – but it is enormously rewarding, as are all the means of helping people to lead more rewarding lives, or assisting them to disentangle their problems, face them, and find solutions (always remembering that it is not the astrologer's job to tell people what they should and should not do, but rather to reveal alternatives, to make suggestions, to guide and comfort).

Becoming a professional astrologer

It may well be that when you have worked your way through this book, you will feel that you would like to become a professional astrologer. No matter how much work you have done so far, the chances are that you are nowhere near ready to work in a professional capacity. It is important that you are properly trained, and advisable that you obtain a diploma of professional competence; this will greatly assist you when you begin to practice – the astrologer with a qualification from a recognized teaching body is always at an advantage over the amateur who has just "picked up" the skill, no matter with how much hard work. For finding a reputable teaching body, see p.404.

These teaching bodies will not only teach you astrological techniques, together with astronomy and the history of astrology to a greater degree of detail than we have been able to provide, but they will ensure that you study, to some extent, counseling techniques, so that you know enough about psychology to recognize, early on, when a client can be helped by you and when he or she needs more specialist psychiatric help. Never be tempted to exceed your grasp: you are dealing with people's lives, and untold harm can be done by overambitious amateurs. A really competent astrologer knows when to stop and knows where the boundaries are.

Learning through writing

We have always felt that the best way to strengthen your interpretative technique is through writing – you need the discipline of being able to organize the material at your disposal into a written essay rather than simply talking about a chart, which can lead to vagueness, repetition, and other evils. Writing concentrates the mind and ensures you acquire a disciplined way of interpreting a chart and putting that interpretation into a readable shape.

Writing constructively

At first you will be able to write very little about the charts you study, but as you progress and realize in just how many different ways planetary placings and aspects can be built into interpretation, so your reports will grow in length. You will probably then go through a period of development when they will be too long, and as a result become boring. Once over that hurdle you will swing back a little and eventually get the length about right.

Many people find writing tedious. If you really feel you cannot face the discipline, the next best thing is probably to make notes and then record your report on tape. But those notes should be as full as you can make them: do not simply jot down two words and embroider them into a 10-minute sprawl of pauses, repetitions, interruptions and technical references which will be pure nonsense to the layman.

In all astrological work the less you mention the planets and their aspects, the better. If your subject is interested in the technicalities, take them through the chart technically at the end of your session, or write a short technical description either at the beginning or end of your written analysis.

Helping people with interpretations

Many of the people who ask you to "do their charts", either when you are starting to study or much later, will have specific problems. They must put you fully in the picture. They will probably be glad to unburden, in any case, and it will be helpful to them. The best approach in these situations is for you and your subject to get together, and for you just to listen. You then take the birth-data and that of the partner or anyone else involved in the problem, calculate the chart or charts and make copious notes – including a list of questions you want to ask, the answers to which will help the subject to come to conclusions about the problem. You can then, when you get together for a second time, give constructive astrological help.

Do not be put off by those who accuse you of gleaning information during these first talks, which you can use later. Just as a doctor needs to know the symptoms before making tests, so you must know the context of a problem before you consider it. The chart fills in the detail, and an assessment of the trends will reveal how the future looks – not exactly what will happen, but how the person concerned can make the most of the planetary influences and energies that will surround him or her.

Know when to stop. In most cases this won't be a problem – your subject will "speak her chart", and together you will reach constructive conclusions. But always remember that certain people need a prop – and if you let them, will lean on you as they would otherwise lean on a psychiatrist or a priest or just a friend.

Demands on you as an astrologer

Astrology is not something to lean on: it shows us our strengths and weaknesses, and, most importantly, how we can develop strengths. If a subject keeps telephoning you for yet more advice, the chances are that you have failed – you have not been sufficiently firm or succinct. Start again: go back to the chart and do some more study. Any subject who persists may need more help than you can give: refer them to other professional help.

The chances are that you will be tempted to work on a great many charts. Once someone knows you are getting interested in astrology you will find that a constant plea is "do my chart – please do mine". All in due course. It is all too easy to get superficially involved with a great many charts. This does not usually help in the gradual development of the necessary technique. Work in depth on a few charts, getting everything you possibly can out of each before moving on to the next. This will also help you build up your confidence.

Remember that it is very important that you keep all your notes, and a drawing of each of the charts you work on. If your subject wants a drawing of their chart, take a carbon or make a photocopy for your file. If you write a report, do the same. In this way you will see your progress – and your files will be invaluable when your subject needs more work.

Dealing with scepticism

Finally, you will always find yourself surrounded by sceptics – and (perhaps more dangerously) by people who misunderstand what astrology is about. Sometimes the two are combined.

As to scepticism: there is no short answer. You will find over the years that – quite apart from the statistical evidence collected by other people, quite apart from the many cases about which you will read or hear – your own files will increasingly convince you that astrology is in fact an empirical science based on a great body of knowledge. You will, of course, at times have doubts; you will want to test theories, to ask questions. But you will find that you will convince yourself (should you need convincing!) of the basic and valuable truths to be found in the birth chart. As for those sceptics who cannot bother to examine the evidence, remember the retort made by Sir Isaac Newton: "Sir – I have studied the matter. You have not." That remains a very good answer.

Julia Parker.

Derek Parker

How To Use This Book

The way in which you use this book depends on how much you know about the subject. If you have previously been aware only of the kind of Sun sign astrology you read about in magazines, it will be best for you to start at the very beginning with "The Astronomical Background" (see p.14). You will certainly know something about the signs of the zodiac (see p.26), but the solar system (see p.20) may well open out the subject for you.

If you already know something about solar system astronomy and astrology, then turn to "Calculating the Birth Chart" (see p.42); if you follow the instructions, using the tables at the back of the book when you need to do so, you should end up with your first complete chart.

Now you must start learning how to interpret a chart – perhaps after drawing several complete charts to make sure you are in command of that technique. Start now with "Interpreting the Birth Chart" (see p.130), then go on to the section on "Progressing the Chart" (see p.60). Having mastered that, move on to "Interpreting the Progressions" (see p.142).

Set out like this, your journey through the book may sound easy; however, you will find that the more time you are able to give to it, the more completely you will be in command of the material. You will find that as you work your way through the sections, unless you are very well aware of the general "meaning" of a chart, you may have to turn from time to time to the basic pages which define various areas of it – "The Ascendant and Midheaven" (see p.36), or "The Houses" (see p.38).

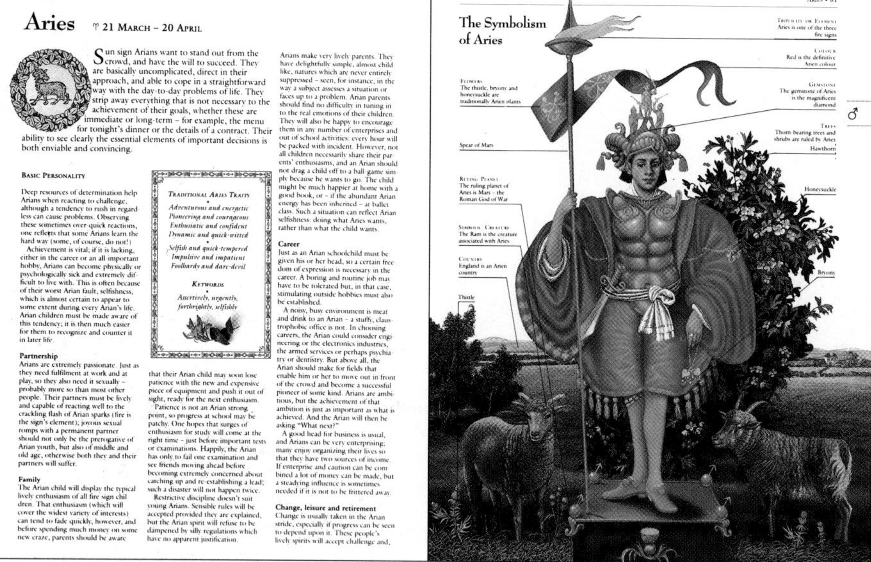

Understanding the Sun Signs
Over the centuries, certain associations have developed with each Sun sign – myths, colors, animals – as well as personal characteristics (see pp.78-127). But you will learn that subtler areas of the personality will be attributable to other areas of the birth chart.

The Astronomical Background
It is very important that as you begin your study into the fascinating and wide-ranging subject of astrology, you should be familiar with the astronomical background (see pp.14-23) – after all, one word was originally used for both these sciences, which share a preoccupation with the skies.

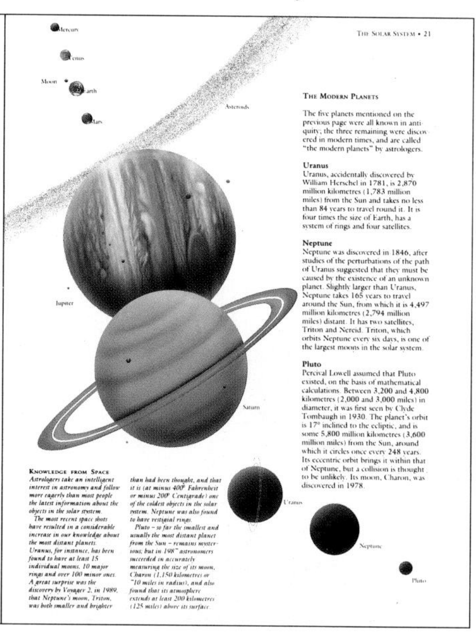

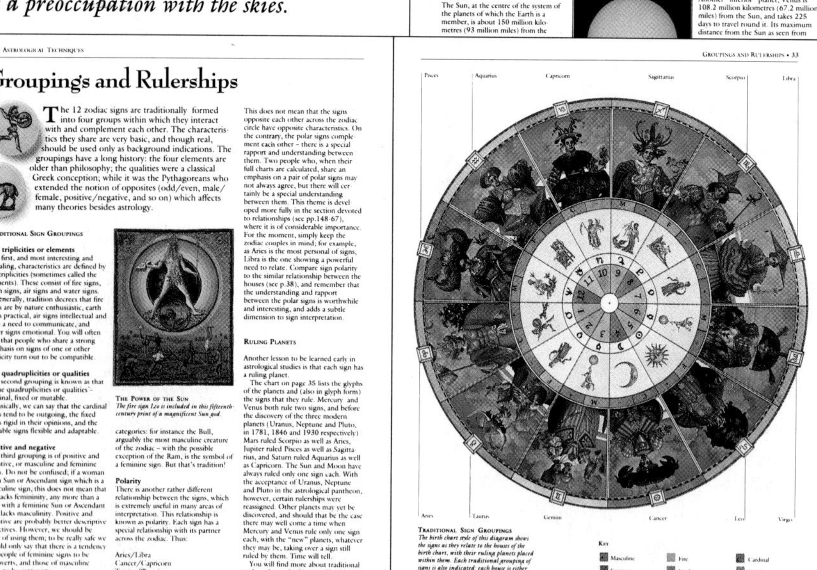

The Zodiac and the Planets
The signs of the zodiac and their relationship with the planets lie at the heart of interpretation (see pp.26-35). Forget the ideas of popular astrology: study the traditional groupings and rulerships (see pp.32-5) and refer to "The Planets at Work" (pp.208-347) to build up a more accurate picture.

Other sections in the book will begin to teach you how to refine your technique, dealing, for instance, with "Additional Techniques" (see p.73) or with synastry – the comparison of two charts (see p.152). We also detail a number of sample case histories which will show you how a practicing astrologer uses the techniques of interpretation in specific consultations.

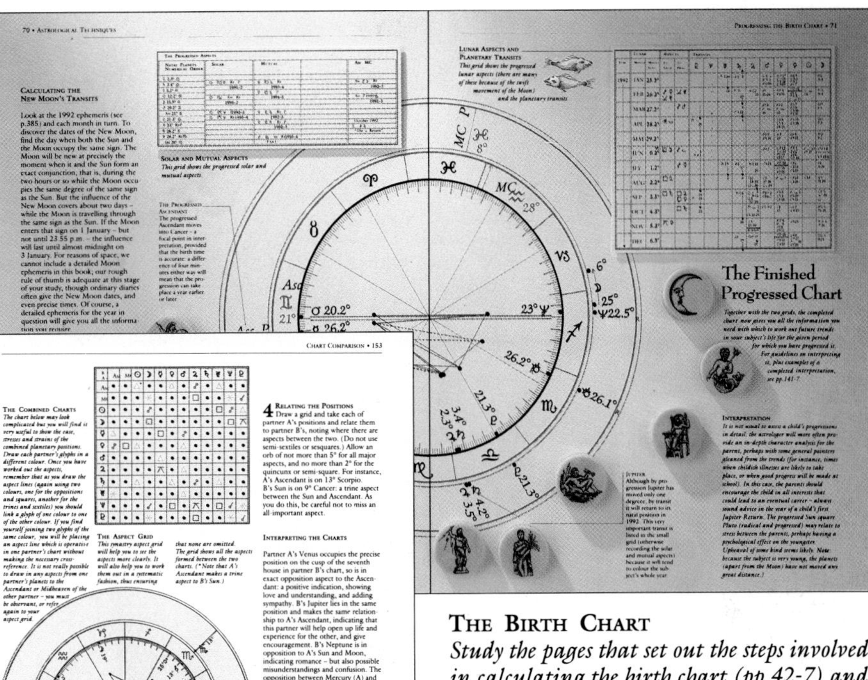

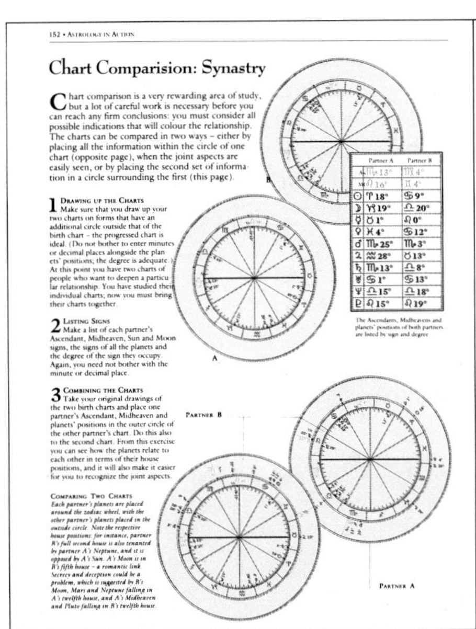

The Birth Chart

Study the pages that set out the steps involved in calculating the birth chart (pp.42-7) and follow the instructions for drawing up the chart (pp.48-59), before you move on to progressing the chart (pp.60-72). As you work, refer to the tables at the end of the book (pp.348-400) which will give you all the data you need to make accurate calculations. Then you will be ready to start your own interpretations (see pp.130-47).

Do not expect that this will be a quick process: at first, it will take you several hours of study. We also strongly recommend that you should thoroughly understand the basic influences of the planets and aspects (described in detail in "The Planets at Work", pp.208-347), before you attempt any interpreting work.

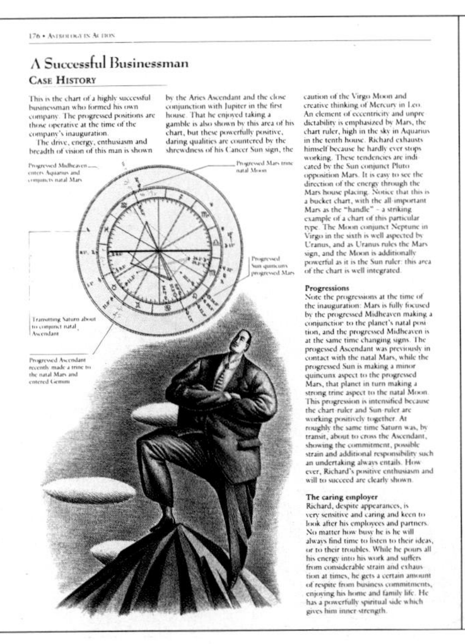

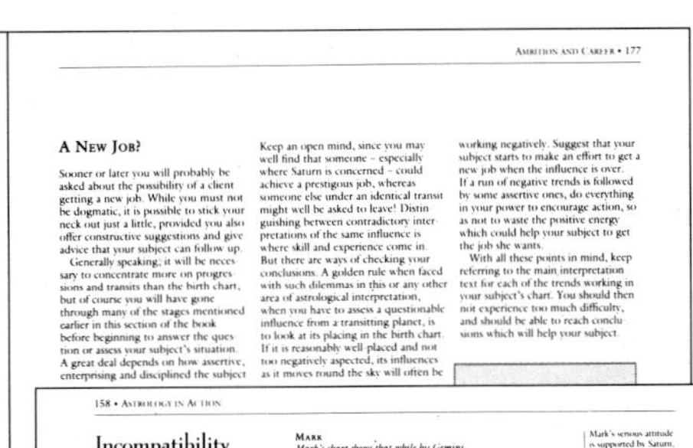

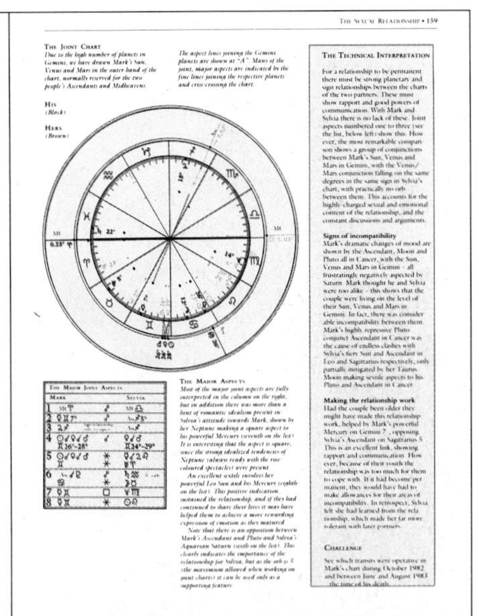

Astrology in Action

Once you are familiar with the processes of calculations and interpretion, you can begin to look at the work of the astrologer in daily action. We describe case histories that have been taken from Julia's own files: they will guide you as you begin your own journey into the complex area of human problems.

SHARP
Scientific calculator EL-553
10 DIGIT 99
MEMORY SAFE GUARD / AUTO POWER OFF
CNST
S.CALC
DRG TAB STAT
2ndF CNST DRG FSE OFF ON/C
arc hyp sin⁻¹ cos⁻¹ tan⁻¹ L.C.M. n!
hyp sin cos tan G.C.M. CE
MDF
log
EXP
S.CALC
CD
RM
DATA
M+
RND QUOT/REM

·1·

Astrological Techniques

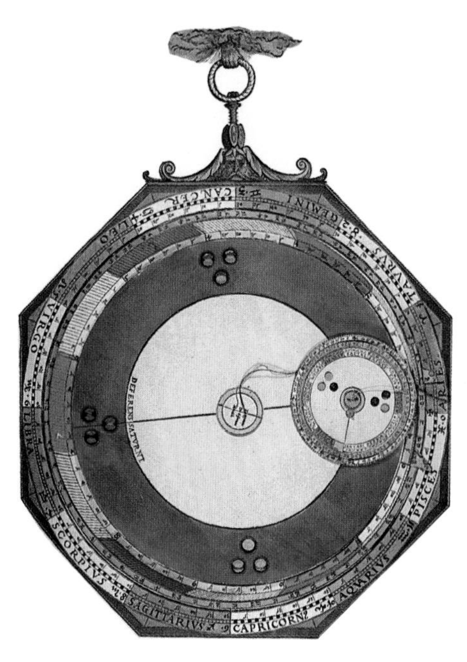

The Astronomical Background

Solar-system astronomy forms the basis of the astrological discipline (it is important to remember that modern Western astrology has nothing to do with the stars; the only star used in astrology is the Sun). Here we set out the basic astronomical facts about the solar system. Assimilate them, along with the instructions on calculating the birth chart, for these are the bare bones of astrology; if you make an error in these early stages then the whole of your birth chart will be inaccurate – and so will your interpretation.

All astrologers should understand certain elements of astronomy, so here we give the simplest possible explanation of certain phenomena and terms that you will need to understand.

Astronomy and astrology went hand in hand for many millennia. Man's preoccupation with the skies began long before the invention of writing, so we can only guess at the extent of the early astronomical knowledge. But as long as 6,000 years ago Chaldean priests used watchtowers to make maps of the skies, and clay tablets dating from 3800 BC record with extraordinary accuracy the motions of the Sun and the Moon.

Early Knowledge
A thirteenth-century astrologer/astronomer examines the heavens.

Astronomy and astrology (and one word was originally used for both sciences) no doubt began out of a marriage of curiosity and the belief that the heavens influenced the Earth. It seems rational to suppose that the Moon, the largest heavenly body, attracted much attention from the beginning, and that quite apart from such obvious lunar effects as those upon the tides and the menstrual cycle, Man soon noticed the effect of the Moon on sexuality.

The Largest Planet
This bright "star" is the planet Jupiter, in the constellation of Cancer.

Then came, however, the realization that among the fixed stars – which seemed to revolve about the Earth but were stationary in relation to each other – five rogue stars rambled in what must at first have seemed illogical motion. Some lumbered slowly about the sky, some seemed almost to dart between their fellows, each revolving about the Earth in the same direction as the fixed stars, but confined to a narrow lane – the ecliptic – which looped around the Earth at an angle of about 23° to the Equator.

Gradually (and the history of the zodiac is a fascinating study of its own) astrologers divided the belt of the ecliptic into 12 sections, naming each after the constellation of fixed stars which stood "behind" it. Furthermore, it was realized that when a planet passed through one of the sections, certain effects occurred: babies born at that time seemed to share common characteristics, and certain events seemed more likely to occur.

Early astronomers

For the next 4,500 years or more, astrologers/astronomers studied the nature of the solar system and the apparent relationship between events in the heavens and events on Earth: the great civilizations of Egypt and Greece contributed to the theory and elaborated on it, working at the same time on purely astronomical theory and on astrology. (The great astronomer Claudius Ptolemy, for instance, not only compiled an astounding catalogue of no less than 1,022 stars, but left us the earliest surviving astrological textbook, the *Tetrabiblos*, written between AD 161 and 139.)

From the earliest times until about the beginning of the eighteenth century, it scarcely ever occurred to astronomers not to study astrology as well – although they had differing notions of its application and the extent of its influence. Those great astronomers of the sixteenth century who so enlarged man's understanding of the solar system – scientists that include Galileo, Kepler, Copernicus and Tycho Brahe – all regarded astrology as an important part of their discipline. The break came, substantially, with the understanding that the Sun, and not the Earth, stands at the center of the solar system.

The Copernican Revolution
Copernicus was the first to place the Sun at the center of the Universe.

This theory was accompanied, during the Age of Enlightenment, by the increasing doubt that human life was affected by planetary influences.

STUDYING THE SOLAR SYSTEM
A stylized view of the astronomer at work at the beginning of the seventeenth century.

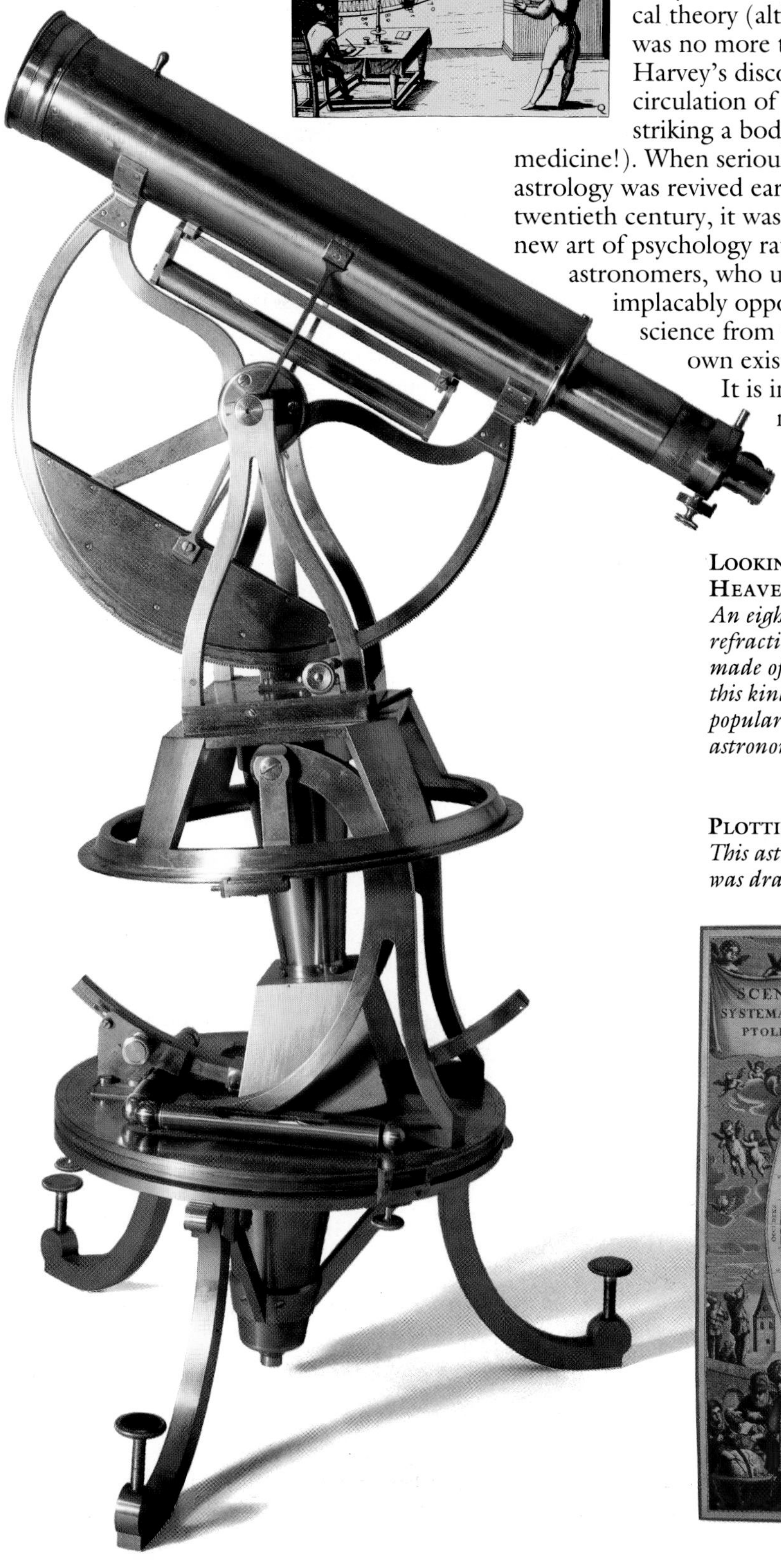

The discovery of the "modern" planets – Uranus, Neptune and Pluto, all first sighted since the middle of the eighteenth century – seemed to direct another body blow at the astrological theory (although this was no more the case than Harvey's discovery of the circulation of the blood striking a body blow at medicine!). When serious interest in astrology was revived early in the twentieth century, it was fuelled by the new art of psychology rather than by astronomers, who usually remain implacably opposed to the science from which their own existence sprang.

It is interesting to note that criticism of astrology by modern astronomers springs almost entirely from ignorance; few trouble to study the subject before condemning it. With a few honorable exceptions, astronomers criticize astrology on absurd grounds, supposing, for instance, that astrologers have no knowledge of astronomy and such phenomena as the precession of the equinoxes (see p.18), or that they believe the effects of the planets are connected with gravity.

On the contrary, astrologers must, of course, understand how the solar system works, and the following pages should be studied closely.

STARS AND PLANETS

The simplest explanation early Man devised of how the solar system worked was to suppose that Earth stood in the center of a revolving sphere, upon the interior surface of which the stars were somehow stuck, and that the planets moved between those stars and observers on Earth. Although we know that this, of course, is nonsense, it is a useful concept to remember when studying the movements of the planets: the stars which seem to move around us because of the revolution of the Earth indeed seem to be stationary when viewed in relation to each other, and so we can use them to make measurements of planetary movements.

LOOKING AT THE HEAVENS
An eighteenth-century refracting telescope made of brass: models of this kind were very popular with amateur astronomers.

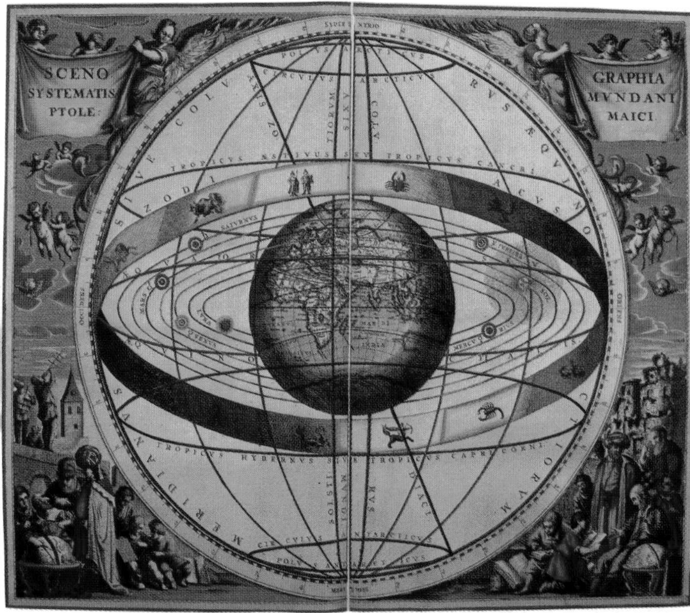

PLOTTING THE STARS
This astrological map was drawn in 1660.

The Three Circles

Three "great circles" are used by astrologers to fix the positions of the planets, relative to the Earth. They are the horizon, the equator and ecliptic. When we project the equator on to the imaginary celestial sphere, it becomes the celestial equator (it is, of course, right above the Earth's equator), dividing the heavens into two hemispheres, northern and southern, with the celestial poles at the center of each – just as the North and South Poles mark the center of the Earth's hemispheres.

Two imaginary circles – the equator and the ecliptic – make it possible for us to fix the positions of the planets, relative to the Earth. The celestial equator is simply the Earth's equator projected upon the surface of our imaginary sphere: so it stands immediately "above" the Earthly equator, dividing the sky into the northern and southern hemispheres, in the center of which stand the celestial poles, above the Earth's North and South Poles.

The ecliptic
The ecliptic is another imaginary circle, which is marked out by the Sun as it seems to travel around the Earth. It lies at an angle to the celestial equator; so their paths meet twice – once at the first point of the sign Aries (this is called the Vernal Equinox) and again at the first point of Libra (called the Autumnal Equinox). In northern latitudes, the Sun reaches those two points at the official beginning of spring and fall; in southern latitudes, the first point of Aries indicates the coming of fall.

The highest points of the ecliptic – furthest from the equator – are known as the solstices. The Sun reaches the summer solstice when it enters Cancer, and the winter solstice at the beginning of Capricorn. (Again, the reverse is true in southern latitudes.) At the point when the Sun reaches either the summer or winter solstice – its furthest distance from the equator, either north or south – it seems to stand still before resuming its journey in the opposite direction. At the June solstice it traces a circle known as the Tropic of Cancer, and in December as the Tropic of Capricorn: the terms do not refer to the zodiac signs, but simply mark the Sun's maximum declination.

Along the ecliptic we measure the 12 equal divisions of 30° which indicate the zodiac signs. The equator (or equinoctial) is divided into 24 parts of 15° each, which we call hours, so one section of 15° of the sky apparently passes over a particular spot every 60 minutes of the day.

The Sun's motion
Because the Earth circles the Sun once a year, from our vantage point it seems to move around the ecliptic once every 12 months, passing through each sign of the zodiac in turn.

The meridian
The meridian is an imaginary line running over the surface of the Earth from pole to pole, and passing through any chosen location. The meridian of your place of birth is the imaginary line running through it from north to south.

Declination
The angular distance of a heavenly body either north or south of the celestial equator is measured in degrees of declination – the equivalent of degrees of latitude on Earth.

The MC (Medium Coeli) or Midheaven
The Midheaven is the point at which the ecliptic meets the meridian of the place of birth.

The IC (Imum Coeli)
The IC is the point exactly opposite the Midheaven. When Placidus and other house division systems (see p.38) are employed it forms the cusp of the fourth house as the Midheaven forms the cusp of the tenth. This is not so when the Equal House system is used; it can then fall in any one of a number of houses, as can the Midheaven.

Nonagesimal
The nonagesimal is the point at 90° from the Ascendant. Note that it is *not* the same as the Midheaven.

The Ascendant
The Ascendant (or Asc.) is the degree of the sign rising over the eastern horizon at any given moment.

The Descendant
The Descendant is the point which is opposite the Ascendant. It is always to be found on the cusp of the seventh house, whichever method of house division is employed.

THE SUN AND THE SOLAR SYSTEM

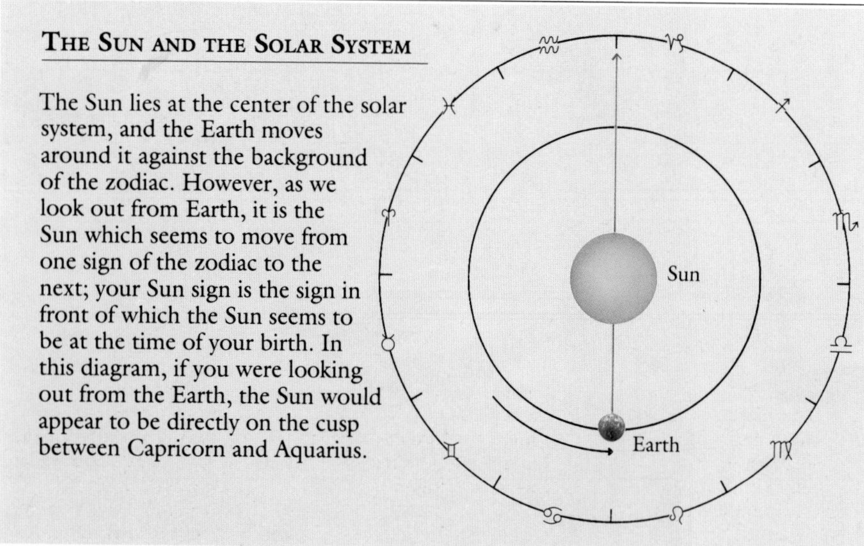

The Sun lies at the center of the solar system, and the Earth moves around it against the background of the zodiac. However, as we look out from Earth, it is the Sun which seems to move from one sign of the zodiac to the next; your Sun sign is the sign in front of which the Sun seems to be at the time of your birth. In this diagram, if you were looking out from the Earth, the Sun would appear to be directly on the cusp between Capricorn and Aquarius.

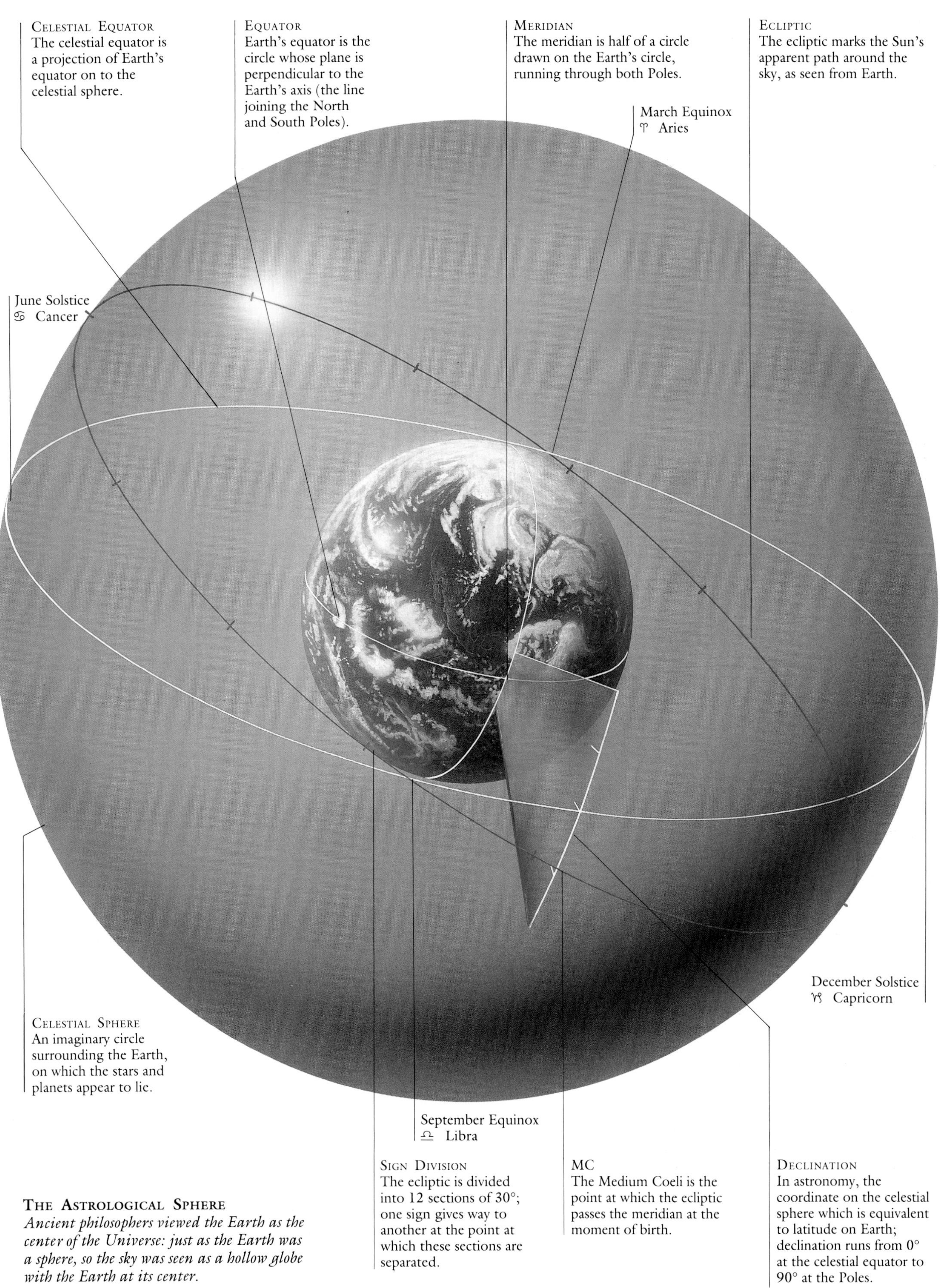

CELESTIAL EQUATOR
The celestial equator is a projection of Earth's equator on to the celestial sphere.
EQUATOR
Earth's equator is the circle whose plane is perpendicular to the Earth's axis (the line joining the North and South Poles).
MERIDIAN
The meridian is half of a circle drawn on the Earth's circle, running through both Poles.
ECLIPTIC
The ecliptic marks the Sun's apparent path around the sky, as seen from Earth.
March Equinox
♈ Aries
June Solstice
♋ Cancer
December Solstice
♑ Capricorn
CELESTIAL SPHERE
An imaginary circle surrounding the Earth, on which the stars and planets appear to lie.
September Equinox
♎ Libra
SIGN DIVISION
The ecliptic is divided into 12 sections of 30°; one sign gives way to another at the point at which these sections are separated.
MC
The Medium Coeli is the point at which the ecliptic passes the meridian at the moment of birth.
DECLINATION
In astronomy, the coordinate on the celestial sphere which is equivalent to latitude on Earth; declination runs from 0° at the celestial equator to 90° at the Poles.

THE ASTROLOGICAL SPHERE
Ancient philosophers viewed the Earth as the center of the Universe: just as the Earth was a sphere, so the sky was seen as a hollow globe with the Earth at its center.

The Zodiac

The zodiac originated as a device for measuring time; no one knows how it first became involved in the classification of personalities or attempts to predict the future, although the first known personal horoscope was drawn up in 410 BC, and the zodiac certainly existed by 500 BC. The Babylonian zodiac had 18 irregular signs, but it was easier to divide a circle of 360 degrees into 12 sections, and there is evidence that the "modern" zodiac was in place long before the birth of Christ. When Plato wrote about astrology in 365 BC the signs were still ruled by gods and goddesses and were linked to myths from Babylon, Egypt and Assyria.

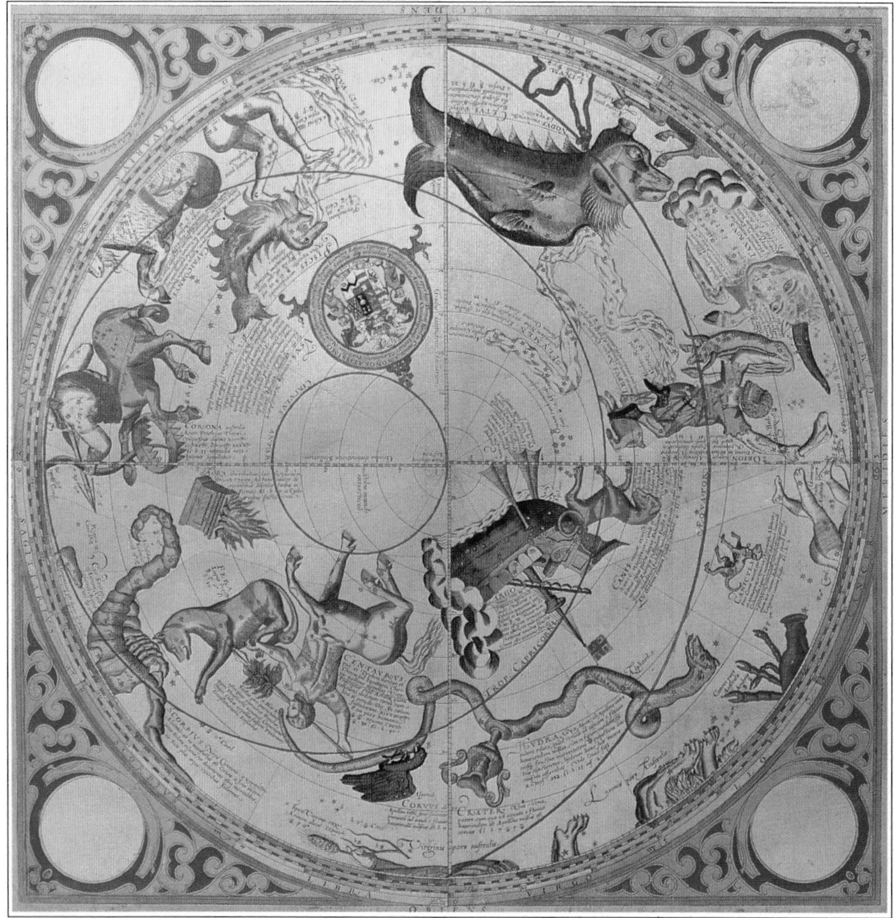

Ancient Views of the Zodiac

The ancient astrologers believed that the Earth had a birthday and that when it was born "Aries was in the Midheaven, and because the Midheaven is, as it were, the vortex of the world, Aries was therefore held to be the first of all the signs, the one which appeared like the head of the world at the beginning of light" (Macrobius, 500 BC).

The myths connected with the signs of the zodiac came from a variety of sources – the ram, for instance, came from Egypt, the bull is associated with Babylon, while the goat came from Assyria.

This map is typical of the graphic representations of the zodiac that are to be found in numerous manuscripts. It includes two constellations that were listed by Ptolemy (in his catalogue of stars of c. AD 150) but are not now officially classed as zodiacal: Ophiuchus, the Serpent-bearer, and Cetus, the Whale. The general view today is that these two constellations are not significant.

The solar system is rather like a gigantic plate, spinning through space. The planets revolve around the Sun on the same plane as the Earth – Pluto, exceptionally, is at 17° from the Earth's plane, but the rest of the planets are under 7°. This explains the fact that, when we observe them from the Earth, the planets seem to move in a fairly constricted path – the ecliptic (see p.16). The zodiac signs are all set within this path (in fact, to the 12 signs with which we are familiar, should be added Ophiuchus, the Serpent-bearer, and Cetus, the Whale, but these signs are not considered to be astrologically significant).

The role of the signs

It cannot be too strongly emphasized that the constellations or signs are merely a convenience to astrologers. They are simply an easy way of naming the 30° segments of the sky within which the Sun, Moon and planets move (the Sun being the only star of significance in astrology). While the symbolic creatures or beings of the zodiac – the Crab, the Archer, the Twins and so on – no doubt played their part in the evolution of the theory, they have no other significance.

Precession of the equinoxes

It is important to note that, because of an astronomical phenomenon called the precession of the equinoxes, these 30° divisions no longer coincide with the constellations. Today, the astrological point Aries 0° is to be found in the astronomical constellation of Pisces. However, this does not affect the astrological theory, which is geared to the relevant segments of the sky rather than the constellations which appear in them, and after which they are named.

Signs of long and short ascension

Because the Earth's axes are oblique in relation to the ecliptic, some of the constellations (the astrological "signs") take longer than others to rise over the horizon. In northern latitudes, the signs of long ascension are Cancer, Leo, Virgo, Libra, Scorpio, Sagittarius and Capricorn. The signs of short ascension are Aries, Taurus, Gemini, Aquarius and Pisces. The opposite applies in southern latitudes.

THE ZODIAC SIGNS
The zodiac signs surround the Earth, each marked and identified by a clutch of stars which over the centuries have been assembled into patterns that roughly outline the symbols of each sign – some more credibly than others.

The Solar System

Five of the planets – Mercury, Venus, Mars, Jupiter and Saturn – have been known ever since man began looking at the heavens. They immediately drew his attention by their brightness and their movements (the word "planet" comes from the Greek word for "wanderer"). Three planets – Uranus, Neptune and Pluto – were discovered after the invention of the telescope. Astrologers were excited to find that their influences filled gaps in interpretations made by ancient astrologers who knew nothing of them.

The Sun

The Sun, at the center of the system of the planets of which the Earth is a member, is about 150 million kilometers (93 million miles) from the Earth and is so large that 109 Earths could be placed side by side inside it.

The Moon

The Moon, the Earth's only natural satellite, is (for convenience) treated as a planet. However, unlike the "real" planets, it circles the Earth (once every 27 days, 7 hours, 43 minutes and 11 seconds), while the Earth and Moon together circle the Sun. Lit by the Sun's light, it appears to grow and decrease in size – wax and wane. It is "new" when it is between the Earth and the Sun, and therefore cannot be seen, and is "full" 14 $\frac{1}{2}$ days later, when in full sunlight.

Because the Moon moves eastwards against the background of the stars, it rises later each night – on average about 50 minutes later, although sometimes it is only 15 minutes and sometimes as much as an hour late. A full Moon always rises at sunset and sets at sunrise. When the Moon passes precisely in front of the Sun, there is a solar eclipse – this is a dramatic event which the ancients believed to be of great astrological significance. However, many modern astrologers consider it of somewhat lesser importance.

Mercury

Mercury is the nearest planet to the Sun, and astronomically it is referred to as an "inferior" planet – that is, its orbit lies between those of Earth and the Sun. It is the smallest of the known planets (only 4,880 kilometers, or 3,000 miles in diameter), and has a year of 88 days – that is the time that it takes to travel round the Sun. So, apart from the Moon, it is the fastest-moving of the bodies used by astrologers, and its movements are comparatively eccentric, for its orbit sometimes takes it to within 47 million kilometers (29 million miles) of the Sun, and sometimes whirls it 70 million kilometers (43 million miles) away. As seen from the Earth, however, it is always relatively close to the Sun and never further away than 27°.

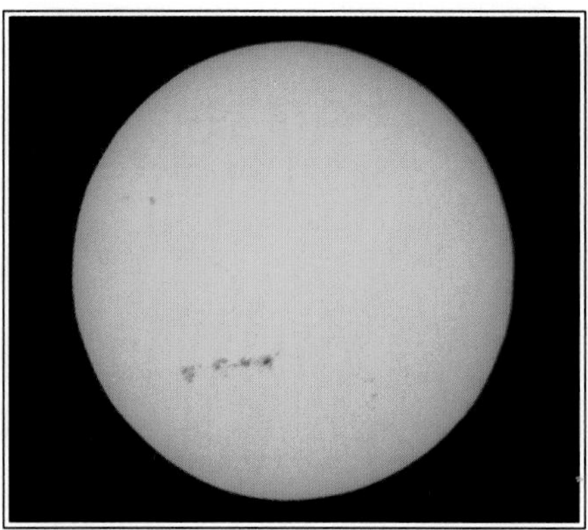

THE SUN
Astrologers call the Sun a planet: it is, in fact, the only star that is used in astrology.

> **MINOR AND HYPOTHETICAL BODIES**
>
> There has been much speculation about the possible astrological effect of minor bodies in the solar system; the asteroids, for instance, of which there are over 40,000. The largest of these is Ceres. Vesta, Pallas and Eros have also been studied, and ephemerides of their movements published. In 1977 a tiny planet (only about 482 kilometres, or 300 miles in diameter) was discovered circling the Sun between the orbits of Saturn and Uranus, but there are no astrological speculations about its possible effect.
>
> **Hypothetical bodies**
>
> Speculation has also been made about Lilith, said to be a satellite of the Earth, one-quarter the size of the Moon. It is unlikely that this "planet" actually exists; eighteenth-century astrologers were probably looking at an asteroid. Astronomers and astrologers have also hypothesized a real planet – sometimes called Vulcan – which may yet be discovered within the orbit of Mercury.

Venus

Another "inferior" planet, Venus is 108.2 million kilometers (67.2 million miles) from the Sun, and takes 225 days to travel round it. Its maximum distance from the Sun as seen from Earth is 48°, so, unlike Mercury, it is usually visible at night.

Mars

Mars is the first planet on the far side of Earth from the Sun, and so is known as a "superior" planet. It has a very eccentric orbit, and can pass as close to the Sun as 208 million kilometers (129 million miles), or be as distant as 228 million kilometers (142 million miles). It circles the Sun once every 687 days.

Jupiter

The largest body in the solar system (143,000 kilometers, or 89,000 miles in diameter), Jupiter is 778 million kilometers (484 million miles) from the Sun and orbits it once every 11.86 years. It has a magnetic field 20,000 times stronger than that of Earth, and sends out radio waves. It has 15 moons; of these, Ganymede, Callisto, Io and Europa are visible from Earth through even a small telescope (they were discovered by Galileo in 1610, with the earliest practical telescope).

Saturn

Saturn is the second largest planet in the solar system (120,000 kilometers, or 74,600 miles in diameter); its orbit around the Sun, from which it is 1,426 million kilometers (886.7 million miles) distant, takes $29\frac{1}{2}$ years. Its rings – three main ones, but hundreds, perhaps thousands, of others – were first studied in 1655, and are now known to be made of ice and rock, whirling around the planet. Saturn has 12 moons, the largest being Titan.

Mercury

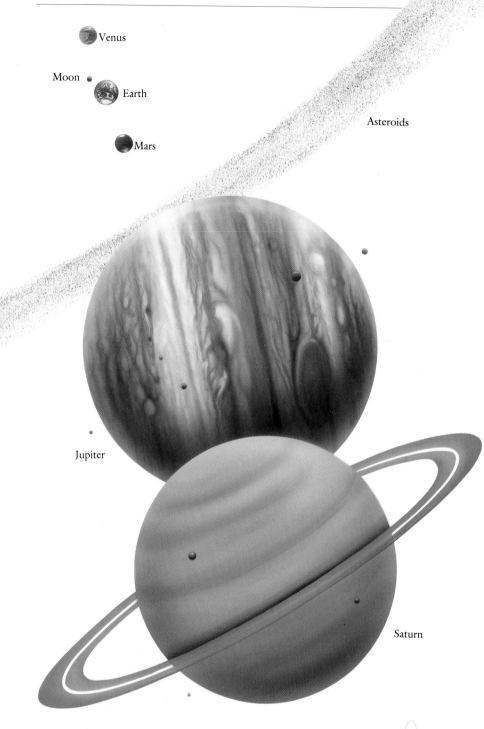

Venus

Moon

Earth

Asteroids

Mars

Jupiter

Saturn

THE MODERN PLANETS

The five planets mentioned on the previous page were all known in antiquity; the three remaining were discovered in modern times, and are called "the modern planets" by astrologers.

Uranus

Uranus, accidentally discovered by William Herschel in 1781, is 2,870 million kilometers (1,783 million miles) from the Sun and takes no less than 84 years to travel round it. It is four times the size of Earth, has a system of rings and four satellites.

Neptune

Neptune was discovered in 1846, after studies of the perturbations of the path of Uranus suggested that they must be caused by the existence of an unknown planet. Slightly larger than Uranus, Neptune takes 165 years to travel around the Sun, from which it is 4,497 million kilometers (2,794 million miles) distant. It has two satellites, Triton and Nereid. Triton, which orbits Neptune every six days, is one of the largest moons in the solar system.

Pluto

Percival Lowell assumed that Pluto existed, on the basis of mathematical calculations. Between 3,200 and 4,800 kilometers (2,000 and 3,000 miles) in diameter, it was first seen by Clyde Tombaugh in 1930. The planet's orbit is 17° inclined to the ecliptic, and is some 5,800 million kilometers (3,600 million miles) from the Sun, around which it circles once every 248 years. Its eccentric orbit brings it within that of Neptune, but a collision is thought to be unlikely. Its moon, Charon, was discovered in 1978.

KNOWLEDGE FROM SPACE

Astrologers take an intelligent interest in astronomy and follow more eagerly than most people the latest information about the objects in the solar stystem.

The most recent space shots have resulted in a considerable increase in our knowledge about the most distant planets. Uranus, for instance, has been found to have at least 15 individual moons, 10 major rings and over 100 minor ones. A great surprise was the discovery by Voyager 2, in 1989, that Neptune's moon, Triton, was both smaller and brighter than had been thought, and that it is (at minus 400° Fahrenheit or minus 200° Centigrade) one of the coldest objects in the solar system. Neptune was also found to have vestigial rings.

Pluto – so far the smallest and usually the most distant planet from the Sun – remains mysterious; but in 1987 astronomers succeeded in accurately measuring the size of its moon, Charon (1,150 kilometers or 710 miles in radius), and also found that its atmosphere extends at least 200 kilometers (125 miles) above its surface.

Uranus

Neptune

Pluto

Modern View of the Solar System
These are the orbits of the planets as we know them today (but without their eccentricities). The planets which are further away than the Earth is from the Sun are known as the superior planets, while those within the Earth's orbit are the inferior planets (see smaller circle, right). The figures by each planet's name are the average distances from the Sun.

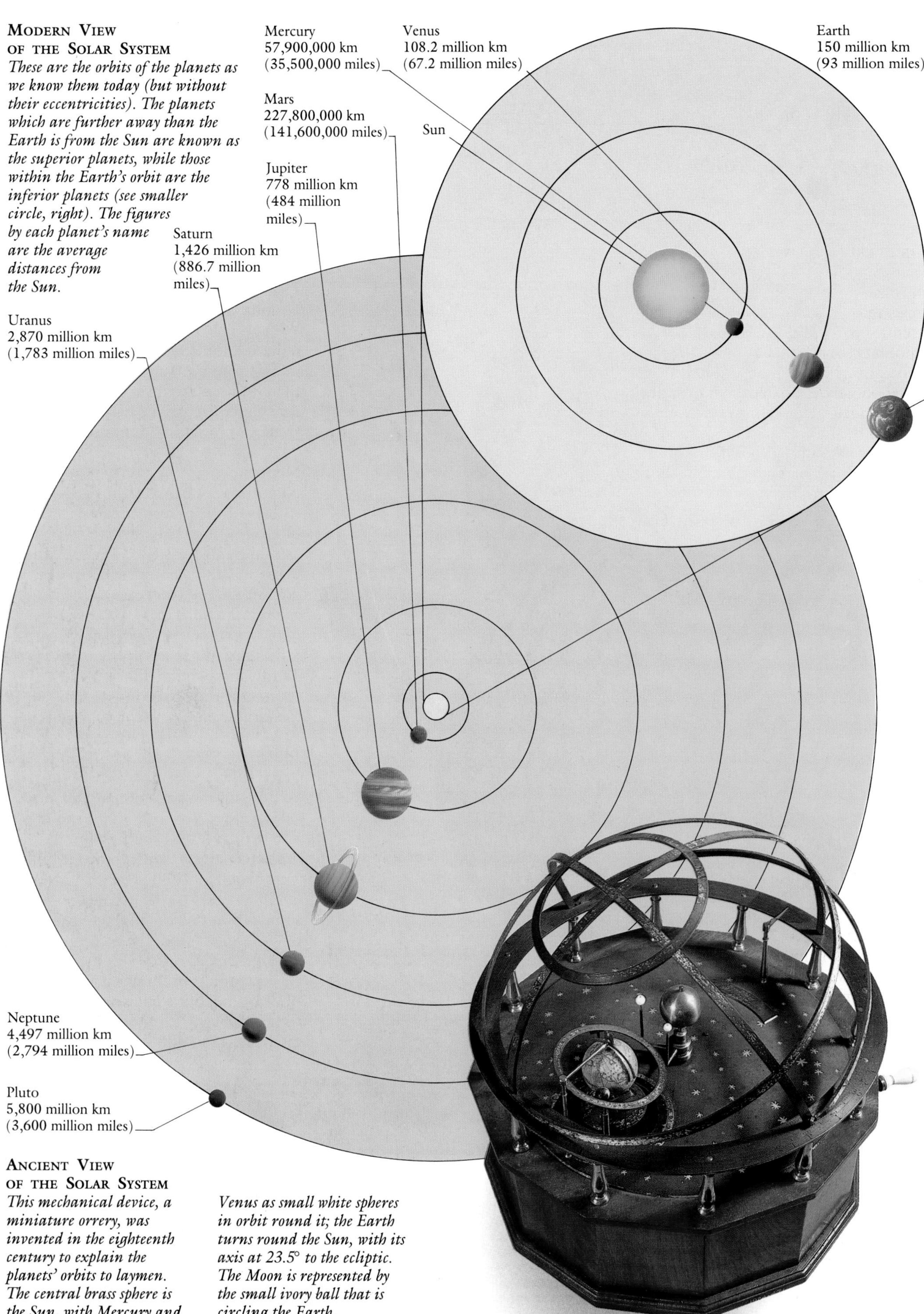

Ancient View of the Solar System
This mechanical device, a miniature orrery, was invented in the eighteenth century to explain the planets' orbits to laymen. The central brass sphere is the Sun, with Mercury and Venus as small white spheres in orbit round it; the Earth turns round the Sun, with its axis at 23.5° to the ecliptic. The Moon is represented by the small ivory ball that is circling the Earth.

CHANGING VIEWS OF THE PLANETS
Copernicus shocked sixteenth-century contemporaries by maintaining that the Sun lay at the center of the solar system; in this map the Earth is no longer in the central position.

THE PLANETS' MOVEMENTS

The planets do not move in perfect circles around the Sun. While the eccentricity of their orbits is more important to astronomers than to astrologers, we must note one phenomenon: as we look at them from the Earth, planets may seem to hesitate, stop and then move backwards for a time before resuming their forward motion. A planet moving backwards in this way is said to be in retrograde

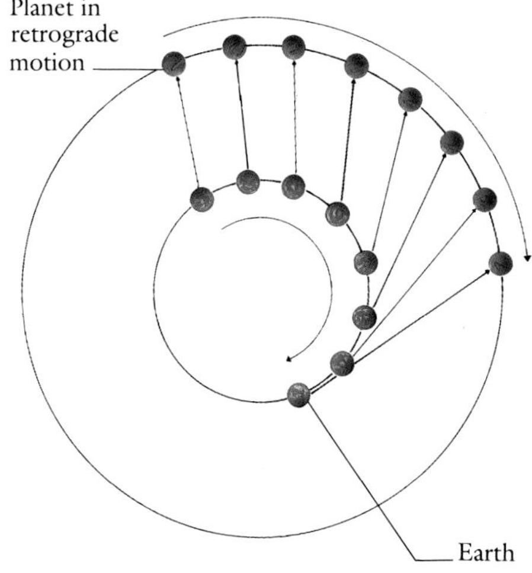

motion, and the optical illusion is the result of the Earth overtaking the planet in question (as when, in a car overtaking another car, you see the overtaken car falling behind, although it is still moving forward). The point at which a planet goes retrograde is marked in astronomical tables with the capital letter "R", and its return to direct motion is marked by a "D". Some astrologers vastly overestimate the effects of a retrograde planet.

Conjunctions

A conjunction occurs when two planets or more (remember that to astrologers the Sun is a planet) are in line, as seen from the Earth. Mercury and Venus can be in either superior or inferior conjunction: inferior when they are between the Sun and the Earth, and superior when they are behind the Sun, as seen from the Earth.

CONJUNCTIONS

In the large diagram (below) Venus and Neptune and also Mars and Uranus appear to be very close together, when seen from Earth – they are in conjunction. In the smaller diagrams (right, from the top) Mars is directly opposite the Sun, as seen from the Earth and is therefore in opposition; Mars and Neptune are in superior conjunction both with the Sun and with each other; Venus, directly between the Earth and Sun, is in inferior conjunction; and Mercury and Venus, on the other side of the Sun (as seen from the Earth) are in superior conjunction. A conjunction of two planets is a crucial factor in the birth chart and will affect its interpretation, according to the different characteristics of the houses and signs involved.

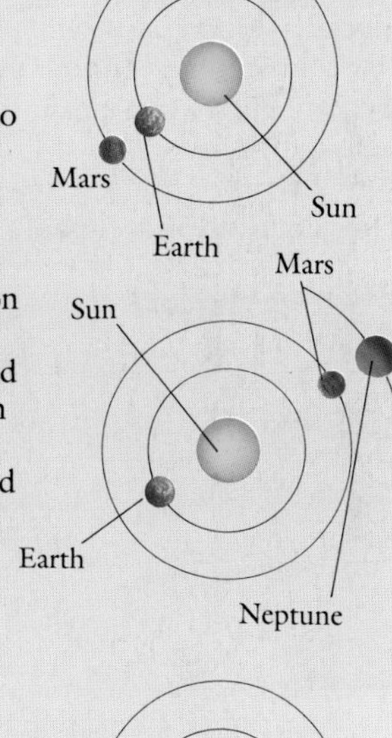

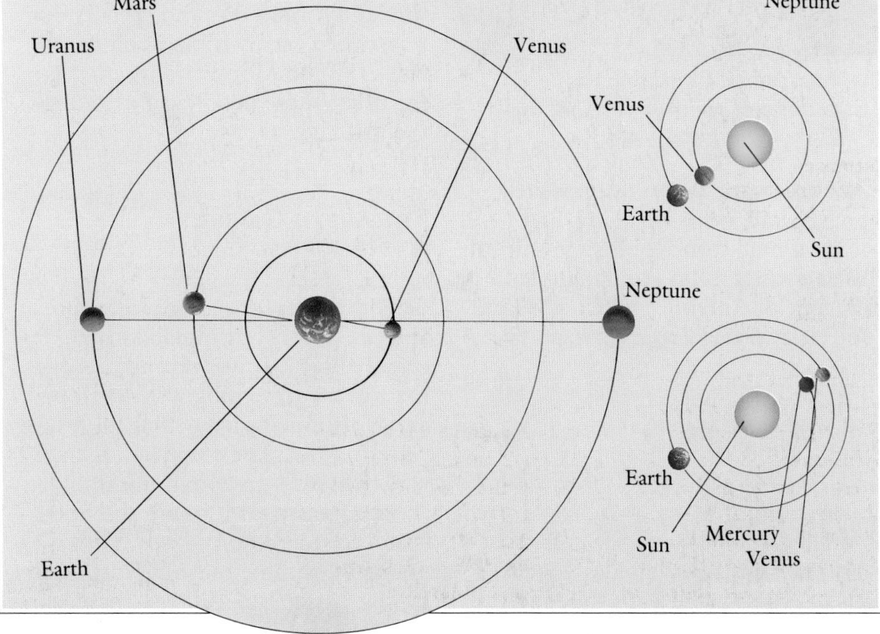

The Great Year

The Earth takes 25,868 years to pass, in retrograde motion (see p.23), through the 12 constellations. It takes approximately 2,500 years to travel through each sign of the zodiac, and these periods are known as "ages". We can trace seven of these ages that have elapsed since Man inhabited the Earth, and relate them to their signs. The dates we offer are highly approximate; the constellations vary in size and overlap, so we cannot know precisely when one age gives way in favor of the next.

The Age of Leo
10000 – 8000 BC

This is the earliest age about which we can speculate. Interestingly, it is prehistoric cave paintings that have survived as the first signs of Man's involvement with art, for Leo is the sign of creativity and has a special association with painting. The importance of the Sun in those distant times was crucial, for at this period it increased in strength, heralding the end of the Ice Age. There is always an element of the influence of the polar, or opposite, sign in evidence in astrology, and some original stone tools survive from this age which echo accurately the influence of Aquarius, which gives its subjects a certain originality and flair.

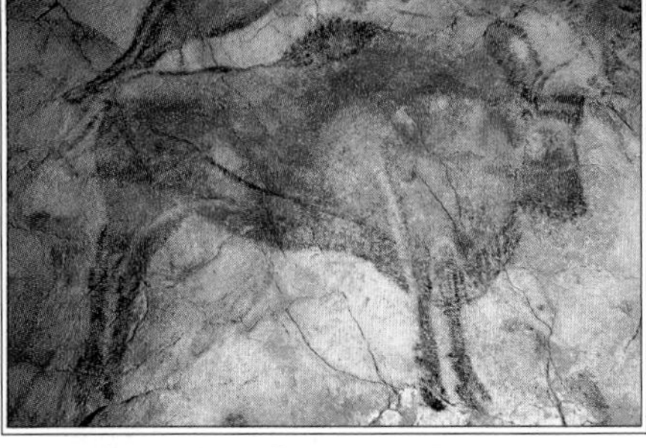

Evidence of a Creative Past
This painting of a bison was found in caves at Altimira, Northern Spain.

The Age of Cancer
8000 – 6000 BC

It was during this age that Man started to build dwellings, and the emphasis on home and family life developed. Cancer is associated with this, and the Moon (its ruling planet) with motherhood. Fertility carvings survive, as do the remains of early communities in China, Mesopotamia, India and many other locations. This shows an increasing need for and awareness of protection – against the elements, wild animals and human enemies. Considering the polar influence of Capricorn, an earth sign, it was also at this time that we have evidence of the beginnings of agriculture and fishing. We can speculate on how much early people watched the phases of the Moon and its effects on the tides; these people were among the first fishermen.

Fertility Figure
An Asian carving from the sixth millenium BC.

The Age of Gemini
6000 – 4000 BC

Gemini represents communication, and is a powerfully intellectually oriented sign. It was during this age that the art of writing was developed, and it also seems likely that the wheel was invented. The emphasis, then, was very definitely on communication. Writing began with rough symbols that were carved on stones. They gradually became more sophisticated so that by around 4000 BC there is evidence of Chinese and Egyptian cuneiform writing (like the tablet, left). Man was at this time ready to develop intellectually, and was motivated to move away from his local environment. Considering the polar influence of Sagittarius, it seems likely that the first explorers were now making sea voyages, and as the intellectual qualities of Gemini complement those of Sagittarius, here are some extremely lively influences at work in an age when civilization took considerable strides forward. Trade, too, was developing, for by now the oldest town, Jericho, was in existence – commerce is something very much associated with Gemini's ruling planet, Mercury.

The Age of Taurus
4000 – 2000 BC

The solid, somewhat heavy characteristics of Taurus, along with its need for security and identification with beauty and luxury, are all highlighted in the evolving early Egyptian dynasties. Their massive and beautiful temples, built for permanence, and the bull cults, provide interesting evidence which closely mirrors the characteristics of the sign. The polar influence of Scorpio is profoundly marked, for the ancient Egyptians were much concerned with death and the after-life. Their development of techniques of embalming

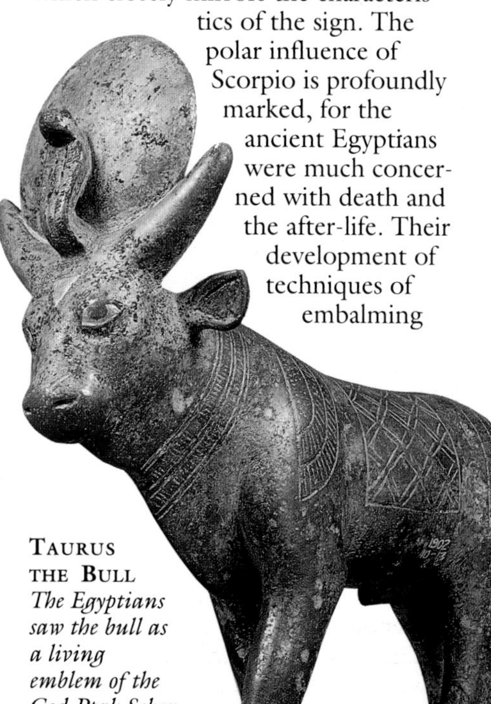

Taurus the Bull
The Egyptians saw the bull as a living emblem of the God Ptah Seker Asari; this is a bronze bull from the thirtieth dynasty.

and mummification, and their tombs, full of artefacts, supply abundant evidence of this. It was during this age that observation of the skies by early priest astrologers/astronomers took place. In these latitudes they found that the clear skies were a source of considerable inspiration.

THE AGE OF ARIES
2000 BC – AD 0

PHYSICAL PROWESS AND BEAUTY
A detail from a Greek vase of c.540 BC depicts Achilles slaying Penthesileia.

During this period Greece came into its own, with the influence of the Aries/Libra polarity interestingly accentuated. The aggressive, assertive qualities associated with Aries show vividly in the behavior of the war-like Greeks. Their physical prowess and concern with fitness and sports is also sympathetic. Perhaps even more interesting is the polar influence from Libra. One of this sign's qualities is the passion for democracy, the desire to see justice done – the Greeks evolved the first democratic government. Balance and harmony are also a part of the Libra syndrome, and what could be more balanced and harmonious to the eye than the stunningly beautiful Parthenon and other Classical Greek buildings? Note the striking difference between the Taurean influence on architecture of the previous age and the Libran polar influence here. Both are beautiful – and with Venus ruling both signs that is to be expected!

THE SYMBOLIC FISH
A graceful dolphin from a Roman mosaic of the third century AD, in Utica, North Africa.

THE AGE OF PISCES
AD 0 – 2000

With the birth of Christ came the age of Pisces. Interestingly enough, the early secret Christian symbol was the fish, which was scrawled on catacomb walls to indicate to believers where the next meetings were to be held. But more importantly, the kind, charitable, forgiving Christian qualities, which feature so strongly in the teachings of Christ, exactly parallel those attributed to Pisces, as indeed does the certain vagueness of thought present both in some aspects of Christianity and in those of this sign. The cloistered lives of monks and nuns show, too, the reclusive qualities of Pisces, and those groups of people who have over centuries made, and today still make, considerable sacrifices for their faith and for the benefit of less fortunate people in the community, are quintessentially Piscean. But yet again in this age we have a very striking polar influence. Virgo, the Pisces polar sign, is constantly to the fore, as represented by the cult of the Virgin Mary. Indeed, it is also reflected in many respects by the modest and restrictive Christian attitude to sex.

THE MODERN AGE
A jet-propelled back pack allows an astronaut to float in space during the 1984 shuttle mission.

THE AGE OF AQUARIUS
AD 2000 – 4000

The 1960s American musical *Hair* had a song, "The Age of Aquarius", that gave people not only an interest in astrology but also the idea that they were on the brink of some new era. Astrologers were often asked what the "New Age" was, and when it would start – as if one day we would wake up to find ourselves in it. No one knows precisely when a new age begins or old age ends. The constellations are widely spaced and some overlap each other; astronomically, the overlap can last as long as 500 years! However, influences of the new age now abound. The development of technology, of space travel and science are all essentially Aquarian in concept. Thinking of the humanitarian qualities of the sign on a world scale, we have the United Nations and many conservation organizations. But what of the polar sign, Leo? Could the eventual outcome of the Age of Aquarius be benevolent world government? Will we see it in our time? Or will we have to leave it to future generations to assess the influence of this age – as we have done up to now?

The Signs of the Zodiac

It is impossible to know how the 12 signs of our modern zodiac became associated with the characteristics attributed to them by astrologers. They were certainly not named on that basis: Gemini takes its name, for instance, simply from the twin stars that shine in that portion of the sky – though the stars in Leo suggests a crouching beast, and those in Virgo have always suggested the outline of a human body. The signs got their names and the myths associated with them from ancient civilizations – the study of their history is fascinating and extremely complex. In the fourth and third centuries BC, for instance, parts of the human body had been allocated to zodiac signs, beginning at the head (at the vernal equinox) with Aries, and ending with Pisces at the feet. This association was probably made by the Greeks, who also associated plants with various signs; Egyptian medical men associated animals with some signs, and stones, too, were linked to signs (the Egyptian astrologers linked "magic" stones with days of the month and decans). For astrologers, however, the importance of the signs is the characteristics with which, over several thousand years, they have been associated.

ASTROLOGY MEETS ASTRONOMY
This sixteenth-century brass nocturnal and quadrant(below), which was used for determining latitude and measuring altitudes, is engraved with the signs of the zodiac.

ZODIAC SIGNS AND ACTIVITIES
Traditionally the signs of the zodiac have been associated with particular activities, relevant to their time of year: the illustrations on this and the next page are from a French Book of Hours of 1423.

ARIES

The entry of the Sun into Aries on or around 21 March marks the beginning of the astrological New Year. The characteristics accurately mirror new beginnings. Here is the most personally oriented of all the signs, and the psychological signal "me first" is synonymous with the forthright, bursting energy of spring growth. It is unlikely that we will fail to notice an Arian in our midst; their enthusiasm and youthful approach is admirable, along with their uncomplicated and hopeful attitude to life.

Aries is the first sign of the fire element and the cardinal quality – all force, all outgoing, all for moving ahead, but also for putting the self first. The fire emphasis ignites enthusiasm and keenness, but that enthusiasm can die quickly. Learning to sustain interest and developing patience is essential. Virtually all Arians have a selfish streak. It is when Aries is the rising sign that this tendency is often at its most negative; when Aries is the Sun sign, Venus can mitigate it. The influence of Mercury can make Arians more thoughtful and soften the harsher Arian characteristics.

TAURUS

The second sign of the zodiac. Stability, security and patience are strong characteristics. Risks are taken only when and if they are essential, and then only after careful consideration. Here is a sign that encourages a steady routine in life.

More than anything else, Taureans need emotional security in their relationships and must have material security.

Taurus is the first sign of the earth element and the first fixed quality. Earth people are practical – literally down to earth! Venus, the planet of love, rules this sign and her influence ensures that Taureans have a great love of beauty, are sensual lovers and enjoy luxury. Taureans have a strong possessive streak and even the loved one may become just another possession. It is when Taurus is the rising sign that this tendency is most powerful, since when the Sun sign is Taurus it is likely that the influence of Venus, which will not be far away, will add another group of characteristics which will help counter the tendency. Indeed, the influence of the fixed quality of the sign adds to the abundant stability of Taurus, although it may also make its subjects a little stubborn.

GEMINI

The third sign of the zodiac – the sign of the heavenly twins. These celestial bodies bestow an element of duality which emerges on many levels. Geminians never seem to do only one thing at a time. But it is up to us to remind them that this tendency can get a little out of hand. Their quick wit and need to communicate comes from the influence of their ruling planet, Mercury.

This is the first air sign of the zodiac and the first of the mutable quality. Both features complement Gemini, for the mental attributes and quickness of mind are allowed plenty of freedom of expression when released into the air. The mutable quality complements the duality of Gemini – again encouraging free and positive expression. Changeability and superficiality are faults that can emerge when Gemini is rising; when Gemini is the Sun sign, the influence of its rising planet, Mercury, will often add stabilizing, practical or intuitive qualities which will counter flightiness and that tendency to be rather shallow.

CANCER

The fourth sign of the zodiac is ruled by the Moon. Think of a Cancerian, and you will see the connection. Does this person have a certain facial roundness and paleness, suggesting the full Moon? Is he or she moody and changeable, but kind and sympathetic? This is the sign of motherhood; Cancer is the home- and family-builder of the zodiac.

Cancer is the first water sign and the second of the cardinal quality. Powerful emotions are blended with an equally strong imagination and intuition. These resources must be nurtured, but also controlled and channelled. The cardinal quality of this sign, however, offers control and discipline, often giving the ability to express love and emotion, and enabling Cancerians to spring to the defence of those they love and themselves. When Cancer is the rising sign there is always additional support for the partner, but worry may not be as well countered as when Cancer is the Sun sign, as the influence of nearby Mercury and Venus often helps to control emotions and take a more relaxed attitude. When Cancer is emphasized by Sun or rising sign, we must note the Moon's sign and its influence in the birth chart.

LEO

Leo is the fifth sign of the zodiac, ruled by the Sun. Here that star – which astrologers for convenience call a planet – shines at its most powerful from the only sign it rules. The Lion can rule and, yes, at times roar, but Leos will retreat when injured. Here is a powerful, but usually well-hidden, sensitivity. Here, too, is the urge to create. Any Leo who isn't expressing creativity will not be truly fulfilled, and an unfulfilled Leo can be extremely disruptive.

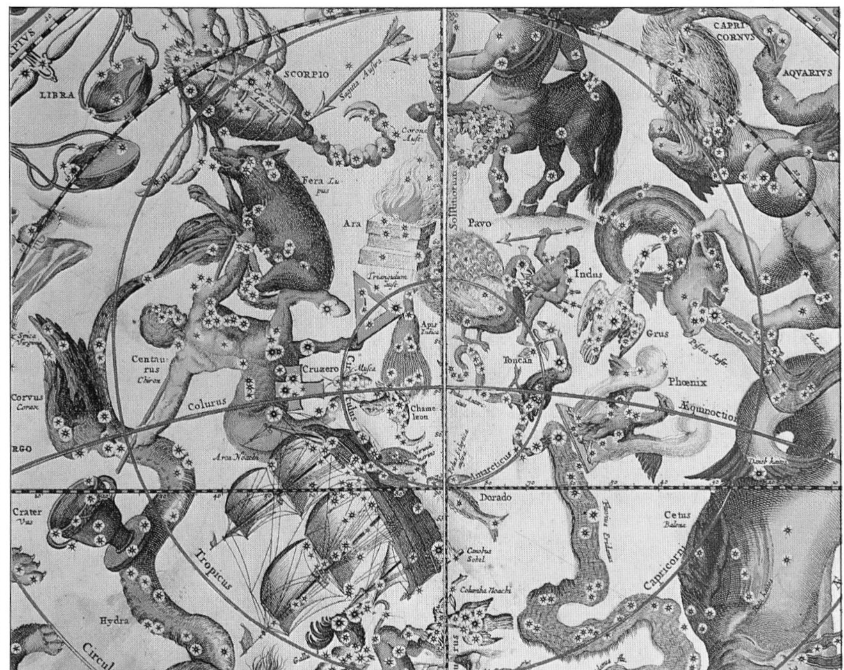

ANCIENT CELESTIAL VIEW
Looking at the patterns in the sky, Man found that they reminded him of various figures or objects, which were superimposed on early star maps – like this one dating from 1650.

Leo is the second sign of the fire element, and the second of the fixed quality. Fiery emotion and enthusiasm crackles and burns brightly. The fixity of the sign can lead to stubborness and haughtiness, but on the positive side it adds determination. Because the Sun is in its own sign the characteristics of Leo will outshine all others in the chart – in a way which is perhaps rather different to those of other Sun signs. Should Mercury or Venus be in Leo with the Sun we sometimes have to help our Leo friends to develop less Leonine characteristics, for in such situations there can be an element of imbalance in their personalities. When Leo is the rising sign, pomposity and bossiness can all too sadly be expressed towards the partner.

VIRGO

Virgo, the sixth sign of the zodiac, is the second to be ruled by Mercury. Here are the practical workers, but also the critics of the zodiac. They have excellent intellects but lack self-confidence. These days, because their Sun sign characteristics are so well-known, Virgoans may try to develop different characteristics in order to live down a prissy reputation.

Here is the second sign of the earth element and the second of the mutable quality. The practical, steady qualities of earth are not very complementary to the mutability of the sign. The influence of Mercury, the ruling planet, gives Virgoans excellent brains but makes them worriers. If Virgoans are creative they will have excellent potential. Those of this Sun sign may also have their ruling planet in Virgo with the Sun – when they will indeed be extremely Virgoan. However, when Mercury is in either Leo or Libra there are some interesting contrasting indications that help give Virgo a broader outlook on life and even greater potential in different fields. When Virgo is the rising sign, the Virgoan characteristics will be countered, but the influence of the Mercury sign will play an important part in the psychological make-up of the subject.

LIBRA

Libra is the seventh sign of the zodiac. As Aries, the first sign, is the most personal, so this, its polar or opposite sign across the zodiac, is the one most concerned with relating to a partner. Fairness, diplomacy, and a sense of justice are very strong indeed, and having a permanent relationship is essential. But there is often an element of resentment, and indecision can cause trouble.

Libra is the second sign of the air element and the third of the cardinal quality. These influences work well within the context of the sign, adding lightness and charm, and an outgoing ease. But underlying these characteristics are sterner ones. Many Librans have an aggressive streak, and most do not deserve their reputation for laziness. The influence of Venus, not far away from the Sun sign in the birth charts, is vital, adding an important dimension to their psychological make-up if it is not in Libra with the Sun. If it is, then Libra will be very Libran indeed. When Libra is the rising sign, its characteristics may be overshadowed by other, stronger elements in the birth chart.

SCORPIO

The eighth sign of the zodiac, and the one with the highest energy level. Its resources of both physical and emotional energy are second to none. Until Pluto was discovered and accepted into the astrological pantheon, Mars, the ruler of Aries and an important factor

THE BODY
This fifteenth century manuscript shows the astrological associations with parts of the body.

in physical energy level, ruled Scorpio. But Pluto rules Scorpio now, and its influence develops and energizes the emotional content of that sign. So here is a force to be reckoned with and one that must be understood and channelled.

Scorpio is the second sign of the water element and the third of the fixed quality, so here the emotion of water is stilled and intensified. Its force must be positively expressed and directed toward the fulfillment of the individual. An unfulfilled Scorpio can become jealous and restless. When Scorpio is the rising sign we see the emergence of the polar influence from Taurus. This will add warmth and charm, expressed towards the partner – but a possessive element can also emerge, which is not evident when Scorpio is the Sun sign, since it is then often mitigated by the nearby influence of Mercury or Venus.

SAGITTARIUS

The ninth sign – the sign of horse and man. A combination of physical strength and energy, and powerful intellect. Here is the second "dual" sign of the zodiac. Versatility will be present, and mind and body should act as one. Rest and relaxation come through both. Jupiter, the ruling planet, encourages both mind and body, along with the need for challenge, and Sagittarians must be aware of this.

Here is the third and last of the fire element signs, and the third of the mutable quality. The fire burns strong and bright, with lively enthusiasm and an infectious emotional level. It gives the individual the ability to grasp overall situations very quickly. Optimism abounds. The Sagittarian Centaur is an Archer with a need for room in which to breathe and for a diversity of interests. Sagittarians must always be aware that intellectual and physical stagnation will lead to the restlessness which is their real enemy. While the Sagittarian polar sign, Gemini, is intellectually oriented, there is an accent on the higher mind, which helps develop philosophical traits and quells the tendency to take risks.

CAPRICORN

The tenth sign of the zodiac. Saturn rules the sign and bestows ambition, a need always to do the right and proper thing, and a love of tradition. But Capricorns do have the capacity for enjoyment and always possess a marvelously offbeat sense of humor.

This is the third and last sign of the earth element, and the fourth and last sign of the cardinal quality. The practical side of earth combines with an outgoing, expressive quality, giving common sense and the ability to express it in a forthright manner. This is a sign with a rather low emotional level, but often the placing of Venus – especially when in either Scorpio or Pisces – will help warm the rather distant Capricorn heart and encourage faithfulness. This may not be as much of a help when Capricorn is the rising sign, but because of the intervention of an influence from Capricorn's polar sign, Cancer, there will be a caring quality, with an instinctive motivation to protect the loved one and family. However, there may be a conflict between working long hours and spending time with the partner and children.

AQUARIUS

The eleventh sign of the zodiac, which shows us true individualists. Aquarians are usually glamorous, always friendly, but they are private people who tend to surround themselves with an air of mystery. This is in defense of a specific lifestyle that can lead to conflict when the question arises of deepening an emotional relationship. The ruling planet, Uranus, adds a certain eccentricity and unpredictability, which is not easy for others to cope with.

Aquarius is the last sign of the air element and the fourth of the fixed quality. This makes for an enquiring mind which can ossify once opinions are formed. Like Capricorn, Aquarius does not bestow a generous emotional level (it once shared Saturn with Capricorn as ruling planet). The influence of Venus will help in the expression of feelings towards partners, while Mercury helps reduce stubbornness. The influence of the polar sign, Leo, comes into its own when Aquarius is the rising sign, adding a passion that blends beautifully with Aquarian originality and is best expressed through art or scientific work.

PISCES

The twelfth and last sign of the zodiac. Here is the recluse who nevertheless has stunning potential, when it is allowed to blossom – although often lack of self-confidence prevents a full expression. The ruling planet, Neptune, while encouraging inspiration, sensitivity and vision, can cloud issues. You will know the kindness of Pisceans, but may find them deceptive. Give them encouragement and they will develop greater confidence and belief in what they can do.

This is the third and last sign of the water element, and the fourth and last sign of the mutable quality. The emotion of water is encouraged by the mutable quality, and is a powerful force that needs shaping and controlling if it is to work in a rewarding and satisfying way. Pisceans often have a powerful spiritual faith, which can, however, be diverted into some unconventional cult. A Piscean Sun sometimes bestows weakness of character, but the nearby presence of Mercury and Venus may counter these tendencies. When Pisces is the rising sign, a critical quality can emerge in the attitude towards the partner.

The Planets and You

The asssociations astrologers make between the planets and human characteristics – Venus and love, Mars and energy, and so on – are well over 2,000 years old. For instance, associations with various plants existed as early as 400 BC. These associations are also specifically Western, though there are often universal similarities. In ancient Chinese astrology, for example, Mars is associated with fire and Saturn with earth. Ancient astrologers dealt only with the planets whose movements they could see with the naked eye – five of them. Though the idea of astrology is immeasurably old, a rational and scientific astrology only became possible at about the end of the fifth century BC, substantially because of the intelligent study the Greeks gave to it. And the discovery of the three modern planets – Uranus, Neptune and Pluto (see p.21) – has highlighted new influences. It is possible that more "new" planets may be discovered, and then the astrological fraternity would need to decide their field of influence and sign rulership.

The Sun

***Keywords:** Self-expression, vitality*

Almost every known civilization has had its own Sun god. In the West, Apollo, the son of Zeus, is perhaps the most prominent Sun god. He is thought to have orginated in Asia, and to have reached Europe via Greece. Not only does he mirror the brightness and purity of the Sun, but he is also the perfect man, depicted in paintings or carvings as a naked and guileless youth. In astrology the Sun – technically a star rather than a planet – is associated with the sign Leo and represents generosity of heart, affection and magnanimity, creativity and simple joy. However, it can encourage self-esteem to the point at which it becomes pomposity.

The Moon

***Keywords:** Response, instinct, intuition, fluctuation, emotion*

The myths that are associated with the Moon (which rules the sign Cancer) tend to show her as feminine and beautiful – but often also as a cruel seductress. As Circe she seduced Odysseus; as Hecate she rewarded her favourites with riches; as Selene she was seen riding her chariot through the night sky. Both in myth and in astrology she is associated with natural childbirth. Perhaps more importantly she encourages natural, instinctive behaviour in a personality. There is a close connection with the emotions, and also with the digestive system. The Moon can make one patient, or changeable and narrow-minded, or imaginative and sympathetic, or perhaps unreliable.

Mercury

***Keywords:** Mind, communication – mental and physical*

Mercury is a direct descendant of Hermes, the messenger of Zeus, and the god of travelers. Mercury invented the lyre, and he was a marvelous athlete. He is usually shown stripped for sports, clad only in winged sandals and helmet. His characteristics are typically those of Gemini, which is a sign he rules: he is intellectual, perceptive, reasonable, versatile and argumentative, but an excellent communicator. This planet stimulates the mind, but it can make a subject argumentative and critical, nervous and tense – all possible traits of Virgo, with which this planet is also associated.

Venus

***Keywords:** Harmony, unison, love*

Venus, the legendary beauty, inherited the attributes of Aphrodite, and so she became the goddess of love – ideal, familial and sexual. In the grounds of her temples were groves in which worshippers could make love. In astrology the planet, associated with Taurus and Libra, is also concerned with love and personal relationships, and with the feminine side of a subject's nature, as well as with art and fashion. Venus encourages gentleness, friendliness, tact and the social graces – but under stress can make one indecisive, careless, over-romantic and dependent on others.

Mars

***Keywords:** Physical energy, initiative*

This planet is associated with the Greek god Ares, fortunate in war but unfortunate in love. Mars was originally a god of farming; however, he is better known as the god of war, to whom Roman soldiers paid tribute before going off to do battle. Powerfully built, Mars is always shown, even when engaged in one of his amorous adventures, dressed for the battlefield. The planet's astrological association is with Aries: Mars is concerned with the masculine side of a subject's nature, with the muscular system and with aggression. Strongly sexual, it can make one aggressive as well as decisive; hasty and rude as well as positive and energetic.

Jupiter

***Keywords:** Expansion – intellectual and physical*

Jupiter protected the city of Rome, and he both blessed warriors before going off to do battle and greeted them when they returned afterwards. He had the power to punish as well as reward them, and was a frequent hurler of thunderbolts. Astrologically associated with Sagittarius (once also Pisces), the planet Jupiter is concerned with learning, philosophy and languages. Its influence can encourage optimism, loyalty and justice – but can make a subject over-optimistic, extravagant, self-indulgent and conceited.

Saturn

***Keywords:** Stability, restriction, limitation, control*

Saturn, like Mars, was originally an agricultural god, but in Rome he presided over the Saturnalia, a highly enjoyable public holiday. The Christians adopted this feast, and renamed it Christmas. Astrologically, the planet originally ruled Capricorn and Aquarius, but now only the former. In ancient times Saturn marked the limit of the known solar system, so it is associated with limitation, but also with perseverance and tenacity. It can make one practical and cautious, but perhaps selfish, narrow-minded and even cruel..

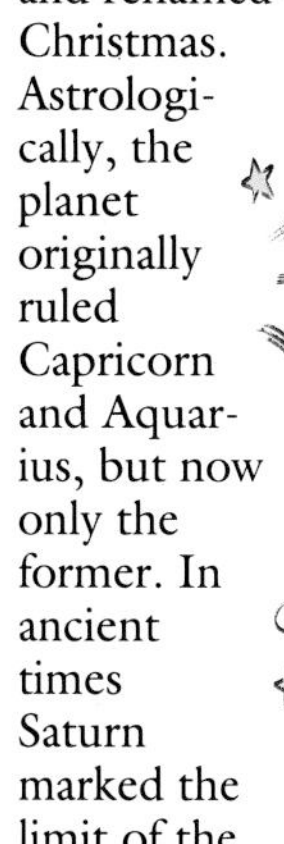

Uranus

***Keywords:** Change, disruption, shock*

Uranus was born of Earth, then mated with her, and from their incestuous union all living things were born. Saturn led a rebellion against him, and he was castrated. From his severed genitals, Aphrodite (later Venus) was born. This unattractive mythical figure names a planet associated with Aquarius, and is concerned with sexual excesses, deviation and possible nervous breakdown. Uranus has also become connected with science fiction and space exploration. At best, it encourages originality, versatility and independence; at worst, it encourages eccentricity, perversion and rebellion.

Neptune

***Keywords:** Cloudiness, unreality*

Neptune inherited his lordship of the sea from the Greek sea-god Poseidon, and he also administered all lakes and rivers. Water-horses drew his chariot when he rose from his palace in the depths. Neptune became a stallion in order to woo the beautiful Demeter when she became a mare; perhaps this is why he is said to have invented horse-racing. The planet bearing his name is associated with the sign Pisces (the most watery of water signs) and is much concerned with the arts – particularly poetry and dancing. It can encourage idealism, imagination and sensitivity – but also carelessness, indecision and deceit.

Pluto

***Keywords:** Elimination, eruptive change*

Pluto, yet another of the agricultural gods, ruled over the Underworld; no creature was ever known to have escaped transportation to his land of death beyond the river Styx. He often wore a helmet which made him invisible, and this must have been of great asssistance in his many campaigns of seduction. The planet that bears his name is associated with the sign Scorpio, and perhaps for that reason it is associated with the genitalia and human reproduction. But it is also concerned with the unconscious (buried emotions), and while it encourages subjects to overcome obstacles, it can also tend to make them sly, critical, secretive and cruel.

Groupings and Rulerships

The 12 zodiac signs are traditionally formed into four groups within which they interact with and complement each other. The characteristics they share are very basic, and though real, should be used only as background indications. The groupings have a long history: the four elements are older than philosophy; the qualities were a classical Greek conception; while it was the Pythagoreans who extended the notion of opposites (odd/even, male/female, positive/negative, and so on) which affects many theories besides astrology.

Traditional Sign Groupings

The triplicities or elements

The first, and most interesting and revealing, characteristics are defined by the triplicities (sometimes called the elements). These consist of fire signs, earth signs, air signs and water signs.

Generally, tradition decrees that fire signs are by nature enthusiastic, earth signs practical, air signs intellectual and have a need to communicate, and water signs emotional. You will often find that people who share a strong emphasis on signs of one or other triplicity turn out to be compatible.

The quadruplicities or qualities

The second grouping is known as that of the quadruplicities or qualities – cardinal, fixed or mutable.

Basically, we can say that the cardinal signs tend to be outgoing, the fixed signs rigid in their opinions, and the mutable signs flexible and adaptable.

Positive and negative

The third grouping is of positive and negative, or masculine and feminine signs. Do not be confused; if a woman has a Sun or Ascendant sign which is a masculine sign, this does not mean that she lacks femininity, any more than a man with a feminine Sun or Ascendant sign lacks masculinity. Positive and negative are probably better descriptive adjectives. However, we should be wary of using them; to be really safe we should only say that there is a tendency for people of feminine signs to be introverts, and those of masculine signs to be extroverts.

To make matters even more complicated, the characters of the sign symbols do not always seem to fit their categories: for instance the Bull, arguably the most masculine creature of the zodiac – with the possible exception of the Ram, is the symbol of a feminine sign. But that's tradition!

The Power of the Sun
The fire sign Leo is included in this fifteenth-century print of a magnificent Sun god.

Polarity

There is another rather different relationship between the signs, which is extremely useful in many areas of interpretation. This relationship is known as polarity. Each sign has a special relationship with its partner across the zodiac. Thus:

Aries/Libra
Cancer/Capricorn
Taurus/Scorpio
Leo/Aquarius
Gemini/Sagittarius
Virgo/Pisces

This does not mean that the signs opposite each other across the zodiac circle have opposite characteristics. On the contrary, the polar signs complement each other – there is a special rapport and understanding between them. Two people who, when their full charts are calculated, share an emphasis on a pair of polar signs may not always agree, but there will certainly be a special understanding between them. This theme is developed more fully in the section devoted to relationships (see pp.148-67), where it is of considerable importance. For the moment, simply keep the zodiac couples in mind; for example, as Aries is the most personal of signs, Libra is the one showing a powerful need to relate. Compare sign polarity to the similar relationship between the houses (see p.38), and remember that the understanding and rapport between the polar signs is worthwhile and interesting, and adds a subtle dimension to sign interpretation.

Ruling Planets

Another lesson to be learned early in astrological studies is that each sign has a ruling planet.

The chart on page 35 lists the glyphs of the planets and (also in glyph form) the signs that they rule. Mercury and Venus both rule two signs, and before the discovery of the three modern planets (Uranus, Neptune and Pluto, in 1781, 1846 and 1930 respectively) Mars ruled Scorpio as well as Aries, Jupiter ruled Pisces as well as Sagittarius, and Saturn ruled Aquarius as well as Capricorn. The Sun and Moon have always ruled only one sign each. With the acceptance of Uranus, Neptune and Pluto in the astrological pantheon, however, certain rulerships were reassigned. Other planets may yet be discovered, and should that be the case there may well come a time when Mercury and Venus rule only one sign each, with the "new" planets, whatever they may be, taking over a sign still ruled by them. Time will tell.

You will find more about traditional and modern rulerships in "The Planets at Work" (pp.208-347). Certainly, it is reasonable to bear in mind their influence when you are interpreting.

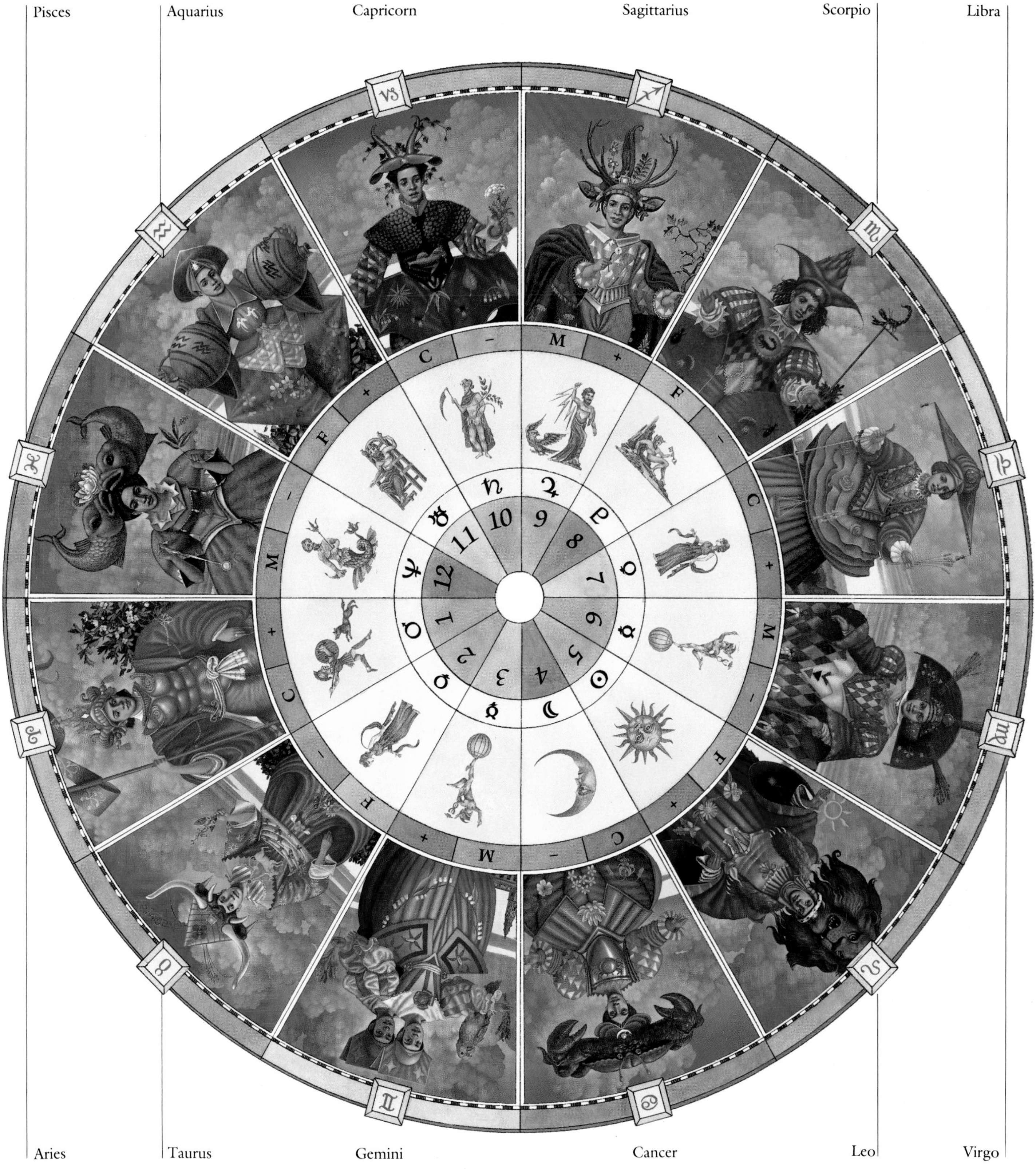

Pisces
Aquarius
Capricorn
Sagittarius
Scorpio
Libra
Aries
Taurus
Gemini
Cancer
Leo
Virgo

TRADITIONAL SIGN GROUPINGS
The birth chart style of this diagram shows the signs as they relate to the houses of the birth chart, with their ruling planets placed within them. Each traditional grouping of signs is also indicated: each house is either "masculine" or "feminine", shown in the middle ring; this ring also shows the qualities or quadruplicities; the elements or triplicities are shown in the outer and inner rings.

KEY

+ Masculine	Fire	C Cardinal
– Feminine	Earth	F Fixed
	Air	M Mutable
	Water	

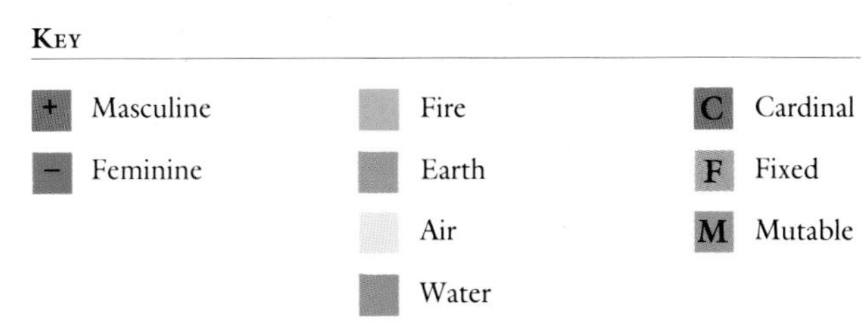

Planetary Traditions

The chart on the opposite page shows when planets are personalized (and so increased in strength), which sign they rule, and other traditional relationships they have with the signs.

Personal planets

The personal planets are: the Sun; the Moon; the planet ruling the Ascendant sign (the chart ruler); the planet ruling the Sun sign (the Sun ruler); and the planet ruling the sign occupied by the Moon (the Moon ruler).

Traditional relationships

Each planet rules one or two signs of the zodiac. These rulerships were decreed way back in the distant past. Each planet is exalted in a particular sign, from which it works well, and with the characteristics of which it has a sympathetic rapport. When a planet is placed in its sign of exaltation, its importance in an interpretation is marginally increased.

Each planet has a sign of detriment. This is the sign of the zodiac opposite the one it rules (its polar sign). Traditional astrology decrees that the planet works less well from this sign.

Each planet has a fall sign. This is the sign directly across the zodiac (again, the polar sign) from that in which it is exalted. Here, again, the planet was once thought to work less well. As with the signs of detriment, this is a factor to be kept in mind when interpreting a chart.

The modern planets

Since the discovery of the three modern planets (see p.21) – Uranus in 1781, Neptune in 1846 and Pluto in 1930 – there has been much discussion concerning the attribution of their rulerships, and the signs in which they may be exalted or in fall.

The signs of rulership, and therefore detriment, have, apart from the planet of Pluto (see p.35), long since been debated and finalized. As will be seen from the chart:

1. Uranus rules Aquarius, so the sign of its detriment is Leo.
2. Neptune rules Pisces, so the sign of its detriment is Virgo.
3. Pluto rules Scorpio, so the sign of its detriment is Taurus.

The Glyphs of the Signs and What They Represent

Sign	Glyph	What it Represents
Aries	♈	The Ram's Head
Taurus	♉	The Bull's Head
Gemini	♊	The Twins
Cancer	♋	Breasts
Leo	♌	The Lion's tail
Virgo	♍	Female Genitals
Libra	♎	A Pair of Scales
Scorpio	♏	Male Genitals
Sagittarius	♐	The Centaur's Arrow
Capricorn	♑	The Goat's Head and Fish's Tail
Aquarius	♒	Water Air Waves – the Ether
Pisces	♓	Two Fish

Planet	Glyph	Rulership
Sun	☉	♌ Leo
Moon	☽	♋ Cancer
Mercury	☿	♊ ♍ Gemini Virgo
Venus	♀	♉ ♎ Taurus Libra
Mars	♂	♈ Aries
Jupiter	♃	♐ Sagittarius
Saturn	♄	♑ Capricorn
Uranus	♅	♒ Aquarius
Neptune	♆	♓ Pisces
Pluto	♇ ⯓*	♏ Scorpio

* The alternative glyph for Pluto is sometimes used

There is more difficulty in determining the signs of exaltation. While most astrologers feel that Uranus is exalted in Scorpio (fall, Taurus), and that Neptune is exalted in Leo (fall, Aquarius), Pluto is still not finally placed.

Placing Pluto

Virgo, however, is a strong contender. Pluto was very much to the fore when in that sign and forming a conjunction with Uranus in the 1960s. Pluto's investigatory tendencies complement Virgoan analytical, researching qualities. Therefore we, and many others, feel that in spite of Mercury also being exalted in Virgo (its own sign), it is fair to place Pluto in that sign. Pluto's fall sign must therefore be Pisces (the polar sign of Virgo).

MUTUAL RECEPTION

Mutual reception occurs when Planet A is in a sign ruled by Planet B, and Planet B is in a sign ruled by Planet A. So, the Moon may be in Scorpio and Pluto in Cancer, or – as here – Mercury in Sagittarius and Jupiter in Gemini (or Virgo). The planets involved are in harmony and if they also make aspect to each other, the strength of that apect is slightly increased. Should the aspect be a square, opposition or minor negative aspect, any tension indicated will be mitigated, since the planets will strengthen the psychological integration of the subject. If both are personal planets the relationship between them will be more important.

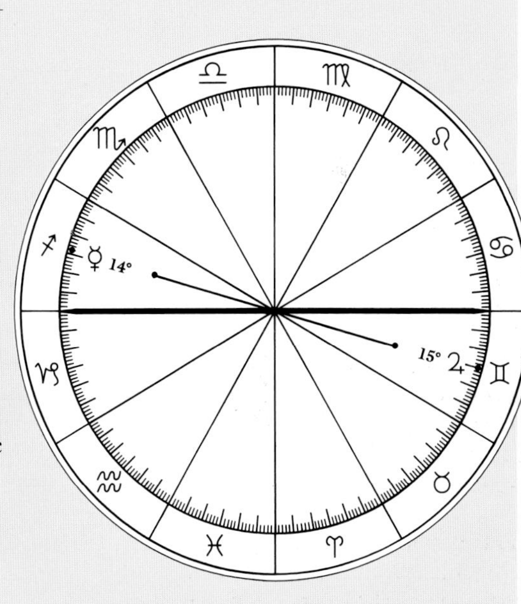

THE STRENGTH OF THE PLANETS

PLANET	WHEN PERSONALIZED	DOUBLY POWERFUL	INCREASED IN STRENGTH	RULES	EXALTED	DETRIMENT	FALL
☉	Always personal	If ☌ Asc from 1st or 12th house If ☉ and Asc are same sign Even more powerful if ☉ Asc are ♌	☉ in ♌ (greatly) ☉ in 5th house	♌	♈	♒	♎
☽	Always personal	If Asc is ♋ or ☽ ☌ Asc from 1st or 12th house If ☉ ☌ ☽ in ♋	☉ in ♋ ☽ in ♋ ☽ in 4th house	♋	♉	♑	♏
☿	If ☉, ☽ Asc = ♊ or ♍	If ♊ or ♍ Asc and ☿ ☌ Asc from 1st or 12th house	☿ in ♊ or ♍ ☿ in 3rd or 6th house	♊ ♍	♍	♐	♓
♀	If ☉, ☽ Asc = ♉ or ♎	If ♉ or ♎ Asc and ♀ ☌ Asc from 1st or 12th house	♀ in ♉ or ♎ ♀ in 2nd or 7th house	♉ ♎	♓	♈	♍
♂	If ☉, ☽ Asc = ♈	If ♈ is Asc and ♂ ☌ Asc from 1st (especially strong) or 12th house (less so)	♂ in ♈ (considerably) ♂ in 1st house	♈ *♏	♑	♎	♋
♃	If ☉, ☽ Asc = ♐	If ♐ is Asc and ♃ ☌ Asc from 1st or 12th house (especially strong)	♃ in ♐ ♃ in 9th house ♃ in ♓ (somewhat)	♐ **♓	♋	♊	♑
♄	If ☉, ☽ Asc = ♑	If ♑ is Asc and ♄ ☌ Asc from 1st or 12th house	♄ in ♑ ♄ in 10th house ♄ ☌ MC, ♄ in ♒ (somewhat)	♑ ***♒	♎	♋	♈
♅	If ☉, ☽ Asc = ♒	If ♒ is Asc and ♅ ☌ Asc from 1st or 12th house (births 1912–9 approx.)	♅ in ♒ ♅ in 11th house	♒	♏	♌	♉
♆	If ☉, ☽ Asc = ♓	There is no one alive with ♆ in ♓	♆ in ♓ (after AD 2012) ♆ in 12th house	♓	♌	♍	♒
♇	If ☉, ☽ Asc = ♏	If ♏ is Asc and ♇ ☌ Asc from 1st or 12th house	♇ in ♏ (those born 1984–95) ♇ in 8th house	♏	♍	♉	♓

* Before Pluto was discovered Mars also ruled Scorpio

** Before Neptune was discovered Jupiter also ruled Pisces

*** Before Uranus was discovered Saturn also ruled Aquarius

The Ascendant and Midheaven

Although there now exist computer programs from which finished birth charts can be printed, almost every professional astrologer prefers to draw or at least re-draw the chart to be studied. In that way, a picture of the client emerges as the chart slowly grows before one's eyes – almost as a portrait sketch slowly becomes recognizable as the major characteristics fall into place on the paper. The business of interpretation begins almost with the first lines which are drawn. And those first lines will be the Ascendant and Midheaven: these are the crucial calculations that you will find will affect the interpretation of the whole birth chart.

THE ASCENDANT

The Ascendant – the degree of the ecliptic rising over the eastern horizon at the moment of birth – is the starting point of an astrological chart interpretation. It indicates the foundation of the personality, and shows how a subject adapts to his or her environment. The effect of the Ascendant has been compared to that of dawn – the approaching light which begins to illuminate the complexities of a human landscape. Just as one's birthday (or solar return, as astrologers call it) represents an individual New Year's Day, so the Ascendant represents the start of that day. It is by it, and the influence of any planet or planets about to rise at the same moment, that we must gear our interpretation.

Revealing the traits of close friends

The Ascendant shows us as we really are. When you are working on your first few charts (which ideally should be of people you know really well) it is a good idea to talk about the personality traits suggested by the Ascending sign to people who don't know the subjects concerned very well. The chances are that they will neither agree with you nor even understand what you are getting at – for the traits suggested by the Ascendant emerge only when one really knows the person concerned. A few experiments along these lines will make the difference between the Ascendant and Sun sign perfectly clear.

If you consider the chart of someone who is a mere acquaintance rather than a close friend, you will find outer expression and image revealing itself very clearly, in almost every case, through the Sun sign. It has been pointed out that this fact is underlined, in our own time, because most people grow up with a knowledge of what "a Taurean" or "a Geminian" is "supposed to be like", and can tend to start behaving – perhaps unconsciously – in a way characteristic to the sign.

Noticeable characteristics

Some astrologers argue that it is the characteristics of the Ascendant which are immediately noticeable. But to take a superficial example, a Sun sign Leo woman with Sagittarius rising is far more likely to go to the supermarket in her smartest winter coat (Leo image) than to a formal occasion dressed very casually (Sagittarius motivation and personality trait). If Sagittarius were the Sun sign and Leo rising, the image would be casual, but those who knew the person will would probably be aware that, in spite of an excellent sense of humor and an informal approach, she could well be autocratic and bossy (Leo rising).

Changes by progression

When the Ascendant changes signs by progression, the subject will tend to absorb some of the personality traits of the new sign, adding them very subtly to those of the original Ascendant. For instance, someone born with Gemini rising will probably become more caring, intuitive and emotional when the Ascendant progresses into Cancer. Asked about this, they would probably say that they now feel differently about things, and find that (for the first time ever) they are beginning to trust their instincts. Geminian scepticism and mistrust of the emotional responses will ease, and there will be a strengthening of intuition and insight; Geminian curiosity will be spiced with a "knowing" quality which the individual will find hard to explain.

The importance of the Ascendant

To sum up, the general rule when drawing up interpretations must be always to remember the Ascending sign. When a trait emerges from another area of the chart which is similar to, or complements, one associated with the Ascendant, it will be a really important attribute. Without the Ascendant – that is, when no birth time is available – astrology is limited; an essential element of the structure is missing.

THE MIDHEAVEN

The Midheaven or Medium Coeli (MC) marks the degree of the zodiac that is, quite simply, at the top of the sky at the moment and place of birth.

To understand fully this angle of the chart, one must know something about the way in which astrologers divide space. There are several systems (see p.38); whichever system is used, it is the Midheaven that tells us what our subject identifies with in life. The characteristics of the sign on the Midheaven will be important to him or her – they will be recognized and admired, and a subject will consciously or unconsciously aim to express them. They are not necessarily part of the sign on the Midheaven: a Libran MC does not give someone the characteristics of a Libran, but that person would identify with the qualities that are most important to Librans.

Progressions or transits

Here, too, is the area of the chart that is usually activated by progression or transit when events or developments occur as a direct result of the intervention of other people. In simple terms, if we decide we want a new job and apply for one, it would probably be as a result of the influence of the psychological motivation marked by our

Ascendant. But if we are unexpectedly offered a job, it will be shown by an important progression or transit to the Midheaven. Remember that we have some control over the events in our lives, and that if an offer is made to us it is probably because our efforts, achievements and reputation are known to and recognized by others. Whilst this is a simplification of this area of the chart, it gives an indication of what it means.

THE IMUM COELI

The Imum Coeli, or IC, marks the point in the sky (above the surface of the Earth immediately opposite us on the other side of the globe) immediately beneath us at the moment of our birth. It symbolizes our roots, and relates strongly to the matters governed by the fourth house.

THE DESCENDANT

This is the degree of the ecliptic which is setting below the western horizon at the moment of birth. It is always the cusp of the seventh house, the house of partnerships, and therefore invariably relates to it. The IC and Descendant are often omitted from conventional chart drawings.

CHANGES IN THE BIRTH CHART

As a general rule, as we grow older and our birth charts age with us, the Ascendant and Midheaven will in time move from one sign to the next. Provided the birth time is really accurate (and this is vital – an error of four minutes represents a 12-month difference in a progressed chart) the periods during which the Ascendant and Midheaven change signs will mark the key years in a lifetime.

Likely changes

Personal development and a change of emotional attitude will be likely to occur when the Ascendant progresses into a neighboring sign, while external changes, perhaps relating to the career, will be likely to occur when the Midheaven changes signs.

The Houses

There are many systems of house division – ways of artificially dividing up the space surrounding the Earth. The most common was devised by Placidus in c.1688, which is based on the time taken for each degree of the ecliptic to move from Ascendant to Midheaven. But this system becomes worthless when dealing with births in extreme northern latitudes, for it becomes impossible to calculate a rising degree. Other systems occasionally used are those of Regiomontanus and Campanus; but the oldest and simplest system is the Equal House system, which we use in this book.

Each house represents a sphere of human life, so it is by using the houses that we can discover in which field of everyday life the planets' movements are likely to affect us. Very roughly,

- The planets represent motivation.
- The signs show how we will direct or use that motivation.
- The houses show in which sphere of life that motivation and effort will be manifested.

Personalized planets

The houses have another significance, however, for if a planet is personalized (see p.34) there will be an additional psychological effect. So, someone with a Virgo Sun sign and with Mercury in Libra in the fifth house will probably have a love of beauty (Libra), the ability to use their hands creatively (Mercury in Libra) and creative potential (fifth house). In addition, because Mercury is the ruling planet of Virgo, there will be a strong psychological need to express that creativity.

This kind of "personalization" is not unusual, and it is important for would-be astrologers not to regard the Sun sign, planet and house as the only indications of motivation, direction and sphere of life. Sometimes a personal planetary placing merely offers an additional emphasis, but more often there is a deep-rooted psychological implication. Planet, sign and house will "shine brightly" in such cases.

Some houses have greater importance than others, and add greater strength to any planets inhabiting them. The main focus falls on the first, fourth, sixth, seventh, tenth and twelfth houses, and the one containing the Midheaven. But in practice the astrologer must, of course, concentrate on the houses relevant to a particular problem. For instance, if there are difficulties at work, and the sixth house is covered by Gemini (ruled by Mercury), the reaction would probably be to discuss it and resolve it in that way.

Usually, several houses in any chart will be empty, unoccupied by planets. The spheres of life they cover are still important: the sign covering the house should be observed, and the planet ruling that sign considered – it will give a good lead as to how the subject reacts to the affairs of the house concerned.

What the houses represent

A traditional rule concerning the houses is that the first six have a personal application, whereas the others relate to more external matters and other people. For instance, as the first house is the most personal, so the seventh (its polar house right across the chart) represents the subject's attitude toward partners. The second house represents possessions, whereas the eighth represents invested and inherited money. The fourth house relates to home, the tenth to matters outside the home, and career and ambition.

1 The First House

The house of Aries and Mars
Keywords: Psychological motivation, well-being

This is the most important house of the birth chart, since it covers the Ascendant, or rising sign. It is through this house that personality will be shown. Health and well-being, attitude and temperament will be revealed here, and physical characteristics are also disclosed by this house and the Ascendant. If there is a planet here, especially within 8 or 10° of the Ascendant, it will exert a powerful influence on the personality and strongly color both the characteristics of the Ascendant and matters affected by the first house itself. The planet is also likely to influence strongly the subject's appearance and behavior patterns – the whole of the persona.

When planets progress into or transit the first house the planet involved will lay a powerful emphasis on all personal matters, particularly health, physical and psychological. The Moon (by progression) can indicate a minor new cycle. Saturn by transit could indicate the beginning of a period when the individual's vitality might be low. Events concerning the individual on a personal level will be in focus. The individual must be encouraged to take advantage of the ways in which different planets will work for them from this house.

2 The Second House

The house of Taurus and Venus
Keywords: Possessions, feelings

The subject's attitude towards security, possessions and partners are second house matters (although love affairs are the domain of the fifth house). By studying the second house you may find it possible to glean some

indication of how the subject copes with partners. Is there a tendency to think of a lover or child as a possession? To answer this, look to the sign on the cusp of this house or to any planet placed in it. Remember that money and love are closely connected (see Venus, p.149) and that this connection will probably make its presence felt when you are interpreting the house. Similarly there is a powerful link between emotional and financial security.

Make quite sure that the emotional needs (vis-à-vis security) are not obscured or stifled by the financial and material ones, and remember they usually complement each other – indeed it is often the case that one need cannot be fully satisfied unless the other is, too. This is particularly important when assessing progressed planetary positions and transits. Be alert to the possibility that if your subject has, for instance, developed a weight problem, it could well be due to a gap in the emotional life. If on the other hand the subject has become over-generous and "silly" with money or possessions, ask yourself whether this is the result of an impulse to "buy" love, friendship and affection.

3 THE THIRD HOUSE

The house of Gemini and Mercury

KEYWORDS: Brothers, sisters, transport, environment, early education

This house is concerned with near relatives (other than parents): with brothers and sisters, uncles, aunts and cousins. It also has a bearing on the subject's response to school life, and on his or her powers of communication and day-to-day traveling. If the subject wants to change cars, then you should look to the third house of the chart. Mental attitude is also under the rulership of this house, and it can be used to support the way in which the subject finds full self-expression. It is worth assessing this house from the point of view of personal environment, since the decision to live in the town or the country, and how subjects cope with noise, crowds or isolation, are concerns of the third house. Speech, the chief means of communication, is also a third house issue. When planets progress into or transit this house the individual will often experience a change of mind and may adopt new attitudes. If a young person has been having a bad time at school, that could change under such a transit or progression because his efforts to think differently will be stimulated. For anyone in a deadlock situation, a positive third house influence will put them in a better position to move forward and make mental adjustments. Problems with close relatives may be traced to the third house, but this is not the house that relates to parents or one's children, though there is a connection between it and young people, so your children's friends would be a third house matter.

4 THE FOURTH HOUSE

The house of Cancer and the Moon

KEYWORDS: Home, domestic life, parents (especially the mother)

Here we move into the important realm of home and family background, and here, too, the role of the subject's parents is focused (as it is to some extent in the tenth house). It is from the fourth house that we can see how subjects regard their parents. It is important to be cautious in any comments to a subject on this matter, for unless the full birth charts of the parents are available it is of course impossible to discover their astrological background. When working on the charts of children for their parents (in which case you should always take the parents' birth data) a study of the fourth house may enable you to offer some hints as to how the child will see the parents, and indeed how the child will react to each individual parent – though again, to get the full picture you must refer back to a the full family profile as shown in the charts of the different generations.

Homes and land are also among fourth house concerns. It is likely that when there are progressions or transits through this house the individual's home life will be in focus. Most planets work in a variety of ways to bring about changes, so ask your subject whether change in this sphere of the life is possible, inevitable, or simply longed for. A strong emphasis on this house in either birth or progressed chart can also mean that the subject is concerned with the past. It may be necessary to encourage a more forward-looking outlook.

5 THE FIFTH HOUSE

The house of Leo and the Sun

KEYWORDS: Creativity, pleasure, children, love affairs, risk-taking, father

Here is the house of creativity. Creativity is not only related to the arts; it can be expressed through the application of such practical skills as cooking or car maintenance – so do not under-estimate what creative potential is shown through the fifth house, especially if the chart as a whole shows, say, mathematical or scientific flair: both these can be spiced with lively creativity. Perhaps one of the most important aspects of creativity relates to parenthood – the parents' relationship with their children, rather than the childrens' relationship with the parents, which is governed by the fourth house. Look also at this house for indications of the subject's reaction to procreation. This lively, positive house also relates to pleasure, speculation, and the way in which we express instinctive affection.

This, too, is the domain of lovers. When a new affair begins, the chances are that the event will be observable in the fifth house. (It is to the seventh we must look for signs of deep emotional involvement or commitment). The dangers inherent in some fifth house emphases can include over-optimism or a devil-may-care attitude. Such tendencies will show up clearly in the progressed chart, as indeed in the birth chart. Do not hesitate to warn your subject if there is an emphasis on speculation, either by progression or transit – or should that particular trait emerge in the assessment of the birth chart. A love of risk is not difficult to interpret from the sign on the cusp of the fifth house, or if certain planets (like Mars and Jupiter) are tenanted in it.

6

The Sixth House

The house of Virgo and Mercury

Keywords: *Health, diet, exercise, hobbies, routine work*

This house is related to health, diet and exercise, and therefore has an important influence on our general well-being. Its influence is not the same as that of the first house, which is more physical. It is as if this house shows us how we treat our bodies. It also relates to our daily round of work – what we must do, whether in a busy career or in the running of a home and the bringing up of a family. From this house it is possible to ascertain how disciplined and systematic your subject is – whether a slave to routine or a victim of disorganization.

Old astrological books include servants among the sixth house concerns. We now say that the sixth house governs our attitude to the people we summon to help us: the plumber, the electrician, the decorator. Transits and progressions to planets in this house focus on all of these matters. Keeping in good physical shape is important: from the sixth house it is possible for you to assess times when your subject will benefit most from new exercise schedules and regimens, or perhaps some sort of change of diet.

7

The Seventh House

The house of Libra and Venus

Keywords: *Partnerships, relationships*

It is not only emotional relationships that are focused here, though the prime function of the house is to comment on these. Here we also see the individual's attitude to colleagues and one-to-one relationships. Planets placed in this house will have a powerful effect on this attitude, especially if the planet is within 8 or 10° of the cusp of the seventh house – in other words if it forms an opposition aspect (see p.54) to the Ascendant. It is important to stress the relationship between the fifth house – the house of love affairs – and the seventh house – the house of partnerships. The seventh is the house of commitment, and reflects the deep-rooted needs of the individual in this area, often giving a vital clue to what the subject needs most from a partner. This house can indicate what sort of partner the subject will look for, and – because of its relationship to Libra – the harmony, balance and fairness within the relationship can be studied here: how much is needed, or how independent and self-contained the subject may be.

As hinted above, it is to this house you must also look when your subject is considering setting up a business partnership, or if there is a question of hiring a personal assistant, but only as far as rapport and personal understanding are concerned. Indeed, rapport is one of the most vital factors of this house, as will be seen when you study the section of the book covering the huge question of relationships in detail (see pp.148-67). Be alert whenever you discover a progression or transit to the seventh house, for the question of relationships will almost certainly be focused. Even if your subject is happily unattached, you may find that some surrogate partner, or perhaps a pet or an all-consuming hobby, may be uppermost in their mind or life-style.

8

The Eighth House

The house of Scorpio and Pluto

Keywords: *Sex, inheritance, investment*

The second house represents money acquired by the individual's efforts; the eighth house is linked to endowments and inheritance. But this is also very much the house of self-searching, with clues to the subject's attitude to death and the after-life. "Death" can also mean change; re-birth can also be assessed here – new beginnings that occur when the individual has come to terms with deep-rooted psychological problems after periods of psychotherapy, or, even more poignantly, self-analysis.

The eighth is also the house of the life force, so sexual instincts and needs are also in focus here. Tradition decrees that it is also the house of crime, research and investigation. Pluto should always be studied with reference to this house, and the eighth sign of the zodiac, Scorpio, but do not forget that Pluto is a "generation influence". On a practical as opposed to a psychological level, it is this house that should be studied when a subject is considering investment or the acquisition of insurance policies. From the sexual point of view it is not the simple,

Traditional Astrology
This astrologer's wheel, which shows the planets, signs and houses all revolving round the Earth, formed the title page of an astrological treatise by Georg von Purbach published in 1515.

pleasurable fun-and-games aspect of sex that is in focus, but the most deep-rooted sexual urges. It is possible to assess whether these are being fulfilled, although you may find that this will challenge your interpretative skills. Transits and progressions to planets in the eighth house will more than likely focus on issues that have a deep meaning and significance to the individual. The outlook on problems could change as a result, especially if the subject is distressed – particularly if they have been having ongoing psychological difficulties. If the transits are favorable you could perhaps suggest therapy or specific professional help to try to resolve these difficulties.

9

THE NINTH HOUSE

The house of Sagittarius and Jupiter
KEYWORDS: Higher education, long-distance travel, ideals, dreams, challenge

The ninth house focuses on further education, and the abilities to communicate and extend our minds. Here are clues to our idealistic and philosophical outlook and opinions on spiritual questions. Long-distance travel is also a ninth house matter. The law, publishing and literature are covered by this house, as are long-distance communications and areas of the media relating to foreign countries. Language skills, dreams and inspiration are accented here, as are moral code and conscience. This house should be carefully studied in the case, for instance, of someone leaving school and deciding about further education.

The ninth house could help if there is a question of travel for a young person, although you should consider whether any psychological problems will be resolved by "getting away from it all". If the influences from this house in the birth chart are positive, this is an excellent indication for someone who wants to live abroad, work in the travel industry or export trade, and for teaching – usually at university level. Sportsmanship and the capacity for study are also to some extent concerns of this house, and often a sense of vocation is indicated. Such indications are enhanced if there are strong aspects to Jupiter.

10

THE TENTH HOUSE

The house of Capricorn and Saturn
KEYWORDS: Aspirations and ambitions

Note: In many systems of house division the cusp of the tenth house is always on the Midheaven. This is not the case when using the Equal House system (as in this book).

This is the house of aspiration and worldly progress. Here also is authority – how we cope with it when it is delegated to us, and how we express it to others. There is also accent on social status, the family, tradition, the sense of duty and all matters outside the home. How the individual copes with responsibility and power can be assessed. If a personal planet is placed in this house there is usually a powerful need for emotional involvement in a career. Although modern astrology is anything but fatalistic, this house is sometimes sharply in focus by progression or transit when "destiny" (whatever the individual means by that) takes a hand, and what can seem like burdensome responsibility is in fact increased prestige and status. It is to the tenth house that one must look when career changes are likely, and any change that will increase a subject's status or involve additional responsibility.

11

THE ELEVENTH HOUSE

The house of Aquarius and Uranus
KEYWORDS: Social life, objectives, social conscience, friends

This is the house of friends and our social life. Objectives in life – those which are not career oriented – are eleventh house concerns. So is our attitude to the suffering in the world, ecology and so on. By assessing the state of this house it is possible to ascertain how much energy an individual is willing to spend furthering good causes, and whether the reasons for doing so are self-centered or altruistic. Consider this house when assessing how well the individual will cope with membership on a committee or has to assume some important office. Transits of, or progressed aspects to, planets in this house may well focus on these matters; it is not a very powerful house, but adds an extra dimension when one is assessing a personality in relation to other people. Do not underestimate it if Aquarius or Uranus is personalized.

12

THE TWELFTH HOUSE

The house of Pisces and Neptune
KEYWORDS: Seclusion, escapism, faith, institutions

This is the house of seclusion and escapism. By tradition it is linked to hospitals and prisons, but there are equally if not more important areas under its rulership. Here is often a powerful indicator of the nature of the unconscious, and of the root of psychological problems. As the eighth house represents the means by which we can come to terms with such difficulties, the twelfth will help us decide their fundamental nature. This is particularly the case if a planet is within 10° of the Ascendant, when the concerns of the planet in question are "buried" and perhaps need to be externalized. Planets transiting the twelfth house or progressions to planets in it may have an inhibiting effect, but at their best encourage us to be reflective, giving serious constructive thought to important issues. Sometimes such influences herald good work done behind the scenes, or perhaps work for a charity. Sacrifice is a twelfth house matter, and can be a theme when the house is in focus; in the end the individual will usually benefit, since strengthening of the character and the realization that psychological problems must be resolved will often be the result.

Calculating the Birth Chart

When drawing up a birth chart you must calculate the positions of the Sun, Moon and planets at the exact moment for which the chart is required. This was once done with logarithms, but pocket calculators now make it easier, although it can be hard to find ones which translate decimals into degrees and minutes. The ephemeris in this book (p.350) therefore gives the planetary positions in degrees and decimal points, and we show how to calculate these positions to a good level of accuracy.

1 PREPARING THE BIRTH CHART

First, trace or photocopy the birth chart, using the example on p.408.

2 CALCULATING THE ASCENDANT AND MIDHEAVEN

The process differs slightly according to whether the place of birth is east or west of Greenwich.

West of Greenwich

For our sample birth chart we have chosen a fictitious person born in Washington DC, USA, on 4 July 1981 at 4.19 a.m. local time. Enter the birth place, date and time on the chart.

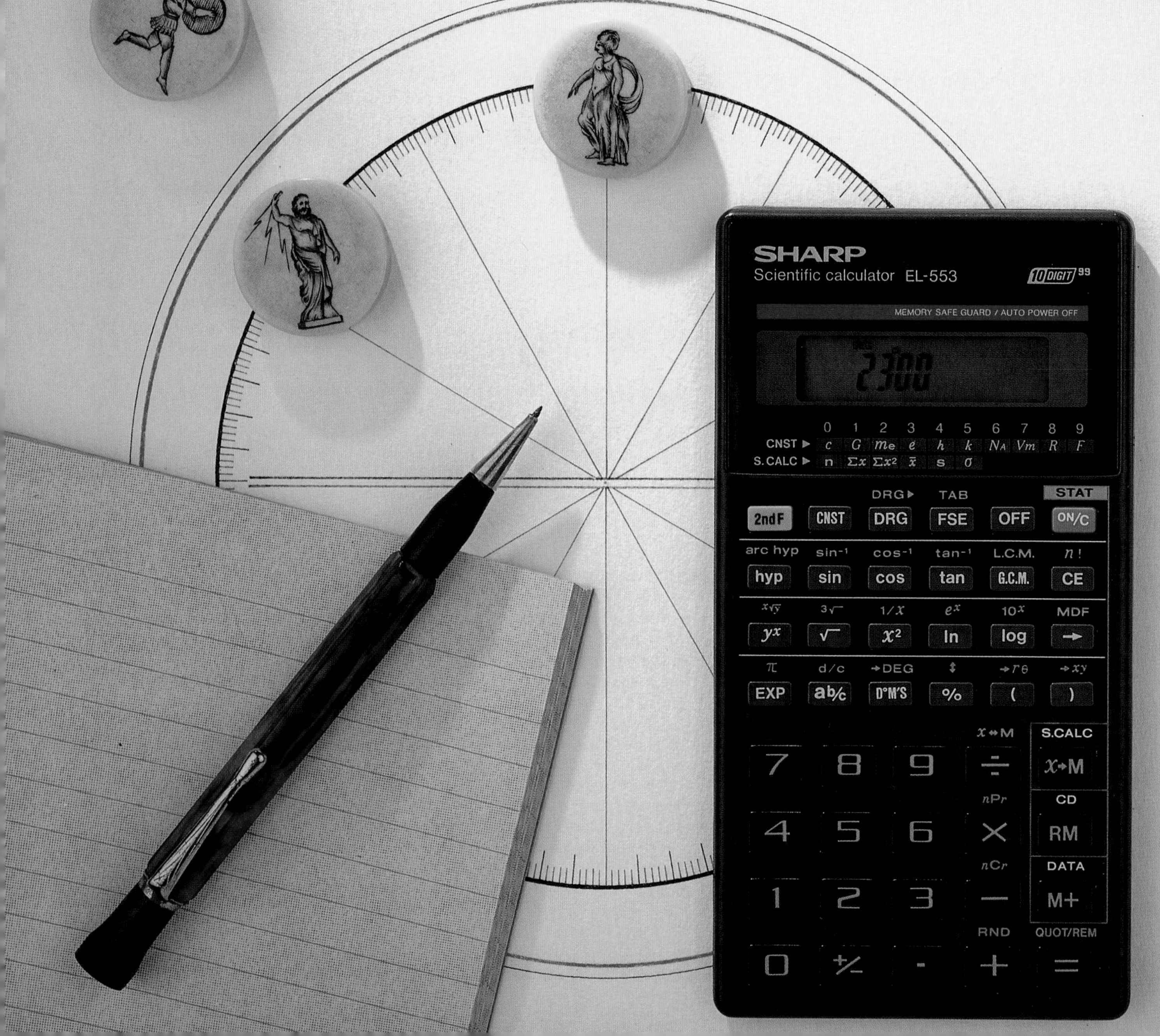

LONGITUDE TIME CORRECTION

DEGREES									MINUTES		
°	h	m	°	h	m	°	h	m	m	m	s
1	0	4	61	4	4	121	8	4	1	0	4
2	0	8	62	4	8	122	8	8	2	0	8
3	0	12	63	4	12	123	8	12	3	0	12
4	0	16	64	4	16	124	8	16	4	0	16
5	0	20	65	4	20	125	8	20	5	0	20
6	0	24	66	4	24	126	8	24	6	0	24
7	0	28	67	4	28	127	8	28	7	0	28
8	0	32	68	4	32	128	8	32	8	0	32
9	0	36	69	4	36	129	8	36	9	0	36
10	0	40	70	4	40	130	8	40	10	0	40
11	0	44	71	4	44	131	8	44	11	0	44
12	0	48	72	4	48	132	8	48	12	0	48
13	0	52	73	4	52	133	8	52	13	0	52
14	0	56	74	4	56	134	8	56	14	0	56
15	1	0	75	5	0	135	9	0	15	1	0
16	1	4	76	5	4	136	9	4	16	1	4
17	1	8	77	5	8	137	9	8	17	1	8
18	1	12	78	5	12	138	9	12	18	1	12
19	1	16	79	5	16	139	9	16	19	1	16
20	1	20	80	5	20	140	9	20	20	1	20
21	1	24	81	5	24	141	9	24	21	1	24
22	1	28	82	5	28	142	9	28	22	1	28
23	1	32	83	5	32	143	9	32	23	1	32
24	1	36	84	5	36	144	9	36	24	1	36
25	1	40	85	5	40	145	9	40	25	1	40
26	1	44	86	5	44	146	9	44	26	1	44
27	1	48	87	5	48	147	9	48	27	1	48
28	1	52	88	5	52	148	9	52	28	1	52
29	1	56	89	5	56	149	9	56	29	1	56
30	2	0	90	6	0	150	10	0	30	2	0
31	2	4	91	6	4	151	10	4	31	2	4
32	2	8	92	6	8	152	10	8	32	2	8
33	2	12	93	6	12	153	10	12	33	2	12
34	2	16	94	6	16	154	10	16	34	2	16
35	2	20	95	6	20	155	10	20	35	2	20
36	2	24	96	6	24	156	10	24	36	2	24
37	2	28	97	6	28	157	10	28	37	2	28
38	2	32	98	6	32	158	10	32	38	2	32
39	2	36	99	6	36	159	10	36	39	2	36
40	2	40	100	6	40	160	10	40	40	2	40
41	2	44	101	6	44	161	10	44	41	2	44
42	2	48	102	6	48	162	10	48	42	2	48
43	2	52	103	6	52	163	10	52	43	2	52
44	2	56	104	6	56	164	10	56	44	2	56
45	3	0	105	7	0	165	11	0	45	3	0
46	3	4	106	7	4	166	11	4	46	3	4
47	3	8	107	7	8	167	11	8	47	3	8
48	3	12	108	7	12	168	11	12	48	3	12
49	3	16	109	7	16	169	11	16	49	3	16
50	3	20	110	7	20	170	11	20	50	3	20
51	3	24	111	7	24	171	11	24	51	3	24
52	3	28	112	7	28	172	11	28	52	3	28
53	3	32	113	7	32	173	11	32	53	3	32
54	3	36	114	7	36	174	11	36	54	3	36
55	3	40	115	7	40	175	11	40	55	3	40
56	3	44	116	7	44	176	11	44	56	3	44
57	3	48	117	7	48	177	11	48	57	3	48
58	3	52	118	7	52	178	11	52	58	3	52
59	3	56	119	7	56	179	11	56	59	3	56
60	4	0	120	8	0	180	12	0	60	4	0

SOUTHERN LATITUDES

A small conversion allows us to use northern latitude tables to give the Ascendant and Midheaven of births in southern latitudes. If we use the same birth time, but set it for Perth, Western Australia (31° 57' S, 115° 52' E), the calculation goes:

3.08 + 7.40 + 0.03 = 10.51.

10.51 is the true ST of birth. The calculations which follow are given merely to enable you to use northern tables in southern latitudes.

The Midheaven is at 11° Virgo, but to find the Ascendant for a southern latitude add 12 hours to the ST, then turn to the table of houses (see pp.396-9) to find the Ascendant degree. The sign involved will be the opposite of the one shown. Therefore, for 10.51 take 22.51, which gives us an Ascendant of 29° Gemini – the true Ascendant is therefore 29° Sagittarius.

(i) Consult an atlas for the latitude and longitude of the place of birth. For Washington this is 38° 52' N, 77° 01' W. Enter the latitude and longitude on the birth chart form.

(ii) Convert the local time to Greenwich Mean Time (GMT). Local summer time (Daylight Saving Time) may have been in force during the time of year that your subject was born. The Bibliography (see p.405) lists some reference books which will help you check this.

In our example, summer time was in force, so the clocks were an hour ahead and the local standard time was therefore 3.19 a.m. You must now convert this to GMT. Consult the table of zone standard times on p.401. This shows that Washington is five hours behind Greenwich, so you must add five hours to the local standard time – the GMT time of birth becomes 8.19 a.m. Enter this on the birth chart form.

When converting the local birth time to GMT, the birth date may change, either moving forwards to the next day, or back to the previous day. Check this, and place the corrected GMT date in the space on the form.

From now on, we will use the GMT time and date in our calculations.

(iii) The Ascendant and Midheaven are found by converting the GMT birth time into sidereal time (ST).

Turn to the table on pp.392-5. This will show you the sidereal time for the date in question. However, this must be slightly corrected for each year: the extra minutes you must add to the sidereal time are shown in the small table. In our example, the sidereal time for 4 July is 18.45.50. The correction is 1.51. Therefore, ST = 18.47.41. Enter this on the form.

(iv) This is, however, the ST for midnight (the beginning of the day) at Greenwich. You must now convert the ST to the time of birth (still at Greenwich) by adding the time of birth to the ST. So, enter 8.19, and add this to the first figure:

18.47.41 + 8.19 = 27.06 (remember, there are 60 minutes to the hour!)

(v) Sidereal time represents a clock that appears to gain about four minutes a day. The technical term for this is the "acceleration of the time interval". It is normally necessary to take account of this, though if the interval is three hours or less you can ignore it.

If the interval is between:
3 and 9 hours – add 1 minute;
9 and 15 hours – add 2 minutes;
15 and 21 hours – add 3 minutes;
21 and 24 hours – add 4 minutes.

The precise rule is to add 10 seconds per hour, 1 second per 6 minutes, but generally the above suggestion will be accurate enough.

In our example we will add one minute; so that the ST becomes 27.07.

(vi) The ST result we now have is the true sidereal time of birth – had the subject been born at Greenwich! However, since that is not the case we must now adjust this ST to become the ST for the place of birth – in our example, Washington DC.

The table on this page is used to convert the degrees and minutes of the longitude of the place of birth into time – the hours and minutes you must add to or subtract from the ST. To do this, *subtract* for places west of Greenwich and *add* for places east of Greenwich. (This is known technically as the longitude equivalent.)

In our example, the table for the degrees gives 5.08, and the table for the minutes gives 0 minutes. Enter the longitude equivalent in time on the birth chart form.

So, ST = 27.07 – 5.08 – 0.00 = 21.59, which is the true ST of birth for Washington DC. Enter this on the birth chart form.

For northern latitudes, calculation of the local ST is now complete. If the birth place is south of the Equator, refer to the box on the left.

Note: If the ST exceeds 24 hours, deduct 24 hours from the total. If the longitude equivalent must be subtracted and is greater than the ST (giving a minus figure), add 24 hours to the ST before doing your subtraction.

(vii) The Midheaven and Ascendant are found by referring to the table of houses (pp.396-9). In the column next to the ST that is closest to the one calculated, you will find the Midheaven (MC). Now refer to the relevant latitude column and, where it intercepts the appropriate ST, you will find the Ascendant.

Note: When finding the Midheaven and Ascendant, we round both figures to the nearest whole degree – i.e. 2.3° becomes 2°, 3.5° becomes 4°. In our example, the Midheaven is 27.8° Aquarius, which we will round up to 28° Aquarius, and the Ascendant is 21° Gemini.

East of Greenwich

If the birth takes place east of Greenwich, e.g. in Moscow (55° 45' N, 37° 35' E), but at the same GMT on the same date, there is only one adjustment that you should be make to your calculations. This affects the longitude equivalent, which is *added* in this case.

So, the ST calculation is now:

3.07 (i.e. 27.07 – 24) + 2.28 + 0.02 = 5.37.

Referring to the table of Houses for Northern Latitudes (see pp.396-9), we find that the Midheaven is 25° Gemini, and the Ascendant is 26° Virgo. (Note the difference the latitude makes to the positions of the Midheaven and Ascendant.)

3 CALCULATING THE PLANETS' POSITIONS

Our ephemeris (see pp.350-89) gives the positions of the Sun, Moon and planets for each day at 0 hours GMT (midnight), expressed in degrees and decimals rather than in degrees, minutes and seconds.

The necessary calculations thereby become much simpler and are identical for the Sun, Moon and each of the planets. Using a pocket calculator, follow this process:

(i) Discover the diurnal proportion: i.e. the birth time expressed as a fraction of the day of birth. To do this, on a typical pocket calculator:

Divide the minutes by 60, add the number of hours and divide the result by 24. Store the final result in the calculator's memory.

In the example we are using, you should enter 19 ÷ 60 + 8 = ÷ 24 to give an answer of .346527. Store this in the memory. Note that it is the diurnal proportion, a constant, which is used in the following calculations, but it is not otherwise important.

The following steps apply to Sun, Moon, Mercury, Venus and Mars.

(ii) From the position for the day after the GMT date (call this *tomorrow*), deduct the position for the GMT date (call this *today*), multiplying the result by the constant and adding the today position.

In terms of your calculator, this can be written as tomorrow – today = constant in memory + today = result.

In our example (for 4 July 1981) the calculation for the Sun is:

12.9 – 11.9 = memory (.346527) + 11.9 = 12.24: i.e. 12.2° Cancer.

For the Moon:

24.8 – 11.2 = memory + 11.2 =15.91: i.e. 15.9° Leo.

(iii) The positions of Jupiter, Saturn, Uranus, Neptune, and Pluto are taken straight from the ephemeris. If a planet is retrograde (see p.23) the above formula still applies, but remember to mark the position with an "R".

(iv) Occasionally, and quite often in the case of the Moon, a planet will change signs between one day and the next. This requires a small change in the formula. For example, were the subject born at the same time on 10 July, the Moon would have moved from 27.5° Libra to 9.4° Scorpio during the day. The degrees would then be counted as though there were no division between the signs.

In our example, although the Moon would be on 9.4° Scorpio at the end of the day, we will call the position 39.4°. So it is from 39.4° that you deduct 27.5°. The calculator formula will be:

39.4 – 27.5 = memory + 27.5 = 31.62°

But there are 30° in every sign, so subtract 30° to make the Moon's position 1.6° Scorpio.

Having calculated the positions of the planets and Ascendant, check them once again for accuracy.

(v) Referring to the list of planets' groupings (see p.35), enter the planets, Ascendant and Midheaven in their traditional groupings (see p.45).

CALCULATING THE ASCENDANT

To check the accuracy of the Ascendant calculations note the points described below.

Note: When checking the accuracy of the Ascendant calculations, you must use the birth time of the birth location, not the GMT position. Do not forget to make allowances for British Summer Time or Daylight Saving Time if it was operative at the time of birth.

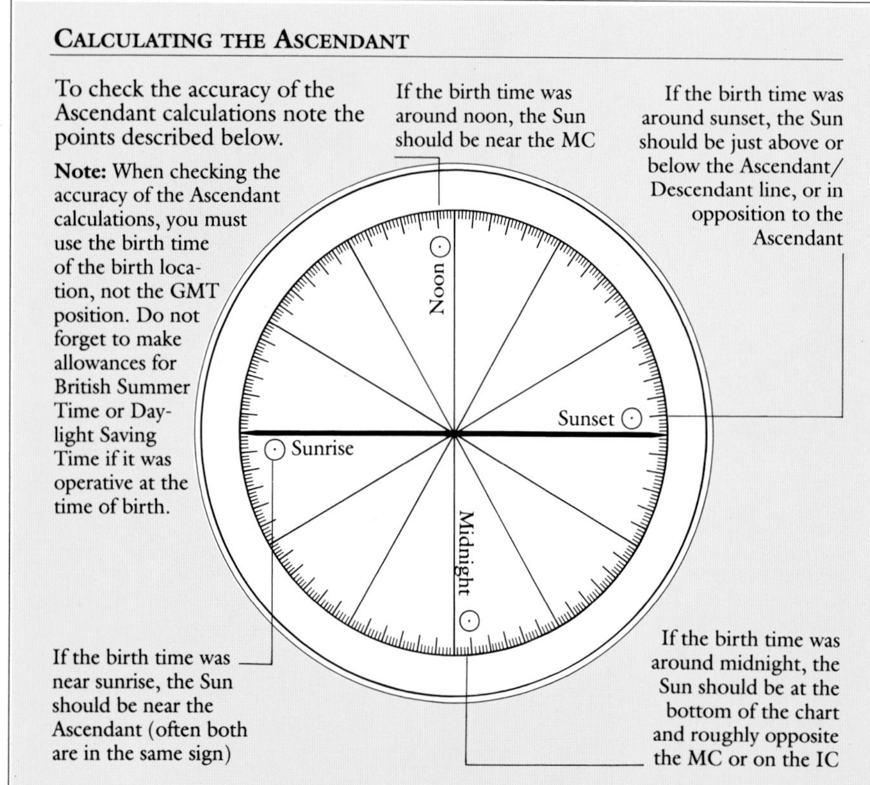

If the birth time was around noon, the Sun should be near the MC
If the birth time was around sunset, the Sun should be just above or below the Ascendant/ Descendant line, or in opposition to the Ascendant
Noon
Sunset
Sunrise
Midnight
If the birth time was near sunrise, the Sun should be near the Ascendant (often both are in the same sign)
If the birth time was around midnight, the Sun should be at the bottom of the chart and roughly opposite the MC or on the IC

TRADITIONAL FACTORS

Although over the centuries astrology has constantly moved forward, it is important for students and professionals alike not to ignore ancient tradition. Traditional factors can still be used to map out excellent, even if somewhat oversimplified, basic routes towards the assessment of influences in the individual birth chart and should be carefully studied. Here we examine those of the chart that was used to illustrate the calculations (see p.47).

RULING PLANET
Mercury is the ruling planet because Gemini is the Ascendant and Mercury rules Gemini.

RULER'S HOUSE
The ruler's house is the first house because Mercury was in the first house for this time and location.

POSITIVE SIGNS
Eight planets are in *positive signs*:
Mercury and Mars in Gemini;
the Moon and Venus in Leo;
Jupiter, Saturn and Pluto in Libra;
Neptune in Sagittarius.

NEGATIVE SIGNS
Two planets are in negative signs:
Sun in Cancer;
Uranus in Scorpio.

RULING PLANET ☿

RULER'S HOUSE 1ST

RISING PLANET ☿ ♂

POSITIVE 8 | NEGATIVE 2

ANGULAR ☿ ♂ ♆

MUTUAL RECEPTION ☉/☽

TRIPLICITIES	QUADRUPLICITIES
Fire 3	Cardinal 4
Earth 0	Fixed 3 MC
Air 5 ASC/MC	Mutable 3 ASC
Water 2	

ANGULAR PLANETS
In addition to Mercury and Mars being "rising" planets they are also angular because they are within 8° of the Ascendant. To this we can add Neptune which is setting, i.e. within 8° of the Decendant (the angle directly opposite the Ascendant, or in opposition to the Ascendant).

RISING PLANETS
Both Mercury and Mars are rising planets because both are in conjunction with the Ascendant, i.e. within 8° of the Ascendant:
Ascendant = 21°;
Mars = 20° in the twelfth house;
Mercury = 26° in the first house.
You may consider a planet to be rising if it is within 15° of an angle, but its effect will be less powerful than if it forms a conjunction.

MUTUAL RECEPTION
The Sun and Moon are placed in each other's signs. This is known as "mutual reception", i.e. the Sun rules Leo; the Moon rules Cancer.

TRIPLICITIES (ELEMENTS)
Three planets are in *fire signs*:
the Moon and Venus in Leo;
Neptune in Sagittarius.

There are no planets in *earth signs*.

Five planets are in *air signs*, also the Ascendant and Midheaven:
Mercury and Mars Ascendant in Gemini;
Jupiter, Saturn and Pluto in Libra
(Midheaven in Aquarius).

Two planets are in *water signs*:
the Sun in Cancer;
Uranus in Scorpio.

QUADRUPLICITIES (QUALITIES)
Four planets are in *cardinal signs*:
the Sun in Cancer;
Jupiter, Saturn and Pluto in Libra.

Three planets are in *fixed signs*:
the Moon and Venus in Leo;
Uranus in Scorpio and the Midheaven Aquarius.

Three planets are in *mutable signs*:
Mercury and Mars in Gemini and the Ascendant;
Gemini and Neptune in Sagittarius.

4 CALCULATING THE ASPECTS

Planets are in aspect to each other when there are specific angular distances between them (see pp.56-7).

(i) Refer to the chart on page 54 showing the various orbs permissible when calculating aspects. Always use the shortest distance between the two planets – if your aspect is over 188° you must go the other way round the signs. Remember the opposition is the most distant aspect (180°), so allowing the accepted orb of 8°, 188° is the maximum. The orb can be lesser or greater than the exact number of degrees for the aspect, i.e. a trine is exact when there are 120° between the planets, but will be operative when planet A is, say, on 10° Aries and planet B is on 18° Leo – or on 2° Leo. Work through each planet in turn from the Sun to Pluto.

(ii) Again, using the Washington chart for 4 July, examine the Sun in relation to all the other planets, the Ascendant and the Midheaven and, using the appropriate glyph, enter the aspects we find (see the grid below).

The Sun is on 12° Cancer. First, we compare its position with that of the Moon, which is on 15° Leo. There are 33° between them. Every sign of the zodiac spans 30°, so the sum is:

30° – 12° = 18° Cancer + 15° Leo = 33°

This is just too wide to form a semi-sextile aspect (exact at 30° with a 2° orb), so we put a dot in the square relating the Sun to the Moon. This shows there is no aspect, but that we have made the calculation.

(iii) Next, compare the Sun's position to that of Mercury. The Sun is on 12° Cancer, and Mercury is on 26° Gemini. There are 16° between them.

30° – 26° = 4° Gemini + 12° Cancer = 16°

Here again, there is no aspect. There would have to be 8° or less between the planets for them to be in conjunction. So place another dot in the grid.

(iv) Next, we study the Sun and Venus (at 5° Leo):

30° – 12° = 18° Cancer + 5° Leo = 23°

Again, there is no aspect.

(v) The Sun makes no aspects, indeed, until we reach Uranus (at 26° Scorpio). Three signs separate the Sun and Uranus – Leo, Virgo and Libra:

Three signs = 90° + the last 18° of Cancer + the first 26° of Scorpio = 134°

The Sun and Uranus must be 135° apart to form a sesquare, so this aspect is within orb. Draw it in on the grid.

(vi) The only other aspect made by the Sun here is to the Midheaven, and again it is a sesquare. This time the degrees are counted from Gemini back through Taurus, Aries, Pisces and the end of Aquarius, numbering 134° in all. Enter it on the grid.

(vii) We don't have to compare the Moon's position to that of the Sun as we studied it when assessing the Sun's relationship to the Moon. So, next look at the Moon and Mercury. The Moon occupies 15° Leo, Mercury 26° Gemini. So:

4° Gemini + 30° Cancer (which separates them) + 15° Leo = 49°

A semi-square aspect requires 45°, and the orb is only 2°, so this is too wide. Place another dot on the grid.

(viii) The Moon and Venus are separated by 10° – too much for a conjunction (orb allowance 8°).

(iv) Mars occupies 20° Gemini, so:

10° Gemini + 30° Cancer (which separates them) + 15° Leo = 55°.

We allow an orb of 6° for a sextile (exact at 60°), so the Moon and Mars form a sextile. Write it on the grid.

(x) The Moon and Jupiter are separated by 47°, so there is a semi-square aspect between them.

(xi) The Moon and Saturn are separated by 48°. As the Moon occupies 15.9° Leo, the actual distance between them is really just over 47°, so we can allow a semi-square aspect.

(xii) There is no aspect between the Moon and Uranus, but because just over 127° separate the Moon and Neptune, here is a wide trine aspect.

(xiii) Calculate all aspects between the planets, as well as those made to the Ascendant and Midheaven.

THE ASPECT GRID

While it is not difficult, with practice, to see the important aspects in a birth chart, even the experienced astrologer finds it much easier to rationalize and synthesize these when they are placed in a formal grid such as the one shown below. When you have entered all the aspects in such a grid, you can easily see them at a glance. Among other things, such grids make it easier to compare chart with chart when doing synastry work (see pp.152-5).

PLANET		ASPECTS									
		☉	☽	☿	♀	♂	♃	♄	♅	♆	♇
SUN	☉		•	•	•	•	•	•	⚼	•	•
MOON	☽			•	•	⚹	∠	∠	•	△	⚹
MERCURY	☿				•	☌	□	□	⚻	☍	△
VENUS	♀					•	⚹	⚹	•	•	•
MARS	♂						•	•	•	☍	△
JUPITER	♃							☌	⚹	•	•
SATURN	♄								•	•	•
URANUS	♅									•	•
NEPTUNE	♆										⚹
PLUTO	♇										
ASC	Asc	•	⚹	☌	•	☌	•	•	•	☍	△
MC	MC	⚼	•	△	•	△	•	•	□	•	△

The Finished Calculation

The chart on this page includes all the calculations which we have made in the previous pages. Because the ephemeris (see pp.350-89) was specially generated for this book, to show the positions of the planets in decimal points rather than minutes and seconds, it was not at hand when the text was written. There is therefore a slight discrepancy between the precise results arrived at in the text (and shown in the charts) here and on pages 60-71, and the results if the calculations are re-worked using the positions shown in the ephemeris. *The method of calculation, however, is correct and should be followed.*

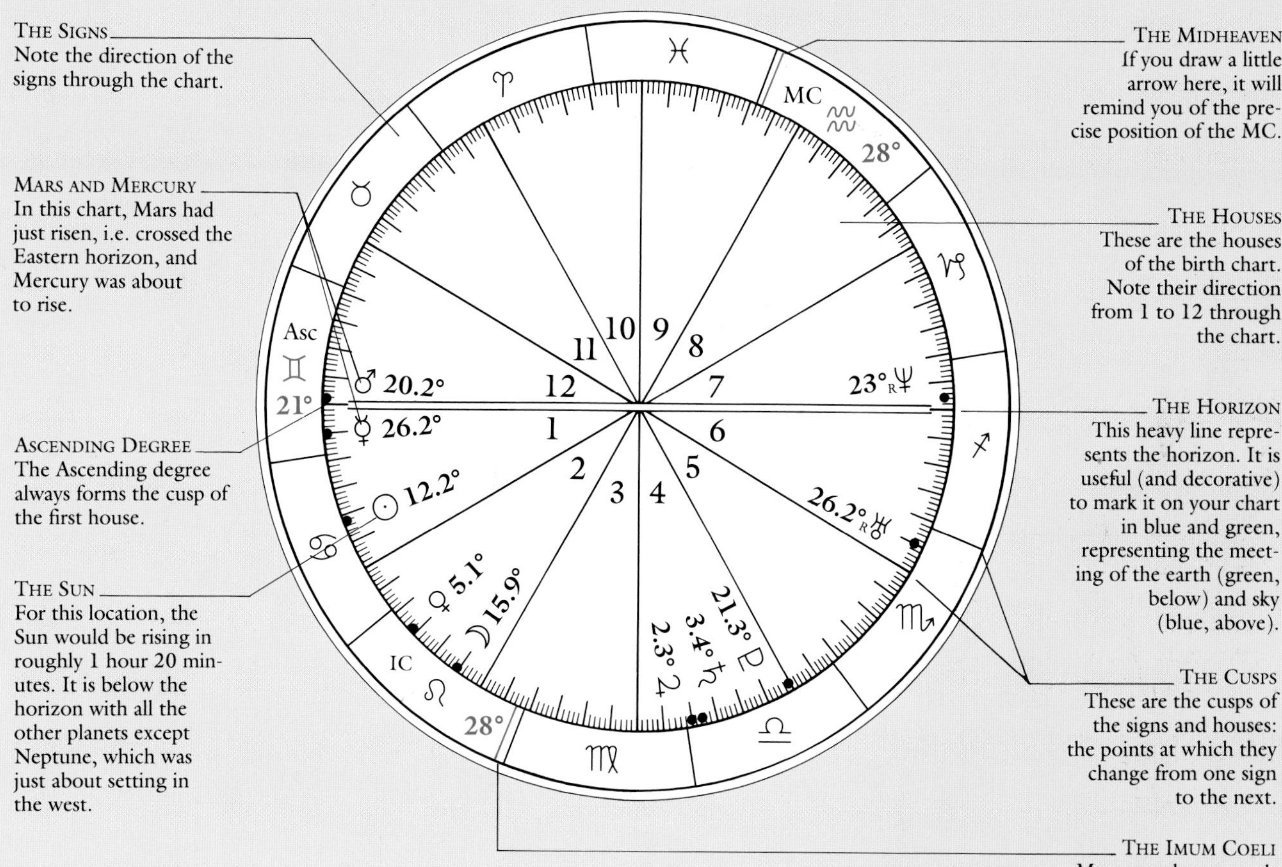

The Signs
Note the direction of the signs through the chart.
Mars and Mercury
In this chart, Mars had just risen, i.e. crossed the Eastern horizon, and Mercury was about to rise.
Ascending Degree
The Ascending degree always forms the cusp of the first house.
The Sun
For this location, the Sun would be rising in roughly 1 hour 20 minutes. It is below the horizon with all the other planets except Neptune, which was just about setting in the west.
The Midheaven
If you draw a little arrow here, it will remind you of the precise position of the MC.
The Houses
These are the houses of the birth chart. Note their direction from 1 to 12 through the chart.
The Horizon
This heavy line represents the horizon. It is useful (and decorative) to mark it on your chart in blue and green, representing the meeting of the earth (green, below) and sky (blue, above).
The Cusps
These are the cusps of the signs and houses: the points at which they change from one sign to the next.
The Imum Coeli
Many astrologers mark the Imum Coeli (IC), the opposite point to the MC, on their birth charts. As it is not easy to see, it is not really necessary, but this sensitive part of the chart must not be forgotten.
MC
28°
Asc
21°
IC
28°
20.2°
26.2°
12.2°
5.1°
15.9°
21.3°
3.4°
2.3°
26.2° R
23° R
10
9
11
8
12
7
1
6
2
5
3
4

Challenge

For practice, complete the drawings of the Moscow and Perth charts. The planets will be in the same signs and occupy the same degrees, but will be in different houses. Go on to recalculate the aspects made to the Ascendant and Midheaven, which will be different.

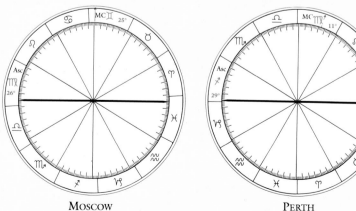

MC 25° Asc 26°

Moscow

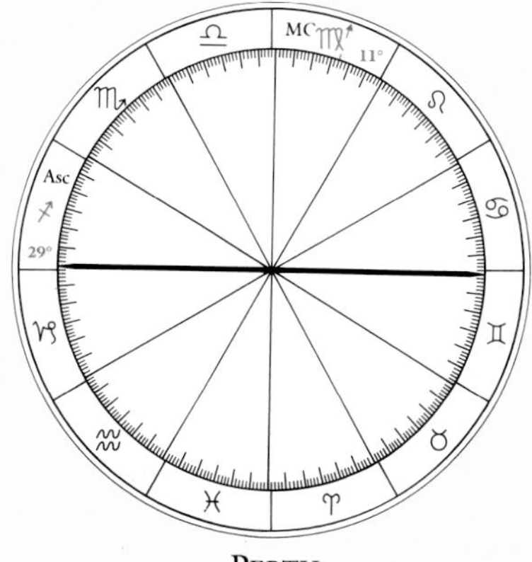

Perth

Name

Reference No.

Chart Calculated on

Referencing
Always write your subject's name in the space provided, give him or her a file number, and add the date.

Drawing a Birth Chart

There is no mystery about the preparation of a birth chart or horoscope. The process certainly calls for patience and application, but it is a matter of mathematical calculation, cool observation and synthesis. Do not be dismayed by the prospect of the mathematics involved. These, as we have shown, are mildly tricky rather than difficult, and now cheap pocket calculators and even computer programs have simplified the process. However, many astrologers will redraw the chart from the computer printout.

1 PREPARING THE CHART
First, photocopy the blank birth chart at the end of the book (p.408). Make sure, as you are working, that the results of the calculations for the birth date in question are near to hand.

2 WRITING IN THE HOUSES
Working counterclockwise from the horizon line, number the segments of the inner circle from 1 to 12.

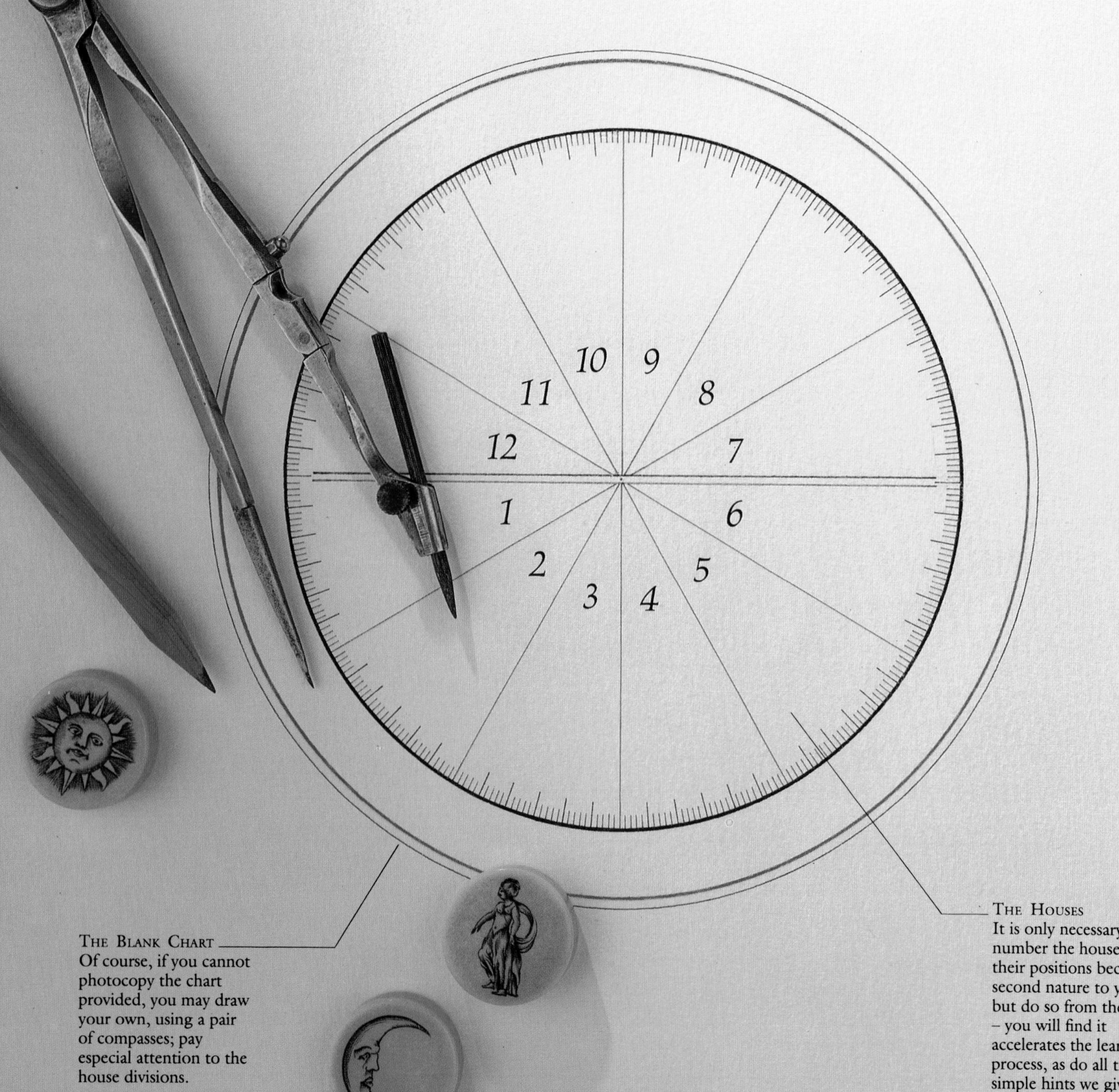

THE BLANK CHART
Of course, if you cannot photocopy the chart provided, you may draw your own, using a pair of compasses; pay especial attention to the house divisions.

THE HOUSES
It is only necessary to number the houses until their positions become second nature to you: but do so from the first – you will find it accelerates the learning process, as do all the simple hints we give.

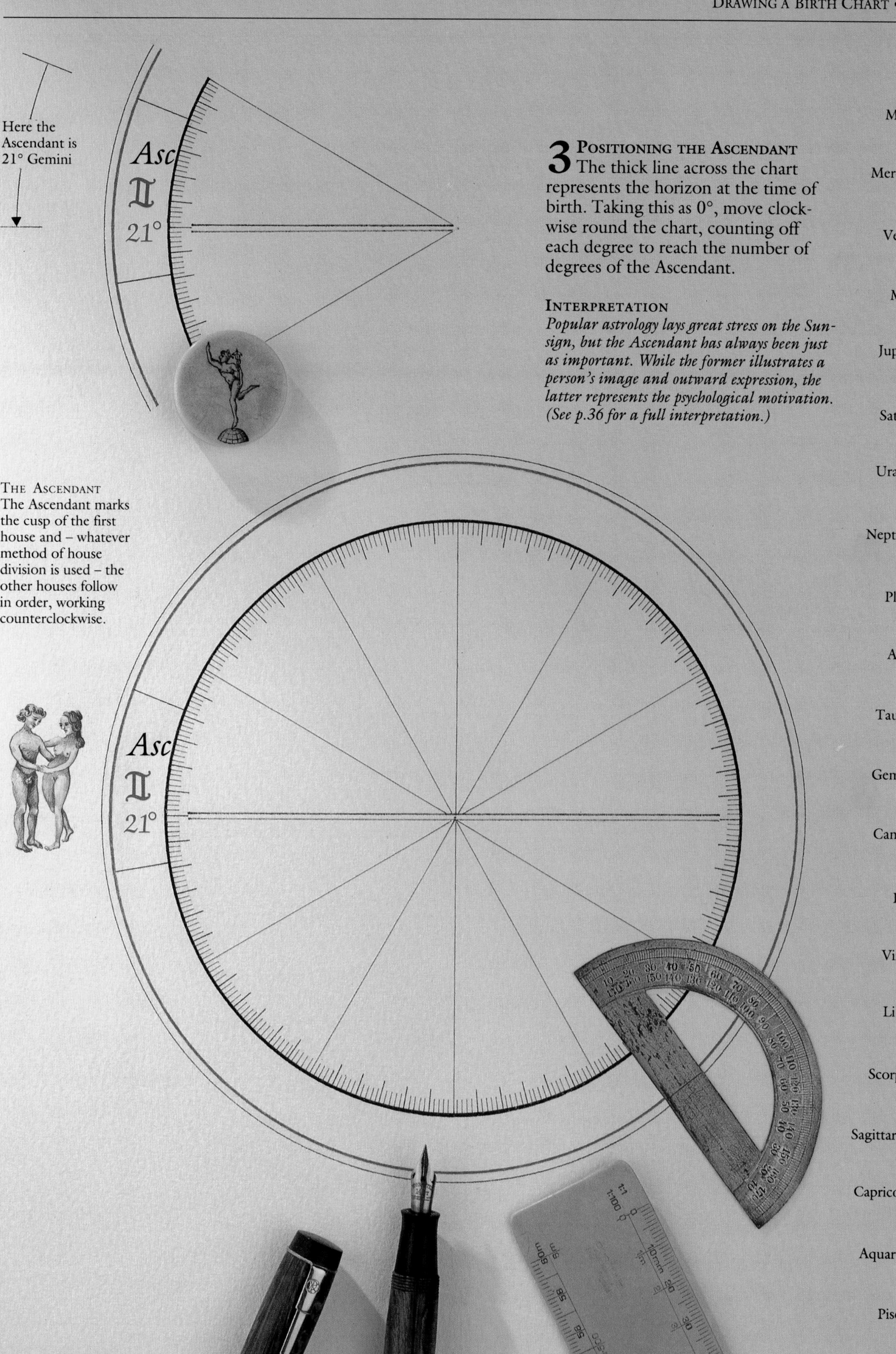

3 Positioning the Ascendant The thick line across the chart represents the horizon at the time of birth. Taking this as 0°, move clockwise round the chart, counting off each degree to reach the number of degrees of the Ascendant.

Interpretation

Popular astrology lays great stress on the Sun-sign, but the Ascendant has always been just as important. While the former illustrates a person's image and outward expression, the latter represents the psychological motivation. *(See p.36 for a full interpretation.)*

The Ascendant

The Ascendant marks the cusp of the first house and – whatever method of house division is used – the other houses follow in order, working counterclockwise.

4 Drawing in the Sign Divisions
Starting at the Ascendant, count 30° in a counterclockwise direction. This is the division (cusp) of the second sign. Continue in this way round the chart until all of the sign divisions have been marked.

5 Writing in the Signs (Glyphs)
Working counterclockwise from the Ascendant in the outer circle, write in the signs or glyphs (that appear down the side of the previous page). The glyphs are written vertically; do *not* turn the paper so that each glyph faces outward.

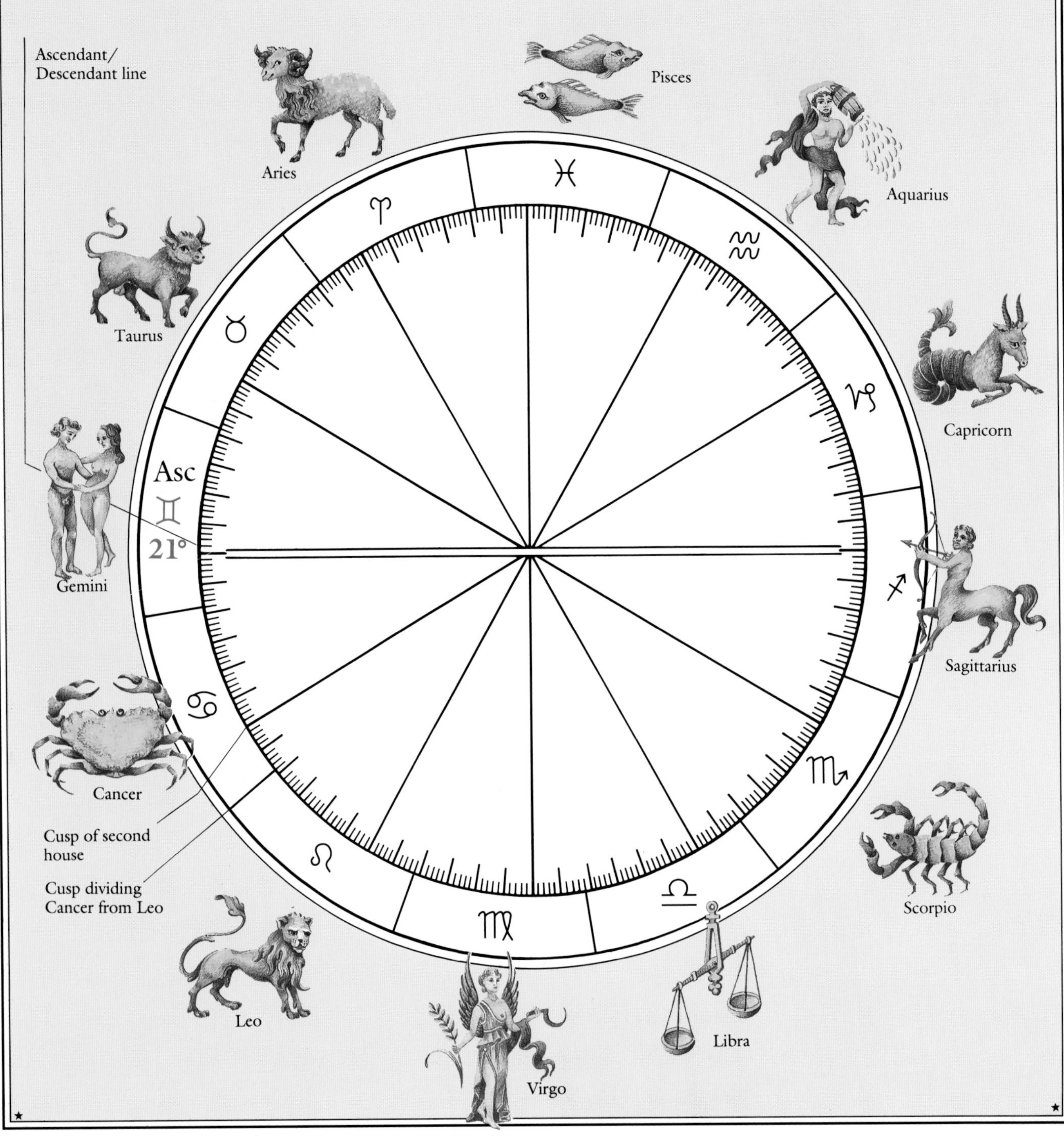

6 DRAWING IN THE MIDHEAVEN

Next, draw in the Midheaven – the part of the sky that was directly overhead at the time of birth (see p.36). For clarity, it is worth drawing the glyphs of the Ascendant and Midheaven in a different color.

INTERPRETATION

The subject will identify with the qualities of the sign on the Midheaven (or MC). A planet stationed on or near the MC in a chart will be strongly focused in interpretation. The point opposite the MC is the Immum Coeli (or IC); some astrologers relate this to our attitude to earth, to environmental or "green" issues.

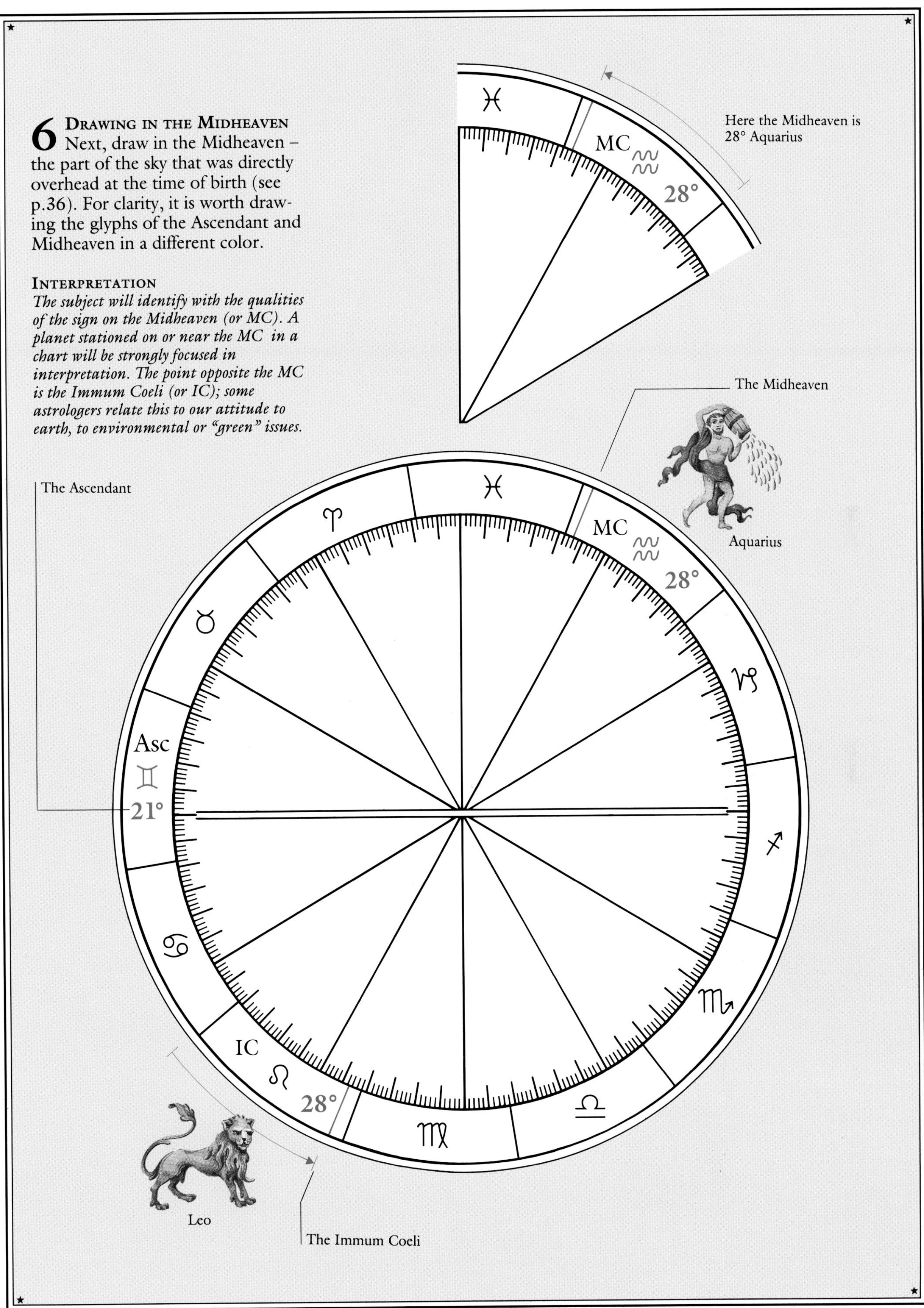

7 POSITIONING THE SUN AND MOON

The Sun is now placed in its sign and house (here, it is on degree 12.2 of Cancer in the first house). Next in importance is the Moon (in this example it is on degree 15.9 of Leo in the second house).

INTERPRETATION

Remember that the Sun represents the subject's image, or outward expression – the face that is presented to the world. The Moon indicates the subject's reactions to the various situations of life, and also underlines traits inherited from parents.

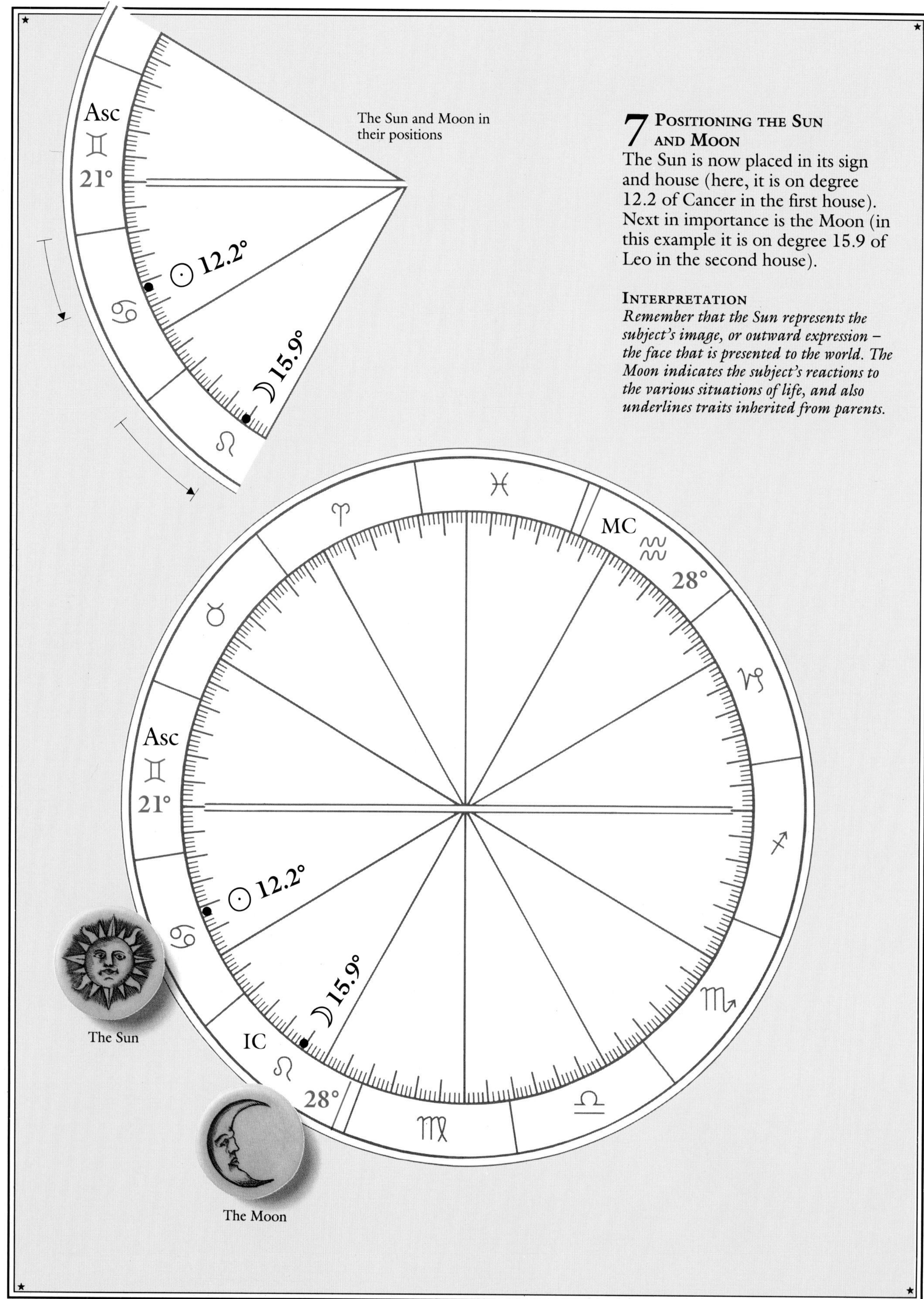

The Sun

The Moon

8 THE REMAINING PLANETS The remaining planets are now drawn into the birthchart, as shown below: you should always, of course, write in the precise position of each planet next to the relevant glyph. Cultivate the habit of writing them in in the order in which they extend outwards from the Sun, i.e. Mercury, Venus, Mars, Jupiter, Saturn, Uranus, Neptune and Pluto.

INTERPRETATION
After considering the Sun, Moon and ruling planet, an interpretation is best built by considering the remaining planets in their proper order.

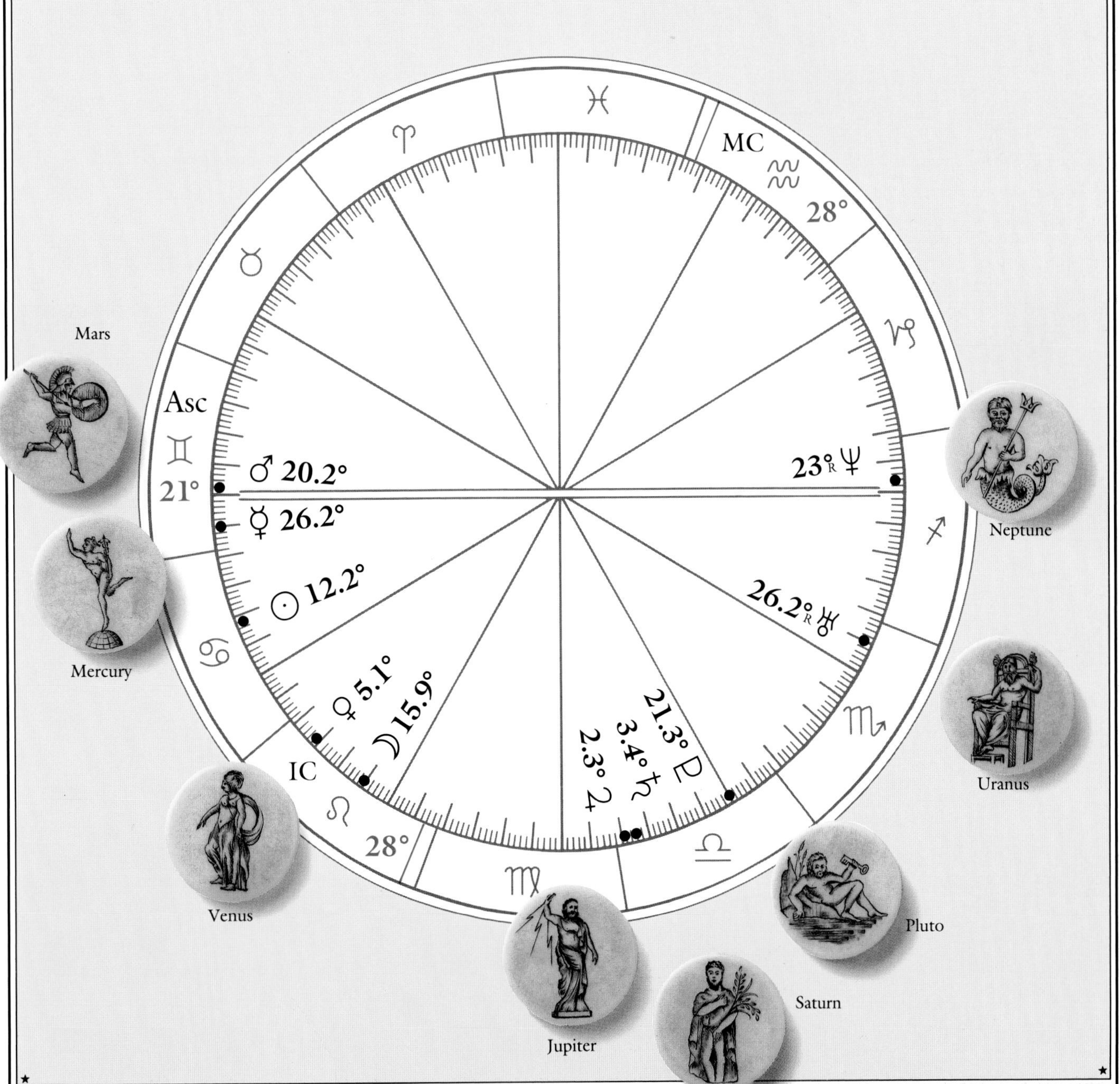

Understanding the Aspects

This is another set of astrological glyphs to be memorized. The aspects are drawn on the birth chart as lines connecting the planets "in aspect" to each other, but it is often necessary to list these in a grid, or in the margin of a written interpretation – hence the glyphs. Astrologers divide the aspects into groups: positive, negative and weak.

Types of aspects

A *conjunction* is the most powerful of all aspects. The negative aspects – the *square* and *opposition* – are powerful, and while considered negative, give us strength of character and make us fight for what we want. The *semi-square* and *quincunx* are often a cause of stress and tension, but are not as strong as the square or opposition and must not be over-interpreted. The quincunx can be rather unpredictable – approach its interpretation with great caution.

The positive aspects, especially the *trine* and *sextile*, help to make life easier, and also help us to express the qualities of signs and planets freely, without stress. The minor *sesquare* and *semi-sextile* are weak aspects but can, like the semi-square and quincunx, be a source of tension or some form of negativity (according to the planets involved). They are background, supporting factors and must not be isolated in interpretation or overinterpreted.

The orbs

An aspect is only considered, in astrology, if it is "in orb" – that is, if the planets are aligned to each other within a certain number of degrees. The chart, above right, shows the maximum number of degrees which should separate two planets forming an aspect.

Positive and Negative Aspects

Aspect	Glyph	Type	Distance	Orb
Conjunction	☌	Positive or Negative	0°	8°, up to 10° with ☉ and ☽
Trine	△	Positive	120°	8°
Sextile	⚹	Positive	60°	6°
Opposition	☍	Negative	180°	8°, up to 10° with ☉, ☽ or ruling planet
Square	□	Negative	90°	8°
Semi-square	∠	Negative	45°	2°
Quincunx	⚻	Negative	150°	2°, up to 3° with ☉, ☽ and personal planet
Sesquare	⚼	Weak – Negative	135°	2°
Semi-sextile	⚺	Weak – Negative	30°	2°

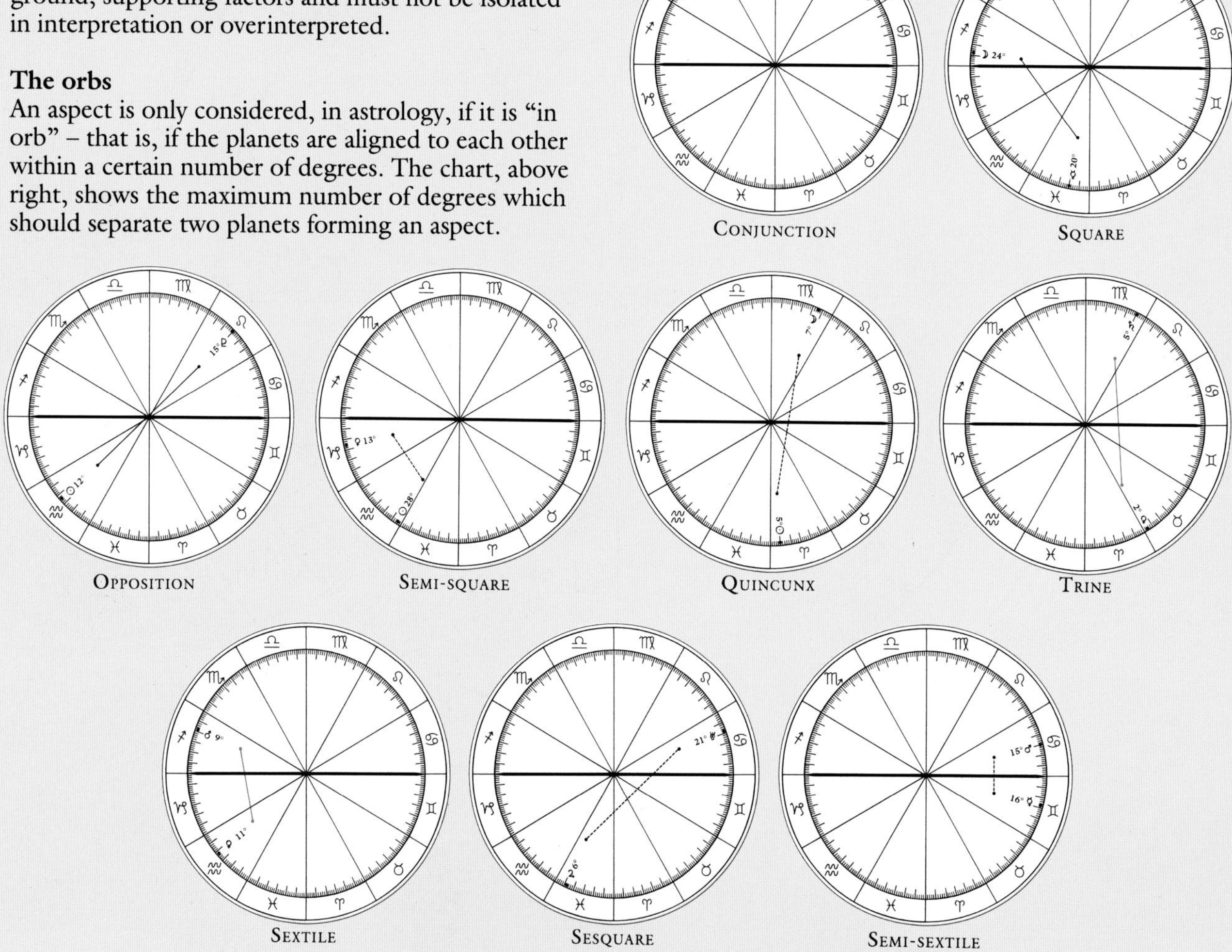

Conjunction

Square

Opposition

Semi-square

Quincunx

Trine

Sextile

Sesquare

Semi-sextile

9 Drawing the Aspects

Take your pair of compasses and place the point at the center of the chart, making dots with the pencil about halfway between the center and the position of each planet. After calculating the aspects, these points will help you draw the lines indicating them. We draw oppositions and squares with a solid, black line; trines and sextiles with a solid red line; semi-sextiles, semi-squares, sesquares and quincunxes with dotted black lines. You may choose different colors if you wish.

Grid Chart
As well as drawing the aspects on the chart, they are also shown in this grid form. It is not usual to draw aspects from the planets to the Ascendant or Midheaven.

Planet		Aspects									
		☉	☽	☿	♀	♂	♃	♄	♅	♆	♇
Sun	☉	╲	•	•	•	•	•	•	⚼	•	•
Moon	☽		╲	•	•	⚹	∠	∠	•	△	⚹
Mercury	☿			╲	•	☌	□	□	⚻	☍	△
Venus	♀				╲	•	⚹	⚹	•	•	•
Mars	♂					╲	•	•	•	☍	△
Jupiter	♃						╲	☌	⚹	•	•
Saturn	♄							╲	•	•	•
Uranus	♅								╲	•	•
Neptune	♆									╲	⚹
Pluto	♇										╲
Asc	Asc	•	⚹	☌	•	☌	•	•	•	☍	△
MC	MC	⚼	•	△	•	△	•	•	□	•	△

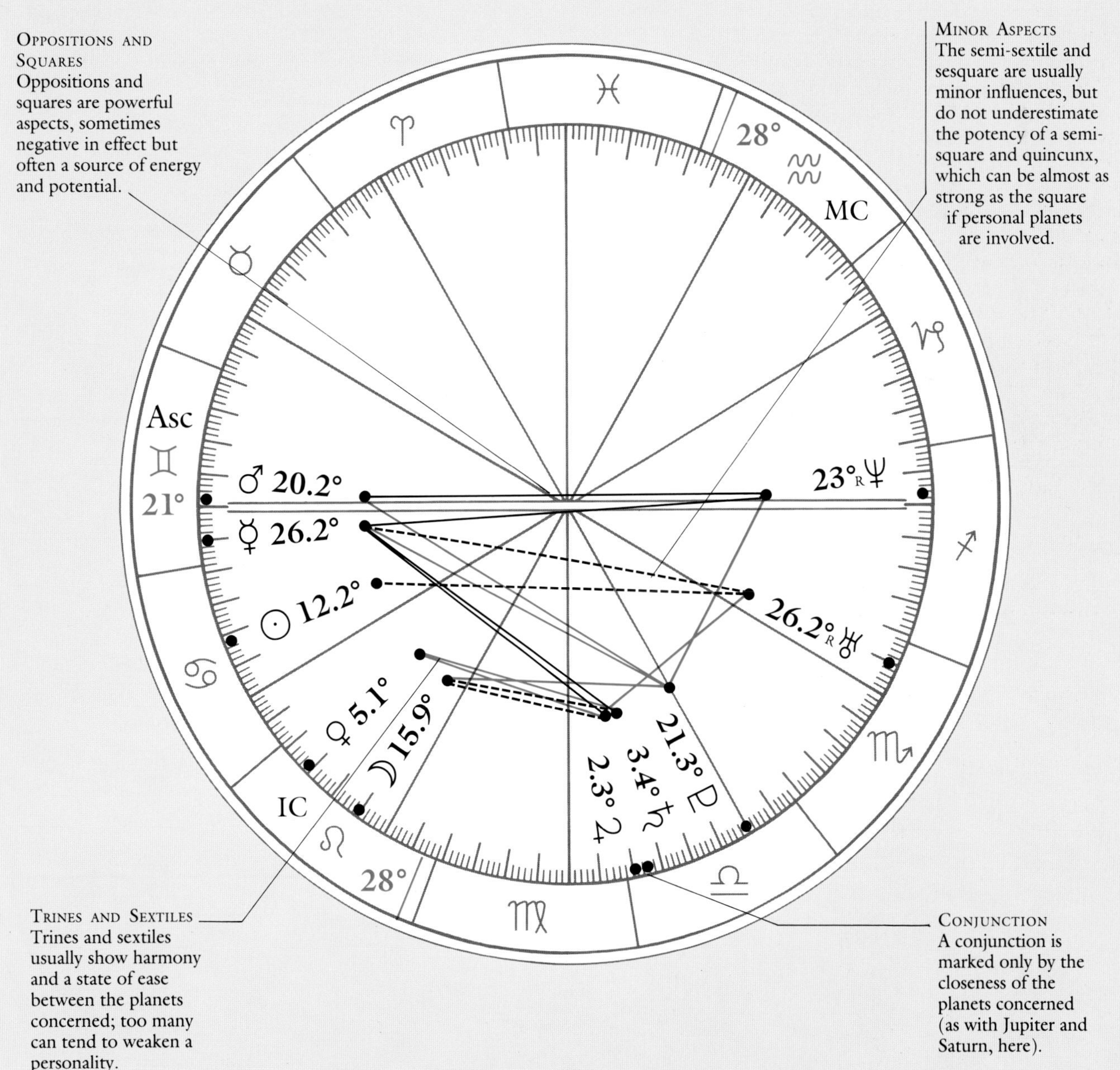

Oppositions and Squares
Oppositions and squares are powerful aspects, sometimes negative in effect but often a source of energy and potential.

Minor Aspects
The semi-sextile and sesquare are usually minor influences, but do not underestimate the potency of a semi-square and quincunx, which can be almost as strong as the square if personal planets are involved.

Trines and Sextiles
Trines and sextiles usually show harmony and a state of ease between the planets concerned; too many can tend to weaken a personality.

Conjunction
A conjunction is marked only by the closeness of the planets concerned (as with Jupiter and Saturn, here).

The Aspect Patterns

In some charts, planets in aspect to each other form patterns. These have powerful influences on the personality of the subject, working positively or negatively. The major aspect patterns are the tee-square, the grand trine, and the grand cross; and less important, but nevertheless a striking feature, the pointer.

The first two patterns involve three planets in the birth chart, while the third and fourth involve four – though it is often the case that (as in the second tee-square and the grand trine diagrams below) other planets join in the configuration, thereby strengthening the effect, so that while we often get a grand trine or a tee square involving only the basic three planets, any of these patterns may be joined by many more planets.

Unaspected Planets

This is not as common as it may seem. Recheck your calculations if you think you have found an unaspected planet in a chart, for the chances are that it may be making an aspect to one of the angles, and perhaps you have missed it. If it is present, it is a very powerful focal point indeed, and usually means that the individual is very much aware of the planet's influence, but may not be able to integrate its qualities psychologically into the personality, so sometimes psychological problems result. If you think your subject is at all distressed, this is a time when you should advise professional counseling.

The Tee-Square

This consists of two planets in opposition aspect, joined by a third making square aspects to both of them. This is a tense and dynamic pattern. It can be enormously energizing, and it usually gives strength to the individual, in spite of all the aspects formed being negative ones (and see p.206 about all the best people having the worst charts!)

However, in certain cases it can cause considerable inhibiton. Much depends on the planets involved; if any of them are personalized the tee-square's effect will be increased. If the chart is generally energetic and forceful, then you will find that the subject will definitely push against obstacles – both psychological and material – to achieve desired goals.

The Grand Trine

Here a group of three trine aspects links planets in a positive and easy way, but beware: this may be less beneficial than it might seem, especially if more than the three basic planets are involved.

The individual may well be extremely charming, but sometimes the pattern will inflict a certain weakness. Tendencies towards a lackadaisical, laid back attitude must be countered. If there are multiple grand trines (these very occasionally form a "star of David" pattern) your subject may tend to "ride" people and take too much for granted, thinking that they can "get away with murder" – and all too often they do. A grand trine is best when accompanied by a tee-square, creating a balance, or by several independent squares and oppositions, adding "grit" to the personality.

The Grand Cross

This does not occur in many charts, but when it does it is an overwhelmingly powerful feature. It consists of four planets roughly spaced at 90°, forming two opposition aspects and making a cross on the chart. At the same time all four make square aspects to each other. Here again sometimes additional planets can join in the configuration, either by square or opposition.

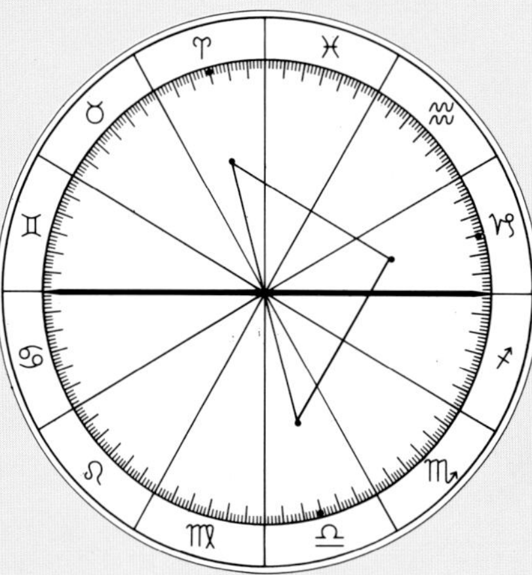

Tee-square

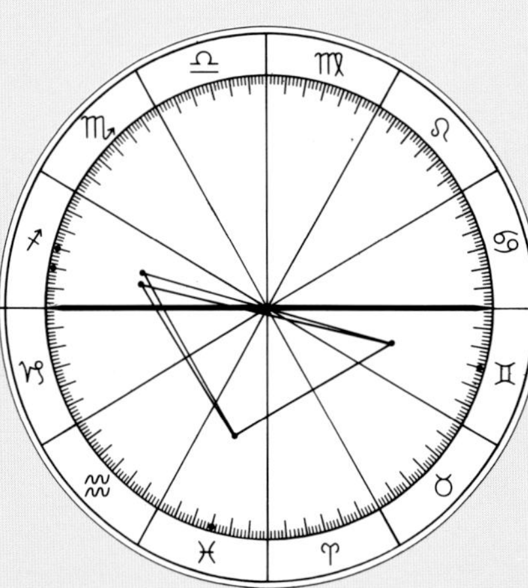

Double Tee-square

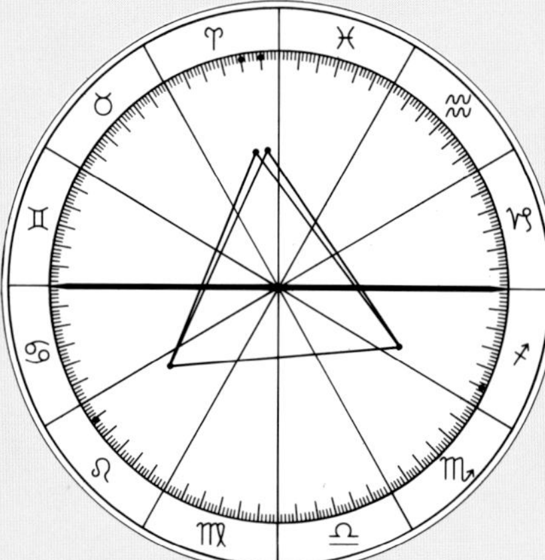

Double Grand Trine

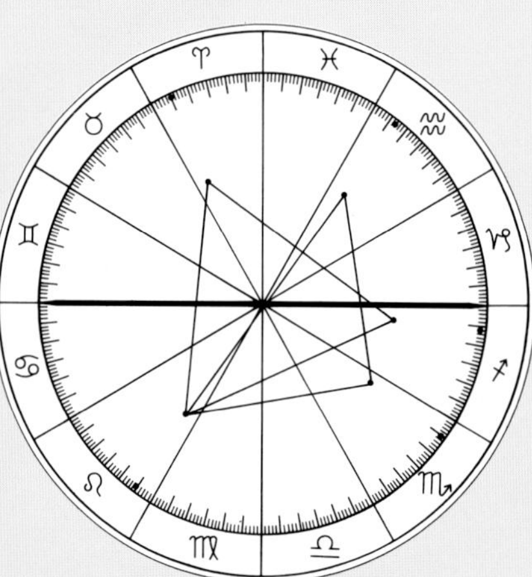

Tee-square and Grand Trine

The grand cross usually involves one quality. This is known as the "make or break" pattern, since people having it are either extremely brave, energetic, powerful and successful often overcoming great obstacles to win – or they cannot cope with the powerful effect, and crumble. The "quality" involved is certainly influential.

The cardinal grand cross
A cardinal grand cross is inhibitive, since subjects will want to release their energies and be outgoing, but are prevented from doing so. If they overcome lack of self-confidence they will prove to be very strong and often become big achievers.

The fixed grand cross
Here we have people who are all too often their own worst enemies because of stubborness. Rather differently, they may well have been "put down" so much by parents that all initiative and confidence has been drained from them. Again, if they can rebuild and develop flexibility and perhaps, too, an open mind, they will achieve much.

The mutable grand cross
The mutable grand cross often causes confusion since subjects will want to be adaptable and live easy, uncomplicated and fulfilling lives, but for a variety of reasons may well not feel in a position to do so – perhaps because of a strong sense of duty, which is sometimes used as an excuse for lack of self-confidence. Nevertheless, there is the potential here to fight through these barriers, and in overcoming obstacles subjects will achieve a great deal.

If the presence of these obstacles for all three types of grand cross are consciously realized, determination often overcomes them and the result is someone definitely to be admired.

GRAND CROSS

In some cases you will find that the tee-square and the grand cross involve more than one quality; as a result the powerful effects may be mitigated to some extent. The same thing applies to the grand trine, where there is usually an emphasis on one of the elements. In these circumstances they are then known as "dissasociated".

THE POINTER

This is a stressful configuration: a planet in an opposition is contacted by quincunx aspects from two others, forming an arrow-head shape. It is also possible for these two planets to form semisextiles to the "base" planet.

This configuration might symbolically be said to "show the way", indicating the direction the subject should take by centering on the affairs of the house in which the "point" of the pattern falls. Do not rely completely on this theory, but remember that the pointer planet always marks a very stressful area of the subject's chart, and the more negative side of all the aspects' influences will be present in the personality.

CHAIN REACTIONS

Later on, when you work on progressions and transits, remember that if any of these planets in any of these patterns are contacted by transiting planets or progressions, they will start a "chain reaction" of influence. If there is little orb between them in the birth chart the period will be important – you will find that it will be eventful, progressive or difficult, according to the planets involved. If the orbs are greater, the effect of any transits or progressions will be spread out over a longer period of time and therefore less intensive.

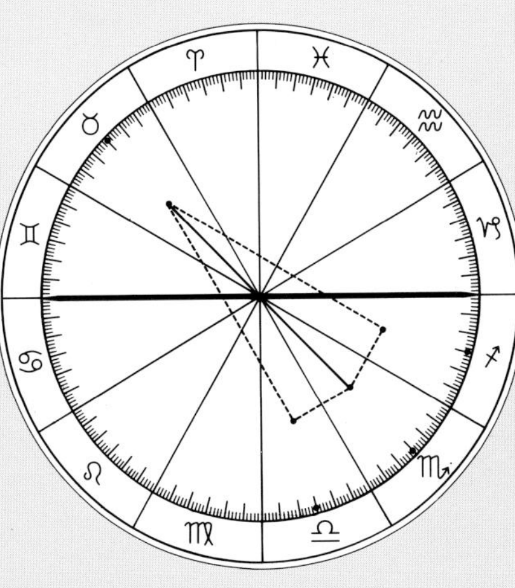

POINTER

THE STELLIUM

This is the name given to a group of planets – three or more – in one sign or house: from time to time there are "traffic jams" of planets in the solar system. Generally speaking, they lay a great deal of stress on the characteristics of the sign or concerns of the house which is so heavily tenanted. The individual is "very Sagittarian", or whatever. It is usually the case that the Sun sign is involved: it is fairly common to have Sun, Mercury and Venus in the same sign (so that the individual will not only have the characteristics of the Sun sign, but will think and love in the manner of that sign) but when they are joined, perhaps by the Moon (the subject would have been born at the time of the New Moon), the responses and reactions to all situations will also be of that sign. Other planets will follow in the same way: for example, Mars will represent the physical energy, and so on.

These powerful stelliums cause imbalance – not only in the solar system (sadly, they are all too often the cause of earthquakes) but in the individual, too, so that the positive and negative qualities of the sign involved are terribly dominant in the personality. Concentrate on other planets and signs to encourage your subjects to achieve the necessary balance in their life.

The Finished Chart

You have now plotted the positions of all the planets in the birth chart, which can tell you a great deal. The Sun indicates the way the subject expresses him or herself; the placing of the Moon shows the subject's reactions to all situations in life. Mercury represents the mental capacity, and Venus shows the needs in relationships. Mars rules the physical energy, and Jupiter, breadth of vision, intellect, and the philosophical and spiritual attitude. Saturn influences responsibility and worldly progress, and Uranus the need for power and capacity to cope with sudden changes. Neptune influences the individual's idealism and also any escapist tendencies, while Pluto represents the reaction to deep-rooted psychological problems.

Mars and Mercury in Gemini
Mercury is the chart ruler: its influence is crucial, not only because it rules Gemini from its own sign, but because it conjuncts the Ascendant from the first house. Mars in Gemini is also powerful: a strong but tense energy source which, because it is in the twelfth house and opposed by Neptune, will make the subject secretive and imaginative.

Sun in Cancer
The Cancerian Sun is a strong psychological influence, given additional strength from the first house; it accentuates Cancerian health vulnerabilities.

Venus and Moon in Leo
From Leo the Moon gives the ability to respond authoritatively and to be a good organiser. The emotional level is positively heightened. Venus in Leo adds warmth and generosity; from the second house it prompts the subject to enjoy luxury and good living. The expression of love for a partner is also enhanced.

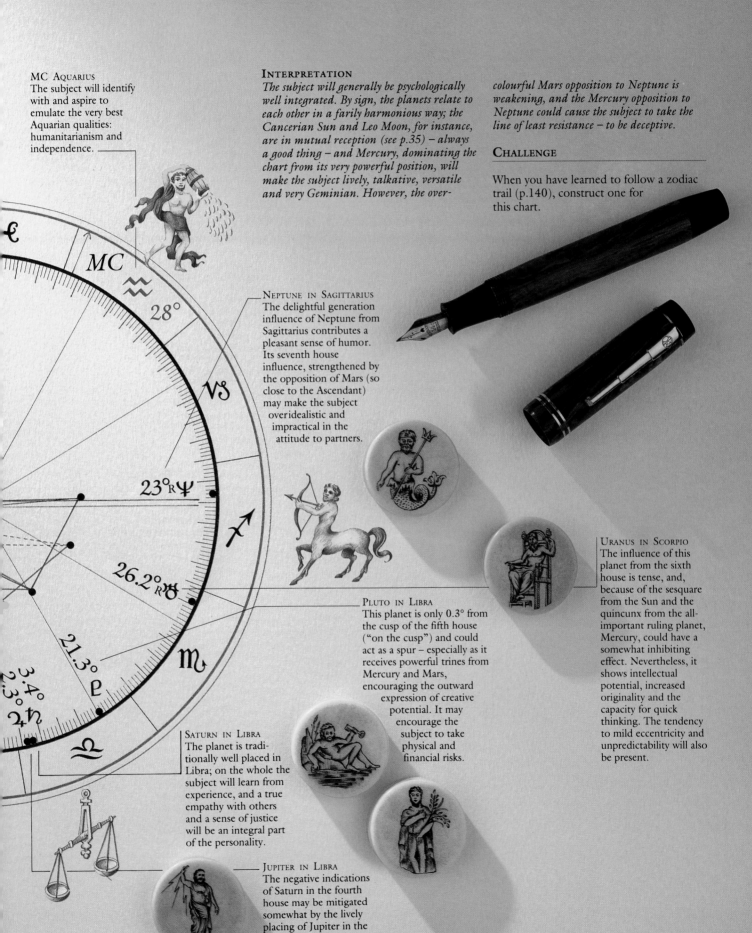

MC AQUARIUS
The subject will identify with and aspire to emulate the very best Aquarian qualities: humanitarianism and independence.

INTERPRETATION

The subject will generally be psychologically well integrated. By sign, the planets relate to each other in a farily harmonious way; the Cancerian Sun and Leo Moon, for instance, are in mutual reception (see p.35) – always a good thing – and Mercury, dominating the chart from its very powerful position, will make the subject lively, talkative, versatile and very Geminian. However, the over-colourful Mars opposition to Neptune is weakening, and the Mercury opposition to Neptune could cause the subject to take the line of least resistance – to be deceptive.

CHALLENGE

When you have learned to follow a zodiac trail (p.140), construct one for this chart.

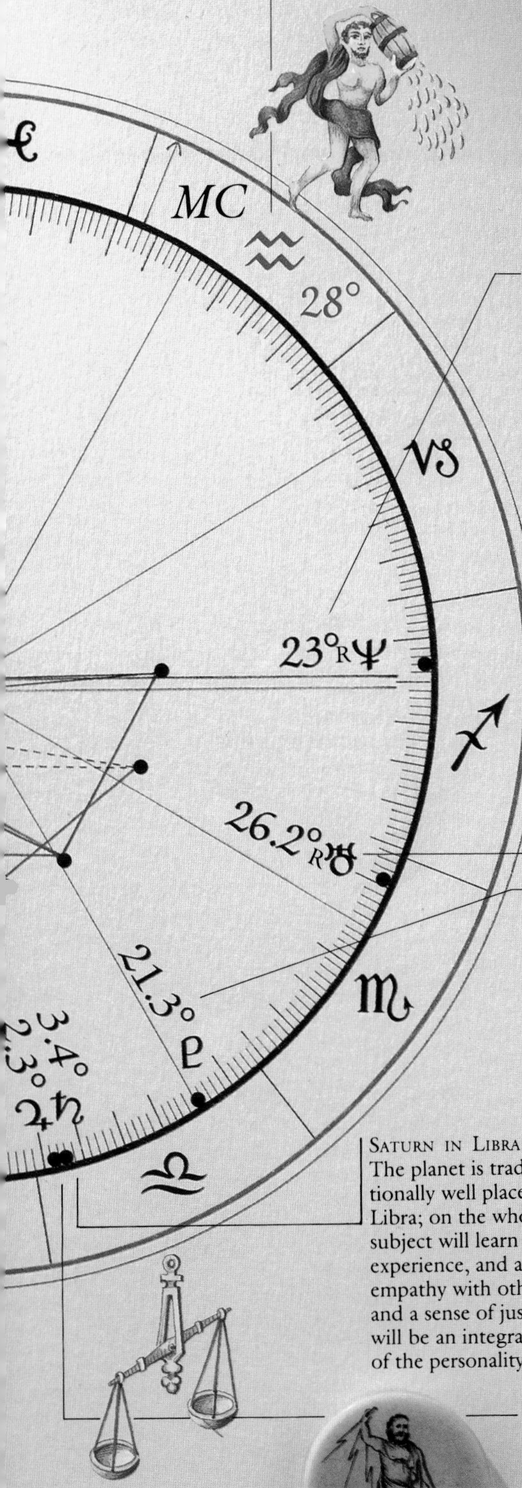

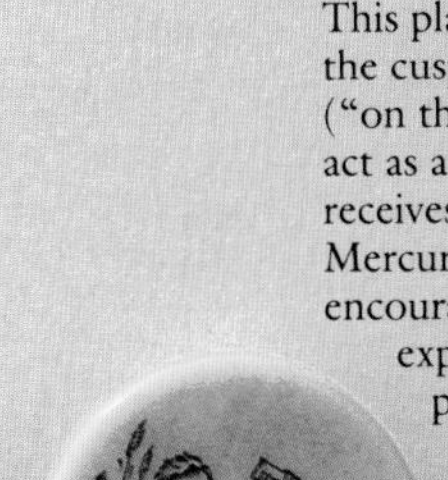

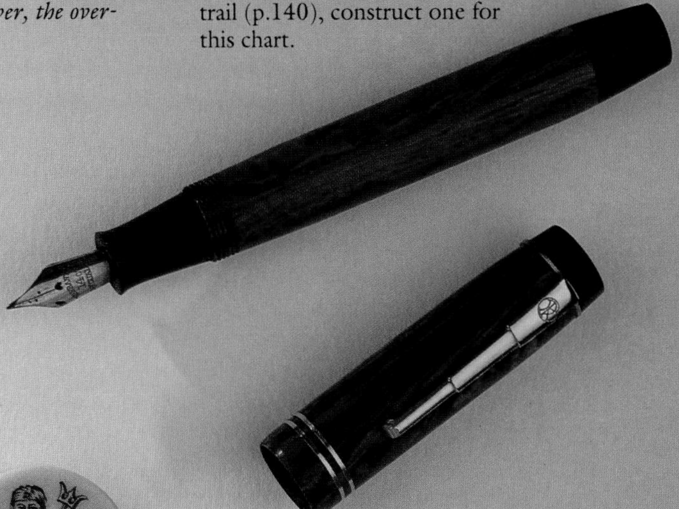

NEPTUNE IN SAGITTARIUS
The delightful generation influence of Neptune from Sagittarius contributes a pleasant sense of humor. Its seventh house influence, strengthened by the opposition of Mars (so close to the Ascendant) may make the subject overidealistic and impractical in the attitude to partners.

URANUS IN SCORPIO
The influence of this planet from the sixth house is tense, and, because of the sesquare from the Sun and the quincunx from the all-important ruling planet, Mercury, could have a somewhat inhibiting effect. Nevertheless, it shows intellectual potential, increased originality and the capacity for quick thinking. The tendency to mild eccentricity and unpredictability will also be present.

PLUTO IN LIBRA
This planet is only 0.3° from the cusp of the fifth house ("on the cusp") and could act as a spur – especially as it receives powerful trines from Mercury and Mars, encouraging the outward expression of creative potential. It may encourage the subject to take physical and financial risks.

SATURN IN LIBRA
The planet is traditionally well placed in Libra; on the whole the subject will learn from experience, and a true empathy with others and a sense of justice will be an integral part of the personality.

JUPITER IN LIBRA
The negative indications of Saturn in the fourth house may be mitigated somewhat by the lively placing of Jupiter in the same house.

Progressing the Chart

In order to assess the trends in the life of a subject, astrologers "progress" the birth chart. There are various ways of doing this: the best known is the "day-for-a-year" system. It involves the simple process of assuming that the position of the planets 24 hours after birth suggests the trends in the life of that baby during its second year. The planets' positions for the time of birth five days after birth suggest the circumstances of its life from the ages of five to six; the positions for the time of birth 27 days on from the birth suggest the circumstances which will affect the subject between the ages of 27 and 28, and so on. To calculate the necessary charts, first calculate a birth chart (see pp.42-7).

It is extremely important to realize that we do not and cannot predict events. We can most certainly assess trends that are working in people's lives, and give our subjects a very great deal of help in such matters as when to make an important change – perhaps in a career – to buy a house, to deepen an emotional relationship, to start a business, and so on. But we never say that, for instance, on 27 May you will meet a gorgeous man, fall instantly in love, and get married on 27 July! That is simply not how astrology works: apart from anything else, fatalism of that sort would deny us free will. We can, however, go as far as to suggest that at a particular time there is a possibility of a deepening emotional relationship, and that this sphere of the life is likely to be emphasized.

Assessing trends

When it comes to the assessment of trends, the astrologer can point out when specific planetary energies are working for or against the subject, so that these can be guarded against or used to full advantage. There are times when moves and changes are likely to take place with as little hassle as possible; others when the subject could well be swimming against the tide, so that proposed changes of direction should be postponed to avoid frustration.

The whole area of progressions (as we call our means of "prediction") is of enormous practical help, both psychologically and practically. In the former case the astrologer can do much in a counseling role to encourage the development of potential and psychological wholeness, and in the latter an assessment of the birth and progressed charts enable us to discover times when the individual will be best able to make progress on all fronts.

Discovering trends

There are two ways of discovering future trends in a subject's – or of course one's own – life. One concerns the actual movements of the planets in the sky during the coming months or years; by considering these we can assess the effects they will probably have (we describe how to do this on pp.68-70). The other is purely symbolic. Over the centuries astrologers have devised and tested many ways of attempting to assess future influences, and we describe here a method which appears entirely irrational, but which is remarkably revealing and accurate. It is perhaps the most commonly used by western astrologers, and is known as the "day-for-a-year" system.

A day for a year

Very simply, one day's planetary motions are taken to symbolize a year in the subject's life. If you wish to assess the way in which the planets will be working for you when you are 35 years old, you count 35 days on from your birthday, and consult the planetary tables for that day. (For example, if your birthday was on 1 January 1955, the planets' positions on 4 February that year would symbolize the astrological atmosphere which will dominate 1990 for you.) The planetary aspects shown for that day will have their influence, and so will the angular relationships between the positions of the planets on that day and the positions they occupied on the day of your birth. The planetary pattern thus revealed symbolizes the working background theme of your life for about a year, although it is often the case that influences tend to "fade in" during the previous year, to be at their strongest when they are exact, and then to "fade out" during the following year.

The progressed birth chart

The chart on the opposite page shows how this works: outside the normal circle of the birth chart is a second ring in which the planets' positions and the Ascendant and Midheaven are repeated, but in different places: the places they were in 35 days after the subject's birth. Remember that the Ascendant and Midheaven positions can still be used only if you are confident of the accuracy of the birth time; they are then extremely significant. But when a chart is progressed, if the birth time is as little as four minutes out, then the timing of the interpretation will be inaccurate by as much as 12 months!

Because the Moon moves more quickly than any other "planet", its aspects symbolize only a three-month effect. But this influence is, like the more powerful transits, very important. (For the additional calculation necessitated by the Moon's quick motion, see pp.64-5).

Transits and the future

The transits are extremely important in assessing future trends. These are discovered by considering the movements of the planets during the time which is under consideration. The ephemeris lists these; some computer programs will also provide them. Having noted them, the astrologer works out what aspects each planet makes to itself and its fellows as they are shown in the birth chart. These are the transits. They can be very powerful influences indeed, and when two or more planets are symbolically in aspect in this way, the events those planets represent are very strongly in focus.

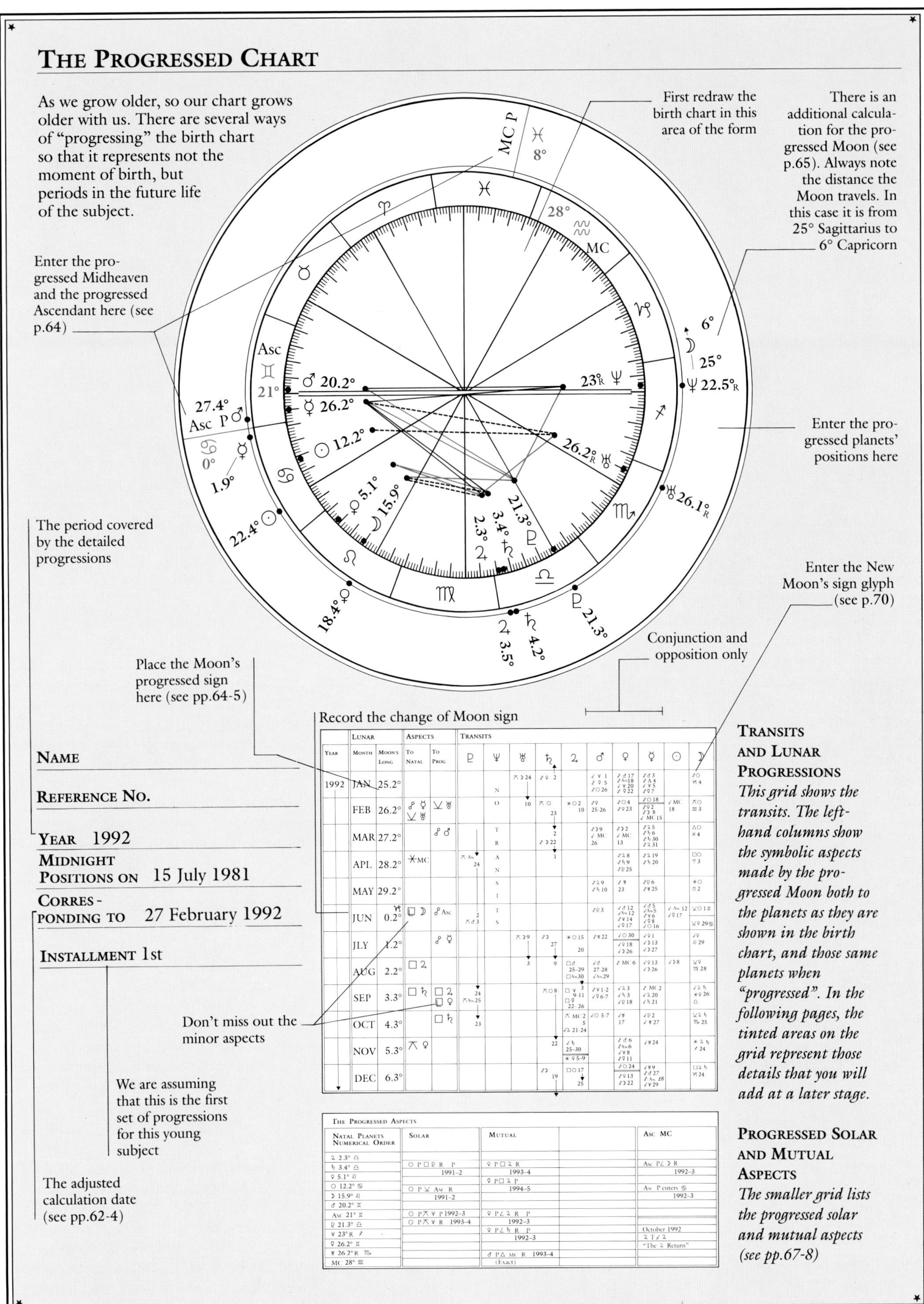
THE PROGRESSED CHART
As we grow older, so our chart grows older with us. There are several ways of "progressing" the birth chart so that it represents not the moment of birth, but periods in the future life of the subject.
First redraw the birth chart in this area of the form
There is an additional calculation for the progressed Moon (see p.65). Always note the distance the Moon travels. In this case it is from 25° Sagittarius to 6° Capricorn
Enter the progressed Midheaven and the progressed Ascendant here (see p.64)
Enter the progressed planets' positions here
The period covered by the detailed progressions
Enter the New Moon's sign glyph (see p.70)
Conjunction and opposition only
Place the Moon's progressed sign here (see pp.64-5)
Record the change of Moon sign
NAME
REFERENCE NO.
YEAR 1992
MIDNIGHT POSITIONS ON 15 July 1981
CORRES-PONDING TO 27 February 1992
INSTALLMENT 1st
Don't miss out the minor aspects
We are assuming that this is the first set of progressions for this young subject
The adjusted calculation date (see pp.62-4)
TRANSITS AND LUNAR PROGRESSIONS
This grid shows the transits. The left-hand columns show the symbolic aspects made by the progressed Moon both to the planets as they are shown in the birth chart, and those same planets when "progressed". In the following pages, the tinted areas on the grid represent those details that you will add at a later stage.
PROGRESSED SOLAR AND MUTUAL ASPECTS
The smaller grid lists the progressed solar and mutual aspects (see pp.67-8)
LUNAR
ASPECTS
TRANSITS
YEAR
MONTH
MOON'S LONG
TO NATAL
TO PROG
1992
JAN 25.2°
FEB 26.2°
MAR 27.2°
APL 28.2°
MAY 29.2°
JUN 0.2°
JLY 1.2°
AUG 2.2°
SEP 3.3°
OCT 4.3°
NOV 5.3°
DEC 6.3°
NON TRANSIT
THE PROGRESSED ASPECTS
NATAL PLANETS NUMERICAL ORDER
SOLAR
MUTUAL
ASC MC
1991–2
1993–4
1994–5
1992–3
1991–2
1993–4
October 1992
"The ♃ Return"
(Exact)

Adjusted Calculation Date

Date of Birth

	1	2	3	4	5	6	7	8	9	10	11	12
1	1	32	60	91	121	152	182	213	244	274	305	335
2	2	33	61	92	122	153	183	214	245	275	306	336
3	3	34	62	93	123	154	184	215	246	276	307	337
4	4	35	63	94	124	155	185	216	247	277	308	338
5	5	36	64	95	125	156	186	217	248	278	309	339
6	6	37	65	96	126	157	187	218	249	279	310	340
7	7	38	66	97	127	158	188	219	250	280	311	341
8	8	39	67	98	128	159	189	220	251	281	312	342
9	9	40	68	99	129	160	190	221	252	282	313	343
10	10	41	69	100	130	161	191	222	253	283	314	344
11	11	42	70	101	131	162	192	223	254	284	315	345
12	12	43	71	102	132	163	193	224	255	285	316	346
13	13	44	72	103	133	164	194	225	256	286	317	347
14	14	45	73	104	134	165	195	226	257	287	318	348
15	15	46	74	105	135	166	196	227	258	288	319	349
16	16	47	75	106	136	167	197	228	259	289	320	350
17	17	48	76	107	137	168	198	229	260	290	321	351
18	18	49	77	108	138	169	199	230	261	291	322	352
19	19	50	78	109	139	170	200	231	262	292	323	353
20	20	51	79	110	140	171	201	232	263	293	324	354
21	21	52	80	111	141	172	202	233	264	294	325	355
22	22	53	81	112	142	173	203	234	265	295	326	356
23	23	54	82	113	143	174	204	235	266	296	327	357
24	24	55	83	114	144	175	205	236	267	297	328	358
25	25	56	84	115	145	176	206	237	268	298	329	359
26	26	57	85	116	146	177	207	238	269	299	330	360
27	27	58	86	117	147	178	208	239	270	300	331	361
28	28	59	87	118	148	179	209	240	271	301	332	362
29	29		88	119	149	180	210	241	272	302	333	363
30	30		89	120	150	181	211	242	273	303	334	364
31	31		90		151		212	243		304		365

Time of Birth

Hours	Days	Minutes	Days	Minutes	Days
1	15.2	1	0.2	24	6.1
2	30.4	2	0.5	25	6.3
3	45.6	3	0.7	26	6.6
4	60.8	4	1.0	27	6.8
5	76.0	5	1.3	28	7.1
6	91.2	6	1.5	29	7.3
7	106.5	7	1.8	30	7.6
8	121.6	8	2.0	35	8.9
9	136.8	9	2.3	40	10.1
10	152.1	10	2.5	45	11.4
11	167.3	11	2.8	50	12.7
12	182.5	12	3.0	55	13.9
13	197.7	13	3.3		
14	212.9	14	3.5		
15	228.1	15	3.8		
16	243.3	16	4.0		
17	258.5	17	4.3		
18	273.7	18	4.6		
19	288.9	19	4.8		
20	304.2	20	5.1		
21	319.4	21	5.3		
22	334.6	22	5.6		
23	349.8	23	5.8		

Notes:
Greenwich Mean Time is always used, if using a Greenwich-based ephemeris.

Deduct one day if a leap year is indicated (i.e. if the year includes 29 February).

1 Preparing the Progressed Chart

We are going to progress the chart drawn for Washington on 4 July 1981, to cover in detail the period 1992-3, and to look in general at a rather longer period. First, redraw (or photocopy) the two progressed chart forms (see pp.408-9). Now calculate the adjusted calculation date.

2 The Adjusted Calculation Date

When progressing a chart by the "day for a year" method, we can take a short cut which avoids recalculating the planets' positions for every year.

The progressed date can be discovered simply by counting the relevant number of days on from the date of birth. To be accurate, we need the precise positions of the planets at the *time* of birth, but for this new *date.* As one day equals a year, any given proportion of a day will equal a corresponding proportion of a year. The planets' positions are listed in the ephemerides for midnight; their relationship to the progressed date will be in proportion to their relationship to a whole year, and as shown will correspond to a different date, according to the time of birth.

Making the calculations
To find the adjusted calculation date, write down the birth date and the birth time for GMT. Consult the day of the year chart to find the day number of the date of birth. Count the number of hours back to midnight, then look in the hours and minutes chart to find the corresponding day number, and subtract this from the number of the date of birth. More often than not, you will have to add 365 in order to reach your result. Then find the resulting number in the day of the year chart; this will give you the adjusted calculation date.

Note: When calculating, you should delete one day if 29 February (in a leap year) enters the calculations.

Accurate calculations
To check the accuracy of the adjusted calculation date, calculate the position of the Moon exactly as if you were calculating it for a birth chart, but for the

ADJUSTED CALCULATION DATE EXAMPLES

To arrive at the adjusted calculation date, the following directions must be observed:

Adjusted calculation date for subject born on 4 July 1981 at 8.19 GMT

1. It is necessary to convert the birth time into days, using the table on page 62:

8 hours = 121.6 days
19 minutes = 4.8 days
121.6 + 4.8 = 126.4
Rounding this down, call it 126 days.

2. Using the table on page 62, discover on what day of the year the subject was born: in this case, 4 July is the 185th day of the year.

3. Now subtract the birth-time number from the birth-date number. In many cases (though not in this example) you will have to "borrow" 365.
185 (number of day) – 126 (birth-time number) = 59.

4. Look up the number you have arrived at in the table on page 62 in order to convert it into a date: in this case it is 28 February. This subject's adjusted calculation date is therefore 28 February 1981.

Therefore:
4 July 1981 =
28 February 1981

5 July 1981 =
28 February 1982

6 July 1981 =
28 February 1983
and so on.

Golden Rule
If it is necessary to add 365 days, the adjusted calculation date will always fall back into the previous year (see examples 1, 3 and 5 below).

EXAMPLE 1

Birth date: **27 July 1932**
Birth time: **16.00 hours GMT**
16 hours = **243.3 days (say 243 days)**
27 July = **day 208**

Since 243 is larger than 208, we must "borrow" 365.
208 + 365 = 573 – 243
= **day 330**
Day 330 = **26 November**
Adjusted calculation date =
26 November

Therefore:
27 July 1932 =
26 November 1931 (the Golden Rule applies)

28 July 1932 =
26 November 1932

29 July 1932 = 26 November 1933
and so on.

EXAMPLE 2

Birth date: **27 May 1932**
Birth time: **1.50 hours GMT**
1 hour = **15.2 days**
50 minutes = **12.7 days**
15.2 + 12.7 = **27.9 (say 28 days)**
27 May = **day 147**

147 – 28 = 119
Day 119 = **April 29**
Adjusted calculation date =
29 April

Therefore:
27 May 1932 =
29 April 1932

28 May 1932 =
29 April 1933

29 May 1932 =
29 April 1934
and so on.

EXAMPLE 3

Birth date: **2 January 1948**
Birth time: **15.15 hours GMT**
15 hours = **228.1 days**
15 minutes = **3.8 days**
228.1 + 3.8 = **231.9 (say 232 days)**
2 January = **day 2**

Borrow 365: 2 + 365 = 367
367 – 232 = 135
Day 135 = **15 May**
Adjusted calculation date =
15 May

Therefore:
2 January 1948 =
15 May 1947 (the Golden Rule applies)

3 January 1948 =
15 May 1948

4 January 1948 =
15 May 1949

EXAMPLE 4

Birth date: **21 November 1970**
Birth time: **17.30 hours GMT**
17 hours = **258.5 days**
30 minutes = **7.6 days**
258.5 + 7.6 = 266.1 **(say 266 days)**
21 November = **day 326**

326 – 266 = 60
Day 60 = **1 March**
Adjusted calculation date =
1 March

Therefore
21 November 1970 =
1 March 1970

22 November 1970 =
1 March 1971

23 November 1970 =
1 March 1972
and so on.

EXAMPLE 5

Birth date: **1 February 1942**
Birth time: **3.00 hours GMT**
3 hours = **45.6 (say 46 days)**
1 February = **day 32**

32 + 365 = 397 – 46 = 351
Day 351 = **17 December**
Adjusted calculation date =
17 December

Therefore
1 February 1942 =
17 December 1941 (the Golden Rule applies)

2 February 1942 =
17 December 1942

3 February 1942 =
17 December 1943
and so on.

year for which you want the progressions. Its position should be identical to that on the adjusted calculation date. The adjusted calculation date is constant, and will apply to any year under consideration, as you will see from the examples given opposite.

3 The Progressed Ascendant

To fix the progressed Ascendant, we must find the distance the Sun has moved from its position at birth. Here, we are progressing the chart for 1992, giving the trends for the subject between the ages of 11 and 12. We therefore count on 12 days from the date of birth, counting the birth date as day one. For this example, this gives us the date of 15 July 1981.

Look up this progressed birth date in the ephemeris and note the position of the Sun, then subtract that from its natal position. Here, the progressed Sun occupies 22.4° Cancer and its natal position is 12.2°, so it has moved 10.2°. Now note the natal position of the Midheaven – here it is 28° Aquarius – and then move it 10.2° around the chart, matching the motion of the Sun. (This distance is the solar arc.) This will move it to 8.2° Pisces, so round it down to 8°.

Finding the Ascendant

Referring to the table of houses for northern latitudes (see pp.396-9) find the Ascendant relating to that Midheaven position – in this case, 0° Cancer. Now enter the progressed Ascendant and Midheaven positions, plus the progressed positions of the other planets (but not the Moon) on 15 July 1981, on the outer rim of the chart. If you are really certain of the time of birth, you could calculate the Ascendant to a tenth of a degree, matching the accuracy of the rest of the chart – a change of Ascendant, for instance, can be significant.

Enter the progressed date (15 July 1981) and the adjusted calculation date (27 February 1992) on the progressed chart.

4 Calculating the Progressed Moon

Now we must calculate the Moon's positions in detail. This calculation is necessary because the Moon moves so quickly through the signs, usually covering more than 1° a month in the progressed chart. Look now at the top grid opposite. Enter the year for which the progressions are to be made in the first column. Write the months in the second column.

Making the calculations

The Moon's position at midnight on the progressed date (15 July 1981) is 27.2° Sagittarius. This position represents the Moon as it will be operative on 27 February 1992 (the adjusted calculation date) in the progressed chart. Usually we would enter this position in the column for the Moon's longitude column opposite February, that being the month belonging to the adjusted calculation date. However, because this date falls so near the end of the month, it is advisable to place it opposite March, as the lunar influence will be at its most potent then. So write 27.2° opposite March.

We must now discover the Moon's positions for January and February. To do this we must first find its position on the day before the progressed date, i.e. 14 July 1981. On that day the Moon occupied 15.1° Sagittarius.

Now calculate the Moon's motion during those 24 hours:

27.2 – 15.1 = 12.1°

This figure represents the Moon's motion during a 12 month period, so divide it by 12 to find the motion during a progressed month:

12.1° ÷ 12 = 1°

Positioning the Progressed Ascendant and Midheaven

Now that you have the progressed positions of the Ascendant and Midheaven, place them in the chart at the appropriate points in the ecliptic.

When progressing the Ascendant and Midheaven, rounding up decimal points to whole numbers can affect timing, sometimes quite radically. So it is useful to keep a note of the position of the Midheaven to two decimal points, and checking with it.

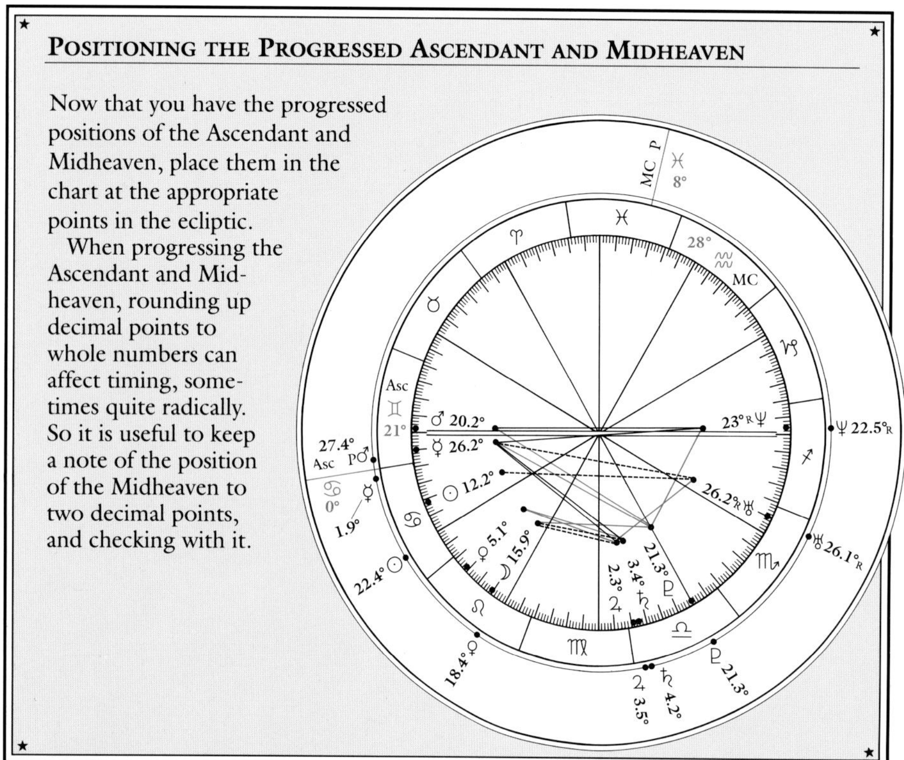

Births in Southern Latitudes

To progress the angles of a southern latitude birth, follow this example for a birth in Perth, Western Australia, latitude 31° 56' S.

Calculate the progressed Midheaven in the usual way (follow the instructions in step 3, above). Here, we will assume that the progressed Midheaven is 2° Virgo.

Refer to the nearest degree in the table of houses for northern latitudes (see pp.396-9), but because this is a southern latitude chart, look up the Midheaven Pisces (the opposite sign to Virgo), i.e. 2° Pisces. This gives an Ascendant of 20° Gemini but, again, reverse the signs to give a progressed Ascendant of 20° Sagittarius.

So the Moon has moved 1° per month. During February it occupied 26.6° Sagittarius; during January, it occupied 25.2° Sagittarius. Enter these positions on the chart. Because the actual motion was 12.1° during 12 months, we must allow for the extra 0.1°. Assume this correction has been made for September 1991, i.e. halfway between the two adjusted calculation dates.

Note: There is often a fraction of a degree to be allowed for. In the case of several decimal points, space these out as evenly as possible throughout the months of the progressed year. For accuracy, work out your division sum to two decimal points, and round up (i.e. 2.77 = 2.8, 2.72 = 2.7).

The remaining months
Now calculate the Moon's progressed positions for the remaining nine months we are to cover in detail. Work from 15 July 1981 to 16 July 1981; on 15 July the Moon is on 27.2° Sagittarius; on 16 July it is on 9.3° Capricorn:

30° – 27.2 = 2.8°

The Moon, then, will travel through 2.8° Sagittarius before entering Capricorn, then move to 9.3° by midnight on 16 July. It will reach that position in our progressions by March 1993. The motion for the 24 hours between midnight on 15 July and midnight on 16 July is 2.8° (the remaining degrees of Sagittarius) plus the 9.3° it travels through Capricorn. Add these, and you get 12.1°. (The motion is unchanged during this period.)

2.8° + 9.3° = 12.1°

Divide this by 12 to find the motion during each progressed month. As before, it is 1° per month, with an extra 0.1° to be added in September.

April = 28.2° Sagittarius
May = 29.2° Sagittarius
June = 0.2° Capricorn
July = 1.2° Capricorn
August = 2.2° Capricorn
September = 3.3° Capricorn
October = 4.3° Capricorn
November = 5.3° Capricorn
December = 6.3° Capricorn

Now turn back to the first (top) chart form and on it enter the progressed Moon's positions.

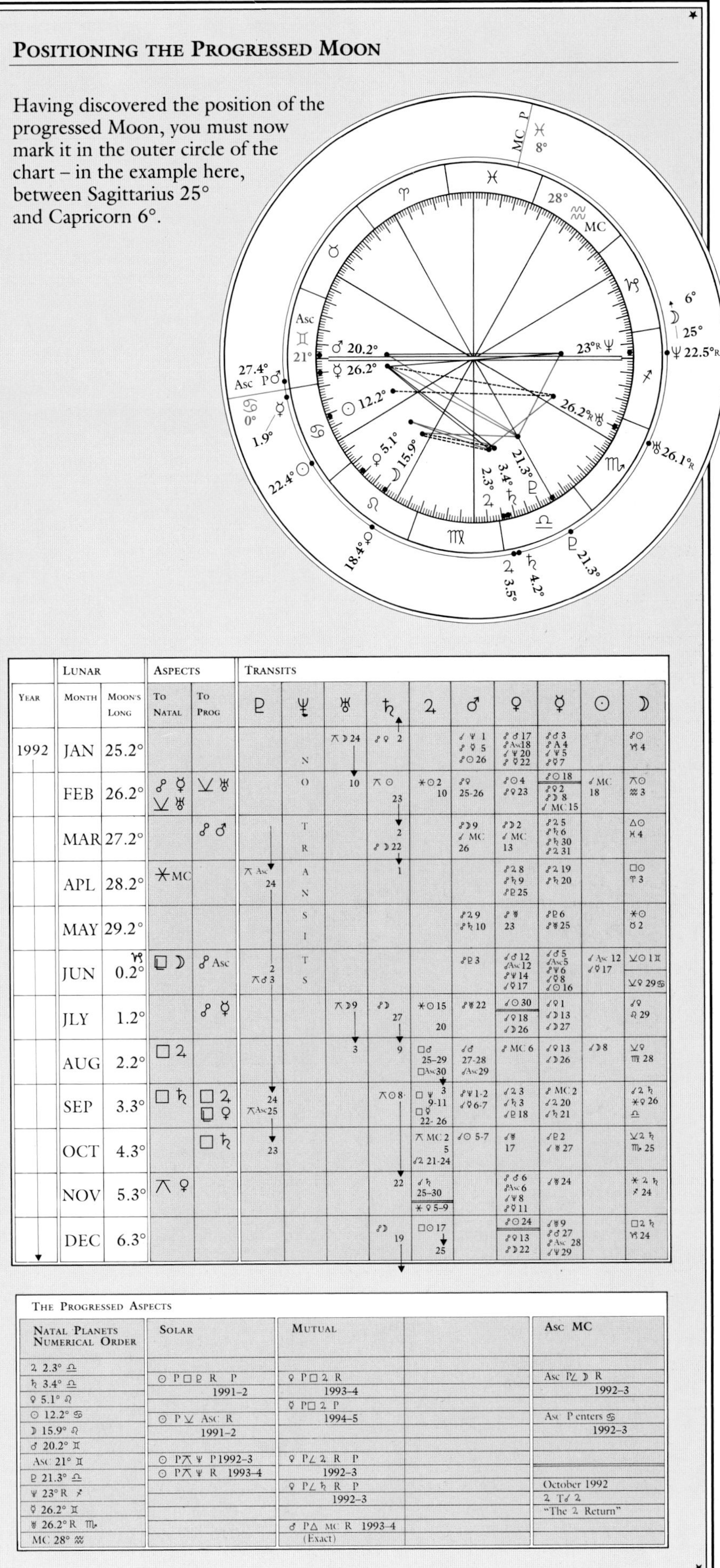

The Moon's Aspects

The Moon's aspects are listed in the chart below, in the "Natal" and "Progressed" columns. The column at the extreme right shows the aspects the New Moon makes to the natal planets as it moves around the sky during the period under consideration.

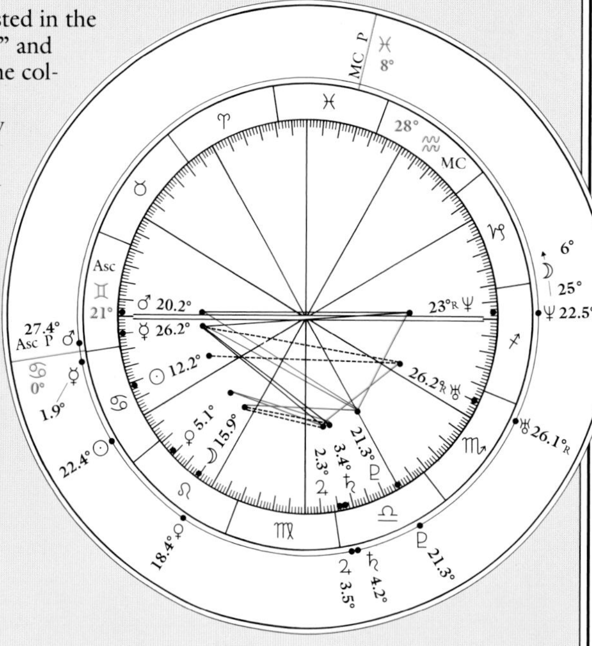

Year	Lunar: Month	Lunar: Moon's Long	Aspects: To Natal	Aspects: To Prog	Transits: ♇	♆	♅	♄	♃	♂	♀	☿	☉	☽
1992	JAN	25.2°				N	⚻☽24	☍♀ 2		☌♆1 ☍☿5 ☍☉26	☍♂17 ☍Asc18 ☌♆20 ☍☿22	☍♂3 ☍A4 ☌♆5 ☍☿7		☍☉ ♑4
	FEB	26.2°	☍ ☿ ⚺ ♅	⚺ ♅		O	10	⚻☉ 23	✶☉2 10	☍♀ 25-26	☍☉4 ☍♀23	☍☉18 ☍♀2 ☍☽8 ☌MC15	☌MC 18	⚻☉ ♒3
	MAR	27.2°		☍ ♂	↓	T R		↓ 2 ☍☽22		☍☽9 ☌MC 26	☍☽2 ☌MC 13	☍♃5 ☍♄6 ☍♄30 ☍♃31		△☉ ♓4
	APL	28.2°	✶MC		⚻Asc 24	A N		1			☍♃8 ☍♄9 ☍♇25	☍♃19 ☍♄20		□☉ ♈3
	MAY	29.2°				S I				☍♃9 ☍♄10	☍♅ 23	☍♇6 ☍♅25		✶☉ ♉2
	JUN	♑ 0.2°	⚼ ☽	☍ Asc	2 ⚻♂3	T S				☍♇3	☌♂12 ☌Asc12 ☍♆14 ☌☿17	☌♂5 ☌Asc5 ☍♆6 ☌☿8 ☌☉16	☌Asc12 ☌☿17	⚺☉1♊ ⚺♀29♋
	JLY	1.2°		☍ ☿			⚻☽9	☍☽ 27	✶☉15 20	☍♅22	☌☉30 ☌♀18 ☌☽26	☌♀1 ☌☽13 ☌☽27		☌♀ ♌29
	AUG	2.2°	□ ♃				3	9	□♂ 25–29 □Asc30	☌♂ 27-28 ☌Asc29	☍MC6	☌♀13 ☌☽26	☌☽8	⚺♀ ♍28
	SEP	3.3°	□ ♄	□ ♃ ⚼ ♀	24 ⚻Asc25			⚻☉8	3 □♆ 9-11 □☿ 22-26	☍♆1-2 ☌☿6-7	☌♃3 ☌♄3 ☌♇18	☍MC2 ☌♃20 ☌♄21		☌♃♄ ✶♀26 ♎
	OCT	4.3°		□ ♄	23				⚻MC2 5 ☌♃21-24	☌☉5-7	☌♅ 17	☌♇2 ☌♅27		⚺♃♄ ♏25
	NOV	5.3°	⚻ ♀					22	☌♄ 25–30 ✶♀5–9		☍♂6 ☍Asc6 ☌♆8 ☍☿11	☌♅24		✶♃♄ ♐24
↓	DEC	6.3°						☍☽ 19	□☉17 25		☍☉24 ☍♀13 ☍☽22	☌♅9 ☍♂27 ☍Asc28 ☌♆29		□♃♄ ♑24

The Progressed Aspects

Natal Planets Numerical Order	Solar	Mutual		Asc MC
♃ 2.3° ♎				
♄ 3.4° ♎	☉ P □ ♇ R P	♀ P □ ♃ R		Asc P∠ ☽ R
♀ 5.1° ♌	1991–2	1993–4		1992–3
☉ 12.2° ♋		☿ P □ ♃ P		
☽ 15.9° ♌	☉ P ⚺ Asc R	1994–5		Asc P enters ♋
♂ 20.2° ♊	1991–2			1992–3
Asc 21° ♊				
♇ 21.3° ♎	☉ P⚻♆ P 1992–3	♀ P∠♃ R P		
♆ 23°R ♐	☉ P⚻♆ R 1993–4	1992–3		
☿ 26.2° ♊		♀ P∠♄ R P		October 1992
♅ 26.2°R ♏		1992–3		♃ T☌♃
MC 28° ♒				"The ♃ Return"
		♂ P△MC R 1993–4 (Exact)		

5 Calculating the Moon's Aspects

To speed up the calculation of the lunar aspects, and later the transits, we now list on the second progressed form the natal planet's positions, the Ascendant and Midheaven, in numerical order. These are entered in the left-hand section of the top grid. The planet occupying the earliest degree of a sign is Jupiter, on 2.3° Libra. Next comes Saturn, on 3.4° Libra.

You may find it useful to make a full list on a piece of rough paper, then double check it for accuracy.

Making the calculations

We are now ready to calculate the aspects the progressed Moon makes to the natal and progressed planets' positions, Ascendant and Midheaven. As well as referring to the column headed "Natal Planets in Numerical Order", we must check the progressed planets' positions from their placings in the outer rim of the first progressed chart.

Lunar aspects through the year

No lunar aspects are exact during January. However, in February, the progressed Moon's position is 26° Sagittarius, so it is in opposition to the natal Mercury and semi-sextile to the natal Uranus. Because the progressed Uranus has not moved on from 26° Scorpio, the progressed Moon also makes a semi-sextile aspect to the progressed Uranus. In March, the progressed Moon makes an opposition to the progressed Mars.

The next aspect it makes is during April, when it forms a sextile to the natal Midheaven. In June, it makes an opposition to the progressed Ascendant (which was moving from Gemini into Cancer at this period). Note, too, that this month the progressed Moon moves into Capricorn. In July it makes an opposition to the progressed Mercury. Continue in this way until you have calculated all the lunar progressions.

In September the progressed Moon makes a sesquare aspect to the progressed Venus. The sesquare (135°) and the semi-square (45°) are easy to miss; always double check for them. As you calculate each aspect, enter it in the aspects column of the large progressed aspects grid.

Now we must calculate the aspects of the progressed planets (other than the Moon), the progressed Ascendant and Midheaven to the natal planets' positions and to each other. These indicate the background conditions operative for the period under consideration.

6 CALCULATING THE SOLAR ASPECTS

Any aspect the progressed Sun makes is very important. It was on 22° Cancer between March 1992 and March 1993. No other planet, natal or progressed, falls on that degree, but during 1991-2, the Sun (on 21° Cancer) made a square aspect to the natal and progressed Pluto. This is listed in the solar column. While no longer exact, it is still operative.

Radical and progressed aspects

Note here two more pieces of astrological shorthand: the "R" and "P" following Sun P square Pluto in the solar column. These letters stand for Radical and Progressed. Radical is another word for natal; be careful not to confuse it with the same letter "R", standing for retrograde. Note, too, the progressed Sun's aspects to Neptune progressed, in 1992-3, and to Neptune radical, in 1993-4.

7 CALCULATING THE MUTUAL ASPECTS

As we have already calculated the lunar aspects, we now calculate those of the progressed Mercury. During 1992-3 this planet occupies 1° Cancer. During 1993-4, it moves on to 2°, whence it will make a square aspect to the radical (natal) Jupiter. Venus makes minor, semi-square aspects to Jupiter and Saturn while Mars will make an exact trine to the radical Midheaven during 1993-4. (This aspect was just within orb in the birth chart.) Finally, we enter the progressed Ascendant in semi-square aspect to the radical (natal) Moon, and note the very important indication that the progressed Ascendant is entering Cancer.

Covering longer periods

This completes calculations for the day for a year background progressions. It is, of course, not difficult to cover far

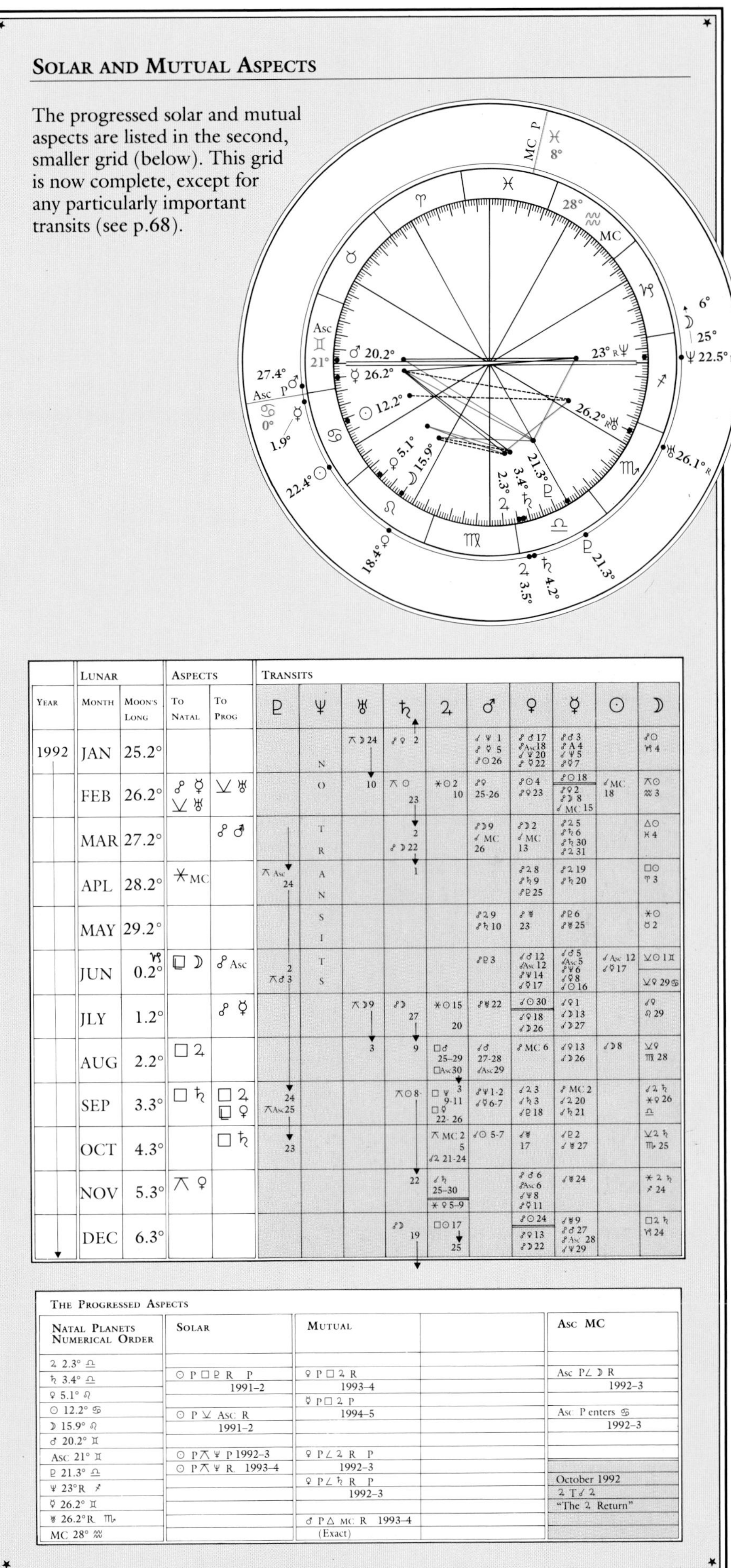

LUNAR			ASPECTS		TRANSITS									
YEAR	MONTH	MOON'S LONG	TO NATAL	TO PROG	♇	♆	♅	♄	♃	♂	♀	☿	☉	☽
1992	JAN	25.2°				N	⚻☽24	☍♀ 2		☌♆1 ☍☿5 ☍☉26	☍♂17 ☍Asc18 ☌♆20 ☍☿22	☍♂3 ☍A4 ☌♆5 ☍☿7		☍☉ ♑4
	FEB	26.2°	☍☿ ⚺♅	⚺♅		O	10	⚻☉ 23	✱☉2 10	☍♀ 25-26	☍☉4 ☍♀23	☍☉18 ☍♀2 ☍☽8 ☌MC15	☌MC 18	⚻☉ ♒3
	MAR	27.2°		☍♂		T R		2 ☍☽22		☍☽9 ☌MC 26	☍☽2 ☌MC 13	☍♃5 ☍♄6 ☍♄30 ☍♃31		△☉ ♓4
	APL	28.2°	✱MC		⚻Asc 24	A N		1			☍♃8 ☍♄9 ☍♇25	☍♃19 ☍♄20		□☉ ♈3
	MAY	29.2°				S I				☍♃9 ☍♄10	☍♅ 23	☍♇6 ☍♅25		✱☉ ♉2
	JUN	♑ 0.2°	□☽	☍Asc	2 ⚻♂3	T S				☍♇3	☌♂12 ☌Asc12 ☍♆14 ☌☿17	☌♂5 ☌Asc5 ☍♆6 ☌☿8 ☌☉16	☌Asc 12 ☌☿17	⚺☉1♊ ⚺♀29♋
	JLY	1.2°		☍☿			⚻☽9	☍☽ 27	✱☉15 20	☍♅22	☌☉30 ☌♀18 ☌☽26	☌♀1 ☌☽13 ☌☽27		☌♀ ♌29
	AUG	2.2°	□♃				3	9	□♂ 25–29 □Asc30	☌♂ 27-28 ☌Asc29	☍MC 6	☌♀13 ☌☽26	☌☽8	⚺♀ ♍28
	SEP	3.3°	□♄	□♃ □♀	24 ⚻Asc25			⚻☉8	3 □♆ 9-11 □☿ 22-26	☍♆1-2 ☌☿6-7	☌♃3 ☌♄3 ☌♇18	☍MC2 ☌♃20 ☌♄21		☌♃♄ ✱♀26 ♎
	OCT	4.3°		□♄	23				⚻MC 2 5 ☌♃ 21-24	☌☉5-7	☌♅ 17	☌♇2 ☌♅27		⚺♃♄ ♏25
	NOV	5.3°	⚻♀					22	☌♄ 25–30 ✱♀5–9		☍♂6 ☍Asc6 ☌♆8 ☍☿11	☌♅24		✱♃♄ ♐24
	DEC	6.3°						☍☽ 19	□☉17 25		☍☉24 ☍♀13 ☍☽22	☌♅9 ☍♂27 ☍Asc28 ☌♆29		□♃♄ ♑24

THE PROGRESSED ASPECTS

NATAL PLANETS NUMERICAL ORDER	SOLAR	MUTUAL		ASC MC
♃ 2.3° ♎				
♄ 3.4° ♎	☉ P □ ♇ R P	♀ P □ ♃ R		Asc P∠ ☽ R
♀ 5.1° ♌	1991–2	1993–4		1992–3
☉ 12.2° ♋		☿ P □ ♃ P		
☽ 15.9° ♌	☉ P ⚺ Asc R	1994–5		Asc P enters ♋
♂ 20.2° ♊	1991–2			1992–3
Asc 21° ♊				
♇ 21.3° ♎	☉ P⚻ ♆ P 1992–3	♀ P∠ ♃ R P		
♆ 23°R ♐	☉ P⚻ ♆ R 1993–4	1992–3		
☿ 26.2° ♊		♀ P∠ ♄ R P		October 1992
♅ 26.2°R ♏		1992–3		♃ T☌ ♃
MC 28° ♒				"The ♃ Return"
		♂ P△ MC R 1993–4		
		(Exact)		

longer periods of time – the process is exactly the same. But we feel that because our lives and circumstances change so abruptly, it is all too easy to become apprehensive or overoptimistic about long-term trends. Here, we have the structure to interpret several years in a general way.

8 Calculating the Transits

As they move around the solar system, the planets constantly make relationships to the positions they occupied at the moment of birth.

The influence of transits

Often these relationships provide very potent influences, which sometimes have the effect of highlighting the background day-for-a-year progressions. More importantly, they also produce a variety of energies of which advantage should be taken. Most, though not all, astrologers use only the transiting planets' relationships to the natal planets, Ascendant and Midheaven, and not to the progressed planets, Ascendant and Midheaven. When you are more experienced, you will probably want to discover for yourself how effective the latter can be. For more on the transits, see p.60.

Making the calculations

This stage of progressing the chart is not as complicated as it may seem from looking at the transit section of the large, lower grid.

Mercury, Venus and Mars move much more quickly through the sky than their fellows, so when relating the positions of the transiting planets – the ones at present moving through the sky – to the positions of the planets in the birth chart, we do not use the squares, trines, sextiles or quincunxes because these transits pass so quickly. So for the three fast moving planets we need to look out for conjunctions and oppositions only. For the other planets, we use all aspects except the weak semi-sextiles, sesquares and semi-squares. For solar transits, see pp.76-7.

To work out which transits are operative during 1992, turn to the relevant section of the ephemeris on p.386. (Always double check – are you on the right page, and looking at the right month and year?)

Calculating Pluto's Transits

First look at Pluto. You will see that on 1 January 1992, Pluto is on 22° Scorpio. Referring to the list of planets in numerical order on the form, we find no natal planet occupying that degree of a sign. On 27 April, Pluto moves back to 21° Scorpio. Looking again at the list, we see that the natal Ascendant occupies 21° Gemini, and Pluto itself (in the birth chart) is on 21° Libra. So Pluto makes a quincunx transit to the Ascendant, and a semi-sextile to its own position (which, however, we ignore – see above). In the square allotted to April and to Pluto, enter Pluto ⊼ Ascendant 27. (The "27" refers to the date when this transit is first exact.) Turn back to the ephemeris to find how long Pluto will occupy 21° Scorpio – it stays there until 2 June. Write "2" in the square allotted to Pluto and June. As this is a lengthy influence, it is as well to draw a line connecting the two dates.

Transits through the year

On 3 June, Pluto moves back once more to 20° Scorpio. In the natal chart, Mars falls on 20° Gemini, so here is another quincunx. Record this transit on the grid. Look through the ephemeris to see how long Pluto stays on 20° Scorpio – it will be there until 24 September. (Note that Pluto, which went retrograde in January, turns to direct motion on 30 July while it is on 20° Scorpio.)

On 25 September it moves on to 21° Scorpio, thus again making the quincunx aspect to the Ascendant. Enter this on the grid. The transit is operative until 23 October. Between then and the end of 1992, Pluto occupies 22°, 23° and 24° Scorpio, while in the birth chart Neptune occupies 23° Sagittarius. However, this transit is a semi-sextile and therefore not powerful enough for consideration.

Pluto makes no more transits during the rest of 1992.

Calculating Neptune's Transits

We now turn to Neptune, which on 1 January is on 16° Capricorn. Note that there are no planets on this degree in the birth chart. During 1992, Neptune occupies 16°, 17° and 18° Capricorn, and so makes no transits to any natal planets, or to the Ascendant or Midheaven. Enter this on the grid.

Calculating Uranus' Transits

Moving on to Uranus, we find that on 24 January it occupies 15° Capricorn and (because, of course, that sign is five signs – 150° – on from Leo) will make a quincunx transit to the Moon, which is on 15° Leo. Because Uranus turns retrograde in April, it will make the same transit again between 9 July and 3 August. Uranus does not make any more transits during 1992.

Calculating Saturn's Transits

Saturn occupies 5° Aquarius on 2 January, and already makes an opposition transit to Venus, then moves on to 6° on 3 January. Note this transit on the grid, but to show that the influence was already operative before the New Year, draw a small arrow pointing upwards, as a reminder. Calculate the remaining Saturn transits for the rest of 1992 with the ephemeris and the list shown on the transit grid. Note that the opposition to the Moon continues into 1993 – as shown by the small arrow pointing downwards.

Calculating Jupiter's Transits

While Jupiter makes a sextile transit to the Sun between 2 and 10 February, it does not really get busy until mid-July, when not only is that transit repeated, but a number of Jupiter transits are operative until the end of November. Follow them through for practice. There are two points to note in the October transits: first, as there are rather a lot of them, they take up more than the allotted space on the grid allows. To show that all the indications occur during October, draw an additional line showing where October ends. Secondly, that month the transiting Jupiter conjuncts the natal Jupiter – the subject experiences a Jupiter Return (see pp.296-7). This important transit should be noted in the small grid, as it can colour the whole year.

CALCULATING MARS', VENUS' AND MERCURY'S TRANSITS

The fast moving planets – Mars, Venus and Mercury – provide many more transits. However, the technique of calculating them is rather different – remember, we only use conjunctions and oppositions – so we only need refer to the drawing of the birth chart in the centre of the progressed chart.

Turn to January in the ephemeris. On 1 January, Mars occupies 23° Sagittarius, and on that day makes a conjunction to Neptune. Look now at the birth chart. You know that Mars is on 23° Sagittarius, forming a conjunction to Neptune. Visualize it in that position and look across the chart – in this case to Gemini (the opposite sign to Sagittarius). There you see Mercury, on 26° Gemini. This will be Mars' next transit. Check in the ephemeris: Mars will reach 26° on 5 January, when the opposition is formed. Looking at the chart, it is clear that the next opposition will be between Mars and the Sun, which is on 12° Cancer. Again, look at the ephemeris to find out when Mars will reach 12° of Capricorn (because Capricorn is opposite Cancer); it will do so on 26 January.

You must now discover when Mars (this time from Aquarius) will make oppositions to the Moon and Venus in Leo, and a conjunction to the Aquarian Midheaven. These are listed. As there are no natal planets in either Pisces or Virgo, Mars will now remain dormant until it occupies 2° Aries, making an opposition to Jupiter, and then 3° Aries, making an opposition to Saturn). As you will see, these transits occur on 9 and 10 May respectively.

The remaining transits

Check the remaining Mars transits, then the Venus and Mercury transits, in the same manner – always carefully referring to the sign they occupy and relating it to that sign and the polar, or opposite, sign in the birth chart.

Exact transits

Sometimes you may find that it is difficult to decide when a transit of Mars, Venus or Mercury is exact. For example, on 17 January 1992, Venus occupies 19.9° Sagittarius, and by 18 January has moved to 21° Sagittarius.

THE COMPLETED GRIDS

You now have a completed grid for the progressed planets and the aspects they will make during a future year in your subject's life. This is your major tool for interpretation of the future trends. For an example of an interpretation of a progressed chart, see pp.141-7.

	LUNAR		ASPECTS		TRANSITS									
YEAR	MONTH	MOON'S LONG	TO NATAL	TO PROG	♇	♆	♅	♄	♃	♂	♀	☿	☉	☽
1992	JAN	25.2°				N	⚻☽24	☍♀ 2		☌♆1 ☍☿5 ☍☉26	☍♂17 ☍Asc18 ☌♆20 ☍☿22	☍♂3 ☍Asc4 ☌♆5 ☍☿7		☍☉ ♑4
↓	FEB	26.2°	☍☿ ⚺♅	⚺♅		O	↓ 10	⚻☉ 23	⚹☉2 10	☍♀ 25-26	☍☉4 ☍♀23	☍☉18 / ☍♀2 ☍☽8 ☌MC15	☌MC 18	⚻☉ ♒3
	MAR	27.2°		☍♂	↓	T R		↓ 2 ☍☽22		☍☽9 ☌MC 26	☍☽2 ☌MC 13	☍♃5 ☍♄6 ☍♄30 ☍♃31		△☉ ♓4
	APL	28.2°	⚹MC		⚻Asc 24	A N		↓ 1			☍♃8 ☍♄9 ☍♇25	☍♃19 ☍♄20		□☉ ♈3
	MAY	29.2°				S I				☍♃9 ☍♄10	☍♅ 23	☍♇6 ☍♅25		⚹☉ ♉2
	JUN	♑ 0.2°	□☽	☍Asc	2 ⚻♂3	T S				☍♇3	☌♂12 ☌Asc12 ☍♆14 ☌☿17	☌♂5 ☌Asc5 ☍♆6 ☌☿8 ☌☉16	☌Asc 12 ☌☿17	⚺☉1♊ / ⚺♀29♋
	JLY	1.2°		☍☿			⚻☽9	☍☽ 27	⚹☉15 20	☍♅22	☌☉30 / ☌♀18 ☌☽26	☌♀1 ☌☽13 ☌☽27		☌♀ ♌29
	AUG	2.2°	□♃				↓ 3	↓ 9	□♂ 25–29 □Asc30	☌♂ 27-28 ☌Asc29	☍MC6	☌♀13 ☌☽26	☌☽8	⚺♀ ♍28
	SEP	3.3°	□♄	□♃ □♀	↓ 24 ⚻Asc25			⚻☉8	↓ 3 □♆ 9-11 □☿ 22-26	☍♆1-2 ☌☿6-7	☌♃3 ☌♄3 ☌♇18	☍MC2 ☌♃20 ☌♄21		☌♃♄ ⚹♀26 ♎
	OCT	4.3°		□♄	↓ 23				⚻MC2 5 ☌♃ 21-24	☌☉ 5-7	☌♅ 17	☌♇2 ☌♅27		⚺♃♄ ♏25
	NOV	5.3°	⚻♀					↓ 22	☌♄ 25–30 / ⚹♀5–9		☍♂6 ☍Asc6 ☌♆8 ☍☿11	☌♅24		⚹♃♄ ♐24
↓	DEC	6.3°						☍☽ 19 ↓	□☉17 ↓ 25		☍☉24 / ☍♀13 ☍☽22	☌♅9 ☍♂27 ☍Asc 28 ☌♆29		□♃♄ ♑24

THE PROGRESSED ASPECTS

NATAL PLANETS NUMERICAL ORDER	SOLAR	MUTUAL		ASC MC
♃ 2.3° ♎				
♄ 3.4° ♎	☉ P □ ♇ R P	♀ P □ ♃ R		Asc P∠ ☽ R
♀ 5.1° ♌	1991–2	1993–4		1992–3
☉ 12.2° ♋		☿ P □ ♃ P		
☽ 15.9° ♌	☉ P ⚺ ASC R	1994–5		Asc P enters ♋
♂ 20.2° ♊	1991–2			1992–3
ASC 21° ♊				
♇ 21.3° ♎	☉ P ⚻ ♆ P 1992–3	♀ P ∠ ♃ R P		
♆ 23°R ♐	☉ P ⚻ ♆ R 1993–4	1992–3		
☿ 26.2° ♊		♀ P ∠ ♄ R P		October 1992
♅ 26.2°R ♏		1992–3		♃ T ☌ ♃
MC 28° ♒				"The ♃ Return"
		♂ P △ MC R 1993–4		
		(Exact)		

In the birth chart, Mars occupies 20° Gemini. In such a case, note the transit as being exact on the earlier date, since these minor transits tend to become effective earlier rather than later.

Note, too, the repeated series of transits from Mercury to Jupiter and Saturn during March and April, to Venus and the Moon during August and September, and to Uranus between October and December. These occur because Mercury turns from direct to retrograde motion, then from retrograde to direct (see p.23). This is, of course, also why Pluto's transits to the Ascendant, and Uranus' transits to the Moon, recur. Such phenomena are very common; be careful you do not miss them when you are calculating transits.

CALCULATING THE SUN'S TRANSITS

There are now just a few solar transits to calculate. Because Leo is not emphasized in this chart (see the note on the table on p.72), we only use conjunctions to the Ascendant, Midheaven, ruling planet and Moon. If Leo is emphasized in the chart, calculate the oppositions as well.

The Progressed Aspects				
Natal Planets Numerical Order	**Solar**	**Mutual**		**Asc MC**
♃ 2.3° ♎				
♄ 3.4° ♎	☉ P □ ♇ R P	♀ P □ ♃ R		Asc P∠ ☽ R
♀ 5.1° ♌	1991–2	1993–4		1992–3
☉ 12.2° ♋		☿ P □ ♃ P		
☽ 15.9° ♌	☉ P ⚺ Asc R	1994–5		Asc P enters ♋
♂ 20.2° ♊	1991–2			1992–3
Asc 21° ♊				
♇ 21.3° ♎	☉ P⚻ ♆ P 1992–3	♀ P∠ ♃ R P		
♆ 23°R ♐	☉ P⚻ ♆ R 1993–4	1992–3		October 1992
☿ 26.2° ♊		♀ P∠ ♄ R P		♃ T☌ ♃
♅ 26.2°R ♏		1992–3		"The ♃ Return"
MC 28° ♒		♂ P△ MC R 1993–4 (Exact)		

Solar and Mutual Aspects
This grid shows the progressed solar and mutual aspects.

Calculating the New Moon's Transits

Look at the 1992 ephemeris (see p.385) and each month in turn. To discover the dates of the New Moon, find the day when both the Sun and the Moon occupy the same sign. The Moon will be new at precisely the moment when it and the Sun form an exact conjunction; that is, during the two hours or so while the Moon occupies the same degree of the same sign as the Sun. But the influence of the New Moon covers about two days – while the Moon is travelling through the same sign as the Sun. If the Moon enters that sign on 1 January – but not until 23.55 p.m. – the influence will last until almost midnight on 3 January. For reasons of space, we cannot include a detailed Moon ephemeris in this book; our rough rule of thumb is adequate at this stage of your study, though ordinary diaries often give the New Moon dates, and even precise times. Of course, a detailed ephemeris for the year in question will give you all the information you require.

Making calculations

Look at the list of planets in numerical order and you will discover whether the New Moon makes an aspect to any of them. Use the Sun's position as your guide, and allow an orb of two degrees. (See also the chart on page 72.)

In our example, at the time of the January New Moon, the Sun occupies 12° Capricorn. So the transiting New Moon makes an opposition to the Sun, in the natal chart. Enter this on the form. Follow this procedure for the whole year.

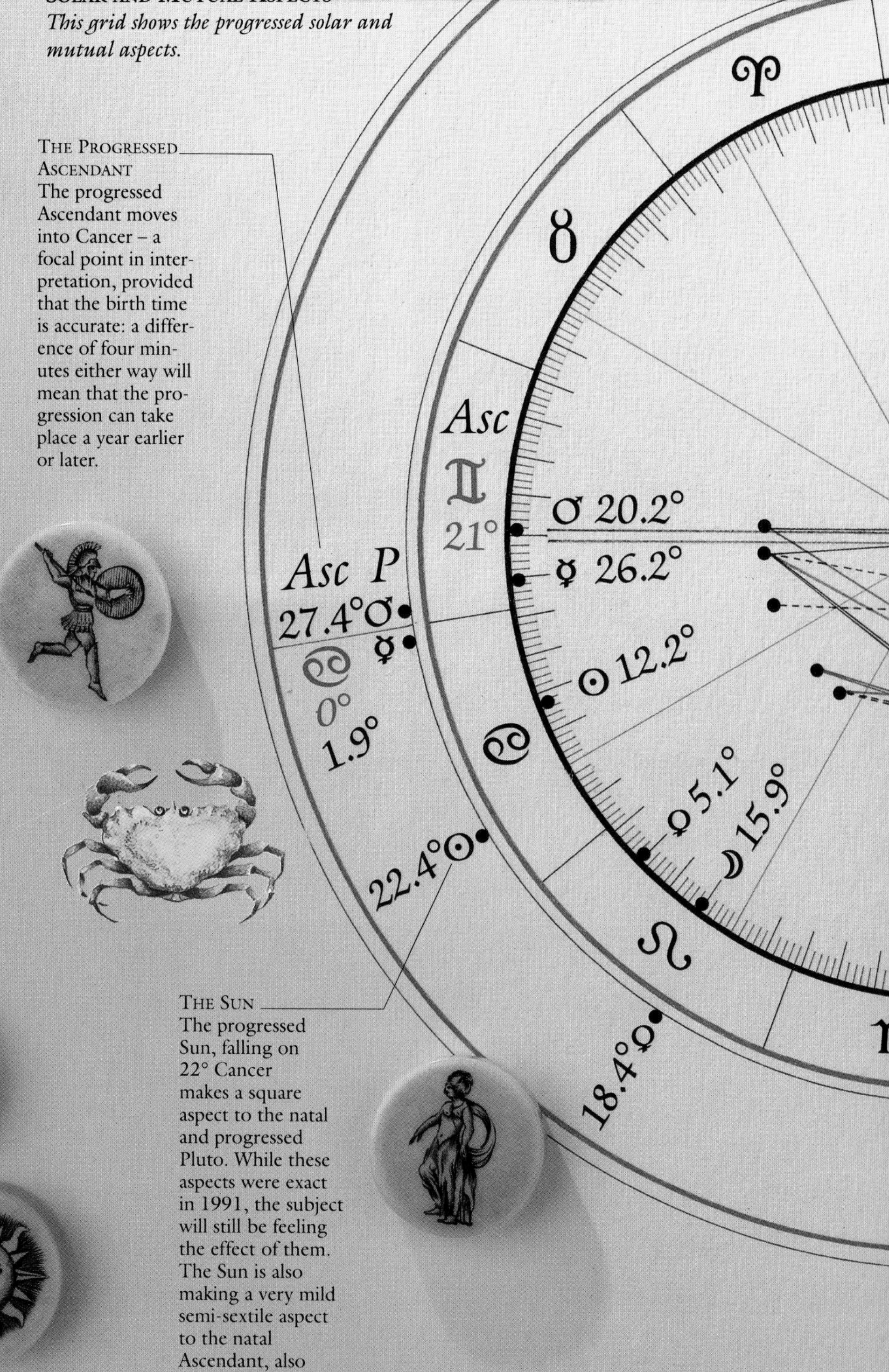

The Progressed Ascendant
The progressed Ascendant moves into Cancer – a focal point in interpretation, provided that the birth time is accurate: a difference of four minutes either way will mean that the progression can take place a year earlier or later.

The Sun
The progressed Sun, falling on 22° Cancer makes a square aspect to the natal and progressed Pluto. While these aspects were exact in 1991, the subject will still be feeling the effect of them. The Sun is also making a very mild semi-sextile aspect to the natal Ascendant, also exact in 1991.

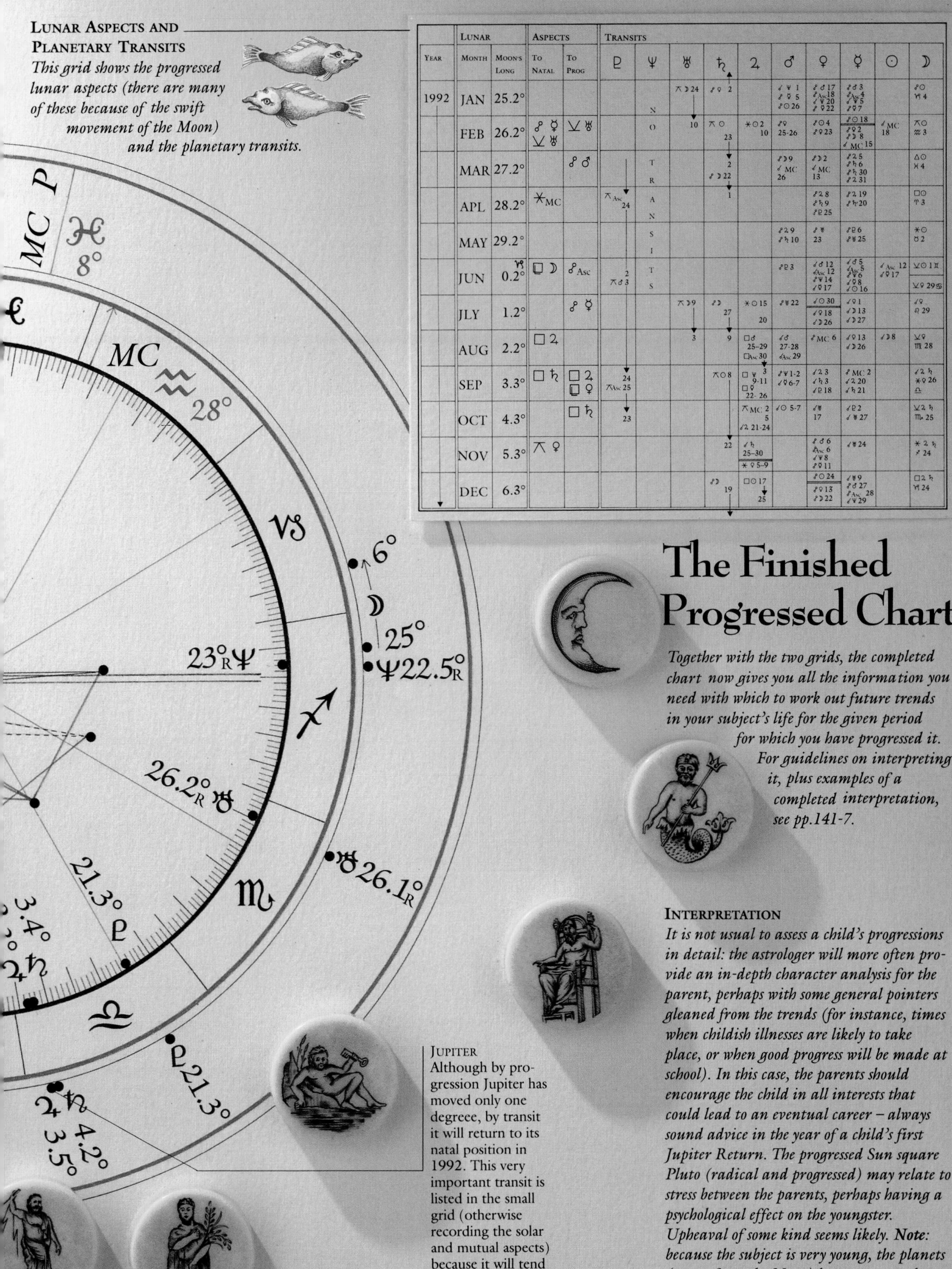

LUNAR ASPECTS AND PLANETARY TRANSITS

This grid shows the progressed lunar aspects (there are many of these because of the swift movement of the Moon) and the planetary transits.

	LUNAR		ASPECTS		TRANSITS									
YEAR	MONTH	MOON'S LONG	TO NATAL	TO PROG	♇	♆	♅	♄	♃	♂	♀	☿	☉	☽
1992	JAN	25.2°					⚻☽ 24 ↓	☍♀ 2 ↑		☌♆ 1 ☍☿ 5 ☍☉ 26	☍♂ 17 ☍Asc 18 ☌♆ 20 ☍☿ 22	☍♂ 3 ☍Asc 4 ☌♆ 5 ☍♀ 7		☍☉ ♑ 4
	FEB	26.2°	☍☿ ⚺♅	⚺♅		N O	10	⚻☉ 23 ↓	⚹☉ 2 10	☍♀ 25-26	☍☉ 4 ☍♀ 23	☍☉ 18 ☍♀ 2 ☍☽ 8 ☌MC 15	☌MC 18	⚻☉ ♒ 3
	MAR	27.2°		☍♂	↓	T R		2 ☍☽ 22 ↓		☍☽ 9 ☌MC 26	☍☽ 2 ☌MC 13	☍♃ 5 ☍♄ 6 ☍♄ 30 ☍♃ 31		△☉ ♓ 4
	APL	28.2°	⚹MC		⚻Asc 24 ↓	A N		1			☍♃ 8 ☍♄ 9 ☍♇ 25	☍♃ 19 ☍♄ 20		□☉ ♈ 3
	MAY	29.2°				S I				☍♃ 9 ☍♄ 10	☍♅ 23	☍♇ 6 ☍♅ 25		⚹☉ ♉ 2
	JUN	♈ 0.2°	□☽	☍Asc	2 ⚻♂ 3	T S				☍♇ 3	☌♂ 12 ☌Asc 12 ☍♆ 14 ☌☿ 17	☌♂ 5 ☌Asc 5 ☍♆ 6 ☌☿ 8 ☌☉ 16	☌Asc 12 ☌☿ 17	⚺☉ 1 ♊ ⚺♀ 29 ♋
	JLY	1.2°		☍☿			⚻☽ 9 ↓	☍☽ 27 ↓	⚹☉ 15 20	☍♅ 22	☌☉ 30 ☌♀ 18 ☌☽ 26	☌♀ 1 ☌☽ 13 ☌☽ 27		☌♀ ♌ 29
	AUG	2.2°	□♃				3	9	□♂ 25–29 □Asc 30 ↓	☌♂ 27-28 ☌Asc 29	☍MC 6	☌♀ 13 ☌☽ 26	☌☽ 8	⚺♀ ♍ 28
	SEP	3.3°	□♄	□♃ □♀	24 ⚻Asc 25 ↓			⚻☉ 8 ↓	3 □♆ 9-11 □☿ 22- 26	☍♆ 1-2 ☌☿ 6-7	☌♃ 3 ☌♄ 3 ☌♇ 18	☍MC 2 ☌♃ 20 ☌♄ 21		☌♃ ♄ ⚹♀ 26 ♎
	OCT	4.3°		□♄	23				⚻MC 2 5 ☌♃ 21-24	☌☉ 5-7	☌♅ 17	☌♇ 2 ☌♅ 27		⚺♃ ♄ ♏ 25
	NOV	5.3°	⚻♀					22	☌♄ 25–30 ⚹♀ 5–9		☍♂ 6 ☍Asc 6 ☌♆ 8 ☍☿ 11	☌♅ 24		⚹♃ ♄ ♐ 24
↓	DEC	6.3°						☍☽ 19 ↓	□☉ 17 ↓ 25		☍☉ 24 ☍♀ 13 ☍☽ 22	☌♅ 9 ☍♂ 27 ☍Asc 28 ☌♆ 29		□♃ ♄ ♑ 24

The Finished Progressed Chart

Together with the two grids, the completed chart now gives you all the information you need with which to work out future trends in your subject's life for the given period for which you have progressed it. For guidelines on interpreting it, plus examples of a completed interpretation, see pp.141-7.

INTERPRETATION

It is not usual to assess a child's progressions in detail: the astrologer will more often provide an in-depth character analysis for the parent, perhaps with some general pointers gleaned from the trends (for instance, times when childish illnesses are likely to take place, or when good progress will be made at school). In this case, the parents should encourage the child in all interests that could lead to an eventual career – always sound advice in the year of a child's first Jupiter Return. The progressed Sun square Pluto (radical and progressed) may relate to stress between the parents, perhaps having a psychological effect on the youngster. Upheaval of some kind seems likely. ***Note:*** *because the subject is very young, the planets (apart from the Moon) have not moved any great distance.)*

JUPITER

Although by progression Jupiter has moved only one degreee, by transit it will return to its natal position in 1992. This very important transit is listed in the small grid (otherwise recording the solar and mutual aspects) because it will tend to color the subject's whole year.

Progressions and Transits

Transits				Progressions
Planet	**Length of Astronomical Influence**	**Astro-logical "Timing" Transits**	**Length of Astrological Influence**	**Length of Influence of Progressed Planets when in Aspect to Natal or Progressed Planets, the Ascendant or Midheaven**
♇	Average stay on degree = 1 month. Up to 4 months when planet is stationary, retrograde, changing from direct to retrograde or retrograde to direct	Easy	Usually coincides with astronomical positions	♇ Does not form progressed aspects
♆	Average stay on degree = 1 month. Up to 4 months when planet is stationary, retrograde, changing from direct to retrograde or retrograde to direct	Very difficult	Influence tends to build slowly, usually 2-3 weeks before planet is on relevant degree, and fade over similar period of time	♆ Does not form progressed aspects
♅	Average stay on degree = 2 1/2 weeks. Up to 10 1/2 weeks when planet is stationary, retrograde, changing from direct to retrograde or retrograde to direct	Moderately easy	Usually coincides with astronomical positions	♅ Does not form progressed aspects
♄	Average stay on degree = 9 days. Up to 2 months when planet is stationary, retrograde, changing from direct to retrograde or retrograde to direct	Difficult	Influence builds slowly, usually starting 2-3 weeks before transit is exact and will take 3 weeks or so to ease afterwards	It is unlikely that Saturn would form a progressed aspect during a lifetime
♃	Average stay on degree = 4-5 days. Up to seven weeks when planet is stationary, retrograde, changing from direct to retrograde, or retrograde to direct	Moderately easy	Usually about 10 days when planet is direct. Allow an additonal week before and after transit is exact if planet is retrograde, etc.	These do not occur very often. When they do the influence will be in the background for about a decade – and would, from time to time, tend to strengthen Jupiter transits
* ♂	Average stay on degree = 2 days. Up to 2 weeks when planet is stationary, retrograde, changing from direct to retrograde or retrograde to direct	Easy	Influence usually lasts as long as transit is exact, but it is advisable to allow two days either side of exactitude, 3 or 4 if planet is retrograde, etc.	These will form a background influence which will probably be operative for about 4 years; longer if Mars is personalized
* ♀	Average stay on degree = 1-2 days. Up to 2 weeks when planet is stationary, retrograde, changing from direct to retrograde or retrograde to direct	Easy	Influence will color about 5 days. Allow 2 days either side of exactitude if planet is retrograde, etc.	These influences will be operative for about 3 years; longer if Venus is personalized
* ☿	Average stay on degree = 1 day or less. Up to 8 days when planet is stationary, retrograde, changing from direct to retrograde, or retrograde to direct	Easy	Influence will usually color 3 days, allow 1 day either side of exactitude if planet is retrograde, etc.	These influences will be operative for about 2 years; longer if Mercury is personalized
** ☉	Average stay on degree 1 day. The Sun is never retrograde	Easy	One day, but influence can color about a week if Leo is the Sun, Ascendant or Moon sign. These influences occur on the same dates – or thereabouts – every year	These are usually important influences which "fade in" the year preceeding exactitude and "fade out" the year after exactitude
☽	Any aspects the New Moon forms to natal planets will last about 3 days, but remember that very often similar themes recur over a period of several months.			These are easy to time. The average lunar progression is usually operative for 3 months, but often the Moon will make a progressed aspect to a natal planet's position, then a few months later make the same aspect to the planet's progressed position. What is focused is either carried over or recurs

This plan gives an idea of the lengths of influences of both transits and progressions, from an astronomical as well as an astrological point of view. Remember, however, that it is only a general guide. The planets influence us very individually and you will come to realize their strengths and weaknesses in every chart the longer you work on it.

* Calculate conjunction and opposition only

** Calculate conjunction only to Moon, Ascendant, Midheaven and ruling planet. If Leo is Sun, Moon or Ascendant, calculate conjunction or opposition to all planets and angles

Additional Techniques

In addition to the conventional birth chart, astrologers use a number of well-tried techniques to examine the relationship between the moment and place of birth and the personality and character of a subject. Astrologers disagree about the viability of these techniques, but as you become more confident in your interpreting skills, you may well find different techniques offer new insights. Here, we outline two of the most important techniques: midpoints and harmonics. You can also use horary astrology to answer specific questions.

Individual astrologers sometimes make use of other indications: for instance, the effect of asteroids, comets, eclipses, hypothetical planets, parallels, stations and degree areas. Some of these may be useful, but there is one obvious drawback: insert enough allegedly important factors into a chart and you can find in it whatever you wish! Dr Geoffrey Dean, in his *Recent Advances in Natal Astrology* (1977), reproduces a chart into which have been inserted 3 angles, 10 planets, 4 asteroids, 30 hypothetical planets and all the corresponding nodes and parts. There are over 120 factors in the chart, and to make sense of it an astrologer would have to consider 6,000 aspects, 50,000 midpoints and over a million and a half aspects between midpoints.

Midpoints

Students of astrology will come across what appears to be a modern technique sometimes referred to as the "Ebertin method", sometimes as "Cosmobiology". The reference is to midpoints, or "half-sums", as they are sometimes called. This system – much studied today – has been in use since the thirteenth century.

The theory of midpoints is that the degree of the ecliptic falling halfway between any two planets, a planet and the Ascendant or Midheaven, or between those two, is important and should be used in interpretation. It can be activated by transit, lunar progression or major progression; or a natal planet may fall on the midpoint of two other planets in the birth chart itself.

It is not difficult to find the midpoint between two planets: it is merely a question of counting the number of degrees separating them and then halving it. So if there is, for instance,

Direct Midpoints

In this example Venus falls on Leo 5° and Mars on Gemini 5°. The midpoint of these two planets is therefore Cancer 5° – this is the point of the zodiac circle halfway between them. But it is most important to remember that this direct midpoint is also picked up right across the zodiac by the polar or opposite degree, Capricorn 5°, and that a transit to either of these two degrees will energize Venus and Mars in the chart. Should there be a planet on Cancer or Capricorn 5° in the birth chart, the three planets will form a strong midpoint structure.

Orbs and midpoints
In this example, the Midheaven stands at Cancer 19°, but while this is near the Venus/Mars midpoint, it is considerably out of orb, and therefore will not have an influence. This is because an orb of only 2° must be used for birth chart midpoints. For progressions and transits to a midpoint the planet contacting it should generally speaking have no orb (i.e. strike at the same degree, when its effect will be felt).

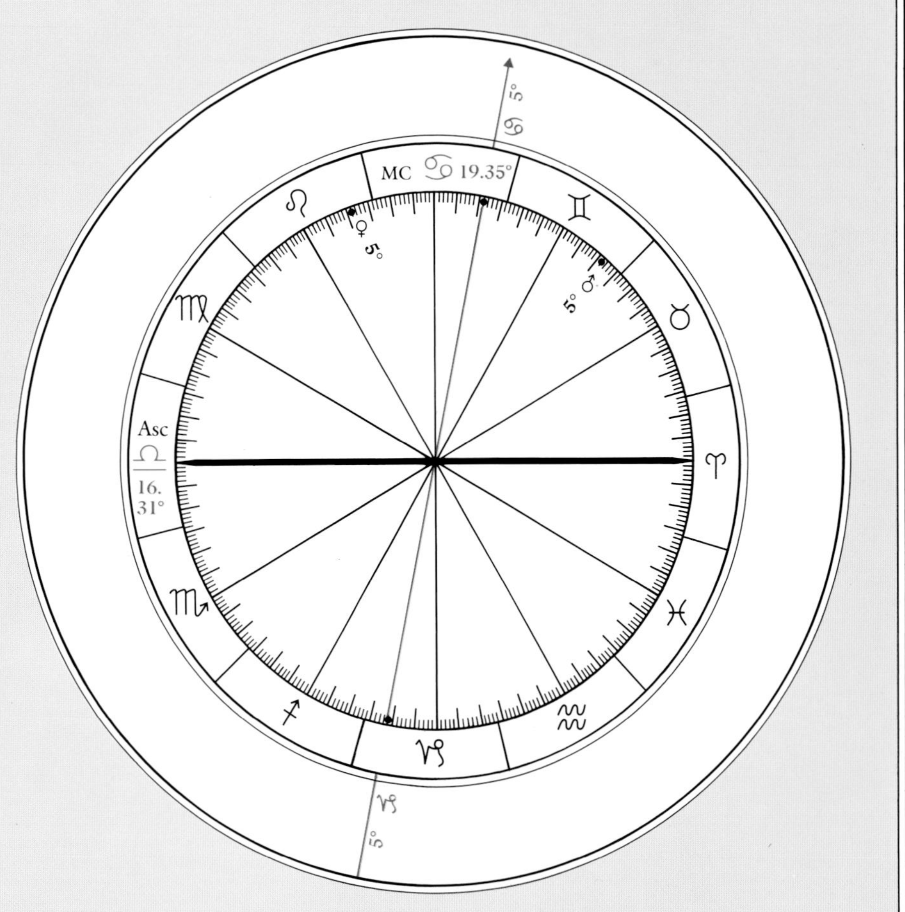

one planet at 5° Gemini and one at 5° Leo, the midpoint between the two will fall at 5° Cancer.

Other midpoints may also be considered, for instance those between the angles and between each angle and each planet. These are known as "direct midpoints". "Indirect midpoints" mark degrees of the ecliptic said to be sensitive because they fall at points of the charts that are semi-square, square or sesquare to the Ascendant, Midheaven, planets or other important points of the chart – including the direct midpoints.

Not all the midpoints in a chart will be of interest. The midpoint between the Ascendant and Midheaven is usually considered most sensitive, and is a good one with which to begin experimental interpretation. Consider its polarity as well as its native position.

Although the houses are not taken into account when working with midpoints, the interpretation of midpoints is identical with that of conventional astrology. If there is a planet on the midpoint between two other planets, its influence is considered with theirs.

Midpoints in interpretation

If we take all the conventional indications noted in a chart and then add all the direct and indirect midpoints, the number of separate factors open to interpretation is greatly increased. For the student this can be confusing. So while some astrologers use midpoints exclusively in the interpretation of a chart, we urge caution, while admitting that the information midpoints offer is extremely valuable when building up a full interpretation.

Harmonics

The theory of harmonics is one of the very few modern astrological conceptions to have become respectable. It provides a wider range of aspects than those conventionally used, and was elaborated by the British astrologer John Addey (1920-82).

When interpreting harmonic charts, those who have found the theory most interesting have turned to the East (whence many astrological theories originally came), and, to some extent, to the tenets of numerology. People who regard numerology as a mere superstition need not reject harmonics. That would be to ignore the deep psychological significance of numbers, which is seen in ancient religious texts. And there is little doubt that harmonics provide a new way of exploring the subtleties of the birth chart.

Dividing the chart

The conventional aspects studied in a birth chart rely – as does so much in astrology – on a numerical basis: the trine has the quality, as it were, of the number three (one planet being one

Indirect Midpoints

This chart shows Jupiter at 0° Aries and Mercury at 15° Leo. To find the indirect midpoint it is necessary first to discover the direct midpoint. This stands at Gemini/Sagittarius 7.5°. An indirect midpoint aspect for Mercury and Jupiter is therefore found on the exact square to that point – at 90° either side of it, on Virgo 7.5° and Pisces 7.5° (emphasizing the mutable qualities in the chart). When planets transit these points, the influence of Mercury and Jupiter will be activated.

Other indirect midpoints fall at the semi-square and the sesquare, i.e. 45° and 135° away from Gemini 7.5°, so they are at Aries, Cancer, Libra and Capricorn 22.5° (emphasizing the cardinal qualities of the chart).

1 Direct midpoint

2 Most commonly used indirect midpoints

3 Other indirect midpoints

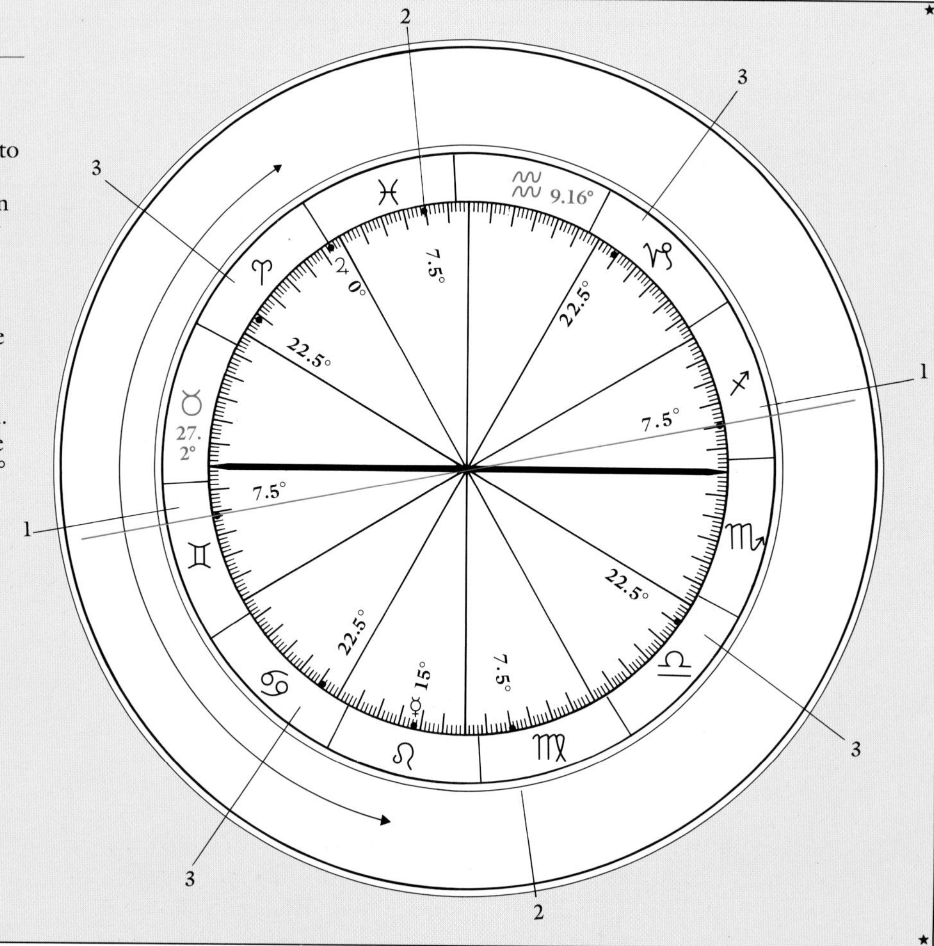

third of the way around the chart from the one to which it makes a trine aspect); the opposition and square that of two; the sextile, that of six.

Essentially, we use harmonics to look more closely into the chart by dividing it into equal segments, then looking at each segment individually. A fifth harmonic chart divides the circle into five segments, the fourth into quarters; the ninth into nine parts, and so on. So far, astrologers have concentrated on examining the fourth, fifth, seventh and ninth harmonics.

Making calculations
It is becoming difficult to buy pocket calculators that have a key which converts decimals into degrees, minutes and seconds. So here we give the manual calculations. (Astrological computer programs can be bought, of course, which produce harmonic charts in a matter of seconds.)

To find a planet's harmonic position, follow these calculations, which are to find the fifth harmonic position of a planet on Leo 11°20':

1. Convert its zodiac position into absolute longitude. This is done simply by counting the number of degrees around the circle from Aries 0° to its position (see the chart, right). A planet which is on Leo 11°20', for instance, is therefore at 131°20' absolute longitude: there are 120° between Aries 0° and Leo 0°, but you add the 11° of Leo, making 131°.

2. Multiply the absolute longitude by the number of the harmonic position you wish to find. In our example: 131 x 5 = 655.

But you have also to deal with the 20': 20' x 5 = 100' = 1°40' (100 – 60), which you add to 131. So the planet's absolute longitude position is 132°40'.
(**Note**: if the answer is greater than 360, subtract 360, and if necessary go on doing so until you arrive at a number less than 360.)

3. Convert the absolute longitude position back into zodiacal longitude: divide 132 by 30.

5 x 30 = 120; the fifth sign on from Aries is Leo, so the planet's fifth harmonic position is Leo 12°40'.

Here is another example. To find the seventh harmonic position of a planet on Gemini 27°14':

1. 27°14' Gemini = 60° + 27°14' = 87°14'

2. 87° x 7 = 609°.
14' x 7 = 98' = 1°38'
609° + 1°38' = 610°38'

3. 610°38' – 360 = 250°38'
– 8 x 30 = 240°38'

So the seventh harmonic position of a planet on Gemini 27°14' (zodiacal position) is Sagittarius 10°38'.

Interpretating harmonic charts
Generally, harmonic charts can be said to reilluminate relationships between planets that already have a relationship in the "ordinary" birth chart, and also reveal new, perhaps more refined relationships between them and other planets. Most of the information that can be gleaned from a harmonic chart is already present in the original, "radical" chart; but you will discover that it provides a way of "fine tuning" it. The aspects you will find in a harmonic chart should be used to expand your understanding of what you have already found – or, perhaps, to help you to resolve contradictions or understand anomalies.

The importance of orbs
Orbs (see p.54) are very important when working with harmonic charts. There is a moderately complex system of graduating the orbs allowed for the various aspects. It is unnecessary to explain this here, but note that the orbs allowed for aspects in harmonic charts are:

Conjunction	12°
Opposition	6°
Trine	4°
Square	3°
Sextile	2°
Semi-sextile	1°3'
Semi-sextile and quincunx	1°

Close aspects or unaspected planets
When looking at harmonic charts, pay attention to close aspects and unaspected planets. Close aspects in the radical chart will be strongly supported in the harmonic charts; interpret them first as you find them in the radical chart, then look at them as they are echoed in the harmonic charts.

Unaspected planets, or weakly aspected planets in the radical chart may, of course, be important, and the way in which they work in the personality of the subject can often be found by studying one or other of the harmonic charts. Look especially for patterns of aspects in the harmonic charts – more than three planets in aspect to each other. The more exact an aspect, the stronger its effect.

Using harmonics
It should be remembered that, while there has been much discussion of harmonics as a system, it is still in its infancy, and must be used cautiously. When the so-called "modern planets" were discovered, it took astrologers many years to work out the nature and

LONGITUDE POSITIONS

The following table shows the absolute longitude position for 0° of each zodiacal sign:

♈	0° Aries = 0°
♉	0° Taurus = 30°
♊	0° Gemini = 60°
♋	0° Cancer = 90°
♌	0° Leo = 120°
♍	0° Virgo = 150°
♎	0° Libra = 180°
♏	0° Scorpio = 210°
♐	0° Sagittarius = 240°
♑	0° Capricorn = 270°
♒	0° Aquarius = 300°
♓	0° Pisces = 330°

extent of their influence; a similar process continues with the theory of harmonics. Until you have done a lot of work on the subject, it is wise to use only the most notable patterns in support of the conclusions drawn from your study of the radical chart.

The fourth harmonic
The fourth harmonic is related to the opposition, square and semi-square, generally considered to be somewhat strenuous aspects. The fourth harmonic chart seems to relate to some kind of dearth in the subject's life – a requirement which is not being fulfilled, or perhaps failure to reconcile some elements in the personality – generally a longing for wholeness in some area of life where at present there is conflict or vacancy.

Elements which are not integrated may be shown by a conjunction or opposition; squares or semi-squares may represent a blockage of some kind – or perhaps an outside force against achievement. The more conjunctions, oppositions, squares and semi-squares in the fourth harmonic chart, the more effort will be needed to overcome obstacles in the pursuit of wholeness.

The fifth harmonic
The effects of the fifth harmonic remain somewhat mysterious. It relates to a numerical idea foreign in western astrology, where the number five has no reference; so astrologers have had more difficulty in conceiving an interpretation of it. John Addey believed that this chart could reveal the artistic side of an individual – by which is probably meant the creative urge, however that is expressed, and the energy with which it is expressed. You may certainly find this chart useful when, for instance, attempting to find new.fields of interest for someone whose horizons need expanding, and to that extent it may be especially interesting when you are advising people who are unemployed or retired, or for some other reason have hours to fill without ideas of how to fill them.

The seventh harmonic
As with the fifth harmonic, the area of personality illuminated by the seventh harmonic chart is somewhat conjectural. Astrologers have linked it to the conception of the divine, to the devleopment of spiritual values, to imaginative creativity, and also to the idea of romance (embracing not only romance expressed in personal relationships, but also a romantic view of the world).

The ninth harmonic
There is general agreement that the ninth harmonic chart reveals the capacity for sheer enjoyment of life, both within a subject and in his relationships with other people.

Horary Astrology

In the days when astrology was considered to be chiefly a means of prediction, horary astrology provided the answers to a great number of everyday questions. It was the means used, for instance, by the seventeenth-century astrologer William Lilly to reveal the answers to such questions as whether a seaman would return safely from a dangerous journey, where a thief had hidden stolen goods or whether someone would be successful in a planned seduction.

Although horary astrology has enjoyed a certain vogue in recent years, most modern practicing astrologers now regard it as a symbolic system which – much like the I Ching or the Tarot – can offer a useful overview of a problem or situation, but is emphatically not a means of divination or prophecy. We briefly describe the process here so that the student can experiment with it, but do not recommend it as a process which should be used in consultation.

Asking questions
The author of a modern textbook on the subject includes such questions as "Will I get married this year?" "Will I pass my driving test?" and even "Will I get pregnant?" Most astrologers would consider attempts to answer such questions with a "yes" or "no" as fortune-telling, and eschew them, although it is fair to say that a minority will entertain such queries.

Horary astrology works on the premise that a chart is erected for the moment when a question is asked – the birthchart of that question, if you like; it is believed that examining that chart will give an answer to the question. If you are asking yourself a question, the chart is drawn for the moment it occurs to you and the place where you are. If you are asked by someone else, set up the chart for the moment the question is asked, but for the place where the questioner is, i.e. if on the telephone, the chart should be drawn for the place from which the questioner is speaking; if by letter, for the place from which it was writtten (but for the time when you first read the question). It is usually thought that the Placidus system of house division is best for horary astrology.

Rules of horary astrology
Those contemporary astrologers who interest themselves in horary astrology base many of their conclusions on ancient rules, most of which were set out in the earliest major English textbook, William Lilly's *Christian Astrology* of 1647. Although in general the planets and houses have the same significance as they do in the interpretation of birth charts or in mundane astrology, there are various other rules, some of which are more complex than others. It is believed, for instance, that there are some conditions under which a chart will offer no answer to a question (a strange attitude that is surely entertained only out of overrespect for tradition?)

Apart from the usual contents of the chart, there are four others which are particularly useful: they are the Part of Fortune, the Part of Change (or Part of Death), the Part of Sickness and the Part of Marriage. The use of these in horary astrology is complex, and we have not the space to describe them here, but the means of placing them in the chart are as follows (we ignore the minutes of arc):

The Part of Fortune
This is discovered by counting the number of degrees from Aries 0° to the position of the Ascendant, adding to the total the number of degrees between Aries 0° and the position of the Moon, and then deducting the number of degrees between Aries 0° and the position of the Sun (in other words, the Ascendant plus the Moon minus the Sun.)

Looking at the example below:

There are 354° between Aries 0° and Pisces 24°, the position of the Ascendant (i.e. 30° in each sign, so 11 x 30 = 330, + 24 = 334).

There are 334° between Aries 0° and Pisces 4°, the position of the Moon (i.e. 11 x 30 = 330, + 4 = 334).

There are 65° between Aries 0° and the position of the Sun (i.e. 30 x 2 = 60, + 5 = 65).

So 354 + 334 = 688 – 65 = 623. Therefore the Part of Fortune for the chart shown is 623° from Aries 0°.

But, of course, there are only 360° in the chart, so deduct 360; you are left with 263°. Sagittarius 0° = 240°; deduct 240 from 263 and you are left with 23°: therefore the Part of Fortune stands at Sagittarius 23°.

The Part of Change

For the other elements, the calculations are similar. For the Part of Change, add the position of the Ascendant to the position of the cusp of the eighth house, and deduct the position of the Moon. In this example 354 + 204 (180 + 24) = 558 – 334 = 224, therefore Scorpio 14°.

The Part of Sickness

To find the Part of Sickness, add the position of the Ascendant to the positon of Mars, then deduct the position of Saturn. Here, 354 + 40 = 394, – 304 = 90, therefore Cancer 0°.

The Part of Marriage

The Part of Marriage is found by adding the position of the Ascendant to the position of the Descendant, and deducting the position of Venus. In this example 354 + 174 = 528 – 103 = 425. This is over 360°, so 425 – 360 = 65, therefore Gemini 5°.

The use of horary astrology

There is one perfectly valid way of using horary astrology. This is to draw up the chart and to use it just as an interpreter of the I Ching would use the trigrams and hexagrams: that is, to illuminate, rather than answer, the question. Use it to suggest new ways of analysing a problem, and to hint at new viewpoints from which it may be considered. In this way the chart for the moment of asking a question is valuable – it presents a snapshot of that moment, and how you feel about the problem that confronts you (on the basis suggested by Jung, that "whatever is born or done this moment has the qualities of this moment of time"). It is well worth experimenting with a horary chart from this point of view.

If you are tempted to experiment with horary astrology as a means of prediction, always bear in mind the famous dictum that "the stars incline, they do not foretell".

The Horary Chart

An horary chart shows the positions of those Parts described above. So in the chart here:

- \+ The Part of Fortune is at 23° Sagittarius
- C The Part of Change is at 14° Scorpio
- S The Part of Sickness is at 0° Cancer
- M The Part of Marriage is at 5° Gemini.

There are many other Parts, besides these, which probably originated in Greece and were adapted by the Arabs; these other Parts are known as the Arabian Parts.

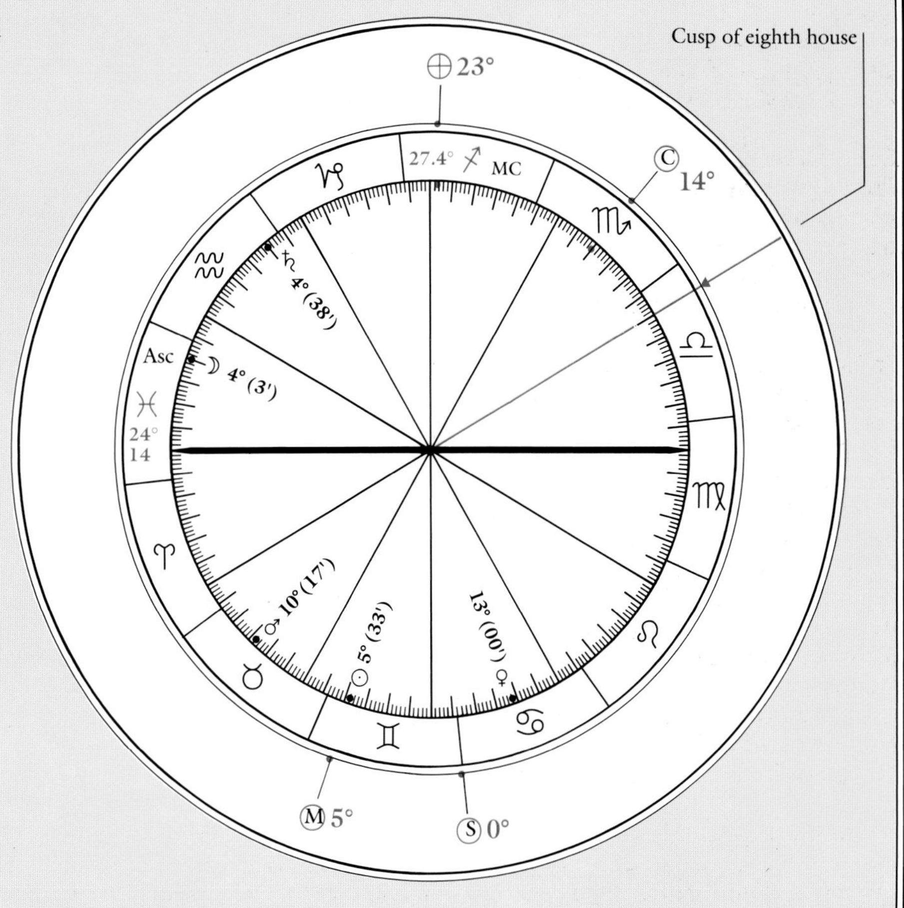

HÆMISPHÆRIUM
AUSTRALE.
SAGITTARIUS
SCORPIUS
LIBRA

·2·

Understanding the Sun Signs

Aries ♈ 21 March – 20 April

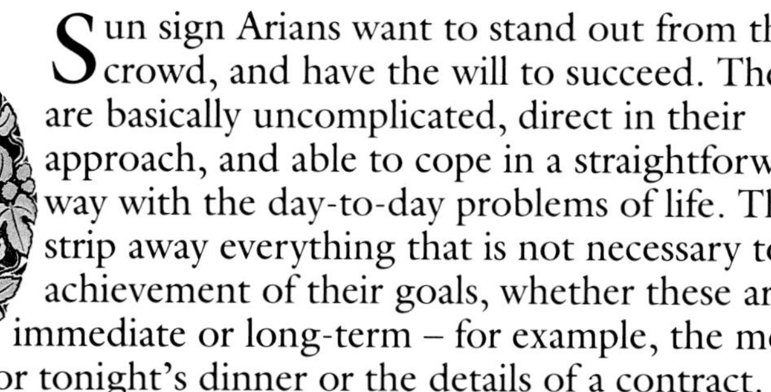

Sun sign Arians want to stand out from the crowd, and have the will to succeed. They are basically uncomplicated, direct in their approach, and able to cope in a straightforward way with the day-to-day problems of life. They strip away everything that is not necessary to the achievement of their goals, whether these are immediate or long-term – for example, the menu for tonight's dinner or the details of a contract. Their ability to see clearly the essential elements of important decisions is both enviable and convincing.

Basic Personality

Deep resources of determination help Arians when reacting to challenge, although a tendency to rush in regardless can cause problems. Observing these sometimes overquick reactions, one reflects that some Arians learn the hard way (some, of course, do not!)

Achievement is vital; if it is lacking, either in the career or an all-important hobby, Arians can become physically or psychologically sick and extremely difficult to live with. This is often because of their worst Arian fault, selfishness, which is almost certain to appear to some extent during every Arian's life. Arian children must be made aware of this tendency; it is then much easier for them to recognize and counter it in later life.

Partnership

Arians are extremely passionate. Just as they need fulfillment at work and at play, so they also need it sexually – probably more so than most other people. Their partners must be lively and capable of reacting well to the crackling flash of Arian sparks (fire is the sign's element); joyous sexual romps with a permanent partner should not only be the prerogative of Arian youth, but also of middle and old age, otherwise both they and their partners will suffer.

Family

The Arian child will display the typical lively enthusiasm of all fire sign children. That enthusiasm (which will cover the widest variety of interests) can tend to fade quickly, however, and before spending much money on some new craze, parents should be aware

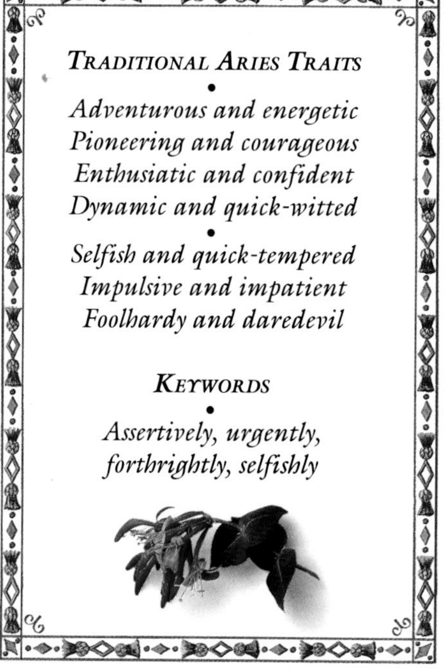

that their Arian child may soon lose patience with the new and expensive piece of equipment and push it out of sight, ready for the next enthusiasm.

Traditional Aries Traits
•
Adventurous and energetic
Pioneering and courageous
Enthusiatic and confident
Dynamic and quick-witted
•
Selfish and quick-tempered
Impulsive and impatient
Foolhardy and daredevil
Keywords
•
Assertively, urgently, forthrightly, selfishly

Patience is not an Arian strong point, so progress at school may be patchy. One hopes that surges of enthusiasm for study will come at the right time – just before important tests or examinations. Happily, the Arian has only to fail one examination and see friends moving ahead before becoming extremely concerned about catching up and reestablishing a lead; such a disaster will not happen twice.

Restrictive discipline doesn't suit young Arians. Sensible rules will be accepted provided they are explained, but the Arian spirit will refuse to be dampened by silly regulations which have no apparent justification.

Arians make very lively parents. They have delightfully simple, almost childlike, natures which are never entirely suppressed – seen, for instance, in the way a subject assesses a situation or faces up to a problem. Arian parents should find no difficulty in tuning in to the real emotions of their children. They will also be happy to encourage them in any number of enterprises and out of school activities: every hour will be packed with incident. However, not all children necessarily share their parents' enthusiasms, and an Arian should not drag a child off to a ball game simply because he wants to go. The child might be much happier at home with a good book, or – if the abundant Arian energy has been inherited – at ballet class. Such a situation can reflect Arian selfishness: doing what Aries wants, rather than what the child wants.

Career

Just as an Arian schoolchild must be given his or her head, so a certain freedom of expression is necessary in the career. A boring and routine job may have to be tolerated but, in that case, stimulating outside hobbies must also be established.

A noisy, busy environment is meat and drink to an Arian – a stuffy, claustrophobic office is not. In choosing careers, the Arian could consider engineering or the electronics industries, the armed services or perhaps psychiatry or dentistry. But above all, the Arian should make for fields that enable him or her to move out in front of the crowd and become a successful pioneer of some kind. Arians are ambitious, but the achievement of that ambition is just as important as what is achieved. And the Arian will then be asking "What next?"

A good head for business is usual, and Arians can be very enterprising; many enjoy organizing their lives so that they have two sources of income. If enterprise and caution can be combined a lot of money can be made, but a steadying influence is sometimes needed if it is not to be frittered away.

Change, leisure and retirement

Change is usually taken in the Arian stride, especially if progress can be seen to depend upon it. These people's lively spirits will accept challenge and,

The Symbolism of Aries

Triplicity or Element
Aries is one of the three fire signs
Color
Red is the definitive Arien color
Gemstone
The gemstone of Aries is the magnificent diamond
Trees
Thorn-bearing trees and shrubs are ruled by Aries
Hawthorn
Honeysuckle
Bryony
Flowers
The thistle, bryony and honeysuckle are traditionally Arien plants
Spear of Mars
Ruling Planet
The ruling planet of Aries is Mars – the Roman God of War
Symbolic Creature
The Ram is the creature associated with Aries
Country
England is an Arien country
Thistle
♂

while many will look forward to relaxing once they have retired, after a week or two they will revive an old interest or establish a new one. By then, they may have cultivated more patience and can even end up with a new career rather than merely a new hobby! In any case, they will not want their standard of living to drop when they retire.

Health, diet and exercise
Arians need plenty of exercise to keep their systems in good condition. This is necessary for everyone, of course, but for Arians it is as vital as breathing. They will, in general, be so enthusiastic that you may have to remind them to modify exercise routines and sporting interests as time passes, if their systems are not to be overstrained.

The head is vulnerable; a tendency to knock and bump the head when young will probably result in early visits from the Tooth Fairy. Arians' natural tendency to rush about carelessly may result in cuts, bruises and even minor burns. The motto "More haste, less speed" is a valuable one for these people; they enjoy working with all kinds of tools, and again carelessness may court disaster. Arians enjoy spicy food, but it is not usually good for them. They have hearty appetites, and thrive on traditional, rather than elaborate, dishes.

Aries as Ascendant

Psychological motivation
Arians want to win, and their energetic driving force almost unconsciously stimulates them into action. Powerful ambition and a remarkable flow of physical energy will be devoted to achieving whatever goal is in sight. Their urge to win will enable Arians to outstrip competitors, and runs parallel with a need to be noticed. This sometimes emerges within the context of the family and, especially if the child with Aries rising is a younger sibling among more successful brothers and sisters, ruthlessness may sometimes be a problem – though competition can be an excellent spur. If ruthlessness does emerge, the natural Arian sense of humor should be invoked, and that innate awareness of others which is a most happy characteristic.

Adapting to any environment, whatever the social circumstances, is easy for those with Aries rising. If these people can be a little more low-key they will be excellent at self-analysis, and the resulting self-knowledge will help them to channel their many positive, strong, extrovert qualities.

Their view of themselves may be rather slap-happy. While in a Sun sign Arian this attitude might lead to slight accidents; with Aries rising it may be expressed on a psychological level – perhaps causing an over-simplification of problems which, in youth, could make it harder to solve them swiftly and easily.

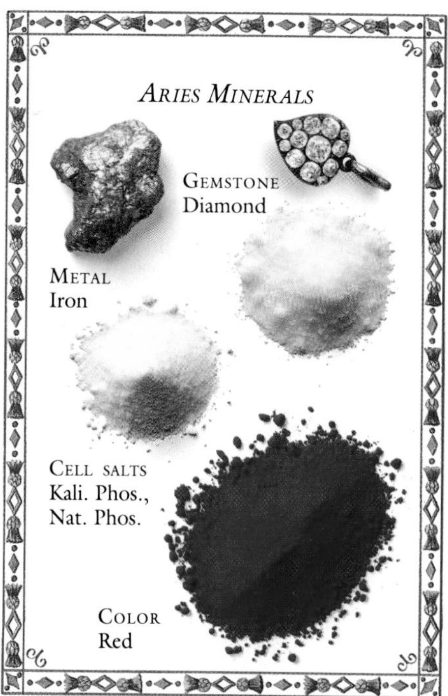
Aries Minerals

Gemstone
Diamond

Metal
Iron

Cell salts
Kali. Phos., Nat. Phos.

Color
Red

The emphasis on the head may lead to rather frequent headaches, perhaps caused by a slight kidney problem or imbalance as opposed to overwork, or eyestrain. With Aries rising such pain is more likely to be the result of a physical condition than circumstances provoked by the subject herself.

The reaction to partners is interesting: there will be great need for a permanent emotional relationship, no matter how many affairs or experiments take place – or, indeed, however independent the spirit. An Arian Ascendant brings not only a need to relate, but also a strong desire to understand and be fair to the partner. These qualities will emerge at the deepest and most personal level; mere acquaintances or even quite close friends may never be aware of them.

Aries Progressed to Taurus

Arian enterprise is emphasized when the Sun progresses to Taurus, but the individual's attitude to finance and possessions will be stabilized. Many Arians buy their first house or flat at this time, especially if they were born during the first few days of the Arian Sun sign (the progression will then occur in their late twenties, at which time many people begin to think about the long-term future).

The Arian image, tending toward the casual, may also change somewhat, and they often develop a liking for more expensive, well-cut and rather formal clothes. This may, of course, relate to a better lifestyle and increased prestige. When this progression takes place, Arians should guard against becoming rather possessive, especially toward their partners. It should not be too difficult to moderate this, for it is always possible to appeal to the independent Arian spirit – once it is pointed out, the subject will realize the pitfalls of trying to possess another human being.

Aries rises very quickly in the northern hemisphere, and even if an early degree of that sign was on the horizon at birth, the changes signaled by the Ascendant progressing into Taurus will occur quite early in life. (This does not apply to southern hemisphere births.) It will probably give the individual a more serious and practical view of life; the psychological effect will be to steady and stabilize the personality. If the person concerned is committed to a permanent relationship, what were always passionate feelings will become considerably more intense, and care must be taken that outbursts of jealousy do not have a negative effect.

The volatile metabolism usually characteristic of an Arian Ascendant is likely to slow down. This will be of positive help if the individual is past middle age, and it is wise to moderate strenuous sports and exercise routines. If there is a sudden, unexplained, weight gain, it might well be due to a thyroid problem.

The Traditional Associations of Aries

Dates
21 March – 20 April

The Origin
The Ram appeared for the first time in Egypt, alternating with a goose's head as the symbol of Aries; its origin is a mystery

Ruling Planet
Mars

Trees
Thorn-bearing trees, some types of fir

Cayenne pepper

Red chillies (dried)

Black and white mustard seed

Hawthorn

Herbs and Spices
Capers, mustard, cayenne pepper

Capers

Positivity/Gender
Positive, masculine

Triplicity or Element
Fire

Quadruplicity or Quality
Cardinal

Body Area
The head

Honeysuckle

Flowers
Honeysuckle, thistle, bryony, peppermint

Hops

French tricolor

Foodstuffs
Onions, leeks, hops, most strong-tasting foods

Thistle

Countries
England, France, Germany, Denmark

Cities
Naples, Capua, Verona, Florence, Marseilles, Krakow, Leicester and Birmingham (UK)

Shallots

Leeks

Wool

Animals
Sheep and rams

Taurus ♉ 21 April – 21 May

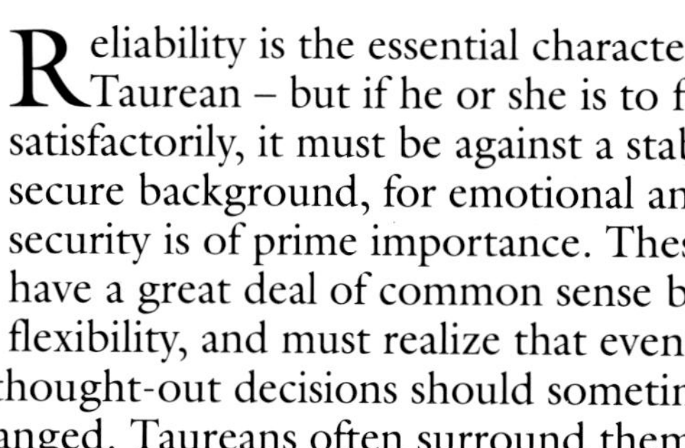

Reliability is the essential characteristic of a Taurean – but if he or she is to function satisfactorily, it must be against a stable and secure background, for emotional and material security is of prime importance. These people have a great deal of common sense but can lack flexibility, and must realize that even well thought-out decisions should sometimes be changed. Taureans often surround themselves with possessions as an outward sign of their achievements, and to convince them of their progress and position in society.

Basic Personality

Possessiveness, shown in many areas of life, is indeed the worst Taurean fault. Sadly, the partner can often become just another well-guarded possession – loved and admired, certainly, but stubbornly regarded as the property of an owner, rather than as a free agent.

The Taurean mind works methodically, carefully and decisively. Perhaps the most marked potential is for the steady building of a life and career. Short cuts are not for these people, and should be avoided. One of their most endearing characteristics is natural charm, expressed in a variety of ways. For instance, Taureans usually have soft, gentle voices, and always seem able to find the time to listen to and encourage anyone who needs help. Their shoulders are always available to those who wish to cry on them, but they are also very good at offering practical advice.

Partnership

Taurus is ruled by Venus, so a successful partnership is of above-average importance; like their Libran cousins, Taureans need peace and harmony in their relationships. Emotional security is vital, and any threat to it may cause serious damage, making the Taurean emotions get out of hand, and the possessiveness, which will certainly be present on some level of the personality, may turn into obsessive jealousy. When there is tension in the home, normal placidity may be shaken by sudden flares of temper.

Under normal, stable circumstances, however, Taureans are extremely loving and kind, eager to express their affection generously and abundantly.

Traditional Taurus Traits

•

Patient and reliable
Warm-hearted and loving
Persistent and determined
Placid and security-loving

•

Jealous and possessive
Resentful and inflexible
Self-indulgent and greedy

Keywords

•

Possessively, permanently

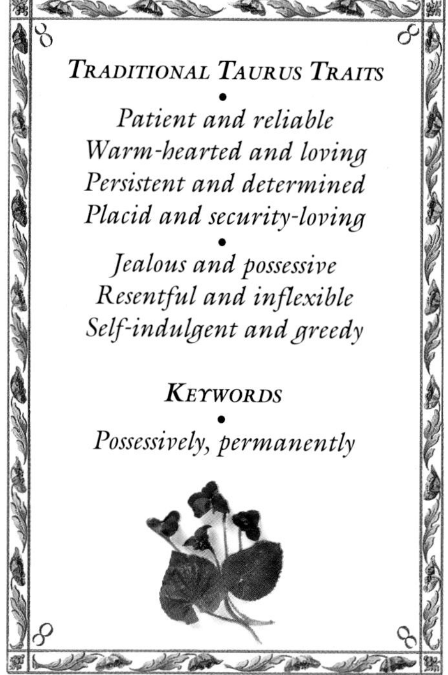

Their generosity is emotional and financial, for as well as being highly-sexed they make excellent, caring and considerate lovers. There will be no lack of sensual pleasure nor, usually, any lack of physical comfort, to which Taureans are devoted – to such an extent, perhaps, that they may even grow complacent, and if partners accuse them of being boring, it may be because they have become slaves to a chosen routine.

Family

A contented child, smiling from its crib and always greeting mealtimes with enthusiasm, is quite likely to be a Sun sign Taurean. There may be some delay when these children learn to walk – indeed, they will even be lazy about crawling, let alone walking. Even so, caring for Taurean babies is usually a pleasure. Slow development need not give rise to concern; when this baby learns something, it does so thoroughly and for good. But despite all the charm, discipline is important, for the Taurean baby needs to live within a firm structure, knowing that things will happen at a particular time. Taureans are at heart conventional, and need rules; parents who themselves might be happier in a more liberal atmosphere should remember this.

Taureans want to set up a comfortable and secure home before they have a family. But their plans will probably involve children, for a strong family life and tradition is important to them: in this sense they are natural conservatives. When children do arrive, their parents will want them to be happy and comfortable, but ironically this can lead to difficulties, for they may work so hard to this end that they deny themselves time to get to know and enjoy their family. If this happens, the trouble will get worse when the children reach adolescence, and a damaging generation gap may result.

Career

Taureans are ambitious, and quite enjoy setting up a sound career plan and following it through to success. However, there can be problems if this involves any kind of risk, because Taureans function best when steady work is available, with the resulting regular income. They should think very carefully before embarking on any career where the income (however great) is unpredictable. The material security offered by money is very important to them. Thus many will accept work that they don't really enjoy, or aren't really interested in, just because the income is a large one, or because it seems assured.

This interest in finance is not only emotional: Taureans are highly practical about it, and are therefore very good in careers connected with money – including banking, insurance and the stock exchange. Although any risks involved will pain them, and they should carefully weigh probable worry against possible eventual benefits, they can succeed in building up very successful businesses from small

The Symbolism of Taurus

GEMSTONE
The clear green emerald is the Taurean gemstone
COLORS
Pink, pale blue and green (and pastel shades in general) are Taurean colors
FLOWERS
The foxglove, rose (especially pink varieties), poppy, columbine, daisy and violet are typical Taurean flowers
Violets
RULING PLANET
Venus is the ruling planet of Taurus
COUNTRY
Switzerland is one of the countries ruled by Taurus
ANIMALS
All cattle are Taurean animals
FOODSTUFFS
Taurus governs cereal crops, especially wheat
Poppy
♀
MYTHOLOGY
In mythology, Taurus was a bull
Foxglove
HERBS AND SPICES
Herbs and spices associated with Taurus include sorrel, as here, cloves and spearmint
FRUITS
Taurean fruits include the apple and pear and berry fruits
Yellow mountain violet
Daisy
Crab apple
Dog rose

beginnings, for they have a natural, strong business sense.

Many Taureans are very happy indeed working in agriculture and horticulture. The open air life is good for them, and contact with the soil seems to give them special satisfaction. They often have musical talent, too, and there are a great many professional Taurean musicians – especially singers.

Change, leisure and retirement
Taureans are not very good at dealing with change; they need a steady routine, and having got into a rut will continue to plough through it. Change seems to threaten their security, and can be emotionally disturbing. However, they are excellent planners, and if a change is necessary they will at least prepare themselves well for it. They greatly enjoy their leisure hours, and their generosity means they will spend lots of money entertaining friends. They may be rather lazy, however, and can all too easily waste time.

Retirement will be viewed with considerable pleasure, especially if there is an adequate pension. If they have a great deal of spare time, they should develop an interest which will occupy it – perhaps something they have enjoyed throughout their lives, and can now explore more fully. If this is not the case, they should be encouraged to take up new and interesting occupations, otherwise lethargy may age them. Gardening and golf spring to mind; the women of the sign particularly enjoy sewing and embroidery (patience is a Taurean virtue).

Health, diet and exercise
Taureans love their food, so can put on weight very easily. Members of this sign are reputed to be extremely good-looking, but too much extra weight does nothing for their figures. A reasonable diet is essential, but not always easy for them. Long hours at an office desk, business lunches and an ever-growing appreciation of good wines will not help their waistlines.

Heavy exercise is no problem; many young Taureans enjoy team games, and some enjoy weight-training. They tend to move slowly: aerobics or dancing will help them to speed up a little, as will brisk country walks, which will also be more aesthetically rewarding.

Taurus as Ascendant

Psychological motivation
When Taurus rises the basic impulse is acquisition, and is even stronger than with a Taurean Sun. As their self-confidence grows, it will be reflected in the possessions with which these people surround themselves. It seems they will never be psychologically whole until they can see around them material proof of their success. (This, of course, is true for Taureans at every economic level.) Established in their own kingdom, they will often feel uneasy if they have to step outside it: once more, it is a signal of the importance of routine and security. Other Sun sign characteristics – stubbornness and possessiveness – are equally deep-rooted; these people will know they are right, and find it very hard to see anyone else's point of view unless it is identical to their own. Self-knowledge will be acquired the hard way.

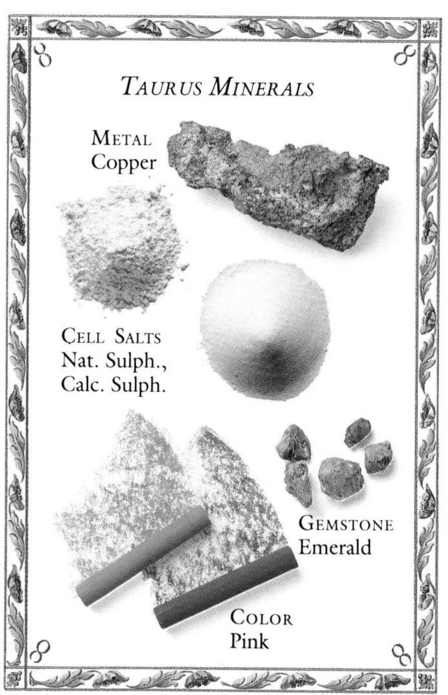

The Taurean body area is the throat, but when Taurus rises there can be difficulties with the thyroid gland (ruled by Venus). Any inordinate weight gain not obviously due to diet may be traced to this.

Relations with partners will be very intense and passionate. These people make very demanding partners, with a high emotional energy that must be "earthed" through the relationship. Sexual fulfillment will be of prime importance, and must be borne in mind when the subject is embarking on an emotional relationship. On the other hand, it is equally important that the commitment is not solely sexual; friendship between partners will make it easier to cope with problems whenever they arise. There may be considerable achievement, especially with the help of the partner.

Taurus Progressed to Gemini

When the Taurus Sun progresses into Gemini, these people can become more talkative or more argumentative, expressing their opinions more openly and taking life less seriously. They will be happier to exchange ideas, rather than suspecting that theirs are the only views worth considering.

The thinking processes will probably speed up, and the whole mental attitude will be far more flexible. A flirtatious tendency may develop; coupled with Taurean charm, this can be quite delightful. They will more readily enjoy getting out and about, and be less preoccupied with their creature comforts. There might be an increased interest in fashion; convention may be enlivened by a slightly trendier image.

Taurus rises very quickly in the northern hemisphere, so it is likely that a Taurean Ascendant will progress into Gemini when the subject is very young. This will be extremely helpful, making the outlook freer and more objective and positive, and less concerned with security. Altogether, he or she should become more adaptable, and much more able to assess psychological problems. A more rational outlook should make stubbornness less offensive, and if the subject is very young, parents should find that there will be better progress at school as the result of an increased interest in study and use of the mind.

If the individual was born in the southern hemisphere and is quite mature when the Ascendant changes signs, a more youthful outlook will develop. There will be an identification with the younger generation, and the need for intellectual challenge will enliven the stable Taurean personality.

The Traditional Associations of Taurus

Dates
21 April – 21 May

The Origin
The Egyptian Horus was the Bull of Heaven, and a white bull was sacrificed in Babylonia at the New Year to placate Ramman, the god of thunder and lightning

Trees
Ash, cypress, vine, apple, pear, fig

Cloves

Cypress

Apple

Sorrel

Fig leaf

Herbs and Spices
Cloves, sorrel, spearmint

Animals
Cattle

Artichokes

Asparagus

Mixed spices

Grapes

Foxglove

Violet

Irish harp

Ruling Planet
Venus

Positivity/Gender
Negative, feminine

Triplicity or Element
Earth

Quadruplicity or Quality
Fixed

Body Area
The throat and neck; the thyroid gland

Foodstuffs
Wheat and other cereals, berry fruits, apples, pears, grapes, artichokes, asparagus, beans; most spices

Flowers
Rose, poppy, foxglove, daisy, primula, violet, columbine

Countries
Ireland, Switzerland, Iran, Cyprus, the Greek Islands, Parma, Capri, Ischia

Cities
Dublin, Lucerne, Mantua, Leipzig, Palermo, St Louis

Gemini ♊ 22 May – 21 June

Versatility is the hallmark of Sun sign Geminians. This is the first dual sign of the zodiac, and its subjects find it essential to pursue several courses of action at once. They also need to communicate on all levels. Their potential can be expressed in many ways, but especially through the media. This need for communication is so strong that they'll telephone their local radio station with comments on every conceivable subject and will even chat to someone in a bus line if no one else is available at the time.

Basic Personality

Superficiality is the worst Geminian fault and should be controlled - these people tend to know a little about many subjects, and sometimes fail to acquire truly deep knowledge of the things that really interest them. An ability to quickly assimilate knowledge can work well under certain conditions (see below), but it is important for this type to realize the necessity for deep thought and seriously based opinions on some matters.

A tendency to inconsistency is another problem; the Geminian need for variety and change makes it all too easy for these people to start a great many different projects but leave most of them unfinished. Once more, awareness of this element in their characters will help counter it.

Geminians are very logical, rational people and, generally speaking, their minds work very quickly, but the influence of their ruling planet, Mercury, is important and must be carefully considered (see pp.239-53).

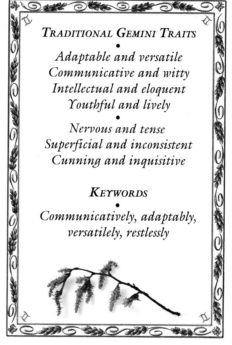

Traditional Gemini Traits

•

Adaptable and versatile
Communicative and witty
Intellectual and eloquent
Youthful and lively

•

Nervous and tense
Superficial and inconsistent
Cunning and inquisitive

Keywords

•

Communicatively, adaptably, versatilely, restlessly

Partnership

Geminians unquestionably need a lively, intellectual rapport with their partners. Shared interest are important, and the partner should have his or her own definite opinions, which will be enjoyably discussed and argued over. All of this will add lively spice to the partnership.

Geminians often don't entirely trust their emotions. When overwhelmed by feelings they will immediately bring their rational, logical minds into play, trying to explain their emotions to themselves in order to give them a coherent perspective. This can cause problems, especially when Geminians are still young and coming to terms with the expression of emotion.

Family

A Geminian child will start talking, and probably crawling, then walking, at a very early age. The parents of such a child should make quite sure that their youngster has plenty with which to keep happily occupied, as boredom will not be tolerated – indeed, Geminians almost fear it. To get to grips very early on with the tendency to inconsistency and superficiality, the child should be encouraged to finish all tasks that are started, although it would be wrong to insist that he or she tackle them one at a time. This simply doesn't work with Geminians, who obtain their best results when able to move from one project to another as the mood takes them and their interest waxes and wanes.

Geminian children usually do quite well at school, but they can bluff their way through tests. Really clever teachers will soon recognize this and be able to stay several steps anead of their Geminian students; less shrewd instructors will be taken for elaborate rides. At examination time the Geminian will probably write reams and reams of opinion, backed up by too few essential facts: they usually find facts boring!

It goes without saying that Geminians are lively parents, filling their children's out-of-school hours with activity. They must be careful, since their children may not be as versatile, or have such quick minds, as they themselves. They should consider the basic needs and true qualities of their children, which may not coincide with their own. There is a very powerful critical streak in every Geminian, which can be more damning than they realize and may badly deflate and upset their children; it should be softened with humor and tempered by praise.

Career

The Geminian versatility and communicative skills should ideally be used in a career. Many Geminians do very well working in the media and are also the natural salespeople of the zodiac, doing well in department stores, advertising and as commercial travellers. Their need for change and variety must definitely not be ignored: predictable routine is inimical to them. So is solitary work, but at least when a Geminian acquires a lonely top job, he or she will never fail to listen to former colleagues, although this doesn't always mean that their advice will be accepted! A full and free interchange of ideas, and the batting to and fro of different opinions, is important.

In business, Geminians can be highly shrewd and cunning, and if they apply these characteristics to making money they often do extremely well, although sometimes a faulty decision, perhaps too hastily made, will result in financial collapse. This is not an overly ambitious sign, but the Gemini imagination will happily enjoy success before it is actually achieved, which acts as a spur!

The Symbolism of Gemini

GEMSTONE
Agate is the Geminian gemstone
BIRDS
Talking birds, especially parrots and parakeets, are ruled by Gemini
Lavender
Lily-of-the-valley
RULING PLANET
The ruling planet of Gemini is Mercury
ANIMAL
The monkey, quick-witted and full of tricks, is a Geminian animal
SYMBOLISM
The two stars represent the sign's duality
COLORS
Of all the colors, Gemini has the closest affinity with yellow
HERBS
Bittersweet is one of the herbs associated with Gemini
FLOWERS
Lily-of-the-valley, lavender and myrtle are true Geminian flowers
Bog myrtle
TREES
The trees ruled by Gemini are those that bear nuts
COUNTRY AND CITY
Wales is a Geminian country and its capital city, Cardiff, is also ruled by the sign

Change, leisure and retirement
Continual change is a way of life for Geminians; as we have suggested, their chief fear in life is being bored, so will continually find new ways of keeping themselves interested. If they don't then their nearest and dearest must, at the slightest sign of twitchiness, do it for them. Leisure? They don't have time for any – every moment is filled with activity, even if that is just writing or conversation. The thought of retirement won't dismay them, because there are many interests they want to pursue (probably all at once!) when they eventually find the time.

Health, diet and exercise
Although not necessarily strong, these people are almost certainly wiry and apparently perpetually young, so should not have too much trouble with their health. Any difficulties that do arise may perhaps be for psychological rather than physical reasons – Geminians have vast amounts of nervous energy which must be burned off. They are usually too individual really to enjoy team games, and they can quickly grow bored with the strict routine of formal exercise. The best solution is to join a health club but to use it in combination with other, individual, forms of exercise, such as running, jogging, walking, squash and tennis.

Gemini rules the lungs, and Sun sign Geminians must watch carefully for signs of breathlessness, or when a cold goes to their chests. It is vital that, if possible, they should refrain from smoking, which, while bad for everybody, is particularly lethal for them. They thrive best on a light diet of fresh salads and fruit, fish and white meat.

GEMINI AS ASCENDANT

Psychological motivation
Surprisingly for such a volatile zodiac type, people with Gemini rising want to keep their feet firmly planted on the ground. However interested they may be in the occult or the spiritual, they will question every concept that is put to them, and may reject it unless it can be proved either by argument or evidence. They also question every attitude of their own, wanting to know precisely why they have adopted it. They can get bogged down if they undergo psychoanalysis, because the deeper they explore their own personalities, the more twists and turns they will notice and want to follow, adding question to question until they get lost in the thicket. One even asks whether they really want to know themselves.

Some interesting characteristics emerge in relationships. A warm, passionate enthusiasm and optimism will delight the partner; but as well as the Sun Geminian's need for friendship, those with Gemini rising will always challenge their partners, encourage them to achieve more and endow the relationship with *joie de vivre*. Shared interests help to cement their relationships: the couple will gain much intellectual satisfaction from each other. The partner may develop more versatility, while the Geminian may complete more activities.

GEMINI MINERALS
GEMSTONE
Agate
COLOR
Most colors, particularly yellow
METAL
Mercury
CELL SALTS
Kali. Mur. and silica

A strongly independent streak is likely, and these people can't cope with jealousy or possessiveness. They hate jealousy partly because they can't understand it: it's natural for them to be interested in other men or women, as well as the one they are with. This might develop into a sexual interest, but it isn't inevitable. The situation should be watched, but it is unwise to nag unless it becomes really necessary. The hands are vulnerable – perhaps, in later years, to arthritis. Any signs of this should be checked with a doctor at the earliest possible moment. Most Geminians (Sun or Ascendant) like to use their hands in various forms of craftwork and keep them mobile, but those with Gemini rising should consciously exercise their fingers.

Nervous tension can easily build up, and may exacerbate an asthmatic tendency. If the subject is very young, he or she will probably grow out of it; in older people, that may be more difficult, and the answer may lie in treating the tension rather than the asthma.

GEMINI PROGRESSED TO CANCER

A surprisingly sentimental streak may appear when the Sun progresses into Cancer; the emotions will also flow more readily and fluently. If the Sun changes signs in or just after adolescence, it will give an excellent extension to Geminian logic and rationality, increasing intuition and instinct. Subjects may suddenly want to rent or buy a place of their own, and develop an interest in handicrafts or do-it-yourself projects. Sometimes the versatility and need for change can be linked to changes of mood, with drastic results.

The Geminian critical faculty may also grow, becoming negative and hurtful. The usually fashionable and trendy Geminian image might be modified by a feeling for nostalgia: the individual will get great pleasure from hunting out antique clothes in street-markets, and creating a more gentle, somewhat romantic look.

When a Geminian Ascendant progresses into Cancer, most of the above possibilities hold good. There can be an increased sensitivity to the feelings of other people: Geminian argument will be less inclined to steamroller their opinions or attitudes. More time will be given to thought and reflection. This may cause moodiness, and sometimes irrational worry (a new experience for Geminians), which will puzzle and disturb them. A tendency to nostalgia may also join the usual forward-looking optimism. Most important is the fact that the new-found intuition should be accepted and used, and these Geminians must learn to trust their emotions.

The Traditional Associations of Gemini

DATES
22 May – 21 June

THE ORIGIN
Castor and Pollux, peculiarly bright stars, were probably the original heavenly twins (actually called, in Egypt, the Two Stars)

FOODSTUFFS
Nuts, those vegetables grown above ground (except cabbage), carrots

ANIMALS
Small birds, minah birds and parrots, butterflies, monkeys

HERBS AND SPICES
Aniseed, marjoram, caraway, balm, bittersweet

TREES
Nut-bearing trees

COUNTRIES
Wales, Belgium, USA, Lower Egypt, Sardinia, Armenia

CITIES
London, Plymouth (UK), Cardiff, San Francisco, Melbourne, Nuremburg, Bruges, Cordoba, Versailles

POSITIVITY/GENDER
Positive, masculine

TRIPLICITY OR ELEMENT
Air

QUADRUPLICITY OR QUALITY
Mutable

BODY AREA
Shoulders, arms, nerves

RULING PLANET
Mercury

FLOWERS
Lily-of-the-valley, lavender, maidenhair, myrtle, fern

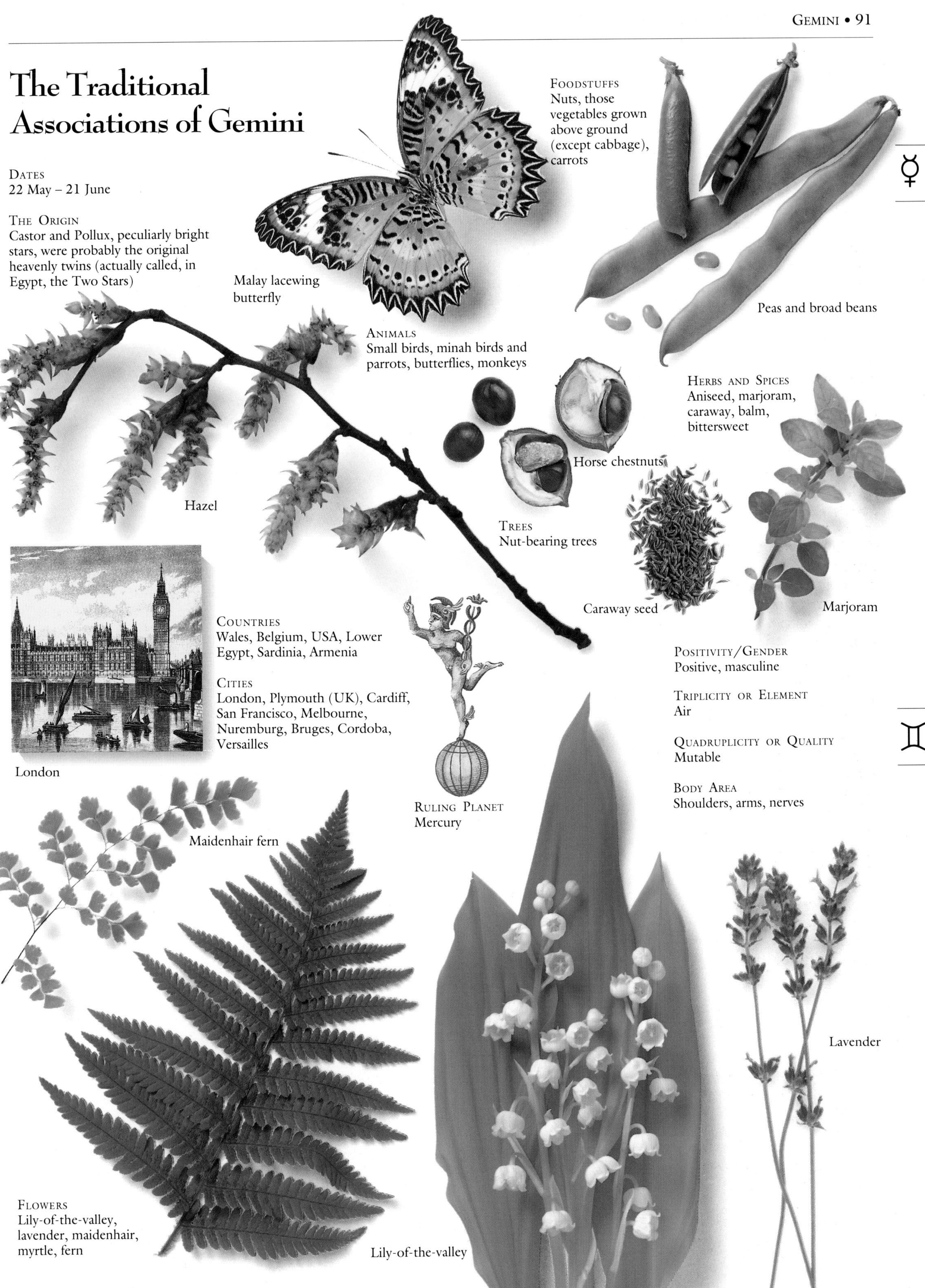

Malay lacewing butterfly

Peas and broad beans

Hazel

Horse chestnuts

Caraway seed

Marjoram

London

Maidenhair fern

Lily-of-the-valley

Lavender

Cancer ♋ 22 June – 22 July

The need to protect the self and the family from threat is one of the chief Cancerian characteristics. Challenge a Cancerian in argument and a remarkable self-defense system springs into action. The expression tightens and clouds, a frown quickly appears between the eyes and there is an instant, rather snappy answer. This is a rather enigmatic zodiac type, but familiarity with a Cancerian reveals loving kindness and caring beneath an unpromising surface. A high emotional level is married to very considerable intuition.

Basic Personality

The imagination is strong and vivid, but emotion and imagination combined, if not carefully governed, can result in almost continual worry, especially over loved ones. Cancerians are certainly high on the list of zodiac worriers, but their intuition and instincts, if trusted, are sound, and can be used to mitigate any resulting problems. However, a sense of logic must also be developed, to work in conjunction with the natural intuition.

The Cancerian mind is at its best when allowed to work instinctively, and this should be most useful when making decisions as there is then no need for procrastination. Even if there are problems, their natural tenacity and bravery in the face of difficulties will see these people through. The worst Cancerian fault is moodiness: one moment they are on top of the world, the next they are sunk into a deep, black depression.

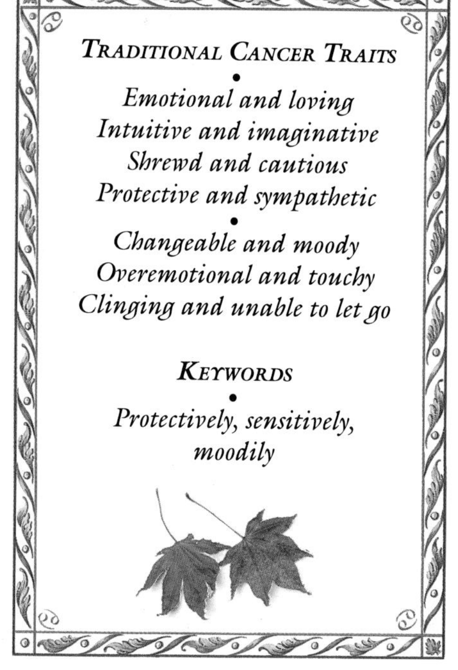

Traditional Cancer Traits

•

Emotional and loving
Intuitive and imaginative
Shrewd and cautious
Protective and sympathetic

•

Changeable and moody
Overemotional and touchy
Clinging and unable to let go

Keywords

•

Protectively, sensitively, moodily

Partnership

Cancerians make wonderfully caring partners; they are very emotional, and have a great deal of pure love to express. They should realize that they can hurt their lovers, releasing their own tension or worry in sharp, even cruel, remarks. However, if their partners respond in a similar fashion, they don't like it at all!

A delightfully sentimental streak is shown towards loved ones: Cancerians will hunt out beautiful old birthday or valentine cards, and are inventive present givers, but they should avoid being too cloying or oversentimental towards their partners. They also tend to look to the past, and may be reluctant to move a relationship forward. They are marvelously sensual lovers, but can be disproportionately upset by the slightest insensitivity. Once in a permanent relationship, they will be firmly committed to family life, including children.

Family

Sensitivity will emerge very early in life, and even Cancerian babies are remarkably intuitive. Changes in the home atmosphere will immediately be reflected in the personal mood – and baby Cancer will (much more than other youngsters) be all smiles one moment and all tears the next. As young Cancerians grow up they will develop a strong memory; sometimes they seem to know more about the past than the present. They can be picky eaters, so the iron hand in the velvet glove may be needed here. The Cancerian digestion does tend to be sensitive, but giving way to food fads can lead to problems later on.

If a Cancerian child is naughty, the best reaction is to say "You've hurt Mommy by doing that" and appeal to his or her inherent sensitivity. It is also important that parents encourage young Cancerians to be tidy! The sign is notorious for untidiness and hoarding; there will be a battle whenever the toy chest is sorted out – even rubbish will be deemed to have great sentimental value.

Cancerian children can be shy and wary when they first go to school. It is from this age that their instinctive, protective and defensive shells begin to develop, supporting the bravery and tenacity with which they can move forward in life.

The need for parenthood is instinctive and strong. Cancerians adore their children and, if anything, tend to cosset them, becoming overconcerned and worried at the slightest provocation. The security of the home and family unit is vital to them, and when their children leave home these parents probably suffer more than most.

Career

The typical Cancerian tenacity and determination is perhaps the greatest asset of these people. In many ways they enjoy variety and change, but their careers must also have a certain continuity. They can then take advantage of past experience and apply it to the present. Cancerians are usually extremely shrewd, and this sign often confers an excellent business sense: another area in which their instinct and intuition serve them well.

The caring professions attract, including teaching, particularly of young children. Nursing and gynecology are also popular. It is also good for them to develop and express their vivid imaginations. Any work involving the past – such as the antiques business or museum work – will appeal to them. Cancerians are also natural cooks.

Fulfillment is more important to them than ambition, but they are keen to make money, and sometimes the Cancerian hoarding instinct can mean they are reluctant to part with it.

The Symbolism of Cancer

ANIMALS
Animals with a shell exterior, such as the crab itself, are Cancerian creatures
GEMSTONE
The pearl is the Cancerian gemstone
METAL
Silver is the metal of Cancer
TRIPLICITY OR ELEMENT
Cancer is a water sign
COLORS
Cancer is linked with smoky-gray and silvery-blue colors – the sheen of the Moon, its ruler
FLOWERS
White flowers, especially white roses, acanthus and convolvulus are associated with Cancer
HERBS
Saxifrage, verbena and tarragon are Cancerian herbs
Water lily
Lily
Mountain saxifrage
COUNTRY AND CITY
Holland is one of the countries ruled by Cancer; Amsterdam, the capital of Holland, is a Cancerian city
Field rose
Convolvulus
RULING PLANET
The ruling planet of Cancer is the Moon

Change, leisure and retirement

Changes of mood are very much part of the Cancerian makeup, but these people are much less ready to change their lifestyles – usually because of the disruption involved. Nevertheless, when faced with the prospect of retirement they will consider moving to another area, but should think carefully about this: they may be parted from their family, and if they buy a smaller property it may not be large enough for everyone to come and stay. Retirement will allow them to enjoy a new rhythm of life, and they will enjoy following their many spare-time interests, which may include a specialized collection of some kind.

Losing a job is hard to accept; a Cancerian's determination to find a new job should be supported to the hilt, so that the effort eclipses the worry of being out of work (which may demolish the self-confidence).

Health, diet and exercise

Keeping the sensitive Cancerian system in good order requires regular, rhythmical exercise. Swimming (from as early an age as possible) is strongly recommended, as is dancing.

The digestion will almost certainly suffer from time to time – especially when the individual is at all worried. A diet rich in fish and dairy produce (provided the cholesterol level is not too high) is usually beneficial, and will help stabilize the system. The sign Cancer, it must be emphasized, has nothing to do with the disease of the same name. However, because Cancer rules the breasts, women of this sign should ensure they regularly examine them and have periodic checkups with their doctors. Cancerian men should not ignore any minor ailment, if only to prevent undue worry.

CANCER AS ASCENDANT

Psychological motivation

When Cancer rises, great satisfaction is gained from caring for and cherishing others. Sometimes this instinct is so strong that the world outside the Cancerian's immediate and cozy circle can be viewed as a threat. Even so, the attitude is protective, not possessive. Cancer is a cardinal sign, the keyword for which is "outgoing". This suggests a conflict, but that is not necessarily so: Cancerians give out an enormous amount of energy and vitality – to those in an immediate circle. If people with Cancer rising do not live within or create a family environment, their powerful caring motivations will be expressed towards an ideal, burning interest, often personalized in a real sense of vocation: they will make the chosen cause very much their own.

People with Cancer rising will be fascinated to explore their own personalities, but if they enter psychotherapy they should remain aware of their self-defense systems, otherwise they may too readily accept the suggestions of the analyst.

CANCER MINERALS

GEMSTONE
Pearl

CELL SALTS
Calc. Flour.,
Calc. Phos.

METAL
Silver

COLOR
Silver gray

Particular ambition is shown for their partners, maybe even to the extent of social climbing on their behalf. They should recognize that a hint of coldness and distance can mar the closest long-term relationship; this should not be a problem, but ought to be watched if it is not to be harmful. Any difficulties should be discussed as honestly as possible.

Illogical worry about the health is likely, causing a vicious circle – worry will lead to digestive problems that cause more worry. Cancerians will search medical dictionaries for imagined diseases – it can be a hobby! This must be recognized, for peace of mind as well as physical well-being.

When Cancer is rising the person concerned very easily takes on the color of any powerful influence. Therefore, any planets in the first house of the birth chart, especially if conjunct the Ascendant, will have a profound effect on the personality.

CANCER PROGRESSED TO LEO

When a Cancerian Sun progresses into Leo, the individual will reap the benefit of positive, extrovert Leonine traits. It will be easier to have an optimistic and outgoing outlook, helping to mitigate Cancerian worry and apprehension. Money will be spent more freely, even if the financial situation has not changed; more pleasure will be gained from buying the occasional luxury. More pride will also be taken in the appearance, with greater attention to detail. Self-confidence (not always a Cancerian strong point) should increase, partly because the value of the subject's past experience will be recognized, and opinions will be expressed with greater confidence.

A new tendency to be bossy and autocratic must not create problems, especially within the family. Any interest in collecting should not be allowed to become obsessive, while a new interest in collecting more valuable and interesting objects should be carefully geared to the financial position.

When a Cancerian Ascendant becomes Leonine, the basic motivation to cherish will be blended with a strongly creative instinct. Cancer is the sign of motherhood and Leo the sign of fatherhood – a first baby seems almost inevitable. At a different level, new-found creativity may be shown through the development and full expression of artistic potential. Leo's influence will strengthen organizational ability, so these people's lives may take on a more coherent air. As with the progressed Sun sign, there will be additional self-confidence, and the powerful Cancerian emotional level will be heightened by the fiery, passionate emotion of Leo. These people will also be less easily hurt, and less ready to hurt others. Fixity of opinions should, however, be avoided.

The Traditional Associations of Cancer

Dates
22 June – 22 July

The Origin
Cancer the Crab probably originated in Babylon; but twin turtles were associated with this sign in Egypt, where Thoth, among other things the god of astronomy, ruled the constellation

Ruling Planet
The Moon

Trees
All trees, particularly those that are rich in sap

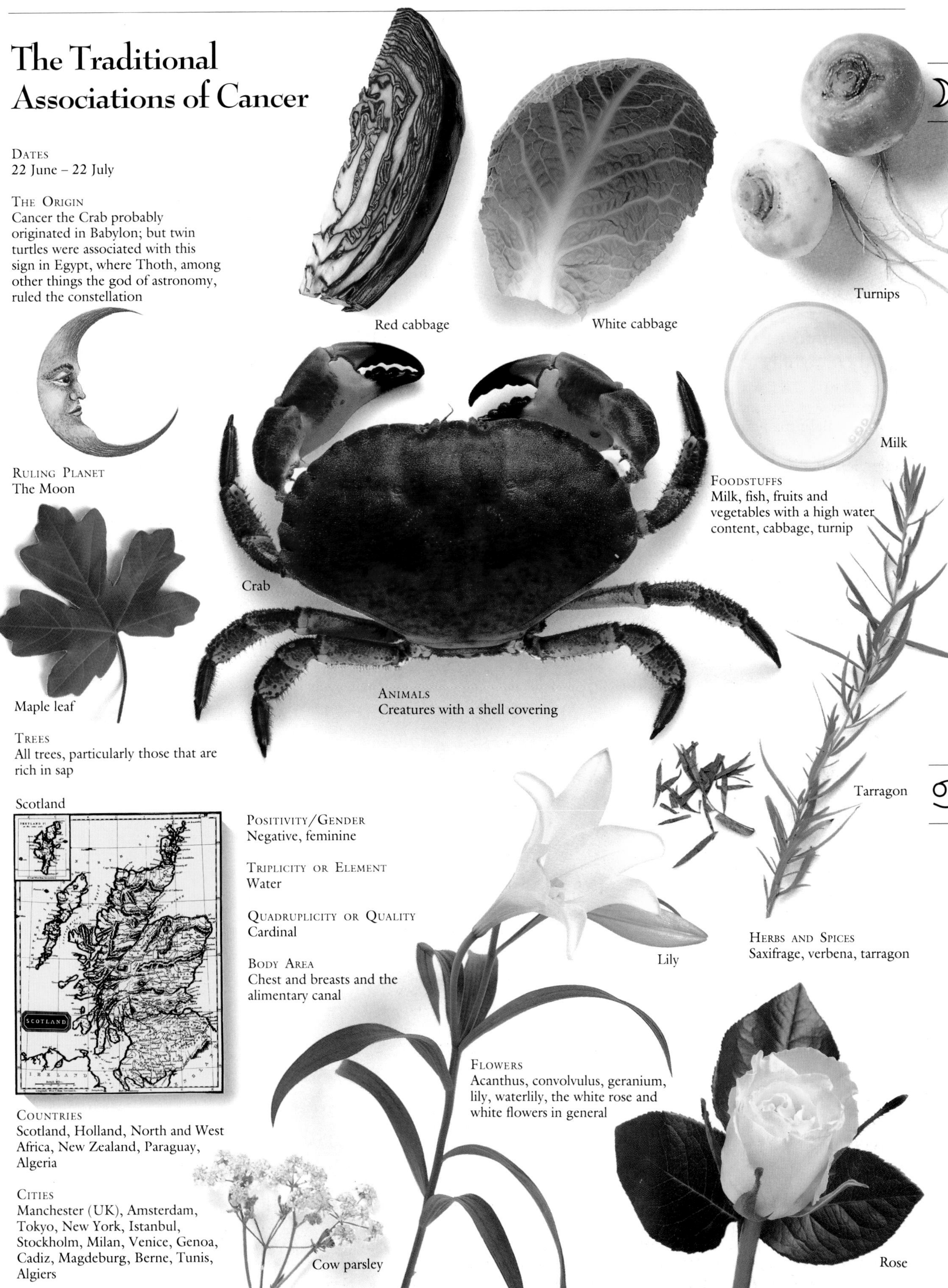

Red cabbage

White cabbage

Turnips

Milk

Crab

Maple leaf

Tarragon

Lily

Scotland

Cow parsley

Rose

Foodstuffs
Milk, fish, fruits and vegetables with a high water content, cabbage, turnip

Animals
Creatures with a shell covering

Positivity/Gender
Negative, feminine

Triplicity or Element
Water

Quadruplicity or Quality
Cardinal

Body Area
Chest and breasts and the alimentary canal

Herbs and Spices
Saxifrage, verbena, tarragon

Flowers
Acanthus, convolvulus, geranium, lily, waterlily, the white rose and white flowers in general

Countries
Scotland, Holland, North and West Africa, New Zealand, Paraguay, Algeria

Cities
Manchester (UK), Amsterdam, Tokyo, New York, Istanbul, Stockholm, Milan, Venice, Genoa, Cadiz, Magdeburg, Berne, Tunis, Algiers

Leo ♌ 23 July – 23 August

Organization is essential for Leos, who need control in their lives. With the slightest encouragement, their organizational ability will spill over into the disordered lives of others. The risk lies in their taking over, because they hate to see ability wasted. Their worst fault is in assuming they always know best. Leos may also be extremely dogmatic, and so must cultivate flexible minds and respect for others' opinions. The characteristic Leonine warmth, generosity and desire to understand others can then be fully indulged.

Basic Personality

A powerfully creative urge is present in every Leo and must be expressed, otherwise a very great deal of potential will be wasted. This does not mean all Leos are painters, actors or sculptors: creation can take place in the kitchen, at the sewing machine, in the garden or at the workbench. The innate Leo enthusiasm is expressed in other areas of life, too: the Sun, ruling this sign, gives Leos an infectious vitality. They must live life to the full, and like to see others doing so as well. They have an inner sun which not only illuminates their own lives and activities, but also lights up the lives of others, or perhaps gives them energy. Leo days should be full, with not a moment wasted, since lack of fulfillment, professionally or personally, can totally destroy them and cloud their personalities.

Partnership

Domination of partners is a possibility that cannot be underestimated. It may be well meant, as when they long to bring out the best in the other person, but nevertheless, Leos shouldn't always be allowed to wear the trousers!

They are surprisingly sensitive, and can be hurt very easily – partly because they are often emotionally idealistic. While this makes them wonderfully supportive and often real powers behind the throne, few people can be safely worshipped, and invariably Leos are disappointed in the end. Leos can also take criticism very much to heart.

Exuberant enjoyment and pleasure are gained from sex, but Leos don't like their love to be rough and ready. They almost demand to be wined, dined and then seduced in luxury!

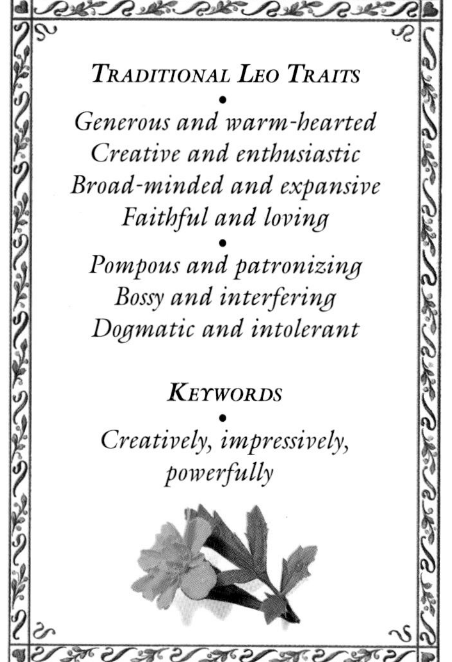

Traditional Leo Traits

Generous and warm-hearted
Creative and enthusiastic
Broad-minded and expansive
Faithful and loving

Pompous and patronizing
Bossy and interfering
Dogmatic and intolerant

Keywords

Creatively, impressively, powerfully

Family

The sunny disposition and ready enthusiasm of a Leo child appears at a very early age, and is always quite delightful. Natural organizational ability soon shows itself, but parents should watch for any tendency towards bossiness in their Leo offspring, who may be seen putting the whole playschool in its place.

Managing the lives of siblings is a distinct possibility when the Leo child is older than them. This self-assertion, however, is not quite as strong as it seems, and it is surprisingly easy to deflate young Leos – perhaps when a well-meaning adult severely criticizes a piece of work. If you must criticize a Leo child do so with affection and humor, otherwise you will severely crush his or her self-confidence. Listening to the opinions of others, even if the child does not accept them, should be actively encouraged. He or she is then less likely to become entrenched in fixed ideas and beliefs. The Leonine stubborn streak must also be discouraged. Try to distinguish it from determination, which should, of course, be welcomed and encouraged.

Leo enthusiasms last a lifetime: if a Leo child is interested in a particular subject or hobby, it is unlikely that it will ever be completely rejected, so it is worthwhile and most important to nurture early interests.

Leo parents are excellent at recognizing and encouraging their children's potential, but they must beware of forcing their own interests and enthusiasms on them. They will insist on the highest standards, but must not expect more than can be given. Challenge is good, but incessant pressure is not.

Career

Emotional involvement in a career is essential if Leos are to feel fulfilled. They are found, of course, in all walks of life, but basically are at their best when able to use their excellent creative potential and organizational abilities. Their natural sense of drama should also be expressed. The theater is an obvious possibility, but they can be equally at home in trades associated with luxury and glamor. Many Leos are in their element in a courtroom or in the operating theater: taking centerstage comes naturally to them.

Innately ambitious, Leos are interested in money chiefly for the luxury it can bring. They love buying and enjoying beautiful things and quality clothes, and they also love to travel – just as long as it can be done in comfort! When Leos reach the top of the tree they usually contrive to stay there, and to make quite sure they are seen!

Leos make excellent employers, due to their good powers of leadership. However, they must retain their natural enthusiasm for life and their desire to improve the lives of others. As they deplore anything second-rate or of a low standard, their employees will be well looked after – but also expected to give of their best. For this reason, Leo bosses can appear difficult and must subdue any autocratic tendencies.

The Symbolism of Leo

Animals
The lion, king of the jungle, and other members of the cat family are ruled by Leo
Ruling Planet
The Sun is Leo's ruling planet
Gemstone
The resplendent rich red ruby is the Leo gemstone
Trees
Among the trees ruled by Leo are the bay and the olive
City and Countries
Rome is a Leo city, and Italy one of the Leo countries, together with Romania, Czecho-slovakia and Lebanon
Colors
Most Leos enjoy wearing the opulent colors of their sign – those of the Sun (the ruling planet)
Metal
The precious metal gold is linked with Leo
Flowers
Yellow flowers, like the celandine and marigold, are associated with Leo
Corn marigold
Greater celandine
Herbs
Leo herbs include saffron, peppermint and rosemary
Bog rosemary
Triplicity or Element
Leo is a fire sign

Change, leisure and retirement
Leos never rush into change in a foolhardy way, because they are not over-fond of it. However, if they can learn to view important periods of change as a succession of challenges and a means to progress, they will cope well.

Leisure is an alien concept to Leos, who prefer to fill every moment with activity. They are *amateurs* in the true sense, since they have no hobbies as such: all their interests are taken to a professional standard. However, they must not be self-satisfied, as self-criticism is important.

Retirement will open new doors for Leos: they will already have many interests to follow up and develop. They will very likely turn some hobbies into moneymaking concerns, for they won't want to accept a standard of living that is lower than the one they have been used to.

Health, diet and exercise
Keeping an even tenor in their lives is important. Otherwise, their usually excellent vitality may be burned out now and again through exhaustion.

The heart is the Leo organ, so Leos would do well to prevent possible heart disease by careful diet and regular exercise. The back is also vulnerable and should be carefully exercised as well. Dancing, ice-skating and forms of exercise with a creative element are especially rewarding. A love of rich foods should be curbed.

LEO AS ASCENDANT

Psychological motivation
The organizational ability of any individual is powerfully enhanced when Leo rises. Unfortunately, so is the likelihood of pomposity and the conviction that the Leo knows better than anyone else. This unattractive assumption should be controlled. The desire to succeed is also very strong, but may lead to the stifling of creative instincts in favor of success in the career, which will be sought after so as to enhance the lifestyle of the Leo and his or her family. This is wholly admirable, but may well be damaging if the vital creative urge is not given some expression: Leos need to create as well as to prosper.

The well-balanced Leo will be psychologically secure, and provided ambition is balanced by a degree of humility, the inner strength of this dynamic sign is of the greatest advantage. But the inherent desire for psychological wholeness will not always be accompanied by a willingness to face up to negative personality traits (such as vanity), and disasters may follow.

The ideal partner has a strong and independent mind, against which the subject can sharpen his or her wits: someone with different and stimulating ideas and ambitions would be perfect to keep the mentally active Leo on the ball. If a partner is outstanding in his or her own right, either because of success or some other characteristic, such as great beauty, then so much the better. The subject can then bask in the reflected glory.

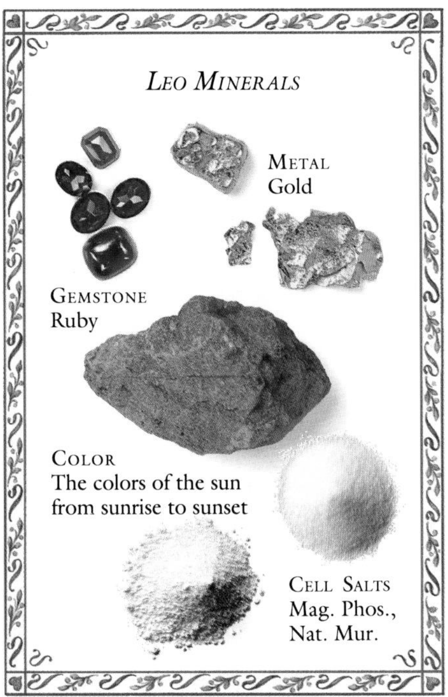

LEO MINERALS
METAL
Gold
GEMSTONE
Ruby
COLOR
The colors of the sun from sunrise to sunset
CELL SALTS
Mag. Phos.,
Nat. Mur.

Vulnerability to psychological disorders is fairly common, and these ailments frequently show themselves externally. A bad back or neckache may be caused, for instance, by a blow to the self-esteem or some overly harsh criticism that has been taken too much to heart. Apparently inexplicable backpain can be a more or less regular circumstance; if it becomes really disabling, these people should look to their lifestyles and try to find a possible psychological cause.

LEO PROGRESSED TO VIRGO

Coping with fussy or pedantic details is usually difficult for Leos. However, when the Sun progresses from Leo into Virgo these people are able to assess situations more carefully, and are far less likely to adopt sweeping generalizations. They can also be more successfully self-critical, recognizing any tendencies to self-satisfaction (especially over creative work) and take a much more objective and logical attitude to life.

Don't forget that worry is second nature to Virgoans, so it will be a pity if it clouds the normally positive Leonine outlook. They should watch for this, and enjoy adding Virgoan analysis and concern for detail to their considerable organizational abilities. Leo enthusiasm and optimism will not be dimmed, but they may become slightly more cautious and a little less dramatic.

Those whose creative bent has been expressed in craftwork, or who enjoy working with their hands, should find their dexterity and practical ability increases. This will also be seen in other areas of life, stabilizing the Leonine outlook and perhaps adding some caution and discrimination about money. This will be welcome, especially if it comes at a time when the Leo's earning ability is growing. The additional common sense will help them when they think of long-term savings, insurance, mortgages or similar projects.

When a Leo Ascendant progresses to Virgo there is a good chance that some of the Leo dogmatism will be modified. Introspection will appear instead and strengthen the self-critical element – always welcome where Leo is a strong influence. A need to serve and help others may also emerge and, allied to the Leonine organizational ability, this may well result in positive, down-to-earth contributions to organizations or charities.

The overweening self-confidence of Leo may diminish. The Leo will then find it easier to see past errors and learn from them, and will be less ready to accept his or her lightest thought as God-given. In this way, the Virgo influence is positive and should help temper the innate egotism.

The Traditional Associations of Leo

Dates
23 July – 23 August

The Origin
The lion is associated with the pattern of stars in its constellation, and may originally have been suggested by it; it was probably born in Egypt at least 3000 years BC

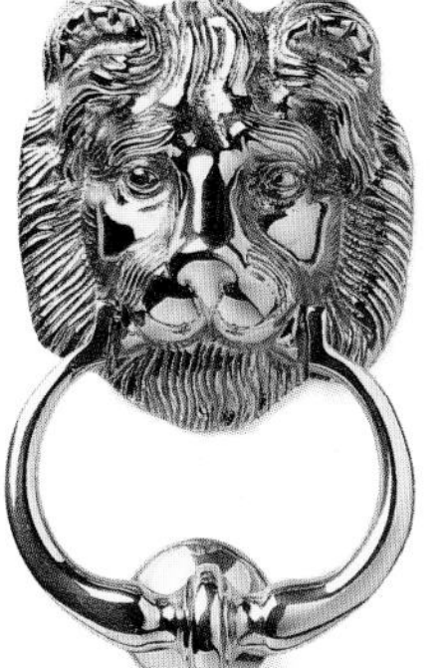

Animals
Big game, especially the cats

Laurel leaf

Rosemary

Saffron

Herbs and Spices
Saffron, peppermint, rosemary, rue

Positivity/Gender
Positive, masculine

Triplicity or Element
Fire

Quadruplicity or Quality
Fixed

Body Area
The heart, spine and back

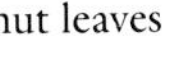

Walnut leaves

Ruling Planet
The Sun

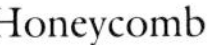

Honeycomb

Marigold

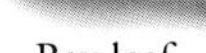

Bay leaf

Italy

Trees
Palm, bay, laurel, walnut, olive, citrus trees

Rice

Flowers
Sunflower, marigold, celandine, passion flower

Watercress

Spinach

Cereals

Countries
Italy, Romania, Sicily, Czechoslovakia, southern Iraq, Lebanon, the South of France

Cities
Rome, Prague, Bombay, Madrid, Philadelphia, Chicago, Los Angeles, Bath, Bristol, Portsmouth, Syracuse, Damascus

Foodstuffs
Meat, rice, honey, crops and vines in general; vegetables with a high iron content

Virgo ♍ 24 AUGUST – 22 SEPTEMBER

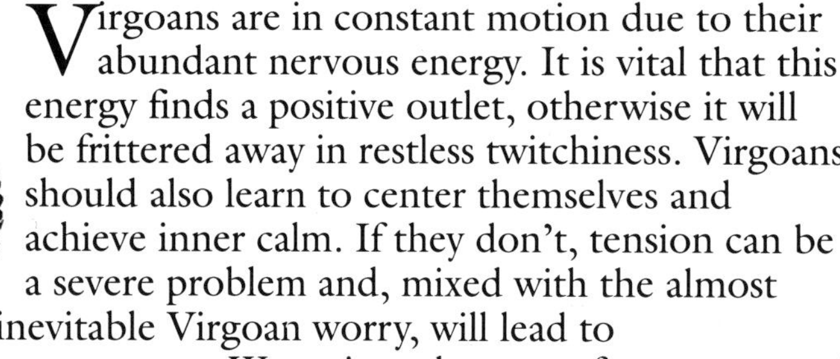

Virgoans are in constant motion due to their abundant nervous energy. It is vital that this energy finds a positive outlet, otherwise it will be frittered away in restless twitchiness. Virgoans should also learn to center themselves and achieve inner calm. If they don't, tension can be a severe problem and, mixed with the almost inevitable Virgoan worry, will lead to nervous upsets. Worry is at the root of most personal problems for these individuals and is best countered by their analytical, critical and practical qualities.

BASIC PERSONALITY

Most Virgoans are practical, but those who aren't can all too easily become bogged down in the small details of problems. This, indeed, is one of their chief difficulties: that their critical acumen can be overapplied, both to themselves and to other people, causing problems in personal relationships. Relentless, carping criticism is their worst fault.

What is needed is a positive synthesis of these qualities, producing people who are hard-working and practical, and who will stand no nonsense, deal sensibly with problems (their own, or other people's), and are most likely to realize their full potential.

Virgoans are talkative, lively in argument and, like their Mercury-ruled cousins Geminians, enjoy communicating their ideas, which are usually without frills, and clearly and economically expressed. Here again, however, a penchant for detail can trap them into overelaboration; they must learn to see the broader outline of things.

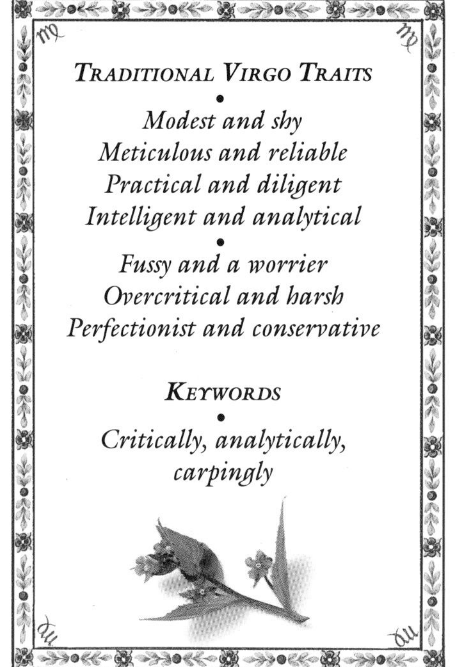

TRADITIONAL VIRGO TRAITS

•

Modest and shy
Meticulous and reliable
Practical and diligent
Intelligent and analytical

•

Fussy and a worrier
Overcritical and harsh
Perfectionist and conservative

KEYWORDS

•

Critically, analytically, carpingly

Partnership

Self-denigration can often get in the way when a Virgoan is thinking of deepening a personal relationship: "What does he/she see in me? – I'm not good enough for him/her." This can be genuine modesty, which (especially in a young person in love for the first time) can be charming – but more often the problem is deeper, and Virgoans should strive for the self-confidence which will allow them to accept compliments gracefully, and (most important) to believe them. Kind and willing to do anything for their partners, their natural modesty can stop them fully expressing both their physical and emotional love. They must learn to relax, and if (in some cases) they have taught themselves to regard sex with suspicion, learn to see it as a happy expression of that emotional devotion which they should allow themselves to show to a partner. The other most inhibiting factor is their tendency to nag, which they must curb.

Family

The Virgo child is neat, clean and a very willing worker at school. Exercise books will be totally devoid of dirty smudges, and the handwriting will be clear and legible. Willing workers who truly enjoy being given things to do, these children can earn a reputation as teachers' pets; this is not the case. They simply like being kept busy. Rather shy, so that the playground can seem threatening, they may be seen as standoffish. Parents should do everything possible to help them develop self-confidence, especially at examination time. The Virgoan tendency to worry will otherwise be overwhelming, and mysterious illnesses will appear.

Virgoans will work from dawn to dusk to build and maintain their family home in a way that satisfies their own highly critical standards. Career women will make time for domestic work, but mustn't spend so much time cleaning and polishing that they never enjoy the environment they so lovingly create. If a partner accuses them of an obsession with spit and polish, they should take note! Similarly, both sexes should try to avoid bringing work home, otherwise they'll never have time for their family.

Career

To work at their very best, Virgoans probably need supervision. Not only is it often difficult for them to see what should be done, but even if they can do so they may be apprehensive about taking matters into their own hands, fearing themselves incompetent or wondering how other people will receive their efforts. But given an instruction they will follow it to the very best of their abilities. They make excellent personal assistants and here, too, are the natural formal critics of the zodiac. As writers they have a sharp incisive style which is of great advantage if they are working in the media. Many make excellent teachers, and others do well in the medical profession, both in conventional or complementary medicine.

Virgoans are not frantically ambitious; in top jobs they must watch their tendency to carp if they want to be popular as well as efficient. A high salary will be carefully managed, but they should try to enjoy spending money as well as investing it.

Change, leisure and retirement

Virgoans, in general, look forward to retirement as an opportunity to cultivate and develop the hobbies with which they have always filled their spare time. These will almost certainly including gardening, for they are

The Symbolism of Virgo

GEMSTONE
The Virgoan gemstone is the reddish-brown sardonyx
FLOWERS
All brightly colored, small flowers are Virgoan
Hop trefoil
DECORATION
Virgoans usually enjoy wearing small detailed patterns
Walnut leaves
RULING PLANET
Mercury is Virgo's ruling planet
CITY
Paris is by tradition a Virgoan city
TRIPLICITY OR ELEMENT
The sign has an affinity with harvest time and the fecundity of the earth – its triplicty or element
COLORS
Green and dark brown are favorite Virgoan colors
ANIMALS
All domestic pets – in particular, cats and dogs – fall under the rulership of Virgo
TREES
Nut-bearing trees, such as the hazel, are Virgoan trees
☿

natural and enthusiastic gardeners. Any diminution of income, provided it is not massive, will be greeted with equanimity; careful with money, they are not devoted to it. Lack of self-confidence can make changes at work rather difficult to cope with. The threat of being fired is frightening; out of work, they are peerless in their effort to find a new job and, willing and hard workers, they should do so more easily than most.

Health, diet and exercise

It is essential for Virgoans to spend as much time as possible in the fresh air and, if possible, in the country. Children of nature, their spirits are revived by long walks and cycle rides. This is also a sign much related to wholefood diets and vegetarianism. The Virgoan diet must contain plenty of fiber: this Sun sign rules the bowels, and constipation can cause problems, usually because of an unbalanced diet.

Medically administered drugs don't suit many Virgoans, and they should always watch carefully for any allergy. Holistic and homeopathic treatments are often favored, with excellent results. Balance is the best answer to Virgoan health problems, plus exercise and fresh air; it is a mistake to sacrifice these for family or work. These people also benefit considerably from relaxation techniques such as yoga; meditation is especially good if they are prone to worry, although resulting introspection may exacerbate the problem.

As a result of worries (perhaps about the career or family), Virgoans are often vulnerable to severe headaches or even migraines. A change of diet may help more than they realize, so they should seek medical advice if they do have painful headaches.

VIRGO AS ASCENDANT

Psychological motivation

Quite frequently when Virgo rises we find the other Mercury-ruled sign, Gemini, on the Midheaven. This offers unique psychological potential for the individual concerned: the principles of Mercury – the need to examine every situation in life in great detail – are handsomely united to the need to communicate. These individuals will have a natural instinct that helps them identify with all Mercury-ruled characteristics as well as the basic principles of Gemini. As a result, they are usually very well integrated psychologically, and provided their potential is constructively and positively directed, there is a good chance that their lives will be splendidly fulfilled.

The Virgoan tendency towards worry and hypercriticism may be turned inwards on the self. This is likely to give rise to the same problems of headaches and migraines that we have mentioned above. The same solution applies – particular care with diet, and proper medical advice. Very often these people need to work harder to establish a reasonable degree of self-confidence than do Sun Virgoans. (To assess this fully, other planetary positions and relationships in the chart must be examined.) Conflicts relating to self-criticism must be worked through; an important way of building up confidence is to allow some self-praise, rather than invariably denigrating personal achievements. Success in this respect will depend to a large extent on upbringing and the attitude of parents; if this was highly critical, the problems will be more intractable.

VIRGO MINERALS

CELL SALTS
Kali. Sulph., Ferr. Phos.

METAL
Mercury and nickel

GEMSTONE
Sardonyx

COLOR
Navy blue, dark brown, green

In one-to-one relationships, in spite of the tendency to nag, a remarkable emotional response will be seen. An inner warmth and sensitivity will dull the slightly brittle edge of their reactions and attitudes, and tender, loving sentiments will be characteristic. These people may take the easy way out of arguments and problems.

Worry is more likely to affect the systems of these people, for example causing constipation and similar problems. Hypochondria is very likely, in which case they should assess any health problems logically and not make mountains out of molehills.

VIRGO PROGRESSED TO LIBRA

When a Virgoan Sun progresses into Libra, life may be taken a little more easily, and more time may be set aside for leisure. More money will probably be spent on simple pleasure. It will be easier for these people to realize they must control their tension, and find ways of doing so. They will be less hard on themselves and their partners.

The change of Sun sign may occur at a time when the individual is coming to terms with his or her emotional life and needs. If so, it will now be easier for them to show their love and affection, and their natural Virgoan modesty will be tempered. The Libran need for peace and harmony will become evident, and as a result the individual will be able to take a more balanced view of life. The characteristic neat, businesslike Virgoan image may give way to a softer, more romantic look: dark colors and small patterns becoming pastel shades and large, floral designs. Venus' sign placing in the natal chart will assume greater importance, and its influence on the individual will now be more marked.

When a Virgo Ascendant progresses into Libra the need to relate in depth to a partner, and to develop a really close and satisfactory rapport with him or her, is strongly enhanced. If these people are unattached, care must be taken that in their anxiety to express themselves in this way they don't rush into a relationship, ignoring their natural Virgoan critical sense. They will also be able to take a more relaxed view of life, and the whole personality should develop a potential inner calm which will do much to ease away tension, worry and nervous restlessness.

The Traditional Associations of Virgo

DATES
24 August – 22 September

THE ORIGIN
Nidaba, Egyptian goddess of grain, was probably the original of the Virgin (the Egyptian harvest began when the Moon was in this constellation). In Sumeria the figure, far from being a virgin, was that of the Great Mother, whose daughter was sometimes the guardian of the harvest

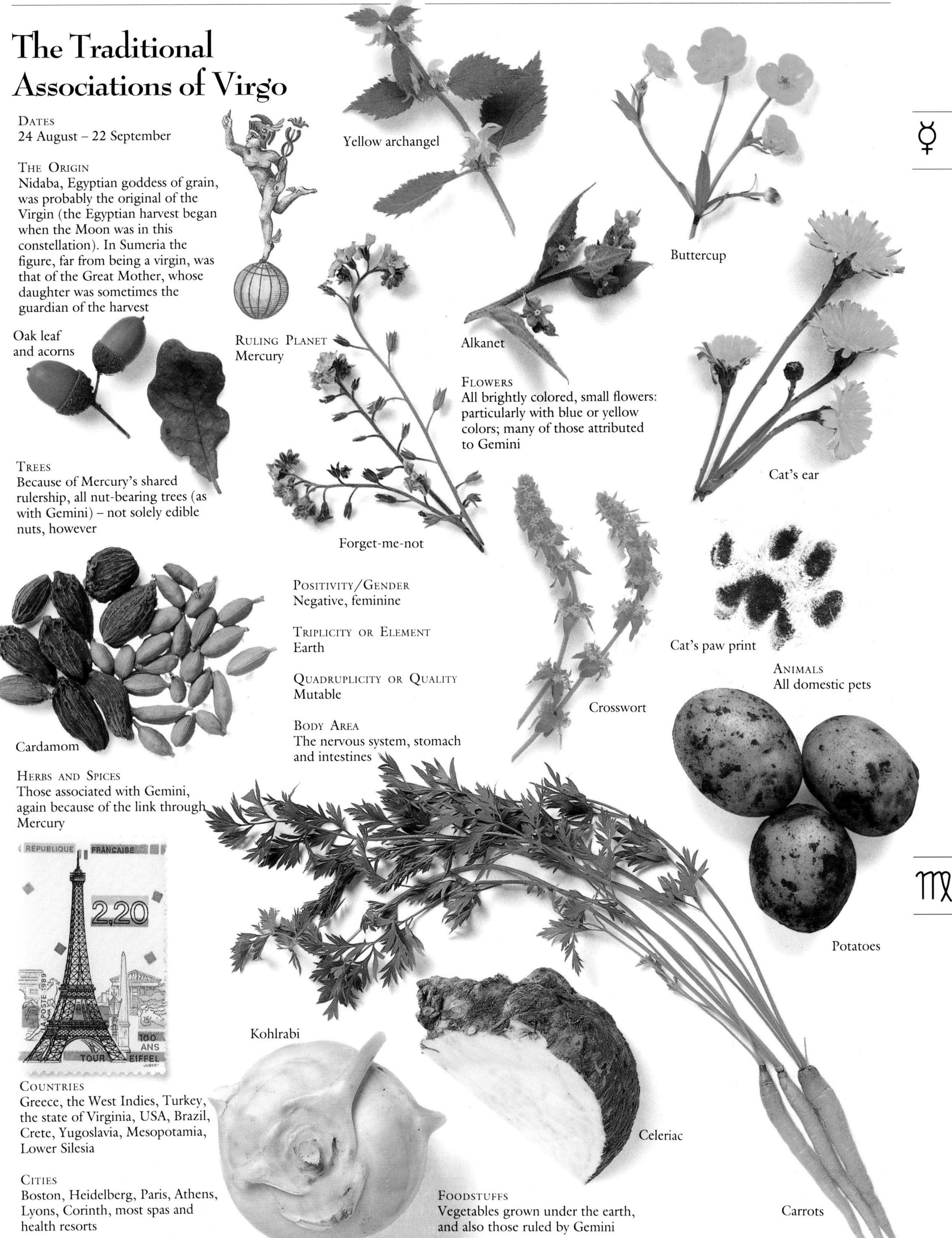

Yellow archangel

Buttercup

Oak leaf and acorns

RULING PLANET
Mercury

Alkanet

FLOWERS
All brightly colored, small flowers: particularly with blue or yellow colors; many of those attributed to Gemini

Cat's ear

TREES
Because of Mercury's shared rulership, all nut-bearing trees (as with Gemini) – not solely edible nuts, however

Forget-me-not

POSITIVITY/GENDER
Negative, feminine

TRIPLICITY OR ELEMENT
Earth

QUADRUPLICITY OR QUALITY
Mutable

BODY AREA
The nervous system, stomach and intestines

Cat's paw print

ANIMALS
All domestic pets

Crosswort

Cardamom

HERBS AND SPICES
Those associated with Gemini, again because of the link through Mercury

Potatoes

Kohlrabi

COUNTRIES
Greece, the West Indies, Turkey, the state of Virginia, USA, Brazil, Crete, Yugoslavia, Mesopotamia, Lower Silesia

CITIES
Boston, Heidelberg, Paris, Athens, Lyons, Corinth, most spas and health resorts

Celeriac

FOODSTUFFS
Vegetables grown under the earth, and also those ruled by Gemini

Carrots

Libra ♎ 23 September – 23 October

The scales, the symbol of this sign, have a deeply symbolic meaning for Sun sign Librans, since the need for balance and harmony in their lives is paramount. They need a harmonious background, free of undue pressure and argument, in order to be happy. They will sometimes even make sacrifices for the sake of peace and quiet, giving in too easily to pressure from others, and when confronted with a problem they will sit on the fence until the problem goes away, rather than commit themselves to one side or the other.

Basic Personality

Decision-making, or supporting one side of an argument, often involves taking one person's side against another, and Librans have a deep dislike to hurting other people. Indecision is the worst Libran fault.

Librans find it more difficult to cope with loneliness than any other sign of the zodiac. Complete happiness for them means sharing their lives, although when they are alone, other areas of their birth charts may show qualities which enable them to come to terms with this problem.

Laziness and relaxation are often associated with this sign but that is not entirely fair. While Librans may not enjoy heavy, dirty jobs, they certainly don't lack physical energy, especially if the work has a creative element; indeed, recent research has shown that those born within the first five or six days of this Sun sign period may seem relaxed because they make time to listen to friends' problems and sympathize in sorrow or share joy, but actually they are very active and anything but time-wasters.

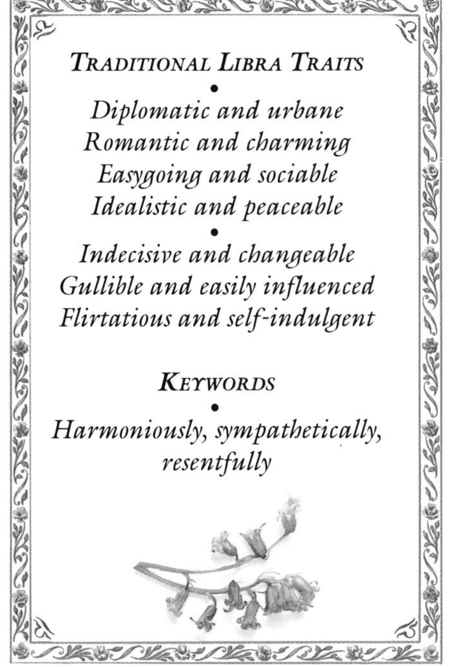

Traditional Libra Traits

•

Diplomatic and urbane
Romantic and charming
Easygoing and sociable
Idealistic and peaceable

•

Indecisive and changeable
Gullible and easily influenced
Flirtatious and self-indulgent

Keywords

•

Harmoniously, sympathetically, resentfully

Partnership

The most important sphere of a Libran life, whether Libra is the Sun sign or Ascendant, is the one-to-one relationship. Librans are not psychologically whole until this has been successfully achieved, and their usual indecision may well take a back seat when it comes to romantic commitment. Sun sign Librans are pure romantics, and will be starry-eyed for months when planning their wedding, without, perhaps, giving sufficient thought to what comes after the ceremony.

Although usually peace-loving, Librans sometimes provoke arguments (even quite serious ones) with their partners to test their affections and reassure themselves that the partnership is really loving. They should be aware of this tendency; repeatedly upsetting the boat just in order to be rescued can be irritating to others. Librans can be extremely generous, but should recognize the moment when their motives become not the giving of pleasure but the purchase of affection.

Family

The Libran child is charming and eager to please. Parents should watch for any tendency to procrastination or laziness, which can develop into serious problems later in life. It is essential that the child is encouraged to be decisive (see above); given a choice, Libran children will often ask "What would you choose, Mommy?" Don't give in to this ploy! Point out the various options, and do all you can to make young Librans have the confidence to think for themselves.

Happiness at school is important for all children, but a Libran child treated unfairly ("It's not fair!" is a common complaint) will magnify the injustice to such an extent that it will interfere with the teaching process, and upset the child for much longer than might be expected. Creative potential should be recognized and encouraged; there is often real talent here, but if left to itself it may not develop as quickly as with some other Sun signs.

Libran parents are kind, loving and gentle, but must beware of being outwitted by a quicker-minded child playing on the Libran tendency to give in rather than insist on the course they know to be best. It is too easy to spoil a child for the sake of peace and quiet, especially by offering bribes! It is also all too easy to allow oneself to be worn down by a child's pleas for an expensive toy or piece of equipment; don't give in too quickly (if at all), especially if fashion is involved. A Libran parent's indecision can infuriate his or her children: decisions should not be shelved or handed over to the partner ("Wait until Daddy comes home").

Career

Librans enjoy luxury and a comfortable lifestyle, so they need to earn plenty of money. They can also be overly generous, which can act as a spur to often impressive careers. Their working environment is not of great importance to them, but their colleagues are – they dislike fussy people, slave drivers and employers who won't allow them to work at their own pace. Their need for harmony is shown here: like-minded colleagues are a boon.

Any profession calling for tact and diplomacy offers them great opportunities. The luxury trades (fashion, beauty, cosmetics) are popular, while the qualities of their polar sign, Aries, sometimes attract them to the armed services, where they may attain rank. They are ambitious, but should think carefully before taking a lonely top job: isolation does not agree with them.

The Symbolism of Libra

Gemstones
Sapphire and jade are Libran stones
Metal
Copper is the metal chiefly associated with Libra
Flowers
Large, opulent roses and any blue flowers, such as bluebells, are related to Libra
Roses
Symbolic Sign
The scales of Libra
Ruling Planet
Venus is Libra's ruling planet
Countries
Burma, Tibet and Indo-china are countries ruled by Libra
Burma
Sapphire
Snakes
Jade
Colors
Libran colors include pink, pale green and various shades of blue
Foodstuffs
Libra, like Taurus, is associated with cereals
Animals
Lizards and other small reptiles are Libra-ruled creatures
Tree
The ash and poplar are related to Libra
Poplar

Change, leisure and retirement
Moving from one district to another will be very disturbing to a Libran, so changes of this kind should be minimized unless the individual is certain of their many benefits. The idea of approaching retirement will be blissful – in theory nothing is more attractive than the thought of not having to rise early, go to work, cope with the petty problems of a working life. However, without a compelling interest in life, retirement will be less fulfilling than these people imagine, and they may even find themselves aging quickly. New and enjoyable hobbies or activities will release fresh areas of potential.

Health, diet and exercise
It is all too easy for Librans to dismiss the idea of regular exercise, but they really do need it. Indeed, it should be an integral part of their life. It is excellent for them to join a health club that offers a good social life and a pleasant ambience, so they can not only work out but also meet congenial people. The exercise itself should be steady rather than spasmodically energetic. The Libran liking for rich, sweet food should be resisted whenever possible; a lighter diet is best, and inaction can encourage weight gain. The kidneys are the Libran organs, and tension or worry can provoke headaches. If these persist, medical advice is needed.

Libra as Ascendant

Psychological motivation
Libra is not one of the strongest signs of the zodiac; any other powerful influence in the birth chart can sap its positive characteristics, especially when it is the rising sign. However, many typically Libran elements will be a part of the personality, especially the all-important need to relate which under these circumstances becomes the basic psychological motivation. Very often the whole personality is geared to this end, with people rushing into permanent relationships. Sadly, such premature commitments can end in heartbreak and divorce. The notorious Libran tendency to fall in love with love is here, however, spiced with lively sexuality and a greater enthusiasm for the physical aspects of love than is often the case with a Libran Sun. The individual should be aware of his or her uncharacteristic leaning towards selfishness in close relationships.

A tendency to ignore personal faults rather than recognize and come to terms with them is also likely: self-satisfaction is not foreign to these people. Natural charm may at first disguise this, but not for long. Self-analysis is the best way for those with Libra rising to see clearly their character weaknesses and correct them. It is almost essential to involve a partner or friend with whom they can talk things through, and who is able to be severely critical when necessary.

Libra Minerals

Color
Shades of blue from pale to ultramarine; pink and pale green

Gemstone
Sapphire, jade

Metal
Copper

Cell Salts
Nat. Phos., Kali. Phos.

Worry or tension don't usually afflict those with Libra rising, so are unlikely to be the cause if the subject often has headaches. If these persist, medical advice should be sought as they may be due to a slight kidney disorder.

Many charts will reveal people born with Neptune close to the Ascendant. If in the first house of the birth chart, it can weaken the personality by increasing the Libran tendency to take the line of least resistance. The gentler, softer qualities of these people will then be strengthened by Neptune's sign placing; very pleasant, no doubt, but full of inherent problems. These individuals must learn to face up to reality and not resort to negative escapism. If Neptune is in Libra in the twelfth house, there can be an inclination to experiment with drugs. The need to escape is better released through art, or perhaps religious or spiritual interests.

Libra Progressed to Scorpio

When the Libran Sun progresses into Scorpio, the individual will have new determination and purpose. The Libran emotions, meaningful but rather lightweight, will now intensify, and the rather diffused personality will gain focus and a cutting edge. Scorpio is the most energetic of signs, so the Libran energy level is likely to be strengthened. Considering Scorpio's enjoyment of the good life and what it has to offer, it won't be surprising if Libra's love of easy living and self-indulgence is even more clearly shown. If ungoverned, this can obviously have an adverse effect on the health.

In a business career, Scorpio's influence on a Libran personality can be an enormous asset: its powerful business sense will be more than useful. In more domestic circumstances the romantic Libran image will become sexier; the wardrobe may now contain more black, and women may sport a deeper décolleté. The sex life should improve because it will assume greater importance, but Scorpio jealousy may appear and should be guarded against.

A Libran Ascendant progressing into Scorpio gives objectivity and a sense of purpose, which will help in decision-making. Indecisiveness will start to take a back seat, countered by the Scorpio determination and strength of will. Scorpio's strength will be a positive contribution to the personality, provided that (as with the progressed Sun sign) jealousy and suspicion do not become obsessions.

Emotional satisfaction within a career may become more important, and so the subject will be less complaisant about work which offers only an income rather than job satisfaction. In personal relationships, this person will want more than just a romantic association – there will be a need for a little grit, some challenge, a sense of purpose and a feeling that the partnership is going somewhere.

The Traditional Associations of Libra

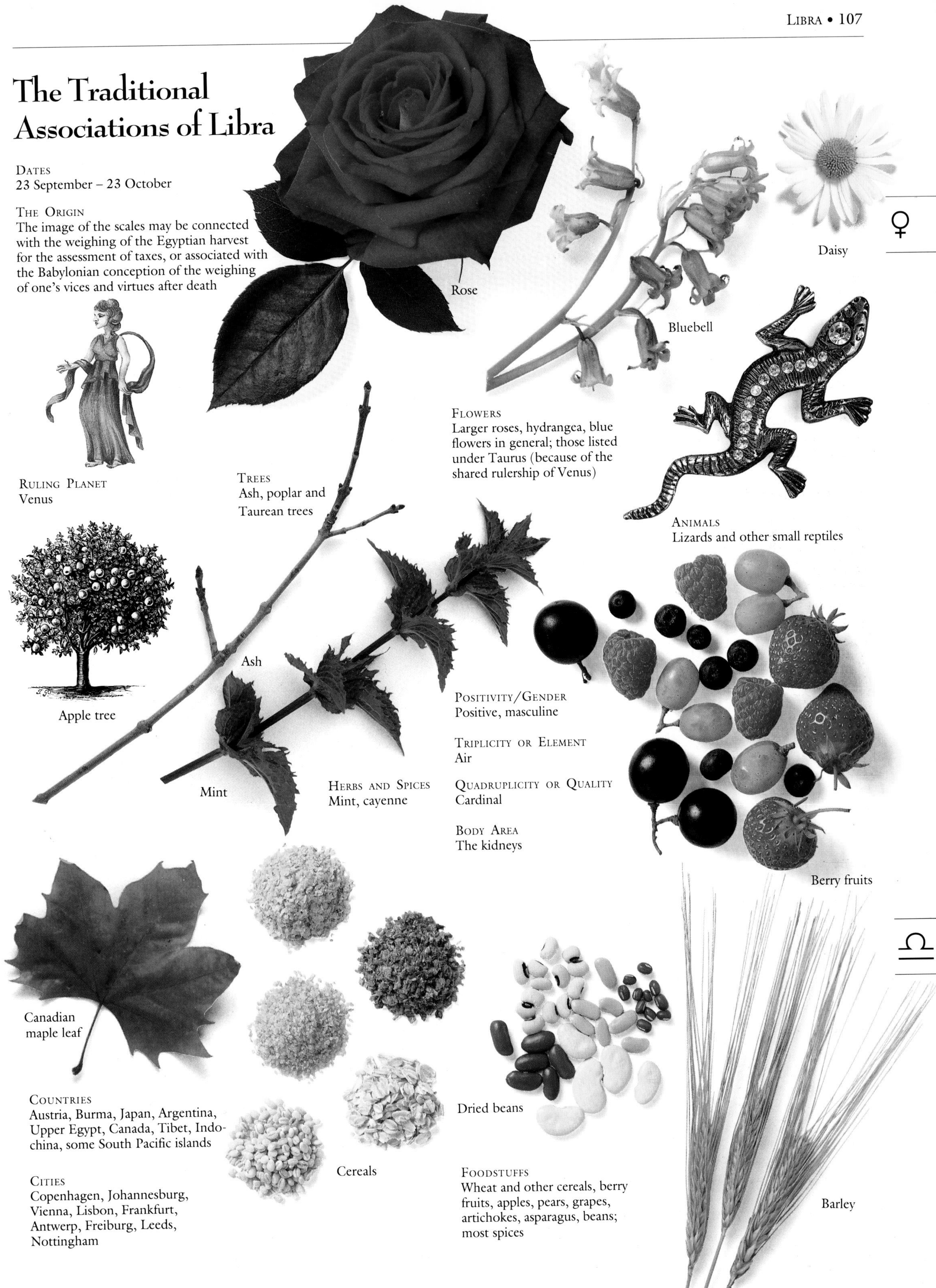

DATES
23 September – 23 October

THE ORIGIN
The image of the scales may be connected with the weighing of the Egyptian harvest for the assessment of taxes, or associated with the Babylonian conception of the weighing of one's vices and virtues after death

Rose

Daisy

Bluebell

RULING PLANET
Venus

TREES
Ash, poplar and Taurean trees

FLOWERS
Larger roses, hydrangea, blue flowers in general; those listed under Taurus (because of the shared rulership of Venus)

ANIMALS
Lizards and other small reptiles

Ash

Apple tree

POSITIVITY/GENDER
Positive, masculine

TRIPLICITY OR ELEMENT
Air

QUADRUPLICITY OR QUALITY
Cardinal

BODY AREA
The kidneys

Mint

HERBS AND SPICES
Mint, cayenne

Berry fruits

Canadian maple leaf

Dried beans

Cereals

COUNTRIES
Austria, Burma, Japan, Argentina, Upper Egypt, Canada, Tibet, Indo-china, some South Pacific islands

CITIES
Copenhagen, Johannesburg, Vienna, Lisbon, Frankfurt, Antwerp, Freiburg, Leeds, Nottingham

FOODSTUFFS
Wheat and other cereals, berry fruits, apples, pears, grapes, artichokes, asparagus, beans; most spices

Barley

Scorpio ♏ 24 October – 22 November

The chief characteristic of a Sun sign Scorpio is a remarkable reserve of energy. It is often said that this is the "worst" of the Sun signs. Of course, this isn't true: the sign's energies are so strong they can seem over-powering, even inhibiting; the Scorpio can feel driven by them. But if they are fully and positively expressed, both physically and emotionally, the individual will be a big achiever. However, if the energy flow is inhibited or uncontrolled it can be disastrous, with typical resentfulness, jealousy and broodiness.

Basic Personality

Jealousy is the worst Scorpio fault, and not only in relationships: Scorpios can be jealous of colleagues and of other people's possessions. This can, however, act as a spur: seeing the progress of others, Scorpios may be inspired to do equally well or better.

The Scorpio body area is the genitals, and this may partly explain the sign's overly sexy reputation. Sun sign Scorpios need just as much sexual fulfillment as everyone else and may suffer more if they don't achieve it, but that certainly doesn't mean every Scorpio is a putative sex-maniac! A great many of them express their sex drives through sport; the women may even devote themselves to becoming perfect housewives. The important thing is that the drive is properly directed and fully extended, and not allowed to stagnate and waste.

Most Scorpios are capable of deep, incisive and analytical thought; they have a powerful urge to get to the root of any problem. They also want to get the most out of life, cramming every day with work and demanding spare-time interests. They may force themselves to extremes of action, and so should try to release their energy as evenly as possible.

Between 1984 and 1995, Pluto, the ruling planet of Scorpio, is traveling through its own sign. This underlines all the most typical characteristics of Scorpio, which will be specially strong in those born during this period.

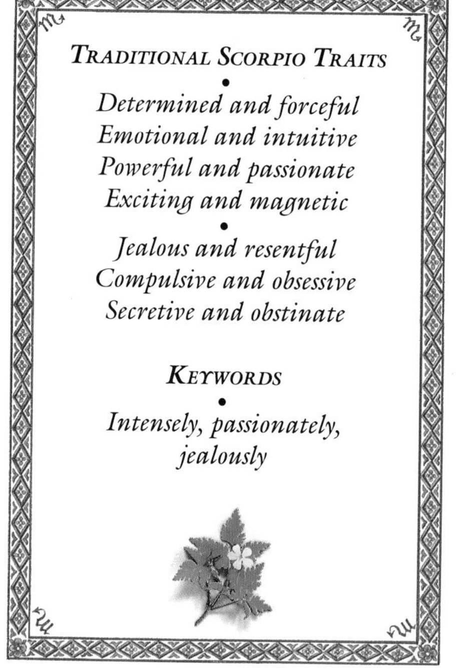

Traditional Scorpio Traits

•

Determined and forceful
Emotional and intuitive
Powerful and passionate
Exciting and magnetic

•

Jealous and resentful
Compulsive and obsessive
Secretive and obstinate

Keywords

•

Intensely, passionately, jealously

Partnership

A Scorpio, who is all energy, needs a conductor. If the energy is not able to strike home and be received and used in some way there will be problems, so it is most important in a personal relationship that the partner is not cold or undemonstrative. Scorpios, overwhelmed by the attractions of a possible partner, can put all their energy into the chase, and persist even when it is obvious that the object of their affections is unsuitable. Difficulties will follow. In the stressful periods of a relationship the Scorpio's tendency to be secretive and vindictive (even to the point of cruelty) may emerge, but other areas of an individual birth chart may modify these characteristics.

Family

When something is wrong with a Scorpio child he or she will become extremely quiet, and probably reject even favorite food. The sooner young Scorpio can be encouraged to talk over any problems, the better; the tendency to bottle things up can lead to serious difficulties in later life, when he or she may suffer unnecessarily. All children need compelling interests, but young Scorpios do so more than most; they should be encouraged to take up a hobby, preferably one that deeply interests them, and will burn up emotional as well as physical energy. This teaches them how to use that energy evenly. They will probably enjoy heavy team games, water sports or, for the more creative types, skating and dancing.

Fulfilled Scorpio parents demand much of their children – sometimes too much. They will be especially eager to encourage their children to take the path they have followed, and become successful in their own right. Deeply interested in their children and their development, they may go too far in their desire to know everything about them, and should remember that children need privacy, too. The intense relationship they desire should include fun and humor. Naturally rather strict, Scorpio parents must realize that some children react better to less stringent discipline. Their tendency to insist on what they think best can make them seem intractable to their children and incapable of sensible discussion and argument.

Less than successful Scorpios whose children are doing really well must be exceptionally careful that jealousy, perhaps their chief fault, doesn't spoil the relationship. They should remember that the children's success is their success, too; they brought them up!

Career

Above all else, and more than most other signs, Scorpios really need to be emotionally involved in their careers. Like those of their polar sign, Taurus, they need emotional and financial security, and are willing to work hard to achieve and maintain it, and to improve their standard of living. Their energy can sometimes seem entirely devoted to making money, and these Scorpio businessmen or women will have found the way in which to direct their keen sense of purpose. Others may have to strive a little harder to discover ways of using their abundant

The Symbolism of Scorpio

Colors
Scorpio has a special link with the dramatic tones of deep red and maroon

Gemstone
The iridescent opal is the gemstone connected to Scorpio

Mythology
The scorpian rose up from the earth and attacked Orion

Ruling Planet
Pluto is Scorpio's ruling planet

Trees
Because Scorpio was ruled by Mars until Pluto was decreed its modern ruler, many Scorpio traditions are similar to those of Aries: Scorpio trees, for instance, are also those which bear thorns, such as the hawthorn

Flowers
Dark red flowers, especially geraniums and rhododendrons, are associated with this sign, as well as those associated with Aries (because of the traditional rulership with Mars, who ruled Scorpio before Pluto)

Rhododendron

Animals
Insects and other invertebrates fall under the rulership of Scorpio

Countries
Syria is a typical Scorpio country, sharing similar barren landscapes to the other countries related to Scorpio – Algeria, the Transvaal, Morocco, Korea, Norway and Uruguay

energy and achieving their potential.

When out of work, Scorpios lack a daily outlet for their energy and must seek somehow to expend it – even, perhaps, in part-time, unpaid work. Otherwise, it is all too easy for the forces to be negatively used, perhaps even in crime. Scorpios need to be under pressure – they must have something against which to test their muscles, mental or physical. They do well in engineering, the mining industry, the navy, the wine trade; they are natural researchers and detectives.

Change, leisure and retirement

Scorpios will probably resist enforced change; their natural stubbornness will rise to the surface. However, there will be times when they feel that change is absolutely vital, and then nothing will stop them seeking it. Sweeping, drastic changes may result, after which they will settle happily into a new lifestyle, ready to accept new responsibilities. Care is needed, of course, that such changes are made for the right reasons and that valuable experience and hard work are not thrown away.

Sitting about doing nothing not only isn't the average Scorpio's idea of pleasure, but may even be bad for them. These people will welcome retirement as a chance to do all the things for which there hasn't yet been time, although they may still lack time to do everything they've got planned. But at all events (however unlikely it is) Scorpios shouldn't look forward to days of sitting in the sun. They need a compelling interest instead.

Health, diet and exercise

Just as Scorpio energy must be evenly spent and controlled, so the physical system needs a regular, controlled diet. That may not be easy; there is a tendency towards self-indulgence in food and drink, which often provokes stomach upsets or constipation. Moderation doesn't come easily to Scorpios but they must cultivate it, both in diet and exercise, for what starts out as a keen interest in sport and exercise can get out of hand, causing strain. They must not hesitate to slow down when necessary. The martial arts will interest them, not only for the physical aspect, but also for their spiritual and esoteric qualities. Swimming is very beneficial.

Scorpio as Ascendant

Psychological motivation

Scorpio's powerful personality traits will color the whole chart when this sign rises, and other elements will in most cases be subservient. The characteristics attributed to the Sun sign are likely to be deeper and more meaningfully expressed when Scorpio rises. There will be a stronger sense of purpose and need to question every action and the tendency to be secretive can become an obsession.

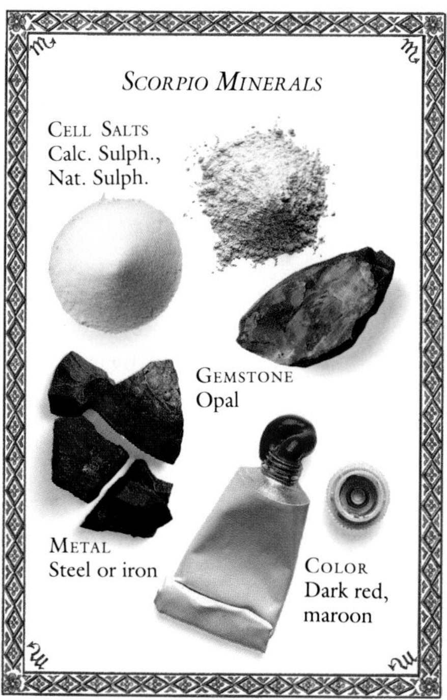

When Scorpio rises and Leo is on the Midheaven, Scorpio's drive and emotional resources are enriched by Leo's organizational and leadership powers. The combination is formidable, but can result in a real need for power and a tendency to dominate others for good or ill. A source of remarkable potential, it can also make the individual highly autocratic and sometimes even power-mad.

People with Scorpio rising generally feel a strong need to know themselves. They don't care to reveal themselves to others but their ability for self-analysis is considerable, and they are usually capable of seeing their own problems clearly and honestly. This introspective tendency may result in the feeling that they do not like themselves very much; they should not discount their positive qualities, nor forget that they have the ability really to enjoy life.

In partnership, those with Scorpio rising will show their affection in a charming and tender way that will be very private and not always discernable to outsiders. Emotional security will be as important as financial security, but jealousy is possible and may be exacerbated by possessiveness. If this is allowed to take hold, a claustrophobic atmosphere may develop which some partners will find extremely trying. An inability to discuss problems, with consequent worry about them, may provoke physical symptoms – notably a lessening of the sexual drive.

Scorpio Progressed to Sagittarius

When a Scorpio Sun progresses into Sagittarius, determination is spiced with a lively, extrovert, enthusiastic attitude to challenge. It will be easier for the subject to be open, and less of a tendency to be secretive and bottle up problems and emotions. Sagittarius, also a sign that likes to enjoy life, won't make it any easier for Scorpios to watch their diets – especially since these people may earn plenty of money to spend on expensive meals and other indulgences. Weight gain and indigestion may become problems.

Sagittarius may persuade the Scorpio person to take more risks, both physical and financial, than normal, but they may find it much easier to study in depth. The Scorpio image, usually rather sexy and often expressed in dark colors, will now become more casual; sometimes conventional in outlook, the individual may cultivate a more relaxed, perhaps sportier look.

When the Scorpio Ascendant progresses into Sagittarius, the psychological outlook will be less intense, with the individual becoming more philosophical. As a result, there will be less obsessive worry about personal problems, which are therefore less likely to provoke physical ailments. If an early degree of Scorpio was rising at birth, the progression will possibly occur when a permanent emotional relationship is being formed, in which case the Scorpio problems of possessiveness and jealousy will happily be less apparent.

The Traditional Associations of Scorpio

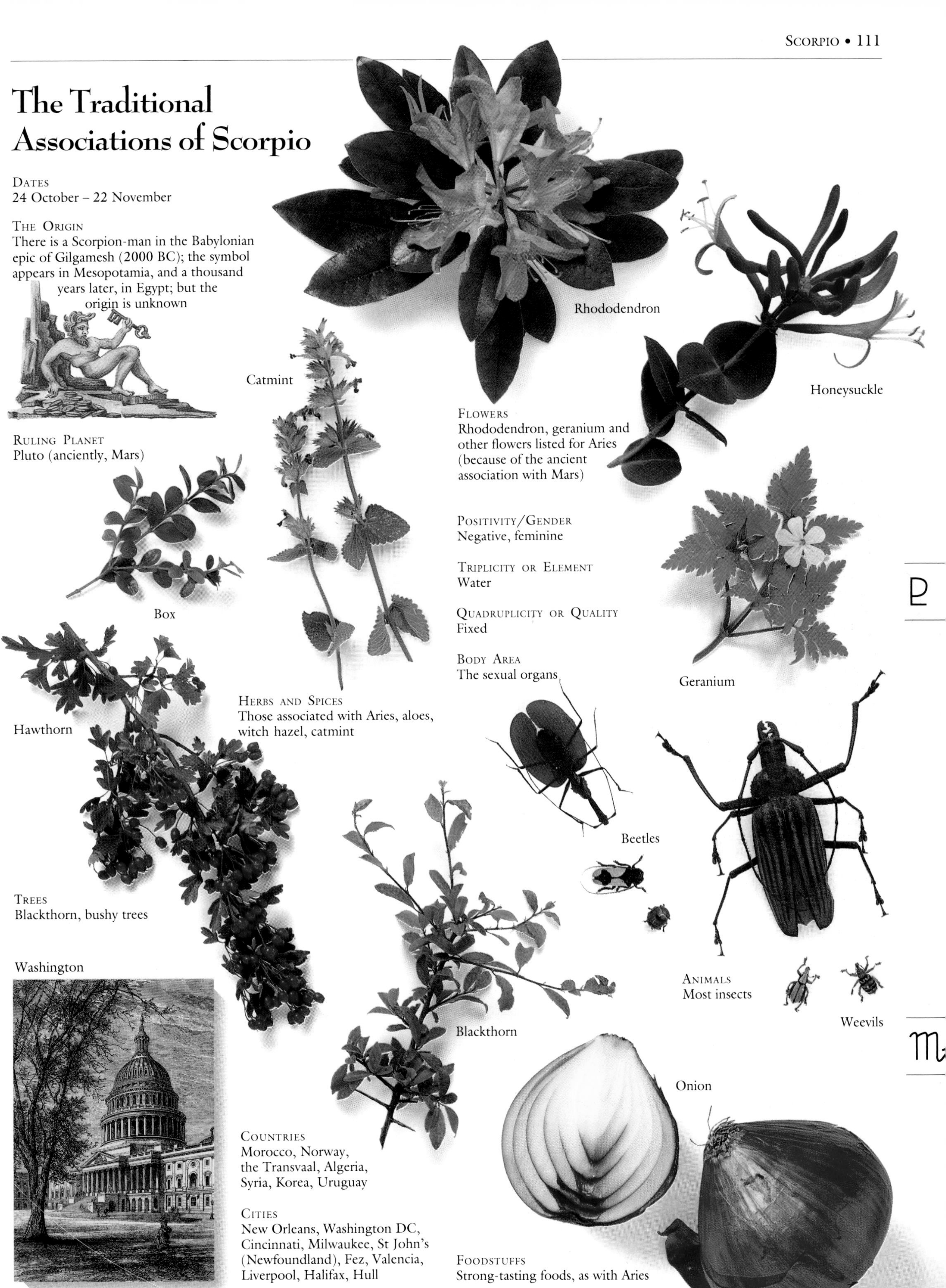

Dates
24 October – 22 November

The Origin
There is a Scorpion-man in the Babylonian epic of Gilgamesh (2000 BC); the symbol appears in Mesopotamia, and a thousand years later, in Egypt; but the origin is unknown

Ruling Planet
Pluto (anciently, Mars)

Flowers
Rhododendron, geranium and other flowers listed for Aries (because of the ancient association with Mars)

Positivity/Gender
Negative, feminine

Triplicity or Element
Water

Quadruplicity or Quality
Fixed

Body Area
The sexual organs

Herbs and Spices
Those associated with Aries, aloes, witch hazel, catmint

Trees
Blackthorn, bushy trees

Animals
Most insects

Countries
Morocco, Norway, the Transvaal, Algeria, Syria, Korea, Uruguay

Cities
New Orleans, Washington DC, Cincinnati, Milwaukee, St John's (Newfoundland), Fez, Valencia, Liverpool, Halifax, Hull

Foodstuffs
Strong-tasting foods, as with Aries

Sagittarius ♐ 23 NOVEMBER – 21 DECEMBER

Challenge is important in a fulfilling Sagittarian life. When an achievement is accomplished, Sagittarius soon begins work on the next one. The compulsion to set new targets and meet them is so strong that it can become all-engrossing, with present activities being skimped because the eye is always on future plans. Sagittarian enthusiasm, optimism and zest for life are second to none but must be controlled. The worst fault, restlessness, can be a severe problem, for Sagittarians don't always see projects through to the end.

BASIC PERSONALITY

Natural excitement and enthusiasm can feed the innate Sagittarian tendency to take risks, which can become real foolhardiness, especially when young. Developing their inherent intellectual powers will enable these people to avoid unnecessary risks. They should also cultivate a more philosophical outlook. If their natural exuberance isn't controlled it will become boisterous. Their enjoyment of life and sense of humor are charming but can sometimes get out of hand – they should remember that practical jokes are rarely funny for their victims.

One of the dual signs of the zodiac, Sagittarius gives versatility which may contribute to the Sagittarian tendency to move too quickly from one task to another, or to be involved in too many things at once. Greater satisfaction will come from steadily working through one project towards the next, which, after all, they can ensure is as different as possible.

This sign confers great breadth of vision and the ability to assimilate quickly what may be a complex situation. However, these people are not usually good at coping with detail, which bores them. In ignoring the minutiae, they can run into difficulties, so should always read the small print.

Partnership

No true Sagittarian can cope with claustrophobic conditions (they must have a room with a view, for instance), particularly within personal relationships. A possessive, suspicious or jealous partner will not last long: their independent spirits won't tolerate any restrictions on personal freedom.

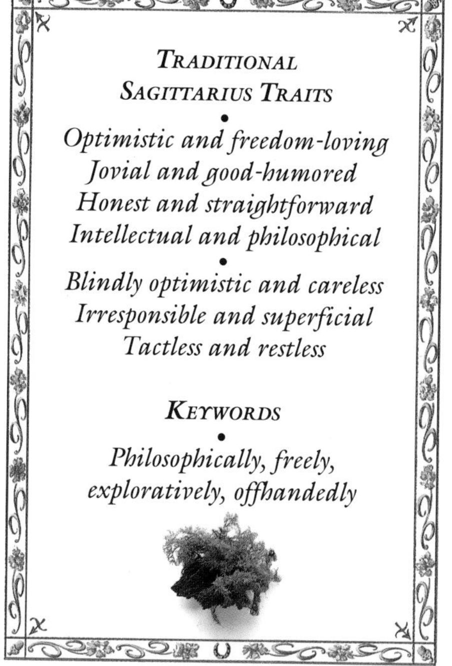

TRADITIONAL SAGITTARIUS TRAITS

•

Optimistic and freedom-loving
Jovial and good-humored
Honest and straightforward
Intellectual and philosophical

•

Blindly optimistic and careless
Irresponsible and superficial
Tactless and restless

KEYWORDS

•

Philosophically, freely, exploratively, offhandedly

Sex is greeted with customary Sagittarian enthusiasm and exuberance; when they are very young, a possible partner's sexual attractions can be irresistible. With experience they will look for other qualities: someone whose intelligence at least matches their own, and with whom they can be friends as well as lovers.

Family

Enthusiasm is a wonderful element in any child, but in young Sagittarians it can be so generous that it needs to be channeled and not frittered away. Similarly, boisterousness may need to be calmed. The parents should discover as early as possible in the child's life where his or her true interests lie. There is tremendous potential here, but it must be properly led (without the child's knowledge). Achievement will feed enthusiasm, whether in class, on the sports field or during out-of-school hours. Sagittarian children find it difficult to obey school rules but aren't blind to reason, and sensible restrictions will be accepted. Their reading and language skills should be encouraged from an early age.

As parents, Sagittarians are admirable: they respond in a lively way to their children, encourage their interests and help them build up good libraries. However, it is vital that a Sagittarian mother doesn't sacrifice her own interests entirely to those of her family but tries to set time aside for herself. No matter how much she loves her children, their limited conversation is not always sufficiently engrossing; restlessness is certain if she has no means of escape. Ideally, new projects should be started as soon after the birth of a child as possible.

Career

Once again, challenge is essential, and boring, repetitive work must be avoided if at all possible. Environment is also important: small, stuffy offices or crowded workshops are equally intolerable. Acquiring money is not in itself very important; Sagittarians usually manage to find it when necessary. Hard-earned cash is more likely to be spent on study, books and travel than on impressive material possessions. A spirit of adventure (not always physical) is important; work which takes these people out of their own environment is good for them. Taking short cuts to success can lead them into serious errors, usually because they haven't attended to enough detail.

While not resting on their laurels, Sagittarians aren't overweeningly ambitious – at least as far as worldly progress or status are concerned. Meeting intellectual demands, or seeing their own decisions bearing fruit, will be much more important; they like to see people profiting from their good work or influence. Publishing, the law and even the church can attract them; teaching at university is perhaps even more satisfying. There is a traditional link between this sign and sport, but while some Sun sign Sagittarians make the grade professionally, this connection should not be overstressed.

The Symbolism of Sagittarius

Gemstone
Topaz is regarded as the gemstone for Sagittarius
Flowers
Dandelions and carnations are Sagittarian flowers
Dandelion
Carnation
Ruling Planet
The ruling planet of Sagittarius is Jupiter
Symbolic Sign
Sagittarius is the archer; half animal and half human
Country
Australia is considered to be a Sagittarian country
Ash
Antlers
Trees
The birch, oak and ash are trees related to Sagittarius
Oak
♃
Colors
Rich purples and dark blues are Sagittarian colors
Fruits
The mulberry and bilberry are Sagittarian fruits
Bilberry
Animals
Hunted animals, such as deer, are ruled by this sign

Change, leisure and retirement
Change, or the need for it, will arouse Sagittarian enthusiasm, and these people cope particularly well with conditions that other, more settled, zodiac types may find very disruptive. Their love of change is so strong that they'll provoke it for its own sake, sometimes due to momentary boredom. Partners should encourage them to think carefully when considering change, which may not always be as progressive as they imagine: the grass isn't always greener on the other side. Retirement will offer exciting possibilities, and Sagittarians will be sure to use the extra time available – perhaps for physical or intellectual travel.

Health, diet and exercise
A love of hearty food and drink means that biliousness is highly likely if the diet isn't watched carefully. Although Sagittarians need and enjoy exercise they can still to put on weight, and most Sagittarian women will at some time notice an accumulation around the hips. The daredevil trait found in most Sagittarians suggests that the interest in sports may result in slight accidents: pulled muscles, for instance, are common, especially hamstrings and thigh muscles. They must remember this particularly as they grow older; they will want to exercise just as violently at sixty as they did at twenty, but this would be unwise.

Any form of sporting activity is usually welcome, but if there is no interest whatsoever in sport (which occasionally happens), they must take sufficient exercise in some other way, for they will almost certainly be intellectuals whose minds need to be relaxed, probably with the help of some moderate physical fatigue. Similarly, those whose work is physically exhausting should try to relax through more intellectual spare-time pursuits.

SAGITTARIUS AS ASCENDANT

Psychological motivation
The need for challenge, so important to a Sun sign Sagittarian, is even greater when Sagittarius rises. These people have what it takes to exploit their potential to the full and, provided early encouragement was given, will move forward with ever-increasing self-confidence, and the great expectations with which a positive, optimistic outlook endows them will probably be accomplished.

Strongly aware of the world about them, a consciously developed depth of character – perhaps through a true assessment of their own shortcomings – will enable these people to achieve personal harmony which might otherwise be denied by their volatile natures. They are objective and eager to know more about themselves, and unlike some people will not shy away from the trail to self-knowledge: in fact, it will fascinate them. However, they must allow time for thought; their downfall can lie in thinking they have all the answers, when in fact important details are missing through a lack of thoroughness. At their most highly developed, these people are the philosophers of the zodiac, with a peerless intellectual capacity.

A healthy level of friendship and intellectual rapport is needed in relationships. There is sexual exuberance, but a partner who only satisfies their sexual needs will very soon bore them. Intellectual challenge is also essential; a claustrophobic lifestyle will have disastrous psychological effects. The individual may go on eating or drinking binges, for instance, or develop psychosomatic liver-related illnesses.

When life offers no challenge, the usual optimistic, enthusiastic outlook will be clouded, and uncharacteristic depression will set in. A change of lifestyle and perhaps of scene is probably best, but escapism must be avoided and physically running away is not a long-term solution. A full assessment of the problem should be made, however tedious this might seem.

SAGITTARIUS MINERALS
GEMSTONE
Topaz
CELL SALTS
Silica, Kali. Mur.
METAL
Tin
COLOR
Dark blue, purple

SAGITTARIUS PROGRESSED TO CAPRICORN

Sun sign Sagittarians are unconventional and usually lack worldly ambition, but when the Sun progresses into Capricorn they become more conventional, more traditional and perhaps more ambitious. They will notice status symbols, and may even start to buy some of them. A young Sagittarian may put a relationship on a more formal footing at this time. The casual Sagittarian image, often a hangover from student days, may sober up and become much neater. For those born on the first or second day of the Sagittarian Sun sign period, this progression will coincide with the first Saturn Return (see p.312), so an important period of change and development is almost inevitable.

When a Sagittarian Ascendant progresses into Capricorn, the wilder areas of the psyche will be tamed, with the individual becoming more reflective and better able to absorb the implications of important issues and think more seriously about them. Blind enthusiasm is less likely, or will be tempered with caution; inner restlessness will be calmed by greater patience.

If the individual has been much involved in sport, exercise or physical activity, very great care should be taken that joints don't start to stiffen, or arthritis develop. The need to keep moving is, of course, paramount.

Sagittarian ambition, which is mostly personal, will be an even stronger motive when the Ascendant progresses into Capricorn, and it may be made more effective by being more clearly and narrowly directed. In general, the subject will become selective in choosing those personal priorities which are at the top of any list of objectives.

The Traditional Associations of Sagittarius

DATES
23 November – 21 December

THE ORIGIN
Of unknown origin; there was an early confusion between Sagittarius and Scorpio, for we find Centaur figures with Scorpio tails in Babylonia

ANIMALS
Horses, hunted animals

FLOWERS
Pink and carnation, dandelion

RULING PLANET
Jupiter

POSITIVITY/GENDER
Positive, masculine

TRIPLICITY OR ELEMENT
Fire

QUADRUPLICITY OR QUALITY
Mutable

BODY AREA
Hips and thighs, and the liver

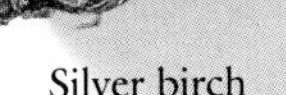
Silver birch

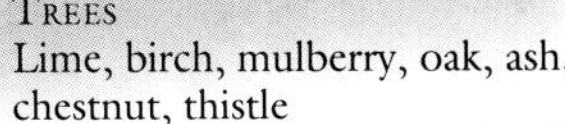
TREES
Lime, birch, mulberry, oak, ash, chestnut, thistle

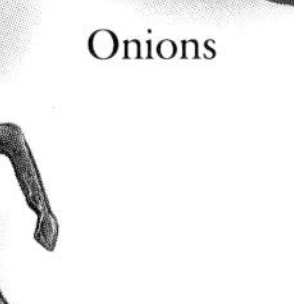
Onions

Currants and sultanas

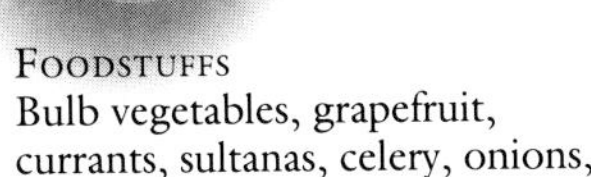
FOODSTUFFS
Bulb vegetables, grapefruit, currants, sultanas, celery, onions, leeks

Celery

Garlic

Carnations

Sage

Cinnamon

Borage

Bilberry

HERBS AND SPICES
Sage, aniseed, balsam, balm, bilberry, borage, cinnamon, dock, mosses

COUNTRIES
Spain, Australia, Hungary, South Africa, Arabia, Yugoslavia

CITIES
Toledo, Stuttgart, Budapest, Cologne, Sheffield, Avignon, Toronto, Naples

♃

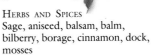

Capricorn ♑ 22 December – 20 January

This is a sign of contrasts. There is a great potential for success in every Capricorn, though sometimes they refuse to recognize it and their outlook can be pessimistic, so the potential may remain undeveloped. On the one hand, some members of this sign are ambitious and aspiring, with the energy and will to succeed in whatever they set themselves to do; on the other, there are those who may have the desire to do well, but are hindered by inhibition and lack of self-confidence (sometimes disguised by a feigned laziness).

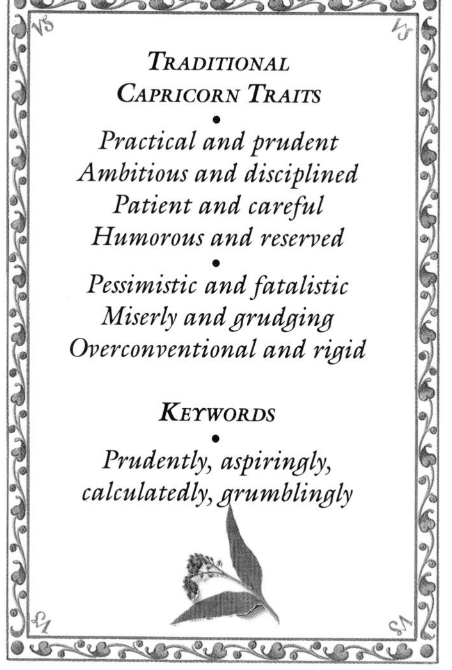

Traditional Capricorn Traits

•

Practical and prudent
Ambitious and disciplined
Patient and careful
Humorous and reserved

•

Pessimistic and fatalistic
Miserly and grudging
Overconventional and rigid

Keywords

•

Prudently, aspiringly, calculatedly, grumblingly

Basic Personality

Both types of Capricorn are conventional and sometimes even slaves to convention; they want always to be seen to do "the right thing". Both have a splendidly offbeat sense of humor, vividly contrasting with a strong tendency to grumble. Both are prudent and methodical. Sometimes the successful Capricorn achievers suffer a lack of confidence, while the less confident and successful may snap out of their negativity and make themselves enjoy life in a remarkably lighthearted way. (The influence of Mercury may be seen under such circumstances: when that planet is in Sagittarius, for instance.)

One of the most endearing characteristics is the dour sense of humor already mentioned: even at their most serious and formal, this can suddenly erupt. Patience is one of their virtues, as is insight, but the less self-confident may not believe this and should be persuaded to develop the ability and rely on it in long-term planning. Confident, aspiring Capricorns are usually very disciplined, but again lack of self-confidence can result in discipline being thrown to the winds. It is not easy to find lovable, tender traits in a Sun sign Capricorn. Fortunately, this is only one side of the character; other elements in the full birth chart will without doubt add warmth to this apparently rather chilly personality.

Partnership

Capricorns abhor starting married life in a garret and may postpone emotional commitment until they are firmly established in a career – perhaps quite late in life. They may then choose someone who is a parent figure, or at least commands admiration and respect. They can also marry for money or social status. They have a rather low emotional level and may find it hard to show their true feelings, especially in intimate relationships. They should realize this, and accept that very often their partners need reassurance that they are still loved, especially if the Capricorn is much involved with a career and time at home is at a premium.

Family

Capricorn children are very loyal and need to express natural pride in their parents, who in turn must realize that these children are highly conventional, and need a secure, structured and disciplined background. They also need well-reasoned encouragement – one of the best reward is extra responsibility and pocket money. Their self-confidence, sense of fun and especially their sheer enjoyment of life need constant bolstering if they aren't to grow too serious and old before their time. It shouldn't be depressing if the child hovers near the bottom of the class as long as steady progress is made; sudden leaps towards the top are not likely. The sense of ambition should always be cultivated and encouraged.

Capricorn parents are eager for their children's success, but should always remember to show their love, affection and appreciation openly – not just with impressive presents, but also by giving the children their time. Ambitious Capricorns can be so involved in their careers and in making money (albeit for the benefit of the family) that they have no time to enjoy their home lives, and in extreme cases – especially if the children went to boarding school – they will suddenly find themselves sharing a home with adults they don't know very well. The importance of moral discipline goes without saying, but Capricorn parents can be over-strict and heavy-handed, especially during the teenage years when children naturally rebel against parental control. An unbridgeable generation gap must not be allowed to develop.

Career

While members of many zodiac signs find it hard to cope with responsibility because of the loneliness that is often involved, self-confident Capricorns may welcome the chance to sit in their own offices at their own desks, keeping even their closest colleagues at a distance. They may of course still have to seek and take advice but they can find this rather irksome, probably because they feel they should know everything, and don't like being reminded otherwise. It is, once again, a question of self-confidence: they find it distressing if anything tends to undermine this. Not all Capricorns may be as autocratic as we suggest, but there is almost always an element of autocracy somewhere in their character.

The Capricorn ladder to success must be steadily climbed; attempts to scale several rungs at once may be disastrous. On the other hand, the top of

The Symbolism of Capricorn

Gemstones
Amethyst and turquoise are the gemstones commonly associated with Capricorn
Turquoise
Metal
Lead is the metal of Capricorn
Trees
Willow, pine and elm are trees linked to Capricorn
Willow (shared with Pisces)
Pine
Pansy
Field pansy
Amethyst
Ruling Planet
Saturn is the ruling planet of Capricorn
Country
India is one of the countries ruled by Capricorn
Flowers
Ivy and pansy are Capricornian plants
Colors
Capricornian colors are generally subdued and include dark green, gray, black and brown
Herbs
Comfrey, hemlock and henbane are associated with Capricorn
Hemlock
Comfrey
Mythology
While the goat is the animal of this sign, it is always represented with a fish's tail – illustrating the myth that relates to Capricorn
Animals
Goats and other animals with cloven hoofs, such as pigs, are governed by Capricorn
♄
Peter Lawman 1990

the ladder is always achievable, and they should set their sights at least as high as its topmost rung.

The attitude to money is a careful one and yes, that may be a synonym for meanness! Early in their careers these people will probably subscribe to savings schemes, and if they are free with their money it will often be spent on people who can help them with their careers, entertaining them to dinner, perhaps. Although Capricorns are found in all walks of life, of course, many do particularly well in local government, banking and finance, estate management, the building trades, the dental profession and in osteopathy. The self-made businessman is often a Capricorn.

Change, leisure and retirement

The Capricorn ability for long-term planning should mean that periods of change will be anticipated. Typically, each change should result in positive material progress, adding to the individual's self-confidence and positive outlook. Prudent saving and investment will ensure a good standard of living on retirement. These people should have no problems in filling their well-earned free time with all the activities they have looked forward to tackling. An earth sign, Capricorn persuades its denizens into the garden – or certainly into the fresh air. But this is also a very musical sign, and a literary one, so music and books will help to fill the days.

Health, diet and exercise

Capricorns are on the whole very sensible about their diets, recognizing the drawbacks of self-indulgence, but they should perhaps watch their calcium levels. Perhaps the most important advice one can give them is to keep moving, for many spend long hours behind a desk and can easily develop stiffness in the joints, leading to arthritic conditions. They must take particular care of their knee-joints (this is the Capricorn body area). Teeth and skin are also concerns of this sign and need special care. Rather like their partners across the zodiac, the Cancerians, they should be very careful of their skin when in strong sunlight; a high-grade sun-screen filter should always be used when sun-bathing.

Capricorn as Ascendant

Psychological motivation

The most crucial problem can be wavering self-confidence: one moment these people think they can rule the world and the next they doubt their ability to write a note for the milkman. This can mean they are very confident in some spheres and very nervous in others: they may be quite sure they can cope with their job, but have no confidence that they can sustain a close personal relationship – or even establish one. This often arises from an inability to see themselves clearly, so they underestimate their own achievements. They must take themselves at others' valuations, accepting compliments gracefully and believing them.

Capricorn Minerals
Gemstone
Turquoise, amethyst
Cell Salts
Calc. Phos.,
Calc. Fluor.
Metal
Silver
Color
Dark gray, black,
dark brown

Perhaps surprisingly, once these people settle into a permanent relationship they become very caring, very sensitive to their partners' needs and often their emotions flow more positively. These traits will be most noticeable to the partner, and even close friends may not discern them. A tendency to worry may increase with their natural concern for their partners.

Problems may cause digestive difficulties which in extreme circumstances will lead to ulcers or skin disorders. To avoid this build-up of internal tension they need a routine which allows time for leisure activities, relaxation and some physical exercise. They can be too easily depressed, even by minor setbacks; pessimism can be a problem. Physical activity can be a great antidote and music can help to calm and cheer them, but above all, they should use their inherent rational qualities. They should also make room in their lives for the spiritual as well as the material.

Capricorn Progressed to Aquarius

When the Sun progresses into Aquarius, the Aquarian need for independence joins the Capricorn's devotion to going it alone. However, Capricorn is the most conventional sign and Aquarius the most unconventional, so the outlook could radically change. If the Sun enters Aquarius when a young Capricorn is coming to terms with his or her personality, this will be very beneficial and encourage greater freedom of expression. Even so, care is obviously necessary, especially if the signs change in childhood; rebelliousness may then make him or her uncharacteristically difficult.

There is often scientific and mathematical potential, in which case these talents could develop in an interesting and original way when the Sun enters Aquarius and so should be encouraged, since they could eventually lead to a successful career or at least a rewarding spare-time interest. The influence of Aquarius will modify the conventional Capricorn image into a liking for very trendy or antique clothes, adding a dash of welcome brilliance to the Capricorn outlook. A tendency to unpredictable and stubborn behaviour will sometimes arise.

When a Capricorn Ascendant becomes Aquarian, the psychological outlook will be freer and less conventional. More extrovert qualities will appear, the subject will become more objective and optimistic, and perhaps minor matters which once seemed very important will now assume their true perspective. The Capricorn need to keep moving will be even more important, for Aquarius is linked with the circulation; the subject must keep warm during cold weather. There may be a sneaking regard for glamor.

The Traditional Associations of Capricorn

Dates
22 December – 20 January

The Origin
The Babylonian god Ea wore a cloak designed as a fish's skin complete with head and tail: among his names was "Antelope of the Seas" – what better description of a fishtailed goat? He came from the oceans to teach wisdom to land-strolling man

Aspen leaves

Pine cone

Trees
Pine, elm, yew, willow, aspen, poplar

Animals
Goats and all cloven-footed animals

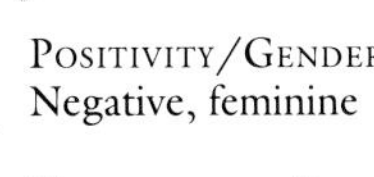

Willow leaf

Elm leaves

Positivity/Gender
Negative, feminine

Triplicity or Element
Earth

Quadruplicity or Quality
Cardinal

Body Area
The knees, skin, bones and teeth

Ruling Planet
Saturn

Knapweed

Malt

Cornflour

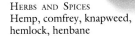

Herbs and Spices
Hemp, comfrey, knapweed, hemlock, henbane

Comfrey

Dried comfrey

Taj Mahal

Flowers
Ivy, heartsease, amaranthus, pansy

Pansies

Pasta

Countries
India, Mexico, Afghanistan, Macedonia, Thrace, Albania, Saxony, Bulgaria, Lithuania, the coast of Yugoslavia, Orkney and Shetland

Cities
Oxford (UK), Delhi, Mexico City, Ghent, Port Said, Brussels, Constanta, Mecklenburg; but the administrative centres of all capital cities are traditionally ruled by Capricorn

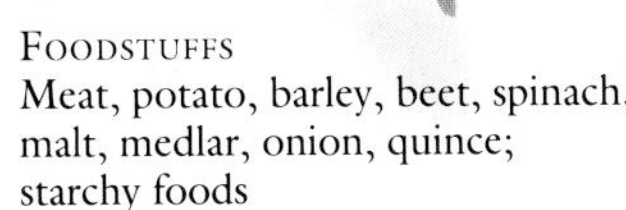

Foodstuffs
Meat, potato, barley, beet, spinach, malt, medlar, onion, quince; starchy foods

Aquarius ♒ 21 January – 18 February

The Aquarian need for independence can't be underestimated, and it is essential that Aquarians develop and sustain the right lifestyle. Although they have the reputation of being particularly friendly, in many ways they are very private and dislike having their privacy invaded. Their natural friendliness is linked to a genuine desire to be helpful, so anyone in trouble will always find them ready to help, approaching others' problems as they approach their own – logically, detached and without undue emotion.

Basic Personality

Aquarians have an original, idealistic streak and the more positively this is shown, the more fulfilled they will be. However, this originality must not become too idiosyncratic or perverse as others can then be at best embarrassed and at worst seriously annoyed.

Aquarius is an air sign, and its inhabitants need air, both physically and metaphorically. They must realize how very stubborn they can be and should try to counter the tendency. When young, they are usually leaders of their generation, but sometimes they continue to cling to youthful opinions, so that what was once a splendidly forward-looking nature becomes ultraconservative. Again, awareness of the problem will go far to counter it.

Positive and optimistic even when life gets difficult, Aquarians rarely lose hope, and their natural humanity always reminds them that many others are less fortunate (in every sense) than themselves. Their chief fault is usually unpredictability, but their independence can also make them very remote, causing emotional problems. Partners and friends may be justified in suspecting that sometimes Aquarians act out of sheer perversity.

Traditional Aquarius Traits

- *Friendly and humanitarian*
- *Honest and loyal*
- *Original and inventive*
- *Independent and intellectual*

- *Intractable and contrary*
- *Perverse and unpredictable*
- *Unemotional and detached*

Keywords

Independently, humanely, distantly

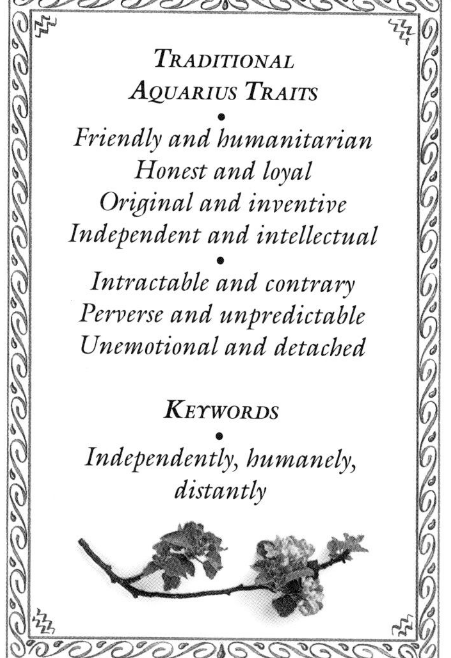

Partnership

Of all the Sun signs, Aquarians can find it most difficult to settle into and sustain a close emotional relationship. Their powerful need for independence makes it particularly hard for them to let others into their lives, for they realize this will mean modifying their lifestyles and tolerating an invasion of their living space – psychological as well as physical. They often decline to enter into a relationship until they are so set in their ways that it all seems impossible, so remain permanently single. Even so, there is a strongly romantic streak in many Aquarians, who like the glamor of romance, and once committed are – like their Capricorn cousins – very loyal. The placing of Venus will color this aspect of an Aquarian's life, and may modify the attitude considerably.

Family

Aquarian originality and the need to be different will soon emerge in children of this sign, who on the whole will be happy and positive, with a great desire to do their own thing. Parents should watch for waywardness; the best antidote is to suggest that they do the opposite of what you really desire! Bear in mind they will truly need to be unconventional, so a school devoted to rigid discipline, with very strong or obsessive academic aims, may not be suitable. They are rational, however, and always listen to reason. This will be a distinct asset in later life.

Aquarian children are naturally friendly, but alas this means they may be overtrusting and too ready to wander off with passing strangers who take advantage of that friendliness. It must be very firmly impressed on them from an early age not to do this. It is particularly good for young Aquarians to become involved in charity work; it will help them develop their strong humanitarianism which is likely to be one of their strongest and most positive traits. Creative and scientific flair should be eagerly encouraged when and if it develops. These children often have an interesting sense of drama, but it can be exaggerated.

Aquarian parents can have a very individual attitude to the education of children. They must remember that a child may be more conventional than the parents, and it is a mistake to force him or her into a particular mould just because they wish it. Security and discipline may be really important to a child, and the parents, however adventurous, should accept this. Aquarian parents should always ask themselves whether they have moved with the times. Their immediate reply will be yes; but they should realize it is unlikely (especially for them), and should not assume automatic and complete understanding of their children. They must learn to really listen to them. Despite possible problems, they usually make lively parents, always ready to bring out their children's potential and make the most of it.

Career

Aquarians must have a free rein to do whatever is expected of them in their own way, uninhibited by continual advice or the insistence on a particular regime. They have to express their inventiveness in their work, whether creative or scientific (or both). They may become inventors of some kind. Some do extremely well working in communications – the airlines, or the technical areas of television or radio, for instance. Despite their keen sense

The Symbolism of Aquarius

Gemstone
Aquamarine is this sign's gemstone
Colors
Electric blue and turquoise are the key Aquarian colors
Flower
The orchid is an Aquarian plant
Triplicity or Element
Aquarius is an air sign and many astrologers feel that he is pouring life-enhancing spirit into the ether
Trees
Most fruit trees fall under Aquarian influence
Apple blossom
Birds
Aquarius governs birds capable of long-distance flight, such as the albatross
Pear tree
Ruling Planet
Uranus is the ruling planet of Aquarius
Country
Russia is an Aquarian country, while its capital, Moscow, is an Aquarian city

of ambition they enjoy and are good at work which allows them to express their concern for humanity. They make excellent field or social workers or administrators for large charitable organizations. Not obsessive about income, they must avoid wasting their money on trendy fripperies.

Change, leisure and retirement
Aquarians are often quite seriously disturbed if they are kept waiting for final decisions, or feel some change hovering over them without knowing precisely when it will happen. A sudden decision (whether their own or someone else's) is not nearly as difficult for them. Their quick reactions may even make them sweep out of a well-established job given enough provocation. They should try not to let the prospect of retirement make them miserable for ten years before the event, instead gradually building up new areas of interest which can fill more of their lives when the time comes. If their work has been dull, uninteresting or too conventional, they should surely look forward to being able to express fully their originality and creative or scientific flair. They should give special thought to any necessary adjustments they may have to make, perhaps thinking of ways in which spare-time work can bolster their retirement income.

Health, diet and exercise
The circulation can be vulnerable. Aquarians are often at their best in cold weather and, like Capricorns, usually enjoy it, but they should keep warm, wearing light but windproof clothes which won't restrict their movements. Regular exercise should be creative rather than dull or repetitive. Like all air signs, Aquarians thrive best on a light, nourishing diet. The ankles are ruled by this sign and can be vulnerable; exercises to strengthen them, perhaps shoes with good ankle support, are desirable, especially if skiing or winter sports are enjoyed.

AQUARIUS AS ASCENDANT

Psychological motivation
As with Sun Aquarians, the need for independence is very great and the personality may seem to be distant; it is difficult to feel close to the enigmatic person with Aquarius rising. The difference between independence and isolation must be recognized: no man is an island. Psychological wholeness is likely to come through awareness that their best qualities are shown through kindness towards and appreciation of other people. When these are reciprocated, they should not push them away or put up barriers, but accept them. Eager for self-knowledge, they are very stubborn and may resist the realization that they should change, even when they accept it intellectually. Pigheadedness and vanity do not become them.

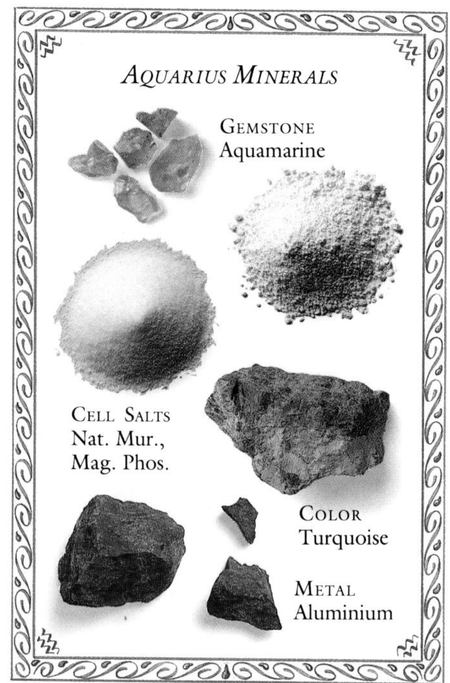

The problems of sacrificing independence for a permanent relationship are never far away. The ideal partner may be one willing to take a back seat and play a purely supportive role. They will certainly need to be proud of their partners, and to see some very special qualities in them (partly because they think these reflect their own qualities?) They are normally very generous, but an underlying need to be boss can be hard to live with, and inflexibility can cause extra problems, so it is vital that these people learn to compromise. Every meaningful relationship to some extent involves sacrifice, and if they feel unable to modify their own needs to take account of their partner's, they should think twice before embarking on the relationship; do they really want a partner, or just a partnership?

Aquarians who grow too inward-looking can become hypochondriacs. However, perversity could drive them in the other direction, so that they ignore their symptoms; they can also be attracted to the latest fashionable health cure. As the circulation is Aquarius-ruled, and the heart is the Leo organ (Leo is the polar sign), the latter should be kept healthy through regular exercise. Psychological problems or even simple worry may cause otherwise inexplicable back pain.

AQUARIUS PROGRESSED TO PISCES

When the Sun progresses into Pisces, Aquarians feel confused because their emotions flow more easily and are more openly shown. They will also rely rather more on intuition. There is a great contrast between the warm, emotional approach typical of the Piscean and the much cooler, distant, logical Aquarian. It's not surprising that Aquarians feel the ground shaking under their feet when the Piscean qualities begin to make themselves felt. Don't forget that the temperamental changes will be gradual, nor that they will be of considerable advantage. The trendy and slightly eccentric Aquarian image may also be softened, and the romantic element, often buried, will now appear, especially in the clothes which may be softer and more delicate.

In the northern hemisphere, Aquarius and Pisces rise fairly quickly, so even if an early degree of Aquarius is rising at birth, the subject may be quite young when the Ascendant progresses into Pisces. Parents should look out for subtle personality changes and ensure that these are positively expressed and contribute to the psychological development. The Aquarian openness and frankness may be clouded by a rather secretive tendency. If, for instance, the change takes place when the child is very young, such an event as the birth of a younger sibling could result in the negative side of Pisces provoking deception, worry and confusion. The increased sensitivity of Pisces will, however, greatly soften anyone with Aquarius rising, making them more personally sympathetic.

The Traditional Associations of Aquarius

Dates
21 January – 18 February

The Origin
The Egyptian god Hapi watered the earth from two jugs; but there seems also an association with Ea (see under Capricorn), sometimes called the God with two Streams

Ruling Planet
Uranus (anciently, Saturn)

Herbs and Spices
Those with sharp, unusual flavors

Foodstuffs
Foods which preserve well: frozen food, apples, citrus fruits, dried fruits

Flowers
Orchid, golden rain

Positivity/Gender
Positive, masculine

Triplicity or Element
Air

Quadruplicity or Quality
Fixed

Body Area
The shins and ankles; the circulation

Animals
Large birds which fly afar

Cities
Moscow, Salzburg, Bremen, Hamburg, St Petersburg

Countries
USSR, Sweden, Poland, Abyssinia, Israel, Iran

Trees
Fruit trees

Pisces ♓ 19 FEBRUARY – 20 MARCH

The symbol of Pisces – two fishes swimming in opposite directions – suggests the main tension in the Piscean character: a natural perversity. Kindness joins with keen intuition to make Pisceans the best sort of friends. They are friendly, charitable and self-sacrificing, but their willingness to help others has a drawback in that they too often make it an excuse for failing to exploit their own high potential; they are so busy using their energy on behalf of their family and friends that they have little left for their own affairs.

BASIC PERSONALITY

It is often very difficult for Pisceans to learn to face reality; stronger, caring people should encourage them to do so at every opportunity. The belief that "whatever will be, will be" can become a veritable trap for them, in the worst cases resulting in complete inaction. Taking the line of least resistance, and deceiving themselves because they don't want to face up to harsh reality, are major faults.

The colorful Piscean imagination, creatively and positively expressed, is an enormous asset, but Pisceans must learn not to allow their imaginations to work negatively, magnifying small problems into major ones. The negative Piscean characteristics will then take over. If they channel their imaginations creatively, finding a specific outlet for them (perhaps in some form of art or craft), they can achieve results which will surprise themselves. Traditionally, Pisces is known as the poet of the zodiac, but take this in the broadest sense – it applies to the creative use of the imagination in any area of life.

The refusal to face reality can emerge in an inability to see things as they really are. This kind of self-deception can be a really dangerous fault, persuading Pisceans to lie because (they tell themselves) the truth will hurt those they love. On the contrary, of course, they are usually only making matters worse. Sun sign Pisceans should strive to develop minds of their own, thus avoiding evasion and indecision whenever major decisions must be made. The position of Mercury (which rules the mind) in the complete birth chart must be carefully studied.

TRADITIONAL PISCES TRAITS

•

Imaginative and sensitive
Compassionate and kind
Selfless and unworldly
Intuitive and sympathetic

•

Escapist and idealistic
Secretive and vague
Weak-willed and easily led

KEYWORDS

•

Nebulously, impressionably, deceitfully

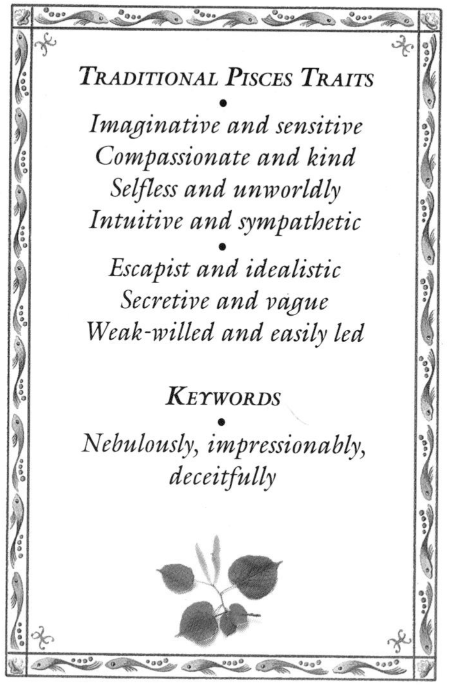

Partnership

Piscean emotion is readily poured into an emotional partnership, and loved ones may even be overwhelmed with affection. Provided their emotions are kept under control, Pisceans can bring something very special to a partnership but their feelings are always very close to the surface, and surprisingly trivial matters can sometimes trigger a scene. Romantic and sentimental, when they fall in love Pisceans wear permanent rose-colored glasses; they will only dispense with them as the result of bitter experience, when the partner's faults are ruthlessly exposed. A clear view of reality, however, usually enables them to build the relationship on firmer foundations. Not overly passionate, their romantic view of sex can be tenderly and handsomely expressed.

Family

It is vital that the parents of a Piscean child train him or her to be honest and straightforward. This may not be easy, but the tendency to embroider the truth with plenty of imaginative color can mean the less desirable Piscean traits do serious damage. Any interest which fires the imagination positively should be encouraged and praised from an early age. This may also be difficult – Pisceans always know someone who can do things better than them. It is no use denying this; but point out that some children will do things less well. Their confidence must be bolstered at all times and their powers of concentration must also be sharpened if dreaminess is not to hinder progress. Any scientific flair should certainly be encouraged; science is potentially a good field for them to work in, provided other areas of the chart show the necessary meticulous concern for detail can be added to their own imagination and inspiration.

Piscean parents are eager to encourage their children but they can be too easygoing with them; parental vagueness can be even more infuriating to a child than overstrictness. They put their children first, wanting them to develop their potential to the fullest.

Career

Ideally, a Piscean's career should bring out the talent for caring which is one of the sign's strongest attributes, so they are admirably suited to work in the caring professions. They are not very good at organization and usually work selflessly in the background, yet they are often excellent and successful actors. This is because, on stage, they can conceal their own personalities behind those of their characters.

Being so aware of the suffering of others they can make exceptional counselors, and a true sense of vocation often takes them into religious orders. But glamor attracts too – they love designing and making beautiful clothes. This is one of the dual signs of the zodiac, so Pisceans often have two jobs at the same time – with a spare-time occupation which (if they have help with the organization) can be successful and remunerative. Variety and flexibility are needed; strict routines and time-keeping are tricky for them.

The Symbolism of Pisces

Symbolic Sign
The fish of Pisces
Triplicity or Element
Water is the fish's element – Pisces is one of the water signs
Herbs
Chicory is one of the herbs associated with Pisces
Gemstone
The colorless, magical moonstone is the gem associated with this sign
Countries
North Africa, and the Gobi desert in particular, are places ruled by Pisces
Water lily
Plants
The water lily and willow, together with other plants growing near water, are naturally Piscean
Willow
Color
The color of Pisces is a soft sea-green and flowers in that shade are typically Piscean
Animals
Any animals that are at home in water are Piscean – all fish are ruled by this sign; they are usually shown joined together, holding a cord in their mouths
Ruling Planet
Neptune is the ruling planets of Pisces
♆

Sun sign Pisceans are not strongly ambitious but can, of course, be financially successful. However, they should seek professional advice in money matters, for as well as not being especially good at organizing their own finances, they are soft touches, and can give more money away than they can really afford (or than is fair to their families).

Change, leisure and retirement
Faced by change, Pisceans can all too easily work themselves up into a confused and apprehensive state. Not only will their imaginations work overtime, but their lack of real organizational talent can prevent them seeing clearly what must be done to cope with the new situation, whether emotionally or physically. Pisceans who enter retirement with a special interest will find the extra time available a sheer delight, but if there is no such interest, a desert of unoccupied time can disorientate them, and enforced retirement can age them all too rapidly. They should find a hobby with which to fill their hours; work in the community or local charity work are obvious antidotes.

Health, diet and exercise
Pisceans easily pick up vibrations in the atmosphere around them so can be physically affected by such things as an unkind word, world disasters, rows or even depressing weather. This sensitivity can very easily disturb the Piscean constitution, upsetting their stomachs or causing headaches. Being aware of this may not stop the problem, but at least it will set their minds at rest whenever they are laid low by what are really emotionally-based ailments.

This sensitivity to atmosphere also means they can comfort themselves by eating or drinking too much, and they are particularly susceptible to nicotine. It is another aspect of the Piscean tendency to find the easy way out of a situation or even an emotion. This can even apply to simple medical remedies: they will reach for the aspirin bottle at the least provocation but should be very careful, for they often react badly even to medically prescribed drugs. (Many Pisceans, however, regard drugs with deep suspicion and are much happier with holistic medicine. Provided they don't rely on it obsessively, it is much safer for them.) Sometimes practical help can alleviate the suffering which has provoked their sympathy in the first place, and this is an obvious way of avoiding difficulties. They must be rational, however, and try not to get too anxious over problems for which there is no solution.

The religious Piscean will take refuge and comfort in prayer; spiritual comfort can also often be found in the inspirational aspects of some forms of exercise, such as yoga. Gentle, rhythmical exercise is good for Pisceans, helping them both psychologically and physically. Finding comfortable shoes can be a problem (Pisces rules the feet); going without shoes is fine, but care should be taken out-of-doors.

PISCES MINERALS
COLOR
Soft sea-green
GEMSTONE
Moonstone, bloodstone
METAL
Platinum, tin
CELL SALTS
Ferr. Phos., Kali. Sulph.

PISCES AS ASCENDANT

Psychological motivation
When Pisces rises, the people concerned can become so much a part of their surroundings that they almost vanish. Others may take them for granted and even deny them proper recognition. But without their help, a considerable gap will appear, for the work they do is usually of real value. They must not undervalue themselves, but recognize their own worth and value to the community. It would be a mistake, however, for someone with Pisces rising to try to see himself as an unfulfilled Rambo and decide to be a world leader (even in a local context). Pisceans should be very careful before accepting any leadership role, for they are really at their best working – very valuably – in the background.

It is valid to ask whether Sun Pisceans really want to know themselves, but when the sign is rising such doubts are even stronger. It often seems that they invent a persona and devote all their considerable imaginative powers to fitting themselves into it, rather than really trying to discover what truly makes them tick. This is not necessarily disastrous, especially as they do it with such conviction; but if they really achieve self-knowledge, it gives them a sense of self-confidence and power which will be of more benefit to them than to any other zodiac type. They must also beware of being too critical of their partners, as this can sometimes, unfortunately, be destructive. The tendency to hypochondria is considerably increased.

PISCES PROGRESSED TO ARIES

When the Sun moves from Pisces into Aries the physical energy level will increase, and it will be easier to be assertive and accept challenge. For instance, sensitive, creative Pisceans will find it less difficult to show their work to people who may appreciate it. The Piscean image may become smarter, with a sudden liking for well-cut blazers, pleated skirts and bright wool sweaters. The pace of life could speed up, and there might be a tendency to accidents. More seriously, a hint of Arian selfishness may show itself – about which the caring, sensitive Piscean will feel guilty. The development of what is usually considerable Piscean potential, so often underestimated, is perhaps the best thing that can occur.

When the Ascendant progresses into Aries (usually early in life) the subject will make strides in personal development and psychological problems may be resolved. The way ahead will be clearer. A sense of ambition will also appear, the sex drive will be more positive and there will be added fire in the Piscean emotion and talent.

The Traditional Associations of Pisces

Dates
19 February – 20 March

The Origin
On its earliest appearance in the Babylonian zodiac, Pisces was called the constellation of the Tails; the two fishes were associated with the goddesses Anunitum and Simmah, one symbolizing the river Tigris and one the Euphrates

Ruling Planet
Neptune (anciently, Jupiter)

Pussy willow

Trees
Willow, fig, trees growing near water

Fish

Lettuce

Animals
Mammals that like water; fish

Positivity/Gender
Negative, feminine

Triplicity or Element
Water

Quadruplicity or Quality
Mutable

Body Area
The feet

Melon

Cucumber

Foodstuffs
Cucumber, pumpkin, lettuce, melon

Jaggery

Moss

Lime

Chicory

Herbs and Spices
Saccharin, chicory, lime, mosses

Countries
Portugal, Scandinavia, many small Mediterranean islands; the Gobi and Sahara deserts

Cities
Jerusalem, Warsaw, Seville, Alexandria, Santiago de Compostella

Waterlily

Flowers
Water lily; those blooming in Piscean colors

♆

♓

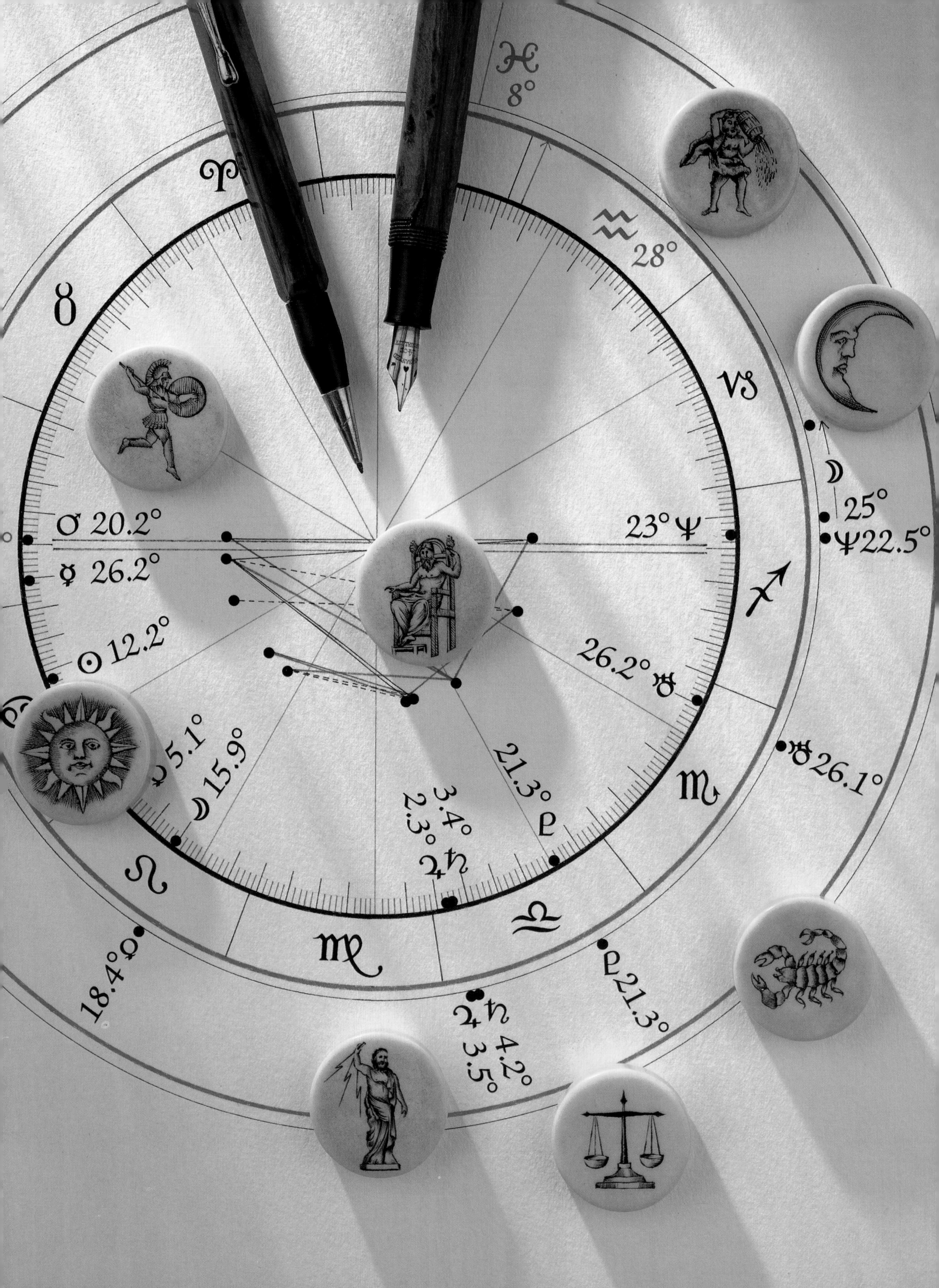

♓ 8°
♒ 28°
♂ 20.2°
☿ 26.2°
☉ 12.2°
23° ♆
♆22.5°
☽ 25°
26.2° ♅
♅26.1°
♀ 5.1°
☽ 15.9°
21.3° ☊
3.4°
2.3°
♃♄
18.4° ♀
☊21.3°
♃♄ 4.2°
3.5°

·3·

Astrology in Action

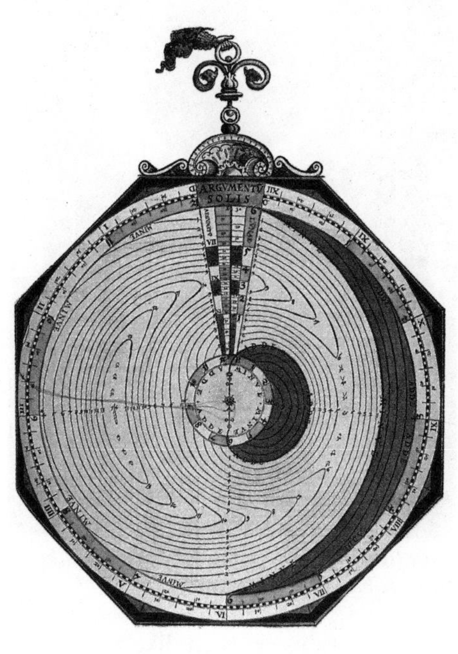

Interpreting the Birth Chart

Having learned how to calculate birth and progressed charts (see pp.42-7 and 60-72), now is the time to move on to the fascinating business of learning how to interpret them. First it is necessary to come to grips with the birth chart. No doubt you have already looked up elements of your birth chart – your Ascendant characteristics, those of your Moon sign and perhaps a few house placings and aspects. But this is not the way to learn how to interpret properly, which will require a much more systematic approach.

Most astrologers start their journey into interpretation by working on their own charts, then those of their partners, children and friends. However, it is very difficult indeed to be objective and impartial about oneself, one's partners and one's children. As we have already suggested, you will get far more out of this book, and far further along the road to becoming a truly competent astrologer, if you work with a friend. If you are doing this already, and studying the calculation process together, you will probably have resolved problems which might have been rather more difficult if you were working alone. Now you should work on your friend's chart and they on yours, before moving on to the charts of each other's partner and children.

There is something else to be gained from this process; you will at once begin to feel what it is like to work with, and indeed for, other people – and this will help you to avoid becoming introspective, which is a real danger with student, and indeed some advanced, astrologers.

Surprising characteristics

As you work systematically through the indications, a characteristic may crop up again and again, in different areas of the chart, which you cannot believe applies to your subject. It just seems wrong. The chances are that when you question your subject, they will accept that characteristic as accurate (maybe reluctantly!), so don't ignore such an indication. (This is another reason why it is as well not to get bogged down in a study of your own chart – if an unpleasant characteristic is suggested, you may ignore it rather than discover how to counter it!)

Just like a work of architecture, it will take time to build your interpretation.

Interpretations are built; like an architect, you have to apply basic rules of construction. There are plans (the charts). There are walls and floors (the Sun, Moon and rising signs). There are windows to let in the light, and buttresses (helpful planets). There are dark passages (difficult planets). Most important, there are stresses and strains, revealed by the difficult aspects; and supports, represented by constructive aspects. And we must not forget the foundations, as shown by the anchorages – of which there are many.

Your first interpretations will be small constructions – like a simple shed. It will take time to build a cathedral or palace, but with patience and care, you will eventually do so.

Beginning Your Interpretation

1 Keywords

Interpretation is built up in several stages. A convenient and helpful start is to learn a system of basic keywords. These give you a short, instant appreciation of the influence of every planet in each of the signs and houses. In their respective sections you will find the keywords for each house (see pp.38-41), Sun sign (see pp.80-127) and planet (see pp.30-1), which you should always use in the following way.

How to use the keywords

Make a list of the following:

a. The Ascendant sign (this always relates to the first house).
b. The Sun's sign and house position.
c. The Moon's sign and house position.
d. The ruling planet's sign and house position.
e. List all the other planets in the same way: i.e. Mercury, Venus, Mars, Jupiter, Saturn, Uranus, Neptune, Pluto. One of these, or the Sun or Moon, will be the ruling planet.

Writing keyword interpretations

Now refer to the keywords for each planet, house and sign, and construct simple sentences using them. For example, Sun in Cancer in the seventh house: "You will express yourself (Sun) very protectively and sensitively (Cancer) towards your partners (seventh house)"; or Mercury in Scorpio in the fifth house: "Your need to communicate (Mercury) will be intensively and passionately (Scorpio) expressed through creative work or the concerns and interests of children (fifth house)".

When you are writing a keyword interpretation of the Midheaven sign remember that the positive keywords indicate the area of life with which the subject will most strongly identify. For example, to someone with a Libran Midheaven you could say: "You will identify with all that is harmonious". Such statements are, of course, very bland and general, and a long way from any in-depth interpretation, but you will find them fun, and they are revealing. List them carefully, since they will have to be used again, later on in your interpretation.

2 THE ELEMENTS OR QUALITIES

The next step is to list how many planets there are in fire, earth, air and water signs (see p.33), and the relative elements of the Ascendant and Midheaven. These add a further basic keyword interpretation level. If there is a preponderance of one element, it will add another dimension to your subject's personality.

The keywords for the elements are:

- *Fire* – enthusiasm.
- *Earth* – stability and practicality.
- *Air* – intellectuality.
- *Water* – sensitivity and intuition.

In many cases the planets are fairly evenly distributed among the elements, but one element often emerges as a leader, and this will add another dimension to your interpretation. For instance, perhaps you will find several indications elsewhere in the chart that your subject is enthusiastic: a number of planets in fire signs will definitely support this. Or perhaps you will discover that your subject is very sensible and down-to-earth: planets in earth signs will suppport this inclination. However, sometimes the planets' positions and aspects reveal someone who is not terribly sensible – perhaps a bit of a dreamer. Here a couple of planets in earth signs will help counter this tendency and give stability.

3 THE QUALITIES OR QUADRUPLICITIES

The same approach to interpretation applies here.

The keywords for the qualities are:

- *Cardinal* – outgoing.
- *Fixed* – inflexible.
- *Mutable* – adaptable.

We feel that this grouping is often rather less revealing than the elements. Try not to allow the strong characteristics they suggest overinfluence you in your interpretation.

4 POSITIVE AND NEGATIVE SIGNS

The next stage in interpretation is to work out whether planets, the Ascendant and Midheaven are in positive or negative signs. This grouping will suggest, even if rather tentatively, that your subject will veer towards extroversion (the positive signs) or introversion (the negative signs). But be careful not to base your conclusions about your subject on this evidence alone: you will find that the in-depth interpretation will be far more revealing. Again, it is more sensible to treat this grouping as a supportive factor.

5 THE STRENGTHS OF THE PLANETS

Now is the time in your interpretation to study the chart which shows rulerships of the signs (see p.35). Make a point of noting which planets shine most brightly in the chart you are interpreting – these are the personalized planets – and keep them in mind all the time you are working.

SOME GOLDEN RULES

◆ Don't throw yourself in at the deep end and start working at once on a great many charts. Because astrology is such a fascinating subject, you will be sorely tempted, in your initial enthusiasm, to do this. It is far, far better to work in as much depth as possible on each chart, rather than darting from one to the next. It is essential that you get as much as you possibly can out of each birth chart before moving on to the next.

◆ Check and recheck your calculations, then check your friend's while he or she checks yours – independently of each other. You have probably done this already, but a further check won't do any harm. If the chart is wrong, the interpretation will also be wrong. Look again at the position of the Sun in the chart. Is it roughly where it should be according to the birth time? If not, go back to square one, and recalculate.

◆ The very best way to learn to interpret is to write your interpretation. Many students dislike doing this, but don't worry if you feel you have no talent for writing and can't spell or construct an elegant sentence. It is very important indeed, if you are to make progress, to start by getting your conclusions down on paper, where you can see and evaluate them, balance them and get them in the proper order of importance. Rough notes will not do. You will find that your first effort will be very short indeed. As your ability for basic interpretation grows, what you get out of each element also grows. Soon you will find, for instance, that you can use the same aspect in more than one area of interpretation. Eventually you may go through a stage of writing a great deal about each chart. This will pass, and when it does you will have moved into a more knowledgeable phase when you can be more concise.

◆ A great many professional astrologers do not write reports for their clients, preferring to record them on tape or merely in conversation. Writing reports is time-consuming and many professionals do not find it economically viable. But it is really the only way to learn the art of interpretation – and actually, it is fun as well as being challenging. Aim to write at least 20 basic birth chart analyses, as fully as possible, before you can feel you are really on your way to being a serious student!

◆ When you have written your interpretation, pass it over to your friend and let him study it for a while. Then go through it with him, discussing each statement and your reason for making it. In this way you can test just how accurate you are, whether you have over- or underinterpreted some of the indications or, hopefully, succeeded in assessing them correctly.

◆ You will be very keen to talk to your subjects about their charts – to give consultations, in fact. This is, of course, an important and necessary aim, but it is equally important to ease yourself gradually into the role. We will be giving a great deal of advice on approaches to various problems later. At this stage it is best to confine yourself to talking to people who are not under any particular strain, but just want to know about their basic characteristics and the way they tick. This is no short cut, however. You should prepare yourself for such a session just as carefully as if you were about to deal with a really taxing human problem. And do not think that merely chatting about a birth chart is any substitute for written work. Persevere with this side of things.

6 More Points to Remember

A birth chart will reveal certain aspects of the subject's:

- *Motivation.*
- *Potential.*
- *Energy level* – physical, emotional and nervous.
- *Response* – to all situations.

As you make your notes on the chart you will soon see which areas are emphasized by which planets' positions and their aspects. It is very easy, when one is learning to interpret, to group the characteristics of the Ascendant, Sun and Moon signs together. However, we are a combination not only of these three, but of all twelve signs. Think about these three signs in their very distinct ways, right from the start.

The Ascendant

The Ascendant represents our real self – known to family and close friends.

The Sun

The Sun represents the face we present to the world – our image. We express ourselves in the manner of the Sun.

The Moon

The Moon represents the way in which we react and respond to situations, and our instinctive level.

The Decanates

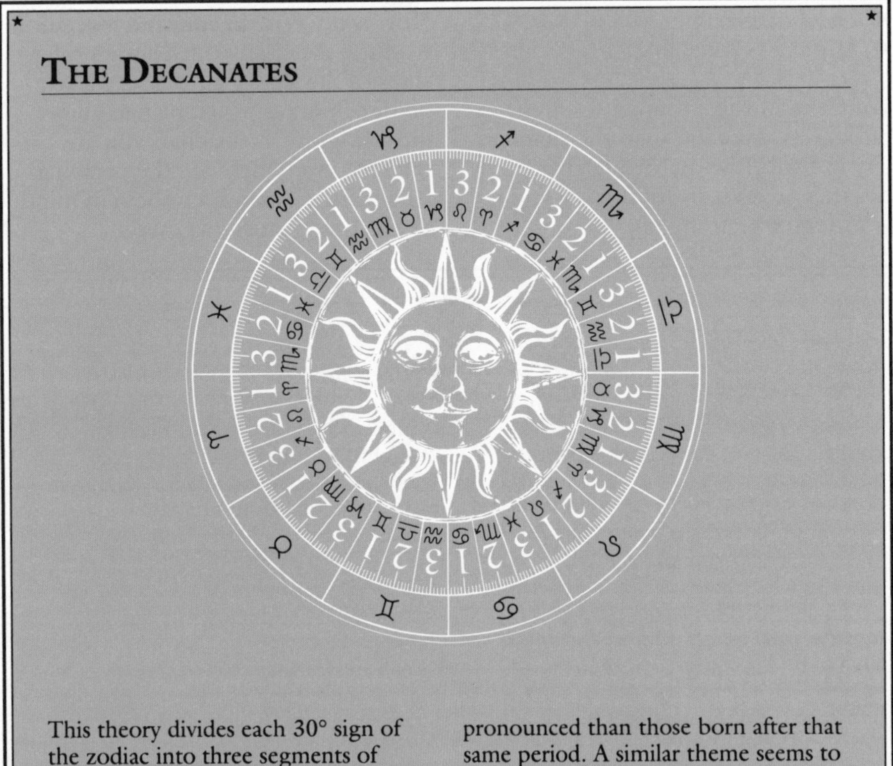

This theory divides each 30° sign of the zodiac into three segments of 10°, and relates to the triplicities. Each "decanate" is ruled by a sign of its own triplicity, so that the decanates of all the fire signs relate to each other, as do those of earth, air and water signs. The first decanate of a sign is ruled by its own sign, the second by the next sign of the same triplicity, and the third by the third sign of the same triplicity.

Although you should be aware of this theory, it is not especially relevant, apart from when it concerns the characteristics of the Sun and the Ascendant sign. Those born during the first 10 days of the period of the Sun sign seem to have its traits more powerfully pronounced than those born after that same period. A similar theme seems to emerge where the Ascendant is concerned. We do not think that the two later decanates are much influenced by the other two signs of their triplicities.

Challenge

See if people you know support this theory. If, for instance, they are Taureans born within the first 10 days of the Taurus Sun sign period, do they look like Taureans, perhaps having low curls on their foreheads? Or if their Ascendant degree is within those first 10 degrees, are they powerfully motivated in the manner of their Ascendant?

You may meet astrologers who believe that the Ascendant represents our outward expression, and the Sun sign characteristics are only revealed to our intimates. We totally disagree! This may have been the case in the past, but since Sun sign astrology became popular in the late 1920s, most people today have at least some basic knowledge of their Sun sign characteristics and tend, whether consciously or unconciously, to match their behavior to them, especially in their choice of clothes and general image.

Recognizing Sun sign traits

You can check this theory: talk to your friend about a mutual acquaintance on whose chart you have worked, alone. Mention some of the subject's Ascendant characteristics, and some of their Sun sign characteristics. Unless the subject is intimately known to your friend, you may find that they will only totally recognize those traits that are attributed to the Sun sign.

The houses

Don't forget that a planet in the first house is a strong focal point; remember, too, that if it is within 8° (or 10° at most) of the Ascendant degree it also makes a powerful conjunction to the Ascendant. You should study the relevant planet in that sign with particular care.

Do not be confused by those houses in a chart with no planets placed in them. This doesn't necessarily mean that there is little or no concern or interest in the affairs of that "empty" house. Look to the sign on the cusp of the house (that is, the sign where the house starts) and the planet that rules that sign. From this you will be able to get some idea of your subject's attitude to the affairs of untenanted houses. You may then discover that there will be other emphases of a similar nature relating to the concerns of these houses, revealed quite independently by aspects.

Contradictory indications

As you work your way through each element of the chart and begin to construct your analysis, you may well find contradictory indications emerging. If so, consider which group of indications is the stronger – decide

THE SEVEN CHART TYPES

There are seven types of chart, relating to the way in which the planets are distributed through the signs and houses, and therefore around the birth chart circle. The best-known system of categorizing them was devised by the American astrologer, Marc Edmund Jones. We describe it because it has considerable relevance, even if the basic interpretations used in isolation are not always totally accurate. When they are supported by certain prominent signs, however, they spring into sharp focus, and their accuracy is much enhanced.

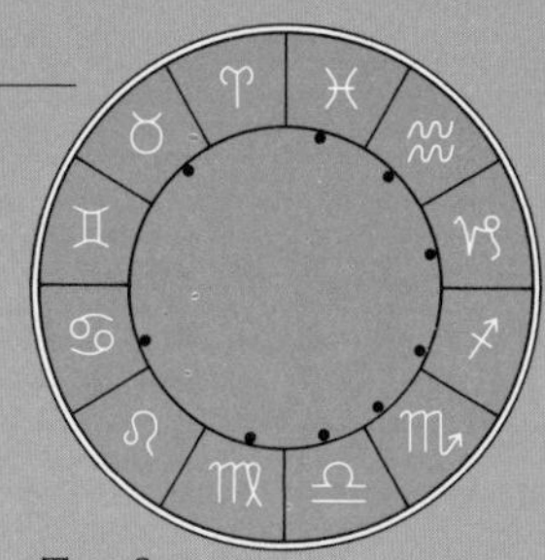

THE SPLASH
The planets are distributed throughout the signs. Subjects will have varied interests, but may be superficial and inconsistent. Particularly relevant to Gemini, perhaps Sagittarius.

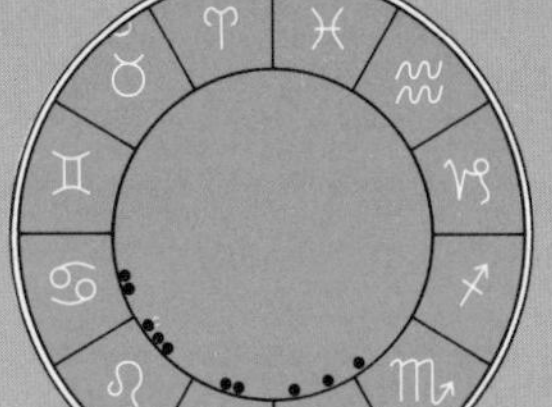

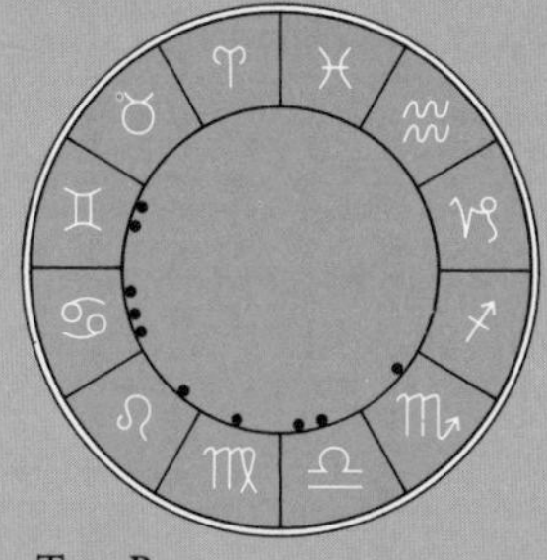

THE BUNDLE
Here the planets are very close together. Subjects will do well as specialists, finding variety within the confines of that subject. Particularly associated with Cancer, perhaps Capricorn.

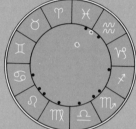

THE LOCOMOTIVE
Jones relates this type to the locomotive's driving wheel. Subjects will have a fund of energy at their disposal as and when it is required. Particularly associated with Aries, sometimes Leo.

THE BOWL
Bowl subjects are self-contained and scoop up experience. The houses in which the planets are tenanted will be especially relevant. Associated with Virgo and Scorpio.

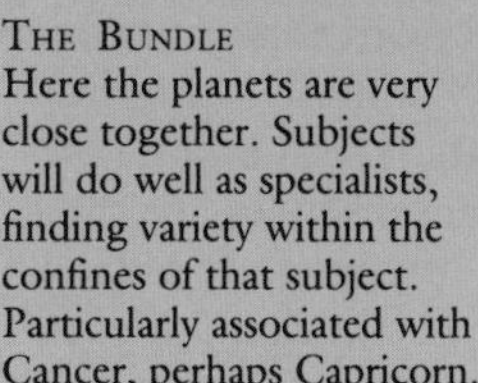

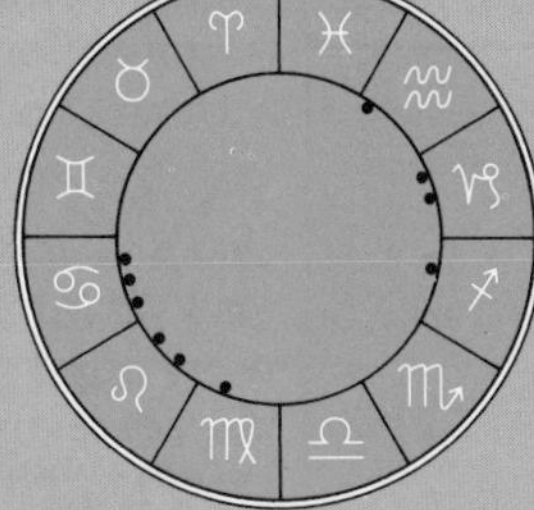

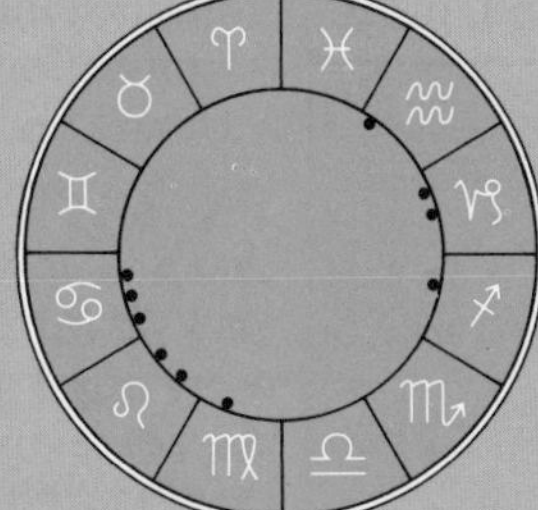

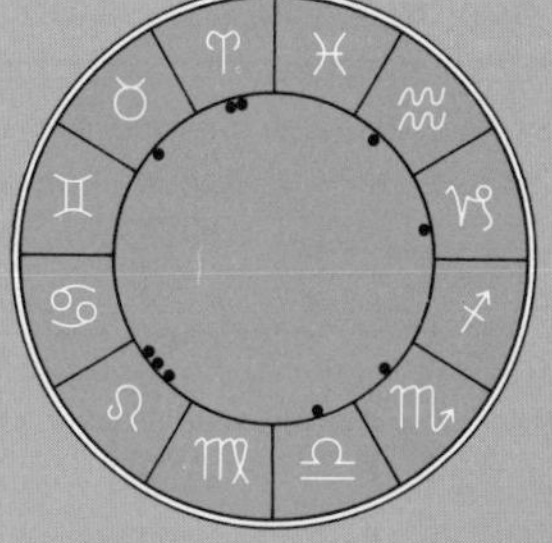

THE BUCKET
Nine planets are in one half of the chart; the tenth is the bucket's handle, making an anchorage. Usually achievement is more important than the end product. Associated with Sagittarius.

THE SEE-SAW
The planets are in two groups on opposite sides of the chart. Subjects weigh up every possibility before coming to decisions. Particularly associated with Libra, often Pisces.

THE SPLAY
The planets are spread all over the chart, but in very uneven groups. These subjects are individualists, disliking routine or discipline. Associated with Aquarius, sometimes Pisces.

whether personal planets influence one of the characteristics. If this is the case, there is a good chance that this trait will dominate. But if the contrasting indications are both supported by personal planets, remember that no one is the single person he or she may appear to be. We are all several people: we react differently to different people, in different ways and in different situations. At work we may be one sort of person; we may be quite another at home with our loved ones. Do not be afraid of these contradictions. Be bold. You may be accused of being vague and inconclusive, but people are complex. Remember the words of the US poet, Walt Whitman:

"Do I contradict myself?
Very well then I contradict myself
(I am large, I contain multitudes)."

CONSTRUCTING YOUR ANALYSIS

You are now ready to begin to construct your analysis. First, make your index chart (see p.134), to assist you when you begin to write your analysis.

Now look up each element of your subject's birth chart, to see what all the individual indications actually mean. This is the order you should follow:

1. Type of chart (i.e. bucket, etc).

2. The dominating triplicity (there may be two).

3. The dominating quality (there may be two).

4. Planets in positive and negative signs (there are usually more in one than the other), including Ascendant.

5. The characteristics of the Ascendant sign.

6. If there is a planet conjunct the Ascendant from the first or twelfth house consider this next, its house position influence and the aspects it makes. This placing will definitely color the personality and the characteristics of the Ascendant sign, acting as a kind of overlaying influence.

7. The Sun sign, its house position and aspects.

8. The Moon sign, its house position and aspects.

9. The ruling planet, its sign, house position and aspects. (You may have already listed some of the latter if the Sun or Moon makes aspects to it: such aspects will be very important.)

10. The influence of the sign on the Midheaven and its house position. (If you use the Placidus house system, this will always be the tenth house cusp, but it can vary considerably with the Equal House system.) Here you should also list any planet making a conjunction to the Midheaven.

11. The Mercury sign, its house position and aspects.

12. The Venus sign, its house position and aspects.

13. The Mars sign, its house position and aspects.

14. The Jupiter sign, its house position and aspects.

15. The Saturn sign, its house position and aspects.

16. The Uranus sign, its house position and aspects.

17. The Neptune sign, its house position and aspects.

18. The Pluto sign, its house position and aspects. (These will only be to the Ascendant and Midheaven, of course, since all other aspects to Pluto will already have been listed.)

Now look again to see what type of chart you are working on. As this is your first note, and will be written on page one of your notes (which will make quite a bundle by the time you reach Pluto!) take your index chart and write the number "1" in the narrow margin and "1" under the wider margin (not forgetting of course also to put a "1" on your written notes, and at the top of your first sheet of paper). What you discover about the chart type may relate to psychological motivation or characteristics.

Next look up the influence of the triplicities. This will be your second note, but (unless you have written reams about the type of chart or have very large handwriting), it will still be on page one of your notes. Again what you discover will probably come under the psychological/characteristics heading. Do the same for the qualities and the positive and negative signs.

The basic interpretation

Soon you will be referring to the main body of basic interpretation. First, follow through the interpretations of the Ascendant, then work through the others as listed above. You should not expect to rewrite everything you discover there, of course, but do make reasonably detailed notes. The way the book is arranged will help you to be careful and systematic; we teach you from the start to consider every planet, its sign and house position and, most important, the influence of the aspects in turn. (While working on the birth chart do not include the influence of the progressed planets' positions and aspects in your interpretation. These interpretations come later.)

By the time you have done all this you will have everything you need to construct your analysis. While making your notes don't hesitate to add your own thoughts about what you are discovering: "Possibly", "Wouldn't have thought so", "That's it!", "Can't be true", and so on. Some elements of the chart will refer to more than one section; if this is the case, list them in your index under each heading, duplicating or even triplicating information wherever necessary.

Assembling the information

Now you must put all these individual elements together. Refer to the keyword lists, and from those make a basic – probably very stilted – sentence about each planet, sign and house position. These sentences are the bare bones of your interpretation. Don't worry how artificial or stilted your sentences seem; they will help you to understand the basic character and motivation of your subject. Now, basing your interpretation on these simple statements and referring to all the various indications, correlate the information gleaned from the rest of your extensive notes.

A systematic approach

Again, be very systematic. First put together all your findings relating to the psychological/characteristic column of your index. Then move on to mind, intellect and emotion, and so on, until you have synthesized all your notes from all the respective headings. You should by then have a pretty concise picture of your subject, ready for them to read before you get together and go through it in detail to see how accurate you have been.

Remember that you may not write much at first. Don't worry; you will get more out of the chart as you progress. However, the more thorough you are with your note-taking and the use of our extensive interpretations, the more detailed your report will be, no matter how inexperienced you are. It is patience and care that really count.

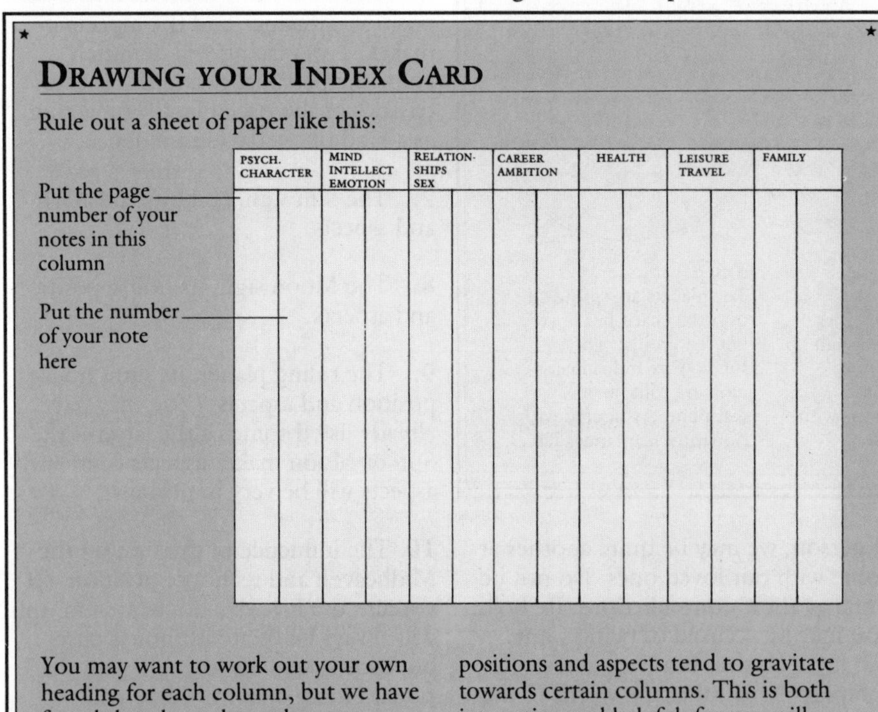

DRAWING YOUR INDEX CARD

Rule out a sheet of paper like this:

You may want to work out your own heading for each column, but we have found that those shown here are concise, reliable and easy to follow through. As you make your notes you will discover that certain planets, house positions and aspects tend to gravitate towards certain columns. This is both interesting and helpful, for you will begin naturally to associate the various planets and aspects with specific spheres of life and areas of the personality.

Complete Birth Chart Notes

EXAMPLE STUDY

These are notes on the chart of a client called Kenneth. Refer to his birth chart and aspect grid on p.136, and the index card on p.137.

Chart type: locomotive, with Venus as leading planet on cusp of eighth.

1. **Career/Ambition:** has driving power but could use it erratically. Aquarian interest emphasized. Venus positively placed financially; could use charm to assist progress in life.
Quadruplicities: 5 mutable, 4 fixed.
Qualities: 4 air, 3 earth.

2. **M/I/E:** good intellectual emphasis; adaptable, but may have fixed opinions, perhaps stubborn. Conflict here.
Positive/negative signs: 6 positive.

3. **Psy/Char:** extrovert leanings – supported by Aries Sun, Gemini Moon.

11 FULL ELEVENTH HOUSE

4. **Relationships:** good at mixing. Needs a wide circle of friends. Good link with Venus in Aquarius leading loco chart, plus Uranus strong in eleventh house, working well with Moon in communicative Gemini, also in eleventh.

♋ ASCENDANT CANCER

5. **Psy/Char:** strong self-defensive system. Brave, determined. May tend to hoard. Will want to explore own personality and motivation. Outgoing, and (because of Aries Sun) positive.

6. **M/I/E:** sensitive, easily hurt, worries, perhaps takes evasive action. Strong imagination. Instinctive, but Moon in Gemini adds logic. Mood changes. Emotional (supported by Aries Sun; mitigated by Gemini Moon).

7. **Relationships:** caring, loving; mood changes can be damaging. Will defend loved ones. Watch for coldness towards partner, who may be older, more socially advanced, since Capricorn on cusp of seventh; but a romantic streak present. May be easily offended.

8. **Health:** recommend steady, rhythmical exercise: swimming, dancing. Digestive problems due to worry. Needs diet rich in fish and dairy products, provided cholesterol intake is controlled. Perhaps sensitive skin.

9. **Family:** will be close to parents, would make excellent parent. Maybe lack here, for strong Venus in Aquarius is dominating, and he is unattached.

10. **Leisure/Travel**: suggest forming interesting collection of unusual artifacts. Travelling can spark off worry; will find being by water restorative – sailing? Could be good at cooking.

♈ SUN SIGN: ARIES IN NINTH HOUSE

Keyword sentence: "You will express yourself assertively and forthrightly when confronted with a challenge." As Sun is within first 10° of the sign, the characteristics will be strong.

11. **Psy/Char:** straightforward, uncomplicated? Overquick reactions (supported by Cancer and Gemini Moon). Selfish? Hasty, assertive. Enthusiastic. Temper?

12. **Relationships:** strong sex drive, passionate. Will enjoy love life.

13. **Health:** needs plenty of exercise. Possible accidents due to carelessness. Headaches. Must avoid spicy food.

14. **Career/Ambition:** ambitious, will want to win, needs freedom of expression and to be stimulated by challenge; achievement is important. Good head for business, supported by Ascendant and Gemini Moon. Enterprising.

15. **M/I/E:** quick-thinking, decisive, impatient, emotional (fire sign).

16. **Family:** would make lively, enthusiastic parent.

17. **Leisure/Travel:** will cope well with change. Encourage development of new interests as retirement approaches.

☉ SUN IN NINTH HOUSE

18. **Psy/Char:** an idealistic and philosophical outlook. Will do well living abroad. Emphasis on long-distance communications, the media; good dream recall; can be inspired.

☉ SUN SEMI-SQUARE VENUS

A powerful aspect, due to Venus being strongly placed.

19. **Relationships:** Breakdown in relationships. Kenneth has no permanent partner. Difficulties here.

☉ SUN SEXTILE URANUS

20. **Psy/Char:** originality and independence, alertness, powers of leadership (complementing Aries).

21. **Relationships:** sexual attraction, charm, popularity, personal magnetism.

☉ SUN OPPOSITION NEPTUNE

22. **Psy/Char:** tendency to deceive, to take easy way out of difficult situations (which will weaken his character); negative escapism; danger of falling back on drugs/drink under stress.

☉ SUN TRINE PLUTO

Powerful aspect as Pluto in first house, though different sign from Ascendant.

23. **Psy/Char:** ability for self-analysis; strong need to explore in-depth subjects of interest; talent for research.

24. **Career/Ambition:** will make advantageous changes in life resulting in psychological development.

☽ MOON (CHART RULER) IN GEMINI IN THE ELEVENTH HOUSE

Keyword sentence: "When dealing with other people and your objectives, you will respond to situations in a instinctively communicative way."

25. **M/I/E:** quick verbal response to all situations; verbose, versatile, will argue and rationalize. Conflict between emotion and logic; may not trust emotions but will speak up. A chatterbox. Must use resources of nervous energy positively.

26. **Psy/Char:** impatient, may need to develop stability and calm.

27. **Health**: strain and tension can build up, resulting in digestive problems; lungs vulnerable, so discourage smoking (smokes heavily). Will worry.

☽ MOON IN ELEVENTH HOUSE

28. **Relationships:** a tendency to rely on friends and acquaintances too much, to lean on "the group". Must develop ability to be independent (Sun in Aries, Venus in Aquarius will help). Must always take independent action. Is a private person; may be difficult to get close to? (Cancer Ascendant may mitigate). Will want to be loved.

☽ Moon Square Mercury

An important aspect, since Moon in Mercury sign.

29. M/I/E: sharpness of response, critical acumen, heightened intellectual power. Liking for gossip.

30. Health: possible digestive problem.

☽ Moon Trine Venus

31. Relationships: adds charm, warmth, affection.

32. Psy/Char: a liking for good living.

33. M/I/E: adds intuition, optimism, good perception.

☽ Moon Conjunct Mars

This is a key aspect since it links the chart ruler, the Moon, with the Sun ruler, Mars.

34. M/I/E: increases emotional level, quickens responses to all situations, adds direct approach. Will take emotional and physical risks. Could be reckless.

☽ Moon Conjunct Jupiter

35. Relationships: adds kindness and softens attitude towards other people; generosity. Satisfaction from encouraging others. Good judge of people.

☽ Moon Square Midheaven

36. Career/Ambition: difficulty in finding real satisfaction in career, even discovering what is really wanted out of life. (While Kenneth knew what he wanted, he has had trouble achieving it.)

MC The Influence of the Midheaven Sign, Pisces

There will be identification with the best Piscean aspirations, but also a tendency to be vague or overidealistic about aims and objectives; this might cloud important issues, in spite of Arian directness and Cancerian shrewdness. Kenneth may be a dreamer – though not liking to think of himself as such!

Note

In this chart no planet makes a conjunction to the Midheaven, though Mercury is extremely near (less than 1° outside orb – if the birth had been a few minutes later it would have been in conjunction). The Geminian influence means that Mercury's influence is therefore quite strong, adding a need for psychological involvement in the career (Mercury rules the Moon, Mars and Jupiter signs.) The communications areas of Kenneth's career are nicely emphasized by Mercury's placing near the Midheaven.

Kenneth's Birth Chart and Aspects

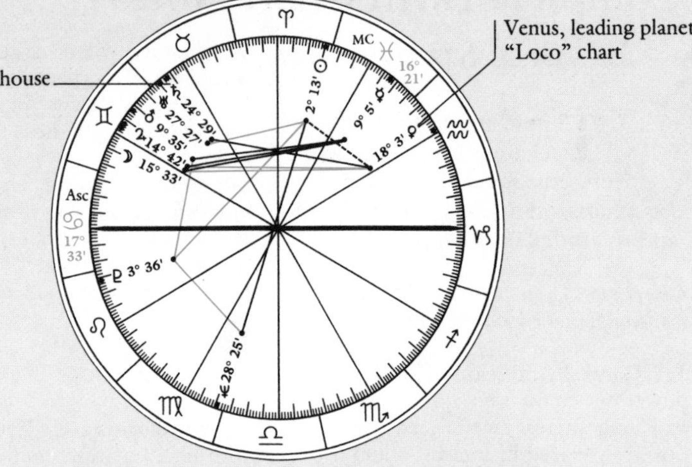

Planet		☉	☽	☿	♀	♂	♃	♄	♅	♆	♇
Sun	☉		•	•	∠	•	•	•	⚹	☍	△
Moon	☽			□	△	☌	☌	•	•	•	•
Mercury	☿				•	□	□	•	•	•	•
Venus	♀					•	△	□	•	•	•
Mars	♂						☌	•	•	•	⚹
Jupiter	♃							•	•	•	•
Saturn	♄								☌	△	•
Uranus	♅									△	•
Neptune	♆										⚹
Pluto	♇										
Asc	Asc	•	•	•	⚻	•	•	•	•	•	•
MC	MC	•	□	•	⚺	•	□	•	•	•	•

Fire planets = 2
Earth planets = 3
Air planets = 4
Water planets = 1, Asc/MC

Cardinal planets = 1, Asc
Fixed planets = 4
Mutable planets = 5, MC

Positive planets = 6
Negative planets = 4

☿ Mercury in Pisces, with Sun sign Aries

Keyword sentence: "You could be easily impressed by moneymaking schemes; beware deception."

37. Psy/Char: Arian assertiveness is softened. Forgetfulness can cause problems. Less decisive than most Aries Sun sign types. May take line of least resistance. Deceit possible.

38. M/I/E: worry, emotional level and intuition increased, but less likely to be angered. Adds kindness.

☿ Mercury in the Eighth House

39. M/I/E: tendency to brood over serious matters; often psychic gifts (supported here by Cancer Ascendant, Sun opposition Neptune); care very necessary in development of these. Increased imagination and intuition. Possible preoccupation with sex.

40. Career/Ambition: Shrewdness in investment, but because Pisces is Mercury sign could be gullible.

☿ Mercury Square Mars

41. M/I/E: quick-thinking, sharp-tongued; tendency to backbite and to be irritable. May make overhasty decisions.

☿ Mercury Square Jupiter

42. M/I/E: good intellect; absent-minded; sceptical. Care needed when signing documents; may ignore details.

43. Health: possible digestive problems.

♀ Venus in Aquarius

Keyword sentence: "You need a rewarding sexual relationship, but must retain your independence."

44. Relationships: contributes movie-star glamor; an independent attitude towards love life. Partnership desired – but perhaps not a partner. Committed, will nevertheless be romantic, idealistic and faithful. Kind and helpful.

♀ VENUS IN EIGHTH HOUSE

45. Relationships: heightens the feelings and passions; needs to beware of jealousy (Venus sign will mitigate). Sex life should be rich and rewarding, but Venus squares Saturn so there could be some cramping and inhibitive factors.

46. Career/Ambition: a good placing for finance and inheritance (perhaps from a partner). Shrewd investor.

♀ VENUS TRINE JUPITER

47. Psy/Char: adds popularity; a pleasant and amusing turn of phrase.

♀ VENUS SQUARE SATURN

48. Relationships: an inhibitive factor influencing the love life. But (because of Aries Sun sign) determined to overcome problems, and (because of the analyzing ability) face any difficulties.

♀ VENUS QUINCUNX ASCENDANT

Not a powerful influence; most of the negative traits listed will not be present.

49. Relationships: he may well feel insecure in emotional relationships, so this aspect may underline the effect of the square between Venus and Saturn.

50. Health: must beware of comfort eating and overindulgence, which could lead to weight gain.

♀ VENUS SEMI-SEXTILE MIDHEAVEN

We are certain of Kenneth's birth time, so can count this very minor aspect.

51. Career/Ambition: complements the involvement with the glamor industries, and connections with many of its stars, with whom he identifies.

♂ MARS IN GEMINI

Keyword sentence: "You will use your initiative and physical energy with versatility in the attainment of objectives; but beware of restlessness."

52. Health: this placing may lower the physical energy level, usually high when the Sun is in Aries. He could dissipate energy and become restless; as a result his well-being will suffer. He may find physical exercise dull. Arms and hands are vulnerable to minor accidents.

53. M/I/E: the intellectual energy is increased, with quickness of mind and intellect. Could become ill-tempered.

54. Career/Ambition: the need for change can provoke feelings of unfulfillment; versatility may need controlling.

55. Relationships: a lively influence on the sex life: an urge to experiment and enjoy sex well into old age.

♂ MARS IN ELEVENTH HOUSE

56. Relationships: a group-leader among his peers, but may quarrel with them. Will want to give practical help. Can be cool in emotional relationships.

♂ MARS CONJUNCT JUPITER

57. Career/Ambition: adds enterprise, enthusiasm and the ability to take the initiative. Ability to concentrate on objectives. Remember risktaking and daring present (Aries Sun).

58. Psy/Char: love of life and good living. Will say what he thinks.

♂ MARS SEXTILE PLUTO

59. Health: physical energy enhanced. Needs physical exercise to burn surplus.

60. M/I/E: emotional energy increased.

61. Psy/Char: motivated to make beneficial changes in life. Hard worker.

♃ JUPITER IN GEMINI

Keyword sentence: "Adaptability in pursuit of objectives and in dealing with other people will help to expand your intellect; beware restlessness."

62. M/I/E: intellectual restlessness, changes of opinion – advise consistency. Broad-minded, up-to-date in outlook. Bright responses to criticism.

♃ JUPITER IN ELEVENTH HOUSE

63. Relationships: a socializer. Large circle of friends and acquaintances. The "just good friends" tendency associated with this placing may be relevant here, due to Venus in Aquarius.

♃ JUPITER SQUARE MIDHEAVEN

64. Psy/Char: may identify with the grand and pompous, and think he is more important than he actually is.

65. Career/Ambition: indicative of success and the attainment of objectives.

♄ SATURN IN TAURUS

Keyword sentence: "You may have to accept certain restrictions and limitations to your objectives if you want stability."

PSYCH. CHARACTER		MIND INTELLECT EMOTION		RELATION-SHIPS SEX		CAREER AMBITION		HEALTH		LEISURE TRAVEL		FAMILY	
135	3	135	2	135	4	135	1	135	8	135	10	135	9
135	5	135	6	135	7	135	14	135	13	135	17	135	16
135	11	135	15	135	12	135	24	135	27	138	68	138	78
135	18	135	25	135	19	136	36	136	30	138	73		
135	20	136	29	135	21	136	40	136	43				
135	22	136	33	135	28	137	46	137	50				
135	23	136	34	136	31	137	51	137	52				
135	26	136	38	136	35	137	54	137	59				
136	32	136	39	137	44	137	57						
136	37	136	41	137	45	137	65						
137	47	136	42	137	48	138	81						
137	58	137	53	137	49								
137	61	137	60	137	55								
137	64	137	62	137	56								
138	66	138	76	137	63								
138	69	138	77	138	67								
138	70	138	79	138	74								
138	71	138	80										
138	72												
138	75												
138	82												

ORGANIZING YOUR ANALYSIS

This chart will help when you are bringing together the various elements of the chart. It is vital to be systematic: you can build each area in a coherent way by following through the notes as listed under each section of the analysis.

66. Psy/Char: adds caution and patience. Tendency to social climbing. Liking for luxury and comfort may clash with more frugal tendencies. Ability to be disciplined.

♄ SATURN IN ELEVENTH HOUSE

67. Relationships: few close friends, and often of the older generation.

68. Leisure/Travel: interests are taken serious and are long-lasting.

69. Psy/Char: conventional in outlook; strong sense of social justice.

♄ SATURN CONJUNCT URANUS

70. Psy/Char: a powerful driving force affecting the psychological need to achieve ambitions and objectives.

♄ SATURN TRINE NEPTUNE

71. Psy/Char: the ability to channel ideas so they can be expressed constructively. Saturn will keep him in check when his aspiration and inspiration may make too ambitious. The indication of a flair for photography turns him toward his filming interests.

♅ URANUS IN TAURUS

Keyword sentence: "You must be prepared for disruptive changes which may cause clashes in ties of permanent friendships; beware possessiveness."

72. Psy/Char: stubborn, but will add stability and originality. Clash between the conventional and unconventional.

73. Leisure/Travel: likes unusual possessions. (This could influence any "Cancerian collection" he may have.)

♅ URANUS IN ELEVENTH HOUSE

74. Relationships: friendly, but keeps his distance. The need of a wide social life could clash with professional contacts. Sudden breaks in friendship due to changes of heart. May be purposely disruptive on committees.

75. Psy/Char: loathes complacency.

♅ URANUS TRINE NEPTUNE

While this is an aspect that was in orb for a long time when Kenneth was born, it is relevant because of the very full eleventh house (the Uranus house) and the fact that Pisces is the Midheaven sign – the Neptune-ruled sign.

76. M/I/E: a good blending of originality and imagination. Intuition and logical thinking are also enhanced.

♆ NEPTUNE IN VIRGO

Keyword sentence: "You may lose touch with reality when analyzing your attitude towards your environment, or in your relationship with brothers or sisters." (Although a generation influence, this placing can be used since Neptune rules the Midheaven.)

77. M/I/E: will stimulate the imagination, which may be expressed through literary work. Could undermine self-confidence, resulting in lack of inner fulfillment. Sometimes discontent and restlessness is present.

♆ NEPTUNE IN THIRD HOUSE

78. Family: early education may have been disrupted; idealized, possibly jealous of brothers and sisters. May not have concentrated very well at school.

79. M/I/E: imagination enhanced by this placing.

♆ NEPTUNE SEXTILE PLUTO

This aspect, although common to many charts, is more important here, since Neptune is the Midheaven ruler and Pluto is in the first house.

80. M/I/E: intuition and emotions are enhanced by this contact.

♇ PLUTO IN LEO

Keyword sentence: "You will cope impressively with disruptive changes, especially if they relate to your psychological development." (Pluto is powerfully placed in the first house, albeit well away from the Ascendant and in a different sign; its influence may have a psychological effect.)

81. Career/Ambition: powers of leadership enhanced; complements the strong Arian characteristics.

♇ PLUTO IN FIRST HOUSE

82. Psy/Char: the need to explore everything in depth – including his own personality. Ability for research. Possible tendency to dominate others.

83. M/I/E: emotional energy intensified and passionately expressed. (Re-check Sun trine Pluto, which complements this placing very well.)

Analysis of a Birth Chart

The analysis that follows was produced from the above notes and put in the form of an analysis which could be presented to the subject. It was written for Kenneth while Julia was still a student. It is included to show the sort of standard it is possible to reach after only a few months of careful, constructive study.

Because we cannot expect other people to be familiar with astrological terms, it is a good rule to omit these wherever possible – though for the student, the significators are printed here, in the margin of the text, by the statements that they prompt. Due to lack of space, we cannot reproduce the whole report.

Kenneth, born with Cancer ascending, the Sun in Aries and under the Midheaven of Pisces.

1. Loco chart	You have in your basic personality an enormous amount of drive, thriving on problems that must be solved, and on hard work. Your objectives may be somewhat unusual. It is likely that you may be moved by external influences rather than being motivated by aspects of your own personality.
5. Asc ♋ 14. ☉ ♈ 58. ♂ ☌ ♃	You are tenacious, and go all-out in pursuit of what you want from life; you have plenty of determination. You wish to get as much enjoyment out of life as possible.
6. Asc ♋ ☉ ♈ 25. ☽ ♂ ♊ 29. ☽ □ ☿ 62. ♃ ♊	While giving the impression of self-assurance and toughness, you may well be sensitive and at times easily hurt. As well as plenty of physical energy (I bet you never stop rushing around!), you have enormous nervous energy and mental alertness. It is possible that you are rather restless and nervously excitable.

Using energy wisely

52. ♂ ♊	In spite of your determination and drive you must be careful that you do not dissipate your energy – your liking for variety and change could mean you go after things only to discover that they are not what you thought they were, and consequently change course mid-stream.
35. ☽ ☌ ♃ 31. ☽ △ ♀ 21. ☉ ⚹ ♅	You have excellent judgement and are able to sum up people quickly. Added to this you have masses of charm, which contributes to your popularity. You have originality and a certain amount

of magnetism, which will be of
use to you both in your personal
life and in your career.

Avoiding extremes

2. Mut- While you are adaptable, it may
able 5 be that you can be a little too
Fixed 4 fixed in your basic opinions,
though you have plenty of
spontaneity and are frank and
34.☽ ♊ direct. You could be erratic, and
11.☉ ♈ tend to go to extremes of action –
partly because you like quick
results. Try to avoid any tendency
to be careless.

Strong You are talkative and excitable
♊ and may tend to give the impression that you know a lot about
different subjects, but your
knowledge may be superficial and
64. ♃ □ you may at times exaggerate – and
MC think that you are rather more
important than you really are.

Good critical faculties

7. Asc ♋ While you are extremely kind and
generous, and possibly somewhat
sentimental, you are also shrewd
– and it may be that you tend to
11.☉ ♈ be somewhat quick-tempered
3/Earth and impatient. Practicality and
♄ ♅ ♉ good critical faculties help you in
your work. Change and variety
6./7.☉ are of the utmost importance to
♈ you – and it is excellent that you
25.☽ ♊ do not have a career which is
monotonous and repetitive. You
♇ ♌ 1st can cope well with changes in
your life – and these may be
drastic, at times. It is possible
that during unsettled periods
♆ ⚹ ♇ you come in for more than your
fair share of confusion.

46.♀ There are in your chart some
8th excellent indications of financial
success. You are sensible in your
attitude to money, and being
57. enterprising will work hard for
♂ ☌ ♃ material advancement.

12.☉ ♈ You are very emotional and pos-
38.☿ ♓ sess a wide range of extremely
34. powerful, active emotions; you
☽ ☌ ♂ are capable of experiencing the
60. highest elation and the deepest
♂ ⚹ ♇ despair. You may respond too
MC♓ readily to outside influences,
without due thought.

Love relationships

You probably give the impres-
44.♀ ♒ sion of being rather light-
(☽ ♊) hearted and somewhat coolly
affectionate and fickle when it
comes to love. You also need to
keep a strong measure of independence in this sphere of your
12.☉ ♈ life. But you are really very
7. emotional, protective and
Asc ♋ tender, with a romantic streak
adding to that touch of sentimentality I have mentioned. You
48.♀ □ are also passionate and sensual,
♄ and your desires are easily
19. stimulated. It is possible that you
☉ ∠ ♀ may have suffered from some
slight strain and shyness which
49.♀ ⚻ may in the past have limited the
Asc demonstration of your feelings.
You may have become depressed
about your love life and this may
7. Asc ♋ have led to periods of moodiness
which your partners may not
have understood; or perhaps
they may, without realizing it,
have said or done something
that has upset you.

The importance of friendships

Full There is a strong emphasis on
11th friendship in your chart: it is
63.♃ essential that you should con-
11th stantly mix and communicate
with other people. You are
47.♀ △ popular and, being friendly and
♃ affectionate, are well equipped to
31.(☽ get on well with other people.
△ ♀) You have a sensible attitude to
your friends, many of whom will
67.♄ perhaps be older than you.
11th There is also an indication that
(♅ your friends will be unusual,
11th) clever and influential – and of
great help to you. Because there
is such an emphasis on friendship, you should be a little
28.☽ careful not to rely too much on
11th others. You could also be
56.♂ changeable towards your friends;
11th try to avoid rashness, and use
patience, tact and willpower to
keep your friends.

Family relationships

9. Asc ♋ The relationship between you
and your family seems a happy
one. You are probably very close
to your mother – but I wonder
whether she has had to contend
(♀ □ ♄) with certain setbacks in her life?
♄ ♉ And was your father over-
anxious for you to grow up? If
78.♆ you have brothers or sisters you
3rd are probably very fond of them.

Creative and healthy pursuits

79.♆ You have plenty of imagination:
3rd it might be worth taking up
(Asc♋) creative writing: short stories,
(☽ ☌ ♊) perhaps with a touch of fantasy,
39.☿ might be especially rewarding. I
8th expect you like to collect things.
10. Asc This could prove profitable.
♋ Because you are a Sun sign
Arian, you are prone to head-
13.☉ ♈ aches which could be rooted in
slight kidney upsets. You should
watch your digestion, and
8. Asc ♋ because of marginal accident-
30.☽ □ proneness may find that your
☿ arms and hands are particularly
vulnerable to damage.

☉ 9th Time spent abroad will be
extremely beneficial to you, and
links with foreigners will also be
successful. You will find being by
water, and taking sea voyages,
psychologically restorative.

COMMENTARY

At the time this analysis was written Kenneth had been to drama school but had given up the idea of becoming an actor and was working with two partners as a researcher and assistant producer of television documentaries. These much older partners were a very powerful influence on Kenneth's development.

In due course both partners died, and Kenneth left the UK to settle in Los Angeles in the hope of breaking into the television and film industries. After long years of struggle he succeeded, and is now involved in the production of television films. His ninth house Sun is indicative of success abroad.

My comments in the analysis on his potential for writing were to prove accurate; he has successfully written film scripts. For his daily income Kenneth produces a vastly successful trade journal – the strong Geminian communicative influence being fully expressed. Kenneth has no regular emotional relationship but he is definitely more than just on the fringe of the Hollywood scene.

It is not usually possible to use in the final analysis every indication or note you may have made – in fact, selectivity is very much at the centre of the art of interpretation. When certain traits recur in independent areas of the chart, these are your "backers". In Kenneth's case, for instance, note the references to restlessness.

This report is very basic and over-simplified, but is an example of a sound beginning in the art of interpretation. We reproduce it with Kenneth's permission.

CHALLENGE

Write your own report from the notes and index provided. Work through each section, perhaps developing some themes that Julia, who constructed her notes as a student, may have missed.

The Zodiac Trail

Here is a further aid to interpretation, based on an old theory by which the strengths and weaknesses of planets were assessed. It helps you see which planets "shine the brightest" and also how psychologically well-integrated the subject is.

We use Kenneth's chart as an example, since by now you will be accustomed to it. When working on your own charts it is helpful to go through this process after you have made your notes and before you write your analysis.

To construct a diagram like this one, always start with the Ascendant and ruling planet. The chart itself will then take you on. The more dead ends you reach, the less well-integrated the person may be.

Ruling Planet
From Gemini move on to that sign's ruling planet, Mercury, in this case in the eighth house. By sign and house position it relates to Neptune in Virgo in the third house as well as to the ruling Moon, Mars and Jupiter. (Note too that Neptune is also the ruler of the Midheaven sign, Pisces.)

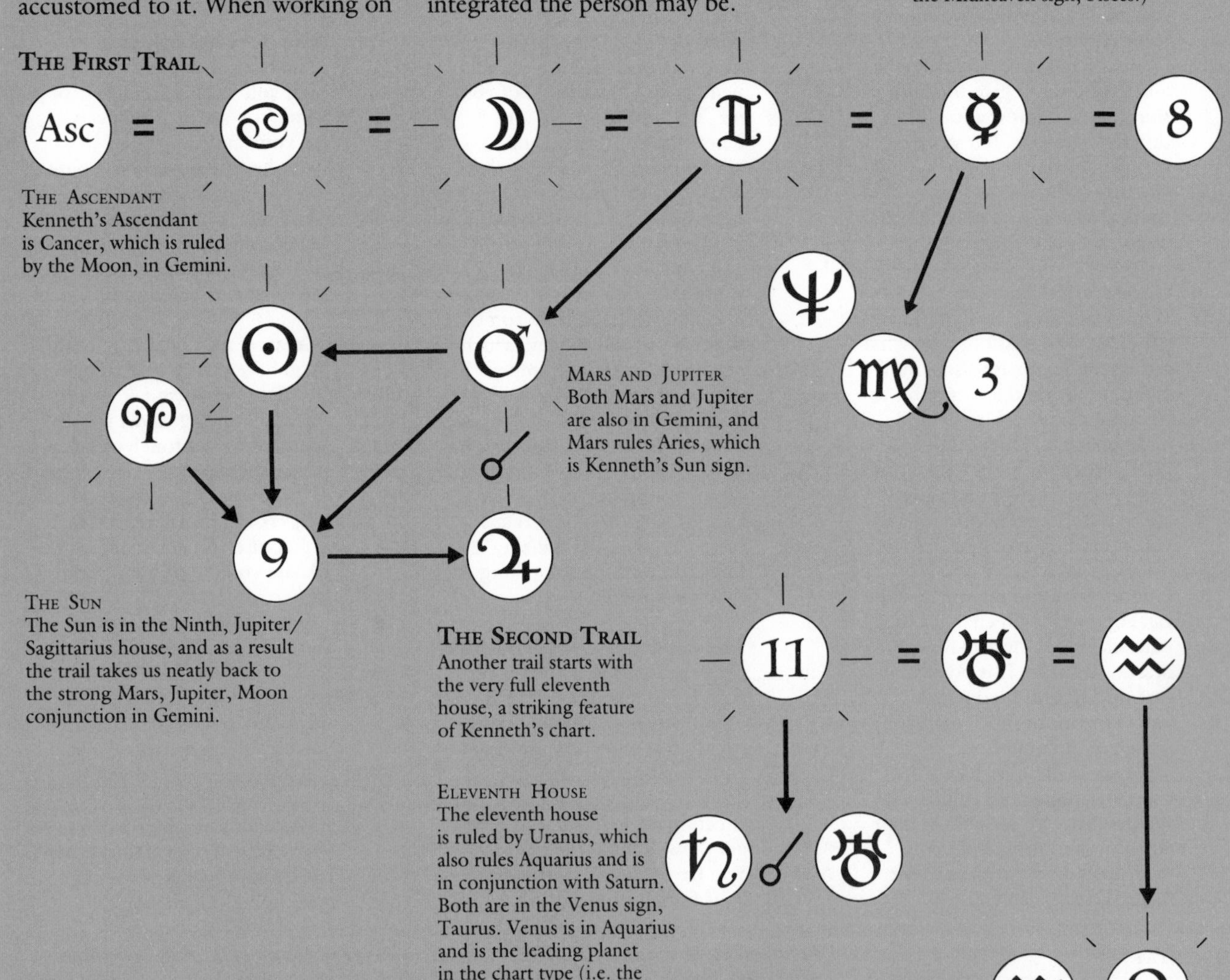

The Ascendant
Kenneth's Ascendant is Cancer, which is ruled by the Moon, in Gemini.

Mars and Jupiter
Both Mars and Jupiter are also in Gemini, and Mars rules Aries, which is Kenneth's Sun sign.

The Sun
The Sun is in the Ninth, Jupiter/Sagittarius house, and as a result the trail takes us neatly back to the strong Mars, Jupiter, Moon conjunction in Gemini.

The Second Trail
Another trail starts with the very full eleventh house, a striking feature of Kenneth's chart.

Eleventh House
The eleventh house is ruled by Uranus, which also rules Aquarius and is in conjunction with Saturn. Both are in the Venus sign, Taurus. Venus is in Aquarius and is the leading planet in the chart type (i.e. the locomotive). In addition, Venus is in the eighth house, along with Mercury.

Eighth House
The eighth house is the Pluto/Scorpio house, so from it we can look to the placing of Pluto – in Leo in the first house.

Commentary
Kenneth is well-integrated – it takes only two trails to go through the chart, and even these are related because of the strength of Mercury (especially) and Venus. Note how well the Aries Sun relates to Mars and Jupiter. Saturn has little to offer; it makes a strong conjunction to Uranus, but the only cross-reference to Saturn is that the sign it rules (i.e. Capricorn) is on the cusp of the seventh. The Saturn principle could be a source of integration problems. Saturn represents our destiny, and Kenneth, although enjoying work, feels he is pushing against the tide. Wary about any commitment in a relationship, Kenneth's independence has Saturnine overtones (the influence of independent Venus in Aquarius is similar). His Aries Sun, however, makes him warm and positive, and his Cancer Ascendant ensures he is caring and kind. The Sun in the ninth house (well-integrated with Jupiter) shows his love of Los Angeles.

Interpreting the Progressions

This is a fascinating area of astrology, and one with which the beginner is usually very eager to become acquainted. However, it is essential to develop not only a good technique, but the right attitude toward progressions. It is all too easy to dramatize certain trends and to assume that, as a result of them, events will take place, so that the astrologer either becomes a prophet of doom or, at the other extreme, a blind optimist.

Always approach indications with an open mind. The planets work differently for all of us, and it takes time to discover their individual moods. Never be fatalistic; it is not good astrology, and the prediction of events is impossible. Progressions are meant to add extra perspective to our lives and be constructive and positive.

There are two categories of progressed influences – symbolic background day-for-a-year progressions, and physical transits. There are other systems, but the day-for-a-year is the most commonly used.

Constantly refer to the interpretation pages of progressed aspects and transits as you build your interpretation. It is advisable to take detailed notes, adding comments regarding your subject's lifestyle, commitments and present concerns and problems.

THE BACKGROUND PROGRESSIONS

These are of two kinds: the aspects the progressed planets make to the natal planets, Ascendant and Midheaven (i.e. those in the birth chart); and the aspects the progressed planets, Ascendant and Midheaven make to each other. Some astrologers think events surface under the influence of one progressed planet to another, while the aspects from progressed to natal planets, Ascendant and Midheaven work on our psychological and instinctive levels. But the planets work very individually for all of us, and it takes time to know precisely how they work for each of our subjects. There are, however, a few general rules to follow:

◆ Aspects from the progressed Sun are the most important, especially if they are formed to the natal chart ruler or its progressed position.

◆ Aspects to or from the ruling planet are also very important.

The planets work differently for all of us and it will take patience to discover their moods.

◆ Aspects formed between two planets, the Ascendant or Midheaven, if they are in aspect in the birth chart, will also be powerful. In this case it is advisable to read all text relating to the aspect, since its influence will be operative in the birth chart as well as having an effect on the subject's current life.

◆ Sometimes a progressed planet will form an aspect to a planet or planets involved in a tee-square, grand trine or grand cross. This will energize the aspect pattern, and if the natal aspect pattern is a very close one – i.e. the orb between the planets involved is tiny – then it is likely that the subject will have an important period when long-term problems may be resolved, or the subject may make important changes. However, the progression may cover a long period, during which the progressed planet completes aspects to all the other planets in the tee-square, in which case the influence will be more subtle and any developments or changes will be very gradual. (Transits to a tee-square or any aspect pattern will have the same effect, but will last for the duration of the transits.)

Eventful and placid periods

It is important to consider the listed planets in numerical order. If several planets occupy the same degree of different signs, then a progressed or transiting planet will make a cluster of aspects or transits at one time. People with planets grouped this way will have very eventful then very placid periods. This pattern will show up both in long periods of time and during briefer periods. A solar progression to several planets at once could indicate a period of about three years when everything seems to happen at once. A transit of, say, Jupiter to the cluster of planets could make for an extremely eventful time. A lunar progression to the cluster might indicate about three months when life is especially eventful. In such cases all these natal planets will also be in aspect in the birth chart and also supporting the theme – the progessions and transits will form a chain reaction. But individuals may well experience bland periods; during these you should encourage them to take life smoothly and calmly while they can!

Lunar progressions

The progressed Moon seems to form a bridge between the day-for-a-year progressions and the transits. These are usually operative for about three months, and if the progressed Moon makes aspects to any planet or planets in aspect in the background progressions there is a good chance that the concerns and effects of those aspects will be highlighted during the periods of the lunar progression. (There may be transits that emphasize the theme, in which case the period will be a key one.) The lunar progressions also help link the two groups because of the length of their influence, which is much shorter than the influences of the other planets.

Some subjects feel and notice the effects of lunar progressions more than others. If Cancer rises, the Moon is in Cancer or Taurus, or perhaps in the fourth house, then the strength of the already powerful Moon in the chart is increased. As the Moon affects our emotions and instinctive level, its influence works subtly on our feelings, and some people, perhaps because they are not intuitive or sensitive, detach themselves from it. This can also be the case if the Moon is negatively aspected in the birth chart. This is something you must discover with each subject you work on – bear it in mind.

THE TRANSITS

For now, ignore the transits of Mars, Venus, Mercury, the Sun and the New Moon. Look across the grid at the slow-moving, or heavy, planets. There may well be a great deal of activity during some months and very little in others. Think of the grid as a kind of graph, and relate it to your subject's life. When the planets are busy, life may be eventful – either because things are happening to your subject (perhaps because the Midheaven is activated by planetary influences – see Jupiter's transits conjunct the Midheaven, p.296, which explains something of particular relevance) or perhaps because the subject is making progress psychologically, changing their attitude towards important issues, and so on. There will be times when the transits complement background and lunar progressions: look out for these.

OTHER METHODS OF PROGRESSIONS

There are two other methods of progressions – one symbolic, the other physical. The one-degree system entails moving all the entities of the chart forward one degree for each year of the life, and assessing the relationships the progressed positions make to the natal positions. This is an interesting (and effective) system and one that you may care to experiment with a little later on. The other system is the solar return chart. This involves calculating a chart for the precise moment when the Sun returns to its natal position each year, and assessing the planets' positions and influence as shown in terms of the subject's life.

Recurring themes

Very often, because of retrograde motion, a transit will recur three times. When a transit is exact for the first time you will probably be able to see how the transit will operate. The project or problem will surface again during the planet's second transit, and will probably be resolved during the third. Frequently the third transit is the most potent influence. Sometimes the first two cause us to feel uncertain or unsettled, and we take matters into our own hands during the last period.

Transits of the fast-moving planets

These provide a guide to day-to-day matters, although their influence is increased if they are personalized or ruling planets. Read the interpretations of these transits to get the feel of them. Mercury and Venus add a lot of color to our lives, the way we communicate, our social life, and so on. Mars is important because it tends to make us unduly hasty and perhaps accident-prone. These minor transits fill the aspect grid but aren't too important, despite being very worthwhile.

The solar transits are quite constant each year. These influences are usually good and can be used in any way your subject desires (see the interpretation pages, 130-40). The same applies to the New Moon's aspects, which form a longer-term theme and can be included as a general tendency when interpreting background trends if the string of aspects to a natal planet goes on for several months.

Interpreting a progression or transit

It is easy to over- or underinterpret a progression or transit. If you are uncertain, admit it, saying that you could be viewing the influence in the wrong perspective; don't dramatize! The planetary energies are at our disposal, and even negative ones can be used effectively – perhaps prompting us to hold back and be patient, or to take health precautions. Practice in interpretation is essential. The longer you work on a chart, the better you will know it and the moods of all the planets.

A Complete Interpretation

LAURA CAMPBELL: BORN 20 OCTOBER 1946 4.37 AM, PORT CHESTER, NEW YORK, USA

Laura is married to an English man (Roger) and lives near Oxford in the UK; she has a daughter (Bronwen), born in 1981. She had an arts training and has been teaching arts and crafts in girls' schools. During 1989 she was thinking of giving up teaching to concentrate on her own creative work; she also had ideas about starting craft workshops and writing a book on screen-printing techniques. The set of progressions Julia prepared for her covered the 12-month period from May 1989 in detail, and rather longer in a more general way.

Laura's birth chart

Notice the position of Neptune, vulnerably placed immediately beneath the Ascendant, and the fact that Laura is a double Libra, with that sign both as Ascendant and Sun sign. Stabilizing and excellent contrasting factors are the Moon in Virgo, and the powerful and very close conjunction between Mercury and Mars in Scorpio. Jupiter is also in that sign, and Venus in Sagittarius adds a nice, glowing fire element and is in delightful contrast to the Libran and Virgoan elements. Venus's placing is a powerful one, since it is both chart- and Sun-ruler.

Highlighted characteristics

Laura's independence and originality is marked by the Sun making a trine aspect to Uranus in the ninth house. There is an element of inhibition, since the long-term and potent Saturn conjunct Pluto in Leo squares her lively Mercury/Mars conjunction; however, the effect of this is two-way, for Laura is well in command and aware of the force of her emotionally charged Mars in Scorpio. Indeed, the conjunction as a whole is well-integrated, since Mercury is ruler of the Virgoan Moon.

The aspect grid

The progressions are dominated by the extremely stabilizing solar trines to the radical, or natal, and progressed position of Saturn. While these are no longer exact they are still operative.

In contrast to these, between 1989 and 1992 the Sun is also in aspect to

Neptune, radical and progressed, and the effects of these aspects will of course hover around for rather longer. The natal conjunction of Neptune to the Ascendant (p.332) – especially from Libra – may tend to weaken the personality. It is likely that with the strong Sun/Saturn link and the fact that the progression between the Sun and Neptune is a sextile (positive) aspect, Laura will progress psychologically and use her Neptune influences in an imaginative way. The minor quincunx between the progressed Mercury and natal Uranus adds originality, bright ideas and inventiveness. Remember that while this is a negative aspect, it is minor; Uranus is well-aspected in the natal chart and Mercury is a powerful planet for Laura. There will be tensions from time to time, especially when this progression is sparked into action by transits, but it is not a truly difficult progression.

Ideas for the future

The very long-term progression from Venus to the Mercury/Mars conjunction is fascinating and focuses beautifully on what Laura wants to do. The tiny semi-sextile progression from the Ascendant chimes in very well with the solar aspects to Neptune, while the Midheaven progression to Uranus supports the Mercury/Uranus progressions and highlights Laura's objectives and ideas for her future. The powerful progression from Mars to the progressed Uranus, exact in 1991, is extremely dynamic, but tricky; it may well need reassessing nearer the time of its exactitude. It could work very well or very strenuously for Laura.

The fact that Laura's progressed Moon is traveling through the sixth house is a good integrating link, since her natal Moon is in Virgo and the sixth house is the "Virgo" house

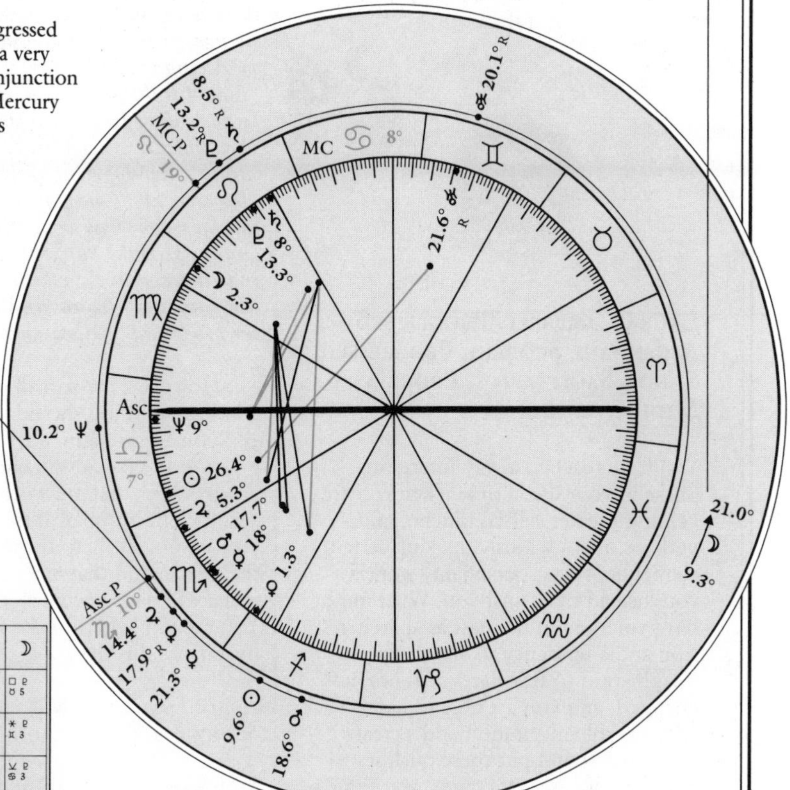

Here the progressed Venus makes a very long-term conjunction to the natal Mercury conjunct Mars

Year	Lunar: Month	Moon's Long	Aspects: To Natal	To Prog	Transits: ♇	♆	♅	♄	♃	♂	♀	☿	☉	☽
1989	MAY	♓ 9.3°	⚻ ♆	□ ☉	□ ♇		✶ ♃ 8	⚻ ♇ 27	△ ♆ 3 ✶ ♇ 18 20	☌ MC 13	☍ ☿ 1 ☍ ♂ ☍ ☿ 12 ☌ ♅ 29	☍ ♀ 1 ☍ ♀ 26		□ ♇ ♉ 5
	JUN	10.4°		⚻ ♆ △ Asc	4				⚻ ☿ 3–8 ⚻ ☌ ♅ 21–24	☌ ♄ 30	☌ MC 12	☍ ♀ 15	☌ MC 30	✶ ♇ ♊ 3
	JLY	11.4°					△ ☽ 4 31	□ ♆ 12 25 ☍ MC ⚻ ♄ 26	△ ☉ 13–16	☌ ♇ 8	☌ ♄ 6 ☌ ♇ 10 ☌ ☽ 26	☌ ♅ 1 ☌ MC 10 ☌ ♄ 24 ☌ ♇ 28		⚺ ♇ ♋ 3
	AUG	12.5°				□ ♆ 14		□ ♆ 12 13	⚻ ♀ 5-10 ✶ ☽ 11–15 △ ♃ 27	☌ ☽ 7–8	☌ Asc 24 ☌ ♆ 26	☌ ☽ 6	☌ ☽ 26	☌ ♄ ♌ 1 ⚺ Asc ♍ 29
	SEP	13.5°	⚻ ♇	⚻ ♇	□ ♇ 9				□ Asc 9-15 ☌ MC 16–24 □ ♆ 25		☌ ☉ 9 ☌ ♃ 17 ☌ ☿ 28	☌ Asc 3 ☌ ♆ 7 ☌ ♆ 17 ☌ Asc 20		☌ Asc ♎ 29
	OCT	14.6°			9	28	△ ☽ 20	10 ☍ MC ⚻ ♄ 11 27	5	☌ Asc 1 ☌ ♆ 4 ☌ ☉ 30	☌ ♀ 16 ☍ ♅ 28	☌ Asc 17 ☌ ♆ 18 ☌ ☉ 28	☌ Asc 1	⚺ Asc ♏ 29
	NOV	15.7°					13	□ ♆ 28 10	□ ♆ 22	☌ ♃ 12 ☌ ☿ 30 ☌ ♂ 30	☍ MC 14	☌ ♀ 10 ☌ ♂ ☌ ♀ 19	☌ ♀ 24	✶ Asc ♐ 28
	DEC	16.7°			☌ ☿ ☌ ♂ 29		✶ ♃ 20	⚻ ♇ 10 16	2 ☌ MC 3 10 □ Asc 11 18	☌ ♀ 20		☍ ♅ 2 ☍ MC 13		□ Asc ♑ 28
1990	JAN	17.8°	△ ☿ △ ♂	△ ♀		⚻ ♇ 28	□ Asc 4 23	✶ ☿ ✶ ♂ 13 21	△ ♃ 27 2 ✶ ☽ 19	☍ ♅ 18				△ Asc □ ♃ ♒ 26
	FEB	18.9°		□ ♂ ⚻ MC		28	10 ☍ MC 11 ⚻ ♄	⚻ ♅ 18 27	28 ⚻ ♀ 29 15	☍ MC 10		☍ ♄ 18 ☍ ♇ 21		⚻ Asc △ ♃ ♓ 25
	MAR	20°		□ ♅			□ ♆ 7 8		⚻ ♀ 8–24 ✶ ☽ 25	☍ ♄ 23 ☍ ♇ 30	☍ ♄ 15 ☍ ♇ 20	☍ ☽ 5 ☍ Asc 23 ☍ ♆ 24		☍ Asc ⚻ ♃ ♈ 26
	APL	21°	□ ♅	△ ☿	15				3 △ ♃ 19 26	☍ ☽ 24	☍ ☽ 9	☍ ☉ 2 ☍ ♃ 8 ☍ ☿ ♂ 20–27		☍ ♃ ♉ 25

NAME Laura Campbell

MIDNIGHT POSITIONS ON 2.12.46

REFERENCE NO. 378

CORRESPONDING TO 27.5.89

YEAR 1989–90

INSTALLMENT 2

Laura's progressed date

Laura's adjusted calculation date

This shows that this is the second time Julia has worked on Laura's chart in detail

Laura's birth time is accurate, and while the semi-sextile is a very minor progression, because the natal Ascendant conjuncts Neptune, its influence is increased

THE PROGRESSED ASPECTS

Natal Planets Numerical Order		Solar	Mutual		Asc MC
♀ 1.3	♐				
☽ 2.3	♍	☉ P △ ♄ R and P 1988–9	☿ P ⚻ ♅ R 1989–90	♂ P ☍ ♅ P 1991	Asc P ⚺ ♆ P 1989 – 90
♃ 5.3	♏				
7.01	♎	☉ P ✶ ♆ R 1989–90			MC P ✶ ♅ P 1990–1
♄ 8	♌		♀ P ☌ ☿ ♂ R 1989–2001		
8	♋				
♆ 9	♎	☉ P ✶ ♆ P 1991–2			
♇ 13.3	♌				
♂ 17.7	♏		♀ P ⚺ ♂ P 1989–90		
☿ 18	♏				
♅ 21.6	♊				
☉ 26.4	♎				

Because Mercury and Mars form such a close conjunction it is fair to calculate progressions and transits to them together

An especially long influence from the progressed Venus which turns from retrograde to direct motion on 17° of Scorpio, indicating a trend that will be operative for Laura for many years

The Interpretation

Here is an interpretation of Laura's progressed background conditions as interpreted from the aspects already described. Julia's comments, giving astrological reasons for her interpretations, are printed in italic.

Laura Campbell, Progressed Ascendant Scorpio, Progressed Sun in Sagittarius, Progressed Midheaven Leo.

You have reached a very interesting phase in your life, a time when you are gaining greater self-confidence and, perhaps unconsciously, making certain elements of your personality work for you instead of against you. What might have emerged in the past as apprehension and a tendency to allow your imagination to fear the worst, has now changed, and you are able to harness considerable inspiration and a creative imagination and put these qualities to constructive use. Of course, you came to terms with your personality many years ago, but there are times during all of our lives when we continue to take further steps forward. This is the case with you at the present time.

I am combining the powerful solar progressions to Saturn and Neptune.

Because of your increased self-confidence, you are now feeling the need to strike out on your own. Indeed, your intuition and instincts are suggesting that you should do so – these feelings coming, as they do, from really deep levels of your personality. With this and an element of independence, it is not surprising that you are at present having several really bright ideas concerning your future and, in particular, concerning your career. It seems as if you could very easily feel somewhat claustrophobic if you continue to work as a full-time art teacher – you need pastures new.

The progressed Sun is in Sagittarius – remember that Sagittarius always hates to feel claustrophobic!

It is interesting that you are in need of this change of direction, for while your long-term background progressions are strong and positive they do not indicate very drastic changes. . . .

This last statement speaks for itself up to a point, but what is interesting is that while Laura wants to make certain changes, there is no "milestone" indication of change, such as a progression of the Sun or Ascendant into a new sign, nor indeed is the Midheaven changing signs. All of Laura's ideas fall within the confines of her present interests and the development of those interests. However, all of the planets do show some change in one way or another, and in some respects the Sun/Saturn contact is indicative, as is the relationship between Mercury and Uranus and the direction of the progressed Midheaven to Uranus.

. . . However, the sort of developments you have in mind should work out well, and you are in many ways in an excellent position to take advantage of the progressions that are working for you. A sufficient number of trends show that you are not likely to throw caution to the winds, and that any changes you make will have been well considered. You are unlikely to make any serious mistake at this time.

Again I am using the strength of the Sun/Saturn contacts.

Your ideas for the future that you put to me are most interesting, and the accent on wanting to develop your screen printing, both to make it commercially viable and to start weekend workshops for those wishing to learn the technique, is excellent. All kinds of craft and creative work should flourish for you, and there is one trend starting for you at present that is going to be influencing you for more than the coming decade, showing that a project of the sort you have in mind could well be with you for that extremely long period of time. Your involvement and enthusiasm for such a project looks unlikely to fade.

This is the conjunction of Venus (double ruler) to the Mercury/Mars conjunction – a beautiful influence. Mercury and Venus often give flair for all kinds of craftwork, and as Mars is involved Laura has the energy and (because Mars is in Scorpio) the determination to make a go of it. The "station of Venus" shows the extreme length of the influence.

It may be that rather later on the pressures of your work could build up and become a problem. If so, be constantly on the lookout for any of the tell-tale signs of pressure, because you could become rather more tense than you may realize, and you could take on too much and not be able to relax.

This is an interpretation of the Mars opposition to Uranus, exact in 1991. At the time of writing it is a little difficult to assess the effect of this particular progression, but it is necessary to warn Laura. The progression might indeed work well for her, but there will almost inevitably be stress, especially when or if there are transits of a similar nature.

Your idea of writing a book about your screen-printing techniques is excellent, and looking at the short-term trends working for you during the coming 12 months, there are certainly times when you might care to present your ideas to a publisher. I will point these out in the monthly summaries. Meanwhile, make a lot of notes and maybe take photographs of your various products.

There are no long-term indications with a special bearing on your health, nor does it seem likely – from the examination of your chart only, of course – that either Roger or Bronwen will give rise to difficulties that cause you serious concern. Any short-term trends affecting them will be covered in the summaries.

Initially, I had some thoughts about the possiblity of interpreting the solar progressions to Neptune from a health standpoint because the Sun represents our vitality, and Neptune is in the first house. The progression does in some ways suggest some kind of health problem, but since I know Laura's chart fairly well, and remembering that Neptune conjunct the Ascendant always seems to affect the subject psychologically, especially when in Libra, I opted instead for the interpretation set out here.

The question of cash must surely arise if you decide to stop teaching full-time. Of course it will mean a smaller income, at least while you are getting started on your various projects. But because of the tenor of the trends working for you, you should be quite able to plan ahead with caution and common sense, and if necessary be able to take a philosophical attitude to this, and indeed, all other spheres of your life. You should be decisive and determined, and your projects should work well.

We now move on to the interpretation of the transits and lunar progressions, remembering the general influence of the long-term background progressions, and watching for points at which the two complement each other.

What I have written so far is an interpretation of the long-term background trends working for you. What follows is an interpretation of the influences of the planets as they move round the sky, and the relationships they make to the positions of the planets as they were when you were born.

On the whole, the transiting planets, as they are known, are fairly active, and I think you will discover that there are one or two times during the coming 12 months which will turn out, in retrospect, to be key periods for you.

The most important time period seems to be centered around January 1990, and I think you will discover just how the trends are going to work for you a few weeks before that time – perhaps even from close to the beginning of December. September 1989 could prove to be eventful, as could April 1990, but see the individual summaries of these months for the details.

In the indications for January, notice that the progressed Moon makes trine aspects to the Mercury/Mars conjunction and to the progressed position of Venus. This is homing in on that interesting very long-term progression. The results of this influence should prove to be dynamic, lively and interesting. I mention September because it is then that the progressed Moon is in contact with Pluto, and Pluto itself squares its own position: a negative trend. The month of April 1990 should be really excellent, for then the progressed Moon is in aspect (albeit a tense square) to the natal Uranus and makes a nice trine to the progressed Mercury – again emphasizing the background progressions.

THE MONTHLY SUMMARIES

May 1989

It may be that you could feel a little less certain of your position for a few weeks. If you have not as yet finally decided to leave your teaching post this may not be a particularly good time to commit yourself, unless for practical reasons you really have to. If this is the case you may need additional support from Roger to help you reach your decision. There may well be some side issue that has been causing a problem, and it could all too easily rear its head again at this time. The chances are that it may well go away after the first week of June, but final resolution is not likely for a while – only respite. The pace of your life at work is likely to speed up for a few days around the 13th. The first few days of May would be a good time to entertain, or arrange a family outing.

The uncertainty is likely because of the negative progressions from the Moon to Neptune and the Sun. The problem I refer to is a possible interpretation of the transit from Pluto to its own position, though this might be working on a more psychological level. The busy period mid-month is due to the Mars transit to the Midheaven, while the suggestion to arrange a family outing relates to the Venus and Mercury transits.

June 1989

The indications show that you will feel more positive. If you wish to make decisions about your future it might be as well to concentrate on these matters at present. The most enjoyable period of the month is likely to occur as a result of influences working for you between the 12th and the 15th or thereabouts – here are days on which to enjoy life thoroughly, expressing all your kind, loving and affectionate Libran qualities. During the last few days of June don't be afraid to tell those who matter what you want to do careerwise. The last day or so of June is a positive date for you in any year – one of four which are worth remembering and using to do anything you feel is worthwhile and memorable.

The transits for June are more positive, so Laura is in a stronger position all round. The enjoyable period relates to the Venus transits, and the solar transit to the Midheaven is also interpreted.

July 1989

Two themes are now working for you. One of the themes beautifully highlights your need for change, and supporting it is an extremely positive and progressive indication, a period during which you should in theory make excellent progress. However, it is possible that there may be some problems to clear up, and your way forward may not be as clear as you would like. An element of confusion is likely and there is also a possibility that someone might try to do you dirt in some way. It is possible that you might have to cope with some sort of an annoying delay. Patience will pay off, as will making quite certain that if you do have problems everything is well and truly above board. These somewhat negative trends are exact during the second half of the month, but remembering that positive indications are very active, it may be that I am tending to overinterpret the possible outcome of the negative indications. This looks as if it will be generally a very busy month for you, with many kinds of unrelated activities crying out for your attention all at the same time. Through them you could get a great deal of fun and pleasure.

The two main themes mentioned are the negative Saturn transits, countered by the lively Uranian trine to the Moon and the excellent Jupiter trine to the Sun. The fast-moving planets are likely to speed up the pace of Laura's life and act as an excellent diversion, especially if there are complications with important issues.

August 1989

It seems as if some of your plans and activities will make excellent progress, and there's a good chance that you will be experiencing a very rewarding time, especially as far as the development of your ideas and projects are concerned – though some indications similar to those for you last month suggest certain delays and complications. Could they relate to a totally different sphere of your life? That is possible. You will know by now how these trends are working. I can only repeat the warning I put forward in last month's summary. These themes are hovering around for a while, but should clear by the end of October. Do not feel downcast or apprehensive about them; any problem may not be constantly with you. If, for instance, it relates to a house repair, or even something infuriating like not getting a response from the manufacturer of a defective household product, you will find that it won't be the main focus of attention the whole time. Be patient – resolution will come. The busiest period of the month is likely to be toward the end of the first week, while time in which to enjoy yourself with Roger and Bronwen will be the last week of August. If you have to take your vacation this month because of the school holidays you might like to plan to go during the second half of the month, when as far as your chart is concerned the indications for travel are good (but we should, of course, also refer to Roger's chart!)

The contrasting trends from Neptune to its own position, and from Saturn to Neptune, are difficult to interpret. It may well be that Laura is perhaps unconsciously working particularly hard on the the basic influence that Neptune has had on her personality, and perhaps fighting some inner battle with herself to sort it out once and for all. On the other hand, trends such as this can very often focus on the kind of household confusion I've mentioned. I have known such instances when Neptune is busy – especially involving washing machines, the drains, the deep freeze, and so on. The positive indications are excellent for the general progress of her ideas. A family holiday could work well at this time, due to the Jupiter influence and the lively little trends from the fast-moving planets.

September 1989

While both progressive and confusing indications can still be seen in your chart, it will be as well for you to concentrate on making good use of the positive indications. If possible you should try to concentrate on ideas for your book and the workshop. Constructive plans made now could work out very well later on. You may find that there are some career developments in store: an interesting trend which is exact for you now, and again later on (toward the end of the year) could result in your being on the receiving end of a very interesting offer. I don't think I am overinterpreting the trend, and since we do not and cannot predict events, consider my comments as only a possibility to bear in mind. In spite of the more confusing negative indications shown this month I think that this will be in many ways a very interesting time for you; a great deal of planetary energy is working in your favour, and it will act as an excellent counter to any negative indications.

The lunar aspects to Pluto, plus Pluto making a transit to its own place, and the ongoing Neptune square to its own position are mixed indications, but the strength of the Jupiter transits, especially the conjunction to the Midheaven, are excellent. The fast-moving planets are extremely active; those tiny influences will add considerable liveliness to the month as a whole.

October 1989

There is a great deal of planetary activity working for you this month. Overall your mood should be energetic, but during the first few days of October a tendency to be overhasty could very easily cause you to be slightly accident-prone. You should consciously slow down, and take special care when driving, working with sharp tools or handling hot dishes.

After a certain amount of frustration and perhaps annoyance, feeling that projects aren't moving forward as quickly as you would like, it seems likely that by the end of October you should be progressing quite well. But remember that – as was the case earlier in the month – a sense of urgency might cause you to act impulsively; try to curb this. There is a return of an influence that was exact for you during July, so you could well see the finalization of plans laid then. A cluster of minor influences around the middle of the month will offer the opportunity to enjoy life socially, and if you are thinking about making a purchase of some kind (perhaps a new outfit?) this would be a good time to visit your favorite boutique. Venus is involved, so a specially pampering beauty treatment or a new hairstyle wouldn't come amiss. Incidentally, 1 October is, in any year, a rather special day for you. Think of it as a kind of "unbirthday" – a day to use, on which to do something special or to start some kind of new work project.

There are some heavy transits from Saturn, and a return of the Uranus contact to the Moon. These form the most important influences of the month. Mars is very active, especially while conjunct the Ascendant on the 1st. The jolly influences from Mercury and Venus, mid-month, add lightness and a good opportunity for Laura to take up my suggestions about fashion and beauty.

I never use any technicalities in reports of this kind, but everyone knows that Venus represents beauty (and this is such a powerful planet for Laura) so a light-hearted comment adds a nice contrasting touch, especially when there are rather heavy influences working in a contrary manner. The reference to 1 October is to the solar transit to Laura's Ascendant.

November 1989

Very gradually as the month gets under way, the pattern of your life could become a little more settled, and you will, I think, be in a strong position from the middle of the month, when you should perhaps take the initiative. If there's something you want or something you feel isn't right, speak up – but only when you are really sure of your ground, for a tendency to act prematurely might otherwise work against you. Don't ignore details, especially if by chance you find you have to sign a contract. During the last few days of November you may get a hint of some new developments that are likely to come more clearly into focus a little later on. These could well have financial overtones.

Astronomically, some trends end this month. The action from Mars to Jupiter could be helpful. The suggestion of new developments is taken from the contacts from Mars to the Mercury/ Mars conjunction. I attach a certain importance to it since later there is a very long transit of Pluto to that conjunction. I mention finance because the conjunction falls in Laura's second house, and Pluto often has an influence on finance.

December 1989

There are several really very good indications working for you this month – indeed, it may be that you will make extremely good progress, and that new developments could very easily have financial overtones. However, I do not think that these will really make their presence felt until just after Christmas, when life could become very eventful. The influences should work very positively for you, especially if some new business project is a possibility – certainly there is a possible emphasis on finance. The trend is exact for you between 29 December and mid-April 1990. You should have an enjoyable and interesting Christmas and New Year.

Notice that Laura has another transit of Jupiter to her Midheaven and Ascendant. Just as important, Pluto conjuncts her Mercury/Mars conjunction in Scorpio. The conjunction is ruled by Pluto, and the planet is stationary on it. This is an important trend and has terrific back-up from some positive Saturn transits next month and some excellent lunar progressions which also contact the progressed Venus. This surely is a key period for

Laura and will probably be very eventful. The nice trine transit of Jupiter to its own position, at the end of December, adds another positive trend. Notice that I mention some specific dates. I can do this because Pluto is usually easy to time (see p.343). However, Pluto doesn't usually make life really easy, so it is important not to be overoptimistic in interpretation – now read on!

January 1990

The trends this month increase in strength, and it looks very much as if you will be experiencing a key period when a great deal will happen. You should make excellent progress, and when you later look back on this period you will certainly see why. But be cautious, and while you will probably be quite right to think that good progress is being made, be prepared for some delays or frustrations which may at the time be irritating, but which could, again in retrospect, turn out to be all to the good. It won't be surprising if you feel pretty tense at times, and you may not sleep as well as usual.

This is a time at which to control any immediate or emotionally impulsive response to situations. By all means listen to and follow up hunches or intuitions, but control the emotional flow – particularly if you are feeling impatient. You will then be channeling a great deal of positive, emotional energy and making it work for and not against you. If you are very busy, try to make quite sure you take time out to enjoy Bronwen's company and interests, since if business developments occupy most of your time and energy, she could feel rather left out of things. This is particularly so if any new venture is a joint one between you and Roger.

The caution is due to the Saturn transits. These trends are positive – hence my comment that any delay should prove worthwhile in retrospect. It is also important to remember that Pluto is somewhat unpredictable, even when working positively. While interpreting Pluto's influence on the Mercury/Mars conjunction jointly, if we look at the basic interpretation of each planet it is not difficult to see that Pluto is working very powerfully indeed for Laura. Again, the influence should work out well, but because so many factors are involved – the emotional level relating to Mars and the second house plus Scorpio – it is fair to advise caution and control.

February 1990

Similar themes continue to work for you, but to maintain good progress you should still heed my warning about controlling impulsiveness. Keep your cool and be patient (though this will be difficult, even for a double Libra, since the planetary energy is rather too strong for such an attitude; nevertheless, try!)

There is very little change in the indications working for Laura during February. The lunar progressions will still be operative, and are given a boost (as is her tendency to be impulsive) by the square to the progressed Mars. The new transits follow a similar theme – of progress plus impatience and an element of frustration.

March 1990

Along with a continuation of existing influences, a new trend accentuates careful thought and circumspection. You may well feel yourself under greater pressure than may actually be the case. There is a possiblity of a certain amount of confusion for you, and someone else may be able to see the situation more clearly – thus assisting you to see the wood through the trees. Overall, I think the main stream of events will work out very well for you, and whatever goes on could easily be extremely exciting; but do consider every move very carefully. The last week of March should prove the most progressive.

The progressed Moon makes a square to the progressed Uranus. Circumspection is all-important. A square transit from Uranus to Neptune starts on the 8th. This is not easy: Laura could have a tricky time for a few weeks. But it does seem that she will come through well and achieve what she wants. She's had transits of Jupiter over her Midheaven, and the constructive energy of her background solar progressions to Saturn should be very stabilizing.

April 1990

It is likely that by mid-April you will be in a good position, and any growing pains or problems relating to projects or business developments will have been eased or resolved: you will feel satisfied with what you have achieved. There are some lively indications working for you for the next two or three months, and it is good to be able to end on a positive note. You really could be taking off. . . .

The indications for April are good. The long Pluto transit eases, and the conditions relating to this transit will ease almost to the day. There is also an excellent lunar progresion to the progressed Mercury (Mercury rules the natal Moon), and the excellent trine transit from Jupiter to its own position recurring for the third time – yet another culmination.

The New Moons

On the large grid (see p.143) the last column refers to "New Moons", and marks tiny relationships that the New Moon makes to the positions of some of the planets when you were born. The number in each square shows the date of the New Moon. During the 12-month period I am covering the influence of the New Moon seems to chime in well with the short-term trends interpreted above. If you wish to use these dates to start any new work, do so. Then from August to the end of the year the New Moon will work on a more personal level, helping you integrate your instincts and reactions with your personality. During the early months of 1990 the New Moon's influence could relate to your general progress, so it might be good to use these dates if you have moves to make that could affect your ideas and projects.

As I had not mentioned the New Moons in the interpretation of each month I decided to cover them in this way. I have not interpreted every indication. This would make the report impossibly long. It is best to be selective, trying to achieve some kind of cohesion – difficult though this often is. It is also extremely difficult to know precisely which line of interpretion to take, because every trend can be viewed in a variety of ways. Assess your subject's lifestyle carefully and try to discover the apposite area or sphere of life before you start your interpretation.

***Note:** It is extremely important for your subjects to learn to assess the outcome of trends for themselves. When a trend recurs they may well know the area of their life that was affected the first time. Encourage them to take notes on your interpretations, so that between you, you build up information on how the planets work for them. They must note how accurate or otherwise you have been in the timing of trends, especially if the birth time is uncertain. You will then become more accurate in the assessment of influences, and could even arrive at a very precise Ascendant. The influence of Mars is extremely useful – if someone cuts themself two days after you gave them a warning, there's a good chance that their Ascendant is a degree further on from the one you arrived at!*

Relationships

This fascinating and important branch of astrology is known as "synastry". Basically it is the comparison of two people's charts to assess compatibility in any or all areas of their personalities and lifestyles. The conclusions will help them reassess their relationship if it runs into difficulties, or, if the couple are thinking about deepening a new relationship in some way, perhaps with a view to marriage, it will help them look at their respective partners more objectively.

Synastry is not applied simply to emotional relationships. It is quite common for an astrologer to give advice to two or more people forming, or already involved in, a business partnership. Sometimes, for a variety of reasons, two friends may require a synastry report. Synastry is also widely used when assessing the vital and very sensitive relationship between parents and children, but that particular area of the technique we deal with in the section on the family (see pp.168–71).

Seeking reassurance

The first question to ask yourself when someone requests a piece of synastry is why they actually need it – indeed, this is an excellent starting point for all astrological work. Very often one partner needs reassurance because they are uncertain whether a relationship should be further developed. It is a good general rule to assess the subject's chart with this in mind – decide just how forthright and decisive they are when not at a crossroads in their life. Ask yourself whether a lack of good judgement is shown in their chart. Are they inhibited or fearful of love or sex, or lacking in self-confidence when it comes to making any kind of commitment? Most importantly, are they trying to use you as a prop – a surrogate mother/father figure who will tell them what to do? If so, will they want this kind of support from their partner in an emotional or working relationship?

Impartiality and ethics

Whatever the nature of the relationship, it is essential that you do not make up people's minds for them. Impartiality is of prime importance. Sometimes, too, a question of ethics arises. This is very often the case where there is an eternal triangle. The injured wife, for instance, will approach an astrologer with her own, her husband's and his girlfriend's data. (Astrologers down the ages have been confronted with the question "Will he come back to me?") You carry a special responsibility in such a case, for it is unlikely that the husband will know anything of the consultation. Discretion and tact are of prime importance.

However, often the partner requesting the work will want it directed at themself only. Try to encourage joint participation, either by preparing a written report addressed to both partners or suggesting a joint consultation/counseling session. In this way a better balance is achieved, and you can encourage better communication between the partners – something that may have been lacking and may even have been at the root of the difficulty. By involving both partners it is possible to achieve a fuller awareness of contrasting personality traits, which will result in greater give and take in the relationship. If only one partner is involved you can only directly help that partner, who will interpret your findings on the other partner subjectively.

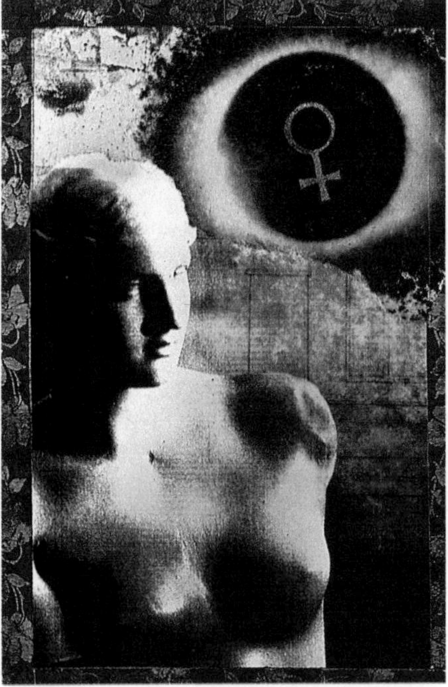

Venus represents love and affection, as well as the way we feel about our possessions.

Recognizing limitations

Sadly, there is all too often a lack of full birth data, and our work is therefore limited. If this is the case, point out to your subject that there is no all-important Ascendant or Midheaven to blend into the interpretation, and that there can also be doubt about the Moon's sign, should it have changed signs on the birth date, and that while you can be of some help, that help will necessarily be limited.

Synastry and Popular Astrology

The general public has it fixed in its head that certain signs go well together and others are badly matched. This generalization simply does not work. The theory is linked to the elements and makes excellent fodder for a popular magazine article, but many people take what is written too seriously: we have heard young people say "I can't go with him – he's an Aries and I'm a Taurus." That's nonsense!

There is an element of truth in the theory that those of the same Sun sign element tend to get on well together as friends, but it is only when the full birth charts of both people have been calculated and interpreted that any real conclusions can be reached about a more serious relationship. Even then, no astrologer ought to say that one person should or should not form a relationship with another – that would be quite wrong and unethical.

What is needed in a compatible relationship if it is going to work is:

- Rapport.
- Good communication.
- Sympathy.
- Empathy.
- Tolerance.
- Give and take.

THE PLANETS

There are specific areas of a birth chart that will show how people react in partnership. Having looked at these in both of the charts you have before you, you can then begin to compare them and come to your conclusions about how the two people will relate to one another, concentrating on the areas of life in which they will be joined. For instance, there is no need to spend too much time and energy working out how the partners will react to parenthood when they are about to open a business – although, interestingly, you should think of that business as their baby!

First, remember that the planets represent the same principles in this area of astrology as in all kinds of general interpretation, so refer to pp.208-347 to guide you through your study of this branch of astrology as well as all others.

To recap and realign the principles to synastry, you may find that the following notes are helpful:

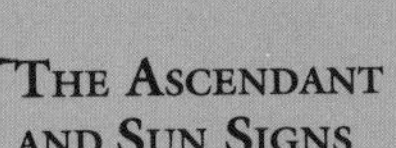

THE ASCENDANT AND SUN SIGNS represent our personalities. From them you will be able to assess temperament and, in particular, tolerance – both vitally important in all kinds of relationships.

THE MOON represents our instincts, reactions and responses to all situations. In synastry, the Moon will tell you how your subject responds to the other partner – this will help you assess how moody or changeable the partners will be when relating to each other.

MERCURY represents our mind, intellect and powers of communication. In synastry, concentrate on each partner's ability to communicate their thoughts, ideas and feelings.

VENUS represents love and affection – and also possessions. These are very closely linked, especially in synastry. If love is withdrawn by one partner, the other will often claim as much as possible of their joint material possessions. Many upsets between partners have financial implications. Some people tend to think of a partner as "theirs".

MARS represents our physical energy – the "get up and go" element in business partnerships, the sexual urge in emotional ones. Whoever has the most powerful Mars may well dominate the sexual side of an emotional relationship. Sexual fulfillment and rapport are often shown by the relationship between the two Mars in the joint charts, but at its best also needs intervention from Venus.

JUPITER represents expansion in general astrology – here, how one partner will help open up life for the other, and the element of challenge in the relationship. The planet also shows how encouragement, joint enthusiasms and intellectual growth develop as a result of one partner becoming involved in the other's interests.

SATURN signifies limitation, control and stability – all are well represented in chart comparison. The Saturn influence between charts will be revealing, especially if Saturn makes a powerful aspect to the Sun, Ascendant or personal planets of the other. Sometimes Saturn in one is seen as a kind of destiny or "hand of fate". This is rather archaic, but not without relevance.

URANUS, with its associations of disruption and change, is often active at either end of a dynamic love affair. While it brings about magnetic attraction, its influence is not to be trusted, unless it is a personal planet – and even then proceed with caution, since it is a potential source of tension.

NEPTUNE, the romantic mystical planet, takes us up to cloud nine. It can bring great happiness but also cause misunderstandings and deceit, throwing a relationship totally out of balance as a result.

PLUTO helps us sort out psychological problems. When it is operative in this area of astrology it will influence the ability of those concerned to sort out their problems, and help them put their relationship on a new footing. At best it acts as a probe, but there will be cases where its action causes a total blockage of progress – either in communication or advancement of the relationship.

Note: *Uranus, Neptune and Pluto stay in each same sign for a long time, and it is likely that these planets will fall in the same signs in both charts. Unless one or more is personal for one partner their influence must not be over emphasized.*

All these can be assessed from the birth chart. There is also the question of contrasting characteristics, and it is important that weaknessess shown in one partner's chart should emerge in the other's as strengths. For instance, it seems a good idea if one partner is basically introverted and the other extroverted. In certain cases this will work quite well and – again, in certain cases – the introvert partner will function to the best of his or her potential within the security that such an arrangement brings. But it is not that simple, for the extrovert could be domineering and crush the introvert, causing that person to retreat further into a psychological shell. An extrovert can, in different circumstances, try to push a shy, self-conscious partner into the limelight, and such action may cause considerable damage.

In spite of all this, some excellent contrasts of this type often show up in successful business partnerships – one partner may be quite happy to be working behind the scenes, perhaps poring over the books, while the other is out and about seeing clients, selling or making contacts.

THE HOUSES

The seventh house

This is the most important area of the chart when interpreting how your subject will relate to other people. The sign on the cusp of the seventh house is an important clue, and the influence of any planet or planets within this house is also extremely important. Do not be concerned if there are no planets in the house – the sign itself is an excellent guide. It is, of course the polar, or opposite, sign to the Ascendant. Here the subject's needs and requirements from a partner are present. It is almost uncanny how clearly people respond to their most intimate partners in the manner of this sign, though this form of expression will be apparent only (and we do mean only!) to the partners themselves. Other people, even quite close friends and certainly relatives, will be totally unaware of these reactions.

For instance, someone with Pisces rising will of course have all the personality traits of Pisces, but within the context of his or her closest partnership an extremely Virgoan reaction will emerge. The sensitivity and tender, emotional attributes of Pisces will be qualified by a sharply critical attitude, of which only the most intimate partners will be aware.

Look out for this indication in your own chart and that of your partner – it is perhaps one of the most fascinating theories of this area of astrology. Describe it to your subjects and you will certainly make them sit up – simply because this attitude is apparent only in the most intimate of situations!

The fifth house

This is the house of love affairs. It is also the house of risk taking. Every love affair that is embarked upon contains an element of risk. Here the risks are emotional. Will the people involved get hurt? Will love be equal on both sides, or will one partner want more from the relationship than the other? Will the affair last, or will it be just one of those things? Astrologically speaking, will the relationship progress from the fifth to the seventh house?

All these questions concern fifth house matters. This is also the house of creativity, which in this case can relate to our attitude towards children (as opposed to parenthood, which is more a fourth house matter).

The second and eighth houses

These are the houses of money and possessions, but they also have a say in each partner's attitude towards sexual expression and the flow of emotion. Because of the financial implications, these houses are, like the Midheaven, very important when it comes to business relationships.

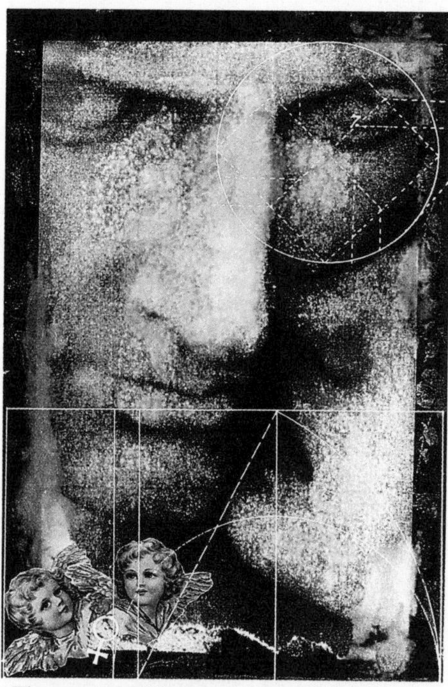

There are specific areas of a birth chart that will show how people react in a partnership.

The fourth house

This is the house of family, home and domesticity. It shows how settled we want to be, what our attitude is towards family life and our feelings about parenthood.

OTHER FACTORS

The polarities

You will find that in many charts you compare there is an emphasis on polar, or opposite, signs. For instance, partner C's Sun is in Taurus while partner D's Ascendant is Scorpio. While there is often an aspect formed between these two and similar elements, it is very useful indeed to compare the sign polarity, even if the planets or angles concerned are not in aspect. Such a polarity will most certainly add strength and permanence to any relationship between two people and therefore should not be ignored. It is important to remember, though, that the influence is naturally much stronger if these features of the charts are in aspect. However, it is advisable to apply this technique only to Ascendants, Midheavens, Suns, Moons and ruling planets.

The elements and qualities

The strengths of the elements (or triplicities) and qualities (or quadruplicities) in individual charts can be used in synastry. They will add yet another factor to help you judge compatibility between partners.

The Midheaven

This is relevant because it represents our identification of aspirations and ambitions and the attitudes we have towards them. You will find that if planets from one chart make aspects to the Midheaven of the other chart, then this is an excellent indication. It is especially important in business relationships (see p.166).

SYNASTRY AND PROGRESSIONS

Very often a relationship begins when the need for or possibility of one is indicated in an individual's chart. For instance, when:

◆ The progressed Sun, Ascendant or ruling planet makes an aspect to the natal or progressed position of Venus, or vice versa.

◆ The progressed Venus makes an aspect to the natal Moon. (The progressed Moon making an aspect to the natal or progressed Venus would be operative only for a few weeks, and while such a trend might put the subject "in the mood for love", unless the Moon is the chart ruler or in Cancer these indications may not be powerful enough.)

◆ There is a transit of Uranus or Neptune to the natal Venus (although if it is a square or opposition the subject could have difficulties).

However, it is necessary to examine the positions of one partner's progressed chart in relation to the other partner's natal and progressed planets. Very often at the start of a new relationship partner C's progressed Ascendant, Sun, Venus or Mars will be in aspect to partner D's Ascendant (and the cusp of the seventh house), Sun, Venus, Mars, Uranus or Neptune. Or there will be an aspect showing the attraction, developing friendship or business potential of the partners. All indications like this are excellent, but in order for such a relationship to last there must be indications joining the respective birth charts, for this will show long-lasting rapport.

What to look for

If there are only a few joint aspects and house positions this does not necessarily mean that a relationship will be unrewarding or dead. It will work well in the areas emphasized by those aspects and planets' positions which are present. (See the interpretation of planets in synastry, pp.154-5.)

The strongest link is an exact opposition between one partner's Sun and the other's Ascendant. In really good relationships we often find this present to the same degree. For instance, if one partner's Ascendant is Libra 22°, the other partner's Sun falls on Aries 22°. Sun opposition Sun is also excellent.

When there is an emphasis on one sign (i.e. shared Ascendants, Sun or Moon signs) the people concerned share the characteristics of that sign on either the Sun, Moon or Ascendant level of their personalities. There is a risk that one partner may grow to dislike or become intolerant of what is seen as the other partner's faults, since consciously or unconsciously she recognizes them in herself. The comment, under stress, may be "We are too much alike".

ASSESSING RELATIONSHIPS

The panel on this page suggests questions that you can ask. Having sorted out the answers, you will be well equipped to cope with your couple when they come and see you, or if you write a report or make a tape for them.

SYNASTRY QUESTIONS AND ANSWERS

Here are some basic questions to ask yourself. Is either partner:

Q Jealous?

A Scorpio, strong Pluto.

Q Freedom-loving?

A Aquarius, Sagittarius, Aries, strong Uranus or Jupiter.

Q Extravagant?

A Leo, strong Venus or Jupiter.

Q Mean?

A Capricorn, Virgo, Cancer with no Leo planets, strong Saturn.

Q Possessive or clinging?

A Taurus, Cancer, strong Venus or Moon.

Q Resentful?

A Libra, Cancer.

Q Very emotional?

A Prominently fire or water signs.

Q Highly sexed and passionate?

A Aries, Scorpio, strong Mars.

Q Very cool and distant?

A Sun, Moon or Venus in Capricorn or Aquarius.

Q Obsessively disciplined?

A Virgo, Capricorn, Scorpio.

Q Overtalkative, gossipy?

A Gemini, Virgo – powerful Mercury.

Q Eager to have children?

A Cancer, Taurus, Capricorn; powerful Moon.

If the answer to any of these questions is yes, you must decide how the other partner will cope with the characteristics shown. Then ask yourself the following, and the answers to these points will give you most of your answers:

Q Do they have compatible personalities?

A Compare respective Sun, Ascendant, Moon and ruling planet.

Q Will there be sympathy and understanding?

A Compare respective Moon and Venus.

Q Do they have a similar attitude towards money (a frequent cause of clashes)?

A Compare second and eighth houses and Venus, also Pluto by house position, Midheaven.

Q How sexually compatible are the partners?

A Compare respective Venus, Mars and Uranus.

Q Have they decided or discussed how many children they wish to have, if any?

A Compare respective Sun, Moon, fourth and fifth houses.

Q What about careers/work?

A Compare Midheaven, sixth house and respective charts as a whole.

Q What are their shared interests and how well will they adapt to each other's views of them?

A Compare respective fifth house and elements.

CHALLENGE

These lists of questions are reasonably comprehensive, but it would be useful to see if you can devise some additional questions for your own use. When you are doing so, bear in mind the sort of relationship the couple will be sharing. Here we are covering mostly emotional relationships, but there will be different questions you can ask for friendships, business relationships, etc.

Chart Comparision: Synastry

Chart comparison is a very rewarding area of study, but a lot of careful work is necessary before you can reach any firm conclusions: you must consider all possible indications that will color the relationship. The charts can be compared in two ways – either by placing all the information within the circle of one chart (opposite page), when the joint aspects are easily seen, or by placing the second set of information in a circle surrounding the first (this page).

1 Drawing up the Charts
Make sure that you draw up your two charts on forms that have an additional circle outside that of the birth chart – the progressed chart is ideal. (Do not bother to enter minutes or decimal places alongside the planets' positions; the degree is adequate.) At this point you have two charts of people who want to deepen a particular relationship. You have studied their individual charts; now you must bring their charts together.

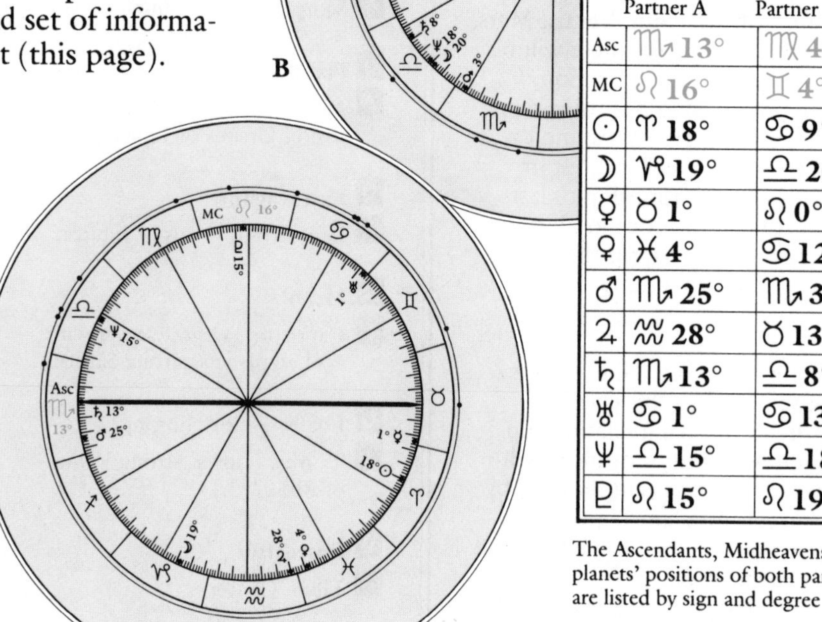

	Partner A	Partner B
Asc	♏ 13°	♍ 4°
MC	♌ 16°	♊ 4°
☉	♈ 18°	♋ 9°
☽	♑ 19°	♎ 20°
☿	♉ 1°	♌ 0°
♀	♓ 4°	♋ 12°
♂	♏ 25°	♏ 3°
♃	♒ 28°	♉ 13°
♄	♏ 13°	♎ 8°
♅	♋ 1°	♋ 13°
♆	♎ 15°	♎ 18°
♇	♌ 15°	♌ 19°

The Ascendants, Midheavens and planets' positions of both partners are listed by sign and degree

2 Listing Signs
Make a list of each partner's Ascendant, Midheaven, Sun and Moon signs, the signs of all the planets and the degree of the sign they occupy. Again, you need not bother with the minute or decimal place.

3 Combining the Charts
Take your original drawings of the two birth charts and place one partner's Ascendant, Midheaven and planets' positions in the outer circle of the other partner's chart. Do this also to the second chart. From this exercise you can see how the planets relate to each other in terms of their house positions, and it will also make it easier for you to recognize the joint aspects.

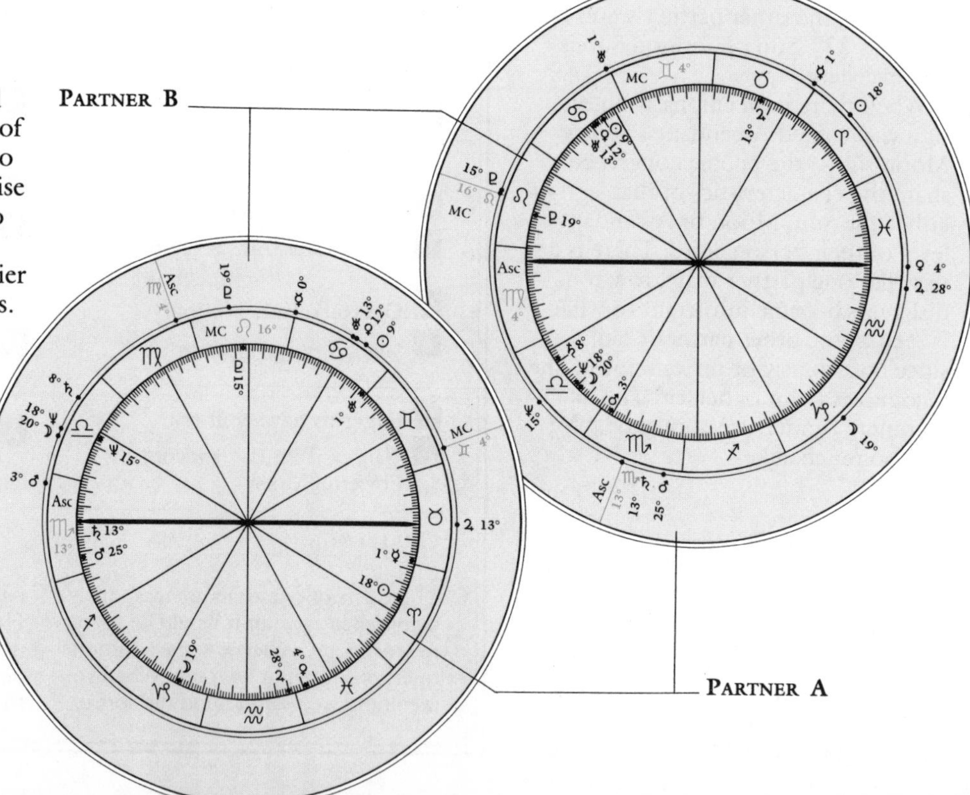

Comparing Two Charts
Each partner's planets are placed around the zodiac wheel, with the other partner's planets placed in the outside circle. Note the respective house positions: for instance, partner B's full second house is also tenanted by partner A's Neptune, and it is opposed by A's Sun. A's Moon is in B's fifth house – a romantic link. Secrecy and deception could be a problem, which is suggested by B's Moon, Mars and Neptune falling in A's twelfth house, and A's Midheaven and Pluto falling in B's twelfth house.

THE COMBINED CHARTS
The chart below may look complicated but you will find it very useful to show the ease, stresses and strains of the combined planetary positions. Draw each partner's glyphs in a different color. Once you have worked out the aspects, remember that as you draw the aspect lines (again using two colors, one for the oppositions and squares, another for the trines and sextiles) you should link a glyph of one color to one of the other color. If you find yourself joining two glyphs of the same color, you will be placing an aspect line which is operative in one partner's chart without making the necessary cross-reference. It is not really possible to draw in any aspects from one partner's planets to the Ascendant or Midheaven of the other partner – you must be observant, or refer again to your aspect grid.

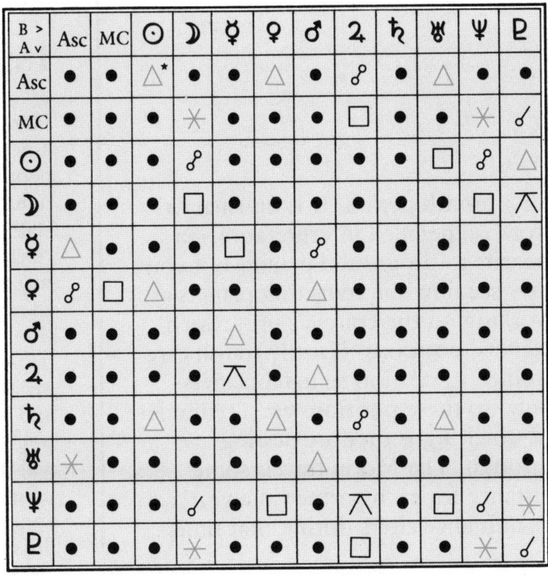

B > A v	Asc	MC	☉	☽	☿	♀	♂	♃	♄	♅	♆	♇
Asc	●	●	△*	●	●	△	●	☍	●	△	●	●
MC	●	●	●	⚹	●	●	●	□	●	●	⚹	☌
☉	●	●	●	☍	●	●	●	●	●	□	☍	△
☽	●	●	●	□	●	●	●	●	●	●	□	⚻
☿	△	●	●	●	□	●	☍	●	●	●	●	●
♀	☍	□	△	●	●	●	△	●	●	●	●	●
♂	●	●	●	●	△	●	●	●	●	●	●	●
♃	●	●	●	●	⚻	●	△	●	●	●	●	●
♄	●	●	△	●	●	△	●	☍	●	△	●	●
♅	⚹	●	●	●	●	●	△	●	●	●	●	●
♆	●	●	●	☌	●	□	●	⚻	●	□	☌	⚹
♇	●	●	●	⚹	●	●	●	□	●	●	⚹	☌

THE ASPECT GRID
*This synastry aspect grid will help you to see the aspects more clearly. It will also help you to work them out in a systematic fashion, thus ensuring that none are omitted. The grid shows all the aspects formed between the two charts. (*Note that A's Ascendant makes a trine aspect to B's Sun.)*

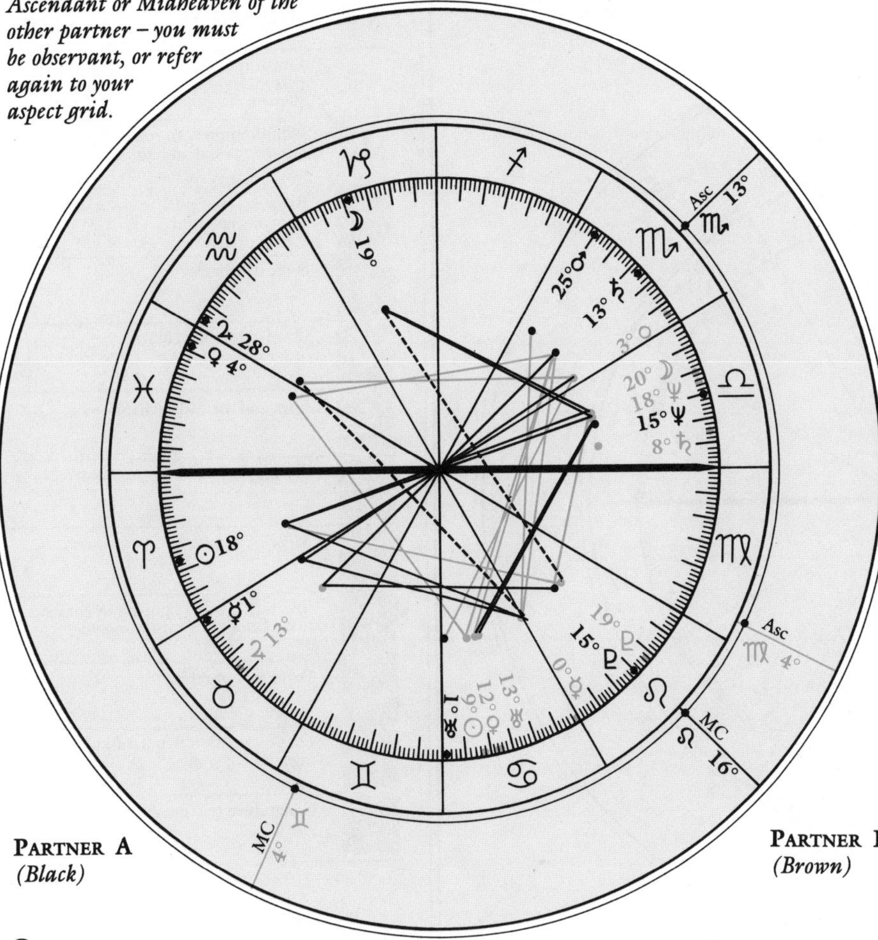

PARTNER A
(Black)

PARTNER B
(Brown)

CHALLENGE

Look up each aspect in these sample charts, and work out a full interpretation. Make up your own case history before you start – inventing the circumstances that have led to the decision for the couple to consult you. You can give your imagination free rein, so long as you also use your practical skills as an astrologer!

4 RELATING THE POSITIONS
Draw a grid and take each of partner A's positions and relate them to partner B's, noting where there are aspects between the two. (Do not use semi-sextiles or sesquares.) Allow an orb of not more than 5° for all major aspects, and no more than 2° for the quincunx or semi-square. For instance, A's Ascendant is on 13° Scorpio. B's Sun is on 9° Cancer: a trine aspect between the Sun and Ascendant. As you do this, be careful not to miss an all-important aspect.

INTERPRETING THE CHARTS

Partner A's Venus occupies the precise position on the cusp of the seventh house in partner B's chart, so is in exact opposition aspect to the Ascendant: a positive indication, showing love and understanding, and adding sympathy. B's Jupiter lies in the same position and makes the same relationship to A's Ascendant, indicating that this partner will help open up life and experience for the other, and give encouragement. B's Neptune is in opposition to A's Sun and Moon, indicating romance – but also possible misunderstandings and confusion. The opposition between Mercury (A) and Mars (B) and the square between Sun (A) and Uranus (B) shows tension.

The most important joint aspects between these two charts (listing A's planets first) are:

Venus opposition Ascendant +
Ascendant opposition Jupiter +
Ascendant trine Sun +
Sun opposition Moon +
Sun opposition Neptune –
Moon square Moon –
Mercury square Mercury –
Ascendant trine Venus and Uranus –
Sun square Uranus –
Saturn opposition Jupiter –
Midheaven square Jupiter –

The remaining squares show potential strain, but could add strength and drive, while trines and sextiles unlisted will add flexibility and ease. Most oppositions give rapport, but here the opposition between the Sun and Neptune is negative, probably leading to misunderstandings and confusion.

An Additional Technique

This is another technique for comparing birth charts. Take a chart form and in the inner circle place one partner's progressed Ascendant, Midheaven and progressed planets' positions. In the outer circle, place the same positions for the other partner. You may draw a circle outside the second and place in this the positions of the transiting slow-moving planets (i.e. Jupiter to Pluto inclusive) and the distance they travel in degrees during, for instance, a 12-month period. It is unusual to work on detailed interpretations of transits to progressed planets but you may see how the transiting planets are working on the couple's progressed planets' positions. Usually transits are studied in relation to natal planets only, so these positions are a reminder of which signs they are passing through. The Moon travels some distance for each partner in a year, so its influence alters during that time.

A Combined Progressed Chart
This chart will give you a clear view of the couple. The influences relate to the present and not their personalities, which are shown in their birth charts. When working out progressed aspects you can, if you think it will help you, draw a combined progressed chart in the same manner as the chart on p.153. But if you draw aspect lines between the couple's planets you must allow only 1° of orb at most. If 5° are allowed the influences will not be operative at that time – they could be over by several years, or still a long way in the future. You can also ignore any joint aspects between Jupiter, Saturn, Uranus, Neptune and Pluto, which are more than likely to be present in your subjects' birth charts.

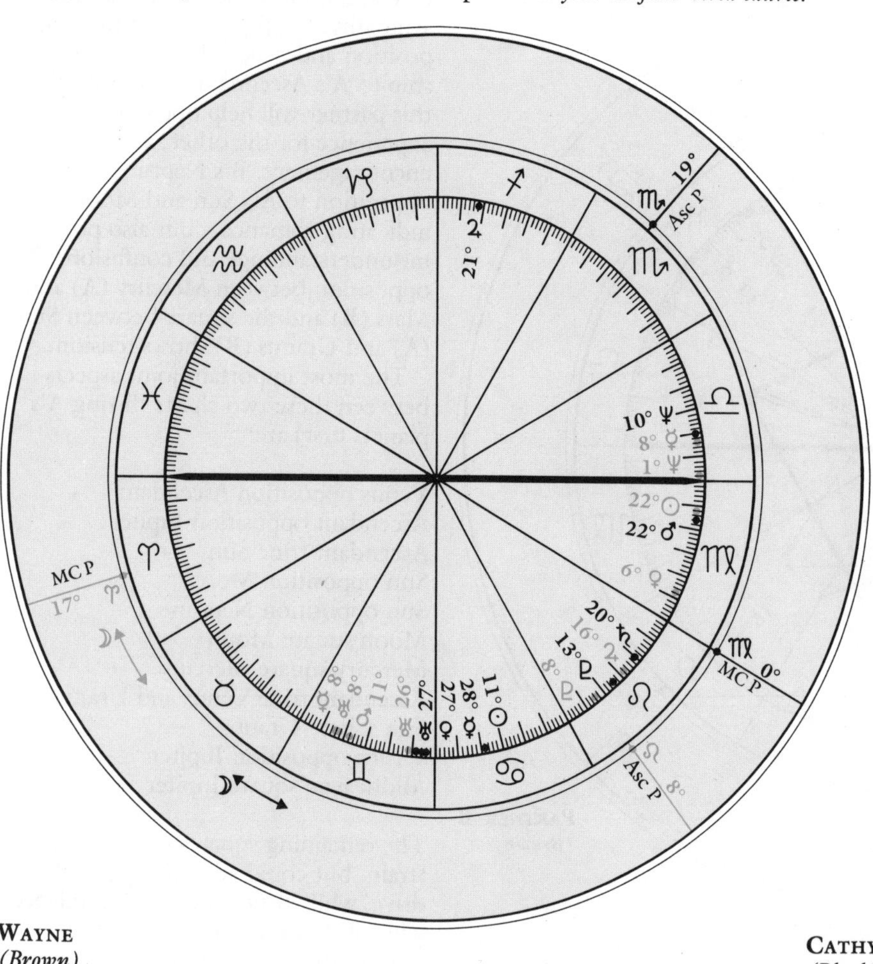

Wayne
(Brown)

Cathy
(Black)

Interpreting Aspects

Here is a brief interpretation of every aspect that can be formed between two peoples' charts. Many of the interpretations give positive and negative statements. Usually the positive ones refer to trines and sextiles, and the negative to squares; but it is important to remember that very often oppositions make for increased rapport between people. This does not necessarily mean that they will entirely and invariably agree, or be willing to give way to each other, but there will be mutual understanding, and excellent feedback within situations concerning the planets or spheres of life involved.

Where there is only one interpretation, you can assume that there is no contrasting influence, unless, having studied the two charts in detail, you think that the planets involved are a potential source of strain or trouble, or the reverse, between your couple.

Asc	**Ascendant**
Asc	Empathy and understanding or personality clashes, refer to respective elements
MC	Identification with respective aspirations and ambitions
☉	Rapport – but refer to signs and elements involved
☽	Sympathy or discord
☿	Good communication
♀	Love and friendship, harmony
♂	Strong physical attraction, quarrelsome
♃	Sense of humor
♄	Inhibiting, style cramping or constructively helpful – a strong shoulder
♅	Dynamic but tense
♆	Possible confusion and misunderstandings but romantic
♇	Compulsive relationship

MC Midheaven

MC	Will work towards joint objectives and aspirations – or rivalry
☉	A supportive partnership will achieve goals
☽	Sympathy and understanding (Moon) will support partner's goals (Midheaven)
☿	Intellectual interest and exchange of ideas about goals
♀	Shared aspirations and goals
♂	Joint hard work but possible disagreement over goals
♃	Encouragement (Jupiter) will make challenges for partner (Midheaven)
♄	(Saturn) A wet blanket or will stabilize partner's ambition
♅	(Uranus) Indifference to partner's goals or will contribute brilliant ideas
♆	(Neptune) Will contribute inspiration or simply cause confusion and get in the way
♇	(Pluto) Will force issues or block progress (Midheaven)

☉ Sun

☉	A powerful link, but refer to signs and elements
☽	A blending of self-expression (Sun) with instinct and intuition – but refer to signs
☿	Excellent for communication
♀	Love or rivalry – usually the former
♂	Sexual attraction, heightened emotions – will work hard together
♃	Jupiter will encourage Sun to broaden horizons intellectually and to accept challenge
♄	Adds permanence, but can cause inhibition
♅	Adds an exciting, dynamic dimension, but a source of tension
♆	Romantic, sentimental but deception likely
♇	A searching, powerful, compulsive relationship

☽ Moon

☽	The couple will "pick up" each others' moods, or will counter them, according to signs
☿	Increases empathy and sympathy. A tendency to worry about each other in above average way
♀	Usually positive expression of feeling – sometimes overdone!
♂	Increases the emotional level of relationship
♃	Good for joint expansion. Might overestimate problems and difficulties
♄	Often a constructive link, but a lowering, heavy and depressing influence
♅	Increases excitement between partners, but also tension
♆	Romantic but often unrealistic
♇	Increased emotional expression, or inhibition

☿ Mercury

☿	Intellectual rivalry, usually well meaning – excellent communication – chatty
♀	Excellent for friendship in all kinds of relationships
♂	Argumentative, sometimes tense, usually fun and active
♃	Intellectual challenge will be infectious
♄	Could stabilize a relationship but Saturn will frustrate Mercury
♅	A lively, intellectual rapport but tension if a negative aspect
♆	Inspirational but misunderstandings likely
♇	Usually causes frustration

♀ Venus

♀	Harmony, romantic love – sometimes resentfulness
♂	Strong sexual attraction
♃	Joint pleasure in life and each others' company
♄	Emotionally restrictive – sometimes disappointments within relationship
♅	Dynamic, magnetic attraction
♆	Pure romance, but beware "rose colored glasses"
♇	Emotionally highly-charged, good for business partnerships

♂ Mars

♂	Highly charged sexually, quarrelsome, energetic
♃	Lively, energetic, enterprising, but "devil may care"
♄	Saturn will be a source of annoyance and frustration to Mars
♅	Adds exciting tension
♆	Romantic, colorful, escapist – often eventual disappointment
♇	Difficult, frustrating

♃ Jupiter

♃	Enjoyable, fun – could be intellectually stimulating
♄	Good blending of common sense and optimism
♅	Uranus will add exciting original ideas when Jupiter accepts challenge
♆	Inspirational
♇	Excellent for finance/business arrangements

♄ Saturn

♄	A heavy, serious side to the relationship – perhaps "destiny" at work
♅	Rivalry for power and domination or partnership
♆	Saturn may frustrate Neptune's inspired ideas – or will channel them constructively
♇	Frustrating and inhibiting

♅ Uranus

♅	Adds dynamic attraction, but source of tension
♆	Possible tension as result of confusing misunderstandings
♇	Tense blockages due to breakdown in communication

♆ Neptune

♆	Ignore unless Neptune personalized in one chart then adds romance, idealism but possibly deception
♇	Usually the sextile – increases romance, and heightens sexual attraction

♇ Pluto

♇	Ignore unless Pluto personalized in one partner's chart – then adds a compulsive element

The Sexual Relationship

Human relationships are composed of so many different factors that it would be foolish ever to judge people's compatibility on the basis of their Sun signs alone. Instead, one must study their birth charts separately and together, assessing the positions of the planets and their aspects, before attempting to build up an astrological picture of the joys, potentials, stresses and strains in the relationship.

A considerable amount of work has been undertaken on astrological indications of sexuality, but on the whole only by individual astrologers. Not many conclusions have been sufficiently supported by statistical evidence to be accorded textbook status. The attempts to link planetary positions or particular aspects in the birth chart to specific areas of sexuality remains tentative, yet there are some general rules that seem supported by enough evidence to be recorded here.

Treading carefully

However, even if one of these strong indications does show up clearly in a chart that you are examining for one of your clients, be sure to take time to approach it with great care. The fact is that it may not be as clear-cut an indication as you think it is at first. When comparing two charts, your care should be doubled. It is important that you should always remember that in this exceptionally sensitive area of emotional life any commentary that you put forward may weigh too heavily with your clients, especially if they are already distressed or worried.

The astrologer's role

As always, it is necessary not to forget that you are in business to sustain and counsel those who seek your astrological guidance and advice: any mistake that you make as a result could have disastrous effects, not only on your clients but also on their partners.

THE PLANETS

◆ Sexual attraction exists when one partner's Venus aspects the other partner's Mars. Conjunctions are the most potent; trines and sextiles make for easy and rewarding expression; squares often promote an excitable, lively tension; and oppositions indicate a powerful rapport.

◆ There is a dynamic, magnetic attraction if the Venus in one chart makes aspects to the Uranus in the other. The panel (right) shows in more detail the strength of each aspect. However, when there is a square or opposition, the Uranus partner may play a game of hard to get or perhaps even resist the magnetic pull.

◆ There is a certain sexual attraction when the Mars of one partner forms aspects to the other's Neptune, but they can sometimes cause an over-romantic attitude in the Neptune partner and perhaps an oversexual approach from the Martian one. This may be particularly true in cases where the Martian partner shows a strong need for independence.

◆ When Mars and Uranus are linked in two charts there will almost inevitably be a certain amount of tension between the couple. They will gain much pleasure if this can be expressed through sexual rapport, but there must also be considerable compatibility in other areas of the charts if the relationship is to work. Without this, the relationship may possibly deteriorate into real cat-and-dog sparring, with the partners draining each other both emotionally and physically.

VENUS CONJUNCT MARS
Positive, passionate and dynamic attraction

VENUS SQUARE MARS
Harmonious, vivacious and rewarding

VENUS SQUARE URANUS
Possible tension, but a lively relationship

VENUS CONJUNCT URANUS
Strong rapport, with emotional differences

VENUS TRINE/SEXTILE MARS
Possible fickleness if the signs are mutable

VENUS OPPOSITION MARS
A lively relationship full of spontaneity

VENUS TRINE URANUS
Dynamic attraction that may be erratic at times

VENUS OPPOSITION/SEXTILE URANUS
Impulsiveness may cause problems at times

THE HOUSES

The fifth, seventh and eighth houses have sexual overtones, and should be studied when assessing the strength of sexual attraction between two people.

First, look at each partner's chart in turn. If Venus or Mars are in any of the following houses they will show:

◆ In the fifth, a lively, not-too-serious attitude towards love and sex.

◆ In the seventh, enjoyment of all aspects of a relationship. A responsive, consistent bedfellow, but may tend to quarrel, should Mars be there.

◆ In the eighth, an intense, smoldering attitude to sex; a hint of jealousy.

If Venus and Mars are not in any of these houses, glean information from any other planet tenanted in them. If the houses are untenanted, look to the sign on the cusp of the house and to the planet ruled by that sign. Carefully compare the two charts and the aspects formed between them. Look for signs of sexual compatibility or tension.

POSITIVE ASPECTS

◆ If the ruling planet of one chart is in positive aspect to the Venus and/or Mars of the other, this will enhance the sexual areas of the relationship and may lead to a fulfilling permanence. The effect will be similar if the Sun and/or Moon of one partner aspects the Venus or Mars of the other.

◆ One partner's Ascendant aspecting the other's Venus or Mars helps to make the relationship sexually rewarding over a long period.

NEGATIVE ASPECTS

◆ The Saturn in one partner's chart may make a square or opposition to the other's Venus or Mars.

◆ Also negative is one partner's Saturn conjuncting or opposing the other's Ascendant, or making an aspect to his Sun, Moon or Uranus if these are in the fifth, seventh or eighth house.

WILL THE RELATIONSHIP LAST?

It may well be that a couple will approach you to compare their charts when they have just passionately fallen in love. You will calculate their birth charts and may find little indication of basic compatibility or rapport (see pp. 148-55) – even sexual attraction. It is at this point that you have to move on to work on their progressed charts, and then you may well find there is a different picture.

The first stage is to calculate the progressed planets' positions, the progressed Ascendant and Midheaven in each chart.

◆ Are there any progressions between Venus and Mars? That is, does the progressed Venus make an aspect to the natal or progressed position of Mars? Does the progressed Mars make an aspect to the natal position of Venus? Is Venus in contact, by progression, to Neptune? If any of these possibilities apply, then one partner is certainly in the mood for love, and may consciously or unconsciously be searching for a partner, for whatever reasons. If there are no contacts, you can assume that neither partner is attempting to force the issue with the other.

◆ Now compare the positions of the progressed Sun, Venus, Mars and the ruling planet with those of the natal and progressed planets in the partner's chart. Then reverse the process. Does the progressed position of one make an aspect to the natal or progressed position of the other? For example, does his progressed Mars make an aspect to her Venus, either natal or progressed? Has her Mars reached the progressed position of his natal or progressed Ascendant or perhaps that of his Sun or Moon?

◆ Do the Venus and Mars of one partner link up the Uranus and Neptune of the other?

If any of these combinations appear in the two progressed charts, the chances are that the couple should certainly enjoy a pleasant relationship. However, if they are thinking of making their relationship more permanent in some way, and if there are very few or fragile indications of permanent rapport in their birth charts, you should advise them to wait a while before they make a strong commitment. The relationship, even if it seems very meaningful, may well not last beyond the period of influence of the progressions.

The progressed Moon
An affair can be even shorter in length, though just as lively, when the progressed Moon in one partner's chart makes a strong aspect to the Venus, Mars or Uranus in the other's. The progressed Moon aspecting the other partner's Neptune can indicate a romantic reverie, with the Moon subject dwelling on cloud nine.

Powerful transits
Sometimes a dynamic sexual relationship can be sparked off by powerful transits. For instance, the man could have Mars on Leo 15°, while the woman's Venus is on or near Aries 15°, making a nice joint trine. Along comes transiting Uranus either to Leo or Aries 15°, and sparks off an affair between them! The same thing could happen if Uranus came to Sagittarius 15° – always supposing, of course, that the couple either already know each other, or the planets show sympathy by bringing them together by circumstance or chance!

Finding permanence
To look for permanence, you must assess all planetary relationships between the two birth charts. Examine all aspects that color every sphere of their lives – do not restrict your assessment just to the sexual areas.

Incompatibility

Case History

Mark and Sylvia met when he was 15 and still at school and she was a 19-year-old art student. He looked a great deal older and was in many ways extremely mature for his age. They shared a compulsive, dynamic and highly-charged relationship for just over a year. Sylvia was very even-tempered and patient with Mark's dramatic and extreme swings of mood.

The couple were passionately in love in the way that only very young people can be, but Mark's volatile changes of mood became a considerable strain on Sylvia. They would talk about and discuss every kind of subject, which was very stimulating and positive for both of them. However, all too often the discussions became arguments and, on his part, aggressive quarrels. There was also great rivalry between them, especially intellectually, and they constantly tried to outwit one another. Mark would frequently say "We're too alike, we could never be friends." He was right – they couldn't.

The end of the relationship

The relationship ended very abruptly when Mark hit Sylvia in the street in broad daylight.

Years later, when both were remarried, they saw each other in a theater. They spent the whole evening glaring at each other and, meeting in the bar during the intermission, did not speak a word!

Mark died of a heart attack in 1983.

Mark

Mark's chart shows that while his Gemini planets meant he was flirtatious and good company, his Cancerian Moon made him caring and sensitive. His expressions of deep, sensual and passionate emotion tended to be shrouded in a miasma of words, but it surfaced more openly through his Cancerian Moon which, along with Pluto in that sign and exactly conjunct the Ascendant, also caused his very sudden changes of mood.

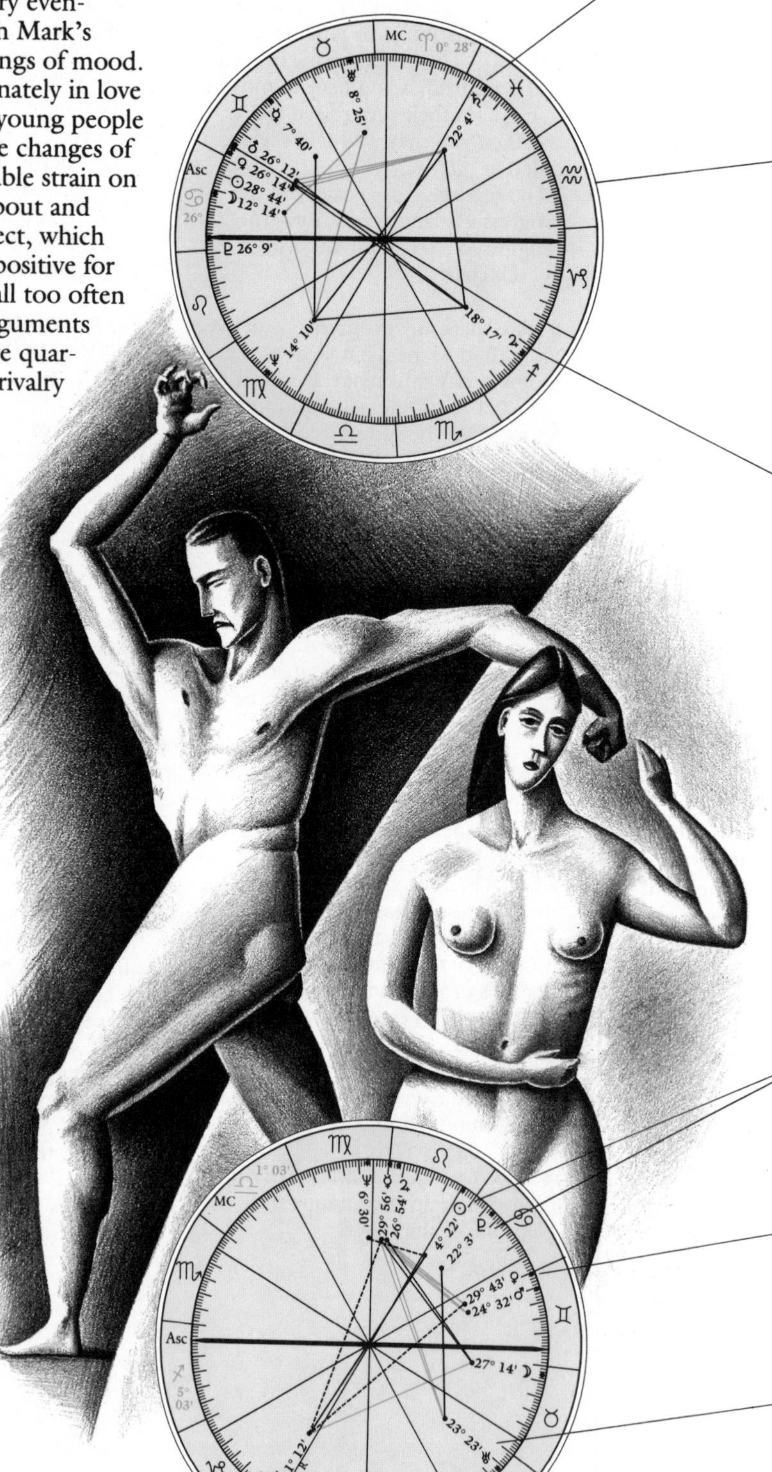

Mark's serious attitude is supported by Saturn, the ruler of Capricorn, tenanted in emotional Pisces in the eighth house. The flow of emotion is, however, seriously blocked, since the planet is at the apex of a heavy tee-square, and receives square aspects from his Sun, Venus and Mars conjunction in Gemini

There are no planets in Mark's seventh house, and as Capricorn is on the cusp of the seventh we can say that he took his relationships very seriously. He wouldn't commit himself quickly or easily, and would be constant and faithful once he did so

Jupiter is powerfully placed in its own sign, Sagittarius, in the fifth house. However, because it is seriously afflicted and at the apex of the second tee-square, its influence was not good, adding an exaggerated sense of drama and tendency to lose his sense of proportion and perspective in his love life

Sylvia

Sylvia's chart is of the bucket type, and if we interpret this in relation to her love life, remembering that Sagittarius is rising, we can fairly say that she will enjoy the chase just as much as the achievement of her heart's desire!

Both the Sun and Pluto are in the eighth house, adding an intense, positive flow of emotion in Sylvia's sexual expression

Sylvia's seventh house is covered by Gemini and tenanted by a conjunction of Venus and Mars. This indicates a positive, but not too serious, attitude toward love and sexual relationships

Sylvia has dynamic, magnetic Uranus in the fifth house, which governs love affairs. She likes this sphere of her life to have a certain amount of glamor

THE JOINT CHART
Due to the high number of planets in Gemini, we have drawn Mark's Sun, Venus and Mars in the outer band of the chart, normally reserved for the two people's Ascendants and Midheavens.

The aspect lines joining the Gemini planets are shown at "A". Many of the joint, major aspects are indicated by the fine lines joining the respective planets and crisscrossing the chart.

HIS
(Black)

HERS
(Brown)

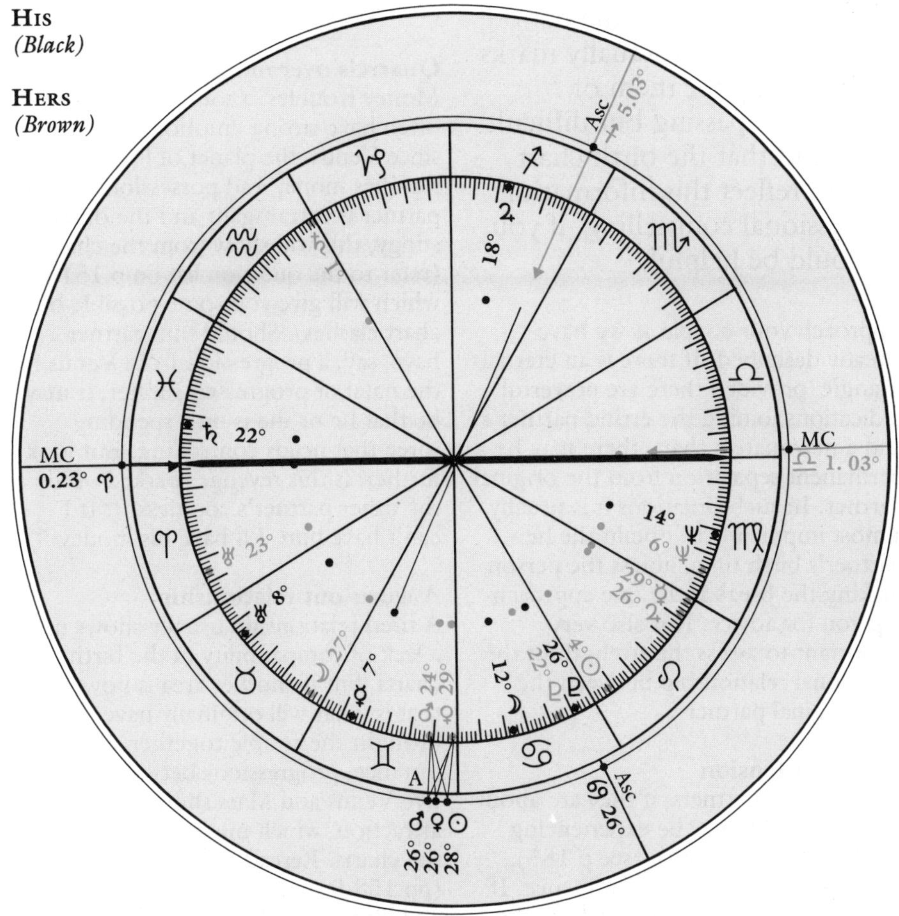

THE MAJOR JOINT ASPECTS			
	MARK		SYLVIA
1	MC♈	☍	MC♎
2	☿♊7°	☍	Asc♐5°
3	♃♐	Sign relationship only, no aspect	Asc♐
4	☉☌♀☌♂ ♊26°–28°	☌	♀☌♂ ♊24°–29°
5	☉☌♀☌♂ ♊	⚹ ⚹	☿☌♃♌ ♅♈
6	Asc☌♇ ♋	☍ ⚹	♄♒ (5° orb) ☽♉
7	☿♊	□	♆♍
8	☿♊	⚹	☉♌

THE MAJOR ASPECTS
Most of the major joint aspects are fully interpreted in the column on the right, but in addition there was more than a hint of romantic idealism present in Sylvia's attitude towards Mark, shown by her Neptune making a square aspect to his powerful Mercury (seventh on the list). It is interesting that the aspect is square, since the strong idealized tendencies of Neptune (always ready with the rose-colored glasses) were present.

An excellent sextile involves her powerful Leo Sun and his Mercury (eighth on the list). This positive indication sustained the relationship, and if they had continued to share their lives it may have helped them to achieve a more rewarding expression of emotion as they matured.

Note that there is an opposition between Mark's Ascendant and Pluto and Sylvia's Aquarian Saturn (sixth on the list). This clearly indicates the importance of the relationship for Sylvia, but as the orb is 5° (the maximum allowed when working on joint charts) it can be used only as a supporting feature.

THE TECHNICAL INTERPRETATION

For a relationship to be permanent there must be strong planetary and sign relationships between the charts of the two partners. These must show rapport and good powers of communication. With Mark and Sylvia there is no lack of these. Joint aspects numbered one to three (see the list, below left) show this. However, the most remarkable comparison shows a group of conjunctions between Mark's Sun, Venus and Mars in Gemini, with the Venus/Mars conjunction falling on the same degrees in the same sign in Sylvia's chart, with practically no orb between them. This accounts for the highly-charged sexual and emotional content of the relationship, and the constant discussions and arguments.

Signs of incompatibility
Mark's dramatic changes of mood are shown by the Ascendant, Moon and Pluto all in Cancer, with the Sun, Venus and Mars in Gemini – all frustratingly negatively aspected by Saturn. Mark thought he and Sylvia were too alike – this shows that the couple were living on the level of their Sun, Venus and Mars in Gemini. In fact, there was considerable incompatibility between them. Mark's highly repressive Pluto conjunct Ascendant in Cancer was the cause of endless clashes with Sylvia's fiery Sun and Ascendant in Leo and Sagittarius respectively, only partially mitigated by her Taurus Moon making sextile aspects to his Pluto and Ascendant in Cancer.

Making the relationship work
Had the couple been older they might have made this relationship work, helped by Mark's powerful Mercury on Gemini 7°, opposing Sylvia's Ascendant on Sagittarius 5°. This is an excellent link, showing rapport and communication. However, because of their youth the relationship was too much for them to cope with. If it had become permanent, they would have had to make allowances for their areas of incompatibility. In retrospect, Sylvia felt she had learned from the relationship, which made her far more tolerant with later partners.

CHALLENGE

See which transits were operative in Mark's chart during October 1982 and between June and August 1983 – the time of his death.

Breakdown in Relationships

It is important to learn the practical reasons for the breakdown of a partnership before assessing the astrological indications. In this way it is possible to discover whether the period of difficulty experienced by your subjects actually marks the end of the relationship for them or whether it is merely a passing but difficult phase. You will find that the birth chart should be able to reflect this information. Do advise professional counselling, if you think that it would be helpful.

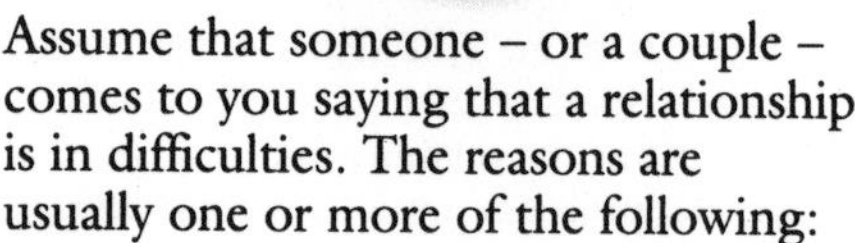

Assume that someone – or a couple – comes to you saying that a relationship is in difficulties. The reasons are usually one or more of the following:

- One partner is having an affair.
- The relationship is worn out – there is now no positive communication between the couple.
- The partners are simply getting on each other's nerves.
- One partner is too much caught up with work or children to have any time and energy left for their partner.

Astrological assessment
Your first step is to calculate and progress their charts and work out their transits. Here are some of the influences that might indicate the cause of the trouble.

A time of evaluation
One or both partners may be experiencing a Saturn Return (see p.185) – most likely their first. If so, their relationship may have reached stalemate. Perhaps they married too young, and now feel that they have far less to offer each other. This is common when this powerful astrological trend is operative. Maybe they should part. It is up to you to point out that they could be experiencing a genuine change of feeling for each other. Assess and interpret their full birth charts to see where they could begin to rebuild their relationship, should they decide to do so.

Changes in the relationship
One or both partners may be experiencing their progressed Sun or Ascendant (sometimes Midheaven) signs moving from one sign to the next. This indicates important changes and often psychological developments.

Approach your couple as we have already described. If there is an eternal triangle, provided there are powerful indications joining the erring partner's and a new mate's chart, there may be a permanent separation from the original partner. In such situations it is usually almost impossible to obtain the new partner's birth time, unless the person making the break is the one approaching you for advice. It is also very important to assess the strength of the emotional relationship between the two original partners.

Causes of tension
One or both partners, if they are about forty years old, may be experiencing the Uranus Half-return (see p.185), which is a very disruptive influence. If they are behaving uncharacteristically – perhaps indulging in a lighthearted affair – the difficult, stressful period may pass, but it will be as well for you to point out how this potent influence can be made to work for, instead of against, the subject. It might be time for the partner not under the Uranian influence to seek some rejuvenation – such as a change of image or a new hairstyle – to show the Uranian partner just how attractive they are.

There can also be tension and difficulties between partners if either or both are suffering from tense transits from Uranus, Neptune or Pluto to the Ascendant, Sun, Moon or Venus – sometimes Mars, natal Saturn, Uranus or Neptune. When these cease to be operative, the permanent relationship will probably settle down, but try to help the partner see reason. Just how easy this will be depends not only on that partner's progressions, transits and lunar progressions but also on the strength of the basic relationship between them, and whether one is simply getting at the other as an excuse to hasten a long-wanted, and probably much-needed, break.

Quarrels over money
Money troubles, a source of difficulty, often have strong emotional overtones, since Venus, the planet of love, also signifies money and possessions. If one partner is extravagant and the other stingy, this will show from the chart (refer to the question list on p.151, which will give you some possible birth chart clashes). Should one partner have, say, a progression from Venus to the natal or progressed Jupiter, it may be that he or she is on a spending spree that needs controlling. But look further: is this revenge sparked off by the other partner's coolness? ("If I can't have him, I'll have his money!")

A worn-out relationship
A tired relationship usually shows up as a lack of compatibility in the birth charts, but if another area is powerful, that is what will originally have brought the couple together. For instance, progressions between respective Venus and Mars show sexual attraction, which might be present in the charts. Reread "Mark and Sylvia" (pp.158-9), a case of sexual, emotional and intellectual fireworks with no meaningful psychological rapport.

Getting on each other's nerves
Each partner will criticize the other if there are too many shared signs and too much psychological recognition of mutual faults and annoying habits. The "hate" is of the area of the self reflected in the partner.

Preoccupation with children
While the maternal or paternal instinct shows up strongly in birth charts, it could – perhaps by the progressed Moon travelling through Cancer – be over-emphasized, making the woman a "baby bore" or unexciting bedmate. Acute tiredness is shown by heavy Saturn transits to the Sun, Moon or Ascendant, as is depression – often present at such times. Try to bring out the man's sympathy – you may have to suggest medical advice or further counselling, especially if the mother is prominently Cancerian. (For similar problems, see pp.168-71.)

Divorce

Case History

This chart shows Wayne's and Cathy's progressed planets at the time they decided to split up and divorce. One of Cathy's reasons for wanting to part from Wayne was that she was totally fed up with their lifestyle, which, though prosperous and very comfortable, had become dull for her. She left Wayne for a man with far less money, who in her eyes was more exciting. Note her progressed Midheaven was changing signs at this time. Of equal importance, her progressed Mars was conjuncting Wayne's progressed Sun: this was a flashpoint. Interestingly, in many cases the contact could easily infer heightened sexual activity, but in her case it was anger and an increasingly aggressive attitude towards Wayne. The general sense of being fed up is also indicated by her progressed Mercury and Venus close to the conjunction of Wayne's progressed Saturn and her progressed Uranus.

Disruption and change

Looking at Wayne's progressed positions, it is worth noting that although he had a group of progressed sextiles and trines operative at the time, the planets show great disruption in his life, affecting him personally and psychologically. Not only is the progressed Ascendant in conjunction with the progressed Pluto (Leo 8°), but progressed Uranus (Gemini 8°) and progressed Mercury (Libra 8°) are also conjoined in the configuration.

All these indications show the level of disruption and change. As stated in the description of the additional technique (see p.154), the transiting planets' positions are merely an aide-memoire, but you could assess them in relation to the couple's progressed positions. Remember, however, it is usually the case that transits apply to natal planetary positions only.

Wayne and Cathy
Wayne's chart is shown with Cathy's planets' positions, Ascendant and Midheaven placed in the middle ring.

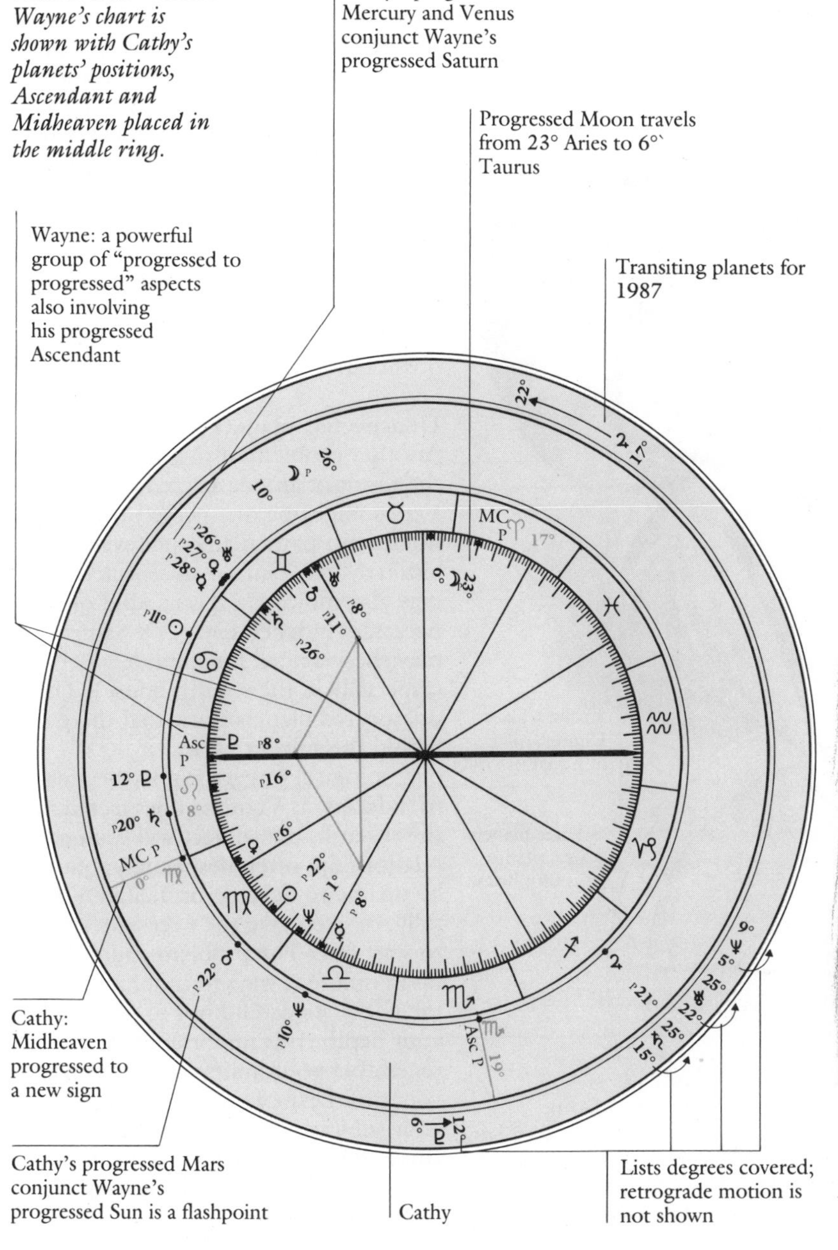
Cathy's progressed Mercury and Venus conjunct Wayne's progressed Saturn
Progressed Moon travels from 23° Aries to 6° Taurus
Wayne: a powerful group of "progressed to progressed" aspects also involving his progressed Ascendant
Transiting planets for 1987
Cathy: Midheaven progressed to a new sign
Cathy's progressed Mars conjunct Wayne's progressed Sun is a flashpoint
Cathy
Lists degrees covered; retrograde motion is not shown
MC P
Asc P
MC P
Asc P

The Subject Alone

There are many people who do not share a relationship – sometimes for deep psychological reasons, which can be externalized in a number of ways. Some spend years caring for an elderly relative, then find they have missed the boat emotionally. But often this is a coverup for more complex reasons. You may not persuade them to reveal these reasons, but it may help to suggest that they do.

Most people who live alone are extremely independent, and three signs are in general related to independence. But remember that when we refer to a sign we are not simply referring to the Sun sign. The emphasis on a sign can be by Sun, of course, but the Ascendant or Moon sign, or a sign with a stellium, or cluster of planets, in it can be equally relevant. Aries and Sagittarius are fiercely independent signs; those with these signs emphasized are warm and need the response and interaction of partners, and on the whole relate extremely well. But the most independent sign of all is Aquarius; the prominently Aquarian person will develop an independent lifestyle that they find difficult to sacrifice. At the same time many are extremely romantic, and will say they desperately want a partner. It seems that what they really want is a partnership – without the partner. This does not prevent them enjoying a rewarding love and sex life, as long as they can hang on to their individuality and their own important lifestyle.

The Aquarian influence

Two contrasting factors emerge here. One is the fact that Aquarius, although an air sign, is also a fixed sign, so that an element of stubbornness is present. The other is that the Aquarian will be extremely friendly, willing to help, but a most private person. Other folk are not allowed to overstep their deliberately drawn boundary lines. As a result, this group often has the most difficulty in developing relationships.

If you are approached by someone with this kind of problem, there may be a striking emphasis on Aquarius in their charts, or it may be that Uranus is powerfully placed and heavily aspected, especially by Venus and Saturn. Only your subjects themselves can reach conclusions about their problems, but you may help if you point out the possibilities we have mentioned.

Unaspected planets

Another problem of this kind may be the result of an unaspected planet. Venus might be unaspected – in any house, but particularly the seventh. Similarly, if Uranus is unaspected that may also indicate a special kind of necessary independence. Or Saturn may show a need for solitude (especially in the twelfth house). These unaspected planets show that there is, within the subject, a lack of psychological integration in the area of friendships. If Venus is unaspected in the seventh, the subject will want a relationship, often desperately, but will be unable to develop or maintain one fully, or even take the necessary steps to start one. The problem could show up in different ways in other areas of the chart. Be careful not to get out of your depth. It is important that you remember your limitations, even when you are an experienced astrologer. If your subject is unhappy you must advise therapy – analysis, if it can be afforded, otherwise perhaps some sort of group therapy.

Marie

Case History

This chart shows an extremely powerful Aquarian influence. It is interesting that the stellium falls in the fifth house, since Marie (who is an attractive woman), enjoys a fulfilling love and sex life but has no permanent partner. Her strong need for independence is also shown by Uranus in the seventh house, closely opposing her Libran Ascendant. In many ways Marie's Libran Ascendant is well-expressed, but the conflict of the Libran need for a permanent relationship fights her Aquarian characteristics. Marie often says she wants to be married, but having to share her life permanently with someone could be anathema to her. In true Aquarian spirit she is kind and always ready to help – a good friend, but an extremely private person.

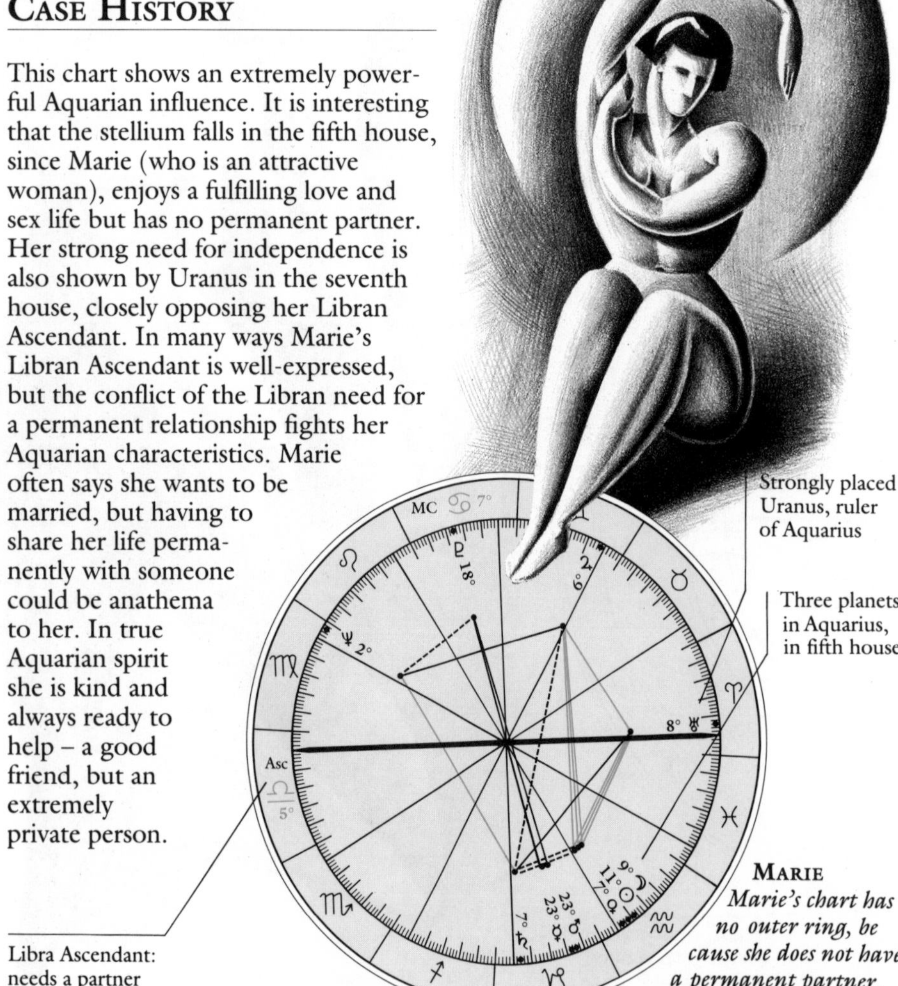

Marie
Marie's chart has no outer ring, because she does not have a permanent partner.

Marriage and Remarriage

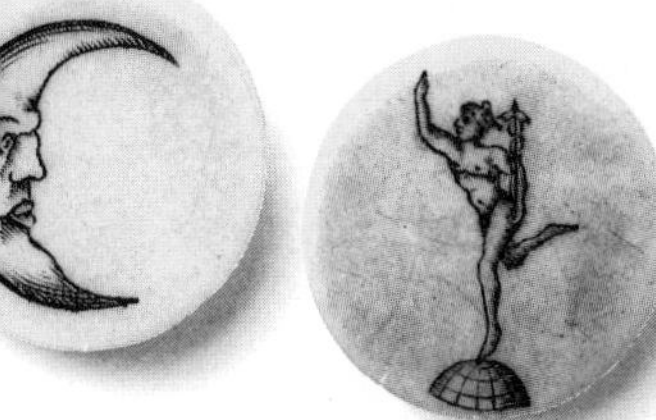

The strengths and weaknesses of a partnership – whether formalized in marriage or not – should appear in the charts of the couple concerned. Never make any difficulty you see here an excuse for warning against marriage, or arguing for it. Once more, simply suggest where possible problems may arise. When you are looking at the chart of a new partner after the departure of an old one, consider whether indications of difficulty in the first reappear in the second.

Toby, Linda and Milly

CASE HISTORY

Toby was first married to Linda. The marriage failed and after a few years they divorced. Later Toby met Milly and remarried. They are extremely happy and have two children and very successful careers.

T > L v	Asc	MC	☉	☽	☿	♀	♂	♃	♄	♅	♆	♇
Asc	•	•	•	⚹	△	•	•	•	•	•	•	•
MC	•	•	•	☍	☌	•	•	□	•	△	•	•
☉	⚻	•	•	•	•	•	□	•	•	•	•	•
☽	•	•	•	•	•	•	•	•	•	•	⚹	☌
☿	•	•	•	☍	☌	•	•	□	•	△	•	•
♀	•	□	•	•	⚹	•	•	•	•	⚹	•	•
♂	•	⚻	•	•	⚹	•	•	⚻	•	•	•	•
♃	•	•	•	•	•	•	•	•	•	•	⚹	☌
♄	•	•	□	•	•	□	☌	•	•	•	•	•
♅	□	•	⚻	⚹	•	•	•	•	•	•	•	•
♆	☌	•	△	•	•	•	•	•	•	•	□	⚹
♇	•	•	☍	•	•	•	•	•	•	•	⚹	(☌)

THE RELATIONSHIP
Toby and Linda's aspect grid.

Toby and Linda's charts
There are some powerful relationships between Toby's and Linda's charts, but most are not conducive to a harmonious relationship. His Uranus in the same position as her Ascendant shows a dynamic attraction, but it is a tense indication. In addition, his Moon opposing her Midheaven and Mercury is also tense and indicative of different emotions about the direction of their lives. Her Saturn squares his Sun and Venus, and her Uranus his Ascendant, while conversely, her Venus is well placed in his seventh house. Often aspects between Saturn and Venus give relationships permanence and fidelity; but because there are squares here, not only involving Saturn and Venus but also an Ascendant and Uranus, the result is a depressing influence.

Friendship is indicated between his Mercury and her Venus and both their Mercurys in conjunction in Pisces (they are still on good speaking terms!). The strong conjunction between his Ascendant and her Neptune made its mark when an idealistic, romantic relationship turned to misunderstanding and disillusionment.

Toby's Midheaven and Pluto share Leo with Linda's Moon, Jupiter and Pluto. These are powerful and highly charged indications, but it seemed that Pluto's influence, intensified by the Moon and Jupiter, had a blocking effect, supported by Toby's Sun creating opposition to Linda's Pluto. Here an opposition works negatively, instead of bringing out the best of a polarity.

Toby and Milly
When we compare Toby's and Milly's charts we find a different picture. First is the conjunction between Toby's Moon and Milly's Sun; in addition there is Toby's Mercury (the Moon ruler) and Milly's Sun, and his Sun opposes her Midheaven. There is also opposition

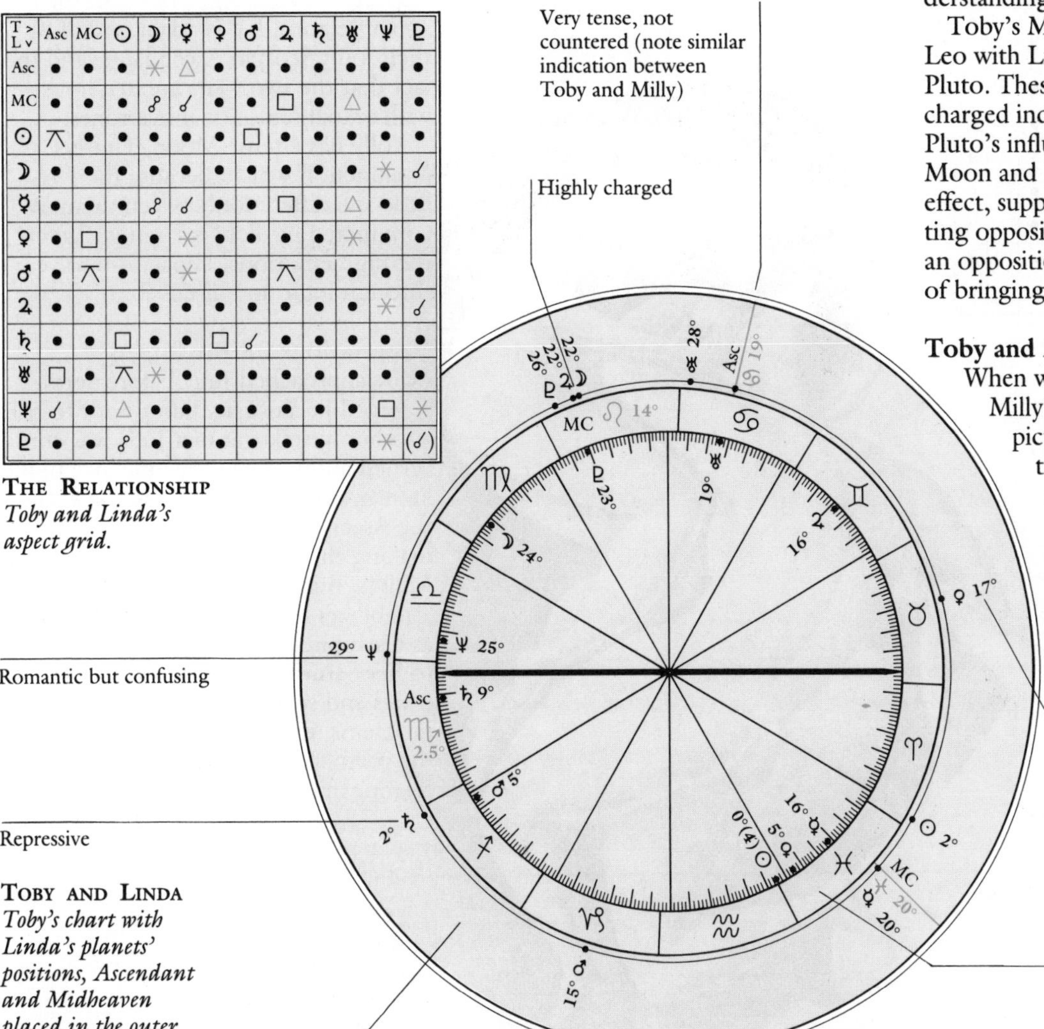

TOBY AND LINDA
Toby's chart with Linda's planets' positions, Ascendant and Midheaven placed in the outer ring.

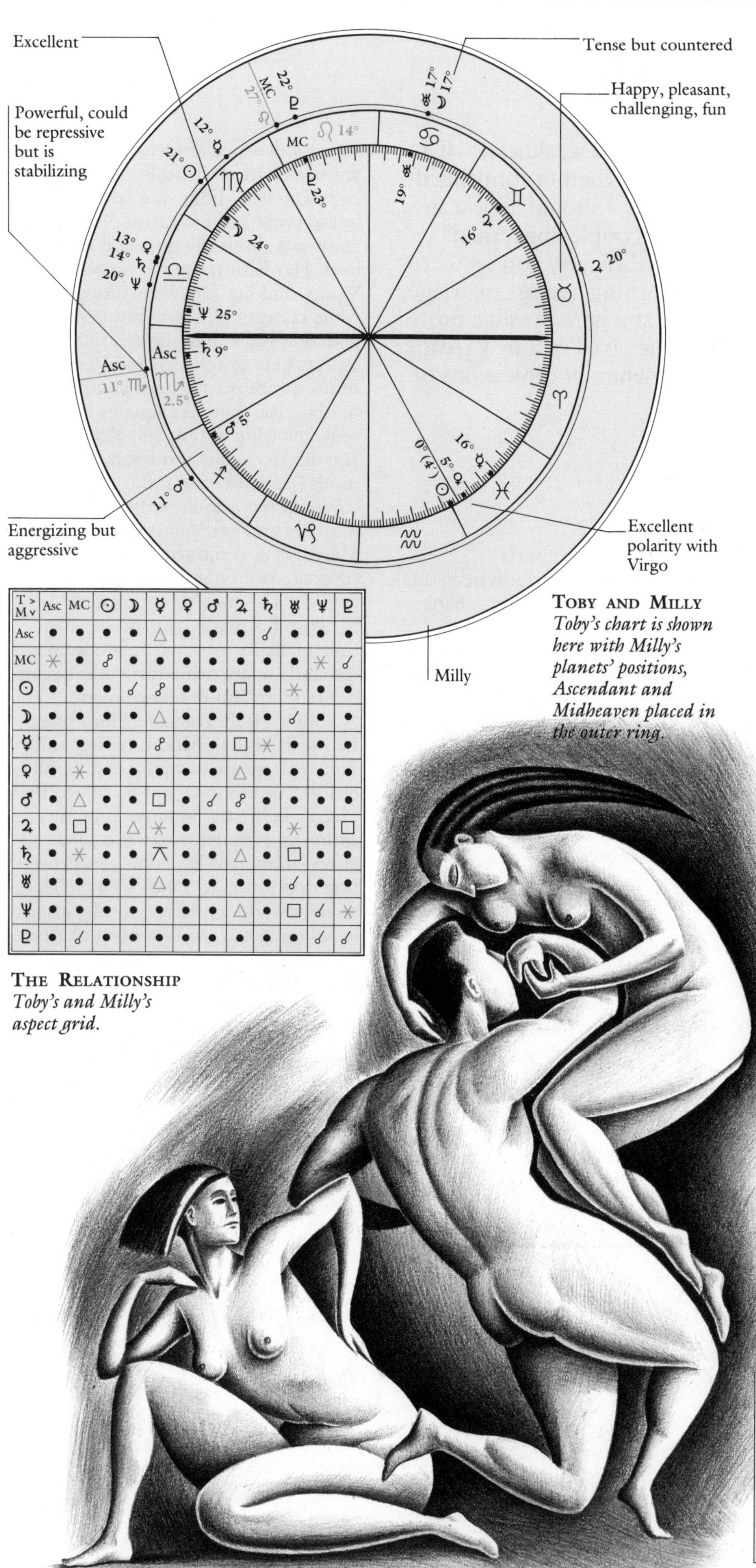

Toby and Milly
Toby's chart is shown here with Milly's planets' positions, Ascendant and Midheaven placed in the outer ring.

T > M v	Asc	MC	☉	☽	☿	♀	♂	♃	♄	♅	♆	♇
Asc	•	•	•	•	△	•	•	•	☌	•	•	•
MC	⚹	•	☍	•	•	•	•	•	•	•	⚹	☌
☉	•	•	•	☌	☍	•	•	□	•	⚹	•	•
☽	•	•	•	•	△	•	•	•	•	☌	•	•
☿	•	•	•	•	☍	•	•	□	⚹	•	•	•
♀	•	⚹	•	•	•	•	•	△	•	•	•	•
♂	•	△	•	•	□	•	☌	☍	•	•	•	•
♃	•	□	•	△	⚹	•	•	•	•	⚹	•	□
♄	•	⚹	•	•	⚻	•	•	△	•	□	•	•
♅	•	•	•	•	△	•	•	•	•	☌	•	•
♆	•	•	•	•	•	•	•	△	•	□	☌	⚹
♇	•	☌	•	•	•	•	•	•	•	•	☌	☌

The Relationship
Toby's and Milly's aspect grid.

between their joint Mercurys. These indications show empathy and excellent communication.

Emotional compatability
There is also a strong Virgo/Pisces polarity at work and three striking indications are the shared Ascendant, Midheaven and Mars signs. The couple recognize each other's faults, but the negativity that might arise is countered by their ability to communicate.

The emotional content of the relationship is high (controlled by the rational Virgo influence, however) and both are fully aware that quarrels could cause problems, because the joint Mars fall in Toby's second house. The enterprising opposition between his Jupiter and her Mars is another controlling factor, as is the pleasant trine between her Jupiter and his Moon.

There are no aspects between their respective Venus and Mars, but their sexual relationship is taken care of by their joint Scorpio Ascendants, and the fact that the two Mars are in a house with sexual/emotional overtones.

Milly has a tense Moon/Uranus conjunction which, because there is little age difference between them, is conjuncted by Toby's Uranus. Again the high emotional impact is resolved through logic and discussion.

Expectations for the future
Toby approached Julia before getting engaged because he didn't want to risk another mistake; at first Julia was concerned about the heavy influence of his Saturn, not only in conjunction with the Ascendant in his chart, but also making the same relationship to Milly's. But this planet seems to act as a stabilizer for both of them, especially as his Jupiter makes a contrasting trine to her Saturn; in addition many minor trines and sextiles add ease. Despite problems, there is enough rapport for the partners in this energetic relationship to overcome difficulties.

Challenge

Draw Toby's and Linda's, and Toby's and Milly's, combined charts, not forgetting to rule in the appropriate aspect lines, as shown in the chart on p.153.

EXTRACTS FROM JULIA'S REPORT FOR TOBY AND MILLY

One fine indication – something that has been remarked on by countless generations of astrologers – is the fact that Milly's Sun sign is Virgo, and the Moon was in that sign when Toby was born. This indicates sympathy and empathy between you. In some respects you share quite a few characteristics and no doubt when you think about it you'll say, "Well, yes, up to a point we are rather alike". That's fine, but obviously it doesn't end there, or anything like it!

Strong partnership
Also in your favor seems to me to be a good possibility that you share the same sort of aspirations, and at once you can see what the other is trying to achieve – you share an identification of ambitions and respect for what the other wants. That is far more important than many people realize, and helps to lay down a strong foundation for a partnership. Even if you are not working together, with this kind of integrating link you will work for joint objectives without any aggro or difference of opinion as to what you want out of life, or where your hard work is taking you.

Because there is a really strong emphasis on the opposite signs, Virgo and Pisces, I am sure that there is excellent rapport between you. You will not necessarily always agree with each other, nor will you always see eye to eye; but no matter how much you differ, there is likely to be excellent sympathy, so your response to each other in disputes will be "Well, I don't agree with you, but I see what you're getting at". You will find, when you get that far, that stalemate will never occur, as it could with many couples. You should rather find that you can progress from that point and develop other aspects of the situation so that resolution will come. This is, I feel, very much your approach in discussion and if you take it you'll not find it too difficult to come out of even the trickiest of situations. There is too, in all this, a marvelous indication that you'll not find it difficult to communicate with each other. Again, this is an important factor in an emotional, or any, relationship. The level of friendship between you is also very high, which is vital, for no matter how powerful our sexual attraction for our partners, we cannot spend all our time in bed!

Intuition and criticism
You will intuitively know when something is wrong, or what the other partner needs, and this too, while usually achieved in a long-term partnership (when the partners get to know each other really well) is something in which you have a considerable head-start! Recognize that you both have quite a strong critical edge. This is a natural part of Milly's personality; probably she always says what she thinks, which is no bad thing. It works rather differently with Toby, who has more of a critical approach to situations. You'll understand these traits, and of course sympathize with them, and because individually you have plenty to counter them, they shouldn't get the better of you. But try if possible to remember, should you have cause to criticize each other, that sweeping general criticism won't go down at all well with either of you, and you should be specific in any criticism you make. And don't, in an argument or discussion, get bogged down in silly, time-consuming detail; you both have better things to do than "pick" at each other.

The restless urge
There is an indication which shows you may both be prone to restlessness – and may tend to catch it from each other. Do watch out for this, since it could ignite quarrels, sometimes over money. I do not think the indication of this possibility will cause you serious problems, since there is too much going for the partnership to allow this to happen, but you should nevertheless be aware of the possibility.

COMPOSITE CHARTS

Once you are familiar with synastry you may want to learn another technique that will help you to gain even greater insight into this area of astrology. If so, we strongly advise you to learn to calculate and interpret composite charts.

Briefly, these are midpoint charts. The positions of the two partners' Ascendants, Midheavens, planets, and sometimes other areas of their charts, are combined, then halved to find their "composite" position in the zodiac. For instance, Toby's Sun is on Pisces 0°, Milly's on Virgo 21°. The composite position of the Sun is therefore Sagittarius 11°.

This calculation is applied to each "pair" of planets, and so on. While it has been found that the influence of the signs has not a great deal of relevance, the house positions and the aspects made are extremely revealing, and often show a very accurate picture of the couple's experience of their relationship.

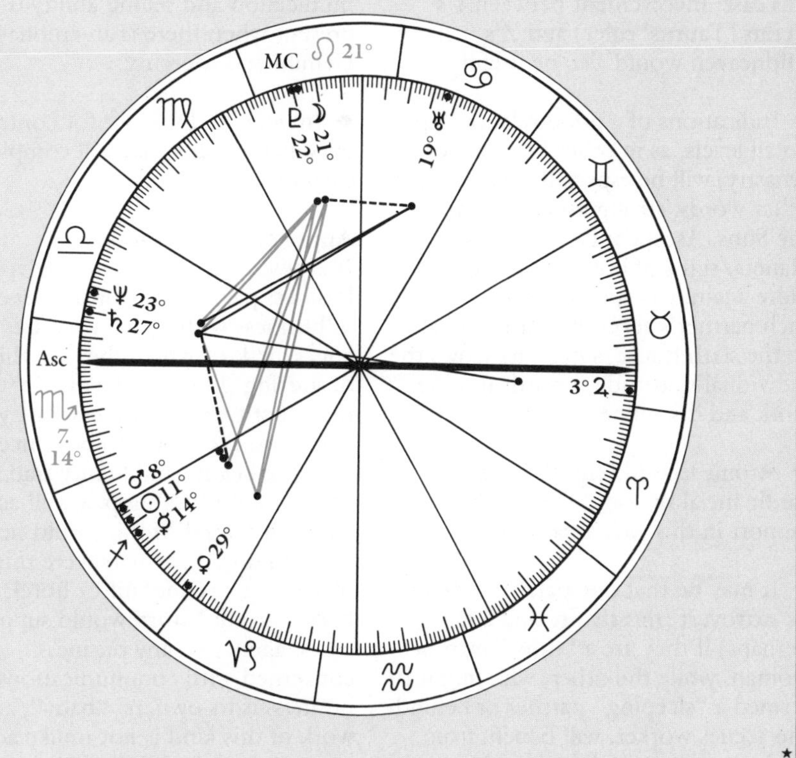

Business Relationships

The approach taken to the synastry of business relationships is very similar to the approach that might be taken to any other area of synastry or chart comparison. However, there are particular indications that may occur in the charts of one or both of the business partners that will add strength to a working relationship, and of course these are of great worth and benefit to the individuals that are involved. The charts of the individuals do not need to be too similar. Indeed, it can often be extremely useful for one of the partners to be an extrovert and for the second partner to be an introvert; the former being concerned primarily with the mechanics of the running of the business, and the latter with the actual "selling" of the business to customers.

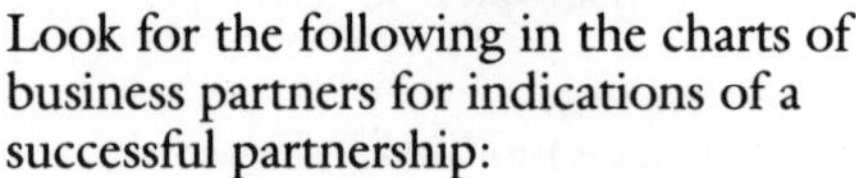

Look for the following in the charts of business partners for indications of a successful partnership:

◆ The two partners need to share their ambitions and hopes for the project, so it is an excellent indication if one partner's Midheaven and Midheaven ruler is in opposition or trine aspect to, or the polar sign of, the other's Ascendant, Midheaven or personal planets. For instance, partner Y's Midheaven is Scorpio and the Midheaven ruler Pluto; partner Z's Sun, Moon or Ascendant is Taurus. In this case, involvement between Y's Venus (Taurus' ruler) and Z's Midheaven would also be useful.

◆ Indications of a good relationship on all levels, as in other branches of synastry, will be especially helpful. In other words, strong aspects between the Suns, Ascendants, Moons or ruling planets/signs of both of the partners. Here again, pay special attention to each partner's seventh house, and also to the sixth house, since this shows the individual's attitude towards routine work and discipline.

◆ Strong second/eighth house links, for financial reasons. These will show rapport in this vital area of business.

◆ It may be that one partner needs to be extrovert (mostly fire and air, perhaps) if they are a "front" man or woman, while the other, who might be termed a "sleeping" partner or behind-the-scenes worker, will benefit from having a strong, well-aspected Saturn, indicating common sense and a practical outlook. A predominance of the earth element is also very useful.

◆ One partner may well need to have an eye for practical detail – if, for instance, the business involves factory work or production. This trait is also essential when contracts have to be drawn up and signed. An emphasis on Virgo or Scorpio, for example, will be an asset. The other may need to enjoy challenge and cautious risk-taking. Aries, or a strong Mars, Sagittarius or a strong Jupiter will help. Good communication and selling ability is usually present when there is an emphasis on Gemini and Mercury.

◆ In general, look out for contrasting personality traits that will complement each other.

Appropriate businesses
It is always necessary when advising business partners to consider the kind of business with which they are concerned, or which they are thinking of starting. Look to the planet which rules that type of business: i.e., you would expect Venus to be concerned with the beauty and luxury trades, or perhaps a florist's shop; a well-aspected and well-placed Moon would be encouraging if partners were thinking of starting a restaurant or hotel; a good, strong Saturn would support an estate agency or any business concerned with communications. A business is its owners' "baby", and work of this kind is not unlike advising parents about a child's chart.

Friends and Business Partners

Case History

Tony and Peter worked together for over 20 years and were friends for much longer. The chart opposite clearly indicates their friendship. The materialistic side of the partnership is emphasized by the extremely potent second/eighth house polarity involving shrewd Cancer and aspiring Capricorn.

The contributions of each partner
The couple sparked each other into action, but Tony was the dominant partner. His Saturn, right on Peter's Ascendant, expresses this. However, Peter's Aries Sun and fiery Leo Ascendant were also strong forces, and while he responded to Tony's ideas and suggestions through his sensitive, subtle Cancerian Moon level, he added balance and energy to the relationship.

There are several more interesting polar influences: Tony's Mars opposes Peter's Mercury. The sparks flew, but Tony's sense of humour, and Taurus/Scorpio love of life, were excellent balancing factors, and between them the two men were great achievers.

Evidence from sign polarities
Although we must be cautious when interpreting sign polarities, it is worth noting (because here personal planets and the angles of the two charts are involved) that by sign Tony's Jupiter opposes Peter's Mars, and Tony's Uranus opposes Peter's Ascendant. Tony's Midheaven opposes Peter's Mercury and Uranus. Original ideas for furthering their work were abundant and they combined business with pleasure, but often worked a 20-hour day. They also travelled extensively – sometimes to countries to which other people had considerable difficulty in obtaining entry. They enjoyed fighting bureaucracy and were adept at reaching the ears of important people – like heads of governments – whom they met to further their business interests.

Mars in Sagittarius in the fifth house in Peter's chart indicates a very strong gambling streak. Because Mars was the Sun- and Midheaven-ruler, this trait needed particularly stringent control – which Tony was able to provide for Peter. Upon Tony's death, gambling became an increasingly important activity for Peter, and with quite disastrous results, as might be imagined. The weakness in Peter's character is shown by Neptune conjuncting the Ascendant, and Mercury being not well placed in Pisces.

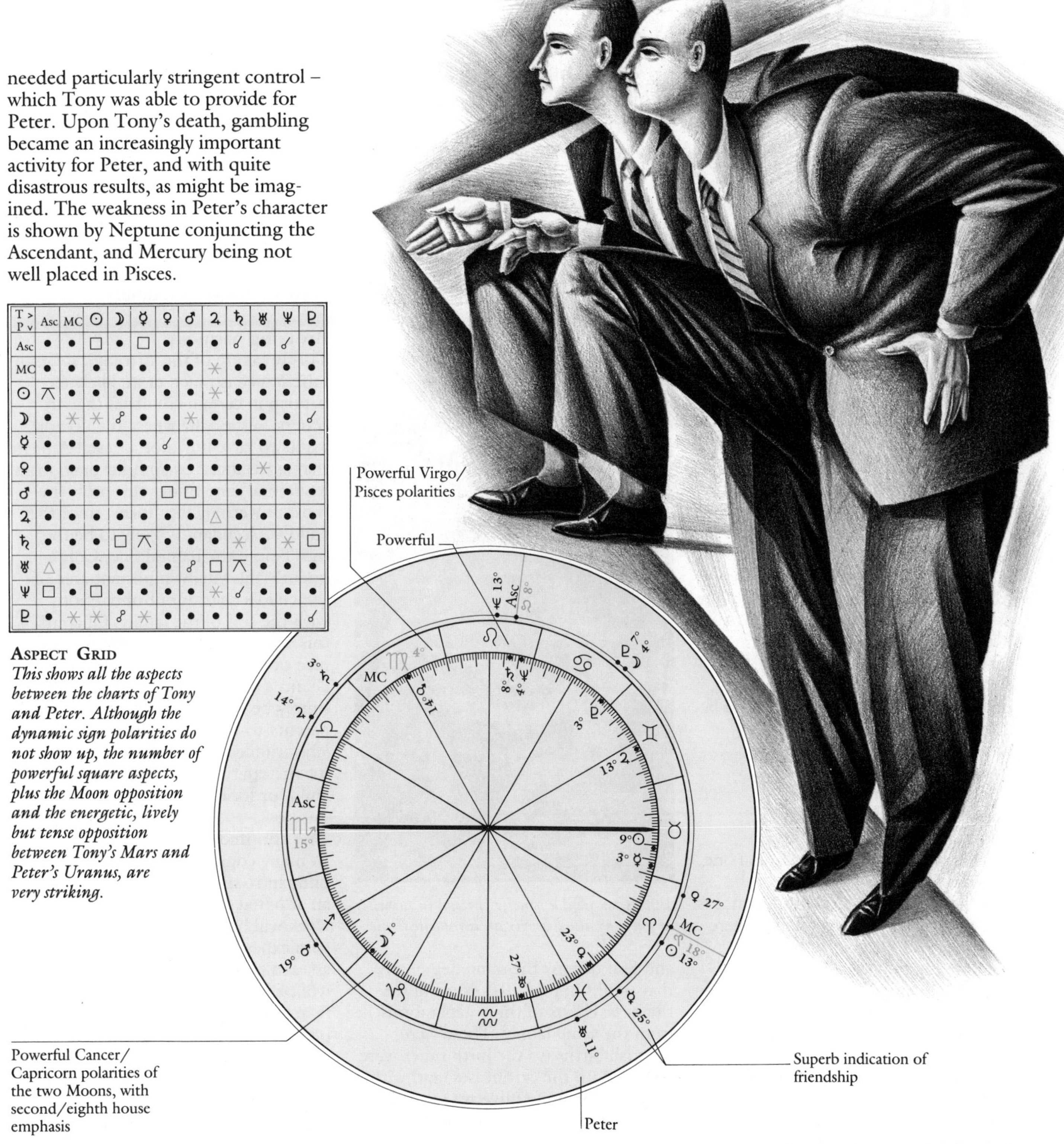

T > P v	Asc	MC	☉	☽	☿	♀	♂	♃	♄	♅	♆	♇
Asc	●	●	□	●	□	●	●	●	☌	●	☌	●
MC	●	●	●	●	●	●	●	⚹	●	●	●	●
☉	⚻	●	●	●	●	●	●	⚹	●	●	●	●
☽	●	⚹	⚹	☍	●	●	⚹	●	●	●	●	☌
☿	●	●	●	●	●	☌	●	●	●	●	●	●
♀	●	●	●	●	●	●	●	●	●	⚹	●	●
♂	●	●	●	●	●	□	□	●	●	●	●	●
♃	●	●	●	●	●	●	●	△	●	●	●	●
♄	●	●	●	□	⚻	●	●	●	⚹	●	⚹	□
♅	△	●	●	●	●	●	☍	□	⚻	●	●	●
♆	□	●	□	●	●	●	●	⚹	☌	●	●	●
♇	●	⚹	⚹	☍	⚹	●	●	●	●	●	●	☌

ASPECT GRID
This shows all the aspects between the charts of Tony and Peter. Although the dynamic sign polarities do not show up, the number of powerful square aspects, plus the Moon opposition and the energetic, lively but tense opposition between Tony's Mars and Peter's Uranus, are very striking.

A POWERFUL RELATIONSHIP
The centre of the chart shows Tony's natal planets' positions, Ascendant and Midheaven. Peter's are placed in the outer ring. The strength of the relationship, both in friendship and more materially is very pronounced. The ideal indication of friendship is Tony's Venus (strengthened by the fact that it is his Sun ruler) in conjunction with Peter's Mercury. Although we only allow an orb of 5° in synastry, Tony's Mercury is only 6° away from Peter's Venus. These configurations involve the fifth and sixth houses, indicating a creative friendship with joint risks (fifth house) and with much hard work (sixth house). Note that the materialistic side of the partnership is emphasized not only by the potent second/eighth house polarity but also by their Moons being in opposition and by Pluto – here in an extremely financial mood.

CHALLENGE

Look up all the other aspects shared by Tony and Peter. You may decide that some do not apply but consider the ones that do, and from them write your interpretation as if for Tony and Peter, remembering not to use any technical astrological jargon!

The Family

Interpreting children's charts is extremely rewarding, and you will probably find yourself doing it early in your studies. Perhaps your first missionary work as an astrologer will be to encourage parents-to-be to make quite certain that their children's birth times are accurately recorded. Try to do this even if they are not interested in astrology; who knows, when the child is older he or she may wish to consult an astrologer and, of course, the work is very severely limited if the birth time is unknown.

Fortunately in a great many countries the birth time is noted on the birth certificate, though sadly this is not the case in England, Wales or Northern Ireland. Scotland fares better, as do many other European countries and the USA. Even so, it is important to remember that these birth times are usually rounded up to the nearest quarter of an hour, and when we are working on the timing of trends in our lives, we need greater accuracy than that. However, many more fathers are now attending births, so give all the encouragement you possibly can to ensure the birth time, which should be taken from the baby's first cry, is accurately timed.

The astrological family tree

Just as there is a genetic pattern running through generations of families, so there is an astrological one. This does not usually emerge at the superficial Sun sign level (although it is true to say that in many families there are clusters of birthdays), but if we examine the fully calculated charts of several generations, we find that it can clearly be seen. In particular, the relationship between grandparents' and grandchildren's charts is well worth studying. So often a grandchild has a special affinity with a grandparent, which shows up in a quite remarkable way when their charts are calculated.

If you spend some time working on this theory, especially if the birth times of the older generation are known to you, you will make some very revealing discoveries. For instance, if a child has a very close relationship with her grandmother, you may well discover that the child's Ascendant sign is the same as the grandmother's Sun sign. Very often the respective Ascendant and Sun occupy the same degree of that sign! On pp.170-1 you will see the birth charts of three generations from the same family. These were Scottish births, so the birth times were recorded on the certificates, and with the aid of a family Bible we were able to trace the grandparents' birth times.

Just as you find a genetic pattern in families, so you may also discover an astrological one.

Premature babies

How do premature babies fit into the astrological family tree? In recent years medical science has discovered that it is the baby that signals to the mother when it is ready to be born, and in all genuine premature births the astrological inheritance is unbroken. However, when we come to Caesarian and induced births it is a different story. Firstly you must reassure the parents, or mother-to-be who knows she is to have a Caesarian, that everything will be well from an astrological point of view. However, some of the more potent astrological links between the members of the family may be broken. While as an individual the child will be fine, he may not fit into the family pattern as well as others who were born at their chosen time.

Breaking harmony

This breaking of the astrological family inheritance is much more likely to happen in certain countries than in others – especially where the doctor wants to have lunch or a siesta! A birth that is advanced by an hour or so from its natural time brings this problem most powerfully into focus, since that child's Ascendant is likely to be the sign before the natural one. Consequently this vitally important area of the child's chart is out of harmony with the rest of the family. Of course this doesn't make the child any less nice or clever than his siblings: the chances of his fully integrating will simply be less. Try to encourage the parents-to-be not to allow induction of labour unless, of course, it is essential for the safety of the mother or the child, or for other medical reasons.

The adopted child

In many countries it is even more difficult to discover the birth time of an adopted child. In such a case your work will be limited, though as you gain experience you may be able to assess a possible birth time; but this will be only speculative at best. It will take a considerable amount of patience over a long period of time to come to any conclusions, but it will be an intriguing trail to follow.

Suggestions, not statements

Especially when a baby has just made its appearance, parents are usually sufficiently starry-eyed to grasp enthusiastically at any suggestion about its talents. Always be careful to suggest rather than make definite statements. Instead of telling them they have an infant Leonardo, suggest that if the child shows an early love of art, she might be given some paints or modelling clay and encouraged to use them.

HOW TO CONSTRUCT AN ANALYSIS FOR A CHILD

There are certain rules you should follow when working on children's charts for their parents.

1 ADOPT A SYSTEMATIC APPROACH

Construct your analyzes by making notes, and following the zodiac trail precisely (see pp.140).

2 WRITE THE REPORT

You will write the report for the baby's parents, of course, rather than for the child – and "write" is the operative word. A written report is much better than merely talking about the child. If you find typing or word-processing a bore, then write the report by hand and speak it into a tape recorder. This is important because the parents, while wanting to study it carefully as soon as it arrives, will also want to refer to it as the child grows up.

3 TAKE DATA FROM THE PARENTS

When asked to study a child's chart you should always take the parents' birth data and calculate their charts too. Remember that the child's chart shows the exact transiting planets' positions for the mother at the time of birth. For instance, you may find the Moon and Mars are prominent in the baby's chart and make transiting aspects to the planets' positions in the mother's chart.

4 CONSIDER THE WHOLE FAMILY

You may not need to spend a great deal of time interpreting the parents' charts, but you should have them at hand, since from them not only can you see in what areas the child takes after which parent, but can also make very practical suggestions about the areas of life in which the child will benefit most from the father's guidance, and where the mother will have the greater and more positive influence. It may also be necessary to calculate the charts of brothers and sisters, if there are any, since it can be helpful for the parents to see how the child will relate to them, and indeed how they will relate to the newcomer. In particular, look for any indications of possible jealousy, either in the chart on which you are working in detail, or in the siblings' charts, then make suggestions for combating this.

Here too is more fodder for the astrological heredity game – see just how much the siblings share by way of common signs or planets' positions or aspects, since sometimes some of these will be common to two or more charts in the family.

5 TAKE THE CHILD'S SIDE

It is important to take the child's side in this area of astrology. Try to see the family through his or her eyes. For instance, you may have parents who are very forward-looking and want to bring up their child in a very free and liberal way. But on examining the chart you might discover that the child is very conventional and needs an above-average amount of emotional security, to be told exactly what to do, and will thrive on a rather strict discipline. You will have to convey such points to the parents, which might not be easy. The reverse could also be true: conventional parents with a freedom-loving child, or one who needs a great deal of warmth and affection while the parents are keen to send him off to boarding school. Constantly watch for such problems, and try to make suggestions which you know will make the child happier and therefore more content, fulfilled and eventually successful.

6 SPOTTING TALENT

Some charts will speak very clearly to you, perhaps shouting out that a child has a considerable gift for music. (For such a specific talent to be really marked it must show up in several different and independent areas of the chart.) Don't, as a result of this, tell the proud parents they've given birth to another Mozart, but certainly suggest that, if the youngster expresses a desire to learn to play an instrument, they shouldn't ignore the plea. If real talent exists, this will allow it to materialize though, of course, generous encouragement is necessary once the potential begins to develop.

7 MAKING SUGGESTIONS FOR LEISURE

It is important for parents to fill their children's leisure hours with as many out-of-school interests as possible. Look to the signs and influences of the Moon in both parents' charts to see how they will respond to your suggestions, especially if some seem a little far-fetched! It is worth remembering that involvement in an interest may develop into a career at a later date. However, you will not forget to assess career potential. Make rather general suggestions as to what the child will probably need from a psychological point of view: to be emotionally involved in his work or simply to make money? State whether he is humanitarian and best working for the good of others, or basically creative or scientific.

8 MAKING SUGGESTIONS FOR HEALTH

Assessment of health is also very useful. Don't be afraid to get back to basics. For instance, if the child has a Leo Ascendant or Sun, suggest any form of exercise that will help strengthen the spine and keep the circulation and heart in good order. A child with a Taurus Sun or Ascendant may have a sweeter tooth than most children, making him prone to putting on weight. A prominently Cancerian baby may fret and worry, perhaps crying more than most. He or she will be sensitive to atmospheres, which can also cause problems.

9 USING DETAILED PROGRESSIONS

It is not usual to work on detailed progressions when writing an analysis of a baby's chart, but do look briefly at the coming trends. There may be some heavy transits on the way which suggest the child will develop all those nasty childish illnesses over a year or so. A flurry of help from Jupiter could mean particularly good progress at school. Heavy transits from Uranus might indicate a difficult time, and so on.

However, there is a time when detailed progressions will be an asset: when the parent's relationship is rocky or they thinking of parting. You can see, both from the child's birth chart and by the progressions and transits, how the child will react.

10 ENCOURAGE CHALLENGES

Finally, all children experience their first Jupiter Return around the age of 12. At this time encourage the parents to allow the child to enter competitions, take tests or exams in out-of-school subjects (they could win some sort of prize or scholarship) or, if at all possible, travel abroad or visit some special place which could get their minds moving in an interesting way. They will certainly respond well to challenge or any kind of intellectual stimulation at this time.

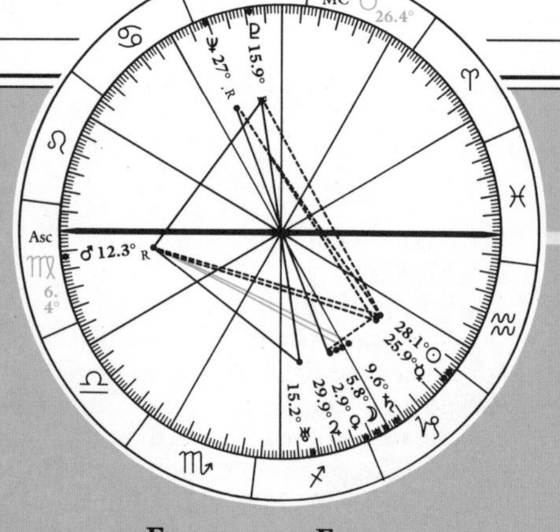

Finlay, his Father

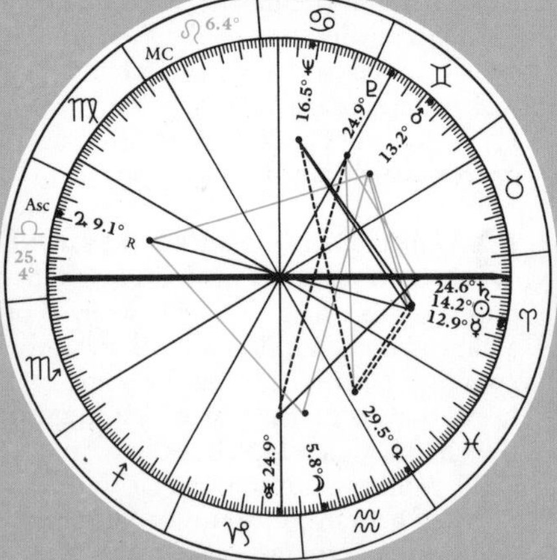

Isobel, his Mother

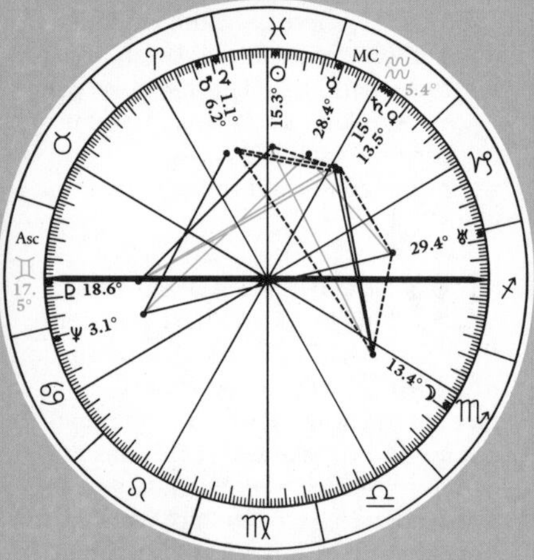

Edward, her Father

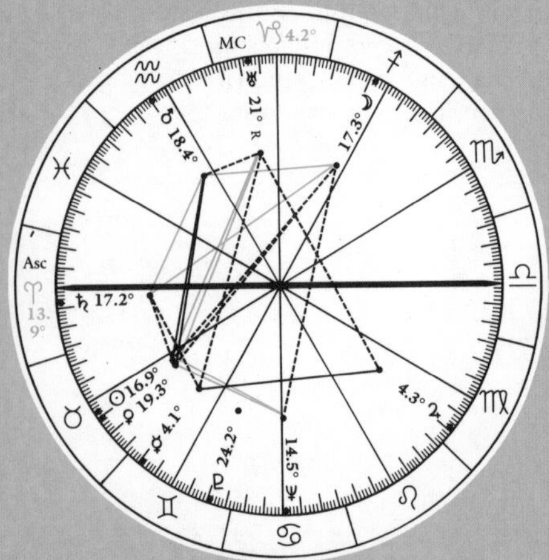

Jane, her Mother

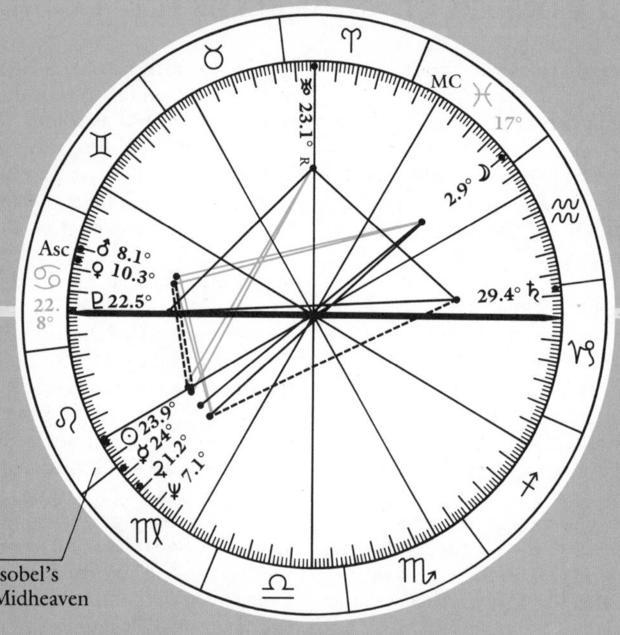

The Father

Following a Family Tree

It is rarely possible for an astrologer to follow an astrological family tree through more than a couple of generations. It can be made extremely difficult because it is not always possible to obtain all of the correct birth-times of the various family members. Those members of the family whose charts are shown here were born in Scotland, where, happily, all birth-times are duly recorded on birth-certificates.

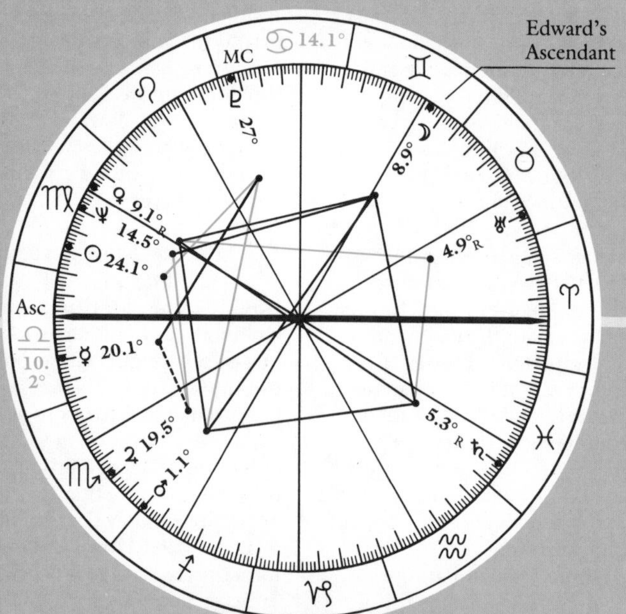

The Mother

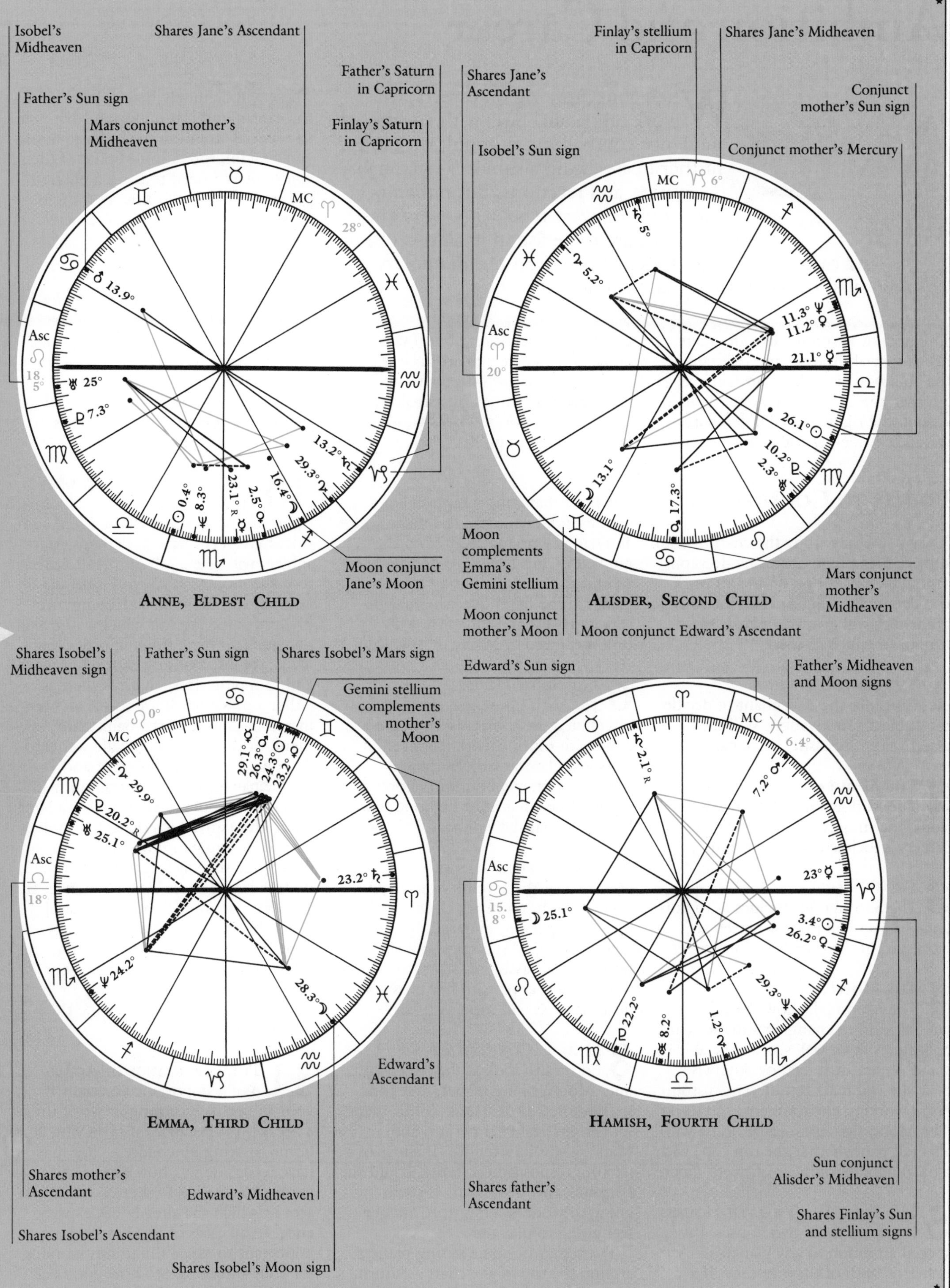
Isobel's Midheaven
Shares Jane's Ascendant
Father's Saturn in Capricorn
Father's Sun sign
Mars conjunct mother's Midheaven
Finlay's Saturn in Capricorn
Moon conjunct Jane's Moon
Anne, Eldest Child
Finlay's stellium in Capricorn
Shares Jane's Midheaven
Shares Jane's Ascendant
Conjunct mother's Sun sign
Isobel's Sun sign
Conjunct mother's Mercury
Moon complements Emma's Gemini stellium
Moon conjunct mother's Moon
Moon conjunct Edward's Ascendant
Mars conjunct mother's Midheaven
Alisder, Second Child
Shares Isobel's Midheaven sign
Father's Sun sign
Shares Isobel's Mars sign
Gemini stellium complements mother's Moon
Edward's Ascendant
Emma, Third Child
Shares mother's Ascendant
Edward's Midheaven
Shares Isobel's Ascendant
Shares Isobel's Moon sign
Edward's Sun sign
Father's Midheaven and Moon signs
Hamish, Fourth Child
Sun conjunct Alisder's Midheaven
Shares father's Ascendant
Shares Finlay's Sun and stellium signs

Ambition and Career

When concentrating on careers, we work on parallel lines with vocational guidance counsellors, although we can go further in asssessing a subject's personality, motivation and reactions. But remember that people of every type, with every kind of birth chart, are to be found in all professions and careers; sweeping statements based on rudimentary astrological knowledge are worse than nonsense.

This area of astrology, like all others, needs special thought and care, and the ability to view the chart from yet another angle. Here we hope to put you on the right track. Of necessity, we make some generalizations – there are always exceptions – but if you proceed with care you are far less likely to fall into the sort of traps to which many popular writers on astrology succumb ("If you're Pisces you must be a monk or a nun"!)

Points to Consider

Always carefully study the chart of your subject before you make any decisions as to which direction or area of work you eventually suggest. The following guidelines will give you a basic structure from which to work:

1 The Ascendant sign
Consider the Ascendant to decide the subject's motivation. Will she be assertive, enthusiastic, work hard?

2 The Midheaven
The Midheaven will show aspirations; the subject will identify with careers associated with that sign.

3 The Sun sign
The Sun sign gives clues as to how your subject will express herself at work and in the context of her career.

4 The Moon
The Moon tells how the subject will respond to changing situations and colleagues; how well she will be able to stand on her own feet, or otherwise; how she will react to different customers, a working environment, and so on. The Moon sign and maybe house will also tell you whether she can cope with a bustling environment or needs quiet.

5 The First and Twelfth Houses
Compare these two houses. Pay special attention to any planets in either or both of these houses. If a personal planet is in the twelfth house, it may be that your subject will get greater fulfillment and feel more secure and happy working away from the public eye, not having to deal with strangers. But if there is a personal planet in the first house she may be very extrovert and therefore will become bored or lonely in isolation.

6 The Sixth House
The sixth house may indicate how disciplined the subject is, how she will cope with routine work (for even in the most glamorous jobs there is usually a certain amount of chores or regular tasks that must be done) and how punctual she will be.

7 The Seventh House
Look at the seventh house, especially if she has to work closely with one other person, undergoing some kind of practical training, or if she is to be a personal assistant. It will show how she will cope with her boss – and how her boss will cope with her!

8 Health Considerations
For health look at the Ascendant, Sun, Moon, ruling planet, first and sixth houses. If demands will be made on her physical energy (Sun and Mars), assess its strength. If she is of a nervous disposition or tense, could she become easily distressed? If she is going to work in a big store are her feet going to play up?

There may be some strong planets around the top of the chart – Saturn, Uranus or perhaps the Sun or Mars. These will definitely have a bearing on the career, and it is important that you pay special attention to the basic house and sign interpretations. Some of them will suggest a need to be in a powerful position; others will show that there must be psychological involvement and fulfillment.

9 The Aspects
As you work through the various areas of the chart, don't ignore the aspects – some may indicate a specific talent. If so, and the planets concerned are personal, what is suggested by them could be worthwhile, especially if a similar or identical theme occurs in other areas of the chart.

10 The Importance of Money
Money is important to all of us, but it can be a crucial factor when considering career matters. Perhaps your subject will take a job simply in order to make money? If so, you must do all you can to encourage a deep involvement in some interest which will make demands on spare time, in order that life is not just a boring routine of work and shopping. In such cases there is either a powerful desire to see an ever-increasing figure in the bank statement, or the individual really wants to do something quite different and maybe pay for expensive training with a view to turning professional at a later date. Alternatively, perhaps the money earned is simply to tide the subject over while she studies, or works to a high standard in sport, for instance. If so, advise an undemanding physical job if the real objective is physically demanding, and an undemanding intellectual job if, for instance, your subject is slaving away at study or perhaps writing a novel outside their working hours.

11 The Importance of Age
Age is important especially if your subject is returning to work after a break – for instance, after staying at home to bring up children. You may have to decide just how easy it will be for her to take a refresher course in an area in which she already has experience. In all cases of this kind it is important to assess the trends working for your subject to see how good the chances are of actually getting a job.

TRAITS TO LOOK FOR IN A CHART

Most professions and careers can be placed under the following headings. One or more will emerge from your study of the chart, and, having paid special attention to the points listed opposite, it should now be possible to move on to this area and discover where your subject's potential will be most rewardingly expressed. Within these sections there will, of necessity, be cross-references. For instance, many creative people need to be scientific in their approach to their work, while scientists need creative flair to move research projects forward; practical people – builders, plumbers, farmers – need good business sense if they are to cope with their book-keeping, and people in the service industries may need to have physical strength.

1 CREATIVE ABILITY

This shows up in a variety of indications, but it is important to remember that creativity covers an extremely wide field. You are just as creative if you are a cook, a hairdresser or a ballet dancer – it is in no way restricted to fine arts. Basically, look for a well-placed Sun – the sign may well tell you the inherent type of creativity. For example, the Sun in Leo suggests painting or colourful design, and acting when in aspect to Jupiter from Leo. A predominantly Cancerian chart suggests cooking. The earth signs show flair for craftwork in natural materials or restoration. Aries suggests all kinds of work with metals. Writing and literature are common with Gemini and Sagittarius, aspects between Mercury and Jupiter, Virgo and sometimes Aquarius. A powerful Venus suggests skill in music, dressmaking and embroidery, though this is more often appreciative than practical. Musical ability is often attributed to a Capricorn or Taurus Sun sign and a strong Saturn. Neptune can give inspiration to creative potential and sometimes skill for poetry writing, dance, lyrical movement and ice skating. The fifth house is also relevant.

2 SCIENTIFIC ABILITY

Saturn and Uranus are the scientific planets, with Saturn also giving flair for mathematics. Look, too, for decisiveness and quick thinking – Mercury and Mars. Those with Pluto strongly placed, often rising in Leo or Virgo, can often show ability with computers and modern technology. The signs of Capricorn and Aquarius can be emphasized. Aquarius/Uranus and Gemini/Mercury influences may steer the individual towards space and telecommunications, and Saturn towards the more traditional sciences.

3 PRACTICAL ABILITY

Most often the earth signs are prominent in this area, especially in the building trades, architecture, agriculture and land management. A strong Mars is good for engineering, whilst prominent Scorpio, Pluto and Mars are good for mining and plumbing. Think in terms of Neptune and Pisces for the fishing industry, boat and shoe trades. A well-aspected Saturn will give practical ability and patience.

4 SERVICE

A flair for teaching young children is often shown by a prominent Cancer or Virgo. Teaching students at the university level is indicated by Sagittarius and a strong Jupiter. For the medical profession, look for Virgo and Scorpio, and sometimes Aries for surgery and psychiatry; Cancer for pediatric work; Capricorn for dentistry and osteopathy; Virgo is often attracted to the complementary medicines and diet. Virgo/Pisces and Cancer are good for nursing. Gemini and a strong Mercury help in selling. Taurus and Libra are useful in all areas of the fashion industry and beauty trades. Aries and Libra often make for good military types; those with a strong Cancer, Moon or water signs do especially well in the navy and working on cruise liners; airline employees are often shown by a combination of air and water signs. The law is Jupiter's domain, although Jupiter with Neptune suggests work of a religious nature. The police force and detective work attracts Aries, Scorpio, sometimes Virgo, Mars and Pluto. The media is rife with predominantly Geminian and Virgoan types.

5 BUSINESS

The highly motivated business magnate is often spurred on towards success by ambition, and so may well prove to have a very strong Saturn. Business sense is usually shown by a well-aspected Moon – often in Cancer or Taurus. The second and eighth houses will be emphasized, as will Pluto, often Scorpio and Virgo. A gambling instinct is shown by Jupiter or Mars in Sagittarius or the fifth house, but these will need controlling. Most money-making types have the need for a feeling of security – that is usually their most basic motivation. This need for security is likely to encompass areas of emotional as well as financial security and again is strongly linked to Taurus and sometimes also to Cancer.

6 HUMANITARIAN

Those in the caring professions are often prominantly Cancerian or Piscean, with the Sun or a personal planet in the twelfth house. They are deeply interested in people and find inner satisfaction in helping them and improving their lot. Be very careful that a subject expressing a desire to enter such a profession is not, in some roundabout way, expressing a power complex. Look for kindness, consideration and sensitivity rather than, say, a strongly placed Pluto, Saturn or Uranus, or any indication of Leo bossiness. However, the Uranus/Aquarius influence at its best can be extremely humanitarian, with these people working in a very practical way – doing fieldwork for international charities, for instance.

7 PHYSICAL

It is essential to assess the individual's physical energy level through the influence of the Sun and Mars. Should there be a desire to take up professional sport or any physically demanding profession, ask yourself just how well the nervous system will cope with the inevitable strain and tension of international competition on the way up, and keeping the necessary level of perfection having "made it".

8 ORGANIZATIONAL

Organizational ability is usually represented by an emphasis on Leo or Capricorn. The Moon in Leo usually high in the sky (i.e. in the tenth house of the chart) shows the ability to cope with large groups of people (many orchestral conductors have this placing). Scorpios are usually well organized, while Virgoans, having the reputation for being tidy (though we doubt that this is the case), need to know precisely what is required before going on to do it, but often lack the confidence to take the initiative. However, as is the case with Scorpios, Virgoans can be obsessional over small details. The go-between – say, an agent who organizes contracts – needs to be assertive and strong, but also to have superb organizing ability; look to Aries for the assertiveness. Positive aspects between the Sun and Moon and Saturn show discipline and order. Conversely, Pisces and Cancer may often be chaotically untidy and disorganized.

Questions To Ask Yourself

Now that you have a general idea of how the vocational possibilities show up in a chart, this is the time to move on to ask yourself how various qualities and characteristics will help your subject to achieve career objectives. Note that a reference to a sign or signs means that the subject can have that sign as Ascendant, Sun, Moon or emphasized by a group of planets. Is your subject:

Q A good communicator?
A Well-aspected Mercury, Gemini or Virgo.

Q Understanding?
A Well-aspected and placed Moon and Venus, Libra.

Q Patient?
A Taurus, aspects of the Sun or Moon to Saturn, often Capricorn.

Q Good at organization?
A Strong Leo or Capricorn.

Q Original and inventive?
A Aquarius, the Sun, Moon, Mercury or Venus in positive aspect to Uranus.

Q Disciplined?
A Taurus, Capricorn, the Sun or Moon in aspect to Saturn.

Q Tactful and diplomatic?
A Libra, Moon, in aspect to Venus.

Q Ambitious?
A A strong well-aspected Mars, or Saturn in the tenth house. Taurus wants to make money.

Q Assertive?
A Aries, strong Mars in aspect to Jupiter, well-aspected Sun or Moon in a fire sign or Capricorn.

Q Caring?
A Cancer, strong Moon in first, fourth or twelfth house or Pisces.

Q Enthusiastic?
A The fire signs, strong Mars and Jupiter.

Q Shrewd?
A Cancer or Scorpio.

Q Open-minded?
A Well-aspected Mercury or Jupiter, usually in air signs.

Q Quick-thinking and decisive?
A Aspects between the Moon, Mercury and Mars; an emphasis on Aries, Gemini, Sagittarius.

Q Physically strong?
A Sun and Mars.

Q Good at detail?
A Virgo or Scorpio.

Q Honest?
A Well-aspected Sun or Moon. Especially Leo and Capricorn – it is beneath their dignity to be otherwise! Often Aries, who can't be bothered with the complications of being dishonest.

Q Intuitive?
A The water signs; the Moon in positive aspect to a water-sign Sun, or to Neptune. Very often, Libra.

Q Good at comprehension?
A Sagittarius, a positively aspected Jupiter.

Challenge

The questions and answers above all relate to positive characteristics and qualities necessary for success. Extend the list – it could easily become a sizeable directory! Conversely, look at our list and work out the parallel negative indications, and the astrological significators applying to them. For instance, the first question concerns a good communicator: what would indicate a poor communicator? We think it might be someone with square aspects to Mercury from Saturn or Pluto, or perhaps a twelfth house Mercury (though the subject might then be very good on the telephone!) Or, to take the third question about patience: an impatient person would probably be an Arien or Geminian type, always wanting everything *now*!

The Next Stage

By now you should have come to some clear conclusions about the practical suggestions you can make to your subject, and be ready to meet her for a question-and-answer session. Below are some questions to which you will know most of the answers, but which it will be helpful for your subject to answer in her individual way. Notice just how much, without prompting, she will speak her chart – something that is of great interest to astrologers.

You will be fully conversant with your subject's personality traits and general characteristics (having assessed them as we suggested in Interpreting the Birth Chart, pp.130-40). You will also know how powerfully motivated she is, and how that inner drive should be expressed in her career. Even so, you should put her to the test.

Motivation

You may feel that she just wants a job for the sake of the money. If so, simply ask her what she wants from her working hours. If she answers as you suspect, perhaps you can lead her towards actually working with money, in banking or insurance; this could be psychologically rewarding. You will also know if she is ambitious, but you need to pursue this further. To do so, play a well-tried game: ask her to think of herself some five years hence. How does she see herself? It is possible that she may well have more than one idea. Excellent: from the reply you should see which is the right course for her, and will give the greatest satisfaction.

Gentle hints

Remember not to be dogmatic. Just drop gentle hints to allow her to collect her thoughts and develop her ideas. In that way she will think she has come to her own conclusions; indeed, that will substantially be the case. If for some reason she is blindly following the wrong track you must come on a little stronger. But if that is so, you will know from the chart that she is self-deceptive – rather like a young person who has always been dreadfully overweight wanting to be a ballet dancer.

There is no need to be evasive. You must have the courage of your convictions, and in the final analysis it may be less difficult than you think to draw up a list of possible careers, though on the whole you should only do this if your subject has absolutely no idea about what she wants to do.

Job satisfaction
It usually follows that the greater the level of psychological integration in a personality, the greater the need for job-satisfaction. Someone who is psychologically strong is far more likely to be upset or disturbed by long working days in which there is no psychological involvement, with work that is soul-destroyingly unrewarding. If circumstance dictates such an existence, the individual will no doubt fill his or her precious spare time with a fulfilling involvement in some sort of consuming interest. But if this is not the case you should make suggestions along those lines. In such a situation, search the chart for potential. There could be a flair for languages, history or perhaps music. Remember, it is up to astrologers to help make their subjects' lives more fulfilling, rewarding and worthwhile. If possible, and if your subject is capable, suggest some kind of study course which could lead to career improvement and in time perhaps secure a release from a dreary job.

The lonely top job
This is one of the most difficult problems to cope with. Very often an ambitious person who is successful has the chance of promotion to a top job. In many ways there will be a natural desire to take it, for the sake of additional prestige, more money and respect from colleagues. However, the individual will be cut off from colleagues, not only responsible for serious decision-making but also all too often given far less opportunity to actually do the work he or she was trained to do. With the job comes administration and more administration. This is particularly so in the teaching profession, or when a senior nursing sister is promoted to matron.

When this happens you must look to the chart in quite a different way, to discover whether your subject can cope with the loneliness – some love it! – or whether, in being cut off, she may become indecisive or even go to pieces due to a lack of rapport with colleagues. Most importantly, if she is really dedicated to the actual work she does, she may be ready to make such a sacrifice. If not, perhaps she will be happier and more fulfilled in not accepting the appointment. But then, if there are family responsibilities, she may well need the extra cash.

Talking things through
These are complicated questions. Often by talking them through with subjects you will help them to see things more clearly and make their own decisions. If this happens you should feel really satisfied. Remember that this is another case when you should very definitely not make up your subjects' minds for them.

The dreadful boss
Sometimes a subject will consult you because she is being plagued by an awful boss; being sexually harassed or imposed upon, given too much work or not enough responsibility. It is most unlikely that you will be able to work on the superior's chart in any detail, though your subject may be able to get hold of a birth date from a personnel file. In such a case you must compare the two charts as described on pp.152-5, but will have to concentrate on your subject's chart to help her gain strength and self-confidence. If you have the superior's chart you will get some idea, even without an Ascendant or Midheaven, of what he or she is like, and should be able to reassure her. But it will probably be a question of her having to prove to herself that she can stand up to her boss, and if necessary ask quite directly for her rights. It may be that there is poor communication between them. Above all, be positive and firm – if you are too kind and sympathetic, you may not get her energy working in the way it needs. If you have had such an experience remember it in your own mind, but don't regale her with it!

COMBINATIONS OF ASCENDANT AND MIDHEAVEN

This diagram lists every combination of Ascendant and Midheaven sign. Note the difference between northern and southern latitude combinations. This occurs because the signs of long ascension in the northern hemisphere become those of short ascension in the southern, and vice versa. For instance Aries, which only takes about an hour to rise (that is, to cross the eastern horizon) in middle northern latitudes, will take roughly two and a half hours to rise in a middle southern latitude: hence the difference in the possible combinations of Ascendant and Midheaven signs for the two hemispheres.

Hemisphere personality differences
If you live in northern latitudes and work mostly on charts of people born north of the equator, you will find that few subjects have Aries or Taurus rising, and more have Libra or Scorpio Ascendants. If you work on charts of people born in southern latitudes the reverse is true; many people have Aries or Taurus rising and few, Libra or Scorpio. We think this widespread difference makes for hemisphere personality differences. Why not follow up this theory in your own way and time?

Asc	MC Northern Latitudes	MC Southern Latitudes
♈	♑	♑ ♒
♉	♑ ♒	♑ ♒ ♓
♊	♒ ♓	♈ ♉ ♒ ♓
♋	♈ ♉ ♒ ♓	♈ ♉ ♊
♌	♈ ♉ ♊	♉ ♊
♍	♉ ♊	♊
♎	♋ ♌	♋
♏	♋ ♌ ♍	♋ ♌
♐	♎ ♍ ♎ ♏	♌ ♍
♑	♌ ♏ ♐	♌ ♍ ♎ ♏
♒	♏ ♐	♎ ♏ ♐
♓	♐	♐

A Successful Businessman

Case History

This is the chart of a highly successful businessman who formed his own company. The progressed positions are those operative at the time of the company's inauguration.

The drive, energy, enthusiasm and breadth of vision of this man is shown by the Aries Ascendant and the close conjunction with Jupiter in the first house. That he enjoyed taking a gamble is also shown by this area of his chart, but these powerfully positive, daring qualities are countered by the shrewdness of his Cancer Sun sign, the caution of the Virgo Moon and creative thinking of Mercury in Leo. An element of eccentricity and unpredictability is emphasized by Mars, the chart ruler, high in the sky in Aquarius in the tenth house. Richard exhausts himself because he hardly ever stops working. These tendencies are indicated by the Sun conjunct Pluto opposition Mars. It is easy to see the direction of the energy through the Mars house placing. Notice that this is a bucket chart, with the all-important Mars as the "handle" – a striking example of a chart of this particular type. The Moon conjunct Neptune in Virgo in the sixth is well aspected by Uranus, and as Uranus rules the Mars sign, and the Moon is additionally powerful as it is the Sun ruler: this area of the chart is well integrated.

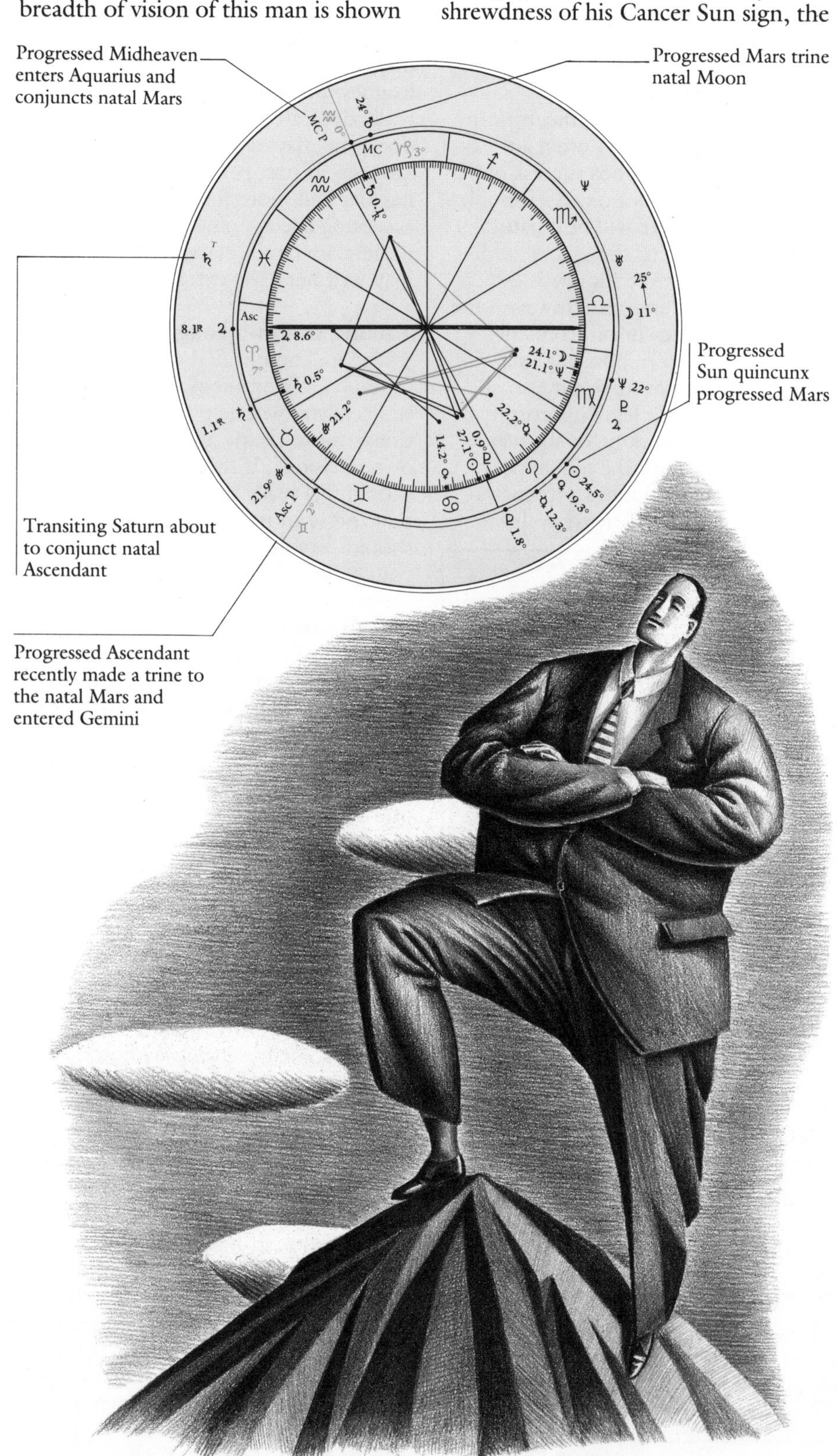

Progressions

Note the progressions at the time of the inauguration: Mars is fully focused by the progressed Midheaven making a conjunction to the planet's natal position, and the progressed Midheaven is at the same time changing signs. The progessed Ascendant was previously in contact with the natal Mars, while the progressed Sun is making a minor quincunx aspect to the progressed Mars, that planet in turn making a strong trine aspect to the natal Moon. This progression is intensified because the chart-ruler and Sun-ruler are working positively together. At roughly the same time Saturn was, by transit, about to cross the Ascendant, showing the commitment, possible strain and additional responsibility such an undertaking always entails. However, Richard's positive enthusiasm and will to succeed are clearly shown.

The caring employer

Richard, despite appearances, is very sensitive and caring and keen to look after his employees and partners. No matter how busy he is he will always find time to listen to their ideas, or to their troubles. While he pours all his energy into his work and suffers from considerable strain and exhaustion at times, he gets a certain amount of respite from business commitments, enjoying his home and family life. He has a powerfully spiritual side which gives him inner strength.

A New Job?

Sooner or later you will probably be asked about the possibility of a client getting a new job. While you must not be dogmatic, it is possible to stick your neck out just a little, provided you also offer constructive suggestions and give advice that your subject can follow up.

Generally speaking, it will be necessary to concentrate more on progressions and transits than the birth chart, but of course you will have gone through many of the stages mentioned earlier in this section of the book before beginning to answer the question or assess your subject's situation. A great deal depends on how assertive, enterprising and disciplined the subject is, how much a job is actually wanted, and so on. Having considered these points, what is the next stage?

How the job offer may appear

You will know from your general study of the meanings of the houses and the earlier comments in this section, that if your subject looks as if she is going to be offered a job out of the blue, the chances are that there will be positive and strong directions to the Midheaven; but if the job comes about through her writing an application, it is most likely that the Ascendant or personal planets are being activated by positive transits, progressions or the short-lived lunar progressions.

Interpreting influences

Do not expect to see only pleasant groups of Jupiter transits, for these expansive trends are not the only indications of such an achievement. Remember that with a new job also comes responsibility and often strain and tension, so there could easily be a conjunction or positive transit from Saturn to the Midheaven at the time of the new appointment, indicating additional responsibility and prestige. Exciting and unexpected career developments can occur when there is a transit of Uranus to the Midheaven. It may be that the ruling planet is one of the fast-moving planets – Mercury Venus or Mars – and quite minor transits from these planets can be significant provided there is some back-up from long-term progressions or other transits. Keep an open mind, since you may well find that someone – especially where Saturn is concerned – could achieve a prestigous job, whereas someone else under an identical transit might well be asked to leave! Distinguishing between contradictory interpretations of the same influence is where skill and experience come in. But there are ways of checking your conclusions. A golden rule when faced with such dilemmas in this or any other area of astrological interpretation, when you have to assess a questionable influence from a transiting planet, is to look at its placing in the birth chart. If it is reasonably well-placed and not too negatively aspected, its influences as it moves round the sky will often be constructive. A negatively aspected Jupiter, perhaps squared by Pluto or even the Moon, will be far less helpful than a well-aspected Saturn which in the birth chart has constructive and positive aspects from the Sun or Moon.

Watch for planetary returns

It may be that your subject is about to experience a Jupiter or Saturn Return, or the Uranus Half-return. If so, apply the same rule. Generally speaking, the chances are that during the year of a Jupiter Return we usually end up with rather more cash than we started – or that some kind of progress is made irrespective of how Jupiter is placed or influenced by other planets in the birth chart. The Saturn Return offers people a period of change and often of psychological development. The Uranus Half-return can persuade many to try to force issues – not always wise.

Other transits and progressions

Look too for strong transits or progressions between Mars and Jupiter; these usually put us not only in an assertive mood but also a good position in which to take the initiative.

If the progressed Moon is making negative aspects to the natal or progressed Saturn, your subject may need to hold back and not force issues. These aspects often make us feel low, dispirited, even hopeless. Advise some quiet research into what is available, the writing of a new resumé, or some refresher studies until the influence has eased. This could also apply if you think Saturn or any heavy planet is working negatively. Suggest that your subject starts to make an effort to get a new job when the influence is over. If a run of negative trends is followed by some assertive ones, do everything in your power to encourage action, so as not to waste the positive energy which could help your subject to get the job she wants.

With all these points in mind, keep referring to the main interpretation text for each of the trends working in your subject's chart. You should then not experience too much difficulty, and should be able to reach conclusions which will help your subject.

The Career Plan

The chart on the following pages lists career possibilities for your subjects. Our suggestions are starting points from which you might begin a discussion with your subject. It may seem odd that there is a considerable variety of careers under each heading, but we have attempted to spread the net widely to cater for the subject's environment, educational background and age.

These suggestions are based on the Sun and Ascendant signs, but in addition to these we need to consider the Midheaven sign. As you see from the chart on p.175, there are several permutations of these for each of the Ascendants, and, while because of space limitations it has not been possible to set out interpretations for each of them, we have taken them into consideration when making our suggestions. Many of the suggestions have been put to Julia's subjects, and often they have proved to be extremely worthwhile. Others are those she would put forward should the specific combination of signs occur.

An open-minded approach

Even so, you must not base your suggestions on this list alone (challenge it every inch of the way, and if you disagree with good reason, you will be making progress and gaining experience). You must also consider the other areas of the chart and the planets' influences relating to career (see pp.30-1). Pay special attention to the Moon's influence with regard to working conditions and environment – a big factor.

SUGGESTED CAREERS: SUN SIGN ARIES ♈

ASC	CHARACTERISTICS	NEEDS	POSSIBLE CAREERS
♈	Brave, energetic, enthusiastic, physically strong	Excitement, challenge, action	Fireman, own business, airlines, the army
♉	Controlled energy, practical	Security but independence	Electronics, scientist, musician, mathematician, finance
♊	Versatile, restless, inquisitive, nervous energy	Variety, movement, intellectual challenge	Motor mechanic, the media, telecommunications, selling
♋	Possibly good with young people, protective emotional energy	To defend and cure others	Gamekeeper, the navy, youth worker, swimming /PE instructor, hotel business
♌	Direct, good organizer, enthusiastic, physical energy, creative	To be in control of situations, to show off	The army, professional sports, painter, dancer, designer
♍	Nervous energy, critical, communicative	To express opinions, security	Literary agent, messenger, researcher, farming, critic, industrial analyst
♎	Lively, affectionate, appreciative of luxury, beauty	To work with other people	The fashion industry, hairdresser, luxury trades, beautician, steward - air or cruise liners
♏	Highly charged emotional/physical energy	To have heavy demands made on him/her	Engineering, psychoanalyst, metallurgist, mining, the marines, accountant, police
♐	Positive outlook, enthusiastic, independent, restless	Challenge, variety, to burn up physical and emotional energy	PE instructor, explorer, expedition organizer, the travel industry, lecturer, publicity
♑	Ambitious, independent	Challenge, to be in control, responsibility	Own business, stock exchange, science, luxury trades
♒	Independent, original, dynamic, inventive	To work in his/her own way	Electrical engineer, glazier, fashion, scientific research
♓	Kind, emotional, sensitive and strong	To work behind the scenes, for good of others	Charity work, nursing, social worker, imaginative writing

SUGGESTED CAREERS: SUN SIGN TAURUS ♉

ASC	CHARACTERISTICS	NEEDS	POSSIBLE CAREERS
♈	Powerful, emotional and physical energy, assertive, stubborn	Security, action	Heavy sports/team game coach, banking, own business
♉	Luxury-loving, good company, excellent business sense	To make money, financial/emotional security	Horticulture, singing, insurance, financial advisor
♊	Communicative, versatile	Variety, within a set routine	Masseur, market management, bartender, the stock exchange
♋	Caring, emotionally strong, shrewd	To see satisfaction in others as result of effort	Grocery, caterer, dairy farmer, insurance agent, nursing, nanny
♌	Appreciates quality, big spender, show off, excellent company	Pleasure, emotional involvement in career	Makeup artist, artist or art teacher, jewelry trades, own business
♍	Practical, methodical, critical	Security, steady growth, a predictable, but not boring routine	Accountant, bricklayer, builder, organic farmer, potter, brewing industry
♎	Could be sybaritic, understanding, eye for beauty	To work with other people, and to make them feel/look good	Painter and decorator, florist, luxury trades, fashion trades, beautician
♏	A hard worker, high emotional energy, determination	A sense of purpose in career, to know what's going on	Banking, the wine trade, mining, detective work
♐	Reliable, broad-minded, enthusiastic	Challenge, possibly "the outdoors"	Farmer, college professor, work with animals, publishing
♑	Practical, cautious, reliable, ambitious	To have a sense of direction and purpose	Executive, official, lumberjack, forester, mason, farmer, musician, own business
♒	Creative, perhaps stubborn, inventive	To be given a free hand	Glassblower, scientist, musician, physical therapist, radiographer
♓	Imaginative, creative	Encouragement, security	Reflexologist, charity work, the shoe trade, specialist journalist, fashion writer/editor, sportswriter

Suggested Careers: Sun Sign Gemini ♊

Asc	Characteristics	Needs	Possible careers
♈	Physical and nervous energy, willing worker, easily bored	Variety, action, to assert him/herself	Publicity agent, sales assistant, reporter, advertising
♉	Versatile, but stubborn	Movement, but security	Retailing, truck driver, car sales, cosmetic trades
♊	Extremely communicative and versatile, restless	To be in touch with other people	Disc jockey, journalist, taxi driver, traveling salesperson, telephone operator
♋	Caring, lively, youthful, sensitive, shrewd	To help others, variety	Nurse, antiquarian bookseller, youth worker, pharmacist, imaginative writer
♌	Usually very extroverted, versatile, creative, bossy, good organizer	To show off, psychological involvement in career	Entertainer, art teacher, the jewelry or fine-art trades, creative journalism/writing
♍	Critical, analytical, versatile, communicative	To investigate and communicate, exchange ideas	Greengrocer, market researcher, traveling salesperson, graphologist, sales assistant, literary critic
♎	A "light" intellectual, good communicator, often caring	Rapport with others	Manicurist, furniture salesperson, telephone operator, receptionist, the hotel trade
♏	Investigative, usually clever, shrewd	To solve problems	Automotive industry, detective work, research, psychology, computer programmer
♐	Enthusiastic, optimistic in outlook, breadth of vision	To communicate with others	Newsdealer, the post office, travel agent, advertising, publishing, the media, teacher
♑	A rational, practical outlook, logical	To have mental challenges	Scientific research or analysis, doctor, osteopath, local government
♒	Quick, original, an individualist, good communicator	Variety, mental stimulation, movement	Radio operator, the airlines, astronomy, space research, radio or TV reporting, sales
♓	Versatile, intuitive, imaginative	Freedom of expression, but to develop sense of direction	Record industry, audiovisual trade, fabric or fashion design, illustrator, teacher

Suggested Careers: Sun Sign Cancer ♋

Asc	Characteristics	Needs	Possible Careers
♈	Good resources of emotional and physical energy, determination	To be confronted with challenge in order to motivate action	Own business, the navy, midwife, doctor
♉	Shrewd, excellent business sense, protective	To make money in order to provide considerable security for family	Restaurant owner, boat builder, own business, banking, stock exchange, beauty business
♊	Changeable, quick witted, argumentative, emotional, logical	Variety, to keep mind active, and use imagination creatively	Kindergarten teacher, nanny, children's story writer, children's clothes/toy trades, antiques trade
♋	Sensitive, caring, emotional, will worry	To care for others or artifacts	Chef, cook, silversmith, child nurse, kindergarten teacher, museum keeper, antiques restorer
♌	Creative, caring, sensitive, bossy	To be in control – sometimes behind the scenes	Hotel trades, headwaiter, harbormaster, cameraman, TV/film makeup artist, art teacher
♍	Critical, a sharp mind, will worry, caring	To give practical help and see the result	Marine biologist, doctor (GP), historian, teacher, conservationist, restorer, dietician
♎	Sympathetic, kind, sometimes weak, sometimes tough	Tranquillity, but must develop assertiveness	Hairdressing, nursing, the army, engineering, catering
♏	High emotional energy, inner strength	A very demanding job, and to use potential fully	Family planning, geneologist, gynecologist, shipwright, parole officer
♐	Has both caution and enthusiasm, emotionally charged motivation	Excitement, variety, to express caring instinct	Dog breeder, stable assistant, travel guide, translator, history teacher/lecturer
♑	Ambitious, shrewd, changeable	To achieve a prestigious position	Poultry farmer, environmentalist, mortgage broker, marine architect, own business, real estate agent
♒	Changeable, original, sometimes eccentric	To develop consistency of effort	Architect, hydrographer, physical therapist, meteorologist, curator
♓	Highly sensitive and emotional, intuitive, imaginative	To be decisive about career, and express natural tenacity	Visiting nurse, counselor, home economics teacher, work on or near the sea, dress design

Suggested Careers: Sun Sign Leo ♌

Asc	Characteristics	Needs	Possible careers
♈	Ambitious, assertive, a go-getter, impatient	To burn up abundant energy during the day's work	Own business, professional sports, any creative work
♉	A powerful personality, sometimes dogmatic, good company	To aquire high standards and earn a lot of money	Luxury trades, real estate, banking, architect, department store buyer
♊	Intellectual, creative, positive in outlook	A happy, lively working atmosphere	Fashion designer, jewelry trades, magazine journalist, trade exhibition consultant
♋	Organizational ability and caring instincts combine	To produce a high standard of goods/service to others	Hotel manager, restaurant owner, the fashion trade, antiques, historian
♌	Creative, showy, enthusiastic, optimistic	To take center stage, to be boss	Theater management, commissionaire, receptionist, own business, model
♍	Self-critical, creative, possibly strict	To know what's going on and to see everything is done	Theatrical agent, school principal, arts and crafts trades or teaching, tailoring
♎	Affectionate, generous, gregarious	Emotional involvement in work – pleasant surroundings, glamor	Advertising, beautician, computer dating agency, the dress hire business
♏	Abundant energy, good sense of direction	To work hard and enjoy every minute	The medical profession, surgeon, the wine trade, the army, banking, criminal investigation
♐	Creative, enthusiastic, optimistic, positive	To express creativity in work	Dance or art teacher/lecturer, the export trades, literary work, translator, publishing
♑	Ambitious, positive, sometimes dictatorial.	To achieve and win respect from the community	Politics, local government, own business, farmer, architect
♒	Originality, creative, scientific	To keep an open mind and express originality creatively or inventively	Innovator, scientific research/design, the airlines, astronomy, jeweler
♓	Sensitive, emotional, creative, positive in outlook	To be consciously practical and control inspiration	Dancer, drama teacher, florist, ice skater, cosmetic trades, work with animals

Suggested Careers: Sun Sign Virgo ♍

Asc	Characteristics	Needs	Possible Careers
♈	Active, nervous, tense energy, keen	To learn to work steadily and calmly	Health club instructor, natural food trades, telecommunications
♉	Practical, hard-working, thorough	To develop self-confidence through gradual acceptance of responsibility	Gardener, personal assistant, banking, accountant
♊	Quick thinking, talkative, good communicator	To work in a lively, busy atmosphere and to be kept on the go	Clerk, carpentry, journalism, retailing, commercial trucker
♋	Will worry, but hard working and protective	To be reassured that what is done is of help to others	Shipping agent, acupuncturist, dietician, teacher, chauffeur
♌	A good – if fussy – organizer, could be very critical	To aquire high standards in work	Traffic police, furniture designer/maker, art/craft teacher
♍	High level of nervous/intellectual energy	To develop inner calm and direct energy constructively	Copywriter, homeopath, microbiologist, the media, horticulture
♎	Hard working, could be "dreamy" at times	Pleasant, clean surroundings and to work with nice people	Model agent, landscape gardener, doctor's receptionist, department store salesperson, dressmaker
♏	Thorough, energetic, hard working, inquisitive	To seek the truth	Employment agent, psychologist, the police/detective work, researcher
♐	Critical, usually intellectual, nervous energy	To stretch the mind and constant challenge, psychological involvement	Editor, librarian, professor, publishing trades, bookseller, travel agent
♑	Very practical, cautious, critical, unadventurous	To seek steady advancement in career	Economist, civil servant, real estate agent, farmer, insurance
♒	Rather tense, perhaps restless, practical, original	To develop consistency of effort and sometimes self-confidence	Research scientist, creative design, nursing, physiotherapist
♓	Kind, considerate, willing, critical	To develop self-confidence and practical ability	Film editor, chiropody, horticulture, the caring professions

SUGGESTED CAREERS: SUN SIGN LIBRA ♎

ASC	CHARACTERISTICS	NEEDS	POSSIBLE CAREERS
♈	Sometimes assertive, sometimes laid back	To be liked and to use energy evenly	Millinery, own business but with partner, hotel work, hairdresser
♉	Very appreciative of beauty and good things of life	To please others and work in pleasant surroundings	Confectioner, household furnishing industry/design, luxury trades, florist
♊	Trendy, versatile, good communicator	Constant rapport with others, social intercourse	Receptionist, china and porcelain trades, department stores, airlines, TV
♋	Very sympathetic and understanding, kind, protective	To develop inner strength	Catering, the antique trade, social worker, dietician
♌	Likes the good life, possibly extravagant	Psychological and emotional involvement in career	Interior decorator, china/porcelain industry, banking, retailing
♍	Practical, critical, but sometimes gullible	A set routine and framework in which to work	Personnel management, personal assistant
♎	Romantic, hates to be alone, diplomatic, charming	To develop self-reliance, to increase metabolic rate	Dress design/making, foreign service, beautician, work with a partner
♏	High emotional and physical energy level, passionate, resentful	An evenly paced but busy working life, to burn up energy	The army, banking, insurance, engineering, the wine trade
♐	Understanding, intellectual, amusing, often clever	Challenge, to constantly broaden horizons	University professor, translator, professional sports, the law, publishing
♑	Diplomatic, very cool for a Sun in Libra!	Status, reassurance of progress in life	Osteopath, local government, landscape gardening, mining
♒	Attractive, friendly, helpful, kind, logical	To relate, but plenty of physical and psychological "fresh air"	Model, cosmetician, magazine journalism, the airlines, scientific research, chemist
♓	Very kind and understanding, sometimes weak, often gullible	To develop skepticism and critical acumen	Lingerie trade/sales, computer dating, medical or beauty salon, receptionist, language teacher

SUGGESTED CAREERS: SUN SIGN SCORPIO ♏

ASC	CHARACTERISTICS	NEEDS	POSSIBLE CAREERS
♈	Very high emotional and physical energy, inner strength	Excitement, challenge, hard demanding work	The army or navy, heavy sports or team game instructor, the police, stunt man/girl
♉	Passionate, often stubborn, emotional, sensual, cautious	Security, to make a lot of money	The wine trade/specialist, tax inspector, the oil industry, engineering, banking, butcher
♊	Inquisitive, logical and emotional, versatile	To get at the root of the problem	Detective, investigative journalist, surgeon, scientific analyst
♋	High emotional energy, protective, brave, intuitive	To channel positively emotional and physical energy into worthwhile work	Deep sea fishing industry, diving, social worker, midwife, gynecologist
♌	Extremely energetic, good company, stubborn, emotional, good organizer	To live life to the full, to be kept very busy, to be boss	Big business, property development, own business, production team leader, psychologist
♍	Investigative, analytical, energetic, thorough, emotional	To work in detail, on all projects	Computer programmer, locksmith, registrar of births and deaths, own business, research, scientific
♎	Excellent potential but could stagnate, persuasive	To get others around to their way of thinking	Beautician, cosmetic surgery, teaching, restaurateur, car sales, advertising
♏	Energetic, obsessional, passionate, emotional	To develop a more open mind and breadth of vision	Detective, police, researcher, the navy, own business, banking, medical profession
♐	Emotional and physical energy, enthusiastic, a go-getter	To achieve ambitions and at once move on to the next	The railroads, literary research, the army or navy, professional sports, anthropology, criminal law
♑	Practical, hard working	Security and gradual materialistic growth	Mining, pathologist, geologist, plumbing
♒	Original, stubborn, strict, sometimes tense and inconsistent	Emotional/psychological involvement in career and to develop flexibility	Scientific or ecological research, the medical profession, charity work
♓	Sympathy, understanding, intuition	To constructively channel and express emotional and physical energy positively	Customs official, prison service, funeral director, mining (oil), the navy, psychotherapist

Suggested Careers: Sun Sign Sagittarius ♐

Asc	Characteristics	Needs	Possible Careers
♈	Independent, energetic, enthusiastic, restless	To control any blind optimism and recklessness, challenge	Fireman, language teacher, translator, dancer, professional sport, exports
♉	Practical, energetic, passionate	To achieve ambitious objectives	Building trades/speculator, architect, the stock market
♊	Excellent intellectual potential, versatile, a fast metabolism	To develop consistency of thought and effort	Lawyer, foreign correspondent, store management, travel industry
♋	Brave and defensive, emotional, independent, conventional	An opportunity to develop caring and intellectual potential	Zookeeper, hotel industry, occupational therapist, industrial design, history teacher
♌	Creative, enthusiastic, broad in outlook	Unclaustrophobic working and living conditions, to show off	The fine arts, teaching, own (luxury) business, the entertainment industry, translator
♍	Critical, versatile, restless, practical, inquisitive	Intellectual challenge, independence, movement	University professor, naturalist, ecologist, truck driver, journalist, printer
♎	Charming, good company, may tend to be lazy	Firm direction/encouragement in order to inspire enthusiasm	Graphic artist, fashion designer, the stationery trade, bookseller, drapery trades
♏	Keen, energetic, controlled optimism, sense of purpose	Must have challenge and express powerful personality in career	Attorney, marine biologist, the merchant marine, the railroads, motor mechanic
♐	Very positive in outlook, restless, over-optimistic, capacity for study	To develop caution and a philosophical outlook	Riding instructor, professional sports, language teacher, the law, exports, geographer
♑	Variable outlook – optimistic/pessimistic, conventional/unconventional	To combine need for challenge with well thought out aims and objectives	Town planning, architect, farming, horse breeding, librarian, teacher
♒	Very independent, freedom loving, original, clever, inventive	To control eccentricity and perhaps to become more disciplined	Experimental scientific research, creative design, space industry, journalism, the air force, airlines
♓	Often spiritual and philosophical, kind, easily influenced by others	To develop a practical more cautious attitude	Veterinary assistant, TV/film cameraman, the church, humanitarian work, occupational therapy

Suggested Careers: Sun Sign Capricorn ♑

Asc	Characteristics	Needs	Possible careers
♈	Determination, toughness, sense of purpose, sometimes aggressive	Psychological fulfillment, and to achieve ambitions	The armed forces, own business, politics, the trade unions
♉	A practical outlook, hard steady worker, ambitious, sometimes boring	A steady climb to success, recognition.	Real estate agent, local government, farming, potter, musician, architecture
♊	Talkative, versatile, practical, conventional, logical	To make voice and opinions heard and to gain respect	Archivist, curator, auctioneer, stockbroker, civil servant
♋	Traditional, changeable moods, caring, will fight emotions	To develop optimism and a positive outlook	The antiques trade, cook, boat building and design, physical therapist
♌	Ambitious, conventional, hard worker, snobbish but enthusiastic	To develop humility and the warm side of personality	Town planner, sculptor, the music industry, makeup artist, own business
♍	Very practical, worry prone, cautious, a hard worker	To develop self-confidence and inner calm	Dentistry, horticulture, accountant, craft worker, financial journalism, stonemason
♎	Practical, ambitious, both hardworking and laid back, resentful at times	To develop consistent use of energy, quality	Interior decorator, concert management, department store buyer, visiting nurse
♏	Tough - copes with difficult conditions, investigative	To have obstacles to overcome and to enjoy work and life	The marines or paratroopers, engineer, mining, medical profession, exploring, own business
♐	Philosophical in outlook, ambitious, learns the hard way, enterprising	Challenge, more material comfort than would care to admit to	Zoologist, geographer, teacher, the law, antique book selling, specialist travel agent
♑	A loner, ambitious, conventional, unemotional	To develop warmth, sometimes self-confidence, and sympathy	Archaeologist, mountaineer, stockbroker, mathematician, own business, real estate agent
♒	Very independent, coolly friendly, a private person	To develop independence, but also warmth and emotional responses	Geologist, mineralogist, scientific research, ortheopedic medicine, astronomy
♓	Emotional and practical, sensitive, caring, sometimes shy	To develop self-confidence, and belief in capabilities	Social worker, creative craft work, homeopath

Suggested Careers: Sun Sign Aquarius ♒

Asc	Characteristics	Needs	Possible careers
♈	Independent, original, adventurous, lively, optimistic	To curb any eccentric tendencies	Electrician, electrical engineer, inventive/experimental scientific work
♉	A striking personal appearance, friendly charm, stubborn	To develop flexibility and not to suppress emotion	The recording industry, model, retailing, fashion, beautician, floristry, welfare work
♊	Communicative, argumentative, perverse, sometimes zany, but fun	To become less unpredictable, variety	Optician, the airlines, astronomer, telecommunications, disc jockey
♋	Sometimes emotional, sometimes cool, caring and protective	To control moodiness, and to come to terms with emotions versus logic	Meteorologist, radiographer, charity work, geriatric nursing, ecology
♌	Romantic, but not always loving, bossy	To show off, but to like others to keep their distance	Theater/TV lighting specialist, display artist, jeweler, performer of some kind, own business
♍	Nervous energy, will show independence as cover-up for insecurity	To aquire a steady pace in life and greater self-confidence	Conservation, yoga teacher, biologist, mathematician, medical/scientific research, tailoring
♎	Likely to be good-looking but vain, charming, romantic	To come to terms with independence and need to relate	Interior decoration, fashion, the airlines, film/TV industry, charity fund raising
♏	Inventive, clever, intense, stubborn, self-analytical	To come to terms with powerful emotional content	TV engineer, the air force, medical profession, psychologist, researcher, genealogist
♐	Communicative, optimistic, breadth of vision	Not to ignore others' needs/feelings when expressing independence	Teacher of literature or languages, exports, veterinary surgeon, publishing, the law
♑	Cool, logical, unemotional, ambitious, friendly	Not to become too distant towards loved ones, due to career involvement	Anthropologist, archaeologist, scientist, mathematician, inventor, business man/woman
♒	Extremely logical, independent, a very private person	To remember that no person is an island	The cut glass/crystal trades, television, airlines, humanitarian work where a level head is required
♓	Humility, creative power, perhaps sense of vocation	To have the courage of convictions and self belief	Creative art or craft work, photography, film making, charity work, the priesthood

Suggested Careers: Sun Sign Pisces ♓

Asc	Characteristics	Needs	Possible careers
♈	Volatile, caring, sometimes dreamy, surprisingly tough	To express positively physical energy and emotions	Working with the mentally handicapped or "difficult" children, photography, computers
♉	Intuitive, practical, creative, luxury-loving	Security, but plenty of self-expression in career	Own business, restaurateur, nursing, the fashion industry, musician, farming
♊	Versatile, inquisitive, sometimes deceitful, clever	Variety, emotional involvement, intellectual challenge	Magician, the media, detective, researcher, scientific analyst
♋	Sensitive, caring, moody, changeable	To help and care for others and to help them care for themselves	Geriatric nurse, cook, cruise liners or navy, hardware sales
♌	Very creative, sensitive, intuitive, sometimes showy	To find some outlet for creativity in career	Photographer, projectionist, makeup artist, dancer, the theater, art teacher
♍	Practical, intuitive, sensible, nit-picking, critical	To combine careful analytical qualities with strong intuition	Film editor, dietician, organic food trade, journalist, advertising
♎	A weak constitution (look for strength from Moon, Saturn aspects)	Encouragement to find sense of direction and develop decisiveness	Jewelry trades, furnishing - production and sales, model, confectionery
♏	Very emotional and intuitive, secretive	To channel emotional energy positively and to work hard	The clergy, wine trade, mining, motor mechanic, the navy, civil service, psychotherapist
♐	Versatile, emotional, broad-minded, sense of humour, self-deceptive	To allow the "fire" of Ascendant to "glow" and have positive expression	Kennel assistant, teaching, tour operator, exporting, geographer, map making, entertainer
♑	Practical, sensitive, ambitious but not always self-confident	Not to lose kind sensitivity as worldly responsibility increases	Building trades, garden planner, plumber, welfare work, geologist
♒	Very original, touchy, sometimes irrational, inventive, imaginative	To have courage of convictions, to be convinced of their potential talent	Any creative or scientific work where originality and imagination combine with independence
♓	Creative, sensitive, understanding, sympathetic	To develop discipline and some sense of order	Priest, photographer, design, the caring professions, shoe sales

Change

There are times when we experience astrological influences that encourage us to rethink our lives – what we have done in the past, what we are doing in the present and where we are heading in the future. As a result of this process, we often make quite striking changes in our lives. While several of these influences occur for every one of us when we reach certain ages, there are other influences which are quite individual and personal and relate to our own individual progressed charts – perhaps when our Ascendant or Midheaven changes signs or when our Sun progresses from one sign to the next.

You will soon discover that the time-honored rule that subjects "speak their charts" couldn't be more relevant at such times. Phrases like "I can't go on any longer as I am", or "I don't know, I somehow feel restless", are very common. It is important to notice whether your subject knows precisely what they want to do, or is hesitant and confused. Also, when you are giving advice – especially about the timing of any change – you should examine very carefully all progressions, especially lunar ones, and important transits that are on the horizon.

Suggesting change

You may have to suggest that your subject would benefit from an immediate change, if the indications are favorable, or that they should wait for a while if, say, Saturn is in a bad mood. If the subject is under some negative influence from Neptune they should also wait, because they are probably confused and uncertain. If they have lunar progressions to Mars or Pluto, or these are prominent in the background progressions, or if they have disruptive transits from Pluto or Uranus, they may be impulsive and make premature decisions. In such cases another kind of warning will be apposite.

The Returns

Periods of reassessment which tend to lead to change and are common to all of us are:

1. The first Saturn Return, when we are 29 plus.

2. The Uranus Half-return, when we are 40 plus.

3. The second Saturn Return, when we approach 60.

If we live long enough we can also experience:

4. The full Uranus Return, when we are about 84.

5. A third Saturn Return, when we approach 90.

The progressed Moon

Another group of indications which relate to the progressed Moon is also relevant. You may find its effects are more potent if the Moon is the ruling planet, in its own sign (Cancer) or house (the fourth), or is in Taurus (the sign of its exaltation). For some subjects these progressions will definitely give rise to a period of rethinking about the self and the attitude to various aspects of life, but the influence may not be very noticeable. However, do not be complacent, for these influences might be having their effect on your subject's inner life – their deepest feelings, intuitions and reactions.

By progression, the Moon travels right round the chart in approximately 28 years, so it returns to its precise natal position when we are about 28 or 29 years old. (By transit, of course, the Moon travels round the chart once a month!) It returns to this position for a second time when we are about 56, and again at 83 plus.

This first progression occurs shortly before the first Saturn Return. The two influences complement each other, the lunar progression causing that stirring of feeling which will very often culminate in practical planning as a result of the Saturn influence.

The second completion of the circuit occurs several years before the second Saturn Return, and often the influence will, despite the time-lag, make people in their mid-50s think about life after retirement. We have found some cases of very elderly people who "shake their feathers" when the Moon comes round for the third time.

To learn more about these "milestone" influences (plus, of course, the extremely helpful Jupiter Returns) refer to the relevant pages in "The Planets at Work" (pp.208-347), under the individual planets.

The personal indications of change

The most powerful indication of change is a progression of the Sun from one sign to the next. If your subject wants to make changes and you discover that they are about to experience a change of Sun sign, this is an excellent portent: the time is precisely right for change. Often if subjects are born during the early degrees of a Sun sign period, you may well find that they marry or settle into a permanent relationship at the time of the first Sun sign change, though this can also indicate a range of different changes. However, there is usually a change of lifestyle, and in the personal life. Sometimes a totally new career is taken on: almost anything can happen.

When the Ascendant changes signs your subject may say that they feel differently about important issues or have made some psychological progess. Sometimes subjects look different – not because they've changed their image (that would be under a Sun sign influence) but due to bodily changes.

Calculating the changing Ascendant

Assessing the precise time of an Ascendant changing signs is difficult; if the birth time is only four minutes out it will make a difference of a year in the timing of the trend. This also applies to a change of Midheaven, which will influence career, ambitions and sense of direction. This, too, can be equally dynamic if the birth time is accurate.

Preparing for retirement

Most people retire, or think about retiring, at the time of the second Saturn Return. Study the comments on

THE RETURNS

During a lifetime a man or woman will experience periods in which all the planets, except for Neptune and Pluto, will make a complete revolution of the zodiac and then return to the position in which they were when the subject was born. The Moon and Sun, Venus and Mercury do this relatively frequently; the other planets less so – you will see from the diagram below that only if you live to the age of 84 will you experience a Uranus Return.

First Progressed Moon Return 28–9

First Saturn Return 29+

Uranus Half-return 40+

Second Progressed Moon Return c. 56

Second Saturn Return c. 60

Third Progressed Moon Return c. 83

Uranus Return c. 84

Third Saturn Return c. 90

this transit if your subject is approaching the age of 60. A change of residence or of the area in which they live could also be under discussion, and you may have to point out the various other factors discussed under the Saturn Return (see p.312).

Planning leisure time

Most importantly, you must discuss with your subjects what they will want to do in their free time. They will probably have many ideas already, but you will find other suggestions in the leisure plan (see pp.188-93). These inevitably provide only a starting point, but you could very easily come to some rewarding conclusions. Try, as well as encouraging a development of existing intellectual and creative interests, to suggest involvement in some new physical activity which will help keep their bodies young-looking and in good shape. Remember that as well as assessing how patient your subjects are, you should consider their state of health: their eyesight may not be quite as good as it was and, as ever, you may have to modify some of the physically demanding suggestions.

PREDICTING DEATH

In our view no astrologer should attempt to predict death. We don't believe that precise events can be predicted; any astrologer who tells you something *will* happen is probably using clairvoyance or some other occult technique, and in any case death occurs under many different influences.

Possible influences

Death may take place under a pleasant transit of Jupiter to Venus or Neptune – which could also mean a pleasant happy experience. It may occur under a Uranian influence, which could certainly mean a shock – but sometimes, too, a surprise. It may be suggested by Saturn, when at other times the same trend can indicate constructive progress, delay or frustration! Sometimes Mars is present, but under other circumstances that planet can merely indicate that the subject is likely to slightly cut or burn themselves, or just act impulsively.

Leisure

We have far more leisure time these days than was the case in the past – partly because we are retiring at an earlier age, and partly because we are now living longer. Many of us also experience periods when we are out of work. Inactivity, physical or mental, is very bad for us – not only psychologically but also physically. Any client who is in this position will need special advice, for discovering the most beneficial ways of spending these leisure hours in a rewarding way is today as important as discovering a worthwhile and fulfilling career.

The approach to finding satisfying leisure activities is in many ways similar to choosing a career. However, there are several other factors to be assessed:

◆ The age of the subject.

◆ The physical type.

◆ Whether the subject simply wants something to do while unemployed, or is in need of some kind of stimulation as an antidote to a dull, repetitive job. Conversely, a soothing antidote to a demanding job might be needed.

◆ How patient the subject is. Are quick results needed? Can the subject plod steadily on, studying or creating something, for a long time?

◆ How much will it cost to set up the new interests? (If the subject is about to retire perhaps retirement presents could be linked with the new, or renewed, interests.)

Spending leisure hours rewardingly is as important as having a fulfilling career.

The leisure plan
If you look at the plan on pp.188-93 you will see that it is divided into three sections. As with the career plan, it is to be used only as a starting-point; something to bridge the gap and stimulate discussion. We have had to cover all ages in this plan so, when working with a 70-year-old, you might find disco-dancing or weight-training suggested! But if so it may be that your subject is physically strong and would benefit from something similar but more sedate such as ballroom dancing. Conversely, you might be working with a teenager and find that bridge is suggested – unlikely to appeal. If so, perhaps that young person is particularly sociable and would enjoy a game like billiards or pool. The scope of the plan is fairly comprehensive, but you could widen it further. For instance, your subject may have Gemini rising and a Libra Sun. Reverse the process, and look up Libra rising and Gemini Sun. This will give you an extended package of suggestions, which might well be fruitful, though you may find some repetitions. While, as you know, the difference of influences between Sun and Ascendant signs is distinctive, as a talking point you could find that the alternative list is helpful.

Different categories
In some cases we have put certain sports under the "general and intellectual" heading, since they don't burn up much physical energy. In others – ice-skating is a good example – we have placed some sports under "creative", and some less inspiring but physically active and marginally creative activities under "physical".

Steer by the Moon
Remember your subject's Moon sign when making your suggestions. You will get an immediate and definite response from someone with an Aries Moon – they will either agree or disagree. To someone with a Cancerian Moon, you could say "Well, I feel that you might like…" Or to someone with a Libra Moon, "Now personally, I think that you would enjoy…Why don't you try it? It would be great fun, and you'd meet a lot of nice people."

Other considerations
The questions of age, physical fitness and metabolism obviously apply to the more physical occupations. We leave it to your good sense to ensure that your subject seeks a medical check-up before spending a lot of money on an expensive health club. In addition, you should in other cases tactfully discover how good a subject's sight is, how mobile the hands – if they are slightly arthritic, something like basket-making might be therapeutic, while someone with shaky hands might not be able to cope with fine, delicate work.

In reaching your conclusions concentrate on two of the planets – the chart-ruler (the planet that rules the Ascendant sign) and the Sun-ruler (the planet that rules the Sun sign). If the same planet appears in both cases – for instance, in the case of a double Leo, or someone born with Virgo rising and a Gemini Sun – that planet's influence will be especially powerful.

There will come a time when you will make a suggestion to someone who is retiring and wants to become involved in a new interest, and will at once see their face light up: "I've always wanted to do that!" This is really terrific – it is what being an astrologer is all about!

The attraction of astrology
You may have noticed that we have not included astrology itself in our plan. There is a specific reason for this. You have by now become quite a

THE PLANETS AND LEISURE INTERESTS

THE SUN
represents creativity, the love of color, a sense of drama and the need to show off.

THE MOON
represents imagination and intuition but sometimes its influence can weaken staying power, since its subjects require changing occupations to fit changing moods.

MERCURY
represents mental processes. It often makes its subjects impatient and restless, and in need of lively, intellectually sympathetic and stimulating friends with whom to share interests.

VENUS
represents a love of beauty and endows patience, but often infers laziness and procrastination, and even self-indulgence. It makes its subjects sociable and relaxed, and suggests a flair for the production of beautiful things.

MARS
bestows impatience and the desire for quick results. It causes flare-ups of great enthusiasm that can all too often die – sudden crazes are common. It also accentuates physical energy, which needs positive expression. Mars makes its subjects brave and daring.

JUPITER
represents the intellect and mind-expanding interests. Its influence, like that of Venus, can suggest self-indulgence, but it is often sport-oriented, with a liking for risk-taking. It bestows, like the Sun, a sense of drama and a tendency to show off.

SATURN
represents patience and determination. Slow, steady progress is likely and should be aimed for, otherwise self-criticism and a lack of self-confidence could blight progress. Sometimes rather solitary occupations are favoured, while conversely these are people who enjoy committee-work and being in charge.

URANUS
represents originality and inventiveness; its subjects usually say they want to do something "different".

NEPTUNE
represents a liking for somewhat reclusive interests and increases the subject's imagination, but because it does not always bestow staying-power and confidence additional encouragement is usually necessary if the potential is to be fully developed. Neptune increases intuition and sometimes gives a sixth sense.

PLUTO
represents a need to research and bring results to the notice of other people. One area of this planet's influence finds the darker, mysterious elements of life fascinating.

LEISURE AND THE HOUSES

Look at the chart on p.33 to see which house each planet inhabits. This will strongly suggest the area of life in which the talents expressed by the planets can best be put to use by your subject in their leisure hours.

In particular, the fifth house is that of creativity – usually artistic – but that does not mean your client has to become a painter or actress: if the Moon is in the fifth, she could become a creative and imaginative cook; if Venus, she might particularly enjoy glamorous dressmaking.

The sixth house is the house of health and discipline, of regular daily work, but it can also be related to hobbies and one's attitudes to them; any planet in this house will help one to work carefully and constructively. Mars or Jupiter here can make one a dedicated sportsperson; Mercury may incline one to language or crossword puzzles, to critical writing – or just to jigsaws.

If there are no planets in the fifth or sixth houses, look to the strongest planets and signs in the chart and see what they suggest.

student of our discipline, and as other people benefit from your study and experience, you will find that some of them will take it up for themselves. As is the case with all professions and interests, astrology attracts people of all types. A few decades ago a brilliant British astrologer and reseacher, Charles E. O. Carter, who worked on thousands of charts, studied specific influences in the charts of successful astrologers. He found that not only were certain signs prominent in their charts, but in many cases specific degrees were emphasized by either an angle or personal planet. These are 10° Virgo/Pisces and 27° Leo/Aquarius. The results of this research and many others are explained in his book *The Encyclopaedia of Psychological Astrology*.

CHALLENGE

Look at Sylvia's chart (see pp.158) and ask yourself what you would suggest as a rewarding and fulfilling interest for her.

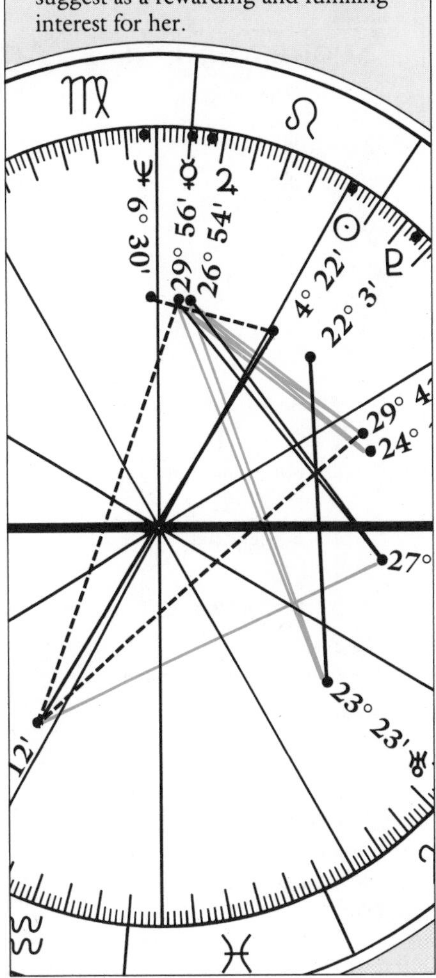

Suggested Leisure Activities: Sun Sign Aries ♈

Asc	Physical	Intellectual/General	Creative
♈	Karate, sprinting, gym	Stock car racing, adventure fiction	Metalwork, DIY
♉	Soccer, football, boxing, weight training	Advanced driving (cars), eating out	Leatherwork, sculpture, painting and decorating
♊	Tennis, athletics, free fall parachuting	Debating, youth clubs, radio ham	Fabric printing, creative writing
♋	Canoeing, baseball	Recreational vehicles, boat building	Machine embroidery, Chinese cookery, painting and decorating
♌	Ballroom dancing, fencing, team games	Cheerleader, zoology, committee work	Collage, music - brass instruments, jewelry
♍	Rally driving, yoga	The Sherlock Holmes Society, the Red Cross, CB radio	Carpentry, weaving, machine knitting
♎	Windsurfing, sailing, judo	Model railways, fashion	Lino cuts and printing, dressmaking
♏	High diving, wrestling, martial arts	Motor cycling, seduction, computers	Model engineering, stained glass
♐	Archery, horseback riding	Competitions, languages, camping	Chinese painting, modern dance
♑	Jogging, mountaineering	Local politics, vintage cars, geology	Music – woodwind instruments, sculpture, pewter work
♒	Skiing, ice hockey	Inventing, astronomy, ecology	Car restoration, amateur theatricals
♓	Water skiing, roller-skating	Helping disabled people	Video making, tap dancing, pressed flowers

Suggested Leisure Activities: Sun Sign Taurus ♉

Asc	Physical	Intellectual/General	Creative
♈	Boxing, team sports	Industrial archaeology, home brewing	Wood-engraving, car restoration
♉	Regular gym workouts	Board games, the stock exchange	Pottery, embroidery, decorative cakes
♊	Basketball, hiking	Fashion, rose growing	Hand knitting, lace making, sketching, creative writing
♋	Swimming, skiing	Treasure hunting, fishing	Decorative cake making, quilting, home improvement
♌	Body building, aerobics	Entertaining, enjoying life!	Landscape painting, sculpture, classic cooking, jewelry, acting
♍	Gardening chores, square dancing, orienteering	Wine/beer making, botany	Weaving, organic cooking, patchwork, wood-carving
♎	Bowling, judo	Music appreciation, entertaining, bridge	Hand embroidery, dress design
♏	Weight training/lifting, underwater swimming	Wine-tasting, erotica, cinema	Soft furnishing, creative dance
♐	Cross-country running	Camping – in luxury! – radio ham	Book-binding, guitar, Country and Western music
♑	Rock climbing, team sports	Reading, biography, coin-collecting, horticulture	Clay modelling, singing in choirs
♒	Ice hockey, yoga	Kite-flying, chemistry, antiques	Horology, singing, piano/keyboards
♓	Cave exploring, rowing	Tarot card reading, fishing	Fabric printing, puppets

Suggested Leisure Activities: Sun Sign Gemini ♊

Asc	Physical	Intellectual/General	Creative
♈	Rallying, gym workouts	Youth clubs, competitions	Appliqué, brass rubbing, machine knitting, percussion instruments
♉	Baseball, football	Treasure hunting, music appreciation	Clay modelling, model-making from kits
♊	Athletics – sprinting, long jump, squash, racquetball	Writers groups, radio ham	Creative writing, machine knitting
♋	Yacht racing, water skiing	CB radio, graphology, baby-sitting	Children's fiction, puppet making, china restoration
♌	Aerobics, roller skating	Chess, entertaining, arranging "events"	Calligraphy, modern dance, fabric design
♍	Hiking, cycling	Ornithology, debating, computer programming	Pottery, hand knitting, patchwork, home improvement
♎	Tennis, karate, aerobics	Quiz games, discussion groups, fashion	Figure drawing, soft furnishing, romantic fiction
♏	Scuba diving, croquet	Backgammon/checkers, neighborhood watch	Model engineering, upholstery
♐	Riding, jogging	Stamp collecting, languages	Landscape painting, photography/video
♑	Mountaineering, horseback riding	Charity fund raising, committee work, board games	Pewter work, paper marbling
♒	Gymnastics, table tennis	Radio ham, inventing	Glass engraving, bead embroidery, modern music
♓	Sailing, synchronized swimming	Book collecting, palmistry	Tapestry, acting, ballet, poetry

Suggested Leisure Activities: Sun Sign Cancer ♋

Asc	Physical	Intellectual/General	Creative
♈	Hiking long distances, running	Collecting model soldiers, local politics	Car maintenance
♉	Gym workouts, golf	Coin collecting, eating out	Confectionery, crochet, carpentry
♊	Canoeing, fishing, jogging	Ephemera and post card collecting	Basket making, model engineering
♋	Rowing, swimming	Collecting antiques – dolls, toys, silver, dowsing	Cooking, working with silver, children's or historical fiction
♌	Ballroom dancing	Visits to stately homes and the theater	Watercolour painting, photography
♍	Yoga, cycling	Organic gardening, recreational vehicles	Patchwork, wood carving, paper marbling, organic cookery
♎	Water-skiing, synchronized swimming	Collecting antique china, bridge	Decorative cake making, dressmaking, interior decoration
♏	Scuba diving, driving, rally driving	Re-enacting historical battles, tarot card reading	String instruments, stained glass
♐	Aerobics, archery, badminton	Languages, cat breeding	Creative writing for children, crochet
♑	Sailing, rock climbing	Industrial archeaology, antique collecting	Singing, book binding
♒	Windsurfing, crosscountry skiing	Astronomy, beachcombing	Restoration of antiques – clothes perhaps, sci-fi
♓	Gymnastics, swimming	Psychic research, magic	Fabric printing, photography

SUGGESTED LEISURE ACTIVITIES: SUN SIGN LEO ♌

ASC	PHYSICAL	INTELLECTUAL/GENERAL	CREATIVE
♈	Square dancing, team sports	Model railways, vintage cars	Metalwork, music – brass or percussion, painting
♉	Body building, golf	Entertaining, shopping, making/spending money	Embroidery, choir singing, gardening
♊	Squash, fencing	Debating, pen-pals, fashion	Model making, creative writing
♋	Swimming, rowing	History, biographies	Watercolor painting, skating
♌	Gym workouts, riding	Chess, theater, visits to art galleries	Jewelry, acting, oil painting
♍	Country/national dancing, cycling	Botany, competitions, biography	Crochet, wood carving, pottery, horticulture
♎	Gliding, golf	Ornithology, crystallography, entertaining	Piano/keyboards, dressmaking
♏	Sailing, team games	Winetasting, computer programming	Car restoration, exotic cooking, modern dance
♐	Archery, athletics	Languages, mythology, geography	Oil painting, ballet, guitar
♑	Cross-country skiing, running, pole-vaulting	Committee work, music appreciation, literature	Clay modelling, book binding
♒	Badminton, tennis	Ballooning, growing orchids, astronomy	Soft furnishings, early or very modern music
♓	Aerobics, gymnastics	Cinema, history of theater or costume	Amateur theatricals, modern ballet, poetry, photography

SUGGESTED LEISURE ACTIVITIES: SUN SIGN VIRGO ♍

ASC	PHYSICAL	INTELLECTUAL/GENERAL	CREATIVE
♈	Basketball, cycling	Advanced motoring, radio ham	Fabric printing, campanology
♉	Soccer/football, karate	The countryside, ecology, horticulture	Weaving, spinning, pottery
♊	Athletics, baseball	Buying and selling, current affairs, radio ham	Short story writing, car maintenance
♋	Roller-skating, sailing, swimming	Historical fiction, the Red Cross or charity work	Toy making, cooking, creative writing
♌	Disco dancing, aerobics, gym	Biography, indoor plants, cat breeding	Photography, creative dance, painting miniatures
♍	Country/national dancing, cycling	Crosswords, gardening	Crochet, knitting, woodwork, vegetarian/Far Eastern cooking
♎	Tennis, golf, cross-country skiing	Fan clubs, ornithology, jigsaws	Dressmaking, pressed flowers, soft furnishings
♏	Boxing, stock car racing, orienteering	Bee-keeping, darts, wine-making	Detective fiction, model making
♐	Fencing, hiking	Chess, languages, philosophy	Florentine embroidery, landscape drawing/painting
♑	Long-distance running, cave exploring	Camping, genealogy, reading	Dressmaking, pewter work, sculpture
♒	Ice hockey, jogging	Reading – science fiction, geology	Candle making, china restoration, Japanese flower arranging
♓	Rowing, yoga	Fishing, psychic research	Mime, ice skating, bookbinding

SUGGESTED LEISURE ACTIVITIES: SUN SIGN LIBRA ♎

ASC	PHYSICAL	INTELLECTUAL/GENERAL	CREATIVE
♈	Hockey, wrestling	Industrial archaeology	Millinery, stained glass
♉	Roller-skating	Entertaining, bridge, music appreciation	Flower arranging, confectionery, model engineering
♊	Tennis, aerobics	Graphology, kite flying, fan clubs	Romantic fiction, fashion, drawing
♋	Sailing, gliding	Romantic fiction, history, antiques	Silverwork, restoring antiques, crochet
♌	Gymnastics, riding	Theater/concert going, socializing, chess, clothes	Chinese painting, stringed instruments
♍	Basketball, jogging	Indoor plants, cosmetic making from natural ingredients	Dressmaking, drawing, lino printing
♎	Hang-gliding, badminton	Quiz games, socializing	Japanese flower arranging, hand knitting, carpentry
♏	Diving, judo, yacht racing	Lepidoptera, detective fiction, entertaining	Photography, engraving, cooking
♐	Gliding, squash	Literature, geography	Writing a diary or romantic fiction, oil painting
♑	Mountaineering, horseback riding	Reading family sagas, music appreciation, politics	Book binding, metal work, stone carving
♒	Parachuting, water-skiing	Egyptology, chemistry, metaphysics	Artificial flowers, science fiction, lace making, machine knitting
♓	Ballroom dancing, synchronized swimming	Poetry appreciation, pet fish, ESP	Patchwork, puppets, guitar

SUGGESTED LEISURE ACTIVITIES: SUN SIGN SCORPIO ♏

ASC	PHYSICAL	INTELLECTUAL/GENERAL	CREATIVE
♈	Canoeing, team sports, karate	War games, skeet shooting	Percussion instruments, campanology
♉	Weight training, rowing	Coin collecting, board games, erotica	Singing, dressmaking, confectionery, engraving
♊	Speed skating, judo	Detective fiction, backgammon/checkers	Horology, stained glass, model engineering
♋	Yacht racing, underwater swimming	Treasure hunting, the Red Cross, detective/romantic fiction	Home improvements, greenhouse horticulture, exotic plants
♌	Gym workouts, soccer football, wrestling	Entertaining, theater/concert going, wine appreciation or making	Creative dance, watercolor or acrylic painting
♍	Yoga, cycling, archery, skiing	Magic, jigsaw puzzles, any kind of research work	Cooking, crime/detective fiction
♎	Swimming, gymnastics	Mixing cocktails, seduction, romantic fiction	Creating exotic clothes, music – piano/keyboard/strings
♏	Martial arts, diving	Amateur detecting, buying and selling, stocks and bonds	Carving, interior decoration, soft furnishings
♐	Polo, fencing, riding, hiking	Backgammon, languages, competitions	Modern dance, poetry, singing – in groups or choirs
♑	Mountaineering, hiking, skiing	Crystallography, genealogy, antiques	Pottery, pebble grinding, music – woodwind instruments
♒	Rock climbing, free-fall parachuting	Cosmology, astronomy, computers	Lace making, skating, electronic music
♓	Yoga, swimming, belly dancing	Psychic research, beachcombing	Photography and processing, mime, acting

Suggested Leisure Activities: Sun Sign Sagittarius ♐

Asc	Physical	Intellectual/General	Creative
♈	Archery, equestrian sports	Adventure fiction, going to dog and horse racing, travel	Landscape painting, photographing animals especially wild ones
♉	Gardening chores	Darts, home-brewing or wine-making	Machine embroidery, leatherwork
♊	Athletics, ballooning, flying	CB radio, pen pals, palmistry	Creative writing, calligraphy, glass engraving
♋	Horseback riding, canoeing	Chess, treasure hunting, party-giving, history	Home improvement, soft-toy making, inventive cooking, children's fiction
♌	Flamenco dancing, riding	Cheerleader, stamp collecting, seduction	Amateur theatricals, oil painting, photography
♍	Jogging, long jump, orienteering	Crosswords, computer programming	Folk/Country and Western music, organic cooking
♎	Tabletennis, skiing	Board games, conversation, entertaining	Oil painting, tapestry, dressmaking
♏	Long-distance swimming or running	War games, fast cars, literary research	Rug making, detective fiction, metalwork
♐	Tennis, riding, baseball	Travel books, languages, youth club leader	Guitar – usually Spanish or classical
♑	Walking, climbing, orienteering	Treasure hunting, antiques, rare books	Book binding, music – perhaps woodwind
♒	Badminton, archery	Radio ham, charity work	Ice skating, china restoration
♓	Competitive swimming	Dog breeding, Egyptology	Ballet, modern or classical poetry, acting

Suggested Leisure Activities: Sun Sign Capricorn ♑

Asc	Physical	Intellectual/General	Creative
♈	Running – possibly marathons	Military history/literature	Campanology, brass rubbing, metal or silver work
♉	Mountaineering, team games	Cosmetic making from natural ingredients	Music – composing and performing, pottery
♊	Athletics – especially sprinting, high jump	Genealogy, debating/lecture societies	Cane work, calligraphy, puppet making
♋	Sailing, rowing, karate	Baby-sitting, investments in antiques, entertaining	Classical cooking, making, dressing or restoring dolls and toys
♌	Roller-skating, hockey, ballroom dancing	Chess, organizing concert and theater going with friends	Jewelry, drawing, sculpture
♍	Yoga, country or square dancing	Archaeology, gardening, conservation of Earth's resources	Wood carving, pottery, weaving upholstery
♎	Skiing, gliding, aerobics	Entertaining, music appreciation, bridge	Lace making, machine knitting, stencilling, soft furnishing
♏	Martial arts, fencing, golf	Anthropology, fishing, board games	Model engineering, engraving, photography
♐	Discus/javelin throwing, jogging, basketball	Book collecting, biography, languages	Video making, collage, landscape gardening
♑	Bowling, rock climbing, hiking	Family sagas, local politics, ecology	Stone carving, basket work, china restoration
♒	Athletics, hang gliding	Science fiction, ornithology, chemistry	Early or very modern music, stained glass
♓	Disco or ballroom dancing, walking	Comparative religion, ESP, pet fish, charity work	Pebble grinding, clay modelling, dried flower arranging

Suggested Leisure Activities: Sun Sign Aquarius ♒

Asc	Physical	Intellectual/General	Creative
♈	Parachuting, martial arts	Inventing, helping disabled people, skeet shooting	Horology, jewelry, acrylic painting
♉	Rally driving, rowing, hiking	Orchid growing, bridge, history of architecture	Wood carving, crochet, soft furnishings
♊	Tennis, ballooning, cycling	Chess, youth clubs, board games	Sci-fi, music (strings), printing
♋	Canoeing, swimming	Collecting curios, dowsing, the Red Cross	Model ships, toy making, painting and decorating, singing
♌	Gym workouts	Committee work, music appreciation, opera	Skating, ballet, dress design and making, acting
♍	Basketball, rock climbing	Cat breeding, kite-flying, charity work	Florentine embroidery, painting miniatures, models from kits
♎	Badminton, tennis	Astronomy, fashion, radio ham	Bead embroidery, piano/keyboard, ancient or very modern music
♏	Speed skating or ice hockey, scuba diving	Local politics, computers, conjuring	Embroidery, classic cooking, stained glass, photography
♐	Squash, table tennis	Exploring, ornithology, billiards	Paper sculpture, landscape painting, calligraphy, vintage car restoration
♑	Cross country skiing or running	Geology, charity fund raising, entertaining	Pebble grinding, campanology, glass engraving
♒	Athletics, gliding, skiing, yoga	Archaeology, science, pet birds	Modern dance, Japanese flower arranging, crochet, model engineering
♓	Gymnastics, sailing	ESP, crystallography, history of the cinema	Lampshade making, guitar, video, mime

Suggested Leisure Activities: Sun Sign Pisces ♓

Asc	Physical	Intellectual/General	Creative
♈	Ice hockey, fencing, squash	Working for animal or children's charities	Carpentry, patchwork, hand knitting, carving
♉	Football, weight training	Entertaining, concert going, ecology	Candymaking, singing, pottery
♊	High diving, skiing, archery	Palmistry, reflexology, languages	Printing, creative writing, fabric design
♋	Rowing, aerobics	Fishing, collecting memorabilia, psychic research	Pottery, pressed flowers, photography
♌	Sailing, riding	Travel to exotic places, dream interpretation, astronomy	Home improvements, jewelry, working with rich fabric or materials
♍	Hiking, canoeing	Bee-keeping, gardening, reading biography	Organic or vegetarian cookery, weaving, poetry
♎	Golf, table tennis	Relaxing/socializing, reading family sagas, shopping	Artificial flower making, Chinese cooking
♏	All water sports	Erotica, beach combing, tarot cards	Video, cooking, figure drawing/painting
♐	Country/national dancing, basketball	Languages, stamp collecting, comparative religion	Skating, paper marbling, lino cuts and printing, home improvement
♑	Golf, hiking, athletics	Maritime history and fiction, philosophy	Clay modelling, music (usually singing), crochet, weaving
♒	Wind-surfing, hang gliding, cycling	Collecting glass, cosmology, inventing	Amateur theatricals, dress design/making, making unusual artifacts
♓	Yoga, gymnastics, boating	Cinema, aromatherapy, pet fish/cats	Poetry, acting, puppet or toy making, cartoon drawing

Health

Association between the planets and signs and areas of the body has been recognized for thousands of years. If you are interested in the history of astrology, you will find many interesting and revealing statements in this area first set down many centuries ago, perhaps by Ptolemy or Manilius, which are still pertinent today, in spite of the advance of both medical science and astrology. These statements show that new medical discoveries are in fact related to traditional astrology, often in a fascinating and revealing way.

Perhaps the best-known relationship is between the signs and various areas of the body (see p.196). There are also powerful connections between the glands and the planets, but this theory is more modern in concept. Both theories are worth memorizing, for they form a basic background to the fascinating area of medical astrology.

The holistic attitude to health is very sympathetic to astrologers; if you lead a fulfilling life and express positive energy – physical, intellectual and emotional – then you are far less likely to become ill. While this is an over simplification, it is an excellent theory and one on which good astrologers concentrate. It is very important that you consider the psychological implications before trying to assess potential illnessess, vulnerabilities and so on.

For instance, someone with a weight problem may be under considerable emotional stress – perhaps there is a lack of affection in their life, so they are comfort eating. But we must never jump to conclusions; the same case might have a thyroid problem, and if that were so then many of the same astrological configurations and indications would present themselves.

Areas of the Chart in Focus

When assessing health and vulnerability to ailments, consider the following:

1. The Ascendant and first house, and any planet or planets that are tenanted in it.

2. The influence of the Sun and Moon, and the ruling planet if the Sun and/or Moon are in aspect to it.

Links between the body and the signs and planets have been made for many centuries.

3. The sixth house and any planet or planets tenanted within it.

4. Sometimes a straight interpretation of an aspect such as Sun square Mars or Saturn has health/ailment implications. Such configurations should be assessed in relation to the general health indications of the birth chart.

In a character analysis remember that the characteristics of the Ascendant and Sun signs, while forming the basis of the personality, emerge on different psychological levels. When assessing the health implications we can usually combine the indications of both the Ascendant and Sun signs. It is advisable to give greater consideration to those connected with the Ascendant, rather than the Sun sign. Sun sign vulnerabilities will emerge as a result of our own actions, while those of the Ascendant seem to be related to our genetic structure. Those of the Moon relate to our reactions to situations. For instance, those with the Moon in Virgo will find that their stomachs react badly when they are under stress, or have had a shock.

Planets in the first house

The closer a planet is to the Ascending degree, the greater is the strength of its influence. At first, you should look up, and gradually learn, the influence each planet exerts when in conjunction with the Ascendant. However, as a general guide, study the brief planet interpretations opposite. The further "down" the house, the less potent the influence – but be careful, for you may have an inaccurate birth time and the strength of the influence may be greater or lesser than first thought: some rectification may be needed.

The list of signs and their relationship to the attitude to health, vulnerability and general needs (see p.198) is another guide. In both cases think constructively and ask yourself questions about the influence of ruling planets and so on; these will refine the possibilities and give a clearer picture.

The sixth house

The way we spend our waking hours, our attitude to routine and what we have to do to make a living, run a home, or whatever, will have a powerful effect on our physical well-being. The body is like a finely-tuned machine. When cared for and used sensibly it will last a very long time. When abused by too much pressure, or even worse when allowed to "rust", it will grind to a halt. Again, to help you come to conclusions see the list on page 199 which sets out the combinations of Ascendants and signs on the cusp of the sixth house. This list will always apply if you are using the Equal House system. If using Placidus, look carefully – the Ascendant and sixth house cusp sign may not be as listed. If so, while some cross-referencing may be helpful, the list will still give an idea of how to structure your interpretation of these two elements of the chart.

PLANETS IN THE FIRST HOUSE

☉ THE SUN

Positive Increased vitality and a positive attitude to health. Usually the Sun and Ascendant signs are the same, making the individual a "double Libran" or whatever. In such cases the general health accent, according to the sign, is also particularly potent; such a placing needs particularly special consideration. Examine the Sun's aspects and those of the ruling planet, whose influence is, of course, also especially powerful.

Negative Negative traits will appear according to the negative aspects from other planets, and the Sun's powerful vitality and positive outlook can be diminished or in some cases exaggerated as a result.

☽ THE MOON

Positive A positive flow of emotion will help the individual to lead a rewarding life, but this placing always sensitizes the subject's skin, whatever its color may be. Worry and intuition can affect the subject's health. Regular breast exams are especially important for women with this placing.

Negative As for the positive, but the tendency to worry is increased. Very often the vitality is lowered and digestive problems occur – again, usually as a result of worry.

☿ MERCURY

Positive There is a heightened metabolism and mental and nervous energy which should find expression in accordance with the characteristics of the Ascendant. Restlessness can become a problem.

Negative Nervous strain and often tension can result, especially if Mercury receives negative aspects from Uranus, the Moon or sometimes Jupiter. Restlessness is increased, and a tendency towards depression can adversely affect the health if Saturn is in square or in opposition.

♀ VENUS

Positive This slows down the metabolism but it can encourage a steady flow of energy if placed in a fire or air sign.

Negative Weight gain is very likely, since this placing will incline the subject to be self-indulgent.

♂ MARS

Positive This heightens the metabolism and physical energy which needs a great deal of positive expression. A tendency to be accident prone is very likely.

Negative As above, but the negative effects are considerably increased. If Saturn contacts Mars there can be an irregular use of energy and a tendency to feverishness and chills. If there is a negative contact from Uranus, tension and stress may lead to physical as well as psychological disorders.

♃ JUPITER

Positive The individual will live life to the fullest; any sort of complication will be due to the enjoyment of far too much rich food and wine, so that even if the planet is well aspected, weight gain is a distinct possibility.

Negative The tendency to overdo things – to eat and drink excessively, not as a result of a need to escape reality, but simply because it is enjoyable to do so, may eventually lead to a degree of liver damage. The hips and thighs are vulnerable, as when Sagittarius rises, and the individual will be likely to put on weight in these areas.

♄ SATURN

There is little that can be said about a positive influence of Saturn on the health from this house. It seems always to lower the vitality, though in a few cases it might act as an anchorage for the personality. It tends to give most individuals a rather negative outlook on life, which does not help their physical well-being. Aches and pains are very common, and sometimes, if Saturn is afflicted by Mercury or Uranus, there is restricted movement. The subject may tend to fall rather frequently and suffer some nasty bruising or more than his or her fair share of broken bones. When the Sun, Moon or ruling planet make negative aspects to Saturn the ailments of the Sun, Moon or Ascendant signs may be present in an above-average way.

♅ URANUS

As with Saturn, there is little that is positive about this placing. It will certainly heighten nervous energy and often the metabolism, but will also add a powerful vulnerability to stress and tension. A proneness to accidents is a distinct possibility, with the subject tending to suffer from sprains if he or she has a fall.

♆ NEPTUNE

Much is said in the psychological section (pp.204-7) about this placing, and in the section on interpretation of the aspects (see Neptune's aspects to the Ascendant, pp.332-3). Its effects seem to veer more strongly towards the psychological than the physical, unless because of psychological problems the subject falls back on drink or drugs in an effort to escape, when it is obvious that these tendencies will have a physical as well as a psychological effect. But it is the psychological area of influence that you must consider rather than the purely or overly physical. A vulnerability to medically administered drugs can also be present, and if the planet is under a Scorpio Ascendant it will slow down the metabolism, thus making the subject very prone to a serious weight problem.

♇ PLUTO

Again there are few positive effects, apart from the possibility that Pluto, if well-aspected, will encourage the elimination of unwanted matter and fluids from the body. If negatively aspected the cramping, inhibiting effect can cause the reverse. As is the case with Neptune, the psychological influence of the planet in this position is very powerful.

THE PLANETS AND THE GLANDS

There is a strong planetary relationship with the glands. If a planet is in the first house, and especially if it conjuncts the Ascendant, the gland it rules may be vulnerable, or at any rate accentuated in some way for the subject. This area of influence is perhaps one of the most important, if not the most important, of such influences. The glandular focus will also be in evidence in relation to the ruling planet, which must also be studied in order to get a full picture.

The Zodiac and the Body

Astrologers have long recognized that the signs seem to "rule" various parts of the body. This was shown by innumerable "Zodiac Men", in which the glyphs of the signs were aligned with that part of the body they ruled. This diagram shows the most commonly recognized associations: the planetary associations are taken from Ptolemy's *Tetrabiblos*, written almost 2,000 years ago; we also add an association between the planets and the human glandular system. Modern astrologers still find that the correspondence works, but as with other areas of the science, use it less fatalistically.

Aries
Aries rules the head, and in particular the cerebrum, where the upper brain lies. A strong emphasis on Aries may involve a tendency to neuralgia or sick headaches. Mars, which rules Aries, is traditionally associated with the left ear, kidneys, veins and genitals. It rules the gonads, or sex glands.

Taurus
The cerebellum or lower brain is associated with Taurus, as are the neck, ears, lower jaw and throat. Taureans also have the reputation of overeating. It affects the parathyroids, which control the calcium level of the body fluids.

Gemini
Gemini rules the lungs, bronchial tubes, shoulders, arms, hands and fingers. Mercury rules Gemini, and there is an emphasis on the mental processes, which are usually quick and bright; Ptolemy connects the planet also with the tongue, and bile and the buttocks. Modern astrologers believe that it helps to control the whole nervous system.

Cancer
Cancer rules the breasts, the stomach and the alimentary canal. The Moon, which rules Cancer, is traditionally connected with the stomach, the womb and the faculties of taste; it also rules the left-hand side of the body. Modern astrologers also associate it with the whole alimentary system.

Leo
Leo rules the heart, spine and back. The Sun, which rules Leo, is said by Ptolemy to rule the brain, heart, sinews and the right-hand side of the body. It is now associated with the thymus and endocrine gland (important at puberty) and connected with the body's immunisation system.

Virgo
Virgo is connected with the intestines, the solar plexus and also the nervous system. The sign is ruled by Mercury (so see under Gemini).

Libra
The kidneys are ruled by Libra; so is the lumbar regions and the loins. There may be a connection with urinary problems. Venus rules the sign, so see also under Taurus.

Scorpio
The sexual organs are traditionally associated with Scorpio (hence its over-stressed reputation as the most sexually active of signs). The bladder, prostate and rectum are also ruled by this sign. The traditional ruling planet is Mars, so see under Aries. But Pluto is the modern ruler, and this planet is linked, like Mars, with the gonads.

Sagittarius
Sagittarius is traditionally associated with hips and thighs; also the blood vessels. Its ruler is Jupiter, which also rules the liver, arteries and semen, and is associated with the pituitary gland, which regulates hormone production and bodily growth.

Capricorn
Capricorn rules the knees, bones and teeth; its ruler is Saturn, which rules spleen, bladder, phlegm and bones, and is associated with the anterior lobe of the pituitary gland, which regulates the sex glands and affects bone and muscle structure.

Aquarius
Aquarius rules the circulation; its traditional ruler is Saturn, so see Capricorn. The modern rulership is that of Uranus, which astrologers associate with the pineal body, the mysterious "third eye".

Pisces
Pisces rules the feet (it is also said to be the ruling sign of all hospitals and medical practice). Its traditional ruling planet is Jupiter, so see under Sagittarius; the modern ruler is Neptune, which affects the thalamus, a brain structure which affects the transmission of stimuli between the sensory organs.

SOME COMMON PROBLEMS, AND HOW TO ASSESS THEM

Perhaps the most important consideration is just how much the subject's mind, outlook and lifestyle affect the health. If the subject is a worrier and lives alone there is a strong possibility that, with little else to worry about, the slightest negative symptom will become emphasized: an attitude of mind will actually causes illness.

These situations will be most common in a prominently Cancerian person – and perhaps one whose family now lives at a distance, or who is a widow. It is not only lonely elderly ladies who are vulnerable in this way: a young man or woman, a student, perhaps, having just left home for the first time, may become mysteriously ill. Again, they could well be prominently Cancerian. Or maybe the Moon conjuncts the Ascendant, or that planet is negatively aspected by another personal planet or by Saturn – in which case the whole outlook may become gloomy. A similar attitude could be present in someone who is prominently Libran, for it is these two signs, along with those who live alone and are strongly Virgoan or Aquarian, who suffer in this way.

Suggesting changes in lifestyle

Before attempting to assess the illness – imaginary or real – approach your subject with what may well be the root cause of the problem. Perhaps their life needs opening up in some way – they need more to occupy their mind. If the subject is very definitely a loner, then that's their pattern and lifestyle, but encourage them to develop potential or maybe become involved in past interests once again.

The young person who is physically ill just after having left home may be feeling very insecure and may simply need encouragement to adapt to the new, less protected, lifestyle. Look to Mars and Jupiter for initiative, and to Uranus to see if any of that planet's independent streak is present. If the fire signs are prominent the symptoms may be very short-lived. If water, the problem could be more tricky and maybe long-term. If earth, he or she must learn to develop a sense of security. If air, then logic, and a logical approach on your part, will be the answer. In any case, if you look at the lunar progressions and transits you may discover what is causing the symptoms and the negative attitude, and be able to assess their possible duration. You may have to proceed very gently and carefully, but sometimes a slight shock can jolt young people out of this "back to the womb" complex. But do remember you cannot prescribe, nor diagnose ailments – unless you are a doctor or qualified homoeopath – so don't overstep the mark.

Neglecting health

From the tendency to be over-concerned or a hypochondriac there is the other extreme; those who bury their heads in the sand. Facing up to reality may be difficult. If so, do everything possible to encourage preventative medicine. The person who tends to veer in this direction is one who shows blind optimism: "Everything's fine." (Look for negative aspects between the Sun and Jupiter, a powerfully placed Jupiter, or conjunct the Ascendant).

There is also the procrastinator who cannot face the idea of having tests (a prominently Libran or Piscean type). You may have a subject who has a strong Mars or is prominently Arien or Sagittarian, and because they like sports and exercise regularly they are stubborn about recognizing symptoms – sometimes until too late.

Remember that you will know the best approach to these different types because you have their charts. Study the position of the Moon, because it is there that you will see how they react to situations. In a difficult case, study your own chart in relation to the subject's to see if there is good rapport between you. In this way you can give them comfort and encouragement.

ASTROLOGY AND DIET

Sometimes people will ask you when it is a good time to start a diet. As ever, study the chart from other points of view before attempting to come up with a suitable time. Ask yourself:

◆ How disciplined is this person? Is he or she strong-willed enough to stick to a diet once it is started? Someone with a well-aspected Saturn should do quite well; someone who shows disorganized tendencies or who is easygoing will need greater encouragement, as will the subject with a very strong Venus or Jupiter and a love of good food (rich, sweet food in the case of Venus) – the chances are they will need to diet more than a well-organized or busy person.

◆ Is the metabolism high or low? If it is fast, there is a good chance that your subject will need to lose only a little weight, and that their body will respond well to the necessary reduction of calories. Also, because they move quickly (and indeed may be something of a fidget) they will shed that weight with little trouble, and will adopt a logical and practical attitude when tempted by unsuitable food. If, however, they have a low metabolism it will take much longer for to lose weight, and they will need much encouragement. However, with subjects with a heavy build, earth signs may dominate their charts, in which case you can appeal to their determination and sense of purpose. If Jupiter gives them a liking for good living you may at least be able to appeal to their intelligence.

◆ When is it a good time to start a diet? Perhaps it is easier to assess when it is not! For instance, a flurry of Jupiter transits, especially to the Sun, Ascendant or Moon, tends to make us put on weight. Transits from Jupiter to Venus, or a cluster of short transits from Venus to Jupiter, the Sun, Moon or Ascendant are also not good for dieting, because at such times we usually find that we have either to entertain other people, or enjoy meals that are far from slimming. Obviously, Christmas and other festivals are not good times; neither is a New Year resolution for those who live in more northern latitudes – in cold weather we do need to eat somewhat heavier food.

Positive indications

Ideally, we should look to transits that give sensible and constructive help. Positive transits from Saturn to the ruling planet are good; those from Saturn to Mercury, which put us in a sensible frame of mind, are also helpful. However, positive lunar progressions to Saturn are surprisingly not

THE SUN SIGNS AND HEALTH

☉	ATTITUDE	METABOLISM	VULNERABLE TO	NEEDS
♈	Hasn't time to worry over health	Usually high	Headaches, accidents due to carelessness – cuts, burns, lost teeth	To counter carelessness, to avoid getting physically and emotionally over heated, spicy food
♉	May worry, but could procrastinate over seeking medical advice	Low	Weight gain, throat infections	To curb self-indulgent eating and drinking – avoid sweet rich food and comfort foods
♊	Will rationalize possible problems	High	Nervous strain and tension, restlessness, arm, shoulder and hand injuries, bronchitis	To counter restlessness through a combination of physical and intellectual activities
♋	May become frightened by minor ailments	Usually low	Digestive problems brought on by worry and serious sunburn due to sensitive skin	To adopt a more rational attitude in order to counter worry and develop an even tenor to life; regular health examination
♌	Furious with self when ill	Steady to high	Back ache and spine injuries	Regular exercise to avoid heart problems and to keep back supple; to keep warm
♍	May run to doctor (or homeopath) at the least provocation	High	Worry, nervous tension, which often leads to migraine; bowel problems, eczema	To develop calm through practice of a relaxation technique
♎	Could procrastinate over seeking a diagnosis	Usually low	Weight gain, physical and psychological headaches	An even tenor to life through regular eating and enjoyable exercise
♏	May attempt self diagnosis to find out what's wrong	If wiry – high; if heavier build – low and getting lower	To avoid psychological and physical stagnation and burn up powerful energy	To avoid excess in all spheres of life, especially in eating and sexual behavior
♐	Will usually ignore symptoms as long as possible	Usually high	Restlessness, which can lead to physical and emotional problems; weight gain around hips and thighs	To make certain that physical and intellectual energy is burned equally and counter one with the other
♑	May well worry	Steady to high	Arthritic conditions and dental problems; knee injuries	To keep moving in order to avoid stiffness in joints; to develop positive attitude to life
♒	May listen to medical advice, but may not take it	Usually high	Arthritic conditions, weak ankles; poor circulation	May need to keep far warmer than he/she feels is necessary; control peverse attitude to ailments
♓	Will tend to worry and to develop imaginary ailments	Usually low	Foot problems, weight gain, sometimes allergic to medically administered drugs	To be aware of tendency towards negative escapism

good. Whatever the season, you can be at least 90 per cent certain that when there are progressed lunar aspects to the natal or progressed Saturn, you will catch a cold or chill (see pp.200-1). The last thing to do at such a time is to eat less. However, if your subject is the sort to go off food when suffering from a cold, they may lose weight, and will not need a diet when well again.

In general, these positive Saturn transits will work well as times for dieting. Otherwise, try to find a time when there is little going on in the progressed chart. This will mean that your subject's life is less likely to have pleasant surprises – such as being taken out to the best restaurant in town!

Sensible approaches to dieting

It is essential that before starting anything like serious dieting your subject consults their doctor. Having done so, if they want to get and keep slim it may well be a question of adjusting to a different eating pattern – in which case they can do no better than attend a local Weightwatchers group; always make sure their address and telephone number is on your file, so that you are able to give the information to a subject who is in the mood to do something about their extra inches!

Always ask yourself whether the reason for a subject's weight problem is related to an unfulfilled emotional life. If so, do what you can to encourage them to unburden. This could indeed be what is needed, rather than a diet; if they can achieve greater serenity and emotional and sexual fulfilment, the chances are they will eat less anyway.

Should a subject start a diet, it is most advisable that they do not cut down on vitamins, and while we never advocate taking vitamins indiscriminately, if they are dieting they may need a supplement to keep a balance.

The fat child

A lack of love is often the reason why a child is over-eating. Perhaps, too, he or she is feeling insecure. Such a child may also steal, possibly because the parents quarrel or because of some petty jealousy due to the birth of a younger brother or sister. On the other hand, a stupidly overindulgent parent can also be the cause.

RECOGNIZING ADDICTIONS

If you have read other sections of the book you will know that certain planets, signs and sometimes aspects, when located in certain areas of a chart, will encourage negative escapism

THE ASCENDANT AND HEALTH

ASC	SIGN ON CUSP OF 6TH HOUSE	POSSIBLE INTERPRETATION
♈	VIRGO	Busy hardworking day, prone to build up of strain and tension – could take on too much
♉	LIBRA	Liking for the easy life, or heavy business lunches will have adverse effect – possibly more physical exercise needed
♊	SCORPIO	Keen to pack as much as possible into working day – could possibly improve work schedule and routines
♋	SAGITTARIUS	Emotional and physical energy may be wasted due to poor organization, worry and "flaps" over what has to be done
♌	CAPRICORN	Usually disciplined and very well organized, sometimes stress and exhaustion due to being too hard on self
♍	AQUARIUS	Would benefit from regular working hours and a predictable routine, but can become stressful and guilty due to being easily distracted
♎	PISCES	Worry and concern over other peoples' reactions to disorganized attitude can cause stress and negative physical symptoms
♏	ARIES	Ascendant Scorpio gives great resources of emotional and physical energy - Aries needs to get on with life. All should be well, but physical exhaustion and too many late nights may cause problems
♐	TAURUS	Will enjoy hard work and pleasure; diet needs to be watched carefully – tendency to weight gain (and restlessness) if physical exercise is neglected
♑	GEMINI	Nervous strain and tension plus possible long hours of concentration may lead to physical stiffness, aches and pains – massage will help
♒	CANCER	Must learn to develop an even pace, and avoid erratic use of physical energy. Worry will cause physical stiffness in joints
♓	LEO	Will often desire a luxurious life-style, but lack of disciplined concentrated effort can lead to discontent – a flexible but well-structured routine is beneficial to mind and body

through drink, drugs or nicotine. So many young people lapse into drug-taking that we find all zodiac types and sign combinations falling into the habit. But it is possible for you to learn a few indications which might show in a chart and perhaps be instrumental in the prevention of an addiction.

Drug problems
An afflicted Neptune is extremely common in the charts of addicts and is often conjunct the Ascendant (usually from the first house, sometimes from the twelfth). If the Ascendant is Libra or Scorpio, there will be even more of a problem. It could be lessened if Neptune is in Sagittarius, since there is an affinity between that planet and sign. Older people born when Neptune was in Virgo could have succumbed, but drug use was less widespread in their youth. The generation born after 1984 and before 1998 has that planet in Capricorn, and will hopefully be less attracted to the drug scene.

A prominent Pluto can add a fascination, and someone with this planet strongly placed in their chart may be hooked simply out of a desire to know what it is all about.

Dealing with drug addition
Specialized counseling is obviously required to wean someone from a heavy drug addiction, and in most cases it is well beyond our ability and training to attempt this. But it is possible to offer help. Look for indications of change in the chart – the Sun or Ascendant progressing into the next sign, for instance; or the Saturn Return, if your subject is old enough (i.e. 29 or 30); strong Saturn transits – especially to the Sun or Moon – will also encourage a more sensible attitude, and perhaps give the inner strength necessary to break the habit. Look always for the individual's strong points, and if you can encourage their development you will undoubtedly give enormous help. It is no good saying "Stop – this is fruitless" but if you are able to point out the subject's strong points, and most importantly where their real potential lies and how they could begin to discover it and concentrate on its development, this could contribute towards a changed attitude, greater determination and eventually the achievement of a more fulfilling lifestyle. Very often those who succumb have suffered from other people not believing in them, so that they decide to opt out.

Smoking
You can apply the same approach, and look for the same kind of trends, if someone is a heavy smoker, but the difference here is that they may well be keen to give up smoking. Indeed, they need to be, for a lack of determination will result in lapses. All the above-mentioned progressions and transits apply, but you could also look for the same kind of indications we mention for the person who wants to start a diet (see pp.197-8). There are similarities – strength of will and determination will be vital, as will the avoidance of situations where the temptation to smoke could weaken the will.

ALLERGIES AND VULNERABILITIES

Many more people today suffer from allergies than in the past, despite members of the medical profession being eager to assure us of the contrary. Some allergic conditions are caused by food additives, although it is now becoming easier to find food which is free from additives. Stress is another contributory factor. If you are working on the chart of someone who suffers from allergies, you may find that they succumb to an outbreak of spots and rashes when they have stressful transits. It is difficult to avoid stress altogether, and you will usually find it indicated in the progressed chart. It will help if you can suggest a relaxation technique, or perhaps yoga, which will increase inner calm and might well have a beneficial effect on the subject's allergy condition.

Many people respond well to homoeopathic medicine, and if your subject is prominently Virgoan (who could be especially prone to these particular ailments) he or she might respond particularly well to homoeopathic remedies. On a practical level, encourage the subject to make careful studies of what is eaten and drunk and to start a slow process of elimination of foods which might cause the trouble.

Cancer and cancer

It is extremely important that you realize, and your subjects realize, that there is absolutely no connection between Cancer the zodiac sign and cancer the disease. A prominently Cancerian person is no more likely to contract the disease than anyone else. Back in the 1970s there was a move among certain members of the astrological fraternity in the United States to change the name of the sign to Moon-Child. This is entirely unacceptable; far better to educate the public than change a term which has been in existence for 2,000 years.

While it is impossible to assess from the chart whether a subject will or will not develop cancer, those known to us who have contracted it do seem to have a particular lifestyle. They have, for a variety of reasons, suppressed their real wishes (sometimes emotional and sexual), often slaving away at an unrewarding job. Some medical research is following this line, although not all cancers conform (those, perhaps, developed in early childhood). But as far as assessing any vulnerability from the chart, it is impossible.

When and When Not to Have Operations

A great deal of astrological research has been done to discover good and not-so-good times at which to undergo surgery. The work is still progressing, and while many sound conclusions have been reached, others seem not quite as pertinent.

Some years ago a group of American surgeons, after a day's work in the operating room, found they had all had difficulties in stopping patients bleeding. Later they realized it was the time of the Full Moon. This interesting revelation is just one of many that reflects the conclusions of astrological research and findings.

As far as operations are concerned, here are a few suggestions which may prove helpful. If possible, try to avoid having an operation:

◆ Five days either before or after the Full Moon.

◆ When the transitting Moon makes a square, opposition or quincunx to the natal position of the Sun, Moon, Ascendant, Mars or Saturn. We do not usually consider the position of the transitting Moon in this book unless we are assessing its influence at the time of the New Moon (see pp.230-1); but Mars is related to bleeding and the act of surgery, so its influence, tiny though it would be, might cause difficulties in this area. Similarly, the influence of Saturn could possibly cause some delays in healing or complications in the operation.

◆ At times when Mercury or Mars are retrograde. There are often misunderstandings and breakdowns in communications when Mercury is retrograde and, as mentioned above, Mars is the planet of surgery. It is as well to have that planet in a good mood at a time when surgery is to be undertaken.

Of course, observing these rules may be extremely difficult – one must often go into hospital when summoned. If your subject has to undergo surgery at a rather unsuitable time, look to the more important progressions and transits working in the progressed chart before becoming concerned about the prevailing atmosphere. Some doctors and surgeons are sufficiently concerned for their patients' well-being to take such preoccupations into consideration at such an important time. It need not be embarrassing to give your reasons for making a request to go into hospital at a particular time.

Good times at which to undergo surgery are:

◆ Five days either side of the New Moon, when bleeding will be at its most controllable.

◆ When the transitting Moon makes a sextile or trine aspect to the natal Venus, Mars or Jupiter; these very minor transits should help your subject to feel at ease.

Many medical astrologers also believe that it is not good to undergo surgery when the Moon is in mutable signs, and that operations should go well when the Moon is in fixed signs. It may be possible for you to consider these positions, but if you observe every astrological suggestion, it does drastically limit possible dates! Generally, we think it is of greater importance to study the individual chart when coming to a decision. Consider the other indications if at all possible (the remarks concerning the New and Full Moons are extremely relevant).

If you are a blood donor, you will find it is more convenient to give your blood just before the Full Moon; it flows more easily and quickly.

Heart attacks and strokes

It is equally impossible to assess a vulnerability to heart disease or strokes from the chart. Obviously a heavy smoker (see Andrew, p.207) is more vulnerable, but one does not need to be an astrologer to realize that. Should you work on a chart where a low metabolism and perhaps some form of escapism are indicated, and you know that the subject takes no exercise, you might well assume that the individual is more susceptible than people who are more regulated in their drinking habits, who don't smoke, and who have a higher metabolism.

All you can do is to encourage the cutting down of smoking, drinking, or whatever; and suggest that your subject starts some kind of exercise programme – after a medical examination, of course. We discuss all kinds of exercise elsewhere; see pp.188-93 for suggestions which might be suitable.

Leo rules the heart, and obviously members of that sign should bear in mind that they especially need exercise, for the heart is a muscle and needs to be made to work. A lethargic Leo is usually an unfulfilled one. This should be considered – but again, as is the case with Cancer and cancer, Sun or Ascendant Leos are statistically no more prone to heart attacks than any other zodiacal group.

Colds and influenza

Here are the most common and miserable of all minor ailments. We hinted above that it is fairly certain that

TRANSITS AND HEALTH

Transitting planets have a variety of effects on heath and well-being, as shown here:

☉ THE SUN

It usually makes us feel more positive when by transit it makes conjunctions or oppositions to our personal planets' positions. While it is travelling through the first house of the chart (for about a month after it has made a conjunction to the Ascendant) it usually gives a boost to our vitality.

☽ THE MOON

It is not usually considered in transit, but if the New Moon makes negative aspects to the Ascendant or to the personal planets we may tend to feel slightly out of sorts, and women may have menstrual problems.

☿ MERCURY

These transits will only affect the health very marginally: there could be a slight increase in nervous tension if the planet contacts a heavily afflicted personal planet, but the trend will only last a day or two.

♀ VENUS

These transits usually bring a great deal of pleasure to our lives. Sometimes we feel slightly irritable because we've enjoyed ourselves and our food a little too much. We can put on weight at such times, but the influence is very temporary.

♂ MARS

Transits of Mars to the Ascendant, Sun, or Moon cause us to be overhasty and all too often slightly accident prone; we tend to cut or burn ourselves. When Mars transits our Midheaven we can all too easily be bumped by another driver when out in our cars. Warn your subjects of these possibilities and tell them to be careful for about a week. Mars increases our energy levels, and we usually feel very fit, but whether the transit is conjunction or opposition we are still at risk.

♃ JUPITER

This is not unlike Venus, but the influence lasts much longer. We are vulnerable to indigestion when the planet makes negative contact to personal planets. Its keyword, expansion, certainly applies to weight gain when it conjuncts the Sun or Ascendant, but there will usually be benefits in other spheres of life.

♄ SATURN

This affects vitality. Depression, colds, flu, aches and pains, and occasionally falls, may occur when it is in contact with the Ascendant, Sun, Moon or ruling planet, by conjunction or negative transitting aspect.

♅ URANUS

We need to be careful that our circulation doesn't suffer, and should take no risks (especially in dangerous sports). Sometimes we receive a shock under the influence of Uranus, but may not notice the physical effects at the time. As with Saturn this is most likely when the planet makes negative transiting aspects, or a conjunction to the Sun, Moon, Ascendant or ruling planet.

♆ NEPTUNE

We can take the easy way out when Neptune is working for us. We should be careful not to drink too much or to fall back on any negative escapism. Sometimes we can suffer from tainted water or get food poisoning, especially when the planet is in contact with Mars. For other influences apply the same rule as Saturn or Uranus.

♇ PLUTO

This planet can cause blockages. If we have a psychological problem we can sometimes talk it through when Pluto is working positively or in conjunction. Pluto either constipates or purges and is most powerful when in contact with the Sun, Moon or Ascendant by conjunction or negative transiting aspect. There could be inflammation or discomfort of the genitals when the planet contacts Mars.

when your subject has lunar progressions to the natal or progressed Saturn they will almost certainly come down with a cold. Warn your subjects of the possibility, suggesting that they should try to avoid crowded places, not touch anyone who has a cold and, as a precaution, take some extra vitamins – vitamin C is usually effective. Even if it is high summer, or the subject lives in a hot climate, there is also a chance that they will feel chilly, so suggest that they keep a warm sweater nearby.

An Anorexic

CASE HISTORY

Lisa is a 17-year-old girl who for several years has suffered from anorexia nervosa. Her parents were divorced when she was seven. Unknown to Lisa or her mother, two months after the divorce her father re-married, and his second wife had a child. When, years later, Lisa found this out about the marriage and discovered the existence of her half-sister, her deep affection for her father, maintained despite the divorce, changed to bitterness, resentment and jealousy of the second wife and half-sister. This seemed to be the origin of her condition, which resulted in long periods in the hospital.

Chart analysis

Lisa's chart (see next page) shows good potential – especially for creative work, or perhaps work in the beauty/fashion world. (Sun conjunct Venus in Leo, Libra Ascendant, Uranus conjunct the Ascendant.)

There is no lack of imagination (Moon conjunct Neptune) which could also be expressed creatively. However, while Venus, the chart ruler, is nicely integrated because of the conjunction to the Leo Sun, the most powerful planet in the chart (because it is being aspected extremely powerfully by seven planets, and makes a trine aspect to the Ascendant) is Saturn. The oppositions between Saturn and the Moon, Neptune and Jupiter totally block the emotional responses, which, if we interpret them by sign and house, show a freedom loving extrovert response to all situations (Moon in Sagittarius), a love of good living

(Jupiter in Scorpio), and a need for emotional security (three or more planets in the second house).

Interestingly, here is Saturn at its most restrictive, saying "Thou shalt not". The situation is exacerbated by Mercury, powerfully placed in its own sign and making tense square aspects to Saturn on the one hand and the Moon and Neptune on the other.

The Moon opposition Saturn indicates periods of depression, while an afflicted Mercury indicates probable cunning and artfulness (common with those subject to addictions). Uranus conjunct the Ascendant, with Mars in Aquarius, suggest a character which may be very perverse and difficult.

It is clear, from studying the birth chart, that Lisa's anorexia has its roots in the powerful Saturn influence. Traditionally, Saturn represents the

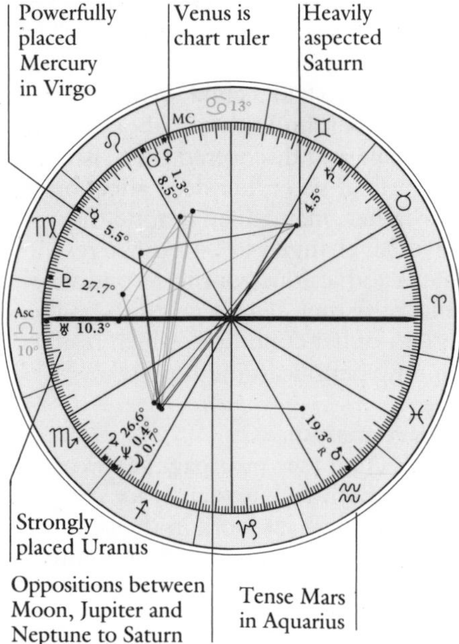

father, and here it shows how Lisa was unbalanced by her father's actions. These planetary influences are supported by Mercury in Virgo – a sign much concerned with diet – and by the perversity of Uranus, in turn strengthened by the brittle, tense characteristics indicated by Mars in Aquarius. The Ascendant characteristics, highly colored by Uranus, give her a need to be different, which at present is not working favorably for her – her condition is an appeal for help. If Saturn did not have such a powerful say in this chart, the chances are that rather than suffering from anorexia, Lisa would have taken the opposite course, and become overweight due to comfort eating binges – perhaps even becoming a bulima sufferer.

Once Lisa has worked through her psychological problem (which is also mirrored in an interesting way by Pluto in the twelfth house), and begins to make use of her creative potential, she should do extremely well.

What to Look Out For

1. A powerful Saturn receiving negative aspects from the Sun, Moon or Ascendant – but note that these could denote a variety of ailments.

2. Indications of undue preoccupation with food and diet – look to aspects between the Moon, Venus and Jupiter, and especially whether a personal planet in Taurus, Virgo or Libra is afflicted by Saturn.

3. Taurus, Virgo or Libra emphasized by the Sun, Moon or Ascendant.

4. A second or sixth house emphasis (by a personal or ruling planet).

5. An afflicted Moon or Venus – especially if either planet is in the sixth house.

6. An emphasis on Cancer – the sign of nourishment – by the Sun, Moon or Ascendant. (In Lisa's case Cancer is the Midheaven "identification" sign – ruled by the Moon, which is strongly involved in the powerfully repressive aspect pattern.)

7. A heavily aspected Pluto in the health houses, i.e. the first, sixth, or the psychological health house, the twelfth. (Again, in Lisa's case, Pluto is in the twelfth house, representing deep-rooted psychological problems. It is heavily aspected, to all intents and purposes helpfully, by trines and sextiles from the vulnerable and afflicted Moon, Jupiter and Neptune, and to Saturn, so the flow of Pluto's energies is positive and works well. Here is both the way she expresses her problem and her escape; but the action she has taken is negative and self destructive – a phrase commonly used to describe the forces of Pluto and, to a certain extent, Neptune.)

A Very Fat Man

Case History

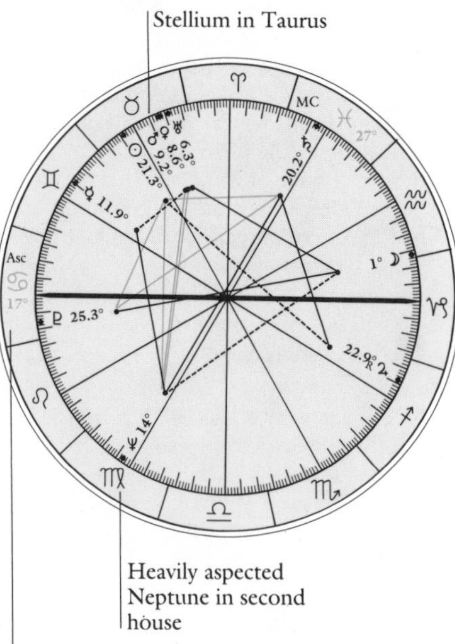

This man, who weighed 378 pounds, was told he had six months to live if he didn't lose weight. He refused to do so because two of his friends had dieted and died.

The powerful stellium in Taurus is symptomatic of a weight problem, and the Cancer Ascendant is not helpful. The heavily aspected Neptune in the second (Taurus) house, making trine aspects to three of the four Taurus planets, shows just how negative trines can be in some cases, for they encouraged him to be undisciplined about his problem. The chart-ruler, the Moon, in Aquarius gave him a perverse, stubborn attitude, which was also emphasized by the extremely potent opposition to Pluto in the first house.

The influence of his friends' experiences is shown extremely clearly because Mercury, in its own sign, Gemini, is in the eleventh house. Jupiter in the sixth has health overtones – especially as it, too, is strongly placed in its own sign. This man might have been able to use Saturn (high in the sky at birth) to help him adopt a more practical attitude (Taurus is, after all, an extremely practical sign), but Saturn's opposition to Neptune is weakening, especially as the planet is in Pisces, the Midheaven sign, which is of course ruled by Neptune.

A Drug Addict

CASE HISTORY

Justin was an extremely wealthy young man with some creative talent, which, however, was entirely inhibited by the influence of drugs and drink. His chart is typical of those of drug addicts of his generation. The strong Libran emphasis (the birth time is very accurate) and the full twelfth house are significant. In addition, Pluto is the most elevated planet and conjuncts the Midheaven.

At an early age Justin's Ascendant progressed into Scorpio, so Pluto's influence is very potent. He wanted to experience every kind of drug and all forms of negative escapism. Sometimes he would come for counseling looking young, well dressed and being extremely positive about life and what he wanted to do. At others he would turn up hours late or not at all, ragged, gray-faced and stumbling. The swings from one extreme to the other are common, but here were emphasized by the mixture of trines and squares. The squares attempted to give stability, but the Mars conjunction to Saturn, with Saturn squaring Neptune, was unhelpful. This aspect also contributed to the way that Neptune worked negatively for Justin from the twelfth house, whereas sometimes it can work well from this, its own house.

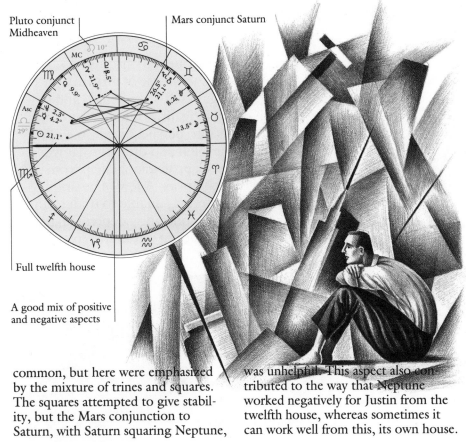

Pluto conjunct Midheaven

Mars conjunct Saturn

Full twelfth house

A good mix of positive and negative aspects

A Positive Life

CASE HISTORY

Bez is one of the most hardworking people we know. Her outlook is positive and forthright. She was for years a professional dancer, and on retirement became a health club aerobics teacher. Her chart is most interesting; here is a fantastic combination of Scorpio and Aries energy. Look at that sixth house – full to capacity; so much so that it is quite difficult to draw the chart clearly! She pours her Aries/Scorpio energy into her day's work, and loves every minute. She is extremely independent – because of the Aries emphasis, Jupiter in Aquarius and the Moon in Sagittarius. The mixture of squares and trines is excellent, for she is very practical and will snap out of any negative lowering effects of the unhelpful Moon square Saturn. Saturn is strong in Leo and the tenth house, and shows that Bez can carry the responsibility of supervising junior staff as well as devising and running physical exercise programs for many people – some of whom are coming to exercise rather late in life.

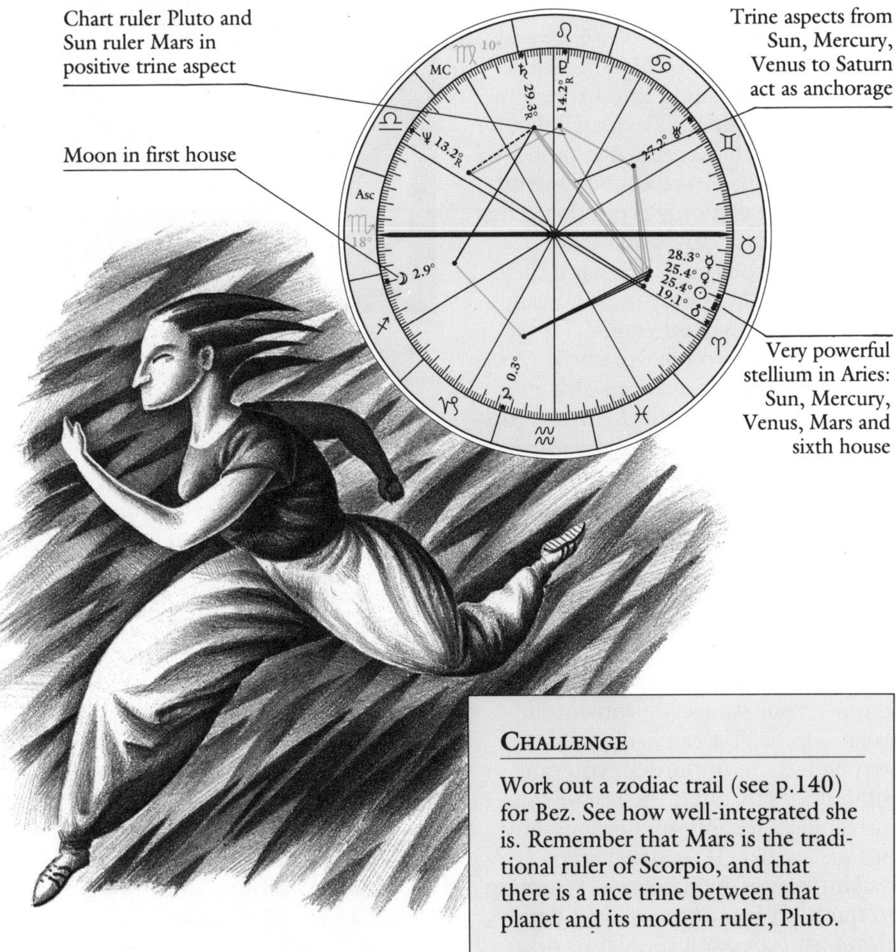

CHALLENGE

Work out a zodiac trail (see p.140) for Bez. See how well-integrated she is. Remember that Mars is the traditional ruler of Scorpio, and that there is a nice trine between that planet and its modern ruler, Pluto.

Psychological Motivation

All of us, in one way or another, work our way through certain psychological problems in the course of growing up and leading our lives. In doing so we gain self-knowledge, and so come to terms with our personalities and get our hang-ups or inhibitions into perspective. Some of us find our problems so difficult that we have to seek professional help from psychotherapists. A few of us simply go on suffering, unable to understand why we are constantly depressed, or seem to be leading unfulfilled lives.

You will know by now that stresses and strains show up clearly in our birth charts, but there are usually areas which show us how we can counter these, and release most blockages. The more you study, the more you will learn to see clear paths through what is often a maze of complicated and sometimes contradictory indications.

However, the assessment of psychologically oriented problems, when we have discovered them through a technical examination of the chart, is extremely difficult, and if we are not careful we find ourselves treading on thin ice – then falling into extremely deep, cold water. It is essential that we don't fall in unintentionally, or indeed dive in wearing some kind of a blindfold, and we can only avoid doing this if we know precisely when to stop – when to tell our subjects that if they need further help they must consult a fully trained psychotherapist. (It is important that you get to know trained analysts so you can give your subject a direct referral. Many psychotherapists are extremely sympathetic to astrology, and quite a few astrologers take full psychotherapy training.)

The role of the astrologer

Remember that however many books on the subject you may have read, unless you have trained as a psychotherapist you are not in a position to explore your subjects' problems in great depth. You can listen to them and help them unburden, you can guide them through the use of your astrological technique, but you must not go further. If a subject starts making too many demands, returning to question you obsessively in detail about attitudes and problems, stop!

The birth chart highlights psychological problems, but may also show the antidote to them.

All you need say is that you are an astrologer and you have helped him as much as you can, and that if he feels further professional help is needed it will be necessary for him to seek it from a qualified psychotherapist.

The danger of overestimating your own value and importance as a counselor has another aspect: your own chart may reveal a love of the dramatic – or perhaps you have many planets in water signs, showing that you are extremely intuitive. You may be very imaginative, or you may be a worrier. You must keep all of that well under control, and don't be carried away: be logical and practical. Don't jump to conclusions – be a down-to-earth astrologer and not a starry-eyed one!

General Rules and Guidelines

Although it will often be obvious from correspondence or conversation with a new subject that some psychological problem exists, you must learn to recognize the indications of any kind of blockage preventing a fulfilling expression of motivation, emotion, or the intellect. In most cases these will emerge quite naturally, but there are a few helpful general guidelines.

Most common problems – lack of self-confidence, shyness, quick temper, worry – show clearly in a chart, and can be assessed as you make notes about each planet's sign and house placing and the aspects it receives. In most cases, too, you will often find the antidote to them within the chart.

Overcoming worry

For instance, prominently Cancerian or Virgoan types will usually be very prone to worry and it is no use telling them to stop. However, because of these particular sign influences we find that the Cancerian type can use intuition to help her – especially if worried about making a decision. The Virgoan who worries needs to learn to counter her difficulties through a logical approach to every aspect of her problems, thereby allowing common sense to hold sway.

An emotional and sexually inhibiting factor

Often when there is an emphasis on Libra and Virgo – a Libran Sun with Venus in Virgo, or a Virgo Sun with Mercury and/or Venus in Libra – there are contradictory factors within the personality. The Sun Libra, Venus in Virgo subject can be very modest and shy, and critical of partners – at the same time longing for love and a settled, permanent relationship. The modest, perhaps not terribly self-confident, Sun sign Virgoan will be very romantic (Venus in Libra), but will find it difficult to let herself go. Either of these two groups of planetary placings when combined in this way can cause considerable distress, not only in the matter of general rapport and the giving and receiving of love and affection, but because of a negative effect on the sexual expression, which might or might not be countered by the position and influence of Mars. If you have a subject suffering from this kind of dilemma look to the Ascendant and Moon signs to see if these offer a corrective factor.

Negative psychological influences
From time to time the "heavy", or slow-moving, planets form either conjunctions or other aspects to each other. These stay in orb for long periods, and while they often act as a kind of generation influence and are for most of the time dormant, when they fall on or straddle the Ascendant or make double conjunctions to the Sun or Moon, they can cause psychological problems. While squares or oppositions can be a source of difficulty, it is usually potent or heavy conjunctions that are most disruptive. For instance, an opposition between Saturn and Uranus could be seriously aggravated by the fact that it crosses the Ascendant/Descendant line, or crosses the chart of someone who has the Sun in opposition to the Moon, thus making two tight oppositions with perhaps the Sun conjunct Uranus on one side of the chart and the Moon conjunct Saturn on the other. Such a configuration would be a potential source of strain and also incline the individual to be depressed, tense and restless. The subject would be under even greater strain when Saturn or Uranus made square aspects (by transit) to each of the four natal positions.

This may seem an extreme example, and an individual may need specialist help that an astrologer cannot give.

Conjunctions between heavy planets
One of the most trying planetary influences is a conjunction between Saturn and Pluto. (For a full description see p.310.) In the late 1940s, when in orb in Leo, and in the early 1980s, when it fell in Libra, it caused considerable psychological problems which have led to inhibition. (These may be seen even in those born during the latter period.) In some cases where Saturn crosses the Ascendant in Leo, subjects have been known to suffer physical symptoms as a result of psychological problems. In other charts, when not personalized by contact with the Ascendant or in conjunction with the Sun or Moon, it is far less potent, but can, when activated by transit, cause difficulties defined by the house in which the conjunction falls.

Other conjunctions between heavy planets will also cause difficulty (defined by the planets' natures). Uranus is indicative of tension, Neptune of negative escapism. Refer to "The Planets at Work" (pp.208-347) for definitions of the various possibilities.

Other negative apects
Indications of psychological problems usually emerge because the planet or planets concerned are negatively aspected by the Sun or Moon or by squares or oppositions in conjunction with the Ascendant, Sun or Moon, or occasionally the ruling planet. Note whether the influence comes from the twelfth or first house: the problem itself may be more difficult to resolve if the planet or planets causing it fall in the twelfth but is usually more easily externalized if they are in the first (though the chance of the negative influence having an additional physical effect is increased). For instance, a heavily aspected Saturn in conjunction with the Ascendant in the first house may indicate a physical disability as much as depression or inhibition. Neptune is the exception. This planet is most trying when conjunct the Ascendant from the first house; it works much better from the twelfth, the Piscean house and its natural home (Neptune rules Pisces).

The Uranus/Pluto conjunction
Sometimes you will work on the charts of people born during the 1960s, when there was a conjunction between Uranus and Pluto in Virgo. The comments above will apply very strongly. In addition, if by chance the Sun is also in Virgo in the birth chart, there is a distinct possibility that the subject will want to assume power over others. If this is so, try to encourage its positive rather than negative expression. (For a full interpretation, see pp.319-26, The Aspects of Uranus.)

The solar system traffic jam
From time to time the planets tend to catch up with one another, causing a considerable traffic jam in one area of the sky, with a great many planets in one sign. For example:

◆ During the period of the above-mentioned Saturn/Pluto conjunction within orb in Leo, those two planets were joined on 15 August 1947 not only by the planets Mercury and Venus, but also by the Sun and Moon. Such an emphasis on one sign (known as a stellium – see p.57) causes a certain imbalance in the individual, with the planets all having their influence channelled through one sign.

◆ On 7 January 1989 not only were the Sun and Moon in Capricorn, but so were Saturn, Uranus and Neptune – a stellium of five planets.

In such cases it only needs someone to be born at or near sunrise to make for an even more powerful emphasis (making the Ascendant belong to the same sign as the Sun). All of the various qualities of the relevant sign, both positive and negative, and those relating to the various levels of the personality as shown by the planets (and possibly also the Ascendant), are geared to that sign influence.

CHALLENGE

Referring to the dates given in the two examples above, assume that your subject was born at sunrise. Without calculating the full chart, place all five, or six, planets in Capricorn or Leo, and follow through the interpretation of each. Look, too, at the clusters of conjunctions (assume that they all fall between 8° and 22° Leo, as they did in 1947, or between 2° and 10° Capricorn, as in 1989).

In each case, first assume that the stellium falls in the first house, then in the twelfth, with a late degree of Leo or Capricorn on the Ascendant. Then move on to place the planets all in the tenth house with a Midheaven falling in about the middle of the stellium. This exercise will show how these indications can cause problems for an individual.

Naturally these are hypothetical cases; in real life there are always other planets to be considered. Nevertheless, the pull in one direction in such charts is powerful and subjects may need help – though in the cases here, as two very powerful signs are involved, the subjects may be too arrogant to accept it!

PERSONALITY TRAITS

Disorganized people

Lack of organization is often the result of integration problems, and you will clearly see these in a chart if you follow the zodiac trail (see p.140). If there are many trails that don't link up, your subject may be inclined to be confused and disorganized, finding it difficult to make decisions. You may notice that two contrasting groups of indications have few links between them so the individual is in permanent flux.

A positive approach is to suggest that your subject accepts that she can express particular personality traits or characteristics at one time, while at others, totally different ones. In all of us there is more than one person, and we can use the contrasting areas in constructive and positive ways. If on some days the subject feels assertive and extroverted, he or she should participate in the kind of activity which demands such an approach. If on others the subject feels sensitive and introverted, he or she should concentrate on work that demands intuition and a sensitive approach, avoiding situations that might induce shyness, nervousness and lack of self-confidence. The problem may particularly affect career choice and attitudes towards children. Of course, every case must be individually assessed.

Laziness and procrastination

Perhaps you will find yourself working on the chart of a subject who keeps saying "I can't be bothered" or "I simply hate to get up in the morning", making a love of ease very plain indeed. This may be a perfectly natural trait, especially if the subject has a powerful emphasis on Libra, Pisces or occasionally Taurus (though many of the latter are very hard disciplined workers), or a strong Venus. However, the chart may show a strong element of Aries, Leo or Capricorn, a well-placed Mars, and so on.

What causes this laziness? In such a potentially energetic chart you must look for other indications for an explanation. These usually show a lack of self-confidence, inhibition or shyness, so that in order to save face – something especially characteristic of Capricorns and when Leo is rising – he or she feigns laziness to cover up a lack of confidence. You will find many references in the aspect interpretations: it is quite common for those with Saturn conjunct the Ascendant, or a negative aspect to the Sun, Moon, ruling planet or Ascendant, to suffer in this way. Sometimes there is a negative aspect between Mars and Saturn, obstructing the flow of energy, thus unbalancing the system.

The chatterbox

Sometimes shyness, especially in young people, is hidden by talkativeness. This is usually the case when Gemini or Virgo are prominent. Sometimes, too, negative aspects between Mercury and Mars or Uranus can spark off such tendencies. If you have a shy, nervous young subject, encourage the use of relaxation techniques or deep breathing exercises; inner calm must be developed. This will take time, but when the gushing nervous energy is controlled and positively channelled it is an extremely good force which can be used to considerable advantage.

Above average sexual needs

Above average sexual activity is often shown by a strong Mars – as ruling planet, Sun or Moon ruler or in Aries. Aspects of all kinds between Venus and Mars usually heighten sexual enjoyment and activity, and the signs and houses involved should also be considered, since these aspects are strengthened if the first/seventh, second/eighth or the fifth are tenanted by either or both planets. If Saturn is involved in a tee-square between them, there is a possibility of sexual frustration. Disappointment, and to an extent inhibition, is often characteristic of those with negative aspects between the Moon and Venus, and Venus and Saturn. Sometimes those with a positive Venus/Saturn aspect prefer a rather older partner – perhaps needing a Father/Mother figure.

Occasionally a marginally sadistic streak is present if Mars and Pluto are in aspect to Uranus, when the sexual implications and energies of Mars are coloured by a need to express power over others. Those with a conjunction or positive aspect between Mars and Neptune will also have an increased and usually rewarding sexual fantasy life but if these planets are in negative aspect and joined by Pluto the individual may have suffered in some way as a result of sexual experiences.

Homosexuality

A great deal of research has gone into finding reliable indications of homosexual tendencies in a chart – but with varying conclusions. Generalization is dangerous; while certain planetary relationships may show a tendency towards homosexuality, they don't necessarily indicate that a subject will find sexual fulfilment with members of the same sex only. Such aspects can equally reveal that there is a greater leaning towards femininity (in the best sense of the word) in men, or a more masculine assertiveness in women.

These characteristics can show up in a variety of ways. In women's charts there may be some particularly feminine aspects, such as the Moon conjunct or trine Venus in a powerfully masculine sign or signs. In men's charts there may be powerfully masculine aspects involving feminine signs.

An indication of same gender sexual preference in men is said to be negative aspects (especially the square) between the Sun and Uranus. For women, the same is alleged to be true of a negative aspect between the Moon and Uranus; again, the square seems to be the most potent influence. However, because of the considerable complexity of the whole area, these indications are in no way conclusive. No definite judgement should be made if they are present in a chart for, on another level, they simply indicate stress and tension.

"The worst people have the best charts"

Every experienced astrologer will agree! Those subjects who seem to have all the right planets in all the right signs, all the nicest, easiest, most auspicious aspects, are usually awful people! They will take advantage not only of your budding astrological experience, but of your time, energy and, if you're not very careful, your money as well! The trouble with them is that they really do seem spectacularly nice, and sometimes generous. They may even arrive with a gift to soften you up. But then, when they've won you over with all the charm in the world they ask their favors. So be on the defensive if you find a subject's chart which is brimming with trines, grand trines, sextiles and lots of lovely conjunctions between all the most friendly, helpful planets. Remember, however, that the symptoms described above will apply only if there is no stabilizing tee-square or other strong indication to balance the overpositive indications. If there is, then your subject will not seek free rides or take advantage of others – the added stability in the chart will give solidity and base to the overwhelming charm, and the chances are that the positivity will be controlled, channelled and constructively expressed.

Indomitable Spirit

CASE HISTORY

Andrew was a much loved and respected ballet teacher who inspired his students, making even the most demanding intricacies of the art seem easy. He always criticized constructively and gave great encouragement.

He was extremely artistic, having attended art school as well as ballet school. He was drafted into the British army early in 1940 and was sent to the Far East, where he became a Japanese prisoner of war, being incarcerated for four years. Rising above his own suffering, the amount he did to relieve his fellow prisoners was remarkable; he made shorts out of the strong pockets of their tattered trousers, having first made a needle from a spoke stolen from a Japanese guard's bicycle. He also encouraged his fellow prisoners to keep physically and mentally alert, in spite of great privation and the work-load imposed by the prison camp regime. He weighed less than 74 pounds on release.

Soon after rejoining his wife, he opened his ballet school. He still suffered psychologically from the war experience and was unable to travel in cars or trains. In the late 1970s he suffered strokes, but bravely forced himself to recover sufficiently to teach from a wheelchair. He died in 1979.

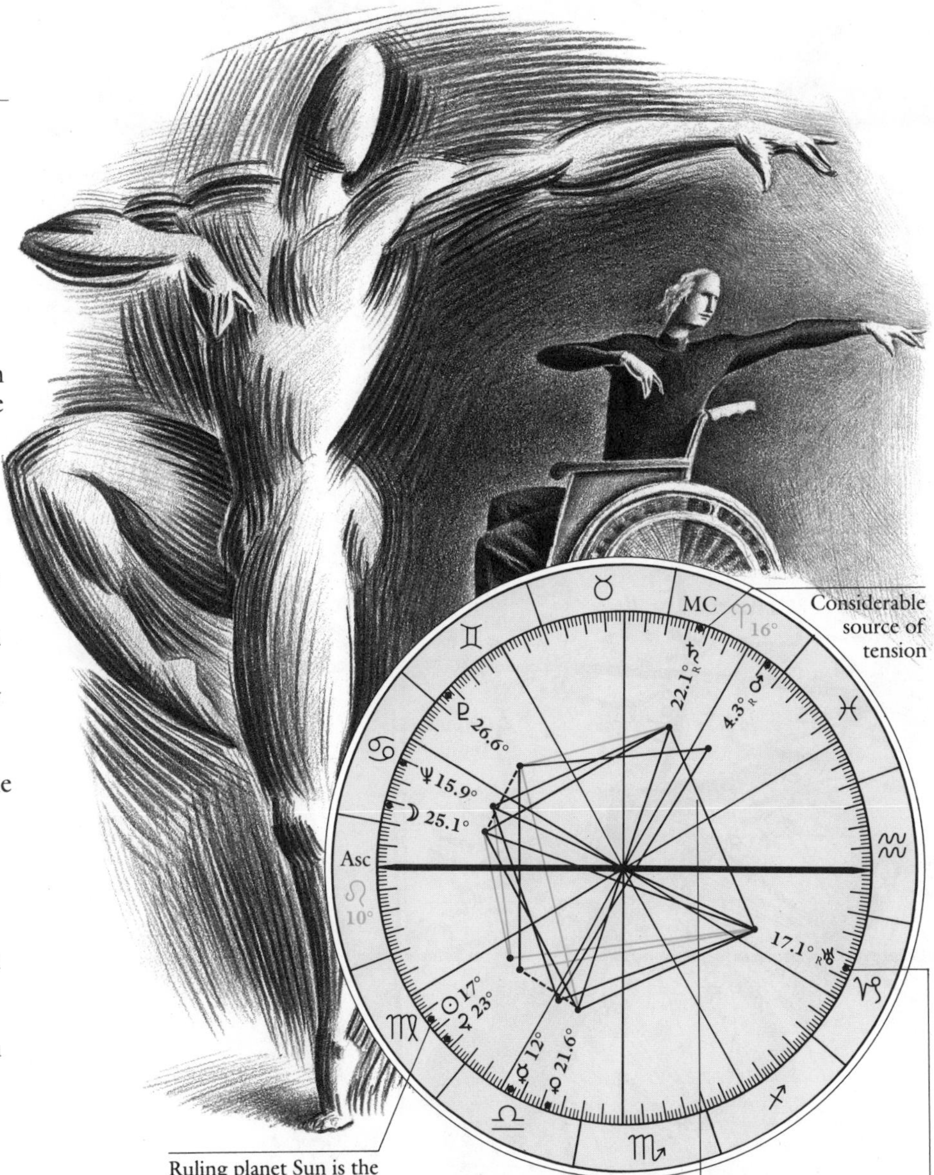

Considerable source of tension

Ruling planet Sun is the only one free of heavy aspects and not involved in grand crosses

Multiple grand crosses in cardinal signs

Considerable source of tension

Chart analysis

The extreme tension shown in his chart could easily have defeated Andrew. Note the way all the planets save the Sun are involved in the multiple cardinal grand crosses. The fact that they fall in cardinal signs shows his eagerness to reach beyond their clutches. Note the inspirational Moon conjunct Neptune in the twelfth house. Although he had been a performer in his youth, he was a much better teacher. He expressed powerfully extrovert tendencies and was a strong and very positive personality. However, he smoked heavily, which contributed to his fatal strokes.

The one essential and powerful escape from the grand crosses is the ruling planet, the Sun in Virgo. The positive trines from the Sun conjunct Jupiter to the very heavily aspected Uranus were also on Andrew's side. Note too Uranus in the sixth (work) house, showing the direction of these energies towards his much-loved, dedicated work. Even so, he had to fight every inch of the way. And we have never known anyone reduce us to such tears of laughter, before or since then! Surely the influence of the Sun conjunct Jupiter?

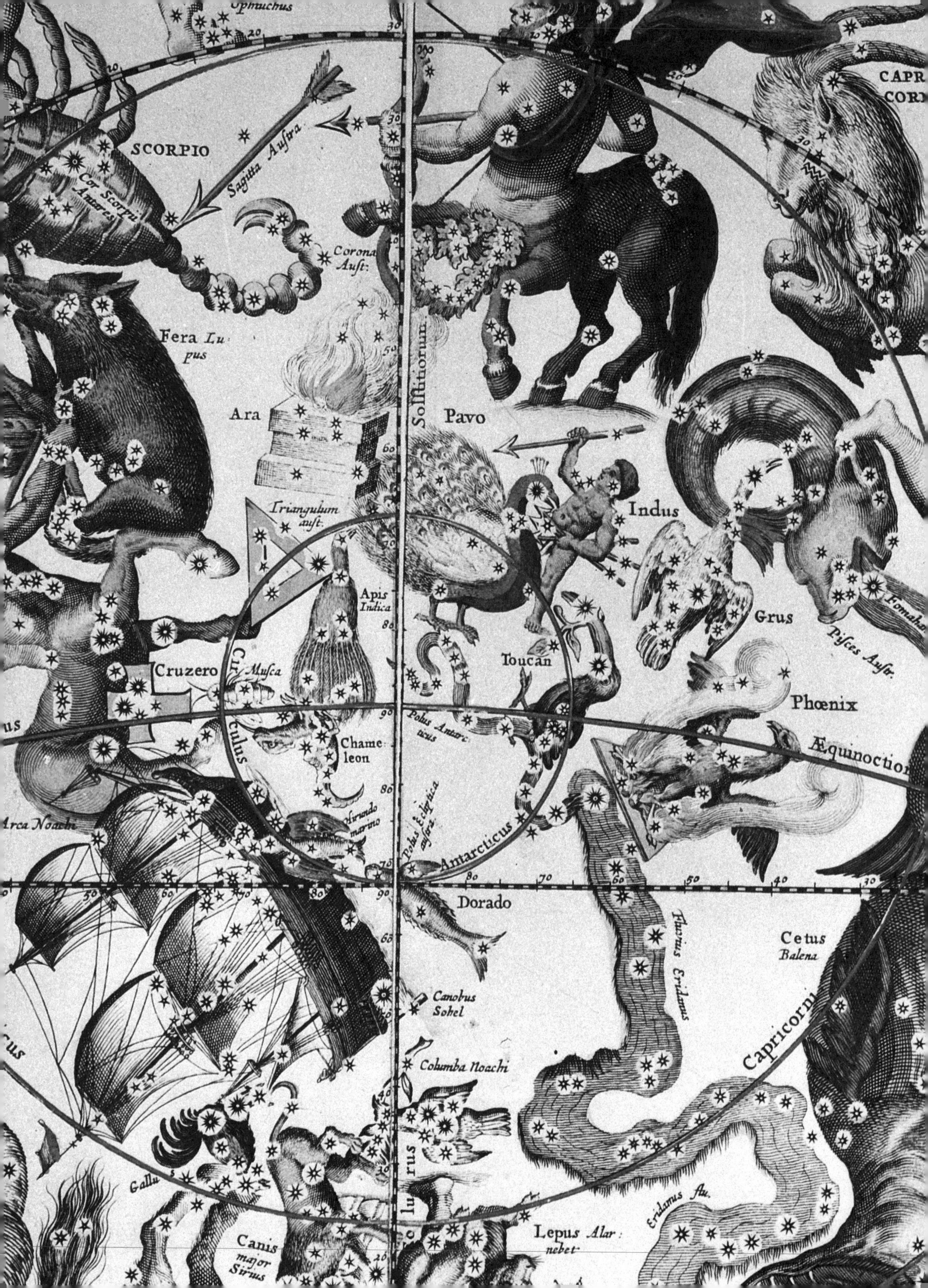
Ophiuchus
SCORPIO
Cor Scorpii Antares
Sagitta Austra
Corona Aust.
Fera Lupus
Ara
Solstitiorum
Pavo
Triangulum aust.
Indus
Apis Indica
Grus
Pisces Austr.
Toucan
Cruzero
Musca
Circulus
Phœnix
Chameleon
Polus Antarcticus
Æquinoctio
Arca Noachi
Hirundo marino
Polus Ecliptica austr.
Antarcticus
Dorado
Cetus
Balena
Fluvius Eridanus
Canobus Sohel
Columba Noachi
Capricorni
Eridanus flu.
Canis major Sirius
Lepus

· 4 ·

The Planets at Work

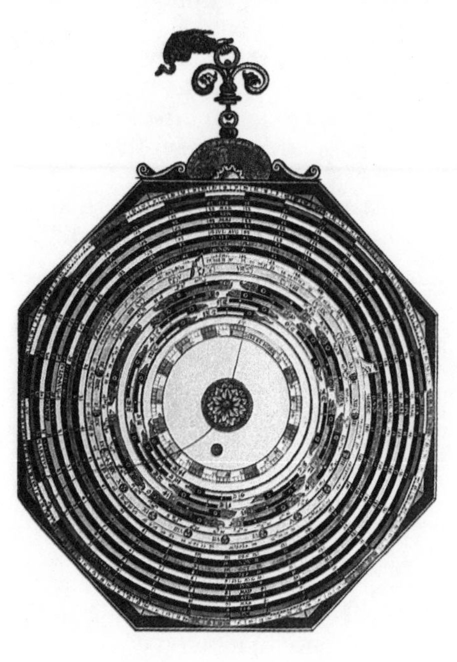

The Sun through the Houses

Because of the great importance of the Sun in both the birth and progressed charts, its sign influence has been covered in detail on pp.78-127. By now you will no doubt have absorbed the interpretations which have special significance both for yourself and for those dear to you. This, therefore, is the time to consider the next level of influence that the Sun exerts in the birth chart – its house position. The Sun represents our vitality and self expression, so its house position will show in which sphere of life those energies will be directed by the individual.

1 The Sun in the First House

This placing is vitally important for the Sun. Because the subject will have been born very near sunrise, it is extremely likely that the Sun and rising signs will be the same. Such people are known as "double Cancerians", "double Librans" and so on, for the Sun sign and Ascendant sign characteristics and motivations will be those of the same sign. The whole chart will be dominated by the influence of the Sun, and the effects of the planet ruling the Sun and Ascending signs will also be considerably increased.

Self-absorption may be a result of this emphasis on the first house, and the individual should be aware of any tendencies towards selfishness, trying to counter them whenever possible.

Health and well-being
Consider the health not only in relation to the sign that the Sun occupies but also to the aspects that it receives. For instance, there may be a tendency to nervous strain and tension (square aspect to Uranus), exuberant physical energy (trine to Mars), digestive problems or biliousness (squares or oppositions to the Moon or Jupiter respectively), and so on.

A certain Leonine coloring is given to the personality when the Sun is in the first house. (Queen Victoria, a double Gemini, is a superb example.) The bearing will be regal, and the back and heart will need the special attention that is advisable for those who have Leo prominent in their birth charts. Equally, because this is the Aries house, the subject will be motivated to win, to be first, and will have the necessary competitive spirit.

2 The Sun in the Second House

The acquisition of possessions is extremely important to the subject, who will feel a great sense of pride in showing these off on every possible occasion. He or she will not simply want to gloat over an ever-increasing bank balance or folio of stocks and shares, but rather will want the world to know of such success.

Generosity is usual unless it is mitigated by other influences (a "careful" Sun sign, for instance). In some cases the acquisitive powers can extend into the personal life, with the partner becoming yet another possession. The Taurean tendency is to own, and when the Sun is in the second house the attitude is "Look – this is mine!" If this happens, problems can arise since the subject is insensitively bulldozing over the real needs of his partner.

A good life
Pleasure is important to the individual, such as a concentration on enjoyment of expensive, rich food in glamorous surroundings. All of these tendencies will be encouraged by positive aspects between the Sun and Jupiter, while either an opposition or a square may make the subject go overboard in second house matters.

Venus will not be very far away if the Sun is in the second house – and do not forget that Venus rules this house. If there is an aspect between the Sun and Venus, the influence of the Sun's house position will be increased, especially in relation to the overall influence of Venus itself.

Hard work will always be undertaken to achieve the subject's ever-increasing materialistic needs – his solar vitality will be powered by the material results of his efforts and he will bask in the light of any glory that comes his way.

3 The Sun in the Third House

The intellectual capacity is exploited to the full with this placing. Whether the subject is bright or slow, there will certainly be a powerful urge to make the mind work, and should the individual feel there was something lacking in his or her early education, the impulse to make up for it will be strong. Having achieved that, she might well go much further, eventually (perhaps rather late in life) gaining some striking academic achievements. If you meet a subject in this position, try to encourage such a development and discourage any tendency to rest on lesser laurels. In such a case, a positive expression of pride and fulfillment will spring from this solar placing.

The need to communicate will be extremely powerful (what is communicated will, of course, depend on the nature of the Sun sign and its attributes). For instance, to oversimplify, someone with a Libran Sun in the third house would be keen to discuss the intimacies of relationships, while another person much involved with her career could, perhaps, make an excellent public relations officer for whatever firm she works for, advertising its products to great effect.

The influence of Mercury
This is the Gemini/Mercury house: Mercury may well occupy the third house with the Sun, in which case this house will be very important in the full interpretation. In any case, Mercury will be nearby, so be sure to consider its placing in relation to the third-house Sun.

4 The Sun in the Fourth House

The vitality and self-expression of the Sun will find a positive outlet in the creation of a good home and happy family life. Parenthood is the essential at the core of this house, but before deciding how the subject will enact the role of father or mother, you must study the Sun sign itself very carefully. An exuberant fire sign Sun will make for an equally exuberant, enthusiastic parent; a sensitive sign, such as Pisces or Cancer, will give a parent who is more intuitive and introspective.

A difficult opposition from Saturn will at worst dampen down the individual's enthusiasm, making him or her feel that children are a burden, or perhaps insist on too much discipline.

The influence of the Moon

This is the Cancer/Moon house, so the placing of the Moon in the birth chart should also be carefully considered, especially if it receives any aspects from the Sun.

Early parental influences are, of course, always vital to the development of every individual, but with the Sun in the fourth house, an in-depth understanding of the background and attitude of the parents is essential to future fulfillment. An element of creative energy will be channeled into redecoration, sewing, and other work that enhances the home.

A need for emotional security

Familiar surroundings will instill a sense of security in the subject, who may be reluctant to stray far from home. However, the influence of the Sun's sign will hold sway. For example, if the sign is extroverted and adventurous, a compromise will be reached when the individual comes to terms with other areas of his personality.

5 THE SUN IN THE FIFTH HOUSE

The Sun shines very brightly indeed from the fifth house, since it is the house of the Sun itself and of its own sign, Leo.

A sense of achievement

Ambition will be very strong, and very probably (unless the Sun is really battered by negative aspects) the individual will not be averse to showing off. He or she may not necessarily take center stage, but will usually enjoy displaying any creative achievements.

This is the house of children, so if the subject is a parent she will tend to push her children to the forefront (sometimes to their embarrassment or reluctance). Care is needed that the parent does not push her offspring in the direction she once wished to take herself, thereby living vicariously through them.

The emotional expression

The love and sex lives are well focused, and while the Sun sign itself will denote the approach and attitude to love, the need for fulfillment and positive, rewarding expression will assume an importance that is greater than average.

Emotional and physical risks are likely to be taken – whether that is blindly or with calculation will depend entirely on the sign placing and the Sun's aspects. Nevertheless there may well be an inherent affection, or even a need, for danger (sometimes to life and limb), which may be satisfied through hazardous sports. The Prince of Wales is a case in point: his Scorpio Sun in the fifth house encouraged this tendency when he was younger (his Ascending sign is Leo). In some extreme cases the urge to gamble can become excessive – especially if the Sun is in Aries or Sagittarius or the Sun and Jupiter make a square or opposition aspect. Creativity and the urge to express it will be present and should always be positively and practically developed.

6 THE SUN IN THE SIXTH HOUSE

Health is strongly influenced by this house, so the Sun's vitalizing force will focus on the well-being of the individual. His or her illnesses and vulnerabilities will be accentuated according to the Sun sign; there can be an overconcentration on ailments, and perhaps undue worry about the general health and diet. Nevertheless, if the Sun is well aspected (especially by the Moon or Mars), the recuperative powers should be excellent and a positive attitude will prevail.

The effect on the health and the whole physical well-being will be accentuated if the Sun makes an opposition aspect to the Ascendant. However, for this to happen the Sun must be within eight degrees (or ten at the most) of the cusp of the seventh house (the point exactly opposite the Ascending degree).

The sense of duty and routine is also emphasized by this placing. Therefore, when interpreting the effect of the Sun in the sixth house it is important to decide whether the individual is a slave to routine and tends to get in a rut or (perhaps because the Sun is placed in a fire or air sign) rebels against such restrictions in daily life.

The influence of Mercury

This is the Virgo/Mercury house, so the influence of Mercury and the sign in which it is placed will be important – the planet won't be very far away in the birth chart. If Mercury shares this house with the Sun, it will increase the possibility of the individual finding satisfaction by developing his intellect and communicative powers. Indeed, work in communications and critical, or perhaps creative, writing could be enjoyed. Being of service to others or perhaps working as a personal assistant might also feature in a positive way and be a source of satisfaction.

7 THE SUN IN THE SEVENTH HOUSE

The need to relate to others is extremely strong when the Sun falls in the seventh house, and there is a possibility that the individual with this placing will live for total commitment to a partner. In fact, care is needed that the subject's identity is not entirely submerged in that of the partner, and self-reliance must be developed if this pitfall is to be avoided. Much will be given to the partner, physically and emotionally, for the Sun's vitality will be expressed in this sphere of life.

The influence of Venus

This is the Venus/Libra house, so the placing of Venus in the chart will be extremely important. If it shares the seventh house with the Sun, it is highly probable that there will be an imbalance in the individual's personality, perhaps to such an extent that a lack of independence will be a real problem for him or her. Conflict will arise if a need for isolation is suggested in other areas of the chart, or if disappointment or unhappiness in the love life is indicated (square aspects from Venus to the Moon and Saturn respectively).

In general terms, the individual must be aware of the need to balance his or her extremely powerful urge to relate to others and the desire for commitment with a proper realization of the self and its fulfillment.

Making partnerships

Taking pride in the partner is essential to the individual, and while at its best this placing can make him or her a wonderful "power behind the throne", the subject must develop a realistic attitude towards loved ones, or high expectations may be cruelly dashed.

Reliance on the partner, moreover, must not be so great that separation presents very considerable psychological problems. When that happens, readjustment to life without the partner will be very difficult to achieve. Recognition of individual worth and the development of confidence in the self are essential.

Tendencies towards emotional dependence will be even stronger if the Sun is in opposition aspect to the Ascendant (i.e. within eight or, at most ten, degrees of the cusp of the seventh house), when the polarity between the Ascending and seventh house signs will also be enhanced.

8 The Sun in the Eighth House

Deep purposeful force and great emotional intensity are shown in this placing of the Sun. It is essential that the powers of intuition are used and controlled (according to the Sun's sign). There will almost inevitably be a need for self-knowledge, but in seeking it the tendency toward introspection is countered.

The drive for satisfaction

Sexual satisfaction will be a powerful outlet for self-expression, and the creative power of the Sun ensures that its achievement will be of paramount importance. The individual will certainly analyze every aspect of his or her sexuality if this fulfillment is lacking, and in extreme cases must counter an inclination to be obsessive about it. The driving force of the Sun may focus completely on sex for some people born with this placing, but for others it may center on money, its growth and the power that it brings. We often find those with this placing in financial careers. In a weak chart, or when the positive nature of the Sun is undermined by negative aspects (a square or opposition to Neptune, perhaps), there may be a tendency to live in hopes of an inheritance.

Understanding change

Transformation is one traditional association of this house, and it is easily seen in the need for self-knowledge, from which the individual can grow, develop and eventually change. The attitude to death should be positive, with the subject regarding it in an objective way as the ultimate and final transformation.

This is the Pluto/Scorpio house, so the influence of that planet should be studied. However, unless Pluto is personalized in the birth chart, remember that its sign placing is a generation influence only.

9 The Sun in the Ninth House

Intellectual growth, the broadening of horizons and the taking of challenging journeys for mind and body are all ways in which the solar energy is directed from the ninth house. This was once known as the "house of dreams" – an interesting description because those for whom it is heavily tenanted may get rather carried away.

If dreams are to become concrete reality, the subject must adopt a practical approach and channel his or her intellect in the necessary directions. The subject will then be able to develop his potential and make the most of the force of the Sun.

Knowledge and ambition

Further education, in the broadest sense, is related to ninth house matters, just as the third house focuses on education in general. We do not necessarily find those with this placing studying for exams well into their sixties, but the drive for the expansion of mind will nevertheless be present, and it is important for the individual to develop his own philosophy of life, with carefully considered religious beliefs based on definite conclusions.

There are few limitations for the individual born with this placing, but nevertheless he should not strive so hard that he misses out on the simple pleasures of life or distances himself from less intellectually inclined or motivated people.

This is the Sagittarius/Jupiter house. Therefore, if there is a sextile or trine between the Sun and Jupiter, the concerns of the house will be well integrated within the individual. If there is a square or opposition, it will be more difficult to control the action of the Sun and, even, to keep a sense of perspective. In any case, look for indications of practicality elsewhere.

10 The Sun in the Tenth House

A powerful need to make a mark on the world is shown by the individual with the Sun in the tenth house. Therefore, it is important that he or she is emotionally involved in the career, ambition or aspiration (after all, it is not everyone who has a career in the strict sense of the word). Worldly progress of one sort or another is of prime importance, and the Sun's vitality confers a driving force.

Attaining personal objectives

If fulfillment is being gained from effort, all well and good, but even so there are important questions to ask. For example, are those efforts misdirected, or totally impossible to achieve? (Neptune in conjunction or opposition to the Sun.) Is the individual motivated by power? (Uranus and/or Pluto in the tenth house with the Sun.) Is that need for power purely selfish or more altruistically oriented? (Mars personalized, Moon well-placed, respectively.) All these considerations must be taken into account, since the placing is, from the point-of-view of the chart itself, a powerful focal point.

If all autocratic tendencies can be controlled, here is a big achiever, and if the Sun shines through a fire sign the individual will have an infectious enthusiasm. If the Sun is in an earth sign, there will be practicality; in air, a lively intellectual rapport; in water, intuition. All these qualities will be expressed in the working life, both in the work itself and in the resulting dealings with others, and will help the subject towards attaining his or her personal objectives. This is the Capricorn/Saturn house: look to the influence and placing of Saturn.

11 The Sun in the Eleventh House

Here is a social animal who needs to make his or her mark within the community. He or she will expend solar energies in the development and enjoyment of group activities, very often with humanitarian overtones.

Charitable fund-raising, for example, will be an important and successful involvement for the individual. Don't forget the purely creative power of the Sun, which here can be expressed as a considerable source of inspiration to others, with group activities making the results well worthwhile. Care is needed, however, that the individual does not try to take control as soon as she comes on the scene. Instead, she should defer to others (and especially older, long-standing members of an organization), even if she thinks she could run things better herself.

Despite needing everything that a full and rewarding social life brings, the subject must be careful not to distance herself from close contact with others. There can be conflict here, but she should be able to look at the situation in a rational and objective way. The life should be divided into compartments, so that there will be good close relationships and an ability to express love, while at the same time the subject aims to fulfill all the needs and expression of the Sun's energies through eleventh house matters.

The influence of Uranus

This is the Aquarius/Uranus house, so you will find some guidance as to how this conflict will be resolved by studying the position of Uranus and its aspects. For the ability to enjoy full emotional relationships, look both to Venus and the seventh house.

12 The Sun in the Twelfth House

A very special perspective is added to the chart when the Sun falls in the twelfth house, for here is someone who needs peace and quiet, space and time alone – whatever those may mean to the individual.

If the Sun sign sympathizes, introversion and a lack of self-confidence will be present. However, creative power still comes from the Sun, even in this, the most withdrawn of all the twelve houses.

A need for security

In working behind the scenes, the individual will be shown at his or her best. If the result is creative, then it is behind these creations that he or she will hide, sometimes getting those who are less introspective and more assertive to do any selling of the end products. It is important for those close to the subject not to try to force her into a more extrovert lifestyle; partners and friends must realize and accept that her familiar environment is the only place in which she feels totally secure and therefore is where she functions best.

Self-interest and understanding

Self-knowledge, and the coming to terms with deep-rooted needs, is essential; it may well be more difficult for others to understand this than the individual herself.

Well-meaning, more extroverted partners may sometimes find it necessary to end the relationship with these individuals, and allow them to live their lives uncluttered by what they believe to be unnecessary commitments that can become devitalizing burdens. They should be allowed to let the results of their labors speak for them, while at the same time making their feelings clear to loved ones in a way that expresses the strong, positive qualities of their Sun sign.

This is the Pisces/Neptune house, so Neptune will now be personalized, thereby increasing that planet's importance in the birth chart. Don't gloss over its sign and house placing or the aspects it receives, as they will all throw a great deal of informative light on to the twelfth-house Sun.

☉ The Sun Progressed through the Houses

As the Sun progresses through the signs, it also, of course, progresses through the houses. On the rare occasions that it moves from one house to the next (and to plot this correctly, the birth time must be strictly accurate), it is likely that the subject will reach a crossroads in life, with the concerns of the new house coming vividly to the fore. When the Sun changes signs, a slight blending of the characteristics of the two signs concerned can be seen.

Changing needs

When the progressed Sun moves from one house to another, the change is sharper, and original concerns which relate to the birth chart house (or, if the individual is older, perhaps to the previous progressed house) will tend to fade fairly quickly into the background – although they will not necessarily disappear altogether. For instance, someone with a tenth house Sun that progresses into the eleventh house may feel that worldly ambitions and aspirations should, to some extent, now give way to a more fulfilled social life. On the other hand, someone with a fourth house Sun might, when it progresses into the fifth house, feel the need of more fun and games, and this person will find greater pleasure and satisfaction in the love life, in creativity and in sport.

Each month, as the Sun appears to move through the zodiac signs, it also moves through the houses of the birth chart. Journalist-astrologers make use of this phenomenon when writing Sun sign columns for the newspapers and magazines, using what is known as the solar chart. This involves placing the Sun sign where the Ascendant of the birth chart would be, and interpreting the Sun's house position for each sign.

In natal astrology this is not an important factor, but when using astrology in everyday life it is worth remembering that the Sun's hints are always worth taking, and therefore concentrating on the concerns of the house through which it is transitting at any given time. For instance, think of increasing your income when the Sun is in the second house, starting a diet when it is in the sixth, and so on.

The Aspects of the Sun

The aspects made by the Sun to other planets and to the angles of the chart are of extreme importance in interpretation, since the effect of the planets on the Sun gives a very clear indication of the way in which its own influence from sign and house will be expressed in the subject whose chart is being studied.

You will discover occasions when an aspect may complement the Sun sign characteristics, and perhaps others when it may conflict. When this happens it is, of course, important to assess carefully the importance of the aspect. If it is a major one without a wide orb, its influence will be powerful, and should be incorporated into the final interpretation. If the orb is wide (between seven or eight degrees), the chances are that the aspect will be less important. If the aspect is between the Sun and the ruling planet of the chart, it should not be ignored even if it is minor, for it will be strongly personalized and thus play an important role in the birth chart.

The Sun's Aspects to the Moon

Conjunction

This occurs when a subject is born at or very near the time of the New Moon, and is a focal point of the chart. Usually both the Sun and Moon will fall in the same sign and house, therefore the characteristics of the Sun sign will also be present on an instinctive and intuitive level for the individual. He or she will respond to all situations in the manner of the Sun sign concerned.

The influence of the Moon sign and its house position should be carefully related to the characteristics indicated by the Sun's position. These will be similar but, in the case of the Moon sign, will be on the level of the personality while, where the Moon's house placing is concerned, the effects will be expressed in a more physical manner.

Should Mercury or Venus fall in the same sign as this potent conjunction, the individual may show a certain imbalance since the basic Sun sign characteristics, although working at different levels, will be almost too powerful for comfort.

The conjunction does not always fall in the same sign or house. When this occurs the individual concerned can feel the same inner conflict, restlessness or discontent that is often present when a negative aspect exists between these planets.

Positive aspects

These are an integrating factor within the chart, helping the individual to understand and come to terms with his or her personality.

If there is a trine aspect, and both planets are of the same element, the flow of natural enthusiasm (fire), practicality (earth), intellectual ability (air) or emotion (water) will be positive. The blending of the instincts and reactions (as shown by the Moon) will also complement the individual's character (as shown by the Sun).

The sextile is also helpful, and has a similar but less powerfully integrating effect, usually emphasizing either extrovert (when derived from positive signs) or introvert (negative signs) tendencies. The constitution in this case is usually healthy.

Negative aspects

The individual may be prone to inner discontent and restlessness that can be hard to resolve. Changes of mood and the inability to rest content can cause difficulties, sometimes within emotional relationships, where other problems can also arise.

The opposition (which occurs when the subject is born at Full Moon) emphasizes the polarity between the two signs concerned.

The square accentuates the quadruplicity, making the individual rather more outgoing (when cardinal signs are involved), stubborn (fixed signs) or flexible (mutable signs). Worry, or a tendency to emotional restlessness, may tend to cause minor, but ongoing, health problems.

If a minor aspect is present these interpretations will be far less prominent and should not be given too much emphasis in your interpretation.

Progressed Aspects between the Sun and Moon

When the progressed Sun aspects the natal Moon, there will be a gradual period of psychological development that almost inevitably leads to the making of long-term changes, often with an instinctive conviction that the time is right to do so. Sometimes alterations in the career will cause a domestic move, or there will be a desperate need for some kind of change.

If the Sun and Moon form an aspect in the birth chart, its nature will enable you to assess just how easy or difficult the period of change will be. A major aspect will color the life, albeit often subtly, for about three years, and when this symbolic progression is triggered off by powerful transits the individual's life will become eventful. When you offer advice, refer to the complete birth chart to see how well he or she will approach the problems that arise at such a time.

The Sun's Aspects to Mercury

Only a conjunction or minor semi-sextile can be formed between these planets, because (as we see it from Earth) Mercury can never be more than 28 degrees from the Sun. These aspects are best related to the sign placing of the planets concerned.

If the planets fall in the same sign, the individual will think in the manner of the Sun sign. If Mercury is in the preceding or following sign, then the mind will work according to that sign.

If the Sun and Mercury form a close conjunction – less than five degrees – this traditionally indicates that the individual is a slow developer. These aspects, unless hampered by other influences, can give optimism and enthusiasm, and the desire for worldly progress is often enhanced.

Progressed Aspects between the Sun and Mercury

When one of these planets forms progressed aspects to the natal or progressed position of the other, necessary practical changes will take place in the subject's life. Decisions will have to be reached, and he or she should be encouraged to be objective and think of the long-term effects of any actions. Ask yourself how decisive, quick-thinking or not he may be. Sometimes greater intellectual challenge or stimulus is needed, or the inspiration to write becomes evident. While only the conjunction and semi-sextile are possible in the birth chart, because of the progression the Sun and Mercury can make many more aspects to each other in the progressed chart.

If an aspect is negative, some nervous strain and tension may be present but on the whole it will stimulate the intellect. The individual will look at problems critically, but may well need constructive advice about which direction to take. There can be a need to increase the education, for self-improvement, and all Mercurial concerns – from the car to media involvement – may be apparent.

The Sun's Aspects to Venus

Only the conjunction, semi-sextile and semi-square can be formed between these planets, as the Sun and Venus are never more than 48 degrees apart.

Conjunction and semi-sextile

If both planets fall in the same sign, love and affection will be shown. The attitude to money and possessions will be denoted by the Sun sign, but strengthened by the conjunction.

If there is a conjunction, the subject is usually loving and enjoys the more sybaritic pleasures of life, sometimes to the point of self-indulgence (weight gain and other problems may result). Usually there is added kindness and generosity, since the blending of the powerful solar vitality with Venus' sympathy and need to relate gives positive, happy qualities to the individual, who will be charming and (if the sign placing permits) easygoing.

If the conjunction is afflicted by an opposition or square from the Moon or Saturn, there will almost inevitably be disappointment and a certain unhappiness in the emotional life.

The semi-sextile is not a strong feature, but with it and the conjunction there is nearly always an appreciation of beautiful things, such as art and music. If Mercury is involved, there will be a talent for creative craft work.

The semi-square

This is a major aspect between these planets, and tends to increase the possibility of a breakdown in marriage or a permanent relationship.

Progressed Aspects between the Sun and Venus

Positive aspects

These can herald a very happy period, and are the traditional indication of marriage or the development of a permanent relationship. If the emotional life is not affected by these aspects, a prosperous period is likely to occur instead. Life will certainly have its enjoyable moments – especially when transits echo these lively progressions.

Negative aspects

If there is a semi-sextile between the Sun and Venus in the chart, or should either planet progress to form a semi-square to the other, stress may afflict the emotional life. If the difficulties can be lived through and communication between the couple is good, any problems should be resolved, but care will be needed for about a year or so. Alternately, there may be money troubles rather than emotional ones.

The Sun's Aspects to Mars

Conjunction

The individual is fueled by a virtual powerhouse of energetic resources. This is because Mars contributes to our physical energy and the Sun adds to our vitality. It is important for there to be plenty of positive channels for these resources – demanding sporting activities or some kind of hard manual work, for instance.

The emotional energies are often heightened too, especially if the planets occupy a water sign, when the energy can be expressed through the devotion to a cause or an ideal.

Selfishness can be present, and the Arian pioneering spirit and need to win will also emerge – remember that Mars rules Aries and the Sun is exalted in this sign (see p.35).

Headaches may often occur and, because of undue haste, the subject can be slightly accident-prone. Nevertheless, there will be plenty of physical strength and sometimes also a wiry athletic frame.

Daring and bravery are characteristic, and there is often heroism, with considerable dash and panache. The sex life will be lively, to say the least! Care is needed that a tendency to work too hard is countered, and that risk-taking does not become combined with foolhardiness.

Positive aspects

Many of the characteristics of the conjunction are seen in the trine and sextile, but the more extreme tendencies will be better controlled, as these are less potent aspects. There will be excellent resources of energy, but the tendency to take risks or work too hard will be reduced.

The flow of energy, whether emotional or physical, will be well channeled, and the individual will be vigorous, but not too overtly so.

Negative aspects

Strain and tension due to overwork can become a problem, and unless there are counter-indications in the chart, there will be a very strong tendency to sudden anger or even rage. If this can be controlled and the subject made aware of the negative effects such outbreaks can have on loved ones and colleagues, the energy-source, which is as powerful as that of the conjunction (minor negative aspects apart) can be used to advantage.

Nevertheless, help will be needed when the individual comes to terms with his or her personality, or when the anger has been the cause of stress or unhappiness in others. The root cause of such problems might well be identifiable as sexual frustration or an uncooperative partner.

♂ Progressed Aspects between the Sun and Mars

☌ Conjunction

An extremely demanding and hard-working period is highly likely, with plenty of challenge or excitement. The end-product should be considerable personal achievement.

The effects of the conjunction will last for three years, with the middle year being the most important as the influence will then be at its strongest. This is an exciting time: the energies will be stretched, but a positive individual will gain much from these powerfully beneficial planetary energies. There will be periods of strain and tension (not too difficult to detect from the patterns of transits, lunar progressions and so on).

+ Positive aspects

The effects of these are similar to the conjunction. However, the influence is less strong, and while extra demands will be made on the individual, his or her channeling of energy will be steady, so that it can be used as and when it is required. There will be a need to set new, challenging projects or goals and to achieve a great deal. The prevailing mood will be optimistic and perhaps a bit aggressive when dealing with competitors.

− Negative aspects

Impress upon your subject that, while there is no need for apprehension or worry, he or she could simply take on too much during this period, and as a result will work too strenuously and become overtaxed.

Aggravation and petty annoyance caused by others could become disproportionate, simply because the subject is feeling tense. She must learn to conserve energy (not always easy) and pace herself in all spheres of her life.

♃ The Sun's Aspects to Jupiter

☌ Conjunction

Traditionally, this is one of the most fortunate aspects of all. We never use the word "lucky" because of its fortune-telling overtones, but nevertheless the subject with this aspect does seem to have more than a fair measure of good, or at any rate easy, fortune.

Optimistic, the individual usually has a warm sense of humor too. Tradition also suggests that when any money is needed it is usually found, whether or not the subject is well-off. "Expansion", the Jupiter keyword, is relevant, for there is usually a liking for good food and wine, and therefore a tendency to gain weight; sometimes indigestion is a problem.

The intellect is excellent and there is potential for its expansion, resulting in a wonderfully philosophical outlook. There is usually no lack of ambition, but this is not colored by ruthlessness of any kind.

Consider the influence of Jupiter's sign placing – which in most cases will be the same as the important Sun sign – and add this interesting gloss to its other characteristics.

+ Positive aspects

These have a similar effect to that of the conjunction, but there can sometimes be less of an inclination to make a really serious effort to expand horizons and develop intellectual potential to the full. Despite this, such pursuits as chess and literature will be enjoyed.

If Venus is strong, the tendency to take life easily and to give it over to pleasure will certainly emerge – and the outlook will be positive and optimistic. There may be an interest in the law and publishing, and if a flair for teaching emerges in other areas of the chart these aspects will support it. The subject is not particularly competitive.

− Negative aspects

The sense of perspective can all too easily be lost, and this must be realized. There is also a strong tendency to exaggerate and, when viewing the broad, overall concept of a project, to ignore the finer details completely, glossing over them in a way that can cause quite serious problems for the individual at a later date.

A lack of moderation is usually one of the worst faults, and must be countered. Sometimes, gambling and the reckless investment of money (and emotions) is a problem, and if a tendency towards negative escapism through drugs or drink is shown elsewhere in the chart, it will be increased here. If several planets are in earth signs, and other aspects show steadying qualities, the negative indications will be less potent, and the Jupiter sense of humor and bonhomie will shine through.

♃ Progressed Aspects between the Sun and Jupiter

☌ Conjunction

An important period in the subject's life is usually signaled. Should the Sun be personalized, if Sagittarius is on the Midheaven, or if Jupiter and the Sun are in aspect in the birth chart, the chances are that the individual will receive some kind of accolade: an award or prize, or perhaps a grant for further study, if young, may be won through competition.

Note the strength of Jupiter's transits during the period involved (which will be about three years). If a Jupiter Return occurs, or the planet is prominent in any other way, life will definitely be very rewarding for the individual, who must be encouraged to wear any laurel wreath that comes his or her way – and indeed to rest on those laurels for a while afterward!

+ Positive aspects

A progressive and usually happy period is denoted by these aspects. The traffic lights are set at green, so encourage your subject to push ahead with plans and not to indulge in false modesty. This may be hard for less extrovert types, but Jupiter usually helps them to take center stage a little more readily.

− Negative aspects

The subject must assess every move carefully as life will not be easy. This is especially important when legal documents or contracts are to be signed: the small print must be read with great care. Sadly, people are often disinclined to take such precautions under this influence, and a tendency to rush in can lead to considerable difficulties.

Financial advice should be sought and acted upon, and the diet controlled. Caution and moderation must be developed, as all too often silly and sometimes serious mistakes can be made – especially if Neptune forms many transits at the same time.

THE SUN'S ASPECTS TO SATURN

Conjunction

It has been accepted astrologically, for thousands of years, that the Sun and Saturn are "enemies" – one providing vitality, the other tending to restrain it. Therefore, when they form a conjunction, the Sun's action will be channelled and limited by the powerful intervention of Saturn.

If most of the aspects from other planets are positive, the influence will merely act as a brake and a stabilizer: for instance, a fire sign Sun will be governed and the more extreme characteristics steadied. However, should there be square aspects to the Sun and/or Saturn – especially from the Moon – the Sun sign characteristics will be clouded. If the conjunction is in Capricorn, the qualities attributed to the sign will be enhanced, since it is ruled by Saturn.

There will be shyness and lack of self-confidence, generally speaking, especially when the subject is young, but there is a strong possibility that he or she will come to terms with this later on, and often ambition and determination will be present.

The conjunction is a very powerful focal point in the chart, especially when contacted by transits and progressions from other planets. Rheumatic problems can arise, so exercise of the joints is advisable.

+ Positive aspects

Common sense and a practical, restrained outlook will be evident. Sometimes enthusiasm can be quenched and apprehension heightened, especially when the individual is confronted by a challenge. However, these traits should not seriously hinder the individual, and it is only when shyness and a lack of self-confidence are indicated elsewhere that the effects of the trine and sextile become a problem. In most cases they add a sense of purpose and determination and, as the Sun and Saturn are on good terms, they encourage the subject to achieve ambitions and reach the top in any chosen field.

Caution and circumspection will be present, with risks taken only after the most careful calculation.

– Negative aspects

Here the Sun and Saturn are at loggerheads, and these potent aspects often have a very restrictive effect. The semisextile should not be over-interpreted, but the other minor aspects will have a stronger influence than usual. Sometimes the health is undermined, with frequent aches and pains and a tendency to catch colds and chills easily.

A lack of self-confidence, however, is the real problem, and if the individual suffered from an unsympathetic or over-critical parent, it will not be easy for such early influences to be overcome. At worst there will be a strong sense of deficiency and so (especially if the aspect is exact or has a close orb – say less than four degrees) self-confidence must be built up the hard way.

This influence is not always entirely negative by any means, and the opposition is always less inhibiting than the square. The former, in a chart where there is otherwise much positive enthusiasm (with fire and air present, perhaps where Jupiter and Venus hold court and there are many trines), will be a welcome restraining influence and anchorage, bringing much stability and injecting common sense.

PROGRESSED ASPECTS BETWEEN THE SUN AND SATURN

Conjunction

An extremely important and possibly critical period, likely to last for about three years, is indicated when these planets are in conjunction by progression (whether or not they relate to each other in the birth chart).

Additional responsibilities are likely, plus increased prestige, and the individual will cope well, although the attainment of ambition may mean adopting a rather sober outlook on life for a while. Indeed, the tendency to make sacrifices for an ultimate goal could become exaggerated, and the pleasures of family life should not be forsaken; relaxation must be encouraged. Important changes are probable, perhaps due to new circumstances.

+ Positive aspects

These are similar to the conjunction in effect, but the events and eventual outcome are likely to be less crucially important both at the time and in the long-term. Progress bringing additional responsibilities is very likely, as is planning for the future. This is a serious but constructive influence.

– Negative aspects

A difficult period is indicated, when progress can be slow. A great deal may be learned the hard way, and if mistakes are made they won't be repeated. This is a "Thou shalt not" influence; however, because of lessons learned, the subject will emerge wiser and probably more psychologically whole.

Issues must not be forced – especially when restrictive transits are operative. However, when the transits are positive and steady, cautious moves may be made, giving achievement and satisfaction. The minor aspects add to a slowing down of progress from time to time, and vitality must be watched.

THE SUN'S ASPECTS TO URANUS

Conjunction

This is an extremely powerful aspect that often provokes rebelliousness, eccentric behavior patterns and unpredictability. However, scientific ability or creative flair can also be present, and if a consistency of effort is developed, much will be achieved.

The need for a powerful position incites a near-obsessive driving force in some cases, especially if the conjunction receives aspects from Mars or Pluto, or if both the Sun and Uranus occupy the tenth house of the chart. The subject must consciously develop restraint and control – look to the influence of Saturn, which may help.

+ Positive aspects

Originality, and often personal magnetism, add spice to the Sun's influence. If Venus is well-placed, there can be dynamic sexual attraction and charm. If the Sun occupies an extrovert sign, powers of leadership and popularity will be enhanced.

The emotional and nervous energy is increased and will be shown in positive ways. These aspects, especially the trine, also contribute alertness and a certain enthusiastic driving force which may be somewhat erratically expressed.

Negative aspects
Perversity, stubbornness and other negative traits are often present, especially with the square. Self-willed behavior can cause problems. Periods of tension may occur, and the individual will be "difficult" from time to time, although other indications may be mitigating influences.

The action of the Sun and Uranus can be turned to good, however, since some very powerful planetary energies contribute positive potential. A social conscience should be developed, with the humanitarian side of Uranus allowed to influence the behaviour, which must not become vainglorious.

The individual's sexuality can sometimes be affected. This is especially so for men, who tend to feel the effects of all Sun/Uranus contacts more potently than women. The square has been said to indicate homosexuality.

Progressed Aspects between the Sun and Uranus

Conjunction
An extremely eventful period is indicated, when vitally important changes will be made. There will be a tendency to react suddenly and drastically, and while decisiveness is usually a good quality, care must be taken that the subject's reaction to situations is not so strong that little thought is given to their eventual outcome.

A need to explore pastures new and perhaps for a total change of lifestyle can be characteristic. "Off with the old and on with the new" seems an apt phrase, but caution is essential.

Positive aspects
These are similar to the conjunction, but the positive energies of the Sun and Uranus will ease the possibility of the individual overreacting in a drastic way. New developments will take place, and perhaps important and exciting changes. These aspects are very invigorating and the image, ideas and outlook may change for the better.

Negative aspects
A tense and difficult period is likely, especially when there are strong transits. There must be an awareness that nervous strain and tension can build up, provoking uncharacteristic behavior, perversity and stubbornness, especially with loved ones.

Drastic changes should be carefully considered before being put into effect. For instance, if faced with being fired or a family disruption, plenty of thinking time must be allowed as the reactions will be heightened in a negative way, and as a result serious mistakes may be made which will have a long-term adverse effect.

The Sun's Aspects to Neptune

Conjunction
Considerable sensitivity is present, and the characteristics of the Sun sign will be softened if Neptune also occupies the sign. There is increased intuition and the imagination will be colorful.

If the conjunction is free of negative aspects (from the Moon or Mars in particular), the imagination will often be expressed creatively, perhaps in the arts; the Sun sign will indicate the form this may take. An interest in, and ability for, astrology is often present, and there may be leanings (which must always be very carefully governed) towards the occult.

There may be a tendency to unworldliness; assess other areas of the chart to see just how practical the individual is. Negative escapism may occur if the conjunction is in opposition or square aspect to the Moon. Medically administered drugs can have an adverse or allergic effect.

Positive aspects
The imagination will work well and with inspiration, but there may be a tendency to be lackadaisical, to drift and daydream. This is good if it results in the positive use of creative potential, but sometimes the will to tackle hard work is weak. The vision and intuition are excellent, and these aspects usually add a marvelous insight.

Negative aspects
A tendency to deceive others, and the self, is present. The subject may think that he or she is finding an easy way out of difficult situations, but if such deceptions are successful they can weaken the character. Children with these aspects need special guidance and encouragement to be honest and tell the truth. Deviousness in financial affairs can occur – usually with disastrous results – so professional financial advice should always be taken.

There is a strong tendency to fall back on negative escapism through drink, smoking or other drugs. This is most likely when Neptune falls in Libra or Scorpio, when there is also a high probability (far greater than is the case with the positive aspects) that medically administered drugs will react negatively on the system. Moderation, and the control of all extreme escapist behavior patterns and the faults described above, is essential.

Progressed Aspects between the Sun and Neptune

Conjunction
This is very subtle, and its effects will be barely felt by anyone who is very practical, materialistic and ambitious. However, in one who is sensitive, creative, emotional and intuitive, this aspect will be a great spur to the imagination and inspiration. A serious study of astrology may begin (never to stop!), and spiritual and creative interests can be accentuated. Increased sensitivity may be a stumbling block.

Positive aspects
These are similar to the conjunction but less potent. However, they can bring a greater ability to use creatively the elusive influence of Neptune. Again, they may be hardly felt by a very practical individual. Less worldly and more inspirational areas of life are likely to become increasingly important, so look out for subtle changes even in the most earnest businessman!

Negative aspects
These escapist and psychologically weakening influences are very tricky to cope with, and there may be a two- or three-year period when common sense behavior and reactions are rejected. The square and opposition are particularly problematic, but the minor aspects cause less disruption.

The tendency to live on cloud nine and to do silly things can occur – perhaps because of infatuation mistaken for love. Muddles and confusion can also be allowed to build up because of uncharacteristic behavior. The situation will become even more difficult if there are transits from Neptune to any personal planet or to the Ascendant.

♇ THE SUN'S ASPECTS TO PLUTO

Conjunction
Pluto entered Gemini in 1883 and passes into Sagittarius in 1995, so for people born in this century the conjunction can only occur in those signs or the intervening ones.

The individual needs to explore the depths of his or her personality and to analyze the motives behind every action. These traits will be most pronounced when the conjunction falls in Cancer or Scorpio, and there will be additional intuition present in anyone who is already naturally intuitive.

A tendency towards acute introspection and obsessive behavior patterns must be avoided. From a conjunction in Leo, the subject may wish to exert power over others; from Virgo (and Uranus may be also involved here), she will be in a strong position to lead others, but may tend towards extremism and even political fanaticism.

Positive aspects
An ability for self-analysis is usually present, and there will be meaningful and advantageous changes of direction in life, resulting in psychological satisfaction and growth. There is a need to explore every aspect of whatever fascinates the individual, and very often there is a real talent for research. If medical ability is suggested in other areas of the chart, these are excellent aspects for someone inclined towards psychiatry or psychotherapy.

Negative aspects
It may be very difficult for the subject to open up and to talk through problems with friends and loved ones. If you have a child with one of these aspects, you must try to counter this tendency as early as possible. Psychological blockages can easily occur, and sometimes the individual can even suffer from physical constipation (and will tend to worry about it and thus exacerbate the problem).

Obsessive tendencies may be present, and should be countered through the use of mitigating indications elsewhere in the chart. A Gemini influence, for example, would help, while Venus in one of her own signs, or receiving a trine from the Moon, will prompt a more relaxed and open attitude.

♇ PROGRESSED ASPECTS BETWEEN THE SUN AND PLUTO

Conjunction
Life is likely to become difficult. Either the individual will be unable to move forward due to circumstances beyond his or her control, or there will be a powerful compulsion to make a drastic change because it is impossible to continue along a former course. There is a distinct tendency to throw out the baby with the bath water, and much hard work and achievement may be lost as a result; the subject should be aware that this can happen. Whether it does or not will depend on transits: steadying ones from Saturn will help, tense squares from Uranus will not. Jupiter may bestow material benefits and breadth of vision. An eventful and troublesome period is likely, but when it is over a whole new era may begin.

Positive aspects
Periods of upheaval and change may occur, as with the conjunction, and will be initiated by the individual. Even so there will be setbacks and periods when progress is frustrated, but the overall effect will probably be that of a new broom sweeping clean.

The individual must not follow a trail compulsively and must consciously develop a circumspect attitude, ready to listen to the opinions of others. With this in mind, the period will probably be considered, in retrospect, to have been rewarding, with greater understanding and psychological growth having been gained, as well as more external developments.

Negative aspects
Progress will be extremely patchy and uneven, and may even grind to a halt at times. It is best for the subject not to force issues under such circumstances, but to be patient, if possible. The individual will instinctively know when the storm clouds have lifted. It is important that problems and difficulties should be openly discussed, but even if the subject usually finds this easy, it will now be less so.

ASC THE SUN'S ASPECTS TO THE ASCENDANT

Conjunction
For this to occur, the subject would have been born within about a half an hour of sunrise, so is probably a "double Gemini" or whatever. The Sun must be within eight degrees of the Ascendant, and to use this aspect one must be sure of an accurate birth time.

If the Sun falls in the first house, the individual will be psychologically well-integrated, and the strength of the Ascendant and Sun signs will be considerable (whether or not they are the same). The Sun gives a rather regal disposition, but its vitality will energize the whole personality with a positive, sunny quality that should bring much happiness. If other aspects intervene (such as a square or opposition from Saturn), there will be less self-confidence. A negative aspect from Jupiter will make the subject overbearing.

If the Sun is in the twelfth house the individual may still receive a double impact from one sign, but will need seclusion, or to work behind the scenes. Use the house position (see pp.210-13) in interpretation as it will be extremely relevant in either case.

Positive aspects
These aspects also rely on house position for interpretation, since the house in which the Sun falls will be a focal point of the chart. However, because the aspect to the Ascendant is present, there is a uniting and strengthening link between the Sun and Ascendant. The most potent effect will occur when the Sun is in the fifth house (its natural house), making a trine. Then all fifth house matters will find positive expression and fulfillment.

Negative aspects
Again, be careful to study the house placing. An opposition from the sixth house to the Ascendant may have a bearing on the subject's health and be

a potential source of strain, but if the Sun is also well aspected by the ruling planet, the Moon or Mars, the placing could be invigorating. If an opposition comes from the seventh house, the accent on relationships (as described in relation to the Sun's house position – see pp.211-12) will be emphasized.

Squares to the Ascendant from the fourth house can be domestically disruptive, and perhaps indicate an above-average problem with parents, but much depends on how well aspected the Sun is from the Moon and Saturn. A love of, and pride in, the home is likely. A square from the tenth house shows a strong driving force and ambition, and a desire for worldly progress that will be achieved with effort.

Asc PROGRESSED ASPECTS BETWEEN THE SUN AND THE ASCENDANT

Remember that an accurate birth time is essential if the timing of these trends is to be correct.

☌ Conjunction
The coming together of the Sun's characteristics and the psychological personality traits indicated by the Ascendant will be of considerable benefit to the subject, who will finally be able to resolve inner conflicts.

+ Positive aspects
These are much as for the conjunction, but the positive focusing of the progressed Sun's house concerns will be rather more powerful than before.

– Negative aspects
The eventual outcome will be psychological development and wholeness, but inner conflicts must be fought, and eventually the concerns of the Sun's progressed house position will come more prominently into focus.

MC THE SUN'S ASPECTS TO THE MIDHEAVEN

☌ Conjunction
For this to occur, the individual will have been born around noon. All the solar drive and energy will be channeled into achieving ambitions, and aspirations will be considerable. Generally self-confident, the subject must take care that big-headedness and perhaps pomposity are controlled. (See the effect of the Sun in the tenth house, pp.212-13.)

+ Positive aspects
The identification with the qualities of the sign on the Midheaven will be accepted and aspired to in a very positive way, and ambitions will usually be achieved without ruthlessness.

– Negative aspects
There may be a struggle to achieve objectives and to gain positive expression from the identification with the qualities of the Midheaven sign. Fulfillment will come through effort.

MC PROGRESSED ASPECTS BETWEEN THE SUN AND THE MIDHEAVEN

☌ Conjunction
A time of prime importance is indicated. The subject will either achieve prominence in his or her career, or realize a much desired ambition. However, any achievement will probably be accompanied by resulting additional responsibilities.

Any achievements should be enjoyed by the subject and, especially if there is increased responsibility, care should be taken that an over-serious outlook does not distance him or her from loved ones or enjoyment of life. A great deal is likely to happen over which the subject has no direct control – entirely due to reputation built up over the years, or becoming known in a chosen field. Promotion is very likely.

+ Positive aspects
With regard to ambition and worldly progress, these aspects are a great help and, as with the conjunction, life could become surprisingly eventful. As a result, the period will be both progressive and memorable. Achievement and success are strong possibilities.

– Negative aspects
The eventual outcome will probably be increased prestige and responsibility, but the path leading to it could be difficult, with the possibility of setbacks and perhaps delays *en route*. Study the transits while this progression is active. If Saturn dominates, it will slow down progress, while help from Jupiter will propel things forward very nicely. If under stress or pressure due to commitments, the subject must not allow his or her vitality to be drained.

☉ THE SUN PROGRESSED TO ITS OWN POSITION

There are times when the Sun's progressed position forms an aspect to its own place in the birth chart. The most important of these aspects more or less coincide with the Saturn Returns (see p.312) and their interpretation should blend with the Saturn transits. The aspects that the Sun will make to itself are shown below.

⚺ The semi-sextile
This minor aspect occurs when the subject is approximately thirty years old. It is not in itself very strong, but enhances the characteristics of the natal Sun sign and helps to blend those which are integrated from the Sun's progressed sign. When the Saturn Return is at its most powerful, this progressed aspect will give the individual additional strength to cope with whatever happens.

⚹ The sextile
This is similar in effect to the semi-sextile, and occurs at roughly the same time as the second Saturn Return. It is stronger than the semi-sextile, and will be a considerable help to those who are making changes in their lives.

□ The square
More people now live to be ninety-plus, when the Sun makes a square aspect to its own position. This will coincide with the third Saturn Return. Remember that the progressed aspect is a square, so if the subject is a lively and enthusiastic personality there will be a tendency to overdo things. However, the Saturn influence will give stability.

∠ The semi-square
This occurs when the subject is about 45 years old. By then the Uranus Half-return will have been experienced (see

p.326), and while this is a strenuous aspect it will still revitalize.

Lessons learned during the period between the Uranus Half-return and the Sun's progressed semi-square to its own position may now help the individual to move forward into the next long-term phase of life, bringing out his or her best, as opposed to the extreme characteristics which may have emerged at the time of the Uranus Half-return.

The vitality level may be out of balance – especially if symptoms of the menopause are beginning to have an effect on the subject.

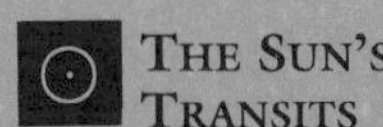

THE SUN'S TRANSITS

Many astrologers do not bother to incorporate solar transits into their schemes of interpretation. However, we find they are useful and fun. There are several other points in their favor, the most important being that they remain more or less constant.

For instance, the Sun as it travels round the sky reaches the precise position of, say, Venus, in a subject's birth chart on or about the same date every year (the only variance will be due to leap years). These tiny solar influences will encourage your subjects to become their own astrologers, as they are easy to follow.

The influence of the solar transits only lasts for a couple of days, but while they are operative they should be considered in the light of the planet the Sun is contacting. However, as they are very minor influences, we suggest that you only calculate the conjunction and opposition transits to the Ascendant, Midheaven, Moon and ruling planet (the planet that rules the Ascendant). Bear in mind that the conjunctions are the most useful of the transits and are also the most likely to work.

There is one exception to this general rule. Because the Sun is so important when there is a heavy Leo influence in a birth chart, you should calculate all the conjunctions and oppositions for someone with any of the following: a Leo Sun sign; a Leo Ascendant; a Leo Moon; or the ruling planet in Leo. This is an area of astrology you can really experiment with. You will notice that we have not listed any solar transits to the Sun's own position. The conjunction occurs on the subject's birthday. This is known astrologically as the Solar Return, and is used in a very important way in the Sun's progressions (see p.67). The opposition occurs exactly six months later, and should be used to full advantage.

Even the oppositions usually do not provoke much stress, unless the Sun in the birth chart is badly afflicted by a great many squares or oppositions. On days when there are solar transits it is sufficient merely to bear them in mind, and if possible the subject should concentrate on the matters listed in the interpretations.

INTERPRETATION OF THE SUN'S TRANSITS

The Sun's transits to the Moon
Family and domestic matters, and also personal problems are emphasized. Time will be well spent on activities associated with home improvements and crafts.

The Sun's transits to Mercury
The subject should take advantage of the media, complain, speak up, try to strike bargains, perhaps buy or sell a car or bike, or make short journeys and telephone calls.

The Sun's transits to Venus
This is a good time to have beauty and hair treatments, buy clothes, entertain, relax and enjoy life.

The Sun's transits to Mars
Hard physical work or sporting activities will be enjoyed. Care is needed to avoid minor accidents and headaches.

The Sun's transits to Jupiter
The accent should be on having fun, and planning or starting vacations abroad. This is a time for signing contracts, studying or writing articles. Possible hangovers or indigestion should be avoided.

The Sun's transits to Saturn
Long-term plans and decisions should be made, and delays expected.

The Sun's transits to Uranus
The subject might act on original, bright ideas and do something different, but should beware of eccentricity.

The Sun's transits to Neptune
Trips to the movies or a concert will be enjoyed. The subject will also enjoy getting out and about with a camera, reading poetry, or being in a romantic and nostalgic mood. However, the intake of alcohol and nicotine should be watched!

The Sun's transits to Pluto
This is a good time to have a purge: for instance, clearing out rubbish from cupboards, getting to work on psychological problems and generally being sleuthlike.

The Sun's transits to the Ascendant
The subject should think of this as an "un-birthday" – an excellent day on which to do something special or start new projects. This is a day to be used to the full.

The Sun's transits to the Midheaven
There may well be a surprise in the offing. Career or parental concerns could be emphasized.

The Moon through the Signs

When interpreting the influence of the Moon and its sign position, remember that the subject will intuitively and instinctively react and respond to all situations in the manner of that sign. The Moon indicates those attributes we inherit from our parents and from earlier generations. We may recognize these, but if we find them inhibiting and undesirable, we often have difficulty in coming to terms with them. However, awareness of these basic reactions is very helpful, and will contribute a great deal to our psychological development and eventual wholeness.

The flow of the Moon's qualities is greatly assisted by positive aspects between it and the Sun and/or ruling planet of the chart: they are strongly supported by a trine or, to a lesser extent a sextile, between the Moon and the planet ruling the sign the Moon occupies. Negative aspects are usually obstructive, while a conjunction adds great strength to the Moon's sign and house position.

The Moon in Aries

Reactions are extremely quick, and the individual will respond emotionally (and sometimes rather too drastically) to issues that arouse passionate feelings. There is much that is positive in this placing, and very little chance that the subject will allow any grass to grow under his or her feet. He or she also has a strongly instinctive need for action, that sometimes results in too much haste.

A very quick temper can be a problem if the Moon receives negative aspects from Mars or Uranus. In this case, the emotional energy level is very strong and needs to be channeled in positive directions.

Impulsive tendencies

The subject may be accident prone, because in dangerous situations, or at times when brave, sudden action is required, he may respond by risking life and limb. It is a good thing, therefore, for him to learn lifesaving, rescue and first aid techniques. An advanced driving course is another good idea, as those with this placing like to drive very fast, and while their reactions to danger are excellent, their driving can become rather aggressive when they are angry.

If impulsive tendencies can be controlled, the subject will be marvelously decisive, and have an excellent broad grasp of most situations. The placing bestows a need for independence and the ability to encourage others to do things for themselves.

The emotional response

Sexually, these people are excellent partners, but as in other spheres of their lives, they can become easily bored, so need to experiment and be adventurous. There is a need for patience, especially when dealing with those who are slower than themselves.

Selfishness, the worst Arian fault, will emerge when subjects are challenged in personal matters: they will instinctively put themselves first. However, once other levels of their personality take over, they may regret what they have said or done, and make amends in the manner of their Sun or rising sign.

The Moon in Taurus

According to tradition, the influence of the Moon is particularly powerful in this sign, because it is exalted (see pp.34-5). Bear this in mind when reaching conclusions about the interpretation of the Moon in Taurus.

A secure background to life is needed by Sun sign Taureans, both materially and emotionally, and those with this placing will respond very quickly and defensively when their background is threatened. Even if they are not particularly concerned with building up a good bank balance, or rely too heavily on their partner for support, their instinct will be to spring into action when in difficulties, and do everything in their power to ensure that their world is kept intact.

A love of convention

The conservatism and conventionality of Taurus may well clash with other areas of the subject's chart. Self-absorption will definitely be seen, and an independent, freedom-loving person can suddenly make a complete about-face.

If a strict adherence to convention is indicated elsewhere in the chart (a Capricorn Sun or Ascendant sign, for instance) the characteristics of this placing will blend into the personality, and the instinctive responses will not be a source of conflict.

The emergence of possessiveness, the worst Taurean fault, may need countering, but this will be hard to do. Practicality will be considerable, and a common sense approach to life will be a great asset, especially if a certain adventurousness is indicated by other planetary positions.

The stubbornness common to this sign will be present, but again this may only be an immediate reaction, with flexibility present on other levels. If there is a preponderance of fixed signs, bloody-mindedness and getting in a rut can become on-going problems.

A love of the good life

The Taurean love of good food and living, and a need to surround the self with beautiful, comfortable objects, may be apparent. Since the Moon is related to the health, it is necessary for the subject to realize that – especially when under stress – he or she is likely to indulge in chocolate bars and other comfort food. Weight gain can be the result. The throat, too, is rather vulnerable – link any such comments in your interpretation to the fact that this area of the subject's body may easily react to stress or general infection.

♊ The Moon in Gemini

A very quick verbal response to situations is characteristic of the subject who has the Moon in Gemini. He or she will, especially when young, often express him- or herself in such a flurry of words that they can sometimes tumble out in an incoherent muddle.

The versatility of Gemini is present, and will be seen particularly when the subject is confronted with several tasks. Rather than consciously deciding on a particular order of preference or importance, the tendency will be to start all of them at the same time.

Sources of emotional conflict

Our emotional responses are powerfully influenced by the Moon, so there can be conflict, when a contrary instinct to rationalize argues with emotion and intuition. The individual must come to terms with the fact that intuition and objective rationalism must merge and flow positively.

The Geminian tendency of not entirely trusting the emotions will be apparent and, because we are dealing with the Moon, the traits will not be far from the surface when the subject is challenged.

The need for action

The natural instinct to speak up will be very strong. For example, the individual will rush to telephone the local radio station in order to join in a discussion on a topic in which she has an interest or firm views. Indeed, this is one of the planetary placings that indicates a chatterbox!

A certain impatience and restlessness will also be obvious. While the individual may well be aware of this and do much to counter it, nevertheless it is to her advantage to realize that her resources of nervous energy are very high and must not be allowed to stagnate. This is where difficulties can be encountered, especially if other areas of the chart suggest a much slower, more stolid personality.

Health and welfare

In theory, there should be the ability to get the best of both worlds, with the Gemini Moon adding a natural quickness of response and the heavier traits contributing stability and patience. Good aspects between the Moon and other personal planets will help, and there could well be a positive or negative link as a result of Mercury's influence.

Sometimes nervous strain and pressure can lead to periods of tension, and digestive problems may be one of the results. In certain cases, because of the Gemini connection with the lungs, asthma (again as a result of tension or worry) may be a problem.

♋ THE MOON IN CANCER

The Moon is always the third most important factor of a birth chart, but because it rules Cancer, its influence is considerably increased when placed in this sign.

The well-known natural defensive system, which is such a prominent characteristic of those with a Cancerian Sun sign, will be equally – if not more powerfully – present. Defensiveness will be the immediate reaction, not only when the individual is challenged but also in less threatening situations.

Instinct and practicality

The emotional and intuitive levels are second to none, and those with this placing should learn to trust and rely on them – their instincts will not let them down. However, it is important that you look for other practical down-to-earth indications in the chart, so that these marvelous facilities can be controlled and not allowed to dominate in a negative way.

The Sun or Mercury in an earth sign, for instance, or perhaps a trine aspect to Saturn from the Moon itself, would be of enormous help. Such a stabilizing influence is necessary because, in addition to a powerful intuition, there is plenty of imagination that, triggered in a negative way, can be expressed through worry.

Expression of anxiety

When worried, the individual will tend to think that the very worst has happened. He or she may not necessarily have a depressive outlook, but apprehension over loved ones can cause these powerful responses to build up out of control. For instance, if a child is unexpectedly late home from school, the subject will soon imagine there has been a serious accident. Nevertheless, both sexes tend to make excellent and loving parents.

From a physical point-of-view, the digestive system will be upset by worry, and it is frequently the case that those with this placing have very sensitive skins, whatever their ethnic coloring. Caucasians will quickly turn beet-red in the sun while the other races will find it difficult to get rid of even quite minor scar tissue. Protection from the sun, and additional care over cuts, insect bites and so on, is absolutely essential.

Attachment to the family

The past is a frequent subject for reflection and nostalgia, and the subject's childhood background may be allowed to dominate his outlook on life. Coming to terms with the attitude and treatment received from parents, whether that was beneficial or difficult, may take longer than for other Moon sign placings.

The family instincts are very powerful indeed, and these people (like those with a Cancerian Sun) often have to face problems when their children have grown up and want to leave home. Such an occurrence runs contrary to much that is of instinctive and genetic importance to them. At such times, they will have to call upon other, more forward-looking, areas of their charts to help them through any period of emotional and physical readjustment that is needed.

The Cancerian tendency to hoard is another strong instinct for the subject with this placing. As a result, clearing out the resulting clutter can be a chore that is avoided at all costs, perhaps because hoarding such items adds to the individual's much-needed sense of security.

Mood and expression

There may be quick changes of mood, which can frequently be disconcerting for loved ones to witness. Women with this placing may suffer in an above-average way from premenstrual tension, but should try hard not to let it dominate their lives.

The face is usually round, with a quite literal moon-like shape and glow to it. When the Moon is placed in Cancer, no matter what its house, it can influence the individual's facial expression: a tiny frown-line may appear between the eyebrows.

♌ The Moon in Leo

The immediate instinct of those with the Moon in Leo is to take over. While there is an active and happy enthusiasm, and a need to express emotions in a positive way, it is all too easy for people with this placing to appear bossy, dogmatic and stubborn. But at best they can be an excellent source of inspiration to others, with the ability to get the most out of them – pack leaders who enjoy the role!

A show of confidence
Their belief that they can do anything as well or better than anyone else is a mixed blessing. While they will inevitably find plenty of outlets for all their potential (indicated by the characteristics of the Sun sign) and will achieve their aspirations (indicated by the Midheaven), they can tend to overstep the mark and become somewhat overwhelming.

If shyness or a lack of self-assurance is shown in other areas of the chart, there will be a conflict which will result in the subject covering up the inhibited areas by showing off, perhaps even feigning extroversion and confidence in a way that can be embarrassing for loved ones. If you are working on the chart of a child with this placing it will be necessary to encourage the parents to steady the youngster's natural exuberance, which at its best is lovely but can become bombastic.

Ability and creativity
There is a special need to make the right impression, especially when these people are young, and as a result a great many of them will learn the hard way. In spite of this, there is determination and a sense of immediacy which is much in their favor. They will cope extremely well in any emergency that arises, for the powers of leadership and organizational ability attributed to the Sun sign Leo are always present and will be called upon and expressed at just a moment's notice.

The emotional forces are strong and the intuition and imagination powerful. These can be expressed creatively through any art form sympathetic to the Sun sign. The tendency to show off, at any age, must be countered by other less extrovert indications in the chart. This is a placing that needs a steadying hand, not only elsewhere in the chart, but also from those with influence over the subject. Even so, this placing is very often found in the charts of big achievers, especially when the Moon is near the Midheaven or situated in the tenth house.

♍ The Moon in Virgo

Some similarities with the characteristics of the Moon in Gemini will be obvious in this placing, inasmuch as the individual will be extremely talkative when nervous or challenged. If anything, however, there will be even greater resources of nervous energy. If this is positively expressed, the individual will have a great deal of practical ability and, because of some extremely quick responses to situations, will be in a good position to keep abreast or ahead of competitors.

Worry and a lack of self-confidence may well be present, and because the worry springs from the deepest instinctive level, the subject can develop rather mysterious stomach upsets or digestive problems without realizing what has caused them. Unconscious concern over a problem will probably be the root cause, affecting the subject in a physical way before he or she is consciously aware of what is wrong. Children with this placing will all too often become ill and have very severe, and indeed real, "schoolitis" when there are problems (perhaps an unsympathetic teacher may be the cause?)

The subject will be fundamentally rational, but this extremely practical approach and her instincts do not always marry. Her reactions are very quick indeed, which is a great asset, as are the characteristic reliability, a great measure of common sense and considerable helpfulness.

A way with words
Literary talent is often present with this placing, and should not be ignored – it is here that any creativity shown in other areas of the chart may be expressed. There is also a critical streak and, especially if the Moon receives a square aspect from Mercury, a tendency to gossip. More positively, because of the sharp reflexes (usually expressed verbally as well as in practical action), there is talent and an incisive quality in debate; in any kind of argument the individual can stand very firmly on her own two feet.

♎ The Moon in Libra

A reputation for bestowing tact and natural diplomacy on the subject accompanies this placing. Here is the peacemaker of the zodiac. There is an immediate response to, and ability to identify with, other people's problems and points of view. This is excellent, but unless strong signs such as Capricorn or Leo are emphasized elsewhere in the chart, or there are indications of the ability to rationalize and detach the self from showing the emotions, the placing can lead to indecision or in some cases may even weaken the character. Its strength lies in the individual's immediate sympathy and very natural understanding. Kindness is complemented by a willingness to listen to people who have problems, encouraging them to relax and calm down.

The ability to take action
Decide for yourself just how much practical, active help your subject would be in a crisis – remembering that the natural reaction is to remain calm rather than join in the fray, and that the tendency to panic is low on the list of characteristic responses to such situations.

Do not forget that the polar, or opposite, sign of Libra is Aries, which will encourage a slightly aggressive tendency in the subject. For example, he can provoke an argument when annoyed, and the Libran Sun sign cry of "It isn't *fair*!" will definitely be heard. Loved ones will usually be called upon to reassure the subject that nothing is seriously wrong and all is well. The Libran identification with balance and harmony is also present, and a need to put matters right, and make amends if necessary, will be an immediate and natural response when there are problems with partners, friends or colleagues.

Bringing out the best in others is a most positive characteristic of this placing. It can be especially strong when the subject meets someone for the first time. She will make strangers feel immediately at ease, partly because she herself is usually relaxed. (However, do look for sources of tension or nervous apprehension in other areas of the birth chart.)

There is an immediate charm which is extremely beguiling, and it is often possible to identify those with this placing because the speech tends to be slow and drawling – something that can also occur with a Libran Sun or Mercury sign.

♏ THE MOON IN SCORPIO

The emotional energy resources, which are strong when the Sun or Ascendant sign is Scorpio, are in some ways even more potent with a Scorpio Moon. They will surface at once when the individual is challenged, and the response to all kinds of situations is influenced in an extremely powerful way. Because the feelings are so instantly on tap, the subject can overreact when provoked; all kinds of reactions, both positive and negative, will be laced with vivid emotion. There may be outbursts which will surprise those confronted with them, since other areas of the personality usually present a very different sort of person.

Not only emotional but also physical energy is boosted by this placing, which adds determination and the instinctive urge to achieve. The subject can also encourage others (particularly loved ones) to achieve more. Laziness in a child, for instance, will be denounced by the Moon-in-Scorpio parent, and in the end the child will be bullied into action. There may also be a tendency to show a certain harsh reaction – such as taking an extreme line in the discussion of the treatment of criminals. Here, the immediate response of the Moon will home in on the cruel streak of Scorpio.

Controlling the jealous impulse

It is very important indeed that the subject realizes how many situations in life will prompt his instinctive response of jealousy. Rather as the individual with a Taurean Moon will react possessively and regret it, so the subject with the Moon in Scorpio may well loathe expressing any form of jealousy, but will simply not be able to help it. Again, it is the powerful influence of the Moon encouraging an immediate response and reaction. It will not be easy for the individual to control this negative trait, and the feelings will most certainly be heartfelt.

An awareness that jealousy can be very easily aroused, however, is essential, and will help the subject to cope with it. This will also enable the partner to fully understand the reaction of the loved one, and if you, as the astrologer, can explain this both to your subject and his or her partner, you will be fulfilling your role very well indeed. If these extremely powerful sources of emotional energy and intuition can be channeled in positive directions, there will be great inner strength and resourcefulness.

♐ THE MOON IN SAGITTARIUS

People with this placing will respond in a very positive, optimistic and enthusiastic way to circumstances (especially those that are challenging), for the sheer enjoyment and need of challenge is a quintessential Sagittarian characteristic. These people give the impression that they will not worry or bother too much with the pros and cons of a situation. In fact, they are not very good at recognizing small details or problems, and will tend to ignore them when they are pointed out by others.

A sense of progression

The urge to move forward physically and intellectually is very strong – impatience when waiting in traffic jams, for instance, is common! These individuals will enjoy feeling that their intellect is being stretched, but can sometimes give the impression of knowing and understanding much more than is really the case.

Hope and optimism run high, until other more sober elements of the personality take over (if they are present elsewhere in the birth chart). Balance is needed if the individual is not to incline towards bluster, with blind optimism clouding common sense. Nevertheless, he or she has general keenness and enthusiasm, and is the complete reverse of the "wet blanket"!

A need for care and consistency

A tendency to be off-hand is a fault that often emerges with this placing, however. "See if I care" is the sort of statement that is characteristic of the Moon in Sagittarius, usually followed by a turn and toss of the head, with the individual already thinking of something, or someone, else.

Sagittarian restlessness will almost inevitably be present, and must be countered, or recognized at the very least. There is marvelous potential, especially intellectually, and it is up to the individual to develop a consistency of effort by fully using other areas of her personality. She must aim to calm her reactions, even though these are positive, so that the Sagittarian sage-like qualities and the subject's own sound, possibly even unique, philosophy of life can be used to their full and best advantage.

Digestive problems and biliousness can affect the health, as those with this placing like to enjoy food which is a little too rich for their systems.

♑ THE MOON IN CAPRICORN

There is a very cool, calm reaction to situations for individuals with this placing, and the emotional responses are rather low, or at least very much under control. There can also be a tendency to aloofness, which gives the impression that these people want, for reasons of their own, to distance themselves from other (sometimes, in their eyes, lesser) mortals. However, the marvelously offbeat Capricorn sense of humor surfaces very spontaneously, and does much to soften this unfortunate impression.

The urge to fulfill aspirations and ambitions is considerable, and if this need is supported by practical and intellectual flair (shown in other areas of the chart), there will be considerable ability to achieve those aims, with success being the eventual reward.

Reactions and responses

The Capricorn tendency to moan will be evident, as will lunar moodiness, and sometimes the subject's immediate reaction to a situation will be negative. This may be due to a lack of confidence (especially if the Moon makes a square or opposition aspect to Saturn, or the weakness shows up in other areas of the chart). In this case, someone close to the individual must always attempt to inspire her by encouraging her to think positively about her ambitions and aspirations, which will no doubt be formidable. If the negative attitude is immovable, the subject will tend to live safely but unadventurously.

There is also an inner desire to impress other people, and a sense of pride, making the subject unwilling to accept help when it is offered. This is because it could be considered charity, and so acceptance may be seen as a sign of weakness.

When the Moon is working in a positive way for the subject (with trine aspects to lively Mars, Saturn, the Ascendant, Sun or chart ruler), this placing will work extremely well. All the strong, practical qualities (including common sense, determination, ambition and the ability to enjoy the good things of life) will then be used at a moment's notice, and to full advantage. There is a natural tendency to self-preservation, and usually only well-calculated risks will be taken.

♒ The Moon in Aquarius

Those with this placing are magnetically attractive, yet send out signals suggesting they are cool and distant, and don't want the rest of us to come too close. This is their immediate reaction, and it is only when we break through this brittle, bright but somewhat frosty barrier that we actually experience the characteristics of the Sun, and eventually the Ascendant, sign. It is as if, in some ways, the subject is on the defensive, and wants to appear enigmatic and mysterious.

The flow of emotion is very controlled, although if anyone needs help the subject will immediately respond and want to do as much as possible, just like his or her Aquarius Sun sign cousins. The subject's reasons for helping will be severely practical, and he will at once see a way through any difficulties that may cloud the issue for the person in trouble.

Acting on impulse

The unpredictability of Aquarius will be seen when the subject is confronted with any aspect of life that could be considered controversial. His reaction may be totally unexpected, and quite different from what was anticipated. Similarly, the subject may take an unexpected line of action, on the spur of the moment, that is completely out of character with other areas of his personality. In retrospect, he may well have problems attempting to justify this to himself.

Anything glamorous will strongly appeal to the subject who, interestingly, also has a romantic streak. However, this is detached, and the way emotions are expressed, especially in love (as opposed to strong feelings relating to worldly issues) must be assessed from the positions of Venus and Mars, and their strength in the chart as a whole.

A possibility of conflict

Originality and often a spark of genius are present. Sudden bright ideas should be acted upon and carried through to completion. If stubbornness is shown in the positions and aspects of the other planets, it could become a serious problem, for it will not blend happily with a tendency to unpredictability. Nervous tension can also cause problems, the likelihood of which will be affected by the influence of Uranus in the birth chart.

The humanitarian qualities of Aquarius, linked with kindness, will be very evident and contribute much that is positive in the subject.

♓ The Moon in Pisces

This placing of the Moon shows the coming together of two forces that are extremely highly-charged. The emotional content of Pisces is powerful, and when the Moon falls in this sign, the responses to all situations will also be emotional. This is not the type of emotion found, for instance, in fiery Aries: it is a very different force, discharged through very different channels and for different reasons.

Emotional responses

The individual is easily moved, whether to great happiness or sadness. He or she may be moved to tears by a piece of music that rings nostalgic bells or affected in an above-average way when scenes of disasters flash on to the television screen. The response will be to do something kind and charitable, perhaps sending hard-earned cash to aid those in distress, even to the point of self-denial.

If creativity is shown in other areas of the chart, this placing will add sensitivity and imagination to the way in which it is expressed. However, the Moon in this sign may weaken the character, encouraging the subject to take the line of least resistance, especially when challenged. As a result, there will be a tendency to tell lies and to be very deceptive – not only towards others but to the self as well.

When the subject does deceive others, her excuse will be that lies are less hurtful than the truth, and those lies will be told with an astonishing spontaneity. Parents with children who have this placing must be kind and understanding, but very firm indeed, in making their offspring realize that truthfulness is essential.

Negative tendencies

A warning should be given to the subject that, like those with a Piscean Sun sign or Ascendant, she may react adversely to medically administered drugs. When under stress, she must be strong enough to resist the extra cigarette or drink. Giving way to any form of negative escapism can become a habit that is hard to break.

A positive contribution

The positive, caring, sacrificial qualities of this placing will contribute much if the individual has a sense of vocation. They are also valuable traits if she is involved in any of the caring professions, since the subject will have an understanding of those needing help, and an ability to give a favorable and sympathetic impression to anyone who is underprivileged.

The Moon through the Houses

The affairs and spheres of life governed by the Moon's house will be of special importance to the subject – and an important focal point of the chart. The more aspects the Moon receives, the greater its prominence; if Cancer is emphasized by the Sun sign or Ascendant, the influence will be increased, as it will to a certain extent if Taurus is the Sun sign or Ascendant.

A good business instinct may be present, and if other sign placings support it, then the individual will do well to give full rein to his intuitions and instincts when investing money. A trine from the Moon to Saturn will help, but squares or oppositions to Jupiter or Neptune will not!

1 The Moon in the First House

The nearer the Moon is to the Ascending degree, the stronger its influence will be. If is it within eight degrees and you are sure of the birth time, the conjunction it makes with the Ascendant will be a very important factor of the chart.

Emotional investment

With or without the conjunction, the placing of the Moon in this house is a focal point, softening the personality and endowing the subject with a great urge to care for other people. There is also a need to protect both the self and the loved ones, and it is only when the individual is quite certain of his or her position that he or she will open up and be self-expressive.

The basic psychological motivation of the Ascendant sign and its personality traits are colored by this placing; you won't go far wrong if you read the characteristics of Cancer Ascending (see p.94). Do remember, however, that despite the very personal position of the Moon and its effect on the personality, it still represents the individual's reactions and responses. These will be heightened, and the intuition and emotions will be forces with which to reckon.

If a sign with a low emotional content is rising, the flow of emotions will be restrained. If the Moon is well aspected by trines and sextiles, the flow will be channeled; if it receives squares or oppositions, however, emotional inhibition may cause problems.

Outer and inner health

The skin is sensitized, so a powerful sun filter cream is essential in strong sunshine. The vitality may fluctuate and the diet should be carefully controlled, since the digestive, and in women, the reproductive, system can be sensitive. Try to discuss the subject's relationship with his mother; there may have been difficulties at birth, rejection by her or some specific problem in the mother/child relationship. Many cases where the subject has been adopted have been documented.

2 The Moon in the Second House

The need for security, both emotional and financial, is very pertinent here, and the Moon's attributes, shown by its sign placing, will flourish against a much needed secure background.

There is a strong instinct to save and to collect possessions, since these will add to the subject's sense of security. At times, the hoarding instinct could become obsessive. However, peaks and troughs may occur in the financial situation from time to time, and whenever the coffers are low, the individual will become unduly concerned, perhaps allowing his or her imagination to run wild. At such times you should look for practicality in the chart in order to counter any such negative reactions. Constant worry about money can be a serious problem, even if the individual is well-off. Every fluctuation of the Stock Exchange can affect the subject's mood, and you may find that the materialistic side of life may assume too great an importance if the birth chart as a whole is that way inclined.

Money management

If the subject is more spiritually or creatively oriented, and this tendency is supported by the Moon sign, money may easily slip through his fingers, with much of it given to charities or needy friends. If so, every act of that kind will drain the individual emotionally and even lead to an imbalance, since it is working against his basically acquisitive lunar instinct.

3 The Moon in the Third House

The need to communicate is paramount and will be expressed in the manner of the Moon's sign. The individual should move around and keep in touch with other people, both through conversation and the media. His or her ideas are spiced with a strong intuition as to the way in which they will evolve. The basic fluctuations of the Moon's influence will probably relate to many changes in education at school, as opposed to college.

A communicative subject

An instinctive need for knowledge is very strong but is often linked to the superficial – too much notice may be taken of what is read in newspapers or seen on television, for instance. The knowledge gained may not be permanent, either, as the subject will have a constant need to move on to the next item of interest. The need to know, as opposed to a desire for real knowledge, perhaps sums up best this placing. In addition, the subject needs to pass on her knowledge to others, and to have good powers of communication with her children. Dealings with children will reflect a very positive influence, for here we may have the parent who tells interesting bedtime stories, especially if the Moon sign bestows imagination.

A sense of cunning colors the instincts, and a certain shrewd cleverness will emerge, especially when the subject is challenged in argument, since her replies will have a sharp edge. Feelings and emotions are easily put into words, unless the Moon's aspects indicate otherwise.

In essence, this is a good position for the Moon as far as the ability to talk through emotional problems is concerned. Only a close square or opposition from Saturn or Pluto will prevent this, or a Scorpio Moon sign, which may block the feelings and thus cause problems for the subject with a third-house Moon.

4 THE MOON IN THE FOURTH HOUSE

The Moon works well and powerfully from this house, and according to the sign, there can be a very vital urge to create a home and family. Security in domestic life will be most important, and when it is undermined the individual will function badly in other areas of his or her life. Indeed, the instinct will be to fight back every inch of the way. Sometimes, as is the case when the Moon or Sun is in Cancer, problems will arise when the subject's children grow up and want to leave home, for this will be seen as undermining his or her basic security. There will also be worry because the young birds will have flown the nest and are no longer safely under the parental eye.

In building a secure home for himself, the subject must recognize that he may be creating claustrophobic conditions for his loved ones. Study the positions of the other planets in the chart, especially the Sun, to see how he can counter this tendency and apply some logic to such a very powerful instinct.

A tendency to introversion
The caring, protective qualities of this placing can turn inward, so that over-cossetting the self leads to introversion and a fear of the unknown. This can cause problems in someone shy and perhaps inhibited – he may shut up like a clam, and introspection can lead to imaginary illnesses, with small problems seeming mountainous. If the Moon makes an opposition to the Midheaven it will also form a conjunction to the IC (see p.238), and may increase such pensive tendencies. If the Moon is well aspected, the maternal instinct and love of the domestic life are enhanced.

There is a focus on the mother, for the Moon's sign will show in a remarkable way how she is viewed by the subject (as opposed perhaps to what she is or was really like), and these points are especially apt here. It is too easy to say that she is the most powerful influence in the subject's life, as this applies to most people. Instead, consider this placing as an extra comment on her maternal influence.

5 THE MOON IN THE FIFTH HOUSE

Unless this placing occurs in a chart where creative ability is strongly indicated, the Moon's creative urge will be directed towards the procreation of children, with great joy gained from parenthood. Doing the right thing for the child will be quite instinctive, and the individual will know the best course of action without reference to books or other guidance.

This is the house of lovemaking. While the placing will make for a responsive sexual partner, the purely creative side of lovemaking must be expressed, as opposed to indulgence in sexual pleasure for its own sake.

There is a frequent instinct to show off, with times when the individual will be overtly showy and extrovert. Then, as a result of a quick change of mood, the introspective areas of the Moon's influence will assert themselves and the individual will recoil from previous actions. Just how far he or she goes in either direction will be shown by the Moon sign; for example, a Sagittarian Moon in the fifth house may make the subject more extrovert, while a Piscean Moon will suggest introversion.

Dealing with risk factors
There will be a similar reaction to taking risks, both financial and emotional. The subject will realize that there is more at stake than the situation itself, for if things go wrong the very fact that a risk was taken can damage his sense of security, and the result will be retrograde both personally and psychologically. His ability to cope will be shown by the Sun and Ascending signs, indicating the general level of common sense and logic.

THE MOON IN THE SIXTH HOUSE

This placing will have an important effect on the health and well-being. The health influence will be especially relevant if the Moon is conjunct the Descendant (see p.237) – i.e. within eight degrees of the cusp of the seventh house – in which case it will also be in opposition to the Ascendant.

Maintaining a personal routine
It is important that the subject develops good steady habits and overcomes such negative ones as smoking, drinking or drug-taking, which will all have a more than usually adverse effect. Just how easy it is to exercise such restraint will be shown by the Moon sign and its aspects. Squares between the Moon and Neptune, and to a certain extent Jupiter or Venus as well, will not make the process an easy one, while a trine from the Sun or Saturn will help, and a Martian influence will invigorate. Tension and stress will be present if the Moon is in difficult aspect to Uranus and, to a certain extent, Mercury (a planet strongly linked to this house). A steady work routine should also be aimed for, so the Moon's emotional forces and responses can develop into a steady rhythm and a balance can then be maintained.

Diet is influenced by the sixth house and this, too, must be regulated, for in adverse conditions there may be a tendency to binge on comfort food, or perhaps to become anorexic. The likelihood that these possibilities may occur is especially pronounced when the individual needs to retreat from difficult situations.

The Moon works well from the sixth house, if this placing can be controlled. If the Moon is in an earth sign, for instance, there is often a considerable adherence to routine, and a common sense reaction to situations.

THE MOON IN THE SEVENTH HOUSE

While in many ways this placing adds to the individual's ability to respond well and sensitively to the partner's needs, there is a tendency to submerge the self totally in him or her. The resulting need for continuous rapport and togetherness with the partner, cultivated for emotional security, may lead to a lack of self-sufficiency.

The way in which the emotions are expressed towards the partner may not be constant, since the lunar tendency to changes in mood can at times cause emotional scenes. Sometimes they are provoked just to attract the partner's attention, and increase the warmth of his or her affection, but the subject must realize the damage that can be done by such outbursts. She can also concede to the wishes of the partner too easily, further weakening her position. The Moon sign will determine how often this happens; the subject will be at her most vulnerable if the Moon is in Libra (although if Aries is the rising sign you will have to balance this with Arian self-centeredness).

Balance in partnership
The caring qualities of the Moon's influence will be apparent, again according to its sign placing, and its protective instinct will also focus on the partner. Ask yourself if your subject is constant and true, or are the attitudes and feelings for the partner changeable and unstable? Is she content and happy, or does she feel inadequate and inferior in relation to the partner? All such problems must be resolved if the Moon's placing is to work in a balanced and positive way.

8 THE MOON IN THE EIGHTH HOUSE

Here, the instinctive Moon is in a house where intuition, emotion and deep-rooted feelings are emphasized. In some cases, the subject may have a "sixth sense", especially if other areas of the chart suggest this (for example, a strong, positive Neptune or an overall accent on Scorpio or Pluto).

The subject's basic instincts must be fulfilled through a strong sexual expression, but this will only happen when he or she is in total rapport with the partner, who must have similar needs and express them in more or less the same way. The emotional resources are considerable, but the way in which they flow and are satisfied will be shown by the Moon's sign and aspects. Building up complete trust in loved ones and partners is vital. Jealousy and suspicion – both likely emotions here – will have a cancerous effect on his ability to love securely and permanently and so should always be countered. Otherwise, they will erode the permanence and stability of the relationship, plus the sexual satisfaction and release, that are so essential for him.

If the Moon's action is inhibited, the result could be psychological problems that are not easily expressed and can affect the subject for long periods. If they do, therapy may be beneficial.

Financial security
Money in relation to inheritance and investment is also influenced by this house. As a result, having a good, growing life assurance policy and a regularly updated insurance policy for the house and its contents will give a subtly increased sense of security.

9 THE MOON IN THE NINTH HOUSE

While the subject may have an instinctive need to stretch his or her intellect through study, the powers of concentration may fluctuate, so that the long-term goal may never be reached. A strong Moon sign and good aspects to Mercury and Jupiter will help, but determination is essential.

Too many emotions about what is being undertaken can cloud the issue, and the individual may have great flights of fancy. "When I qualify..." or "If only I could..." are the sort of musings heard when his emotions are moved by a challenging situation. However, if he has as strong a grasp of reality as emotional flow, the two should merge with positive results. The ability to keep both feet on the ground is essential, and the Moon's sign will reveal whether this quality is present or, at least, attainable.

There is an attraction to travel, with long journeys in the imagination and the wish that they could become reality. The intellect is philosophical, but moral decisions are often taken instinctively. The subject will search after the truth and usually finds it.

10 THE MOON IN THE TENTH HOUSE

This often indicates someone who has the potential for fame in a chosen field. There will also be the ability to govern large groups, and the two sometimes combine. In fact, this is a fascinating placing to research, if you eventually find that you enjoy studying the charts of famous people. See how many of them have the Moon high up in their charts – you will not be bored!

There is usually a sympathy and understanding of those over whom the individual has authority, and very often he or she is widely loved, or even idolized, by many people. The flow of intuition and emotion extends into taking care of others, who can respond very powerfully. However, in interpreting this placing, the Moon's sign will show how the individual expresses these basic instincts; dogmatically, for instance, if the Moon is in Leo, with a cold authority in Capricorn, and so on.

"I love the world" is the motto here, and the instinct to put it to rights could be a channel for the Moon's action, eliminating cruelty and fostering the best of the maternal instinct, in the broadest sense of the word.

Personal progress
The need for change and variety is most likely to be shown in the career, so even if the individual becomes famous, he will still have a variety of accomplishments. Other areas of the chart must show a positive channeling of energy and strong ambition if he is to benefit fully from this placing; a sense of general direction is essential. An instinctive ability for choosing the best time to make changes will be an asset, and a good sense of timing is usually present.

11 THE MOON IN THE ELEVENTH HOUSE

Here the instincts of the Moon are expressed towards groups. It is as though the individual will always want to be part of a group, whatever it may mean to him or her. Sometimes this may happen because the subject was not accepted by her peers when a child. This can cause long-term damage, and in later life she will do everything to compensate. It is important for her to recognize the real reason for her need to identify with a group, otherwise she may lose part of her sense of identity.

Friends and acquaintances, and what they stand for, may be so heavily relied upon (albeit happily so) that the subject can find it hard to stand alone and take any independent action.

Difficulty in getting close

Can the subject express deep-rooted feelings easily and freely? It may be that, as is the case with an Aquarian influence (and this is the Aquarius house), she is so private that getting close to her will not be easy, in spite of her instinct to belong and be accepted by others.

Another possibility is the person who wants to be loved. Sometimes, because this need is so strong, she will express such a powerful plea for affection that it puts off the very people she is trying to attract. She will have simply tried too hard, and if she had an unsympathetic or unhappy childhood, she may find it difficult to reciprocate real love completely when she does find it.

12 The Moon in the Twelfth House

No matter how extroverted and outgoing the subject may be, it is important for him or her to acknowledge that there is a strong need to withdraw and to spend some time alone.

This withdrawal is instinctive, and both psychologically and spiritually restorative. He must not ignore the necessity for peace and quiet, the best means of which he should decide for himself. For instance, one person with this placing may take a spiritual retreat from time to time, while another will prefer to listen to loud rock music alone in his room.

There is natural kindness and an emotionally sensitive response and, according to the Moon sign, the instincts and intuitions will be powerful forces that can be directed charitably and beneficially towards others. The urge to make sacrifices is present and the Moon sign will indicate whether this is shown through hard work, contemplation or material help.

The secret self

A tendency to deceive is possible, and negative escapism must be guarded against. The subject may have hidden depths and an instinctive secrecy that acts as protection from the outside world. At times he or she can find it hard to discuss problems with loved ones, so look for the ability to communicate in the rest of the chart. The Moon sign will help (Gemini, for instance) or hinder (Scorpio).

If the Moon and Ascendant signs are the same, the Moon level is likely be well-integrated with the personality so that, although secretive traits will be present, he will be aware of them and perhaps put them to good use.

The Moon Progressed through the Houses

If you use the Equal House system (see p.38), the progressed Moon will take roughly two-and-a-half years to travel through each house of the chart. If you use other house systems, including system devised by Placidus, this journey time may vary, since the houses cover a varying number of degrees within the chart circle.

The influence of the Moon from the houses is a subtle one, and will not be fully in focus during the whole period in question. Even so, it is useful, especially when backed up by sympathetic transits or lunar progressions to the natal or progressed planets' positions.

When the progressed Moon first enters a house, you should make your subject aware of its influence, since he or she will then be able to concentrate, to a certain extent, on the concerns of that house. For instance, while the Moon is traveling through the ninth house, the individual may gain special satisfaction from a challenging study course – learning a language, perhaps. Maybe when there are transits which harmonize with the Moon, extended journeys will be particularly beneficial. When the Moon travels through the fourth house, it is advisable for the subject to concentrate on home improvements or, if other indications support this trend, to move house or buy a new home. Most importantly, when the Moon crosses from the twelfth to the first house and conjuncts the Ascendant (see also Moon conjunct the Ascendant, p.237), the subject may begin a new cycle of life in one way or another.

New and Full Moons

Everyone, whether or not they are interested in astrology, is aware of the many influences the waxing and waning Moon has on human, animal and natural life. Ask a receptionist, for instance, or anyone dealing with public inquiries, if their phone constantly rings at the time of the New Moon and the answer is likely to be "yes". It is also true that a great many of us tackle outstanding tasks at this time. These days are usually good ones on which to start new work – it is as if our energies are given a boost and our will to move forward is heightened.

The impact of the Full Moon

Just before a Full Moon there is a very different influence, for this is a period of frustration and all too often of violence. At the very least we can expect traffic to be snarled up more than usual; but in areas of the world where there is unrest, violence tends to break out in a spectacular way at this time. We have discovered that the worst tragedies in Northern Ireland, for instance, have occurred at or near these tense times.

This is an area of astrology you must study for yourself; your findings will not only enhance your own understanding, but may even be of use to astrology as a whole.

Eclipses

It is not difficult to discover when eclipses will take place. They are clearly listed in ephemerides, and often in calendars and almanacs. Eclipses are physically extremely dramatic, and it is not surprising that in the past a great many (mostly unfounded) superstitions grew up around them. However, many astrologers feel that when an eclipse falls on or very near a planet (within two or three degrees) or an angle of the birth chart, its effect will be extremely powerful. An eclipse may activate the area of the chart involved and, according to the aspects the planet or angle receives and its relative strength in the chart (whether it is a personal planet or otherwise) the outcome can be positive or negative –

usually negative. Considerable difficulties arise when we consider the timing of developments. Some astrologers say the effect will color many months, and it has certainly been known to do so; but when it stretches so far, we think that other more powerful trends may be the real cause, with the eclipse itself being only a contributory factor.

If an eclipse falls within two degrees of an important planet in a chart, observe the subject in relation to the areas ruled by the planet concerned, with the above possibilities in mind. If the eclipse contacts the Ascendant, Sun, Moon or chart ruler, the personal life and even the health may be under strain, while if the Midheaven is affected, the career can be under stress, or enforced changes may occur. We suggest that you bow to tradition, and do not plan important events, such as weddings, the opening of a new business and so on, at the time of an eclipse. Another theory suggests that solar eclipses are more important to men, lunar ones to women. We don't agree, but why not put it to the test?

Political implications

It is in Mundane Astrology – the astrological study of countries, their governments and leaders – that eclipses are important and widely used. This is a fascinating and extremely complex area of astrology which has its own specialists; it is outside the confines of this book. Those interested should read Charles E. O. Carter's *An Introduction to Political Astrology*; but see also the Bibliography, p.405.

Note: An eclipse of the Sun occurs at the time of the New Moon, while an eclipse of the Moon is at Full Moon.

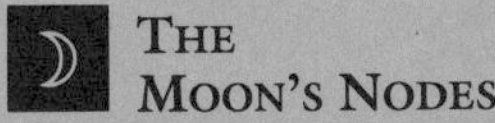

THE MOON'S NODES

The Moon's orbit is at an angle of five degrees to the ecliptic, and the points where it intersects are called the Moon's nodes. The line joining them is the nodal line, and it travels westward along the ecliptic, taking eighteen-and-a-half years to pass right around it in retrograde motion – that is, backwards through the signs. When the Moon moves north and crosses the Earth's orbit, the point of crossing is the ascending or north node, also known as the Dragon's Head; when the Moon moves south the crossing point is the descending, or south, node – the Dragon's Tail. The nodes are an interesting minor element of the chart, but we don't feel justified in devoting space to a full ephemeris of them here. As you progress and no doubt invest in more detailed ephemerides you will find the nodes clearly listed in them.

Interpretation of the Moon's nodes

This area is rather controversial, but there are two main schools of thought. The first suggests that the south node represents (by its house position) the area of life from which we can best give our experience or personal qualities, while the north node represents the qualities for which we should strive. Someone with the south node in the third house, for instance, has plenty of basic education and the power to communicate knowledge, and because the north node will be in the ninth house, will strive to develop the basic education through further study, thereby working towards a higher standard of achievement in this sphere of life. The majority of astrologers, however, probably believe that the nodes have a strong influence on our attitude towards other people, and when interpreting their position concentrate on their aspects to the Ascendant, Midheaven and planets. These are very valid, and they fall into three categories – powerful, positive and negative. As the north and south nodes are always directly opposite each other, the aspects which the planets make to them are therefore categorized rather differently.

- **Powerful:** A conjunction to one node and therefore an opposition to the other.
- **Positive:** A trine to one, therefore a sextile to the other.
- **Negative:** A square aspect to both nodes.

Bear this in mind when interpreting the principle of the planets in relation to the nodes. The powerful aspects will add an emphasis and are strong. The positive aspects will make for easy relationships (as influenced by the nature of the planet), while the negative ones will cause difficulty in the type of relationship (indicated by the nature of the planet involved). Here is a brief interpretation of the nodes' effects when in aspect to the planets:

- **Sun:** A physical or intellectual rapport with others.
- **Moon:** An instinctive response and rapport with others.
- **Mercury:** The sharing of ideas and mental rapport with others.
- **Venus:** An adaptability in emotional relationships.
- **Mars:** Sexual attraction dominates the attitude towards others.
- **Jupiter:** A general adaptability and ease toward others.
- **Saturn:** Isolation and a lack of adaptability toward others.
- **Uranus:** An interestingly different or eccentric attitude to others.
- **Neptune:** Willing to help others but not always reliable.
- **Pluto:** An urge to exert power over others, or feel frustrated by them.
- **Ascendant:** A helpful or disruptive family member. (Those with the nodal line very close to the Ascendant/Descendant line are often very tall or very short!)
- **Midheaven:** An identification and need to associate with people who express the characteristics of the Midheaven sign – or resentment of them and their achievements.

NEW MOONS AND THE PROGRESSED CHART

New Moons are used quite differently in progressions (see p.70). They often make a series of contacts to natal planets, and are in fact the transits of the New Moon. It may be that the New Moon will first make a square aspect to say, Mars, a trine the next month, a month later a quincunx, and finally an opposition. These are tiny influences, but can herald a theme which will be suggested by the planet or planets involved, and as a result something, perhaps a project, lasting roughly for the time of the run of aspects, will occur. These little trends should not be ignored and are always worth calculating; they add another dimension to the current progressions.

The Aspects of the Moon

These will be of considerable importance because the Moon tends subtly to personalize whichever planets it contacts. In interpreting these aspects remember they will have a bearing on these areas of the personality – sharpening the reactions (Mars), adding a more cautious response (Saturn), or perhaps a more immediate enthusiasm (Jupiter). It is reasonable to allow a slightly increased orb on any aspect the Moon makes to the Sun, ruling planet, Ascendant or Midheaven – not more than two extra degrees for a major aspect and not more than one for a minor aspect. You may allow up to ten degrees for a conjunction to the Sun, Ascendant or Midheaven. The Moon's house and sign should also be borne in mind in relation to the planet concerned.

Aspects between the Moon and the Sun

The natal aspects between these two planets have been fully interpreted under the section The Sun's Aspects to the Moon (see p.214), so if they are in aspect in the birth chart you will have already studied the effects. However, as you begin working on progressions, you will learn that the progressed Moon travels fairly quickly through the chart, and will from time to time make aspects to the Sun both in the birth and the progressed charts. Because of this, we must consider the relationships differently: they are not as long-term, nor do they have such a dynamic effect, as the Sun's progressed aspects to the Moon in the birth chart.

Progressed Moon's Aspects to the Sun's Progressed or Natal Position

Conjunction

This will probably herald a key period lasting for three or four months. It is a good time in which to make changes, provided that restlessness and, perhaps, uncharacteristic changeability can be controlled.

Positive aspects

These will help the individual to come to terms with any on-going psychological problems, but should there be a negative aspect between the Sun and Moon in the birth chart, it is possible that a certain amount of strain and tension will be present. However, the aspect will help the subject work on any troubles of this kind. Otherwise, the emotions and intuitions will be heightened and there should be feelings of inner contentment, even if other trends indicate a difficult time. All-round progress will be made if the life is relatively free from problems; indeed, problems may well be sorted out under this influence.

Negative aspects

There may be feelings of discontent and restlessness. This is not a very good time in which to make important decisions, since the emotions are susceptible to considerable fluctuation. However, if there is a trine or sextile between these two planets in the birth chart, this subtle influence will be much less harmful. Nevertheless, long-term changes, especially in the home life, should not be encouraged.

Note: All aspects between the progressed Moon and the Sun (again, whether natal or progressed) will tend to lower the vitality, so additional rest, and perhaps a tonic or course of vitamins, will be helpful at times.

The Moon's Aspects to Mercury

Conjunction

This is a powerfully invigorating influence on the mind, and unless the conjunction is frustrated by a square or opposition from Saturn, there will be good intuition, instinct and logic.

The Moon sign will be spiced with the thinking processes of Mercury, giving excellent potential that can be expressed through literary work that will be imaginative or practical, according to the nature of the sign in which the Moon and Mercury are placed. There will be a cross-fertilization of influences should Mercury be positioned in one sign while the Moon is in another.

When the conjunction falls in the same sign as the Sun, look out for an over-emphasis of that particular sign's characteristics, since these will work not only on the level of the Sun, but also on the instinctive level of the Moon, as well as on the mental level of Mercury.

Positive aspects

The shrewdness of the Moon and the cunning of Mercury are controlled by these aspects, and the individual's powers of concentration will be good.

These aspects add common sense and, usually, a practical outlook. Decisions will be made both logically and intuitively, so the individual in this case will have the best of both worlds in this respect.

Negative aspects

There will be a sharp response to any challenging situation or comment. There may be a tendency to enjoy gossip, although the intellectual powers are heightened by this influence and critical acumen is direct, somewhat cutting and, in certain circumstances, can be sarcastic. Digestive problems or nervous upsets can beset the individual from time to time, especially if Mercury is a personal planet.

Progressed Aspects between the Moon and Mercury

Conjunction

This indicates a period of intense mental activity. It will be a good time in which to revise for examinations, since the memory is usually retentive, and there is an instinctive desire to commit facts and ideas to paper in a businesslike manner.

Changes are often made under this influence. For instance, there may be a move to another department at work or, more domestically, a change of decoration or simply the rearrangement of some furniture.

Positive aspects
The effects of these are very much as for the conjunction. Any projects started at this time, or already underway, should move forward extremely well. This is also a good period for making opinions known and gaining the support of the public. Speaking up about any issue that is important to the self or the community is particularly desirable.

Negative aspects
While it is not seriously disruptive, care is needed during this time that tactlessness, or simply speaking out of turn, does not cause problems – especially within the family.

Nervous tension may be present, and if the individual tends to be highly strung, additional rest or time spent in some soothing relaxation technique will be restorative.

Note: During all progressions between the Moon and Mercury, the time is right for the subject to change cars, or whatever form of transport he or she happens to own.

♀ The Moon's Aspects to Venus

Conjunction
This is a delightful influence, helping to make the individual popular, affectionate, calm and serene. There is a taste for luxury and good living. The aspect will also enhance an instinctive awareness of the partner's needs in any relationship that may be formed.

Carefully relate the conjunction to the sign it occupies, remembering that the flow of emotion and affection will be influenced by the sign placing. Art appreciation is usual.

Positive aspects
These add natural charm and sensitivity. Sometimes if there are a great many trine aspects in the birth chart the individual will tend to take life a little too easily and perhaps, at worst, "ride" people, getting away with rather too much. An awareness of this fault is most desirable.

In a chart with a good balance of strenuous and easy aspects, however, all the positive traits described for the conjunction will be present, as will optimism and good perception. These aspects also add intuition, especially if the Moon occupies a water sign.

Negative aspects
There can be an above-average number of disappointments in personal relationships, usually due to incompatibility. The individual will have a powerful store of love and affection to express, but the way in which this is done may be a cause of difficulty with the partner. Perhaps there will be a tendency to rush into relationships, and a glossing over of minor problems which then become more serious as time passes.

Check the position of the Moon and Venus: if either planet is in Virgo or Capricorn, or if Saturn intervenes, there can be shyness and a lack of self-confidence in the attitude towards the opposite sex. Lessons of love will be learned the hard way. Any tendencies toward a lackadaisical attitude must be controlled.

♀ Progressed Aspects between the Moon and Venus

Conjunction
This will be a happy time for the individual involved in a permanent relationship, and a good period during which to concentrate on improving matters with the partner.

If other indications show an emphasis on love, this progression could herald a new romance. However, look to other long-term background progressions to decide whether it is likely to be permanent or a relationship that will not last. The general outlook will be optimistic.

Positive aspects
These will enhance other positive trends, especially beneficial transits from Jupiter. This is a time in which the subject can enjoy him- or herself, and is good for entertaining at home.

Negative aspects
Caution is needed when dealing with loved ones or business partners. If he or she is making investments, your subject should seek independent professional advice whenever possible. If transits show frustration, the individual could experience difficulties relating to love or money. This is not a time for taking financial or emotional risks, since it is likely that rejection or loss of money can occur.

♂ The Moon's Aspects to Mars

Conjunction
This is an invigorating and powerful influence, heightening the subject's emotions and responses to various situations, and encouraging a directness of approach.

A liking for risk-taking is also present, and the energy level – both emotional and physical – is decidedly increased. The conjunction can cause recklessness or rebelliousness if it receives aspects from Uranus.

Positive aspects
Here the emotional and physical energies work well together. Since they are very invigorating, these aspects can act in a positive way for people who are not very well organized, or perhaps tend to be lazy.

A willingness to help others is present, and the influence usually generously supports good health and a physical robustness.

Negative aspects
Shortness of temper and over-volatile responses can occur with these aspects. Sometimes there is nervous and emotional tension, and impulsiveness can cause misjudgement. Any tendency towards the taking of premature and hasty action must be recognized and then countered.

♂ Progressed Aspects between the Moon and Mars

Conjunction
This period will last for about three months, during which the pace of the subject's life will increase. He or she will have plenty of physical and emotional energy with which to tackle life, and both mind and body will be invigorated by this influence. However, make sure that there are no negative transits from Saturn or Pluto

(which would frustrate), or from Uranus (which would cause tension), to interfere with the energies from the Moon and Mars.

Positive aspects
The effect of these is much as for the conjunction: again, a busy period seems likely, and the streams of emotional and physical energy will be compatible, so that a great deal should be achieved at this time.

The subject will be decisive, instinctively seeing and then taking the correct line of action. This characteristic will be a considerable asset to any individual who normally tends to be rather indecisive.

Negative aspects
Impulsiveness and premature actions can cause problems while these progressions are in force. It is necessary for the individual to pace him- or herself, since mistakes can be made, especially if important decisions are to be taken.

Encourage delaying tactics, if at all possible, since a consciously calm attitude and extra time for serious thought are essential during this period. However, the subject will not in the least want to approach life that way! This influence can also cause a flurry of headaches and occasionally insomnia, which will ease as the progression passes.

♃ The Moon's Aspects to Jupiter

Conjunction
This adds a kindness and gentleness to the personality and will soften the subject's attitude towards other people. There is usually a charitable generosity, and energy, time and money will all be given freely.

Encouragement should be offered to the individual to pass on his or her experience to those who are able to benefit from it. Much inner satisfaction will be gained from doing so, since a happy knack of being able to give strong, positive encouragement is also present. Sometimes a tendency toward slight pomposity can occur – especially if the conjunction falls in Leo or Capricorn.

Positive aspects
The sympathy, kindness and general helpfulness of the conjunction is just as likely to be present with these aspects, and especially with the trine.

The imagination is heightened by these aspects, which also give the mind the potential for philosophical thought, sometimes progressing it along new avenues.

There is an instinctive sympathy and identification with people of other countries and cultures, and those with this placing will often do extremely well, while also gaining significant spiritual or psychological fulfillment, from living abroad.

Negative aspects
These are extremely tricky, adversely affecting the judgement and causing the individual to dramatize and overreact to situations – even if both planets are placed in practical, stable earth signs. An awareness of these traits is essential in order for them to be countered by the subject through the development of a positive, practical attitude (if this possibility is shown in other areas of the chart).

A trine from the Moon to Saturn will help, as will positive aspects between the Sun and Saturn. Sometimes indigestion can occur, especially if the individual enjoys rich food – both characteristics are synonymous with these aspects!

♃ Progressed Aspects between the Moon and Jupiter

Conjunction
During this period the intellect could be enlightened in some way. The individual may make considerable progress as a result of this, since his or her mind will be receptive to new, meaningful concepts.

This influence is basically fortunate, and a good one under which to take long-distance travel. An excellent grasp of situations will go hand in hand with breadth of vision and a very positive, optimistic outlook.

If the conjunction occurs at a time when there are also assertive and positive transits, the effects may last for several months and will be progressive and rewarding.

Positive aspects
The influence of these is much as for the conjunction, with the judgement being particularly finely tuned. This is a good time for finalizing contracts and for undertaking travel.

Generosity may have to be curbed by the individual, since he or she could be moved into parting with too much money at this time – albeit for the most altruistic of reasons.

Negative aspects
Mistakes may be made during these progressions, a possibility that should always be borne in mind, especially if important decisions have to be reached or contracts signed.

There will be a strong tendency (perhaps uncharacteristic) to overreact to situations, and it may be quite hard to maintain a balanced attitude and approach to whatever is happening at the time. Conscious steadying of the emotions and reactions is obligatory. It is a good idea to keep a supply of bicarbonate of soda to hand, since high living will almost inevitably lead to abnormally persistent hangovers.

♄ The Moon's Aspects to Saturn

Conjunction
The outlook on life will be extremely serious, and sometimes can even be rather gloomy. The individual is hardworking and will have a practical, matter-of-fact attitude, but his or her emotional flow will be restrained. Sometimes there may be an almost manic striving for perfection, especially if the conjunction falls in Virgo, Scorpio or Capricorn.

Expressions of affection are often limited, but loyalty and faithfulness are usually present. The conjunction can act as an anchorage in a chart where fire and air dominate, but must be carefully studied, as its contrasting influences can be a source of conflict.

Positive aspects
Here we have common sense, determination and a sensible attitude. The mind and outlook are conventional. This influence will help to restrain any impulsiveness which may be shown in other areas of the chart.

An ability to work hard in a disciplined and practical way will be present, and success will be achieved by gradually building up a reputation for reliability and thoroughness. The instinctive reactions are controlled.

Negative aspects

There are times when the outlook will become negative and depression will set in. It is vital that other areas of the birth chart should be carefully searched for any characteristics that will help the individual to counter this pessimistic tendency.

Inhibition and a lack of self-confidence are sometimes present. These aspects can weaken the constitution, making the subject especially susceptible to colds and flu. In certain cases he or she may be unpopular – perhaps because of a tendency to grumble and moan.

Progressed Aspects between the Moon and Saturn

Conjunction

Long-term plans may be under consideration at this time. While progress in finalizing them may be slow, mistakes are not often made. Planning could lead to important change, and even to extra responsibility and prestige within the career or domestic life. The health should be given special care.

Positive aspects

The effect of these is much as for the conjunction: progress will be slow but steady. The individual should be encouraged to think about the long-term future, especially in relation to his or her family commitments or career ambitions and aspirations.

Negative aspects

These indicate a period lasting about three months during which the individual may become dispirited or uncharacteristically depressed. This negative time will pass, but for as long as it lasts loved ones will be hard-pressed to find different ways of cheering up the subject.

Should there be problems in the career or with unemployment, the time is right for quiet background research to improve prospects, rather than for actual job applications. Subjects should put their resumés in order, watch out for new developments in any specialist field, and so on. This is not a period in which the individual should try to push him- or herself forward or try to force issues – usually this will be a waste of time.

Note: When the progressed Moon contacts Saturn, either natal or progressed, the vitality will be low and (whether it is summer or winter) the tendency to catch a bad cold is greatly increased. Crowded places should be avoided and the diet supplemented with extra vitamins.

The Moon's Aspects to Uranus

Conjunction

This potent planetary relationship provides a powerful element of emotional tension: whether it is discharged positively or negatively will depend on other influences.

Magnetic and dynamic, this aspect contributes originality, brilliance and intuitive thought and ideas. However, Uranian perversity will color the reactions to situations and the expression of feelings, and add a need to be different and unconventional. If the conjunction receives squares from the Sun, Mars or Saturn, or squares the Ascendant, tension and nervous strain will be a source of considerable difficulty, and one that will not be easy to resolve.

Positive aspects

These are powerhouses of emotional tension, but the individual should be able to use such a force positively and originally, whether in a scientific or creative manner.

Parents of children with one of these aspects may find it easiest to persuade them do to things by telling them to do the exact opposite!

Negative aspects

In many ways the square is more difficult to cope with than the opposition, but in both cases emotional tension and strain are present. Just as the Sun's negative aspects seem to work more adversely for men, so the Moon's tend to have a more potently negative effect on women, being for instance a source of migraine or preventing total relaxation. There will be a tendency in both sexes to be extremely self-willed; if this can be determinedly channeled the aspects will be made to work in a more positive manner.

Being very active is good for the subject, since this will burn off tension and energy; involvement in sport as well as intellectually demanding projects is important. Very often, as with the conjunction, real flair and talent are present.

Progressed Aspects between the Moon and Uranus

Conjunction

An eventful period is likely, but this will also be a time when the demands made upon the individual can give rise to an excitable tension. In this period new developments, sometimes unexpected, will occur.

Positive aspects

A great deal may happen during this time, and there will be a desire to do something new and different. This could be a passing phase, so while encouraging your subject to give serious thought to any new project, advise delaying for a few weeks the spending of large sums of money on its pursuit. When the progression has eased and the situation has stabilized, the individual can then spend money on special lessons, some tools, a musical instrument or whatever else has captured his or her imagination.

Negative aspects

The individual will probably experience tension during this time. Advise him or her to take life as calmly as possible, although this won't be easy. Drastic emotional responses and reactions to situations must be controlled, since they could easily be regretted in the long run.

Careful thought, circumspection and a practical approach are essential; stubbornness (sometimes bordering on the ridiculous) and perversity could have a long-lasting damaging effect, especially when an emotional relationship hits stormy waters.

The Moon's Aspects to Neptune

Conjunction
These planets sensitize the reactions and fertilize the imagination. There will be an idealistic streak and much genuine kindness and sympathy. Sometimes these qualities can be so apparent that they enable others to take advantage of the individual.

The spiritual or religious areas of life are often important, and there is a need to retreat from the world. Because of kindness and a desire not to hurt others, the negative, deceptive side of Neptune will cause a tendency to tell lies. This is a trait to be corrected at all ages, and must be especially watched for in children. If the imagination can be creatively used it is a marvelous source of potential; the idealism is very strong indeed.

Positive aspects
Both planets work well in these aspects, adding imagination and emotional force. However, these qualities must be channeled and restrained if vagueness and confusion are not to mar their expression. Sometimes there are psychic gifts: if the individual feels an inclination in this direction it is important for him or her to seek reliable advice from someone of experience. These aspects are often present in the charts of astrologers.

Negative aspects
The tendency to take the easy way out of difficult situations is likely here, and many muddles and an impractical attitude towards life will seriously hamper real progress.

Considerable talent and imaginative potential can be present, but other areas of the chart should be studied to see if these qualities will be fully exploited. A strong Saturn, and indications of practical ability, will help enormously to counter the wistful weakness that these contacts seem to bestow.

Progressed Aspects between the Moon and Neptune

Conjunction
There will be a tendency to become dreamy and unworldly under this influence. If this happens after the individual has experienced a particularly busy period when material concerns have been to the fore, the time will be right for a relaxing holiday – perhaps in a watery site such as by the sea, a river or lake.

The mood may also become very romantic, and while it is important that any tendency to dwell on cloud nine is countered, some pleasant experiences can occur under this progression. The accent is on escape and restoration of the spirit.

Positive aspects
These are very much as for the conjunction, but the individual may have some inspiring and imaginative ideas. It is advisable to sit on them for a while, since he or she may be too inspired and therefore impractical, needing to rethink the ideas in a subsequent period under more practical influences.

Great care is needed that the subject does not enter a fool's paradise, convinced that everything is marvelous, when in fact he or she is becoming out of touch with reality.

Negative aspects
The individual must be very careful not to allow self-deception or escapism (through a reliance on drink, cigarettes or drugs) to get the better of him or her at this time, especially if life in general is stressful or complicated.

The emotions may well be highly negatively charged, so avoiding making important decisions and attempting to take life calmly, with a steady routine and plans that are as simple as possible, is the most desirable course of action.

Note: It is important to realize that there will be many people who will not consciously feel any effects during these progressions from the Moon to Neptune – especially if they tend to be greatly concerned with the material side of life.

Imaginative, sensitive and creative people, on the other hand, will feel these subtle influences more markedly, and must consciously control them, for the Moon and Neptune, while inspirational, can insidiously harm and weaken the character.

The Moon's Aspects to Pluto

Conjunction
The emotional level of the individual is considerably heightened by this aspect, and at times emotional outbursts will occur and be very passionately and forcefully expressed. However, unless the conjunction is negatively aspected by Saturn or Uranus, squared by the Sun, or Pluto squares the Ascendant, they will act as a very necessary purge, and the individual will get a great deal off his or her chest. The feelings will then be expressed in a more serene way once more, until the next time that the emotional forces build up inside the subject.

If the conjunction is inhibited by other planets, the subject may well find it difficult to express his true feelings. Look for this in children's charts, as encouragement of a controlled flow of emotion, as opposed to emotional storms, is obviously desirable.

Positive aspects
The emotional force is increased, and in many cases there will be scenes, but they usually occur for a good reason when the aspect is positive. The individual should be aware, however, that he or she may be overreacting to someone's casual remark or reaction, or to personal jealousy.

A desire to rid the immediate environment of clutter will be present, and the subject will enjoy large clearing-out binges. It is worth remembering that this may not simply be the result of a mania for tidiness, but could have deeper psychological roots. Perhaps there is a need for the subject to get someone out of his system, or for the physical expression of an emotional attitude towards them.

Negative aspects
The expression of emotion can be blocked, and the resulting frustration and inhibition can have a long-term adverse effect; it is necessary to look to other areas of the chart to see if this trait can be countered.

For the problem to become really serious there would have to be other indications of shyness or inhibition, and a lack of self-confidence in the chart as a whole. Nevertheless, the individual with a square or opposition between these two planets can find it virtually impossible to express him- or herself emotionally, even under circumstances that are ideal. These aspects are tricky to interpret, and are a source of trouble for those afflicted with them.

Progressed Aspects between the Moon and Pluto

Conjunction

The individual will probably experience a very unsettled period – a time when he or she will feel like making drastic changes.

It is important to encourage the subject to take time before throwing away too much, since she may overreact under any kind of provocation, sacrificing much that has been built up over a long period of time. It is important for her to control both her emotions and reactions.

Positive aspects

The time will probably have come for a purge of some sort. Clearing out cupboards and drawers, or more ambitious general spring cleaning, are examples of the practical expressions of these progressions.

As with all Pluto contacts, there may well be deeper psychological reasons for these activities, but nevertheless the positive aspects usually allow a clean start to be made in some way.

Negative aspects

The emotions may be under a great deal of stress during this period, and much as the subject may want to reveal an aspect of his or her personality, this will not be possible for a variety of reasons. Usually external difficulties will be cited as the justification for the inhibition, but in fact it will spring from the inner psyche, prompted by apprehension or fear.

If there are no negative aspects between the Moon and Pluto in the birth chart, the situation will more than likely become easier as the power of the progression eases. Encourage your subject to relax and avoid trying to force the issue – whether interior or exterior – while the influence of this progression is operative.

The Moon's Aspects to the Ascendant

Conjunction

This is an extremely important aspect. However, remember that an accurate birth time is essential in assessing the potency of the conjunction. You should also consider very carefully the Moon's house position (the conjunction can be formed when the planet occupies either the first or the twelfth house). Usually the Ascendant and the Moon are placed in the same sign, in which case the individual will have a double influence of the Ascending and Moon sign. As a result, the level of intuition, instinct and response will be identical to that of the psychological reaction. The moodiness and changeability that are so much a part of the Moon's influence will be powerful, and the subject may be easily swayed by the prevailing atmosphere and the reactions of other people.

There will be a secretive and perhaps reclusive quality to those with the Moon conjunct the Ascendant from the twelfth house, and lunar sensitivity will be present. If the Moon falls in the first house, the skin will react adversely to strong sunlight, and the digestive system can also cause problems. The face is usually round and pale, and the forehead really will seem to reflect the glow of the Full Moon! The appearance of a line between the eyebrows (a common feature with Sun sign Cancerians) will also be present.

Positive aspects

Here is a marvelously integrating link; the individual will have fewer problems than most when coming to terms with his or her personality. The level of instinct and intuition, and the lunar emotions, will harmonize with the personality of the Ascendant, thereby helping the individual to make the most of all these qualities. These aspects often give common sense, an adaptable nature and an innate ability to get on easily with other people.

Negative aspects

There can be inner restlessness and discontent, and even sometimes a huffy and impatient attitude towards others. These tendencies can mar much that is positive and pleasant in the personality, and as a result may put other people off on first acquaintance. There might also be some inner discontent (not unlike that which occurs when the Sun and Moon are in opposition).

If the opposition is present and the Moon is in the seventh house, this can lead to problems and restlessness within any permanent relationship. When the Moon is in the sixth house and opposes the Ascendant, vulnerable health (indicated by the Moon sign) will make its presence felt rather more potently than would otherwise be so.

Progressed Aspects between the Moon and the Ascendant

Conjunction

The effects of this aspect will vary in strength. When the Moon's conjunction is to the natal Ascendant, the subject may instinctively feel the need to make changes or a new beginning in some way. This is a good thing, and provided the Moon's influence does not cause an overreaction to what is happening and there is no exaggerated view of what is desired, the fresh start can be extremely beneficial, often heralding a new cycle in the life. Remember that here we have the Moon progressing from the reflective and passive twelfth house to the assertive first house. The same thing will occur when the Moon makes a conjunction to the progressed Ascendant, but then a change of house position at the same time is unlikely.

Positive aspects

This is a period when the qualities of the Moon and Ascendant will work well together and the individual will instinctively make the best decisions for him- or herself and other loved ones. Action will follow, and progress will usually be made. A feeling of being at one with the self is common.

Negative aspects

These can herald a trying period when the subject feels pulled in two directions at once and does not know what to do. Restlessness and dissatisfaction may build up as a result. It is not a good time to instigate changes, and the physical well-being, in addition to the psychological reactions, may be negative, so that the individual will act uncharacteristically or hastily when in a bad mood, and take actions which will be regretted later.

The tendency to overreact is very likely, especially if Mars is personalized or making its presence felt by receiving adverse transits, or receiving progressed aspects to the Moon. If any of these possibilities apply, encourage your subject to make time to relax and to shelve important matters for those few weeks.

The Moon's Aspects to the Midheaven

Conjunction

The house placing of the Moon is important in this aspect, so give it additional consideration. Traditionally, the conjunction shows someone who will either become famous or be in charge of a large number of people. It makes for a strong ego, provided that the Moon is uninhibited by negative aspects. If not, allowances must be made according to the planet or planets involved. There will be a magnetic appeal which will encourage others to respond well to the subject – perhaps even hysterically so.

The potential this placing endows is considerable, and the astrologer should encourage its development and expression. However, there is a tendency for the subject to be changeable – sometimes to the detriment of his or her progress and popularity.

Positive aspects

There is increased identification with the characteristics attributed to the Midheaven sign, and an instinctive urge to express them.

Negative aspects

The subject may well have some difficulty in deriving real satisfaction from his or her career, or in deciding what is truly wanted out of life.

There will be complications and perhaps barriers to the aspirations and ambitions, and identification with the characteristics of the Midheaven sign will be present but not allowed immediate or easy expression. The tendency will be to say of someone "I wish I could be like that", without making any great or sustained effort to emulate the admired person.

Encouragement to overcome these negative factors should be given; and help will be gained from other areas of the birth chart where no such problematic blockages exist.

MC Progressed Aspects between the Moon and the Midheaven

Conjunction

This is a very interesting aspect, and one to watch for. People who have it may be in the public eye for one reason or another – many will be interviewed on television. A change in the career can also occur, so that the subject will be in charge of more people than was previously the case.

Certainly there will be a boost to the ego, but it may not be totally recognized at once. In fact, the importance of any change may only be realized in retrospect. We suggest that you conduct your own research on this fascinating conjunction.

Positive aspects

The individual will feel at one with him- or herself, and under these unifying influences will move forward psychologically, perhaps as a result of job satisfaction. Past incidents and efforts will have added to the emotional security and self-confidence of the subject, and such effects will now be given full recognition.

Negative aspects

There may be problems at work, especially with colleagues' reactions to the individual, and his or her attitude toward them. Care is needed particularly if the subject holds a position of authority, since personal insecurity could result in the persecution of subordinates.

If career interests are not at stake then a general dissatisfaction with one's lot is likely, but it is not a good time at which to make changes. Sometimes, however, they may have to be made due to external influences. If this is the case, make sure that decisions are as unrushed and calmly planned as possible.

The Moon's Progressed Aspects to its Own Position

Conjunction

This is the most important of these aspects. It occurs at roughly the age of 28, again at 56-plus and also at 83-plus. The first conjunction is usually in evidence just prior to the all-important first Saturn Return (see p.312). The need for change and psychological readjustment is a major factor, and all the emotion, intuition, and instinct denoted by the position of the Moon will be keenly in focus.

Other aspects

These either positively or negatively accentuate the Moon's natal characteristics, but also bring with them some influence of the sign and house through which the Moon is progressing at the time. Everything that the Moon represents will be emphasized according to the nature of the aspect.

These progressed lunar aspects add to the current important transits mirroring the response of the subject to events at the time in question.

The Transits of the Moon

These recur every 28 days so only someone who is obsessive about planetary influences will bother to follow them with unmitigated regularity. However, the Moon's position is, of course, very important when setting up a chart for a specific occasion or event, in which case it should harmonize with its position in the individual's birth chart and with other important areas of his or her chart.

Mercury through the Signs

Mercury's area of influence is the mind. From this planet's placing and aspects we can form a good picture of how our minds work and at what speed, whether we think in a logical, practical way or use our minds intuitively. We can also assess how we reach decisions and communicate with others.

Mercury's orbit lies between the Earth and the Sun (so is known as an "inferior" planet); as seen from the Earth the planet always appears near to the Sun. Indeed, for astrological purposes, the planet cannot be more than 28 degrees away from the Sun, so will always be either in the preceding sign, the same sign as the Sun or the following one. In interpretation Mercury has a special relationship with the Sun, so we align our sign interpretation of Mercury with that of the Sun sign, as shown on these pages.

MERCURY IN ARIES

This gives decisiveness, quick thinking, and the ability to assess problems in a straightforward way. If Mercury is in negative aspect to Mars there may be impulsive thinking and hasty actions. Usually, however, the natural decisiveness works well, with the individual making the right choice and taking positive, assertive action. There is a love of argument and debate, with a tendency towards stimulating and provocative remarks. Generally fools are not suffered gladly; the individual comes straight to the point, and his or her outlook is both positive and optimistic. The overall grasp is excellent but help is advisable when making plans, for he is bored by detail and prefers the broad sweep of a project. It can be difficult to concentrate for long, so study may be erratic. Here is someone who will stay up all night before an exam – and often this is no bad thing, since he is more concerned with the here and now than with facts he tried months before to memorize.

Sun Sign Pisces with Mercury in Aries

This adds necessary decisiveness, a more positive outlook, and to a certain extent more self-assurance. The imagination will be ignited, and as a result creative potential will be expressed positively when in other cases it can lie dormant due to lack of self-confidence. The high emotional level of Pisces will be expressed, and the ability to communicate feelings enhanced, although if Mercury is negatively aspected by the Moon or Uranus there can be an above-average amount of tension, and excitable, positive moods can alternate with periods of uncertainty. Piscean strength of will is increased.

Sun Sign Aries with Mercury in Aries

The Arian need for action, and to be out in front, is spiced with extremely quick thinking processes. There is a general hastiness, with patience almost non-existent, unless the Moon or Ascendant suggest otherwise. Directness of approach, decisiveness and positive, uncomplicated thinking are splendidly in tune with Arian characteristics, and if they can be tempered (look for positive help from Saturn) the individual will certainly make his or her mark on the world. Impulsive, hasty actions with unnecessary risk-taking and selfishness due to a lack of thought must be controlled.

Sun Sign Taurus with Mercury in Aries

Speed and vivacity are added to the stable Taurean type, making him or her less cautious but more assertively decisive. However, the individual will also be less patient and may even show some irritation when others do not greet his ideas or suggestions in the right way. Problems and projects are approached with realism and enthusiasm, and the Taurean need for careful planning will be enhanced by the ability to grasp a situation quickly and concisely. A spirit of enterprise blends with the Taurean business ability.

MERCURY IN TAURUS

Thinking is steady, but the subject may be rather slow to learn. Parents of children with this placing must not worry if they think the child is not responding to teaching, for if gradual progress is maintained, what is learned will be remembered and form a good foundation for the future. Stubbornness (to a greater or lesser degree) is almost inevitable, and flexibility must be cultivated, otherwise opinions can become so entrenched that the individual may become proud of them, perhaps saying "Once my mind's made up that's it." Conversely we find others who pretend to be very fixed in their opinions, and go all out to shock people in the way they express them! However, caution and much practical common sense are always present, sometimes coupled with a conservative and conventional outlook. The ability to plan constructively is considerable, with a methodical and disciplined approach to problems and to work. Obsessional tendencies are possible, and perhaps an inclination to get in a rut because it offers security. She will usually express herself with considerable charm.

Sun Sign Aries with Mercury in Taurus

This acts as an excellent stabilizer to the impetuous Arian. The ability to think slowly and constructively is an asset, and the chances of impulsive or reckless decision-making are very much mitigated. There is plenty of common sense and the individual will have no difficulty in pacing him- or herself when making plans or preparing for any kind of examination or test. Sometimes Arian selfishness can be exacerbated by stubbornness, and there will be an inclination to reject both faults when they are mentioned.

Sun Sign Taurus with Mercury in Taurus

Here is a "salt of the earth" type – what is said is meant, so the individual is reliable. However, quick responses and the ability to get moving, both physically and mentally, must be developed. Taurean stubbornness and dislike of change will certainly be present. Every opinion will be cautiously and carefully considered, as this is the strong, silent type, only speaking when he or she has something really worthwhile to say. The grasp of situations and acquisition of knowledge will be slow but comments will be deliberate; thoughts are charmingly expressed. Time is needed to assimilate new ideas.

Sun Sign Gemini with Mercury in Taurus
Because Mercury rules Gemini, this placing has a considerable effect on the subject's Sun sign characteristics as well as his or her mental outlook and thinking processes. Considerable stability is added to this lively, quick, versatile type, and will greatly assist her to think more carefully and constructively, even adding a little patience at times. Practical common sense is usual and the individual will assimilate facts well; brightness of personality is not diminished. Geminian restlessness is less likely to be a problem, and the need to communicate will remain strong. This is an excellent anchorage for Sun sign Geminians.

Mercury in Gemini

Here Mercury is placed in one of the signs it rules, strengthening its influence. It gives a considerable need to exchange ideas and opinions, and generally the subject likes to be heard and really needs to communicate with others – from talking to the next person in a line to participating in public debates. He or she is able to think very quickly and be involved in more than one task at a time, perhaps talking on the telephone while making notes on a quite different matter! Quick decisions will be made, but not necessarily adhered to, for the mind is often changed – sometimes with the individual denying that this has happened. Facts will be a bore, so in an exam, for instance, there is a tendency to show off opinions at great length without the support of real knowledge or long, hard study. Often, too, there is a flair for selling. Impatience – especially with people of a slower turn of mind – is common, and the individual will easily be able to talk his way out of tricky situations. Adaptability is a great asset, but at all times superficiality of thought and action must be guarded against. Look for other elements in the chart to counter such traits. Cunning and craftiness may also be present.

Sun Sign Taurus with Mercury in Gemini
The slow, steady Taurean type will be aided by quick thinking and be far less stubborn than those with Mercury in other signs. While still liking routine there is less chance of getting into a rut, since the strong influence of Mercury will add considerable adaptability and some versatility without sacrificing the excellent Taurean sense of purpose and determination. The subject will take a less conventional, more up-to-date outlook on life, and be able to reassess his or her opinions with the passing of time. Any Mercurial superficiality is unlikely.

Sun Sign Gemini with Mercury in Gemini
The subject has many Geminian characteristics, especially those strongly relating to Mercury – i.e. the need to communicate, quick thinking, changeability of mind, versatility, and the ability to talk his or her way out of difficult situations. Geminian faults (superficiality and restlessness) must be guarded against. Very often there is a tendency to question the self when the emotions are aroused, since they can be mistrusted; he must justify these reactions to his own satisfaction. If the speedy thought patterns can be controlled there is more than a touch of brilliance. Inquisitiveness is common.

Sun Sign Cancer with Mercury in Gemini
Cancerian changes of mood will be exacerbated by Mercurial changes of mind, but this placing will counter the Cancerian tendency to over-sentimentality, endowing the individual with more forward-looking thinking and planning ability. The high emotional content always present in Cancerians will be spiced with an element of scepticism, so that the out-and-out romanticism and sometimes over-colorful imagination is less likely to get out of hand. The Cancerian memory, which is usually excellent, should not be impaired, and this Gemini/Mercury influence will speed up decision-making, and, most importantly, help mitigate the overwhelmingly powerful Cancerian tendency to worry.

Mercury in Cancer

An excellent memory and imagination is likely, but there is a tendency to look to the past – sometimes too nostalgically – so that forward thinking and planning can cause apprehension and worry because of having to consider and accept the unknown. It is important that the individual realizes that his or her imagination tends to work overtime, all too often negatively, so that when things go wrong (or appear to do so) they are turned from molehills into mountains. If creativity is indicated elsewhere in the chart the imagination can be made to work in this way, perhaps through writing or telling stories. A love of the past may be seen in a fascination with history, so long historical/romantic novels or family sagas will be enjoyed – or even written. There is usually tenacity, especially when studying, but the subject may change his mind, perhaps mostly when emotional reactions clash with logical thinking and the assessment of situations. The Sun and Moon signs often show which response will dominate.

Sun Sign Gemini with Mercury in Cancer
Considerable intuition and a powerful instinct are added to the Gemini traits. The imagination is likely to be expressed through writing or perhaps some form of handicraft. The placing adds a measure of sensitivity –- especially when the individual is assessing other people's reactions – making him or her more sympathetic than critical. It can cause even the most rational Geminians to worry, but nevertheless logic should eventually rule the day. The individual should recognize that a changeable mind can cause problems to loved ones as well as herself.

Sun Sign Cancer with Mercury in Cancer
The Cancerian imagination is increased and must be given positive or creative expression. Undue worry is extremely

likely, and if pessimism or depression are hinted at elsewhere this placing will increase such possibilities. Intuition and love of the past will be enormously enhanced, as will moodiness. The thinking process is almost totally intuitive and ideas, thoughts and decisions will be made quite instinctively, which is right for this combination.

Sun Sign Leo with Mercury in Cancer

Here, intuition and sentimentality are heightened, with the imagination put to excellent use. Leo optimism will help overcome the Cancerian tendency to worry, but Mercury adds kindness, consideration and sympathy, making the subject less dogmatic and bossy. Mental flexibility will also be an asset and caution and shrewdness act as a good counter to Leo's fire. The high emotional level of Leo is increased by the more sensitive, emotional element of Mercury in Cancer, increasing, for instance, Leonine appreciation of splendid theatrical or musical performances, and allowing a full expression of feeling toward loved ones.

MERCURY IN LEO

Mercury in Leo contributes excellent planning and organizational ability. Tasks of all kinds are approached in a practical and rather conventional way, and while there is often considerable ability to think creatively there is a tendency to be stubborn and inflexible, which often emerges in the young. The subject has plenty of determination, and considerable mental and nervous energy. Usually there are good powers of concentration, especially when studying. Speech can be dramatic, sometimes with a tendency to exaggerate. There is no lack of enthusiasm and unless a pessimistic outlook strongly emerges from other areas of the chart (negative aspects between Moon and Saturn, for instance) the individual will be very optimistic. Powers of communication are good, but can at times be marred by a rather condescending manner, which should be mentioned to the individual since usually he or she is totally unaware of it. This placing, because it assists the organizational ability, encourages helpfulness to others, giving much flair in assessing and helping to solve their problems. However, dogmatic tendencies and bossiness can also be present.

Sun Sign Cancer with Mercury in Leo

The outlook is positive and organizational ability is increased. There will be less tendency to worry irrationally, but the subject can be surprisingly bossy. Tenacity is enhanced, with the individual able to make long-term plans and stick to them. The thinking processes will be less purely intuitive, with ideas formulated constructively and then acted upon when the time is right. The Cancerian tendency to look to the past is kept under control – there will be no nostalgic longing for "the good old days" – but there will be sentimentality. Enthusiasm will help the subject to overcome apprehension.

Sun Sign Leo with Mercury in Leo

Leo fiery enthusiasm and optimism will be enhanced by positive thinking and increased organizational ability. However, the individual must be aware that bossiness and a dogmatic attitude can mar many of his or her positive qualities. The powers of leadership and ability to get things done are strong points, and dramatic flair when communicating ideas, expressing opinions and describing events will be very colorful and often exaggerated. Flexibility must be developed since stubbornness can be quite a problem.

Sun Sign Virgo with Mercury in Leo

The strong Virgoan tendency to worry will be countered here, and because Mercury rules Virgo it will work very powerfully for the individual, in many cases also helping to temper the Virgoan lack of self-confidence and giving him or her a more positive and optimistic outlook. The Virgoan preoccupation with detail is less dominant, and there is usually a better grasp of an overall situation. Critical carping – a common Virgoan fault – can be colored by bossiness, but there is the ability to think creatively and often considerable potential for creative craftwork. Literary flair can be present.

MERCURY IN VIRGO

This is the second sign that Mercury rules, so its influence is increased. The ability to analyse and critically assess every aspect of a situation or problem is a dominant feature of this placing, which also gives much common sense and a very practical approach – yet this does not usually prevent the individual suffering to a certain extent from worry. Learning to think for oneself is important as sometimes the organizational ability is undermined, and there is a tendency only to feel totally safe and at one's best when knowing precisely what to do and what is expected. Preoccupation with detail can sometimes mean the overall grasp of a situation is poor, so this trait should be countered. (Often the placing of Jupiter and its aspects will be helpful.) The subject can think practically and constructively, and is very able to cope with demanding intellectual work. There is a great deal of highly-charged nervous energy which must be burned off if stomach upsets, bowel problems or even migraines are to be avoided.

Sun Sign Leo with Mercury in Virgo

Mercury acts as a brake to many of the over-exuberant, enthusiastic and optimistic qualities of Leo. Its influence will add some practical down-to-earth common sense, preventing the Leo from over-reacting when excited, and causing him or her to think twice before bragging, or perhaps buying showy clothes. Here is an excellent blend of the ability to assess situations in detail and the broader Leonine approach. The nervous energy of Mercury will complement the fiery emotional and physical energy of Leo and, if other planets do not inhibit, a great deal should be achieved, since creative flair (Leo) will work with the careful, critical development of potential (Mercury in Virgo).

Sun Sign Virgo with Mercury in Virgo

The individual will seem very Virgoan, with a great many of the known attributes of that sign, but must guard against being over-critical or a born worrier. This critical streak will often be turned on the self, causing a lack of self-confidence and shyness. But here is an excellent mind, capable of detailed, analytical work and research of all kinds. Nervous haste can sometimes cause surprisingly careless mistakes, and the ability to relax is almost nonexistent. Yoga is often beneficial.

Sun Sign Libra with Mercury in Virgo
Libran procrastination and indecisiveness is mitigated, with the subject able to assess problems more critically, due to an active, versatile mind. Common sense is also present, and the stimulation it brings will certainly encourage the development of all kinds of Libran potential (usually considerable). Libran laziness is not usually a problem, and there is a liking for social intercourse; sometimes, too, there is a love of gossip. This is a good combination, provided Venus is not also in Virgo.

Mercury in Libra

The thinking processes tend to be slowed down here, and although there is always increased sympathy, understanding and a desire to communicate with friends and loved ones, procrastination and indecisiveness are likely. The powers of concentration are not usually very good (positive aspects between the Sun, Moon and Saturn will help), and sometimes a lackadaisical attitude is taken towards important issues. The speech can be slow and drawling, with plenty of time taken when answering questions or responding in conversation. The Libran need to keep the peace is also present, making the subject avoid discussing anything remotely controversial. Even so, there is plenty of charm and a delightful turn of phrase. Sometimes the attitude is "*Que sera sera*", with the subject spurred into action by loved ones. Studying does not come easily or naturally, and a desire to achieve results without much effort is likely.

Sun Sign Virgo with Mercury in Libra
Hastiness, a sense of urgency, and to a certain extent nervous tension, are all eased here, and the ability to unwind is also present. The attitude to life and its problems will be quite calm, with less Virgoan worry, although sometimes the powerful critical acumen of Virgo will cause undue carping or even nagging at loved ones. But there will be a sense of fairness, and partners should learn to appeal to it. Indecisiveness must be recognized and countered.

Sun Sign Libra with Mercury in Libra
This tends to make the Libran more indecisive and often mentally lazy – sometimes giving the erroneous impression of a lack of intelligence. If there is a lack of self-confidence, laziness will be feigned as a cover-up. The subject should weigh up every aspect of a situation before reaching conclusions. Gentle encouragement from parents to children with this combination, making quite sure they realize they have made progress, is important if intellectual potential is to be developed; nagging will have an adverse effect. Procrastination will be a problem – especially for loved ones.

Sun Sign Scorpio with Mercury in Libra
This takes some of the harsh, deeply incisive edge off the Scorpio Sun sign traits, and gives the ability to listen sympathetically. There is greater flexibility of thought, so stubbornness is less of a problem. Popular and charming, the subject communicates well. The tendency to brood, especially over personal problems, is not as apparent, since he or she will find it easier to talk to friends and loved ones. The mind works well but in a relaxed way.

♏ Mercury in Scorpio

Scorpionic intuition and intensity combine with Mercurial logic and a rational approach. Determination is a strong point, and the individual will have a sleuth-like mind, leaving no stone unturned to discover the truth of a situation and root out every aspect of it. Here is someone with the mind of a researcher: one who perhaps could become a psychotherapist, psychiatrist, or a detective. While the placing usually works well, there can be obsessional tendencies, especially if Mercury makes a negative aspect to Pluto. Mercury is not very communicative in Scorpio because the necessary outgoing qualities are not sympathetic to that sign. The subject will be more inward-looking, going in for a great deal of self-analysis, perhaps tending to hug psychological problems, and finding it very hard to open up. This must be countered, especially during stressful periods. There is much intellectual and imaginative potential, and sometimes a fascination with the occult, crime and mystery.

Sun Sign Libra with Mercury in Scorpio
This adds considerable determination and sense of purpose; Libran indecisiveness will not be such a problem. The individual may seem indecisive, but will intuitively know what line of action to take, even if he or she procrastinates over actually making a move! Natural Libran charm will be expressed, but there can be a minor or major tendency to plot and scheme. However, if determination and a sense of purpose can be directed positively towards the attainment of objectives and a more rewarding lifestyle, this is a good combination.

Sun Sign Scorpio with Mercury in Scorpio
The thinking processes of Mercury will be as powerfully intense and intuitive as they can be, with formidable determination and sense of purpose. The intellectual powers are usually excellent, but the individual could become obsessive – perhaps over attaining an objective or a compelling interest. There will be a fascination with mysteries, which will be relentlessly pursued and researched. It is important for there to be a compelling objective of this kind, otherwise these powerful qualities can go sour and turn into Scorpio jealousy or resentfulness.

Sun Sign Sagittarius with Mercury in Scorpio
This acts as a good counter to the Sagittarian dislike of detail. It reduces the hastiness of Sagittarius and endows natural enthusiasm with a little caution. Any tendency to over-optimism is also controlled, and Mercury in this

position generally adds depth to someone who is basically more concerned with the overall breadth of problems and situations. Sagittarius is a fiery, emotional sign, and Mercury's placing gives some dampening emotion to the intellect, making for an individual who is a force to be reckoned with and has a sense of humor.

MERCURY IN SAGITTARIUS

Traditionally, Mercury works badly here. However, provided restlessness, superficiality and some over-optimism can be controlled, much can be made of this placing. The subject will always be studying something and should do so, since he or she truly needs intellectual stimulation. Consistency of effort must be developed, and interests should not be changed too often as restlessness and a lack of satisfaction will be inhibiting. Breadth of vision is considerable, as is a quick grasp of situations, giving the appearance of brilliance, but this may be a bluff! All will be well if a philosophical outlook and attitude can be developed. There can be a flair for languages, and travel is of great importance. If physical travel is impossible, reading about or studying far-flung countries may compensate.

Sun Sign Scorpio with Mercury in Sagittarius

Here the heavy intensity of Scorpio gets a lively fillip from Mercury, and encourages the individual not to take him- or herself quite so seriously, nor to become so obsessive over personal or psychological problems. A certain openness will be very refreshing. There is broad-mindedness and an optimistic outlook. A controlled enthusiasm will be shown and the emotional and intuitive content of Scorpio will be positive and reasoned, generally allowing free expression of the true feelings. Important interests or hobbies will give full scope to the imagination.

Sun Sign Sagittarius with Mercury in Sagittarius

This is perhaps rather too lively a combination which needs steadying from other elements in the chart if natural Sagittarian enthusiasm and breadth of vision are not to overwhelm the subject, making it hard for him or her to cope with details. Optimism can get out of hand, too, and there will be gushing enthusiasm that fizzles out after an initially strong start. Despite these exaggerative tendencies, this placing has a lot to offer if the individual recognizes the pitfalls and ensures that restlessness (especially the mental kind) is countered. Changing to a physically demanding activity can help.

Sun Sign Capricorn with Mercury in Sagittarius

Here optimism and a more positive outlook are added to the rather serious Capricorn traits. The Capricorn offbeat sense of humor is also enhanced. The "wet fish" element (as seen from the Capricorn goat's fishtail) is less likely to emerge, thereby giving a lively and aspirational subject. He or she will be less single-minded and doggedly persistent, and more relaxed and easy, able to cope with setbacks philosophically and without grumbling. A controlled and enthusiastic attitude can be both amusing and endearing!

MERCURY IN CAPRICORN

Although the mind usually works fairly slowly, the subject thinks in a constructive and practical way, able to form a rational and cool view of every situation. Mathematical ability is likely, but he or she will be slow when studying, and progress may be more steady than rapid. What is said is meant, and there is usually no time for idle gossip, with the subject seeming the strong and silent type. Pessimism is likely, especially if the Moon and Saturn form negative aspects, but there is often strong ambition and achievement. The approach is very matter-of-fact, and long-term planning presents few problems. Determination and decisiveness will be present unless other natal influences make the outlook bleak and depressed, when excuses may be made to cover up procrastination or lack of self-confidence. In any case, every move is calculated and made with great caution. A liking for quality and tradition is common. Achievements are often underestimated.

Sun Sign Sagittarius with Mercury in Capricorn

Sagittarian over-enthusiasm and blind optimism are steadied here. Common sense and a practical, cautious streak are added, plus the ability to cope with details. The broad Sagittarian sense of humor is spiced with the off-beat Capricorn slant, making the subject very funny at times. Sagittarian restlessness will be less of a problem but versatility may be reduced.

Sun Sign Capricorn with Mercury in Capricorn

This adds lively ambition and often a positive outlook. The subject enjoys coping with rivals, and careful planning and forethought come easily. The mind works in a very calculated and careful way, with plenty of common sense and usually excellent mathematical and scientific potential. Sometimes there is also musical ability. A measured, steady yet slow pace is common, but what is learned is done so very thoroughly indeed.

Sun Sign Aquarius with Mercury in Capricorn

Aquarian originality and perversity are steadied by the ability to think in a practical way, and stubbornness can be less of a problem. However, some conventionality will be added to Aquarian unconventionality, so the subject's opinions may swing between the two extremes. Some caution will be a counter to the Aquarian need for individuality and independence. A flair for science is present, and imagination will be shown in all intellectual pursuits.

MERCURY IN AQUARIUS

The mind is quick, and the individual usually has considerable originality, especially in opinions and ideas. There will be an intellectual approach to problems and dynamism, most apparent when communicating with others. However, he or she can be stubborn and perverse, and perhaps slightly hysterical under stress. Nervous tension can cause problems and it may be hard to unwind (either or both are likely if Mercury is negatively aspected by Mars or Uranus). Consistency of effort must be developed. The subject is usually very friendly and helpful, with the quick mind necessary to assess problems succinctly and speedily. Unusual studies or hobbies often fascinate, and there may be an attraction to the deep past or distant future. The Aquarian humanitarian traits are present, and the subject may do well when raising money or bringing injustice to light. Creative ability can also be increased if shown elsewhere in the chart.

Sun Sign Capricorn with Mercury in Aquarius
In the blending of originality of thought and Capricorn conventionality, a burning need to be an individualist (where ideas are concerned) may clash with love of tradition and the Capricorn need to do the "right and proper thing". Hopefully, such problems will be resolved when the individual comes to terms with his or her personality. The ambitious Capricorn will use an original approach to achieve objectives, but progress may be erratic – as is the case when the subject is studying. This placing adds a lively spark to the sometimes rather serious Capricorn. There is considerable objectivity, with the ability to detach the self from personal problems.

Sun Sign Aquarius with Mercury in Aquarius
While considerable originality is likely, stubbornness and often perversity are present and under extreme circumstances it can be hard for the subject to accept that he or she is being difficult. This group is usually at the forefront of its generation, but as individuals get older they can be reluctant to reassess opinions, so tend to fall behind the times. There is great objectivity, personal detachment, friendliness and helpfulness, but Aquarian unpredictability will be spiced with unexpected statements and opinions. Flexibility of mind must be developed.

Sun Sign Pisces with Mercury in Aquarius
Piscean emotions will be countered by the ability to think objectively. The subject can be detached from his or her feelings, so is not usually overwhelmed by them. Natural intuition is also controlled by more logical thinking processes. Piscean sympathy and kindness blends well with the humanitarian element of Mercury in Aquarius – help is given because it is seen to be needed, as well as because the individual is moved by a surge of emotion. The imagination is good and can be used originally and creatively, but Piscean self-confidence needs boosting if the most is to be made of this potential. Again, Mercury will help, since it enables Pisces to think positively.

Mercury in Pisces

The mind works in a disorganized and intuitive way; decisions and opinions will emerge rather than be consciously taken. Kindness, sympathy and empathy for others is considerable, but often there is forgetfulness and even carelessness, leading to confusing situations that the individual finds hard to resolve. It is difficult to develop constructive thinking and practicality. However, a practical approach is not entirely necessary, for the subject's strong intuitions are usually right. Much care is needed when coping with worry, for there is vivid imagination which can make the subject fear the worst. A tendency to take the line of least resistance is sometimes combined with deceitfulness. Usually when untruths are told it is in order not to hurt others, but cunning is not altogether absent. The placing does not support self-confidence, and shyness or self-effacement is sometimes present.

Sun Sign Aquarius with Mercury in Pisces
The rather brittle Aquarian traits are softened and the humanitarian qualities of Pisces are warmed and sympathetically expressed. The creative and very original imagination must find specific areas of expression, perhaps through some unusual, off-beat hobby or career. There is much more flexibility of mind and opinion, and usually the emotional level is greatly heightened, perhaps with less ability to be detached from the feelings. Aquarian perversity and unpredictability are less evident, since Mercury in Pisces contributes considerable sensitivity towards other people's feelings.

Sun Sign Pisces with Mercury in Pisces
The subject often becomes rather scatter-brained, surrounded by confusion and muddle. However, here is also great kindness and sympathy, and a wonderful imagination which must be channelled and constructively used. When under stress, there may be a tendency to deceive the self and others by falling back on negative escapism. Parents whose children have this placing must gently but very firmly encourage truthfulness. Any indication of creative potential should be encouraged, as self-expression though the arts (especially photography) is desirable.

Sun Sign Aries with Mercury in Pisces
Here Arian assertiveness is softened, and selfishness is less likely to be a problem (but consider the Venus sign in this respect). Arian decisiveness will not be quite so strong and forgetfulness, especially over small matters, can cause great annoyance to the active energetic Arian. This is most likely when he or she is being unduly hasty. The increased intuition of the placing is a help, particularly when assessing competitors' actions and reactions to situations. The emotional level of Aries is increased, but the subject is less likely to be easily roused to anger.

☿ Mercury Progressed through the Signs

Mercury is likely to progress through three or four signs during a lifetime. The individual will feel a mental stimulus when the progression occurs, tending to think differently about all kinds of things. Not only will the mind and opinions be changed, but the actual thinking processes themselves will gain a new dimension. The influence of the natal Mercury sign will still be evident, but another layer will be added. Mercury turns retrograde quite frequently, and there are times (when using the "day for a year" system of progressions) when it returns to a natal sign for a few years. Watch out for this – the above process may be reversed: "I now think I was right when I was younger." Do your own research: it will be very amusing!

Mercury through the Houses

The concerns and sphere of life represented by the house that Mercury occupies will be given much thought by the individual. Whether he or she thinks constructively or intuitively, worries or becomes blindly optimistic or pessimistic will, of course, depend on Mercury's sign and, to some extent, the aspects it receives. However, when interpreting the influence of Mercury's house position, consider too whether the subject will plan constructively and sensibly, or be carried away by ideas.

1 MERCURY IN THE FIRST HOUSE

The influence of Mercury will be very powerful, adding an extra dimension to the Ascendant, and will give the subject a bright personality.

The need to communicate will be very strong. Here is someone with a quick repartee, who is talkative and changeable. There will be a tendency to generous gesticulation, and the individual will have a rapid, nervous hastiness.

The aspects that Mercury receives must be considered with great care, since they will color the outlook on life, for example making the subject optimistic or pessimistic. Mercury's sign placing is also influential.

Versatility will be considerable, but the superficiality and restlessness of Mercury must be countered. Quickness of mind is very likely, with witty, sharp answers coming thick and fast. If there are negative aspects from the Moon, Mars or Uranus, nervous tension could cause migraines or stomach upsets. A tendency to worry unduly may lead to hypochondria. The nearer Mercury is to the Ascending degree, the more it will influence the Ascendant and the whole chart. If Mercury is within eight degrees of the Ascendant, refer to Mercury conjunct the Ascendant (see p.252).

2 MERCURY IN THE SECOND HOUSE

There will be a quick and clever attitude toward money, with perhaps a flair for investment, and the individual may be attracted to, or become involved in, get-rich-quick schemes. Just how well or badly these work will entirely depend on the sign placing and the aspects that Mercury receives.

Positive aspects from Saturn will be a steadying influence, while negative ones from Neptune could lead to confusion, complications, deceit and even fraud – in which case the astrologer should sound a tactful warning.

Bargaining ability will be good, and certainly the subject will enjoy finding, or striking, a bargain. Financial wheeling and dealing, from bartering to big money markets, could prove fascinating. Often two or more sources of income will be enjoyed. A liking for trendy or kitsch possessions is likely.

The gentle touch

This is the Venus/Taurus house and as Mercury rules the hands, texture is often important, with the feel of silk, velvet or the touch of beautiful skin being much appreciated.

3 MERCURY IN THE THIRD HOUSE

This is the Mercury/Gemini house, so the planet's influence will be strong. Great curiosity, a need to communicate and mobility are all important to the subject, who will spend a lot of time on the telephone, writing letters, and expressing his or her thoughts.

Ways of communicating

Words usually come thick and fast, and sometimes the subject will be more interested in the manner in which his or her opinions are stated than in what is actually said! If Mercury is in an air or fire sign, a certain provocativeness in argument and debate can occur and, like Mercutio in *Romeo and Juliet*, here is someone who speaks more in a minute than he listens to in a month!

Mental agility and the powers of perception are usually good, and the subject is mentally and intellectually alert. There is a strong need to know of events in the family and immediate environment, and keeping up with news stories is almost obligatory; newspapers and magazines will be read voraciously. Although there is a quest for knowledge it can be on a very superficial level, so try to encourage a deepening and broadening of the intellect, and the development of a more consistent mental effort and more serious in-depth achievements.

Skill is usually shown in work involving communication, so there may be the potential for a career in the media, or work with telephones, computers or facsimile machines.

4 MERCURY IN THE FOURTH HOUSE

The home and family will be of above-average importance to the individual, whose mental attitude towards them will relate to that of the sign in which Mercury is placed. Ask yourself whether he or she will worry unduly about the family, be relaxed in their company or feel stifled by them.

A constant need to change the place of residence, or at least the home's decorative schemes, may be very obvious. Often the subject is unable to rest content in one place for long. This may be the result of some inner conflict that prevents him or her from feeling totally secure in the home and will be most likely if the Sun and Moon are in negative aspect to each other, thus indicating an inner discontent.

This is the Cancer/Moon house, so it is sometimes possible to glean facts about the subject's mother, whose intellectual influence may well have been particularly stimulating. Research into family history might prove to be of great interest to the individual and be a rewarding and worthwhile study.

5 MERCURY IN THE FIFTH HOUSE

A risk-taking, perhaps gambling, instinct may be strong. Remember that it will be intuitive, logical, practical or whatever, according to the sign in which Mercury is placed.

This house has an important bearing on love affairs, so the feelings are often expressed in a way that will achieve precisely the right reaction from the object of affection. What is said under such circumstances may prove to be simply flattery, but nevertheless it will have the desired effect! Every aspect of an intended love affair will be planned in advance, but the changeability of Mercury will almost certainly encourage some duality in this sphere of life.

Mental and physical dexterity
Games of chance may also attract the individual, as will leisure pursuits that challenge the intellect, such as chess (if Mercury is placed in a sign endowing patience). If creativity is indicated in other areas of the chart this placing could enhance it. This will be especially so in literary or craft work, where the dexterous use of the hands is an essential part of the process.

6 Mercury in the Sixth House

Mercury's influence is considerably strengthened in this placing, since the planet occupies its own Virgo house. Diet will be of particular interest and there may be a sympathy for vegetarianism or natural foods. However, sometimes the concentration on diet can be excessive, with the individual constantly trying new and different eating plans. Faddishness in eating can occur in children with this placing.

If worry is suggested, either by Mercury's sign or in other areas of the chart, this placing will increase that tendency, perhaps resulting in stomach or bowel troubles. Over-concern with the problem may make it worse, irrespective of the ailment or the subject's vulnerability, for he or she may dwell on it (as can be the case when Mercury is in the first house). Encourage a practical approach, and perhaps a more philosophical attitude. Very often people with this placing respond particularly well to homeopathic remedies and holistic medicine.

A useful role
There is often a liking for routine and for serving others, since the individual will be sympathetic towards a well-organized existence. However, this does not necessarily mean that these people are good at organizing themselves! Knowing what is expected and carrying it out to perfection is more likely. This is, for instance, a good placing for a personal assistant.

The powers of communication are excellent, but very often a sharp critical edge will be quite forcibly expressed according to Mercury's sign placing. There is also an ability to analyze every aspect of each task and project undertaken, and to talk through any resulting problems, thereby contributing a great deal of practical assistance to the eventual outcome.

7 Mercury in the Seventh House

A good level of friendship is very necessary within personal relationships, and while the individual will have an excellent ability to communicate with the partner, this must be reciprocated.

Gullibility, and a tendency to fall into the partner's way of thinking, can sometimes cause problems. The sign occupied by Mercury should therefore be considered to see how well the subject can counter these tendencies. If Mercury is in Libra or Pisces, for instance, there will be a leaning towards credulity. However, the Ascendant (probably Aries or Virgo respectively) would in either of these cases lend sufficiently strong qualities to allow the individual to keep such a vulnerability under control.

Good business relations
This is a lively house placing for anyone in a business partnership, and the individual may be a gifted salesperson, or able to convey ideas to partners, customers or clients. There may also be a good ability to bring together prospective partners – a possible matchmaker, in other words! Or we may have a natural agent, a go-between, to negotiate between parties who are otherwise occupied. If the law is indicated in other areas of the chart (a powerful Jupiter, Sagittarius Sun or Midheaven, for instance), this placing might make for a talented lawyer. Should earth signs be prominent, a job as a real estate agent is suggested.

8 Mercury in the Eighth House

There can be a tendency to brood over such serious issues as life after death, and the individual may well have psychic gifts. However, before encouraging the development of these talents, it is essential to study the influence of Neptune and the Moon in the birth chart. If they are adversely aspected to each other or to the Sun, the potential is probably best left undeveloped, since such a basically sensitive individual may easily be overwhelmed by feelings of this sort. In this case the flow of imagination and sensitivity should be developed in other ways. If there are no adverse indications, and especially if earth signs are prominent, all should be well, as long as the subject is given careful guidance from a thoroughly attested expert. Nevertheless, this placing must be supported by other indications of psychic ability in the chart.

A fantasy life
An above-average preoccupation with sexuality is often present, and there may even be a very active and strong fantasy life. At best, this placing denotes an inquisitive, searching mind. The individual will probably be capable of research and the solving of mysteries, the type of which will be indicated by Mercury's sign placing.

A good ability for investment and the study of capital growth is also possible. If Mercury is in a water sign, the intuitive powers will be used to advantage; fire will add a natural enthusiasm (which could cause over-investment); air will denote a rational approach; and earth will indicate a practical one.

9 Mercury in the Ninth House

As this is the house of the higher intellect, Mercury is placed sympathetically here and is also attuned to the spheres of life ruled by the ninth house.

The mind needs constant challenge but it is important that consistency of effort and powers of concentration are developed, for the subject may be very restless, with an ever-present need to move on to new pastures. While the mind should be able to cope with daunting projects, the ability to grasp details will be dictated by the sign in which Mercury is placed, with some signs faring much better than others.

"The house of dreams" was once the traditional name for this house, so when Mercury occupies it there can be a tendency to daydream. An especially common dream may be of "getting away from it all"; usually to attractive-sounding far-off countries. Fascination with travel, either in the mind or physically, is compulsive, and the subject will follow up every possible lead in order to do so – often resorting to plotting and scheming to get abroad. Sometimes, for instance, a career will be chosen simply because it offers the opportunity to travel.

Acquiring knowledge

A hunger for intellectual expansion will be present in others with this placing, and an individual may enjoy work in libraries, bookstores or a university, in order to become part of the sort of life that is so admired and desired.

The need to learn is always present, and as for those with a Sagittarian Sun or Ascendant, there is a strong element of the eternal student. There may be a flair for foreign languages.

10 MERCURY IN THE TENTH HOUSE

It is very likely that there will be many changes of career. If no career is followed, there will be changes of direction in life with regard to the aspirations and objectives. All these matters will be given much thought and planning because progress will often become a preoccupation.

Responsibility to self and others

If the Mercury sign is sympathetic to this house placing, the individual will be able to carry responsibility, but awareness of it will be present whatever the sign. How well the subject copes will depend on the Mercury sign and the aspects it receives.

For the career to have an overall shape there should be as much variety in the daily work as possible. If a good mix of intellectual stimulation, responsibility and mobility can be achieved, then so much the better, since the chances are that boredom leading to restlessness (and dissatisfaction, if it is shown in other areas of the chart) will otherwise hamper long-term progress.

There are connections between this house and the father, and it is worth discussing this with the subject. On one level, perhaps, the individual will think and plan in a style reminiscent of his father; on a deeper psychological level the "father" will be an inner voice representing authority, saying what the subject should or shouldn't do.

11 MERCURY IN THE ELEVENTH HOUSE

There will be a great need of many friends and acquaintances, and a desire to communicate ideas and become involved in conversations and arguments at social gatherings. Unless Mercury is restricted by an opposition or square from Saturn, initiating discussions will be easy. The subject may well be a natural committee member.

A need for sociability

Deep and meaningful friendships may not be all that important to him or her, but social intercourse will be, and the spare time will be used to the full, with every moment thoroughly enjoyed. If ever a need to get out and about and to mix freely is expressed, it is here. Perhaps a certain amount of free time will be spent on humanitarian causes. Try suggesting something of this sort to the subject, since there could be much fulfillment in charity work or, for example, in writing letters for Amnesty International, thus involving the intellect.

"The group" will be important, as is the case with most eleventh house planets. Remembering, however, the close proximity of the Sun to Mercury, this placing may conflict with the Sun's house position (if it is in the twelfth). If so, encourage your subject to make the most of peace and quiet and working alone (Sun in the twelfth house) as well as outgoing, social activities (Mercury in the eleventh house). If the Sun is in the tenth, there will be few problems, other than persuading the subject to slow down, for the energy channeled into career and social life will call for a nonstop schedule!

12 MERCURY IN THE TWELFTH HOUSE

There may be conflict between the logical elements of Mercury and the intuition and emotion of the twelfth house, especially if Mercury is in a water sign. It will be excellent if the subject can rationalize his or her intuition and channel the emotions, expressing them with all the positive communicative abilities of Mercury. Another conflict can sometimes be felt when solitude is demanded yet there is also a need for communication and social intercourse. Perhaps hours will be spent talking on the telephone!

A love of literature (especially poetry) can be present, plus considerable critical acumen. Sometimes people who work in the media, especially the radio, have this placing. If there is a flair for technology, the engineering side of broadcasting can be worthwhile. In other cases the subject's work may speak for itself – for example, that of a photographer who develops his prints alone in a darkroom. For those with religious faith there is usually a great belief in the power of prayer, and a deeply-held conviction that positive thought always has its desired effect.

☿ MERCURY PROGRESSED THROUGH THE HOUSES

Like the Sun, Mercury will probably travel through three houses in the progressed chart during an average lifetime. If Mercury progresses into the house that contained the Sun in the birth chart, that house will be brought to prominence by the Mercury influence, and the subject will give extra thought to the concerns of that house. In any case, the focus of the progression into a "new" house is an intellectual and communicative one, with Mercury picking up the house influence as described above. Bear this in mind, and look out for key periods when Mercury either makes a progressed aspect to the natal Sun, or the progressed Sun makes an aspect to Mercury's natal or progressed position. Short key periods will occur when the progressed Moon makes aspects to Mercury – again, either to its natal or progressed position.

The Aspects of Mercury

These aspects can intellectualize any planet that Mercury contacts. Negative aspects will sharpen the receiving planet, but can also produce tension and stress, especially where contacts to Uranus are concerned. However, it is usually possible for the individual to use any Mercury influence positively, since there is good potential for a lively expression of the mind.

For Mercury's aspects to the Sun, see the Sun's aspects to Mercury, pp.214-15.

For Mercury's aspects to the Moon, see the Moon's aspects to Mercury, pp.232-3.

While you can use the interpretation set out for the Moon's progressions to Mercury, when interpreting Mercury's progressed aspects to the Moon, other factors should be taken into consideration. Bear in mind that, when Mercury makes a progressed aspect to the Moon, its influence will add background conditions to the life lasting for about a year, as opposed to the progressed Moon's aspects to Mercury, when the influence will only last for about three months at most.

♀ Mercury's Aspects to Venus

Note: Because the two planets can never be more than 76 degrees apart, they can only form the conjunction, semi-sextile, semi-square and sextile, although the progressed Mercury can form many more aspects to the natal position of Venus.

Conjunction

In this placing, love, natural sympathy and understanding are shown to the partner, with empathy toward friends and colleagues. There are good powers of communication, according to the joint Mercury and Venus sign. There is usually harmony rather than conflict if the conjunction crosses two signs, with the thoughts of Mercury and the feelings of Venus working well together.

The semi-sextile

This promotes harmony between the subject's thoughts and feelings. However, the semi-sextile is very weak, and unless Mercury and/or Venus is personalized, it is unwise to use this aspect much in your interpretation.

The semi-square

Sometimes there is a sharp, biting criticism of the partner. If this does not apply, because the planets are in amenable signs, there will be extra friendliness and a willingness to see eye-to-eye with friends and lovers.

The sextile

Friendliness and openly expressed affection are usual. If the chart shows creative potential, this aspect is a marvelous boost as it nearly always bestows a considerable ability for craftwork of all kinds. There is a great appreciation of texture, and the hands are used with dexterity. When Venus or Mercury are in earth signs, the love and creative use of natural materials – such as wool, linen, silk, stone or wood – should be encouraged.

♀ Progressed Aspects between Mercury and Venus

The expression of feelings and sense of companionship within a love-relationship will be enhanced. If partnerships are not relevant, there may be a considerable surge of activity instead, with the individual acquiring skills in an arts or crafts technique. This activity will become important – a different sort of love affair. Sometimes there is the strong desire to play a musical instrument. Literary talent, possibly of a romantic nature, may also be evident.

Little strain and tension will arise even if Mercury makes a square aspect to Venus (this would have to be the progressed Mercury to the natal Venus). However, if Venus is heavily aspected in the birth chart, there could be problems relating to that aspect. For example, the subject may be disappointed or inhibited in love (Venus square or opposition Moon or Saturn), or be carried away to a fool's paradise (Venus square or opposition Neptune). Otherwise, the best influences of both planets will provide a pleasant background to the year or so during which the aspect is exact, with the progressed conjunction and sextile (or trine, if your subject is older), being the best.

Mercury's Aspects to Mars

Conjunction

Whatever the sign, this aspect accelerates and energizes the mind, making the individual very quick-thinking and decisive. He or she can keep well ahead of rivals, and assertiveness and competitiveness in business, study and sport will be present. There is a capacity for hard mental work and sometimes a liking for satire, which can emerge in the sense of humor. If aggressiveness is shown elsewhere there will be a tendency to quarrel, although usually this is channeled into lively and provocative opinions that will be forcibly voiced in discussions.

Positive aspects

These are much the same as the conjunction, with the same lively, quick-thinking and decisive mind. The nervous system is also strengthened, enabling the subject to cope well in situations that would induce strain and tension in others. He or she may even thrive on such an atmosphere, perhaps having a very demanding job in the money markets, and will act positively whenever the going gets tough.

Negative aspects

The mental energy is increased in much the same way as described above, but there is a risk of tension due to overwork, perhaps resulting in a breakdown. This would be most likely if either Mercury or Mars also make negative aspects to Uranus.

The great risk, however, is a tendency to act prematurely, since in making snap decisions, undue consideration may be given to the details of a problem or situation. There is a distinct tendency for fools to rush in; look for qualities of common sense and mental stability in other areas of the chart. The Sun or rising sign in an earth sign may help, as would a well-aspected Saturn.

♂ Progressed Aspects between Mercury and Mars

☌ Conjunction

The individual may face additional intellectual demands for about a year. Involvement in one specific project lasting for the duration of the progression's effect is likely. The challenge will be exciting, and an excited nervous energy will ignite the subject's enthusiasm for the job in hand.

Premature action and over-hasty decision-making must be guarded against; if these tendencies are kept under control, the results should be extremely satisfying. Transits from Jupiter will help this progression.

+ Positive aspects

The effects of these are much as for the conjunction, but there may not be quite the same frenetic pace or powerful concentration on one project. Certainly the general rhythm of life will increase, resulting in demanding intellectual or mental work.

Enthusiasm and energy channeled into all kinds of work or ambitions will be rewarded. This progression could also work well for an athlete training for a specific event, since he will be in the right frame of mind to cope, and the nervous and physical energies should complement each other.

− Negative aspects

For about a year, the individual may be vulnerable to nervous strain and tension, but will be most at risk when (and if) there are negative transits from Uranus either to the natal Mercury or Mars. Impatience is likely, and should plans be frustrated (perhaps due to Saturn's or Pluto's influence on other areas of the chart), the tendency will be to overreact by making hasty and rash decisions that could, in the long run, only make matters worse.
The subject may tend to become rather sarcastic or even slightly bitter at times, due to strain and tension. However, such extreme reactions would only be provoked by additional stress from other planets, as mentioned above.

♃ Mercury's Aspects to Jupiter

☌ Conjunction

There is excellent intellectual potential here which, if creativity is shown in other areas of the chart, can be expressed through writing and all kinds of literary work. In a chart where there is scientific or mathematical potential, this aspect is also an extremely powerful and useful focal point, since the mind should work well and the capacity for learning will be quite considerable.

The sign placing must be very carefully considered since this shows how the mental energies will develop and what the intellectual outlook and attitude will be.

+ Positive aspects

The level of intellectual potential may be very strong, and the subject is usually good-natured and optimistic. He or she may lean toward an over-philosophical outlook and as a result be rather too easy-going. The more mental demands that are made the better, since this aspect will work well for the subject if he or she accepts mind-stretching challenges.

− Negative aspects

These usually cause few problems and are as indicative of good intellectual potential as the conjunction and positive aspects. However, the subject may have a tendency to be somewhat absent-minded.

A healthy element of scepticism, a tendency to exaggerate and occasional carelessness are usually present and can lead to complications. Under some circumstances the nervous system can suffer, especially if Mercury or Jupiter are negatively aspected by Uranus, or Mercury is in Virgo. If biliousness is shown in other areas of the chart this aspect will exacerbate the problem.

Special attention should always be paid to the small print when signing contracts or legal documents, for the individual will tend to gloss over and ignore such details.

♃ Progressed Aspects between Mercury and Jupiter

☌ Conjunction

This can be very exciting, especially if the individual has always had a yearning to write or travel extensively. It will also be of enormous help to anyone studying or taking examinations.

Look to the transits of Jupiter during the year in which the progression is exact, as there will be plenty of key periods to use for such occupations which, unless Mercury or Jupiter are heavily afflicted in the birth chart, should be very successful.

+ Positive aspects

The areas mentioned above will all flourish, with the mind working well and accepting all sorts of intellectual challenges. Perhaps a language will be studied, or comparative religions. (Remember that Jupiter has a relationship with religion.) Overall, life should expand for the individual, who must keep an open mind but whose outlook will be hopeful and optimistic.

− Negative aspects

Some nervous strain and tension is likely, but considerable success can be achieved provided blind optimism is avoided. Contracts must be studied very carefully, as mistakes could easily be made. Extra time should be allowed for decision-making.

♄ Mercury's Aspects to Saturn

☌ Conjunction

This is a powerful aspect, bestowing a serious outlook and practical thinking. There is an ability to make and carry out long-term plans, but the individual will tend to be pessimistic. Usually there are good powers of concentration and perception, and if Mercury is a personal planet there can sometimes be a liking for solitude. The mind works meticulously, with plenty of common sense and caution.

Parents who have a child with this conjunction must not expect him or her to make rapid progress at school. Rather, the child will be a steady plodder – especially if the conjunction falls in the same sign as the Sun. If the conjunction is in a fire or air sign it will act as a stabilizer to fiery energy and airy, lively intellectuality. It will calm the emotions when in a water sign and may lead to a certain obstinacy and self-will if in an earth sign.

+ Positive aspects
These can act as an excellent anchorage in a chart showing a great deal of lively, positive enthusiasm. There is an ability to think in a careful and concentrated way, and usually the mind works very methodically. What is said is meant, and the individual will have an element of reliability as a result of this aspect (look for other indications of that positive characteristic elsewhere in the birth chart).

– Negative aspects
Sometimes these aspects cause obsessional tendencies and a passion for neatness and order. The individual will be extremely hard on him- or herself, and is often critical of others. The subject can also be shocked surprisingly easily, and may have a narrow-minded streak.

Pessimism (especially if the Moon and Saturn form a negative aspect to each other) and depression can occur. Look to other areas of the chart for a counter to this. Suspicion and cunning are also possible traits, and sometimes the individual is rather shy, lacking in self-confidence especially at large social gatherings.

♄ Progressed Aspects between Mercury and Saturn

☌ Conjunction
This important trend should be used positively, since the time is right for the subject to make long-term plans. The astrologer must encourage him or her to understand that such plans cannot be expected to fall into place very quickly, as the presence of Saturn means delays and frustrations are almost inevitable.

The mind will be working along very constructive and practical lines, and should there be a possibility of promotion, the subject will carry any additional responsibilities extremely well. Positive transits from Saturn to the Sun will encourage these themes.

+ Positive aspects
These aspects are much as above, but will not be quite as strong unless Mercury and Saturn are personal planets. They will give the subject a sensible, practical outlook on achievements, and while progress may be slower than hoped, it will still be very sound.

– Negative aspects
The individual may experience a period when progress is very slow. Delays and frustrations can cause disproportionate annoyance. If the progression occurs at the time of a Saturn Return (see p.312), encourage your subject to believe that whatever changes or decisions are made will be the right ones. However, patience is essential.

Look to positive transits – perhaps from Jupiter to Mercury, the Sun or Ascendant – to counter depression, negative thoughts and any feelings of hopelessness that may arise during this tricky period.

♅ Mercury's Aspects to Uranus

☌ Conjunction
This is a dynamic configuration that contributes originality and adds speedy brilliance to the mind. It also gives some independence and perhaps stubbornness and self-will, lending considerable support to these characteristics if they are shown elsewhere.

The need for independence may become important to the subject, who can be a very private person, liking to go his or her own way uninhibited by the demands of others. The positive originality of this aspect is marvelous and will be of considerable use to the subject if it is properly encouraged.

+ Positive aspects
Talent, and a liking, for somewhat unusual interests is probable. Originality and bright ideas are common and – especially if Leo or Jupiter is prominent – there will be a well-developed sense of drama. An inventive imagination can be used in creative or scientific work.

Independence will be necessary, especially if either Mercury or Uranus is a personal planet or if Mercury falls in the same sign as the Sun.

– Negative aspects
These will contribute the same bright, original mind, but there is a possibility of nervous tension, especially if Mars makes negative aspects to either planet. There can be tactlessness, with the individual suddenly speaking out of turn or being known for letting the cat out of the bag! Sometimes the subject will think he or she has special gifts, with a particular message for mankind. This will be most likely if Neptune receives negative aspects from the Sun or Moon, or squares the Ascendant.

Note: Aspects between Mercury and Uranus are often found in the charts of professional astrologers.

♅ Progressed Aspects between Mercury and Uranus

☌ Conjunction
Mental activity will be increased, and the subject will have at least one bright idea, or maybe even a series of them. Encouragement should be given to follow these ideas through, albeit with the warning to avoid undue haste. This aspect could also spark off the study of a fascinating or unusual subject.

If Jupiter is prominent by transit, the chances are that the project, or projects, will be successful, but look for positive Saturn influences to indicate increased powers of concentration, or delays (negative Saturn).

+ Positive aspects
These are very much as above, but there will be less compulsive, dynamic force. Other progressed aspects will either encourage the development of original ideas or hamper them. It is really up to you to help your subject to develop his or her ideas in the way that will provide the greatest amount of inner satisfaction.

– Negative aspects
Periods of nervous strain and tension may be likely, especially if other progressed aspects show these tendencies, or transits indicate delay or frustration. In either case it is important that you consider whether or not your subject is being his or her own worst enemy, since stubbornness to a ridiculous degree may be present, thus

causing an even greater build-up of tension. However, if this doesn't apply, the individual may be able to use this energy positively, in the manner suggested in the descriptions of both the conjunction and positive aspects.

MERCURY'S ASPECTS TO NEPTUNE

Conjunction

Here, the mental attributes of Mercury combine with the imagination and inspiration of Neptune, so if the conjunction is free of negative aspects from Saturn, these two planets will add an interesting quality. They do not give common sense, however, and the subject may sometimes drift off into a private fantasy world, or simply daydream. This will be most obvious if the conjunction falls in Libra or Scorpio, when the imagination may center on romantic or sexual fantasies.

The conjunction will be an asset for those who have it in Leo, Virgo or Sagittarius, since then the intellect and imagination will be expressed positively, and probably creatively; encourage development of this potential. Increased sensitivity and intuition can be marked if they are shown in other areas of the chart, and sometimes the individual has psychic powers, but these must also be indicated elsewhere. Usually this aspect is a delightful influence, but one that must be controlled.

Positive aspects

The effect of these is much as above, with the subject being kind, gentle and sensitive. He or she will know intuitively what the other person is thinking – sometimes, indeed, thinking imaginatively ahead.

The occult may attract, as with the conjunction, but much depends on the other aspects Neptune receives. As always, sound a note of caution to your subjects if they want to become involved in such activities.

Negative aspects

These contribute an element of cunning and a tendency to scheme. Sometimes deception and lying may even be practiced. If either planet is personal there may well be self-deception, with the individual unable, or unwilling, to see reality or face facts. Just how much of a problem this can be will depend on the amount of practicality indicated elsewhere in the chart.

Help will be given if the Sun, Moon or Ascendant fall in an earth sign, as will positive aspects of the Sun or Moon to Saturn, or a positive aspect from Saturn to the Ascendant. If Neptune rules the Sun or the chart, these tendencies will be a stumbling block. Parents of children with these aspects must always encourage truthfulness.

PROGRESSED ASPECTS BETWEEN MERCURY AND NEPTUNE

Conjunction

If other progressed aspects are positive and there are encouraging transits from Jupiter, this will be an interesting year or so. Imaginative, creative work will be achieved, and there is a good chance that the individual will look back on this period with nostalgia, especially if Venus is involved in the progressions. Concrete form should be given to all ideas at this time.

Positive aspects

These are much as above, with the additional possibility that the imagination and mind will work well together, with interesting and unusual results.

Negative aspects

Self-deception can occur and the individual may not want to face up to reality. There can be an attraction to cults, but much practical thought must be given before the subject becomes over-involved. Keeping a balanced outlook on such topics will be difficult, and firm, constructive advice is needed. However, it may be hard to make the subject accept such counsel, especially if he or she is very young and prone to fascinating but negative influences.

MERCURY'S ASPECTS TO PLUTO

Conjunction

This placing gives an ability to think deeply and intuitively and to work through psychological problems and inhibitions with the aid of self-analysis. However, there will also be a tendency to hold on to such problems if either Mercury or Pluto receives square aspects from the Moon, Saturn, or any personal planet. If the aspects are positive, there should be an ability to talk through such problems with friends once the subject has reached his or her own conclusions. Here is a sleuth-like mind that enjoys solving mysteries.

Positive aspects

No details of any topic will be glossed over, and once his or her interest is ignited, the individual will be fascinated to explore any subject in depth. If Mercury or Pluto are personal planets, the need to explore the self will be just as powerful as with the conjunction, but a result may be more easily achieved.

Negative aspects

There can be difficulty in discussing personal problems, and secretiveness is common. Sometimes obsessive tendencies and stubbornness are present if the fixed signs are involved. If nervous tension is shown in other areas these aspects may have an adverse effect on the health, causing constipation, stomach upsets or even ulcers, especially if the individual is prone to worry – which will almost inevitably be "bottled up". Encourage your subject to relax into talking through his or her problems. This will be difficult, but you will learn a great deal about counseling skills if and when you succeed.

Note: Aspects between Mercury and Pluto often give an individual a flair for computer technology.

PROGRESSED ASPECTS BETWEEN MERCURY AND PLUTO

Conjunction

While this progression is operative there is a possibility that the individual will suffer considerable frustrations every now and then. The time will be right for him or her to come to terms with ongoing psychological problems. A course of therapy will work very well, and result in the ability to make a fresh start with greater self-confidence. If Mercury or Pluto are personalized, then it is highly likely that this will be an important period for your subject, but one that will need support from strong, positive transits to the Sun, Ascendant or Moon.

+ Positive aspects
Sometimes sweeping changes are made, with the individual needing to reshape his life in some way. There may be a radical change of opinions. As with the conjunction, psychological hang-ups can be positively resolved.

– Negative aspects
Warn your subject that during this period (and remember that Mercury may first aspect the natal position of Pluto and then move directly on to that planet's progressed position, so extending this aspect's duration to about two years), there will be times when progress will be blocked and he or she may come up against metaphorical brick walls. If this happens, the solution is to try not to force issues. The blockage usually only occurs when there are negative transits backing up the Mercury/Pluto progression, and once these have passed the subject will be able to move on again. This is not an easy trend and patience is needed.

Asc Mercury's Aspects to the Ascendant

☌ Conjunction
Here, Mercury adds lively, bright and intelligent qualities. There will usually be quick-thinking and considerable versatility, but restlessness is often present. The individual will be talkative and have a powerful need to communicate his or her ideas and opinions. The nervous system will be sensitive, working well and without problems if Mercury is positively aspected by other planets, but causing nervous strain and tension if it receives negative aspects.

If Mercury falls in the twelfth house, the subject may be secretive. The imagination and intuition can be heightened. The closer to the Ascendant this aspect is, the stronger its effects, but an accurate birth time is necessary for a reliable interpretation.

+ Positive aspects
These are much as for the conjunction, with the house position of Mercury having an increased personal effect on the subject. Unless Mercury falls in the Sun sign its effects will be noticeable but not very powerful; they will help the individual towards an integration of the mind and personality.

– Negative aspects
The subject will be inclined to talk too much when nervous, and some tension may well be present which will quicken the mind. There may be a tendency toward hypochondria, especially if you find that worry is shown elsewhere in the chart.

Asc Progressed Aspects between Mercury and the Ascendant

☌ Conjunction
This indicates a period of change, when the individual will reassess his or her opinions and ideas, perhaps even totally rethinking the lifestyle. Look to Mercury's natal aspects to see how the subject will cope with this interesting but unsettling period. Do not forget Mercury's influence on the nervous system, and if necessary advise relaxation techniques. This period is very important if Mercury is personalized.

+ Positive aspects
The effect of these is very much as for the conjunction. The progression will provide a light but stimulating background theme over a period of about a year or so. New interests will be taken up, and mental challenges readily accepted. This is a lively progression; advise your subject to make the most of its intellectually revitalizing effects.

– Negative aspects
There will be a marked tendency to succumb to worry or nervous tension, with the possibility of small problems becoming disproportionately large. The influence is not very strong unless Mercury is personalized, but decision-making may cause tension and the subject must not act prematurely.

A flurry of stomach upsets can occur, or perhaps there will be skin rashes as a result of tension: these are most likely if the progression coincides with tense transits from Uranus, or perhaps with the Uranus Half-return (see p.326). The subject will find that relaxation techniques and exercises can help.

MC Mercury's Aspects to the Midheaven

☌ Conjunction
The individual will need and enjoy many changes in his or her career, or in objectives. There will be a flair for work in communications of all kinds and the media. Teaching, the travel industry or the airlines may appeal, but the need for variety should be expressed within the confines of a carefully chosen career, otherwise there will be a tendency to move around so much that real progress is inhibited. The importance of this placing is increased if Mercury occupies the same sign as the Sun, or is personalized.

+ Positive aspects
These have much the same effects as the conjunction, but will be less powerful. There will be an added emphasis on the positive Mercury areas and in the subject's ability not to allow restlessness in the career or objectives to become overwhelming.

– Negative aspects
Above-average nervous strain, tension and worry may plague the subject when there are problems at work or decisions to be made as to his or her direction in life. Look to other areas of the chart to see how your subject can come to terms with such problems. The negative aspects will only be a contributory factor in these problems unless Mercury is a personal planet.

MC Progressed Aspects between Mercury and the Midheaven

☌ Conjunction
Assuming that the birth time is accurate, your subject will experience some very interesting and lively changes, thanks to his or her reputation and known experience. There may be the chance to change jobs (sometimes within the current employment), take a sabbatical or some additional study course, maybe abroad, or to express opinions by writing articles for trade journals or the media.

Life is likely to be eventful when there are lively, progressive transits from Jupiter or Uranus to the Sun or the personal planets. The individual should be encouraged to take up any offer that comes along, but not to act in a hasty or premature way. Restlessness and impatience may well have to be controlled, so look for a cluster of stabilizing, positive Saturn transits too.

+ Positive aspects
These have much the same effect as the conjunction, but are not such a dynamic trend. There can be opportunities for positive changes, but they may not be as all-engulfing as those of the conjunction. This progression needs even more back-up from positive transits, and will be so colored by them that they may exert the strongest influence. Nevertheless, these are useful and lively progressions.

− Negative aspects
These may cause stress and tension in the career or the attainment of objectives. It may be necessary for the subject to make changes, perhaps against his or her wishes – at work, for instance, a company take-over may mean moving to a less congenial department or area. Much depends on personal circumstance, of course, and, as with the positive progressions, these can be irritated by negative transits and soothed by positive ones.

☿ Mercury's Progressed Aspects to its Own Position

These occur every now and then during a lifetime. Mercury can make any aspect to itself up to the square, and if you are working on an elderly person's chart you may find a trine! The emphasis is totally on Mercury, so the way this planet works in the birth chart will be particularly important – look again at Mercury's natal aspects.

The progressed house position of Mercury will also be important, and whether the aspect is positive or negative will show whether or not the trend will help or hinder.

These progressions will give an intellectual stimulus to other background themes working for the individual, but if Mercury is making a negative aspect to itself and was negatively aspected in the birth chart, worry and tension may be a problem. Excitement, bright ideas and a particularly well-tuned mind and nervous system will be present if most other indications are positive.

☿ The Transits of Mercury

Many astrologers do not bother to calculate or interpret these tiny influences, but we think they are quite worthwhile, for they add color to the life for two or three days and, since several transits often occur one after the other, it is well worth taking advantage of these brief energies.

Only conjunctions and oppositions need be calculated, and as Mercury is a harmless planet there is little difference in interpreting either contact. Nevertheless, do remember that if any negative Mercury trait is indicated in the birth chart, or when Mercury makes an opposition transit to its own position, the Sun, Moon, chart-ruler, Ascendant or Midheaven, there will be a slight tendency for it to be apparent in the subject's attitude of mind. The strength of the transits will be slightly increased if Mercury is prominent in the progressions or if it is also contacted by other slower-moving transitting planets.

Roughly speaking, it is good to make telephone calls, write letters, arrange meetings or conduct business discussions while these transits are operative. They also provide good communicative back-up when other stronger transits or progressed lunar aspects are working.

Mercury's transits to the Sun
An effort should be made to catch up on letter-writing, put ideas to other people, and get out and enjoy life.

Mercury's transits to the Moon
Intuition should be combined with practical thinking. Minor changes to domestic routine should be considered. The subject ought to initiate family discussions and sort out any problems associated with children, parents or other relatives.

Mercury's transits to Mercury
All of Mercury's natal influences should be used to their best advantage.

Mercury's transits to Venus
This is a good time to arrange pleasant, chatty meetings or parties with friends. Looking for bargains and visiting favorite department stores can also be enjoyable.

Mercury's transits to Mars
The subject should be decisive, making his or her opinions known and, if necessary, telling other people a few home truths. This is a time for being firm but keeping one's cool.

Mercury's transits to Jupiter
These lively influences are particularly good for all kinds of intellectual work or study. They can also be used to plan or take long journeys, or to make contact with foreigners.

Mercury's transits to Saturn
Plans and important decisions should be made, although feelings of optimism may be less strong than usual. Mail delays or frustration when trying to make telephone calls can be expected.

Mercury's transits to Uranus
Original ideas could come thick and fast. The subject should not act impulsively, but give him- or herself time to think things through. There may be a flash of brilliance. Tense, nervous excitement is likely.

Mercury's transits to Neptune
Feelings of inspiration may occur. This is a good time for getting out and about with a camera. Careful lists should be made of everything the subject has to do, since forgetfulness may easily be a stumbling block.

Mercury's transits to Pluto
The subject may feel like exploding with rage, and will probably be right in doing so. This is a good time to clear out any clutter – especially old papers, magazines and so on.

Mercury's transits to the Ascendant
This is a time for thinking about oneself and what one wants. Any problems should be talked over with partners.

Mercury's transits to the Midheaven
New developments and a change of plans should be expected.

Venus through the Signs

The orbit of Venus, like that of Mercury, lies between us and the Sun. Venus is known, astronomically, as the second inferior planet, and it can never be more than 48 degrees from the Sun as seen from the Earth. It will therefore share the same sign as the Sun or be in one of the two signs either side of it. For instance, in a chart with a Gemini Sun sign, Venus will be in Aries, Taurus, Gemini with the Sun, Cancer or Leo.

Venus influences the way in which we relate to other people, both socially and economically. Our attitudes to money and possessions are also the concern of this planet. When reading this section, first look up the relevant sign placing of Venus, then read the ensuing paragraph relating it to the Sun sign in question.

Venus in Aries

The individual is passionate, falling in love quickly, and will be demonstrative. Sexual fulfillment is of above-average importance, and an uncooperative partner will not be tolerated. Although an element of Arian selfishness may well cause problems occasionally, the individual will be generous to a loved one, making sure there are many occasions of joint enjoyment. Here is a lively friend and energetic colleague. The attitude to money is extremely enterprising, but a risk-taking element can cause financial losses. Often, there is an enjoyable second source of income, but money can still slip through the fingers.

Sun Sign Aquarius with Venus in Aries
This adds warmth and passion to the cool detachment of the Aquarian Sun. There will be powerful emotional relationships, but sometimes conflict can arise when the subject has to decide whether to deepen one of these through home-sharing or marriage, and there may be a delay in making an emotional commitment. Independence is most important, as is the Aquarian lifestyle; there will be an active social life and many like-minded friends. There is an erratic attitude to money, with a liking for unusual possessions.

Sun Sign Pisces with Venus in Aries
The sensitive watery emotion of Pisces combined with the fiery passion of Aries makes these individuals ardent but caring and tender lovers. At times they will be confused by their own emotional intensity, and apprehension and a lack of self-confidence (Pisces) may clash with a desire for the loved one (Venus in Aries). Nonetheless, the striving for a rewarding relationship is important, as are friends with shared interests. Money will be enjoyed, so saving may well be difficult. The subject may find that impulsive generosity could cause problems.

Sun Sign Aries with Venus in Aries
Here is a very passionate and enthusiastic partner who needs to maintain independence within a permanent relationship. Although selfish at times, he or she will be generous to loved ones, wanting them to enjoy the relationship. Rivalry can occur in friendship, with the subject needing to take the lead. Money is often made from sidelines as well as a main source, and investment will be enjoyed. Impulse-buying can lead to cashflow problems.

Sun Sign Taurus with Venus in Aries
The passions are very powerful, and while this subject makes an excellent, sensual lover, the emotional level is so high that storms may well arise. At such times possessiveness (Taurus) and selfishness (Venus in Aries) can cause serious problems, but the highs will be marvelously romantic as well as fulfilling. Over-emotional reactions can sometimes cause difficulties with friends. In money matters, the individual is clever, but a liking for luxury will prove expensive.

Sun Sign Gemini with Venus in Aries
The Geminian mistrust of emotion can cause problems with this passionate placing, but there will be good rapport and friendship, and sexual fulfillment once the tendency to rationalize is overcome. This is a lively friend with many varied interests, wanting to do a great deal and travel widely. Spendthrift tendencies must be countered.

Venus in Taurus

Venus rules this sign so its influence will be increased by this placing. The individual is loving, warm and affectionate and makes a passive, sensual and romantic partner, but the Taurean possessiveness will incline him or her to think of the loved one as another much-cherished belonging. Material possessions will be extremely important, since they contribute a measure of security and stability. There will be much hard work to achieve luxury and comfort, but if it is possible to make money easily, the subject will be keen to do so, since a liking for relaxation is common. Often there is a talent for, and appreciation of, music, combined with a general love of beauty, art and good living – especially for food.

Sun Sign Pisces with Venus in Taurus
This adds stability, and is a good counter to Piscean elusiveness. The emotions are steady and tempered with common sense and fiscal ability. A practical approach both to love and financial matters is often present, and the placing will add to the creative flair of Pisces, helping to give it concrete form. As a friend, the subject is more reliable than most Sun sign Pisceans, but an element of possessiveness may emerge within relationships.

Sun Sign Aries with Venus in Taurus
This will increase the affection and add seething passion. The subject approaches love affairs with surprising caution, but must realize that selfishness and possessiveness can cause more damage than might be imagined. Enthusiasm and prudence should be

combined to get the best of this placing, both emotionally and materially. Here is an excellent friend who is good company, with an infectious enjoyment of life. Financial enterprise is combined with care.

Sun Sign Taurus with Venus in Taurus

The Taurean characteristics are very prominent and could outweigh the power of the Ascendant. Love and the attitude towards money and its making are as described under Venus in Taurus (see left), with all Sun sign characteristics complementing, enhancing or exaggerating those of Venus in Taurus. The metabolism could be slow and Taurean ailments may be present. The weight should be strictly controlled by restricting the intake of rich food. Financial and emotional security are of vital importance.

Sun Sign Gemini with Venus in Taurus

This increases the Gemini emotional level, but can cause problems, since the individual must learn to express his or her emotions and not over-rationalize them. The subject will try very hard to counter any possessive tendencies. Here is a lively, talkative friend who will enjoy organizing events. A liking for luxury will prove expensive. Quick Gemini wit will complement the Taurean business ability.

Sun Sign Cancer with Venus in Taurus

There is marvelous potential for being a caring, sensitive and extremely sensual lover. However, the Cancerian tendency to cherish and protect, combined with a Taurean leaning toward possessiveness, can create highly claustrophobic conditions within a relationship and have an adverse effect on family life. This is a friend who is faithful but easily offended. Business potential is superb, with Cancerian shrewdness adding to Venusian flair.

♊ VENUS IN GEMINI

Lively and fun-loving, the individual can communicate well with partners. There will also be an important need both for friendship and an intellectual rapport within emotional relationships. The subject is flirtatious and may even indulge in dual relationships, having the cunning necessary to talk his or her way out of any tight spots when the need arises! The sharing of joint interests is vital if a relationship is to be enjoyed and therefore sustained, as is a stimulating partner who will present welcome challenges, both intellectually and sexually. The emotional level is low but is very much governed by the Sun sign (see below). Many of the qualities expressed towards the lover will be evident in ties of friendship too, and this positive, enthusiastic individual will do much to encourage friends to share these traits. There is a flair for moneymaking and a knack for finding, and striking, bargains.

Sun Sign Aries with Venus in Gemini

The ardent passion of Aries is tempered with light-hearted affection and an attractive expression of feelings. Infidelity and getting the best of both worlds are common, often hurting the permanent partner. Arian selfishness and a quick response to tricky situations will be seen when the subject is challenged! Partners with good minds as well as bodies are essential. Intellectual competitiveness is welcome within friendships. Arian financial enterprise is increased here, sometimes giving the ability to sell well.

Sun Sign Taurus with Venus in Gemini

The love, passion, intensity and natural charm of Taurus are enhanced. As Venus rules this sign the whole personality will be lightened, possessive tendencies reduced, and the overall Taurean slowness corrected, both intellectually and physically. Here is a friend who enjoys intelligent conversation and good living. The need for possessions as material security will be tempered. Alertness and quick-thinking in business will be an advantage.

Sun Sign Gemini with Venus in Gemini

The powerful influence of Venus in Gemini (see left) will be very apparent, and any tendency to over-rationalize the emotions should be countered as it can cause inhibition. The emotional level must only be assessed in relation to other areas of the chart, especially the Ascendant and the Moon sign and their aspects. Making money will be easy for the individual.

Sun Sign Cancer with Venus in Gemini

This adds a much-needed rational streak to near-torrential Cancerian emotion, and steadies the tendency to worry unduly about loved ones. The subject must not be swayed only by love when choosing a partner; intellectual rapport and friendship are essential, as is mental stimulus (outside the family for women, once children are born). Views will be freely and even sharply expressed but Cancerian faithfulness will still be evident. Shrewdness will be shown in business deals.

Sun Sign Leo with Venus in Gemini

Enthusiasm and the need for love and affection are spiced with flirtatiousness, while friendship and a progressive relationship are essential. There is a good blend of well-expressed emotion and a rational approach to joint problems. The partner must be able to enjoy life and be generous both emotionally and financially. Bossiness should be countered, especially towards friends. Extravagance and a clever financial flair are usually complementary.

♋ VENUS IN CANCER

Kindness, sympathy, the expression of true love and affection and a high level of emotion are characteristic. A powerful protective instinct can at times create a claustrophobic atmosphere within a relationship. A tendency to look nostalgically to the past is also frequent, and this may need conscious correction if the subject is not to reach stalemate due to his or her fear of progressive changes. Killing with kindness and moodiness are sometimes present, and the need for a secure relationship is of above-average importance. Ties of friendship will be long-lasting. Love and affection will be focused on the home, and a great deal of money will be spent carefully to make it comfortable – although often cluttered and untidy. Creative cooking and home crafts will be displayed with flair. A safe, steady growth of capital is preferred, and shrewd investments will be made when possible.

Sun Sign Taurus with Venus in Cancer
Passion and sensuality are heightened, with love and affection actively shown. Possessiveness may mar the relationship. The emotional level is extremely high and there may be storms and scenes at times. The subject must learn not to cling to loved ones after a relationship has ended. Look for logic in other areas of the chart – the position of Mercury, perhaps. This is an affectionate but possibly demanding friend. Financial ability and an excellent business sense are likely.

Sun Sign Gemini with Venus in Cancer
This heightens the level of Geminian emotion and, provided the subject doesn't overrationalize the feelings, these will be marvelously and romantically expressed, showing kindness and a cherishing quality. The sex life must be lively and stimulating. The subject is considerate and a good communicator both with friends and loved ones. Financial security can be gained from collecting old or unusual artifacts.

Sun Sign Cancer with Venus in Cancer
The emotional force and expression of love are very powerful, but the inclination to worry over the partner and family is immense, and the Cancerian capacity for caring may also get out of hand with friends. Here the qualities are very much as for Venus in Cancer (see p.255). Shrewdness in business matters is a strong asset.

Sun Sign Leo with Venus in Cancer
The emotional level is very high, and the subject needs a partner to look up to and admire, otherwise there will be a tendency to dominate with a Leo bossiness that can be extremely harmful. Leo sensitivity is greatly increased; this individual will suffer more than seems possible. There will be a great appreciation of quality and the beautiful things in life, with a lot of money spent on them. Comfort, security and quality are important. The sex life will be rich, rewarding and imaginatively expressed. Here is a caring friend with excellent organizing ability.

Sun Sign Virgo with Venus in Cancer
Although there will be considerable emotional resources, there may be shyness and reserve in expressing the feelings. The imagination will be rich, but worry over the loved one's reactions can be inhibiting, especially in young people. There may be a tendency to criticize the partner or be very moody. The household chores or hobbies can be used as an excuse for failing to enjoy the intimacies of a relationship. A clever business sense is likely, but sometimes meanness is present.

♌ Venus in Leo

The fiery, passionate emotion of Leo is expressed to the loved one, and the subject will want to be proud of the partner. Great encouragement will be given to the development of his or her potential, but a tendency to be bossy must be watched. Here is big-heartedness, generosity of spirit and an enjoyment of all aspects of life. The sex life is usually exuberant and must be fulfilling. Loyalty and faithfulness are also usual. An enjoyment of quality and luxury will be shared with loved ones; appreciation of the arts, and even creative potential, will also be present. A tendency towards showiness and a sense of drama may need controlling. This placing encourages a desire to earn a lot of money, principally to add to the richness and enjoyment of life. However, the sense of owning a part of large companies through shares gives considerable satisfaction. Here is a faithful friend whose enthusiasm and optimism are infectious.

Sun Sign Gemini with Venus in Leo
Emotion is heightened, with the subject aiming for a fulfilling and rewarding relationship. He or she may be boastful towards, and about, the partner. Generous, with a sense of occasion and a need for sexual and social variety, this is a fun-loving, if not always faithful, partner. Leo loyalty, however, will help counter Geminian duality. Here is a rewarding and lively friend. Extravagance and impulse-buying can cause financial problems.

Sun Sign Cancer with Venus in Leo
In this placing an extrovert exuberance is added to the Cancerian expression and emotional needs. Constancy and loyalty are important, but Cancerian moodiness and snappiness may combine with Leo bossiness and must be controlled if the individual is to relax and enjoy this sphere of life. Nevertheless, this is a caring and warm-hearted friend. Special collections, maybe of silver, are good investments.

Sun Sign Leo with Venus in Leo
If an over-extravagant expression of emotion can be controlled so that dramatic scenes do not cause problems, here is someone who will look up to and admire a partner, giving much encouragement and support. If bossiness can be exchanged for diplomacy and tact, partnerships should be rewarding. There is usually no lack of sexual enthusiasm, and the sign interpretation (see left) is especially applicable. Money will be spent to enhance the quality of the subject's life.

Sun Sign Virgo with Venus in Leo
This placing bolsters the self-confidence of the rather shy Virgoan. The tendency to be over-talkative when nervous should be controlled. Natural Virgoan modesty can easily clash with Venus in Leo showiness, both sexually and image-wise. This is a lively friend who will want to organize occasions for everyone's benefit. Occasional extravagances should be enjoyed rather than viewed as reasons for guilt.

Sun Sign Libra with Venus in Leo
Venus rules Libra, so there will be some Leonine traits, and the influence of Venus will be strong. Generosity is usual, and if love and affection are lacking the subject may try to buy them with elaborate presents. At his or her best, the individual is romantic with a love of good living, and will give much to a partner both through warm-hearted affection and sex. This is a considerate and sympathetic friend. Although extravagant, money is usually managed quite well.

♍ Venus in Virgo

The critical acumen of Virgo will often be directed towards the partner, and awareness of any tendency to nag or carp is essential if emotional fulfillment is to be achieved. Nevertheless, there is a delightful, natural, unassuming and totally genuine modesty which is charming, whatever the age of the subject. Sexual inhibitions and tensions must be overcome so that the individual can enjoy all aspects of emotional relationships. Just how easy or difficult this is will depend on the signs of Sun, Moon and Ascendant, and to some extent on the influence of Mars. There will be willingness to give practical help to friends and partners whenever necessary. The financial situation may frequently be viewed in a pessimistic way (whether justified or not), with a resulting stinginess. Sometimes, career and emotional relationships are sacrificed for the care of an elderly relative.

Sun Sign Cancer with Venus in Virgo
The Cancerian tendency to worry will be directed toward the partner, and the subject may find it a little difficult to express feelings as freely as is desired. Cancerian moodiness and the critical tendencies of Venus in Virgo should be recognized, and the individual must learn to relax into relationships and derive real pleasure from them, especially as Cancerians have so much to give in this sphere of life. This is a kind, if somewhat critical, friend. Reluctance to part with money is a common characteristic.

Sun Sign Leo with Venus in Virgo
Leo emotions and exuberance are toned down and occasionally aloofness can mask sexual inhibition. Leo bossiness and Virgoan critical tendencies can cause problems, so must be consciously recognized and controlled. There are usually good powers of communication within relationships, and aiming to use these positively will be rewarding. Shared interests and work projects are particularly stimulating. The subject makes a lively and rewarding friend. Flair for investment is common, but the modest needs of Virgo will clash with Leonine extravagance.

Sun Sign Virgo with Venus in Virgo
Self-confidence, especially related to sexual appeal, is not strong. Virgoan modesty will present a charming challenge to prospective lovers, but the subject should learn to break down any barriers that may come between the self and fulfillment in all aspects of relationships. The description of the sign interpretation (see left) is very applicable. Money will be spent with some degree of caution.

Sun Sign Libra with Venus in Virgo
This is not an easy combination, for Libra needs love and harmony while Virgo will tend to be shy of expressing feelings and responding to love. As Venus rules Libra, there will be a powerful element of Virgo present in the individual, and any resulting conflicts must be evaluated and countered. The subject is a lively, talkative, albeit indecisive, friend. Financial affairs are approached in a practical way.

Sun Sign Scorpio with Venus in Virgo
This powerful but tricky combination can make the subject obsessive about sex. Conversely, there may be a clinical attitude, or a feeling that sex is dirty and undesirable. Much will depend on how the Scorpio Sun is aspected, and on the Moon, Ascendant and Mars signs. At its best, this placing makes for an energetic friend and thoughtful partner. Financial flair is considerable.

♎ Venus in Libra

Libra is the second sign ruled by Venus, the influence of which is increased when placed in this sign. The attitude to love is romantic, affectionate and idealistic. The subject may even fall in love with love, but here is someone with such a strong need for a loving relationship that his or her potential may not be fully developed when alone. There is much kindness, sympathy and understanding, with time spent listening to the problems of others and lending moral support. Tact and diplomacy are usual, as is a great love of beauty and a comfortable (sometimes luxurious) lifestyle. Rich food eaten in congenial surroundings can make life worthwhile for someone with this placing. Negatively, there may be resentment, indecision and sybaritism (if laziness is shown elsewhere in the chart). Money will be spent openly and freely, but may be used to buy affection.

Sun Sign Leo with Venus in Libra
This placing will tend to make the subject rather laidback. Leonine generosity is increased, and there will be a tendency to put the loved one a pedestal, increasing the possibility of hurt should the partner fail to measure up to the exacting standards required. The pleasures of the good life will be important and enjoyed, and creative flair may be shown in design or music. As a friend, he or she will make quite sure that every event is an occasion. A great deal of money must be earned, so that it can be spent!

Sun Sign Virgo with Venus in Libra
This placing often helps the shy, not so self-confident Virgoan to relax and enjoy love relationships and other luxuries. It will also ease the harsher, more critical side of Virgo. There is often flair for creative handiwork such as woodcarving or dressmaking, and all such potential must be fully developed. Here is a helpful, sympathetic friend who will enjoy doing good turns for others. The subject will want to work hard for every penny earned, but will not be averse to enjoying the pleasures that extra money can bring.

Sun Sign Libra with Venus in Libra
The influence of Venus is very strong in this placing, adding all the qualities and negative traits mentioned in the sign interpretation (see left). All the attributes of Libra will be considerably strengthened by this placing, especially if the Sun and Venus are in conjunction (see p.215). Money may be extravagantly spent.

Sun Sign Scorpio with Venus in Libra
This adds a colorful, romantic side to the intense passion of Scorpio, increasing sympathy and understanding of partners and encouraging the warm expression of feeling. The liking for comfort and luxury is enhanced, but the resentfulness of this placing can

combine with Scorpio jealousy and must be controlled. Here is a good friend, but one who may become suspicious. Generosity and financial flair will be present.

Sun Sign Sagittarius with Venus in Libra
This gives a sense of romance to the exuberant, enthusiastic Sagittarian who will enjoy the relationship as much as the chase. (Not always the case for people with this Sun sign!) The power of Venus will help to quell Sagittarian restlessness and encourage a philosophical outlook. Financial security is of above-average importance, since creature comforts are sought more than is usual for most Sagittarians.

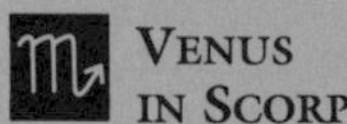

Venus in Scorpio

The need for a rewarding, harmonious and loving relationship is intensified by the passion of Scorpio: sexual desire and romance are both fulfilled and seen to be fulfilled. The jealousy of Scorpio will make itself felt from time to time, and it is possible that an element of resentfulness or an inability to forgive and forget can cause quite serious problems. Even if Venus is the only planet in Scorpio, its energy will need a positive outlet, not only through sex and mutual affection, but also more aesthetic interests. If Neptune shares Scorpio with Venus, romanticism can be disproportionate, as can negative escapism under stress. At best, here is Venus working at its sexiest. A certain rivalry, not to mention occasional jealous scenes, will occur in friendship. Financially, this is an excellent placing, for security is important and there is usually a flair for investment and business, although spending is often considerable.

Sun Sign Virgo with Venus in Scorpio
A conflict can arise between Virgoan modesty and the sexual desires of Venus in Scorpio. While the subject is extremely sexually attractive, he or she may not want to appear so! If self-confidence and relaxation into sexual enjoyment can be developed, the influence of Venus will do much good for the possibly sexually inhibited Virgoan. This is a wholehearted friend who may become overcritical at times. Money is managed well.

Sun Sign Libra with Venus in Scorpio
On the whole, Librans should gain much from this placing of the planet that rules their Sun sign. It will give them an air of romantic mystery, making the women inclined to be femmes fatales! The increased sexuality of this combination weakens the otherwise wholly romantic Libran outlook on love, and adds an intensity and sense of purpose that can otherwise be lacking. This is a friend who wants to enjoy all aspects of life, and will have the capacity to do so. The individual will make money – and spend it!

Sun Sign Scorpio with Venus in Scorpio
The passion of Scorpio will have some very romantic overtones, which will add to the sexual attraction of the subject. Scorpio jealousy will be increased, as will a tendency to become obsessive about the partner's every action. The description of Venus in Scorpio (see left) will apply. Moneymaking acumen will be present.

Sun Sign Sagittarius with Venus in Scorpio
The lively, fiery passion of Sagittarius is increased, with the need for independence clashing somewhat with the Scorpionic intensity of feeling. The individual will probably feel pangs of jealousy from time to time and loathe them, doing everything possible to rationalize these difficult feelings. Awareness of the conflict will help to counter it. The Sagittarian enjoyment of life will be enhanced; here is a friend who will be a marvelous host, full of suggestions for enjoyable experiences. Financial risks will be taken, with mixed results.

Sun Sign Capricorn with Venus in Scorpio
The love life will be taken very seriously, and perhaps the individual will refuse to realize that he or she has some deep, intense and very powerful feelings. There will be loyalty once committed, but there can sometimes be a conflict between emotion and a practical approach to life, resulting in the delaying of commitment. Friends will be put to the test in some way before being fully accepted. Steady financial growth is important and will be achieved.

Venus in Sagittarius

Although considerable enthusiasm and lively emotions will be warmly expressed towards partners, the Sagittarian need for independence may make the individual loath to be too tied to one person. The duality present in this sign will be evident, and more than one relationship may be experienced at any given time. Certainly, love will be enjoyed, and the subject will make life rewarding and exhilarating for the partner, both in bed and out. In turn, the partner needs to respond well, not only sexually but also intellectually. Eventually a philosophical, idealistic element will develop and have its effect on the partner, doing a great deal to instill a more meaningful expression. However, intellectual rapport and friendship, as well as the willingness to enjoy sex, are essential. This is a lively friend who will make life fun. The attitude toward finance may be "Easy come, easy go", perhaps with the emphasis on "go"!

Sun Sign Libra with Venus in Sagittarius
The subject may not seem to care about love, but he or she needs just as much romance as others. This placing helps to rationalize the feelings, however, and the need for intellectual rapport and good friendship, as well as pure romance, is very healthy. This combination is excellent for friendship, easing any Libran tendency to take too much from other people. Professional financial help is advisable.

Sun Sign Scorpio with Venus in Sagittarius
This influence lightens the steamy, rather heavy Scorpio attitude to love and sex, adding a need for intellectual rapport. Much will be expected of partners, but much will be contributed. Scorpio jealousy can clash

with the Sagittarian independence, and a resolution of this conflict is important. Here is a friend who needs to share interests and challenges. Investments will be enjoyed, but a gambling spirit should be controlled.

Sun Sign Sagittarius with Venus in Sagittarius
Sagittarians are the hunters of the zodiac, so when Venus joins the Sun in this sign much attention is given to the emotional chase. Fickleness must be countered. All the attributes of Venus in Sagittarius (see p.258) will be present. If Neptune is also in Sagittarius there will be idealism and romantic reverie. Money may easily slip through the subject's fingers.

Sun Sign Capricorn with Venus in Sagittarius
Although the loyalty and faithfulness of Capricorn is less evident, this is a good placing for those with rather serious Capricorn qualities, helping them to enjoy life and warming their cool emotions. There will be less social climbing in the love life, but a good mind will be deemed important, and the partner will spur on the Capricorn ambitions and aspirations. Friends must share demanding interests. Moneymaking is less important than for other Capricorn groups.

Sun Sign Aquarius with Venus in Sagittarius
The Aquarian spirit will be sympathetic to the independence of Venus in Sagittarius, while the fire of that sign will warm the distant but dynamic attraction of Aquarius. Nevertheless, the liking for individuality will not encourage even the most romantic Aquarian to rush into a long-term commitment. Sexual experiment is usual. There is a wide circle of friends, who often share philanthropic or intellectual interests. Money will be spent erratically, often on silly, trendy things.

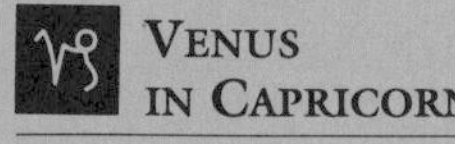

VENUS IN CAPRICORN

Although the worldly ambition associated with Capricorn does not easily blend with the Venusian need to relate and love, when the planet is placed in this sign it gives someone who will, once committed, want to remain faithful and constant. Because of the differing characteristics of the sign and principles of the planet, there can be inhibition in the full expression of feeling, so it is important that, while there may be no desire to gush forth with affirmations of love, the partner really knows how much he or she is loved. Sometimes, in order to make worldly progress, a partner will be chosen as a status symbol of some kind. However, true, constant love should be the aim, with the Capricorn ambition geared towards joint development of the partnership, materially and emotionally. Here is the faithful friend who likes to create an impression. Money is spent in a calculated way, often to show off, yet a careful streak will also be evident.

Sun Sign Scorpio with Venus in Capricorn
This links the deep intensity and passion of Scorpio with the cool calculation of Capricorn. Here are people who will get what they want, but may not consider a partner's feelings carefully or sympathetically. They are demanding friends who will encourage others in their ambitions. Ruthlessness in all areas of life must be countered. Business- and moneymaking abilities are excellent.

Sun Sign Sagittarius with Venus in Capricorn
This calms the passion of Sagittarius, and the love life is taken seriously. The subject is thoughtful and fairly constant (more so than other members of this Sun sign), but there can be conflict between the Sagittarian need for freedom of expression within a relationship and the Capricorn urge to do the right thing. Here is a friend who enjoys demanding challenges. Financial growth can occur through clever and calculated risk-taking.

Sun Sign Capricorn with Venus in Capricorn
Faithfulness and loyalty join with a reserved expression of feeling. The characteristics of Venus in Capricorn (see left) will be very evident. Ambition for material progress must not be so great that the partner and children are neglected as a result.

Sun Sign Aquarius with Venus in Capricorn
The very independent Aquarian lifestyle will cause a reluctance to be committed to an emotional relationship. The romantic tendencies often present in this Sun sign may be suppressed. The impression given is cool and distant, but there are magnetic powers of attraction. Here is a good, faithful friend but someone who will be difficult to know really well. The management of finances may or may not be good, so a balance is needed.

Sun Sign Pisces with Venus in Capricorn
The blending of earth (Capricorn) and water (Pisces) is excellent, since Venus will help steady the gush of Piscean emotion. If a practical approach to love can be achieved there should be no conflict, but the coolness of Venus must be recognized as a positive factor, helping to channel and give an element of caution and common sense in this sphere of life. Here is a kind friend who will offer plenty of sensible suggestions when called upon to help. There will be some fiscal ability but, if Mercury is also in Pisces, professional financial advice is to be recommended.

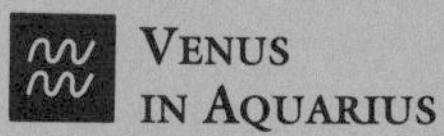

VENUS IN AQUARIUS

This placing contributes more magnetic, film star glamor than any other. Admiration will be thoroughly enjoyed, but conflict can arise between the need for a relationship and the sacrifices that must be made accordingly. At times, these may seem too great, and sometimes a partnership is desired but a partner isn't. Conversely, there is plenty of enjoyable romance here. The individual who uses other areas of his or her chart (Sun, Moon and Ascending signs in particular) and resolves the complexities of this placing will be able to love with idealism and fidelity. Nevertheless, the feelings are coolly expressed and the emotional level must be finally judged by other planetary influences. If there is an aspect between Venus and Mars, sexual expression and enjoyment may be increased. Here is a very kind and helpful friend. He or she is usually good with money but too much may be spent on glitzy, expensive clothes and items for the home.

Sun Sign Sagittarius with Venus in Aquarius
This considerably increases the Sagittarian love of independence yet cools the ardent passions of that sign. However, there is increased fidelity once the subject is committed emotionally. The Sagittarian love of the chase and its challenge is carefully disguised. This placing can also glamorize the usually very casual Sagittarian image. This is a rewarding, warm-hearted friend who will give plenty of positive encouragement. Financial risks may be enjoyed and taken erratically, without due thought.

Sun Sign Capricorn with Venus in Aquarius
This placing can make the aspiring Capricorn type seem rather haughty. Budding relationships may be damaged because the subject feels that no prospective partner is good enough. This may be an excuse to delay commitment and the full expression of emotion, which can be difficult. (The Moon's influence may help.) Here is a faithful and helpful, yet unpredictable, friend. Financially, caution may clash with a desire to live it up.

Sun Sign Aquarius with Venus in Aquarius
This is what Julia calls the "Snow Queen" combination. The subject has dynamic and magnetic powers of attraction, but may be very difficult to know really well. Independence is necessary, but love and admiration are also needed. All the traits described for Venus in Aquarius apply (see p.259). Expensive items may be hard to resist.

Sun Sign Pisces with Venus in Aquarius
Piscean emotion is controlled here, and there is also a good ability to distance the self from the feelings, with the individual relying on intuition. Look, too, for indications of practical common sense. The image is spiced with originality – and too much sparkle at times. Great kindness and charity often result in personal sacrifices. This is a superb, if occasionally forgetful, friend. Professional financial advice is recommended unless business ability is shown elsewhere.

Sun Sign Aries with Venus in Aquarius
Here, the fiery Arian passion is quenched by the cool detachment of Venus, but the Arian need for independence will be complementary. The desire for a permanent relationship may clash with the wish to be fancy-free. A compromise must be reached, helped by a sympathetic partner. Here is a very lively friend who is enthusiastic about joint interests. Financial flair may be present, but hastiness when investing could cause problems.

VENUS IN PISCES

The emotional level is greatly increased and the individual is entirely swayed by emotion in all spheres of life. The subject can all too easily be taken advantage of, and as a result usually learns the hard way, often tending to make the same mistakes (especially emotional ones) time and time again. Look for other indications of a practical approach and rational outlook – Mercury in Capricorn or Aquarius will help. The need to express love and affection is powerful and sincere, albeit sentimental at times. Care is needed that self-deception or a tendency not to face facts is countered. Parents of a child with this placing must firmly encourage truthfulness. Taking the easy way out of difficult situations is common, especially in relationships. Self-confidence may be undermined, especially with regard to the powers of attraction. Charity can become a fault, leading to cashflow problems. This is a tender and caring friend.

Sun Sign Capricorn with Venus in Pisces
This warms the Capricorn heart and softens the attitude towards partners. Social climbing is less pronounced, and time will be spent enjoying relationships and children, rather than worrying about material matters. Capricorn characteristics will counter the gullible emotion of Pisces, adding common sense to the extreme fluidity of the Piscean emotion. Here is a practical and sympathetic friend. In financial affairs, and particularly investments, the intuition should be followed.

Sun Sign Aquarius with Venus in Pisces
This adds to the kind, humanitarian and charitable qualities of Aquarius and warms the emotions, making the subject more responsive and less distant. Emotional involvement is increased, yet Piscean emotion will blend with Aquarian independence. This is an understanding and sympathetic friend. Money may be handled badly – advise professional help.

Sun Sign Pisces with Venus in Pisces
There is a great deal that is beautiful about this placing, but the individual must realize that his or her emotions can dominate all too easily. Too much kindness and sympathy may exist, plus a tendency to become a doormat. Sacrifices may be made to the considerable detriment of the subject. All indications described for Venus in Pisces (see left) will apply very strongly. Financial problems can occur through excessive generosity.

Sun Sign Aries with Venus in Pisces
Here the fire and water emotions are combined, but the fire of Aries gives a natural assertiveness so that inner strength will be added to warmth, kindness and passion. The placing softens the selfishness of Aries and adds understanding and sympathy. There is great sexual exuberance, making for an enthusiastic partner. Both partners and friends will be given positive encouragement. Money-making ideas can sometimes be harmed by an overly enterprising spirit. Look for other indications of practical common sense.

Sun Sign Taurus with Venus in Pisces
This is a delightful combination, giving a gentle but nonetheless deep and meaningful expression of feelings. Taurean possessiveness is less likely to be a stumbling block, but emotional security is important. The emotion of Venus is controlled, creating an individual who is a very caring, passionate and sensual lover. Too much money can be spent on creature comforts.

Venus through the Houses

Venus' influence is increased from the second and seventh houses – the Taurean and Libran houses respectively. Consider the house position of Venus in relation to that of the Sun, since the two planets are always fairly close together. The individual will need to relate to others within the sphere of life ruled by the house in which Venus is placed in the birth chart.

1 VENUS IN THE FIRST HOUSE

The individual has considerable charm and a compelling need to relate to a partner – in other words, to love and be loved. He or she can move gracefully and is socially desirable, due to innate sympathy and kindness. Sometimes laziness is present, or at any rate a laidback attitude to life, which may be feigned. Time will always be made for good, relaxed conversation. The need for harmony and to relate in depth on a one-to-one basis is crucial, and (as is the case when Libra is prominent) psychological wholeness may only be fully achieved once a permanent relationship is established.

The metabolism may be slow, and there will be a languid, rhythmical walk and perhaps a dislike of exercise. If so, interest should be stimulated by stressing the social angle of workouts and so on. As Venus rules the thyroid glands and the metabolism is slow, a weight problem is very possible.

In most respects, the individual is easygoing, but resentfulness can occur. Parents of children with this placing must take care not to spoil them. The closer Venus is to the Ascending degree, the greater the influence that the planet will have.

2 VENUS IN THE SECOND HOUSE

Venus' influence is increased by its presence in the Taurus/Venus house. Acquiring possessions that give aesthetic pleasure and some material security is very important. There is a great love of beauty, and the subject will want to feel and look good, so as to attract love and attention from others.

Taurean possessiveness and the tendency to regard loved ones as belongings should be countered. Generosity is usual but can be used to gain attention and adoration. This is more likely in a basically showy sign such as Leo, and less so in a modest one such as Virgo. There is also a need to improve the financial situation, thereby strengthening the material security that is so essential. Good business sense is likely and investing money will be both intriguing and enjoyable.

3 VENUS IN THE THIRD HOUSE

There is an ability to communicate sympathetically, and a mutual and natural understanding will develop between the subject and his or her close relations. Intellectual challenge is a great pleasure, and difficult topics are often studied slowly and carefully, with considerable success. Large, glossy encyclopedias will be appreciated.

Socializing is important to the subject, who will also enjoy entertaining in a pleasant, relaxed, but mentally stimulating atmosphere.

4 VENUS IN THE FOURTH HOUSE

Great pride is taken in the home, with the subject very keen to make it look beautiful and comfortable and be a haven of peace. Love of the immediate family is also enhanced and increased, but disruption when grownup children leave home can cause problems. There may be a tendency to spoil offspring and to lavish affection and expensive gifts on them.

An above-average identification with, and adoration of, the mother can be present, since the inner child may very much want to be like the subject's mother. He or she will have to come to terms with this in later life, as it can inhibit the personality's development.

5 VENUS IN THE FIFTH HOUSE

Appreciation of the arts is present, and if the birth chart shows creative ability (perhaps for music, fashion design or painting), this placing will certainly enhance it.

The love life will be colorful and is most important, with the subject enjoying much romantic reverie. There will be a tendency to put the loved one on a pedestal, and consequently pain is possible when things go wrong.

A love of luxury and the chance of the subject being stylish and elegant is high, but just how extravagant or trendy he or she is will depend on Venus' sign placing. For instance, if it is in Sagittarius, the clothes will be up to the minute and elegant, but very casual. A fascination with financial risk-taking can be disastrous – advise control of any gambling instincts. Skillful games, such as chess or bridge, can be played with talent and enjoyment.

6 VENUS IN THE SIXTH HOUSE

The desire for exercise is not usually increased but the need may be, since rich food and wine will be enjoyed. There is also a distinct possibility of weight problems which may be thyroid-related, since the metabolism could be slow. The individual will either be very good at following a constant work routine or languid, tending to procrastinate over regular jobs. A steady routine is best, as it can stabilize or even increase the metabolism.

There will be a dislike of working in dirty or unpleasant conditions, although these may be tolerated if the end-product is aesthetically pleasing. For instance, pottery or horticulture could attract. Good manners are important, and the subject will set an excellent example to others but be quick to criticize them over any lapses.

7 VENUS IN THE SEVENTH HOUSE

The planet's influence is increased by its position in this, the Venus/Libra house. The need to share the life with a partner is extremely important, and in order to fulfill it the subject may rush into emotional commitments. The way in which he or she relates to the partner will be in the manner of Venus' sign placing, but this will only emerge in the personal relationship.

The influence of the partner must not encroach upon the subject's own personality. This is because, at times, the identity will be lost or merged with that of the partner, through pure love, affection and admiration. The manner of this will depend on the Venus sign. A well-rounded relationship should be aimed for, encompassing friendship, good communication and some element of working together for joint progress as well as love, harmony and a happy sex life.

If Venus is inhibited by the Moon, Saturn or Uranus, the subject should be encouraged to work harder at the relationship – there may be a tendency to give up when it goes wrong. Again, the manner and likelihood of this will be shown by Venus' sign placing.

8 Venus in the Eighth House

This placing increases the intensity of the individual's emotions and passions and sometimes jealous feelings can disrupt partnerships. The sex life is usually rich and rewarding unless Venus is inhibited by Saturn or Pluto, in which case it may be cramped by psychological problems that can only be resolved by in-depth discussion with a partner, or, if really persistent, a sex therapist.

If Venus is in a water sign the intuition will be considerably increased, but in all cases there is insight and sympathy. The subject may also identify with other people's problems and be able to analyze them, or indeed, his or her own difficulties. By tradition this is a fortunate placing for inheritance, and there is often a shrewd business sense and flair for investment.

9 Venus in the Ninth House

There will be a great love of and need for travel, with the subject tending to fall in love with foreign countries and daydream about them. Quite often romantic episodes occur abroad. Tradition also decrees that the subject will marry someone from overseas and live abroad, and this is often the case.

A wisely relaxed and pleasantly philosophical attitude toward life is very apparent, and the individual will want to live in an idealistic world that is beautiful and peaceful. If he or she is well-motivated and energetic (look to the Ascendant and Mars), action will be taken along these lines – campaigning for peace, for example. The college years will be enjoyable and rewarding, although not necessarily as a result of hard work. Instead, the experiences undergone there will have an above-average impact on the subject. Sometimes a love relationship with a professor can prove colorful.

10 Venus in the Tenth House

This is excellent for developing good relationships with colleagues. If the subject holds a managerial or administrative position he or she will be less likely to be a lonely figure. However, coping with onerous responsibilities can be daunting. This should be borne in mind when promotion is offered, for here is someone who is better at working with others than alone, although prestige is enjoyed, and there is usually an ability to delegate.

Great pride in the profession is common, and the subject needs a near-emotional relationship with the career in order to feel fulfilled. Financial gain is very important but must not be the only motivation. Sometimes this placing is not very good for freelance workers, who can become lazy and undisciplined. Those who are not in a profession will have some idealistic aspirations that blend with those of the partner. The ability to identify with the partner's ambitions, giving much support and encouragement, is also likely.

11 Venus in the Eleventh House

The social life will be much enjoyed and very important to the individual, who will have a great many friends and a very large number of acquaintances. Committee work will be sincerely enjoyed, as will furthering the aims of the particular groups and societies which develop the subject's special interests. He or she will thrive on the admiration of others when praised for special efforts.

There is a genuine desire to please, and a flair for entertaining or organizing social events which not only give pleasure to the participants but also raise money for the relief of suffering and give the subject much satisfaction.

12 Venus in the Twelfth House

There can be great secrecy about love relationships and often, due to inhibition and shyness, the subject is unable to express his or her feelings, resulting in silent passion and adulation from a distance. If this happens, a tendency to fantasize will develop and, while this is usually very healthy for most people, it may get out of hand in this case. The subject can also become isolated. Under stress, comfort may be sought from eating or drinking too much.

Religious faith is sometimes strengthened, with a love of the Deity and a sense of vocation being used to suppress sexual and emotional relationships. An aesthetic or creative interest which is carried on in peace and quiet will be good for the individual, especially if it brings concrete results. The influence of Venus is strengthened considerably if it is in conjunction with the Ascendant.

♀ Venus Progressed through the Houses

At most, Venus will progress through three houses during a lifetime. The effect of its progress from one house to the next will be very subtle, with the subject perhaps merely becoming more aware of, and attracted to, the concerns of the house into which the planet has progressed. There should be enhanced enjoyment in the sphere of life influenced by the house. For instance, when Venus enters the tenth house, the career will become more fulfilling and happier than before.

The Aspects of Venus

Venus is a beneficial planet, so its effect is totally negative unless it exaggerates the action of the planet it contacts. Some caution is needed, however, since Venus can bestow too much charm, laziness and a tendency to "ride" others. On the whole these aspects will enhance the subject's expression of love and ability to cope with money and possessions.

For Venus' aspects to the Sun see the Sun's aspects to Venus, p.215.

For Venus' aspects to the Moon see the Moon's aspects to Venus, p.233.

For Venus' aspects to Mercury see Mercury's aspects to Venus, p.248.

♂ Venus' Aspects to Mars

Conjunction

This aspect enhances the sexual appeal and enjoyment of sexual relationships. Traditionally, Mars tends to coarsen the influence of Venus while Venus refines that of Mars, and this is often true. Even so, these two polar planets seem to work well in conjunction, adding exuberance, sexual appetite and enthusiasm while helping the individual to be sensitive to the partner's wishes and making him or her truly affectionate.

Note the sign influence: the attitude toward love and sex will be very much in the manner of the sign in which the conjunction falls. It will considerably strengthen the characteristics of the Sun sign should it fall in the same sign as that of the Sun.

Positive aspects

These work in much the same way as the conjunction, often with an emphasis on the element concerned. You should therefore consider whether the subject will tend to take an intellectual, rather detached attitude towards love and sex (air), will need security and perhaps be fairly conventional (earth), be enthusiastic and passionate (fire), or be very emotional and sensual (water).

Negative aspects

These also enliven the attitude towards love and sex and often increase the desire – but sometimes there is tension and, as a result, the ability to relax and really enjoy love and sex will depend on some effort being made. In some cases emotional problems may be suppressed, especially if the Moon receives negative aspects from Saturn, Uranus or Pluto. Sometimes the individual is a victim of undue unkindness from others and has to develop a thick skin in order to cope with this.

It will be easier if Mars is the stronger planet in the chart as a whole, and more difficult if Venus dominates (this may increase the subject's sensitivity to the statements and reactions of others).

♂ Progressed Aspects between Venus and Mars

Conjunction

Almost inevitably, there will be an emphasis on the love life under this planetary influence. Sometimes this means an enjoyable love affair that does not last, and at other times it can be something more permanent.

Should the conjunction occur when important indications of change are also working in the progressed chart, there is a likelihood that the relationship will last. If the progression is unsupported by, say, a change of Sun sign or Ascendant, or perhaps the Saturn Return, then the relationship may be short-lived, "just one of those things". Nevertheless, an enjoyable period seems likely.

Positive aspects

The effects of these are very much as described for the conjunction, with the possibility that things will go according to plan provided there are no really disruptive transits or other indications of long-term delays or frustrations. Assess whether any new relationship formed at this time is likely to last or not (see above).

Negative aspects

These herald a tricky period as far as the love life is concerned. Warn your subject that there may be some strain and tension causing problems; there could be upsetting quarrels from time to time.

Some steadying positive transits from Saturn to the Moon, or progressed aspects from the Moon to Saturn, could be really beneficial during these progressions, since they will cool the emotions, countering any tendencies to premature action which may otherwise be likely during this period.

♃ Venus' Aspects to Jupiter

Conjunction

This contributes charm and generosity and makes the subject warm and affectionate – and popular! Sometimes there is a tendency to be sybaritic and, especially if the chart has a preponderance of trine and sextile aspects, this configuration will add to an existing inclination to be too charming. As a result, the individual will tend to "ride" other people.

At its best this gives a philosophical and idealistic outlook. If the conjunction falls in a sign which bestows creativity, the influence will support it. Sometimes there is a leaning towards literature. This aspect is also good for business deals between the sexes.

Positive aspects

The subject will be very popular and attractive, and may also have a pleasant and amusing turn of phrase. These aspects are particularly useful for those who deal with the general public. They also increase the chance of the individual living to a ripe old age. Usually there are few financial problems.

Negative aspects

Because both Venus and Jupiter are said to be beneficial planets, little strain should result from any negative aspects between the two. However, restlessness and sometimes discontent will mar the subject's happiness from time to time. Recklessness, sometimes in investments, can occur, and overindulgence in food or drink may lead to indigestion and weight gain.

Progressed Aspects between Venus and Jupiter

Conjunction
This should herald a period of prosperity and happiness, but warn the subject of any tendencies towards over-generosity or extravagance should extra good fortune come along.

Look at Jupiter's transits. This progressed aspect will be most powerful if it coincides with Jupiter transits to the Sun, Moon, Ascendant or Midheaven, or a Jupiter Return. Even so, a friendly caution will not come amiss, especially if the tenor of the chart is generally extroverted. A progressive period seems very likely, and will be almost certain if Venus or Jupiter are personalized in the birth chart.

Positive aspects
These are almost as powerful as the conjunction, but there is less chance of restlessness or over-extravagance, since the influence may not be quite as strong (unless either planet is personalized in the birth chart). Supporting influences from a transitting Jupiter will assist these aspects enormously.

Negative aspects
Care is needed that in a weak moment large sums of money are not wasted or lent to others with disastrous results. There will also be tendencies towards restlessness and perhaps lapses of judgement when making decisions about love or money. Steadying influences from Saturn – especially transitting trines to Sun or Moon – will help.

Look out for any negative lunar progressions to Jupiter during the year or so that these aspects are exact, as they could magnify the above weaknesses. The diet should be carefully checked from time to time, since irritability – perhaps due to over-eating or drinking when problems become oppressive – can add to existing difficulties.

Venus' Aspects to Saturn

Conjunction
This is a focal point as far as the individual's attitude to personal relationships is concerned, and as a result the affections will be cooled. There can often be shyness and inhibition, so that being forthcoming and responsive in a naturally relaxed way will not be easy. Often there is above-average disappointment in the love life.

To counter these lowering traits it will help if the subject is certain of his or her ground before commitment, since emotional security is essential. Sometimes there is an attraction to an older partner. A powerful sense of duty can prevent the formation of a permanent relationship, for instance with the subject devoting love, time and energy to looking after an elderly parent instead. The real reason, however, may be a deep-rooted inhibition.

Positive aspects
These are less difficult than the conjunction, but often they contribute financial hardship so that whatever is greatly desired (Venus) is frustrated (Saturn). This energy will be particularly active if Venus occupies a luxury-loving sign such as Taurus, Leo or Libra. Once emotional security is established, the individual will develop the ability to be very faithful. Even so, these aspects are inhibiting.

Negative aspects
These will have the same restrictive effect, if not an even greater one, than the conjunction. However, if drive and emotional energy are shown in other areas of the chart the subject will have sufficient strength of will to overcome the problem. Should the Sun or Moon make a positive aspect to Pluto, or Pluto make one to the Ascendant, the overcoming of inhibition through therapy will be worth encouraging.

Progressed Aspects between Venus and Saturn

Conjunction
All aspects between these two planets will have a rather depressive effect on emotional relationships. With the conjunction it is possible that the subject will come through a difficult period, but in the end he or she will benefit from the experience. However, the long-term effect can very often be mitigated by powerful, positive transits from Jupiter to Venus, any personal planet, or the Ascendant. This will be a key period if Saturn makes contact by transit with the natal Venus. The subject should be encouraged to take things calmly and to be practical.

Very often this progression means that a couple will be separated for a while, usually due to career or family commitments. The end result may be more money and increased prestige.

Positive aspects
These may evoke in the subject a more serious attitude towards his or her relationships. Sometimes they herald a long-term commitment – especially if they coincide with a change of Sun sign, Ascendant, or a Saturn Return.

Plans could be delayed, perhaps those concerning house purchase or finance. This is not the happiest of progressions, but it can stabilize and cool over-ardent, impulsive and passionate feelings, adding common sense just when it is most needed.

Negative aspects
If transits and lunar progressions show a preponderance of Saturn, Uranus or Pluto, the subject is likely to experience quite a lot of frustration and delay during this period. Sometimes he or she will make important changes.

Assess just how practical and decisive the subject is, since these qualities will be called upon. If a worrier (with Cancer or Virgo as Sun, Moon or Ascendant signs), encourage the use of positive traits (see the sign interpretations) as steadying influences. Obviously, if transits are positive – i.e. help from Jupiter – and there are invigorating progressed lunar aspects to Mars and the personal planets, the heaviness of the Venus/Saturn contact will be greatly reduced.

Venus' Aspects to Uranus

Conjunction
There is usually a high level of excitable emotional tension that needs to be positively expressed – perhaps creatively or through some unusual and original interest.

Considerable personal magnetism and sex appeal are likely, but the subject will tend to distance him- or herself from a deep and fulfilling commitment. Self-will can be present, and perhaps an element of perversity. If foolhardiness is shown in other areas of the chart (look to Mars) this aspect will exacerbate it. When the conjunction is activated by transits life is likely to become unexpectedly and very suddenly eventful.

Positive aspects
These are similar to the conjunction in effect, but less forceful, adding much originality and sometimes creativity (which may be expressed in a very trendy way, with an emphasis on literature, music or design). Eccentricity is possible, and a hint of perversity and self-will is not unknown. The emotions will definitely be cooled by these aspects, with the subject subtly distancing him- or herself from partners.

Negative aspects
These usually show considerable strain and tension, expressed in the subject's attitude towards his or her relationships. It is often almost impossible for the individual really to relax, and as a result he can be difficult at times, showing self-will to the point of saying one thing and then proceeding to do precisely the opposite.

Parents of children with this aspect may do well, when correcting them, to suggest the exact opposite of what they really want, in order to obtain the desired result. Relaxation techniques such as yoga are helpful when the subject is under stress.

Progressed Aspects between Venus and Uranus

Conjunction
This is a dynamic force which may well focus on the love life, with the subject falling in love at first sight. However, when interpreting, do look for indications of long-term change and some steadying transits.

It is always wise to advise delaying marriage or a permanent commitment until the progression has passed; especially if the above-mentioned indications are not giving long-term support, the chances are that the relationship will be sweet and exciting, but not really enduring (unless Venus or Uranus are personal planets).

Positive aspects
The effect of these will be much as above, with the possibility of greater fun and memorable experiences, and an accent on excitement rather than tension. The chances of a lasting commitment being made, however, are not increased, unless the support is present (see above) or Venus and/or Uranus are personal planets.

Negative aspects
These could indicate a very tricky period; a time when the individual might go off the rails – usually for fun, and sometimes with disastrous consequences. Care is needed, then: the highly-powered, tense, excited mood inspired by these aspects can lead to drastic action which may well be regretted at a later date.

Encourage your subject to be calm (it won't be easy!); any tendency to take drastic or perverse action will lead to strain. Look to the transits to see whether the progression will be strengthened or eased.

Venus' Aspects to Neptune

Conjunction
A very romantic and idealistic attitude towards love, but also an increased sensitivity, means there will often be an above-average number of heartbreaks which the subject must learn to ameliorate by using other, stronger planetary indications. These tendencies are most likely when the conjunction falls in Libra. There will also be an appreciation of beauty, art, and all things aesthetic, and many astrologers have noted a particular fondness for animals (this seems most likely for those with the conjunction in Sagittarius).

The constitution may be weakened by this aspect, perhaps because it reduces the will, so that fondness for certain favorite foods or drinks will be difficult to resist.

Positive aspects
These contribute a great deal of sympathy and kindness, and will have a softening effect on the personality – especially if the chart shows the subject to be down to earth, practical and materialistic. He or she will tend not to admit to these qualities, which may be considered rather soppy!

If artistic ability is shown in other areas, these aspects – especially the trine – will definitely increase that potential, which may be expressed musically. An inclination to daydream, perhaps in a somewhat visionary way, can also be present.

Negative aspects
If restlessness is indicated in other areas of the chart, these contacts will increase it, burdening the character with inner discontent. It is important to consult the positions of the Sun and Moon: should they also be in negative aspect these traits could be quite a serious problem for the subject, who may tend to drift from job to job, perhaps from home to home, never resting content but always staying hopeful.

The sensitivity shown in the conjunction is increased, and while there will still be an idealistic attitude to love, the emotions tend to overwhelm the individual, sometimes in a rather misguided way. This is most likely if Neptune is in Scorpio.

Progressed Aspects between Venus and Neptune

Conjunction
If there are not any really heavy, negative transits, this progression promises a happy period when romance is in the air. But while enjoying considerable romantic reveries and experiences, the subject must try not to get too carried away because, by the very nature of the conjunction, the feelings will be heightened and sensitized. Try to encourage the keeping of at least one foot on the ground.

Positive aspects
The effect of these is very much as for the conjunction, although it may be even more romantic and enjoyable – again look to the transits. If indications of change are operative – such as the progressed Sun or Ascendant changing signs, or the Saturn Return – then according to one astrologer, life will be "as merry as a wedding bell"!

If none of these indications apply, and due to other stronger influences the individual is not experiencing a progressive period, perhaps he or she should try not to give up or make excuses for this lack of progress.

Negative aspects

Care is needed that the individual does not insist on wearing rose-colored glasses, especially with regard to emotional relationships or misplaced feelings of love. Things may not be as they seem, and although there could be considerable happiness great care is needed, since much disappointment might be the eventual outcome. There may also be financial confusion.

There really is a need for caution, especially over love and money. Taking the easy way out simply won't work, and self-deception and coverups must be avoided.

Venus' Aspects to Pluto

Conjunction

The individual will tend to fall in love very deeply and passionately. This will be fine, provided that his or her powerful emotions can be positively channeled and love is reciprocated.

The need for sexual fulfillment is also very high, but all will be well if it can be given full and rewarding expression with the help of a sympathetic partner. However, there may be problems should the conjunction be aspected by Saturn, or if Uranus joins the conjunction of Venus and Pluto (in which case all three planets will probably be in Virgo). The subject may find that therapy is necessary in order to clear any psychological blockages.

Venus and Pluto have a bearing on finances, so this powerful conjunction sometimes gives a flair for investment, and a financial ability which may be usefully employed by the individual in his or her career.

Positive aspects

The emotional level is high and fulfilling expression of this is essential. In addition there are considerable powers of attraction and often a seductive, smolderingly sexy look, especially if Venus is in Scorpio. (We go hot all over to think of the effect these aspects will have on the looks of the young people with Pluto in Scorpio!)

Negative aspects

These are difficult and can sometimes prevent a positive flow of emotion. Intensity and passion are present, but it may be difficult for the subject to talk problems over with sympathetic friends, so professional counseling is sometimes necessary.

Other planetary influences may overrule the effect of this aspect; study the chart very carefully with this in mind. If there are indications of inhibition, shyness or worry, sympathetic advice and counseling may be needed.

Progressed Aspects between Venus and Pluto

Conjunction

This is a difficult trend; the individual may fall in love, but perhaps the feelings will not be reciprocated. There is little that can be done except to try to develop a philosophical attitude and divert the mind by concentrating on meaningful interests of quite a different nature. Easy transits will give periods of relief, and it is during these times that progress will be made – but usually not towards the object of the affections. As ever, time will be the best healer.

Positive aspects

The individual will probably be deeply in love during this period, and show extremely intense and meaningful feelings toward the partner. Sexual satisfaction should give the subject considerable pleasure.

However, we never really trust Pluto, so examine what that planet is up to as it moves round the sky; the transits it makes to the subject's natal planets will have a crucial effect during the life of this progression. If these transits block, there could, even with these positive progressions, be difficulties and frustrations ahead. The influence might focus on finance – an inheritance or a good business deal, perhaps. This would also be a good time at which to take out insurance.

Negative aspects

At least one sphere of life will probably grind to a halt at this time. The influence may cause considerable emotional problems, only surfacing when there are transits from Saturn, Uranus or Pluto to the personal planets. There could be financial difficulties, with much-needed money, promised or earned, simply not materializing.

Great care is essential in all financial dealings and contracts, and the commitment of capital must be discussed carefully with knowledgeable and disinterested professionals.

Venus' Aspects to the Ascendant

Conjunction

If Venus falls in the first house its influence will add an important dimension to the personality, and the whole of the Ascendant characteristics will be influenced. The individual will be warm and lovingly affectionate, and will need, and probably create, a peaceful and harmonious life. However, he or she will not become completely whole in a psychological sense until established in an emotionally and, to a certain extent materially, secure partnership.

Everything that is beautiful will be appreciated, and artistic ability will be present, if the rising sign is that way inclined. Sometimes the metabolism is slow and a rather languid manner is projected by the individual.

If Venus is afflicted by negative aspects from Mars, Saturn, Uranus or Pluto, there could be health problems, perhaps linked to mild kidney disorders – these will probably take the form of headaches. If there is a negative aspect from Neptune, care is needed that overindulgence in food and/or drink does not cause weight gain or urinary difficulties, which also originate from the kidneys.

If Venus is in the twelfth house there can be reclusive or escapist tendencies. Reread Venus in the twelfth house (see p.262) since this influence is now increased. On the other hand, if Venus falls in the first house, read the interpretation of that placing (see p.261), since you will find that those tendencies will also be increased.

Positive aspects

These add warm affection and the need to give and receive love. The individual is sympathetic and understanding, with an appreciation of all that is beautiful and luxurious in life. A full and rewarding social life will be enjoyed, and satisfaction gained from giving other people pleasure.

Negative aspects
Sometimes these make the individual extravagant and self-indulgent. The negative Venus traits of resentfulness and indecisiveness can also be present. If the opposition falls with Venus in the seventh house, although the planet is particularly well-placed in this, its own house, there may be a tendency to expect far too much from the partner, and to overindulge him or her with a rather stifling love and generosity. It will be as though the subject has to buy affection to be really assured of the security of the relationship.

If Venus is in the sixth house, look out for health problems due to lack of exercise or an overrich diet that is causing weight gain; comfort-eating may be an expression of the lack of emotional security.

Progressed Aspects between Venus and the Ascendant

Conjunction
This is a time when the emotional life should be particularly rich and rewarding. Very often this indicates a commitment to marriage or to a permanent relationship. If this is not the case, there may be strong involvement in a compelling interest, study or vocation. This is a rewarding and happy period, emotionally, spiritually and often financially.

Positive aspects
The effects of these are very much as those described for the conjunction, but these progressions are less dynamic and therefore need support from other easy, beneficial influences. They should indicate happy, progressive and enjoyable experiences and events for the individual during the period in which they are operative.

Negative aspects
There will be a tendency for the subject to overreact emotionally or to misplace affection. Because the feelings will be so sensitive, he or she can be more easily hurt and upset than usual. Harsh words, especially from loved ones, will hit very hard. Financial problems can also occur, often due to overspending.

The diet should be carefully controlled and the individual must not be allowed to become languid and self-indulgent, or to give up on life in any way during this time. Other progressions, transits and lunar directions may counter or accentuate these negative possibilities.

Venus' Aspects to the Midheaven

Conjunction
This aspect makes for a kind and considerate colleague who, when promoted, will not distance him- or herself from subordinates, but will always listen sympathetically to their opinions and problems. Here is someone who is better working in a team than alone.

If there is no profession, the individual will see to it that aspirations and ambitions are sympathetic to those of the partner or loved ones. The placing is not at all good for the freelance worker, who may find it difficult to keep to a routine or discipline, being far too easily distracted from the job in hand and tending generally to procrastinate over starting work. The Midheaven sign may help counter this tendency – but it will only help, not resolve the problem.

Consider Venus' influence on the choice of career. All luxury trades, the beauty business or creative work may well appeal and be fulfilling. Dirty, unpleasant working conditions will be loathed. There will be an identification with Venusian traits.

Positive aspects
The effect of these is much as for above, but these aspects are easier than the conjunction for those who are self-employed.

Pleasant working conditions are important and the work itself must be enjoyable and satisfying. If it is dull and routine, a good rapport with colleagues will be an excellent corrective, as will a rewarding social life, perhaps organized by the firm. These aspects usually encourage good relationships with parents.

Negative aspects
Sometimes the individual must work in uncongenial conditions or at an unrewarding job. There may be a tendency to overreact to conditions and colleagues' attitudes, sometimes getting matters out of perspective so that discontent and resentfulness mar the working life of the subject. Arrogance and conceit can also cause conflict with colleagues.

Progressed Aspects between Venus and the Midheaven

Conjunction
This should prove to be a very rewarding period when aspirations and ambitions will reach fruition not only in the career but often in the love life too. This will take on a new and rewarding expression, with the admired one reciprocating the subject's emotions in the desired manner.

A progressive, happy and rewarding period is likely, especially if transits and lunar progressions support this tendency. An important milestone may also be indicated by this conjunction, on which the individual will look back with considerable nostalgia.

Positive aspects
These have an effect similar to the conjunction but are rather less potent. Nevertheless, these very positive indications will certainly be beneficial, and are often indicative of progress and happiness in the love life and where the aspirations of the individual are concerned. Ideals can be achieved and relationships should be rewarding and memorable.

Negative aspects
There is a distinct possibility during this time that the individual will be let down – either by a close colleague or a lover. Other people's reactions may become far less sympathetic than usual, perhaps because of the way in which the subject has behaved.

A difficult period seems likely, but one during which faults and maybe indiscretions will be recognized and a certain amount of reformation will take place, the individual having learned his or her lesson the hard way.

♀ The Transits of Venus

Because they are so fleeting, many astrologers do not calculate or interpret the transits of Venus. However, we have found them very useful. Their influence, lasting for two to four days, usually makes for rewarding and enjoyable events and experiences which add a gloss to the social life, and emphasize all manner of the more pleasurable elements of life. Since Venus is such an easy, pleasant planet, most of its minor influences (for so these transits must be considered) do little harm. Where necessary, we suggest the negative indications of these transits.

Calculate only conjunctions and oppositions to all planets, the Ascendant and Midheaven. You will often find that little clusters of these occur quite close together, usually indicating a time when life is more fun than usual, even if, sadly, Venus is not well-placed in the birth chart.

In such cases, where there are negative traits indicated in the birth chart, there is a chance that they will surface when Venus makes an opposition transit to the Sun, Moon, chart-ruler, Ascendant, Midheaven or to its own natal position. It is only fair to warn the subject of this likelihood.

Above all remember that the influences, tiny though they are, are planetary energies to be used, and that if they can be utilized they will be beneficial. Venus, like most planets, seems to enjoy being given a tiny push in the direction in which we want her to go!

Venus' transits to the Sun
This is a time when the subject should show off a little, dress up in his or her best and go out and have fun – he or she will be looking fantastic. Too much money may be spent, but in very enjoyable ways. It is also a good time to entertain others.

Venus' transits to the Moon
The subject will be feeling romantic and nostalgic and will respond well to his or her loved one's suggestions. He should freely express feelings and emotions, put worries aside and relax. Organizing a special dinner for a lover will be enjoyable.

Venus' transits to Mercury
It will be enjoyable to get in touch with friends who have not been seen for some time. A good bargain may be struck under this influence. Long-distance telephone calls could be an expensive, but nonetheless enjoyable, indulgence during these transits!

Venus' transits to Mars
These signify a fun, romantic and sexy interlude, but the individual should be careful not to become possessive or quarrelsome – he or she may feel like rocking the boat, but in doing so it could be completely capsized!

Venus' transits to Jupiter
On several occasions the subject may go out, or be taken out, for rather rich meals. These will be extremely enjoyable but may result in hangovers or indigestion. A good supply of bicarbonate of soda may be needed. This is certainly not the time to start a diet!

Venus' transits to Saturn
Venus is in a serious mood here, but this is a good time for making long-term plans with a partner. Sometimes the individual will be in a rather bad mood for a few days, and should not allow frustration to get the upper hand. Unless there are a lot of negative transits at the same time these feelings will definitely pass. An older person may prove to be demanding and tiring. This is a good time to fast or diet.

Venus' transits to Uranus
The subject will be especially dynamic and attractive to the opposite sex during these transits, and could have a great deal of fun. However, care is needed, as emotional tension can cause unexpected but temporary problems.

Venus' transits to Neptune
These are very romantic influences. However, the individual should be careful not to get too carried away but to keep in touch with reality instead. Old "weepy" films, ballet and poetry will be particularly enjoyable during this time.

Venus' transits to Pluto
During this period the subject may feel frustrated because something or someone is blocking his or her progress. The time may be right for bringing the problem into the open and making a fresh start in a minor way. The influence alone is not strong enough to have a long-term or important effect on big issues, but minor domestic crises could be resolved. The subject should be on the alert for financial problems that are related to tax or insurance matters.

Venus' transits to the Ascendant
This is a time for spoiling oneself, perhaps visiting a favorite department store, buying a new outfit (there may be plenty of choice), having a beauty treatment or even a change of image. It may be difficult to keep to a diet during this enjoyably indulgent transit.

Venus' transits to the Midheaven
Suggest that your subject does nothing, and keeps some time free, since he or she is likely to get a surprise, perhaps being asked out at the last minute or unexpectedly meeting a friend who has not been seen for a long time. If Venus is the ruling planet, this tiny influence could do the subject's career a power of good.

Venus' transits to its own position
Everything that the Venus sign suggests, and all that is influenced by the planet and its house position, will be enjoyably emphasized at this time, so look to the birth chart for more information. Encourage the subject to concentrate on the matters of the house in which Venus is placed.

Mars through the Signs

Because Mars' orbit is further from the Sun than that of the Earth, it can fall in any sign of the zodiac (unlike Mercury and Venus which are always relatively near the Sun). The planet influences our physical energy levels, assertiveness, competitiveness and sex drives. Mars also shows how easily we are roused to anger, for it governs the flow of adrenalin in our systems.

MARS IN ARIES

Aries is the sign that Mars rules, and when in this sign, the planet becomes a strong focal point of a chart. As a result, when interpreting this placing Mars should be considered second in importance to the influence of the ruling planet. It will bestow a powerful physical energy level which must be positively expressed. If there is no outlet through sports or another physically demanding activity, the system will stagnate, with the individual becoming restless and unfulfilled. The need to win, to be first, will be very important, and there should be no lack of drive. However, if Mars makes any aspect to Saturn or negative aspects to Uranus or Pluto, these should be studied with particular care, since they will inhibit the flow of energy.

Assertive action

These possibilities aside, the influence of Mars from its own sign is very pure, and will powerfully invigorate the individual, making him or her very much a "get up and go" type who will encourage loved ones also to take bold, assertive action. If they do not respond, the subject is likely to take the upper hand and force issues. There will, however, be a strong tendency to lack consideration for others' feelings and needs, forcing others (and especially the partner, if he or she lacks confidence and assertiveness) to take what is believed to be the right action. If tact, diplomacy and sensitivity to the needs of others are present elsewhere in the chart they will help counter the overzealous pushiness of this placing. If not, there can be problems, sometimes causing considerable embarrassment to others. So, encouragement is needed to be tactful and thoughtful.

The sex drive is powerfully increased by this placing, which also adds a strong emotional passion – but one that is simple and straightforward rather than seething, smoldering, intense or distorted by psychological twists and turns. The desire for motherhood can also be increased. The individual is usually uncomplicated, reducing apparently complex problems to a few simple components.

When the energy from Mars in Aries is flowing and the individual is happily occupied with plenty of varied interests, all will be well, but the stagnating effect mentioned above will provoke health problems if it is allowed to persist. Usually, however, the subject will not allow this to happen.

Headaches will occur all too often, as will outbursts of Martian anger – a rapid loss of temper and a sudden raging storm that is over as quickly as it began. Resentfulness is not usual.

MARS IN TAURUS

There is plenty of passion here, and an abundant sex-drive will be expressed with Taurean warmth. Here is a sensuous and affectionate lover who is sometimes possessive. If Mars is unafflicted there will be plenty of energy, used in a controlled, steady way.

Once anger is aroused, the rage of these subjects is only too obvious. It will take much provocation to reach this state, for Taurean patience will steady the Martian influence but, because Mars quickens action, once their adrenalin is flowing those angry and heated feelings will be shown in no uncertain terms. These people must understand that, while such outbursts may be justified, they can cause great damage to those on the receiving end, for their feelings may be expressed far more passionately than they realize.

At its best this placing adds determination, firmness and the ability to work very hard and tenaciously at both career and spare-time interests. Sometimes these qualities can develop into stubbornness, and Mars will definitely increase it if this trait is indicated elsewhere. In a chart dominated by earth signs, the more adventurous side of Mars is slowed down, so it is important to look out for any tendency to get stuck in a rut. Overadherence to routine (even with a lively planet like this) and a Taurean need for emotional and financial security will both be evident. A great deal of energy will be spent in making and spending money.

Strength and fitness

This is a marvelous placing for those who participate in heavy team games or the heavier sports in general – boxing, wrestling or weightlifting, for instance. Thinking of the Venus influence on Taurus, this will be a good, strong placing for a dancer, since discipline and routine are essential for such a profession and, for the men, a great deal of weightlifting is involved – ballerinas are, after all very much flesh and blood! The effect on health will be a tendency to feverishness and a vulnerability to throat infections.

MARS IN GEMINI

This placing stimulates the mind, although many astrologers have found that Mars is not well placed in this sign, as it is not physically invigorating. We do not necessarily agree, provided that some kind of intellectual motivation for physical action is shown. It is important for the individual to exercise the body as well as the mind (as is the case with everyone), but he or she may not be particularly inclined to do so unless some sort of intellectual challenge is involved. Many forms of exercise will be tried, but most will be deemed boring. Encourage your subject to find one which satisfies his intellectual and physical needs, and to stick to it. If this does not happen, restlessness will build up, bringing a rather sharp bad temper and irritability that will be directed not only towards others but also to the self, through considerable self-criticism. Energy may be dissipated through too many changes of direction, both in life in general and on a day-to-day basis. This will obviously lead to feelings of dissatisfaction, so look to other stabilizing areas of the chart for a steadier approach and sense of discipline; this influence can then be expressed in a more controlled and practical way.

Active occupation
Quite a strong element of versatility is usually present, and the key to getting the very best out of this placing is to remember that, because total relaxation is not usually enjoyed (again because it is considered boring), a change of occupation will be most beneficial. If heavy physical demands are made on the subject during the working day he or she should invite intellectual challenges in the evening, or vice versa, remembering, of course, that the inclination to make too many changes must be controlled.

The arms and hands are vulnerable so the subject should be encouraged to wear protective gloves when gardening or doing rough chores, and to be very careful when handling sharp tools or hot dishes – especially when Mars is making transits to the personal planets or the Ascendant.

As far as the sex life is concerned, here is a lively, experimental partner who will enjoy a rewarding sex life from youth right through to old age. The attitude towards sex will be lighthearted: it is fun, and to be enjoyed. This placing tends to take some of the steamy passion out of this sphere of life, but the subject will nevertheless be an energetic and often athletic lover, which in turn will help to keep the partner equally energetic, youthful, and athletic!

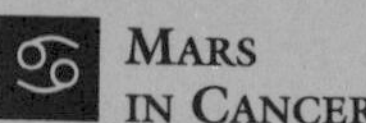

MARS IN CANCER

The energy of Mars is expressed emotionally and passionately in this sign. There will be physical stress and tension if Mars receives negative aspects from the Moon in particular, the Sun or Uranus. There is great tenacity, and any demanding project, whether it calls for the expenditure of physical or emotional energy, will be seen through to its end.

The love and sex lives are powerfully influenced, making for a very sensuous and caring partner who instinctively knows the lover's needs. However, he or she will sometimes create a rather claustrophobic atmosphere, in a sense working too hard at the relationship and expending much emotional and physical energy upon it – even to the point of exhaustion. The temper is short, with some very harsh, and occasionally cruel, remarks being hurled in moments of anger. Such rage may not be as easily assuaged as when Mars is in other signs and, because Cancer enhances the memory, resentfulness will not be easy to cleanse from the emotions, even though the individual will dislike this trait in himself.

Considerable impetus to family life is present, and the acquisition of a home and (often most importantly) children will be enthusiastically pursued. If a woman is pregnant and has Mars in this sign, look at the planet's aspects to see how easy or tricky the pregnancy and labor are likely to be. If there are strenuous aspects to Mars, relaxation classes will be advisable. Sometimes this placing speeds up labor.

Health and well-being
The best forms of exercise are water sports, when the physical body and emotions can be restored, water being so closely related to the emotions. It is also important for the subject to talk through problems freely, especially when upset or annoyed. In any case there may be a tendency to worry and bottle up problems; this will start a spiral of physical and emotional difficulties that could considerably affect the individual's well-being.

♌ MARS IN LEO

The fiery enthusiasm, energy and assertiveness of Mars are well complemented in Leo, and this placing gives excellent organizational ability and powers of leadership. Nevertheless, the individual must guard against becoming too pushy, especially with others who are less extrovert.

The emotions are positively increased, and there will be a great love of life; special pleasure will be gained from enabling others to be happy and enjoy themselves. The sex life will be full, rewarding and colorful, but if Mars is negatively aspected by Saturn, energy will be spent more unevenly than is usual when these two planets are at loggerheads. There is usually a sense of drama, and while this can be fun, it must be controlled – as must a tendency to exaggerate and show off, which can become bombastic at times. There is a genuine hatred of small-mindedness and petty behavior. The temper is generally quick (almost as much as when Mars is in Aries), but Leo magnanimity means all will be forgiven and forgotten equally quickly.

A passion for art and creativity is often shown. If painting or design is enjoyed there is usually a flair for color – especially hot, sunny shades. If the Sun sign complements the Mars placing (being another fire sign, for instance), the subject will look for such colors when choosing clothes, which will also allow plenty of movement.

A need for exercise
If overenthusiasm is consciously controlled, or is countered by other somewhat more sober elements in the chart, this placing is a marvelously invigorating one. It adds a certain robustness to the health, but look to the spine, which could be prone to strain especially if the subject is confined to an office desk for long hours at a time. A backrest chair would be an excellent and perhaps necessary investment. As Leo rules the heart, you should also encourage steady exercise, whatever the age of the subject. This does not mean that he or she will be prone to heart attacks, but it is as well to remember that the heart is a powerful muscle – a machine – and, like all machines, will work better and longer if it is kept well oiled and sensibly used. For exercise, all kinds of dancing are to be recommended, as are workouts at a well-equipped health club.

♍ MARS IN VIRGO

Here is a hard and willing worker. In order to counter tension, Mars needs positive aspects from the Sun, Moon,

Mercury or Venus, since the Virgo influence on Martian energy is inclined to tighten it and, while there is a chance of a powerful level of nervous energy, this placing can easily make the individual edgy, tense and rather restless. There is often a need for constant activity; if that can be expressed in a controlled, practical way by devising and keeping to a steady routine or timetable, all will be well. Should Mars receive, say, negative aspects (especially squares) from the Sun, Mercury or Uranus, the ability to relax completely and unwind can be severely inhibited. In time this can lead to nervous stomach upsets and sometimes migraines. Skin allergies, again as a result of tension or perhaps an unacceptable diet, can occur occasionally.

Attention to detail

On the positive side, the individual usually works hard and willingly, and although we cannot ever say that Mars bestows patience, he or she is often able to work in a detailed way, leaving no stone unturned in attaining a particular objective.

The passion of Mars is reduced and, while the individual may feel very strongly about such important issues as the environment and nature conservancy (and can spend a great deal of time and energy in furthering such causes), the Martian influence on the sex life is uneasy, since Virgo and Mars are not very happy bedfellows. The discrimination of Virgo versus the sexual needs of Mars can clash, so look to Venus (it will be particularly helpful in this respect if it makes a positive aspect to Mars) and to the Venus sign to see if there is a counter to this tendency. The lunar influence may help, since the emotions are not increased by Mars in Virgo.

A secret ambition is sometimes nurtured, but a lack of self-confidence can prevent its fruition and may even intervene when the subject has to carry responsibility for any length of time. Emotional tension can be relieved by relaxation – yoga usually works well. Ingenuity is present, perhaps shown in modelmaking or the development of machines, but too much attention to detail, with a poor grasp of the overall plan, may cramp the style. The influence of Jupiter, or an emphasis on Sagittarius, may well help here. If recommending exercise, cycling, hiking or jogging will prove rewarding.

MARS IN LIBRA

The need for love, harmony and a good relationship are spiced by an increased sexuality in this placing. Even so, the energy of Mars is not at its best in Libra since, while sometimes the individual will be energetic and enthusiastic, at others he or she will take an extremely relaxed attitude, saying "I can't be bothered". That will be the truth, although other excuses may be made for not getting moving. Venus and Mars are so often bracketed together that one would expect Mars to work well from this sign, but the tradition is that its energy is weakened when it is placed in Libra, the willpower is reduced, and there is less inclination to use the physical energy. However, Mars will certainly stimulate the sexuality of Libra, and should there be other planets in this sign (you will find a lot of people with Neptune in Libra, for instance) the quintessentially Libran sense of romance and idealism will be enlivened and expressed in a more physical way.

The Libran tendency to fall in love with love should not be forgotten. When Mars is placed in this sign the inclination is also to fall in love at first sight, and as a result the subject will suffer considerable heartbreak and learn lessons the hard way. Look for steadying influences to control the emotions – a trine between the Moon and Saturn, for instance.

Relating to others

Good perception is usually present, and often considerable intuition, so the subject should be encouraged to develop these qualities – especially when considering a new relationship. It is important for the individual with this placing to accept that he or she tends to quarrel very easily. It is no bad thing to express our feelings when something annoys or upsets us, but there can be a tendency to overdo this, so encourage the subject to think twice before being too verbally aggressive, especially toward a lover.

As far as the health is concerned, there can be a preponderance of headaches, the reason for which may be slight kidney upsets. All the same, we have a sneaking feeling that at times these might be feigned when the individual isn't in the mood, or is feeling too lazy, for sex. On the whole, exercise may not be popular, but some form of lyrical movement can be attractive, as can a health club where there is a pleasantly relaxing social scene after workouts. Encourage an interest in tennis, badminton or squash which will strengthen the flow of Martian energy and generally speed up the metabolism, which may otherwise be rather slow.

MARS IN SCORPIO

This placing will be a focal point of the chart, since Mars was the ruler of Scorpio before Pluto was discovered. Old textbooks may declare that Mars (rather than Pluto) rules Scorpio, but this is out of line with modern astrological thought. Nevertheless, the influence is a powerful one, and should be given full attention.

The heavy emotion of Scorpio is intensified by the passion of Mars, and it is essential that someone with this placing finds rewarding and satisfying sexual expression. Do not dismiss this statement as a generalization; while we all need sexual fulfillment, if this is not forthcoming for someone with Mars in Scorpio there will be resentfulness and a brooding unhappiness which may be hard to pin down if the individual is not consciously aware of his or her problems – sometimes obsessive tendencies emerge.

A tendency to excess

There is marvelous potential in this placing, and if the emotions related to all spheres of life are allowed to flow positively, we find brilliant engineers, miners, specialists in the wine trade and many other professions who have Mars in Scorpio. On the negative side, jealousy can be a problem, and in extreme circumstances the subject may show vengeful tendencies. There will be a love of good food and sometimes a liking for really living it up!

Here are the whole-hoggers; for instance, when they decide they need to lose weight they will go on a severe crash diet – then have a large and calorific celebration once they have achieved their goal! If the love of food and drink gets out of hand it may be that they are compensating for a lack of emotional fulfillment. Try to talk problems through; there may well be a tendency to gloss over difficulties, for the subject can be very secretive. It is vital that these people are emotionally involved in their careers because, while moneymaking is immensely important to them, the forceful and highly-charged energies of Mars should be fully expressed through work.

The physical energy of Mars will be plentiful, and as the placing adds considerable determination (often stubbornness), heavy exercise – and sometimes martial arts – are usually enjoyed. Water sports are also very popular. As the genitals are governed by Scorpio, any inflammation or slight problem in that area should not be ignored. Mothers of babies with this placing should take particular precautions to avoid diaper rash, which could cause above-average discomfort.

MARS IN SAGITTARIUS

While this is a very lively and exciting placing for Mars, because it increases the physical energy level so much, it is very important that the individual is encouraged to enjoy some form of demanding exercise in order that these powerful resources are positively exploited. In most cases where there are planets in Sagittarius or when the sign rises there is a tendency towards restlessness, and it is certainly very likely indeed when Mars is tenanted in this sign.

Intellectual energy will also be present, and the individual will devour challenges that make a heavy demand on the mind as much as those that make physical demands on the body. There will be breadth of vision and plenty of surprising ideas set out with terrific enthusiasm. Provided staying-power and determination are shown in other areas of the chart, such plans will be carried though to a satisfactory conclusion, but the individual must always beware of restlessness and of simply getting fed up with the project in hand. These feelings are particularly likely because he will always feel that the grass is greener on the other side. There will be a considerable liking for risk-taking, and sometimes a sneaking enjoyment of gambling – especially at sporting events.

Responding to challenge

If leanings toward the unconventional are shown in other areas, this placing will contribute to them, because Mars likes to be out in front and to win. Anything new and different will attract – this individual will want to be the first to express an opinion, and will often enjoy slightly shocking other more conventional types. Versatility is usually an asset, but it will need to be controlled, because if the individual is involved in too many different projects this could encourage restlessness; moving from one job to another without completing anything must be avoided.

The liking for adventure, excitement, and to some extent danger, can make the individual vulnerable to accidents. Taking care will be considered boring; but at least do your best to advise the subject to wear the necessary protective clothing when involved in such hazardous sports as horse-riding, motor-cycle racing and so on, and also to develop advanced driving techniques. Those with this placing must maintain a balance between great physical activity and equally demanding intellectual challenges; in this way the fiery energy of Mars in Sagittarius will burn wonderfully brightly and steadily. They must take aim when directing their Sagittarian arrows, otherwise they will dance through life shooting them hither and thither without a care, but also with little real effect and less eventual fulfillment.

MARS IN CAPRICORN

Tradition decrees that Mars is exalted in Capricorn (see p.35). We have always found this rather difficult to understand, because in many ways the sign influence of Capricorn is slow and steady, practical and earthy, while Mars is all speed, fire and extrovert enthusiasm. However, we should not ignore the ancients who certainly knew what they were talking about, so at least we must say that Mars is strongly placed in Capricorn.

Ambition and achievement

Increased ambitions are usually indicated by this placing, and will be of help to the subject where the attainment of objectives is concerned. Where it also scores well is in increasing the powers of endurance; those with this placing will cope in physically demanding situations of the sort that are encountered on expeditions. If the career makes physical demands on the subject, or he or she has to work where there is danger, the likelihood of silly risktaking, which can so easily occur when Mars is in other signs, is certainly minimized. As far as exercise is concerned, the endurance of the placing will be of considerable help to anyone who wishes to run marathons or swim long distances. Rock climbing and mountaineering often prove to be rewarding and enjoyable.

The Martian preoccupation with being first and winning may be expressed in the career, especially if ambition is shown in other areas (look to the influence and sign placing of Saturn). The chances are that the individual will be highly motivated toward success, and it is in this direction that the Martian energy will be directed, especially if it harmonizes with the Ascendant and with the aspirations of the Midheaven sign. There can often be a liking for power. Here is someone who could be a self-made businessman or woman, or who can spring from humble beginnings to win scholarships and succeed academically. For this potential to be fully expressed, however, the individual will need considerable support from other areas of the chart, unless Mars or Saturn are personal planets.

If very ambitious it will be important to realize that the risk of sacrificing partners and loved ones for objectives is omnipresent, and that it is all too easy to work to breaking point. This will be particularly likely if Mars receives negative aspects from Uranus, in which case the need for power will also be increased. Apart from eventual exhaustion due to overwork, the joints may be prone to inflammation, especially after heavy exercise.

Extremes of temperature may have an overly negative effect on the body; when making long-distance flights it is vital that time is allowed to acclimatize to any vast change of temperature as feverish complaints and sudden chills may otherwise result. Protection against malaria and similar tropical diseases is essential. The individual will take sex very seriously, giving great consideration to the choice of a partner before making a first move.

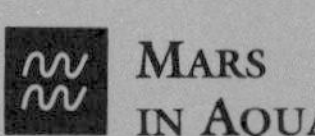

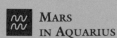

MARS IN AQUARIUS

The independence and need for freedom often present with a Martian influence is very evident when that planet is placed in Aquarius, and nicely complements many Aquarian characteristics. There is a decidedly unconventional streak – indeed, we think that this planetary placing contributes more zaniness than any other. Although this can be extremely amusing and entertaining to friends and loved ones, it can also result in embarrassment at times.

There is often stubbornness, and the energy of Mars is spent rather unevenly, so that there will be considerable bursts of activity followed by times when the individual will want to get on with the usual demands of living but may be unable to do so, perhaps because of tension or sheer eccentricity in the shape of perversity.

Seeking individual solutions

It is vitally important that the aspects Mars receives are studied with great care: if the planet is afflicted by the Moon, Saturn or Uranus, the likelihood of nervous strain and tension is considerable, and ways of releasing them must be sought. Because the placing contributes considerable individuality it is difficult to make positive suggestions along these lines, so look to other areas of the birth chart which might suggest some energetic and demanding sporting activity or, as a contrast, something much more introspective, such as yoga.

An element of the pioneering spirit of Mars is combined with the humanitarian side of Aquarius in this placing; as a result the subject will do much to relieve suffering, perhaps even a certain amount of fieldwork in places that have suffered a famine or flood.

There is no very highly-charged emotional influence from this sign; in fact, while the subject will enjoy sex and may want to experiment, the need for freedom could delay commitment. Look out for complications in this sphere of life if other areas of the chart contradict these tendencies, but in all probability, unless Mars or Uranus are personal planets, the Sun, Moon and Ascending signs, plus the influence of Venus, will overrule.

Energy and invention

Considerable originality is often indicated by this placing, and can be expressed through scientific experimentation, inventiveness or simply an interest in offbeat and unusual subjects. Exercise and sporting activities should contribute to a steady and regular expenditure of energy, with the additional benefit that they also encourage good circulation.

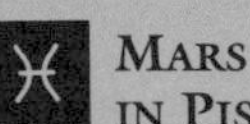

MARS IN PISCES

This considerably raises the emotional level, sometimes to a torrent! There must be some channel for all this emotion so that it can be positively used and not allowed to stagnate or be blocked by psychological problems.

Here is a very sensual, passionate lover who will make great sacrifices for love – but who will sometimes sacrifice love itself in order to follow, with equal fervor, a vocation geared to helping those in need. The sexual desires are usually more considerable, and should be expressed imaginatively. The placing needs planetary influences which give practical ability and discipline if the individual is not to get into complicated, long-term muddles, excused by the phrase "Everything will be fine when I've got myself sorted out." He or she never does!

If Mars is afflicted by Neptune there could be indecision and a tendency not to face up to reality. Great care is needed that during stressful periods reliance is not placed on tranquilizers, medically-administered drugs, alcohol or nicotine. In addition, the subject may be allergic to shellfish.

Creative expression

This placing underlines a very colorful imagination which should be used creatively, for here is considerable potential. If such qualities are indicated in other areas of the chart, give encouragement along these lines – there could be some very surprising results, although this placing does not usually enhance either self-confidence or assertiveness.

The physical energy of Mars does not come through all that powerfully, and heavy exercise may not be beneficial. However, if it is linked to some form of lyrical or creative expression it will appeal, and the individual will benefit. Skating, dance, synchronized swimming or (if there is aggression which the subject may tend to suppress, since it is repulsive to him or her) some of the Far Eastern martial art disciplines may be rewarding. Gullibility, secretiveness, and sometimes self-deception can be present.

MARS PROGRESSED THROUGH THE SIGNS

You may discover that Mars, by progression, moves from one sign to the next. This provides a subtle background influence that will probably color the way in which the subject expends his or her energy. There will be a tendency to concentrate on areas that are ruled by the new sign; for instance, if Mars progresses into Taurus, there may be a sudden and long-lasting urge to make more money (because the need for financial and emotional security will become far more important). The energy of Mars will also be expressed more deeply and passionately. There could be a desire to sing or an increased interest in rich food – in which case you should encourage the subject not to neglect any exercise routine that he will probably have followed fairly rigidly over the years, since prior to the progression Mars would have been in the very active and energetic sign of Aries!

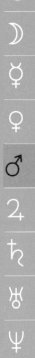

Mars through the Houses

Mars' action is to energize, and it will have that effect on the affairs of the house it occupies in the birth chart. The individual will expend considerable energy on the sphere of life denoted by this house, but in the manner suggested by the sign in which Mars falls. It is important to decide whether the energies will be expressed positively or aggressively; and you must consider all the aspects that Mars receives in the chart (see pp.277-82).

1 Mars in the First House

Since this, the first/Aries house, is the most important house of any chart (Mars rules Aries), Mars will dominate the chart, especially if it falls within about 10 degrees of the Ascendant. The physical energy of the planet will enliven the characteristics of the Ascending sign, and the individual will have tremendous willpower and be motivated by the need to win and to be first in his or her particular field.

An air of constant hastiness surrounds the subject, who will have little patience with those who have a slower metabolism; fools will not be suffered gladly. There will be considerable enjoyment of challenge and competitiveness. However, in putting the self and much-cherished objectives first, the selfishness and self-centeredness of Mars can cause difficulties, and the individual may be totally unaware of some of them. Recognition of such problems is essential, however, if his relationships, both emotional and impersonal, are to be fulfilling.

Energy and vitality
Plenty of physical energy is usually apparent, and the individual will need and enjoy exercise, which must form part of his regular routine. Bravery and daring are also present, and expressed in the manner of the Ascendant. These qualities will form part of the subject's general motivation, so once objectives are formed nothing will hold him back; going all-out in a really pioneering way is the essence of this placing.

Good vitality generally accompanies the subject's abundant energy, and while undue haste and carelessness can lead to accidents, the recuperative powers are excellent. The complexion is usually fresh and the expression open and unclouded by frowns or intensity. The subject can generate enthusiasm in others and can achieve much, but must be careful not to burn himself out through over-activity.

2 Mars in the Second House

Here, the Martian energy will be directed towards the acquisition of wealth and possessions. However, the subject will also be a big spender who wants to enjoy his or her hard-earned cash and, equally, will want to allow others to share it. Whether capital is acquired through careful investment, sheer hard work or clever financial dealing will depend on the Mars sign.

The emotions are also intensified and will be expressed passionately, with a great deal of sensual pleasure given to partners who, if they do not respond in the desired manner, will not remain partners for long! This placing also adds determination which, combined with strong physical resources, makes for a drive that thrives on opposition.

Check the Mars sign: if it is Taurus, Cancer or Scorpio, the subject will have a temper that may erupt rarely but very fiercely – it may not be easy for the target of such an outburst to forgive and forget. The subject should be aware of possible possessiveness, which will be more likely with some Mars signs than with others.

3 Mars in the Third House

Very often, the individual will have been keen to make good progress at school, and will have enjoyed his or her school days, provided the instructors were enthusiastic and encouraging. Parents of children with this placing must watch carefully for any aggressiveness directed toward weaker classmates. The child will be extremely competitive, especially in sport, and must be encouraged to participate in competitions that will further progress in subjects that are enjoyed and in which talent is shown. An interest in education may stay with the individual, who will enjoy mental challenges.

An argumentative tendency is usually present, so that discussions – often very heated at times – will give much pleasure. If the subject has a burning cause or interest, he or she will do everything possible to communicate those opinions and ideas in order to arouse the enthusiasm of others.

Inquisitiveness is also common. The individual will be fired by a sense of urgency, with a need to know the answers to questions at once, and usually a lack of patience when kept waiting about. There is also an instinct to take a rather warrior-like stance in the protection of brothers and sisters! Advanced driving tuition is advisable, as the subject may drive very fast indeed, irrespective of Mars' sign.

4 Mars in the Fourth House

A great deal of Martian energy will be rewardingly spent on improving and redecorating the home. Some people with this placing can periodically become bored with their homes, so that they move house many times. This restlessness can be profitable if it coincides with do-it-yourself skills.

The influence of the family
Family life is usually greeted with enthusiasm, and parenthood is often welcomed. On a deeper psychological level, this placing gives some indication of the way in which the subject sees his or her mother. The image and influence of the mother may well be that of a woman who knew what she wanted from her children and brought them up in a somewhat masculine way. She may have been rather tomboyish, enthusiastic and energetic and, perhaps due to circumstance, had to stand in for the father, either because he was absent in some way or dead, or because he was rather weak. While you

shouldn't be at all dogmatic about this, it will nevertheless be an interesting and revealing topic for discussion, especially when you add the dimension of the Mars sign to the interpretation.

5 Mars in the Fifth House

An extremely active and rewarding love life is highly likely, with an additional emphasis on sexual pleasure. The subject is an assertive lover who wants to take the lead sexually, and who will need plenty of response from his or her partner. Passion will be shown in a very positive way, and there will be much fun and enjoyment. Pleasure will be taken in children – either the subject's own or others – and perhaps in groups such as Girl Scouts, Boy Scouts, and so on.

A flamboyant temperament
An inclination for risktaking may be evident, and perhaps the individual will have something of a gambling spirit. The sign in which Mars is placed will decree how such a tendency can be controlled, and there may even be some conflict between the need for this kind of excitement (Mars) and the need to restrain it (the relevant sign).

A colorful flair will be added to any creative talent shown in other areas of the chart, but there will not be much patience in its execution. Enthusiasm and energy will be poured into any interest, creative or otherwise. This is also an excellent influence on sporting activities, as it is another house placing that encourages competitiveness.

6 Mars in the Sixth House

If there is little or no indication of nervous strain and tension elsewhere in the chart, and if Mars is free from negative aspects from the Moon, Mercury or Uranus, this placing can help to invigorate the nervous system and gives a sharply critical, incisive attitude.

On a more physical level, there could be a tendency to suffer from skin complaints, with rashes or allergies causing annoyance when the individual is under stress or coping with any tense situation. If Mars receives positive aspects from the Sun, Moon or ruling planet, this placing will help to speed recovery and, as mentioned above, the nervous system will also be enhanced. Rather differently, here is someone who is probably one of the world's workers, and while there will be little patience with dreary, boring routine, he or she is energetically disciplined and aims to carry out the daily round of work with military precision.

The assertive side of Mars may not be quite so noticeable here, but a willingness to serve and be energetically helpful will be present. There may be a tendency to nag when annoyed.

7 Mars in the Seventh House

Much positive energy will be directed towards the subject's partnerships and he or she will use some strength of will to make them work. Sometimes these people may push their partners to the fore, to their own detriment, but this should be countered (it will often be modified by the Mars sign). However, they must realize that their relationships are progressive and have a sense of purpose and direction.

If the harsher, quarrelsome side of the Martian influence is controlled, this placing can be helpful not just for couples who live together but also for those who work together, since their joint objectives are encouraged by the influence of Mars.

The connection between Mars and sexual activity is so strong that it might seem the sex life will dominate any love relationship. However, there is room for the other factors mentioned. Indeed, they are vital, as the need to keep the relationship alive, active and rewarding is essential. Energy and passion will, of course, ensure a happy and demonstrative sexual experience.

8 Mars in the Eighth House

This house placing is a powerful one for Mars because, before Pluto was discovered and brought into the astrological structure, Mars was the traditional ruler of Scorpio. An extremely powerful sex drive will be present and expressed with intensity. In fact, fulfillment in this sphere of life is essential if the subject is to find satisfaction in other areas. There is a fascination with investigation which is often self-involved (especially if Mars receives aspects from the personal planets or Pluto). This usually works out well, but there can be tendencies toward obsession, in which case the subject's self-analysis will be unending.

The choice of career can sometimes be influenced by this placing: there may be an attraction to surgery or psychiatry, or perhaps police and detective work. The individual can often show a deep and abiding interest in finance and big business, with a keen, positive attitude to investment. However, you should look to the Mars sign to see how careful and controlled, how reckless, or indeed how successful, he or she will be in this sphere of life.

Powerful intuition
The intuition is increased by this placing, and will be especially well-tuned when it comes to assessing prospective partners and financial opportunities. There can be an above-average concern with death. Occasionally (especially if Neptune is in Scorpio), this house placing may stimulate psychic ability if, and only if, it is shown elsewhere in the chart, and such an indication is unrelated to the sign in which Neptune is placed.

9 Mars in the Ninth House

Provided the subject shows good intellectual potential (look to the influence of Mercury and Jupiter), this placing will encourage involvement in, and excitement with, intellectual challenge. If powers of concentration are good (look for positive aspects from the Sun or Moon to Saturn), he or she should enjoy the experience of further education, and the attainment of a qualification will be especially rewarding.

An adventurous spirit flows through the subject who will – sometimes with very little money – travel to the ends of the earth either just for the sake of it, or as part of an expedition. Generally there is a ready acceptance and enjoyment of all kinds of challenge, and he will certainly ensure that he has a good and sporting chance of success in whatever he attempts.

The brave influence of Mars is increased by this house placing, and the way in which it is eventually expressed will no doubt be seen in the sign placing (i.e. there will be sympathy and caring for others if Mars is in Pisces, a rather eccentric quality if Mars is in Aquarius, and so on).

The constant need to move further and further forward may cause restlessness, especially if plans are frustrated. The subject should be warned of this, and it is important for you to assess the chart to see whether he is patient or otherwise. If nervous tension is present, a relaxation discipline will help, encouraging a calmer and perhaps more philosophical outlook on life.

10 Mars in the Tenth House

This placing will make the subject a force to be reckoned with in his or her career and professional life. The ability to work hard and to achieve objectives will be extremely important, and the possibility of success high. There should be emotional involvement in the career, and a sense of urgency as to its progress will be inherent in the individual, who may sometimes have to slow down a little and be patient, since overhasty decisions and a lack of tolerance with slower colleagues can cause problems.

A tendency to argue and to be quarrelsome may be present, especially if Mars receives negative aspects from the personal planets or from Uranus, since the individual will be prone to a build-up of tension in any sphere of her life. Nevertheless, at its best, Mars contributes considerable enthusiasm for worldly progress, and there will be a great deal of ambition and high aspirations present, especially if Mars conjuncts the Midheaven.

Signs of rebellion

The tenth house has a certain connection with the father, and the subject may have viewed him as strong and perhaps someone who exerted an over-assertive influence. As a result, there may be inner anger that can be given expression in the form of rebellious behavior against society, particularly during the teenage years.

If this is the case, it will be up to you to talk to your subject very calmly and firmly about these possibilities. If you find this prospect at all formidable, keep in mind that you are an astrologer and not a psychoanalyst, and there could even be a need for you to recommend specialized professional help if the individual is in any way aggressive. As always, other areas of the chart will either underline this tendency or help to soften it, but look out for indications of tension, or a blocking of the ability to talk problems through, due to negative aspects involving Pluto.

11 Mars in the Eleventh House

The pioneering spirit of Mars, when placed in the eleventh house, will make its presence felt in the individual's social life. Here is the pack-leader among a group of friends, spurring them into action and injecting them with enthusiasm and energy for the development and furtherance of a joint interest or cause.

Friendship is of above-average importance, but this is a sphere of life that will experience some rocky periods since the aggressive, argumentative side of Mars will tend to cause upsets between the subject and his or her friends. This will be especially so when others challenge his reasons or motives for certain actions.

Variable sensitivities

The humanitarian side of the eleventh/Aquarius house will be present, and it seems very likely that the individual will become extremely combative when moved by suffering. He will at once want to take positive action to do something that will help to alleviate it.

The emotional level of Mars, which will be so fervently expressed toward the subject's interests and hobbies, may however be somewhat cool when it comes to human relationships. This is because the independence of the eleventh house will add an element of personal detachment to the subject, damping down a really warm expression of feeling.

12 Mars in the Twelfth House

The individual may be rather secretive, and it can be very difficult for him or her to unburden problems on to sympathetic friends or counselors, even though there can often be the ability to help other people in this respect. There is a colorful fantasy life, and the subject's resources of emotional energy will be strengthened, even in a chart where this level is below average.

A caring role

An identification with human suffering is one of the best possible characteristics of this placing, with the tendency to take on other people's burdens and work hard to help lighten them. Alternatively, an interest in counseling will bring out his or her support on a more psychological level.

If the chart shows sympathy for, and empathy with, other people, this is an excellent placing for the caring professions – especially social work or the prison service. For Mars to work well, however, it should not receive negative aspects from the Moon or Neptune, since then there would be escapist tendencies and an inclination towards self-deception. This will be heightened if Mars forms a conjunction with the Ascendant from this house.

♂ Mars Progressed through the Houses

You may find that Mars will progress from one house to the next during the course of a lifetime. As a result, the subject may take a new and energetic interest in the concerns of the new house. If the planet progresses into the sixth house and the individual is over- or underweight, a sensible diet or the restructuring of eating habits will have a long and beneficial effect. Someone whose Mars progresses into the third house may become more communicative and find it easier to speak up, expressing opinions more dynamically and forcefully than before.

The Aspects of Mars

Any planet contacted by Mars is invigorated and energized physically, emotionally or intellectually, but its positive and negative influences are very different. This is so with all planets, of course, but it is especially important for you to decide whether Mars is giving a positive energy, released through action and achievement, or causing tension or stress. If the latter applies, it is equally vital to discover ways in which your subject can channel this energy rewardingly by controlling it or, if aggression is present, by sublimating it in demanding physical exercise.

For aspects between Mars and the Sun see the Sun's aspects to Mars, pp.215-16.

For aspects between Mars and the Moon see the Moon's aspects to Mars, pp.233-4.

For aspects between Mars and Mercury see Mercury's aspects to Mars, pp.248-9.

For aspects between Mars and Venus see Venus' aspects to Mars, p.263.

♃ Mars' Aspects to Jupiter

☌ Conjunction

It is best to describe this aspect as the "get up and go" configuration. The individual will show initiative and be forthright and decisive. There is usually considerable enterprise, and no opportunity will be missed due to procrastination. Instead, there is great enthusiasm for, and the ability to concentrate on, objectives which may seem horrendous to less assertive people. Financial ability is often present, as is a daring attitude toward investment, which may need a steadying influence from other less invigorating indications.

Those with this conjunction will say what they think – not too bluntly or harshly, although sometimes a tendency to be combative in arguments causes problems, especially with colleagues. See if there are steadying, more cautious indications to counter this tendency.

Usually there is a love of life and good living. If the conjunction falls in Aries or Sagittarius, risk-taking and a devil-may-care attitude can be present. The physical and intellectual energies are increased, but both should be spent evenly, because much can be achieved as a result of this dynamic influence.

+ Positive aspects

These are excellent influences, contributing optimism, enthusiasm and many of the attributes of the conjunction, but in a less forcible manner. Any tendency to express feelings and opinions overassertively will be controlled in a way that is not usual in those who have the conjunction. These aspects contribute toward a lively mind and active body, and this will be particularly so if either planet is personalized in the birth chart. Either way, here is an excellent source of potential that can be used to enhance talent for sport or intellectual pursuits.

− Negative aspects

If restlessness is shown in other areas of the chart these aspects will add to it considerably, and indeed will cause it (even if it is not indicated elsewhere). The intellectual and physical energy is increased, but there will be a tendency to overdo things and to exaggerate. Encourage your subject to work hard in a disciplined way, otherwise the expenditure of energy and the will to work will be very uneven.

An inability to do anything in moderation characterizes those with this placing, and this tendency can undermine the health, especially if either planet is personalized. If the influence is countered by positive help between the Sun and Saturn the influence, which is a powerful one, can be controlled and put to good use. Gambling can be attractive but may sometimes get out of hand.

♃ Progressed Aspects between Mars and Jupiter

☌ Conjunction

The individual is in a very powerful position to take the initiative, and will probably be in the mood to forge his or her way forward in exactly the required direction.

Success will result: but study the transits carefully for key periods when the taking of bold action seems most desirable. The influence, which will be operative for about three years, indicates an important and exciting time.

+ Positive aspects

These contribute towards considerable success, suggesting an enterprising mood when, if transits are supportive, the initiative should be taken. If the progression occurs at or near the time of a Jupiter Return, or any other important indication of change, the period will probably be an extremely progressive and successful one, with much being achieved that is important and meaningful to the subject.

− Negative aspects

There will be a tendency to take premature action and to be overoptimistic at this time. Moderation should be exercised in all areas of life. Restlessness and impatience must also be controlled, and the subject must think several times before investing any large sums of money. Financial risks may be taken, perhaps through get-rich-quick schemes.

♄ Mars' Aspects to Saturn

☌ Conjunction

This is very potent and exerts a powerful effect on the individual's energy, which will often be expressed very unevenly. As a result there will be times when, in a determined assertive mood, he or she will work to breaking point while at others the energy expenditure will be low, resulting in lack of action and a sense of frustration. There are usually deep-rooted psychological reasons for these tendencies. The outlook can become gloomy and negative, while at other times resourcefulness will motivate action.

☉ ☽ ☿ ♀ ♂ ♃ ♄ ♅ ♆ ♇ ♈ ♉ ♊ ♋ ♌ ♍ ♎ ♏ ♐ ♑ ♒ ♓

Often there is self-will, and if obstinacy is shown in other areas, this too will be increased. Sometimes there is a tendency to be accident-prone – the subject may be slightly hurt or injured, perhaps due to carelessness. Exercise that keeps the joints free of rheumatic aches and pains is to be recommended.

+ Positive aspects
These contribute considerable powers of endurance and determination. The individual can usually cope with, and enjoy, working in difficult conditions or traveling on expeditions. The will to succeed is present, but again it is necessary to achieve a balance in the expenditure of physical energy.

– Negative aspects
These contribute a serious, rather stern outlook; the individual can sometimes be enthusiastic and positive, then negative and depressed. Some writers call it the "blow hot, blow cold" influence. We think this is apt and – as is the case with the conjunction – the expenditure of energy must be consciously controlled, since the tendency to work with the grimmest determination until exhaustion sets in, then relax into lethargy (due perhaps to a sudden lack of self-confidence, or to depression) may do quite serious, long-term damage to the constitution.

If the individual can devise a steady exercise routine and keep to it, this will be of enormous help, but it will only be possible if he or she is able to ignore an inner voice that says "can't be bothered".

♄ Progressed Aspects between Mars and Saturn

☌ Conjunction
For about three years or so, determination and patience must be called upon, for the individual will have to cope with frustration – especially when Saturn is active by transit. Progress will be uneven so caution, good constructive work, and if necessary background research into what is proposed, must be very thorough.

If there is promotion the subject must learn to be very patient with subordinates and to keep an even temper. He or she must remember that a steady pace is essential and should not undermine the health when having to work under pressure.

+ Positive aspects
Determination and powers of endurance will be evident at this time and will be of enormous help to the subject who is trying desperately hard to make progress in his or her chosen field. Patience and sheer hard work will pay off, but as is always the case when Saturn is activated, quick results are not the order of the day.

– Negative aspects
Considerable frustration is likely at times, during which the individual must try not to force issues. These periods will occur when there are transits from Saturn, Pluto or Uranus usually to personal planets, the Ascendant or Midheaven. Action should be taken when these transits are not exact, but even then the individual must only make cautious well-calculated moves. Steady exercise and additional vitamins, especially calcium, are recommended, as is Vitamin C when the weather is cold or the subject is likely to catch a cold or chill.

♅ Mars' Aspects to Uranus

☌ Conjunction
This very powerful aspect contributes great determination and self-will. Usually there is obstinacy, but the ability to achieve objectives is considerable. The individual is very frank and outspoken and, if the aspect falls in a fixed sign, stubbornness and intolerance can also be present. There is an air of hastiness and as a result accidents can frequently occur.

It is important that the individual does not become fanatical in opinion, for extremist tendencies can be possible. Consider carefully whether your subject is inclined to enjoy being in a powerful position: if so, make sure that he or she understands that advantage should not be taken of such a privilege. This would be most likely if the conjunction falls in the tenth house, or either or both planets are conjunct the Midheaven. Strenuous situations will often provoke nervous tension.

+ Positive aspects
These add a highly motivated nervous energy which subjects will use to advantage and when furthering their objectives. There is often considerable originality, with a flair for science, engineering or technology. These people will react very quickly in an emergency, and their potent sources of energy will give great support and strength at such times.

Independence is very characteristic, and nervous energy usually abundant. If the individual is leading an interesting, independent life this energy will be burned off very positively, but even so there will be periods of stress.

– Negative aspects
These are a source of considerable nervous strain and tension, and if such traits emerge from other planetary positions in the birth chart, Mars and Uranus will exacerbate the condition. Migraines sometimes occur. Self-will, argumentativeness and perversity are likely, and the individual will always want his or her own way. Parents of children with these aspects may have to suggest the opposite of the desired effect to get the child to do what they want. Awareness of other people's feelings and sensitivity to the hurt that can be caused is important.

There is a terrific desire to win, and often considerable success, but don't underestimate the tendency to stress and, in extreme cases, breakdown. Sometimes these individuals are their own worst enemies, but look for other, more sympathetic, indications to counter the harshness of these aspects.

♅ Progressed Aspects between Mars and Uranus

☌ Conjunction
A period of both stress and achievement is indicated – one in which the individual will probably have to put up a tremendous fight to achieve the desired goal. In retrospect, however, the effort will have been worthwhile. This progression will cover a period of about three years or so, and life will become extremely eventful when Uranus is active by transit.

Action should be encouraged when there are Jupiter transits, and thought, careful planning and patience needed when Saturn is busy. Often important and unexpected changes will be made, but the subject must keep calm and not take premature action.

+ Positive aspects

Life will at times become exciting and eventful, with the individual feeling strong, positive and assertive. There will be a great desire to win, and an original approach will pay off. It is, however, important that your subject does not become headstrong, and he or she should be encouraged to listen to good advice when it is proffered. Keeping reasonably calm, even when life is exciting, is also important. Opportunities are most likely when Jupiter makes transits to the Midheaven or to its own position.

− Negative aspects

Some very difficult times are likely but just how hard they are will depend on the strength of the transits. With negative intervention from transitting Uranus, Saturn or Pluto, life could become very demanding, taking a heavy toll on nervous and physical energy, and any tendency to worry will surface at such times. There may be an inclination to act very stubbornly or willfully. This does not usually work out well, and may even be uncharacteristic of your subject, who should be reprimanded if this occurs.

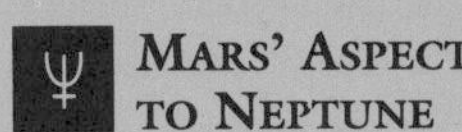

Mars' Aspects to Neptune

Conjunction

This interesting aspect increases the imagination, which is extremely colorful; the individual will probably have a fascinating and rich fantasy life. It also heightens the emotions and adds a sensual air to the way in which the sexual desires are expressed. However, it tends to deflate physical energy, making the subject rather languid in other spheres of life. If the sex life is unsatisfying or there is no positive or creative outlet for the imagination, there will all too often be an ongoing dissatisfaction and restlessness, the reasons for which cannot exactly be pinpointed by the subject.

Parents of children with the conjunction or negative aspects must give them special guidance on the dangers of drugs, drink and smoking, since once hooked on any of them it may be extra-difficult to give them up.

+ Positive aspects

If creativity or originality are shown in other areas of the chart, these aspects will help your subject to combine a rich imagination with his or her individual talent. As a result there is often, for instance, a superb color sense or an original approach to design, whether creative or technical.

The emotions and feelings are increased and should be shown in a positive way, although other influences such as those of the Moon and Venus (planets that exert such an important effect on this area of the personality) will dominate. The contacts will enhance the expression of sex and give it intensity and sensitivity, but the individual must keep both feet on the ground, especially when falling in love.

− Negative aspects

These can cause a falling back on negative escapism, especially when the subject is under stress. The individual may want to retreat, and fail to cope, so look for stronger indications to see what sort of a fight he or she will be able to put up under such conditions. There will be a tendency towards discontent and sometimes moodiness, especially if either planet is placed in a water sign.

Progressed Aspects between Mars and Neptune

Conjunction

This subtle but colorful progression will enhance the individual's imagination, and the result may be some very colorful and creative work. If this is not the case he or she may experience a period during which a particular dream or fantasy comes true – such as a long-desired visit to a place that has been a source of fascination since childhood. There will be no lack of inspiration which can be used to advantage and will blend in very well with any creative activity.

If your subject is under stress due to other progressions or transits warn him or her of an inclination to fall back on tranquilizers, drugs or drink – all of which will be harmful in an above-average way.

+ Positive aspects

The effects of these are much as for the conjunction, but there is an even better chance of the subject being able to use the influence in a practical way, so that there will eventually be concrete results. A tendency to drift off into a dream world can occur and the powers of concentration may be less strong than usual.

− Negative aspects

These are tricky and may cause your subject to feel discontented with his or her lot in life, and not be strong or positively assertive enough to take decisive action. Sometimes the self-confidence is more easily sapped than usual, and any harsh words from other people can cause disproportionate hurt. The risk of negative escapism is considerable when under stress, and additional care is advisable in the preparation of food – especially shellfish – since there is an increased vulnerability to food poisoning.

The effects of this influence will not always be felt for the whole of the three years during which it is operative, but will surface when there are Neptune transits to the personal planets, the Ascendant or the Midheaven, or when there are lunar progressions of a similar nature. The subject should be aware of any tendencies to negative escapism and perhaps uncharacteristic secretiveness.

Mars' Aspects to Pluto

Conjunction

This is a very powerful influence. If it is well aspected by the Sun or Moon there will be a strong driving force and determination, although stubbornness is usually present. If the conjunction receives squares or oppositions there may be a lot of pent-up energy which the subject will find difficult to release in a positive way. The force is so strong that, if you decide your subject is tense or perhaps restless, it would be useful to suggest he or she takes up judo or karate in order to release this energy in a very controlled way. The psychological effect, combined with the physical one, will be most beneficial.

Obsessive tendencies can be present and, when angry, the individual has a fierce temper. This will be most likely for those who have the conjunction in Scorpio (at the time of writing they will be very young, so it is an influence for parents to consider and watch for very carefully), or if the conjunction falls in Virgo and is joined by Uranus. This aspect considerably increases the emotional level, and a cruel streak can also be present.

+ Positive aspects

Here the levels of physical and emotional energy are greatly increased and must be recognized. What is more, they must be positively expressed through a demanding sport or exercise regime. Involvement in one of the martial arts could be as rewarding for this group as for those with the conjunction (see above).

Sweeping changes will be made at times, often because the individual is compulsively led to make them. This placing increases the ambition and the individual is usually a hard worker – sometimes becoming a workaholic.

– Negative aspects

As with the conjunction and positive aspects, both the emotional and physical energies are increased, but there will be a tendency to work to breaking point and the attainment of objectives can become an obsession.

Desperate attempts will be made to overcome obstacles, but all too often these seem to increase in proportion and size, so that a satisfactory conclusion is not always achieved.

♇ Progressed Aspects between Mars and Pluto

☌ Conjunction

This heralds a period when a great deal of emotional and physical energy will be expended. Frustrations and blocked progress are possible when this conjunction coincides with difficult transits, but the eventual outcome may be a fresh start in some area. Sometimes this is as a result of overcoming psychological problems through therapy or an improvement in finances. Plans should be pursued when the transits are positive and there is support from lunar progressions.

This is a demanding period that is often not easy but is eventually rewarding. It will more or less color the life for about three years, but will not be of prime concern all the time.

+ Positive aspects

These indicate a time when the individual may make a clean sweep of some kind. Getting rid of worn-out conditions, making changes to the home, moving house or – if there are indications of change in other areas of the chart – perhaps ending a relationship and starting fresh with a new partner are just some of the possibilities.

At times progress may be blocked, even with these positive aspects, especially if Pluto is busy by transit, but overall the outcome will be very satisfactory and the subject will feel refreshed and ready for the next phase in life. However, be careful not to overinterpret this trend as it needs some pretty powerful back-up to be really strong – in particular, if Mars or Pluto are personal planets.

– Negative aspects

Here is a period when there will be a series of frustrations, especially if changes are being made. This is not a time to force issues, especially if there are negative transits from Saturn to personal planets or Pluto. Advise your subject to be assertive when there is help from Jupiter, or even if Mars is active by transit, remembering that these influences only last a few days (see pp.281-2).

Asc Mars' Aspects to the Ascendant

☌ Conjunction

If Mars is in the first house reread the relevant section (see p.274), remembering that this information will apply very powerfully indeed, and the closer Mars is to the Ascending degree the stronger the influence will be. However, do bear in mind that an accurate birth time is necessary. If Mars is in the twelfth house reread that house placing for Mars (see p.276) since these indications will apply most powerfully. The physical energy will be enhanced (Mars in the first house) or the emotional energy increased (Mars in the twelfth house).

The inclination to be self-centered and selfish will be more potent if Mars is in the first house than the twelfth. If in the latter, however, while the individual will make sacrifices and be helpful to others, there will be a deeply secretive tendency. Irrespective of the house placing, a tendency to accidents is increased due to hastiness.

+ Positive aspects

These increase the physical energy level, so the subject should be involved in demanding sporting activities so as to give such energy plenty of positive release. This is less necessary, however, if he or she has a physically active job. The need for action, and plenty of it, is present and an independent streak is usually evident along with the need to be in the winning team.

– Negative aspects

There may be a tendency to overwork which can lower the vitality, especially if Mars is placed in the sixth house. A lively, sexually rewarding relationship is necessary if Mars occupies the seventh, but also warn your subject of quarrelsome tendencies (particularly applicable if the aspect is a square).

As with the conjunction, use the sign and house placing of Mars quite prominently in your interpretation since any of these aspects add to the strength of the planet.

Asc Progressed Aspects between Mars and the Ascendant

☌ Conjunction

The individual will set some very demanding and brave objectives during the three years that this progression is operative. The will to win and achieve such aims will be very strong. Make sure that the energy is burned positively and evenly, thus avoiding the temptation to overwork.

A tendency to put oneself first and perhaps not listen to partners will be present. Usually the subject will be right in doing so, since with energy and determination comes decisiveness, but in the majority of cases selfish behavior must be controlled.

+ Positive aspects
These will give terrific support to any projects in which the individual is involved and will help him or her to cope with demanding tasks and the attainment of goals. The health and vitality should be especially good at this time. This trend is excellent if extra demands are to be made on the body, since both inner and physical strength are usually increased.

− Negative aspects
There will be a tendency to work too hard, and as a result fatigue will build up. From time to time there could well be shortness of temper, especially if things aren't going according to plan. Patience is necessary and must be developed, but this will be difficult due to an inclination to be hasty and very impatient. The subject may also behave in an uncharacteristic fashion.

If the progression occurs at or near the Uranus Half-return (see p.326) the subject may become involved in a lighthearted love affair that could get out of hand, since the need to prove that he or she is still sexually attractive will be very strong.

MC Mars' Aspects to the Midheaven

☌ Conjunction
The will to succeed is paramount, and ambition and independence will also be strong qualities. Above all, the individual must be emotionally involved in his or her career or, if no career is followed, then the same devotion should be aligned to a compelling interest. Either way, a great deal of energy will be expended on the day's work. Reread the house positions of Mars (see pp.274-6) to gain further insight into this prominent placing.

+ Positive aspects
There will be much the same direction of energy as with the conjunction, and Mars will support the individual's efforts. Enthusiasm for work will be infectious, and there is usually an ability to spur colleagues into action.

− Negative aspects
Although a hard worker, sometimes to breaking point, there is often an argumentativeness with colleagues. As a result, patience must be developed, especially with those who work at a slower pace. Whether or not that is easy will be determined by other areas of the chart.

MC Progressed Aspects between Mars and the Midheaven

☌ Conjunction
This is very likely to herald a period of intense activity and the attainment of objectives. The ease or difficulty of this time will depend on two factors: how well Mars is placed and aspected in the birth chart, and whether the current transits indicate a progressive period or one fraught with setbacks and problems. Nevertheless, there is a good chance of the individual achieving whatever he or she sets out to do.

+ Positive aspects
These will give considerable back-up to any demanding project undertaken at this time. Indeed, the individual should become involved in any activity that he or she would very much enjoy, for this trend increases self-confidence, assertiveness and the will to succeed.

− Negative aspects
Overwork and strain usually occur, and the subject may have to make a particularly great effort to achieve whatever he or she sets out to do. If care is taken to control the temper and to be patient, all should be well, but this will not be easy. Look to other areas of the birth chart to see if rashness, premature action and unnecessary risktaking can be controlled.

♂ Mars' Progressions to its Own Position

Everything that Mars stands for in its natal position will be emphasized at this time. Mars' progressed sign and house will also be activated in a rather energetic way.

These progressions are interesting, contributing assertiveness and the will to get on with projects. Mars is unlikely to make any aspect beyond the square in a lifetime, so remember that the semi-sextile, because it is weak, will not be very strenuous, the semi-square will cause some tension and the sextile will be very energetic. The square, which could occur for someone very elderly, may be tense, but if the natal Mars is well placed it could have an invigorating influence.

♂ The Transits of Mars

Like the transits of Mercury and Venus, these are short-lived but even so they can have quite strong effects. They increase our energy and need for action, making us assertive or impatient, quarrelsome or decisive. These are planetary energies to be used, but also to be controlled. Generally speaking, they will have a positive effect, but we have to consider the negative side of Mars too, so both positive and negative interpretations are given. Read both, remembering that the negative interpretations will tend to apply to the oppositions. The effects of these transits will be felt for between three or four days. Only the conjunctions and oppositions should be calculated.

☉ Mars' Transits to the Sun

+ Positive transits
Vitality and energy are increased, so demanding tasks should be set. The demeanour is decisive and assertive.

− Negative transits
A tendency to overwork should be controlled and the temper watched carefully. This is a time for pacing oneself. Care should be taken when handling sharp tools and hot dishes, and also when driving.

☽ Mars' Transits to the Moon

+ Positive transits
The emotions are heightened at this time, perhaps causing passionate feelings about someone or something that should be ardently expressed.

Negative transits
Care should be taken not to overreact to situations. Patience is needed at all times, especially when the subject is dealing with children.

☿ Mars' Transits to Mercury

Positive transits
This is a time for speaking one's mind, for then important points will be made and listened to.

Outdoor exercise may be of benefit, such as a long bracing walk or perhaps an invigorating bicycle ride.

Negative transits
Verbal aggression may be more pronounced than is realized, and complaints could be overstated, possibly thus causing distress to loved ones or work colleagues.

♀ Mars' Transits to Venus

Positive transits
There should be a lively and positive accent on the sex and love life. This is a particularly good time for the subject to arrange a special occasion for him- or herself and a lover.

Negative transits
Care should be taken not to make many sexual demands or to pick silly, unnecessary quarrels. Accusations of selfishness may be well-founded at this time.

♃ Mars' Transits to Jupiter

Positive transits
This is a very good time at which to take the initiative and not let the grass grow under one's feet. Although other, more long-term transits should be considered, these may easily be a few very progressive days.

Negative transits
Care is needed to avoid premature action or any tendency to ignore the details in contracts or any other on-going work.

♄ Mars' Transits to Saturn

Positive transits
The tendency to work too hard and then feel drained and lethargic should be countered. Sudden changes of temperature must be avoided.

Negative transits
These will be a tricky few days, when issues should not be forced or too much work tackled. Feelings of depression or annoyance will soon ease.

♅ Mars' Transits to Uranus

Positive transits
There is a strong need for action, but this is likely to be followed four days later by exhaustion!

Negative transits
Much tense, nervous strain may be experienced for a few days, which might lead to headaches. Important decisions should be avoided.

♆ Mars' Transits to Neptune

Positive transits
A romantic, nostalgic mood will never be far away and life will become colorful, but disappointment or confusion could occur.

Negative transits
Disappointments, usually minor but nevertheless annoying, will almost inevitably occur. For instance, an appointment may be missed due to a confusion over the date, place or time.

♇ Mars' Transits to Pluto

Positive transits
If the air needs to be cleared with a few home truths or an argument, this is the time to do it.

Negative transits
Life may be at a temporary stalemate but it will not be worthwhile forcing issues for a day or two. Any resulting aggression can be usefully channeled by having a purge on any personal clutter and throwing it away.

Asc Mars' Transits to the Ascendant

Positive transits
Energetic and positive feelings will be evident. This is a time for action but not for always putting oneself first.

Negative transits
A tendency to be quarrelsome should be avoided. Care should also be taken when exercising, as muscles could be pulled through over-exertion.

Note: With either transit of Mars to the Ascendant, the tendency to be accident-prone is increased, so especial care should be taken when driving or handling hot dishes or sharp tools. This influence is very similar to that of Mars' transits to the Sun.

MC Mars' Transits to the Midheaven

Positive transits
These will be a very hardworking but rewarding few days, usually producing excellent results.

Negative transits
Work may result in exhaustion. Making suggestions to others might also cause fatigue and there may not be full cooperation from colleagues. Any outbursts of temper should be controlled, since the emotional energy will be highly charged. Accidents as a result of others' actions is possible.

♂ Mars' Transits to its Own Position

Positive transits
The sign and house position of Mars will be emphasized in a very positive and assertive way, but any extreme feelings should be controlled.

Negative transits
These will be a very hectic and tiring few days, especially if issues have had to be forced.

Jupiter through the Signs

The largest planet of the Solar System, Jupiter takes about twelve years to travel round the Sun and through all twelve signs of the zodiac. It is connected with physical and intellectual expansion and associated with the acquisition of knowledge; it helps develop a philosophical outlook on life and encourages our understanding of foreign countries and people. Those with this planet strongly placed or emphasized will, according to its sign, generally be optimistic and broad-minded, and direct their mental energies very positively. The negative side of Jupiter encourages blind optimism, exaggeration, extravagance, a gambling instinct, and sometimes wastefulness and an overdeveloped sense of drama.

JUPITER IN ARIES

The positive, fiery enthusiasm of Aries is very sympathetic to Jupiter's lively and optimistic influence. Here is someone who is assertive, broad-minded and enthusiastic. A love of freedom is important, but care is needed that it is not expressed selfishly, without due consideration for the partner or for other people's feelings. There may be a rather devil-may-care attitude, especially if Jupiter is negatively aspected by the Sun, Moon or Mars, so look for indications of stability and common sense elsewhere in the chart.

The pioneering spirit characteristic of Aries will surface and be expressed – perhaps through pure adventurousness, wanting to travel to faraway or dangerous places, or maybe through a new development of some kind that will call for enterprise, which is another characteristic of this sign placing. Sometimes Jupiter's influence will encourage sportsmanship and a competitive spirit. This is marvelous while the subject is young, but intellectual potential and the development of a philosophical outlook should also be encouraged. Powerfully extroverted children with this placing may need correction, since bullying tendencies sometimes develop. A liking for risk-taking will also need to be controlled.

Self-confident action

There is decisiveness, sometimes leading to premature action, generosity to the point of extravagance, and an ability to ignite enthusiasm in others. In many ways this placing encourages individuals to be very full of themselves. It will give considerable extroversion, and the subject won't be at all backward in coming forward, blowing his or her own trumpet at every opportunity. This is fine in many respects, but these individuals must consciously recognize that it can be rather overdone at times. A tactful warning may help them achieve a desirable balance. Any emphasis in the natal chart on Virgo, or planets in that sign, will act as a powerful counter. A course of advanced driving instruction, once the legal license has been granted, will be beneficial, as these subjects may drive in a reckless way.

JUPITER IN TAURUS

Jupiter is at its most jovial here, thus contributing plenty of bonhomie. There is usually a great love of life and appreciation of good food and wine, so it is vital for the individual to understand that the basic principle of Jupiter, which is expansion, is very likely to encourage an ever-expanding waistline! If Jupiter is afflicted by the Sun, Moon, Venus or Neptune, this attraction to good food may border on self-indulgence and greediness. If this is the case remember that the subject may be comfort-eating to counter a lack of real love, whether given or received, and the joviality may be clown-like, disguising introversion and unhappiness. If the individual is overweight it will be necessary for you to warn him or her of possible liver damage, especially if the intake of alcohol is above the generally recommended level.

Material success

The motivation to make money is encouraged by this placing, and often brings great success, since the individual will invest cleverly, with flair and a good sense of timing. A healthy bank balance is necessary, since those who enjoy good food and wine often also thoroughly appreciate all the other creature comforts. There is, however, considerable generosity and great pleasure is taken in entertaining others and seeing them enjoying themselves. Jupiter in this position contributes reliability, and common sense will prevail whenever intellectual challenges or demanding problems are faced.

There should be no difficulty in developing the more philosophical attributes of Jupiter, and a warm sense of humor, plus a true sincerity, are among the other positive qualities of this sign placing.

JUPITER IN GEMINI

Traditionally, Jupiter is not very well placed in Gemini and this is true to a certain extent, since this placing can cause intellectual restlessness. Changes of opinion and too much versatility may interfere with real progress, especially when at college or university. There can also be a scattering of intellectual energy so that the mind becomes serendipitous. Consistency of effort must be encouraged and also sought in other areas of the chart. A generally stabilizing influence, such as positive aspects from the Sun, Moon or Mercury to Saturn, will help.

The individual will be broad-minded, up-to-date in outlook and often very clever, but should be aware of the benefits of in-depth knowledge in one or two areas at least. Alas, this can seem very boring, but his or her eventual success may depend on it, for despite getting away with murder for 99 per cent of the time, he or she will be caught out in the end, no matter how quick the arguing skills nor how brightly criticism is countered. There can be considerable craftiness, but sadly not much discretion! This placing is an excellent one for teachers working with children in the eleven-plus age group.

JUPITER IN CANCER

Jupiter is traditionally well-placed in this sign, and its influence is somewhat strengthened. The intuition and the emotional level are both increased. There is a marvelous natural kindness and sympathy, plus an understanding of other people's problems and difficulties. The caring, charitable and protective instincts common to Cancer are enhanced and often expressed on a broad, humanitarian level as well as a personal one; concern, consideration and often cash will be given to alleviate mass suffering. The changeability of Cancer is shown in an uncertainty of opinion, and there can be changes of direction in religious thought or belief.

The imagination certainly benefits: look to other areas of the chart to see how it may best be expressed. It may be in writing or literature if the chart shows creativity, or in inventiveness if the bent is scientific, when the imagination will combine with intuition, helping the subject to assess the possible outcome of an experiment.

Learning and achievement

The home and family life also gain by this placing, which will enhance the parents' ability to be objective about their children. The home will probably be full of books (perhaps rather untidily so!) and a special kind of encouragement will be given to children to develop their minds in exciting and imaginative ways.

Natural shrewdness is a Cancerian characteristic, and here it will enhance any indication of a good business sense. If the subject wants to start a small business enterprise, you might suggest something connected with antiques, for the acquisition of knowledge of a chosen period or type of artwork will be as stimulating as the making of extra money. Here is someone who enjoys good food, and may also be a superb cook.

JUPITER IN LEO

Optimism, enthusiasm and generosity are common with this placing, and the individual is often intelligent and ambitious. However, the measure of extroversion that this placing gives will, especially if the rest of the chart is that way inclined, tend to encourage showiness and sometimes too much dramatic projection. There will be a need to take center stage – but also the talent to encourage others to achieve their full potential.

Every day must be lived to the full, and time-wasting may be deemed to be sinful. Subjects with this placing should certainly realize that they can become too exuberant and flamboyant, especially in dress. However, if they can control bombastic tendencies and let their natural enthusiasm and zest for life invigorate others, they will be expressing themselves in a marvelous way. Sometimes they need to be taken down a peg or two; they can be very pompous. Quality is important, with well-made clothes and real jewelry thoroughly appreciated. There is usually a great love of tradition, and loyalty to loved ones and, more generally, to their country.

Finding a creative outlet

Self-satisfaction and an inflated ego are sometimes present, especially if the Sun makes a negative aspect to Jupiter. The sense of drama and a tendency to exaggerate are usually evident if there is a negative aspect between the Moon and Jupiter. At best there will be excellent organizational ability and convincing powers of leadership.

Acting can be a good outlet for this dramatic sense, and a love of painting and the theater is common. If creative flair is shown elsewhere, Jupiter in Leo will definitely help it to be expressed fully and enthusiastically. This placing is excellent for individuals who enjoy working with children or young people, either as a teacher or simply in passing on their own skills. It is marvelous for them to be involved in intellectually expanding projects, which will be a constant source of pleasure as well as a challenge.

JUPITER IN VIRGO

There is something of a contradiction in terms about this placing, for while Jupiter encourages expansion of the intellect in particular, Virgo is related to small, narrow detail and critical acumen. Sometimes as a result there is conflict and apprehension when the individual is confronted with a situation or project that demands a broad sweeping approach. He or she will want to take it, but may feel a lack of self-confidence and fail to commit him- or herself as boldly as might be wished. The outlook will definitely be matter-of-fact, and it is to this characteristic that the subject should appeal at such times. You must also encourage reflection on past achievements and successes, for it is in that way that confidence will be gained and a broader perspective taken.

Precision and practicality

Considerable literary skill often accompanies this placing. Here is the patience and dedication of a meticulous writer with the intelligence to develop the technique necessary if he is to put down on paper precisely and directly just what is in his mind. This placing also contributes technical and scientific ability, along with tremendous practical flair for working with machinery. Healthy scepticism and critical acumen are also present.

If Jupiter is afflicted by the Moon or Neptune there can be considerable absent-mindedness. This will infuriate the individual, who will consider it stupid and annoyingly time-consuming when he or she leaves keys in the wrong place, for instance, or mislays a vitally important piece of paper or book! Sometimes there can be constipation, especially if rich food is enjoyed, and digestive problems are also common.

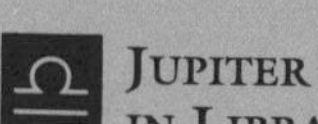

JUPITER IN LIBRA

Here is a kind, sympathetic and charming individual, hospitable and very charitable. There is a natural friendliness and an easy expression of warm affection, and the attitude to life is somewhat laid-back. "*Que sera sera*" may be a motto!

There is a great love of luxury, especially if Jupiter receives a negative aspect from Venus. In this case, the positive qualities mentioned above will be present but the subject can very easily become sybaritic and lazy; unless Mars is really strong there may well be little get-up-and-go.

Money-making will be of great importance, and the results will be spent on pleasure and entertaining friends in a hospitable and extravagant way. The individual may well have a very good mind but the motivation to stretch it and accept demanding intellectual challenges will probably not be especially noticeable. He or she may prefer to relax with some long, exciting romantic fiction or a family saga rather than actually getting round to writing one, even if inspired to do so.

A need for self-fulfilment

A loathing of loneliness indicates the Libran influence, and so the individual will be more fulfilled when living and, indeed working, in partnership. She will have a great deal of love and affection to give to a partner, together with encouragement and enthusiasm – this is a positive and rewarding factor in a business relationship. On the negative side, the placing does not contribute much to independence. Indeed, there may even be tendencies to rely too heavily on loved ones, and if Jupiter receives negative aspects from the Sun, Moon or ruling planet there is often self-indulgence and conceit.

It is important that these individuals are encouraged to develop their potential and to increase their expenditure of physical energy. Look to the Mars sign to see which sporting or exercise regime would be most rewarding, and encourage action along those lines. The suggestion that chess or intellectually demanding games could be satisfying may be greeted with enthusiasm. This is another Jupiter sign that likes its food, so suggest a little moderation in eating and drinking, otherwise indigestion may cause problems.

JUPITER IN SCORPIO

The powerful emotional energy force of Scorpio will inject Jupiter's influence with determination and willpower. There is a need for progress, and a strong emotional involvement in interests or career is essential if the subject is to feel fulfilled. In a chart where enterprise and the motivation to develop potential is present, this placing will give plenty of staying-power.

The Jupiterian trait of living life to the full is encouraged by this placing: Scorpio knows nothing of half-measures and, at its most assertive, Jupiter is a whole-hogger, so it is easy to see the potency of this placing. However, care is needed that the subject does not burn him- or herself out when pursuing objectives or simply living it up; moderation must be encouraged, and hopefully a restraining factor will be present elsewhere in the chart. The subject will be vulnerable to overdoing things if the Sun or Moon squares or opposes Jupiter, in which case you should look out for mental strain in particular. The individual may be naturally suspicious, and must not allow this tendency to become obsessive.

If there is an inclination to write, detective fiction will probably be successful and/or rewarding – certainly pleasure will be gained from reading this particular genre. Here, too, is the ability to research thoroughly anything of interest. This placing is excellent for a criminal lawyer or judge. There is often financial flair and a good eye for a calculated financial risk, and sweeping generosity is also usually present. The subject may need to be warned against possible vanity and pride, and sometimes of verbal aggression too.

JUPITER IN SAGITTARIUS

Jupiter rules Sagittarius, so the planet will be a very powerful element of the chart when it is in this sign. We suggest rereading the Sun sign characteristics of Sagittarius (see pp.112-15), since you are very likely to see some of them in your subject. In addition, he or she will have some superb intellectual potential, although this may not emerge in early life, for this placing also contributes a very happy-go-lucky attitude, and one which, when the individual is adventurous, encourages him or her to take risks and be rather careless. The outlook is optimistic and there will be abundant enthusiasm – both extremely positive traits unless they are overexpressed and become blind optimism. This is most likely if Jupiter is afflicted by opposition or square aspects from the Sun, Mercury or Mars. This is certainly a placing that needs countering by some steadying influence from Saturn, or perhaps a personal planet in an earth sign.

Continual learning

As these subjects grow a little older, both intellectually and physically, they will become wiser and develop an ever-strengthening philosophical attitude. It is essential for them always to study something as there is a strong element of the eternal student here, and this trait must be fulfilled. There may also be a wonderful sense of justice, a flair for languages and a love of travel.

Note: During the whole of 1983 Jupiter traveled through Sagittarius with Uranus and Neptune. This stellium (see p.57) creates a particularly fascinating focal point in the charts of children born during that year. It is something to look out for, making them individual, original and very intuitive people with great potential, which will be expressed according to their Sun, Moon and Ascending signs. (See also the influence of Uranus and Neptune in Sagittarius, p.315 and p.328 respectively.)

JUPITER IN CAPRICORN

This gives a blend of positive, extrovert qualities (Jupiter) with powerfully negative, introvert ones (Capricorn). Together they produce a set of remarkable characteristics. The individual is ambitious and determined and will not shirk responsibility. He or she is able to work very hard and persistently, and usually has excellent powers of concentration. Parents of children with this placing must not expect their offspring to make meteoric leaps to the top of the class. Nevertheless, they will make very steady gradual progress, and what is learned will be remembered. This is generally the pattern throughout life.

The outlook is extremely sensible, neither shirking the acceptance of challenge nor being blindly optimistic. Common sense and some caution

should dominate, and hard-earned success will be the eventual outcome. There can be times when the more serious side of Capricorn will be to the fore, resulting in a tendency toward a rather bleak and marginally pessimistic attitude or outlook; the generosity and flamboyance of Jupiter will not often be evident when the planet is in this sign. However, the jolly Jupiter sense of humor combines with the offbeat Capricorn one to emerge when it is least expected, to the great amusement of those present; it is most certainly something to look for!

The individuals are usually kind and thoughtful, but sometimes pigheadedness and the tendency to think that they are always right can be evident. At times this will tend to make them their own worst enemies, but these more extreme tendencies usually only occur if Jupiter receives a square aspect from the Sun or Moon. Pay extra attention to the placing and influence of Saturn since, if that planet is heavily aspected or personalized, the Capricorn influence on Jupiter (i.e. the more serious personality traits) will tend to dominate.

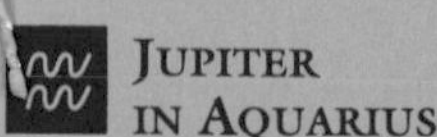

Jupiter in Aquarius

There is usually a splendid imagination and no lack of originality with this placing. The effect of an Aquarian Jupiter will be to endow the subject with powerfully humanitarian qualities, and give him or her the need to express them in a positively helpful way. The sense of justice is also very prominent and this individual, by taking positive action, will see to it that justice is done and seen to be done.

A social subject

Here is someone who is impartial and tolerant, and who can be very sympathetic in a totally unsentimental way. Many of these fine qualities are often expressed through an attraction to humanitarian causes, with plenty of hard work done on their behalf. The independence of Aquarius will certainly be present, and while this sign may make the subject cool and distant, that is not so when Jupiter occupies it, for the planet's warmth and general cheerfulness will melt the crackling ice which is usually characteristic of every Aquarian. The social life is extremely important, and the subject will no doubt have a wide circle of friends and acquaintances who will be encouraged to become involved in, for instance, his concern to improve the lot of those who are less fortunate than himself.

Scientific or technological ability can be present, and originality and imagination will be expressed very inventively. Sometimes there is literary or musical talent but control your enthusiasm if this emerges here. The potential may well be present, but unless Jupiter is personalized, you should see if these abilities emerge independently elsewhere in the chart; and even then you should be rather restrained in your statements! In some cases the sense of humor may border on the eccentric. If Jupiter is afflicted there can be a lack of tact, and sometimes a sort of stubborn intolerance and an element of unpredictability. The intuition is usually increased by this placing.

♓ Jupiter in Pisces

Before the discovery of Neptune and its acceptance into the astrological pantheon, Jupiter was the ruler of Pisces. As a result, its influence from this sign is increased and indeed it is very well placed here.

The philosophical, spiritual and reflective elements of both sign and planet are beautifully blended and will be prominent in the subject, for he or she will be kind, sympathetic and caring. There will be a compassionate spirit and a natural friendliness; she will always listen to what is being said, and build up a marvelously sympathetic rapport with other people. This placing is often found in the charts of those working in the caring and medical professions. It can also bestow a great love of animals (and an excellent rapport with them), and will help anyone wanting to become a vet or to work with animals in some other way.

A sense of commitment

The emotional level is considerably enhanced, and the imagination and intuition are also greatly heightened, sometimes to the point that these tendencies will be much increased should worry show up in other areas of the chart. Here too is someone with the best kind of religious faith – and who practices what she preaches. Identification with suffering is also present, and while many will take positive action to help alleviate it (much as Jupiter in Aquarius does), the caring can sometimes be expressed less directly through contemplation, meditation or prayer. There may also be powers of healing.

Self-indulgence may be present if Jupiter is afflicted by the Sun or Moon, and these people may be unreliable, with a tendency toward deceptiveness or self-deception. They will make sacrifices, sometimes of their personal success or happiness, giving up much to look after a sick relative or perhaps forsaking a successful career to turn to something that is considered to be more worthwhile.

♃ Jupiter Progressed through the Signs

It is rare for Jupiter to move from one sign to the next by progression unless it occupies an early or late degree of a sign in the birth chart. If it is in an early degree it may, during the course of a lifetime, turn from direct to retrograde motion, and re-enter the previous sign. If Jupiter is at the end of a sign it is just possible that it may progress into the next sign, turn retrograde and eventually re-enter the sign in which it is placed in the birth chart.

These changes, if and when they occur, will take place over a long period of time and be very subtle. However, remember that while, as is always the case, the birth position of the planet will still hold good, there will be some influence from the new sign, with the subject perhaps becoming more extrovert and optimistic if Jupiter progresses into a fire sign, or more practical and maybe materialistic if it moves into an earth sign. You will find that there will be greater intellectual stimulation if the new sign is air, and more intuition and thoughtfulness, with an increased philosophical outlook, if the new sign belongs to the water element.

Jupiter through the Houses

Expansion is Jupiter's keyword, so relate this potential to the spheres of life covered by the house placing. In simple terms, unless Jupiter is very negatively aspected in the birth chart, the subject generally does well or experiences little difficulty in these matters. Consider the more exaggerative and overoptimistic side of Jupiter when interpreting its house position.

1 JUPITER IN THE FIRST HOUSE

The closer Jupiter is to the Ascendant, the stronger its influence will be. If it is within 8 or 10 degrees (at most), see also Jupiter conjunct the Ascendant, pp.291-2.

This is an extremely powerful placing, and the characteristics and motivations of the Ascendant sign will be strongly influenced by Jupiter's presence in this house. It adds a strongly positive and enthusiastic outlook on life, which will be lived to the full, and the individual will be warmhearted and optimistic. There is often considerable breadth of vision, and even if a meticulous sign, such as Virgo, rises the subject can assess situations very broadly and wisely.

Positive qualities

Here is someone open and honest, who accepts others at face value, unless deception, dishonesty and craftiness are shown elsewhere. If Jupiter is afflicted by the Sun, Moon or Mars, there will be a tendency to exaggerate, and perhaps some boisterousness or a love of risk-taking and gambling. Usually, however, the positive qualities dominate, including the ability to give encouragement to others – partly because the subject's own enthusiasm is infectious.

A more philosophical attitude and outlook will emerge with age and experience, and the individual should be encouraged to develop an excellent intellectual potential, especially if the more racy, risk-taking side of Jupiter seems to color the personality.

Weight can be gained because of a liking for good food and drink, and indigestion can occur. The individual may also suffer badly from hangovers, so advise care of the rather vulnerable liver, and encourage better treatment of it. Sometimes, as is the case when there is a Sagittarian influence, there may be a tendency to put on weight around the hips and thighs.

2 JUPITER IN THE SECOND HOUSE

The materialistic side of Jupiter is prominent here. There will be a considerable urge to make money and often marked success in this area, with the individual taking financial risks that pay off more often than not. However, if Jupiter is afflicted (especially by a square or opposition from Venus), the subject may go too far and overinvest his or her money in a flurry of blind optimism. Creature comforts are both greatly liked and deeply needed, and the subject will spend money entertaining friends and making the home extremely luxurious and comfortable.

This is the Taurus/Venus house, so don't forget its connection with relationships. The subject is a generous partner, showing love flamboyantly by giving expensive and beautiful presents, sometimes when he can't really afford them. There may be a tendency to buy love and affection, especially if that will boost the ego. This is most likely if Jupiter falls in a very extrovert sign, such as Leo or, perhaps, Libra.

3 JUPITER IN THE THIRD HOUSE

This is the Gemini house and has strong connections with the mind. Jupiter is also the planet of the intellect, so Jupiter's influence will enhance the need to exercise the mind, and intellectual challenge will be taken up with the greatest possible enthusiasm.

The need to share opinions, and even impose them, will be powerful, and the individual's ability to communicate is excellent. He or she may do much good when exercising these qualities, since his or her sense of justice will ensure that actions follow words, especially if the chart shows a strong Mars or Uranus in positive aspect to Jupiter. This is a good placing for children, who will probably enjoy school and its challenges.

A need for mobility

Restlessness is almost inevitable if the Moon or Mercury make negative aspects to Jupiter (although some Jupiter signs fare better than others). There can sometimes be an inability to rest content, but this must be supported elsewhere in the chart.

The desire to continue to learn and sometimes to educate oneself will last well after the school years have ended, and the subject will have a great desire for both physical and mental mobility. Encourage very careful training when learning to drive a car, ride a bicycle, motorcycle or horse, since a certain wildness may take over at such times.

4 JUPITER IN THE FOURTH HOUSE

A happy childhood is often indicated, when the subject had a positive relationship with parents who were always encouraging and enthusiastic. As a result, there is an excellent chance that he or she in turn will create a marvelous home atmosphere when building his or her own family life.

The attitude toward children will be considerate and philosophical, and the family unit will generally have a great deal of fun. The placing conjures up the picture of a wise and but young Santa Claus figure, filling a rather chaotic home with lovely books and goodies that the children will enjoy, but which will also be of benefit to them. Sometimes there will be some sentimentality apparent in the attitude toward the family. From a more materialistic point of view, money doesn't seem to be of prime importance. Nevertheless, if the subject is keen to invest money, the added security of home ownership, and an increase of the house's value by building on extensions and the like, may well prove to be the most beneficial course, both financially and emotionally.

5 Jupiter in the Fifth House

This is something of a mixed blessing. At its best it will certainly bestow great optimism and enthusiasm, and if the chart shows creative flair in other areas Jupiter will definitely enhance any talents, especially for acting or painting. However, Jupiter can get rather carried away here and needs stabilizing if the subject is to gain the most from this placing. Enthusiasm and optimism can run wild, and as a result the individual will tend to take risks. That is fine providing these are calculated (this will show in other areas – a well-aspected Saturn would help enormously), but if Jupiter is squared or opposed by the Sun, Moon or Mars, there can be considerable recklessness when taking risks of all kinds.

A liking for gambling (which Julia has known in many cases to become obsessive) must be guarded against. The individual will love life and live it fully. He or she will be marvelous company and a source of inspiration and encouragement to friends and family. There will be a strong tendency to show off, and a well-developed sense of drama: again, if these traits are controlled, all will be well.

Rewarding relationships
There is a powerful influence on the love life (which will also be enjoyed with gusto), and over the years the subject may have more partners than most! Great generosity will be shown to them, both emotionally and materially. There is also especial joy in parenthood, and the relationship with children will be positive and rewarding. Nevertheless, this is a rather exaggerated placing and needs firm handling if Jupiter is to act at its best.

6 Jupiter in the Sixth House

Here, the Jupiter keyword, "expansion", can have physical effects. Depending on the sign, weight gain (and a difficulty in subsequently losing it) can often cause problems, not simply because the subject enjoys food a little too much, but also because the metabolism may be rather slow. You must warn your subject that he or she can overdo things all too easily.

Too much work, too much food or too much inaction can have a serious effect on the body and/or liver. If there is awareness of what is being done to the system, and bad eating, drinking, or smoking habits (the worst of all) are gradually corrected, long-term damage will be averted. Ideally, a disciplined lifestyle is needed, and the subject will gain a sense of security from its steady rhythm; a tendency to harmful excess may then be avoided.

Being of help to others comes naturally to these individuals, who will hurry to someone's aid as soon as it is requested. Generosity is shown by serving others, and they will freely give time, and often money, plus a natural cheery optimism; it is easy for them to tell when and where help is needed.

7 Jupiter in the Seventh House

Relationships are often embarked upon at an early age by people with this placing, due to the challenge of developing an emotional relationship, great enthusiasm and, most of all, high hopes. Unfortunately, expectations of the partner are frequently far too high, so that when they are not fulfilled there is a tendency to give up, sometimes all too quickly. The subject may take a rather superficial attitude to this sphere of life, and the Jupiter inclination to think that the grass is always greener on the other side may be the basic reason for such downfalls.

Mental compatibility
Encourage your subject to think more seriously and to practice plenty of self-analysis. Most importantly, he or she should discover what the partner really needs, for with this placing comes great potential if the positive, enthusiastic side of Jupiter is fully expressed.

Intellectual rapport is important, and the partners should be of equal intelligence and intellectual and educational development. If the subject is further ahead in these areas than the partner, the gap between them will definitely widen. However, if they are equal or, better still, if the partner is ahead, this will stimulate the subject as opposed to fostering a sense of frustration.

Here is a very assertive business partner, if natural enthusiasm is controlled, who will not lack ideas for company expansion. He or she may make a good front man or woman, working with a steady behind-the-scenes associate who can attend to the details while the individual exercises his or her boundless breadth of vision.

8 Jupiter in the Eighth House

Financial gain through investment is indicated here, and if Jupiter is well aspected, the individual should have a good business sense. The planet's influence, however, needs a great deal of controlling, and the ease or difficulty of this will depend largely on Jupiter's sign. If this is an earth sign, he or she should be able to invest wisely and intelligently, but this is less likely if it is in any other element.

Considerable sexual exuberance will be evident, and it is particularly important for the partner to be responsive and willing to experiment in the sex life. It may be that the subject is over-demanding and must become more aware of the partner's needs, consciously developing consideration for them. Sometimes too much is expected of the partner, and the individual will find satisfaction elsewhere. There is a freedom-loving element which will be expressed very naturally and openly, but the damage it can do to the regular partner is considerable, so restraint may have to be developed.

Tradition once decreed that Jupiter in this house was beneficial for inheritance, but this is an oversimplification not to be taken literally. In considering the more intellectual and philosophical side of Jupiter, the subject will give serious thought to life after death and may arrive at wise conclusions that will give a sense of stability.

9 Jupiter in the Ninth House

Jupiter's influence is strong here, for this is the Sagittarius/Jupiter house. There is considerable intellectual potential, which should be developed in accordance with the sign in which Jupiter is placed. The outlook on life is very positive, with great breadth of vision. The imagination will also be enhanced, with the ninth house love of travel, both intellectual and physical, emphasized in the best possible way.

The acquisition of knowledge and the need to study will be very important, and in order for the individual to feel fulfilled there should be constant opportunity for this. Should your subject be a young mother, do everything possible to encourage her to have a couple of hours away from her children at least once a week for she will find their constant chatter frustrating, no matter how much she loves them.

A variety of experience

Considerable versatility is usually present, but with it may come restlessness. This is more likely if Jupiter is in a fire or air sign, or is negatively aspected by Mercury, Mars or perhaps Uranus. Parents of children with this placing should remember that further education must be positively encouraged, and if the youngster wants to travel extensively, such an experience will contribute considerably to the development of his or her personality. There is often flair for languages, and time may be spent living abroad.

10 JUPITER IN THE TENTH HOUSE

If Jupiter is within eight degrees of the Midheaven, see also Jupiter conjunct the Midheaven, p.292. Whatever Jupiter's degree, dramatic flair is usually present, and these subjects will certainly attract attention in their chosen fields. If in a position of power, this will be wielded very fairly and with understanding and kindness, although they may be pompous at times. They will seize opportunities as they come along and will also create them; no grass will grow under these feet.

There is real strength in the ability to take in the broad perspective of situations, and to view the long-term philosophically and practically. Aspirations are high, and as they are conquered, worldly wisdom will grow and lessons be learned, which will be born in mind whenever the need arises.

Successful actors and actresses frequently have this placing, although a sense of drama and the tendency to show off are usually present even in those who do not become actors. There may be a talent for the law, publishing or any job where the individual is able to take center stage!

11 JUPITER IN THE ELEVENTH HOUSE

Here is someone who is a great socializer, who gathers together a large circle of friends and acquaintances and who contributes much to his or her set, or to any group interest. He or she may well serve on committees and eventually hold an important office.

Working with others

There is a natural inclination and ability to generate much energy and enthusiasm, and the chosen interest will move forward as a result of the subject's much-enjoyed hard work and effort. It will not be difficult for him to inspire others, and willing workers will give their all under his leadership.

The humanitarian side of the Aquarius/eleventh house will be present, with the subject perhaps being an excellent fundraiser, or one who takes action to help fight injustice – maybe working for famine relief or animal welfare. If he is creative, the chosen interest might be amateur dramatics.

Here is an excellent friend, always giving others encouragement to develop their potential, and throwing out challenging suggestions and ideas in order to keep the friendship alive, even when separated by many miles. An interesting consideration for you may be whether those with this placing tend to extend the friendship period of any developing romantic relationship, since the attitude to love and romance can be somewhat cynical: "We're just good friends" seems to be a typical statement here!

12 JUPITER IN THE TWELFTH HOUSE

Because Jupiter ruled Pisces until Neptune was taken into the astrological pantheon, this placing is a very important one. If Jupiter lies within eight or ten degrees of the Ascendant, see also Jupiter conjunct the Ascendant, pp.291-2.

There may be a true sense of vocation, perhaps religious but possibly also geared to fully developing the potential in some chosen subject that needs great dedication. There can also be reclusive tendencies, and usually the individual needs to work alone in peace and quiet. (Remember, however, that "quiet" means different things to different people!)

A creative contribution

The attitude to life is very philosophical, and the mind an excellent one. It will be up to the subject not just to drift into his or her own little world and opt out of reality, since the potential is excellent and must be used wisely and practically. A marvelous compromise can be reached if the individual finds work that has a concrete end-product, and it is this that is shown off to the public, rather than the individual himself. For instance, here we may have a solitary writer, potter or perhaps inventor, whose work speaks for itself rather than the person who projects his own personality. Indeed, the individual may wear a psychological mask in public, and be truly known by few people.

Esoteric subjects and religion, perhaps in the broadest sense, may be important. This is a good placing for the medical or caring professions, or for work in institutions.

♃ JUPITER PROGRESSED THROUGH THE HOUSES

Because Jupiter moves very slowly, it is not often that it moves by progression from its natal house to the next one. The change is only likely to occur if Jupiter is near the cusp of a house, although it may also happen that the planet turns from direct to retrograde motion, and as a result backs into the previous house; or if at birth it was retrograde, turns to direct motion and moves forward into the next house. The influence of Jupiter from its new house will offer fresh opportunities relating to whichever sphere of life concerns that house.

The Aspects of Jupiter

A well-aspected Jupiter – one receiving trines from the Sun, Moon, Mars or Saturn – can considerably enhance the individual's personality. However, it is easy to underestimate the effect of a badly-aspected Jupiter. We are dealing here with Jupiter's aspects to the outer planets, which remain in orb for several days, so relate them to their house and sign positions. Unless the planets are personalized, they may have a more general effect than those Jupiter receives from the Sun to Mars inclusive.

For Jupiter's aspects to the Sun see the Sun's aspects to Jupiter, p.216.

For Jupiter's aspects to the Moon see the Moon's aspects to Jupiter, p.234.

For Jupiter's aspects to Mercury see Mercury's aspects to Jupiter, p.249.

For Jupiter's aspects to Venus see Venus' aspects to Jupiter, pp.263-4.

For Jupiter's aspects to Mars see Mars' aspects to Jupiter, p.277.

Note: It is rare that Jupiter makes a progressed aspect to another planet with which it is not in aspect in the birth chart, but there will be times when such aspects become exact – i.e. when there is no orb between them (see p.54). Whenever these aspects are exact, bear their influence in mind when interpreting the progressions of the planets in question.

If Jupiter forms an aspect to the natal or progressed position of Saturn, Uranus, Neptune or Pluto, look up the relevant transit interpretation, remembering that although the influence will be less potent, it will last while Jupiter is on the relevant degree, and will give support to important transits as and when they are operative. Base your interpretation on the most apt paragraph, i.e. conjunction, positive or negative aspects.

If Jupiter forms a progressed aspect to the natal Sun, Moon, Mercury, Venus or Mars, read the interpretation for that planet's progressions to Jupiter, and pay especial attention to the relevant paragraph, i.e. conjunction, positive or negative aspects.

If Jupiter makes a progressed aspect to the Ascendant or Midheaven in either the birth or progressed chart, refer to the interpretation of Jupiter's transits to the Ascendant or Midheaven. These progressions will be powerful and operate over several years, but their effects will be the same as Jupiter's transits.

Jupiter's Aspects to Saturn

Conjunction

Here the two giants of the Solar System join forces. At its best this will bestow optimism and common sense, a balanced outlook on life and the ability to be enthusiastic or restrained, as and when necessary. However, the planets don't always exert an equal influence, and we often find that Saturn wins – the subject will be optimistic and hopeful, but with occasional gloom or depression. Even so, there is always a sense of purpose, with a serious and practical attitude to whatever has to be done. There can also be staying-power.

Decide which of the two is the stronger planet in the chart as a whole. If one is personalized, it will dominate this aspect. If neither is personal, look at each planet's sign and house position to discover which is dominant. If, once again, the answer is neither, you may find that the subject shows Jovian optimism at times and Saturnian pessimism at others. A steady physical and emotional pace must be achieved if this conjunction's influence is to be kept in balance, and that may not be easy.

+ Positive aspects

These have a steadying influence, with the common sense, practical attributes of Saturn blending well with the extrovert enthusiasm and optimism of Jupiter. Breadth of vision will combine with caution. The individual's inner voice gives good advice and boosts the self-confidence. There is an ability to plan constructively for the future and to carry out such plans. He or she has good judgement and can put problems into a coherent perspective.

– Negative aspects

There is usually an element of discontent, with the subject feeling that he or she is achieving, or has achieved, very little. Restlessness is common, with a tendency to blame circumstance or background for lack of success or fulfillment. In fact, inner discontent and a lack of will or self-confidence are often the cause of the problem. It is vital to discover what the individual's inner voice is saying; it may emerge that he had to cope with many put-downs as a child, which is the reverse of the effect of positive aspects between Jupiter and Saturn. Listening to himself, the subject gains no confidence but hears only a negative authoritarianism that convinces him that he isn't much good at anything, so why should he bother?

Look elsewhere in the chart to see where the real potential lies, and to find any indications that will counter this heavy influence, helping your subject to build up self-confidence and the strength of will to move forward. Stress the positive qualities of the Ascendant, Sun and Moon signs and the influence of the personal planets. A well-aspected Mars will also help. If either Jupiter or Saturn is personalized, its influence will be emphasized.

Jupiter's Aspects to Uranus

Conjunction

This is a powerful focal point in a chart. The individual will be very positive in outlook, have an excellent and original mind, and be extremely forward-looking, with humanitarian kindness and benevolence. In recent years the conjunction was formed in Sagittarius – a lively and positive placing for it. It is endowing these young people not only with the qualities already mentioned, but also a delightful, warm sense of humor, and is marking them with pleasant, slightly offbeat characteristics that will enhance their personalities throughout their lives.

Generally speaking, it is only if the conjunction is negatively aspected that it will be a source of tension and restlessness, and even then these can be discharged positively and dynamically through work and other interests.

Positive aspects

The subject has a powerful element of originality and many of the qualities of the conjunction. There is usually a lively sense of humor and a friendly willingness to help others. Popularity is also likely, especially if the chart shows that the individual is extrovert.

Determination is increased but there can be a certain eccentricity, which if controlled will do no real harm, unless it is indicated elsewhere in the chart. These aspects will help the subject to develop his or her potential and make it possible to attract the attention of others.

Negative aspects

There is usually considerable restlessness and eccentricity, especially if either planet is personalized. Sometimes, too, there can be discontent and little ability to sustain strong but fleeting enthusiasms, with the subject often spending much money on whatever will further the interest, which is then cast aside as suddenly as it began.

Independence can be carried to extremes – for instance, by refusing help when it is seriously needed. This in turn can lead to excessive stubbornness, and is not admirable. Vanity and pomposity can also be present. Don't over-interpret these aspects; use them as supporting factors unless the planets are personalized.

Jupiter's Aspects to Neptune

Conjunction

As Jupiter traditionally ruled Pisces and Neptune is the modern ruler of the sign, there is considerable affinity between these two planets. Here, they give idealism and some humility. There is often a subtle, caring instinct, and sympathy and empathy with others.

A certain spirituality may also be evident, not necessarily linked to conventional religion, but often to a more universal faith. The individual is also optimistic. The fantasy life is rich, and there is a certain dreaminess which is most creative when supported by practical elements elsewhere in the chart. Otherwise the subject can become simply a dreamer of dreams. (Personal planets in earth, or a well-aspected Mars and/or Saturn will provide more stimulus.) If this aspect is part of a chart that shows the subject is very materialistic and ambitious, its subtle influence can be lost – although it may help to soften any inherent harshness.

Positive aspects

These are similar to the conjunction in effect, but may be swamped by other, stronger elements, unless the subject is prominently Piscean or Sagittarian, or very sensitive. Nevertheless, the subtle, gentle qualities will add delicacy and sympathy to even the strongest of charts. The aspect also inspires the subject to do his or her bit to make the world a better place in which to live.

Negative aspects

As with the above aspects, there is kindness, sympathy and sensitivity to suffering. Unfortunately, the individual can easily become forgetful and rather dreamy, getting lost in his or her own little world at every opportunity.

The emotional level is increased, and there is a colorful imagination, but neither are always be expressed positively. Any tendencies to dishonesty or self-deception may be increased. Many writers suggest that there is a vulnerability to gas fumes or fish poisoning, especially when either Jupiter or Neptune are negatively contacted by transitting planets. Again, this aspect can get lost among stronger indications, so don't over-interpret it.

Jupiter's Aspects to Pluto

Conjunction

There is a compelling desire for power, especially if the aspect falls in the tenth house, or either or both planets form a conjunction with the Midheaven. The need to make material progress is strong, with a near-obsessive enthusiasm for objectives of all kinds. Sometimes fanaticism is present. If controlled, these powerful qualities are a marvelous source of potential. Otherwise, the individual can be overwhelming and ruthless in the pursuit of aims. There are powers of leadership, and others can be magnetically attracted. The organizational abilities are usually superb, but if the subject is wrong-minded he or she can over-influence weaker personalities.

Positive aspects

These give a great deal of inner strength and the determination to pursue objectives. Organizational ability and leadership powers are present, and we usually find an ability to use the intelligence to achieve what is planned.

Negative aspects

There can be total adherence to the pursuit of fanatical objectives, and if considerable dynamism is shown in other areas of the chart the individual will have the power to mislead others. This is most likely if Uranus conjuncts Pluto in Virgo (births between 1963 and 1969) and Jupiter negatively aspects both planets. Watch out for such tendencies in your subject, and encourage him or her to develop other positive and sensitive qualities derived from the Sun, Moon or rising sign.

Jupiter's Aspects to the Ascendant

Conjunction

If Jupiter is in the first house the subject is enthusiastic, positive and open-minded; there is optimism, breadth of vision and an excellent intellect. He or she gets along well with other people and is popular. Life is enjoyed in a fun-loving way, but the outlook is philosophical, with a sense of justice. Sometimes there is a tendency to exaggerate, and a liking for risk-taking, both emotional and physical. She will put on weight very easily, often around the hips and thighs. Slight indigestion can also occur. Constant exercise is very important and is usually enjoyed.

If Jupiter is in the twelfth house, the influence will not be as extrovert, since the more spiritual, reflective side of the planet is working. A sense of vocation is possible, and sacrifices can be made.

In either case, the respective house-placing of Jupiter is powerfully enhanced. Do remember that if Jupiter is within one degree of the Ascendant the birth time need only be inaccurate by four minutes to change the planet's house position. As you gain experience you will be able to tell whether your subject is a first-house or twelfth-house Jupiter person: the difference in the effect will be striking.

+ Positive aspects
These are similar in effect to the conjunction when it falls in the first house, but Jupiter's influence will be less powerful and the characteristics of the aspect will enhance or counter those of the Ascendant. The health is unlikely to be affected.

− Negative aspects
A tendency to exaggerate and show off may alienate other people and thereby weaken the subject's position, both personally and in material advancement. In some cases these traits will make him or her rather a bore. The chances are that these extreme characteristics will be mitigated by other more desirable ones, but warn the subject of their presence if they emerge – pride comes before a fall!

MC JUPITER'S ASPECTS TO THE MIDHEAVEN

☌ Conjunction
As Jupiter is likely to be the highest planet in the birth chart sky, its effect will be very strong. The individual will potentially be very successful and well-liked, and inner contentment is usual. All Jovian vocations and careers may fascinate and be very rewarding and successful; the subject won't ever allow the grass to grow under his or her feet. The outlook on life is very optimistic, with considerable enthusiasm for any project undertaken.

There may not be much interest in detail (although this could emerge from the Jupiter/Midheaven sign or from other areas of the chart) and a sense of justice will color the natural powers of leadership. Here is someone who usually sets a good example to others, especially if in charge of them. Reread the house placing for Jupiter as it will add another dimension to this interpretation. Self-confidence is increased and the subject usually has a powerful, but not overinflated, ego.

+ Positive aspects
The positive Jupiter traits of optimism and enthusiasm, plus the ability to take calculated risks, will influence the subject's attitude toward aims and ambitions. There is usually success in achieving challenging objectives and self-confidence is increased, with a sense of pride in achievement.

− Negative aspects
There is a tendency to show off and to exaggerate, especially where accomplishments are concerned. An identification with all things grand and pompous is usual, as is an excessive devotion to the Establishment and all that it stands for. Nevertheless, since Jupiter is a beneficial planet, the subject will be successful in the career and in attaining objectives – but may not be as popular as he or she thinks.

♃ THE TRANSITS OF JUPITER

The transits of the Sun, Mercury, Venus and Mars are of very short duration. While they often have striking effects on our day-to-day lives, they do not influence important trends which can lead to changes, developments, opportunities and so on. Jupiter is the first planet to be considered in this way. The contacts it makes to the natal positions of the planets, the Ascendant and the Midheaven are important and can be used in a variety of beneficial ways. To calculate these and the influences of all the slow-moving planets, and to fully understand their duration and how they affect us, reread Progressing the Chart (see pp.60-9) and the general hints on interpretation (see pp.130-47).

When working on the transits of the the Sun and the other fast-moving planets you will only have calculated the conjunctions and oppositions, but with Jupiter and the other slow-moving planets (i.e. Saturn, Uranus, Neptune and Pluto) all the aspects should be used.

Generally speaking, Jupiter's influence is positive and useful; opportunities often occur when the planet is working well for us. We also have enjoyable experiences, sometimes travel and sometimes study to advantage. Sometimes we put on weight, or overreact. The interpretations of these transits are dealt with in the same way as for the aspects, being divided into the conjunction, positive and negative aspects. Again, as with aspect interpretation, we recommend that you read all three categories first to gain the general idea of the influence.

If Jupiter is aspected negatively in the birth chart the transit influence – even if it is a trine – will be less beneficial, but the subject should use Jupiter's energy in whichever ways are of most help. Of all the planets, Jupiter provides the greatest encouragement and help when given a gentle but firm push in the direction in which we want it to go!

The transits of Jupiter to its own position are especially relevant and, as with the fast-moving planets, we place that interpretation at the end of the section. In addition, you will find a full explanation and interpretation of the Jupiter Return, which is one of the most exciting and fascinating of all transits (see p.297).

☉ JUPITER'S TRANSITS TO THE SUN

☌ Conjunction
This happens once every 12 years, marking a period of opportunity and heralding an especially rewarding time. But it is vital that the individual makes a concentrated effort, taking center stage, showing off a little, and ensuring that those people who can help know of his or her potential.

If out of work, this is the time to apply for more jobs. Travel and study will be particularly rewarding, and there is a sense of being on a winning streak. All the Sun sign characteristics will be enhanced, and feelings of optimism and enthusiasm usually predominate. This is an influence to exploit fully.

+ Positive transits
These have a similar effect to the conjunction, but the sextile will not be quite as strong and can be overruled by other more powerful transits,

especially if they are negative. Nevertheless the sextile and the trine are very helpful for general progress, study and travel, and indicate good times for holidays. Opportunities must be looked for and acted upon.

Negative transits

Any tendency to exaggerate and overdramatize situations must be avoided. Financial or emotional risks or gambles may also be taken. An overoptimistic outlook and blind enthusiasm can be disastrous, so caution is very necessary.

In some circumstances good advice could fall on deaf ears. Biliousness due to high living is common, and a good supply of hangover remedies may be needed. If the natal Sun and Jupiter are in negative aspect to each other, important decisions should be delayed until the influence has passed, for mistakes can be made due to the ignoring of small print or over-optimism.

Jupiter's Transits to the Moon

Conjunction

This enhances the emotions, intuitions and feelings. The influence is excellent if the Moon is well-aspected in the birth chart, but if it receives mostly squares or oppositions the judgement may not be sound and Jupiter's influence might bring out these less helpful traits. However, in most cases the reactions to situations will be sensible, and the decisions taken will be correct.

Life may be viewed in a more philosophical light, with situations assessed instinctively and fairly. The subject will be in a generous mood and will probably want to improve his or her social life – something you might care to suggest. Enterprise should be definitely encouraged.

Positive transits

Considerable personal success is likely. Encourage your subject to listen to his or her instincts and intuitions. The influence is like that of the conjunction and could herald a very rewarding period, especially where the home and family life are concerned. These are excellent transits to use for family vacations or concentrating on projects involving parents and children. Those who enjoy do-it-yourself activities might like to start redecoration or home extension work at such times. If creative work is enjoyed, the imagination and intellect will combine to give rewarding results. The judgement should be sound, so this is the time to make decisions.

Negative transits

These can cause more trouble than is realized but unfortunately the subject will probably not know that anything is wrong, or that mistakes are being made. There will be a tendency to overreact to situations and to dramatize them. If upset, extreme action may be taken so that mountains are made out of molehills, resulting in quite serious damage, especially to loved ones, which might be difficult to put right. This is not a good time in which to make important decisions since misjudgement is likely.

Care is needed when dealing with money, rental agreements or anything to do with the law. The diet should be kept simple, since the system can be more easily upset by rich food and drink than usual. On the whole a consciously logical outlook and perspective must be kept at this time.

Jupiter's Transits to Mercury

Conjunction

This is an excellent influence, when the time is right to travel for pleasure or business, to study, to learn to drive or take the driving test. Here the two planets of the intellect are working well together, so concentration on any project or area requiring mental dexterity or an extension of the mind is excellent. However, these planets do not always increase the powers of concentration, so you will find that the transit will be at its best if Saturn is making one or two positive transits to the Sun, Moon or Mercury.

The time is right for embarking on a new study course or any interest which is intellectually challenging or develops the potential. The outlook will be optimistic and enterprising. Those with a flair for business could easily set up some good deals, and as a result considerable progress will be made. The Sun and Mercury are always reasonably close together in the birth chart, so Jupiter's conjunction to the Sun will either have preceeded its conjunction to Mercury or will follow it within about twelve months. The two influences may therefore give a beneficial theme to a year or so. (It may be interesting to ask how your subject fared twelve years previously, when Jupiter was last in this position). These influences, especially the Mercury contact, is of enormous assistance to school children, who may well rise several places in class as a result.

Positive transits

These present the ideal time for taking an exciting vacation abroad. They are also a good period in which to start a new study venture – learning a language perhaps – as the mind is ready for intellectual challenge. There will be a notably increased desire to communicate ideas, perhaps on radio phone-ins! Articles may be written for trade or specialist journals and, as hinted above, the time is also right to take a driving test or some advanced driving lessons.

There is scarcely a better influence under which to take examinations, provided the powers of concentration are naturally good or enhanced by stabilizing transits. Any inclination to restlessness must be controlled.

Negative transits

Uncharacteristic absentmindedness is very common, and the inability to take life sufficiently seriously can cause problems. Sometimes the subject will gloss over difficulties or fail to keep promises. A lack of caution is likely and common sense can be badly lacking so that mistakes are made, sometimes due to blind optimism.

Important decisions affecting the long-term future should not be taken at this time; for example, taking on too large a mortgage or other monetary commitment can lead to severe financial difficulties.

If the subject is a student approaching examinations there will be a tendency to think that there's no need to revise and that his or her answers to examination questions are marvelous. They might not be! Advise him or her to take life a little more seriously.

♀ Jupiter's Transits to Venus

Conjunction

This is a lovely influence which makes us generous, kind, affectionate, understanding and happy – and often happy to see others enjoying themselves at our expense. Popularity will increase, with life enjoyed to the full. However, as with all contacts between these planets there will be a tendency to put on weight, since rich food is nearly always eaten – here is another influence that often requires bicarbonate of soda! The time is right to think about making extra money, either by starting an enterprising project or by investing (albeit with a certain restraint).

This can be a memorable time if the transit supports positive long-term progressions or lunar progressions. Sometimes (but don't over-stress the possibility) people become engaged when Jupiter and Venus meet up. The emotions and intellect work well together. Remember that traditionally Jupiter is the most beneficial planet in the Solar System, while Venus is the next in line for that happy position.

Positive transits

These transits are almost identical to the conjunction but can work in even more positive ways, since there is less likelihood of Jupiter and Venus getting out of hand and encouraging the subject to overdo things or spend too much on entertaining! They are positive influences that can be used to further his or her interests and future enterprises.

Purchases, especially investment buys, will give long-lasting pleasure (as well as a good return if they have to be sold later). There will be an increased appreciation of luxury and comfort, which probably won't go away as the indication eases. After all, having experienced the best it's difficult to settle for a star or two less when choosing an hotel. The same goes when boosting one's wardrobe: a taste for designer labels is easily acquired at this time!

Negative transits

These tend to cause a period of laziness, of "couldn't care less" – or of untoward extravagance. If the subject is going through a difficult period in a personal relationship, there will be a tendency to give up, or make a rash decision that may be regretted later.

The emotions and intellect are under strain, and reason and common sense will not prevail. Watch out for any inclinations to eat too much or to starve; either will be the result of feeling unloved. Usually this is quite the wrong impression, as will be seen when the influence has passed. The whole trend is to exaggerate the feelings and to be excessive in action, so it is important to keep on the straight and narrow. Professional advice should be taken over financial problems, with the reduction of any investments or financial risk-taking, since mistakes are all too easily made at this time.

♂ Jupiter's Transits to Mars

Conjunction

This is a marvelously positive transit, heralding a period when the subject should take the initiative and be assertive. He or she will be in a very strong position, and as a result of putting these energies to work will make excellent progress. Boldness and brave action is encouraged, especially if that means being powerfully decisive and determined. There is increased willpower, and the subject will want to fill every moment with action.

Under this influence we should make opportunities for ourselves as opposed to simply taking them if they come our way, but there will be the desire to create them. Any apprehension should be discouraged – action taken under this lively influence will pay off, and progress will almost certainly result. The influence is marvelous for anyone involved in competitive projects – sporting activities, for instance, or anything that demands the expenditure of physical as well as intellectual energy.

Positive transits

These influences are almost identical to those of the conjunction, although the powerful drives and energies will be expressed with more consideration for other people. Success is just as likely, especially if the transit is a trine. The sextile is very useful and will give support to other positive trends, but will not of itself promote such powerfully energetic conditions or have the drive of the conjunction or trine. The same decisiveness will be present, as will the ability to cope with protagonists in a just and reasonable way.

Both intellectual and physical energy is increased by this transit, as is the desire to win. A new, invigorating exercise regime or renewed interest in sports may be taken up, doing much to brush away any cobwebs, whether mental or physical, that are lingering.

Negative transits

These can make the individual somewhat rebellious and devil-may-care. Recklessness is common, and should be consciously guarded against, as should the inclination to take financial risks or other big gambles. The tendency to exaggerate will be present here, as will over-hastiness, both physical and mental. Warn the subject of all these possibilities. Thoughtlessness, usually because the individual is being uncharacteristically self-centered, can also cause problems, especially with loved ones.

There is a positive side to these rather extreme transits. If there have been quarrels and upsets, this influence will finally resolve them, bringing "peace among the planets" and to the subject and his or her close associates, for Jupiter will have aligned with Mars, and as a result the dust will settle.

♄ Jupiter's Transits to Saturn

Conjunction

Some dissatisfaction is usual when Jupiter contacts Saturn. However, because Jupiter's influence is positive and this is the most powerful of the contacts, the will and determination to do something about what is wrong is equally likely. Once the individual has decided precisely where the root of the discontent lies, he or she will develop a need for challenge. There will, for instance, be a desire to make a greater effort or earn more money. Sometimes the subject realizes that his or her mind is stagnating, and there is room for improvement, so that as the influence becomes stronger so the commitment to study or to concentrate on some mentally stimulating and involving interest will develop. Sometimes there is a general discontent with lifestyle, relationship or surroundings: encouragement from you might motivate your subject. He or she may not follow your suggestions precisely, but on thinking about what you have said may come up with an idea which wouldn't have otherwise occurred.

If the individual is extremely practical and down-to-earth, you may have to beat him into action. If so, shock tactics might pay off; statements like "You'll be old before your time if you don't do something about all this" are enough to start Jupiter rolling toward him in the best possible way!

Positive transits

These contacts will bring out the individual's common sense and practical approach to life. Determination is increased, as is the realization that his or her perseverance will pay off.

Decisions about the long-term future can be made during this period, even if plans laid down now do not have to be put into operation for some time. The influence will, for instance, complement changes made at the time of a Saturn Return, stabilize the attitude toward developments and opportunities that may arise during a Jupiter Return, or as the result of other exciting or dynamic progressions or transits. This is a time for thinking carefully about important issues – the conclusions gained will be correct under this stabilizing influence.

Negative transits

Considerable frustration is possible, especially when the individual thinks he or she is making good progress. The trend acts as a brake, and while this can be most annoying at the time, in retrospect it may be realized that all was for the best. However, he may be very dissatisfied, restless and easily infuriated while under this stop/go influence, so must be calmed down. There will be less patience than usual, but unfortunately it will be necessary if he is to take problems and setbacks in his stride. One possibility is that Jupiter is working overtime and causing overoptimism, so that there is an exaggerated sense of being let down when things go wrong.

♅ Jupiter's Transits to Uranus

Conjunction

This is an exciting influence that often brings about unexpected developments which open up new horizons. The urge for independence is strengthened, and while this is enough to motivate action or the making of changes, because we are dealing with the conjunction there is little likelihood of selfish, irresponsible or unpredictable actions. To make sure of this, see how both planets are aspected in the birth chart. Are they receiving squares or oppositions from the personal planets? Are they in aspect to each other? If the former, there could be tension, which is also likely if they are in negative aspect to each other. If well-aspected, the transit will have a splendid effect.

Here is a surge of powerful nervous and intellectual energy which should get plenty of positive expression. The influence will probably bring some exciting and maybe memorable events.

Positive transits

These will also bring unexpected and exciting events, and as a result some new elements may begin to build in the subject's life. As to which sphere will be affected, look at the house position of Uranus, which may give you a clue. Only suggest the possibility – you must not predict an event, remember. Sometimes under this influence people are keen to stretch their minds, and as a result take a new and wiser attitude to life, or acquire some specialist knowledge. There may be an inclination to study a very offbeat or unusual subject.

Negative transits

The individual will probably experience a period when at least one sphere of life, or an important project, is a source of tension, and he or she may want to break away from whatever is the source of the trouble. However, action must not be taken prematurely, for hastiness or even stubborn obstinacy may mean a loss of perspective. If there are problems with tension and nerves, a course of relaxing exercises would be beneficial and help to calm the nervous tension (Uranus) and refresh the spirit (Jupiter).

♆ Jupiter's Transits to Neptune

Conjunction

This is a marvelously subtle influence that will do much for sensitive, intuitive, creative people, but when it occurs in the charts of very practical, materialistic subjects it can have very little outward effect.

There will be increased sensitivity and an awareness of the finer elements of life – often spiritual, mystical and idealistic areas. The emotions are considerably heightened and there is a tendency to fall into very contemplative moods.

Sometimes there can be a need to get away from it all, perhaps with a quiet weekend by the sea or river, or whichever landscape is most restorative. If of a religious nature, this is a superb influence under which to make a retreat. Afterwards, the individual will feel refreshed and much restored, well able to cope once more with his or her job or family.

Positive transits

The effects of these are very similar to those of the conjunction, although the sextile may get a little lost in the mists if it coincides with more worldly and assertive transits. It may be that the individual will be inspired in some way, with new, probably beautiful, creative work being the outcome. It is always good to suggest that time will be well spent making notes or photographic records of whatever appeals and is observed; there will be especially interesting and original results.

The influence also inspires a dreamy, perhaps overromantic mood; remember that cloud nine should not be dwelled on for too long!

Negative transits

Care is needed at this time, since it can be all too easy to be negatively overinfluenced by other people's opinions and actions. Mistakes can be made, usually when the individual is feeling particularly carefree and happy. Sometimes the wrong thing is said, causing misunderstandings and confusion. It is vital to keep a firm grip on reality but that may not be easy. The powers of concentration won't be very good, either. This is not a favorable time in which to make important decisions, and caution is necessary when listening to advice – something, of course, that you may well have to bear in mind!

♇ Jupiter's Transits to Pluto

☌ Conjunction

The individual will push forward, taking a stronger line of action and a more dominant position. Self-confidence grows and often he or she becomes more materialistic, with a greater interest in investment, insurance and finance generally. The desire for power is increased and all will be well provided that the subject is not too fanatical.

The craving for power will probably be most pronounced if Pluto is in Leo in the birth chart, or if the subject was born in the sixties, when Uranus and Pluto were in conjunction in Virgo. Remember that Jupiter's influence is a fine and positive one, and on the whole progress and the attainment of objectives seem the most likely outcomes. An event or action may boost the subject's ego, but she should not become big-headed as a result!

+ Positive transits

Here again, material progress will be made and the bank balance be improved. As a result, there could be real flair for investment, and provided common sense overrules any blind optimism, this should work out very well. Again, the individual will probably move up the ladder and find him- or herself in a stronger position. She will be listened to more readily, and will find that her opinions are taken more seriously.

− Negative transits

Care is needed that a tendency to form fanatical opinions or take extreme action is avoided. If money is involved, there will be an inclination to over-invest or to spend carelessly. Much money has been lost by people under this particularly trying influence, and all forms of gambling should definitely be avoided while it persists. Any financial decisions should be shelved until the transit has passed (allow at least three clear weeks).

Asc Jupiter's Transits to the Ascendant

☌ Conjunction

Here, Jupiter ends a transit of the twelfth house and enters the first, so this aspect marks a period when that planet's influence changes from encouraging contemplation, retrospection and reflection to proposing that the individual should take center stage, show off and create opportunities. He or she should feel refreshed and rejuvenated, be as self-expressive as possible and seek challenge and action. This is an excellent time in which to look for a job that is more rewarding, both financially and intellectually. There will be enjoyable times but weight gain and indigestion must be guarded against. Enjoyment of life is to be encouraged.

+ Positive transits

These have much the same effects as the conjunction, but look at the house through which Jupiter is transiting, since its concerns may blossom. For instance, if there is a trine transit and Jupiter is in, or about to enter, the fifth house, there may be a new love affair or a second honeymoon. Creative interests will also flourish.

− Negative transits

There will be a strong tendency to view problems out of perspective and to over-react. The individual may become unbearably self-important and pompous for no reason at all, then once the transit has passed realize how foolish he or she has been. Caution is necessary in what is said or written, and any inclination to exaggerate must be controlled if possible.

MC Jupiter's Transits to the Midheaven

☌ Conjunction

The accent is on opportunities, but there is a distinct difference between what happens when Jupiter conjuncts the Midheaven and when it conjuncts the Ascendant. For example, Jupiter conjunct the Ascendant: subjects get a new job they applied for; Jupiter conjunct the Midheaven: they are offered a new job because people have heard about their abilities, so the offer comes out of the blue. Opportunities and new developments will further the subject's progress. Sometimes there is the chance to travel (perhaps at someone else's expense?)

In general, you will find that all things connected with Jupiter will flourish and much may happen unexpectedly – often a nice surprise or a win of some kind.

+ Positive transits

These are much as the conjunction, but any new developments are unlikely to be as important unless Jupiter is a personal planet, in Sagittarius, or that sign is on the Midheaven. Even so, this should be a very rewarding period.

− Negative transits

Hopes may be dashed to the ground at this time, so a sceptical and cautious attitude should be adopted. The subject may be easily influenced by others who could, for their own reasons, be doing everything possible to boost his or her ego. Caution is needed all the way, especially if contracts or legal documents are being drawn up; the small print must be read. It is all too easy to be swept along on a tide of over-optimistic enthusiasm at this time.

♃ Jupiter's Transits to its Own Position

Generally speaking, when Jupiter forms a positive transit to its own position the subject will experience a time in which life moves forward very progressively and the outlook is optimistic and positive. When Jupiter forms a negative transit the subject can be overoptimistic, perhaps getting small problems out of perspective. Sometimes unnecessary risks are taken, with financial and emotional gambling. In addition, the period is not conducive to the signing of contracts or legal documents, since the small print may be ignored or too much money signed away in a flurry of enthusiasm.

When calculating a transit of Jupiter to its own position you must study the planet's natal aspects, its sign and house position, since their effects will be to the fore in the life of the individual concerned. Even if the transit itself is positive, some of its beneficial nature will be lost if Jupiter has more negative aspects than positive ones. If the transit is negative but Jupiter is well-aspected natally, the negativity of the transit will be mitigated although, while things will go well, the subject may take on too much or be too optimistic. To decide the eventual outcome, it is best to calculate and interpret any planetary transits that follow the Jupiter contacts.

♃ The Jupiter Return

In essence, this is the conjunction transit of Jupiter to its own position. As Jupiter takes 12 years to complete a journey around the Sun and through all 12 signs of the zodiac, the planet takes 12 years to return to the position it occupies in the birth chart. So we have a Jupiter Return when we are approximately 12, 24, 36, 48, 60, 72, 84 and 96 years of age. These are periods to which we should look forward, and when we should take full advantage of every opportunity that arises.

After a Jupiter Return year we should be in a stronger position financially, and have taken a step or two up the career ladder or in any interest that means a lot to us. It is important not to miss any opportunities; they must be confidently seized – and the more they challenge us, the better. Sometimes we must work very hard indeed during the year of a Jupiter Return, but we usually enjoy what we do in the expectation that it will be worthwhile in the long run. This is especially so if we are studying, traveling or working in any of the areas ruled by Jupiter.

Referring to past experience

A little retrospective astrology is interesting when considering the influence of a Jupiter Return. If the subject is due for one, ask what he or she was doing 12 years ago. Which sphere of life was most to the fore?; was she making special progress?; did she pass an examination, or travel more extensively than previously? All such things may have happened, and while history is unlikely to repeat itself exactly, it may well affect the same sphere of life with the same sort of conditions. Care is necessary when retracing Jupiter's influence; your subject may have had a ghastly time, when everything went wrong! If so, you must delve more deeply into the planetary influences of that time – if the subject was suffering from stress, other even stronger indications were probably the source of the trouble, with much of Jupiter's positive influence being overruled. Even so, you may decide that things might have been even worse without Jupiter's help! Just how good the influence was will by now largely depend on Jupiter's natal position and aspects; but even so this really is a strong influence, and there should (in theory, and nearly always in practice) be some excellent developments. As we have said, do remember that Jupiter likes to be given a little push in the direction we want it to go – particularly so during a Jupiter Return. It is therefore a time to be very assertive – to apply for jobs, make suggestions to people who matter, and so on.

Early years

Parents of children approaching their first Jupiter Return should heartily encourage them to put this strong planetary energy to use. They should enter competitions, take tests or examinations (especially in specialist extra-curricular subjects such as music or athletics) or increase their study of any compelling interest. Progress made at this particular time can often spark off interest in a specialist subject that is later studied in depth, or which becomes a career after college is over.

Later life

The Jupiter Returns occurring later in life are progress points along the way. Life often becomes a little easier, due to extra money, and is more rewarding and worthwhile. However, we cannot stress too strongly that Jupiter's energy should be put to good use and not wasted. The Jupiter Return that occurs when we are about 60 often coincides with the second Saturn Return (see p.312), which is a particularly important one. Similarly the Jupiter Return, which occurs at around 84, can coincide with the extraordinary Uranus Return (see p.326). These are all of special interest and often more potent than usual. Not everyone is affected by the Jupiter Return in the same way, nor, of course, do we all take sudden steps forward at precisely the same point in our lives. In interpreting the influence it is important to consider the subject's Ascendant, Sun, Moon and Midheaven signs, as well as that of the ruling planet. They will indicate how he or she will react and respond to this interesting transit.

The extent of the influence

How long does the influence last? In astronomical terms, if Jupiter is moving steadily forward through the zodiac it can be exact (i.e. rest on the degree it occupies in the birth chart) for as few as four days. However, having passed over its precise natal position, Jupiter may turn to retrograde motion and then later return to direct motion and conjunct its natal position for a third time. This can take as long as nine months. Even so, it seems that no matter how often Jupiter conjuncts its natal position, its astrological return will cover most of a year. It is unlikely for things suddenly to fall into place when Jupiter is exact. However, the time when Jupiter is exact could be the centre of a key period relating to the influence as a whole, and the sphere of life that progresses as a result may be emphasized. By this time the subject will be aware of what is happening.

The chances are that the Jupiter Return will work rather more powerfully for those who have one or more of the following in their birth charts:

- Sagittarius Ascendant.
- Sun in Sagittarius.
- Sagittarius Midheaven.
- Moon in Sagittarius.
- Jupiter in Sagittarius.
- Jupiter conjunct the Ascendant from the first or twelfth house.
- Jupiter conjunct the Midheaven.
- Jupiter conjunct the Sun.
- Jupiter in Cancer (traditionally, Jupiter is well-placed here).
- Jupiter in Pisces (Jupiter ruled this sign before the acceptance of Neptune as the ruler of Pisces).
- Jupiter in the first, ninth, or twelfth house.

Saturn through the Signs

Saturn represents authority; here is our inner father figure. Often his authoritarianism says "Thou shalt not", and he definitely inhibits. At such times we must decide whether to accept the situation or whether, because we have been on the receiving end of put-downs as children, we should fight his inner authoritative voice. When this process is working, we either gain self-confidence because we have taken a prudent line of action, or regress because we have blindly and stupidly gone against a sensible inner voice or are crushed by the effect of our relationship with our parents, upbringing and early environment. Conversely, at other times Saturn says "Thou shalt", and we do what usually turns out to be the right thing, difficult though it may be at the time.

SATURN IN ARIES

The positive, energetic force of Aries is at total variance with the caution and restriction of Saturn, and on the whole the two are not happy bedfellows. The individual will be very strong, brave and assertive at times, but at others will show inhibition and even weakness. A balance should be consciously developed, as possible extremes of action and inaction will then be governed and the energetic force of Aries used with common sense and practicality. When the subject has come to terms with the Saturn influence, he or she will be determined, persistent and able to cope when life is difficult. Physical and emotional energy must be evenly used, however, if strain is not to occur during demanding periods.

When the pace slows, the reverse happens and stagnation, or restlessness and discontent, can build up. Any inclination toward depression should be worked off with a change of occupation – sporting activities, or workouts at a health club, may be the best kind of antidote. The authoritative inner voice can cause confusion and restlessness – at times goading the subject into action when he or she knows that inaction would be better, and at others sapping the self-confidence.

SATURN IN TAURUS

The patience of Taurus, plus the ability to be careful and cautious which is so much a part of Saturn's influence, complement each other here. The individual is long-suffering and will patiently cope and plod on to accomplish whatever most concerns him or her. However, the combination of the luxury-loving side of Taurus and the prudence of Saturn (too often turning into meanness or frugality) can cause considerable conflict.

Finding the right approach
How is it possible, then, for subjects to take advantage of this placing? There is little doubt that they are ambitious and want to make money. Saturn also brings a tendency to social climbing within the context of its ambitious qualities. As a result, this placing can encourage a steady (and no doubt comfortable!) climb toward the objectives in life. However, Saturn's negative inner voice will sound accusations of being extravagant, of eating too much and too expensively, and will constantly ask "Do you really need that?" Individuals must come up with their own answers, but must also learn to enjoy the Taurean side of this placing. If, on the whole, the chart is extrovert in influence, this should not be too hard, but if the subject is rather shy and generally inhibited this will be far more difficult, as feelings of guilt will recur and must be tempered by stronger qualities. Usually, a justification of pleasure should not be necessary; perhaps a lesson that those with this placing must learn.

Caution, patience, persistence and sometimes an overrigid routine and discipline are common. Parents with this placing, while wanting to give their children the best, may tend to be overstrict with them. The way in which the emotions are expressed may also be inhibited, although the individual is usually very kind. Generally, objects that are functional will be preferred to those that are beautiful.

SATURN IN GEMINI

The intellectual ability and stability are usually increased by this placing, which often contributes scientific flair. It is a marvelous supporting factor if this potential is shown in other areas of the chart. However, it is not particularly helpful from the creative point of view, although it is of use to people with a musical talent.

The mind is steadied, and the subject has the ability to be impartial yet profound. He or she will be economical with words, sometimes saying a great deal in a very few sentences – the opposite effect from that of the usual Geminian influence! Children with this placing may be rather slow to speak, and so can be deemed quiet. Parents should not worry; the chances are that their children's powers of observation are high, and they are missing nothing.

Ways of communicating
If Saturn is negatively aspected by personal planets, or the planet itself is personalized, very occasionally there can be a slight speech impediment. If the individual is accused of being non-communicative he should take heed of the criticism, since it may well be true. A harshness, often bordering on the cynical or sarcastic, can emerge. Again, he should be aware of these traits and encouraged to counter them by giving full rein to what can be an interesting and offbeat sense of humor. If he holds a position of authority you may have to suggest, tactfully, that there may be misunderstandings at times if memos and directives are worded rather too brusquely. Although he may be expressing his opinions and directions tongue-in-cheek, that may not be the way in which they are received.

Positive thinking and an optimistic outlook must be cultivated if they are not present in other areas of the chart; look to the influences of Mercury and Jupiter. The inner authoritative voice will be carping and argumentative, so when opportunities arise or the self-confidence is at stake, there will often be considerable hesitation before any brave moves are made.

♋ Saturn in Cancer

The need for emotional security is very strong, with the subject usually keen to build a stable family life. Questions about the family background will produce some revealing answers. If the father was very strict or there was some kind of breakdown or deprivation, the subject may have suffered greatly and been unable to take things as much in his or her stride as other children.

If a tendency to worry is indicated elsewhere this placing will increase it, and the outlook is often rather pessimistic, perhaps with suspicion and a tendency to self-pity (most likely if the Moon is in negative aspect to Saturn). More positively, there is usually considerable shrewdness and the ability to make and save money very cleverly. A sense of purpose and tenacity are characteristic, but it is very easy indeed for individuals to creep into their shells and hide there, particularly when challenged. However, this trait may be countered by the influence of Mars or Jupiter, especially if either is placed in a fire sign and/or well aspected.

A freer expression of the emotions is needed, since inhibition and the tendency to be timid with loved ones can be at the root of problems in emotional relationships. The inner authoritative voice may subtly undermine the subject's self-confidence when she wishes to take bold, assertive action; "If you do that, you know what'll happen, and you won't like it, will you?" This is because she may have suffered emotional blackmail as a child, and unless she has come to terms with it, will have to try not to pass her reactions on to her children.

♌ Saturn in Leo

Strength of will, determination, excellent organizing ability and loyalty are present here. The individual will take life very seriously, and the warm fiery qualities of Leo will not emerge unless other planets also occupy this sign. Even then, Saturn will cloud the Leonine Sun. The worst faults are autocracy and a total inability to accept limitations; pride very often does precede some pretty heavy falls for this subject. There will be self-inflicted restrictions – perhaps because of the need to succeed in a burning ambition. Once a line of action has been decided upon, there is little or no let-up of effort. Nevertheless, the ability to cope with situations and to organize (and strictly discipline) others, especially in an emergency, is second to none.

Positive and negative expression

If these qualities can be positively expressed, much that is admirable can result. However, loyalty can be misplaced and the individual's sense of values may lose their perspective. When the negative side of the placing is evident it can be because the childhood was organized along military lines, with the strictest of routines and disciplines, so that it is difficult for the subject to forsake this early training. Formality and general tightness may also be characteristic.

The authoritative inner voice will probably be like that of a martinet nurse, schoolmaster or Sergeant Major, forcing the individual to take certain lines of action because they are what is expected, even if it would be better to respond more sympathetically both to his or her own needs and feelings and to the situation in question. If the negative traits are most apparent, try asking whether the subject was brought up very rigidly and conventionally, perhaps spent time in care or was sent to a very strict boarding school.

Since Leo rules the back and spine and Saturn the bones, encourage your subject to take special care of his spine. Sitting well when at a desk, sensible exercise to strengthen the spine, and so on, are most desirable.

♍ Saturn in Virgo

Adherence to routine and practical activity are present with this placing. A sense of duty is common and the individual will not shirk from this, since it is natural for most of those with this Saturn sign to work hard and methodically. As is the case with most Virgoan emphases there is careful attention to detail and, because Saturn encourages caution, an element of patience, with the individual not being fond of short cuts. There is also considerable prudence and modesty.

The self-confidence is usually undermined and, especially in young people, causes shyness. Even in an otherwise exuberant and positive chart, the individual with this placing can lapse into shyness from time to time. If he or she can realize that this placing provides an anchorage, its more inhibitive elements can be countered and the practical caution it endows will be used in positive ways.

A need for constructive criticism

If the individual holds a position of authority over others, you may have to warn him that being too strict and demanding could alienate employees. Adherence to discipline, a powerful critical sense and a liking for perfection will set in him high standards, and he will expect the same from others. Excellent! – but unless he is kind and sensitive, with a good sense of humor, he may seem distant, cool, rather sarcastic and sometimes prone to carping. All of which is, indeed, a way to describe the inner authoritative voice, which may criticize the self at every opportunity, thereby eroding self-confidence. If this is so, you could ask the subject whether his parents were very critical of him when he was little. He should also realize that obsessive tendencies may build up, especially in times of stress, but that such habits must be broken if possible.

♎ Saturn in Libra

Saturn is traditionally well-placed in this sign, and there certainly seems to be a subtle harmony between the sign and the planet. There is a natural sense of justice, and the individual has an above-average sympathy and understanding of other people. Kindness and practical common sense are also present; tact and diplomacy will color any advice that is given. He or she is usually impartial, flexible and fair, and the need to see fair play, so characteristic of any Libran emphasis, will certainly be present with this placing.

Negative tendencies

If Saturn receives mostly negative aspects, particularly from the personal planets, or makes a square or opposition to the Ascendant, some intolerance may be shown toward partners or colleagues, especially if Saturn is in the seventh or tenth house. If in the fourth house, there may be a tendency to be discontented with the home and domestic situation, and/or perhaps a desire to move very frequently. However, attention must always be given to Saturn's house position.

Despite the longing for a permanent emotional relationship, it may be avoided or sacrificed for some reason, perhaps due to sexual inhibition or an inability to express the emotions freely. Any external reason will probably be mere justification – the real one will definitely go much deeper.

Saturn's inner authoritative voice from this sign will sharpen the subject's conscience by arousing a guilty sense of shame; "If you do that you will be treating me very badly, after all I've done for you. You are totally selfish and if you do this dreadful thing I'll never forgive you." Ask if the subject had a parent who always grumbled in this way and was never satisfied with what his or her child produced or did.

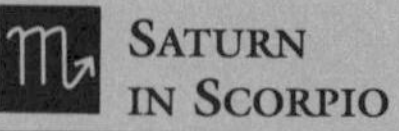

SATURN IN SCORPIO

This gives an element of dark, brooding intensity which will make its presence felt even in charts where other indications show extrovert and enthusiastic qualities. There is a tremendous sense of purpose and determination, and emotional energy will be generously spent on attaining objectives.

An excellent and shrewd business sense is perhaps one of the most powerful qualities of this Saturn placing. These people do extremely well in big business or the international money markets. A certain heaviness is usually countered by a marvelously offbeat sense of humor, and in spite of the usual Saturnian caution, often in relation to overspending, Scorpio knows how to live it up and enjoys excellent food and wine. As a result, some of this may be present in the subject, especially if a liking for these pleasures in shown elsewhere in the chart (look to Venus and Jupiter in particular).

On the negative side obsessive tendencies are all too likely, with determination becoming extreme stubbornness. Sadly, we sometimes find a rather cruel streak; once really set on achieving a demanding objective, the subject may be ruthless in attaining it. If you think this possible, encourage the cultivation of sympathy and greater consideration of others. Much hard work will be carried out, and an emotional involvement in the profession is often essential – even if the basic motivation is to make money, this is enough to put the subject on the road to success.

Combating jealousy

The sex life can be complex: sometimes a full and rewarding expression is inhibited, and as a result the subject feels dissatisfied in this sphere of life. It may be that the inner authoritative voice will instill jealousy and envy, and if this is not fought against with tooth and claw it will have a very negative effect on the individual's personality and, sometimes, physical well-being.

SATURN IN SAGITTARIUS

Jupiter and Saturn are essentially polar planets, for Jupiter represents expansion and Saturn restriction. As a result, it may seem that Saturn is not well-placed in Sagittarius. However, much good can come from this placing.

Saturn heightens concentration and encourages the desire to study so that the intellectual potential is fully developed. The outlook is philosophical, and in some respects children with this placing have old heads on young shoulders, so don't be surprised at the words of wisdom which are spoken seriously but quite naturally.

Meeting a challenge

Honesty and straightforward speech are increased by this placing. Here too is the ability to speak up, sometimes bravely, uttering opinions that may be at variance with the mainstream consensus. However, challenges often cause conflict, for on the one hand there will be a desire to accept them and push forward fearlessly with whatever is proposed, and on the other there can be caution and a certain fearfulness which may frustrate the desire, so that the enthusiasm of Sagittarius may not be given the full expression it needs. To determine whether Sagittarius or Saturn will gain the upper hand, look at the planet's aspects. If they are positive, and the chart contains quite a lot of fire and air, the chances are that the individual will not be held back. If, however, the chart shows someone rather shy and sensitive, then no doubt the more cautious Saturn influence will dominate. Here, the authoritative inner voice will be quite straightforward: it will simply state that the subject is incapable of coping with the smallest challenge!

SATURN IN CAPRICORN

As Saturn rules Capricorn, the planet is at its most powerful in that sign, unless it is personalized, in which case its influence is redoubled (see the table on p.35). There is nearly always caution, determination, ambition and practical ability. Sometimes the individual will make rather too many personal sacrifices in order to achieve objectives. The hardworking father will spend long hours at the office, then bring work home, so that there is little or no time for relaxing and having fun with the children. This is done with the best of intentions because he will be very keen indeed to give those children a better start in life than he himself had. Nevertheless it is up to you to encourage a balance, for in being materialistic he will miss out on a very great deal.

Children may be treated very strictly, and both sexes must realize that they can err in this direction. Parents of children with this placing (born between November 1988 and February 1991) may find that their offspring will be interestingly serious at times, with an excellent capacity for hard and steady work. However, it is vital that their self-confidence is built up gradually, for it may not come naturally. There is usually a tendency to grumble, which will alternate with a very Saturnine sense of humor.

If Saturn is negatively aspected the outlook can be rather grim and pessimistic, but there is no lack of fortitude. "I must grin and bear it" seems a characteristic statement, with the subject turning down the corners of the mouth as it is uttered! Very differently, there is a liking for power – sometimes political – and the Capricorn tendency to social climbing is also present. Money will be spent to impress, rather than for pure pleasure. Again, if Saturn is badly aspected we often find meanness. In spite of all this, the strong positive qualities usually dominate.

The subject must keep moving, so he or she should be encouraged to exercise regularly: Saturn rules the skin and bone structure, and stiffness in the joints must be avoided. The skin may be particularly sensitive to strong sunlight. The young children now being born with this placing should enjoy athletics or winter sports.

The inner authoritative voice will be like the wrath of God! Here Saturn's influence is at its most dictatorial. The subject may have had very strict, formal, conventional parents who always expected nothing less than the correct behavior on all occasions. Just how well or how poorly he coped will be seen from other areas of the chart. However, it seems very likely indeed that there was, and still is, a considerable lack of self-confidence, due to constant criticism.

Saturn in Aquarius

This is an interesting, positive placing for Saturn. The planet works powerfully from Aquarius because it ruled that sign before Uranus was accepted into the astrological pantheon. There is considerable determination, which is shown by the achievement of ambitious objectives. The mind has a strong element of originality, but very often, especially in the young, once opinions are formed they can be adhered to rather too rigidly.

The real conflict lies between taking a conventional line and a totally opposite, unconventional one – something the subject will have to resolve in his or her own way. Often it is not easy to do so since the conscience will want to be safe and secure, operating from a position that is familiar and acceptable to others, whereas the need for adventure, originality and independence will be equally strong. This is a dilemma that is usually helped by the influence of the Ascendant, Sun and Moon signs and the personal planets.

Privacy and independence

Some Aquarian humanitarianism is present, and if scientific potential is shown elsewhere it will be considerably boosted by this placing. The individual may have an obstinate and rather cunning streak if Saturn is negatively aspected. There may be a tendency to distance the self from other people, although the subject is also friendly. Some of the Aquarian inclination to be a very private person can emerge. Independence is often very important to the subject, although at times it can bring loneliness.

The inner authoritative voice will tend to say "Do as you like – I don't care – please yourself." The chances are that the individual won't be able to do so, and as a result there will be a crushing psychological conflict to be resolved. Ask whether his or her parents were perverse, or were cold and/or unpredictable.

Saturn in Pisces

The self-sacrificing qualities of Pisces will be present in those who have Saturn in this sign. There is humility, sympathy and increased intuition, which should be controlled and expressed with caution, but definitely not ignored. Often there is also very little self-confidence, and it may be that the subject will be his or her own worst enemy, since the inclination to hold back may become disproportionate. As a result she will constantly do herself down.

At its best, this trait makes a person attractively self-effacing, but sadly its influence is usually too strong, so that shyness and inhibition dominate. Sometimes the outlook on life is rather depressing, and under stress there can be an inclination to give up hope. Despite this, the influence of the rest of the chart may act as a strong counter to these negative tendencies, so be very careful not to overinterpret them. They will probably only be present if a negative outlook is indicated in other totally independent areas of the chart.

It is important for the subject to realize that she possesses a powerful imaginative force which should be put to creative use. It certainly needs to be given some sort of concrete shape, and the nature of a suitable means of expression may be indicated in other areas of the chart – a flair for handicrafts, perhaps, or writing skills. If not, and your subject is hesitant about developing this excellent source of potential, it may be that long-term encouragement given by the partner will help her find a suitable outlet and eventually develop it to the full.

Quite severe changes of mood are usual, as is a tendency to worry (especially if this is shown in other areas of the chart, or if Saturn receives negative aspects from the Moon). One result can be hypochondria. The inner authoritative voice can sound like the Ugly Sisters talking to Cinderella! If that rings a bell with your subject, don't forget to say that Cinderella did, after all, marry her Prince!

Saturn Progressed through the Signs

It is very rare indeed that Saturn moves from one sign to the next by progression. Should this happen, the effect will be very slow and subtle, even allowing for the fact that the change will occur, astronomically, during only one day's motion (remember that this will represent a whole year in the individual's life). As a result, the subject will probably develop some Saturn-influenced characteristics in the area indicated by the new sign. Should this occur, especially if he or she is well-known to you, watch out for these developments. If you should see them, discuss them with him or her, first studying carefully the interpretations of Saturn in both its natal and progressed signs.

Saturn through the Houses

The house in which Saturn is placed is a considerable focal point of the chart, since the sphere of life affected will be taken very seriously and will, in some respects, be a burden to the subject. While there is no reason for this area of life to be entirely unsuccessful or an on-going source of difficulty, progress will usually only be made after a special effort. When it is made, however, great satisfaction will be taken in personal development; the subject will have learned lessons, often the hard way. Here, Saturn is certainly a taskmaster. It is vitally important to remember that the aspects the planet receives will be a powerful indication as to just how easy or difficult it is for the subject to make Saturn work for him- or herself, and if it is a personal planet, the characteristics it indicates will be a key to the whole personality.

1 Saturn in the First House

Here, a great deal depends on how close Saturn is to the Ascending degree. The closer it is, the more potent the influence will be. If it is within eight or ten degrees, see Saturn conjunct the Ascendant, p.307.

The overall effect will be to inhibit the personality, often causing shyness and a lack of self-confidence. Nevertheless, there is natural caution and a great deal of common sense. The way in which Saturn influences the characteristics of the Ascendant sign will, of course, be shown in the planet's sign interpretation, which must be studied very carefully since those characteristics will be very powerful. At times, the individual can feel unable to cope with the problems and responsibilities of life, and the whole outlook may become pessimistic. Again, such feelings may well be rooted in a lack of self-confidence.

Sources of inhibition

Adherence to what is expected and a strong sense of duty, plus a conventional and conservative outlook, are present, and it may be that inhibiting tendencies relate to a restrictive environment in childhood. If you have an accurate birth time it will be a good idea to question your subject about what happened when the progressed Ascendant made an exact conjunction to Saturn. There may have been a traumatic event: the death of the father, a breakup of family life which had a very negative effect on the subject, or perhaps he or she was involved in an accident which had a nasty physical effect, such as broken bones or a long stay in the hospital.

The effect on the health of Saturn in this house can be to lower the vitality, but it is very important indeed for your subject to realize that such conditions are likely to be based on hypochondria, and that pessimism and depression are his worst enemies.

2 Saturn in the Second House

There is no doubt that Saturn in this house indicates that the subject will work very hard indeed for every penny earned. That is not to say he or she will not make a lot of money, but it does mean that wins, monetary prizes or sudden gains are likely be very thin on the ground, and even such simple triumphs as winning a raffle will be most unlikely.

The way to make money is by investment in the safest, most secure stock available. However, the sense of achievement and inner fulfillment when, for instance, a long-standing mortgage has been repaid will particularly increase the individual's self-esteem and sense of pride. This is chiefly because she will realize that it has been achieved by a great deal of blood and sweat (she will be too practical and sensible for tears!)

The emotional overtones of this house should not be forgotten: Saturn's presence may inhibit the flow of feelings. If this does not apply, it may be that the attainment of sensual pleasure at its most perfect will come more slowly than for most people, but will continue for much longer.

3 Saturn in the Third House

The chances are that there were disruptions to your subject's school days, or that he or she hated school and was very unhappy there. However, maybe such difficulties were overcome, resulting in the individual developing some very special qualities which eventually led to a position of responsibility and prominence – becoming first in his class, perhaps. In that case, Saturn was working positively, but at the same time placing the subject in a remote and somewhat isolated position.

Encouraging practicality

There may be a tendency to blame weaknesses and failures on the education. If this occurs you will must discover the truth of the matter; look to see how well or otherwise the personal planets are working, and whether there is real justification in your subject taking this attitude; it may be simply an excuse, in which case a change of attitude is most desirable.

This house is connected with the mind, so there is a good chance of the individual being sensible and practical, with the ability to make cautious long-term plans. He may also have an inner need to fill any gaps in his education.

4 Saturn in the Fourth House

The subject's family life and home atmosphere were probably rather severe when he or she was growing up. The parents may have been strict, perhaps distant and cold, and might have placed an overemphasis on discipline.

Perhaps the father was ineffective or simply not there, whether physically or psychologically, so that the mother had to play both roles. This need not have resulted in anything as straightforward as the one-parent family, but may have had more complicated implications. It is very important for the subject to realize how difficult it can be to come to terms with such indoctrination. As a result, not only may he find it hard to express himself very freely, but he may also imitate his parent's attitudes.

This is the Cancer/Moon house so there is an emphasis on intuition, which will be increased but controlled by Saturn. Usually, this force will probably be positively channeled and used to great effect but even so, the subject must realize the potential of his intuition, and learn to trust it.

5 Saturn in the Fifth House

Since this is the Leo/Sun house it has a bearing on the father, and when Saturn occupies it, the chances are that he was very domineering and dogmatic, making the subject feel inhibited. Rather differently, when the subject becomes a parent he or she will be very ambitious for the children, spending much time and money on what is considered best for them. Sometimes there is a tendency to push them into areas into which they do not want to go, and for which they have no real talent, simply because the parent sees the child as a clone of herself.

Creative talent is often present. It will be slow to develop, and the subject might not be sure what to do, but the urge to make and create may be strong. Suggest that the subject works with natural materials, should you get no hint from the Saturn sign.

A need for commitment

The attitude to love affairs is deadly serious. Despite a powerful need for them, the desire to do the right thing will probably act as a sobering force, so that the subject will experience few relationships before making a total commitment to a partner. In a roundabout way, the father's influence may make its presence felt here, especially for men, and in women's attitude towards, and their feelings about, men.

6 Saturn in the Sixth House

While there is an ability to work very carefully and hard, there may be an obsessive adherence to routine, and perhaps even a tendency to grumble continually about one's lot in life, since the work being carried out may not be what the subject really wants.

There is often a reluctance to change, however, since risk-taking can be rather frightening. ("Better the devil you know than one you don't" is a typical belief.) Such an approach will, of course, relate to a lack of self-confidence and an overcritical attitude toward what is being achieved, which will be thought of as slender. Encourage the development of self-esteem, and suggest that the subject gives him- or herself a pat on the back from time to time by considering what actually has been achieved. There is dogged persistence (which in itself will surely give results) in whichever area is suggested by the Saturn sign.

Care of the health

This is a house of health, so Saturn's placing here may indicate a weakness towards the ailments attributed to the Saturn sign. More generally, there may be rheumatic aches and pains, and perhaps a particular vulnerability to damp weather conditions. Especial care should be given to the teeth, and perhaps the subject should take extra calcium to strengthen teeth and bones. (Calcium is also good for all women after menopause, and particularly for those with this placing.) If Saturn is within eight degrees of the Descendant, and therefore in opposition to the Ascendant, carefully consider the latter aspect as it will increase the emphasis on health in this case.

7 Saturn in the Seventh House

At its best, this encourages a serious attitude towards permanent relationships. The subject won't rush into marriage or a serious relationship, but will be a constant and faithful partner once committed in love.

If Saturn is in opposition to the Ascendant, commitment is often delayed and sometimes, for deep-rooted psychological reasons, relationships won't be formed at all. While the subject may grumble at being single, the responsibility of a partnership will be a greater burden. There may be considerable differences in age in a relationship, with the subject needing a much older partner – a father- or mother-figure. A common outcome is the desire to marry for prestige or money, and the taking of a purely calculated attitude in doing so. Love and romance will not be present, only the rising of the social status and mounting figures in the bank balance.

At its worst, this placing causes a certain heaviness in relationships, sometimes creating poor communication between partners. This usually occurs, however, when Saturn not only opposes the Ascendant but is also negatively aspected by other planets – especially the Sun, Moon or Venus.

8 Saturn in the Eighth House

Determination and good powers of concentration are likely here. The outlook is usually serious, with a tendency towards depression and sometimes obsession. This placing is excellent for someone who carries financial responsibility for other people, or who has a career in insurance, banking or perhaps the engineering or mining professions.

A rewarding and fulfilling sex life is not denoted by this placing, since there are often sexual inhibitions or a form of sexual expression that makes the subject either repress these urges or feel guilty about them. There can be a fascination with, and sometimes a concentration on, the darker elements of life – an interest in criminology, for instance – and almost certainly a great deal of serious thought will be given to the possibility of survival after death.

Difficulties in relationships

The individual may be suspicious and untrusting of others – all too often partners in intimate relationships. Care is therefore needed that jealousy does not mar the relationship, especially where sex or money are concerned. In time, the subject will learn from his or her mistakes, and this negative tendency will gradually ease.

Since this is the Scorpio/Pluto house, and related to the water element, the intuitions will be quite strong. Encourage the subject to learn to trust them.

9 Saturn in the Ninth House

There is usually an ability to think seriously and deeply about important issues, and there can be good powers of concentration. The mind is unlikely to be very adventurous or inventive, however, unless these traits are shown up quite strongly in other areas (through the influence of Jupiter, for instance). As a result, the subject's opinions and conclusions will be conventional and perhaps a bit unimaginative. There will be a considerable desire to improve his or her mind, and once a study course is undertaken it will probably be completed, even if it is more taxing than was expected.

Challenges will be approached with extreme caution. The prospect of physical travel can arouse all kinds of inhibitions and fears of the unknown, such as a terror of flying. If we extend this possibility to a more psychological dimension, it can mean a fear of taking off, intellectually and perhaps emotionally, as well as from the standpoint of beginning to achieve objectives and ambitions. So, here again, Saturn can cause inhibition and apprehension.

If Saturn is negatively aspected from any of the personal planets, there will be shyness and a lack of self-confidence. The resulting inferiority complex will be most noticeable when the subject is mixing with people whom he believes to be of a higher intellectual or academic level than himself.

10 Saturn in the Tenth House

Here, Saturn is in its own house, so its influence is much strengthened. The individual may have to shoulder much responsibility as a result of circumstances. They will be carried well, however, and there will be plenty of ambition and very high aspirations.

Sometimes the individual can set a distance between him- or herself and loved ones, and a preoccupation with achieving objectives is very likely. If you think this is happening to the subject, do warn that he may be sacrificing many good things in life as a result, and that in extreme cases there can be a loss of love and family happiness.

Any characteristic coldness may spring from childhood influences, since he might have been strictly disciplined to do the right thing as a child. Check the position of Saturn: if it is within eight degrees of the Midheaven it is in conjunction with that point, so its influence is further strengthened and may even dominate the chart.

11 Saturn in the Eleventh House

Saturn is well-placed here because of its special relationship with Aquarius (see Saturn in Aquarius, p.301). However, the subject may have few close friends. Sometimes, too, friends of an older generation are preferred. If not older in years, then perhaps they may be more distinguished intellectually or more worldly wise.

Here is a focus on the social life, which he or she may take rather seriously. Nonworking hours will definitely be enjoyed, but there is usually little time for anything that is deemed flippant. However, once she develops an interest it will usually last a lifetime. Very often she is asked to serve on committees and almost as often can be elected chairperson or president. This may be a cause of complaint, but equally she grumbles if she has to suffer someone else in that role, slowing up the proceedings and the progress of the concerns of the association.

Taking a stand

A powerful humanitarian streak is present, and while Saturn is conventional in outlook, this placing nevertheless instills a sense of justice, so the individual will do a great deal to right what is wrong in the world. Those with this placing will, for instance, be natural supporters of Amnesty International but won't want to court trouble by taking any militant action!

12 Saturn in the Twelfth House

At its most potent, this tends to make the individual something of an isolationist, and at its least powerful gives a need to retreat from worldly concerns. Sometimes the subject may only feel safe within his or her own little world. He will do an excellent job during the day, then look forward to returning to the security of his own home at night. It is not a good idea to try to nag him out of this pattern, for it will only encourage him to enclose himself further. Instead, someone with this placing should learn to enjoy quiet hobbies – music appreciation, reading and handicrafts, for instance.

Too much introspection should not be encouraged, since it can lead to hypochondria and perhaps other phobias. Even so, it is excellent if the subject can accept that the warmth and security of his own home is restorative, since that is where he will gain psychological and physical refreshment. If Saturn conjuncts the Ascendant from this house the subject will be shy, introspective and lacking in confidence, as is the case when Saturn is in the first house, but here the reclusive tendencies will be even stronger.

A need for self-expression

Creative exercise through some form of expressive dance or movement is excellent therapy, but yoga and such contemplative disciplines are not as rewarding in the long-term. That is because they may increase the subject's introspection which, if anything, needs to be countered.

A very meaningful sense of vocation may be present. The subject might identify with suffering or with those confined to institutions, and can derive considerable psychological reward from helping such people.

♄ Saturn Progressed through the Houses

Since Saturn progresses so slowly, it moves from one house to the next only very rarely. As is the case when Saturn changes signs by progression, astronomically the change will be completed during the course of 24 hours, but the astrological effect will be noticeable for about one year. If a house change occurs in a progressed chart, its effect will be very subtle, so don't overinterpret it. Very gradually the concerns and sphere of life indicated by the new house will increase in importance for the individual.

The Aspects of Saturn

Here we deal with the aspects Saturn makes to planets beyond it in the Solar System – Uranus, Neptune and Pluto, all discovered in modern times. Until the discovery of Uranus in 1781 Saturn was at the edge of the known universe, which may be a reason for one of its keywords, limitation. The aspects interpreted below will be within orb for quite long periods of time, and therefore appear in many charts, but must not be ignored; they can inhibit but they also stabilize the individual.

For Saturn's aspects to the Sun see the Sun's aspects to Saturn, p.217.

For Saturn's aspects to the Moon see the Moon's aspects to Saturn, pp.234-5.

For Saturn's aspects to Mercury see Mercury's aspects to Saturn, pp.249-50.

For Saturn's aspects to Venus see Venus' aspects to Saturn, p.264.

For Saturn's aspects to Mars see Mars' aspects to Saturn, pp.277-8.

For Saturn's aspects to Jupiter see Jupiter's aspects to Saturn, p.290.

If Saturn forms an aspect to the progressed Jupiter, Uranus, Neptune or Pluto, look up the particular transit interpretation, remembering that although the influence will be less potent, it will last while Saturn is on the relevant degree, and will support important transits as and when they are operative. Base your interpretation on the relevant paragraph – conjunction, positive or negative transits.

If Saturn forms a progressed aspect to the natal Sun, Moon, Mercury, Venus or Mars, read the relevant interpretation for that planet's progressions to Saturn, and pay special attention to the paragraph in question – conjunction, positive or negative transits. If Saturn makes a progressed aspect to the Ascendant or Midheaven in the birth or progressed chart, refer to the interpretation of Saturn's transits to the Ascendant or Midheaven (see p.311). These progressions are powerful, and will operate over several years. The effects will be the same as those of Saturn's transits to these areas of the birth chart.

SATURN'S ASPECTS TO URANUS

Conjunction

(See also Saturn conjunct Neptune, right.) This potent conjunction occurred in the 1940s in Taurus, and is now to be found in the birth charts of children born between December 1986 and December 1989 – the years during which it was in orb. Earlier in that period the conjunction occurred in Sagittarius, later in Capricorn, and in some cases Saturn was in Capricorn while Uranus was in Sagittarius.

Here is a very powerful energy source which will color the mass characteristics of a whole generation. If the two planets contact the subject's Sun, Moon, Ascendant or Midheaven you are probably working on the chart of someone who will be a leader of his or her generation, who will put forward its views very potently and make a mark in some important way.

When the conjunction occurs in Sagittarius it contributes towards a broad mind with considerable potential for hard and serious work, and at the same time is strongly tinged with originality. When the conjunction crosses the signs, Saturn's influence is likely to dominate since Saturn rules Capricorn; the outlook will then be more serious, less adventurous, and less open to the acceptance of challenge. When both planets are in Taurus or Capricorn there will be an adherence to the concepts and idealism of the subject's generation, and within that the outlook will be conventional, although it may not conform to the ideas of older generations.

The powerful driving force of this conjunction may also be expressed in some people as a power complex, especially if Scorpio is also emphasized by a personal planet. Those with this conjunction who also have Pluto in Scorpio (see p.339) have another generation influence which chimes in very powerfully with this aspect. The children of this generation need to know precisely where they stand; they need freedom of expression, but also guidance as to how to express themselves, and will benefit from firm but logical discipline. Alternating bouts of nervous tension and depression may need countering but the potential is terrific.

Positive aspects

There is usually a blending of conventional behavior and outlook with a sympathy for the unconventional. The mind is serious. Some natural caution is present but it is accompanied by an ability to develop original ideas and concepts. The subject has willpower and determination, and often patience too. However, unless Saturn and Uranus are personalized, think of these traits as supporting those of a similar nature in other areas of the chart.

Negative aspects

The pessimism of Saturn being at loggerheads with the tension of Uranus can cause problems if these tendencies appear in other areas of the chart. You may need to warn against stubbornness, which may at times become extreme. This influence can be unhelpful to people who are in a position of power, since they may express themselves coldly and in a very authoritative way that can distance them from subordinates. Encourage patience when life is stressful. If the planets are personalized, developing a relaxation technique may be of benefit.

SATURN'S ASPECTS TO NEPTUNE

Conjunction

(See also Saturn conjunct Uranus, above.) This conjunction occurs every 36 years or so. It was within orb in Leo in 1917, in Libra in the 1950s and is present in the charts of most children born between March 1988 and November 1990. However, during the whole of this latter period Uranus is traveling though the last degrees of Sagittarius and the early degrees of Capricorn (the sign in which this conjunction occurs), and lies between Saturn and Neptune. It is therefore almost impossible to interpret this conjunction without considering the intervening influence of Uranus.

You may have read some dramatic stories about this potent placing in the press, or perhaps heard it discussed on television. It is certainly very powerful, and although everything that is stated above concerning the conjunction of Saturn and Uranus applies most strongly, while Neptune is between these two planets its confusing, rather dreamy influence may affect these young people's determination and originality, perhaps fogging their outlook and clouding their judgement with regard to their objectives in life.

In charts where this double conjunction (as it is known) is positively aspected by personal planets, the Neptune influence will no doubt work well, softening and making more idealistic the rather harsher, more strident characteristics of Saturn and Uranus. The three planets will, we think, help this generation to save planet Earth, partly because they all occupy an earth sign, and partly because of the humanitarian side to Uranus' influence (i.e. the positive Uranus) and the sensitivity and idealism of Neptune. Together they may not be strong enough to encourage the young people to carry out the reforms so necessary for the continuing existence of our planet, but with Saturn's cautious, careful and practical intervention, which will channel the inspiration of Neptune and control the originality of Uranus, all should be well. These aspects are affecting a whole generation, and such a powerful planetary force should be successfully used for the good of mankind. See if your child's chart shows that he or she will be among the generation's leaders.

+ Positive aspects

There is usually the ability to channel high ideals and inspirations so that these qualities can be positively expressed. Kindness and sympathy are usual, and at the same time practical help is offered to those in need. Saturn will keep dreamy up-in-the-clouds Neptune down to earth, and if the chart shows creative inclinations this aspect will be of enormous help. There can often be flair for photography, pottery or, very differently, scientific ability expressed through chemistry or the development of medical drugs.

− Negative aspects

If either Saturn or Neptune are personal planets, these negative aspects will considerably weaken the subject, since they usually denote someone who can be a confused thinker and is all too often very impractical. The emotional content is high but Saturn will inhibit its flow. Unfortunately any creative potential shown elsewhere can be thwarted, since the individual has little confidence in expressing his or her talents. A tendency always to undermine the self is present, so that lack of self-esteem can occur, but if none of these traits appear in other areas of the chart, don't emphasize them in your interpretation. If your subject is very shy or overmodest, this aspect will exacerbate the tendencies. Interpret with considerable care.

Saturn's Aspects to Pluto

Conjunction

This occurred for a long period during the late 1940s when both planets were in Leo, and again during the early 1980s when they were in Libra.

In Leo: This is an extremely powerful energy source, and its effects tend to be negative rather than positive. It has a strong inhibiting influence, and if the two planets form a conjunction to the Sun, Moon or Ascendant, or are negatively aspected by them, there can be adverse psychological effects. The subject may nurse deep-rooted psychological problems that are difficult to resolve, and indeed in most cases therapy has been advised to do just that. Very often there are physical effects, with the individual suffering rheumatic pain as a result of what are really inhibiting psychological problems. In most cases, of course, the conjunction is not personalized, so these extreme indications are not always present. However, the conjunction falls in the charts of many people born over a long period, and they will experience frustration and an inability to progress at times when transitting planets activate the conjunction. Be careful, when interpreting this powerful influence, not to place too much stress on it. If your subject suffers from inhibition, however, or you think there are deep-rooted psychological problems, remember you are an astrologer and not a psychiatrist; recommend therapy if you think it will help.

In Libra: The conjunction is less pungent in this sign: the more positive side of Saturn adds caution and determination while the Pluto influence gives a certain intensity and driving force. There is a more relaxed attitude towards any psychological problems or hang-ups. The energies of these two strong planets need to be positively expressed though a compelling interest, whether spare-time or professional: there is powerful potential here.

+ Positive aspects

These give additional determination and a driving energy force, and stubbornness will be increased. Even so, the aspect will only be really powerful if either planet is personalized. The subject should be able to come to terms with any deep-rooted problems or phobias, once having worked on them. Indeed, whenever transits contact either planet is an excellent time in which to externalize any ongoing problems and eventually resolve them.

− Negative aspects

There may be some obsessional behavior-patterns or psychological problems which can be difficult to resolve. Perhaps there will be a tendency to avoid doing so – with the excuse that the subject "cannot be bothered". In reality, it will be the fear of facing up to any such problem that will cause procrastination. If encouragement can be given to work on such difficulties it will be to advantage in the long run. He or she will admit to feeling "lighter", "much better", and so on but, as is the case with the Saturn/Pluto conjunction, do not take too much on yourself. Also remember that these rather extreme tendencies will only occur if there are indications of repression elsewhere in the chart, or if Saturn and/or Pluto are personal planets. Interpret with great care.

Asc Saturn's Aspects to the Ascendant

Conjunction

If Saturn is in the first house it will lower the subject's self-confidence and cause shyness, especially in the young. Despite this, he or she is practical, with a great deal of common sense, and gradually confidence will build up so that ambition and high aspirations will eventually become driving forces.

If Saturn receives negative aspects from the Sun or Moon the outlook can be limited, however, and it will be a struggle for the individual to develop enough confidence to be able to fully realize her potential. Depression is possible, especially if the Moon aspects Saturn. The placing tends to darken the expression and encourage a brooding intensity, but this can be countered by the well-known offbeat Saturnine sense of humor.

The vitality is often lowered too, and regular exercise is needed to avoid stiffness in the joints.

When Saturn is in the twelfth house there are reclusive tendencies which will be of benefit to the subject if she expresses them positively through contemplative interests. Sometimes, too, many sacrifices will be made (in following a vocation or helping an elderly parent, for instance). She will feel most secure, both emotionally and physically, at home, surrounded by familiar items. Reread the house position of Saturn as it is especially important (see pp.302-4).

Positive aspects

On the whole, these contribute practical ability, caution and common sense. They are a good anchorage for anyone who has a lively fire or air chart, or when there is an abundance of emotion which may need steadying.

Negative aspects

These can cramp the style and inhibit the more extrovert areas of the personality. The vitality may be lowered, and at times the outlook can become pessimistic or rather gloomy. These indications seem to jostle for position with the more powerful characteristics of the Sun and Ascendant signs, but nevertheless they will be present. Look out for grumbles and moaning! It may be that you can tease your subject into an awareness of these negative and boring tendencies.

MC Saturn's Aspects to the Midheaven

Conjunction

If Saturn conjuncts the Midheaven from the tenth house it will be a very important planet indeed. The individual will carry a great deal of responsibility, and more than likely will do so extremely well. Events over which he or she has no direct control may bring him or her to prominence, but such a position will have been attained because of experience and reputation (or maybe due to inheritance, perhaps of a family business). There is a tendency to distance the self from others, and often the ambitions and aspirations are so powerful that he misses out on a great deal of fun – the joy of time spent with the partner and children, for instance, and other simple but meaningful pleasures. Everything that is written about the house position of Saturn will be very pertinent.

Remember that this placing, both in the tenth house and in conjunction with the Midheaven, puts Saturn at its "home base". The planet will certainly make its presence felt from there by playing a part in the subject's destiny. The influence is only slightly less powerful if Saturn is in another house.

Positive aspects

The individual will identify with all the positive Saturn qualities. He or she will aspire to be practical, to show common sense and to be a disciplined, careful worker. There will be no lack of caution – or ambition. This influence will help the individual to reach the top in whichever way is most desirable.

Negative aspects

The individual will suffer more than his or her fair share of setbacks, and efforts to achieve objectives may be frustrated. However, he should learn a great deal from each experience. It must be realized that the achievement of goals will be slow and steady. This may be difficult to accept if the subject is, for instance, a predominantly Arian type, or an impatient Geminian. There can be a lack of self-confidence in relation to the career: "I can't take that job – so-and-so will do it far better than me." This is really a sign of overcaution and an inability to accept challenge or to take the initiative. Look to Mars and Jupiter for help.

♄ The Transits of Saturn

The transits of Saturn, like those of Jupiter, are an important part of the influences that are working in our lives. When Saturn is traveling around the zodiac at its normal pace, uninhibited by changes from direct to retrograde motion or vice versa, it takes roughly ten days to traverse one degree of a sign. However, very often we find that, as we see it from Earth, it slows down, or even turns retrograde, often staying for as long as two months on one degree, or crossing a degree three times. This applies to all the planets, but the effect is more noticeable in those from Saturn to Pluto, as the timescale is much longer.

It is easy to assess how long the astrological influence of some planets will last (and it is always easy to work this out astronomically). However, with Saturn the effects of a transit can be much longer than the time the planet spends on the degree from which it contacts a planet's natal position. Very often the effects will be felt for several months, sometimes as much as a year – especially if there are a number of Saturn transits to other planets in the birth chart, following one after the other. Now that you are beginning to study Saturn's influence by transit, it as well to reread the general introduction to the planet (see p.31), remembering that the influence is not entirely gloomy; it makes us practical and sensible. Yes, it will often frustrate, but it is from Saturn's influence we learn the lessons of life.

☉ Saturn's Transits to the Sun

Conjunction

This will probably mark a key period for the subject, who may well experience a taxing time. There is a tendency to think that progress is slow and frustrating – and on the surface it may be. In retrospect, however, quite a lot that is positive may result. Certainly, the individual will have "been through the mill", but perhaps will have made a worthwhile commitment. Often additional responsibilities are taken at this time, such as promotion, house purchase or marriage.

Setbacks and a slowing down of progress must be prepared for, but increased prestige and often a considerable climb up the ladder toward personal objectives usually occurs. The vitality must be carefully watched, and if necessary the subject could take additional vitamins.

+ Positive transits

These are excellent influences under which either to make long-term plans or take important decisions. Steady, constructive progress will be made but the pace of life may be slow, so quick responses should not be expected, especially from those in authority. As with the conjunction, increased prestige and responsibilities, or even promotion, are likely. Much hard, steady work will be done. If there are rather dull periods they provide the chance to catch up on any backlog of work.

– Negative transits

These can be the cause of considerable frustration, so the subject should try to be as patient as possible. It is very important that the vitality is watched, since tiredness or inexplicable aches and pains may occur, or the individual may feel unusually chilly, especially if there are lunar progressions to Saturn at roughly the same time.

A pessimistic outlook may be justified at this time. A philosophical attitude and the making of well-calculated moves will pay off, however. Look to the house through which Saturn is transitting: this will indicate the sphere of life that may be under pressure.

☽ Saturn's Transits to the Moon

☌ Conjunction

There may be uncharacteristic changes of mood, some of which will be gloomy and perhaps negative. At such times, however, the intuition should be working well, putting the subject in a good position to make well-calculated and reasoned, as well as intuitive, decisions. The attitude will be very serious. Usually, this is not a good time for taking the initiative, so while Saturn's influence can be put to good use for forward planning, it is as well to advise waiting until the transit is truly over (by two weeks at least), before making any moves.

+ Positive transits

Solid, constructive progress may be made under this influence, especially if there are plans for house purchase, home extensions and so forth. Again, accentuate the making of plans rather than the taking of action, although if cautious moves are made they should not result in too much frustration. Sometimes help and support is received from parents or older people. This is also a time when young people really benefit from the advice of their parents, and might even respond to it!

– Negative transits

The outlook will be pessimistic, and a general sense of being fed up will last for several weeks. The individual should hold back and not take decisions or try to make important moves at this time, for progress will be slow, and his or her frame of mind inappropriate to any kind of assertive action.

Note: Under any transit of Saturn to the Moon, the vitality should be carefully monitored, since there is considerable vulnerability to colds, chills or influenza. It is always advisable to suggest to subjects that they take their favorite, well-proven course of vitamins. If they do not have one, Vitamin C is usually worthwhile, especially in cold weather, but this rule also applies to those who live in mild climates.

☿ Saturn's Transits to Mercury

☌ Conjunction

This is excellent for study or difficult and demanding mental work, since the powers of concentration are greatly enhanced. The outlook is serious and cautious: the right decisions should be made. If contracts or rental agreements are to be signed, there is little likelihood of the subject ignoring the small print, even if this is characteristic. Levelheadedness on every level is accentuated at this time. Very assertive get-up-and-go types may feel slightly fed up under this influence; however, increased patience will do them no harm and they could learn a lot!

+ Positive transits

The effects of these are much as for the conjunction, but even sounder progress will be made. Should the subject be consulted by superiors it is very likely that what is said will be listened to, and promotion will be the result. This is, however, very much the kind of influence under which to work quietly at home, since it is reflective and introverted rather than outwardly expressive. It is not a time for showing off but, when it is over, the subject will feel pride and satisfaction at the amount of work that has been done.

– Negative transits

There is a tendency to feel rather depressed and miserable, sometimes for no apparent reason. It is a time in which to relax and take consolation from such quiet interests as reading and listening to favorite music – or anything else that lifts the spirit. (The bottle should be avoided, however, as that may badly upset the stomach!). Friends can sometimes be a burden under this influence, and great patience must be exerted if they are not to become "hair shirts". As hinted above, the digestive system can also cause problems.

♀ Saturn's Transits to Venus

☌ Conjunction

This will promote serious thought regarding relationships. Emotional ones will mostly be affected but sometimes business partnerships or working relationships with colleagues are also influenced by this transit. If there have been problems, there is a good chance that the individual will start to sort them out, once and for all.

Sometimes this heralds the end of a relationship, or an important change.

However, there is no need to be apprehensive of the outcome of such an influence since it can often have a calming and serene effect, especially if there have been storms in the past. Certainly the accent is on serious thought, and any sensible conclusions that are reached are usually beneficial in the long-run.

Positive transits

As with the conjunction there is often a concentration on the constructive development or resolution of problems concerning all kinds of relationships. Sometimes (especially with the positive transits) there is an accent on older friends who may prove helpful and supportive should the subject be in any sort of difficulty. The outlook will be serious and constructive. This can be a good time in which to overhaul investments or insurance policies, especially those covering personal possessions.

Negative transits

These often indicate a difficult period regarding relationships of all kinds. Sometimes there is simply a rather dreary atmosphere, with poor communication. If the individual feels unable to continue his or her current situation, it is as well to encourage waiting until the transit is over by at least a couple of weeks before making any final decision. If Saturn turns retrograde and the subject experiences the transit three times in all, the whole period may be gloomy emotionally. Consider whether or not the subject is responding as well as usual to the partner, since this could easily be the source of indifference or coldness – a lack of sexual desire is common at this time. The influence sometimes has a restricting effect on finance, and prudence in this area is also recommended. Tradition says that this transit indicates a loss of personal possessions, so advise the checking of locks, and additional home security.

♂ Saturn's Transits to Mars

Conjunction

This indicates a rather tricky period when there will be a tremendous outpouring of energy alternating with lethargy – optimistic assertiveness, then no desire for action whatsoever.

It won't be easy to keep a balance and all the subject can do is try to work steadily and not be too enthusiastic about any projects. It is important for him or her to keep calm and listen carefully to what is suggested, then allow plenty of thinking time before making a commitment. In this way some sort of balance will be achieved. If it isn't, the chances are that the resulting frustration and annoyance will be even more upsetting. In theory, this influence should encourage determination, but that is not always so.

Positive transits

Here is some ability to balance the energy level, and if steady determination is aimed for, progress will be maintained. If Mars is personalized Saturn will have a calming effect; if Saturn is the stronger planet in the birth chart the energies should be boosted. If the going gets difficult the individual will usually cope well.

Negative transits

This surely is the influence which must have always dominated the lives of many fictional characters! Constant rage and equally constant frustration is the quintessential expression of Saturn and Mars at loggerheads with each other. Of course, in books adventures caricature what really happens, but the chances are that something – perhaps an on-going difficulty with a builder, for instance – will make the individual want to scream with frustration.

All that can be done is to suggest that the subject blows off steam and then tries to be calm and rational, perhaps writing serious and moderately expressed letters of complaint rather than staging a verbal or aggressive showdown! Care is needed that physical strain is avoided. It is at such times that the subject may have to readjust exercise regimes due to increasing age.

♃ Saturn's Transits to Jupiter

Conjunction

The natural optimism and enthusiasm of Jupiter are somewhat sobered by this contact. At the same time, however, the steadying effect on the intellect will probably mean that the subject reaches sound decisions, and if studying will make excellent progress, especially along conventional or traditional lines. The aspect will not do much for original thinking, nor will it encourage brilliant ideas, but it will work well for someone following a strict syllabus.

More generally, periods of optimism and pessimism will occur and sometimes the subject may experience a certain inner restlessness. As with Saturn's contacts to Mars, keeping a balance is essential. At its best there can be both opportunities and promotion plus additional responsibility, especially if both planets are well-aspected on the whole and well-placed in the birth chart. A natal trine or sextile between them would work wonders for this powerful transit.

Positive transits

These have much the same effect as the conjunction, but are less likely to cause an imbalance in the outlook or mood of the individual. Both the cautious and the adventurous characteristics of the subject are highlighted if this strong planetary energy is used to its full advantage.

Progressive and practical decisions may be taken at this time and, as is the case with the conjunction, the individual could well experience an eventful and rewarding period. This certainly is not a time for letting grass grow under the feet.

Negative transits

Restlessness and discontent are almost certain. There will be a strong desire to make progress and take up adventurous challenges, but at the same time the subject may feel that something – perhaps a restricting responsibility – is likely to prevent it. If the subject can be patient and wait for the transit to ease, the frustrated sphere of life will also become easier and the subject will find that progress will be made.

In the meantime, it is as well to concentrate on areas that are not being frustrated by Saturn, for the more emotional and physical energy that is given to the problems arising under such negative influences, the worse they seem to become.

♅ SATURN'S TRANSITS TO URANUS

☌ Conjunction

This very powerful influence will more than likely mark an important period. As these planets are rather heavy in their effect, life may become both eventful and strenuous; new developments and/or important changes are very likely. During the period as a whole, progress may be rather uneven.

On a psychological level, the individual may suffer a dilemma. On the one hand he or she will want to do the "right" and conventional thing, responding to a natural sense of duty and loyalty – perhaps to the family (Saturn), but on the other there will be a powerful need to strike out independently and maybe to act somewhat unconventionally or even unpredictably (Uranus).

If either planet is personalized, it is that planet's dictates that will be followed. Sometimes the subject will seek a compromise, but will usually err towards Saturn. In any case, if unexpected developments occur it is wise to take full advantage of them since Saturn's influence will steady decision-making and boost caution. Sometimes increased power and additional responsibilities result from this potent transit. In many respects there is a certain sympathy between these two planets, because Saturn is the traditional ruler of Aquarius, which is the sign now ruled by Uranus.

+ Positive transits

These are similar in effect to the conjunction, but will be less powerful. Nevertheless, new and often unexpected developments are likely, and because the influence is easier there is less possibility of a build-up of tension, perhaps because there will be less at stake. Again, if either planet is personalized there will be a tendency to follow the direction it suggests – i.e. practical, cautious and conventional (Saturn) or unexpected, possibly unconventional and exciting (Uranus).

– Negative transits

A great deal may be happening in the individual's life, with resulting strain and tension. If tendencies to be a natural worrier are shown elsewhere in the chart (with Cancer or Virgo prominent signs), encouragement must be given to approach these worries in the most appropriate way. No decision should be taken rashly (which may happen if the situation is very serious) and, if possible, the cautious Saturn side of the transit should be encouraged. If in doubt, advise waiting until the influence has passed (by at least two or three weeks) and the influence has eased. However, while the individual may go through hell and high water, what is afoot should be to his or her advantage in the long run and advance him or her several rungs up the ladder, either with regard to the career or the personal prestige.

Note: With all the transits from Saturn to Uranus, even if the latter is personalized in the birth chart there will be a tendency for Saturn to dominate, since it is this planet that is exerting its power over Uranus. In some cases, the planets will be more or less evenly matched in strength.

♆ SATURN'S TRANSITS TO NEPTUNE

☌ Conjunction

For someone who is sensitive, idealistic and perhaps creative, this influence will be a good one. It will help to consolidate ideas and steady the emotions, perhaps to the point that such statements will be made as "I've not known what to think about that, but now I'm certain." The subject in question may be esoterically or religiously inclined. If so, the influence will help to realize his or her creative potential in a constructive way.

The influence is good, too, for those interested in any kind of abstract or occult work. With practical people who might not usually have much time for such vague ideas, Saturn may encourage them to think again and review their opinions. With everyone, inspiration or unusual ideas should be considered seriously, with a view to developing them in practical ways.

+ Positive transits

These have much the same effect as the conjunction although the influence is more subtle, and if it is only a sextile it can pass unnoticed by practical people. Very sensitive loved ones will know that something has happened, even if the person concerned doesn't think so, or doesn't care to admit it!

There could, for instance, be a sudden and uncharacteristic interest in poetry or any Neptune-related interests. Watch for these apparent changes in your down-to-earth business orientated friends and, of course, give all encouragement to the development of ideas by those who are more sensitive and creative.

– Negative transits

These are nasty. Sometimes the individual is done down in some way, resulting in endless confusion and delay. Rather differently, he or she may pay a very high price for any misdemeanor, especially if it was deception, lying, or attempting to take the easy way out of a demanding or difficult situation. Lessons are often learned in a very hard way indeed.

♇ SATURN'S TRANSITS TO PLUTO

☌ Conjunction

This is a difficult and very trying influence. While it is operative little or no progress is likely to be made, and there is a tendency to be confronted by brick walls. This trend may not affect every sphere of life, and it is a good idea to discover in which areas there is progress and fulfillment, for it is essential to concentrate on those, rather than attempting to push forward, wasting time and emotional and physical energies on what is likely to be essentially blocked.

During this period, and for a few weeks before and after it has passed, special care should be taken of the health. Saturn may cause some kind of limiting pain or perhaps uncharacteristic constipation.

Psychologically, the outlook may be negative, with feelings of frustration creeping up from time to time. These conditions will clear within a couple of weeks of the influence easing. If it recurs due to retrograde motion, the interim periods are likely to provide the subject with considerable and welcome respite.

+ Positive transits
Although some sound conclusions will be reached during this time, and the individual will perhaps be released from a problem in his or her life, even these positive transits can cause difficulties. Nevertheless, once the influence is over it will be found that progress has been made, whether in the reassessment of some area of life or in the making of an important change. Even so, these trends aren't much fun. Advise holding back if the subject seems to be swimming against the tide.

– Negative transits
These have similar effects to those of the conjunction, with perhaps an even greater slowing down of progress. Follow the interpretation as given above, but in addition a philosophical attitude should be adopted, with a falling-back on restorative interests and hobbies – it will be a sheer waste of time to attempt to force issues.

Asc SATURN'S TRANSITS TO THE ASCENDANT

☌ Conjunction
This is an extremely important trend. For the last two and a half years or so Saturn's transit through the twelfth house will have been experienced (read the interpretation of Saturn in the twelfth house, p.304). This influence may have led to a reassessment of spiritual, metaphysical and inspirational values and opinions but now, as Saturn enters the first house, a change of direction may follow. Perhaps it will be a more serious attitude to life, or a long-term commitment – often the best outcome of this serious transit.

Note the health emphasis of the Ascending sign since Saturn's influence may cause problems.

Often this is a turning point during which the life is reassessed in some way – sometimes with regard to relationships. Lessons are learned, especially if any mistakes are made, but these will relate to the influence of other planets rather than to Saturn.

+ Positive transits
The house through which Saturn is transiting will dictate the way in which this trend affects the individual – sometimes in parenthood or when a love affair becomes more serious (perhaps Saturn in the fifth house), or when making a safe investment (Saturn in the second), and so on. You will find that steady, slow progress but sound decisions and practical actions are usually the outcome.

– Negative transits
As with the positive transits, the house through which Saturn is transiting will be important. Look out for Saturn opposing the Ascendant, when a permanent relationship will be under discussion and changes may be made – often to the eventual good of both parties, who may put their life together on a new footing, or at least come to realize what was previously lacking. Sometimes this is the time when a business partner is taken on.

A square transit can mean problems at work (Saturn in the tenth house) or difficulties in the domestic or family life (Saturn in the fourth). This is not an easy time but, as ever, in the final analysis the hard taskmaster side of Saturn can bring about the benefits of personal development and increased stability of the subject.

MC SATURN'S TRANSITS TO THE MIDHEAVEN

☌ Conjunction
Study Saturn in the tenth house (see p.304). This is an extremely important influence that will have a powerful effect on the career or profession, with the distinct possibility of promotion or maybe a striking change of job. If no career is followed, some ambition or objective will be achieved – not easily, but in a manner which will make the eventual outcome seem well-deserved. It could certainly mark a turning point in the life, and events over which the subject has no direct control, but which came about as a result of his or her reputation, are most likely to occur. Sometimes there is promotion to a lonely top job.

+ Positive transits
Events concerning the house through which Saturn is transitting will occur, but, as above, these will not be as a direct result of the individual's own actions or motivation. Again, steady progress is likely, and the outlook will be practical – especially if any decisions have to be made regarding loved ones as well as the subject concerned.

– Negative transits
These bring frustration and delay and sometimes the loss of a job (perhaps due to redundancy). These are not easy influences, and patience and caution are needed. The best outcome arises in situations when issues have not been forced.

Other transits very often ease the situation, and help from Jupiter is particularly useful. The influence can also mean that the subject is working particularly hard on extremely demanding yet prestigious work.

♄ SATURN'S TRANSITS TO ITS OWN POSITION

There will be times when Saturn makes positive and negative transits to its own position. When it makes a positive transit, gradual progress and additional responsibility will usually result, with the subject gaining prestige and often accepting extra responsibility. Usually in retrospect there is the inclination to say "I'm so glad I did that – things have worked out so well, although at the time it was a difficult decision to make." The difficulty of the decision was probably caused by the subject questioning his or her own confidence and ability to cope. Once having taken the step, Saturn would have ensured that progress was made.

When the transit is negative there will be frustration and delay, and it is all too easy to become disheartened and pessimistic. Sometimes, too, there are losses of one kind or another. (Personal property should be guarded with special care.)

Sometimes changes are made within relationships, or they are even ended, but look to other progressions and transits to counter this side of the influence. All in all, when Saturn transits its own position the planet's sign and house position in the birth chart will be affected, and the ways in which Saturn is aspected there will have a powerful influence on the eventual outcome of the influence.

♄ THE SATURN RETURNS

In essence, these are the conjunction transits of Saturn to its own position. Together, they form one of the most fascinating and easily understood of all the planetary influences. They are, along with the Jupiter Returns (see p.297) and the Uranus Half-return (see p.326), influences about which you can enthuse with friends who up to now only know their Sun sign. And they certainly work!

It is common knowledge that as we approach thirty, and later sixty, we think about our progress in life and whether we should make any important changes. At thirty we may become rather gloomy and even begin to feel old, despite realizing that we have gained a certain amount of experience. Again at sixty most of us begin to think about the stage, fast approaching, when we will no longer be fully involved with our careers, and will at last have more time in which to do the things we really want to do. Our families are grownup and we can enjoy ourselves.

Even people with no knowledge of astrology accept these well-known facts; astrologers assign these turning points to Saturn's influence. Saturn takes twenty-nine-and-a-half years to complete a journey round the Sun and through all the signs of the zodiac, so that as we approach thirty and sixty it "returns" to its natal position. If we live long enough, we get a third Return as we reach ninety.

The first Saturn Return

Someone approaching this important period may feel apprehensive and perhaps depressed at the prospect of moving into the next decade of his or her life. However, this is quite unnecessary. Often the individual will want to make some important changes, which are usually quite in order and very beneficial. Sometimes a subject will say "I simply cannot go on any longer as I am." If this is so, ask him what he wants to do: in most cases he will have a pretty clear idea and should follow it, whatever it is.

Sometimes there is a desire to end a youthful relationship, even a marriage, which began before he was ready for such a commitment. On the other hand, someone who has perhaps been living with a partner will want to take on the commitment of marriage. Others buy their first house or start a family. Here, Saturn encourages the acceptance of extra responsibility but also, of course, gives the added prestige of a new home, new husband/wife, new baby and so on.

The long-term future is set, and there is greater stability and security. Anyone dissatisfied with his career is not too old to make quite a drastic change (although there are one or two exceptions these days). In any case, drastic changes can be, and often are, made, which is exactly as it should be.

As Saturn is working full blast, however, a warning is needed that the subject may be suffering from slightly lower vitality than usual – often due to additional physical and emotional demands. As is the case with most serious Saturn influences, careful thought should be given to each possibility, for then the right decision will usually be reached; we seldom make serious mistakes during a Saturn Return. It usually colors most of a year, even if Saturn only inhabits its natal degree once, and only then for a week or so.

The second Saturn Return

As this approaches, people make decisions about life after retirement. They develop new interests, some of which become professional, so that new careers are started, often in areas which have only concerned spare-time occupations or hobbies before. Such interests are usually very fulfilling and rewarding, so should be encouraged.

However, before giving advice you should reach some very vital conclusions about your subjects. They may say that all they want is a nice, lazy time with their feet up. Decide from their charts whether this is so, or whether, after a week or two of doing nothing much, they will be unbearable to live with! If they are given a retirement present, encourage them to choose something that will further a real interest – perhaps an expensive camera, quality sewing machine or a telescope. Fixing on this may give them a considerable sense of direction.

Another question that often arises at this point is whether the couple (if the subject is one half of a partnership) should move to a smaller house or to a district in which they have spent happy holidays, or where the climate is easier. Here you should be extremely careful. If one partner is prominently Taurean or Cancerian they will have many possessions that have been collected over the years. Will they want to part with them? If there are children and grandchildren will there be room for them to come and stay? Both important questions must be answered.

Even more vital is the question of a move to a strange town. You must decide how self-contained the couple are, whether they are communicative and will make new friends easily or are less adaptable, so that they will soon miss old friends and familiar surroundings. A pleasant seaside resort can be very bleak in the damp and cold of winter, and in some areas locals resent the intrusion of so-called outsiders. On the other hand, if the couple are excellent organizers and find a lack of the clubs and facilities they require, they will put this sorry state of affairs to rights. All such questions will arise when you work on the charts of subjects who are coming up to their second Saturn Return.

A Jupiter Return often coincides with the second Saturn Return. This is extremely useful, for it makes the subject buoyant and optimistic. Plans for the future are likely to progress well under such a joint influence, and the individual should be encouraged to make the most of both these powerful planetary forces.

The third Saturn Return

For those who reach their third Saturn Return (an increasing number every year) more research is needed if they are to be given the necessary encouragement. This is a step further from the full Uranus Return that is discussed in detail (see p.326) and complements it.

Generally, you can encourage your ninety-year-old subject to talk about the past, and for your own researches try to pinpoint dates in the long life, and do some retrospective astrology to see just what was happening in the progressed chart at the time. You can find exciting, real evidence of the planetary influences.

Uranus through the Signs

Uranus spends about seven years in each sign as it moves around the zodiac, so is in that sign for everyone born during that period. All planets are important in the birth and progressed charts, but a sign influence which is identical for so many people does not indicate personal characteristics which will dominate an individual unless, of course, Uranus is a personal planet. Instead, it is what is known as a "generation" influence.

Uranus in Aries

This is a powerful and positive placing, with the energy and assertiveness of Aries complementing the forthright, nervous energy of Uranus. Unless negatively aspected, Uranus should endow plenty of originality and the motivation to use it in positive ways. There will be erratic tendencies, however, and patience is not enhanced; look elsewhere in the chart to see if this and more cautionary qualities are present.

In a chart showing creative potential, the influence will strengthen originality and often gives a lively color sense. The pioneering spirit of Aries also complements the search for what is new, out-of-the-ordinary and different – all powerful Uranian traits. The placing also heightens self-confidence and reinforces the individual's powers of leadership. However, possible foolhardiness must be checked, since it can surface in an extremely eccentric way with the individual becoming involved in silly and daredevil feats (if often with good intentions, such as raising money for charity). As always with this placing, caution must be developed. If Uranus is negatively aspected, especially by Mars, these daring tendencies will be increased. If Uranus is generally negatively aspected, its characteristic nervous and emotional tension will be particularly noticeable.

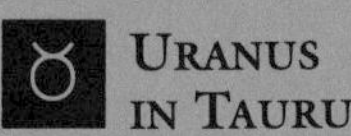

Uranus in Taurus

Here the stubborn area of the Uranian influence makes its presence felt. It will definitely strengthen any lack of flexibility of opinion, and if other fixed signs are prominent the subject may proudly say "Once I've made up my mind I don't change it." If so, he or she should be encouraged to develop a more flexible outlook. However, if the chart tends towards indecision, with a powerful emphasis on Libra or perhaps Pisces, this is a good placing, since it gives a combination of stability and Uranian originality.

Opposing tendencies

Stubbornness is common but again, if it is really damaging it will also appear in other areas of the chart, or be emphasized by Uranus' house position and aspects. Sometimes there is a clash between taking conventional action (Taurus) and being unconventional or slightly out on a limb (Uranus). If a balance is achieved, we often find an original and practical individual, which is when Uranus in Taurus is at its best. There may be an attraction to collecting unusual possessions, and the attitude to money may also be slightly eccentric. Perhaps he or she can be extravagant, spending much on glamorous evenings out but then pulling back and living rather frugally.

Uranus in Gemini

This is an excellent, very dynamic and lively placing, endowing originality, quick thinking and often brilliant ideas which the subject should be encouraged to think through carefully and eventually develop to the full. Here is excellent potential. If the chart veers towards the intellectual, with Mercury and Jupiter well-placed by sign as well as aspect, this influence will blend in, adding spiciness, a sharp attitude and quick responses, especially in argument and debate. It is also good for the subject who works in the media or follows any sort of literary or academic career. The technical areas of communications will also be of interest.

The restless, nervous side of Gemini and the tension of Uranus can cause problems. See if these are indicated elsewhere in the chart, if Uranus receives squares or oppositions from the Sun, Moon or Mercury, or if it is in negative aspect to the Ascendant. If so, such an aspect, plus this sign placing, will be a potential source of tension and sometimes distress, since the individual will become very worried when finding it difficult to relax, sleep properly or put problems to one side; a relaxation technique or yoga may help. If Mars is involved there may be migraines, or nasty headaches at the very least. However, on the whole Uranus is in an excellent mood here.

Uranus in Cancer

The changeable moodiness of Cancer, combined with the unpredictability of Uranus, may at times cause problems. While, of course, planets in more powerful positions will hold sway over this generation sign influence, when Uranus is contacted by transit the influence of its natal position may emerge, and perhaps at times the subject will be a little confused at some of his or her quirky and even uncharacteristic behavior patterns. However, if Cancer is a prominent sign or Uranus a personal planet, these indications will definitely make their mark, and must be controlled if the individual is not to heap problems on herself because loved ones and colleagues never know where they stand with her. At its best, however, this placing enhances the imagination, which will have a wonderfully original slant. In a creative chart it is definitely an asset, while more generally the trait is useful.

Uranus is a cold, unemotional planet, always encouraging logical, clear-cut action, while Cancer is all intuition and very emotional. Unless Uranus is personalized or Cancer is the Sun, Moon or Ascending sign, this dilemma is unlikely to surface. However, when Uranus is a personal planet it can be quite a source of tension, with the individual not knowing which area to develop. It is obvious that she should let one complement the other, but because they are such opposing factors this will be difficult, and there may be persistent conflict. She should decide whether her emotions and intuitions overrule logic or vice versa, and allow the stronger to take precedent.

♌ URANUS IN LEO

There is increased energy here, and a dynamic driving force. Sometimes, too, some autocracy and a liking for power are present. If the latter can be positively expressed, the talent for leadership will be such that others will gladly follow. Nonetheless, don't forget that Leo is a fixed sign, and since Uranus increases stubbornness, the subject may well become an immovable object. Leo is also a warm, enthusiastic fire sign while Uranus, albeit friendly, likes to keep its distance and is cool, calculating and unemotional. However, conflict will only emerge if Uranus is a personal planet, or if it is negatively aspected by the Sun.

Self-confidence is certainly boosted, especially in a chart in which this tends to be lacking. It is a lively, colorful placing, and will give a rather glitzy glamor if Uranus is aspected by the Moon or Venus. There may also be a sense of the dramatic which is used to excellent effect. This will be apparent if, for instance, Uranus is in the fifth house, and it would be combined with a need for power and a desire to influence the masses if Uranus were high in the sky in the tenth house.

Since Leo is a creative sign there is often creative flair which may be developed through a hobby, thus encouraging the personal potential. This would be an excellent form of original expression in someone who is perhaps rather shy and apprehensive, lacking in self-confidence. However, if we reverse the coin, all the overwhelming, power-loving, showy tendencies of this planet may have to be countered.

♍ URANUS IN VIRGO

This is a potential source of tension, especially if the subject is rather nervous or apprehensive, or if tension is evident in other areas of the chart. These energies can be put to good use as they will inject the mind with the ability to analyze and research, and will also encourage a certain originality of approach to any problem or project that is under consideration. Since Virgo is an earth sign it tends to be conventional – the familiar and well-tried is preferred, yet Uranus' influence is quite the reverse, encouraging original thoughts and actions, and often unconventional behavior.

The influence of Pluto
People who have Uranus in Virgo will also have Pluto in that sign, and many have the strikingly powerful Uranus/Pluto conjunction (see pp.319-20). Check this possibility, as it could be very revealing and, because of these additional influences it is difficult to divorce the effect from that of Pluto. However, while Virgo is generally anything but power-loving, the energy force of this placing, plus Pluto's intervention, have endowed this particular generation with some dynamic, forceful qualities. They have what it takes to make world-shattering changes, but refer to the aspect interpretation for a fuller explanation of the conjunction. To put this on a personal level, the individual may be a seeker and questioner, unable to rest content, and with the ability to scrutinize every aspect of a situation. If these attributes can be positively used, and are supported elsewhere in the chart, he or she may have a considerable talent for investigative or research work that is often medical. Scientific flair is possible, but the subject must accept his originality since there may sometimes be an inclination to suppress it.

♎ URANUS IN LIBRA

Although Uranus shines in a glamorous way from this sign, and often gives increased powers of attraction and a sneakingly romantic streak, its independence can cause difficulties when fighting Libra's compulsive need to relate. In most cases a thread of independence, and perhaps occasional coolness, will emerge in the attitude toward the partner; but if either Venus or Uranus are personal planets, or if they are in aspect to each other, these very contrasting indications will have a considerable effect on the relationship as a whole. If Aquarius is the Sun, Moon or Ascendant sign the subject will have to admit that he or she may want a partnership but not a partner. It is obviously important to come to terms with this attitude if the partner is not to be adversely affected.

Here is an excellent, caring and helpful friend who will give much time and energy when called upon to do so and who will be sympathetic and kind – traits that should be developed by the subject if she has the above-mentioned negative attitude to her intimate relationships. Even so, this placing will help to stabilize and rationalize the emotions, and can therefore be constructive and positive for someone with a very high emotional level.

♏ URANUS IN SCORPIO

Here Uranus is perhaps at its most weighty and complex. Remember that the planet's influence is increased since it is exalted in this sign; the dynamic force of Uranus, added to the emotional intensity of Scorpio, gives considerable extra power to the subject. He or she is brave and daring, but tends to avoid showing the emotions and may even try to reject them. As a result, he will appear calm while much is boiling up on deeper levels of his personality. He must accept that the gradual release of emotional tension and energy is good, and when channeled they can be used positively and rewardingly so that inner satisfaction accompanies achievement.

Potential for power
A need for power is sometimes present. People with this placing will have been born between 1975 and 1981 and are still, at the time of writing, young; if older generations do not give them careful, sound guidance they will waste some powerful potential and energy. The influence will be at its most dynamic if the Sun, Moon or Ascendant sign is Scorpio, or if that sign and Uranus were on or near the Midheaven. These youngsters need to feel they are in a powerful position –

often to help the world or to make it think in the same way that they do. If their parents realize they have potential and give firm guidance they will do well, but association with the seamier sides of life may drag them down.

URANUS IN SAGITTARIUS

Here Uranus is in lively, dynamic mood, giving an original slant to the intellect and opening up the mind. The Sagittarian need for challenge is complemented by an attraction to all things new and unusual. Uranus traveled through Sagittarius between 1981 and 1988, and Jupiter, the ruler of Sagittarius, made a transit of that sign in 1983 – a delightful joint influence, adding liveliness, an attractive sense of humor and very good brains.

A green future
Generally speaking, the splendid influence of this placing alone will make these children intellectually and physically adventurous. They will be humanitarian and be able to contribute fully to the greening of the Earth, for they will be entirely aware of world ecological problems yet have a very different approach from those of the previous generation who have Uranus in Scorpio. Parents of young children with this placing should try to always increase their awareness of the beauty of the world. These traits will be particularly pronounced if Sagittarius is prominent or Uranus is personalized.

URANUS IN CAPRICORN

Here Uranus will give a rational, cool outlook and the ability to put problems into a coherent and logical perspective. However, Capricorn is the sign most sympathetic to conventional behavior and to doing "the right and proper thing" and Uranus is exactly the opposite, often encouraging shock tactics and perverse and unpredictable actions. Conflict will be the result. In most cases, hopefully, there will be a weighing up of the contrasting possibilities when the occasion demands, and the subject will take the sensible line of action, neither causing embarrassment nor cramping his or her style. This is a generation influence, so these traits will not be strongly emphasized in everyone born over a seven-year period. Nevertheless, if someone of this generation consults you for astrological advice in a few years' time, and you mention something along these lines, he or she will understand and perhaps may be able to add some additional and incisive comments.

A certain hardness is present, but the humanitarian side of Uranus will emerge in a very practical, down-to-earth way, and this generation will continue to improve the environment and cope with the problems of their time. Study the power of the Uranian influence in the child's chart to see if she will be a leader of her generation. You should also refer to both Saturn and Neptune in Capricorn (see pp.300-1 and p.328 respectively), and to the Saturn/Uranus conjunction (see p.305). All these planets' positions, and possibly the above-mentioned conjunction, could be present in the chart on which you are working.

URANUS IN AQUARIUS

Here Uranus is in the sign that it rules, giving these people a certain Aquarian air. They are friendly, kind and humanitarian, usually with an independent streak, and may be rather private. As they get older they must be encouraged to keep their independence, and will probably want to. However, Uranian unpredictability and intractability will surely emerge, so the rest of the chart should be examined to find the best solution to such deadlocks. If air signs are emphasized, this placing's influence will be somewhat increased.

There is considerable inventiveness and originality, and a certain flair in whichever area of self-expression is most fulfilling. Many will look glamorous well into the later years of their lives, but poor circulation and stiffness or arthritic conditions in the joints is likely – exercise should be encouraged.

Kindness and the Aquarian/Uranian humanitarian traits are usually present. Here is someone who likes to raise money for charity, or at least ease suffering in a practical way. As Uranus is in its own sign here its influence is enhanced, and will be even more potent if it is also a personal planet.

URANUS IN PISCES

The principles of Uranus and the characteristics of Pisces couldn't be more different, yet this subject has inspired idealism and can sometimes view problems with objectivity and even vision, but with real human kindness and sympathy. It is here that we see a rapport between the planet and the sign: Pisces sacrifices much for the good of others, and Uranus is the most humanitarian of planets.

Creative potential
Here is originality, imagination and inspiration – marvelous for someone who is creative or inventive. Any emphasis on Pisces may cause evasive or escapist action – a possibility even with the increased logic of this placing, especially if the subject is quite gullible and likes to be considered fashionable. There will then be an instinct to follow the trend, which may be a negative drug- or drink-taking one. If so, the tense side of Uranus will emerge, causing emotional strain and tension. However, this is only likely for very sensitive people with escapist or self-deceptive tendencies elsewhere in their charts. At its best this is an interesting placing, contributing some fascinating and helpful characteristics, even to those who do not have the planet very powerfully placed in their charts.

URANUS PROGRESSED TO A NEW SIGN

This is most unlikely to happen unless your subject was born at the time, once in seven years, when Uranus was about to change signs. In the event of your coming across this progression, reread the interpretation of the natal (i.e. the original) Uranus sign, and study also the characteristics of the new sign. If Uranus is personalized these traits may begin to have an effect on your subject. If not, this trend can be virtually ignored.

Uranus through the Houses

The concerns of the house in which Uranus falls can cause unexpected developments and sudden changes. The individual may force issues, especially if the planet is personalized or aspected by personal planets. As this is a potential stress factor, try to find ways of turning tension into positive energy.

1 Uranus in the First House

The presence of Uranus here will powerfully affect the influence of the Ascending sign's traits. The individual will be fiercely independent, original and with perhaps more than a dash of brilliance shown through the potential of the Ascendant sign. A strong element of perversity and unpredictability is also possible, and if the planet is negatively aspected the subject is likely to suffer from emotional tension.

A golden rule is to study the characteristics of the Uranus sign, for unless that differs from the Ascendant sign, the indications listed there will form a very vital and vibrant part of your subject's personality. If the signs differ, you must blend their characteristics with care, concentrating where possible on those that complement each other. If Uranus is within ten degrees of the Ascendant, its influence conjunct the Ascendant from the first house will definitely apply.

Note: With such a planet in the first house you will learn much about Ascendant progressions if you ask whether the subject had an accident when the progressed Ascendant made an exact conjunction to Uranus, or was directly affected by a drastic event in the parents' lives, such as divorce. The age of your subject at that time will have been approximately the number of degrees between the Ascendant and Uranus. If not, the birth time is inaccurate or the Ascendant is progressing at less than one degree a year.

2 Uranus in the Second House

The attitude towards money will be more than a little zany. The individual may often make what are thought to be clever investments, but these are likely to be too clever by half, and as a result financial problems will arise that will be his or her own fault! However, if the chart veers powerfully towards the material (and if, for instance, an earth sign is prominently emphasized – we include the Midheaven here), the brilliance of Uranus could work very well, with considerable and unexpectedly sudden gains being made. In most cases the subject must realize, before it is too late, that he can make serious financial mistakes, often because he is attracted to an investment that sounds glamorous and unusual.

Uranus will work badly if negatively aspected, especially by the Sun, Moon or Venus. This emotions may be expressed in a cool way, although the powers of attraction will be undimmed. Uncharacteristic possessiveness may clash with the Uranian need for independence – something partners will find hard to swallow.

3 Uranus in the Third House

This adds brilliance and originality to the mind. The individual will make somewhat erratic progress at school and may not take very easily or kindly to discipline. Parents of children with this placing should consider these characteristics: too much restriction at school will cramp what is probably a lively, free-ranging mind that needs plenty of stimulation.

If Uranus is positively aspected, the planet's cool logic and rational outlook will be present and the individual will definitely want logical answers to his or her questions. This trait will emerge from a very early age, and will persist throughout life. If Uranus is in a fixed sign and negatively aspected, the stubbornness and perversity so typical of its influence will certainly be apparent, and in many cases it is likely that some willful contrariness will be present. Anyone conducting a discussion or argument with the subject should present the opposite opinion in order to achieve the desired action or response!

4 Uranus in the Fourth House

"We must make allowances for *her* – she's *different*!" Such a statement is often made of a child with this placing. He or she may be brilliant and clever but might also be rather perverse and if Uranus is negatively aspected (especially by the Moon), also moody and very unpredictable. The originality and brightness of intuitive ideas should be noted and developed to the full.

The importance of the home
An inner conflict may exist between the need for, and love of, a stable, comforting home life and an equal desire to live freely, without domestic responsibilities. If this causes problems, consider the most prominent signs in the chart. If one is Sagittarius, or perhaps Aries, the subject's freedom-loving side must be given greater expression. If Cancer, Pisces or a similarly introverted sign is emphasized, the subject should concentrate on the security of the home life.

Circumstances surrounding the home background may also be revealed. Was it disruptive? Were there drastic changes? Was the mother out of the ordinary in some way? Perhaps she was not a mother figure as such, but too glamorous or simply uncaring? Care is also needed that, because of such an influence, the individual does not repeat this pattern in his domestic life or attitude toward children.

5 Uranus in the Fifth House

Uranus is well-placed here, since the spheres of life connected with this house mostly benefit from the planet's influence (unless it is negatively aspected by personal planets, especially the Sun). In someone who has and expresses creative potential, it encourages originality and adds brilliance to the end product, which will probably be colorful in every way. There will be a positive and lively attitude toward love affairs, with the subject usually fairly fearless of emotional risks. Sometimes, especially if fire signs are prominent in the chart, there is a tendency to take risks. Warn your subject of this inclination; if Uranus is negatively aspected the risks will not be calculated, and the individual may at times be more than usually in danger.

Uranus' influence on the subject's children infers that they will be clever and unusual, with excellent potential. However, they will not be easy to cope with, since they will have many different interests and therefore exert more demands on their parents' time, energy and money (for special lessons and so forth). Such efforts will probably be very worthwhile in the long run.

6 URANUS IN THE SIXTH HOUSE

When placed in the sixth house, the brilliance of Uranus will have an exciting effect on the intellect, probably giving some flair for innovation.

The health may not always be particularly strong and robust, and the subject can frequently be laid low by a minor infection or simply feel out of sorts. The real reason for this may easily be strain and tension, but worry and an inability to relax are also distinct possibilities. The diet should be very carefully watched: he or she may eat erratically and not very sensibly. If Uranus is negatively aspected, especially by an opposition to the Ascendant, or it receives a square or opposition from Mercury, these negative influences will certainly make their presence felt and worry may prove to be an especial problem, often leading to stomach upsets.

Constructing a pattern of work

The attitude towards routine work will be complex. The Virgo/sixth house likes and needs a steady routine and some security at work, but the Uranian influence here is disruptive, often causing the individual to become fed up with routine tasks. Encourage the even flow of both physical and nervous energy, and the establishment of an overall pattern to the life. In order that he or she avoids stress, suggest that your subject introduces plenty of variety, with a different pattern and routine for every day of the week. Adopting such a constructive plan will help her to gain inner fulfillment and complete whatever has to be done.

7 URANUS IN THE SEVENTH HOUSE

This needs particularly close consideration and study. When in this house, Uranus exerts a strong effect on the individual's attitude toward relationships, and a partner who is sympathetic to his or her needs is essential.

Independence versus commitment

It is likely that the subject will be reluctant to commit herself to a permanent relationship; the sign in which Uranus is placed will show whether this is a source of conflict, or simply a straightforward need to be independent. The polarity of the Ascendant and the sign on the cusp of the seventh house will come into play, and you may have to study the Relationships section (see pp.148-67) of this book to clarify this complex placing.

If Uranus occupies a highly emotional sign in the birth chart there may be mixed feelings about some aspects of partnerships, and as result mistakes can be made, so that there is an above-average number of commitments followed by an equally high number of breakdowns. The root of the conflict will stem from the subject being uncertain whether her head rules her heart or vice versa.

A rather romantic outlook may be encouraged by another area of this Uranian influence, which also makes the individual magnetically attractive. If, as is the case when certain signs are prominent, we add a desire for a committed relationship, then the individual may realize too late that her freedom of expression and independence are more important than she originally thought. She must sort out these problems herself; you can help her clarify the situation by assessing which group of characteristics will dominate. Do this by considering the influences of the Ascending, Sun and Moon signs, as well as the influence of Venus and the personal planets.

8 URANUS IN THE EIGHTH HOUSE

From the financial/investment point of view, there may be a simple, couldn't-care-less attitude when Uranus is placed in the eighth house. If the individual has money it will be enjoyed, but if he or she hasn't – so what? If your subject is dominated by this somewhat lackadaisical effect of Uranus, it may be that lessons will have to be learned and a more conventional view adopted (although there is something to be said for such an unmaterialistic outlook). A classic interpretation of someone with Uranus in the eighth house would be the individual giving away an inheritance to a charity that works for the relief of suffering or starvation.

This is a complex placing; as well as having financial overtones, there are deeper references to the sexual attitudes and appetites and the way in which the subject reaches, psychologically, for sexual fulfillment. He will sometimes be very responsive and need much satisfaction, while at other times the cool, unemotional side of this influence will predominate.

The subject may analyze his sexually oriented problems to an almost obsessive degree, yet he may never actually resolve them – perhaps he does not want to. If you think that something like this is happening to your subject, we strongly advise that he seeks help from a psychotherapist in order to place his difficulties, hang-ups or any other complications in a more coherent perspective. This may be most necessary if Uranus is in Virgo and forms a conjunction with Pluto, or if other independent indications in the chart point in this direction.

9 URANUS IN THE NINTH HOUSE

Uranus is in a lively and slightly wicked mood here. At its best, it will add a marvelously original and clever streak to the mind, with the subject making a notable impact at university. There can be scientific flair, or a unique literary talent. Challenges are seized with the greatest enthusiasm and the mind itself knows no restrictions. The placing will considerably enhance the intellectual potential, and there is usually be a constant need for excitement, and for new and different experiences. There is also an ability to resolve problems through lateral thinking.

Broadening the mind
Both intellectual and physical travel will be of considerable importance to the individual, and tradition suggests that the unexpected will occur when he or she is abroad! Sometimes, too, there is an inexplicable and dynamic attraction either to a foreigner or to a remote country whose culture is very different from that of her own.

Uranus in this house can make for some lively and unusual experiences when traveling. However, when your subject is planning to travel under negative transits to Uranus, it may be as well to advise postponing the trip until such an influence has passed, since there can sometimes be complications, and the exciting and unexpected is not always pleasant!

Look to the influence of Jupiter and the Jupiter sign of Sagittarius in the chart. If Uranus is in Sagittarius, the subject (who will be very young) is very bright indeed, and further education should be strongly encouraged in the future, in whichever field is found to be most attractive.

10 Uranus in the Tenth House

Because Uranus was high in the sky at the time of the subject's birth, its influence is increased to a certain extent by this placing, especially if the planet makes a conjunction to the Midheaven (see p.320).

Career choices
The chosen profession is likely to be influenced by Uranus, so the individual may well be attracted to airlines, the space industry, science, astronomy, or perhaps the humanitarian and caring professions. Alternatively, he or she may be drawn to work that has an exciting or glamorous aspect.

Sudden changes of career direction are possible. However, should the subject be confronted by the prospect of such a change (because of having been fired, for instance), there will be a tendency to overreact and to throw away a great deal of hard-earned experience in order to start afresh on the new professional path.

Reactions of this sort will be the result of the more perverse side of Uranus exerting itself, and if you find it happening to your subject, do all you can to encourage him or her to think again and in a much more practical manner.

An involvement in politics or the trade unions sometimes occurs for the individual with this placing. In this or other contexts, a liking for power is also very common.

11 Uranus in the Eleventh House

Uranus is very much at home in the eleventh house, because it is also the Aquarius house, so its influence will be strong from here.

The individual can be extremely friendly, but at the same time he or she will not want to become too close to other people. There is a universality in the outlook, and an abiding need to develop a wide and varied social life which may well vie with the subject's profession in importance – indeed, it often takes precedence.

Social influence
The Uranus sign will show just how the influence of the eleventh house will be best expressed. For instance, Uranus in Leo may create a natural chairman ruling the life of a club or society. Rather differently, this same sign placing may create a sort of workhorse – for instance, a hard-working secretary who takes on every task himself, working indomitably for his much-loved club and never receiving the reward he deserves.

The unpredictability of Uranus will emerge from time to time, however, and there is a good chance that sudden breaks in ties of friendship or in the allegiance to the club or society will occur as a result of the subject's rapid change of heart. Sometimes, too, the individual will be disruptive on purpose, in order to stir the committee and other members into action, due to a loathing of complacency.

12 Uranus in the Twelfth House

This is a very interesting placing for Uranus. Although Uranus and the twelfth/Pisces house are so different, they also come together extremely well in many ways.

Uranus is kind and humanitarian, while the twelfth house represents our need to be charitable and to make sacrifices. Here the flow of feeling and an instinctive urge to be of help is blended with the logical and unemotional approach characteristic of the cool, detached, Uranian influence. Sometimes the subject with this placing will distance him- or herself from a close permanent relationship in order to take up some caring vocation, or to tend an elderly relative.

A deep-rooted psychological motivation may be present, for while the outward expression will be marvelously positive for the person for whom sacrifices are made, the individual himself may well shy away from living a fulfilling existence with a partner. Perhaps the whole childhood background was influenced by a parent's demands? Such motivations are very complex, and we must always be careful not to stretch our astrological technique or overstep the confines of our discipline when we feel that complicated and very deep-rooted psychological problems are present. We must not step into the unknown – it is far better to leave that to psychotherapists and psychiatrists, so suggest that your subject seeks such professional help if you believe that it is necessary.

♅ Uranus Progressed to a New House

It is unlikely that Uranus will move from one house to the next by progression. If this does happen, read the interpretations both of the natal and the new, progressed house. Do not emphasize this progression too much in your interpretation unless Uranus is a personal planet or the chart ruler. This being so, the concerns of the progressed house may be a focus of attention, with the subject regarding the sphere of life it represents in a new and different light.

The Aspects of Uranus

The aspects that Uranus forms to Neptune and Pluto stay within orb for long periods, not only because Uranus moves slowly but also because Neptune and Pluto are even further away from the Sun than Uranus itself. Hence, many aspects between these planets will be operative in the charts of all people born over a very long time. While they must be thought of as generation influences, it is unwise to ignore them.

Look at each planet to see if its strength is bolstered by its sign or house position. If so, the aspect will be rather more personalized and felt in the overall make-up of the individual's personality. In many cases the characteristics described under such an aspect will also occur in other areas of the chart, and therefore be underlined. If this is not so, the aspect may simply make a general statement about the subject's attitude to the concerns of his or her generation. If neither planet is personalized it is important not to single out the influence of the aspect when working through the chart.

For Uranus' aspects to the Sun, see the Sun's aspects to Uranus, pp.217-18.

For Uranus' aspects to the Moon, see the Moon's aspects to Uranus, p.235.

For Uranus' aspects to Mercury, see Mercury's aspects to Uranus, pp.250-1.

For Uranus' aspects to Venus, see Venus' aspects to Uranus, pp.264-5.

For Uranus' aspects to Mars, see Mars' aspects to Uranus, pp.278-9.

For Uranus' aspects to Jupiter, see Jupiter's aspects to Uranus, pp.290-1.

For Uranus' aspects to Saturn, see Saturn's aspects to Uranus, p.305.

In the most unlikely event of Uranus forming, by progression, any aspect to a natal or progressed planet from the Sun to Mars, refer to the above list and study the progressed aspect positions. If Uranus, by progression, forms an aspect to the natal position of Jupiter or Saturn, or (even less likely) a progressed aspect to the natal or progressed Neptune or Pluto, refer to the Uranus transit interpretations (see pp.320-5). Such progressed aspects would stay within orb for decades, and are not generally considered in interpretation, but you may still find them of academic interest.

Uranus' Aspects to Neptune

Conjunction

This recurs roughly every 171 years. It was last in orb, in Sagittarius, around 1818. It first became within orb again in January 1989, is exact in April 1992 and several times during 1993. It will not pass out of orb until 1998. For those born between January 1989 and February 1990, there is an additional influence from Saturn (see Saturn's aspects to Uranus and Neptune, pp.305-6). These are potent influences for this generation, and if we consider the originality, independence and humanitarian qualities of Uranus, combined with the more spiritual, esoteric and sensitive qualities of Neptune, plus the fact that the sign influence is Capricorn, this generation's concerns with the environment will be considerable. They will probably approach such problems very differently from the sixties generation, most of whom have the Uranus/Pluto conjunction in Virgo (see right).

+ Positive aspects

A pleasant blending of originality and imagination is usual. This is an excellent influence for creative people or those involved in inventive scientific work, since intuition and logical thinking are enhanced by these aspects. However, only stress these qualities in your interpretation if they are suggested by other influences, or if you find that Uranus or Neptune are personalized planets.

– Negative aspects

If tension is indicated in other areas of the chart, and the subject tends also to be rather forgetful or scatterbrained, these aspects may increase such inclinations, sometimes (if either planet is personalized) to the point at which he or she may say "I'm so worried and anxious, I don't know which way to turn and I can't sleep." If so, studying a relaxation technique will be most beneficial. Yoga will be good for some, provided they are not particularly introspective by nature.

Uranus' Aspects to Pluto

Conjunction

This extremely potent generation influence only occurs once every 115 years. It was last within orb between 1963 and 1969, in Virgo. It is a vibrant planetary energy source and those who have Virgo personalized, or that sign on the Midheaven, will tend to be leaders of their generation; it encourages change and drastic action. During the working lives of this generation we should see a great deal of injustice swept away – again, often drastically. However, because this influence is so strong and the two planets involved are concerned with power, it also has a destructive and negative side – hence the increase in drug problems and violence.

If the conjunction is personalized and is also negatively aspected, the subject may have had to sort out deep-rooted, psychological problems, and perhaps even fight an addiction. If he or she is still in difficulty, you will be able to help a great deal, but in particularly problematic cases extra treatment from more qualified specialists may be necessary.

This is a generation influence, however. Therefore, in many charts it will not be a dominating feature, although the individual may experience frustration and difficulty in the sphere of life indicated by the house placing of these two planets.

+ Positive aspects
There will be a strong tendency to make drastic changes. These are most likely to occur when either the natal Uranus or Pluto receive transits from Saturn, or from Uranus or Pluto as they move round the sky and contact their own or each other's positions. If these transits are negative there may be an inner compulsion for change, but plans will probably only be carried out with difficulty. Sometimes there is a power complex. Do not overinterpret these aspects unless the planets are personalized in the birth chart.

− Negative aspects
These are a potential source of conflict and tension but usually only when either planet is activated by transits, especially from Saturn. The individual may tend to be disruptive and make changes simply for the sake of doing so, sometimes regretting them later. This will be most likely if Scorpio is a prominent sign in the chart.

Asc Uranus' Aspects to the Ascendant

☌ Conjunction
Here the sign and house placing of Uranus have a vitally important bearing on your interpretation of this aspect. The subject will be fiercely independent, with considerable originality and often personal magnetism. However, if Uranus is negatively aspected, especially by the Sun, Moon or ruling planet, perversity, eccentricity and intractability are likely. Sometimes there is considerable nervous strain and tension, but all is usually well if they can be burned off through a compelling interest, profession or some physical activity. A certain crankiness should be countered.

If Uranus is in the twelfth house its influence is more subtle and the individual may make sacrifices and shun the limelight, perhaps by following a humanitarian vocation.

Rather differently, this placing sometimes occurs in the charts of film technicians or those who work in the technical areas of television or the theater. It is also propitious for adventurous photography or computer graphics, since it increases creative inventiveness. However, there may also be an inclination towards mysticism and cults. Sadly, this is often dangerous and you should therefore sound the appropriate warnings.

+ Positive aspects
Here Uranus works well, adding a lively brilliance to the personality. It increases originality in creative and inventive people and can add dynamic powers of attraction, much as the conjunction does. If Uranus is in the fifth house there may be a lively and rather spicy love life, with a need for some independence, even when in a committed relationship. The affairs of the Uranian house should move forward well – often with unexpected and exciting developments.

− Negative aspects
These are usually a potential source of tension and can make the individual extremely perverse and often unpredictable. The square tends to have a more disruptive and negative affect than the opposition, although with the latter it is important to decide whether Uranus will have a strenuous effect on the individual's health (sixth house), or influence his or her attitude towards relationships (seventh house). Squares from the fourth or tenth houses may cause tensions within the home or career respectively. The subject may be somewhat highly-strung, and magnify out of all proportion problems that arise in these areas of life.

MC Uranus' Aspects to the Midheaven

☌ Conjunction
Drastic changes of direction within the career or professional life are likely with this aspect. From a psychological point of view there may be an identification with power, so that the subject wants to be in a strong or powerful position – perhaps taking up the cause of colleagues through trade union work. Sometimes, too, there is an attraction to politics.

A tendency to be rebellious and a need to work independently are both present, with the individual only functioning at his or her best when unhampered by interfering superiors. Brilliance and great originality are usually shown in the work, and Uranian professions are likely to be attractive.

+ Positive aspects
These operate in much the same way as the conjunction, adding originality to the way in which the career is approached. The individual's natural dynamism will be noticed at work, but care is needed that a tendency to make sudden changes does not impede the long-term progress. The subject will be eager to break fresh ground; especially in the development of new ideas, and to outwit rivals by taking unexpected action.

− Negative aspects
Here the individual will probably suffer from an above-average build-up of tension in his or her working life. This may eventually result in a tendency to become overapprehensive over the slightest problem. Unfortunately, tension and strain will always occur when the subject is put upon by colleagues or an unsympathetic superior. Incompetence is not usually the cause of such reactions, although the attitude towards such problems can become slightly exaggerated, and perverse or unpredictable reactions may produce further setbacks.

Note: Remembering the powerful connection between Uranus and independence, when that planet makes any sort of aspect to the Midheaven it frequently produces people who want to make their own way in the world. Often they will work in a freelance capacity and, if a business sense is indicated elsewhere in their birth charts, may build up their own businesses. Originality can also go hand in hand with good entrepreneurial skills.

♅ The Transits of Uranus

The overall effect of Uranian transits is to make life unexpectedly eventful, so a useful key phrase is "Expect the unexpected". At best, the planet's influence brings excitement and has the effect of jolting us out of complacency; at worst it is a potential source of tension and shock.

The way ahead during these transits should be clear-cut, and we look to the future with renewed hope and the expectation that the changes made will, because of the action we have taken, develop as yet untapped potential and the ability to cope with a totally different set of circumstances. Obviously, not every influence that we receive from Uranus is going to have a drastic effect on our lives and lifestyles but it can and does happen from time to time – especially when we experience the very important Uranus Half-return (see p.326).

When Uranus is moving at its quickest pace as seen from Earth, a Uranian transit lasts roughly two and a half weeks. However, very often the planet seems to slow down, turning to retrograde motion and then reverting to direct motion again (see p.23). It is thus common to see it contacting the precise natal position of a planet three times within a period of perhaps six months. If this happens you will probably find that the planet doesn't contact the natal planet all the time, but there will be three distinct periods when it does.

When Uranus isn't in direct contact, very often the individual concerned will be able to enjoy a certain respite from the new developments or problems that are being influenced by the planet, although it is unlikely that these problems will be finally resolved until the last of the three contacts has been experienced.

This usually marks the key period of the trend, when resolution comes and decisions, changes or moves are made. On the other hand, if Uranus has been working negatively, the pressure is lifted and the subject will find that it is possible to return to his or her more usual lifestyle and routine.

The accurate timing of some planets' influences is extremely difficult to gauge astrologically (although it is easy astronomically, once one has learned to use the ephemeris correctly). What is more, their astrological influence spreads over far longer periods than is indicated astronomically. However, Uranus does not fall into this category and, as with Mars and Pluto, its influence seems to "click" on and off. Having said that, what will actually happen is very unpredictable – hence the general rule, always to "Expect the unexpected".

In the interpretation of these influences in this section you will find some good guidelines as to what is likely. In fact, "likely", "possibly" and "perhaps" are all words you will use more and more as you begin to understand the influences of the progressed chart and transits. Never be dogmatic when you are interpreting these influences, especially when interpreting the actions of Uranus. Remember that it is the planet of surprises – often nice, but sometimes nasty.

Note: When a subject is under the influence of a Uranian transit he or she may act somewhat uncharacteristically by being erratic, unpredictable or even perverse. Sometimes there is stubbornness too. While these rather extreme tendencies are only likely to emerge under powerfully negative transits from Uranus to the Sun, Moon or personal planets, nevertheless it is possible that they can surface with any Uranian contact.

If you think your subject is overreacting negatively, do all you can to encourage him or her to shelve making any vital decisions until the influence has completely passed. If this is not possible because the transit is going to colour a long period, reassess the birth chart to see which stable, cautious characteristics are present in your subject, and encourage him or her to draw on these in order to avoid taking premature or drastic action.

☉ Uranus' Transits to the Sun

Conjunction

This is a very powerful influence, during which the subject may want to make important changes which could affect either the personal life or the career. He or she is likely to be at a crossroads in life and, while any alterations should be made for the better, it is essential to warn against impulsiveness and premature action. Maybe she feels unable to continue in her present pattern (this is very common), and indeed the time may be right to make an important change. It will be especially so if, in her progressed chart, you also see important indications of change, such as the Sun or Ascendant progressing from one sign to the next (affecting her personal life), the Midheaven changing signs (career), or the progressed Moon crossing her natal Ascendant or Midheaven. It is good if this transit is backed up by some sort of progression. If not, then the change, although very important, may not be quite so radical. New unexpected developments might occur, but since this is such a personal transit it is possible that the changes may be self-motivated.

+ Positive transits

These have much the same influence as the conjunction but are far less powerful. However, they usually have an excellent effect, with the subject making a break or a fresh start in some way. Here are interesting, positive transits, which will encourage individuals to take up new interests, perhaps change their image, and make life a little more exciting and stimulating. Mental cobwebs will be brushed away and subjects should experiment in any way that promises to be both beneficial and enjoyable.

− Negative transits

These are difficult trends, during which strain and nervous tension are all too likely to accumulate. The subject may be working under undue pressure and might not have the time or inclination to relax. He or she will prefer to continue working at full tilt and make as much progress as possible. There may also be strain in the personal life or in a relationship, probably as a result of the subject's previous actions or lack of them.

Perversity and uncharacteristic behavior are possible at this time and should be watched for. The subject may enjoy a great deal of what is happening, but her actions can cause considerable disruption. Advise your subject that some delay should be allowed before any important decisions are taken, and also reread the Note about Uranian transits (see left).

☽ Uranus' Transits to the Moon

☌ Conjunction
Here the instincts and intuitions will be influenced by Uranus, so the subject may say "I *feel* the time is right for a change." This is usually true, and such feelings should be followed up by well thought-out action and carefully laid plans. Sudden changes of mind for no practical reason must be viewed with suspicion, however, so warn the subject against acting on impulse when motivated in this way.

Much will depend on the Moon sign and its natal aspects. If, on the whole, it is free of negative aspects from Saturn, Uranus itself, Neptune or Pluto, then all should be well, but if such afflictions are present in the birth chart, the characteristics described under the respective influence are likely to emerge with additional tension. If so, great care is needed. For instance, someone having these transits to his or her Moon, which in the birth chart receives a square from Neptune, may, in a tense moment, try to deceive others or take a deceptively easy way out of a tricky situation, perhaps due to an imagination working overtime.

+ Positive transits
There is a need to do something new and different; to make changes in the domestic environment perhaps, or to move house. Again, the subject will feel instinctively which developments will be most worthwhile. The intuitions should be followed, but even so, careful thought is needed before any drastic action is taken, since mistakes can still be made under these positive influences. For instance, if in the mood to decorate, the subject may begin work with some expensive wallpaper, only to find that it looks awful when on the walls! All being well, however, the planetary traffic lights are usually set at green when the Moon and Uranus are on friendly terms!

− Negative transits
These often bring tricky and tense conditions. The individual is usually working or living under great pressure, which can cause uncharacteristic moodiness and unpredictable actions. "I don't know what's come over him/her" is a frequently heard phrase from loved ones, while the subject may be tense, upset and uncertain, or arrogantly perverse, taking a couldn't-care-less attitude by brushing aside responsibilities and commitments. It is essential that every encouragement is given to cool down and postpone any drastic decisions or actions. In some cases, however, a great deal of very original and brilliant work can be done, but the individual will pay the price through mental or nervous exhaustion when the transit has passed and the work is completed.

☿ Uranus' Transits to Mercury

☌ Conjunction
Encouragement should be given to follow up any bright ideas. They are likely to be original and worthwhile, but it is not easy to work out the fine details of a plan during this transit. Nevertheless, the brilliance of Uranus activating the mind often produces some interesting, lively and original work, be it literary, creative (remember Mercury rules the hands) or perhaps, for those in business, a new money-making scheme (Mercury also has powerful trading connections). There may be a considerable change of opinion during the life of this transit, but if Mercury is in a fixed sign the subject can become totally intractable.

+ Positive transits
These are almost identical to the conjunction in effect, but there is less impulsiveness so any original ideas may not need quite as much fine-tuning before becoming practical propositions. Combining the communication influence of Mercury with the humanitarian and social conscience side of Uranus, this would be an excellent time in which to voice feelings about injustice through the media or by writing to people who are in a position to take steps to right the wrong.

− Negative transits
These usually cause a fair amount of nervous strain and tension, and often the individual will become anxious about other people's reactions, or an external situation. Working for far too long on a mentally demanding project can lead to problems, so try to encourage your subject to pace him- or herself, although this won't be easy. Eccentric behavior is sometimes present; this might be fun or may prove embarrassing.

Note: Uranus is much connected with astrology, and people often start to study it under this planet's influence, whether by transit or progression – especially to Mercury.

♀ Uranus' Transits to Venus

☌ Conjunction
Under this powerful influence the individual often not only holds an increased attraction for the opposite sex but also often falls in love very suddenly. The experience may well be enjoyable, but this is not a good time under which to make a long-term, serious commitment to marriage or to setting up home with the loved one, for all too often such an affair turns out to be "just one of those things".

If this romantic interpretation does not apply, here is an ideal influence under which the individual should revise his or her wardrobe by investing in new outfits which are rather different and perhaps more adventurous than usual, thereby creating a change of image. A new hair style or color will also boost the ego. However, this is yet another Uranian influence under which over-drastic reactions to situations or behavior should be controlled, especially in the love life. Unexpected financial developments may also arise. Advise careful, but not impulsive, investment.

+ Positive transits
These have very similar effects to those of the conjunction, especially as far as reviving the image is concerned. If Venus is a personal planet, the individual will also respond particularly well to a course of beauty treatments, a diet or perhaps a spell at a health farm, since Venus will then exert a psychological and physical effect on the individual. This will be an enjoyable time in the love life, but it is not one in which to make commitments.

Other transits operative immediately after this one may provide a revealing clue as to the eventual outcome or progress of any such love affair. You should also look carefully for any indication of long-term change in the progressed aspects operative at this time. This influence can also have positive financial repercussions.

Negative transits

These usually cause a certain amount of upheaval or tension within an emotional relationship. Sometimes this is due to the subject's suddenly uncharacteristic behavior – perhaps he or she has had a fling or flirtation, or is upset over the partner's conduct. If so, the incident may simply reflect the subject's lack of sexual cooperation (the underlying reason for which could be fatigue, the strain of children, a boring lifestyle or a general feeling of being fed up).

Better communication should be encouraged between the partners, and you may have to study both charts in order to be really helpful (see the Relationships section, pp.148-67). Venus' connections with money mean this is not a good time to make investments, and sometimes unexpected losses are incurred.

♂ Uranus' Transits to Mars

Conjunction

All the characteristics of the Mars sign and its general influence in the birth chart will be powerfully highlighted, so the subject will become brave and daring. Under these conditions the physical and nervous energies will flow and be spiced with adrenalin when required.

A great deal can be achieved under this powerful influence, but all too often the individual becomes very impulsive and erratic, making unconsidered and overhasty decisions. As a result of his or her own actions life is likely to become very eventful indeed. It may reach such a point that loved ones and colleagues will be quite exhausted by all the rather frenetic action, since the subject will want to involve others and such enthusiasm will be infectious.

Care is needed that the outlook doesn't become blindly optimistic, as there will be a strong tendency to overlook possible pitfalls, especially when acting in haste. Jumping in at the deep end usually occurs in one way or another during this transit. This is simply marvelous provided the subject can swim and make progress even against the tide!

A series of tense, nervous headaches are sometimes the result of such a large outpouring of nervous and physical energy. It is usually difficult to relax, and the subject probably won't want to do so.

Excellent results are likely provided that some element of caution and common sense prevails to counteract haste or overenthusiasm. Keep saying "Be careful" to the subject. Your voice might just be heard!

Positive transits

These are an excellent energy source if challenging or difficult work has to be tackled. There is the ability to grasp situations very quickly, and to take sudden and drastic action if necessary. Sometimes these transits are present when the individual is being very brave, whether physically or mentally. Daring in the career and business life is also common; these transits are very similar in effect to the conjunction, but less drastic and impetuous.

Brilliant performances in sport could also occur. Give extra encouragement if the subject is in training, although the chances are you will find that this won't be necessary.

Negative transits

The individual may experience a very tense and stressful period, perhaps feeling angry or aggressive as a result of his or her current situation. It is good to "let fly" at such times, but here again the impulsiveness, perversity and the unpredictability of Uranus can surface, often to the long-term detriment of the individual.

Nervous strain can cause physical effects, especially serious headaches. In addition, the Martian tendency to be careless may make the subject slightly accident-prone while this transit is operative. Advise extra care when driving, working with machines or handling hot dishes.

♃ Uranus' Transits to Jupiter

Conjunction

This should herald an exciting, eventful and progressive period, and a time when a great deal of pleasure (some of which may well be unexpected) will be experienced. The individual can and should show off a little, making certain that others know how clever and original he or she is.

Encourage the dispersion of doubt and anything that is negative in the outlook, for apart from the obvious good results, this transit will help to develop the self-confidence and the realization that a certain amount has been achieved in the past, and certainly at present.

Some special success can occur – a prize perhaps, as a result of the subject's originality and efforts. The influence is excellent for all Jupiter concerns, but especially study or writing papers which contribute an original slant to the individual's favorite specialist subjects or interests.

Positive transits

These have much the same effects as the conjunction, with life becoming eventful, progressive and usually worthwhile, and giving the individual the opportunity to expand his or her fields of interest or take steps which will lead to even further advancement in the future. The acceptance of new projects and challenges is to be highly recommended.

Negative transits

It is easy, under these negative influences, to become too enthusiastic and to make a sudden decision or take impulsive action. As a result, because of blind optimism and perhaps too much faith in a project (or sometimes another person), serious mistakes are made. The stress and tension so common to the negative transits of Uranus will then make their presence felt, and the individual will suffer considerable regret as a result.

While these transits are operative it is all too easy to throw caution to the winds, and the tendency to behave unpredictably will have a negative effect on the subject's judgment and common sense.

Uranus' Transits to Saturn

Conjunction

Very drastic and long-term changes are often considered under this influence. While Saturn will stabilize the decision-making process, it is important that the subject allows practical common sense and a sensible outlook to overcome any tendency to take premature or drastic action. This is not an easy influence.

Sometimes there is conflict between the need to do what is expected and doing what is really desired. Unless the choice is obvious, it is important to decide whether Saturn or Uranus is the stronger planet in the individual's birth chart; the best results will be achieved by following the dictates of that planet. However, because Uranus is making the contact, the chances are that there will be a certain amount of stress. This may be a time when the subject will feel like revolting against superiors (for instance, because of bad working conditions). There is usually just cause for complaint at such times, with the outcome being a considerable improvement. Look to Saturn's house position to see which sphere of life will probably be the most influential source of difficulty while the transit from Uranus is operative.

Positive transits

These will encourage the taking of actions and decisions that are cautious and practical, along with the enlightened acceptance of change. Here, common sense and logic go hand in hand. Constructive progress will be made – if not at once, then later on when those in authority have had the chance to assess the subject's efforts. Sometimes promotion can be offered or, if losses have been incurred, new developments as a result of them will be beneficial, increasing the subject's prestige and standing.

Negative transits

Considerable frustration is likely, with the individual held back by circumstances and a feeling that he or she has no room to breathe. There may be a conflict between the need for greater self-expression and the necessity to cling on to a worn-out lifestyle. This might apply, for instance, to a young person who wants to leave home but cannot do so because of high rents and house prices, and therefore has to live far less independently and in a claustrophobic way with restrictive parents.

Patience and a reassessment of the problem from a totally different viewpoint will certainly help, but it may be that no real developments will occur until this frustrating influence is well out of the way.

To assess times when the subject is most likely to move forward, look to the influences of Jupiter's position once Uranus has stopped attacking Saturn. Positive transits from Jupiter to Mars are especially good, since under these influences we are usually in an excellent position to take the initiative, which is just what is needed after a planetary squabble such as this one.

Uranus' Transits to Neptune

Conjunction

Between the early 1990s and the beginning of the twenty-first century, Neptune is traveling between Capricorn and Aquarius. Since Uranus entered Capricorn at the end of the 1980s and will be completing its journey through Pisces by about 2012, no adults will experience this transit (unless they are 84 or more). Young children born after 1988 will have the conjunction in their birth charts, but the transit of Uranus to Neptune as such is inoperative.

Positive transits

Increased sensitivity and awareness to suffering may develop, but sometimes there is an attraction to the more glamorous aspects of life, and the individual is likely to benefit from a little light relief and some positive romantic escapism.

Negative transits

Here the individual may encounter some strain and tension which may be linked to his or her spiritual or religious beliefs. Again there could be a change of feeling, but watch out for any tendencies toward negative escapism since sometimes there is an attraction to cults; the subject may well be searching for a psychological prop. Point out to her in a careful, down-to-earth way, the positive areas of her personality which will help counter any current negativity; astrology always shows strengths to counter weaknesses in individuals. She must face reality and rely on herself and not you – or any other discipline.

Uranus' Transits to Pluto

Conjunction

Between the 1880s and the early twenty-first century Pluto will have traveled from Gemini through to Sagittarius. Towards the end of the 1980s Uranus entered Capricorn and by roughly 2012 will be completing a journey through Pisces. Therefore as there is no one alive with Pluto in Capricorn, Aquarius or Pisces (or indeed, in several other signs through which Uranus will be traveling in the twenty-first century), this transit will be inoperative.

Positive transits

There will be a strong tendency to throw off existing circumstances and make a fresh start. Such changes should work out well, with the subject coping enthusiastically with new conditions. Sometimes a reassessment of psychological problems leads to a change of attitude and outlook.

Negative transits

Frustration and a blocking of progress can cause some distress, especially if either Uranus or Pluto are personal planets. If this is not the case then a particular project or area of life may cause concern and considerable frustration, such as the very late or non-arrival of a check or goods. Perhaps someone in the subject's circle of friends or a family member is being extremely difficult. If Uranus turns to retrograde motion (see p.23) and the influence is exact three times, the chances are that there will be a respite during the period when it is is not exact. Advise your subject to concentrate on areas in his or her life that are going well, since it is usually fruitless to waste time and energy on problems that arise under this transit.

Asc Uranus' Transits to the Ascendant

Conjunction

This powerful transit will have some exciting and dynamic effects. Often there is tension but changes are made and new lines of action taken. Care is needed that impulsiveness, perhaps as a result of other people's actions, does not lead to hasty decisions which are detrimental in the long run. Certainly the need for change will be in evidence. Encourage the development of as yet untapped potential, especially in interests where the individual's originality and powers of dynamism can be given positive expression. However, as a result of this powerful trend the subject may have to cope with strain and tension, and might have to work under considerable pressure. Nevertheless this is an exciting, if demanding and strenuous, influence.

+ Positive transits

There will be a need to do something new and to make changes, but the compulsive drive for such changes will not be present. These are excellent times during which to start studying, or working on, new creative hobbies, or those which have a scientific slant. Sometimes an attraction to the deep past or the distant future will emerge, especially if Uranus is entering the fifth house and making a trine transit to the Ascendant. A new and exciting, but probably not long-lasting, love affair is also a possibility. In any case the affairs and concerns of the house in which Uranus is entering will be abruptly emphasized.

– Negative transits

During the opposition, the subject may well think about, or make changes to, his or her personal relationships. The influence can be good in clearing up any relationships or situations that have dragged on for too long, so that the partners can make a fresh start. Discourage any hasty decisions, especially if the partners are thinking of parting – there could well be room for compromise, although your subject may be adamant while the transit is exact, due to the intractability of Uranus. In most cases there will be tension and stress in the sphere of life marked by the house that Uranus is entering, yet this is a time in which to place those areas on a new footing.

MC Uranus' Transits to the Midheaven

Conjunction

This is the most powerful of all Uranian influences, during which we must expect the unexpected. Such developments can be absolutely marvelous or very stressful, but almost always cause temporary shock or excitement. For instance, the subject may be offered a totally new exciting and different job, or equally suddenly might be made redundant.

Remember that the Midheaven represents events over which we have no direct control, but which happen to us as a result of reputation and experience – we have done what is necessary to arrive at our present position, but other people motivate the action, and action is what usually happens when Uranus is on the Midheaven!

Prepare the subject for new and unexpected developments. Look again at the sign, house placing and the aspects Uranus receives in the birth chart, and also remember that, if Aquarius is a prominent sign, this transit will be even more dynamic. This is an eventful period (to put it mildly!), one to look forward to rather than be apprehensive about. Even if your subject should lose his or her job or undergo a difficult experience, other events could follow which will counter any negativity.

+ Positive transits

These have much the same effect as the conjunction; the period will be eventful but in less important ways. Life should become exciting and lively, with new developments taking place that either concern the career or the house Uranus is transiting or entering. Again, the subject should expect the unexpected.

– Negative transits

A certain amount of stress and tension is likely at this time, especially concerning the career. Some subjects may remark "So what's new?" If so, you could with justification reply "Quite a lot!" The chances are that difficulties and strains will have positive results once the trend has eased, and from then on the subject may take off along new lines, not only having learned from experience but being all the stronger for it. One demanding project will probably predominate for roughly the overall length of the transit. Advise additional relaxation and suggest your subject "gets away from it all" whenever possible, since the influence is a demanding one.

♅ The Uranus Returns

These influences, which are in essence the transits of Uranus to its own position, are extremely important and mark distinctive phases in our lives. Uranus takes some 84 years to complete a journey round the Sun and through all 12 signs of the zodiac. Therefore, should we live to be 84 years of age we will be fortunate enough to experience a full Uranus Return. When we are in our early twenties the planet completes a quarter of its journey, so we receive the influence of its square transit to its own position. Then as we turn forty we are influenced by Uranus' opposition transit to its own position – in other words, the Uranus Half-return.

The Uranus Quarter-return

This is the square transit of Uranus to its own position. The very early twenties are often rather a tense time, when a great deal is at stake – especially if we have been at college or through a long period of training – and are now in search of recognition. Those who have been working for several years will feel that with a certain amount of experience under their belts they are ready to move on and make certain changes.

The tension so characteristic of Uranus' influence often makes its presence felt through our concern about our progress. This is also a time when we are working out our precise feelings about our sexual and emotional relationships. Hearts may be more painfully broken than before, or perhaps we fall in love in a far more mature way – although no less dynamically – than during our teenage years.

This influence is by no means the most powerful of those felt when Uranus contacts its own position, but nevertheless you should consider it very carefully if you are working on the chart of someone of this age when the influence is either about to become operative or has just passed.

Interestingly, the tradition of independence which is associated with the twenty-first birthday – the "I've got the key to the door" syndrome – is very sympathetic to Uranus, especially since the planet will be making its presence felt within a year of this milestone birthday.

The Uranus Half-return

This is the most powerful of the Uranian transits to its own position. Most people approach the age of forty with considerable apprehension. We feel old, not simply because we are changing decades, but because we realize that there are now many successful people younger than ourselves – the competition is becoming stronger. And not only do we feel old, we begin to think we look old. For many, their children are now young men and women, fast becoming independent, so some parents, women especially, begin to feel that life is over for them. They are also within sight of menopause. It is perhaps at this time that we as astrologers should be at our most helpful and positive.

Remember that one area of influence ascribed to Uranus is change and new beginnings – and that there is a great deal of truth in the old saying that "Life begins at forty"! So your subjects should be encouraged to think again, perhaps about becoming involved in new hobbies and interests. They might also look to their images. Perhaps they haven't previously been very interested in fashion and may have neglected to move with the times, so the women, especially, may be looking and feeling dowdy. A change of hair style or color and experimentation with some new, more fashionable outfits or styles they've not worn before will do a great deal to revitalize them. This might also be a good time to reassess their sex lives and to ask themselves how worthwhile their relationships are, for those too could be tending to stagnate. Starting diets or new exercise regimens is also excellent (but always with medical approval, since your subjects could very easily be out of condition). Remember that much can be done to liven up the life by using the energy from Uranus.

This is also a very tricky period, and it can be extremely difficult for the people concerned to cope with the tension and negativity of Uranus. Many at this point in their lives will overreact to the planet's influence, going to great lengths to convince themselves that they are not growing old. The men will often continue playing heavy team sports long after they should have stopped and revised their fitness schedule, with the result that they strain themselves physically – especially if they are overweight.

Many people will become involved in what they think is a lighthearted love affair (often with someone much younger than themselves) really in order to convince themselves and their friends that they are still attractive to the opposite sex. All too often, however, this gets out of hand and can be very hurtful to the permanent partner. You will see, then, that this extremely dynamic influence is to be used but must be controlled, since the perversity and eccentricity of Uranus can play havoc at this time. At its best it is dynamic and invigorating, but at its worst it can be disruptive and a possible source of strain and trouble not only for the individual but also for his or her loved ones.

Note: Look out for the sextile and trine transits of Uranus to its own position. When these are operative the individual often has the desire and enthusiasm to start new interests and to use the planet positively. The first sextile occurs during the teens, and can be used to shake the young teenager out of apathy.

The Uranus Return

This is one of the most amusing and invigorating of transits and occurs at about 84 years of age. It is fascinating to look at what has happened to many elderly people who have experienced this dynamic influence, and if you know someone who is approaching their 84th birthday it will be great fun to see if they are suddenly spurred into action, starting some new interest, revitalizing an old one, or simply longing to do something totally different.

Between 1982 and 1988 (very roughly) the planet traveled through Sagittarius, and those octogenarians who experienced their Uranus Return had the planet in that sign in their birth charts. This, basically, added a lively liking for challenge to their personalities, and we have plotted some very interesting examples. The most amusing is perhaps that of George Burns, who celebrated his 84th birthday by making his first Country and Western record (though we have no reason to believe that he had had astrological advice to do so!) Many other people have also had their creativity revitalized at this time: Verdi wrote *Falstaff*, his most musically advanced opera; Picasso was still vigorously painting; in the world of the dance Martha Graham, Marie Rambert and Ninette de Valois were all very active in their middle and late eighties, as was the lovely movie actress Lillian Gish, not only still making films but also carrying out extensive lecture tours. These are just a few names and you may be able to add to the list.

If you have an elderly grandparent or relative, the least you can do is present them with a stimulating gift on this special birthday – perhaps a specialist magazine subscription (providing their sight is reasonable). Take them off on some special visit – one case known to us was of a lady who took her first flight in a hot air balloon; another went down in a submarine with Jacques Cousteau to view the hulk of a ship whose wreck she had survived when in her teens! If nothing really dynamic is possible, at least go along with your tape recorder and get your subject to talk about times long past; when she was a flapper and he wore a raccoon coat, or they drank in speakeasies. Both you and they will have a marvelous time!

Neptune through the Signs

Neptune, the second of the "modern" planets, takes 146 years to complete its journey round the Sun and through all 12 signs of the zodiac, staying in each for about 14 years. Neptune works on two levels. Its influence as it travels through the sky is on everyday life, but it also emerges as a mass influence on the lifestyles of people born into each of its generations.

You will see that we have only included detailed interpretations for Neptune through seven signs – those in which that planet is placed for living people. It will not be until the end of 1998 that Neptune moves from Capricorn (the sign it entered in the mid-1980s) into Aquarius. There it will stay for 14 years, moving steadily but very slowly towards Pisces. There are a very few elderly people alive with Neptune in Gemini, but no one living can have Neptune in Pisces, Aries or Taurus.

NEPTUNE IN CANCER (1901/2 – 1915)

Generation influence

In this placing the overall influence was centred on the home. There was confusion and unhappiness due to so many men being killed during the First World War, and the overall grief is shown by the emphasis on Cancer – the most family-oriented sign in the zodiac. It then further occurred that when the people who were born during those years with Neptune in Cancer were adults and bringing up their own families, they had to cope with the difficulties and unhappiness of the Second World War.

Between 1905 and 1911, Uranus made an opposition to Neptune from Capricorn. This generation aspect (which appears in the charts of all the people born during that period) added to the stresses and strains of the time, and was another negative factor in the lives of this generation.

Personal influence

If Neptune is a personal planet in the birth chart it will very powerfully heighten the subject's sensitivity, emotion and intuition. If it receives negative aspects, he or she may well show a tendency to take the easy way out of difficult situations. The imagination can also work overtime. This placing will increase any inclination to worry, but will sensitize and refine any creative work that is carried out by the individual.

NEPTUNE IN LEO (1915 – 1928/9)

Generation influence

While Neptune was traveling through Leo the accent was on the development and power of the movies. The great silent films were being made and, especially as times were hard (this period includes the misery of the First World War and its economic aftermath, plus the financial depression beginning in 1929), the masses sought and enjoyed escape into this wonderful make-believe world, which lifted them straight out of the grim reality they were experiencing in their daily lives.

Personal influence

This placing of Neptune confers glamor and a sense of drama, and also enhances creative work. The emotional flow is both positive and spiced with a lively enthusiasm.

Because Neptune occupies a fire sign and, we think, the sign of its exaltation (although some astrologers do not agree), if you are working on a chart of someone belonging to this generation, you should bear in mind that Neptune's influence is slightly stronger than usual in this placing.

If the planet is personalized and positively aspected, your subject is well blessed, and will probably have imaginative and creative potential. An interest in art is quite a common attribute, and the individual may also have an above-average talent and particular flair for photography.

NEPTUNE IN VIRGO (1928/29 – 1942/43)

Generation influence

Here is the first modern generation seriously to criticize accepted religious beliefs. Neptune, ruler of Pisces – a sign closely linked with Christianity – was at this time traveling through Virgo, which is Pisces' polar sign. Virgo, ruled by Mercury, is analytical and critical. In addition, one of the most interesting generation influences of this planet is that at precisely the time Neptune first entered Virgo, the cinema, which had until then been silent, discovered sound. (Remember that Mercury is the planet that rules communications.) In general, people enjoyed greater and easier communication and the medium of radio also increased this.

Personal influence

If Neptune is personalized or Virgo is a prominent sign in the birth chart, the imagination is stimulated and can be expressed well (perhaps through literary work). Since Virgo is an earth sign, the subject may also have a flair for horticulture.

At worst, Neptune in Virgo tends to lower the self-confidence, since the subject's critical faculty can undermine his or her belief in what is achieved, and this can result in a lack of inner fulfilment. Discontent and restlessness may also be present, especially if these tendencies are indicated in other areas of the chart.

NEPTUNE IN LIBRA (1942/3 – 1956/7)

Generation influence

While these children were being born much of the civilized world was at war, and everyone was longing for peace. (Think of the popular songs of the period.) When these children grew up they became the "flower power" generation of the late sixties and early seventies. "All you need is love" speaks volumes about the prevailing attitude at this time. Many people were opting out of society and experimenting with drugs and a totally relaxed lifestyle – unrealistic, easy, all very beautiful, all very harmonious and peaceful, but also all entirely impractical! One does not have to be a very advanced astrologer to couple the influence of peace-loving Libra with the self-deception and illusory influences of Neptune. We think this is one of the most striking of the Neptune generation influences.

Personal influence
This is a very critical placing and influence. Those with Libra rising are most vulnerable to Neptune. If you find yourself working on a chart with this configuration, consider closely whether Neptune is in the first or twelfth house. Reread Neptune through the Houses (see pp.329-31), and if Neptune conjuncts the Ascendant make careful note of that influence also (see p.332).

If Libra is not a prominent sign, however, and Neptune isn't personalized, its influence will not be very strong in the chart but it does give additional sympathy and kindness. In a chart that indicates the individual is rather laidback and perhaps slightly lazy or lacking in self-confidence, the influence will strengthen these attitudes – sometimes causing the subject to slip into a sybaritic lifestyle.

Neptune in Scorpio (1956/57 – 1970/71)

Generation influence
Think how different the young people born with Neptune in Scorpio are to those with Neptune in Libra! Here are the hard-rock types who are much tougher – or so they would have you think. They often have a very aggressive and formidable image, but have had to fight much harder for what they want out of life.

It is not surprising that in coping with unemployment, many succumbed to the negative, escapist, drug addictive tendencies of Neptune. This drug scene is not the peaceful, loving, easy one often associated with the flower power people; here it is much more intensive, even more poisonous, weird and spooky (adjectives which are very Scorpionic in essence).

On the other hand there are many of this generation who live to make money and enjoy a glamorous life in the fast lane – the Yuppie generation, who are another manifestation of Neptune in Scorpio. Remember that Scorpio is also the sign of big business, so read Pluto in Scorpio, p.339.

Personal influence
There is increased emotional intensity when Neptune is personalized. If the planet is well aspected the emotions will be positively expressed by inspiring the individual's talents and ambitions. Do not single out these trends in interpretation, however, unless similar complementary ones are also present or Scorpio is personalized in the chart.

Neptune in Sagittarius (1970/71 – 1984/85)

Generation influence
Although at the time of writing we are rather too close to this generation to be able fairly to assess the mass influence of Neptune, the children who are known to us do seem to have some very pleasant qualities.

Due to the powerful relationship between Neptune and Jupiter (through Neptune's rulership of Pisces, over which Jupiter traditionally ruled), and because this is heightened by Neptune's journey through the Jupiter sign of Sagittarius, we can expect much that is idealistic, hopeful and positive from this generation. Neptune works well here, and there is a natural ability to distinguish right from wrong.

While these children will have to be tough to cope with the demands of life in the early part of the twenty-first century, they have a kind, sympathetic, idealistic, hopeful side which is both optimistic and enthusiastic. In the young people known to us, we find there is also a fine Sagittarian sense of humor. See if these qualities are present in your subjects.

Personal Influence
If Sagittarius is prominent you will probably have a generation leader on your hands. One emerging indication which could relate to this placing is a growing inclination to vegetarianism. We equate this with a general love of and sympathy for animals (a common Sagittarian characteristic) and more particularly an awareness of the cruelty of battery farming, which may spring from the gentler qualities of Neptune present in this sign.

Neptune in Capricorn (1984/5 – 1998)

Generation influence
Here Neptune is in an earth sign, and so the vital issue of the Earth's resources, of the harm that has been done by their exploitation, is powerfully focused. We hope we can save the planet, but it will be up to the children of the 1970s and early 1980s to do so – to right the wrong of many earlier, less caring generations.

Personal influence
We can only assume what the personal implications will be, but it would seem that for someone with Capricorn prominent in their chart, the sign's rather strident, severe qualities will be softened, and its rather low emotional level will be heightened.

There may be flair for the creative use of natural materials. Here are people who will be determined but cautious, able to control the negative elements of Neptune so that they will be less vulnerable to escapism, self-deception and taking the easy way out of difficult situations.

Neptune in Aquarius (c.1998 – c.2010)

The gentle characteristics of Neptune should marry well with the humanitarian elements of Aquarius, but the detached, independent, loving Aquarian traits are poles apart from the sensitive, intuitive emotion of Neptune. Those with the planet well-placed should be able to get the best of both entirely different worlds.

Neptune Progressed to a New Sign

This is most rare. If it does occur you will have the opportunity to do some original research into how your subject reacted to the change of sign; but on the whole it is not a problem you are likely to encounter.

Neptune through the Houses

The subject's attitude towards the spheres of life and concerns of the house in which Neptune is placed can be rather woolly, indecisive and almost always uncertain. All too often events in these areas are a source of confusion; the subject will tend to take the easy way out of situations, even if the chart shows fortitude and common sense. Neptune can be engrossing on a spiritual, idealistic or creative level and if you can encourage this you will help your subject to make Neptune work for, not against, him or her. Mars and Jupiter will show initiative and energy.

1 NEPTUNE IN THE FIRST HOUSE

If Neptune lies within eight, or at the most ten, degrees of the Ascendant, this planet will have a strong effect on the personality (see Neptune conjunct the Ascendant, p.332). In most cases there is likely to be a weakening of the Ascendant sign's characteristics, with the individual finding it rather difficult to organize him- or herself.

Excuses may be made for not fully exploiting or developing the potential, and the Neptunian tendency to take the easy way out of troubled and challenging situations is very common in the individual with this placing. This may be because Neptune undermines the self-confidence, but the dreaminess, escapist and idealistic implications of the planet's influence will also be powerful forces in the personality.

Neptune through the signs

The sign occupied by Neptune will dictate the complexity, or otherwise, of this house placing. For example, when placed in Virgo (see p.327), Neptune tends to soften the rather harsh critical edge of this sign. Neptune also works quite well for many people who have the planet in Leo (see p.327). Sometimes, however, these people can suffer from escapist problems, as in the case of Marilyn Monroe who had Neptune in Leo in the first house. She, of course, chose the ultimate escape – that of suicide.

Life can be extremely tricky if Neptune is rising in Libra, partly because of an additional interplay from Pluto (which in such cases is often very near the Leo Midheaven). There is then an element of compulsion present which can make the individual lean toward harmful escapism. This is a common negative influence for those born with Neptune in Libra.

Neptune certainly gives potential from the first house when it is placed in Scorpio, but unfortunately it also weakens, or even destroys, the ability and drive to exploit it fully.

The influence of Neptune from this house will have a profound effect on the individual, and the nearer it lies to the Ascending degree, the more powerful that influence will be.

2 NEPTUNE IN THE SECOND HOUSE

When Neptune is in the second house, the subject's attitude to money will not be very sound. There is usually generosity, to the point that far too many people with this placing are such soft touches that their financial situations can be considerable sources of confusion and difficulty.

A great deal of time and sympathy will be given to those who are short of money, and the individual will be extremely vulnerable to bouts of overgenerosity. There may also be a certain gullibility over financial matters, so that the tendency to fall for confidence tricks or make very poor investments must be guarded against with care.

Professional financial advice should always be taken by the subject when important decisions are to be made concerning money. Sometimes those with this placing will take great pleasure in investing in art, and they may even enjoy an element of financial stability as a result. In this way they can make a collection of items they find pleasing, and know that its value is steadily increasing.

Loving expression

The effect of Neptune in the second house on the way in which the individual expresses love and emotion is beautiful, and provided the level of emotional intensity is kept under control, there will be no lack of imagination in this area. Sometimes too, there is a delightful sentimentality, especially if Neptune is placed in Libra.

3 NEPTUNE IN THE THIRD HOUSE

Parents of children with this placing should be on their guard if they wish to have any more children; the influence of Neptune may confuse the elder sibling's attitude towards the younger. For example, there may be an above-average show of jealousy, simply because the child finds the situation bewildering. Other areas of the child's chart will show the way through this possible difficulty – and we wish to stress that it is only a possibility.

Strength of imagination

Early education is often unsettled, and there may have been tendencies to spend time in daydreaming at school, so that concentration on the matter in hand was very poor. As a result, the subject may have gained rather unsatisfactory grades.

This is a house related to the mind, nonetheless, so there is a good chance that the imagination will be heightened by this placing, especially if the chart as a whole shows imaginative flair. Some astrologers believe that this placing enhances the voice; the subject certainly may have the potential for singing, and there is often a subtle delicacy in the tone of the voice, and also good projection.

4 NEPTUNE IN THE FOURTH HOUSE

Neptune's influence in this house may well give a clue to the subject's early childhood. It might have been colorful, or at least have specially stimulated his or her imagination. Perhaps, too, there was a tendency to look upon the mother as a sort of fairy godmother – a magical person.

Hopefully, there will not have been some disastrous disillusion since then, but there is a chance that home conditions were fairly chaotic and undisciplined. Maybe there were no regular meals and no really helpful guidance from the parents, so that since the individual has left home he has had to learn the hard way about what is right and what is wrong.

This is a tricky placing for Neptune: be careful not to overinterpret it. However, the clues it can offer about the individual's background may enable you to help him resolve any ongoing problems.

5 Neptune in the Fifth House

This placing usually adds imagination and flair to the type of creativity suggested by the sign in which Neptune is placed, if not a direct element of creative potential.

As far as the love life is concerned, the individual may tend to fall in love all too easily and to be inordinately starry-eyed over the adored one. This can be so pronounced that his or her overromantic and unrealistic attitude can lead to disaster and heartbreak.

The love and sex lives will definitely be colorful, nonetheless, and tinged with an above-average element of fantasy. Here too, the heart very definitely rules the head; encourage your subject to use all her caution (the position of Saturn?) and practical qualities (any planets in earth signs?) to help counter the likely gullibility in her attitude towards the opposite sex. Both men and women can suffer from the romantic ideals of this placing.

Foolish risks are sometimes taken by people with Neptune in the fifth house. Warn your subject against gambling, since the financial risks often work in tandem with emotional ones.

6 Neptune in the Sixth House

As far as the health is concerned, there can be allergies to particular foods when Neptune is placed here.

The imagination works overtime all too often with this placing, and hypochondria is very common. To be fair, however, the subject may not react well even to medically administered drugs, and may make much better progress relying on homeopathy or, when possible, a cure that positively stimulates the psyche. Encourage your subject to be his or her own healer, and to take a positive attitude toward any ailments – the benefits they may reap could be considerable.

A need for practicality

Where work is concerned, it may well be difficult for someone with this placing to discipline herself into a steady routine. She will get through the necessary day-to-day tasks in her own way, but this personal approach might cause problems with colleagues. Keeping deadlines may also be considered a bore, with the result that they may sometimes be missed.

Look to other more practical areas of the birth chart to see if there is a counter to these tendencies, although there may not be if Neptune is a personal planet.

7 Neptune in the Seventh House

The subject may find it difficult to settle into a permanent relationship. There will be high expectations of partners, and perhaps a tendency to live on cloud nine. Difficulties can arise, however, when the time comes for emotional commitment, as the individual may be unwilling to take such a step. Conversely, those with this placing will sometimes rush into relationships prematurely. Do bear this tendency in mind, especially if your subject has a relationship problem at the time of the consultation.

There is a great love of pure romance, and all being well, the subject will create an especially romantic or particularly imaginative atmosphere for the partner. However, attention must also be paid to the practical areas of life and, whether your subject is a man or woman, his or her partner may have to take care of such responsibilities as bill-paying, and the general organization of the practical side of the relationship. The subject's partner should, in fact, encourage the equal sharing of such tasks, otherwise there can be an upsetting lack of balance and harmony in the relationship.

8 Neptune in the Eighth House

This will be a more than usually powerful placing for those with Neptune in Scorpio, adding intensity and deep, meaningful passion to the sexual nature. This sphere of life will be rich, providing it is able to be expressed in a full and positively rewarding way.

If the subject is at all confused about the form of sexual expression to which he or she is most attracted, it might be advisable for him or her to go into therapy to remove any feelings of guilt, or deal with negative or inhibitive emotions. These tendencies are somewhat less likely should Neptune be in a sign other than Scorpio, although the possibility is still present.

The powers of seduction are certainly endowed by this placing, and the individual will attract members of the opposite (or same) sex like a magnet. As a result, the sexual sphere of his life may well assume an above-average importance; nevertheless, it does need really positive expression.

A careful approach to finance

Generosity will be present, as it is when Neptune is in the other money house, the second, but the individual may take a rather gullible financial attitude toward the partner. Care will be needed here, and professional financial advice is usually to be recommended unless the chart shows considerable business or moneymaking potential, in which case this placing could add imaginative flair. Nevertheless, a strong level of caution should be present in the chart if this talent is to work well.

9 Neptune in the Ninth House

When placed in the ninth house, Neptune will have a considerable effect on the intellect, giving inspiration and an element of idealism that are probably combined with a marvelously philosophical outlook on life.

The natural relationship between Jupiter and Neptune (they are the traditional and modern rulers of Pisces respectively) will work well and powerfully when the latter planet is in this, the Jupiter/Sagittarius house, and the placing will add a wise, inspired element. The subject may, perhaps, have a religious, or at any rate a studious, sense of purpose or vocation. This may emerge as an interest in mysticism or other esoteric subjects.

Mental capacities

The mind may have few limitations, but to harness its qualities and keep them in balance it might be necessary for the individual to develop a logical and practical attitude, and also a healthy measure of scepticism. Astrological tradition decrees that those with this placing will enjoy unusual and perhaps rather weird experiences while traveling abroad.

A particularly vivid dream recall is very possible in the individual with this placing: this is something to discuss with your subject. It is certainly likely if he or she is imaginative and creative, but less so if there are very materialistic tendencies indicated elsewhere in the birth chart.

10 Neptune in the Tenth House

In most of the cases we have come across, the placing of Neptune in this house, high in the sky and often assuming an above-average importance as a result of its position, usually means that not only will the career be colorful but also that there will be many changes of direction in life.

When such changes are analyzed in retrospect, it may well seem that they were brought about because of the subject's inner feelings, or even that the individual was in some way destined to make those moves as and when he or she did.

Ambition and achievement

If Neptune conjuncts the Midheaven (see p.333), the sign in which Neptune is placed must of course be very carefully considered. That is because it will not only show the individual's aspirations and objectives but also – because of Neptune's placing – his or her inspiration, too, which will color this additional ambition to achieve.

Here is a true romantic who can sometimes really allow his imagination to take flight. If, for instance, he signed on as a junior in a department store, he would immediately see himself as president! If the chart is basically practical and shows ambition in other ways, the subject will no doubt make the grade – provided that he can truly keep his feet firmly on the ground while still letting his imagination roam free!

At worst, your subject may lack a sense of direction. If this is the case, consider carefully the potential that is shown by the Sun, Moon and Ascending signs.

11 Neptune in the Eleventh House

Although the individual may enjoy a very lively social life and have a wide circle of friends and acquaintances, it is often the case that he or she is taken in by them and can sometimes be used. Gullibility may well make its presence felt in this sphere of life.

Much enjoyable time will be spent helping to raise money for charity, and the subject will also show skill in such altruistic activities. Other leisure hours may be spent at group poetry readings or photography clubs.

Coping with responsibility

Some reluctance to hold office may be likely, since there might be a dislike of having to cope with the responsibilities involved but at the same time the subject may be too easily persuaded to do so. If this happens, the result could be a source of worry or concern, so decisiveness and a really practical attitude must be developed if he or she is not to be put upon or suffer tension, confusion, or worry in what should, after all, be an enjoyable side of life.

12 Neptune in the Twelfth House

Neptune is at home in this placing, since it is the house of Pisces, the sign that is ruled by this planet. In fact, Neptune usually works well from this house, though often it will add secretive and reclusive tendencies to the personality of the individual.

A need for personal privacy

Probably it will be very necessary for the individual to withdraw and get away from the pressures of life from time to time. At the very least, it is advisable for her to have a room of her own where peace and quiet can be enjoyed. Remember, however, that "peace and quiet" will mean different things to different people; to some it can mean the cloistered weekend religious retreat and to others it can be the donning of earphones and immersion in the confined world of the personal stereo!

Creative work executed well away from other people is also encouraged by this placing. and the subject may even shun the limelight, allowing her talents to speak for her. There can be creative flair, especially if it is shown in other areas of the chart.

This is also an excellent placing for those who wish to follow the caring professions, or who find it rewarding to work in institutions. There is usually considerable sympathy, empathy, understanding and an identification with suffering.

If Neptune is negatively aspected in the birth chart the difficult escapist elements of the planet will be present in the personality, so deception is sadly all too probable. This is usually directed towards the self, but sometimes it can be channeled towards other people as well. If Neptune is within eight or ten degrees at most from the Ascendant, see Neptune conjunct the Ascendant, p.332.

♆ Neptune Progressed to a New House

This is most unlikely, since Neptune progresses very slowly through the chart, moving only a very few degrees – if that – during a lifetime. Should it occur in a chart on which you are working, you may find that its influence will be so subtle as to be hardly noticeable. Even so, by all means study your subject with this change of influence in mind.

The Aspects of Neptune

Apart from the aspects Neptune makes to Pluto, the Ascendant and the Midheaven, it is necessary to lay great emphasis on the *inner* planet – the planet making the contact to Neptune. In most cases where Neptune is involved in aspect you will be looking back through this section of the book. But the aspects to the Ascendant and Midheaven, which can have a subtle but devastating effect, must be carefully interpreted.

For Neptune's aspects to the Sun, see the Sun's aspects to Neptune, pp.218-9.

For Neptune's aspects to the Moon, see the Moon's aspects to Neptune, p.236.

For Neptune's aspects to Mercury see Mercury's aspects to Neptune, p.251.

For Neptune's aspects to Venus, see Venus' aspects to Neptune, pp.265-6.

For Neptune's aspects to Mars, see Mars' aspects to Neptune, p.279.

For Neptune's aspects to Jupiter, see Jupiter's aspects to Neptune, p.291.

For Neptune's aspects to Saturn, see Saturn's aspects to Neptune, pp.305-6.

For Neptune's aspects to Uranus, see Uranus' aspects to Neptune, p.319.

Because of its very slow motion, Neptune will not form an aspect in the progressed chart.

NEPTUNE'S ASPECTS TO PLUTO

During the 1880s and 1890s Neptune and Pluto were in the same sign, Gemini, and from time to time formed a conjunction. Since then Neptune has overtaken Pluto in their long, slow journey round the Sun, and gradually moved ahead by two signs. The planets have been roughly this distance apart since Neptune entered Virgo in 1928 while Pluto was still traveling through Cancer. Playing a sort of cat-and-mouse game out in space, they will stay roughly two signs apart for many years to come and well into the twenty-first century, by which time Neptune will be in Aquarius and Pluto in Sagittarius.

The sextile

This is the only aspect Neptune and Pluto will make to each other, and it is very common, cropping up in a great many charts. It is not very important in the chart unless either planet is powerfully placed or personalized. If the latter applies, that planet's positive influence will enhance intuition and increase the emotional level, both of which should flow positively. If either planet is conjunct the Ascendant from the first house, these resources will be considerably increased, and there may well be a tendency for the subject to have an overabundance of both qualities, so that conscious control and positive expression of them will be necessary. Remember, however, that the sextile is the weakest of the positive aspects; don't be tempted to over-interpret it, no matter how powerfully either planet is placed.

NEPTUNE'S ASPECTS TO THE ASCENDANT

Conjunction

From the first house: This will weaken the characteristics of the rising sign, making the individual veer toward its gentler but rather negative qualities. It will sap determination and, while making for a kind and often sympathetic person, the ability to express the characteristic form of psychological motivation common to the Ascendant will be lacking. In Scorpio, for instance, all the emotional forces of the sign will be present and often increased by Neptune's powerful influence. However, Scorpio's energy, usually such a formidable driving force, can be defused so that the individual's potential is not fully expressed and there is less inner fulfillment and satisfaction on all levels of the personality than there should be. Negative escapism may be a problem.

From the twelfth house: Since this is Neptune's natural home, the planet will work more positively here, and the individual may well benefit from its influence. Sympathy and kindness are usually present and often sacrifices will be made, but for a variety of rather complicated reasons. From a practical point-of-view these will be most altruistic, but the psychological reason for them may be rooted in apprehension – perhaps fear of the "great world outside" or sheer lack of self-confidence. At its best, Neptune will encourage good work carried out well away from the public eye, with individuals preferring to allow the results of their labor to speak for them. The tendency to "escape" is usually controlled, although the need for peace and quiet is very strong. Remember that the aspects Neptune receives from the Sun, Moon, or personal planets must be carefully considered. Reread Neptune in the first and twelfth houses (see pp.329-31) and compare the subtle but nevertheless striking differences of influence between these two placings.

Positive aspects

These are not very powerful, but will soften the rising sign characteristics and give imagination and intuition, plus a sneaking tendency to adopt an air of mystery. All this will add a seductive quality to the subject, especially if Neptune is in Scorpio! The creative imagination is enhanced and can be used in all manner of ways – not only from an artistic point-of-view.

Negative aspects

Here the influence of Neptune, although subtle, will add some self-deception and a tendency to tell untruths. It is often all too easy for the individual to lose touch with reality. An opposition from the sixth or seventh house will powerfully strengthen Neptune's house position. Reread these two house placings (see p.330) and compare them, then concentrate on the relevant one when you build your full interpretation. Apply the same technique if the aspect is a square from either the fourth or tenth house. If the aspect is minor do not over-interpret it, although a tendency towards deception or a slight element of confusion can be present in the personalities of those with the semi-square or quincunx.

MC NEPTUNE'S ASPECTS TO THE MIDHEAVEN

Conjunction

As described for Neptune in the tenth house (see p.331), there is a likelihood of changes of direction in the career – even if Neptune conjuncts the Midheaven from another house. The individual will probably identify with Neptunian concepts and may be successful in them, provided the rest of the chart shows stability and the ability to use Neptune's influence positively rather than allowing the planet to sap inner strength and determination.

Positive aspects

These influences are not strong but will be helpful if the individual happens to follow a career sympathetic to Neptune – i.e. photography, the caring professions, dance, or any work where inspiration and imagination can be put to good use.

Negative aspects

There may be a tendency to fall back on rather devious tactics when attempting to gain promotion, or to try to curry favor with those in authority – Uriah Heep, in *David Copperfield,* must surely have had this aspect (plus, perhaps, another square from Saturn)! An underhanded streak is common, and the subject may pull the wool over other people's eyes – and that's putting it mildly!

THE TRANSITS OF NEPTUNE

Of all the transits, these are the most difficult to interpret, because some people feel their effects very powerfully while others do not. The various complications do not end there, since very often when a powerful Neptune transit is operative the individual can react in one of several different ways. At one end of the scale we have the subject who will reject every suggestion we make in interpretation, while at the other is another type who will suddenly opt out by going on a drinking or eating binge, or becoming totally undisciplined. Some even see visions! Beware! – they need help from a psychotherapist; don't get deeply involved. A common phrase is "I don't know what's come over me, I can't seem to settle down to work; my powers of concentration have gone."

There is a parallel in dream recall: some people say they never dream, but of course they do – they simply don't remember their dreams. Others remember every detail. Those with poor dream recall are usually very materialistic, concerned only with money and attaining a place in society. Those who have excellent recall are sensitive, intuitive, more emotional and often creative in some way. The surface effects of Neptune are not dissimilar, with the materialists swearing that Neptune has had no impact and has struck a dead note; the intuitive types will feel every tiny nuance.

We have to take these reactions even further, however, and for a moment look more carefully at those who claim that Neptune has had no effect. This may well not be true. The materialist, as a result of a negative Neptune transit, may for instance have done a dirty deal on Wall Street or had a secret affair. More psychologically, there may be a very subtle change of feeling if the transit was a positive one – maybe an increased sensitivity to some finer element of life which up to now has gone unnoticed. Perhaps the prosperous business-lunching type of executive cried at a film for the first time ever – or suffered a nasty bout of gout or food poisoning? As far as the sensitive type is concerned, the negative influence could result in the telling of white lies in order not to hurt a loved one – and in doing so, the creation of considerable confusion. At best, with a positive influence, the end product could be some especially impressive and inspired creative work, or perhaps the taking up of some esoteric subject. Could this be astrology? (Neptune is, along with Uranus, often emphasized when we first become interested that subject, especially if that planet is at all prominent in the birth chart.)

The timing of Neptunian transits is difficult. Astrologically, their influence tends to fade in and out because the effects of Neptune are so subtle. When interpreting such a trend it is wise to stress this fact, and in order not to confuse your subject (who may already be in a confused state due to Neptune's influence!) it is advisable to interpret the trend as simply as possible. While mentioning the astronomical timing, point out that the planet is difficult to "time" astrologically, so its influence may last rather longer than the dates you give – maybe beginning earlier and ending later.

NEPTUNE'S TRANSITS TO THE SUN

Conjunction

A great deal will depend on how Neptune is aspected in the birth chart, but it is always reasonable to warn your subject that he or she may slightly lose touch with reality. Experiences under this influence are often quite marvellous, and usually enjoyable but – and it's a big "but" – there is usually a tendency to drift up to cloud nine, and sometimes to do things one wouldn't normally do, thinking that all will be well. We are not going to say they won't be – but they can go decidedly wrong, especially when the influence has eased away, and the individual may return to earth with a bump.

A spate of creative work is often one result of this transit, giving a full expression of the imagination. Above all, it is essential for the subject to steady the emotions consciously, and to practice caution and common sense, although often this isn't easy.

Note: This transit will only be operative for Sun sign Capricorns until 1998, and for Aquarians and Pisceans during the following 28 years.

Positive transits

In essence these are similar to the conjunction, although not as potent. More people will tend to feel there has been no effect from them. Generally the emphasis is on the easier side of Neptune's influence, with positive results occurring, and less of a tendency to get carried away emotionally or to allow life to become confusing.

Negative transits
The more negative possibilities discussed under the conjunction will be likely to occur, but there is often far greater confusion, and care is necessary that the escapist tendencies do not encourage drug-taking. This applies as much to medically administered drugs such as tranquilizers as to the more dangerous, addictive drugs. Obviously, the intake of alcohol must also be watched. Self-deception is also possible and you should be on the alert for such behavior. As always, the effect of these transits will vary considerably according to your subject's personality.

NEPTUNE'S TRANSITS TO THE MOON

Conjunction
There will be a tendency to respond very quickly to the influence of Neptune; the individual will be very easily moved – by suffering, for instance – and want to respond to it in whichever way is considered most helpful. Something quite inconsequential may impress the subject, acting as a potent source of inspiration and prompting dramatic developments; because the subject has reacted to the occurrence so strikingly, he or she will make important changes. This is particularly likely if indications of change show up in the progressed chart or other transits. People sometimes "see the light" under this influence, although it may just be appearing at the end of an unhappy tunnel.

Positive transits
The emotions are in focus, and reaction to them is enhanced; this trend could easily put your subject in a very romantic mood. In theory all should go well, especially if there are some positive progressions involving Venus. However, if there are heavy negative transits involving Saturn or Uranus, the Moon and Neptune will take on the color of these influences. In such circumstances, warn your subject that he or she could be overreacting emotionally and perhaps becoming a little bit starry-eyed – especially if in love. Alternatively, he or she may be overreacting to current problems and getting them out of perspective.

Negative transits
These are difficult to interpret, since to some extent they are unpredictable. Basically, there is usually some kind of emotional stress or self-deception, and perhaps overreaction to another person's actions. The subject could be more easily led by unscrupulous people, and get into all kinds of difficulties. On the other hand, if deception is indicated in the birth chart it may well be the individual who behaves in this way, and deceives loved ones, friends or business associates. Warn against participation in anything that seems remotely shady; suggest a careful and simple diet too, for sometimes food poisoning is likely.

NEPTUNE'S TRANSITS TO MERCURY

Conjunction
This should work well for the subject, who as a result of it is likely to have a bright and inspired idea, or find a source of inspiration in as yet unconsidered subjects. Very often the more critical side of Mercury's influence will be heightened by Neptune, and provided these elements are not expressed in a rather vague and negative way toward loved ones, all should be well. Sometimes the escapist side of Neptune surfaces, with the individual wanting to "get away from it all". If so, suggest a long weekend break to a peaceful, beautiful place that is easy to get to and fairly near home. The transit is useful to those who wish to communicate their ideas to other people, but if they have to give a talk while it is operative they should make very careful notes and stick to them, since the temptation to digress and to go on for too long will be very strong!

Positive transits
These are good influences, especially helpful to those studying esoteric subjects or who are particularly interested in reading or writing poetry – here the poets' planet is in harmony with the planet of communication. The influence will also help to view such topics more objectively.

Negative transits
These influences are very subtle, and tend to make us extremely absent-minded because the powers of concentration suffer. Warn your subject to make very careful checks on what he or she has to do, to keep appointment diaries to hand, to have the right keys before going out and not to lock them inside the car! Forgetfulness causes problems under these influences, as does the tendency to get carried away by what may seem a brilliant idea, but in reality turns out to be totally impractical. Don't be discouraging, but do advise your subject to postpone taking any important decisions or irrevocable actions until the influence has passed by a good three weeks.

Professional advice should certainly be sought if Neptune or Mercury are personal planets or emphasized in some way in the birth chart. Even so, your subject may still continue along this "world-of-make believe" path.

NEPTUNE'S TRANSITS TO VENUS

Conjunction
Neptune works well here and enhances much that is positive about Venus. The way Venus works in the birth chart, and of course its sign and house position, must be considered when assessing how this trend will work, and on which sphere of life. The chances are that the individual will be very happy, and experience several romantic and/or idealistic events. Perhaps he or she will have a very special memorable experience – the romantic night of a lifetime, or perhaps one of those special occasions that stay in the memory for ever. The influence will certainly add a lot of color to a few weeks, and life should be enjoyable at the very least. This would be a delightful trend at the time of a wedding, but the indications of marriage or the deepening of a permanent relationship must to be far stronger than just this aspect (see the Relationships section, pp.148-67).

Positive transits
These are similar to the conjunction but easier; the subject may be in a romantic and sybaritic mood. Ideally, the duration of these transits should be spent on a warm, tropical beach with a lover! They are to be used and enjoyed, so you could suggest the subject plans a special occasion with his or her partner; it will almost certainly be delightful and memorable. These influences are particularly good if they occur just after a stressful period within a relationship, since they will help the couple get back on to an even keel, and romance will be born anew. People often fall in love while Neptune and Venus are in positive contact.

Negative transits
These are decidedly difficult. The subject may not be viewing emotional problems in their true light, and perhaps will react illogically to events. The escapist tendency may also make its presence felt, so try to encourage your subject not to do anything too drastic. Sometimes a short break away from the partner (or other source of the difficulty) is a good thing, but running away from reality isn't.

Look to other indications to see if permanent change is likely, and encourage the individual to consciously draw on his or her common sense and logic. This won't be easy, since the emotions will probably be in some turmoil. However, do reread our comments in the introduction to The Transits of Neptune (see p.333), and remember that some people react more to Neptune than others. The subject may also be succumbing to deceitfulness. The chances of "being found out" are considerable since carelessness due to forgetfulness (often a problem when Neptune is active) may lead to the making of a silly mistake. Too many people may suffer as a result of what may seem, and indeed could well be, an idyllic influence.

♂ Neptune's Transits to Mars

Conjunction
The emotions will be activated in a very colorful and passionate way. Here the accent is on romanticism, and creative potential can also spring into action. All kinds of water-related sporting interests may also develop at this time. Everything that is invigorating and exciting will be particularly attractive to the individual, and the influence could more generally act as a spark to a firework, with a lot of gloriously attractive results.

Positive transits
These have much the same effect as the conjunction. Encourage your subject to use these positive transits to begin work on any Neptunian interest that has always been attractive to him or her. A great deal of potential may emerge as a result of action taken while any of these influences are operative.

Negative transits
These are difficult and, as is the case when experiencing the very minor opposition transit from Mars to Neptune, all too often one has to cope with a disappointment. Obviously we are not going to say that your subject will definitely suffer a disappointment, but nevertheless at this time it is most advisable to suggest that his or her hopes must not be pinned too high, for there may well be a letdown of some kind in the offing.

Like all Neptune transits, these will last several weeks, and if the individual experiences them three times (due to retrograde motion), the overall period may be rather disappointing in some way; assess all other trends to see if there are mitigating influences. (Positive Jupiter transits and/or good lunar progressions will help, as will steadying, positive transits from Saturn to the Sun or Moon.)

♃ Neptune's Transits to Jupiter

Conjunction
This is a very subtle but often rewarding influence, under which the subject may reach some sound conclusions over religion or some philosophical questions. Sometimes the subject will go traveling, often more extensively than previously, and this will be marvelous if it happens, for the impact of foreign countries on him or her will be most impressive and long-lasting. Here is a trend under which to study, provided the powers of concentration are good. (The subject may be so overwhelmed by what he or she is studying at this time that you may find he or she will become starry-eyed or dreamy. As a result it will be difficult to assimilate what is being learned, as it can all seem rather amorphous.)

You will not go far wrong if you think of this influence in terms of the basic keyword for Jupiter, which is "expansion". And, yes, it can mean weight gain too – especially if an expensive cruise or holiday is taken at this time! In spite of the pleasant and, indeed, interesting possibilities of this influence, do gently hint to your subjects that at some time she will have to return to reality!

Positive transits
The effects of these are almost identical to those of the conjunction. Remember the sympathy between Jupiter and Neptune due to their relationship with Pisces (Jupiter was once that sign's ruler). Here the two planets are working well: there will be no lack of inspiration, and the imagination will also be enhanced.

All Jupiter concerns benefit from these transits: inspired intellectual conclusions may emerge, or the subject will have developed intellectually, often along some new and perhaps unusual path. These transits can also help people who are inspired to take up a new study or subject – maybe a foreign language to which they are attracted simply because they like its sound!

Negative transits
The individual may not want to conform to any restrictions at this time. For instance, if a college student, he or she may break away from the study course and tread his or her own somewhat undisciplined path instead. The results are unlikely to be good, and perhaps chances will be missed along the way. Generally the judgement is weak while these negative transits are operative, so important decisions should not be made under them. They can also have an adverse effect on the liver, because the individual may tend to eat comfort food, or perhaps drink too much, as a means of escaping from current problems.

♄ Neptune's Transits to Saturn

☌ Conjunction

At its best this transit may mark quite an important point in the subject's life; reality and idealism come together here. What is more, ambition, the will to succeed and determination are all balanced by the individual's more idealistic attributes, and sound, compassionate and considerate decisions and conclusions will be reached. The process may not be an easy one, since what is known to be right and one's sense of duty do not always go hand in hand with what is considered ideal. This is because the foibles of the individual's personality will intervene, and as a result such negative traits as selfishness, possessiveness and meanness will emerge and must be countered.

Idealism at its highest level may emerge and, due to much soul-searching, the subject will become more rounded, sympathetic and understanding, often concluding that materialism and worldly ambition are less important than he or she previously believed. This is particularly interesting while Neptune is transiting Capricorn; the conjunction will be especially powerful because those born with Saturn in this sign have the planet strongly placed, since Saturn rules Capricorn.

+ Positive transits

These help to steady the emotions and intuition. Often inspiration is positively channeled so that the resulting ideas and conclusions are practical and workable. These transits are excellent for anyone inspired to create something new. Encourage your subject to use fully these controlling and practical, but inspired, trends.

− Negative transits

These are difficult. Very often the subject is pulled in two directions, with the emotions encouraging one line of action and a sense of duty suggesting another. The result can often cause a lot of soul-searching and confusion, sometimes to the point that neither one path nor the other is taken, but a sort of limbo-like compromise is tolerated. This, then, can be a period of indecision and usually it is better not to make a decision under this trend (for the reasons already stated). The subject will one moment be strong, the next weak and confused.

Overall, the outlook tends to be rather gloomy and "I don't know what to think, I'm in a bit of a mess" is a characteristic statement. It is up to you to supply a good strong supportive shoulder (perhaps for your subject to cry on) and to advise postponing any direct action, unless there are a lot of positive progressions and transits to show whether practical or more idealistic lines of action should be taken. Whichever planet is stronger in the birth chart will be the one that has the greatest influence over these transits.

♅ Neptune's Transits to Uranus

☌ Conjunction

Until well into the twenty-first century Neptune is traveling through Capricorn and Aquarius, so will only form conjunctions for elderly people who have Uranus in one of these signs.

This should be an interesting and maybe rewarding period for the individual, who will be thinking in an inspired and original way. Progress will be made if ideas can be given concrete shape and practical application, since the eventual outcome may be dynamic and could put the subject way ahead of competitors. Sometimes there is a change of opinion and outlook on spiritual matters. This transit will work best if there are positive Saturn transits at roughly the same time; if not, the individual may become rather impractical, carried away by the sudden realization that he or she has chanced upon something special. If either planet is negatively aspected in the birth chart stress is likely at this time.

+ Positive transits

These are less powerful than the conjunction but equally rewarding. The subject is likely to produce some original work or ideas. Encourage the development of interests.

− Negative transits

The chances are that the individual will experience a confusing and rather stressful period. If Neptune or Uranus is a personal planet, such troubles will tend to dominate his or her life. If neither planet is personalized or powerfully placed in the birth chart, the individual may be faced by one ongoing, difficult and annoying problem which, although draining, will not be totally dominating. Instead, he or she should be able to put it aside and get on with more important things. Even with these negative transits there can be a flurry of bright and original ideas, but it may be hard for the individual to bring them into reality and they may not be completely practical.

♇ Neptune's Transits to Pluto

☌ Conjunction

Since Neptune takes 14 years to travel through a sign and remains in Capricorn until 1998, while Pluto will be in Scorpio until 1995, and takes between 13 and 32 years to travel through a sign, this transit will not be operative during at least the next 100 years, if not more.

+ Positive transits

These can have a positive and rather exciting effect on the sex life, bringing together emotion and sexual fulfillment. If there have been problems in the past, these can ease away as a result of the contact, especially if either planet is personalized.

− Negative transits

Confusion and a blockage of a positive flow of emotion related to sex will cause a certain amount of stress. There may be physical problems which will inhibit sexual enjoyment, especially if Pluto is in Cancer or Libra. Because of Pluto's connection with big business it is not particularly advisable to make important investments while these influences are operative. There could be difficulties – mild confusion at best, a fraudulent use of funds at worst.

Asc Neptune's Transits to the Ascendant

☌ Conjunction

This is a subtle but nevertheless powerful influence. As stated in the introduction to the Transits of Neptune (see p.333), different types of people feel Neptune's influence in different ways. This must be considered first when interpreting the trend, which will only apply to those with Capricorn, Aquarius or Pisces as Ascendant signs until well into the twenty-first century.

Until Neptune makes the precise conjunction, the planet will have been traveling though your subject's twelfth house. Has this influence had any noticeable effects? To find out, reread Neptune in the twelfth house (see p.331), remembering, of course, that Neptune has been slowly transitting it (and any planets it contains) for over a decade, so the effects will have been very long-term. When it hits the Ascendant, the individual may become less disciplined and very dreamy. If Neptune is negatively aspected in the birth chart there may be deceptive tendencies and uncharacteristic behavior. Sometimes the subject's creative potential gains a new and inspired form of expression, which is marvelous. Much good can come of the transit and it will sensitize the individual, but it can also have a negative effect. It is difficult to interpret, since there are so many possibilities.

Positive transits

Here the best side of Neptune's influence usually emerges, and while the individual may become rather dizzy and forgetful, there will be no lack of inspiration and it should find some positive outlet.

Negative transits

These are very tricky. The opposition may have an adverse effect on a permanent relationship or, if the subject is just forming a new partnership, he or she may not be assessing the lover correctly – being swept away by the whole glorious romance and seeing only what he or she wants to see. Advise delaying a commitment to marriage or to setting up a home together – especially if there are no progressions showing a really strong positive emphasis on this sphere of life. Even if there are some good supportive progressions, your subject may still be ascending too fast and furiously up to cloud nine. The squares will have a similar effect, either on work (Neptune in the tenth house or at the top of the chart), or on home and family life (Neptune in or entering the fourth house). Confusion, losing touch with reality, deception or being deceived (opposition) are very likely.

NEPTUNE'S TRANSITS TO THE MIDHEAVEN

Conjunction

The individual often has some unusual experiences. Sometimes there are interesting career developments or changes, the results of which will allow a freer expression of intuition, imagination and/or inspiration. Occasionally someone who is fed up with the rat race will opt out for a more rewarding and fulfilling career and lifestyle. If Neptune is negatively aspected in the birth chart, some of the planet's less desirable influences may make their presence felt, such as colleagues going behind the subject's back and "doing them dirt". Perhaps unfairness or some sort of underhanded action will occur if promotion is in the air. It is vital that the subject does not become involved in office politics, or succumb to any kind of dishonesty or milder forms of insidious blackmail at such times.

Positive transits

Subtle changes of some kind may be made. These will either effect the career or lifestyle, and may bring about easier and more rewarding conditions.

Negative transits

The effects of these are similar to the negative indications described under the conjunction, but the individual may become more confused and unhappy about the situation. The house that Neptune is transiting may show which sphere of life is involved.

If the transit is a square, for instance, and Neptune is transiting the seventh house, a typical result would be for one partner to be offered an exciting and perhaps glamorous opportunity but for the other partner not to want to cooperate (for instance, refusing to move so that a new job can be taken up). If the transit is an opposition, and Neptune is in the fourth house, parental disapproval or plain and simple emotional blackmail may be directed against the opportunity. In both cases the individual should put up a fight, but may not see any definite results until the trend has eased.

NEPTUNE'S TRANSITS TO ITS OWN POSITION

There are no Neptune Returns as we would have to be 168 years old in order to experience one! As Neptune's influence is so subtle when it transits its own position (notably the square and trine transits) it is not as striking as that of Saturn at the time of the Saturn Return, or Uranus at its Half-return.

The sextile transit of Neptune occurs when we are about 28, and may perhaps spark off thoughts which eventually emerge as changes made at the time of the first Saturn Return. The square transit occurs quite near the tense Uranus Half-return, and may add confusion at that tricky time.

The trine is subtly operative when we are about 56, perhaps encouraging a more philosophical attitude and planting the seeds of some pleasant daydreams about what we shall do half a decade later, when making plans for retirement and the next phase of life. There's no harm in drifting a little at this time – after all, most of us are still working hard and striding purposefully up the ladder to our eventual goal, with the self-confidence that a great deal of experience brings.

Parents of young teenagers may like to glance at the ephemeris when their children are about 14, for it is roughly at that age that Neptune will make a very weak semi-sextile transit to its own position. You may have a starry-eyed teenager on your hands – deeply in love for the first time, unable to concentrate on important studies, or full of passionate feelings for some remote rock star or sports personality.

These are all generalizations, of course, but they are worth considering and assessing to discover more about the way the extremely subtle transits of Neptune to its own position affect your subjects.

Pluto through the Signs

Pluto, the slowest-moving of all the planets, takes 246 years to complete its journey around the Sun and through all 12 signs. Its orbit is eccentric, for it will take only 13 years to travel through some signs and up to 32 years to transit others. It is therefore a generation influence. We do not think it quite so potent in this respect as Neptune, but nevertheless there are some striking examples, as you will see from these interpretations.

There is no one alive with Pluto in Aries or Taurus, and at the other end of the list of signs, the first children to be born with Pluto in Sagittarius will arrive during 1995, when the planet starts its slow journey through that sign. We can only conjecture how its influence will work from Sagittarius; time will tell.

Pluto in Gemini (until 1912/13)

Generation influence
Developments and changes were afoot at this time, and many old concepts and doctrines were swept away. A great deal that had gone unchallenged was now seen in a new light and, due to the development of the automobile and ever-improving communications, the world began to get smaller.

Personal influence
There are still elderly people alive with Pluto in this sign. It has given them inquisitiveness and curiosity – especially about much younger people, since they themselves have lived through so many remarkable changes and developments. Those with good intellects and comprehension are wise, drawing on their long experiences to enrich their own lives and sympathize or argue with the younger generations. Those less gifted are totally confused. All possess Geminian scepticism.

Pluto in Cancer (1912/13 – 1937/38)

Generation influence
As Pluto entered Cancer the First World War got underway. Disruption to family life was notable, and many children, especially those born in the early years of this placing, became fatherless, either temporarily or permanently. This theme was, of course, to continue to influence the children born in the thirties – many of whom had to suffer as a result of the war.

Personal influence
If Pluto is personalized or Cancer a prominent sign, this placing will have a powerful effect on the individual's intuition and emotional level. Both should flow well, and positive use will be made of these heightened levels. If Pluto is negatively aspected by the Sun, Moon, ruling planet or the Ascendant, there can be psychological blockage. If none of these apply, bear in mind that the individual's emotional level is somewhat increased by this placing. If his or her chart shows business acumen, this placing will certainly increase it. Characteristic Cancerian tenacity will also be enhanced. If worry is shown in other areas, look to Pluto to see whether or not the individual is able to come to terms with it, or is inclined to bottle up problems, thereby allowing Pluto to "constipate" the attitude and outlook.

Pluto in Leo (1937/8 – 1957)

Generation influence
Once again a world war broke out as Pluto settled down to a journey through a new sign. Domination and power were highlighted in the worst possible way but as a result of such conflicts some good emerged: while Pluto was still traveling through Leo The United Nations was formed. Another generation influence of this placing has been the development of technology, and many who work in that area have Pluto strongly placed in Leo. This is especially true of computer specialists.

Personal influence
The powers of leadership common to Leo will be somewhat heightened, but only minutely if neither Pluto nor Leo are personal or prominent. If the Sun, Moon or Ascendant are in Leo there can be a power complex. Carefully consider the house position of Pluto, and be especially wary if the planet is at the top of the chart, for here we sometimes have a little – or big! – empire builder. How is the subject achieving his or her objectives? Is he or she becoming power-mad, or able to work extremely well for the good of others as well as him- or herself? Sometimes (again if Leo is prominent) the positive, fiery enthusiasm of Leo is darkened – and the "inner psychological Sun", which is such a feature of this sign, does not shine as strongly. The placing adds business sense, though in a rather different way from Cancer, since there is a greater adventurousness and less intuitive shrewdness.

Pluto in Virgo (1957 – 1971)

Generation influence
It is almost impossible to detach this influence from that of Uranus in Virgo, because that planet was in Virgo with Pluto between late 1961 and late 1968, and together they formed the extremely potent Uranus/Pluto conjunction. There was much student unrest and criticism of the values and standards of the older generation, so that Pluto's upheaval and Uranus' desire for sudden change emerged very strongly indeed. This generation has a very special power – to blast the world to bits or to rid it of much that is selfish and unjust. Thinking of the Virgoan obsession with detail and analytical inclinations, it is also interesting to discover that it was during the sixties that the first pocket calculator was created.

Personal influence
Decide whether the influence of Pluto is a source of obsessional tendencies in your subject. It may not be, but if such traits are suggested in other areas of the chart, this placing will increase such an indication. Again, as with the generation influence, you must reassess

the influence of the Uranus/Pluto conjunction in this sign, and carefully consider its house placing. If the two planets are in conjunction or in the same sign, there will definitely be a sign influence. If they are negatively aspected the ability to talk freely about problems – generally to unburden – will be very limited, and the subject will tend to worry. Look to other areas of the chart to see how this can be tempered. The desire to see problems in a coherent perspective and to resolve them will be present when Pluto is activated by important transits, or indeed when it makes a transit to the Sun, Moon or Ascendant. (See The Transits of Pluto, pp.343-7.) Incidentally, if Pluto is personalized or aspected by the Sun, Moon or ruling planet, there may be a tendency to constipation, since Virgo rules the bowels. If your subject tends to be overcritical in a harsh incisive way, it may be due to the influence of Pluto. Look to other areas to find a counter to this undesirable tendency.

PLUTO IN LIBRA (1971 – 1983/4)

Generation influence
During the seventies there was a great deal of sexual permissiveness. The Pill had brought freedom from unwanted pregnancy and given women the right to decide when to have children. Interestingly, those with Neptune in Libra, the "flower power" generation, were "doing their own thing". The emergence of drugs and "dropping out", the rock festivals and escapism in general were attractive to their generation. The burning of draft cards was synonymous with the War–Peace axis; as was the "balance" of Libra, with love and harmony on one scale and the horrors of Vietnam (Pluto) on the other.

Personal influence
In some ways Pluto puts some spice into Libra, but it does increase the Libran tendency to rock the boat, and especially to instigate quarrels in order to prove the partner's affection or lack of it. This trait emerges powerfully when Libra is prominent or Pluto personalized. If there is a Libra Sun or Moon there will be a particularly active and rewarding sex life, and the pure romanticism of Libra will be less evident. If Pluto is negatively aspected – with the Sun and/or Moon in particular – there can be sexual problems. Your subject may be able to talk them through, but if not you must recommend therapy. Jealousy and possessiveness will also be a problem if Libra is prominent or Pluto personalized.

PLUTO IN SCORPIO (1983/84 – 1995)

Generation influence
Those with Neptune in Scorpio (1956 –1970/1) are making their presence felt in increasingly powerful positions. Why is black so popular in fashion design? Whence came the heavy punk-rock movement in the early eighties? Pluto's entry into Scorpio has had its effect on those with Neptune in Scorpio. This is a powerful trend, but perhaps the most Scorpionic of all effects is in the appearance of AIDS – a sexually-transmitted disease; and Pluto's influence is very much part of our sexuality. Remember that Pluto is at home in Scorpio, so its strength is increased. Hopefully, the situation will be controlled and Pluto's influence, having brought the scourge to the surface, will be curative. Here, lessons are learned the hard way. The light on the horizon is from the influence of the other generation planet, Neptune, working from Capricorn. Uranus is also in that sign, and Saturn transitting Capricorn between 1988 and the end of 1990 is also curative. The developments of the first half of the nineties will be most interesting and probably dramatic. We must not forget the financial implications of Pluto from its own sign. The desire to make more money and the ever-increasing implications of the expansion of world markets are very much part of this physically tiny but important planet.

Personal influence
This adds an intensity and sense of purpose, but if Pluto receives negative aspects from the Sun, Moon or ruling planet there may be psychological problems. These must be resolved if the individual is fully to develop potential and make positive use of increased emotion and intuition. There will be a much stronger source of emotional and physical energy if Scorpio is the Sun, Moon or rising sign, and this must be channeled positively. Make sure your subject's parents are aware of this, since using it through competitive sport and in reaction to very demanding challenges is essential. The earlier parents start to encourage it in their offspring the better, otherwise they could possibly have a difficult, restless and unfulfilled child on their hands. If Pluto is conjunct the Midheaven and/or placed in the tenth house (see p.343 and p.342 respectively), the expression of power and identification with everything that is strong and powerful will be present.

PLUTO IN SAGITTARIUS (from 1995 until well into the twenty-first century)

We can only speculate on the personal and generation influences of Pluto from this sign. In essence, the sign and planet are opposites; Sagittarius is open, freedom-loving, independent, and couldn't be less secretive while Pluto is very secretive, finding it difficult to unburden, intense and possessively jealous. However, when Pluto's influence causes purges, a great deal is brought into the open. Is it in this way that Pluto will act from Sagittarius? Hopefully so, provided of course that there are not such powerful reactions to situations that the disturbance and disruption they cause is a problem in itself. It seems hard to think of any Sagittarian influence causing revolutionary tendencies, so the chances are that reactions will be tinged with wisdom and the sage-like traits of Sagittarius/Jupiter. It is these qualities which we hope will add an interesting dimension to the children born while Pluto is in this sign.

PLUTO PROGRESSED TO A NEW SIGN

It would be extraordinary to find this progression, since it is most unlikely. The influence of the new sign would only be noticeable if Pluto or Scorpio were personalized or prominent.

Pluto through the Houses

The house in which Pluto falls is likely to be a source of difficulty. When the planet is activated by progression or transit the subject can expect progress to be at best uneven, at worst totally blocked, until the trends causing the problem are over. Sometimes the individual will overreact and the Pluto influence will act as a purge, clearing the decks. If Pluto is negatively aspected there is a possibility of the subject becoming obsessional about the affairs of the Pluto house.

1 Pluto in the First House

The nearer Pluto lies to the Ascending degree, the stronger its influence will be. If it is within eight to ten degrees, it will be very powerful indeed, and if the distance is eight degrees or less, Pluto will form a conjunction, the effects of which should be considered very carefully.

Whichever sign Pluto occupies, and in most cases this will also be the Ascendant sign, the planet's influence will darken the personality, adding an incisive and deep, emotionally intense quality. The individual will want to explore in depth anything he or she finds fascinating, and so there can be considerable potential for research.

On a more psychological level, there can be obsessional tendencies and sometimes (especially if Pluto and the Ascendant are in Leo), a need to dominate others. The emotional level will be increased, even if Pluto is in the emotionally restrained sign of Virgo. A zest and inner strength will be added when Pluto is in Libra. The emotional energy will be passionate and often expressed sexually, although it can be positively directed towards achieving ambitious objectives. A marvelous sense of purpose is generally present, and must be expressed and fulfilled, otherwise an inner seething sense of dissatisfaction may afflict the subject.

These energies will be blocked if Pluto is negatively aspected in the birth chart, causing deep-rooted psychological problems that can emerge as physical ailments.

Channelling the energy

Considerable potential is given in this placing, since it is so full of intense emotional energy. However, we cannot stress too strongly just how important it is for these qualities to be given a rewarding outlet. It may be that your subject was born when both Saturn and Pluto were in Leo – if so, study the influence of the Saturn/Pluto conjunction (see p.306). Parents whose young children have this placing must control and discipline them with great care and make sure that they are kept very busy in areas where they can express their powerful traits. Strenuous team games or water sports are excellent. Watch out for any inclinations towards cruelty.

2 Pluto in the Second House

This placing usually denotes excellent business potential. If the chart as a whole veers in this direction, the chances are that your subject will be keen to work in business, perhaps starting from scratch and building up an individual "empire", or will simply make a lot of money. Sometimes, however, this tendency can get out of control, with the individual becoming obsessed with making money.

The powers of concentration are usually good when Pluto is in the second house, and may help to stabilize any individual who tends to have his or her head in the clouds.

An acquisitive attitude

Determination and the will to succeed are usually present, especially if other areas of the chart also indicate these qualities. A great deal of psychological satisfaction will be gained from collecting and owning possessions. This theme will emerge very strongly indeed if Cancer is a prominent sign in the birth chart, or if the Moon is placed in Taurus. Unfortunately this tendency can extend to the subject's attitude towards his or her loved one – who may well be thought of simply as yet another possession.

The emotional life will be intense and passionate. Indeed, Pluto's influence from this house often enhances the sensual expression, thereby making the individual a good lover.

3 Pluto in the Third House

The need to communicate (third house) and the tendency to be secretive and silent (Pluto), is a contradiction in terms, yet the two qualities are combined in this placing.

A powerful element of curiosity and a searching kind of mind are denoted by Pluto's tenancy of the third house. Very little will be missed by the individual, despite the characteristic tendency to wear a blank facial expression, especially when in boring company, thereby giving the impression that he or she is totally cut off from the surroundings. In fact, everything that is happening and being said will be noted – almost nothing will have escaped the subject's attention!

A need for information

If Gemini is prominent in the chart, or Pluto is in Virgo, this placing may be a splendid supporting factor for someone who has inclinations towards investigative journalism or detective work. Parents with children who have Pluto in Scorpio in this house must always make a point of answering their every question very thoroughly indeed, since superficiality or a glossing over of the facts will not be tolerated at any price!

4 Pluto in the Fourth House

If your subject has this placing, he or she is likely to have suffered from an above-average amount of frustration during childhood and adolescence. Perhaps he was not allowed to follow up interests which he found fascinating, he was blocked in some way, or maybe he was unable – either through his parents' stubbornness or a lack of funds – to attend whichever school that would have been most suitable. In fact, he may well have suffered considerably from the force of sheer power exerted by his parents.

The intuition is increased by this placing, however, so it may be that the subject found his own way round any such problems, employing considerable tenacity and determination. If that is the case, he will have used his Pluto influence to its best advantage, perhaps learning difficult lessons the hard way.

Long-term problems

This is a difficult placing for Pluto – you will learn a great deal if you can encourage your subject to unburden his feelings, especially about his childhood (was he ever in contact with an institution, perhaps due to the misdemeanors of one of his parents?) If the childhood background was disturbed and is still a distressing topic for your subject, you should advise that he seeks help through psychotherapy. However, you will find that very often when Pluto is involved the individual concerned is quite capable of practicing self-analysis – especially when the planet is in Virgo.

5 PLUTO IN THE FIFTH HOUSE

If creativity is indicated in other areas of the chart, the individual will strive with considerable determination to exploit his or her potential in this field. Even if the odds are stacked against this, the subject's strength of will and expenditure of emotional energy can often win through in the end. As a result, there is considerable inner psychological fulfillment, even if, technically speaking, what is produced is of a rather low standard. The areas on which the individual will concentrate will be determined by the influence of the prominent signs and the personal planets in her chart.

The love life is also affected by this placing. It will probably be both intense and very rich, but sometimes the subject may expect too much of lovers, so that real satisfaction is not always achieved and the individual is forever seeking perfection. There will almost inevitably be an above-average number of love affairs but, for the reasons already stated, it may not be easy for the individual to be completely logical in her attitude towards such emotional relationships.

A compulsive tendency to take risks may also be present. These will often be emotional, but can sometimes be physically daring or concerned with financial affairs.

6 PLUTO IN THE SIXTH HOUSE

The subject with this placing may be a great stickler for routine and discipline, especially if Pluto is in Virgo. There will be a tendency to be rather hard on the self, however, and as a result whichever tasks have to be tackled can become an obsession.

If these tendencies are controlled, nonetheless, and Pluto can be made to work in a positive way from this house, this placing will enhance the individual's powers of concentration. The result may be that he or she will direct a great deal of energy toward concentrated work, which will prove to be of considerable benefit.

Health problems

A negative effect on the health may be felt by those with this placing. If Pluto is negatively aspected there can be bowel problems (here we get Pluto's characteristic constipating action in the literal sense!), and if the individual suffers from a lack of emotional fulfillment, he or she may tend to overeat for the sake of the comfort that the food gives, thereby putting on too much weight.

As the children with Pluto in Scorpio placed in the sixth house reach their teenage years, their parents should look out for these tendencies. Any extreme is bad for all of us, but is even more so for those with Pluto tenanting the sixth house.

7 PLUTO IN THE SEVENTH HOUSE

Since this house emphasizes the polarity of the Ascendant, a great deal of its effect depends on the Pluto sign, the influence of which should be reread with considerable care (see pp.338-9). It is possible that the subject with this placing needs to be the dominant partner in an emotional relationship. As far as business partnerships are concerned, here we have someone who will probably be excellent at dealing with the business/money side of the company. In fact, this placing works well for such business relationships, but complicates life for emotional partnerships.

Emotional extremes

On a personal level, a great deal of emotion will certainly be expressed through the subject's relationships. As a result, while there will be some marvelous moments, there is an equal likelihood of some pretty severe storms from time to time. The individual must be very careful indeed to preserve a balance within his or her partnerships and not dominate them. In extreme cases, it is possible that she will, probably unconsciously, seek a weaker personality as a partner for that very reason.

On the whole, if the birth chart shows compassion, real sympathy and a good understanding of others, then the emotional forces within the individual with this placing will be enough for both her and her partner, and things will work out very well. Nevertheless, the highs and lows of relationships can make for an uneasy path in this sphere of life.

8 PLUTO IN THE EIGHTH HOUSE

Pluto is at home here, since this is the Scorpio/Pluto house. The intuition is increased by this placing, and the individual will be able to combine it with logic. There is often sympathy for mystical topics and, sometimes, psychic ability may be present. If your subject senses that he or she has such gifts, do encourage the seeking out of sound instruction so that they are developed in the right way – so much can go wrong when these areas are inexpertly tampered with.

A shrewd business sense is another possibility of this placing, especially if Pluto is in Cancer or Virgo. This should also prove to be the case with those youngsters who have the planet in Scorpio. (When it is in Scorpio, and also in this house, it will certainly be a powerful feature of the chart as a whole and must be treated as such.)

The emotional level is increased here, but the feelings and sexual expression may not flow as easily or as positively as the subject would wish. Sexual problems can therefore occur as a result of this placing, and the individual may need to seek help through professional counseling.

9 PLUTO IN THE NINTH HOUSE

This placing may give a compulsive desire to study and to accept mental challenge – sometimes beyond the individual's scope. As a result, considerable strain and tension can build up. It is fair to warn your subject of this particular vulnerability. It may be that he or she has a need for perfection in every area that makes intellectual demands. For example, letters and articles will be written and rewritten many times and he may find it difficult to rest content with the results of labors of this kind.

Such a striving for perfection can sometimes mean that the subject becomes discontented and frustrated by his or her chosen course of study while taking further education. As a result, that course can be terminated – often with disgust. If your subject has reached this critical point, you should do everything you can to dissuade him against such drastic action, since he may be demonstrating the Pluto tendency of throwing the baby out with the bathwater. Making a clean sweep is no bad thing, but it can be taken to extremes! You may receive some interesting replies should you question your subject about events he experienced while traveling abroad. There may well be a fund of unusual, or perhaps slightly weird, stories to tell!

10 PLUTO IN THE TENTH HOUSE

Pluto will assume considerable importance in this house, especially if it conjuncts the Midheaven. The individual will need to be very much emotionally involved in the career or, if no career is followed, it is important that he or she has a particular goal or compelling objective for which to aim.

A power complex is all too often indicated by this placing, unfortunately, especially if Pluto is in Leo. If it falls in Virgo, it may well be in conjunction with Uranus – if so, study the interpretation of that aspect with care (see pp.319-20). Nevertheless, the will to succeed is very strong, but sometimes it can be expressed ruthlessly (for instance, if Pluto is negatively aspected by personal planets). Perhaps your subject is an empire builder, or simply has a great deal of emotional energy to exploit.

A need for constructive action
Every encouragement to expend such energy positively should be given, since there is considerable potential to be used here, and it must be expressed to the full. Otherwise, as is so common with a Pluto/Scorpio influence, it can easily turn sour, and that will be when life becomes complicated and troubled for the individual and his or her immediate circle.

11 PLUTO IN THE ELEVENTH HOUSE

Pluto is not very powerfully placed in the eleventh house, but it does tend to encourage the individual to become too concerned, and perhaps somewhat obsessional, over the attitude of friends and acquaintances. If some small action displeases the subject, he or she is likely to overreact, thus provoking quarrels and upsets.

Outside influences
Other people's attitudes to the individual's actions will also be important. "What will they think if I do that?" may be a frequently uttered phrase – especially in the not-so-young, who might chide their children with similar statements calculated to stop them doing anything that may upset others. Sometimes the objectives of a group or society to which the subject belongs will assume too great an importance – to the detriment of partner and family.

If these powerful traits can be directed towards philanthropic ends much good can be done. However, it is up to the individual concerned to keep such feelings in perspective, and not allow them to take over her life or behavior in any way.

12 PLUTO IN THE TWELFTH HOUSE

When Pluto is placed in the twelfth house it will have a powerful effect on the unconscious. There will be a considerable tendency to be secretive and sometimes even reclusive. It can also be very difficult for the individual to talk freely about his or her problems, which may be rooted in an inability to express the characteristically powerful emotions easily and positively. An air of mystery will surround your subject, and if she is at all canny she will use it to great advantage!

Nevertheless, this placing is a difficult one, especially if Pluto receives negative aspects from the Sun or Moon, or is in conjunction with the Ascendant from this house (see p.343). To delve and analyze will be second nature to the subject, so that her investigatory powers will be heightened in much the same way as they are when Pluto occupies the eighth house. Unfortunately, this placing will give a more powerful tendency to turn these inclinations on the self. Sometimes, if there is a problem, it can be all too easy for the subject to mull it over so often that it becomes a kind of mazelike vicious circle in her mind, from which it is hard to escape. She must also be warned against falling into the habit of taking any sort of drugs when under stress, since tranquilizers may be deemed attractive.

♇ PLUTO PROGRESSED TO A NEW HOUSE

This is a most unlikely progression because of Pluto's very slow motion. However, if by chance you should discover that the planet is moving from one house to the next, the house it is entering may well assume considerably increased importance in your subject's life. He or she must not become too overwhelmed by what is happening, and should try to maintain a logical sense of perspective.

The Aspects of Pluto

Because Pluto (at the time of writing – see p.21) is the most distant planet in the Solar System, here we deal only with its aspects to the Ascendant and Midheaven where, as will be seen, its influence is very powerful indeed. But be careful – an error of a very few minutes in the birth time will either weaken or strengthen the influence of this planet.

For Pluto's aspects to the Sun, see the Sun's aspects to Pluto, p.219.

For Pluto's aspects to the Moon, see the Moon's aspects to Pluto, pp.236-7.

For Pluto's aspects to Mercury, see Mercury's aspects to Pluto, pp.251-2 .

For Pluto's aspects to Venus, see Venus' aspects to Pluto, p.266.

For Pluto's aspects to Mars, see Mars' aspects to Pluto, pp.279-80.

For Pluto's aspects to Jupiter, see Jupiter's aspects to Pluto, p.291.

For Pluto's aspects to Saturn, see Saturn's aspects to Pluto, p.306.

For Pluto's aspects to Uranus, see Uranus' aspects to Pluto, pp.319-20.

For Pluto's aspects to Neptune, see Neptune's aspects to Pluto, p.332.

PLUTO'S ASPECTS TO THE ASCENDANT

Conjunction

From the first house: Reread Pluto in the first house (see p.340). Pluto may have a striking effect on the appearance; the looks will be darkened and given an intense expression. The eyes may also have a piercing, powerful gaze; the subject will need to get at the root of every problem. The emotional force is strong and needs positive expression, and there must always be total involvement in projects. The emotional and physical energy must not be burned, but actually consumed.

From the twelfth house: Pluto may also darken the looks here. The individual may be very secretive with smoldering intensity, so that his or her energies may stagnate. This is most likely if Pluto is negatively aspected by the Sun, Moon or ruling planet. Sometimes much satisfaction can be derived from research and working alone – in libraries or with complicated computer programs, for instance.

Note: In either case encourage your subject to use up energy in sport or another demanding physical activity.

Positive aspects

These will help the individual to come to terms with important changes. Sometimes there is a tendency to be overenthusiastic about what he or she may call "moving on", caused by a deep-rooted, psychological urge for making a clean sweep. Even so, you may have to warn against throwing out the baby with the bathwater. If there are psychological problems, the subject should not be reluctant to solve them.

Negative aspects

Pluto's house position will show where the individual may experience frustration and the inability to move forward. This is most likely during transits to Pluto or other heavy influences. If the opposition falls from the sixth house, there could be bowel complaints or problems with the genitals. Likewise, there can be problems with partnerships for Pluto in the seventh, and so on. The urge to make drastic changes can also get out of perspective, with the subject going overboard. In general, these aspects will block progress whenever they are activated.

MC PLUTO'S ASPECTS TO THE MIDHEAVEN

Conjunction

A power complex is likely, and the individual will almost certainly identify with the stronger characteristics of the Midheaven sign. He or she has potential and may be successfully attracted to any Plutonian career. In fact, emotional involvement with the career or objectives in life is essential. Drastic changes may be made during the working life – throwing away lots of experience in one field so as to turn to something different and begin again.

Positive aspects

Just like the positive aspects to the Ascendant (see left), these help when the subject faces enforced changes. When Pluto aspects the Ascendant, the need for change will be psychologically motivated, but when Pluto aspects the Midheaven, the changes are likely to occur through circumstance. Even so, the subject will be able to cope.

Negative aspects

Circumstances may provoke difficulties and upheavals from time to time. How well the subject copes will depend on the chart as a whole. A practical, tenacious person will manage, while one who is less energetic or confident may crumble. It is up to you to discover where positive inner strength lies (the Moon's position?) and help your subject build up confidence at this time.

THE TRANSITS OF PLUTO

Because Pluto has such an eccentric orbit, its transits to the natal positions of planets are often experienced three times. Generally speaking, Pluto will stay in one degree for about a month when moving forward, but when its motion becomes hesitant, it can sit in one degree for fourteen weeks or more at a time. Pluto's astrological influence is fairly easy to time when working from its precise astronomical position. The trends do not seem to fade in and out over any longer a period than is suggested from its astronomical position, as is the case with Saturn or Neptune. In fact, Pluto's influence seems to "click" on and off clearly; life is eventful or grinds to a halt. In most cases it is usually only one sphere of life or a specific project that is affected when Pluto is working negatively, so you can advise your subject to devote extra time and energy to other areas –

working hard against Pluto is almost always fruitless. But often it urges us to make a clean sweep in one area or have a purge in another. This can work very well, but as Pluto heightens emotional energy, we can easily view problems out of perspective, making overdrastic decisions which we may live to regret.

If there is a run of Pluto transits (especially three identical ones to the same planet), there may be considerable respite whenever they are not operative. So, the impact of the problem or project will be felt during the first period, emphasized during the second, and greatly heightened during the third. Only when the influence has passed can we reach a resolution, and it is then, if possible, that final decisions should be made. During the lulls we may be held up by a third party – or perhaps our concern evaporates. If the influence is very strong or the problem dominates our lives, we may find ourselves in some sort of limbo.

Note: Until 1995 all the conjunction transits of Pluto will be operative only on planets in Scorpio in the birth chart, or on a Scorpio Ascendant or Midheaven. After 1995 the planet will ease into Sagittarius. For many years afterward the conjunction transit will only be operative for natal planets, the Ascendant or Midheaven in this sign.

Pluto's Transits to the Sun

☌ Conjunction

This is very important for Sun sign Scorpios, probably indicating a key period of change and when psychological problems will be exposed and resolved. If the individual is facing difficulties that cramp his or her lifestyle or impede fulfillment, psychotherapy may help considerably. A clean sweep is often made, so the subject can move forward in a new and more rewarding way, perhaps becoming immersed in a long-standing interest; this will be most fulfilling. New developments may also begin under this transit.

+ Positive transits

These are similar to the conjunction, but there will be less blockage and the way ahead should be clear even while the transit is operative. Those prone to worry (Sun signs Cancer, Virgo or Pisces) may feel confused or apprehensive, but if the emotional energy flows well and the urge is to move forward psychologically, or to develop potential, then much good will result. There may be powerful financial overtones, especially for Sun sign Capricorns.

− Negative transits

The "constipating" effect of Pluto is probably strongest here. These transits will cause frustration and block plans, so that progress may be halted. The personal life may be involved in some way and sometimes the individual is unable to express his or her true feelings. If your subject has a psychological problem it could be pronounced at this time. Resistance to therapy is common, but this attitude may change once the transit is over.

Pluto's Transits to the Moon

☌ Conjunction

A Scorpio Moon always increases emotional intensity and energy, and especially when conjuncted by Pluto, so the subject will be spurred into making sweeping changes and fresh starts. These will be worthwhile, but outbursts of temper or overreactions to trivial situations must be avoided. It may always be hard for those with this placing to keep cool and control jealousy, but it will be worse at this time.

+ Positive transits

There will be the same desire for new beginnings following changes as there is for the conjunction, and this basic need will again be emotionally motivated. The intuition is heightened, so the individual should not make any mistakes, but you may have to encourage him or her not to overreact to situations which occur as a result of his or her own actions. The changes will be refreshing and worthwhile; indeed, these transits can be used to clear away clutter, physically or emotionally.

− Negative transits

Emotional stress is likely, sometimes as the result of long-term psychological problems, which may relate to the subject's childhood and perhaps negatively affect his or her sex life. Sometimes jealousy will gain the upper hand. If so, decide whether the reaction is justified or due to an overactive imagination. Action may be neither desired nor possible. If anger is justified, its release is no bad thing – but it is more likely to be bottled up, which may do psychological harm. The natal Moon's aspects should show how easy it is to release the true feelings, which is what is most needed at this time.

Pluto's Transits to Mercury

☌ Conjunction

Here, the deep-thinking and detective-like mind of a Scorpio Mercury will be even more pronounced. Ensure that your subject uses this trend positively, through involvement in a research project that calls upon such skills. If not, the more psychological implications may inhibit good communication, and as a result there may be breakdowns in intellectual rapport between partners, for instance.

When Pluto conjuncts a Sagittarian Mercury the individual may become unusually secretive, or perhaps involved in work about which it will be inappropriate to speak freely.

+ Positive transits

The individual is likely to air problems – sometimes rather overdramatically. The urge to speak out and to do so freely will be underlined, and should be encouraged no matter what sphere of life or views are involved. As a result of such openness the world may learn that your subject has changed his or her opinions or at least thinks differently now about some topics.

− Negative transits

Circumstances may provoke frustrating difficulties over which the individual is powerless. It may seem to you easy for the subject to solve them, but for many reasons he or she will be unable to do so. Is this basically due to fear or lack of self-confidence, or would the consequences of action, real or imagined, be so dire that it would be best for him or her to keep quiet? Appeal to your subject's logic in such cases. It may be that these problems are less traumatic than they seem because Pluto is causing obsessive tendencies.

♀ Pluto's Transits to Venus

Conjunction
The jealousy of a Scorpio Venus may surface, so suggest that your subject may be overreacting to a partner's trivial action or misconduct. The emotional intensity (a powerful force in this placing) must be positively expressed; at its best this transit can enhance the sex life. Sometimes it can cause unrequited love – but those with Venus in Scorpio will no doubt cope!

Those with Venus in Sagittarius can resolve any Pluto heaviness by seeking pastures new. There can be tricky financial overtones. If Venus is well aspected, an investment made at this time should be profitable, but those with a Sagittarian Venus must avoid taking gambles.

+ Positive transits
The emotions are heightened and should flow positively, provided the feelings are reasonably controlled and any tendency to swamp the partner or be too sexually demanding is checked. The transit may be less easy for those with Venus in Virgo, since the subject may be confused by a surge of emotion toward a current or prospective partner. However, it should prove rewarding in the long run.

– Negative transits
These are difficult and may lead to the enforced repression of feelings – or individuals may find they can do nothing to improve a stagnating relationship. There can be an overemotional reaction, but deep-rooted psychological problems may mar a relationship. If these are worked through in discussion, though, the subject can usually make a fresh start.

Any important decisions should be postponed while these transits are operative. If they recur and final conclusions must be reached, advise using the periods of respite for action or decision-taking. Jealousy or possessiveness may affect those whose natal Venus is in Taurus.

♂ Pluto's Transits to Mars

Conjunction
Mars in Scorpio is a strong feature of any chart, and when transiting Pluto conjuncts it the individual will have a strong desire to take some important and compulsive action, so that sweeping changes are made. These usually work out well, but Martian premature action must be avoided. As Pluto and Scorpio are involved the hasty side of Mars is usually repressed, and the subject may have carried out much serious thought and behind-the-scenes research before announcing plans, but warnings must still be given. The rest of the chart should show whether the subject is impulsive, thoughtful or logical; study the Sun, Moon and Ascendant signs. The emotional intensity of this transit is considerable.

+ Positive transits
Increased determination and the will to succeed are likely. The emotional and physical energies are probably enhanced, so the subject must be deeply involved in a project or interest, otherwise this marvelous reservoir of energy will stagnate. Considerable achievements should be the outcome of these influences, but the subject must be warned against acting hastily.

– Negative transits
The desire for achievement and to make changes may be present, but progress is likely to be blocked, and any action taken may be detrimental. Pluto's compulsion and Mars' energy may get the better of the subject, provoking overdrastic reactions. He or she must be encouraged to calm down a little, but frustration and impatience may make this difficult, for it is all too easy to continue knocking one's head against a brick wall at such times.

♃ Pluto's Transits to Jupiter

Conjunction
The mind will be able to cope with depth and detail, but will also possess breadth of vision. When Jupiter is transited by Pluto an intellectually searching process may begin, resulting in a considerable change of opinion on intellectual and even philosophical matters. Whether Jupiter is in Scorpio or Sagittarius, an element of daring may be present, resulting in some kind of risk-taking. This will be emotionally oriented if Jupiter is in Scorpio, and more intellectually or sportively daredevil if in Sagittarius. Jupiter's gambling spirit could also be emphasized, plus a tendency to overinvest emotionally or, more importantly, financially. If your subject is shrewd and has a good business sense he or she may be on to a winner, but if Jupiter is negatively aspected, especially by the Sun or Moon, there may be blind optimism.

+ Positive transits
These should result in changes and general progress. Many of the positive elements of the conjunction are possible, but the effects will be less potent and life is less likely to become very eventful. Any tendency to take overdrastic action or to overrespond to situations must be curbed. Often there is financial gain. A change of attitude and perhaps a clearing away of restricting opinions or beliefs can also occur.

– Negative transits
The individual may feel physically or emotionally claustrophobic, due to an unrewarding lifestyle or because he or she hasn't enough intellectual freedom of expression. Boredom may result from coping with partners or others who are less intelligent or who don't share the subject's interests. The inability to escape from restrictions except through drastic action can be troubling. Advise careful thought and perhaps the delaying of important changes until this transit has passed. By that time feelings will have stabilized and lessons have been learned.

♄ Pluto's Transits to Saturn

Conjunction
Saturn is strongly and heavily placed in Scorpio, so any transit it receives will tend to make the individual introspective, moody and brooding. This inclination will be very much strengthened under Pluto's influence, with periods of depression and perhaps a lack of

self-confidence. You must emphasize that, while your subject may not be exactly buoyant at this time, careful long-term planning can be done, even if action should not be taken until the influence has passed (otherwise there may be frustrating delays); plan in the abstract, wait until later for action. If Saturn is in Sagittarius a restless tendency must be controlled. For either sign the vitality may be lowered or there may be a physical blockage.

+ Positive transits
While these may bring about long-term changes, they are hard to cope with because the planets are individually restrictive and difficult. Common sense will probably prevail and all will be well in the long run, but the subject may have to act in a way that seems less desirable than an apparently easy way out of a situation.

– Negative transits
The best thing to do at this time is nothing. Do not advise your subject to take action or to fight. Speaking one's mind, especially to officials or those in power, is fine, but the subject should wait until the influence is over before making any important moves. Here we have the "constipation" of Pluto hammering away with the frustration and limitation of Saturn – neither pleasant nor helpful. Your subject should keep moving and exercising, since he or she may suffer arthritic aches and pains.

Pluto's Transits to Uranus

Conjunction
Uranus was in Scorpio between 1975 and 1981, and in Sagittarius from 1981 to 1988, so this transit will affect young people. It may be difficult, and normal youthful rebelliousness may emerge very strongly. Parents should sympathize if their children start acting in a difficult and uncharacteristic manner; they may be feeling extremely fed-up and claustrophobic. They will want to make drastic and important changes which they may not have thought through; quite a few will learn the hard way. If the young person has had a fairly stable and disciplined childhood, he or she will use these powerful energy resources positively and gain much from them, but drastic, compulsive and unconventional action, trying to overpower other people emotionally, will not pay off. A lot of guidance is necessary at this time.

+ Positive transits
The urge to break free and start fresh, at least in one area of life, is likely. A change of job or spare-time interests, or taking on a new and compellingly demanding project, should work out well in the long run. However, over-enthusiasm and eccentricity should be monitored! Sometimes the influence puts the individual in a position of power, but such an event or development should not go to his or her head.

– Negative transits
This may be a frustrating and difficult time, although just how annoying or upsetting it is very much depends on other transits and lunar directions. If these are pleasant and easy probably only one project or problem will cause difficulty. If there are heavy transits from Saturn or Uranus to the Sun, Moon, Ascendant or ruling planet, life will not be a bed of roses. Patience, calm and controlled emotions are essential, but complacency is not called for. It is a time for showing one's inner strength, while not fighting back so hard that nervous exhaustion, tensions and adverse effects on the health (severe headaches?) are the result. Sometimes relaxation techniques will help. Life will move forward again when the transit is over, but the situation may not be totally finalized until other influences have also passed.

Pluto's Transits to Neptune

Conjunction
Since the turn of the century, Neptune has moved from Gemini to Capricorn, where it will remain until 1998. Pluto is in Scorpio until 1995, when it moves into Sagittarius, so it will only make the conjunction transit to Neptune for those who have Neptune in Scorpio (until 1995) and for those who have Neptune in Sagittarius (after 1995). There is often some kind of awakening when Pluto contacts Neptune, for here the searching, incisive qualities of Pluto relate to the spiritual, dreamy inspiration of Neptune. In people who are sensitive, creative and very aware of their surroundings, there can be interesting inspirational developments which may contribute much towards psychological progress and enlightenment. As a result, potential for creative or imaginative work will blossom. In weaker people there may be a tendency to negative escapism – opting out, all too often initiating drug-taking. This is perhaps more likely for those with a Scorpio Neptune than for those with the planet in Sagittarius. They should develop under this influence, even if there will be some tension and perhaps a sense of being confused or pulled in two directions at the same time. Sometimes there is an awareness of psychic power, but you should encourage your subject to be cautious and sceptical, since such gifts need careful control and tutelage.

+ Positive transits
The trine will only be operative for very elderly people with Neptune in Cancer, and (towards the end of the century) for those with Neptune in Leo. The effects are much as for the conjunction, but there may be some confusing disruption. Otherwise the influence may encourage a reexamination of beliefs and perhaps a changing viewpoint on such matters. The sextile may occur for those with Neptune in Virgo and later Libra, or for children with Neptune in Capricorn. There is usually a critical element in those with Neptune in Virgo – it will be to the fore when Pluto makes this transit; again there may be a rethinking of spiritual or perhaps esoteric subjects, or confusion over such matters. Unless Pluto or Neptune are personalized the influence does not seem to be very powerful. As for the children (born after 1984/5) here is an area for research; look for any underhandedness, which may be motivated for the most altruistic reasons, but will need firm correction. There could be moodiness or a lack of attention at school because the child has become too fascinated by monsters – whether in prehistory or science fiction! Certainly the imagination will be stirred – make sure it is expressed positively.

Negative transits
The square will affect those with Neptune in Leo and, later, Virgo. Sometimes one sphere of life is thrown into disarray, with the individual experiencing a difficult and very confusing period. There may be a desire to make changes, but of which sort? That could be quite a problem. The influence is tricky to interpret, and it is possible that it may be strengthened by others operative at the time.

Sometimes there are additional burdens and frustrations, with a great deal of time and energy sacrificed in helping others. This influence can have a negative effect on the system, with the individual becoming particularly susceptible to food poisoning, so encourage keeping the diet simple.

PLUTO'S TRANSITS TO THE ASCENDANT

Note: Because Pluto moves so slowly, you may find the timing of the transits to the Ascendant or Midheaven inaccurate. This will not be due to your inexperience, but because the birth time is inaccurate; four minutes' inaccuracy will mean a difference of one degree in the position of the Ascendant or Midheaven. This will throw out the timing of Pluto's influence by several weeks. Needless to say, the less accurate the birth time, the greater the margin of error.

Conjunction
Here is a crucial transit for those with Scorpio rising. The individual may implement important changes, often to the lifestyle and sometimes in a personal relationship. Sometimes the influence will bring about important psychological developments which will have a purging effect and clear much negativity, so the subject can lead a more fulfilling and rewarding life. The transit is especially strong because Pluto is the ruling planet of Scorpio. It seems very likely that, as a result of the individual's own actions, life will become eventful. The trend will also be powerful for those with Sagittarius rising, but study Pluto's strength in your subject's birth chart to assess the potency. It will be more powerful if Pluto is personalized, of course.

Positive transits
The individual will have some kind of clearing-out, making changes and fresh starts. These might be quite simple – a redecorating plan, perhaps. The beginnings of new interests, changes in financial arrangements, can also occur. If there are psychological problems, this is a good time for starting therapy.

Negative transits
These often cause strain and block progress. The subject may feel that every avenue is obstructed. Patience is needed, for as the transit eases the chances are that the way ahead will be cleared– perhaps very suddenly.

MC PLUTO'S TRANSITS TO THE MIDHEAVEN

Conjunction
An upheaval in the career or objectives is almost certain. Sometimes the subject has the chance of a lifetime which can't be missed but causes heart-searching before being accepted. If firing seems likely, the subject's company is to be taken over, or you can see a similar danger, you should warn that this transit can often bring about such a drastic situation, and encourage your subject to start looking for a new job. Life is likely to become eventful, and there may be a considerable shakeup, although not usually as a result of a personal relationship. Sometimes the outcome can be staggeringly rewarding, with considerable financial gain, but a high price may have to be paid, perhaps due to temporary parting from a loved one.

Positive transits
New developments are likely to occur, and as a result changes may be made and new beginnings instigated. These will be due to external forces. Such developments should work out well, but will not be without an element of strain, disruption or upheaval.

Negative transits
There may be quite a lot of stress and tension as a result of upheaval in the career but it may pass without the individual having to make any important changes – especially if indications of change do not show up elsewhere in the progressed chart or through the intervention of other transits. Storms will have to be weathered, but they will stop quite suddenly as Pluto moves out of the way.

PLUTO'S TRANSITS TO ITS OWN POSITION

We do not experience a Pluto Return (we would have to be 246 years old to do so) but there are times when Pluto makes a transit to its own position.

The sextile
This occurs when Pluto has moved on two signs from its natal position. It is hard to say how old we will be when we experience it because of Pluto's erratic orbit. Those with Pluto in Virgo and Libra will be having, or have had, this transit. Think of it as supporting other trends operative at the time. If these indicative changes and new developments, Pluto will encourage and support them. If they do not show up, then the more psychological influence of Pluto may be working, with the individual undergoing some form of self-analysis and making important conclusions about his or her objectives and long-term plans. Those with Pluto in Cancer will be having, or have had, the trine transit. The above interpretation applies, perhaps with more rewarding results.

The square
While Pluto is in Scorpio it will make a square transit to those with the planet in Leo in their birth charts, and when it moves into Sagittarius it will make a square transit to those who have it in Virgo. There is often stress and sometimes a blockage of progress. Much rethinking and inner searching may go on but, as with the positive transits, the way ahead is usually clear once the indication has eased. What appear to be enforced changes may occur, but probably any enforcing is really being motivated by the individual, who may be using circumstance as protection from having to take bold action: "I must stay here because..." But that won't be the case! Sometimes realization dawns after the Pluto influence – but it depends on the inner strength and determination of the subject.

·5·

ASTROLOGICAL TABLES

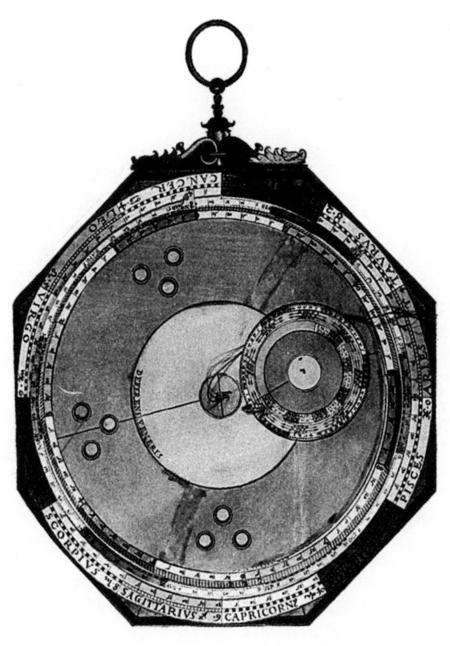

Note: In the following ephemeris, because the decimal points are always rounded up or down (i.e. 12.84 is rounded down to 12.8, and 12.89 up to 12.9), in theory a planet could appear at 0.00 of a sign when it is still in the previous one. In such cases, the planet is *always* shown as at 30.00 of the sign it actually occupies (i.e. a planet on 29.96 of Taurus will be shown as at 30.00 Taurus rather than at 0.00 Gemini).

The date on which a planet changes degrees is always shown, but because of the rounding up or down of the decimal points, the figure given for that date may not indicate the change. Remember that it is *always* to be assumed that a change of degree has taken place if a date is given for such a change.

I

	1	2	3	4	5	6	7	8	9	10	11	12	13	14	15	16	17	18	19	20	21	22	23	24	25	26	27	28	29	30	31
☉	♑ 10.1	11.1	12.1	13.1	14.1	15.2	16.2	17.2	18.2	19.2	20.2	21.3	22.3	23.3	24.3	25.3	26.4	27.4	28.4	29.4	♒ 0.4	1.4	2.5	3.5	4.5	5.5	6.5	7.5	8.6	9.6	10.6
☽	♎ 7.7	20.8	♏ 3.4	15.8	28	♐ 10	22	♑ 3.9	15.7	27.6	♒ 9.5	21.4	♓ 3.4	15.5	27.8	♈ 10.3	23.1	♉ 6.3	19.8	♊ 3.9	18.5	♋ 3.4	18.6	♌ 4	19.3	♍ 4.3	18.9	♎ 3	16.6	29.8	♏ 12.5
☿	♑ 0.8	2.4	3.9	5.5	7.1	8.7	10.2	11.8	13.4	15	16.6	18.3	19.9	21.5	23.2	24.8	26.5	28.2	29.8	♒ 1.5	3.2	4.9	6.6	8.4	10.1	11.8	13.6	15.3	17.1	18.8	20.6
♀	♒ 23.2	24.4	25.5	26.7	27.9	29	♓ 0.2	1.3	2.5	3.6	4.8	5.9	7.1	8.2	9.4	10.5	11.6	12.7	13.9	15	16.1	17.2	18.3	19.4	20.5	21.6	22.7	23.8	24.9	26	27.1
♂	♒ 26.6	27.4	28.2	29	29.8	♓ 0.5	1.3	2.1	2.9	3.6	4.4	5.2	6	6.7	7.5	8.3	9.1	9.8	10.6	11.4	12.2	12.9	13.7	14.5	15.2	16	16.8	17.6	18.3	19.1	19.9

	1	6	11	16	21	26	31
♃	♍ 18.9	18.9R	18.8	18.7	18.4	18.1	17.8
♄	♍ 24.8	24.8R	24.8	24.7	24.5	24.4	24.2

	1	11	21	31
♅	♓ 2.8	3.2	3.7	4.2
♆	♌ 13.2R	13	12.7	12.4
♇	♋ 7.8R	7.6	7.4	7.2

	1	2	3	4	5	6	7	8	9	10	11	12	13	14	15	16	17	18	19	20	21	22	23	24	25	26	27	28	29	30	31
☉	♑ 9.8	10.8	11.8	12.9	13.9	14.9	15.9	16.9	18	19	20	21	22	23.1	24.1	25.1	26.1	27.1	28.1	29.2	♒ 0.2	1.2	2.2	3.2	4.3	5.3	6.3	7.3	8.3	9.3	10.3
☽	♒ 10.8	22.7	♓ 4.6	16.3	28.2	♈ 10.1	22.3	♉ 4.7	17.6	♊ 0.9	14.7	28.9	♋ 13.6	28.5	♌ 13.6	28.6	♍ 13.5	28	♎ 12.2	26	♏ 9.5	22.7	♐ 5.6	18.3	♑ 0.8	13.1	25.3	♒ 7.4	19.3	♓ 1.2	13
☿	♑ 12.4	14	15.6	17.2	18.9	20.5	22.2	23.8	25.5	27.2	28.8	♒ 0.5	2.2	3.8	5.5	7.2	8.8	10.5	12.1	13.8	15.4	17	18.5	20	21.5	22.9	24.2	25.5	26.7	27.7	28.7
♀	♑ 0.4	1.7	2.9	4.2	5.4	6.7	7.9	9.2	10.5	11.7	13	14.2	15.5	16.8	18	19.3	20.5	21.8	23	24.3	25.5	26.8	28.1	29.3	♒ 0.6	1.8	3.1	4.3	5.6	6.9	8.1
♂	♏ 3.2	3.8	4.4	5	5.5	6.1	6.7	7.3	7.8	8.4	9	9.6	10.1	10.7	11.3	11.8	12.4	13	13.5	14.1	14.6	15.2	15.8	16.3	16.9	17.4	18	18.5	19.1	19.6	20.2

	1	6	11	16	21	26	31
♃	♎ 17.2	17.7	18.1	18.4	18.6	18.8	18.9
♄	♎ 7.4	7.5	7.6	7.6	7.6R	7.5	7.4

	1	11	21	31
♅	♓ 6.6	7	7.5	8
♆	♌ 15.5R	15.2	15	14.7
♇	♋ 9.0R	8.8	8.6	8.4

II

	1	2	3	4	5	6	7	8	9	10	11	12	13	14	15	16	17	18	19	20	21	22	23	24	25	26	27	28	29	30	31
☉	♒ 11.6	12.6	13.6	14.7	15.7	16.7	17.7	18.7	19.7	20.7	21.7	22.8	23.8	24.8	25.8	26.8	27.8	28.8	29.8	♓ 0.8	1.8	2.8	3.8	4.9	5.9	6.9	7.9	8.9			
☽	♏ 24.9	♐ 7	19	♑ 0.9	12.7	24.6	♒ 6.5	18.4	♓ 0.5	12.6	24.9	♈ 7.3	20	♉ 2.8	16	29.5	♊ 13.3	27.6	♋ 12.2	27.1	♌ 12.2	27.3	♍ 12.2	26.8	♎ 11	24.7	♏ 8	20.8			
☿	♒ 22.3	24.1	25.8	27.6	29.3	♓ 1	2.6	4.3	5.9	7.4	8.9	10.2	11.6	12.8	13.9	14.9	15.7	16.5	17	17.4	17.7	17.8R	17.7	17.4	17	16.4	15.8	14.9			
♀	♓ 28.1	29.2	♈ 0.2	1.3	2.3	3.4	4.4	5.4	6.5	7.5	8.5	9.5	10.5	11.5	12.4	13.4	14.4	15.3	16.3	17.2	18.1	19	19.9	20.8	21.7	22.6	23.4	24.2			
♂	♓ 20.6	21.4	22.2	22.9	23.7	24.5	25.2	26	26.8	27.5	28.3	29.1	29.8	♈ 0.6	1.4	2.1	2.9	3.6	4.4	5.2	5.9	6.7	7.4	8.2	8.9	9.7	10.4	11.2			

	1	6	11	16	21	26
♃	♍ 17.7R	17.2	16.7	16.1	15.5	14.9
♄	♍ 24.1R	23.9	23.6	23.3	22.9	22.5

	1	11	21
♅	♓ 4.3	4.8	5.4
♆	♌ 12.4R	12.1	11.8
♇	♋ 7.2R	7.1	6.9

	1	2	3	4	5	6	7	8	9	10	11	12	13	14	15	16	17	18	19	20	21	22	23	24	25	26	27	28	29	30	31
☉	♒ 11.4	12.4	13.4	14.4	15.4	16.4	17.4	18.5	19.5	20.5	21.5	22.5	23.5	24.5	25.5	26.5	27.6	28.6	29.6	♓ 0.6	1.6	2.6	3.6	4.6	5.6	6.6	7.6	8.6			
☽	♓ 24.8	♈ 6.6	18.5	♉ 0.7	13.1	25.8	♊ 9	22.7	♋ 6.9	21.5	♌ 6.5	21.7	♍ 7	22.2	♎ 7	21.5	♏ 5.6	19.2	♐ 2.4	15.3	27.9	♑ 10.2	22.4	♒ 4.4	16.3	28.1	♓ 10	21.8			
☿	♒ 29.5	♓ 0.2	0.7	1	1.2	1.2R	1	0.7	0.1	♒ 29.4	28.6	27.6	26.5	25.4	24.3	23.1	22	20.9	19.9	19	18.3	17.6	17	16.6	16.3	16.1	16	16.1D			
♀	♒ 9.4	10.6	11.9	13.1	14.4	15.6	16.9	18.2	19.4	20.7	21.9	23.2	24.4	25.7	26.9	28.2	29.4	♓ 0.7	1.9	3.2	4.4	5.7	6.9	8.2	9.4	10.7	11.9	13.2			
♂	♏ 20.7	21.2	21.8	22.3	22.9	23.4	23.9	24.5	25	25.5	26	26.6	27.1	27.6	28.1	28.6	29.1	29.7	♐ 0.2	0.7	1.2	1.7	2.2	2.7	3.2	3.6	4.1	4.6			

	1	6	11	16	21	26
♃	♎ 18.9	18.9R	18.8	18.6	18.4	18.1
♄	♎ 7.4R	7.3	7.1	6.8	6.6	6.3

	1	11	21
♅	♓ 8	8.6	9.1
♆	♌ 14.7R	14.4	14.1
♇	♋ 8.4R	8.2	8.1

III

	1	2	3	4	5	6	7	8	9	10	11	12	13	14	15	16	17	18	19	20	21	22	23	24	25	26	27	28	29	30	31
☉	♓ 9.9	10.9	11.9	12.9	13.9	14.9	15.9	16.9	17.9	18.9	19.9	20.9	21.9	22.9	23.9	24.9	25.9	26.9	27.9	28.9	29.8	♈ 0.8	1.8	2.8	3.8	4.8	5.8	6.8	7.8	8.8	9.7
☽	♐ 3.3	15.5	27.5	♑ 9.4	21.2	♒ 3.1	15	27.1	♓ 9.3	21.7	♈ 4.2	16.9	29.9	♉ 13	26.3	♊ 9.9	23.8	♋ 7.9	22.2	♌ 6.8	21.4	♍ 6	20.5	♎ 4.8	18.9	♏ 2.5	15.8	28.6	♐ 11.2	23.5	♑ 5.5
☿	♓ 14.1R	13.1	12.1	11	10	9	8	7.1	6.3	5.6	5	4.5	4.1	3.8	3.6	3.5	3.5D	3.6	3.8	4.1	4.5	4.9	5.5	6.1	6.7	7.5	8.3	9.1	10	11	12
♀	♈ 25.1	25.9	26.7	27.5	28.2	29	29.7	♉ 0.4	1.1	1.8	2.5	3.1	3.7	4.3	4.9	5.5	6	6.5	7	7.4	7.8	8.2	8.6	8.9	9.2	9.5	9.7	9.9	10	10.2	10.2
♂	♈ 12	12.7	13.5	14.2	15	15.7	16.5	17.2	17.9	18.7	19.4	20.2	20.9	21.7	22.4	23.2	23.9	24.6	25.4	26.1	26.9	27.6	28.3	29.1	29.8	♉ 0.5	1.3	2	2.7	3.5	4.2

	1	6	11	16	21	26	31
♃	♍ 14.5R	13.9	13.2	12.6	12	11.4	10.8
♄	♍ 22.3R	21.9	21.5	21.1	20.8	20.4	20

	1	11	21	31
♅	♓ 5.9	6.4	7	7.5
♆	♌ 11.6R	11.4	11.2	11.1
♇	♋ 6.9R	6.8	6.8	6.8D

	1	2	3	4	5	6	7	8	9	10	11	12	13	14	15	16	17	18	19	20	21	22	23	24	25	26	27	28	29	30	31
☉	♓ 9.6	10.6	11.6	12.6	13.6	14.6	15.6	16.6	17.6	18.6	19.6	20.6	21.6	22.6	23.6	24.6	25.6	26.6	27.6	28.6	29.6	♈ 0.6	1.6	2.6	3.6	4.6	5.6	6.5	7.5	8.5	9.5
☽	♈ 3.6	15.5	27.5	♉ 9.7	22.2	♊ 4.9	18	♋ 1.5	15.5	29.9	♌ 14.7	29.8	♍ 15	♎ 0.2	15.2	29.9	♏ 14.2	28	♐ 11.4	24.3	♑ 7	19.3	♒ 1.4	13.3	25.1	♓ 6.9	18.7	♈ 0.6	12.5	24.6	♉ 6.8
☿	♒ 16.2	16.5	16.8	17.2	17.7	18.3	19	19.7	20.5	21.3	22.2	23.1	24.1	25.2	26.2	27.3	28.5	29.7	♓ 0.9	2.2	3.4	4.7	6.1	7.5	8.8	10.3	11.7	13.2	14.7	16.2	17.8
♀	♓ 14.4	15.7	16.9	18.2	19.4	20.7	21.9	23.2	24.4	25.7	26.9	28.2	29.4	♈ 0.7	1.9	3.2	4.4	5.6	6.9	8.1	9.4	10.6	11.9	13.1	14.3	15.6	16.8	18.1	19.3	20.5	21.8
♂	♐ 5.1	5.6	6	6.5	7	7.5	7.9	8.4	8.8	9.3	9.7	10.2	10.6	11	11.5	11.9	12.3	12.7	13.2	13.6	14	14.4	14.8	15.2	15.6	15.9	16.3	16.7	17	17.4	17.8

	1	6	11	16	21	26	31
♃	♎ 17.8R	17.4	16.9	16.4	15.8	15.2	14.6
♄	♎ 6.1R	5.7	5.4	5	4.6	4.2	3.8

	1	11	21	31
♅	♓ 9.6	10.2	10.7	11.3
♆	♌ 13.9R	13.7	13.5	13.3
♇	♋ 8.0R	8	7.9	8.0D

IV

	1	2	3	4	5	6	7	8	9	10	11	12	13	14	15	16	17	18	19	20	21	22	23	24	25	26	27	28	29	30	31
☉	♈ 10.7	11.7	12.7	13.7	14.7	15.7	16.6	17.6	18.6	19.6	20.6	21.5	22.5	23.5	24.5	25.5	26.4	27.4	28.4	29.4	♉ 0.3	1.3	2.3	3.3	4.2	5.2	6.2	7.2	8.1	9.1	
☽	♑ 17.5	29.3	♒ 11.2	23.2	♓ 5.3	17.7	♈ 0.3	13.1	26.1	♉ 9.5	23	♊ 6.7	20.7	♋ 4.7	18.9	♌ 3.1	17.3	♍ 1.6	15.7	29.8	♎ 13.6	27.3	♏ 10.6	23.7	♐ 6.5	19	♑ 1.3	13.4	25.3	♒ 7.2	
☿	♓ 13	14.1	15.2	16.4	17.6	18.8	20.1	21.4	22.7	24.1	25.5	26.9	28.4	29.9	♈ 1.4	2.9	4.5	6.1	7.7	9.4	11.1	12.8	14.5	16.3	18.1	19.9	21.7	23.6	25.5	27.5	
♀	♉ 10.3	10.3R	10.2	10.1	10	9.9	9.7	9.4	9.1	8.8	8.4	8	7.6	7.1	6.6	6.1	5.5	4.9	4.4	3.7	3.1	2.5	1.9	1.2	0.6	♈ 30	29.4	28.8	28.2	27.7	
♂	♉ 4.9	5.7	6.4	7.1	7.8	8.6	9.3	10	10.7	11.5	12.2	12.9	13.6	14.3	15.1	15.8	16.5	17.2	17.9	18.6	19.3	20.1	20.8	21.5	22.2	22.9	23.6	24.3	25	25.7	

	1	6	11	16	21	26
♃	♍ 10.7R	10.3	9.9	9.5	9.3	9.1
♄	♍ 19.9R	19.6	19.3	19	18.7	18.5

	1	11	21
♅	♓ 7.6	8.1	8.5
♆	♌ 11.1R	11	11
♇	♋ 6.8	6.9	7

	1	2	3	4	5	6	7	8	9	10	11	12	13	14	15	16	17	18	19	20	21	22	23	24	25	26	27	28	29	30	31
☉	♈ 10.5	11.5	12.5	13.4	14.4	15.4	16.4	17.4	18.4	19.3	20.3	21.3	22.3	23.3	24.2	25.2	26.2	27.2	28.2	29.1	♉ 0.1	1.1	2.1	3	4	5	6	6.9	7.9	8.9	
☽	♉ 19.2	♊ 1.9	14.7	27.9	♋ 11.4	25.2	♌ 9.3	23.8	♍ 8.5	23.4	♎ 8.3	23.2	♏ 7.8	22.2	♐ 6.1	19.6	♑ 2.7	15.4	27.7	♒ 9.8	21.8	♓ 3.6	15.4	27.2	♈ 9.2	21.3	♉ 3.5	16	28.8	♊ 11.7	
☿	♓ 19.3	20.9	22.5	24.2	25.9	27.5	29.3	♈ 1	2.8	4.6	6.4	8.2	10.1	12	13.9	15.8	17.8	19.8	21.8	23.8	25.9	28	♉ 0.1	2.2	4.3	6.5	8.6	10.8	12.9	15	
♀	♈ 23	24.3	25.5	26.7	28	29.2	♉ 0.4	1.7	2.9	4.1	5.4	6.6	7.8	9.1	10.3	11.5	12.8	14	15.2	16.5	17.7	18.9	20.1	21.4	22.6	23.8	25	26.3	27.5	28.7	
♂	♐ 18.1	18.4	18.8	19.1	19.4	19.7	20.1	20.4	20.7	20.9	21.2	21.5	21.8	22	22.3	22.5	22.7	22.9	23.2	23.4	23.6	23.7	23.9	24.1	24.2	24.4	24.5	24.6	24.8	24.9	

	1	6	11	16	21	26
♃	♎ 14.5R	13.8	13.2	12.6	11.9	11.4
♄	♎ 3.8R	3.4	3	2.7	2.3	2

	1	11	21
♅	♓ 11.3	11.8	12.3
♆	♌ 13.3R	13.2	13.2
♇	♋ 8	8	8.1

V

	1	2	3	4	5	6	7	8	9	10	11	12	13	14	15	16	17	18	19	20	21	22	23	24	25	26	27	28	29	30	31
☉	♉ 10.1	11	12	13	14	14.9	15.9	16.9	17.8	18.8	19.8	20.7	21.7	22.7	23.6	24.6	25.5	26.5	27.5	28.4	29.4	♊ 0.4	1.3	2.3	3.2	4.2	5.2	6.1	7.1	8	9
☽	♒ 19.1	♓ 1.1	13.3	25.7	♈ 8.4	21.4	♉ 4.8	18.4	♊ 2.4	16.6	♋ 1	15.4	29.8	♌ 14.1	28.3	♍ 12.3	26.1	♎ 9.8	23.2	♏ 6.4	19.4	♐ 2.2	14.8	27.2	♑ 9.4	21.4	♒ 3.3	15.2	27.1	♓ 9.1	21.2
☿	♈ 29.4	♉ 1.4	3.4	5.5	7.6	9.7	11.8	13.9	16.1	18.2	20.4	22.6	24.8	26.9	29.1	♊ 1.3	3.4	5.5	7.6	9.7	11.7	13.7	15.7	17.6	19.4	21.3	23	24.8	26.5	28.1	29.7
♀	♈ 27.2R	26.7	26.3	25.9	25.5	25.1	24.8	24.6	24.4	24.2	24	23.9	23.9	23.9	23.9D	23.9	24	24.2	24.3	24.5	24.8	25	25.3	25.7	26	26.4	26.9	27.3	27.8	28.3	28.8
♂	♉ 26.4	27.1	27.8	28.5	29.2	29.9	♊ 0.7	1.4	2	2.7	3.4	4.1	4.8	5.5	6.2	6.9	7.6	8.3	9	9.7	10.4	11.1	11.8	12.4	13.1	13.8	14.5	15.2	15.9	16.6	17.2

	1	6	11	16	21	26	31
♃	♍ 9.0R	8.9	9.0D	9.1	9.3	9.5	9.9
♄	♍ 18.3R	18.2	18.1	18	18.0D	18	18.1

	1	11	21	31
♅	♓ 8.9	9.2	9.4	9.6
♆	♌ 11	11.1	11.2	11.4
♇	♋ 7.1	7.3	7.5	7.7

	1	2	3	4	5	6	7	8	9	10	11	12	13	14	15	16	17	18	19	20	21	22	23	24	25	26	27	28	29	30	31
☉	♉ 9.8	10.8	11.8	12.8	13.7	14.7	15.7	16.6	17.6	18.6	19.5	20.5	21.5	22.4	23.4	24.3	25.3	26.3	27.2	28.2	29.2	♊ 0.1	1.1	2	3	4	4.9	5.9	6.8	7.8	8.8
☽	♊ 24.9	♋ 8.3	21.9	♌ 5.7	19.8	♍ 4	18.3	♎ 2.8	17.3	♏ 1.8	16.1	♐ 0.3	14.1	27.6	♑ 10.7	23.4	♒ 5.8	17.9	29.8	♓ 11.7	23.5	♈ 5.4	17.4	29.6	♉ 12.1	24.9	♊ 7.9	21.3	♋ 4.9	18.6	♌ 2.6
☿	♉ 17.2	19.3	21.4	23.4	25.5	27.5	29.4	♊ 1.4	3.2	5.1	6.8	8.6	10.2	11.8	13.4	14.9	16.3	17.7	19	20.2	21.4	22.5	23.6	24.6	25.5	26.3	27.1	27.8	28.5	29	29.5
♀	♉ 29.9	♊ 1.2	2.4	3.6	4.8	6.1	7.3	8.5	9.7	10.9	12.2	13.4	14.6	15.8	17	18.2	19.5	20.7	21.9	23.1	24.3	25.5	26.7	27.9	29.2	♋ 0.4	1.6	2.8	4	5.2	6.4
♂	♐ 25	25	25.1	25.2	25.2	25.2	25.3	25.3	25.3R	25.2	25.2	25.2	25.1	25.1	25	24.9	24.8	24.7	24.5	24.4	24.2	24.1	23.9	23.7	23.5	23.3	23.1	22.8	22.6	22.4	22.1

	1	6	11	16	21	26	31
♃	♎ 10.9R	10.4	10	9.6	9.4	9.2	9
♄	♎ 1.7R	1.5	1.3	1.1	1	0.9	0.8

	1	11	21	31
♅	♓ 12.7	13	13.3	13.5
♆	♌ 13.2	13.2	13.4	13.5
♇	♋ 8.2	8.4	8.6	8.8

VI

	1	2	3	4	5	6	7	8	9	10	11	12	13	14	15	16	17	18	19	20	21	22	23	24	25	26	27	28	29	30	31
☉	♊ 10	10.9	11.9	12.8	13.8	14.7	15.7	16.7	17.6	18.6	19.5	20.5	21.4	22.4	23.3	24.3	25.3	26.2	27.2	28.1	29.1	♋ 0	1	1.9	2.9	3.8	4.8	5.7	6.7	7.7	
☽	♈ 3.6	16.3	29.4	♉ 12.9	26.9	♊ 11.2	25.8	♋ 10.6	25.5	♌ 10.2	24.8	♍ 9.1	23	♎ 6.7	20.1	♏ 3.2	16	28.7	♐ 11.2	23.6	♑ 5.8	17.8	29.8	♒ 11.7	23.5	♓ 5.4	17.4	29.5	♈ 11.8	24.5	
☿	♋ 1.2	2.7	4.1	5.5	6.9	8.1	9.4	10.5	11.6	12.7	13.7	14.7	15.5	16.4	17.1	17.8	18.4	19	19.5	19.9	20.2	20.5	20.7	20.8	20.9	20.8R	20.7	20.5	20.3	19.9	
♀	♈ 29.3	29.9	♉ 0.5	1.1	1.7	2.4	3	3.7	4.4	5.1	5.9	6.6	7.4	8.1	8.9	9.7	10.5	11.4	12.2	13	13.9	14.8	15.6	16.5	17.4	18.3	19.2	20.2	21.1	22	
♂	♊ 17.9	18.6	19.3	20	20.7	21.3	22	22.7	23.4	24	24.7	25.4	26.1	26.7	27.4	28.1	28.8	29.4	♋ 0.1	0.8	1.4	2.1	2.8	3.4	4.1	4.8	5.4	6.1	6.8	7.4	

	1	6	11	16	21	26
♃	♍ 9.9	10.3	10.8	11.3	11.9	12.6
♄	♍ 18.1	18.2	18.4	18.6	18.8	19.1

	1	11	21
♅	♓ 9.6	9.6	9.6R
♆	♌ 11.4	11.6	11.9
♇	♋ 7.7	7.9	8.2

	1	2	3	4	5	6	7	8	9	10	11	12	13	14	15	16	17	18	19	20	21	22	23	24	25	26	27	28	29	30	31
☉	♊ 9.7	10.7	11.6	12.6	13.6	14.5	15.5	16.4	17.4	18.3	19.3	20.2	21.2	22.2	23.1	24.1	25	26	26.9	27.9	28.8	29.8	♋ 0.7	1.7	2.7	3.6	4.6	5.5	6.5	7.4	
☽	♌ 16.6	♍ 0.7	14.8	29	♎ 13.1	27.2	♏ 11.3	25.2	♐ 9	22.5	♑ 5.8	18.7	♒ 1.3	13.7	25.8	♓ 7.7	19.6	♈ 1.4	13.3	25.3	♉ 7.7	20.3	♊ 3.3	16.6	♋ 0.3	14.3	28.5	♌ 12.9	27.2	♍ 11.6	
☿	♊ 30	♋ 0.3	0.6	0.7	0.9	0.9R	0.9	0.7	0.6	0.3	♊ 30	29.6	29.2	28.7	28.2	27.7	27.1	26.5	26	25.4	24.9	24.3	23.9	23.4	23.1	22.7	22.5	22.3	22.2	22.1D	
♀	♋ 7.6	8.8	10	11.2	12.4	13.6	14.8	16	17.2	18.4	19.6	20.8	22	23.2	24.4	25.6	26.8	28	29.2	♌ 0.4	1.6	2.8	4	5.1	6.3	7.5	8.7	9.9	11.1	12.2	
♂	♐ 21.8R	21.5	21.2	21	20.7	20.3	20	19.7	19.4	19.1	18.7	18.4	18.1	17.8	17.4	17.1	16.8	16.5	16.1	15.8	15.5	15.2	14.9	14.6	14.4	14.1	13.8	13.6	13.3	13.1	

	1	6	11	16	21	26
♃	♎ 9.0R	9	9.0D	9.1	9.3	9.5
♄	♎ 0.8R	0.8D	0.9	1	1.1	1.2

	1	11	21
♅	♓ 13.5	13.6	13.6R
♆	♌ 13.6	13.8	14
♇	♋ 8.8	9.1	9.3

VII

	1	2	3	4	5	6	7	8	9	10	11	12	13	14	15	16	17	18	19	20	21	22	23	24	25	26	27	28	29	30	31
☉	♋ 8.6	9.6	10.5	11.5	12.4	13.4	14.3	15.3	16.2	17.2	18.1	19.1	20	21	22	22.9	23.9	24.8	25.8	26.7	27.7	28.6	29.6	♌ 0.5	1.5	2.5	3.4	4.4	5.3	6.3	7.2
☽	♉ 7.5	21.1	♊ 5.1	19.6	♋ 4.4	19.5	♌ 4.7	19.8	♍ 4.6	19.1	♎ 3.2	16.9	♏ 0.2	13.1	25.8	♐ 8.2	20.5	♑ 2.7	14.7	26.7	♒ 8.6	20.4	♓ 2.3	14.2	26.1	♈ 8.2	20.6	♉ 3.2	16.2	29.6	♊ 13.6
☿	♋ 19.6R	19.1	18.6	18.1	17.5	16.9	16.3	15.6	15	14.4	13.8	13.3	12.8	12.3	11.9	11.6	11.4	11.2	11.2	11.2D	11.3	11.5	11.8	12.2	12.7	13.3	14	14.8	15.7	16.7	17.8
♀	♉ 23	23.9	24.9	25.8	26.8	27.8	28.8	29.8	♊ 0.8	1.8	2.8	3.8	4.8	5.8	6.8	7.9	8.9	10	11	12	13.1	14.2	15.2	16.3	17.4	18.4	19.5	20.6	21.7	22.7	23.8
♂	♋ 8.1	8.8	9.4	10.1	10.7	11.4	12.1	12.7	13.4	14	14.7	15.4	16	16.7	17.3	18	18.6	19.3	20	20.6	21.3	21.9	22.6	23.2	23.9	24.5	25.2	25.8	26.5	27.1	27.8

	1	6	11	16	21	26	31
♃	♍ 13.2	14	14.7	15.6	16.4	17.3	18.2
♄	♍ 19.4	19.7	20.1	20.5	20.9	21.4	21.9

	1	11	21	31
♅	♓ 9.5R	9.4	9.1	8.8
♆	♌ 12.2	12.5	12.9	13.2
♇	♋ 8.4	8.7	8.9	9.2

	1	2	3	4	5	6	7	8	9	10	11	12	13	14	15	16	17	18	19	20	21	22	23	24	25	26	27	28	29	30	31
☉	♋ 8.4	9.3	10.3	11.2	12.2	13.1	14.1	15.1	16	17	17.9	18.9	19.8	20.8	21.7	22.7	23.6	24.6	25.5	26.5	27.5	28.4	29.4	♌ 0.3	1.3	2.2	3.2	4.1	5.1	6	7
☽	♍ 25.8	♎ 9.9	23.9	♏ 7.8	21.5	♐ 5	18.4	♑ 1.5	14.5	27.1	♒ 9.6	21.8	♓ 3.9	15.7	27.5	♈ 9.4	21.2	♉ 3.3	15.6	28.3	♊ 11.4	24.9	♋ 8.8	23.1	♌ 7.7	22.4	♍ 7.2	21.8	♎ 6.4	20.6	♏ 4.7
☿	♊ 22.2	22.3	22.5	22.8	23.2	23.6	24.2	24.8	25.5	26.3	27.1	28.1	29.1	♋ 0.2	1.4	2.6	4	5.3	6.8	8.4	10	11.6	13.4	15.1	17	18.9	20.8	22.8	24.8	26.8	28.9
♀	♌ 13.4	14.6	15.8	17	18.1	19.3	20.5	21.7	22.8	24	25.2	26.4	27.5	28.7	29.8	♍ 1	2.2	3.3	4.5	5.7	6.8	8	9.1	10.3	11.4	12.6	13.7	14.9	16	17.1	18.3
♂	♐ 12.9R	12.7	12.5	12.3	12.1	12	11.8	11.7	11.6	11.4	11.4	11.3	11.2	11.2	11.1	11.1	11.1	11.1D	11.1	11.2	11.2	11.3	11.3	11.4	11.5	11.7	11.8	11.9	12.1	12.2	12.4

	1	6	11	16	21	26	31
♃	♎ 9.9	10.3	10.7	11.2	11.8	12.4	13.1
♄	♎ 1.5	1.7	2	2.3	2.6	3	3.4

	1	11	21	31
♅	♓ 13.5R	13.4	13.2	12.9
♆	♌ 14.3	14.7	15	15.4
♇	♋ 9.5	9.8	10	10.3

VIII

	1	2	3	4	5	6	7	8	9	10	11	12	13	14	15	16	17	18	19	20	21	22	23	24	25	26	27	28	29	30	31
☉	♌ 8.2	9.1	10.1	11.1	12	13	13.9	14.9	15.9	16.8	17.8	18.7	19.7	20.7	21.6	22.6	23.5	24.5	25.5	26.4	27.4	28.4	29.3	♍ 0.3	1.2	2.2	3.2	4.1	5.1	6.1	7
☽	♊ 28	♋ 12.8	28	♌ 13.3	28.5	♍ 13.6	28.3	♎ 12.5	26.3	♏ 9.7	22.6	♐ 5.2	17.6	29.7	♑ 11.8	23.7	♒ 5.6	17.5	29.3	♓ 11.2	23.2	♈ 5.3	17.5	29.9	♉ 12.6	25.6	♊ 9	22.8	♋ 7	21.6	♌ 6.6
☿	♋ 19	20.2	21.6	23	24.5	26.1	27.7	29.4	♌ 1.2	3	4.9	6.8	8.8	10.8	12.7	14.8	16.8	18.8	20.8	22.9	24.9	26.9	28.9	♍ 0.8	2.8	4.8	6.7	8.6	10.5	12.3	14.2
♀	♊ 24.9	26	27.1	28.2	29.3	♋ 0.4	1.5	2.7	3.8	4.9	6	7.1	8.3	9.4	10.5	11.7	12.8	13.9	15.1	16.2	17.4	18.5	19.7	20.8	22	23.1	24.3	25.4	26.6	27.8	28.9
♂	♋ 28.4	29.1	29.7	♌ 0.4	1	1.6	2.3	2.9	3.6	4.2	4.9	5.5	6.2	6.8	7.4	8.1	8.7	9.4	10	10.6	11.3	11.9	12.6	13.2	13.8	14.5	15.1	15.8	16.4	17	17.7

	1	6	11	16	21	26	31
♃	♍ 18.4	19.4	20.3	21.3	22.3	23.4	24.4
♄	♍ 22	22.5	23.1	23.6	24.2	24.8	25.4

	1	11	21	31
♅	♓ 8.8R	8.4	8.1	7.7
♆	♌ 13.3	13.7	14	14.4
♇	♋ 9.2	9.4	9.6	9.7

	1	2	3	4	5	6	7	8	9	10	11	12	13	14	15	16	17	18	19	20	21	22	23	24	25	26	27	28	29	30	31
☉	♌ 8	8.9	9.9	10.8	11.8	12.7	13.7	14.7	15.6	16.6	17.5	18.5	19.5	20.4	21.4	22.3	23.3	24.3	25.2	26.2	27.2	28.1	29.1	♍ 0	1	2	2.9	3.9	4.9	5.8	6.8
☽	♏ 18.4	♐ 1.9	15.2	28.2	♑ 11	23.6	♒ 6	18.2	♓ 0.3	12.2	24.1	♈ 5.8	17.6	29.5	♉ 11.6	23.9	♊ 6.5	19.6	♋ 3	17	♌ 1.4	16.1	♍ 1.1	16.2	♎ 1.2	16	♏ 0.6	14.8	28.6	♐ 12.1	25.2
☿	♌ 0.9	3	5.1	7.2	9.3	11.4	13.4	15.5	17.5	19.5	21.5	23.5	25.5	27.4	29.3	♍ 1.2	3.1	4.9	6.7	8.5	10.3	12	13.7	15.4	17.1	18.8	20.4	22	23.6	25.2	26.7
♀	♍ 19.4	20.6	21.7	22.8	23.9	25.1	26.2	27.3	28.4	29.6	♎ 0.7	1.8	2.9	4	5.1	6.2	7.3	8.4	9.5	10.6	11.7	12.8	13.9	15	16	17.1	18.2	19.2	20.3	21.4	22.4
♂	♐ 12.6	12.8	13	13.3	13.5	13.7	14	14.3	14.6	14.9	15.2	15.5	15.8	16.1	16.5	16.8	17.2	17.5	17.9	18.3	18.7	19.1	19.5	19.9	20.4	20.8	21.2	21.7	22.1	22.6	23.1

	1	6	11	16	21	26	31
♃	♎ 13.2	13.9	14.7	15.5	16.4	17.3	18.2
♄	♎ 3.5	4	4.4	4.9	5.5	6	6.5

	1	11	21	31
♅	♓ 12.9R	12.6	12.2	11.8
♆	♌ 15.4	15.8	16.1	16.5
♇	♋ 10.3	10.5	10.7	10.9

IX

	1	2	3	4	5	6	7	8	9	10	11	12	13	14	15	16	17	18	19	20	21	22	23	24	25	26	27	28	29	30	31
☉	♍ 8	9	9.9	10.9	11.9	12.9	13.8	14.8	15.8	16.7	17.7	18.7	19.7	20.6	21.6	22.6	23.6	24.5	25.5	26.5	27.5	28.4	29.4	♎ 0.4	1.4	2.4	3.3	4.3	5.3	6.3	
☽	♌ 21.7	♍ 6.9	21.9	♎ 6.7	21	♏ 4.9	18.4	♐ 1.4	14.1	26.5	♑ 8.6	20.6	♒ 2.5	14.3	26.2	♓ 8.1	20.2	♈ 2.3	14.6	27	♉ 9.7	22.5	♊ 5.7	19.1	♋ 2.8	16.9	♌ 1.2	15.8	♍ 0.6	15.4	
☿	♍ 16	17.8	19.6	21.3	23.1	24.8	26.5	28.2	29.8	♎ 1.5	3.1	4.7	6.3	7.9	9.4	10.9	12.4	13.9	15.4	16.9	18.3	19.8	21.2	22.5	23.9	25.3	26.6	27.9	29.2	♏ 0.4	
♀	♌ 0.1	1.3	2.4	3.6	4.8	5.9	7.1	8.3	9.5	10.7	11.9	13	14.2	15.4	16.6	17.8	19	20.2	21.4	22.6	23.8	25	26.2	27.4	28.6	29.8	♍ 1	2.2	3.4	4.6	
♂	♌ 18.3	18.9	19.6	20.2	20.8	21.5	22.1	22.7	23.4	24	24.6	25.3	25.9	26.5	27.2	27.8	28.4	29.1	29.7	♍ 0.3	1	1.6	2.2	2.8	3.5	4.1	4.7	5.4	6	6.6	

	1	6	11	16	21	26
♃	♍ 24.6	25.7	26.8	27.9	28.9	♎ 0
♄	♍ 25.5	26.1	26.7	27.3	27.9	28.6

	1	11	21
♅	♓ 7.6R	7.2	6.9
♆	♌ 14.4	14.8	15.1
♇	♋ 9.8	9.9	10

	1	2	3	4	5	6	7	8	9	10	11	12	13	14	15	16	17	18	19	20	21	22	23	24	25	26	27	28	29	30	31
☉	♍ 7.8	8.7	9.7	10.7	11.6	12.6	13.6	14.6	15.5	16.5	17.5	18.4	19.4	20.4	21.4	22.3	23.3	24.3	25.3	26.2	27.2	28.2	29.2	♎ 0.2	1.1	2.1	3.1	4.1	5.1	6	
☽	♑ 8	20.6	♒ 3	15.1	27.2	♓ 9.1	20.9	♈ 2.7	14.5	26.3	♉ 8.3	20.4	♊ 2.7	15.3	28.2	♋ 11.6	25.4	♌ 9.7	24.3	♍ 9.3	24.5	♎ 9.7	24.7	♏ 9.6	24	♐ 8	21.6	♑ 4.7	17.5	30	
☿	♍ 28.2	29.7	♎ 1.2	2.7	4.1	5.5	6.9	8.3	9.6	11	12.2	13.5	14.8	16	17.2	18.3	19.4	20.5	21.6	22.6	23.5	24.4	25.3	26.1	26.9	27.6	28.2	28.8	29.2	29.6	
♀	♎ 23.5	24.5	25.6	26.6	27.6	28.7	29.7	♏ 0.7	1.7	2.7	3.7	4.7	5.7	6.7	7.7	8.7	9.6	10.6	11.6	12.5	13.4	14.4	15.3	16.2	17.1	18	18.9	19.8	20.6	21.5	
♂	♐ 23.5	24	24.5	25	25.5	26	26.5	27	27.6	28.1	28.6	29.2	29.7	♑ 0.3	0.8	1.4	1.9	2.5	3.1	3.7	4.2	4.8	5.4	6	6.6	7.2	7.8	8.4	9	9.7	

	1	6	11	16	21	26
♃	♎ 18.4	19.3	20.3	21.3	22.3	23.4
♄	♎ 6.7	7.2	7.8	8.4	9	9.6

	1	11	21
♅	♓ 11.8R	11.4	11
♆	♌ 16.5	16.9	17.2
♇	♋ 10.9	11	11.1

X

	1	2	3	4	5	6	7	8	9	10	11	12	13	14	15	16	17	18	19	20	21	22	23	24	25	26	27	28	29	30	31
☉	♎ 7.3	8.3	9.2	10.2	11.2	12.2	13.2	14.2	15.2	16.1	17.1	18.1	19.1	20.1	21.1	22.1	23.1	24.1	25.1	26.1	27.1	28.1	29	♏ 0	1	2	3	4	5	6	7
☽	♎ 0.2	14.8	29.1	♏ 13	26.5	♐ 9.6	22.3	♑ 4.7	16.9	28.9	♒ 10.8	22.6	♓ 4.5	16.5	28.7	♈ 11	23.6	♉ 6.3	19.3	♊ 2.6	16	29.7	♋ 13.5	27.6	♌ 11.7	26	♍ 10.4	24.7	♎ 9	23.2	♏ 7.2
☿	♏ 1.7	2.9	4	5.2	6.3	7.4	8.4	9.4	10.4	11.3	12.1	12.9	13.6	14.3	14.9	15.4	15.8	16	16.2	16.3R	16.2	16	15.7	15.2	14.5	13.7	12.8	11.7	10.6	9.3	8
♀	♍ 5.9	7.1	8.3	9.5	10.7	11.9	13.2	14.4	15.6	16.8	18	19.3	20.5	21.7	23	24.2	25.4	26.6	27.9	29.1	♎ 0.3	1.6	2.8	4	5.3	6.5	7.8	9	10.2	11.5	12.7
♂	♍ 7.2	7.9	8.5	9.1	9.7	10.4	11	11.6	12.2	12.9	13.5	14.1	14.7	15.4	16	16.6	17.2	17.8	18.5	19.1	19.7	20.3	20.9	21.6	22.2	22.8	23.4	24	24.7	25.3	25.9

	1	6	11	16	21	26	31
♃	♎ 1.1	2.2	3.2	4.3	5.4	6.4	7.4
♄	♍ 29.2	29.8	♎ 0.4	1	1.6	2.2	2.7

	1	11	21	31
♅	♓ 6.5R	6.2	6	5.8
♆	♌ 15.3	15.6	15.7	15.9
♇	♋ 10	10.1R	10	10

	1	2	3	4	5	6	7	8	9	10	11	12	13	14	15	16	17	18	19	20	21	22	23	24	25	26	27	28	29	30	31
☉	♎ 7	8	9	10	11	12	12.9	13.9	14.9	15.9	16.9	17.9	18.9	19.9	20.9	21.8	22.8	23.8	24.8	25.8	26.8	27.8	28.8	29.8	♏ 0.8	1.8	2.8	3.8	4.8	5.8	6.8
☽	♒ 12.2	24.2	♓ 6.1	17.9	29.7	♈ 11.5	23.4	♉ 5.3	17.4	29.6	♊ 12	24.7	♋ 7.7	20.9	♌ 4.6	18.6	♍ 3	17.7	♎ 2.7	17.8	♏ 2.9	17.8	♐ 2.3	16.5	♑ 0.3	13.5	26.3	♒ 8.8	21	♓ 2.9	14.7
☿	♎ 29.9	♏ 0.1	0.2	0.2R	0	♎ 29.7	29.3	28.8	28.1	27.3	26.4	25.3	24.2	23	21.8	20.6	19.4	18.3	17.3	16.5	15.7	15.2	14.8	14.7	14.7D	14.9	15.3	15.8	16.5	17.3	18.3
♀	♏ 22.3	23.2	24	24.8	25.6	26.4	27.1	27.9	28.6	29.3	♐ 0	0.7	1.4	2	2.7	3.3	3.9	4.4	5	5.5	6	6.5	6.9	7.3	7.7	8.1	8.4	8.7	9	9.2	9.4
♂	♑ 10.3	10.9	11.5	12.2	12.8	13.4	14.1	14.7	15.4	16	16.7	17.3	18	18.6	19.3	19.9	20.6	21.3	22	22.6	23.3	24	24.7	25.3	26	26.7	27.4	28.1	28.8	29.5	♒ 0.2

	1	6	11	16	21	26	31
♃	♎ 24.4	25.5	26.6	27.7	28.7	29.8	♏ 0.9
♄	♎ 10.2	10.8	11.5	12.1	12.7	13.3	13.9

	1	11	21	31
♅	♓ 10.6R	10.3	10	9.8
♆	♌ 17.5	17.7	17.9	18.1
♇	♋ 11.2	11.2	11.2R	11.2

XI

	1	2	3	4	5	6	7	8	9	10	11	12	13	14	15	16	17	18	19	20	21	22	23	24	25	26	27	28	29	30	31
☉	♏ 8	9	10	11	12	13	14	15.1	16.1	17.1	18.1	19.1	20.1	21.1	22.1	23.1	24.1	25.1	26.1	27.1	28.1	29.2	♐ 0.2	1.2	2.2	3.2	4.2	5.2	6.2	7.3	
☽	♏ 20.9	♐ 4.4	17.4	♑ 0.2	12.6	24.8	♒ 6.8	18.7	♓ 0.6	12.5	24.5	♈ 6.7	19.2	♉ 2	15.1	28.5	♊ 12.2	26.1	♋ 10.2	24.4	♌ 8.6	22.8	♍ 6.9	20.9	♎ 4.9	18.8	♏ 2.5	16	29.4	♐ 12.6	
☿	♏ 6.7R	5.5	4.3	3.2	2.3	1.6	1	0.6	0.4	0.4D	0.6	1	1.5	2.1	2.9	3.8	4.8	5.9	7	8.3	9.5	10.8	12.2	13.6	15	16.4	17.9	19.4	20.9	22.4	
♀	♎ 14	15.2	16.4	17.7	18.9	20.2	21.4	22.7	23.9	25.2	26.4	27.7	28.9	♏ 0.2	1.4	2.7	3.9	5.2	6.4	7.7	8.9	10.2	11.4	12.7	13.9	15.2	16.4	17.7	18.9	20.2	
♂	♍ 26.5	27.1	27.7	28.4	29	29.6	♎ 0.2	0.8	1.4	2	2.7	3.3	3.9	4.5	5.1	5.7	6.3	6.9	7.5	8.2	8.8	9.4	10	10.6	11.2	11.8	12.4	13	13.6	14.2	

	1	6	11	16	21	26
♃	♎ 7.6	8.6	9.6	10.5	11.4	12.3
♄	♎ 2.8	3.4	3.9	4.4	4.8	5.3

	1	11	21
♅	♓ 5.8R	5.7	5.7D
♆	♌ 15.9	16	16.0R
♇	♋ 10.0R	9.9	9.7

	1	2	3	4	5	6	7	8	9	10	11	12	13	14	15	16	17	18	19	20	21	22	23	24	25	26	27	28	29	30	31
☉	♏ 7.8	8.8	9.8	10.8	11.8	12.8	13.8	14.8	15.8	16.8	17.8	18.8	19.8	20.8	21.8	22.9	23.9	24.9	25.9	26.9	27.9	28.9	29.9	♐ 0.9	1.9	3	4	5	6	7	
☽	♓ 26.5	♈ 8.3	20.2	♉ 2.2	14.3	26.6	♊ 9.1	21.8	♋ 4.6	17.7	♌ 1.1	14.6	28.5	♍ 12.6	27	♎ 11.6	26.3	♏ 11.1	25.8	♐ 10.3	24.5	♑ 8.2	21.6	♒ 4.5	17	29.2	♓ 11.1	23	♈ 4.7	16.6	
☿	♎ 19.3	20.5	21.7	23	24.3	25.7	27.1	28.6	♏ 0.1	1.6	3.2	4.7	6.3	7.9	9.4	11	12.6	14.2	15.8	17.4	19	20.6	22.2	23.7	25.3	26.9	28.5	♐ 0.1	1.6	3.2	
♀	♐ 9.6	9.7	9.8	9.8	9.8R	9.8	9.7	9.6	9.4	9.2	9	8.7	8.4	8.1	7.7	7.3	6.8	6.3	5.8	5.3	4.7	4.1	3.5	2.9	2.3	1.7	1.1	0.5	♏ 29.9	29.4	
♂	♒ 0.9	1.6	2.3	3	3.7	4.4	5.1	5.8	6.5	7.2	7.9	8.6	9.3	10	10.7	11.5	12.2	12.9	13.6	14.3	15.1	15.8	16.5	17.2	17.9	18.7	19.4	20.1	20.8	21.6	

	1	6	11	16	21	26
♃	♏ 1.1	2.2	3.3	4.4	5.4	6.5
♄	♎ 14	14.6	15.1	15.7	16.2	16.7

	1	11	21
♅	♓ 9.8R	9.7	9.7D
♆	♌ 18.1	18.2	18.2R
♇	♋ 11.1R	11.1	10.9

XII

	1	2	3	4	5	6	7	8	9	10	11	12	13	14	15	16	17	18	19	20	21	22	23	24	25	26	27	28	29	30	31
☉	♐ 8.3	9.3	10.3	11.3	12.3	13.3	14.4	15.4	16.4	17.4	18.4	19.4	20.5	21.5	22.5	23.5	24.5	25.5	26.6	27.6	28.6	29.6	♑ 0.6	1.7	2.7	3.7	4.7	5.7	6.7	7.8	8.8
☽	♐ 25.5	♑ 8.1	20.5	♒ 2.7	14.7	26.5	♓ 8.3	20.2	♈ 2.2	14.4	26.9	♉ 9.8	23.1	♊ 6.8	20.9	♋ 5.3	19.9	♌ 4.5	19.1	♍ 3.6	17.8	♎ 1.8	15.6	29.1	♏ 12.5	25.6	♐ 8.6	21.4	♑ 4	16.5	28.7
☿	♏ 23.9	25.4	26.9	28.4	30	♐ 1.5	3.1	4.6	6.1	7.7	9.2	10.8	12.3	13.9	15.5	17	18.6	20.1	21.7	23.3	24.8	26.4	28	29.6	♑ 1.2	2.7	4.3	5.9	7.5	9.1	10.7
♀	♏ 21.4	22.7	24	25.2	26.5	27.7	29	♐ 0.2	1.5	2.7	4	5.3	6.5	7.8	9	10.3	11.5	12.8	14.1	15.3	16.6	17.8	19.1	20.3	21.6	22.9	24.1	25.4	26.6	27.9	29.1
♂	♎ 14.8	15.4	16	16.6	17.2	17.8	18.4	19	19.6	20.2	20.8	21.4	22	22.6	23.2	23.8	24.4	25	25.6	26.2	26.8	27.4	27.9	28.5	29.1	29.7	♏ 0.3	0.9	1.5	2.1	2.6

	1	6	11	16	21	26	31
♃	♎ 13.1	13.9	14.7	15.4	16	16.6	17.1
♄	♎ 5.7	6	6.4	6.7	6.9	7.2	7.3

	1	11	21	31
♅	♓ 5.8	6	6.2	6.6
♆	♌ 15.9R	15.8	15.7	15.5
♇	♋ 9.6R	9.4	9.2	9

	1	2	3	4	5	6	7	8	9	10	11	12	13	14	15	16	17	18	19	20	21	22	23	24	25	26	27	28	29	30	31
☉	♐ 8	9	10	11.1	12.1	13.1	14.1	15.1	16.1	17.2	18.2	19.2	20.2	21.2	22.2	23.3	24.3	25.3	26.3	27.3	28.3	29.4	♑ 0.4	1.4	2.4	3.4	4.5	5.5	6.5	7.5	8.5
☽	♈ 28.5	♉ 10.6	22.9	♊ 5.5	18.3	♋ 1.3	14.6	28	♌ 11.6	25.3	♍ 9.2	23.2	♎ 7.3	21.5	♏ 5.8	20.2	♐ 4.5	18.6	♑ 2.5	16.1	29.4	♒ 12.2	24.8	♓ 7	19	♈ 0.8	12.6	24.4	♉ 6.4	18.6	♊ 1
☿	♐ 4.8	6.4	7.9	9.5	11.1	12.7	14.2	15.8	17.4	18.9	20.5	22.1	23.7	25.2	26.8	28.4	30	♑ 1.6	3.2	4.7	6.3	7.9	9.5	11.1	12.7	14.3	15.9	17.5	19.1	20.7	22.3
♀	♏ 28.8R	28.3	27.8	27.3	26.8	26.4	26.1	25.7	25.4	25.2	25	24.8	24.6	24.6	24.5	24.5D	24.5	24.6	24.7	24.9	25	25.3	25.5	25.8	26.1	26.5	26.9	27.3	27.8	28.2	28.7
♂	♒ 22.3	23	23.8	24.5	25.2	26	26.7	27.4	28.1	28.9	29.6	♓ 0.3	1.1	1.8	2.5	3.3	4	4.7	5.5	6.2	7	7.7	8.4	9.2	9.9	10.6	11.4	12.1	12.8	13.6	14.3

	1	6	11	16	21	26	31
♃	♏ 7.5	8.5	9.5	10.4	11.3	12.2	13.1
♄	♎ 17.1	17.6	18	18.4	18.7	19.1	19.3

	1	11	21	31
♅	♓ 9.7	9.9	10.1	10.4
♆	♌ 18.2R	18.1	17.9	17.8
♇	♋ 10.8R	10.6	10.4	10.2

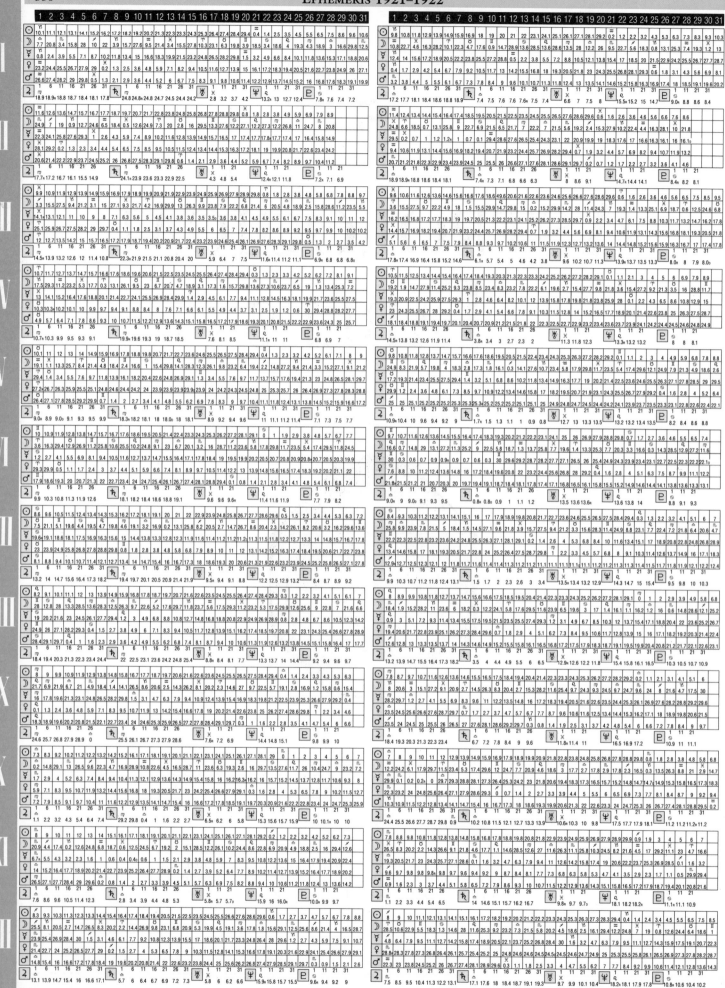

1923

I

	1	2	3	4	5	6	7	8	9	10	11	12	13	14	15	16	17	18	19	20	21	22	23	24	25	26	27	28	29	30	31
☉	♑ 9.6	10.6	11.6	12.6	13.6	14.7	15.7	16.7	17.7	18.7	19.8	20.8	21.8	22.8	23.8	24.8	25.9	26.9	27.9	28.9	29.9	♒ 1	2	3	4	5	6	7.1	8.1	9.1	10.1
☽	♊ 13.8	26.9	♋ 10.3	23.9	♌ 7.8	21.8	♍ 5.9	20	♎ 4.1	18.2	♏ 2.3	16.3	♐ 0.2	14.1	27.8	♑ 11.3	24.5	♒ 7.5	20.2	♓ 2.6	14.8	26.7	♈ 8.6	20.4	♉ 2.2	14.2	26.3	♊ 8.8	21.6	♋ 4.8	18.4
☿	♑ 23.9	25.4	27	28.5	♒ 0	1.5	3	4.4	5.8	7.1	8.4	9.6	10.7	11.7	12.6	13.4	14	14.5	14.9	15	14.9R	14.7	14.3	13.6	12.8	11.9	10.8	9.7	8.4	7.2	5.9
♀	♏ 29.3	29.8	♐ 0.4	1	1.6	2.3	2.9	3.6	4.3	5.1	5.8	6.5	7.3	8.1	8.9	9.7	10.6	11.4	12.3	13.1	14	14.9	15.8	16.7	17.6	18.6	19.5	20.5	21.4	22.4	23.4
♂	♓ 15	15.8	16.5	17.2	18	18.7	19.4	20.2	20.9	21.6	22.4	23.1	23.8	24.6	25.3	26	26.8	27.5	28.2	29	29.7	♈ 0.4	1.2	1.9	2.6	3.4	4.1	4.8	5.5	6.3	7

♃	1	6	11	16	21	26	31
	♏ 13.2	14	14.8	15.5	16.1	16.7	17.2
♄	1	6	11	16	21	26	31
	♎ 19.4	19.6	19.8	19.9	20	20.1	20.1R
♅	1	11	21	31			
	♓ 10.4	10.8	11.2	11.7			
♆	1	11	21	31			
	♌ 17.7R	17.5	17.3	17			
♇	1	11	21	31			
	♋ 10.2R	10	9.8	9.6			

II

	1	2	3	4	5	6	7	8	9	10	11	12	13	14	15	16	17	18	19	20	21	22	23	24	25	26	27	28	29	30	31
☉	♒ 11.1	12.1	13.1	14.2	15.2	16.2	17.2	18.2	19.2	20.2	21.3	22.3	23.3	24.3	25.3	26.3	27.3	28.3	29.3	♓ 0.3	1.3	2.4	3.4	4.4	5.4	6.4	7.4	8.4			
☽	♌ 2.4	16.6	♍ 1.1	15.6	♎ 0.2	14.7	29	♏ 13.2	27.1	♐ 10.9	24.4	♑ 7.6	20.7	♒ 3.6	16.2	28.6	♓ 10.8	22.9	♈ 4.8	16.6	28.4	♉ 10.2	22.2	♊ 4.3	16.7	29.5	♋ 12.6	26.2			
☿	♒ 4.7R	3.6	2.6	1.7	1	0.3	♑ 29.8	29.5	29.3	29.2	29.2D	29.4	29.6	♒ 0	0.5	1	1.6	2.3	3.1	3.9	4.8	5.7	6.7	7.7	8.7	9.8	11	12.1			
♀	♐ 24.4	25.4	26.4	27.4	28.4	29.4	♑ 0.4	1.4	2.5	3.5	4.6	5.6	6.7	7.7	8.8	9.9	10.9	12	13.1	14.2	15.3	16.4	17.5	18.6	19.7	20.8	21.9	23			
♂	♈ 7.7	8.4	9.2	9.9	10.6	11.3	12.1	12.8	13.5	14.2	15	15.7	16.4	17.1	17.8	18.6	19.3	20	20.7	21.4	22.1	22.9	23.6	24.3	25	25.7	26.4	27.1			

♃	1	6	11	16	21	26
	♏ 17.3	17.8	18.1	18.5	18.7	18.8
♄	1	6	11	16	21	26
	♎ 20.1R	20.1	20	19.9	19.7	19.5
♅	1	11	21			
	♓ 11.8	12.3	12.9			
♆	1	11	21			
	♌ 17.0R	16.7	16.4			
♇	1	11	21			
	♋ 9.6R	9.4	9.3			

III

	1	2	3	4	5	6	7	8	9	10	11	12	13	14	15	16	17	18	19	20	21	22	23	24	25	26	27	28	29	30	31
☉	♓ 9.4	10.4	11.4	12.4	13.4	14.4	15.4	16.4	17.4	18.4	19.4	20.4	21.4	22.4	23.4	24.4	25.4	26.4	27.4	28.4	29.4	♈ 0.4	1.3	2.3	3.3	4.3	5.3	6.3	7.3	8.3	9.3
☽	♌ 10.3	24.7	♍ 9.4	24.4	♎ 9.4	24.3	♏ 9	23.4	♐ 7.5	21.3	♑ 4.7	17.7	♒ 0.5	13	25.4	♓ 7.5	19.5	♈ 1.4	13.3	25.1	♉ 6.9	18.8	♊ 0.7	12.9	25.2	♋ 7.9	20.9	♌ 4.4	18.3	♍ 2.7	17.4
☿	♒ 13.4	14.6	15.8	17.1	18.5	19.8	21.2	22.6	24	25.4	26.9	28.3	29.8	♓ 1.4	2.9	4.5	6.1	7.7	9.3	10.9	12.6	14.3	16	17.7	19.5	21.3	23.1	24.9	26.7	28.6	♈ 0.5
♀	♑ 24.1	25.2	26.4	27.5	28.6	29.7	♒ 0.9	2	3.1	4.3	5.4	6.6	7.7	8.9	10	11.2	12.3	13.5	14.6	15.8	16.9	18.1	19.2	20.4	21.6	22.7	23.9	25.1	26.2	27.4	28.6
♂	♈ 27.9	28.6	29.3	30	♉ 0.7	1.4	2.1	2.8	3.5	4.2	4.9	5.6	6.3	7.1	7.8	8.5	9.2	9.9	10.6	11.3	12	12.7	13.4	14.1	14.8	15.4	16.1	16.8	17.5	18.2	18.9

♃	1	6	11	16	21	26	31
	♏ 18.9	18.9R	18.9	18.8	18.6	18.3	18
♄	1	6	11	16	21	26	31
	♎ 19.3R	19.1	18.8	18.5	18.1	17.7	17.4
♅	1	11	21	31			
	♓ 13.3	13.9	14.5	15			
♆	1	11	21	31			
	♌ 16.2R	16	15.7	15.6			
♇	1	11	21	31			
	♋ 9.2R	9.1	9.1	9.1D			

IV

	1	2	3	4	5	6	7	8	9	10	11	12	13	14	15	16	17	18	19	20	21	22	23	24	25	26	27	28	29	30	31
☉	♈ 10.3	11.2	12.2	13.2	14.2	15.2	16.2	17.1	18.1	19.1	20.1	21.1	22.1	23	24	25	26	26.9	27.9	28.9	29.9	♉ 0.9	1.8	2.8	3.8	4.7	5.7	6.7	7.7	8.6	
☽	♎ 2.5	17.7	♏ 2.9	17.9	♐ 2.7	17	♑ 1	14.4	27.4	♒ 10.1	22.5	♓ 4.6	16.6	28.5	♈ 10.3	22.1	♉ 3.9	15.8	27.7	♊ 9.8	22	♋ 4.4	17.1	♌ 0.1	13.4	27.1	♍ 11.3	25.8	♎ 10.7	25.8	
☿	♈ 2.4	4.3	6.3	8.2	10.2	12.3	14.3	16.3	18.4	20.5	22.6	24.7	26.8	28.9	♉ 1	3.1	5.1	7.2	9.2	11.2	13.2	15.1	16.9	18.7	20.5	22.2	23.8	25.4	26.9	28.4	
♀	♒ 29.8	♓ 0.9	2.1	3.3	4.5	5.6	6.8	8	9.2	10.3	11.5	12.7	13.9	15.1	16.3	17.4	18.6	19.8	21	22.2	23.4	24.6	25.8	27	28.1	29.3	♈ 0.5	1.7	2.9	4.1	
♂	♉ 19.6	20.3	21	21.7	22.4	23.1	23.8	24.4	25.1	25.8	26.5	27.2	27.9	28.6	29.2	29.9	♊ 0.6	1.3	2	2.7	3.3	4	4.7	5.4	6	6.7	7.4	8.1	8.7	9.4	

♃	1	6	11	16	21	26
	♏ 17.9R	17.5	17	16.5	15.9	15.3
♄	1	6	11	16	21	26
	♎ 17.3R	16.9	16.5	16.1	15.8	15.4
♅	1	11	21			
	♓ 15.1	15.6	16			
♆	1	11	21			
	♌ 15.6R	15.5	15.4			
♇	1	11	21			
	♋ 9.1	9.2	9.2			

V

	1	2	3	4	5	6	7	8	9	10	11	12	13	14	15	16	17	18	19	20	21	22	23	24	25	26	27	28	29	30	31
☉	♉ 9.6	10.6	11.5	12.5	13.5	14.5	15.4	16.4	17.4	18.3	19.3	20.3	21.2	22.2	23.2	24.1	25.1	26	27	28	28.9	29.9	♊ 0.9	1.8	2.8	3.7	4.7	5.7	6.6	7.6	8.5
☽	♏ 11.1	26.2	♐ 11.2	25.7	♑ 9.8	23.3	♒ 6.4	19.1	♓ 1.5	13.6	25.5	♈ 7.3	19.1	♉ 0.9	12.8	24.7	♊ 6.9	19.1	♋ 1.5	14.1	26.9	♌ 10	23.3	♍ 6.9	20.8	♎ 5.1	19.8	♏ 4.6	19.6	♐ 4.6	19.4
☿	♉ 29.7	♊ 1	2.2	3.4	4.4	5.4	6.3	7.2	7.9	8.6	9.1	9.6	10.1	10.4	10.6	10.8	10.9	10.9R	10.8	10.7	10.4	10.1	9.8	9.4	8.9	8.4	7.9	7.3	6.8	6.2	5.7
♀	♈ 5.3	6.5	7.7	8.9	10.1	11.3	12.5	13.7	14.9	16.1	17.3	18.5	19.7	20.9	22.1	23.3	24.5	25.7	26.9	28.1	29.3	♉ 0.5	1.7	2.9	4.1	5.3	6.5	7.7	8.9	10.1	11.3
♂	♊ 10.1	10.8	11.4	12.1	12.8	13.5	14.1	14.8	15.5	16.1	16.8	17.5	18.1	18.8	19.5	20.1	20.8	21.5	22.1	22.8	23.5	24.1	24.8	25.5	26.1	26.8	27.4	28.1	28.8	29.4	♋ 0.1

♃	1	6	11	16	21	26	31
	♏ 14.7R	14	13.4	12.8	12.2	11.6	11.1
♄	1	6	11	16	21	26	31
	♎ 15.1R	14.7	14.4	14.2	14	13.8	13.6
♅	1	11	21	31			
	♓ 16.5	16.8	17.1	17.3			
♆	1	11	21	31			
	♌ 15.4	15.4	15.5	15.7			
♇	1	11	21	31			
	♋ 9.4	9.5	9.7	9.9			

VI

	1	2	3	4	5	6	7	8	9	10	11	12	13	14	15	16	17	18	19	20	21	22	23	24	25	26	27	28	29	30	31
☉	♊ 9.5	10.4	11.4	12.4	13.3	14.3	15.2	16.2	17.1	18.1	19.1	20	21	21.9	22.9	23.8	24.8	25.7	26.7	27.7	28.6	29.6	♋ 0.5	1.5	2.4	3.4	4.3	5.3	6.2	7.2	
☽	♑ 3.9	18	♒ 1.6	14.8	27.5	♓ 9.9	22	♈ 3.9	15.8	27.6	♉ 9.4	21.4	♊ 3.5	15.8	28.3	♋ 11	23.9	♌ 7	20.3	♍ 3.7	17.4	♎ 1.3	15.4	29.8	♏ 14.3	28.9	♐ 13.5	28	♑ 12.2	26.2	
☿	♊ 5.1R	4.6	4.1	3.7	3.3	3	2.7	2.5	2.4	2.3	2.3D	2.4	2.6	2.8	3.1	3.5	3.9	4.5	5.1	5.8	6.5	7.3	8.2	9.2	10.2	11.3	12.4	13.6	14.9	16.2	
♀	♉ 12.5	13.7	14.9	16.1	17.3	18.5	19.7	21	22.2	23.4	24.6	25.8	27	28.2	29.4	♊ 0.6	1.8	3	4.3	5.5	6.7	7.9	9.1	10.3	11.5	12.7	14	15.2	16.4	17.6	
♂	♋ 0.7	1.4	2.1	2.7	3.4	4	4.7	5.3	6	6.6	7.3	8	8.6	9.3	9.9	10.6	11.2	11.9	12.5	13.2	13.8	14.5	15.1	15.8	16.4	17.1	17.7	18.4	19	19.7	

♃	1	6	11	16	21	26
	♏ 11.0R	10.5	10.1	9.7	9.5	9.3
♄	1	6	11	16	21	26
	♎ 13.6R	13.5	13.4	13.4	13.4D	13.4
♅	1	11	21			
	♓ 17.4	17.5	17.6			
♆	1	11	21			
	♌ 15.7	15.9	16.2			
♇	1	11	21			
	♋ 9.9	10.2	10.4			

VII

	1	2	3	4	5	6	7	8	9	10	11	12	13	14	15	16	17	18	19	20	21	22	23	24	25	26	27	28	29	30	31
☉	♋ 8.1	9.1	10.1	11	12	12.9	13.9	14.8	15.8	16.7	17.7	18.6	19.6	20.5	21.5	22.4	23.4	24.4	25.3	26.3	27.2	28.2	29.1	♌ 0.1	1	2	2.9	3.9	4.9	5.8	6.8
☽	♒ 9.7	22.8	♓ 5.5	17.9	♈ 0.1	12	23.9	♉ 5.7	17.6	29.7	♊ 11.9	24.4	♋ 7.2	20.2	♌ 3.4	16.8	♍ 0.5	14.3	28.2	♎ 12.2	26.4	♏ 10.6	24.8	♐ 9.1	23.2	♑ 7.3	21.1	♒ 4.7	17.9	♓ 0.9	13.5
☿	♊ 17.6	19.1	20.6	22.2	23.8	25.5	27.2	29	♋ 0.9	2.8	4.7	6.7	8.7	10.8	12.8	14.9	17	19.2	21.3	23.4	25.6	27.7	29.8	♌ 1.9	4	6.1	8.1	10.2	12.2	14.2	16.1
♀	♊ 18.8	20	21.3	22.5	23.7	24.9	26.1	27.3	28.6	29.8	♋ 1	2.2	3.4	4.7	5.9	7.1	8.3	9.5	10.8	12	13.2	14.4	15.7	16.9	18.1	19.3	20.6	21.8	23	24.2	25.5
♂	♋ 20.3	20.9	21.6	22.2	22.9	23.5	24.2	24.8	25.5	26.1	26.8	27.4	28	28.7	29.3	30	♌ 0.6	1.3	1.9	2.5	3.2	3.8	4.5	5.1	5.7	6.4	7	7.7	8.3	8.9	9.6

♃	1	6	11	16	21	26	31
	♏ 9.1R	9.1	9.1D	9.2	9.3	9.6	9.9
♄	1	6	11	16	21	26	31
	♎ 13.5	13.7	13.8	14.1	14.3	14.6	14.9
♅	1	11	21	31			
	♓ 17.5R	17.4	17.3	17			
♆	1	11	21	31			
	♌ 16.5	16.8	17.1	17.5			
♇	1	11	21	31			
	♋ 10.7	10.9	11.2	11.4			

VIII

	1	2	3	4	5	6	7	8	9	10	11	12	13	14	15	16	17	18	19	20	21	22	23	24	25	26	27	28	29	30	31
☉	♌ 7.7	8.7	9.6	10.6	11.6	12.5	13.5	14.4	15.4	16.4	17.3	18.3	19.2	20.2	21.2	22.1	23.1	24	25	26	26.9	27.9	28.8	29.8	♍ 0.8	1.7	2.7	3.7	4.6	5.6	6.6
☽	♓ 25.8	♈ 8	19.9	♉ 1.8	13.7	25.6	♊ 7.7	20	♋ 2.6	15.5	28.7	♌ 12.2	26.1	♍ 10.1	24.4	♎ 8.7	23	♏ 7.4	21.6	♐ 5.7	19.7	♑ 3.5	17.1	♒ 0.5	13.7	26.6	♓ 9.3	21.7	♈ 3.9	16	27.9
☿	♌ 18	19.9	21.8	23.7	25.5	27.3	29	♍ 0.8	2.5	4.2	5.8	7.5	9.1	10.7	12.2	13.8	15.3	16.8	18.2	19.6	21	22.4	23.8	25.1	26.4	27.7	28.9	♎ 0.1	1.3	2.4	3.5
♀	♋ 26.7	27.9	29.2	♌ 0.4	1.6	2.8	4.1	5.3	6.5	7.8	9	10.2	11.5	12.7	13.9	15.2	16.4	17.6	18.9	20.1	21.4	22.6	23.8	25.1	26.3	27.5	28.8	♍ 0	1.3	2.5	3.7
♂	♌ 10.2	10.9	11.5	12.1	12.8	13.4	14.1	14.7	15.3	16	16.6	17.2	17.9	18.5	19.2	19.8	20.4	21.1	21.7	22.3	23	23.6	24.3	24.9	25.5	26.2	26.8	27.4	28.1	28.7	29.3

♃	1	6	11	16	21	26	31
	♏ 10	10.3	10.8	11.3	11.9	12.5	13.2
♄	1	6	11	16	21	26	31
	♎ 15	15.4	15.8	16.2	16.6	17.1	17.6
♅	1	11	21	31			
	♓ 17.0R	16.7	16.3	15.9			
♆	1	11	21	31			
	♌ 17.5	17.9	18.3	18.6			
♇	1	11	21	31			
	♋ 11.4	11.7	11.9	12			

IX

	1	2	3	4	5	6	7	8	9	10	11	12	13	14	15	16	17	18	19	20	21	22	23	24	25	26	27	28	29	30	31
☉	♍ 7.5	8.5	9.5	10.4	11.4	12.4	13.4	14.3	15.3	16.3	17.2	18.2	19.2	20.2	21.1	22.1	23.1	24.1	25	26	27	28	28.9	29.9	♎ 0.9	1.9	2.9	3.8	4.8	5.8	
☽	♉ 9.8	21.6	♊ 3.6	15.6	27.9	♋ 10.5	23.4	♌ 6.8	20.5	♍ 4.6	19	♎ 3.6	18.4	♏ 3.2	17.9	♐ 2.3	16.5	♑ 0.4	14	27.3	♒ 10.4	23.1	♓ 5.7	18.1	♈ 0.3	12.4	24.4	♉ 6.2	18.1	29.9	
☿	♎ 4.5	5.6	6.5	7.5	8.4	9.2	10	10.7	11.3	11.9	12.4	12.9	13.3	13.5	13.7	13.8	13.8R	13.6	13.4	13	12.5	11.9	11.2	10.4	9.5	8.5	7.4	6.3	5.2	4.1	
♀	♍ 5	6.2	7.5	8.7	9.9	11.2	12.4	13.7	14.9	16.2	17.4	18.6	19.9	21.1	22.4	23.6	24.9	26.1	27.3	28.6	29.8	♎ 1.1	2.3	3.6	4.8	6.1	7.3	8.6	9.8	11.1	
♂	♌ 30	♍ 0.6	1.3	1.9	2.5	3.2	3.8	4.4	5.1	5.7	6.3	7	7.6	8.3	8.9	9.5	10.2	10.8	11.4	12.1	12.7	13.3	14	14.6	15.2	15.9	16.5	17.2	17.8	18.4	

♃	1	6	11	16	21	26
	♏ 13.3	14.1	14.9	15.7	16.6	17.5
♄	1	6	11	16	21	26
	♎ 17.7	18.2	18.8	19.3	19.9	20.5
♅	1	11	21			
	♓ 15.9R	15.5	15.1			
♆	1	11	21			
	♌ 18.7	19	19.3			
♇	1	11	21			
	♋ 12	12.2	12.3			

X

	1	2	3	4	5	6	7	8	9	10	11	12	13	14	15	16	17	18	19	20	21	22	23	24	25	26	27	28	29	30	31
☉	♎ 6.8	7.8	8.8	9.7	10.7	11.7	12.7	13.7	14.7	15.7	16.7	17.6	18.6	19.6	20.6	21.6	22.6	23.6	24.6	25.6	26.6	27.6	28.6	29.6	♏ 0.6	1.6	2.6	3.5	4.5	5.5	6.5
☽	♊ 11.9	23.9	♋ 6.1	18.6	♌ 1.5	14.7	28.4	♍ 12.6	27.2	♎ 12.1	27.2	♏ 12.4	27.4	♐ 12.2	26.6	♑ 10.6	24.2	♒ 7.4	20.2	♓ 2.7	15.1	27.2	♈ 9.2	21.2	♉ 3.1	14.9	26.8	♊ 8.7	20.6	♋ 2.7	14.9
☿	♎ 3.0R	2	1.1	0.3	♍ 29.7	29.2	28.9	28.8	28.9D	29.1	29.5	♎ 0	0.8	1.6	2.6	3.7	4.9	6.1	7.5	8.9	10.4	11.9	13.4	15	16.6	18.2	19.9	21.5	23.2	24.8	26.5
♀	♎ 12.3	13.5	14.8	16	17.3	18.5	19.8	21	22.3	23.5	24.8	26	27.3	28.5	29.8	♏ 1	2.3	3.5	4.8	6	7.3	8.5	9.8	11	12.3	13.5	14.8	16	17.3	18.5	19.7
♂	♍ 19.1	19.7	20.3	21	21.6	22.3	22.9	23.5	24.2	24.8	25.4	26.1	26.7	27.3	28	28.6	29.3	29.9	♎ 0.5	1.2	1.8	2.4	3.1	3.7	4.4	5	5.6	6.3	6.9	7.6	8.2

♃	1	6	11	16	21	26	31
	♏ 18.4	19.4	20.4	21.4	22.4	23.5	24.6
♄	1	6	11	16	21	26	31
	♎ 21.1	21.7	22.3	22.9	23.5	24.1	24.7
♅	1	11	21	31			
	♓ 14.7R	14.4	14.1	13.9			
♆	1	11	21	31			
	♌ 19.6	19.9	20.1	20.2			
♇	1	11	21	31			
	♋ 12.4	12.4	12.4R	12.3			

XI

	1	2	3	4	5	6	7	8	9	10	11	12	13	14	15	16	17	18	19	20	21	22	23	24	25	26	27	28	29	30	31
☉	♏ 7.5	8.5	9.5	10.6	11.6	12.6	13.6	14.6	15.6	16.6	17.6	18.6	19.6	20.6	21.6	22.6	23.6	24.6	25.6	26.6	27.7	28.7	29.7	♐ 0.7	1.7	2.7	3.7	4.7	5.7	6.8	
☽	♋ 27.4	♌ 10.1	23.2	♍ 6.8	20.8	♎ 5.2	20.1	♏ 5.3	20.7	♐ 5.9	21	♑ 5.7	19.9	♒ 3.6	16.8	29.6	♓ 12.1	24.3	♈ 6.3	18.2	♉ 0.1	11.9	23.8	♊ 5.7	17.7	29.8	♋ 12	24.3	♌ 6.8	19.5	
☿	♎ 28.2	29.8	♏ 1.5	3.1	4.8	6.4	8.1	9.7	11.3	13	14.6	16.2	17.8	19.4	21	22.6	24.2	25.8	27.4	28.9	♐ 0.5	2.1	3.6	5.2	6.8	8.3	9.9	11.4	13	14.6	
♀	♏ 21	22.2	23.5	24.7	26	27.2	28.5	29.7	♐ 1	2.2	3.5	4.7	6	7.2	8.5	9.7	11	12.2	13.5	14.7	16	17.2	18.5	19.7	21	22.2	23.5	24.7	26	27.2	
♂	♎ 8.8	9.5	10.1	10.7	11.4	12	12.7	13.3	13.9	14.6	15.2	15.9	16.5	17.1	17.8	18.4	19.1	19.7	20.3	21	21.6	22.3	22.9	23.5	24.2	24.8	25.5	26.1	26.7	27.4	

♃	1	6	11	16	21	26
	♏ 24.8	25.9	27	28.1	29.2	♐ 0.3
♄	1	6	11	16	21	26
	♎ 24.8	25.4	26	26.6	27.1	27.7
♅	1	11	21			
	♓ 13.9R	13.7	13.6			
♆	1	11	21			
	♌ 20.3	20.4	20.4			
♇	1	11	21			
	♋ 12.3R	12.2	12.1			

XII

	1	2	3	4	5	6	7	8	9	10	11	12	13	14	15	16	17	18	19	20	21	22	23	24	25	26	27	28	29	30	31
☉	♐ 7.8	8.8	9.8	10.8	11.8	12.8	13.9	14.9	15.9	16.9	17.9	18.9	20	21	22	23	24	25	26.1	27.1	28.1	29.1	♑ 0.1	1.2	2.2	3.2	4.2	5.2	6.3	7.3	8.3
☽	♍ 2.6	16	29.8	♎ 14	28.6	♏ 13.6	28.8	♐ 14	29	♑ 13.8	28.1	♒ 12	25.3	♓ 8.2	20.7	♈ 3	15	26.9	♉ 8.7	20.6	♊ 2.5	14.5	26.6	♋ 8.9	21.3	♌ 3.9	16.6	29.5	♍ 12.7	26.1	♎ 9.8
☿	♐ 16.1	17.7	19.2	20.7	22.3	23.8	25.4	26.9	28.5	30	♑ 1.5	3.1	4.6	6.1	7.6	9.1	10.6	12	13.5	14.9	16.3	17.7	19	20.3	21.6	22.8	23.9	24.9	25.9	26.8	27.5
♀	♐ 28.5	29.7	♑ 0.9	2.2	3.4	4.7	5.9	7.2	8.4	9.7	10.9	12.2	13.4	14.7	15.9	17.2	18.4	19.6	20.9	22.1	23.4	24.6	25.9	27.1	28.4	29.6	♒ 0.8	2.1	3.3	4.6	5.8
♂	♎ 28	28.7	29.3	30	♏ 0.6	1.2	1.9	2.5	3.2	3.8	4.4	5.1	5.7	6.4	7	7.7	8.3	8.9	9.6	10.2	10.9	11.5	12.1	12.8	13.4	14.1	14.7	15.4	16	16.6	17.3

♃	1	6	11	16	21	26	31
	♐ 1.4	2.5	3.6	4.7	5.8	6.9	7.9
♄	1	6	11	16	21	26	31
	♎ 28.2	28.7	29.2	29.7	♏ 0.1	0.5	0.8
♅	1	11	21	31			
	♓ 13.7	13.8	14	14.2			
♆	1	11	21	31			
	♌ 20.4R	20.3	20.2	20			
♇	1	11	21	31			
	♋ 12.0R	11.8	11.6	11.4			

1924

I

	1	2	3	4	5	6	7	8	9	10	11	12	13	14	15	16	17	18	19	20	21	22	23	24	25	26	27	28	29	30	31
☉	♑ 9.3	10.3	11.3	12.4	13.4	14.4	15.4	16.4	17.5	18.5	19.5	20.5	21.5	22.6	23.6	24.6	25.6	26.6	27.7	28.7	29.7	♒ 0.7	1.7	2.7	3.8	4.8	5.8	6.8	7.8	8.8	9.9
☽	♎ 23.8	♏ 8.2	22.7	♐ 7.5	22.4	♑ 7.1	21.7	♒ 5.9	19.8	♓ 3.2	16.2	28.8	♈ 11.1	23.1	♉ 5.1	16.9	28.8	♊ 10.7	22.8	♋ 5.1	17.6	♌ 0.2	13.1	26.2	♍ 9.5	23	♎ 6.7	20.6	♏ 4.6	18.8	♐ 3
☿	♑ 28.1	28.5	28.8	29	28.9R	28.6	28.2	27.5	26.7	25.6	24.5	23.3	22	20.6	19.3	18.1	16.9	15.9	15	14.3	13.7	13.2	13	12.8	12.8D	13	13.2	13.6	14	14.6	15.2
♀	♒ 7	8.3	9.5	10.8	12	13.2	14.5	15.7	17	18.2	19.4	20.7	21.9	23.1	24.4	25.6	26.8	28.1	29.3	♓ 0.5	1.8	3	4.2	5.5	6.7	7.9	9.1	10.4	11.6	12.8	14
♂	♏ 17.9	18.6	19.2	19.9	20.5	21.1	21.8	22.4	23.1	23.7	24.4	25	25.6	26.3	26.9	27.6	28.2	28.9	29.5	♐ 0.1	0.8	1.4	2.1	2.7	3.3	4	4.6	5.3	5.9	6.6	7.2

♃	1	6	11	16	21	26	31
	♐ 8.1	9.1	10.1	11.1	12	12.9	13.8
♄	1	6	11	16	21	26	31
	♏ 0.9	1.2	1.5	1.7	2	2.1	2.2
♅	1	11	21	31			
	♓ 14.2	14.6	15	15.5			
♆	1	11	21	31			
	♌ 20.0R	19.8	19.5	19.3			
♇	1	11	21	31			
	♋ 11.4R	11.2	11	10.8			

II

	1	2	3	4	5	6	7	8	9	10	11	12	13	14	15	16	17	18	19	20	21	22	23	24	25	26	27	28	29	30	31
☉	♒ 10.9	11.9	12.9	13.9	14.9	15.9	17	18	19	20	21	22	23	24	25	26.1	27.1	28.1	29.1	♓ 0.1	1.1	2.1	3.1	4.1	5.1	6.1	7.1	8.1	9.1		
☽	♐ 17.4	♑ 1.8	16	♒ 0.2	14.1	27.7	♓ 10.9	23.9	♈ 6.5	18.8	♉ 0.9	12.9	24.8	♊ 6.7	18.6	♋ 0.7	13.1	25.7	♌ 8.5	21.7	♍ 5.2	19	♎ 3	17.1	♏ 1.3	15.6	29.8	♐ 14	28.1		
☿	♑ 16	16.7	17.6	18.5	19.5	20.5	21.5	22.6	23.7	24.9	26.1	27.3	28.6	29.8	♒ 1.1	2.5	3.8	5.2	6.6	8	9.4	10.8	12.3	13.8	15.3	16.8	18.4	19.9	21.5		
♀	♓ 15.2	16.5	17.7	18.9	20.1	21.3	22.5	23.8	25	26.2	27.4	28.6	29.8	♈ 1	2.2	3.4	4.6	5.8	7	8.2	9.4	10.6	11.8	13	14.2	15.3	16.5	17.7	18.9		
♂	♐ 7.8	8.5	9.1	9.8	10.4	11	11.7	12.3	13	13.6	14.2	14.9	15.5	16.2	16.8	17.4	18.1	18.7	19.3	20	20.6	21.3	21.9	22.5	23.2	23.8	24.4	25.1	25.7		

♃	1	6	11	16	21	26
	♐ 14	14.8	15.5	16.2	16.9	17.5
♄	1	6	11	16	21	26
	♏ 2.3	2.3	2.3R	2.3	2.3	2.1
♅	1	11	21			
	♓ 15.5	16	16.6			
♆	1	11	21			
	♌ 19.2R	19	18.7			
♇	1	11	21			
	♋ 10.7R	10.6	10.4			

III

	1	2	3	4	5	6	7	8	9	10	11	12	13	14	15	16	17	18	19	20	21	22	23	24	25	26	27	28	29	30	31
☉	♓ 10.2	11.2	12.2	13.2	14.2	15.2	16.2	17.2	18.2	19.2	20.2	21.2	22.2	23.2	24.1	25.1	26.1	27.1	28.1	29.1	♈ 0.1	1.1	2.1	3.1	4.1	5.1	6.1	7	8	9	10
☽	♑ 12.1	25.9	♒ 9.5	23	♓ 6.2	19.1	♈ 1.9	14.4	26.7	♉ 8.8	20.7	♊ 2.6	14.5	26.4	♋ 8.5	20.8	♌ 3.4	16.4	29.7	♍ 13.5	27.6	♎ 12	26.7	♏ 11.4	26	♐ 10.6	24.9	♑ 9	22.8	♒ 6.3	19.5
☿	♒ 23.1	24.7	26.3	27.9	29.6	♓ 1.3	3	4.7	6.4	8.2	9.9	11.7	13.5	15.4	17.2	19.1	21	22.9	24.8	26.8	28.7	♈ 0.7	2.7	4.7	6.7	8.8	10.8	12.8	14.9	16.9	19
♀	♈ 20.1	21.3	22.4	23.6	24.8	25.9	27.1	28.3	29.4	♉ 0.6	1.7	2.9	4.1	5.2	6.3	7.5	8.6	9.8	10.9	12	13.2	14.3	15.4	16.5	17.7	18.8	19.9	21	22.1	23.2	24.3
♂	♐ 26.3	27	27.6	28.2	28.9	29.5	♑ 0.1	0.8	1.4	2	2.7	3.3	3.9	4.5	5.2	5.8	6.4	7.1	7.7	8.3	8.9	9.5	10.2	10.8	11.4	12	12.7	13.3	13.9	14.5	15.1

♃	1	6	11	16	21	26	31
	♐ 17.9	18.4	18.9	19.2	19.5	19.7	19.9
♄	1	6	11	16	21	26	31
	♏ 2.0R	1.9	1.6	1.4	1.1	0.8	0.5
♅	1	11	21	31			
	♓ 17.1	17.7	18.2	18.8			
♆	1	11	21	31			
	♌ 18.4R	18.2	18	17.8			
♇	1	11	21	31			
	♋ 10.4R	10.3	10.2	10.3D			

IV

	1	2	3	4	5	6	7	8	9	10	11	12	13	14	15	16	17	18	19	20	21	22	23	24	25	26	27	28	29	30	31
☉	♈ 11	12	13	14	14.9	15.9	16.9	17.9	18.9	19.9	20.8	21.8	22.8	23.8	24.8	25.7	26.7	27.7	28.7	29.6	♉ 0.6	1.6	2.6	3.5	4.5	5.5	6.5	7.4	8.4	9.4	
☽	♓ 2.6	15.4	28	♈ 10.5	22.8	♉ 5	17	28.9	♊ 10.8	22.6	♋ 4.5	16.6	28.8	♌ 11.4	24.3	♍ 7.6	21.5	♎ 5.7	20.4	♏ 5.4	20.5	♐ 5.6	20.5	♑ 5.1	19.3	♒ 3.1	16.6	29.7	♓ 12.4	25	
☿	♈ 21	23	24.9	26.9	28.7	♉ 0.6	2.4	4.1	5.8	7.4	8.9	10.4	11.8	13.1	14.3	15.4	16.4	17.3	18.2	18.9	19.6	20.1	20.6	20.9	21.2	21.3	21.4	21.3R	21.2	21	
♀	♉ 25.4	26.5	27.5	28.6	29.7	♊ 0.8	1.8	2.9	4	5	6.1	7.1	8.1	9.2	10.2	11.2	12.2	13.2	14.2	15.2	16.2	17.2	18.1	19.1	20	21	21.9	22.9	23.8	24.7	
♂	♑ 15.7	16.4	17	17.6	18.2	18.8	19.4	20	20.6	21.2	21.9	22.5	23.1	23.7	24.3	24.9	25.5	26.1	26.7	27.2	27.8	28.4	29	29.6	♒ 0.2	0.8	1.4	1.9	2.5	3.1	

♃	1	6	11	16	21	26
	♐ 19.9	19.9	19.9R	19.8	19.6	19.3
♄	1	6	11	16	21	26
	♏ 0.4R	0	♎ 29.7	29.3	28.9	28.5
♅	1	11	21			
	♓ 18.8	19.4	19.8			
♆	1	11	21			
	♌ 17.8R	17.7	17.6			
♇	1	11	21			
	♋ 10.3	10.3	10.4			

V

	1	2	3	4	5	6	7	8	9	10	11	12	13	14	15	16	17	18	19	20	21	22	23	24	25	26	27	28	29	30	31
☉	♉ 10.3	11.3	12.3	13.3	14.2	15.2	16.2	17.1	18.1	19.1	20	21	22	22.9	23.9	24.8	25.8	26.8	27.7	28.7	29.7	♊ 0.6	1.6	2.5	3.5	4.5	5.4	6.4	7.3	8.3	9.3
☽	♈ 7.4	19.6	♉ 1.7	13.7	25.6	♊ 7.5	19.4	♋ 1.2	13.1	25.2	♌ 7.4	19.9	♍ 2.7	16	29.7	♎ 13.9	28.6	♏ 13.7	29	♐ 14.3	29.5	♑ 14.3	28.8	♒ 12.7	26.2	♓ 9.3	22.1	♈ 4.5	16.7	28.8	♉ 10.8
☿	♉ 20.8R	20.4	20	19.5	19	18.4	17.8	17.2	16.6	16	15.4	14.8	14.3	13.8	13.4	13	12.7	12.4	12.2	12.1	12.1	12.1D	12.2	12.4	12.7	13	13.4	13.9	14.4	15.1	15.7
♀	♊ 25.6	26.5	27.4	28.2	29.1	29.9	♋ 0.8	1.6	2.4	3.2	4	4.8	5.5	6.2	7	7.7	8.4	9	9.7	10.3	10.9	11.5	12.1	12.6	13.2	13.7	14.1	14.6	15	15.4	15.8
♂	♒ 3.7	4.3	4.8	5.4	6	6.5	7.1	7.7	8.2	8.8	9.3	9.9	10.4	11	11.5	12	12.6	13.1	13.6	14.2	14.7	15.2	15.7	16.3	16.8	17.3	17.8	18.3	18.8	19.3	19.7

♃	1	6	11	16	21	26	31
	♐ 19.0R	18.6	18.1	17.6	17	16.4	15.8
♄	1	6	11	16	21	26	31
	♎ 28.1R	27.8	27.4	27.1	26.8	26.5	26.3
♅	1	11	21	31			
	♓ 20.3	20.7	21	21.2			
♆	1	11	21	31			
	♌ 17.6	17.6	17.7	17.9			
♇	1	11	21	31			
	♋ 10.5	10.7	10.9	11.1			

VI

	1	2	3	4	5	6	7	8	9	10	11	12	13	14	15	16	17	18	19	20	21	22	23	24	25	26	27	28	29	30	31
☉	♊ 10.2	11.2	12.1	13.1	14	15	16	16.9	17.9	18.8	19.8	20.7	21.7	22.7	23.6	24.6	25.5	26.5	27.4	28.4	29.3	♋ 0.3	1.2	2.2	3.1	4.1	5.1	6	7	7.9	
☽	♉ 22.7	♊ 4.6	16.4	28.3	♋ 10.2	22.2	♌ 4.3	16.6	29.1	♍ 11.9	25.1	♎ 8.7	22.8	♏ 7.3	22.3	♐ 7.4	22.7	♑ 7.9	22.8	♒ 7.4	21.5	♓ 5.1	18.3	♈ 1.1	13.5	25.7	♉ 7.8	19.7	♊ 1.6	13.4	
☿	♉ 16.5	17.3	18.2	19.1	20.1	21.1	22.2	23.4	24.6	25.8	27.1	28.5	29.9	♊ 1.4	2.9	4.4	6	7.7	9.4	11.2	13	14.8	16.7	18.6	20.6	22.6	24.7	26.7	28.8	♋ 1	
♀	♋ 16.1	16.4	16.7	16.9	17.1	17.3	17.4	17.5	17.6	17.6	17.6R	17.5	17.4	17.3	17.1	16.9	16.6	16.3	16	15.6	15.2	14.7	14.3	13.8	13.2	12.7	12.1	11.5	10.9	10.3	
♂	♒ 20.2	20.7	21.2	21.6	22.1	22.6	23	23.5	23.9	24.3	24.8	25.2	25.6	26	26.4	26.8	27.2	27.6	28	28.4	28.7	29.1	29.4	29.8	♓ 0.1	0.4	0.7	1	1.3	1.6	

♃	1	6	11	16	21	26
	♐ 15.7R	15	14.4	13.8	13.2	12.6
♄	1	6	11	16	21	26
	♎ 26.3R	26.1	25.9	25.8	25.7	25.6
♅	1	11	21			
	♓ 21.3	21.4	21.5			
♆	1	11	21			
	♌ 17.9	18.1	18.3			
♇	1	11	21			
	♋ 11.1	11.3	11.6			

VII

	1	2	3	4	5	6	7	8	9	10	11	12	13	14	15	16	17	18	19	20	21	22	23	24	25	26	27	28	29	30	31
☉	♋ 8.9	9.8	10.8	11.7	12.7	13.6	14.6	15.5	16.5	17.5	18.4	19.4	20.3	21.3	22.2	23.2	24.1	25.1	26	27	27.9	28.9	29.9	♌ 0.8	1.8	2.7	3.7	4.6	5.6	6.5	7.5
☽	♊ 25.3	♋ 7.2	19.3	♌ 1.4	13.7	26.2	♍ 8.9	21.8	♎ 5	18.6	♏ 2.6	16.9	♐ 1.5	16.4	♑ 1.4	16.3	♒ 1.1	15.6	29.7	♓ 13.4	26.6	♈ 9.5	22	♉ 4.3	16.3	28.2	♊ 10.1	22	♋ 3.9	15.9	28.1
☿	♋ 3.1	5.3	7.4	9.6	11.8	14	16.1	18.3	20.4	22.5	24.6	26.7	28.7	♌ 0.7	2.7	4.7	6.6	8.5	10.4	12.2	14	15.8	17.5	19.3	20.9	22.6	24.2	25.8	27.4	29	♍ 0.5
♀	♋ 9.7R	9	8.4	7.8	7.2	6.6	6	5.5	4.9	4.4	3.9	3.5	3.1	2.7	2.4	2.1	1.8	1.6	1.4	1.3	1.1	1.1	1.1	1.1D	1.1	1.2	1.3	1.5	1.7	1.9	2.2
♂	♓ 1.9	2.2	2.4	2.7	2.9	3.2	3.4	3.6	3.8	4	4.1	4.3	4.5	4.6	4.7	4.8	4.9	5	5.1	5.2	5.2	5.3	5.3	5.3	5.3R	5.3	5.3	5.2	5.2	5.1	5

♃	1	6	11	16	21	26	31
	♐ 12.1R	11.6	11.2	10.8	10.5	10.3	10.1
♄	1	6	11	16	21	26	31
	♎ 25.6	25.7	25.7	25.9	26	26.2	26.5
♅	1	11	21	31			
	♓ 21.5R	21.4	21.3	21.1			
♆	1	11	21	31			
	♌ 18.6	18.9	19.3	19.6			
♇	1	11	21	31			
	♋ 11.8	12.1	12.3	12.6			

VIII

	1	2	3	4	5	6	7	8	9	10	11	12	13	14	15	16	17	18	19	20	21	22	23	24	25	26	27	28	29	30	31
☉	♌ 8.5	9.4	10.4	11.3	12.3	13.2	14.2	15.2	16.1	17.1	18	19	20	20.9	21.9	22.8	23.8	24.8	25.7	26.7	27.7	28.6	29.6	♍ 0.5	1.5	2.5	3.4	4.4	5.4	6.3	7.3
☽	♌ 10.5	23.1	♍ 5.8	18.8	♎ 2	15.5	29.2	♏ 13.1	27.3	♐ 11.7	26.2	♑ 10.7	25.3	♒ 9.7	23.9	♓ 7.8	21.4	♈ 4.6	17.5	♉ 0	12.3	24.4	♊ 6.3	18.2	♋ 0.1	12.1	24.2	♌ 6.5	19.1	♍ 2	15.1
☿	♍ 1.9	3.4	4.8	6.2	7.6	8.9	10.2	11.5	12.7	13.9	15	16.1	17.2	18.3	19.3	20.2	21.1	21.9	22.7	23.5	24.1	24.8	25.3	25.8	26.2	26.5	26.7	26.9	26.9	26.9R	26.8
♀	♋ 2.5	2.8	3.2	3.5	4	4.4	4.9	5.4	5.9	6.4	7	7.5	8.2	8.8	9.4	10.1	10.8	11.5	12.2	12.9	13.6	14.4	15.2	16	16.8	17.6	18.4	19.2	20.1	20.9	21.8
♂	♓ 4.9R	4.8	4.7	4.6	4.4	4.3	4.1	3.9	3.8	3.6	3.4	3.2	2.9	2.7	2.5	2.2	2	1.7	1.5	1.2	1	0.7	0.4	0.2	♒ 29.9	29.6	29.4	29.1	28.9	28.6	28.4

♃	1	6	11	16	21	26	31
	♐ 10.1R	10.1	10.1D	10.2	10.4	10.6	10.9
♄	1	6	11	16	21	26	31
	♎ 26.5	26.8	27.1	27.5	27.8	28.2	28.7
♅	1	11	21	31			
	♓ 21.0R	20.7	20.4	20			
♆	1	11	21	31			
	♌ 19.7	20	20.4	20.8			
♇	1	11	21	31			
	♋ 12.6	12.8	13	13.2			

IX

	1	2	3	4	5	6	7	8	9	10	11	12	13	14	15	16	17	18	19	20	21	22	23	24	25	26	27	28	29	30	31
☉	♍ 8.3	9.2	10.2	11.2	12.1	13.1	14.1	15.1	16	17	18	18.9	19.9	20.9	21.9	22.8	23.8	24.8	25.8	26.8	27.7	28.7	29.7	♎ 0.7	1.6	2.6	3.6	4.6	5.6	6.6	
☽	♍ 28.5	♎ 12.1	26	♏ 10	24.1	♐ 8.3	22.5	♑ 6.7	20.9	♒ 4.9	18.9	♓ 2.7	16.3	29.6	♈ 12.7	25.5	♉ 8	20.2	♊ 2.3	14.2	26.1	♋ 8	19.9	♌ 2.1	14.5	27.2	♍ 10.3	23.8	♎ 7.6	21.7	
☿	♍ 26.5R	26.2	25.7	25.1	24.5	23.7	22.9	22	21.1	20.1	19	18	17	16.1	15.3	14.5	13.9	13.3	13	12.8	12.7D	12.8	13.1	13.6	14.2	14.9	15.8	16.8	17.9	19.1	
♀	♋ 22.7	23.6	24.5	25.4	26.3	27.3	28.2	29.1	♌ 0.1	1.1	2	3	4	5	6	7	8	9	10	11.1	12.1	13.2	14.2	15.3	16.3	17.4	18.4	19.5	20.6	21.7	
♂	♒ 28.1R	27.9	27.7	27.4	27.2	27	26.8	26.7	26.5	26.3	26.2	26	25.9	25.8	25.7	25.6	25.5	25.5	25.4	25.4	25.3	25.3	25.3D	25.3	25.4	25.4	25.5	25.5	25.6	25.7	

♃	1	6	11	16	21	26
	♐ 11	11.4	11.9	12.4	13	13.7
♄	1	6	11	16	21	26
	♎ 28.8	29.2	29.7	♏ 0.2	0.8	1.3
♅	1	11	21			
	♓ 20.0R	19.6	19.2			
♆	1	11	21			
	♌ 20.8	21.2	21.5			
♇	1	11	21			
	♋ 13.2	13.4	13.5			

X

	1	2	3	4	5	6	7	8	9	10	11	12	13	14	15	16	17	18	19	20	21	22	23	24	25	26	27	28	29	30	31
☉	♎ 7.5	8.5	9.5	10.5	11.5	12.5	13.5	14.4	15.4	16.4	17.4	18.4	19.4	20.4	21.4	22.4	23.4	24.3	25.3	26.3	27.3	28.3	29.3	♏ 0.3	1.3	2.3	3.3	4.3	5.3	6.3	7.3
☽	♏ 6	20.4	♐ 4.9	19.3	♑ 3.5	17.6	♒ 1.5	15.3	28.8	♓ 12.2	25.4	♈ 8.4	21.2	♉ 3.7	16.1	28.3	♊ 10.3	22.2	♋ 4	15.9	27.8	♌ 9.9	22.3	♍ 5.1	18.2	♎ 1.8	15.9	♏ 0.3	15.1	30	♐ 14.9
☿	♍ 20.5	21.9	23.3	24.9	26.4	28.1	29.7	♎ 1.4	3.1	4.8	6.6	8.3	10	11.8	13.5	15.3	17	18.7	20.4	22.1	23.9	25.5	27.2	28.9	♏ 0.6	2.2	3.9	5.5	7.2	8.8	10.4
♀	♌ 22.8	23.8	24.9	26	27.1	28.2	29.4	♍ 0.5	1.6	2.7	3.8	5	6.1	7.2	8.4	9.5	10.6	11.8	12.9	14.1	15.2	16.4	17.6	18.7	19.9	21.1	22.2	23.4	24.6	25.7	26.9
♂	♒ 25.8	25.9	26.1	26.2	26.4	26.6	26.7	26.9	27.1	27.3	27.6	27.8	28.1	28.3	28.6	28.9	29.2	29.5	29.8	♓ 0.1	0.4	0.7	1.1	1.4	1.8	2.2	2.5	2.9	3.3	3.7	4.1

♃	1	6	11	16	21	26	31
	♐ 14.4	15.1	15.9	16.8	17.7	18.6	19.5
♄	1	6	11	16	21	26	31
	♏ 1.9	2.4	3	3.6	4.2	4.8	5.4
♅	1	11	21	31			
	♓ 18.8R	18.5	18.1	17.9			
♆	1	11	21	31			
	♌ 21.8	22	22.3	22.4			
♇	1	11	21	31			
	♋ 13.5	13.6	13.6R	13.5			

XI

	1	2	3	4	5	6	7	8	9	10	11	12	13	14	15	16	17	18	19	20	21	22	23	24	25	26	27	28	29	30	31
☉	♏ 8.3	9.3	10.3	11.3	12.3	13.3	14.3	15.3	16.3	17.3	18.3	19.3	20.4	21.4	22.4	23.4	24.4	25.4	26.4	27.4	28.4	29.4	♐ 0.4	1.5	2.5	3.5	4.5	5.5	6.5	7.5	
☽	♐ 29.6	♑ 14.1	28.3	♒ 12.2	25.8	♓ 9.1	22.1	♈ 5	17.6	♉ 0.1	12.5	24.7	♊ 6.7	18.7	♋ 0.5	12.3	24.1	♌ 6	18.1	♍ 0.4	13.1	26.2	♎ 9.7	23.8	♏ 8.4	23.3	♐ 8.5	23.7	♑ 8.8	23.7	
☿	♏ 12	13.6	15.2	16.8	18.4	19.9	21.5	23.1	24.6	26.2	27.7	29.2	♐ 0.8	2.3	3.8	5.3	6.9	8.4	9.9	11.4	12.9	14.3	15.8	17.3	18.8	20.2	21.7	23.1	24.5	25.9	
♀	♍ 28.1	29.3	♎ 0.5	1.7	2.8	4	5.2	6.4	7.6	8.8	10	11.2	12.4	13.6	14.8	16	17.3	18.5	19.7	20.9	22.1	23.3	24.5	25.8	27	28.2	29.4	♏ 0.6	1.9	3.1	
♂	♓ 4.5	4.9	5.4	5.8	6.2	6.7	7.1	7.6	8	8.5	9	9.5	9.9	10.4	10.9	11.4	11.9	12.4	12.9	13.4	14	14.5	15	15.5	16.1	16.6	17.1	17.7	18.2	18.8	

♃	1	6	11	16	21	26
	♐ 19.7	20.7	21.8	22.8	23.9	25
♄	1	6	11	16	21	26
	♏ 5.5	6.1	6.7	7.3	7.9	8.5
♅	1	11	21			
	♓ 17.9R	17.7	17.6			
♆	1	11	21			
	♌ 22.4	22.5	22.6			
♇	1	11	21			
	♋ 13.5R	13.4	13.3			

XII

	1	2	3	4	5	6	7	8	9	10	11	12	13	14	15	16	17	18	19	20	21	22	23	24	25	26	27	28	29	30	31
☉	♐ 8.5	9.6	10.6	11.6	12.6	13.6	14.6	15.6	16.7	17.7	18.7	19.7	20.7	21.7	22.8	23.8	24.8	25.8	26.8	27.9	28.9	29.9	♑ 0.9	1.9	2.9	4	5	6	7	8	9.1
☽	♒ 8.1	22.2	♓ 5.8	19.1	♈ 2	14.7	27.1	♉ 9.4	21.5	♊ 3.6	15.5	27.4	♋ 9.2	21	♌ 2.9	14.8	26.9	♍ 9.2	21.8	♎ 4.8	18.2	♏ 2.1	16.5	♐ 1.3	16.4	♑ 1.7	17	♒ 2.1	16.8	♓ 1.1	15
☿	♐ 27.3	28.7	♑ 0	1.3	2.6	3.9	5.1	6.3	7.4	8.4	9.4	10.3	11	11.7	12.3	12.7	13	13	13.0R	12.7	12.2	11.6	10.7	9.7	8.5	7.2	5.9	4.5	3.2	1.9	0.7
♀	♏ 4.3	5.5	6.8	8	9.2	10.5	11.7	12.9	14.1	15.4	16.6	17.8	19.1	20.3	21.6	22.8	24	25.3	26.5	27.7	29	♐ 0.2	1.5	2.7	3.9	5.2	6.4	7.7	8.9	10.2	11.4
♂	♓ 19.3	19.9	20.5	21	21.6	22.1	22.7	23.3	23.9	24.4	25	25.6	26.2	26.8	27.4	28	28.5	29.1	29.7	♈ 0.3	0.9	1.5	2.1	2.7	3.3	4	4.6	5.2	5.8	6.4	7

♃	1	6	11	16	21	26	31
	♐ 26.1	27.2	28.4	29.5	♑ 0.6	1.8	2.9
♄	1	6	11	16	21	26	31
	♏ 9.1	9.6	10.1	10.6	11.1	11.6	12
♅	1	11	21	31			
	♓ 17.6	17.7	17.8	18.1			
♆	1	11	21	31			
	♌ 22.6R	22.5	22.4	22.2			
♇	1	11	21	31			
	♋ 13.1R	13	12.8	12.6			

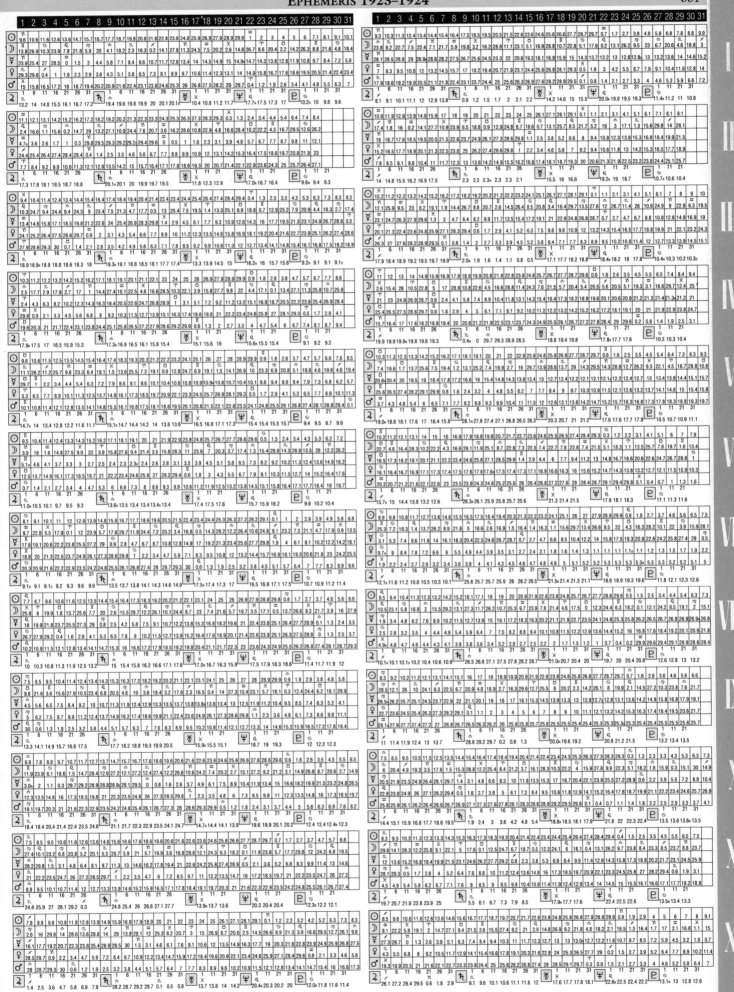

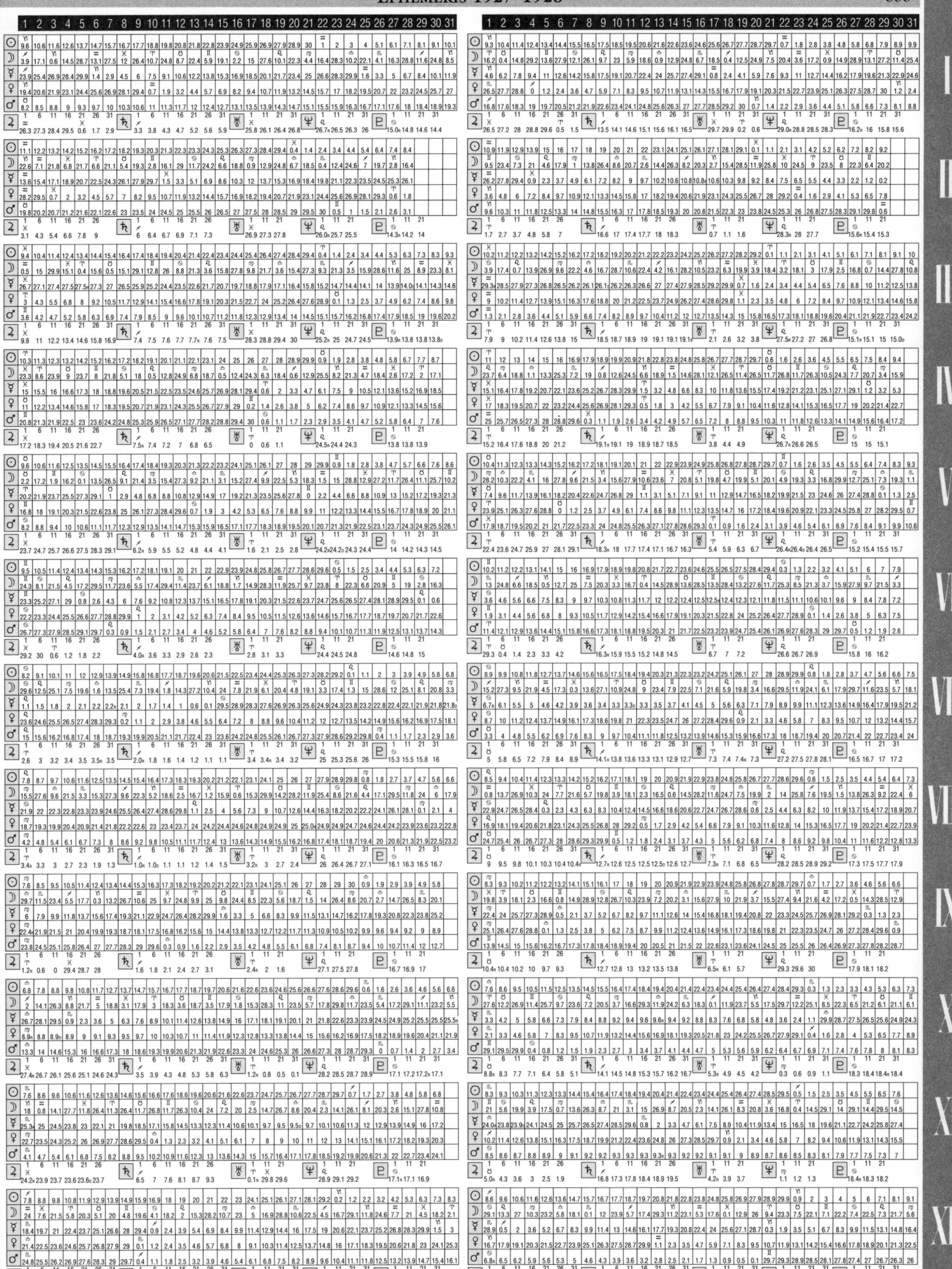

I

1929

	1	2	3	4	5	6	7	8	9	10	11	12	13	14	15	16	17	18	19	20	21	22	23	24	25	26	27	28	29	30	31
☉	♑10.1	11.1	12.2	13.2	14.2	15.2	16.2	17.2	18.3	19.3	20.3	21.3	22.3	23.4	24.4	25.4	26.4	27.4	28.5	29.5	♒0.5	1.5	2.5	3.5	4.6	5.6	6.6	7.6	8.6	9.6	10.7
☽	♍19.1	♎2.1	14.6	26.9	♏8.9	20.8	♐2.5	14.3	26.1	♑8	20.1	♒2.3	14.6	27.2	♓9.9	22.8	♈6	19.4	♉3.1	17.1	♊1.4	15.9	♋0.7	15.6	♌0.4	15.1	29.5	♍13.5	27.1	♎10.1	22.8
☿	♑18	19.6	21.3	22.9	24.6	26.2	27.8	29.5	♒1.1	2.7	4.3	5.9	7.5	9.1	10.6	12.1	13.6	15	16.4	17.7	18.9	20.1	21.1	22	22.8	23.5	23.9	24.3	24.4	24.3R	24.1
♀	♒23.6	24.8	26	27.1	28.3	29.4	♓0.6	1.7	2.9	4	5.2	6.3	7.5	8.6	9.7	10.8	12	13.1	14.2	15.3	16.4	17.5	18.6	19.7	20.8	21.9	23	24.1	25.1	26.2	27.3
♂	♊25.6R	25.3	25	24.7	24.4	24.1	23.8	23.5	23.3	23	22.8	22.6	22.4	22.2	22	21.9	21.7	21.6	21.5	21.4	21.3	21.2	21.1	21.1	21	21	21	21.0D	21	21	21.1

♃ 1: ♉0.5 · 6: 0.7 · 11: 0.9 · 16: 1.2 · 21: 1.6 · 26: 2.1 · 31: 2.6 — ♄ 1: ♐23.7 · 6: 24.3 · 11: 24.8 · 16: 25.4 · 21: 25.9 · 26: 26.4 · 31: 26.9 — ♅ 1: ♈3.6 · 11: 3.8 · 21: 4.1 · 31: 4.5 — ♆ 1: ♍1.2R · 11: 1 · 21: 0.8 · 31: 0.5 — ♇ 1: ♋17.5R · 11: 17.2 · 21: 17 · 31: 16.8

1930

	1	2	3	4	5	6	7	8	9	10	11	12	13	14	15	16	17	18	19	20	21	22	23	24	25	26	27	28	29	30	31
☉	♑9.9	10.9	11.9	12.9	13.9	15	16	17	18	19	20.1	21.1	22.1	23.1	24.1	25.2	26.2	27.2	28.2	29.2	♒0.2	1.3	2.3	3.3	4.3	5.3	6.3	7.4	8.4	9.4	10.4
☽	♑20.9	♒2.7	14.6	26.5	♓8.4	20.6	♈2.9	15.4	28.4	♉11.7	25.5	♊9.8	24.6	♋9.8	25.1	♌10.5	25.7	♍10.5	24.9	♎8.8	22.2	♏5.1	17.7	♐0	12.1	24.1	♑6	17.8	29.7	♒11.6	23.5
☿	♑28.1	29.4	♒0.7	2	3.1	4.2	5.2	6	6.8	7.4	7.9	8.1	8.3	8.2R	7.9	7.4	6.8	5.9	4.9	3.8	2.6	1.3	0	♑28.8	27.6	26.4	25.4	24.6	23.8	23.2	22.8
♀	♑1.1	2.3	3.6	4.9	6.1	7.4	8.6	9.9	11.1	12.4	13.7	14.9	16.2	17.4	18.7	19.9	21.2	22.5	23.7	25	26.2	27.5	28.7	30	♒1.3	2.5	3.8	5	6.3	7.5	8.8
♂	♑1.9	2.7	3.4	4.2	4.9	5.7	6.4	7.2	8	8.7	9.5	10.2	11	11.8	12.5	13.3	14	14.8	15.6	16.3	17.1	17.9	18.6	19.4	20.2	20.9	21.7	22.5	23.2	24	24.8

♃ 1: ♊7.9R · 6: 7.4 · 11: 7.1 · 16: 6.8 · 21: 6.5 · 26: 6.4 · 31: 6.4 — ♄ 1: ♑3.7 · 6: 4.3 · 11: 4.9 · 16: 5.5 · 21: 6 · 26: 6.6 · 31: 7.1 — ♅ 1: ♈7.6 · 11: 7.7 · 21: 8 · 31: 8.3 — ♆ 1: ♍3.4R · 11: 3.2 · 21: 3 · 31: 2.8 — ♇ 1: ♋18.7R · 11: 18.5 · 21: 18.3 · 31: 18.1

II

1929

	1	2	3	4	5	6	7	8	9	10	11	12	13	14	15	16	17	18	19	20	21	22	23	24	25	26	27	28	29	30	31
☉	♒11.7	12.7	13.7	14.7	15.7	16.7	17.8	18.8	19.8	20.8	21.8	22.8	23.8	24.8	25.8	26.9	27.9	28.9	29.9	♓0.9	1.9	2.9	3.9	4.9	5.9	6.9	7.9	8.9			
☽	♏5.1	17.2	29	♐10.8	22.6	♑4.5	16.5	28.7	♒11.1	23.7	♓6.6	19.7	♈3	16.4	30	♉13.7	27.6	♊11.7	26	♋10.3	24.8	♌9.2	23.5	♍7.6	21.4	♎4.9	17.9	♏0.6			
☿	♒23.7R	23.1	22.3	21.4	20.4	19.3	18.1	16.9	15.7	14.6	13.5	12.5	11.6	10.8	10.2	9.7	9.3	9	8.9	8.9D	9	9.2	9.5	9.9	10.4	11	11.6	12.3			
♀	♓28.3	29.4	♈0.4	1.5	2.5	3.5	4.5	5.6	6.6	7.6	8.5	9.5	10.5	11.5	12.4	13.4	14.3	15.2	16.2	17.1	18	18.9	19.7	20.6	21.4	22.3	23.1	23.9			
♂	♊21.1	21.2	21.3	21.3	21.4	21.5	21.7	21.8	21.9	22.1	22.2	22.4	22.6	22.8	23	23.2	23.4	23.6	23.9	24.1	24.3	24.6	24.9	25.1	25.4	25.7	26	26.3			

♃ 1: ♉2.7 · 6: 3.3 · 11: 4 · 16: 4.8 · 21: 5.6 · 26: 6.4 — ♄ 1: ♐27 · 6: 27.5 · 11: 27.9 · 16: 28.3 · 21: 28.7 · 26: 29.1 — ♅ 1: ♈4.5 · 11: 4.9 · 21: 5.4 — ♆ 1: ♍0.5R · 11: 0.2 · 21: ♌30 — ♇ 1: ♋16.8R · 11: 16.6 · 21: 16.5

1930

	1	2	3	4	5	6	7	8	9	10	11	12	13	14	15	16	17	18	19	20	21	22	23	24	25	26	27	28	29	30	31
☉	♒11.4	12.4	13.5	14.5	15.5	16.5	17.5	18.5	19.5	20.5	21.6	22.6	23.6	24.6	25.6	26.6	27.6	28.6	29.6	♓0.6	1.7	2.7	3.7	4.7	5.7	6.7	7.7	8.7			
☽	♓5.5	17.6	29.8	♈12.2	24.8	♉7.6	20.9	♊4.5	18.6	♋3.1	18	♌3.2	18.4	♍3.6	18.6	♎3.1	17.1	♏0.7	13.8	26.5	♐8.8	20.9	♑2.9	14.7	26.6	♒8.4	20.4	♓2.4			
☿	♑22.5R	22.3	22.3D	22.4	22.6	22.9	23.3	23.8	24.4	25.1	25.8	26.6	27.5	28.4	29.4	♒0.4	1.4	2.5	3.7	4.8	6	7.3	8.5	9.8	11.1	12.4	13.8	15.2			
♀	♒10	11.3	12.6	13.8	15.1	16.3	17.6	18.8	20.1	21.3	22.6	23.8	25.1	26.4	27.6	28.9	♓0.1	1.4	2.6	3.9	5.1	6.4	7.6	8.9	10.1	11.4	12.6	13.9			
♂	♑25.5	26.3	27.1	27.9	28.6	29.4	♒0.2	1	1.7	2.5	3.3	4.1	4.8	5.6	6.4	7.2	7.9	8.7	9.5	10.3	11.1	11.8	12.6	13.4	14.2	15	15.7	16.5			

♃ 1: ♊6.4D · 6: 6.4 · 11: 6.5 · 16: 6.8 · 21: 7.1 · 26: 7.4 — ♄ 1: ♑7.2 · 6: 7.7 · 11: 8.2 · 16: 8.7 · 21: 9.1 · 26: 9.6 — ♅ 1: ♈8.3 · 11: 8.7 · 21: 9.2 — ♆ 1: ♍2.8R · 11: 2.5 · 21: 2.2 — ♇ 1: ♋18.1R · 11: 17.9 · 21: 17.7

III

1929

	1	2	3	4	5	6	7	8	9	10	11	12	13	14	15	16	17	18	19	20	21	22	23	24	25	26	27	28	29	30	31
☉	♓9.9	10.9	11.9	12.9	13.9	14.9	16	17	18	18.9	19.9	20.9	21.9	22.9	23.9	24.9	25.9	26.9	27.9	28.9	29.9	♈0.9	1.9	2.9	3.9	4.9	5.9	6.8	7.8	8.8	9.8
☽	♏12.9	25	♐6.9	18.7	♑0.5	12.4	24.5	♒6.8	19.4	♓2.3	15.5	28.9	♈12.6	26.5	♉10.4	24.5	♊8.6	22.7	♋6.8	20.9	♌5	19	♍2.8	16.5	29.9	♎13	25.9	♏8.4	20.7	♐2.8	14.7
☿	♒13.1	13.9	14.8	15.7	16.7	17.7	18.8	19.9	21.1	22.2	23.4	24.7	26	27.3	28.6	29.9	♓1.3	2.7	4.2	5.6	7.1	8.6	10.1	11.7	13.3	14.8	16.5	18.1	19.8	21.4	23.2
♀	♈24.7	25.5	26.2	27	27.7	28.4	29.1	29.8	♉0.5	1.1	1.7	2.3	2.9	3.4	3.9	4.4	4.9	5.3	5.7	6.1	6.5	6.8	7.1	7.3	7.5	7.7	7.9	8	8	8	8.0R
♂	♊26.6	26.9	27.2	27.6	27.9	28.2	28.6	28.9	29.3	29.7	♋0	0.4	0.8	1.2	1.5	1.9	2.3	2.7	3.1	3.5	4	4.4	4.8	5.2	5.6	6.1	6.5	7	7.4	7.8	8.3

♃ 1: ♉6.9 · 6: 7.8 · 11: 8.8 · 16: 9.8 · 21: 10.8 · 26: 11.9 · 31: 12.9 — ♄ 1: ♐29.3 · 6: 29.5 · 11: 29.8 · 16: ♑0 · 21: 0.2 · 26: 0.3 · 31: 0.4 — ♅ 1: ♈5.8 · 11: 6.4 · 21: 6.9 · 31: 7.5 — ♆ 1: ♌29.7R · 11: 29.5 · 21: 29.2 · 31: 29 — ♇ 1: ♋16.4R · 11: 16.3 · 21: 16.2 · 31: 16.2D

1930

	1	2	3	4	5	6	7	8	9	10	11	12	13	14	15	16	17	18	19	20	21	22	23	24	25	26	27	28	29	30	31
☉	♓9.7	10.7	11.7	12.7	13.7	14.7	15.7	16.7	17.7	18.7	19.7	20.7	21.7	22.7	23.7	24.7	25.7	26.7	27.7	28.7	29.7	♈0.7	1.6	2.6	3.6	4.6	5.6	6.6	7.6	8.6	9.6
☽	♓14.5	26.8	♈9.3	21.9	♉4.7	17.7	♊1	14.6	28.5	♋12.7	27.3	♌12.1	27	♍11.8	26.5	♎10.9	25	♏8.6	21.8	♐4.5	17	29.2	♑11.2	23	♒4.9	16.8	28.8	♓10.9	23.2	♈5.8	18.5
☿	♒16.6	18	19.4	20.9	22.4	23.9	25.4	27	28.5	♓0.1	1.7	3.3	5	6.6	8.3	10	11.7	13.5	15.2	17	18.8	20.6	22.5	24.3	26.2	28.1	♈0.1	2	4	6	8
♀	♓15.1	16.4	17.6	18.9	20.1	21.4	22.6	23.9	25.1	26.4	27.6	28.8	♈0.1	1.3	2.6	3.8	5.1	6.3	7.6	8.8	10	11.3	12.5	13.8	15	16.3	17.5	18.7	20	21.2	22.4
♂	♒17.3	18.1	18.9	19.6	20.4	21.2	22	22.8	23.6	24.3	25.1	25.9	26.7	27.5	28.2	29	29.8	♓0.6	1.4	2.2	2.9	3.7	4.5	5.3	6.1	6.9	7.6	8.4	9.2	10	10.8

♃ 1: ♊7.7 · 6: 8.2 · 11: 8.8 · 16: 9.4 · 21: 10 · 26: 10.8 · 31: 11.6 — ♄ 1: ♑9.8 · 6: 10.2 · 11: 10.5 · 16: 10.8 · 21: 11.1 · 26: 11.3 · 31: 11.5 — ♅ 1: ♈9.6 · 11: 10.1 · 21: 10.7 · 31: 11.2 — ♆ 1: ♍2.0R · 11: 1.7 · 21: 1.5 · 31: 1.3 — ♇ 1: ♋17.6R · 11: 17.5 · 21: 17.5 · 31: 17.4

IV

1929

	1	2	3	4	5	6	7	8	9	10	11	12	13	14	15	16	17	18	19	20	21	22	23	24	25	26	27	28	29	30	31
☉	♈10.8	11.8	12.8	13.7	14.7	15.7	16.7	17.7	18.7	19.6	20.6	21.6	22.6	23.6	24.5	25.5	26.5	27.5	28.5	29.4	♉0.4	1.4	2.4	3.3	4.3	5.3	6.3	7.2	8.2	9.2	
☽	♐26.5	♑8.4	20.3	♒2.4	14.7	27.4	♓10.4	23.8	♈7.5	21.5	♉5.8	20.2	♊4.7	19.2	♋3.5	17.8	♌1.8	15.7	29.4	♍12.8	26.1	♎9.1	21.8	♏4.4	16.7	28.9	♐10.9	22.7	♑4.6	16.4	
☿	♓24.9	26.6	28.4	♈0.2	2	3.9	5.8	7.7	9.6	11.5	13.5	15.5	17.5	19.5	21.6	23.7	25.8	27.9	30	♉2.1	4.2	6.4	8.5	10.6	12.7	14.8	16.9	18.9	20.9	22.8	
♀	♉8.0R	7.9	7.7	7.6	7.3	7.1	6.8	6.4	6.1	5.7	5.2	4.7	4.2	3.7	3.1	2.5	1.9	1.3	0.7	0.1	♈29.4	28.8	28.2	27.6	27	26.4	25.8	25.3	24.8	24.3	
♂	♋8.7	9.2	9.7	10.1	10.6	11.1	11.5	12	12.5	13	13.4	13.9	14.4	14.9	15.4	15.9	16.4	16.9	17.4	17.9	18.4	18.9	19.4	19.9	20.4	20.9	21.5	22	22.5	23	

♃ 1: ♉13.2 · 6: 14.3 · 11: 15.4 · 16: 16.5 · 21: 17.7 · 26: 18.9 — ♄ 1: ♑0.5 · 6: 0.5 · 11: 0.5R · 16: 0.5 · 21: 0.4 · 26: 0.3 — ♅ 1: ♈7.6 · 11: 8.1 · 21: 8.7 — ♆ 1: ♌29.0R · 11: 28.8 · 21: 28.7 — ♇ 1: ♋16.2 · 11: 16.2 · 21: 16.3

1930

	1	2	3	4	5	6	7	8	9	10	11	12	13	14	15	16	17	18	19	20	21	22	23	24	25	26	27	28	29	30	31
☉	♈10.6	11.5	12.5	13.5	14.5	15.5	16.5	17.4	18.4	19.4	20.4	21.4	22.4	23.3	24.3	25.3	26.3	27.2	28.2	29.2	♉0.2	1.2	2.1	3.1	4.1	5	6	7	8	8.9	
☽	♉1.4	14.6	27.9	♊11.5	25.3	♋9.2	23.4	♌7.7	22.1	♍6.5	20.9	♎5.2	19.2	♏3	16.4	29.6	♐12.3	24.8	♑7	19.1	♒1	12.9	24.8	♓6.8	19	♈1.5	14.2	27.2	♉10.5	24	
☿	♈10	12	14.1	16.1	18.2	20.3	22.4	24.5	26.5	28.6	♉0.6	2.6	4.6	6.5	8.4	10.3	12.1	13.8	15.5	17.1	18.7	20.2	21.6	22.9	24.1	25.3	26.4	27.4	28.3	29.1	
♀	♈23.7	24.9	26.2	27.4	28.6	29.9	♉1.1	2.3	3.6	4.8	6	7.3	8.5	9.7	11	12.2	13.4	14.7	15.9	17.1	18.3	19.6	20.8	22	23.3	24.5	25.7	26.9	28.2	29.4	
♂	♓11.5	12.3	13.1	13.9	14.7	15.4	16.2	17	17.8	18.6	19.3	20.1	20.9	21.7	22.5	23.2	24	24.8	25.6	26.3	27.1	27.9	28.7	29.4	♈0.2	1	1.8	2.5	3.3	4.1	

♃ 1: ♊11.7 · 6: 12.6 · 11: 13.4 · 16: 14.4 · 21: 15.3 · 26: 16.3 — ♄ 1: ♑11.5 · 6: 11.7 · 11: 11.8 · 16: 11.9 · 21: 11.9 · 26: 11.9R — ♅ 1: ♈11.3 · 11: 11.9 · 21: 12.4 — ♆ 1: ♍1.2R · 11: 1.1 · 21: 0.9 — ♇ 1: ♋17.4D · 11: 17.5 · 21: 17.5

V

1929

	1	2	3	4	5	6	7	8	9	10	11	12	13	14	15	16	17	18	19	20	21	22	23	24	25	26	27	28	29	30	31
☉	♉10.1	11.1	12.1	13	14	15	16	16.9	17.9	18.9	19.8	20.8	21.8	22.7	23.7	24.6	25.6	26.6	27.5	28.5	29.5	♊0.4	1.4	2.3	3.3	4.3	5.2	6.2	7.1	8.1	9.1
☽	♑28.3	♒10.4	22.8	♓5.4	18.4	♈1.8	15.6	29.8	♉14.4	29.1	♊14	28.9	♋13.7	28.2	♌12.4	26.3	♍9.8	23	♎6	18.6	♏1.1	13.3	25.5	♐7.4	19.4	♑1.2	13	24.9	♒6.8	18.9	♓1.2
☿	♉24.8	26.6	28.4	♊0.2	1.9	3.5	5.1	6.7	8.1	9.5	10.8	12.1	13.3	14.4	15.5	16.5	17.4	18.2	19	19.7	20.3	20.9	21.3	21.7	22	22.2	22.4	22.4	22.4R	22.4	22.2
♀	♈23.9R	23.5	23.1	22.8	22.5	22.3	22.1	21.9	21.8	21.7	21.7	21.7D	21.7	21.8	21.9	22	22.2	22.4	22.7	22.9	23.3	23.6	24	24.4	24.8	25.3	25.7	26.2	26.8	27.3	27.9
♂	♋23.5	24.1	24.6	25.1	25.7	26.2	26.7	27.3	27.8	28.3	28.9	29.4	30	♌0.5	1	1.6	2.1	2.7	3.2	3.8	4.3	4.9	5.5	6	6.6	7.1	7.7	8.3	8.8	9.4	9.9

♃ 1: ♉20 · 6: 21.2 · 11: 22.4 · 16: 23.6 · 21: 24.8 · 26: 25.9 · 31: 27.1 — ♄ 1: ♑0.2R · 6: ♐30 · 11: 29.7 · 16: 29.5 · 21: 29.2 · 26: 28.9 · 31: 28.6 — ♅ 1: ♈9.2 · 11: 9.7 · 21: 10.1 · 31: 10.5 — ♆ 1: ♌28.6R · 11: 28.6D · 21: 28.6 · 31: 28.7 — ♇ 1: ♋16.4 · 11: 16.5 · 21: 16.7 · 31: 16.9

1930

	1	2	3	4	5	6	7	8	9	10	11	12	13	14	15	16	17	18	19	20	21	22	23	24	25	26	27	28	29	30	31
☉	♉9.9	10.9	11.8	12.8	13.8	14.8	15.7	16.7	17.7	18.6	19.6	20.6	21.5	22.5	23.4	24.4	25.4	26.3	27.3	28.3	29.2	♊0.2	1.1	2.1	3.1	4	5	6	6.9	7.9	8.8
☽	♊7.8	21.8	♋6	20.2	♌4.4	18.7	♍2.8	16.9	♎0.9	14.7	28.3	♏11.6	24.8	♐7.7	20.3	♑2.7	14.9	27	♒8.9	20.8	♓2.7	14.7	26.9	♈9.4	22.2	♉5.4	18.9	♊2.9	17.1	♋1.6	16.1
☿	♉29.9	♊0.5	1.1	1.6	1.9	2.2	2.4	2.6	2.6R	2.6	2.4	2.2	2	1.6	1.2	0.8	0.3	♉29.7	29.2	28.6	28	27.4	26.9	26.3	25.8	25.4	25	24.6	24.3	24.1	23.9
♀	♊0.6	1.8	3	4.3	5.5	6.7	7.9	9.1	10.4	11.6	12.8	14	15.2	16.5	17.7	18.9	20.1	21.3	22.5	23.7	24.9	26.2	27.4	28.6	29.8	♋1	2.2	3.4	4.6	5.8	7
♂	♈4.8	5.6	6.4	7.2	7.9	8.7	9.5	10.2	11	11.8	12.5	13.3	14.1	14.8	15.6	16.3	17.1	17.9	18.6	19.4	20.1	20.9	21.6	22.4	23.2	23.9	24.7	25.4	26.2	26.9	27.7

♃ 1: ♊17.3 · 6: 18.4 · 11: 19.4 · 16: 20.5 · 21: 21.6 · 26: 22.7 · 31: 23.9 — ♄ 1: ♑11.8R · 6: 11.7 · 11: 11.6 · 16: 11.4 · 21: 11.2 · 26: 11 · 31: 10.7 — ♅ 1: ♈13 · 11: 13.5 · 21: 13.9 · 31: 14.3 — ♆ 1: ♍0.8R · 11: 0.8 · 21: 0.8D · 31: 0.9 — ♇ 1: ♋17.6 · 11: 17.8 · 21: 17.9 · 31: 18.1

VI

1929

	1	2	3	4	5	6	7	8	9	10	11	12	13	14	15	16	17	18	19	20	21	22	23	24	25	26	27	28	29	30	31
☉	♊10	11	11.9	12.9	13.8	14.8	15.8	16.7	17.7	18.6	19.6	20.5	21.5	22.5	23.4	24.4	25.3	26.3	27.2	28.2	29.1	♋0.1	1	2	3	3.9	4.9	5.8	6.8	7.7	
☽	♓13.8	26.7	♈10	23.8	♉8	22.6	♊7.5	22.7	♋7.8	22.9	♌7.7	22.2	♍6.2	19.7	♎2.9	15.7	28.2	♏10.4	22.5	♐4.4	16.3	28.2	♑10	21.9	♒3.8	15.8	28	♓10.3	22.9	♈5.7	
☿	♊22.0R	21.7	21.3	20.9	20.5	20	19.5	18.9	18.4	17.8	17.3	16.7	16.2	15.7	15.3	14.9	14.6	14.3	14.1	13.9	13.9	13.9D	14	14.1	14.4	14.7	15.1	15.6	16.2	16.8	
♀	♈28.5	29.1	29.7	♉0.4	1.1	1.8	2.5	3.2	3.9	4.7	5.4	6.2	7	7.8	8.6	9.5	10.3	11.1	12	12.9	13.8	14.6	15.5	16.4	17.4	18.3	19.2	20.2	21.1	22.1	
♂	♌10.5	11.1	11.7	12.2	12.8	13.4	13.9	14.5	15.1	15.7	16.2	16.8	17.4	18	18.6	19.1	19.7	20.3	20.9	21.5	22.1	22.6	23.2	23.8	24.4	25	25.6	26.2	26.8	27.4	

♃ 1: ♉27.4 · 6: 28.5 · 11: 29.7 · 16: ♊0.8 · 21: 1.9 · 26: 3 — ♄ 1: ♐28.5R · 6: 28.2 · 11: 27.8 · 16: 27.4 · 21: 27.1 · 26: 26.7 — ♅ 1: ♈10.5 · 11: 10.9 · 21: 11.1 — ♆ 1: ♌28.7 · 11: 28.9 · 21: 29.1 — ♇ 1: ♋16.9 · 11: 17.2 · 21: 17.4

1930

	1	2	3	4	5	6	7	8	9	10	11	12	13	14	15	16	17	18	19	20	21	22	23	24	25	26	27	28	29	30	31
☉	♊9.8	10.7	11.7	12.7	13.6	14.6	15.5	16.5	17.4	18.4	19.4	20.3	21.3	22.2	23.2	24.1	25.1	26	27	27.9	28.9	29.9	♋0.8	1.8	2.7	3.7	4.6	5.6	6.5	7.5	
☽	♌0.8	15.3	29.6	♍13.8	27.7	♎11.3	24.7	♏7.9	20.9	♐3.7	16.4	28.8	♑11.1	23.2	♒5.2	17	28.9	♓10.8	22.8	♈5	17.4	♉0.2	13.4	27.1	♊11.2	25.7	♋10.6	25.6	♌10.6	25.4	
☿	♉23.8R	23.8D	23.9	24	24.2	24.5	24.8	25.2	25.7	26.3	26.9	27.7	28.4	29.3	♊0.2	1.1	2.2	3.2	4.4	5.6	6.8	8.2	9.5	11	12.5	14	15.6	17.2	18.9	20.7	
♀	♋8.2	9.4	10.6	11.8	13	14.2	15.4	16.6	17.8	19	20.2	21.4	22.6	23.8	25	26.2	27.4	28.6	29.8	♌1	2.2	3.4	4.5	5.7	6.9	8.1	9.3	10.5	11.6	12.8	
♂	♈28.4	29.2	29.9	♉0.7	1.4	2.1	2.9	3.6	4.4	5.1	5.8	6.6	7.3	8.1	8.8	9.5	10.3	11	11.7	12.5	13.2	13.9	14.6	15.4	16.1	16.8	17.5	18.3	19	19.7	

♃ 1: ♊24.1 · 6: 25.2 · 11: 26.4 · 16: 27.5 · 21: 28.6 · 26: 29.8 — ♄ 1: ♑10.6R · 6: 10.3 · 11: 10 · 16: 9.7 · 21: 9.3 · 26: 9 — ♅ 1: ♈14.4 · 11: 14.7 · 21: 15 — ♆ 1: ♍0.9 · 11: 1 · 21: 1.2 — ♇ 1: ♋18.2 · 11: 18.4 · 21: 18.6

VII

1929

	1	2	3	4	5	6	7	8	9	10	11	12	13	14	15	16	17	18	19	20	21	22	23	24	25	26	27	28	29	30	31
☉	♋8.7	9.6	10.6	11.5	12.5	13.4	14.4	15.3	16.3	17.3	18.2	19.2	20.1	21.1	22	23	23.9	24.9	25.8	26.8	27.7	28.7	29.7	♌0.6	1.6	2.5	3.5	4.4	5.4	6.3	7.3
☽	♈19	♉2.6	16.6	♊1.1	15.9	♋1	16.3	♌1.5	16.5	♍1.1	15.3	28.9	♎12.1	24.9	♏7.3	19.5	♐1.5	13.4	25.2	♑7	18.9	♒0.8	12.9	25.1	♓7.4	19.9	♈2.5	15.5	28.7	♉12.2	26
☿	♊17.5	18.3	19.2	20.1	21.1	22.2	23.4	24.6	25.9	27.3	28.7	♋0.2	1.8	3.4	5.1	6.8	8.6	10.4	12.3	14.3	16.3	18.3	20.3	22.4	24.5	26.6	28.7	♌0.8	2.9	5	7.1
♀	♉23	24	25	25.9	26.9	27.9	28.9	29.9	♊0.9	1.9	3	4	5	6.1	7.1	8.1	9.2	10.2	11.3	12.3	13.4	14.5	15.5	16.6	17.7	18.8	19.9	20.9	22	23.1	24.2
♂	♌28	28.6	29.2	29.8	♍0.4	1	1.6	2.2	2.8	3.4	4	4.6	5.2	5.8	6.4	7	7.6	8.2	8.8	9.4	10.1	10.7	11.3	11.9	12.5	13.1	13.7	14.4	15	15.6	16.2

♃ 1: ♊4.1 · 6: 5.2 · 11: 6.2 · 16: 7.2 · 21: 8.2 · 26: 9.1 · 31: 10 — ♄ 1: ♐26.3R · 6: 26 · 11: 25.7 · 16: 25.3 · 21: 25.1 · 26: 24.8 · 31: 24.6 — ♅ 1: ♈11.3 · 11: 11.4 · 21: 11.4R · 31: 11.3 — ♆ 1: ♌29.3 · 11: 29.6 · 21: 29.9 · 31: ♍0.2 — ♇ 1: ♋17.7 · 11: 17.9 · 21: 18.2 · 31: 18.4

1930

	1	2	3	4	5	6	7	8	9	10	11	12	13	14	15	16	17	18	19	20	21	22	23	24	25	26	27	28	29	30	31
☉	♋8.4	9.4	10.3	11.3	12.3	13.2	14.2	15.1	16.1	17	18	18.9	19.9	20.8	21.8	22.7	23.7	24.7	25.6	26.6	27.5	28.5	29.4	♌0.4	1.3	2.3	3.2	4.2	5.2	6.1	7.1
☽	♍10	24.3	♎8.2	21.7	♏5	17.9	♐0.6	13.1	25.5	♑7.7	19.8	♒1.8	13.7	25.6	♓7.4	19.3	♈1.3	13.4	25.8	♉8.6	21.7	♊5.4	19.5	♋4.1	19	♌4.3	19.5	♍4.7	19.5	♎4	18
☿	♊22.5	24.3	26.2	28.2	♋0.2	2.2	4.2	6.3	8.4	10.6	12.7	14.8	17	19.1	21.3	23.4	25.6	27.7	29.8	♌1.9	3.9	5.9	7.9	9.9	11.9	13.8	15.7	17.5	19.4	21.2	23
♀	♌14	15.2	16.3	17.5	18.7	19.9	21	22.2	23.4	24.6	25.7	26.9	28	29.2	♍0.4	1.5	2.7	3.8	5	6.2	7.3	8.5	9.6	10.8	11.9	13	14.2	15.3	16.5	17.6	18.7
♂	♉20.4	21.1	21.8	22.6	23.3	24	24.7	25.4	26.1	26.8	27.5	28.2	28.9	29.6	♊0.3	1	1.7	2.4	3.1	3.8	4.5	5.2	5.9	6.6	7.3	8	8.6	9.3	10	10.7	11.4

♃ 1: ♋0.9 · 6: 2.1 · 11: 3.2 · 16: 4.3 · 21: 5.4 · 26: 6.5 · 31: 7.6 — ♄ 1: ♑8.6R · 6: 8.2 · 11: 7.9 · 16: 7.5 · 21: 7.2 · 26: 6.8 · 31: 6.5 — ♅ 1: ♈15.2 · 11: 15.3 · 21: 15.4 · 31: 15.3R — ♆ 1: ♍1.4 · 11: 1.7 · 21: 2 · 31: 2.3 — ♇ 1: ♋18.9 · 11: 19.1 · 21: 19.4 · 31: 19.7

VIII

1929

	1	2	3	4	5	6	7	8	9	10	11	12	13	14	15	16	17	18	19	20	21	22	23	24	25	26	27	28	29	30	31
☉	♌8.3	9.2	10.2	11.1	12.1	13	14	15	15.9	16.9	17.8	18.8	19.8	20.7	21.7	22.6	23.6	24.6	25.5	26.5	27.5	28.4	29.4	♍0.3	1.3	2.3	3.2	4.2	5.2	6.1	7.1
☽	♊10.3	24.9	♋9.8	24.8	♌9.9	24.8	♍9.5	23.7	♎7.4	20.7	♏3.5	16	28.1	♐10.1	21.9	♑3.8	15.6	27.6	♒9.6	21.9	♓4.3	16.8	29.6	♈12.5	25.6	♉8.9	22.5	♊6.3	20.4	♋4.8	19.3
☿	♌9.2	11.3	13.3	15.3	17.3	19.3	21.3	23.2	25.1	27	28.9	♍0.7	2.5	4.3	6.1	7.8	9.5	11.2	12.9	14.5	16.1	17.7	19.3	20.9	22.4	23.9	25.4	26.8	28.3	29.7	♎1
♀	♊25.3	26.4	27.5	28.6	29.7	♋0.9	2	3.1	4.2	5.3	6.5	7.6	8.7	9.9	11	12.1	13.3	14.4	15.6	16.7	17.9	19	20.2	21.3	22.5	23.6	24.8	26	27.1	28.3	29.5
♂	♍16.8	17.5	18.1	18.7	19.3	20	20.6	21.2	21.8	22.5	23.1	23.7	24.4	25	25.6	26.3	26.9	27.5	28.2	28.8	29.4	♎0.1	0.7	1.3	2	2.6	3.3	3.9	4.6	5.2	5.8

♃ 1: ♊10.1 · 6: 11 · 11: 11.8 · 16: 12.5 · 21: 13.2 · 26: 13.8 · 31: 14.4 — ♄ 1: ♐24.5R · 6: 24.3 · 11: 24.2 · 16: 24 · 21: 24 · 26: 23.9 · 31: 23.9D — ♅ 1: ♈11.3R · 11: 11.1 · 21: 10.9 · 31: 10.6 — ♆ 1: ♍0.3 · 11: 0.6 · 21: 1 · 31: 1.4 — ♇ 1: ♋18.5 · 11: 18.7 · 21: 18.9 · 31: 19.1

1930

	1	2	3	4	5	6	7	8	9	10	11	12	13	14	15	16	17	18	19	20	21	22	23	24	25	26	27	28	29	30	31
☉	♌8	9	9.9	10.9	11.9	12.8	13.8	14.7	15.7	16.6	17.6	18.6	19.5	20.5	21.4	22.4	23.4	24.3	25.3	26.3	27.2	28.2	29.1	♍0.1	1.1	2	3	4	4.9	5.9	6.9
☽	♏1.6	14.8	27.7	♐10.2	22.6	♑4.8	16.8	28.8	♒10.7	22.6	♓4.4	16.3	28.2	♈10.3	22.5	♉4.9	17.6	♊0.7	14.2	28.2	♋12.7	27.5	♌12.7	27.9	♍13.2	28.2	♎12.8	27	♏10.7	24	♐6.9
☿	♌24.7	26.5	28.2	29.8	♍1.5	3.1	4.7	6.2	7.8	9.3	10.8	12.2	13.6	15	16.4	17.7	19.1	20.3	21.6	22.8	24	25.1	26.2	27.3	28.3	29.3	♎0.2	1.1	2	2.8	3.5
♀	♍19.9	21	22.1	23.3	24.4	25.5	26.6	27.7	28.9	30	♎1.1	2.2	3.3	4.4	5.5	6.6	7.7	8.8	9.9	10.9	12	13.1	14.2	15.3	16.3	17.4	18.4	19.5	20.6	21.6	22.6
♂	♊12	12.7	13.4	14.1	14.7	15.4	16.1	16.7	17.4	18.1	18.7	19.4	20	20.7	21.4	22	22.7	23.3	24	24.6	25.2	25.9	26.5	27.2	27.8	28.4	29.1	29.7	♋0.3	1	1.6

♃ 1: ♋7.8 · 6: 8.9 · 11: 9.9 · 16: 10.9 · 21: 11.8 · 26: 12.8 · 31: 13.7 — ♄ 1: ♑6.5R · 6: 6.2 · 11: 6 · 16: 5.8 · 21: 5.6 · 26: 5.4 · 31: 5.3 — ♅ 1: ♈15.3R · 11: 15.2 · 21: 15 · 31: 14.8 — ♆ 1: ♍2.4 · 11: 2.7 · 21: 3.1 · 31: 3.5 — ♇ 1: ♋19.7 · 11: 19.9 · 21: 20.2 · 31: 20.4

IX

1929

	1	2	3	4	5	6	7	8	9	10	11	12	13	14	15	16	17	18	19	20	21	22	23	24	25	26	27	28	29	30	31
☉	♍8.1	9	10	11	11.9	12.9	13.9	14.9	15.8	16.8	17.8	18.7	19.7	20.7	21.7	22.6	23.6	24.6	25.6	26.5	27.5	28.5	29.5	♎0.5	1.4	2.4	3.4	4.4	5.4	6.4	
☽	♌4	18.7	♍3.4	17.8	♎1.8	15.5	28.7	♏11.6	24	♐6.2	18.2	♑0.1	12	23.9	♒5.9	18.1	♓0.5	13.1	25.9	♈9	22.3	♉5.8	19.4	♊3.2	17.2	♋1.3	15.4	29.7	♌14	28.3	
☿	♎2.4	3.7	5	6.3	7.6	8.8	10	11.1	12.3	13.4	14.4	15.4	16.4	17.3	18.2	19	19.8	20.5	21.1	21.7	22.2	22.6	23	23.2	23.3	23.4R	23.3	23.1	22.7	22.3	
♀	♌0.6	1.8	3	4.1	5.3	6.5	7.7	8.9	10.1	11.2	12.4	13.6	14.8	16	17.2	18.4	19.6	20.8	22	23.2	24.4	25.6	26.8	28	29.2	♍0.4	1.6	2.8	4	5.3	
♂	♎6.5	7.1	7.8	8.4	9.1	9.7	10.4	11	11.7	12.4	13	13.7	14.3	15	15.6	16.3	17	17.6	18.3	18.9	19.6	20.3	20.9	21.6	22.3	22.9	23.6	24.3	24.9	25.6	

♃ 1: ♊14.5 · 6: 15 · 11: 15.4 · 16: 15.8 · 21: 16.1 · 26: 16.3 — ♄ 1: ♐23.9 · 6: 24 · 11: 24 · 16: 24.2 · 21: 24.3 · 26: 24.5 — ♅ 1: ♈10.6R · 11: 10.3 · 21: 9.9 — ♆ 1: ♍1.4 · 11: 1.8 · 21: 2.1 — ♇ 1: ♋19.2 · 11: 19.3 · 21: 19.5

1930

	1	2	3	4	5	6	7	8	9	10	11	12	13	14	15	16	17	18	19	20	21	22	23	24	25	26	27	28	29	30	31
☉	♍7.8	8.8	9.8	10.7	11.7	12.7	13.7	14.6	15.6	16.6	17.5	18.5	19.5	20.5	21.4	22.4	23.4	24.4	25.3	26.3	27.3	28.3	29.2	♎0.2	1.2	2.2	3.2	4.1	5.1	6.1	
☽	♐19.4	♑1.7	13.8	25.8	♒7.7	19.6	♓1.4	13.3	25.3	♈7.4	19.6	♉1.9	14.5	27.3	♊10.4	23.9	♋7.7	22	♌6.5	21.4	♍6.4	21.5	♎6.3	21	♏5.2	19	♐2.4	15.4	28	♑10.3	
☿	♎4.1	4.8	5.3	5.8	6.1	6.4	6.6	6.8	6.8R	6.7	6.5	6.2	5.8	5.3	4.6	3.9	3.1	2.1	1.1	0.1	♍29	27.9	26.9	25.9	24.9	24.1	23.4	22.8	22.4	22.2	
♀	♎23.7	24.7	25.8	26.8	27.8	28.8	29.8	♏0.8	1.8	2.8	3.8	4.8	5.8	6.7	7.7	8.7	9.6	10.6	11.5	12.4	13.3	14.2	15.1	16	16.9	17.8	18.6	19.5	20.3	21.1	
♂	♋2.2	2.8	3.5	4.1	4.7	5.3	5.9	6.5	7.1	7.7	8.3	8.9	9.5	10.1	10.7	11.3	11.9	12.5	13.1	13.7	14.2	14.8	15.4	16	16.5	17.1	17.7	18.2	18.8	19.3	

♃ 1: ♋13.9 · 6: 14.7 · 11: 15.5 · 16: 16.3 · 21: 17 · 26: 17.6 — ♄ 1: ♑5.3R · 6: 5.3 · 11: 5.3D · 16: 5.3 · 21: 5.4 · 26: 5.5 — ♅ 1: ♈14.7R · 11: 14.4 · 21: 14 — ♆ 1: ♍3.5 · 11: 3.9 · 21: 4.2 — ♇ 1: ♋20.4 · 11: 20.6 · 21: 20.7

X

1929

	1	2	3	4	5	6	7	8	9	10	11	12	13	14	15	16	17	18	19	20	21	22	23	24	25	26	27	28	29	30	31
☉	♎7.3	8.3	9.3	10.3	11.3	12.3	13.2	14.2	15.2	16.2	17.2	18.2	19.2	20.2	21.2	22.2	23.1	24.1	25.1	26.1	27.1	28.1	29.1	♏0.1	1.1	2.1	3.1	4.1	5.1	6.1	7.1
☽	♍12.5	26.4	♎10.2	23.6	♏6.7	19.4	♐1.9	14.1	26.1	♑8	19.9	♒1.8	13.8	26	♓8.5	21.3	♈4.4	17.8	♉1.4	15.4	29.5	♊13.7	28	♋12.3	26.5	♌10.6	24.7	♍8.6	22.3	♎5.8	19.1
☿	♎21.7R	21	20.2	19.3	18.2	17.1	16	14.8	13.6	12.5	11.4	10.5	9.7	9	8.5	8.2	8	8.1D	8.3	8.7	9.3	10	10.9	11.8	12.9	14.1	15.3	16.7	18	19.5	20.9
♀	♍6.5	7.7	8.9	10.1	11.3	12.6	13.8	15	16.2	17.4	18.7	19.9	21.1	22.4	23.6	24.8	26	27.3	28.5	29.7	♎1	2.2	3.5	4.7	5.9	7.2	8.4	9.6	10.9	12.1	13.4
♂	♎26.3	27	27.6	28.3	29	29.7	♏0.3	1	1.7	2.4	3.1	3.7	4.4	5.1	5.8	6.5	7.2	7.8	8.5	9.2	9.9	10.6	11.3	12	12.7	13.4	14.1	14.8	15.5	16.2	16.9

♃ 1: ♊16.4 · 6: 16.4R · 11: 16.4 · 16: 16.2 · 21: 16 · 26: 15.7 · 31: 15.3 — ♄ 1: ♐24.8 · 6: 25.1 · 11: 25.4 · 16: 25.7 · 21: 26.1 · 26: 26.5 · 31: 26.9 — ♅ 1: ♈9.5R · 11: 9.1 · 21: 8.7 · 31: 8.3 — ♆ 1: ♍2.4 · 11: 2.7 · 21: 3 · 31: 3.2 — ♇ 1: ♋19.6 · 11: 19.6 · 21: 19.6R · 31: 19.6

1930

	1	2	3	4	5	6	7	8	9	10	11	12	13	14	15	16	17	18	19	20	21	22	23	24	25	26	27	28	29	30	31
☉	♎7.1	8.1	9.1	10	11	12	13	14	15	16	17	17.9	18.9	19.9	20.9	21.9	22.9	23.9	24.9	25.9	26.9	27.9	28.9	29.9	♏0.9	1.9	2.9	3.9	4.9	5.9	6.9
☽	♑22.4	♒4.4	16.3	28.1	♓10	22	♈4.1	16.4	28.8	♉11.5	24.3	♊7.4	20.7	♋4.3	18.1	♌2.2	16.5	♍0.9	15.5	♎0.2	14.7	29.1	♏13.2	27	♐10.4	23.4	♑6.1	18.4	♒0.6	12.5	24.4
☿	♍22.1D	22.2	22.5	22.9	23.5	24.2	25.1	26.1	27.2	28.4	29.7	♎1.1	2.6	4.1	5.6	7.2	8.8	10.5	12.1	13.8	15.5	17.2	18.9	20.6	22.3	23.9	25.6	27.3	29	♏0.7	2.3
♀	♏22	22.8	23.5	24.3	25.1	25.8	26.5	27.3	27.9	28.6	29.3	29.9	♐0.5	1.1	1.7	2.3	2.8	3.3	3.8	4.3	4.7	5.1	5.5	5.8	6.1	6.4	6.7	6.9	7	7.2	7.3
♂	♋19.9	20.4	21	21.5	22.1	22.6	23.1	23.7	24.2	24.7	25.2	25.7	26.2	26.7	27.3	27.8	28.2	28.7	29.2	29.7	♌0.2	0.7	1.1	1.6	2.1	2.5	3	3.4	3.9	4.3	4.7

♃ 1: ♋18.2 · 6: 18.8 · 11: 19.2 · 16: 19.7 · 21: 20 · 26: 20.2 · 31: 20.4 — ♄ 1: ♑5.6 · 6: 5.8 · 11: 6 · 16: 6.3 · 21: 6.6 · 26: 6.9 · 31: 7.3 — ♅ 1: ♈13.6R · 11: 13.2 · 21: 12.8 · 31: 12.5 — ♆ 1: ♍4.6 · 11: 4.9 · 21: 5.1 · 31: 5.4 — ♇ 1: ♋20.8 · 11: 20.9 · 21: 20.9 · 31: 20.9R

XI

1929

	1	2	3	4	5	6	7	8	9	10	11	12	13	14	15	16	17	18	19	20	21	22	23	24	25	26	27	28	29	30	31
☉	♏8.1	9.1	10.1	11.1	12.1	13.1	14.1	15.1	16.1	17.1	18.1	19.1	20.1	21.1	22.2	23.2	24.2	25.2	26.2	27.2	28.2	29.2	♐0.2	1.2	2.3	3.3	4.3	5.3	6.3	7.3	
☽	♏2.1	15	27.5	♐9.9	22	♑4	15.9	27.7	♒9.6	21.6	♓3.8	16.3	29.1	♈12.2	25.8	♉9.7	24	♊8.6	23.3	♋8.1	22.7	♌7.2	21.5	♍5.5	19.2	♎2.6	15.7	28.6	♏11.3	23.7	
☿	♎22.5	24	25.5	27.1	28.7	♏0.3	1.9	3.5	5.2	6.8	8.4	10	11.6	13.2	14.9	16.5	18.1	19.7	21.3	22.9	24.5	26	27.6	29.2	♐0.8	2.4	4	5.5	7.1	8.7	
♀	♎14.6	15.9	17.1	18.3	19.6	20.8	22.1	23.3	24.6	25.8	27.1	28.3	29.6	♏0.8	2.1	3.3	4.6	5.8	7.1	8.3	9.6	10.8	12.1	13.3	14.6	15.8	17.1	18.3	19.6	20.9	
♂	♏17.6	18.3	19	19.7	20.4	21.1	21.8	22.5	23.2	23.9	24.6	25.3	26	26.7	27.5	28.2	28.9	29.6	♐0.3	1	1.8	2.5	3.2	3.9	4.6	5.4	6.1	6.8	7.5	8.3	

♃ 1: ♊15.2R · 6: 14.8 · 11: 14.3 · 16: 13.7 · 21: 13.1 · 26: 12.4 — ♄ 1: ♐27 · 6: 27.5 · 11: 28 · 16: 28.5 · 21: 29 · 26: 29.5 — ♅ 1: ♈8.3R · 11: 8 · 21: 7.7 — ♆ 1: ♍3.2 · 11: 3.4 · 21: 3.5 — ♇ 1: ♋19.6R · 11: 19.5 · 21: 19.4

1930

	1	2	3	4	5	6	7	8	9	10	11	12	13	14	15	16	17	18	19	20	21	22	23	24	25	26	27	28	29	30	31
☉	♏7.9	8.9	9.9	10.9	11.9	12.9	13.9	14.9	15.9	16.9	17.9	18.9	19.9	20.9	21.9	22.9	23.9	24.9	25.9	27	28	29	30	♐1	2	3	4	5	6.1	7.1	
☽	♓6.2	18.2	♈0.2	12.5	24.9	♉7.7	20.6	♊3.9	17.4	♋1.1	15	29	♌13.1	27.2	♍11.4	25.6	♎9.7	23.8	♏7.8	21.5	♐5	18.3	♑1.2	13.9	26.2	♒8.4	20.3	♓2.2	14	25.9	
☿	♏4	5.6	7.3	8.9	10.6	12.2	13.8	15.4	17	18.6	20.2	21.8	23.4	25	26.5	28.1	29.7	♐1.2	2.8	4.3	5.9	7.4	9	10.5	12	13.6	15.1	16.6	18.2	19.7	
♀	♐7.3	7.4	7.4R	7.3	7.2	7.1	6.9	6.7	6.4	6.1	5.8	5.4	5	4.6	4.1	3.6	3.1	2.5	2	1.4	0.8	0.2	♏29.6	29	28.4	27.8	27.2	26.6	26.1	25.6	
♂	♌5.2	5.6	6	6.4	6.8	7.2	7.6	8	8.4	8.8	9.1	9.5	9.9	10.2	10.5	10.9	11.2	11.5	11.8	12.1	12.4	12.7	13	13.3	13.6	13.8	14.1	14.3	14.5	14.7	

♃ 1: ♋20.4 · 6: 20.5 · 11: 20.5R · 16: 20.4 · 21: 20.2 · 26: 20 — ♄ 1: ♑7.4 · 6: 7.8 · 11: 8.2 · 16: 8.7 · 21: 9.2 · 26: 9.7 — ♅ 1: ♈12.4R · 11: 12.1 · 21: 11.8 — ♆ 1: ♍5.4 · 11: 5.6 · 21: 5.7 — ♇ 1: ♋20.9R · 11: 20.8 · 21: 20.7

XII

1929

	1	2	3	4	5	6	7	8	9	10	11	12	13	14	15	16	17	18	19	20	21	22	23	24	25	26	27	28	29	30	31
☉	♐8.3	9.3	10.4	11.4	12.4	13.4	14.4	15.4	16.4	17.5	18.5	19.5	20.5	21.5	22.5	23.6	24.6	25.6	26.6	27.6	28.7	29.7	♑0.7	1.7	2.7	3.7	4.8	5.8	6.8	7.8	8.8
☽	♐6.1	18.2	♑0.3	12.2	24.1	♒5.9	17.8	29.8	♓11.9	24.3	♈6.9	20	♉3.5	17.5	♊1.9	16.8	♋1.8	17	♌2.1	17	♍1.6	15.7	29.4	♎12.7	25.6	♏8.3	20.7	♐2.9	15	27	♑9
☿	♐10.2	11.8	13.4	14.9	16.5	18.1	19.6	21.2	22.8	24.3	25.9	27.5	29.1	♑0.6	2.2	3.8	5.3	6.9	8.5	10	11.6	13.2	14.7	16.3	17.8	19.3	20.9	22.4	23.8	25.3	26.7
♀	♏22.1	23.4	24.6	25.9	27.1	28.4	29.6	♐0.9	2.2	3.4	4.7	5.9	7.2	8.4	9.7	11	12.2	13.5	14.7	16	17.2	18.5	19.8	21	22.3	23.5	24.8	26	27.3	28.6	29.8
♂	♐9	9.7	10.4	11.2	11.9	12.6	13.4	14.1	14.8	15.6	16.3	17	17.8	18.5	19.2	20	20.7	21.5	22.2	23	23.7	24.4	25.2	25.9	26.7	27.4	28.2	28.9	29.7	♑0.4	1.2

♃ 1: ♊11.7R · 6: 11 · 11: 10.4 · 16: 9.7 · 21: 9.1 · 26: 8.5 · 31: 8 — ♄ 1: ♑0.1 · 6: 0.7 · 11: 1.3 · 16: 1.8 · 21: 2.4 · 26: 3 · 31: 3.6 — ♅ 1: ♈7.6R · 11: 7.5 · 21: 7.5D · 31: 7.5 — ♆ 1: ♍3.6 · 11: 3.6R · 21: 3.5 · 31: 3.4 — ♇ 1: ♋19.3R · 11: 19.1 · 21: 18.9 · 31: 18.7

1930

	1	2	3	4	5	6	7	8	9	10	11	12	13	14	15	16	17	18	19	20	21	22	23	24	25	26	27	28	29	30	31
☉	♐8.1	9.1	10.1	11.1	12.1	13.2	14.2	15.2	16.2	17.2	18.2	19.2	20.3	21.3	22.3	23.3	24.3	25.4	26.4	27.4	28.4	29.4	♑0.4	1.5	2.5	3.5	4.5	5.5	6.6	7.6	8.6
☽	♈8	20.3	♉2.9	15.8	29.1	♊12.8	26.7	♋10.9	25.3	♌9.7	24	♍8.3	22.4	♎6.3	20.1	♏3.8	17.3	♐0.6	13.7	26.7	♑9.4	21.9	♒4.2	16.3	28.2	♓10.1	21.9	♈3.7	15.7	28	♉10.6
☿	♐21.2	22.7	24.2	25.7	27.2	28.7	♑0.2	1.7	3.1	4.6	6	7.4	8.8	10.2	11.5	12.8	14.1	15.3	16.4	17.5	18.5	19.4	20.2	20.9	21.5	21.9	22.2	22.3R	22.2	21.9	21.4
♀	♏25.1R	24.6	24.2	23.8	23.4	23.1	22.8	22.6	22.4	22.2	22.1	22.1	22	22.0D	22.1	22.2	22.3	22.5	22.7	22.9	23.2	23.5	23.8	24.2	24.6	25	25.5	26	26.5	27.1	27.6
♂	♌14.9	15.1	15.3	15.5	15.7	15.8	16	16.1	16.2	16.4	16.5	16.5	16.6	16.7	16.7	16.8	16.8	16.8	16.8R	16.8	16.8	16.7	16.7	16.6	16.5	16.4	16.3	16.2	16.1	15.9	15.8

♃ 1: ♋19.6R · 6: 19.2 · 11: 18.8 · 16: 18.2 · 21: 17.6 · 26: 17 · 31: 16.4 — ♄ 1: ♑10.2 · 6: 10.7 · 11: 11.3 · 16: 11.9 · 21: 12.4 · 26: 13 · 31: 13.6 — ♅ 1: ♈11.6R · 11: 11.5 · 21: 11.4 · 31: 11.5D — ♆ 1: ♍5.8 · 11: 5.8R · 21: 5.7 · 31: 5.6 — ♇ 1: ♋20.6R · 11: 20.4 · 21: 20.2 · 31: 20

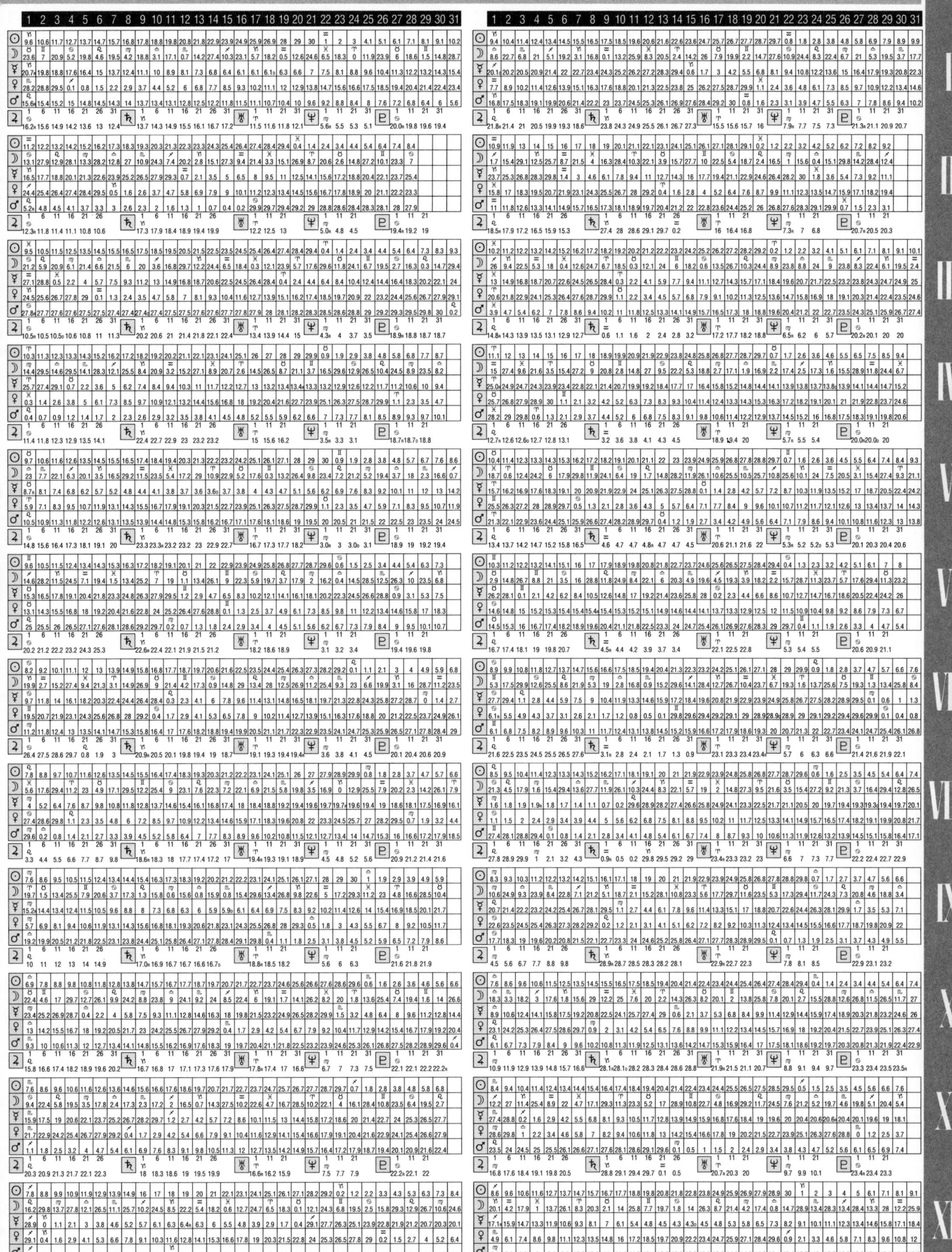

I

II

III

IV

V

VI

VII

VIII

IX

X

XI

XII

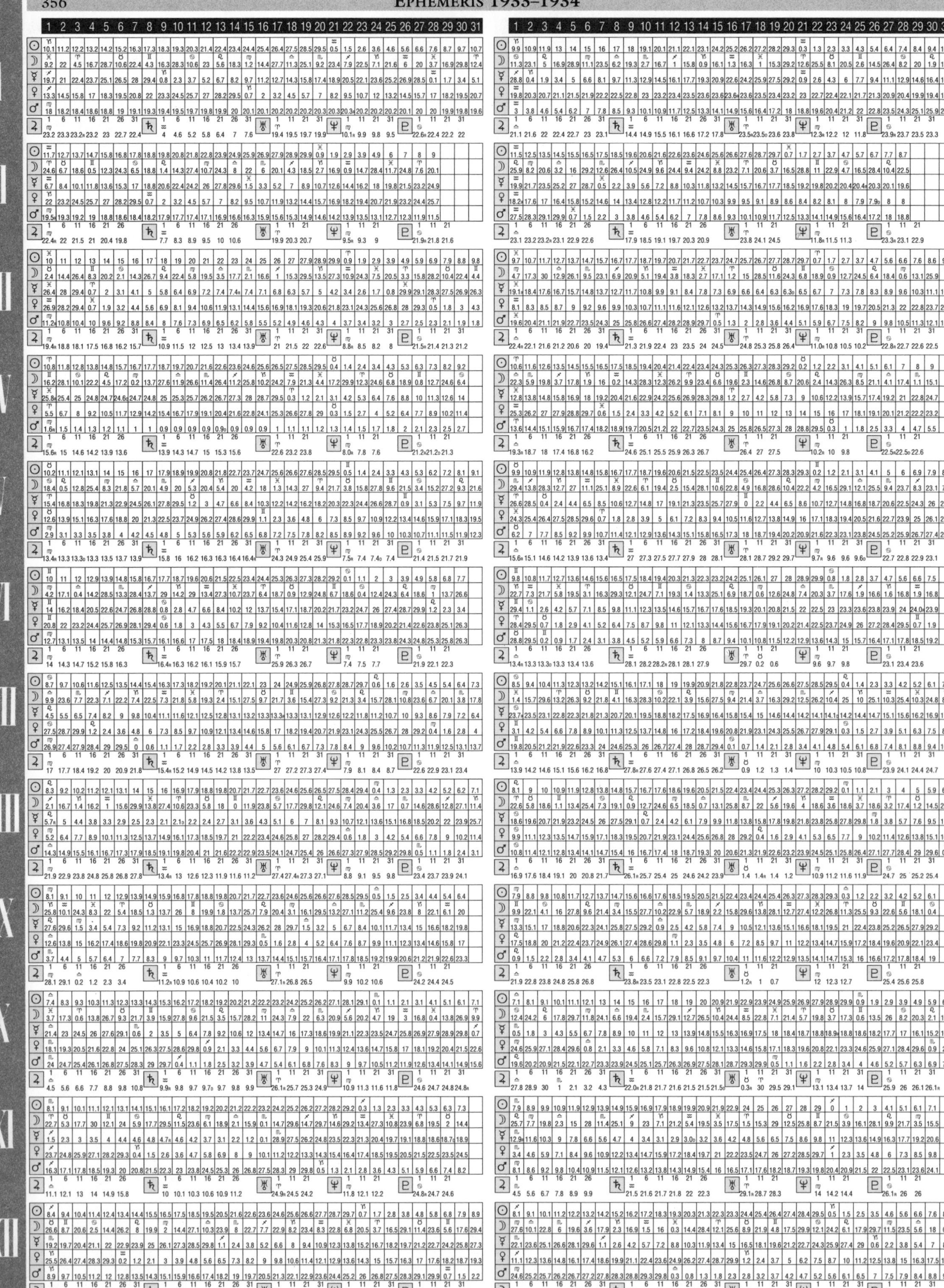

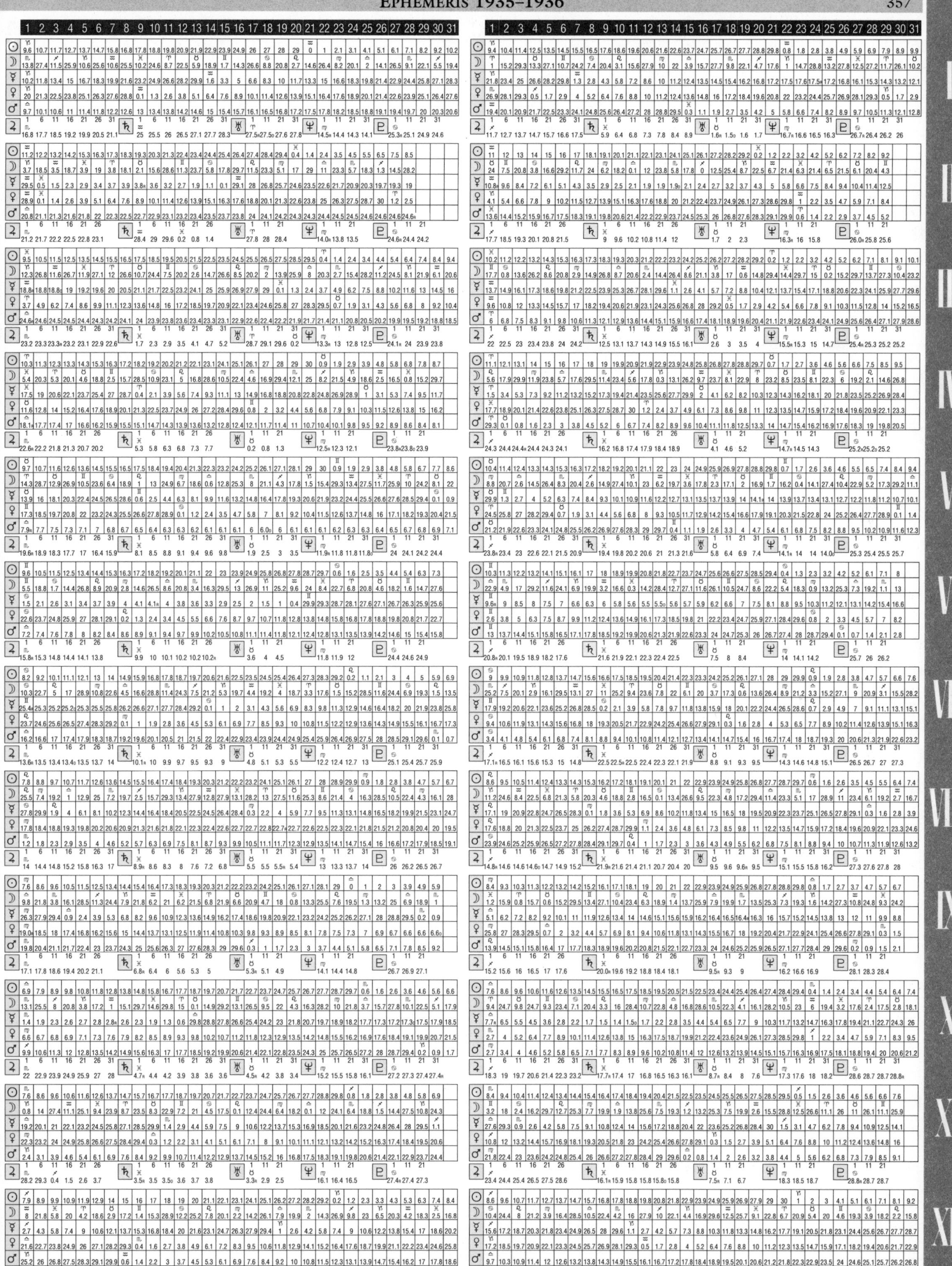

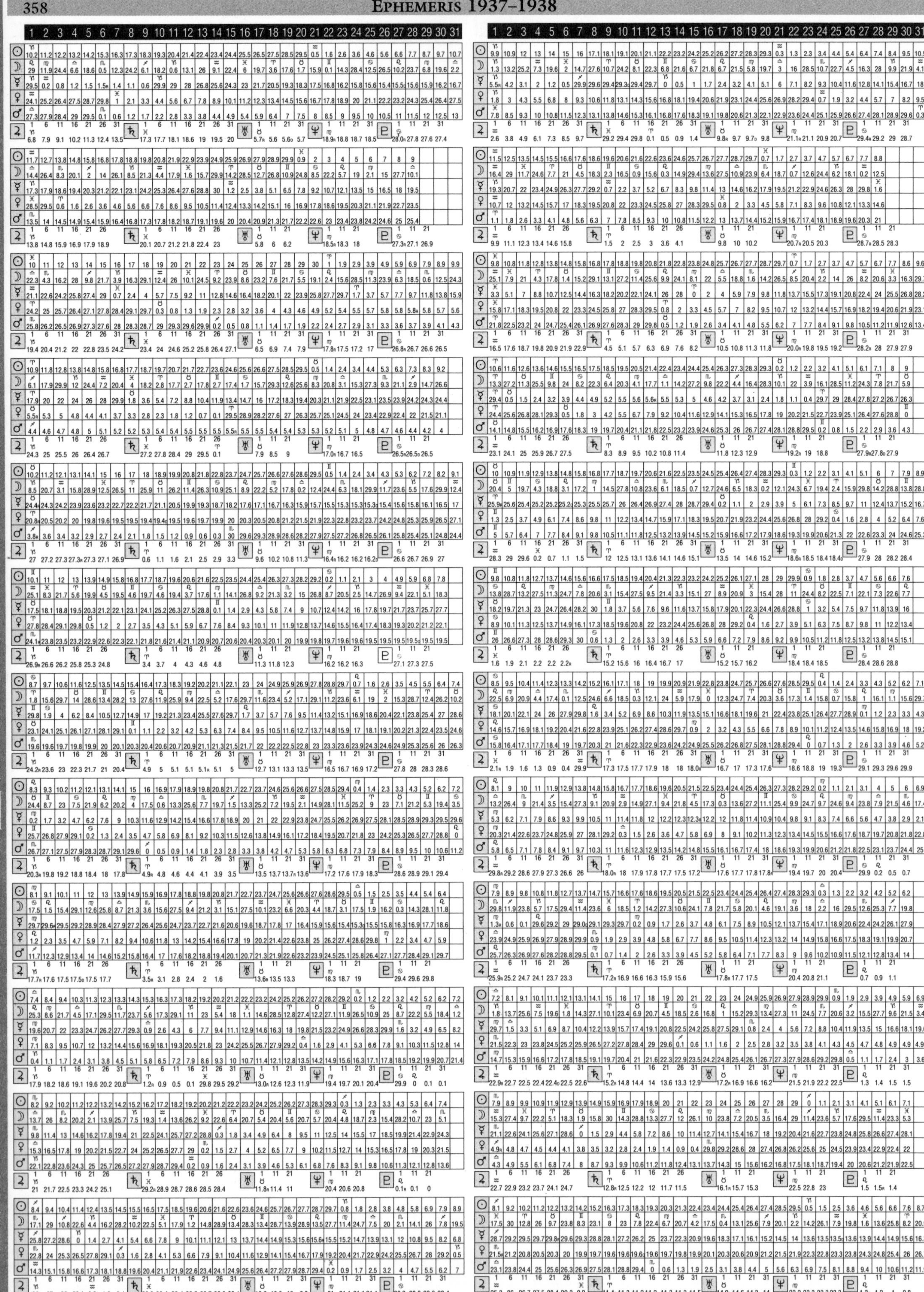

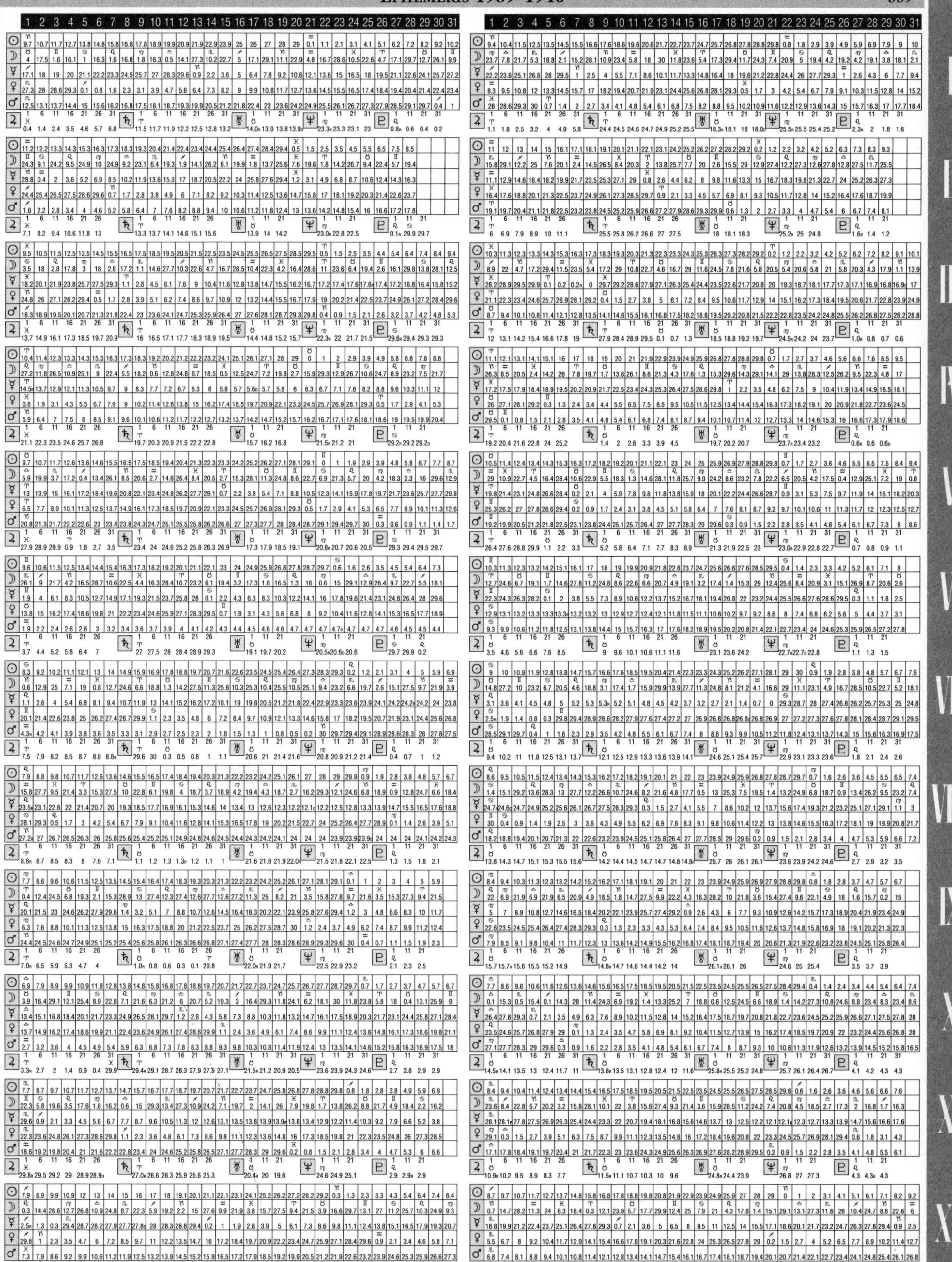

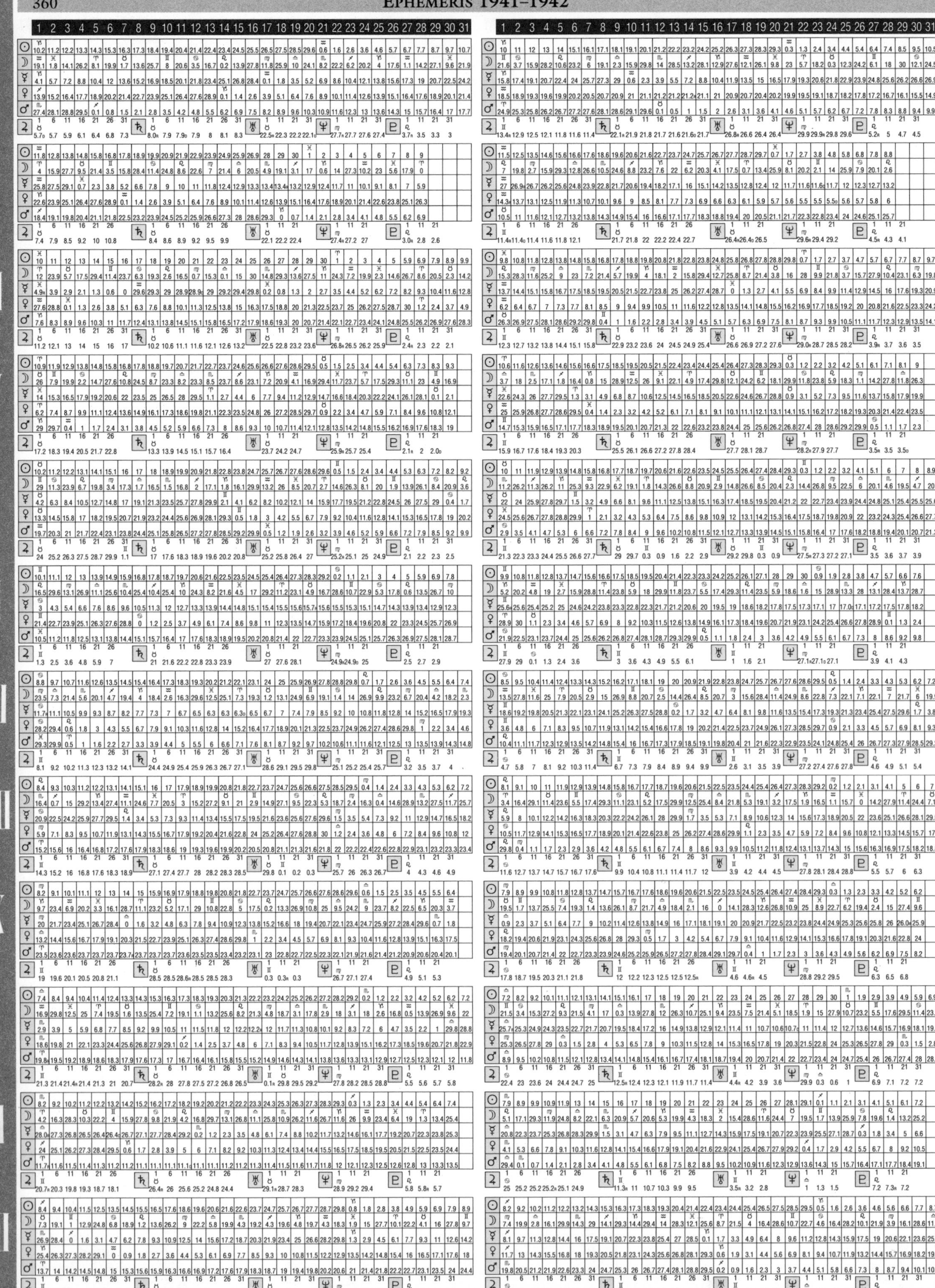

I

1941

	1	2	3	4	5	6	7	8	9	10	11	12	13	14	15	16	17	18	19	20	21	22	23	24	25	26	27	28	29	30	31
☉	10.2	11.2	12.2	13.3	14.3	15.3	16.3	17.3	18.4	19.4	20.4	21.4	22.4	23.4	24.5	25.5	26.5	27.5	28.5	29.6	0.6	1.6	2.6	3.6	4.6	5.7	6.7	7.7	8.7	9.7	10.7
☽	19.1	1.8	14.1	26.2	8.1	19.9	1.7	13.6	25.7	8	20.6	3.5	16.7	0.2	13.9	27.8	11.8	25.9	10	24.1	8.2	22.2	6.2	20.2	4	17.6	1.1	14.2	27.1	9.6	21.9
☿	4.1	5.7	7.2	8.8	10.4	12	13.6	15.2	16.9	18.5	20.1	21.8	23.4	25.1	26.8	28.4	0.1	1.8	3.5	5.2	6.9	8.6	10.4	12.1	13.8	15.6	17.3	19	20.7	22.5	24.2
♀	13.9	15.2	16.4	17.7	18.9	20.2	21.4	22.7	23.9	25.1	26.4	27.6	28.9	0.1	1.4	2.6	3.9	5.1	6.4	7.6	8.9	10.1	11.4	12.6	13.9	15.1	16.4	17.6	18.9	20.1	21.4
♂	27.4	28.1	28.8	29.5	0.1	0.8	1.5	2.1	2.8	3.5	4.2	4.8	5.5	6.2	6.9	7.5	8.2	8.9	9.6	10.3	10.9	11.6	12.3	13	13.6	14.3	15	15.7	16.4	17	17.7

♃ (1, 6, 11, 16, 21, 26, 31): 5.7D 5.7 5.9 6.1 6.4 6.8 7.3 — ♄ (1, 6, 11, 16, 21, 26, 31): 8.0R 7.9 7.9D 7.9 8 8.1 8.3 — ♅ (1, 11, 21, 31): 22.5R 22.3 22.2 22.1D — ♆ (1, 11, 21, 31): 27.7R 27.7 27.6 27.4 — ♇ (1, 11, 21, 31): 3.7R 3.5 3.3 3

1942

	1	2	3	4	5	6	7	8	9	10	11	12	13	14	15	16	17	18	19	20	21	22	23	24	25	26	27	28	29	30	31
☉	10	11	12	13	14	15.1	16.1	17.1	18.1	19.1	20.1	21.2	22.2	23.2	24.2	25.2	26.3	27.3	28.3	29.3	0.3	1.3	2.4	3.4	4.4	5.4	6.4	7.4	8.5	9.5	10.5
☽	21.6	3.7	15.9	28.2	10.6	23.2	6	19.1	2.3	15.9	29.8	14	28.5	13.2	28.1	12.9	27.6	12.1	26.1	9.8	23	5.7	18.2	0.3	12.3	24.2	6.1	18	30	12.1	24.5
☿	15.8	17.4	19.1	20.7	22.4	24	25.7	27.3	29	0.6	2.3	3.9	5.5	7.2	8.8	10.4	11.9	13.5	15	16.5	17.9	19.3	20.6	21.8	22.9	23.9	24.8	25.6	26.2	26.6	26.9
♀	18.5	18.9	19.3	19.6	19.9	20.2	20.5	20.7	20.9	21	21.1	21.2	21.2	21.2R	21.1	21	20.9	20.7	20.4	20.2	19.9	19.5	19.1	18.7	18.2	17.8	17.2	16.7	16.1	15.5	14.9
♂	24.9	25.3	25.8	26.2	26.7	27.2	27.6	28.1	28.6	29.1	29.6	0.1	0.5	1	1.5	2	2.6	3.1	3.6	4.1	4.6	5.1	5.7	6.2	6.7	7.2	7.8	8.3	8.8	9.4	9.9

♃ (1, 6, 11, 16, 21, 26, 31): 13.4R 12.9 12.5 12.1 11.8 11.6 11.4 — ♄ (1, 6, 11, 16, 21, 26, 31): 22.1R 21.9 21.8 21.7 21.6 21.6D 21.7 — ♅ (1, 11, 21, 31): 26.8R 26.6 26.4 26.4 — ♆ (1, 11, 21, 31): 29.9 29.9R 29.8 29.6 — ♇ (1, 11, 21, 31): 5.2R 5 4.7 4.5

II

1941

	1	2	3	4	5	6	7	8	9	10	11	12	13	14	15	16	17	18	19	20	21	22	23	24	25	26	27	28
☉	11.8	12.8	13.8	14.8	15.8	16.8	17.8	18.9	19.9	20.9	21.9	22.9	23.9	24.9	25.9	26.9	28	29	30	1	2	3	4	5	6	7	8	9
☽	4	15.9	27.7	9.5	21.4	3.5	15.8	28.4	11.4	24.8	8.6	22.6	7	21.4	6	20.5	4.9	19.1	3.1	17	0.6	14	27.3	10.2	23	5.6	17.9	0
☿	25.8	27.5	29.1	0.7	2.3	3.8	5.2	6.6	7.8	9	10	11	11.8	12.4	12.9	13.3	13.4	13.4R	13.2	12.9	12.4	11.7	11	10.1	9.1	8.1	7	5.9
♀	22.6	23.9	25.1	26.4	27.6	28.9	0.1	1.4	2.6	3.9	5.1	6.4	7.6	8.9	10.1	11.4	12.6	13.9	15.1	16.4	17.6	18.9	20.1	21.4	22.6	23.8	25.1	26.3
♂	18.4	19.1	19.8	20.4	21.1	21.8	22.5	23.2	23.9	24.5	25.2	25.9	26.6	27.3	28	28.6	29.3	0	0.7	1.4	2.1	2.8	3.4	4.1	4.8	5.5	6.2	6.9

♃ (1, 6, 11, 16, 21, 26): 7.4 7.9 8.5 9.2 10 10.8 — ♄ (1, 6, 11, 16, 21, 26): 8.4 8.6 8.9 9.2 9.5 9.9 — ♅ (1, 11, 21): 22.1 22.2 22.4 — ♆ (1, 11, 21): 27.4R 27.2 27 — ♇ (1, 11, 21): 3.0R 2.8 2.6

1942

	1	2	3	4	5	6	7	8	9	10	11	12	13	14	15	16	17	18	19	20	21	22	23	24	25	26	27	28
☉	11.5	12.5	13.5	14.6	15.6	16.6	17.6	18.6	19.6	20.6	21.6	22.7	23.7	24.7	25.7	26.7	27.7	28.7	29.7	0.7	1.7	2.7	3.8	4.8	5.8	6.8	7.8	8.8
☽	7	19.8	2.7	15.9	29.3	12.8	26.6	10.5	24.6	8.8	23.2	7.6	22	6.2	20.3	4.1	17.5	0.7	13.4	25.9	8.1	20.2	2.1	14	25.9	7.9	20.1	2.6
☿	27	26.9R	26.7	26.2	25.6	24.8	23.9	22.8	21.7	20.6	19.4	18.2	17.1	16	15.1	14.2	13.5	12.8	12.4	12	11.7	11.6	11.6D	11.7	12	12.3	12.7	13.2
♀	14.3R	13.7	13.1	12.5	11.9	11.3	10.7	10.1	9.6	9	8.5	8.1	7.7	7.3	6.9	6.6	6.3	6.1	5.9	5.7	5.6	5.5	5.5	5.5D	5.6	5.7	5.8	6
♂	10.5	11	11.6	12.1	12.7	13.2	13.8	14.3	14.9	15.4	16	16.6	17.1	17.7	18.3	18.8	19.4	20	20.5	21.1	21.7	22.3	22.8	23.4	24	24.6	25.1	25.7

♃ (1, 6, 11, 16, 21, 26): 11.4R 11.4D 11.4 11.6 11.8 12.1 — ♄ (1, 6, 11, 16, 21, 26): 21.7 21.8 22 22.2 22.4 22.7 — ♅ (1, 11, 21): 26.4R 26.4D 26.5 — ♆ (1, 11, 21): 29.6R 29.4 29.2 — ♇ (1, 11, 21): 4.5R 4.3 4.1

III

1941

	1	2	3	4	5	6	7	8	9	10	11	12	13	14	15	16	17	18	19	20	21	22	23	24	25	26	27	28	29	30	31
☉	10	11	12	13	14	15	16	17	18	19	20	21	22	23	24	25	26	27	28	29	30	1	2	3	4	5	5.9	6.9	7.9	8.9	9.9
☽	12	23.9	5.7	17.5	29.4	11.4	23.7	6.3	19.3	2.6	16.5	0.7	15.3	0.1	15	30	14.8	29.3	13.6	27.5	11	24.3	7.2	19.9	2.3	14.6	26.7	8.6	20.5	2.3	14.2
☿	4.9R	3.9	2.9	2.1	1.3	0.6	0	29.6	29.3	29	28.9	28.9D	29	29.2	29.4	29.8	0.2	0.8	1.3	2	2.7	3.5	4.4	5.2	6.2	7.2	8.2	9.3	10.4	11.6	12.8
♀	27.6	28.8	0.1	1.3	2.6	3.8	5.1	6.3	7.6	8.8	10.1	11.3	12.5	13.8	15	16.3	17.5	18.8	20	21.3	22.5	23.7	25	26.2	27.5	28.7	30	1.2	2.4	3.7	4.9
♂	7.6	8.3	8.9	9.6	10.3	11	11.7	12.4	13.1	13.8	14.5	15.1	15.8	16.5	17.2	17.9	18.6	19.3	20	20.7	21.4	22.1	22.7	23.4	24.1	24.8	25.5	26.2	26.9	27.6	28.3

♃ (1, 6, 11, 16, 21, 26, 31): 11.2 12.1 13 14 15 16 17 — ♄ (1, 6, 11, 16, 21, 26, 31): 10.2 10.6 11.1 11.6 12.1 12.6 13.2 — ♅ (1, 11, 21, 31): 22.5 22.8 23.2 23.6 — ♆ (1, 11, 21, 31): 26.8R 26.5 26.2 25.9 — ♇ (1, 11, 21, 31): 2.4R 2.3 2.2 2.1

1942

	1	2	3	4	5	6	7	8	9	10	11	12	13	14	15	16	17	18	19	20	21	22	23	24	25	26	27	28	29	30	31
☉	9.8	10.8	11.8	12.8	13.8	14.8	15.8	16.8	17.8	18.8	19.8	20.8	21.8	22.8	23.8	24.8	25.8	26.8	27.8	28.8	29.8	0.7	1.7	2.7	3.7	4.7	5.7	6.7	7.7	8.7	9.7
☽	15.3	28.3	11.6	25.2	9	23	7.2	21.4	5.7	19.9	4	18.1	2	15.8	29.4	12.7	25.8	8.7	21.4	3.8	16	28	9.9	21.8	3.7	15.7	27.9	10.4	23.1	6.3	19.8
☿	13.7	14.4	15.1	15.8	16.7	17.5	18.5	19.5	20.5	21.5	22.7	23.8	25	26.2	27.4	28.7	0	1.3	2.7	4.1	5.5	6.9	8.4	9.9	11.4	12.9	14.5	16	17.6	19.3	20.9
♀	6.2	6.4	6.7	7	7.3	7.7	8.1	8.5	9	9.4	9.9	10.5	11	11.6	12.2	12.8	13.5	14.1	14.8	15.5	16.2	16.9	17.7	18.5	19.2	20	20.8	21.6	22.5	23.3	24.2
♂	26.3	26.9	27.5	28.1	28.6	29.2	29.8	0.4	1	1.6	2.2	2.8	3.4	3.9	4.5	5.1	5.7	6.3	6.9	7.5	8.1	8.7	9.3	9.9	10.5	11.1	11.7	12.3	12.9	13.5	14.1

♃ (1, 6, 11, 16, 21, 26, 31): 12.3 12.7 13.2 13.8 14.4 15.1 15.8 — ♄ (1, 6, 11, 16, 21, 26, 31): 22.9 23.2 23.6 24 24.5 24.9 25.4 — ♅ (1, 11, 21, 31): 26.6 26.9 27.2 27.6 — ♆ (1, 11, 21, 31): 29.0R 28.7 28.5 28.2 — ♇ (1, 11, 21, 31): 3.9R 3.7 3.6 3.5

IV

1941

	1	2	3	4	5	6	7	8	9	10	11	12	13	14	15	16	17	18	19	20	21	22	23	24	25	26	27	28	29	30
☉	10.9	11.9	12.9	13.8	14.8	15.8	16.8	17.8	18.8	19.7	20.7	21.7	22.7	23.7	24.6	25.6	26.6	27.6	28.6	29.5	0.5	1.5	2.5	3.4	4.4	5.4	6.3	7.3	8.3	9.3
☽	26	7.9	19.9	2.2	14.7	27.6	10.8	24.5	8.7	23.3	8.2	23.3	8.5	23.7	8.6	23.1	7.2	20.9	4.1	16.9	29.4	11.7	23.7	5.7	17.5	29.3	11.1	23	4.9	16.9
☿	14	15.3	16.5	17.9	19.2	20.6	22	23.5	25	26.5	28	29.5	1.1	2.7	4.4	6	7.7	9.4	11.2	12.9	14.7	16.6	18.4	20.3	22.2	24.1	26.1	28.1	0.1	2.1
♀	6.2	7.4	8.7	9.9	11.1	12.4	13.6	14.9	16.1	17.3	18.6	19.8	21.1	22.3	23.5	24.8	26	27.2	28.5	29.7	0.9	2.2	3.4	4.7	5.9	7.1	8.4	9.6	10.8	12.1
♂	29	29.7	0.4	1	1.7	2.4	3.1	3.8	4.5	5.2	5.9	6.6	7.3	8	8.6	9.3	10	10.7	11.4	12.1	12.8	13.5	14.2	14.8	15.5	16.2	16.9	17.6	18.3	19

♃ (1, 6, 11, 16, 21, 26): 17.2 18.3 19.4 20.5 21.7 22.8 — ♄ (1, 6, 11, 16, 21, 26): 13.3 13.9 14.5 15.1 15.7 16.4 — ♅ (1, 11, 21): 23.7 24.2 24.7 — ♆ (1, 11, 21): 25.9R 25.7 25.4 — ♇ (1, 11, 21): 2.1R 2 2.0D

1942

	1	2	3	4	5	6	7	8	9	10	11	12	13	14	15	16	17	18	19	20	21	22	23	24	25	26	27	28	29	30
☉	10.6	11.6	12.6	13.6	14.6	15.6	16.6	17.5	18.5	19.5	20.5	21.5	22.4	23.4	24.4	25.4	26.4	27.3	28.3	29.3	0.3	1.2	2.2	3.2	4.2	5.1	6.1	7.1	8.1	9
☽	3.7	18	2.5	17.1	1.8	16.4	0.8	15	28.9	12.5	26	9.1	22.1	4.9	17.4	29.8	12.1	24.2	6.2	18.1	29.9	11.8	23.8	5.9	18.3	1.1	14.2	27.8	11.8	26.3
☿	22.6	24.3	26	27.7	29.5	1.3	3.1	4.9	6.8	8.7	10.6	12.5	14.5	16.5	18.5	20.5	22.6	24.6	26.7	28.8	0.9	3.1	5.2	7.3	9.5	11.6	13.7	15.8	17.9	19.9
♀	25	25.9	26.8	27.7	28.6	29.5	0.4	1.4	2.3	3.2	4.2	5.2	6.1	7.1	8.1	9.1	10.1	11.1	12.1	13.1	14.1	15.1	16.2	17.2	18.2	19.3	20.3	21.4	22.4	23.5
♂	14.7	15.3	15.9	16.5	17.1	17.7	18.3	18.9	19.5	20.1	20.7	21.3	22	22.6	23.2	23.8	24.4	25	25.6	26.2	26.8	27.4	28	28.6	29.2	29.9	0.5	1.1	1.7	2.3

♃ (1, 6, 11, 16, 21, 26): 15.9 16.7 17.6 18.4 19.3 20.3 — ♄ (1, 6, 11, 16, 21, 26): 25.5 26.1 26.6 27.2 27.8 28.4 — ♅ (1, 11, 21): 27.7 28.1 28.7 — ♆ (1, 11, 21): 28.2R 27.9 27.7 — ♇ (1, 11, 21): 3.5R 3.5 3.5D

V

1941

	1	2	3	4	5	6	7	8	9	10	11	12	13	14	15	16	17	18	19	20	21	22	23	24	25	26	27	28	29	30	31
☉	10.2	11.2	12.2	13.1	14.1	15.1	16	17	18	18.9	19.9	20.9	21.8	22.8	23.8	24.7	25.7	26.7	27.6	28.6	29.6	0.5	1.5	2.4	3.4	4.4	5.3	6.3	7.2	8.2	9.2
☽	29	11.3	23.9	6.7	19.8	3.4	17.3	1.7	16.5	1.5	16.8	2	17.1	1.8	16.1	29.9	13.2	26	8.5	20.7	2.7	14.6	26.3	8.1	20	1.9	13.9	26.1	8.4	20.9	3.6
☿	4.2	6.3	8.4	10.5	12.7	14.8	17	19.1	21.3	23.5	25.7	27.8	29.9	2.1	4.1	6.2	8.2	10.2	12.1	14	15.9	17.7	19.5	21.2	22.8	24.5	26	27.5	29	0.4	1.7
♀	13.3	14.5	15.8	17	18.2	19.5	20.7	21.9	23.2	24.4	25.6	26.9	28.1	29.3	0.5	1.8	3	4.2	5.5	6.7	7.9	9.2	10.4	11.6	12.8	14.1	15.3	16.5	17.8	19	20.2
♂	19.7	20.3	21	21.7	22.4	23.1	23.8	24.4	25.1	25.8	26.5	27.2	27.8	28.5	29.2	29.9	0.5	1.2	1.9	2.6	3.2	3.9	4.6	5.2	5.9	6.6	7.2	7.9	8.5	9.2	9.9

♃ (1, 6, 11, 16, 21, 26, 31): 24 25.2 26.3 27.5 28.7 29.9 1.1 — ♄ (1, 6, 11, 16, 21, 26, 31): 17 17.6 18.3 18.9 19.6 20.2 20.8 — ♅ (1, 11, 21, 31): 25.2 25.8 26.4 27 — ♆ (1, 11, 21, 31): 25.2R 25.1 25 24.9 — ♇ (1, 11, 21, 31): 2.1 2.2 2.3 2.5

1942

	1	2	3	4	5	6	7	8	9	10	11	12	13	14	15	16	17	18	19	20	21	22	23	24	25	26	27	28	29	30	31
☉	10	11	11.9	12.9	13.9	14.8	15.8	16.8	17.7	18.7	19.7	20.6	21.6	22.6	23.5	24.5	25.5	26.4	27.4	28.4	29.3	0.3	1.2	2.2	3.2	4.1	5.1	6	7	8	8.9
☽	11.2	26.2	11.3	26.2	11	25.3	9.3	22.9	6.2	19.1	1.8	14.3	26.6	8.8	20.9	2.9	14.8	26.6	8.5	20.4	2.3	14.4	26.8	9.5	22.5	6	20.1	4.6	19.5	4.7	20
☿	22	24	25.9	27.8	29.7	1.5	3.2	4.9	6.6	8.1	9.6	11.1	12.5	13.8	15.1	16.3	17.4	18.5	19.5	20.4	21.2	22	22.7	23.4	23.9	24.4	24.8	25.1	25.4	25.5	25.6
♀	24.5	25.6	26.7	27.8	28.8	29.9	1	2.1	3.2	4.3	5.3	6.4	7.5	8.6	9.8	10.9	12	13.1	14.2	15.3	16.4	17.5	18.7	19.8	20.9	22	23.2	24.3	25.4	26.6	27.7
♂	2.9	3.5	4.1	4.7	5.3	6	6.6	7.2	7.8	8.4	9	9.6	10.2	10.8	11.5	12.1	12.7	13.3	13.9	14.5	15.1	15.8	16.4	17	17.6	18.2	18.8	19.4	20.1	20.7	21.3

♃ (1, 6, 11, 16, 21, 26, 31): 21.3 22.3 23.3 24.4 25.5 26.6 27.7 — ♄ (1, 6, 11, 16, 21, 26, 31): 29 29.7 0.3 0.9 1.6 2.2 2.9 — ♅ (1, 11, 21, 31): 29.2 29.8 0.3 0.9 — ♆ (1, 11, 21, 31): 27.5R 27.3 27.2 27.1 — ♇ (1, 11, 21, 31): 3.5 3.6 3.7 3.9

VI

1941

	1	2	3	4	5	6	7	8	9	10	11	12	13	14	15	16	17	18	19	20	21	22	23	24	25	26	27	28	29	30
☉	10.1	11.1	12	13	13.9	14.9	15.9	16.8	17.8	18.7	19.7	20.6	21.6	22.5	23.5	24.5	25.4	26.4	27.3	28.3	29.2	0.2	1.1	2.1	3	4	5	5.9	6.9	7.8
☽	16.5	29.6	13.1	26.9	11.1	25.6	10.4	25.4	10.4	25.4	10	24.3	8.2	21.6	4.5	17	29.2	11.2	23.1	4.9	16.7	28.6	10.7	22.9	5.3	17.8	0.6	13.5	26.7	10
☿	3	4.3	5.4	6.6	7.6	8.6	9.6	10.5	11.3	12	12.7	13.3	13.9	14.4	14.8	15.1	15.4	15.5	15.6	15.7R	15.6	15.5	15.3	15.1	14.7	14.3	13.9	13.4	12.9	12.3
♀	21.4	22.7	23.9	25.1	26.3	27.6	28.8	0	1.2	2.5	3.7	4.9	6.1	7.4	8.6	9.8	11	12.3	13.5	14.7	15.9	17.2	18.4	19.6	20.8	22	23.3	24.5	25.7	26.9
♂	10.5	11.2	11.8	12.5	13.1	13.8	14.4	15.1	15.7	16.4	17	17.6	18.3	18.9	19.5	20.2	20.8	21.4	22	22.7	23.3	23.9	24.5	25.1	25.7	26.3	26.9	27.5	28.1	28.7

♃ (1, 6, 11, 16, 21, 26): 1.3 2.5 3.6 4.8 5.9 7 — ♄ (1, 6, 11, 16, 21, 26): 21 21.6 22.2 22.8 23.3 23.9 — ♅ (1, 11, 21): 27 27.6 28.1 — ♆ (1, 11, 21): 24.9R 24.9D 25 — ♇ (1, 11, 21): 2.5 2.7 2.9

1942

	1	2	3	4	5	6	7	8	9	10	11	12	13	14	15	16	17	18	19	20	21	22	23	24	25	26	27	28	29	30
☉	9.9	10.8	11.8	12.8	13.7	14.7	15.6	16.6	17.5	18.5	19.5	20.4	21.4	22.3	23.3	24.2	25.2	26.1	27.1	28	29	30	0.9	1.9	2.8	3.8	4.7	5.7	6.6	7.6
☽	5.2	20.2	4.8	19	2.7	15.9	28.8	11.4	23.8	5.9	18	29.9	11.8	23.7	5.5	17.4	29.3	11.4	23.5	5.9	18.6	1.6	15	28.9	13.3	28	13.1	28.4	13.7	28.7
☿	25.6R	25.6	25.4	25.2	25	24.6	24.2	23.8	23.3	22.8	22.3	21.7	21.2	20.6	20	19.5	19	18.6	18.2	17.8	17.5	17.3	17.1	17	17.0D	17.1	17.2	17.5	17.8	18.2
♀	28.9	30	1.1	2.3	3.4	4.6	5.7	6.9	8	9.2	10.3	11.5	12.6	13.8	14.9	16.1	17.3	18.4	19.6	20.7	21.9	23.1	24.2	25.4	26.6	27.8	28.9	0.1	1.3	2.4
♂	21.9	22.5	23.1	23.7	24.4	25	25.6	26.2	26.8	27.4	28.1	28.7	29.3	29.9	0.5	1.1	1.8	2.4	3	3.6	4.2	4.9	5.5	6.1	6.7	7.3	8	8.6	9.2	9.8

♃ (1, 6, 11, 16, 21, 26): 27.9 29 0.1 1.3 2.4 3.6 — ♄ (1, 6, 11, 16, 21, 26): 3 3.6 4.3 4.9 5.5 6.1 — ♅ (1, 11, 21): 1 1.6 2.1 — ♆ (1, 11, 21): 27.1R 27.1D 27.1 — ♇ (1, 11, 21): 3.9 4.1 4.3

VII

1941

	1	2	3	4	5	6	7	8	9	10	11	12	13	14	15	16	17	18	19	20	21	22	23	24	25	26	27	28	29	30	31
☉	8.8	9.7	10.7	11.6	12.6	13.5	14.5	15.4	16.4	17.3	18.3	19.3	20.2	21.2	22.1	23.1	24	25	25.9	26.9	27.8	28.8	29.8	0.7	1.7	2.6	3.6	4.5	5.5	6.4	7.4
☽	23.5	7.3	21.4	5.6	20.1	4.7	19.4	4	18.4	2.6	16.3	29.6	12.5	25.1	7.3	19.3	1.2	13.1	24.9	6.9	19.1	1.4	14	26.9	9.9	23.2	6.7	20.4	4.2	18.2	2.3
☿	11.7R	11.1	10.5	9.9	9.3	8.7	8.2	7.7	7.3	7	6.7	6.5	6.3	6.3	6.3D	6.5	6.7	7	7.4	7.9	8.5	9.2	10	10.8	11.8	12.8	14	15.2	16.5	17.9	19.3
♀	28.2	29.4	0.6	1.8	3	4.3	5.5	6.7	7.9	9.1	10.3	11.6	12.8	14	15.2	16.4	17.7	18.9	20.1	21.3	22.5	23.7	24.9	26.2	27.4	28.6	29.8	1	2.2	3.4	4.6
♂	29.3	29.9	0.5	1	1.6	2.2	2.7	3.3	3.9	4.4	5	5.5	6	6.6	7.1	7.6	8.1	8.7	9.2	9.7	10.2	10.6	11.1	11.6	12.1	12.5	13	13.5	13.9	14.3	14.8

♃ (1, 6, 11, 16, 21, 26, 31): 8.1 9.2 10.2 11.3 12.3 13.2 14.1 — ♄ (1, 6, 11, 16, 21, 26, 31): 24.4 24.9 25.4 25.9 26.3 26.7 27.1 — ♅ (1, 11, 21, 31): 28.6 29.1 29.5 29.8 — ♆ (1, 11, 21, 31): 25.1 25.2 25.4 25.7 — ♇ (1, 11, 21, 31): 3.2 3.5 3.7 4

1942

	1	2	3	4	5	6	7	8	9	10	11	12	13	14	15	16	17	18	19	20	21	22	23	24	25	26	27	28	29	30	31
☉	8.5	9.5	10.4	11.4	12.4	13.3	14.3	15.2	16.2	17.1	18.1	19	20	20.9	21.9	22.8	23.8	24.7	25.7	26.7	27.6	28.6	29.5	0.5	1.4	2.4	3.3	4.3	5.3	6.2	7.2
☽	13.5	27.8	11.6	25	7.9	20.5	2.9	15	26.9	8.8	20.7	2.5	14.4	26.4	8.5	20.7	3	15.6	28.4	11.4	24.9	8.6	22.8	7.3	22.1	7.1	22.1	7	21.7	6	19.9
☿	18.6	19.2	19.8	20.5	21.3	22.1	23.1	24.1	25.2	26.3	27.5	28.8	0.2	1.7	3.2	4.7	6.4	8.1	9.8	11.6	13.5	15.4	17.3	19.3	21.3	23.4	25.4	27.5	29.6	1.7	3.8
♀	3.6	4.8	6	7.1	8.3	9.5	10.7	11.9	13.1	14.2	15.4	16.6	17.8	19	20.2	21.4	22.5	23.7	24.9	26.1	27.3	28.5	29.7	0.9	2.1	3.3	4.5	5.7	6.9	8.1	9.3
♂	10.4	11.1	11.7	12.3	12.9	13.5	14.2	14.8	15.4	16	16.7	17.3	17.9	18.5	19.1	19.8	20.4	21	21.6	22.3	22.9	23.5	24.1	24.8	25.4	26	26.7	27.3	27.9	28.5	29.2

♃ (1, 6, 11, 16, 21, 26, 31): 4.7 5.8 7 8.1 9.2 10.3 11.4 — ♄ (1, 6, 11, 16, 21, 26, 31): 6.7 7.3 7.9 8.4 8.9 9.4 9.9 — ♅ (1, 11, 21, 31): 2.6 3.1 3.5 3.9 — ♆ (1, 11, 21, 31): 27.2 27.4 27.6 27.8 — ♇ (1, 11, 21, 31): 4.6 4.9 5.1 5.4

VIII

1941

	1	2	3	4	5	6	7	8	9	10	11	12	13	14	15	16	17	18	19	20	21	22	23	24	25	26	27	28	29	30	31
☉	8.4	9.3	10.3	11.2	12.2	13.1	14.1	15.1	16	17	17.9	18.9	19.9	20.8	21.8	22.7	23.7	24.7	25.6	26.6	27.5	28.5	29.5	0.4	1.4	2.4	3.3	4.3	5.3	6.2	7.2
☽	16.4	0.7	15	29.2	13.4	27.4	11.1	24.6	7.7	20.5	3	15.2	27.2	9.1	21	2.9	14.9	27.1	9.5	22.3	5.3	18.7	2.4	16.3	0.4	14.6	28.9	13.2	27.5	11.7	25.7
☿	20.9	22.5	24.2	25.9	27.7	29.5	1.4	3.4	5.3	7.3	9.3	11.4	13.4	15.5	17.5	19.5	21.6	23.6	25.6	27.6	29.6	1.5	3.5	5.4	7.3	9.2	11	12.9	14.7	16.5	18.2
♀	5.9	7.1	8.3	9.5	10.7	11.9	13.1	14.3	15.5	16.7	17.9	19.2	20.4	21.6	22.8	24	25.2	26.4	27.6	28.8	30	1.2	2.4	3.6	4.8	6	7.2	8.4	9.6	10.8	12
♂	15.2	15.6	16	16.4	16.8	17.2	17.6	17.9	18.3	18.6	19	19.3	19.6	19.9	20.2	20.5	20.8	21.1	21.3	21.6	21.8	22	22.2	22.4	22.6	22.8	22.9	23.1	23.2	23.3	23.4

♃ (1, 6, 11, 16, 21, 26, 31): 14.3 15.2 16 16.8 17.6 18.3 18.9 — ♄ (1, 6, 11, 16, 21, 26, 31): 27.1 27.4 27.7 28 28.2 28.3 28.5 — ♅ (1, 11, 21, 31): 29.8 0.1 0.2 0.3 — ♆ (1, 11, 21, 31): 25.7 26 26.3 26.7 — ♇ (1, 11, 21, 31): 4 4.3 4.6 4.9

1942

	1	2	3	4	5	6	7	8	9	10	11	12	13	14	15	16	17	18	19	20	21	22	23	24	25	26	27	28	29	30	31
☉	8.1	9.1	10	11	11.9	12.9	13.9	14.8	15.8	16.7	17.7	18.7	19.6	20.6	21.5	22.5	23.5	24.4	25.4	26.4	27.3	28.3	29.2	0.2	1.2	2.1	3.1	4.1	5	6	7
☽	3.4	16.4	29.1	11.4	23.6	5.5	17.4	29.3	11.1	23.1	5.2	17.5	29.9	12.5	25.4	8.4	21.8	5.3	19.1	3.2	17.5	1.9	16.5	1.1	15.7	0	14.2	27.9	11.4	24.4	7.1
☿	5.9	8	10.1	12.2	14.2	16.3	18.3	20.3	22.2	24.2	26.1	28	29.9	1.7	3.5	5.3	7.1	8.9	10.6	12.3	14	15.6	17.3	18.9	20.5	22	23.6	25.1	26.6	28.1	29.5
♀	10.5	11.7	12.9	14.1	15.3	16.5	17.7	18.9	20.1	21.4	22.6	23.8	25	26.2	27.4	28.6	29.9	1.1	2.3	3.5	4.7	5.9	7.2	8.4	9.6	10.8	12.1	13.3	14.5	15.7	17
♂	29.8	0.4	1.1	1.7	2.3	2.9	3.6	4.2	4.8	5.5	6.1	6.7	7.4	8	8.6	9.3	9.9	10.5	11.2	11.8	12.4	13.1	13.7	14.3	15	15.6	16.3	16.9	17.5	18.2	18.8

♃ (1, 6, 11, 16, 21, 26, 31): 11.6 12.7 13.7 14.7 15.7 16.7 17.6 — ♄ (1, 6, 11, 16, 21, 26, 31): 9.9 10.4 10.8 11.1 11.4 11.7 12 — ♅ (1, 11, 21, 31): 3.9 4.2 4.4 4.5 — ♆ (1, 11, 21, 31): 27.8 28.1 28.4 28.8 — ♇ (1, 11, 21, 31): 5.5 5.7 6 6.3

IX

1941

	1	2	3	4	5	6	7	8	9	10	11	12	13	14	15	16	17	18	19	20	21	22	23	24	25	26	27	28	29	30
☉	8.2	9.1	10.1	11.1	12	13	14	15	15.9	16.9	17.9	18.8	19.8	20.8	21.8	22.7	23.7	24.7	25.7	26.6	27.6	28.6	29.6	0.6	1.5	2.5	3.5	4.5	5.5	6.4
☽	9.7	23.4	6.9	20.2	3.3	16.1	28.7	11.1	23.2	5.2	17.1	29	10.8	22.8	5	17.5	0.2	13.3	26.9	10.8	25	9.5	24.2	9	23.7	8.2	22.5	6.5	20.3	3.7
☿	20	21.7	23.4	25.1	26.7	28.4	0	1.6	3.2	4.8	6.3	7.8	9.4	10.9	12.3	13.8	15.2	16.6	18	19.4	20.7	22.1	23.4	24.7	25.9	27.2	28.4	29.6	0.7	1.8
♀	13.2	14.4	15.6	16.7	17.9	19.1	20.3	21.5	22.7	23.9	25.1	26.3	27.4	28.6	29.8	1	2.2	3.4	4.5	5.7	6.9	8.1	9.3	10.4	11.6	12.8	13.9	15.1	16.3	17.5
♂	23.5	23.6	23.6	23.7	23.7	23.7	23.7R	23.7	23.7	23.7	23.6	23.5	23.5	23.4	23.2	23.1	23	22.8	22.7	22.5	22.3	22.1	21.9	21.6	21.4	21.2	20.9	20.6	20.4	20.1

♃ (1, 6, 11, 16, 21, 26): 19 19.6 20.1 20.5 20.8 21.1 — ♄ (1, 6, 11, 16, 21, 26): 28.5 28.5 28.6R 28.5 28.5 28.3 — ♅ (1, 11, 21): 0.3 0.3R 0.3 — ♆ (1, 11, 21): 26.7 27.1 27.4 — ♇ (1, 11, 21): 4.9 5.1 5.3

1942

	1	2	3	4	5	6	7	8	9	10	11	12	13	14	15	16	17	18	19	20	21	22	23	24	25	26	27	28	29	30
☉	7.9	8.9	9.9	10.8	11.8	12.8	13.7	14.7	15.7	16.7	17.6	18.6	19.6	20.6	21.5	22.5	23.5	24.5	25.4	26.4	27.4	28.4	29.3	0.3	1.3	2.3	3.3	4.2	5.2	6.2
☽	19.5	1.7	13.7	25.5	7.4	19.3	1.4	13.6	26.1	8.7	21.7	4.9	18.4	2.1	16	0	14.1	28.3	12.6	26.8	10.9	25	8.9	22.7	6.2	19.4	2.4	15	27.4	9.6
☿	0.9	2.3	3.7	5.1	6.4	7.7	9	10.2	11.4	12.6	13.8	14.9	16	17.1	18.1	19.1	20	20.9	21.7	22.5	23.2	23.8	24.4	24.9	25.3	25.6	25.8	26	26.0R	25.9
♀	18.2	19.4	20.6	21.9	23.1	24.3	25.6	26.8	28	29.3	0.5	1.7	3	4.2	5.4	6.7	7.9	9.1	10.4	11.6	12.9	14.1	15.3	16.6	17.8	19.1	20.3	21.6	22.8	24
♂	19.4	20.1	20.7	21.4	22	22.7	23.3	23.9	24.6	25.2	25.9	26.5	27.2	27.8	28.4	29.1	29.7	0.4	1	1.7	2.3	3	3.6	4.3	4.9	5.6	6.2	6.9	7.5	8.2

♃ (1, 6, 11, 16, 21, 26): 17.8 18.7 19.5 20.3 21.1 21.8 — ♄ (1, 6, 11, 16, 21, 26): 12 12.2 12.3 12.5 12.5 12.5R — ♅ (1, 11, 21): 4.6 4.6R 4.5 — ♆ (1, 11, 21): 28.8 29.2 29.5 — ♇ (1, 11, 21): 6.3 6.5 6.8

X

1941

	1	2	3	4	5	6	7	8	9	10	11	12	13	14	15	16	17	18	19	20	21	22	23	24	25	26	27	28	29	30	31
☉	7.4	8.4	9.4	10.4	11.4	12.4	13.3	14.3	15.3	16.3	17.3	18.3	19.3	20.3	21.3	22.2	23.2	24.2	25.2	26.2	27.2	28.2	29.2	0.2	1.2	2.2	3.2	4.2	5.2	6.2	7.2
☽	16.9	29.8	12.5	25	7.4	19.5	1.6	13.5	25.4	7.2	19.1	1.1	13.2	25.6	8.2	21.3	4.8	18.7	3.1	17.8	2.9	18	3.1	18	2.6	16.8	0.5	13.9	26.9	9.6	22
☿	2.9	3.9	5	5.9	6.8	7.7	8.5	9.2	9.9	10.5	11	11.5	11.8	12	12.2	12.2R	12	11.7	11.3	10.8	10.1	9.2	8.3	7.2	6	4.7	3.5	2.2	1	29.8	28.8
♀	18.6	19.8	21	22.1	23.3	24.4	25.6	26.8	27.9	29.1	0.2	1.4	2.5	3.7	4.8	6	7.1	8.3	9.4	10.5	11.7	12.8	13.9	15.1	16.2	17.3	18.5	19.6	20.7	21.8	22.9
♂	19.8R	19.5	19.2	18.9	18.6	18.3	17.9	17.6	17.3	17	16.7	16.4	16.1	15.8	15.5	15.2	14.9	14.6	14.3	14.1	13.8	13.6	13.3	13.1	12.9	12.7	12.5	12.3	12.1	12	11.8

♃ (1, 6, 11, 16, 21, 26, 31): 21.3 21.4 21.4R 21.4 21.3 21 20.7 — ♄ (1, 6, 11, 16, 21, 26, 31): 28.2R 28 27.8 27.5 27.2 26.8 26.5 — ♅ (1, 11, 21, 31): 0.1R 29.8 29.5 29.2 — ♆ (1, 11, 21, 31): 27.8 28.2 28.5 28.8 — ♇ (1, 11, 21, 31): 5.5 5.6 5.7 5.8

1942

	1	2	3	4	5	6	7	8	9	10	11	12	13	14	15	16	17	18	19	20	21	22	23	24	25	26	27	28	29	30	31
☉	7.2	8.2	9.2	10.1	11.1	12.1	13.1	14.1	15.1	16.1	17	18	19	20	21	22	23	24	25	26	27	28	29	30	1	1.9	2.9	3.9	4.9	5.9	6.9
☽	21.5	3.4	15.3	27.2	9.3	21.5	4.1	17	0.3	13.9	27.8	12	26.3	10.7	25.1	9.4	23.5	7.5	21.4	5.1	18.5	1.9	15	27.9	10.7	23.2	5.5	17.6	29.5	11.4	23.2
☿	25.7R	25.3	24.9	24.3	23.5	22.7	21.7	20.7	19.5	18.4	17.2	16	14.9	13.8	12.9	12.1	11.4	11	10.7	10.6	10.7D	11	11.4	12	12.7	13.6	14.6	15.7	16.9	18.1	19.5
♀	25.3	26.5	27.8	29	0.3	1.5	2.8	4	5.3	6.5	7.8	9	10.3	11.5	12.8	14	15.3	16.5	17.8	19	20.3	21.5	22.8	24	25.3	26.5	27.8	29	0.3	1.5	2.8
♂	8.9	9.5	10.2	10.8	11.5	12.1	12.8	13.4	14.1	14.8	15.4	16.1	16.7	17.4	18.1	18.7	19.4	20	20.7	21.4	22	22.7	23.4	24	24.7	25.4	26	26.7	27.4	28	28.7

♃ (1, 6, 11, 16, 21, 26, 31): 22.4 23 23.6 24 24.4 24.7 25 — ♄ (1, 6, 11, 16, 21, 26, 31): 12.5R 12.4 12.3 12.1 11.9 11.7 11.4 — ♅ (1, 11, 21, 31): 4.4R 4.2 3.9 3.6 — ♆ (1, 11, 21, 31): 29.9 0.3 0.6 1 — ♇ (1, 11, 21, 31): 6.9 7.1 7.2 7.2

XI

1941

	1	2	3	4	5	6	7	8	9	10	11	12	13	14	15	16	17	18	19	20	21	22	23	24	25	26	27	28	29	30
☉	8.2	9.2	10.2	11.2	12.2	13.2	14.2	15.2	16.2	17.2	18.2	19.2	20.2	21.2	22.2	23.3	24.3	25.3	26.3	27.3	28.3	29.3	0.3	1.3	2.3	3.4	4.4	5.4	6.4	7.4
☽	4.2	16.3	28.3	10.3	22.2	4	15.9	27.8	9.8	21.9	4.2	16.8	29.7	13.1	26.8	11.1	25.8	10.9	26.2	11.6	26.7	11.6	26	9.9	23.4	6.4	19	1.3	13.4	25.4
☿	28.0R	27.3	26.8	26.5	26.4	26.4D	26.7	27.1	27.7	28.4	29.2	0.2	1.2	2.3	3.5	4.8	6.1	7.4	8.8	10.2	11.7	13.2	14.6	16.1	17.7	19.2	20.7	22.3	23.8	25.3
♀	24	25.1	26.2	27.3	28.4	29.5	0.6	1.7	2.8	3.9	5	6	7.1	8.2	9.2	10.3	11.3	12.4	13.4	14.4	15.5	16.5	17.5	18.5	19.5	20.5	21.5	22.5	23.5	24.4
♂	11.7R	11.6	11.5	11.4	11.3	11.2	11.2	11.1	11.1	11.1	11.1D	11.1	11.1	11.2	11.2	11.3	11.4	11.5	11.6	11.7	11.8	12	12.1	12.3	12.5	12.6	12.8	13	13.3	13.5

♃ (1, 6, 11, 16, 21, 26): 20.7R 20.3 19.8 19.3 18.7 18.1 — ♄ (1, 6, 11, 16, 21, 26): 26.4R 26 25.6 25.2 24.8 24.4 — ♅ (1, 11, 21): 29.1R 28.7 28.3 — ♆ (1, 11, 21): 28.9 29.2 29.4 — ♇ (1, 11, 21): 5.8 5.8R 5.7

1942

	1	2	3	4	5	6	7	8	9	10	11	12	13	14	15	16	17	18	19	20	21	22	23	24	25	26	27	28	29	30
☉	7.9	8.9	9.9	10.9	11.9	13	14	15	16	17	18	19	20	21	22	23	24	25	26	27	28.1	29.1	0.1	1.1	2.1	3.1	4.1	5.1	6.1	7.2
☽	5.1	17.1	29.3	11.9	24.8	8.2	22.1	6.3	20.9	5.7	20.6	5.3	19.9	4.3	18.3	2	15.4	28.6	11.6	24.4	7	19.5	1.7	13.9	25.9	7.8	19.6	1.4	13.2	25.2
☿	20.8	22.3	23.7	25.3	26.8	28.3	29.9	1.5	3.1	4.7	6.3	7.9	9.5	11.1	12.7	14.3	15.9	17.5	19.1	20.7	22.3	23.9	25.5	27.1	28.7	0.3	1.8	3.4	5	6.6
♀	4.1	5.3	6.6	7.8	9.1	10.3	11.6	12.8	14.1	15.4	16.6	17.9	19.1	20.4	21.6	22.9	24.1	25.4	26.7	27.9	29.2	0.4	1.7	2.9	4.2	5.5	6.7	8	9.2	10.5
♂	29.4	0.1	0.7	1.4	2.1	2.8	3.4	4.1	4.8	5.5	6.1	6.8	7.5	8.2	8.8	9.5	10.2	10.9	11.6	12.3	12.9	13.6	14.3	15	15.7	16.4	17.1	17.7	18.4	19.1

♃ (1, 6, 11, 16, 21, 26): 25 25.2 25.2 25.2R 25.1 24.9 — ♄ (1, 6, 11, 16, 21, 26): 11.3R 11 10.7 10.3 9.9 9.5 — ♅ (1, 11, 21): 3.5R 3.2 2.8 — ♆ (1, 11, 21): 1 1.3 1.5 — ♇ (1, 11, 21): 7.2 7.3R 7.2

XII

1941

	1	2	3	4	5	6	7	8	9	10	11	12	13	14	15	16	17	18	19	20	21	22	23	24	25	26	27	28	29	30	31
☉	8.4	9.4	10.4	11.5	12.5	13.5	14.5	15.5	16.5	17.6	18.6	19.6	20.6	21.6	22.6	23.7	24.7	25.7	26.7	27.7	28.7	29.8	0.8	1.8	2.8	3.8	4.9	5.9	6.9	7.9	8.9
☽	7.3	19.1	1	12.9	24.8	6.8	18.9	1.2	13.6	26.2	9	22.2	5.8	19.9	4.3	19.2	4.3	19.6	4.8	19.7	4.3	18.3	1.9	15	27.7	10.1	22.2	4.1	16	27.8	9.7
☿	26.9	28.4	0	1.6	3.1	4.7	6.2	7.8	9.3	10.9	12.5	14	15.6	17.2	18.7	20.3	21.9	23.4	25	26.6	28.2	29.8	1.3	2.9	4.5	6.1	7.7	9.3	11	12.6	14.2
♀	25.4	26.3	27.3	28.2	29.1	0	0.9	1.8	2.7	3.6	4.4	5.3	6.1	6.9	7.7	8.5	9.3	10	10.8	11.5	12.2	12.9	13.5	14.2	14.8	15.4	16	16.5	17.1	17.6	18
♂	13.7	14	14.2	14.5	14.8	15	15.3	15.6	15.9	16.3	16.6	16.9	17.2	17.6	17.9	18.3	18.7	19	19.4	19.8	20.2	20.6	21	21.4	21.8	22.2	22.7	23.1	23.5	24	24.4

♃ (1, 6, 11, 16, 21, 26, 31): 17.4R 16.7 16.1 15.4 14.7 14.1 13.5 — ♄ (1, 6, 11, 16, 21, 26, 31): 24.0R 23.6 23.3 22.9 22.6 22.4 22.1 — ♅ (1, 11, 21, 31): 27.9R 27.5 27.2 26.8 — ♆ (1, 11, 21, 31): 29.6 29.8 29.8 29.9 — ♇ (1, 11, 21, 31): 5.7R 5.5 5.4 5.2

1942

	1	2	3	4	5	6	7	8	9	10	11	12	13	14	15	16	17	18	19	20	21	22	23	24	25	26	27	28	29	30	31
☉	8.2	9.2	10.2	11.2	12.2	13.2	14.3	15.3	16.3	17.3	18.3	19.3	20.4	21.4	22.4	23.4	24.4	25.4	26.5	27.5	28.5	29.5	0.5	1.6	2.6	3.6	4.6	5.6	6.6	7.7	8.7
☽	7.4	19.9	2.8	16.1	29.9	14.3	29	14.1	29.3	14.4	29.4	14	28.3	12.1	25.6	8.7	21.5	4	16.4	28.6	10.7	22.7	4.6	16.4	28.2	10.1	21.9	3.9	16.1	28.6	11.3
☿	8.1	9.7	11.3	12.8	14.4	16	17.5	19.1	20.7	22.3	23.8	25.4	27	28.5	0.1	1.7	3.3	4.9	6.4	8	9.6	11.2	12.8	14.3	15.9	17.5	19	20.6	22.1	23.6	25.1
♀	11.7	13	14.3	15.5	16.8	18	19.3	20.5	21.8	23.1	24.3	25.6	26.8	28.1	29.3	0.6	1.9	3.1	4.4	5.6	6.9	8.1	9.4	10.7	11.9	13.2	14.4	15.7	16.9	18.2	19.5
♂	19.8	20.5	21.2	21.9	22.6	23.3	24	24.7	25.3	26	26.7	27.4	28.1	28.8	29.5	0.2	0.9	1.6	2.3	3	3.7	4.4	5.1	5.8	6.6	7.3	8	8.7	9.4	10.1	10.8

♃ (1, 6, 11, 16, 21, 26, 31): 24.7R 24.3 23.9 23.5 22.9 22.3 21.7 — ♄ (1, 6, 11, 16, 21, 26, 31): 9.1R 8.7 8.3 7.9 7.5 7.2 6.8 — ♅ (1, 11, 21, 31): 2.3R 1.9 1.5 1.2 — ♆ (1, 11, 21, 31): 1.7 1.9 2 2.1 — ♇ (1, 11, 21, 31): 7.1R 7 6.9 6.7

I

	1	2	3	4	5	6	7	8	9	10	11	12	13	14	15	16	17	18	19	20	21	22	23	24	25	26	27	28	29	30	31
☉	♑ 9.7	10.7	11.7	12.8	13.8	14.8	15.8	16.8	17.9	18.9	19.9	20.9	21.9	23	24	25	26	27	28	29.1	♒ 0.1	1.1	2.1	3.1	4.2	5.2	6.2	7.2	8.2	9.2	10.2
☽	♎ 24.5	♏ 8.2	22.4	♐ 7	22	♑ 7.3	22.6	♒ 7.7	22.7	♓ 7.2	21.2	♈ 4.9	18	♉ 0.9	13.4	25.6	♊ 7.7	19.7	♋ 1.5	13.4	25.2	♌ 7.1	19	♍ 1	13.1	25.4	♎ 8	20.8	♏ 4	17.5	♐ 1.4
☿	♑ 26.6	28.1	29.5	♒ 0.9	2.3	3.5	4.8	5.9	7	7.9	8.8	9.5	10.1	10.5	10.8	10.8R	10.7	10.4	9.9	9.2	8.3	7.3	6.2	5	3.7	2.4	1.2	♑ 30	28.9	27.9	27.1
♀	♑ 20.7	22	23.2	24.5	25.7	27	28.2	29.5	♒ 0.7	2	3.3	4.5	5.8	7	8.3	9.5	10.8	12	13.3	14.5	15.8	17	18.3	19.5	20.8	22.1	23.3	24.6	25.8	27.1	28.3
♂	♐ 11.5	12.2	12.9	13.6	14.3	15.1	15.8	16.5	17.2	17.9	18.6	19.3	20.1	20.8	21.5	22.2	22.9	23.7	24.4	25.1	25.8	26.5	27.3	28	28.7	29.4	♑ 0.2	0.9	1.6	2.3	3.1

♃ 1: ♋ 21.6R · 6: 20.9 · 11: 20.2 · 16: 19.6 · 21: 18.9 · 26: 18.3 · 31: 17.7
♄ 1: ♊ 6.8R · 6: 6.5 · 11: 6.2 · 16: 6 · 21: 5.8 · 26: 5.7 · 31: 5.6
♅ 1: ♊ 1.2R · 11: 0.9 · 21: 0.7 · 31: 0.6
♆ 1: ♎ 2.1 · 11: 2.0R · 21: 2 · 31: 1.9
♇ 1: ♌ 6.7R · 11: 6.5 · 21: 6.2 · 31: 6

	1	2	3	4	5	6	7	8	9	10	11	12	13	14	15	16	17	18	19	20	21	22	23	24	25	26	27	28	29	30	31
☉	♑ 9.5	10.5	11.5	12.5	13.5	14.6	15.6	16.6	17.6	18.6	19.7	20.7	21.7	22.7	23.7	24.7	25.8	26.8	27.8	28.8	29.8	♒ 0.9	1.9	2.9	3.9	4.9	5.9	7	8	9	10
☽	♓ 15.5	29.7	♈ 13.6	27.2	♉ 10.6	23.7	♊ 6.5	19.2	♋ 1.6	13.9	26	♌ 8	19.8	♍ 1.6	13.4	25.3	♎ 7.3	19.4	♏ 1.9	14.6	27.8	♐ 11.5	25.5	♑ 10	24.9	♒ 10	25.1	♓ 10.1	25	♈ 9.5	23.6
☿	♑ 24.7R	24.4	23.8	23.1	22.2	21.1	19.9	18.7	17.3	16	14.7	13.5	12.3	11.4	10.5	9.8	9.3	8.9	8.7	8.7D	8.7	8.9	9.2	9.7	10.2	10.8	11.5	12.3	13.1	14	14.9
♀	♏ 27.4	28.6	29.8	♐ 1	2.2	3.3	4.5	5.7	6.9	8.1	9.3	10.5	11.7	12.9	14.1	15.3	16.5	17.7	18.9	20.2	21.4	22.6	23.8	25	26.2	27.4	28.6	29.9	♑ 1.1	2.3	3.5
♂	♊ 5.4R	5.3	5.2	5.1	5	5	4.9	4.9	4.9	4.9	4.9D	4.9	4.9	4.9	5	5.1	5.1	5.2	5.3	5.5	5.6	5.7	5.9	6	6.2	6.4	6.5	6.7	6.9	7.2	7.4

♃ 1: ♌ 26.5R · 6: 26.2 · 11: 25.8 · 16: 25.3 · 21: 24.8 · 26: 24.2 · 31: 23.6
♄ 1: ♊ 21.9R · 6: 21.5 · 11: 21.1 · 16: 20.8 · 21: 20.5 · 26: 20.3 · 31: 20.1
♅ 1: ♊ 5.6R · 11: 5.3 · 21: 5 · 31: 4.9
♆ 1: ♎ 4.2 · 11: 4.2R · 21: 4.2 · 31: 4.1
♇ 1: ♌ 8.2R · 11: 8 · 21: 7.8 · 31: 7.5

II

	1	2	3	4	5	6	7	8	9	10	11	12	13	14	15	16	17	18	19	20	21	22	23	24	25	26	27	28	29	30	31
☉	♒ 11.3	12.3	13.3	14.3	15.3	16.3	17.3	18.4	19.4	20.4	21.4	22.4	23.4	24.4	25.4	26.5	27.5	28.5	29.5	♓ 0.5	1.5	2.5	3.5	4.5	5.5	6.5	7.5	8.5			
☽	♐ 15.8	♑ 0.5	15.4	♒ 0.5	15.6	♓ 0.5	15.2	29.4	♈ 13.2	26.6	♉ 9.5	22.1	♊ 4.4	16.4	28.3	♋ 10.1	22	♌ 3.8	15.7	27.8	♍ 10	22.4	♎ 5	17.8	♏ 0.9	14.2	27.7	♐ 11.5			
☿	♑ 26.4R	25.8	25.4	25.1	24.9	24.9D	25	25.3	25.6	26	26.5	27.1	27.8	28.5	29.3	♒ 0.2	1.1	2.1	3.1	4.1	5.2	6.4	7.5	8.7	10	11.2	12.5	13.8			
♀	♒ 29.6	♓ 0.8	2	3.3	4.5	5.8	7	8.3	9.5	10.8	12	13.3	14.5	15.8	17	18.2	19.5	20.7	22	23.2	24.4	25.7	26.9	28.2	29.4	♈ 0.6	1.9	3.1			
♂	♑ 3.8	4.5	5.3	6	6.7	7.5	8.2	8.9	9.6	10.4	11.1	11.8	12.6	13.3	14.1	14.8	15.5	16.3	17	17.7	18.5	19.2	20	20.7	21.4	22.2	22.9	23.7			

♃ 1: ♋ 17.6R · 6: 17 · 11: 16.5 · 16: 16.1 · 21: 15.8 · 26: 15.5
♄ 1: ♊ 5.6R · 6: 5.6 · 11: 5.6D · 16: 5.7 · 21: 5.8 · 26: 6
♅ 1: ♊ 0.6R · 11: 0.6D · 21: 0.7
♆ 1: ♎ 1.8R · 11: 1.7 · 21: 1.5
♇ 1: ♌ 6.0R · 11: 5.8 · 21: 5.5

	1	2	3	4	5	6	7	8	9	10	11	12	13	14	15	16	17	18	19	20	21	22	23	24	25	26	27	28	29	30	31
☉	♒ 11	12	13	14.1	15.1	16.1	17.1	18.1	19.1	20.1	21.2	22.2	23.2	24.2	25.2	26.2	27.2	28.2	29.2	♓ 0.2	1.3	2.3	3.3	4.3	5.3	6.3	7.3	8.3	9.3		
☽	♉ 7.3	20.6	♊ 3.6	16.2	28.6	♋ 10.8	22.9	♌ 4.8	16.6	28.5	♍ 10.3	22.1	♎ 4	16.1	28.3	♏ 10.7	23.4	♐ 6.4	19.9	♑ 3.8	18.1	♒ 2.8	17.9	♓ 3.1	18.3	♈ 3.4	18.2	♉ 2.6	16.5		
☿	♑ 15.9	17	18	19.2	20.3	21.5	22.7	24	25.2	26.5	27.9	29.2	♒ 0.6	2	3.4	4.8	6.2	7.7	9.1	10.6	12.1	13.7	15.2	16.8	18.3	19.9	21.5	23.2	24.8		
♀	♑ 4.7	5.9	7.2	8.4	9.6	10.8	12	13.3	14.5	15.7	16.9	18.1	19.4	20.6	21.8	23	24.3	25.5	26.7	27.9	29.2	♒ 0.4	1.6	2.8	4.1	5.3	6.5	7.8	9		
♂	♊ 7.6	7.8	8.1	8.4	8.6	8.9	9.2	9.5	9.8	10.1	10.4	10.7	11	11.3	11.7	12	12.4	12.7	13.1	13.4	13.8	14.2	14.6	14.9	15.3	15.7	16.1	16.5	16.9		

♃ 1: ♌ 23.5R · 6: 22.9 · 11: 22.2 · 16: 21.5 · 21: 20.9 · 26: 20.3
♄ 1: ♊ 20.0R · 6: 19.9 · 11: 19.8 · 16: 19.7 · 21: 19.7D · 26: 19.7
♅ 1: ♊ 4.9R · 11: 4.8 · 21: 4.9D
♆ 1: ♎ 4.1R · 11: 3.9 · 21: 3.7
♇ 1: ♌ 7.5R · 11: 7.3 · 21: 7.1

III

	1	2	3	4	5	6	7	8	9	10	11	12	13	14	15	16	17	18	19	20	21	22	23	24	25	26	27	28	29	30	31
☉	♓ 9.5	10.5	11.5	12.6	13.6	14.6	15.6	16.6	17.6	18.6	19.6	20.6	21.6	22.5	23.5	24.5	25.5	26.5	27.5	28.5	29.5	♈ 0.5	1.5	2.5	3.5	4.5	5.5	6.5	7.4	8.4	9.4
☽	♐ 25.6	♑ 10	24.5	♒ 9.2	23.9	♓ 8.6	23.1	♈ 7.2	21.1	♉ 4.5	17.5	♊ 0.2	12.5	24.6	♋ 6.5	18.3	♌ 0.2	12	24.1	♍ 6.3	18.7	♎ 1.4	14.4	27.6	♏ 11	24.6	♐ 8.4	22.4	♑ 6.4	20.5	♒ 4.8
☿	♒ 15.1	16.5	17.9	19.3	20.7	22.1	23.6	25.1	26.6	28.1	29.7	♓ 1.3	2.8	4.5	6.1	7.7	9.4	11.1	12.8	14.5	16.3	18	19.8	21.6	23.5	25.3	27.2	29.1	♈ 1	3	4.9
♀	♈ 4.3	5.6	6.8	8	9.3	10.5	11.7	13	14.2	15.4	16.6	17.9	19.1	20.3	21.6	22.8	24	25.2	26.4	27.7	28.9	♉ 0.1	1.3	2.5	3.7	5	6.2	7.4	8.6	9.8	11
♂	♑ 24.4	25.2	25.9	26.6	27.4	28.1	28.9	29.6	♒ 0.4	1.1	1.9	2.6	3.4	4.1	4.9	5.6	6.3	7.1	7.8	8.6	9.3	10.1	10.8	11.6	12.4	13.1	13.9	14.6	15.4	16.1	16.9

♃ 1: ♋ 15.4R · 6: 15.2 · 11: 15.2 · 16: 15.2D · 21: 15.3 · 26: 15.5 · 31: 15.7
♄ 1: ♊ 6.1 · 6: 6.3 · 11: 6.6 · 16: 6.9 · 21: 7.2 · 26: 7.6 · 31: 8.1
♅ 1: ♊ 0.8 · 11: 1 · 21: 1.3 · 31: 1.7
♆ 1: ♎ 1.3R · 11: 1 · 21: 0.7 · 31: 0.5
♇ 1: ♌ 5.4R · 11: 5.2 · 21: 5.1 · 31: 5

	1	2	3	4	5	6	7	8	9	10	11	12	13	14	15	16	17	18	19	20	21	22	23	24	25	26	27	28	29	30	31
☉	♓ 10.3	11.3	12.3	13.3	14.3	15.3	16.3	17.3	18.3	19.3	20.3	21.3	22.3	23.3	24.3	25.3	26.3	27.3	28.3	29.3	♈ 0.3	1.3	2.3	3.2	4.2	5.2	6.2	7.2	8.2	9.2	10.2
☽	♉ 29.9	♊ 12.9	25.5	♋ 7.8	19.9	♌ 1.8	13.6	25.4	♍ 7.2	19.1	♎ 1	13.1	25.3	♏ 7.6	20.2	♐ 2.9	16	29.3	♑ 13	27.1	♒ 11.5	26.3	♓ 11.3	26.4	♈ 11.5	26.3	♉ 10.8	24.9	♊ 8.4	21.5	♋ 4.2
☿	♒ 26.5	28.1	29.8	♓ 1.5	3.3	5	6.8	8.5	10.4	12.2	14	15.9	17.7	19.6	21.6	23.5	25.4	27.4	29.4	♈ 1.4	3.4	5.4	7.4	9.4	11.5	13.5	15.5	17.5	19.4	21.4	23.3
♀	♒ 10.2	11.4	12.7	13.9	15.1	16.3	17.6	18.8	20	21.3	22.5	23.7	25	26.2	27.4	28.6	29.9	♓ 1.1	2.3	3.6	4.8	6	7.3	8.5	9.7	10.9	12.2	13.4	14.6	15.9	17.1
♂	♊ 17.3	17.8	18.2	18.6	19	19.5	19.9	20.3	20.8	21.2	21.7	22.1	22.6	23.1	23.5	24	24.5	24.9	25.4	25.9	26.4	26.9	27.3	27.8	28.3	28.8	29.3	29.8	♋ 0.3	0.8	1.3

♃ 1: ♌ 19.8R · 6: 19.2 · 11: 18.7 · 16: 18.3 · 21: 17.9 · 26: 17.6 · 31: 17.3
♄ 1: ♊ 19.8 · 6: 19.9 · 11: 20 · 16: 20.2 · 21: 20.5 · 26: 20.8 · 31: 21.1
♅ 1: ♊ 5 · 11: 5.2 · 21: 5.4 · 31: 5.8
♆ 1: ♎ 3.5R · 11: 3.2 · 21: 3 · 31: 2.7
♇ 1: ♌ 6.9R · 11: 6.7 · 21: 6.6 · 31: 6.5

IV

	1	2	3	4	5	6	7	8	9	10	11	12	13	14	15	16	17	18	19	20	21	22	23	24	25	26	27	28	29	30	31
☉	♈ 10.4	11.4	12.4	13.4	14.3	15.3	16.3	17.3	18.3	19.3	20.2	21.2	22.2	23.2	24.2	25.1	26.1	27.1	28.1	29.1	♉ 0	1	2	3	3.9	4.9	5.9	6.8	7.8	8.8	
☽	♒ 19	♓ 3.3	17.5	♈ 1.6	15.5	29.1	♉ 12.4	25.4	♊ 8	20.4	♋ 2.5	14.4	26.2	♌ 8.1	20	♍ 2	14.3	27	♎ 9.9	23.2	♏ 6.8	20.7	♐ 4.7	18.9	♑ 3.2	17.4	♒ 1.6	15.6	29.7	♓ 13.6	
☿	♈ 6.9	8.9	11	13	15	17.1	19.2	21.3	23.4	25.4	27.5	29.6	♉ 1.6	3.7	5.7	7.7	9.6	11.5	13.3	15.1	16.9	18.5	20.1	21.7	23.1	24.5	25.9	27.1	28.3	29.3	
♀	♉ 12.2	13.4	14.6	15.8	17	18.2	19.4	20.6	21.8	23	24.2	25.4	26.6	27.8	29	♊ 0.2	1.4	2.6	3.8	4.9	6.1	7.3	8.5	9.7	10.8	12	13.2	14.4	15.5	16.7	
♂	♒ 17.6	18.4	19.1	19.9	20.6	21.4	22.1	22.9	23.6	24.4	25.2	25.9	26.7	27.4	28.2	28.9	29.7	♓ 0.4	1.2	1.9	2.7	3.5	4.2	5	5.7	6.5	7.2	8	8.7	9.5	

♃ 1: ♋ 15.8 · 6: 16.2 · 11: 16.6 · 16: 17.1 · 21: 17.6 · 26: 18.2
♄ 1: ♊ 8.1 · 6: 8.6 · 11: 9.1 · 16: 9.6 · 21: 10.1 · 26: 10.7
♅ 1: ♊ 1.7 · 11: 2.2 · 21: 2.7
♆ 1: ♎ 0.4R · 11: 0.2 · 21: ♍ 29.9
♇ 1: ♌ 5.0R · 11: 4.9 · 21: 4.9D

	1	2	3	4	5	6	7	8	9	10	11	12	13	14	15	16	17	18	19	20	21	22	23	24	25	26	27	28	29	30	31
☉	♈ 11.2	12.1	13.1	14.1	15.1	16.1	17.1	18	19	20	21	22	23	23.9	24.9	25.9	26.9	27.8	28.8	29.8	♉ 0.8	1.7	2.7	3.7	4.7	5.6	6.6	7.6	8.6	9.5	
☽	♋ 16.5	28.6	♌ 10.4	22.2	♍ 4	15.9	27.8	♎ 9.9	22.1	♏ 4.6	17.2	30	♐ 13	26.1	♑ 9.6	23.2	♒ 7.1	21.3	♓ 5.8	20.4	♈ 5.2	19.9	♉ 4.6	18.9	♊ 2.9	16.4	29.6	♋ 12.3	24.6	♌ 6.7	
☿	♈ 25.2	27	28.8	♉ 0.5	2.1	3.7	5.2	6.6	7.9	9.2	10.3	11.4	12.3	13.2	14	14.6	15.2	15.6	16	16.2	16.4	16.4	16.4R	16.2	16	15.7	15.3	14.9	14.4	13.8	
♀	♓ 18.3	19.6	20.8	22	23.2	24.5	25.7	26.9	28.2	29.4	♈ 0.6	1.9	3.1	4.3	5.5	6.8	8	9.2	10.5	11.7	12.9	14.1	15.4	16.6	17.8	19.1	20.3	21.5	22.7	24	
♂	♋ 1.8	2.3	2.8	3.4	3.9	4.4	4.9	5.4	5.9	6.5	7	7.5	8	8.6	9.1	9.6	10.2	10.7	11.3	11.8	12.3	12.9	13.4	14	14.5	15.1	15.6	16.2	16.7	17.3	

♃ 1: ♌ 17.3R · 6: 17.1 · 11: 17 · 16: 17.1D · 21: 17.1 · 26: 17.3
♄ 1: ♊ 21.2 · 6: 21.5 · 11: 21.9 · 16: 22.4 · 21: 22.9 · 26: 23.3
♅ 1: ♊ 5.8 · 11: 6.3 · 21: 6.7
♆ 1: ♎ 2.6R · 11: 2.4 · 21: 2.1
♇ 1: ♌ 6.5R · 11: 6.4 · 21: 6.4D

V

	1	2	3	4	5	6	7	8	9	10	11	12	13	14	15	16	17	18	19	20	21	22	23	24	25	26	27	28	29	30	31
☉	♉ 9.8	10.7	11.7	12.7	13.6	14.6	15.6	16.5	17.5	18.5	19.4	20.4	21.4	22.3	23.3	24.3	25.2	26.2	27.2	28.1	29.1	♊ 0	1	2	2.9	3.9	4.9	5.8	6.8	7.7	8.7
☽	♓ 27.3	♈ 11	24.5	♉ 7.7	20.8	♊ 3.6	16.1	28.3	♋ 10.4	22.3	♌ 4.1	15.9	27.8	♍ 9.9	22.2	♎ 4.9	18	♏ 1.5	15.4	29.7	♐ 14.2	28.8	♑ 13.4	28	♒ 12.3	26.5	♓ 10.5	24.2	♈ 7.7	21	♉ 4.1
☿	♊ 0.3	1.3	2.1	2.8	3.5	4.1	4.6	5	5.3	5.5	5.7	5.7	5.7R	5.6	5.4	5.2	4.9	4.5	4	3.6	3	2.5	1.9	1.4	0.8	0.2	♉ 29.7	29.2	28.7	28.3	27.9
♀	♊ 17.9	19	20.2	21.4	22.5	23.7	24.8	26	27.1	28.3	29.4	♋ 0.6	1.7	2.9	4	5.1	6.3	7.4	8.5	9.7	10.8	11.9	13	14.2	15.3	16.4	17.5	18.6	19.7	20.8	21.9
♂	♓ 10.2	11	11.7	12.5	13.3	14	14.8	15.5	16.3	17	17.8	18.5	19.3	20	20.8	21.5	22.3	23	23.8	24.5	25.2	26	26.7	27.5	28.2	29	29.7	♈ 0.5	1.2	1.9	2.7

♃ 1: ♋ 18.9 · 6: 19.6 · 11: 20.3 · 16: 21.1 · 21: 22 · 26: 22.9 · 31: 23.8
♄ 1: ♊ 11.3 · 6: 11.9 · 11: 12.5 · 16: 13.1 · 21: 13.7 · 26: 14.4 · 31: 15
♅ 1: ♊ 3.2 · 11: 3.7 · 21: 4.3 · 31: 4.9
♆ 1: ♍ 29.7R · 11: 29.5 · 21: 29.4 · 31: 29.3
♇ 1: ♌ 5 · 11: 5 · 21: 5.2 · 31: 5.3

	1	2	3	4	5	6	7	8	9	10	11	12	13	14	15	16	17	18	19	20	21	22	23	24	25	26	27	28	29	30	31
☉	♉ 10.5	11.5	12.4	13.4	14.4	15.3	16.3	17.3	18.2	19.2	20.2	21.1	22.1	23.1	24	25	26	26.9	27.9	28.9	29.8	♊ 0.8	1.7	2.7	3.7	4.6	5.6	6.5	7.5	8.5	9.4
☽	♌ 18.6	♍ 0.5	12.3	24.2	♎ 6.2	18.4	♏ 0.9	13.6	26.5	♐ 9.6	23	♑ 6.5	20.1	♒ 3.9	17.9	♓ 2	16.2	♈ 0.6	14.9	29.2	♉ 13.4	27.4	♊ 11.1	24.5	♋ 7.5	20.2	♌ 2.5	14.6	26.6	♍ 8.4	20.3
☿	♉ 13.2R	12.6	12	11.3	10.7	10.1	9.5	9	8.5	8	7.6	7.3	7.1	6.9	6.8	6.8D	6.8	7	7.2	7.4	7.8	8.2	8.7	9.3	9.9	10.6	11.4	12.2	13.1	14	15
♀	♈ 25.2	26.4	27.7	28.9	♉ 0.1	1.3	2.6	3.8	5	6.3	7.5	8.7	9.9	11.2	12.4	13.6	14.8	16.1	17.3	18.5	19.8	21	22.2	23.4	24.7	25.9	27.1	28.3	29.6	♊ 0.8	2
♂	♋ 17.8	18.4	18.9	19.5	20	20.6	21.2	21.7	22.3	22.8	23.4	24	24.5	25.1	25.7	26.2	26.8	27.4	28	28.5	29.1	29.7	♌ 0.2	0.8	1.4	2	2.6	3.1	3.7	4.3	4.9

♃ 1: ♌ 17.5 · 6: 17.8 · 11: 18.2 · 16: 18.7 · 21: 19.2 · 26: 19.7 · 31: 20.3
♄ 1: ♊ 23.9 · 6: 24.4 · 11: 25 · 16: 25.6 · 21: 26.2 · 26: 26.8 · 31: 27.4
♅ 1: ♊ 7.3 · 11: 7.8 · 21: 8.4 · 31: 9
♆ 1: ♎ 1.9R · 11: 1.7 · 21: 1.6 · 31: 1.5
♇ 1: ♌ 6.4 · 11: 6.5 · 21: 6.6 · 31: 6.8

VI

	1	2	3	4	5	6	7	8	9	10	11	12	13	14	15	16	17	18	19	20	21	22	23	24	25	26	27	28	29	30	31
☉	♊ 9.6	10.6	11.6	12.5	13.5	14.4	15.4	16.4	17.3	18.3	19.2	20.2	21.1	22.1	23	24	25	25.9	26.9	27.8	28.8	29.7	♋ 0.7	1.6	2.6	3.5	4.5	5.4	6.4	7.4	
☽	♉ 17	29.7	♊ 12.2	24.5	♋ 6.7	18.6	♌ 0.5	12.3	24	♍ 5.9	18	♎ 0.3	13	26.1	♏ 9.7	23.7	♐ 8.1	22.9	♑ 7.8	22.8	♒ 7.7	22.4	♓ 6.8	20.9	♈ 4.6	18	♉ 1.2	14	26.6	♊ 9.1	
☿	♉ 27.6R	27.4	27.2	27.1	27	27.1D	27.2	27.3	27.6	27.9	28.3	28.8	29.4	30	♊ 0.7	1.4	2.3	3.1	4.1	5.1	6.2	7.3	8.5	9.8	11.1	12.5	13.9	15.4	17	18.6	
♀	♋ 23	24.1	25.2	26.2	27.3	28.4	29.5	♌ 0.5	1.6	2.7	3.7	4.8	5.8	6.8	7.9	8.9	9.9	11	12	13	14	15	16	17	18	18.9	19.9	20.9	21.8	22.7	
♂	♈ 3.4	4.2	4.9	5.6	6.4	7.1	7.8	8.6	9.3	10	10.8	11.5	12.2	12.9	13.7	14.4	15.1	15.8	16.6	17.3	18	18.7	19.4	20.2	20.9	21.6	22.3	23	23.7	24.4	

♃ 1: ♋ 24 · 6: 24.9 · 11: 25.9 · 16: 26.9 · 21: 27.9 · 26: 29
♄ 1: ♊ 15.2 · 6: 15.8 · 11: 16.4 · 16: 17.1 · 21: 17.7 · 26: 18.4
♅ 1: ♊ 5 · 11: 5.5 · 21: 6.1
♆ 1: ♍ 29.3R · 11: 29.3D · 21: 29.3
♇ 1: ♌ 5.3 · 11: 5.5 · 21: 5.8

	1	2	3	4	5	6	7	8	9	10	11	12	13	14	15	16	17	18	19	20	21	22	23	24	25	26	27	28	29	30	31
☉	♊ 10.4	11.3	12.3	13.2	14.2	15.2	16.1	17.1	18	19	19.9	20.9	21.9	22.8	23.8	24.7	25.7	26.6	27.6	28.5	29.5	♋ 0.4	1.4	2.4	3.3	4.3	5.2	6.2	7.1	8.1	
☽	♎ 2.2	14.3	26.6	♏ 9.2	22.1	♐ 5.3	18.8	♑ 2.5	16.4	♒ 0.5	14.6	28.8	♓ 13	27.2	♈ 11.4	25.4	♉ 9.3	23.1	♊ 6.6	19.9	♋ 3	15.7	28.2	♌ 10.5	22.6	♍ 4.5	16.3	28.2	♎ 10.1	22.2	
☿	♉ 16	17.1	18.3	19.5	20.7	22	23.4	24.8	26.2	27.7	29.2	♊ 0.8	2.5	4.1	5.9	7.6	9.5	11.3	13.2	15.2	17.1	19.2	21.2	23.3	25.4	27.5	29.7	♋ 1.9	4	6.2	
♀	♊ 3.3	4.5	5.7	6.9	8.2	9.4	10.6	11.8	13.1	14.3	15.5	16.8	18	19.2	20.4	21.7	22.9	24.1	25.4	26.6	27.8	29	♋ 0.3	1.5	2.7	4	5.2	6.4	7.6	8.9	
♂	♌ 5.5	6	6.6	7.2	7.8	8.4	9	9.6	10.1	10.7	11.3	11.9	12.5	13.1	13.7	14.3	14.9	15.5	16.1	16.7	17.3	17.9	18.5	19.1	19.7	20.3	20.9	21.5	22.1	22.7	

♃ 1: ♌ 20.5 · 6: 21.1 · 11: 21.9 · 16: 22.6 · 21: 23.4 · 26: 24.3
♄ 1: ♊ 27.5 · 6: 28.2 · 11: 28.8 · 16: 29.5 · 21: ♋ 0.1 · 26: 0.8
♅ 1: ♊ 9 · 11: 9.6 · 21: 10.2
♆ 1: ♎ 1.5R · 11: 1.5 · 21: 1.5D
♇ 1: ♌ 6.8 · 11: 7 · 21: 7.2

VII

	1	2	3	4	5	6	7	8	9	10	11	12	13	14	15	16	17	18	19	20	21	22	23	24	25	26	27	28	29	30	31
☉	♋ 8.3	9.3	10.2	11.2	12.1	13.1	14	15	15.9	16.9	17.8	18.8	19.7	20.7	21.7	22.6	23.6	24.5	25.5	26.4	27.4	28.3	29.3	♌ 0.2	1.2	2.2	3.1	4.1	5	6	6.9
☽	♊ 21.3	♋ 3.4	15.4	27.2	♌ 9	20.8	♍ 2.6	14.5	26.6	♎ 8.9	21.5	♏ 4.6	18	♐ 2	16.4	♑ 1.2	16.2	♒ 1.4	16.6	♓ 1.5	16.2	♈ 0.5	14.4	27.9	♉ 10.9	23.7	♊ 6.2	18.4	♋ 0.5	12.4	24.2
☿	♊ 20.2	21.9	23.7	25.5	27.4	29.3	♋ 1.2	3.2	5.2	7.3	9.4	11.5	13.6	15.8	17.9	20.1	22.2	24.4	26.5	28.6	♌ 0.7	2.8	4.8	6.9	8.9	10.9	12.8	14.8	16.7	18.6	20.4
♀	♌ 23.7	24.6	25.5	26.4	27.4	28.2	29.1	♍ 0	0.9	1.7	2.6	3.4	4.2	5	5.8	6.6	7.4	8.1	8.9	9.6	10.3	11	11.6	12.3	12.9	13.6	14.2	14.7	15.3	15.8	16.3
♂	♈ 25.1	25.8	26.5	27.2	27.9	28.6	29.3	♉ 0	0.7	1.4	2.1	2.8	3.5	4.2	4.8	5.5	6.2	6.9	7.5	8.2	8.9	9.5	10.2	10.9	11.5	12.2	12.8	13.5	14.1	14.8	15.4

♃ 1: ♌ 0 · 6: 1.1 · 11: 2.2 · 16: 3.3 · 21: 4.4 · 26: 5.5 · 31: 6.6
♄ 1: ♊ 19 · 6: 19.6 · 11: 20.2 · 16: 20.8 · 21: 21.4 · 26: 22 · 31: 22.5
♅ 1: ♊ 6.6 · 11: 7.1 · 21: 7.6 · 31: 8
♆ 1: ♍ 29.4 · 11: 29.5 · 21: 29.7 · 31: 29.9
♇ 1: ♌ 6 · 11: 6.3 · 21: 6.6 · 31: 6.9

	1	2	3	4	5	6	7	8	9	10	11	12	13	14	15	16	17	18	19	20	21	22	23	24	25	26	27	28	29	30	31
☉	♋ 9	10	10.9	11.9	12.8	13.8	14.7	15.7	16.7	17.6	18.6	19.5	20.5	21.4	22.4	23.3	24.3	25.2	26.2	27.1	28.1	29.1	♌ 0	1	1.9	2.9	3.8	4.8	5.7	6.7	7.7
☽	♏ 4.6	17.2	♐ 0.2	13.6	27.3	♑ 11.3	25.6	♒ 10.1	24.7	♓ 9.3	23.8	♈ 8.1	22.3	♉ 6.2	19.8	♊ 3.2	16.4	29.3	♋ 12	24.4	♌ 6.7	18.8	♍ 0.8	12.7	24.5	♎ 6.4	18.3	♏ 0.4	12.7	25.3	♐ 8.2
☿	♋ 8.4	10.6	12.7	14.9	17	19.2	21.3	23.3	25.4	27.4	29.4	♌ 1.4	3.3	5.2	7.1	8.9	10.7	12.5	14.2	16	17.6	19.3	20.9	22.5	24.1	25.6	27.1	28.6	♍ 0	1.4	2.8
♀	♋ 10.1	11.3	12.6	13.8	15	16.2	17.5	18.7	19.9	21.2	22.4	23.6	24.9	26.1	27.3	28.5	29.8	♌ 1	2.2	3.5	4.7	5.9	7.2	8.4	9.6	10.9	12.1	13.3	14.6	15.8	17
♂	♌ 23.3	23.9	24.5	25.1	25.7	26.3	26.9	27.5	28.1	28.7	29.3	29.9	♍ 0.6	1.2	1.8	2.4	3	3.6	4.2	4.8	5.5	6.1	6.7	7.3	7.9	8.6	9.2	9.8	10.4	11	11.7

♃ 1: ♌ 25.2 · 6: 26.1 · 11: 27 · 16: 28 · 21: 29 · 26: ♍ 0 · 31: 1
♄ 1: ♋ 1.4 · 6: 2 · 11: 2.7 · 16: 3.3 · 21: 3.9 · 26: 4.5 · 31: 5.1
♅ 1: ♊ 10.7 · 11: 11.2 · 21: 11.7 · 31: 12.1
♆ 1: ♎ 1.6 · 11: 1.7 · 21: 1.9 · 31: 2.1
♇ 1: ♌ 7.5 · 11: 7.8 · 21: 8 · 31: 8.3

VIII

	1	2	3	4	5	6	7	8	9	10	11	12	13	14	15	16	17	18	19	20	21	22	23	24	25	26	27	28	29	30	31
☉	♌ 7.9	8.8	9.8	10.8	11.7	12.7	13.6	14.6	15.6	16.5	17.5	18.4	19.4	20.3	21.3	22.3	23.2	24.2	25.2	26.1	27.1	28	29	30	♍ 0.9	1.9	2.9	3.8	4.8	5.8	6.7
☽	♌ 6	17.8	29.6	♍ 11.5	23.5	♎ 5.7	18	♏ 0.7	13.7	27.1	♐ 10.9	25.1	♑ 9.7	24.6	♒ 9.7	24.9	♓ 10	24.8	♈ 9.3	23.3	♉ 6.9	20.1	♊ 2.9	15.3	27.4	♋ 9.4	21.2	♌ 3	14.8	26.6	♍ 8.6
☿	♌ 22.2	24	25.8	27.6	29.3	♍ 1	2.6	4.2	5.9	7.4	9	10.5	12	13.5	14.9	16.4	17.8	19.1	20.5	21.8	23	24.3	25.5	26.7	27.8	28.9	30	♎ 1	2	2.9	3.8
♀	♍ 16.8	17.3	17.7	18.1	18.5	18.8	19.2	19.5	19.7	19.9	20.1	20.3	20.4	20.5	20.5	20.5R	20.5	20.4	20.3	20.2	20	19.8	19.5	19.2	18.8	18.5	18	17.6	17.1	16.6	16.1
♂	♉ 16.1	16.7	17.4	18	18.6	19.3	19.9	20.5	21.1	21.7	22.3	23	23.6	24.2	24.8	25.4	26	26.5	27.1	27.7	28.3	28.9	29.4	30	♊ 0.6	1.1	1.7	2.2	2.8	3.3	3.8

♃ 1: ♌ 6.8 · 6: 7.9 · 11: 9 · 16: 10.1 · 21: 11.2 · 26: 12.3 · 31: 13.4
♄ 1: ♊ 22.6 · 6: 23.1 · 11: 23.6 · 16: 24.1 · 21: 24.5 · 26: 24.9 · 31: 25.2
♅ 1: ♊ 8 · 11: 8.3 · 21: 8.6 · 31: 8.8
♆ 1: ♍ 30 · 11: ♎ 0.2 · 21: 0.5 · 31: 0.9
♇ 1: ♌ 6.9 · 11: 7.2 · 21: 7.4 · 31: 7.7

	1	2	3	4	5	6	7	8	9	10	11	12	13	14	15	16	17	18	19	20	21	22	23	24	25	26	27	28	29	30	31
☉	♌ 8.6	9.6	10.5	11.5	12.4	13.4	14.4	15.3	16.3	17.2	18.2	19.2	20.1	21.1	22	23	24	24.9	25.9	26.8	27.8	28.8	29.7	♍ 0.7	1.7	2.6	3.6	4.6	5.5	6.5	7.5
☽	♐ 21.6	♑ 5.4	19.6	♒ 4.2	19	♓ 4	19	♈ 3.9	18.5	♉ 2.7	16.7	♊ 0.2	13.4	26.3	♋ 8.9	21.3	♌ 3.5	15.5	27.5	♍ 9.4	21.2	♎ 3.1	14.9	26.9	♏ 9	21.2	♐ 3.8	16.6	29.9	♑ 13.6	27.7
☿	♍ 4.2	5.5	6.7	8	9.2	10.3	11.5	12.6	13.6	14.6	15.6	16.5	17.3	18.1	18.9	19.6	20.2	20.7	21.2	21.6	22	22.2	22.4	22.5	22.5R	22.3	22.1	21.8	21.4	20.9	20.3
♀	♌ 18.2	19.5	20.7	21.9	23.2	24.4	25.6	26.9	28.1	29.3	♍ 0.6	1.8	3	4.3	5.5	6.7	8	9.2	10.4	11.7	12.9	14.1	15.4	16.6	17.8	19.1	20.3	21.5	22.8	24	25.2
♂	♍ 12.3	12.9	13.5	14.2	14.8	15.4	16	16.7	17.3	17.9	18.6	19.2	19.8	20.4	21.1	21.7	22.3	23	23.6	24.3	24.9	25.5	26.2	26.8	27.4	28.1	28.7	29.4	♎ 0	0.6	1.3

♃ 1: ♍ 1.2 · 6: 2.3 · 11: 3.4 · 16: 4.4 · 21: 5.5 · 26: 6.6 · 31: 7.7
♄ 1: ♋ 5.2 · 6: 5.8 · 11: 6.4 · 16: 6.9 · 21: 7.4 · 26: 7.9 · 31: 8.3
♅ 1: ♊ 12.2 · 11: 12.5 · 21: 12.8 · 31: 13
♆ 1: ♎ 2.1 · 11: 2.4 · 21: 2.7 · 31: 3
♇ 1: ♌ 8.4 · 11: 8.6 · 21: 8.9 · 31: 9.2

IX

	1	2	3	4	5	6	7	8	9	10	11	12	13	14	15	16	17	18	19	20	21	22	23	24	25	26	27	28	29	30	31
☉	♍ 7.7	8.7	9.6	10.6	11.6	12.5	13.5	14.5	15.5	16.4	17.4	18.4	19.3	20.3	21.3	22.3	23.2	24.2	25.2	26.2	27.1	28.1	29.1	♎ 0.1	1.1	2	3	4	5	6	
☽	♍ 20.6	♎ 2.8	15.1	27.7	♏ 10.5	23.6	♐ 6.9	20.6	♑ 4.6	18.9	♒ 3.5	18.3	♓ 3.3	18.2	♈ 3	17.5	♉ 1.6	15.3	28.5	♊ 11.4	23.8	♋ 6	17.9	29.7	♌ 11.5	23.3	♍ 5.2	17.3	29.5	♎ 12	
☿	♎ 4.7	5.5	6.2	6.9	7.5	8	8.5	8.8	9.1	9.4	9.5	9.5R	9.4	9.2	8.9	8.5	7.9	7.3	6.5	5.6	4.7	3.7	2.6	1.5	0.4	♍ 29.4	28.4	27.4	26.6	25.9	
♀	♍ 15.5R	14.9	14.4	13.7	13.1	12.5	11.9	11.3	10.7	10.1	9.5	8.9	8.4	7.9	7.4	6.9	6.5	6.1	5.8	5.4	5.2	4.9	4.7	4.6	4.5	4.4	4.3	4.3D	4.4	4.5	
♂	♊ 4.4	4.9	5.4	5.9	6.4	6.9	7.4	7.9	8.4	8.9	9.4	9.8	10.3	10.8	11.2	11.7	12.1	12.5	13	13.4	13.8	14.2	14.6	15	15.4	15.7	16.1	16.5	16.8	17.1	

♃ 1: ♌ 13.6 · 6: 14.6 · 11: 15.6 · 16: 16.6 · 21: 17.6 · 26: 18.6
♄ 1: ♊ 25.3 · 6: 25.6 · 11: 25.9 · 16: 26.1 · 21: 26.3 · 26: 26.5
♅ 1: ♊ 8.8 · 11: 8.8 · 21: 8.8R
♆ 1: ♎ 0.9 · 11: 1.3 · 21: 1.6
♇ 1: ♌ 7.7 · 11: 8 · 21: 8.2

	1	2	3	4	5	6	7	8	9	10	11	12	13	14	15	16	17	18	19	20	21	22	23	24	25	26	27	28	29	30	31
☉	♍ 8.4	9.4	10.4	11.3	12.3	13.3	14.2	15.2	16.2	17.2	18.1	19.1	20.1	21.1	22	23	24	25	25.9	26.9	27.9	28.9	29.8	♎ 0.8	1.8	2.8	3.8	4.7	5.7	6.7	
☽	♒ 12.4	27.3	♓ 12.5	27.8	♈ 13	27.9	♉ 12.4	26.4	♊ 10	23.2	♋ 5.9	18.4	♌ 0.6	12.6	24.6	♍ 6.4	18.3	♎ 0.1	12	23.9	♏ 5.9	18.1	♐ 0.4	12.9	25.7	♑ 8.8	22.4	♒ 6.4	20.8	♓ 5.6	
☿	♍ 19.6R	18.8	18	17	16.1	15.1	14.1	13.2	12.2	11.4	10.6	9.9	9.3	8.9	8.7	8.5	8.6D	8.8	9.1	9.6	10.3	11.1	12	13.1	14.2	15.5	16.9	18.3	19.8	21.4	
♀	♍ 26.5	27.7	28.9	♎ 0.2	1.4	2.6	3.9	5.1	6.3	7.6	8.8	10	11.2	12.5	13.7	14.9	16.2	17.4	18.6	19.9	21.1	22.3	23.6	24.8	26	27.2	28.5	29.7	♏ 0.9	2.2	
♂	♎ 1.9	2.6	3.2	3.9	4.5	5.2	5.8	6.5	7.1	7.8	8.4	9.1	9.7	10.4	11	11.7	12.3	13	13.7	14.3	15	15.6	16.3	17	17.6	18.3	19	19.6	20.3	20.9	

♃ 1: ♍ 7.9 · 6: 9 · 11: 10.1 · 16: 11.1 · 21: 12.2 · 26: 13.3
♄ 1: ♋ 8.4 · 6: 8.8 · 11: 9.2 · 16: 9.5 · 21: 9.9 · 26: 10.1
♅ 1: ♊ 13 · 11: 13.1 · 21: 13.1R
♆ 1: ♎ 3 · 11: 3.4 · 21: 3.8
♇ 1: ♌ 9.2 · 11: 9.5 · 21: 9.7

X

	1	2	3	4	5	6	7	8	9	10	11	12	13	14	15	16	17	18	19	20	21	22	23	24	25	26	27	28	29	30	31
☉	♎ 7	7.9	8.9	9.9	10.9	11.9	12.9	13.8	14.8	15.8	16.8	17.8	18.8	19.8	20.8	21.8	22.8	23.7	24.7	25.7	26.7	27.7	28.7	29.7	♏ 0.7	1.7	2.7	3.7	4.7	5.7	6.7
☽	♎ 24.6	♏ 7.5	20.6	♐ 3.9	17.3	♑ 1	14.9	29	♒ 13.3	27.7	♓ 12.3	26.8	♈ 11.3	25.6	♉ 9.6	23.3	♊ 6.5	19.3	♋ 1.8	14	25.9	♌ 7.8	19.6	♍ 1.4	13.4	25.6	♎ 8	20.7	♏ 3.7	16.9	♐ 0.4
☿	♍ 25.4R	25	24.7	24.7D	24.8	25.1	25.6	26.2	27	27.9	28.9	♎ 0	1.3	2.6	4	5.4	6.9	8.5	10.1	11.7	13.3	15	16.6	18.3	20	21.6	23.3	25	26.7	28.4	♏ 0
♀	♍ 4.6	4.7	4.9	5.2	5.4	5.7	6.1	6.4	6.8	7.2	7.7	8.1	8.6	9.2	9.7	10.3	10.9	11.5	12.1	12.8	13.5	14.2	14.9	15.6	16.4	17.1	17.9	18.7	19.5	20.4	21.2
♂	♊ 17.5	17.8	18.1	18.4	18.7	19	19.2	19.5	19.8	20	20.2	20.4	20.6	20.8	21	21.2	21.4	21.5	21.6	21.8	21.9	22	22	22.1	22.2	22.2	22.2	22.2	22.2R	22.2	22.2

♃ 1: ♌ 19.5 · 6: 20.4 · 11: 21.2 · 16: 22 · 21: 22.8 · 26: 23.5 · 31: 24.1
♄ 1: ♊ 26.6 · 6: 26.6 · 11: 26.6R · 16: 26.6 · 21: 26.5 · 26: 26.4 · 31: 26.2
♅ 1: ♊ 8.7R · 11: 8.6 · 21: 8.3 · 31: 8
♆ 1: ♎ 2 · 11: 2.4 · 21: 2.7 · 31: 3.1
♇ 1: ♌ 8.4 · 11: 8.6 · 21: 8.7 · 31: 8.7

	1	2	3	4	5	6	7	8	9	10	11	12	13	14	15	16	17	18	19	20	21	22	23	24	25	26	27	28	29	30	31
☉	♎ 7.7	8.7	9.7	10.6	11.6	12.6	13.6	14.6	15.6	16.6	17.6	18.5	19.5	20.5	21.5	22.5	23.5	24.5	25.5	26.5	27.5	28.5	29.5	♏ 0.5	1.5	2.5	3.5	4.5	5.5	6.5	7.5
☽	♓ 20.8	♈ 6.1	21.3	♉ 6.4	21.1	♊ 5.3	19	♋ 2.2	15	27.4	♌ 9.6	21.6	♍ 3.4	15.2	27.1	♎ 9	20.9	♏ 3	15.2	27.5	♐ 10	22.6	♑ 5.5	18.6	♒ 2.1	15.9	♓ 0.1	14.6	29.4	♈ 14.5	29.5
☿	♍ 23	24.6	26.3	28	29.8	♎ 1.5	3.3	5	6.8	8.6	10.3	12.1	13.8	15.6	17.3	19.1	20.8	22.5	24.2	25.9	27.5	29.2	♏ 0.9	2.5	4.2	5.8	7.4	9	10.6	12.2	13.8
♀	♏ 3.4	4.6	5.8	7.1	8.3	9.5	10.8	12	13.2	14.4	15.7	16.9	18.1	19.3	20.6	21.8	23	24.2	25.5	26.7	27.9	29.1	♐ 0.4	1.6	2.8	4	5.3	6.5	7.7	8.9	10.1
♂	♎ 21.6	22.3	22.9	23.6	24.3	25	25.6	26.3	27	27.7	28.3	29	29.7	♏ 0.4	1	1.7	2.4	3.1	3.8	4.4	5.1	5.8	6.5	7.2	7.9	8.5	9.2	9.9	10.6	11.3	12

♃ 1: ♍ 14.3 · 6: 15.3 · 11: 16.3 · 16: 17.3 · 21: 18.3 · 26: 19.2 · 31: 20.1
♄ 1: ♋ 10.3 · 6: 10.5 · 11: 10.7 · 16: 10.7 · 21: 10.8 · 26: 10.8R · 31: 10.7
♅ 1: ♊ 13.1R · 11: 12.9 · 21: 12.7 · 31: 12.4
♆ 1: ♎ 4.1 · 11: 4.5 · 21: 4.9 · 31: 5.2
♇ 1: ♌ 9.9 · 11: 10.1 · 21: 10.2 · 31: 10.2

XI

	1	2	3	4	5	6	7	8	9	10	11	12	13	14	15	16	17	18	19	20	21	22	23	24	25	26	27	28	29	30	31
☉	♏ 7.7	8.7	9.7	10.7	11.7	12.7	13.7	14.7	15.7	16.7	17.7	18.7	19.7	20.7	21.8	22.8	23.8	24.8	25.8	26.8	27.8	28.8	29.8	♐ 0.8	1.8	2.9	3.9	4.9	5.9	6.9	
☽	♐ 14.1	27.9	♑ 11.8	25.8	♒ 9.9	24	♓ 8.1	22.2	♈ 6.4	20.4	♉ 4.3	18	♊ 1.4	14.4	27.2	♋ 9.6	21.8	♌ 3.7	15.6	27.4	♍ 9.2	21.2	♎ 3.4	16	28.8	♏ 12.1	25.6	♐ 9.5	23.6	♑ 7.9	
☿	♏ 1.7	3.4	5	6.7	8.3	10	11.6	13.2	14.8	16.4	18	19.6	21.2	22.8	24.4	26	27.6	29.1	♐ 0.7	2.3	3.8	5.4	6.9	8.5	10	11.6	13.1	14.7	16.2	17.7	
♀	♍ 22	22.9	23.8	24.7	25.6	26.5	27.4	28.3	29.3	♎ 0.2	1.2	2.2	3.1	4.1	5.1	6.1	7.1	8.1	9.2	10.2	11.2	12.3	13.3	14.4	15.4	16.5	17.6	18.6	19.7	20.8	
♂	♊ 22.1R	22.1	22	21.9	21.8	21.7	21.5	21.4	21.2	21	20.8	20.6	20.4	20.2	19.9	19.7	19.4	19.1	18.8	18.5	18.2	17.9	17.5	17.2	16.8	16.5	16.1	15.7	15.4	15	

♃ 1: ♌ 24.3 · 6: 24.9 · 11: 25.4 · 16: 25.8 · 21: 26.2 · 26: 26.6
♄ 1: ♊ 26.2R · 6: 26 · 11: 25.7 · 16: 25.4 · 21: 25.1 · 26: 24.7
♅ 1: ♊ 8.0R · 11: 7.6 · 21: 7.2
♆ 1: ♎ 3.1 · 11: 3.4 · 21: 3.7
♇ 1: ♌ 8.7 · 11: 8.8R · 21: 8.7

	1	2	3	4	5	6	7	8	9	10	11	12	13	14	15	16	17	18	19	20	21	22	23	24	25	26	27	28	29	30	31
☉	♏ 8.5	9.5	10.5	11.5	12.5	13.5	14.5	15.5	16.5	17.5	18.5	19.5	20.5	21.5	22.5	23.5	24.5	25.5	26.6	27.6	28.6	29.6	♐ 0.6	1.6	2.6	3.6	4.6	5.7	6.7	7.7	
☽	♉ 14.5	29.1	♊ 13.4	27.1	♋ 10.5	23.3	♌ 5.8	18	♍ 0	11.9	23.7	♎ 5.6	17.5	29.6	♏ 11.8	24.2	♐ 6.8	19.6	♑ 2.5	15.7	29	♒ 12.5	26.3	♓ 10.4	24.6	♈ 9.1	23.7	♉ 8.3	22.8	♊ 7.2	
☿	♏ 15.4	17	18.5	20.1	21.6	23.2	24.7	26.3	27.8	29.3	♐ 0.8	2.3	3.8	5.3	6.8	8.3	9.8	11.3	12.7	14.2	15.6	17.1	18.5	19.9	21.3	22.7	24	25.4	26.7	28	
♀	♐ 11.4	12.6	13.8	15	16.3	17.5	18.7	19.9	21.1	22.3	23.6	24.8	26	27.2	28.4	29.6	♑ 0.9	2.1	3.3	4.5	5.7	6.9	8.1	9.3	10.5	11.8	13	14.2	15.4	16.6	
♂	♏ 12.7	13.4	14.1	14.8	15.5	16.2	16.9	17.6	18.3	19	19.7	20.4	21.1	21.8	22.5	23.2	23.9	24.6	25.3	26	26.7	27.4	28.1	28.8	29.5	♐ 0.3	1	1.7	2.4	3.1	

♃ 1: ♍ 20.3 · 6: 21.2 · 11: 22 · 16: 22.8 · 21: 23.5 · 26: 24.2
♄ 1: ♋ 10.7R · 6: 10.6 · 11: 10.5 · 16: 10.3 · 21: 10 · 26: 9.8
♅ 1: ♊ 12.4R · 11: 12 · 21: 11.6
♆ 1: ♎ 5.2 · 11: 5.5 · 21: 5.8
♇ 1: ♌ 10.2 · 11: 10.3R · 21: 10.2

XII

	1	2	3	4	5	6	7	8	9	10	11	12	13	14	15	16	17	18	19	20	21	22	23	24	25	26	27	28	29	30	31
☉	♐ 7.9	8.9	10	11	12	13	14	15	16	17.1	18.1	19.1	20.1	21.1	22.1	23.2	24.2	25.2	26.2	27.2	28.3	29.3	♑ 0.3	1.3	2.3	3.3	4.4	5.4	6.4	7.4	8.4
☽	♑ 22.2	♒ 6.5	20.8	♓ 4.9	19	♈ 2.9	16.7	♉ 0.3	13.7	27	♊ 10	22.8	♋ 5.3	17.6	29.7	♌ 11.6	23.4	♍ 5.2	17.1	29	♎ 11.2	23.7	♏ 6.6	19.9	♐ 3.6	17.7	♑ 2.2	16.8	♒ 1.6	16.4	♓ 1
☿	♐ 19.3	20.8	22.3	23.8	25.4	26.9	28.4	29.9	♑ 1.4	2.9	4.4	5.8	7.3	8.7	10.2	11.6	12.9	14.3	15.6	16.8	18	19.2	20.3	21.3	22.2	23	23.6	24.2	24.6	24.8	24.8R
♀	♎ 21.9	23	24.1	25.2	26.3	27.4	28.5	29.6	♏ 0.8	1.9	3	4.2	5.3	6.4	7.6	8.7	9.9	11	12.2	13.3	14.5	15.7	16.8	18	19.2	20.3	21.5	22.7	23.9	25	26.2
♂	♊ 14.6R	14.2	13.8	13.4	13.1	12.7	12.3	11.9	11.5	11.2	10.8	10.4	10.1	9.7	9.4	9.1	8.8	8.5	8.2	7.9	7.6	7.3	7.1	6.9	6.6	6.4	6.2	6	5.9	5.7	5.6

♃ 1: ♌ 26.8 · 6: 27 · 11: 27.1 · 16: 27.1R · 21: 27 · 26: 26.8 · 31: 26.6
♄ 1: ♊ 24.4R · 6: 24 · 11: 23.6 · 16: 23.1 · 21: 22.7 · 26: 22.3 · 31: 21.9
♅ 1: ♊ 6.8R · 11: 6.4 · 21: 6 · 31: 5.6
♆ 1: ♎ 3.9 · 11: 4.1 · 21: 4.2 · 31: 4.2
♇ 1: ♌ 8.7R · 11: 8.5 · 21: 8.4 · 31: 8.2

	1	2	3	4	5	6	7	8	9	10	11	12	13	14	15	16	17	18	19	20	21	22	23	24	25	26	27	28	29	30	31
☉	♐ 8.7	9.7	10.7	11.7	12.7	13.8	14.8	15.8	16.8	17.8	18.8	19.9	20.9	21.9	22.9	23.9	24.9	26	27	28	29	♑ 0	1.1	2.1	3.1	4.1	5.1	6.2	7.2	8.2	9.2
☽	♊ 21.2	♋ 4.9	18.2	♌ 1.1	13.7	25.9	♍ 8	19.9	♎ 1.7	13.6	25.6	♏ 7.8	20.1	♐ 2.7	15.6	28.7	♑ 12	25.6	♒ 9.3	23.2	♓ 7.2	21.3	♈ 5.5	19.7	♉ 3.9	18	♊ 2.1	15.9	29.6	♋ 13	26.1
☿	♐ 29.2	♑ 0.4	1.6	2.7	3.8	4.8	5.7	6.5	7.3	7.9	8.4	8.7	8.9	9.0R	8.8	8.5	7.9	7.2	6.3	5.2	4	2.7	1.3	♐ 30	28.6	27.4	26.2	25.2	24.4	23.7	23.2
♀	♑ 17.8	19	20.2	21.4	22.6	23.8	25	26.2	27.4	28.6	29.8	♒ 1	2.2	3.4	4.5	5.7	6.9	8.1	9.3	10.5	11.6	12.8	14	15.2	16.3	17.5	18.7	19.8	21	22.2	23.3
♂	♐ 3.8	4.5	5.3	6	6.7	7.4	8.1	8.9	9.6	10.3	11	11.8	12.5	13.2	14	14.7	15.4	16.1	16.9	17.6	18.3	19.1	19.8	20.5	21.3	22	22.8	23.5	24.2	25	25.7

♃ 1: ♍ 24.8 · 6: 25.4 · 11: 25.9 · 16: 26.4 · 21: 26.7 · 26: 27 · 31: 27.3
♄ 1: ♋ 9.5R · 6: 9.1 · 11: 8.8 · 16: 8.4 · 21: 8 · 26: 7.6 · 31: 7.2
♅ 1: ♊ 11.2R · 11: 10.8 · 21: 10.4 · 31: 10
♆ 1: ♎ 6 · 11: 6.2 · 21: 6.3 · 31: 6.4
♇ 1: ♌ 10.2R · 11: 10.1 · 21: 9.9 · 31: 9.7

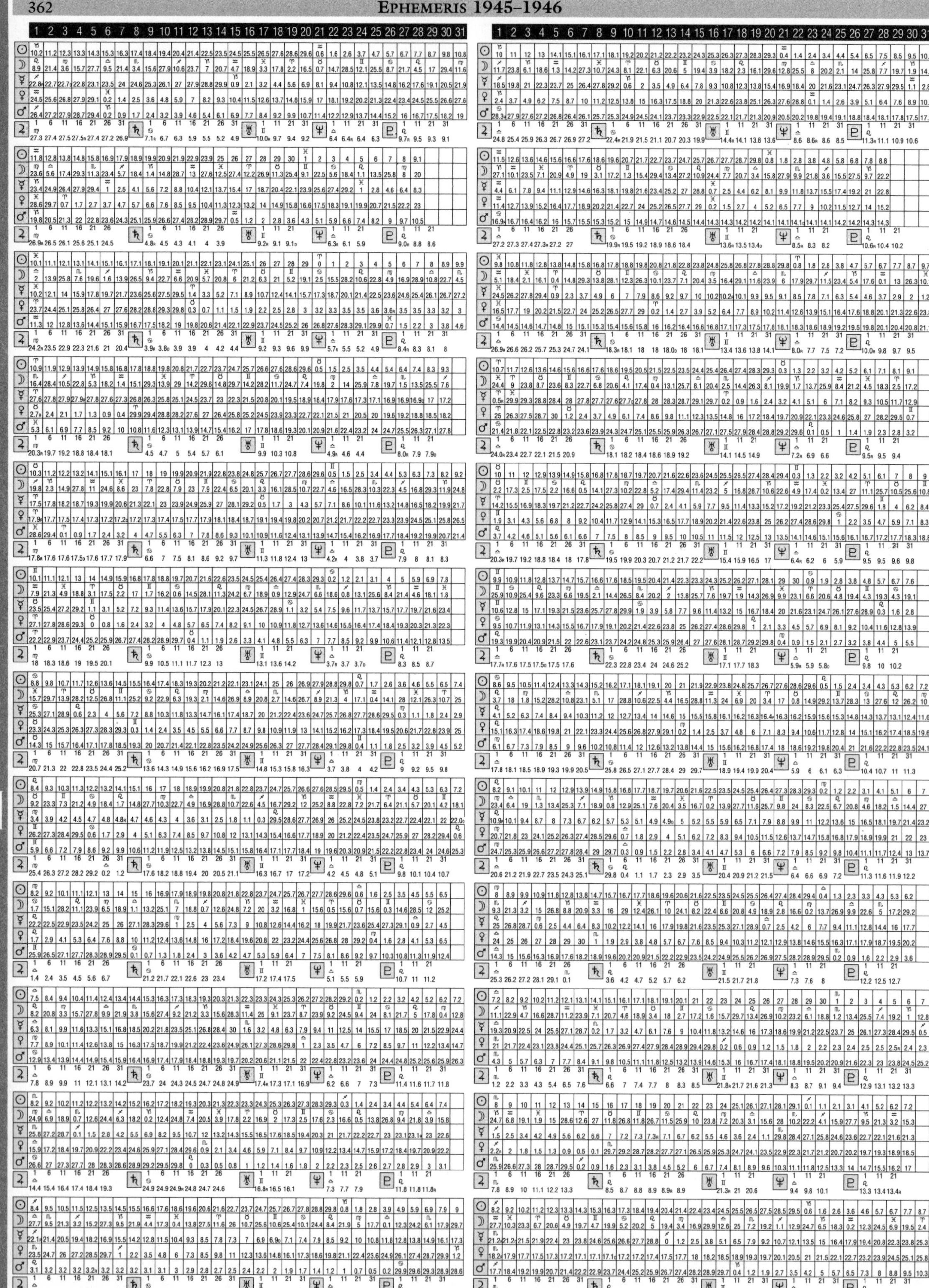

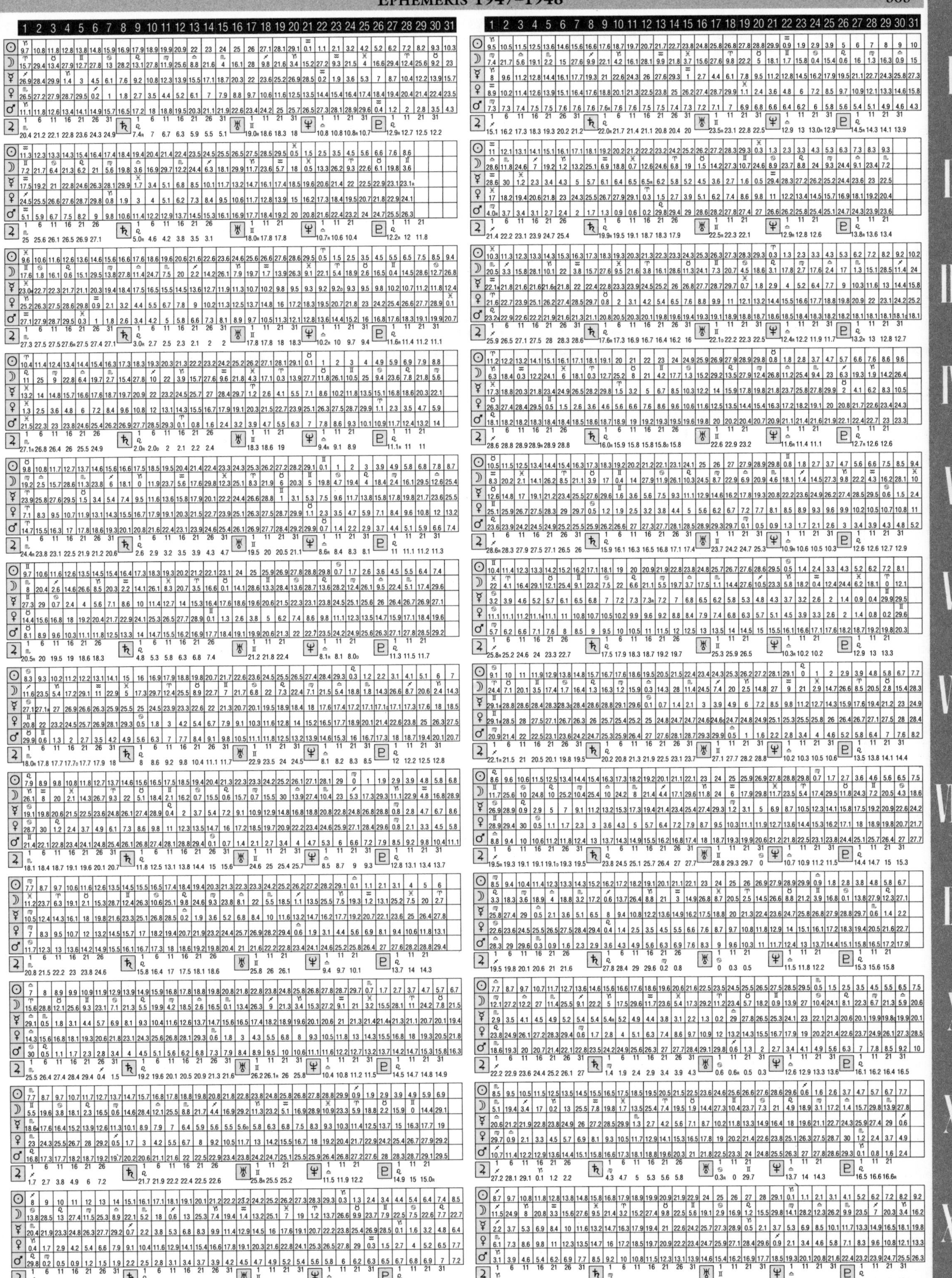

I

II

III

IV

V

VI

VII

VIII

IX

X

XI

XII

1949

I

	1	2	3	4	5	6	7	8	9	10	11	12	13	14	15	16	17	18	19	20	21	22	23	24	25	26	27	28	29	30	31
☉	♑ 10.3	11.3	12.3	13.3	14.3	15.4	16.4	17.4	18.4	19.4	20.5	21.5	22.5	23.5	24.5	25.5	26.6	27.6	28.6	29.6	♒ 0.6	1.7	2.7	3.7	4.7	5.7	6.7	7.8	8.8	9.8	10.8
☽	♑ 28.9	♒ 11.3	23.5	♓ 5.5	17.4	29.2	♈ 11	22.9	♉ 5.1	17.5	♊ 0.3	13.5	27.1	♋ 11.2	25.7	♌ 10.3	25.1	♍ 9.9	24.5	♎ 8.9	23	♏ 6.9	20.5	♐ 3.8	16.9	29.8	♑ 12.5	25.1	♒ 7.5	19.7	♓ 1.8
☿	♑ 21.4	23	24.6	26.2	27.8	29.4	♒ 1	2.6	4.1	5.7	7.2	8.7	10.1	11.5	12.8	14.1	15.2	16.3	17.3	18.2	18.9	19.5	19.9	20.1	20.2R	20.1	19.8	19.3	18.6	17.7	16.8
♀	♐ 14.6	15.8	17.1	18.3	19.6	20.8	22.1	23.3	24.5	25.8	27	28.3	29.5	♑ 0.8	2	3.3	4.5	5.8	7	8.3	9.5	10.8	12	13.3	14.5	15.8	17	18.3	19.5	20.8	22
♂	♑ 27.1	27.9	28.6	29.4	♒ 0.2	1	1.8	2.6	3.3	4.1	4.9	5.7	6.5	7.3	8.1	8.9	9.6	10.4	11.2	12	12.8	13.6	14.4	15.2	16	16.8	17.5	18.3	19.1	19.9	20.7

♃ 1: ♑ 10.4; 6: 11.5; 11: 12.7; 16: 13.8; 21: 15; 26: 16.1; 31: 17.2 — ♄ 1: ♍ 6.0R; 6: 5.8; 11: 5.6; 16: 5.4; 21: 5.1; 26: 4.8; 31: 4.5 — ♅ 1: ♊ 28.1R; 11: 27.7; 21: 27.3; 31: 27 — ♆ 1: ♎ 15.1; 11: 15.2; 21: 15.2R; 31: 15.1 — ♇ 1: ♌ 16.1R; 11: 15.9; 21: 15.7; 31: 15.5

II

	1	2	3	4	5	6	7	8	9	10	11	12	13	14	15	16	17	18	19	20	21	22	23	24	25	26	27	28	29	30	31
☉	♒ 11.8	12.8	13.8	14.9	15.9	16.9	17.9	18.9	19.9	20.9	21.9	23	24	25	26	27	28	29	♓ 0	1	2	3.1	4.1	5.1	6.1	7.1	8.1	9.1			
☽	♓ 13.7	25.5	♈ 7.3	19.1	♉ 1	13.1	25.4	♊ 8.2	21.3	♋ 5	19.1	♌ 3.7	18.6	♍ 3.7	18.9	♎ 3.9	18.6	♏ 3	17	♐ 0.7	13.9	26.9	♑ 9.6	22.1	♒ 4.4	16.5	28.6	♓ 10.5			
☿	♒ 15.7R	14.5	13.3	12.1	10.9	9.7	8.6	7.7	6.8	6.1	5.6	5.1	4.8	4.6	4.6D	4.6	4.8	5.1	5.4	5.9	6.4	7.1	7.7	8.5	9.3	10.2	11.1	12.1			
♀	♑ 23.3	24.5	25.8	27	28.3	29.5	♒ 0.8	2	3.3	4.5	5.8	7	8.3	9.5	10.8	12	13.3	14.5	15.8	17	18.3	19.5	20.8	22	23.3	24.5	25.8	27			
♂	♒ 21.5	22.3	23.1	23.9	24.7	25.5	26.2	27	27.8	28.6	29.4	♓ 0.2	1	1.8	2.6	3.4	4.2	4.9	5.7	6.5	7.3	8.1	8.9	9.7	10.5	11.3	12	12.8			

♃ 1: ♑ 17.5; 6: 18.6; 11: 19.6; 16: 20.7; 21: 21.7; 26: 22.7 — ♄ 1: ♍ 4.4R; 6: 4; 11: 3.7; 16: 3.3; 21: 2.9; 26: 2.5 — ♅ 1: ♊ 27.0R; 11: 26.7; 21: 26.6 — ♆ 1: ♎ 15.1R; 11: 15; 21: 14.8 — ♇ 1: ♌ 15.5R; 11: 15.2; 21: 15

III

	1	2	3	4	5	6	7	8	9	10	11	12	13	14	15	16	17	18	19	20	21	22	23	24	25	26	27	28	29	30	31
☉	♓ 10.1	11.1	12.1	13.1	14.1	15.1	16.1	17.1	18.1	19.1	20.1	21.1	22.1	23.1	24.1	25.1	26.1	27.1	28.1	29.1	♈ 0.1	1	2	3	4	5	6	7	8	9	10
☽	♓ 22.3	♈ 4.1	15.9	27.7	♉ 9.7	21.8	♊ 4.1	16.7	29.8	♋ 13.3	27.3	♌ 11.7	26.6	♍ 11.8	27	♎ 12.3	27.3	♏ 11.9	26.2	♐ 10	23.4	♑ 6.4	19.1	♒ 1.4	13.6	25.6	♓ 7.5	19.3	♈ 1.1	12.9	24.8
☿	♒ 13.1	14.2	15.3	16.4	17.6	18.8	20	21.3	22.6	23.9	25.2	26.6	28	29.4	♓ 0.9	2.3	3.8	5.3	6.9	8.4	10	11.6	13.2	14.9	16.5	18.2	19.9	21.6	23.4	25.2	27
♀	♒ 28.3	29.5	♓ 0.8	2	3.3	4.5	5.7	7	8.2	9.5	10.7	12	13.2	14.5	15.7	17	18.2	19.4	20.7	21.9	23.2	24.4	25.7	26.9	28.2	29.4	♈ 0.6	1.9	3.1	4.4	5.6
♂	♓ 13.6	14.4	15.2	16	16.8	17.6	18.3	19.1	19.9	20.7	21.5	22.3	23	23.8	24.6	25.4	26.2	27	27.7	28.5	29.3	♈ 0.1	0.9	1.6	2.4	3.2	4	4.7	5.5	6.3	7.1

♃ 1: ♑ 23.3; 6: 24.3; 11: 25.2; 16: 26.1; 21: 26.9; 26: 27.7; 31: 28.4 — ♄ 1: ♍ 2.2R; 6: 1.8; 11: 1.4; 16: 1.1; 21: 0.7; 26: 0.4; 31: 0.2 — ♅ 1: ♊ 26.5R; 11: 26.5D; 21: 26.6; 31: 26.8 — ♆ 1: ♎ 14.7R; 11: 14.4; 21: 14.2; 31: 13.9 — ♇ 1: ♌ 14.8R; 11: 14.6; 21: 14.4; 31: 14.3

IV

	1	2	3	4	5	6	7	8	9	10	11	12	13	14	15	16	17	18	19	20	21	22	23	24	25	26	27	28	29	30	31
☉	♈ 10.9	11.9	12.9	13.9	14.9	15.9	16.9	17.8	18.8	19.8	20.8	21.8	22.7	23.7	24.7	25.7	26.7	27.6	28.6	29.6	♉ 0.6	1.5	2.5	3.5	4.5	5.4	6.4	7.4	8.4	9.3	
☽	♉ 6.7	18.8	♊ 1	13.4	26.1	♋ 9.2	22.6	♌ 6.4	20.6	♍ 5.2	20.1	♎ 5.2	20.3	♏ 5.3	20.1	♐ 4.5	18.5	♑ 2.1	15.2	27.9	♒ 10.3	22.4	♓ 4.4	16.2	28	♈ 9.8	21.7	♉ 3.7	15.8	28	
☿	♓ 28.8	♈ 0.6	2.5	4.4	6.3	8.2	10.2	12.2	14.2	16.2	18.3	20.3	22.4	24.5	26.6	28.7	♉ 0.8	2.9	5	7.2	9.2	11.3	13.4	15.4	17.4	19.3	21.2	23	24.8	26.6	
♀	♈ 6.8	8.1	9.3	10.6	11.8	13.1	14.3	15.5	16.8	18	19.3	20.5	21.7	23	24.2	25.4	26.7	27.9	29.2	♉ 0.4	1.6	2.9	4.1	5.3	6.6	7.8	9	10.3	11.5	12.7	
♂	♈ 7.8	8.6	9.4	10.1	10.9	11.7	12.5	13.2	14	14.8	15.5	16.3	17.1	17.8	18.6	19.3	20.1	20.9	21.6	22.4	23.1	23.9	24.7	25.4	26.2	26.9	27.7	28.4	29.2	29.9	

♃ 1: ♑ 28.5; 6: 29.2; 11: 29.8; 16: ♒ 0.3; 21: 0.8; 26: 1.2 — ♄ 1: ♍ 0.1R; 6: ♌ 29.9; 11: 29.7; 16: 29.5; 21: 29.4; 26: 29.3 — ♅ 1: ♊ 26.8; 11: 27.1; 21: 27.5 — ♆ 1: ♎ 13.9R; 11: 13.6; 21: 13.3 — ♇ 1: ♌ 14.3R; 11: 14.2; 21: 14.2

V

	1	2	3	4	5	6	7	8	9	10	11	12	13	14	15	16	17	18	19	20	21	22	23	24	25	26	27	28	29	30	31
☉	♉ 10.3	11.3	12.2	13.2	14.2	15.1	16.1	17.1	18	19	20	20.9	21.9	22.9	23.8	24.8	25.8	26.7	27.7	28.7	29.6	♊ 0.6	1.5	2.5	3.5	4.4	5.4	6.3	7.3	8.3	9.2
☽	♊ 10.5	23.2	♋ 6.1	19.3	♌ 2.7	16.4	♍ 0.5	14.8	29.3	♎ 14	28.8	♏ 13.6	28.2	♐ 12.6	26.6	♑ 10.2	23.4	♒ 6.2	18.6	♓ 0.8	12.7	24.6	♈ 6.4	18.2	♉ 0.2	12.3	24.6	♊ 7.1	19.9	♋ 2.9	16.2
☿	♉ 28.2	29.9	♊ 1.4	2.9	4.3	5.7	7	8.2	9.3	10.4	11.4	12.3	13.1	13.9	14.6	15.2	15.7	16.2	16.6	16.8	17.1	17.2	17.2	17.2R	17.1	16.9	16.7	16.3	16	15.6	15.1
♀	♉ 14	15.2	16.4	17.7	18.9	20.1	21.4	22.6	23.8	25.1	26.3	27.5	28.8	30	♊ 1.2	2.5	3.7	4.9	6.1	7.4	8.6	9.8	11.1	12.3	13.5	14.7	16	17.2	18.4	19.7	20.9
♂	♉ 0.7	1.4	2.2	2.9	3.7	4.4	5.2	5.9	6.7	7.4	8.1	8.9	9.6	10.4	11.1	11.8	12.6	13.3	14	14.8	15.5	16.2	17	17.7	18.4	19.2	19.9	20.6	21.3	22.1	22.8

♃ 1: ♒ 1.6; 6: 1.8; 11: 2; 16: 2.1; 21: 2.2R; 26: 2.1; 31: 2 — ♄ 1: ♌ 29.3R; 6: 29.3D; 11: 29.4; 16: 29.5; 21: 29.7; 26: 29.8; 31: ♍ 0.1 — ♅ 1: ♊ 27.9; 11: 28.3; 21: 28.9; 31: 29.4 — ♆ 1: ♎ 13.1R; 11: 12.9; 21: 12.7; 31: 12.5 — ♇ 1: ♌ 14.2; 11: 14.2; 21: 14.3; 31: 14.4

VI

	1	2	3	4	5	6	7	8	9	10	11	12	13	14	15	16	17	18	19	20	21	22	23	24	25	26	27	28	29	30	31
☉	♊ 10.2	11.1	12.1	13	14	15	15.9	16.9	17.8	18.8	19.7	20.7	21.7	22.6	23.6	24.5	25.5	26.4	27.4	28.3	29.3	♋ 0.2	1.2	2.2	3.1	4.1	5	6	6.9	7.9	
☽	♋ 29.7	♌ 13.3	27.2	♍ 11.1	25.3	♎ 9.5	23.9	♏ 8.3	22.6	♐ 6.9	20.9	♑ 4.8	18.2	♒ 1.4	14.2	26.6	♓ 8.8	20.7	♈ 2.6	14.4	26.3	♉ 8.3	20.5	♊ 3	15.8	28.9	♋ 12.3	26	♌ 9.8	23.9	
☿	♊ 14.6R	14.1	13.5	12.9	12.4	11.8	11.3	10.8	10.3	9.9	9.6	9.3	9	8.8	8.7	8.7	8.7D	8.8	9	9.3	9.6	10.1	10.6	11.1	11.8	12.5	13.3	14.2	15.1	16.1	
♀	♊ 22.1	23.3	24.6	25.8	27	28.2	29.5	♋ 0.7	1.9	3.1	4.4	5.6	6.8	8	9.3	10.5	11.7	12.9	14.2	15.4	16.6	17.8	19	20.3	21.5	22.7	23.9	25.2	26.4	27.6	
♂	♉ 23.5	24.2	25	25.7	26.4	27.1	27.8	28.6	29.3	30	♊ 0.7	1.4	2.1	2.8	3.5	4.3	5	5.7	6.4	7.1	7.8	8.5	9.2	9.9	10.6	11.3	12	12.7	13.4	14.1	

♃ 1: ♒ 2.0R; 6: 1.7; 11: 1.5; 16: 1.1; 21: 0.7; 26: 0.2 — ♄ 1: ♍ 0.1; 6: 0.4; 11: 0.7; 16: 1.1; 21: 1.5; 26: 1.9 — ♅ 1: ♊ 29.5; 11: ♋ 0.1; 21: 0.7 — ♆ 1: ♎ 12.5R; 11: 12.4; 21: 12.4 — ♇ 1: ♌ 14.4; 11: 14.6; 21: 14.8

VII

	1	2	3	4	5	6	7	8	9	10	11	12	13	14	15	16	17	18	19	20	21	22	23	24	25	26	27	28	29	30	31
☉	♋ 8.8	9.8	10.7	11.7	12.6	13.6	14.6	15.5	16.5	17.4	18.4	19.3	20.3	21.2	22.2	23.1	24.1	25	26	27	27.9	28.9	29.8	♌ 0.8	1.7	2.7	3.6	4.6	5.5	6.5	7.5
☽	♍ 8	22.1	♎ 6.3	20.4	♏ 4.5	18.5	♐ 2.5	16.3	30	♑ 13.4	26.7	♒ 9.6	22.2	♓ 4.6	16.7	28.7	♈ 10.5	22.3	♉ 4.2	16.2	28.5	♊ 11.1	24	♋ 7.3	21.1	♌ 5.1	19.4	♍ 3.9	18.4	♎ 2.8	17.1
☿	♊ 17.2	18.3	19.5	20.8	22.1	23.5	25	26.5	28.1	29.8	♋ 1.5	3.3	5.1	6.9	8.8	10.8	12.8	14.8	16.9	19	21.1	23.2	25.3	27.4	29.5	♌ 1.7	3.8	5.9	7.9	10	12.1
♀	♋ 28.8	♌ 0	1.3	2.5	3.7	4.9	6.1	7.3	8.6	9.8	11	12.2	13.4	14.6	15.9	17.1	18.3	19.5	20.7	21.9	23.2	24.4	25.6	26.8	28	29.2	♍ 0.4	1.6	2.9	4.1	5.3
♂	♊ 14.8	15.5	16.2	16.9	17.6	18.2	18.9	19.6	20.3	21	21.7	22.4	23.1	23.7	24.4	25.1	25.8	26.5	27.1	27.8	28.5	29.2	29.8	♋ 0.5	1.2	1.9	2.5	3.2	3.9	4.5	5.2

♃ 1: ♑ 29.6R; 6: 29.1; 11: 28.5; 16: 27.8; 21: 27.2; 26: 26.5; 31: 25.9 — ♄ 1: ♍ 2.3; 6: 2.8; 11: 3.3; 16: 3.8; 21: 4.3; 26: 4.9; 31: 5.5 — ♅ 1: ♋ 1.3; 11: 1.8; 21: 2.4; 31: 2.9 — ♆ 1: ♎ 12.4; 11: 12.5; 21: 12.6; 31: 12.8 — ♇ 1: ♌ 15.1; 11: 15.3; 21: 15.6; 31: 15.9

VIII

	1	2	3	4	5	6	7	8	9	10	11	12	13	14	15	16	17	18	19	20	21	22	23	24	25	26	27	28	29	30	31
☉	♌ 8.4	9.4	10.3	11.3	12.2	13.2	14.2	15.1	16.1	17	18	19	19.9	20.9	21.8	22.8	23.8	24.7	25.7	26.6	27.6	28.6	29.5	♍ 0.5	1.5	2.4	3.4	4.4	5.3	6.3	7.3
☽	♏ 1.3	15.3	29.2	♐ 12.8	26.3	♑ 9.6	22.7	♒ 5.6	18.2	♓ 0.6	12.8	24.9	♈ 6.8	18.6	♉ 0.3	12.2	24.2	♊ 6.5	19.1	♋ 2.1	15.5	29.3	♌ 13.6	28.2	♍ 13	27.9	♎ 12.7	27.4	♏ 11.8	25.9	♐ 9.8
☿	♌ 14.1	16.1	18	20	21.9	23.8	25.7	27.5	29.3	♍ 1.1	2.9	4.6	6.4	8	9.7	11.4	13	14.6	16.1	17.7	19.2	20.7	22.2	23.6	25	26.4	27.8	29.1	♎ 0.5	1.7	3
♀	♍ 6.5	7.7	8.9	10.1	11.3	12.5	13.7	14.9	16.1	17.4	18.6	19.8	21	22.2	23.4	24.6	25.8	27	28.2	29.4	♎ 0.6	1.8	3	4.2	5.4	6.6	7.8	9	10.2	11.4	12.5
♂	♋ 5.9	6.5	7.2	7.9	8.5	9.2	9.9	10.5	11.2	11.8	12.5	13.2	13.8	14.5	15.1	15.8	16.4	17.1	17.7	18.4	19	19.7	20.3	21	21.6	22.2	22.9	23.5	24.2	24.8	25.4

♃ 1: ♑ 25.8R; 6: 25.2; 11: 24.6; 16: 24.1; 21: 23.6; 26: 23.2; 31: 22.9 — ♄ 1: ♍ 5.6; 6: 6.2; 11: 6.8; 16: 7.4; 21: 8; 26: 8.6; 31: 9.3 — ♅ 1: ♋ 3; 11: 3.5; 21: 3.9; 31: 4.3 — ♆ 1: ♎ 12.8; 11: 13; 21: 13.3; 31: 13.6 — ♇ 1: ♌ 15.9; 11: 16.2; 21: 16.6; 31: 16.8

IX

	1	2	3	4	5	6	7	8	9	10	11	12	13	14	15	16	17	18	19	20	21	22	23	24	25	26	27	28	29	30	31
☉	♍ 8.2	9.2	10.2	11.1	12.1	13.1	14	15	16	17	17.9	18.9	19.9	20.9	21.8	22.8	23.8	24.8	25.7	26.7	27.7	28.7	29.6	♎ 0.6	1.6	2.6	3.6	4.5	5.5	6.5	
☽	♐ 23.3	♑ 6.5	19.5	♒ 2.3	14.9	27.2	♓ 9.4	21.4	♈ 3.4	15.2	27	♉ 8.7	20.6	♊ 2.6	14.9	27.4	♋ 10.3	23.7	♌ 7.5	21.8	♍ 6.4	21.4	♎ 6.5	21.6	♏ 6.6	21.4	♐ 5.7	19.7	♑ 3.3	16.5	
☿	♎ 4.2	5.4	6.6	7.7	8.8	9.9	10.9	11.9	12.8	13.7	14.5	15.3	16	16.7	17.3	17.8	18.3	18.6	18.9	19.1	19.1	19.1R	18.9	18.7	18.3	17.8	17.1	16.4	15.5	14.5	
♀	♎ 13.7	14.9	16.1	17.3	18.5	19.7	20.9	22.1	23.2	24.4	25.6	26.8	28	29.2	♏ 0.3	1.5	2.7	3.9	5.1	6.2	7.4	8.6	9.8	10.9	12.1	13.3	14.4	15.6	16.8	17.9	
♂	♋ 26.1	26.7	27.4	28	28.6	29.3	29.9	♌ 0.5	1.1	1.8	2.4	3	3.7	4.3	4.9	5.5	6.1	6.8	7.4	8	8.6	9.2	9.8	10.5	11.1	11.7	12.3	12.9	13.5	14.1	

♃ 1: ♑ 22.8R; 6: 22.6; 11: 22.4; 16: 22.3; 21: 22.3D; 26: 22.4 — ♄ 1: ♍ 9.4; 6: 10; 11: 10.7; 16: 11.3; 21: 11.9; 26: 12.5 — ♅ 1: ♋ 4.3; 11: 4.6; 21: 4.8 — ♆ 1: ♎ 13.6; 11: 13.9; 21: 14.3 — ♇ 1: ♌ 16.9; 11: 17.2; 21: 17.4

X

	1	2	3	4	5	6	7	8	9	10	11	12	13	14	15	16	17	18	19	20	21	22	23	24	25	26	27	28	29	30	31
☉	♎ 7.5	8.5	9.5	10.4	11.4	12.4	13.4	14.4	15.4	16.4	17.4	18.3	19.3	20.3	21.3	22.3	23.3	24.3	25.3	26.3	27.3	28.3	29.3	♏ 0.3	1.3	2.3	3.2	4.2	5.2	6.2	7.2
☽	♑ 29.3	♒ 11.9	24.2	♓ 6.4	18.4	♈ 0.3	12.1	23.9	♉ 5.7	17.5	29.5	♊ 11.6	23.8	♋ 6.4	19.2	♌ 2.5	16.1	♍ 0.2	14.7	29.5	♎ 14.6	29.8	♏ 15	29.9	♐ 14.5	28.7	♑ 12.5	25.8	♒ 8.6	21.1	♓ 3.4
☿	♎ 13.5R	12.4	11.2	10.1	9	7.9	6.9	6	5.3	4.7	4.3	4	4.0D	4.1	4.4	4.8	5.5	6.2	7.1	8.2	9.3	10.5	11.8	13.2	14.6	16	17.6	19.1	20.7	22.2	23.8
♀	♏ 19.1	20.3	21.4	22.6	23.7	24.9	26.1	27.2	28.4	29.5	♐ 0.7	1.8	3	4.1	5.2	6.4	7.5	8.7	9.8	10.9	12.1	13.2	14.3	15.4	16.6	17.7	18.8	19.9	21	22.1	23.2
♂	♌ 14.7	15.3	15.9	16.5	17.1	17.7	18.3	18.9	19.5	20.1	20.7	21.3	21.9	22.5	23.1	23.6	24.2	24.8	25.4	26	26.5	27.1	27.7	28.3	28.8	29.4	30	♍ 0.6	1.1	1.7	2.2

♃ 1: ♑ 22.6; 6: 22.8; 11: 23.1; 16: 23.5; 21: 24; 26: 24.5; 31: 25.1 — ♄ 1: ♍ 13.1; 6: 13.7; 11: 14.3; 16: 14.8; 21: 15.4; 26: 15.9; 31: 16.4 — ♅ 1: ♋ 5; 11: 5; 21: 5.0R; 31: 4.8 — ♆ 1: ♎ 14.6; 11: 15; 21: 15.4; 31: 15.7 — ♇ 1: ♌ 17.6; 11: 17.8; 21: 18; 31: 18.1

XI

	1	2	3	4	5	6	7	8	9	10	11	12	13	14	15	16	17	18	19	20	21	22	23	24	25	26	27	28	29	30	31
☉	♏ 8.2	9.2	10.2	11.2	12.3	13.3	14.3	15.3	16.3	17.3	18.3	19.3	20.3	21.3	22.3	23.3	24.3	25.3	26.3	27.3	28.4	29.4	♐ 0.4	1.4	2.4	3.4	4.4	5.4	6.4	7.5	
☽	♓ 15.4	27.3	♈ 9.1	20.8	♉ 2.7	14.5	26.5	♊ 8.6	20.9	♋ 3.3	16	28.9	♌ 12.1	25.6	♍ 9.4	23.6	♎ 8.1	22.9	♏ 7.9	23	♐ 7.9	22.6	♑ 6.9	20.8	♒ 4.2	17.1	29.7	♓ 11.9	23.9	♈ 5.8	
☿	♎ 25.5	27.1	28.7	♏ 0.4	2	3.6	5.3	6.9	8.5	10.2	11.8	13.4	15	16.7	18.3	19.9	21.5	23.1	24.7	26.2	27.8	29.4	♐ 1	2.6	4.1	5.7	7.3	8.8	10.4	12	
♀	♐ 24.3	25.4	26.5	27.6	28.7	29.8	♑ 0.9	1.9	3	4.1	5.2	6.2	7.3	8.3	9.4	10.4	11.4	12.5	13.5	14.5	15.5	16.5	17.5	18.5	19.5	20.5	21.5	22.4	23.4	24.3	
♂	♍ 2.8	3.4	3.9	4.5	5	5.6	6.1	6.7	7.2	7.8	8.3	8.9	9.4	9.9	10.5	11	11.5	12	12.6	13.1	13.6	14.1	14.6	15.2	15.7	16.2	16.7	17.2	17.7	18.2	

♃ 1: ♑ 25.2; 6: 25.9; 11: 26.6; 16: 27.4; 21: 28.2; 26: 29.1 — ♄ 1: ♍ 16.5; 6: 16.9; 11: 17.3; 16: 17.7; 21: 18.1; 26: 18.4 — ♅ 1: ♋ 4.8R; 11: 4.6; 21: 4.3 — ♆ 1: ♎ 15.8; 11: 16.1; 21: 16.4 — ♇ 1: ♌ 18.1; 11: 18.2; 21: 18.2R

XII

	1	2	3	4	5	6	7	8	9	10	11	12	13	14	15	16	17	18	19	20	21	22	23	24	25	26	27	28	29	30	31
☉	♐ 8.5	9.5	10.5	11.5	12.5	13.5	14.6	15.6	16.6	17.6	18.6	19.6	20.7	21.7	22.7	23.7	24.7	25.7	26.8	27.8	28.8	29.8	♑ 0.8	1.9	2.9	3.9	4.9	5.9	7	8	9
☽	♈ 17.5	29.3	♉ 11.2	23.2	♊ 5.4	17.7	♋ 0.3	13	25.9	♌ 9.1	22.4	♍ 5.9	19.7	♎ 3.7	17.9	♏ 2.3	16.8	♐ 1.5	16.1	♑ 0.6	14.8	28.6	♒ 12.1	25.1	♓ 7.7	19.9	♈ 1.9	13.8	25.6	♉ 7.4	19.3
☿	♐ 13.5	15.1	16.7	18.2	19.8	21.3	22.9	24.5	26	27.6	29.1	♑ 0.7	2.2	3.8	5.3	6.9	8.4	10	11.5	13	14.6	16.1	17.5	19	20.5	21.9	23.3	24.6	25.9	27.2	28.3
♀	♑ 25.2	26.2	27.1	28	28.9	29.8	♒ 0.7	1.5	2.4	3.2	4	4.8	5.6	6.4	7.2	7.9	8.6	9.4	10.1	10.7	11.4	12	12.6	13.2	13.8	14.3	14.8	15.3	15.8	16.2	16.6
♂	♍ 18.7	19.2	19.7	20.1	20.6	21.1	21.6	22	22.5	23	23.4	23.9	24.4	24.8	25.3	25.7	26.1	26.6	27	27.4	27.9	28.3	28.7	29.1	29.5	29.9	♎ 0.3	0.7	1.1	1.5	1.8

♃ 1: ♒ 0; 6: 1; 11: 2; 16: 3; 21: 4.1; 26: 5.2; 31: 6.3 — ♄ 1: ♍ 18.7; 6: 18.9; 11: 19.1; 16: 19.3; 21: 19.4; 26: 19.4; 31: 19.4R — ♅ 1: ♋ 4.0R; 11: 3.6; 21: 3.2; 31: 2.7 — ♆ 1: ♎ 16.7; 11: 16.9; 21: 17.1; 31: 17.3 — ♇ 1: ♌ 18.2R; 11: 18.1; 21: 18; 31: 17.8

1950

I

	1	2	3	4	5	6	7	8	9	10	11	12	13	14	15	16	17	18	19	20	21	22	23	24	25	26	27	28	29	30	31
☉	♑ 10	11	12.1	13.1	14.1	15.1	16.1	17.1	18.2	19.2	20.2	21.2	22.2	23.3	24.3	25.3	26.3	27.3	28.4	29.4	♒ 0.4	1.4	2.4	3.4	4.5	5.5	6.5	7.5	8.5	9.5	10.6
☽	♊ 1.4	13.7	26.3	♋ 9.2	22.3	♌ 5.6	19.1	♍ 2.8	16.6	♎ 0.5	14.5	28.5	♏ 12.7	26.9	♐ 11.1	25.2	♑ 9.3	23.1	♒ 6.7	19.9	♓ 2.8	15.4	27.7	♈ 9.7	21.6	♉ 3.4	15.2	27.1	♊ 9.3	21.6	♋ 4.4
☿	♑ 29.5	♒ 0.5	1.4	2.2	2.9	3.5	3.9	4.1	4.1R	4	3.6	3.1	2.3	1.4	0.4	♑ 29.2	27.9	26.6	25.3	24.1	22.9	21.8	20.8	20	19.3	18.8	18.4	18.2	18.1	18.1D	18.3
♀	♒ 17	17.3	17.6	17.9	18.1	18.3	18.5	18.6	18.7	18.7	18.7R	18.7	18.6	18.5	18.3	18.1	17.9	17.6	17.3	16.9	16.5	16.1	15.6	15.1	14.6	14	13.4	12.8	12.2	11.6	11
♂	♎ 2.2	2.6	2.9	3.3	3.6	4	4.3	4.6	5	5.3	5.6	5.9	6.2	6.5	6.8	7	7.3	7.6	7.8	8.1	8.3	8.5	8.7	9	9.2	9.3	9.5	9.7	9.9	10	10.2

♃ 1: ♒ 6.5; 6: 7.6; 11: 8.8; 16: 10; 21: 11.1; 26: 12.3; 31: 13.5 — ♄ 1: ♍ 19.4R; 6: 19.4; 11: 19.3; 16: 19.2; 21: 19; 26: 18.8; 31: 18.6 — ♅ 1: ♋ 2.7R; 11: 2.3; 21: 1.9; 31: 1.5 — ♆ 1: ♎ 17.3; 11: 17.3; 21: 17.4R; 31: 17.3 — ♇ 1: ♌ 17.8R; 11: 17.6; 21: 17.4; 31: 17.1

II

	1	2	3	4	5	6	7	8	9	10	11	12	13	14	15	16	17	18	19	20	21	22	23	24	25	26	27	28	29	30	31
☉	♒ 11.6	12.6	13.6	14.6	15.6	16.6	17.7	18.7	19.7	20.7	21.7	22.7	23.7	24.7	25.7	26.8	27.8	28.8	29.8	♓ 0.8	1.8	2.8	3.8	4.8	5.8	6.8	7.8	8.8			
☽	♋ 17.4	♌ 0.8	14.5	28.5	♍ 12.6	26.8	♎ 11.1	25.4	♏ 9.5	23.6	♐ 7.6	21.5	♑ 5.3	18.9	♒ 2.2	15.4	28.3	♓ 11	23.4	♈ 5.5	17.5	29.4	♉ 11.2	23	♊ 5	17.1	29.4	♋ 12.2			
☿	♑ 18.5	18.9	19.4	20	20.6	21.3	22.1	23	23.9	24.8	25.8	26.9	28	29.1	♒ 0.2	1.4	2.7	3.9	5.2	6.5	7.8	9.2	10.5	11.9	13.3	14.8	16.2	17.7			
♀	♒ 10.4R	9.8	9.2	8.6	8	7.4	6.9	6.4	5.9	5.5	5	4.7	4.3	4	3.8	3.6	3.4	3.3	3.2	3.1	3.1D	3.1	3.2	3.3	3.5	3.6	3.9	4.1			
♂	♎ 10.3	10.4	10.5	10.6	10.7	10.8	10.9	10.9	11	11	11	11	11.0R	11	11	10.9	10.9	10.8	10.7	10.6	10.5	10.4	10.3	10.1	10	9.8	9.6	9.4			

♃ 1: ♒ 13.8; 6: 15; 11: 16.1; 16: 17.3; 21: 18.5; 26: 19.7 — ♄ 1: ♍ 18.5R; 6: 18.2; 11: 17.9; 16: 17.5; 21: 17.2; 26: 16.8 — ♅ 1: ♋ 1.5R; 11: 1.3; 21: 1.1 — ♆ 1: ♎ 17.3R; 11: 17.2; 21: 17.1 — ♇ 1: ♌ 17.1R; 11: 16.9; 21: 16.7

III

	1	2	3	4	5	6	7	8	9	10	11	12	13	14	15	16	17	18	19	20	21	22	23	24	25	26	27	28	29	30	31
☉	♓ 9.8	10.8	11.9	12.9	13.9	14.9	15.9	16.9	17.9	18.9	19.9	20.9	21.9	22.8	23.8	24.8	25.8	26.8	27.8	28.8	29.8	♈ 0.8	1.8	2.8	3.8	4.8	5.8	6.8	7.7	8.7	9.7
☽	♋ 25.3	♌ 8.8	22.7	♍ 6.9	21.4	♎ 6.1	20.9	♏ 5.5	20.1	♐ 4.4	18.4	♑ 2.2	15.7	29	♒ 12	24.7	♓ 7.3	19.7	♈ 1.8	13.9	25.8	♉ 7.6	19.4	♊ 1.3	13.2	25.3	♋ 7.6	20.2	♌ 3.2	16.7	♍ 0.6
☿	♒ 19.2	20.7	22.2	23.8	25.3	26.9	28.5	♓ 0.1	1.8	3.4	5.1	6.8	8.5	10.3	12	13.8	15.6	17.4	19.2	21.1	23	24.9	26.8	28.7	♈ 0.7	2.7	4.6	6.7	8.7	10.7	12.8
♀	♒ 4.4	4.7	5.1	5.4	5.9	6.3	6.8	7.3	7.8	8.3	8.9	9.5	10.1	10.7	11.4	12	12.7	13.4	14.2	14.9	15.6	16.4	17.2	18	18.8	19.6	20.5	21.3	22.2	23	23.9
♂	♎ 9.2R	9	8.8	8.5	8.3	8	7.7	7.4	7.1	6.8	6.5	6.2	5.8	5.5	5.1	4.8	4.4	4	3.7	3.3	2.9	2.5	2.1	1.7	1.3	0.9	0.6	0.2	♍ 29.8	29.4	29

♃ 1: ♒ 20.4; 6: 21.5; 11: 22.7; 16: 23.8; 21: 24.9; 26: 26; 31: 27 — ♄ 1: ♍ 16.5R; 6: 16.1; 11: 15.7; 16: 15.4; 21: 15; 26: 14.6; 31: 14.2 — ♅ 1: ♋ 1.0R; 11: 0.9D; 21: 1; 31: 1.1 — ♆ 1: ♎ 16.9R; 11: 16.7; 21: 16.4; 31: 16.2 — ♇ 1: ♌ 16.5R; 11: 16.3; 21: 16.1; 31: 15.9

IV

	1	2	3	4	5	6	7	8	9	10	11	12	13	14	15	16	17	18	19	20	21	22	23	24	25	26	27	28	29	30	31
☉	♈ 10.7	11.7	12.7	13.7	14.6	15.6	16.6	17.6	18.6	19.6	20.5	21.5	22.5	23.5	24.5	25.4	26.4	27.4	28.4	29.4	♉ 0.3	1.3	2.3	3.3	4.2	5.2	6.2	7.1	8.1	9.1	
☽	♍ 14.9	29.6	♎ 14.5	29.6	♏ 14.7	29.6	♐ 14.2	28.5	♑ 12.4	25.9	♒ 9	21.8	♓ 4.3	16.6	28.7	♈ 10.7	22.6	♉ 4.4	16.2	28.1	♊ 9.9	21.9	♋ 4	16.4	29	♌ 11.9	25.2	♍ 8.9	23.1	♎ 7.7	
☿	♈ 14.8	16.9	18.9	21	23.1	25.1	27.1	29.1	♉ 1.1	3	4.9	6.7	8.5	10.2	11.8	13.4	14.9	16.4	17.7	19	20.2	21.3	22.3	23.2	24.1	24.8	25.5	26.1	26.5	26.9	
♀	♒ 24.8	25.7	26.6	27.5	28.5	29.4	♓ 0.4	1.3	2.3	3.2	4.2	5.2	6.2	7.2	8.2	9.2	10.2	11.2	12.2	13.2	14.3	15.3	16.3	17.4	18.4	19.5	20.5	21.6	22.7	23.7	
♂	♍ 28.7R	28.3	27.9	27.6	27.2	26.9	26.6	26.2	25.9	25.6	25.3	25	24.8	24.5	24.3	24	23.8	23.6	23.4	23.2	23	22.9	22.7	22.6	22.5	22.4	22.3	22.2	22.1	22.1	

♃ 1: ♒ 27.2; 6: 28.2; 11: 29.2; 16: ♓ 0.1; 21: 1; 26: 1.9 — ♄ 1: ♍ 14.2R; 6: 13.9; 11: 13.6; 16: 13.3; 21: 13.1; 26: 12.9 — ♅ 1: ♋ 1.2; 11: 1.4; 21: 1.7 — ♆ 1: ♎ 16.1R; 11: 15.9; 21: 15.6 — ♇ 1: ♌ 15.9R; 11: 15.8; 21: 15.8

V

	1	2	3	4	5	6	7	8	9	10	11	12	13	14	15	16	17	18	19	20	21	22	23	24	25	26	27	28	29	30	31
☉	♉ 10.1	11	12	13	13.9	14.9	15.9	16.8	17.8	18.8	19.7	20.7	21.7	22.6	23.6	24.6	25.5	26.5	27.5	28.4	29.4	♊ 0.3	1.3	2.3	3.2	4.2	5.1	6.1	7.1	8	9
☽	♎ 22.7	♏ 7.9	23.1	♐ 8.3	23.2	♑ 7.7	21.8	♒ 5.4	18.5	♓ 1.3	13.7	25.8	♈ 7.8	19.7	♉ 1.5	13.3	25.1	♊ 7	19	♋ 1.1	13.3	25.8	♌ 8.4	21.3	♍ 4.5	18.1	♎ 2.1	16.5	♏ 1.2	16.3	♐ 1.4
☿	♉ 27.2	27.4	27.5	27.5R	27.4	27.3	27.1	26.8	26.4	26	25.5	25	24.4	23.8	23.2	22.6	22	21.5	20.9	20.4	20	19.6	19.2	19	18.7	18.6	18.5	18.5D	18.6	18.7	19
♀	♓ 24.8	25.9	27	28	29.1	♈ 0.2	1.3	2.4	3.5	4.6	5.7	6.8	7.9	9	10.1	11.2	12.4	13.5	14.6	15.7	16.8	18	19.1	20.2	21.4	22.5	23.6	24.8	25.9	27	28.2
♂	♍ 22.0R	22	22	22.0D	22	22	22.1	22.1	22.2	22.2	22.3	22.4	22.5	22.6	22.8	22.9	23.1	23.2	23.4	23.6	23.8	24	24.2	24.4	24.6	24.8	25.1	25.3	25.6	25.9	26.1

♃ 1: ♓ 2.7; 6: 3.4; 11: 4.1; 16: 4.8; 21: 5.3; 26: 5.9; 31: 6.3 — ♄ 1: ♍ 12.8R; 6: 12.7; 11: 12.6; 16: 12.6D; 21: 12.6; 26: 12.7; 31: 12.8 — ♅ 1: ♋ 2.1; 11: 2.6; 21: 3.1; 31: 3.6 — ♆ 1: ♎ 15.3R; 11: 15.1; 21: 14.9; 31: 14.8 — ♇ 1: ♌ 15.8; 11: 15.8; 21: 15.9; 31: 16

VI

	1	2	3	4	5	6	7	8	9	10	11	12	13	14	15	16	17	18	19	20	21	22	23	24	25	26	27	28	29	30	31
☉	♊ 9.9	10.9	11.9	12.8	13.8	14.7	15.7	16.6	17.6	18.6	19.5	20.5	21.4	22.4	23.3	24.3	25.2	26.2	27.2	28.1	29.1	♋ 0	1	1.9	2.9	3.8	4.8	5.7	6.7	7.6	
☽	♐ 16.6	♑ 1.6	16.2	♒ 0.4	14.1	27.3	♓ 10.1	22.5	♈ 4.7	16.6	28.4	♉ 10.2	22	♊ 3.9	15.9	28.1	♋ 10.4	22.8	♌ 5.5	18.3	♍ 1.3	14.6	28.2	♎ 12	26.2	♏ 10.7	25.4	♐ 10.3	25.2	♑ 9.9	
☿	♉ 19.3	19.6	20.1	20.6	21.2	21.8	22.5	23.3	24.2	25.1	26	27.1	28.1	29.3	♊ 0.5	1.7	3	4.4	5.8	7.3	8.8	10.4	12	13.7	15.4	17.2	19	20.8	22.8	24.7	
♀	♈ 29.3	♉ 0.5	1.6	2.8	3.9	5.1	6.2	7.4	8.5	9.7	10.8	12	13.1	14.3	15.5	16.6	17.8	19	20.1	21.3	22.5	23.6	24.8	26	27.1	28.3	29.5	♊ 0.7	1.8	3	
♂	♍ 26.4	26.7	27	27.3	27.6	28	28.3	28.6	29	29.3	29.7	♎ 0.1	0.4	0.8	1.2	1.6	2	2.4	2.8	3.2	3.6	4	4.4	4.9	5.3	5.7	6.2	6.6	7.1	7.6	

♃ 1: ♓ 6.4; 6: 6.8; 11: 7; 16: 7.3; 21: 7.4; 26: 7.4 — ♄ 1: ♍ 12.8; 6: 13; 11: 13.2; 16: 13.4; 21: 13.7; 26: 14 — ♅ 1: ♋ 3.6; 11: 4.2; 21: 4.8 — ♆ 1: ♎ 14.7R; 11: 14.6; 21: 14.6 — ♇ 1: ♌ 16; 11: 16.2; 21: 16.4

VII

	1	2	3	4	5	6	7	8	9	10	11	12	13	14	15	16	17	18	19	20	21	22	23	24	25	26	27	28	29	30	31
☉	♋ 8.6	9.6	10.5	11.5	12.4	13.4	14.3	15.3	16.2	17.2	18.1	19.1	20	21	21.9	22.9	23.9	24.8	25.8	26.7	27.7	28.6	29.6	♌ 0.5	1.5	2.4	3.4	4.4	5.3	6.3	7.2
☽	♑ 24.5	♒ 8.6	22.3	♓ 5.5	18.4	♈ 0.8	13	24.9	♉ 6.8	18.6	♊ 0.5	12.5	24.6	♋ 6.9	19.5	♌ 2.2	15.1	28.3	♍ 11.6	25.1	♎ 8.8	22.7	♏ 6.8	21.1	♐ 5.5	19.9	♑ 4.4	18.8	♒ 3	16.9	♓ 0.4
☿	♊ 26.7	28.7	♋ 0.8	2.9	5	7.1	9.3	11.4	13.6	15.8	17.9	20.1	22.2	24.3	26.5	28.5	♌ 0.6	2.6	4.6	6.6	8.6	10.5	12.4	14.3	16.1	17.9	19.7	21.5	23.2	24.9	26.6
♀	♊ 4.2	5.4	6.5	7.7	8.9	10.1	11.3	12.5	13.6	14.8	16	17.2	18.4	19.6	20.8	22	23.1	24.3	25.5	26.7	27.9	29.1	♋ 0.3	1.5	2.7	3.9	5.1	6.3	7.5	8.7	9.9
♂	♎ 8	8.5	9	9.4	9.9	10.4	10.9	11.4	11.9	12.4	12.9	13.4	13.9	14.4	15	15.5	16	16.5	17.1	17.6	18.1	18.7	19.2	19.8	20.3	20.9	21.5	22	22.6	23.2	23.7

♃ 1: ♓ 7.4R; 6: 7.3; 11: 7.1; 16: 6.9; 21: 6.5; 26: 6.1; 31: 5.7 — ♄ 1: ♍ 14.4; 6: 14.8; 11: 15.2; 16: 15.6; 21: 16.1; 26: 16.6; 31: 17.1 — ♅ 1: ♋ 5.4; 11: 6; 21: 6.6; 31: 7.1 — ♆ 1: ♎ 14.6; 11: 14.6; 21: 14.7; 31: 14.9 — ♇ 1: ♌ 16.6; 11: 16.9; 21: 17.2; 31: 17.5

VIII

	1	2	3	4	5	6	7	8	9	10	11	12	13	14	15	16	17	18	19	20	21	22	23	24	25	26	27	28	29	30	31
☉	♌ 8.2	9.1	10.1	11.1	12	13	13.9	14.9	15.8	16.8	17.8	18.7	19.7	20.6	21.6	22.6	23.5	24.5	25.5	26.4	27.4	28.3	29.3	♍ 0.3	1.2	2.2	3.2	4.1	5.1	6.1	7
☽	♓ 13.5	26.3	♈ 8.8	20.9	♉ 2.9	14.8	26.7	♊ 8.6	20.6	♋ 2.8	15.3	28.1	♌ 11.1	24.4	♍ 7.9	21.6	♎ 5.5	19.5	♏ 3.6	17.8	♐ 2	16.2	♑ 0.4	14.4	28.3	♒ 12.1	25.5	♓ 8.8	21.7	♈ 4.3	16.7
☿	♌ 28.2	29.8	♍ 1.4	3	4.5	6	7.5	8.9	10.3	11.7	13.1	14.4	15.7	16.9	18.1	19.3	20.5	21.6	22.7	23.7	24.7	25.7	26.6	27.4	28.2	28.9	29.6	♎ 0.2	0.8	1.3	1.7
♀	♋ 11.1	12.3	13.5	14.7	15.9	17.2	18.4	19.6	20.8	22	23.2	24.4	25.6	26.9	28.1	29.3	♌ 0.5	1.7	2.9	4.2	5.4	6.6	7.8	9	10.3	11.5	12.7	13.9	15.2	16.4	17.6
♂	♎ 24.3	24.9	25.5	26	26.6	27.2	27.8	28.4	29	29.6	♏ 0.2	0.8	1.4	2	2.6	3.2	3.8	4.5	5.1	5.7	6.3	6.9	7.6	8.2	8.8	9.5	10.1	10.7	11.4	12	12.7

♃ 1: ♓ 5.6R; 6: 5; 11: 4.4; 16: 3.8; 21: 3.2; 26: 2.5; 31: 1.9 — ♄ 1: ♍ 17.2; 6: 17.8; 11: 18.3; 16: 18.9; 21: 19.5; 26: 20.1; 31: 20.7 — ♅ 1: ♋ 7.2; 11: 7.7; 21: 8.2; 31: 8.6 — ♆ 1: ♎ 14.9; 11: 15.1; 21: 15.4; 31: 15.7 — ♇ 1: ♌ 17.5; 11: 17.8; 21: 18.1; 31: 18.4

IX

	1	2	3	4	5	6	7	8	9	10	11	12	13	14	15	16	17	18	19	20	21	22	23	24	25	26	27	28	29	30	31
☉	♍ 8	9	9.9	10.9	11.9	12.8	13.8	14.8	15.8	16.7	17.7	18.7	19.6	20.6	21.6	22.6	23.5	24.5	25.5	26.5	27.4	28.4	29.4	♎ 0.4	1.4	2.3	3.3	4.3	5.3	6.3	
☽	♈ 28.8	♉ 10.8	22.7	♊ 4.6	16.5	28.5	♋ 10.8	23.3	♌ 6.2	19.4	♍ 2.9	16.8	♎ 0.9	15.3	29.7	♏ 14.2	28.7	♐ 13	27.2	♑ 11.1	24.9	♒ 8.4	21.7	♓ 4.8	17.6	♈ 0.2	12.7	24.9	♉ 7	18.9	
☿	♎ 2	2.2	2.4	2.4	2.4R	2.2	2	1.6	1.1	0.5	♍ 29.9	29.1	28.2	27.3	26.3	25.2	24.2	23.1	22.1	21.2	20.3	19.6	18.9	18.5	18.1	18	18.0D	18.1	18.5	19	
♀	♌ 18.8	20.1	21.3	22.5	23.8	25	26.2	27.5	28.7	29.9	♍ 1.2	2.4	3.6	4.9	6.1	7.3	8.6	9.8	11.1	12.3	13.5	14.8	16	17.3	18.5	19.7	21	22.2	23.5	24.7	
♂	♏ 13.3	14	14.6	15.3	15.9	16.6	17.3	17.9	18.6	19.2	19.9	20.6	21.2	21.9	22.6	23.3	23.9	24.6	25.3	26	26.7	27.4	28.1	28.7	29.4	♐ 0.1	0.8	1.5	2.2	2.9	

♃ 1: ♓ 1.7R; 6: 1.1; 11: 0.5; 16: ♒ 29.9; 21: 29.4; 26: 28.9 — ♄ 1: ♍ 20.8; 6: 21.4; 11: 22.1; 16: 22.7; 21: 23.3; 26: 23.9 — ♅ 1: ♋ 8.6; 11: 9; 21: 9.2 — ♆ 1: ♎ 15.7; 11: 16; 21: 16.4 — ♇ 1: ♌ 18.5; 11: 18.8; 21: 19

X

	1	2	3	4	5	6	7	8	9	10	11	12	13	14	15	16	17	18	19	20	21	22	23	24	25	26	27	28	29	30	31
☉	♎ 7.3	8.2	9.2	10.2	11.2	12.2	13.2	14.1	15.1	16.1	17.1	18.1	19.1	20.1	21.1	22.1	23.1	24	25	26	27	28	29	♏ 0	1	2	3	4	5	6	7
☽	♊ 0.8	12.6	24.5	♋ 6.5	18.7	♌ 1.2	14	27.3	♍ 10.9	24.9	♎ 9.4	24.1	♏ 9	24	♐ 8.8	23.4	♑ 7.8	21.8	♒ 5.4	18.7	♓ 1.7	14.4	26.9	♈ 9.2	21.4	♉ 3.5	15.5	27.3	♊ 9.2	21.1	♋ 3
☿	♍ 19.6	20.4	21.4	22.4	23.6	24.8	26.2	27.6	29.1	♎ 0.6	2.2	3.8	5.5	7.1	8.8	10.5	12.2	13.9	15.7	17.4	19.1	20.8	22.5	24.2	25.9	27.6	29.3	♏ 0.9	2.6	4.3	5.9
♀	♍ 26	27.2	28.5	29.7	♎ 1	2.2	3.5	4.7	5.9	7.2	8.4	9.7	10.9	12.2	13.4	14.7	15.9	17.2	18.4	19.7	21	22.2	23.5	24.7	26	27.2	28.5	29.7	♏ 1	2.2	3.5
♂	♐ 3.6	4.3	5	5.7	6.4	7.1	7.9	8.6	9.3	10	10.7	11.4	12.2	12.9	13.6	14.3	15	15.8	16.5	17.2	18	18.7	19.4	20.2	20.9	21.6	22.4	23.1	23.8	24.6	25.3

♃ 1: ♒ 28.5R; 6: 28.1; 11: 27.9; 16: 27.7; 21: 27.6; 26: 27.6D; 31: 27.7 — ♄ 1: ♍ 24.5; 6: 25.2; 11: 25.8; 16: 26.3; 21: 26.9; 26: 27.5; 31: 28 — ♅ 1: ♋ 9.4; 11: 9.5; 21: 9.5R; 31: 9.4 — ♆ 1: ♎ 16.7; 11: 17.1; 21: 17.5; 31: 17.8 — ♇ 1: ♌ 19.3; 11: 19.5; 21: 19.6; 31: 19.8

XI

	1	2	3	4	5	6	7	8	9	10	11	12	13	14	15	16	17	18	19	20	21	22	23	24	25	26	27	28	29	30	31
☉	♏ 8	9	10	11	12	13	14	15	16	17	18	19	20	21.1	22.1	23.1	24.1	25.1	26.1	27.1	28.1	29.1	♐ 0.1	1.1	2.2	3.2	4.2	5.2	6.2	7.2	
☽	♋ 14.9	27.1	♌ 9.5	22.2	♍ 5.3	18.8	♎ 2.9	17.3	♏ 2.2	17.4	♐ 2.6	17.8	♑ 2.8	17.4	♒ 1.6	15.3	28.6	♓ 11.4	24	♈ 6.3	18.4	♉ 0.4	12.4	24.2	♊ 6.1	18	29.9	♋ 11.9	23.9	♌ 6.1	
☿	♏ 7.6	9.2	10.8	12.4	14	15.6	17.2	18.8	20.4	22	23.6	25.1	26.7	28.3	29.8	♐ 1.4	2.9	4.4	6	7.5	9	10.6	12.1	13.6	15.1	16.6	18.1	19.6	21.1	22.6	
♀	♏ 4.7	6	7.2	8.5	9.8	11	12.3	13.5	14.8	16	17.3	18.5	19.8	21.1	22.3	23.6	24.8	26.1	27.3	28.6	29.9	♐ 1.1	2.4	3.6	4.9	6.1	7.4	8.7	9.9	11.2	
♂	♐ 26.1	26.8	27.6	28.3	29.1	29.8	♑ 0.6	1.3	2.1	2.8	3.6	4.3	5.1	5.8	6.6	7.4	8.1	8.9	9.6	10.4	11.2	11.9	12.7	13.5	14.2	15	15.8	16.5	17.3	18.1	

♃ 1: ♒ 27.7; 6: 27.9; 11: 28.1; 16: 28.4; 21: 28.9; 26: 29.3 — ♄ 1: ♍ 28.1; 6: 28.6; 11: 29.1; 16: 29.6; 21: ♎ 0; 26: 0.4 — ♅ 1: ♋ 9.4R; 11: 9.2; 21: 8.9 — ♆ 1: ♎ 17.9; 11: 18.2; 21: 18.5 — ♇ 1: ♌ 19.8; 11: 19.8; 21: 19.9

XII

	1	2	3	4	5	6	7	8	9	10	11	12	13	14	15	16	17	18	19	20	21	22	23	24	25	26	27	28	29	30	31
☉	♐ 8.2	9.2	10.3	11.3	12.3	13.3	14.3	15.3	16.3	17.4	18.4	19.4	20.4	21.4	22.4	23.5	24.5	25.5	26.5	27.5	28.6	29.6	♑ 0.6	1.6	2.6	3.7	4.7	5.7	6.7	7.7	8.7
☽	♌ 18.5	♍ 1.1	14.1	27.4	♎ 11.3	25.5	♏ 10.3	25.4	♐ 10.7	26	♑ 11.2	26	♒ 10.4	24.3	♓ 7.6	20.6	♈ 3.1	15.4	27.4	♉ 9.3	21.2	♊ 3	14.9	26.9	♋ 8.9	21	♌ 3.2	15.5	28.1	♍ 10.8	23.8
☿	♐ 24.1	25.6	27	28.5	29.9	♑ 1.3	2.7	4.1	5.5	6.8	8.1	9.4	10.6	11.7	12.8	13.9	14.8	15.7	16.4	17.1	17.6	17.9	18.1	18.2R	18	17.6	17.1	16.3	15.4	14.3	13.1
♀	♐ 12.4	13.7	14.9	16.2	17.5	18.7	20	21.2	22.5	23.7	25	26.3	27.5	28.8	♑ 0	1.3	2.5	3.8	5	6.3	7.6	8.8	10.1	11.3	12.6	13.8	15.1	16.4	17.6	18.9	20.1
♂	♑ 18.8	19.6	20.4	21.2	21.9	22.7	23.5	24.3	25	25.8	26.6	27.4	28.2	28.9	29.7	♒ 0.5	1.3	2.1	2.8	3.6	4.4	5.2	6	6.8	7.5	8.3	9.1	9.9	10.7	11.5	12.3

♃ 1: ♒ 29.9; 6: ♓ 0.5; 11: 1.2; 16: 2; 21: 2.8; 26: 3.6; 31: 4.5 — ♄ 1: ♎ 0.8; 6: 1.2; 11: 1.5; 16: 1.7; 21: 1.9; 26: 2.1; 31: 2.2 — ♅ 1: ♋ 8.6R; 11: 8.2; 21: 7.8; 31: 7.4 — ♆ 1: ♎ 18.8; 11: 19.1; 21: 19.3; 31: 19.4 — ♇ 1: ♌ 19.8R; 11: 19.8; 21: 19.7; 31: 19.5

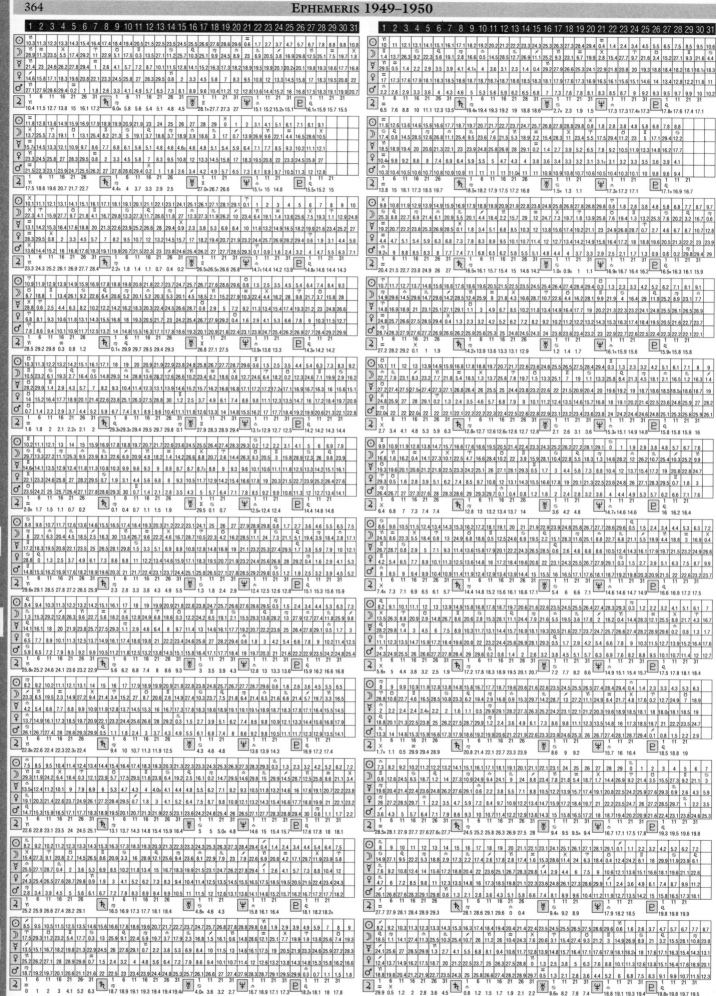

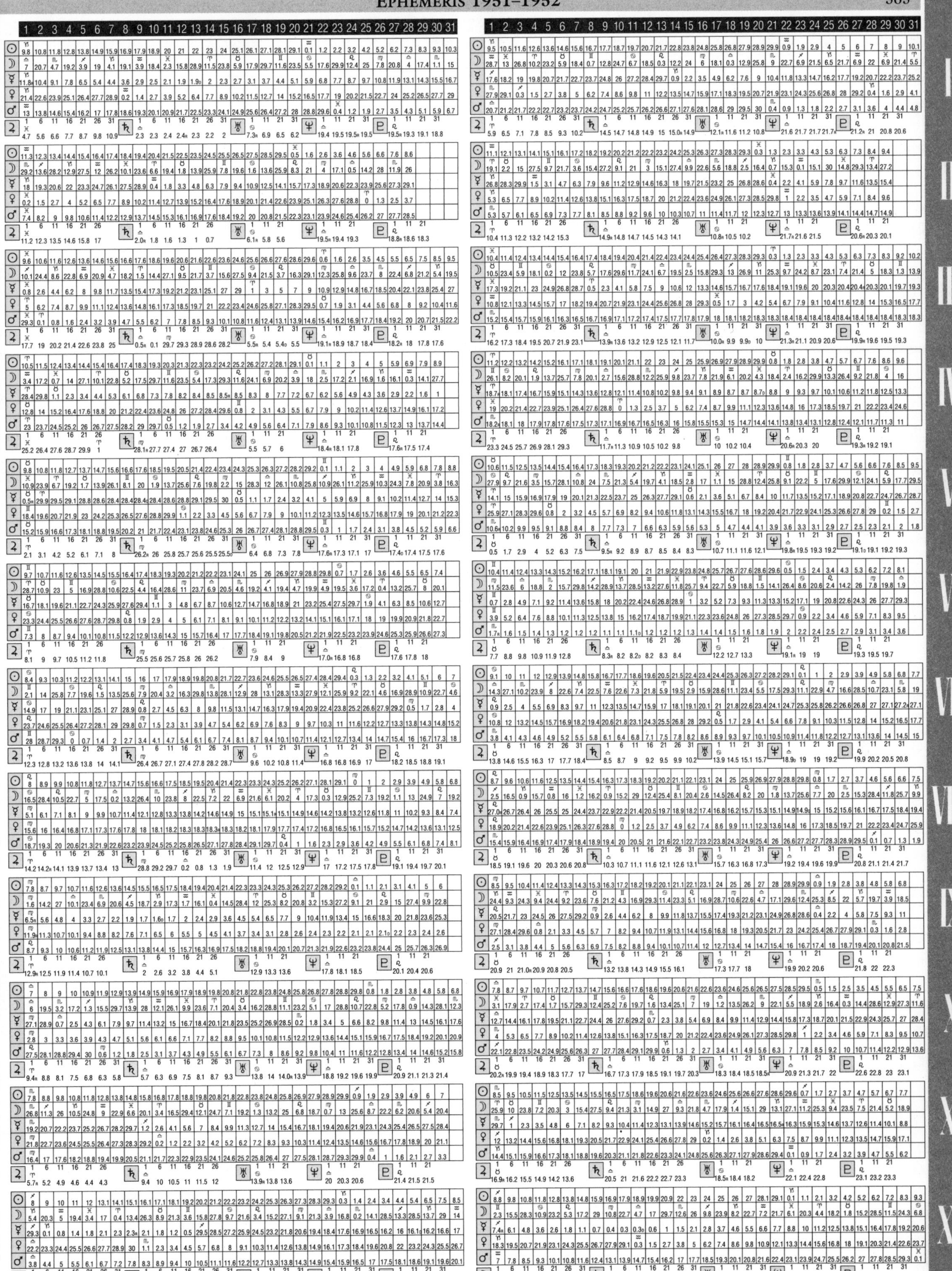

1951

I

	1	2	3	4	5	6	7	8	9	10	11	12	13	14	15	16	17	18	19	20	21	22	23	24	25	26	27	28	29	30	31
☉	9.8	10.8	11.8	12.8	13.8	14.9	15.9	16.9	17.9	18.9	20	21	22	23	24	25.1	26.1	27.1	28.1	29.1	0.1	1.2	2.2	3.2	4.2	5.2	6.2	7.3	8.3	9.3	10.3
☽	7	20.7	4.7	19.2	3.9	19	4.1	19.1	3.9	18.4	2.3	15.8	28.9	11.5	23.8	5.9	17.9	29.7	11.6	23.5	5.5	17.6	29.9	12.4	25	7.8	20.8	4	17.4	1.1	15
☿	11.8	10.4	9.1	7.8	6.5	5.4	4.4	3.6	2.9	2.5	2.1	1.9	1.9	2	2.3	2.7	3.1	3.7	4.4	5.1	5.9	6.8	7.7	8.7	9.7	10.8	11.9	13.1	14.3	15.5	16.7
♀	21.4	22.6	23.9	25.1	26.4	27.7	28.9	0.2	1.4	2.7	3.9	5.2	6.4	7.7	8.9	10.2	11.5	12.7	14	15.2	16.5	17.7	19	20.2	21.5	22.7	24	25.2	26.5	27.7	29
♂	13	13.8	14.6	15.4	16.2	17	17.8	18.6	19.3	20.1	20.9	21.7	22.5	23.3	24.1	24.9	25.6	26.4	27.2	28	28.8	29.6	0.4	1.2	1.9	2.7	3.5	4.3	5.1	5.9	6.7

♃ (1 6 11 16 21 26 31): 4.7 5.6 6.6 7.7 8.7 9.8 10.9 — ♄: 2.3 2.3 2.4 2.4R 2.3 2.2 2 — ♅ (1 11 21 31): 7.3R 6.9 6.5 6.2 — ♆: 19.4 19.5 19.5R 19.5 — ♇: 19.5R 19.3 19.1 18.8

II

	1	2	3	4	5	6	7	8	9	10	11	12	13	14	15	16	17	18	19	20	21	22	23	24	25	26	27	28
☉	11.3	12.3	13.4	14.4	15.4	16.4	17.4	18.4	19.4	20.4	21.5	22.5	23.5	24.5	25.5	26.5	27.5	28.5	29.5	0.5	1.6	2.6	3.6	4.6	5.6	6.6	7.6	8.6
☽	29.2	13.6	28.2	12.9	27.5	12	26.2	10.1	23.6	6.6	19.4	1.8	13.9	25.9	7.8	19.6	1.6	13.6	25.9	8.3	21	4	17.1	0.5	14.2	28	11.9	26
☿	18	19.3	20.6	22	23.3	24.7	26.1	27.5	28.9	0.4	1.8	3.3	4.8	6.3	7.9	9.4	10.9	12.5	14.1	15.7	17.3	18.9	20.6	22.3	23.9	25.6	27.3	29.1
♀	0.2	1.5	2.7	4	5.2	6.5	7.7	8.9	10.2	11.4	12.7	13.9	15.2	16.4	17.6	18.9	20.1	21.4	22.6	23.9	25.1	26.3	27.6	28.8	0	1.3	2.5	3.7
♂	7.4	8.2	9	9.8	10.6	11.4	12.2	12.9	13.7	14.5	15.3	16.1	16.9	17.6	18.4	19.2	20	20.8	21.5	22.3	23.1	23.9	24.6	25.4	26.2	27	27.7	28.5

♃ (1 6 11 16 21 26): 11.2 12.3 13.5 14.6 15.8 17 — ♄: 2.0R 1.8 1.6 1.3 1 0.7 — ♅ (1 11 21): 6.1R 5.8 5.6 — ♆: 19.5R 19.4 19.3 — ♇: 18.8R 18.6 18.3

III

	1	2	3	4	5	6	7	8	9	10	11	12	13	14	15	16	17	18	19	20	21	22	23	24	25	26	27	28	29	30	31
☉	9.6	10.6	11.6	12.6	13.6	14.6	15.6	16.6	17.6	18.6	19.6	20.6	21.6	22.6	23.6	24.6	25.6	26.6	27.6	28.6	29.6	0.6	1.6	2.6	3.5	4.5	5.5	6.5	7.5	8.5	9.5
☽	10.1	24.4	8.6	22.8	6.9	20.9	4.7	18.2	1.5	14.4	27.1	9.5	21.7	3.7	15.6	27.5	9.4	21.5	3.7	16.3	29.1	12.3	25.8	9.6	23.7	8	22.4	6.8	21.2	5.4	19.5
☿	0.8	2.6	4.4	6.2	8	9.8	11.7	13.5	15.4	17.3	19.2	21.2	23.1	25.1	27	29	1	3	5	7	9	10.9	12.9	14.8	16.7	18.5	20.4	22.1	23.8	25.4	27
♀	5	6.2	7.4	8.7	9.9	11.1	12.4	13.6	14.8	16.1	17.3	18.5	19.7	21	22.2	23.4	24.6	25.8	27.1	28.3	29.5	0.7	1.9	3.1	4.4	5.6	6.8	8	9.2	10.4	11.6
♂	29.3	0.1	0.8	1.6	2.4	3.2	3.9	4.7	5.5	6.2	7	7.8	8.5	9.3	10.1	10.8	11.6	12.4	13.1	13.9	14.6	15.4	16.2	16.9	17.7	18.4	19.2	20	20.7	21.5	22.2

♃ (1 6 11 16 21 26 31): 17.7 19 20.2 21.4 22.6 23.8 25 — ♄: 0.5R 0.1 29.7 29.3 28.9 28.6 28.2 — ♅ (1 11 21 31): 5.5R 5.4 5.4D 5.5 — ♆: 19.1R 18.9 18.7 18.4 — ♇: 18.2R 18 17.8 17.6

IV

	1	2	3	4	5	6	7	8	9	10	11	12	13	14	15	16	17	18	19	20	21	22	23	24	25	26	27	28	29	30
☉	10.5	11.5	12.4	13.4	14.4	15.4	16.4	17.4	18.3	19.3	20.3	21.3	22.3	23.2	24.2	25.2	26.2	27.2	28.1	29.1	0.1	1.1	2	3	4	5	5.9	6.9	7.9	8.9
☽	3.4	17.2	0.7	14	27.1	10.1	22.8	5.2	17.5	29.7	11.6	23.5	5.4	17.3	29.3	11.6	24.1	6.9	20.2	3.9	18	2.5	17.2	2.1	16.9	1.6	16.1	0.3	14.1	27.7
☿	28.4	29.8	1.1	2.3	3.4	4.4	5.3	6.1	6.8	7.3	7.8	8.2	8.4	8.5	8.5R	8.5	8.3	8	7.7	7.2	6.7	6.2	5.6	4.9	4.3	3.6	2.9	2.2	1.6	1
♀	12.8	14	15.2	16.4	17.6	18.8	20	21.2	22.4	23.6	24.8	26	27.2	28.4	29.6	0.8	2	3.1	4.3	5.5	6.7	7.9	9	10.2	11.4	12.6	13.7	14.9	16.1	17.2
♂	23	23.7	24.5	25.2	26	26.7	27.5	28.2	29	29.7	0.5	1.2	1.9	2.7	3.4	4.2	4.9	5.6	6.4	7.1	7.9	8.6	9.3	10.1	10.8	11.5	12.3	13	13.7	14.4

♃ (1 6 11 16 21 26): 25.2 26.4 27.6 28.7 29.9 1 — ♄: 28.1R 27.7 27.4 27 26.7 26.4 — ♅ (1 11 21): 5.5 5.7 6 — ♆: 18.4R 18.1 17.8 — ♇: 17.6R 17.5 17.4

V

	1	2	3	4	5	6	7	8	9	10	11	12	13	14	15	16	17	18	19	20	21	22	23	24	25	26	27	28	29	30	31
☉	9.8	10.8	11.8	12.7	13.7	14.7	15.6	16.6	17.6	18.5	19.5	20.5	21.4	22.4	23.4	24.3	25.3	26.3	27.2	28.2	29.2	0.1	1.1	2	3	4	4.9	5.9	6.8	7.8	8.8
☽	10.9	23.9	6.7	19.2	1.7	13.9	26.1	8.1	20	1.9	13.7	25.6	7.6	19.8	2.2	15	28.3	12	26.1	10.8	25.8	10.9	26.1	11.2	25.9	10.3	24.3	7.8	20.9	3.8	16.3
☿	0.5R	29.9	29.5	29.1	28.8	28.6	28.4	28.4	28.4D	28.4	28.6	28.8	29.1	29.5	30	0.5	1.1	1.7	2.4	3.2	4.1	5	5.9	6.9	8	9.1	10.2	11.4	12.7	14	15.3
♀	18.4	19.6	20.7	21.9	23	24.2	25.3	26.5	27.6	28.8	29.9	1.1	2.2	3.3	4.5	5.6	6.7	7.9	9	10.1	11.2	12.3	13.5	14.6	15.7	16.8	17.9	19	20.1	21.2	22.3
♂	15.2	15.9	16.6	17.3	18.1	18.8	19.5	20.2	21	21.7	22.4	23.1	23.8	24.6	25.3	26	26.7	27.4	28.1	28.8	29.5	0.3	1	1.7	2.4	3.1	3.8	4.5	5.2	5.9	6.6

♃ (1 6 11 16 21 26 31): 2.1 3.1 4.2 5.2 6.1 7.1 8 — ♄: 26.2R 26 25.8 25.7 25.6 25.5 25.5D — ♅ (1 11 21 31): 6.4 6.8 7.3 7.8 — ♆: 17.6R 17.3 17.1 17 — ♇: 17.4D 17.4 17.5 17.6

VI

	1	2	3	4	5	6	7	8	9	10	11	12	13	14	15	16	17	18	19	20	21	22	23	24	25	26	27	28	29	30
☉	9.7	10.7	11.6	12.6	13.5	14.5	15.5	16.4	17.4	18.3	19.3	20.2	21.2	22.2	23.1	24.1	25	26	26.9	27.9	28.8	29.8	0.7	1.7	2.6	3.6	4.6	5.5	6.5	7.4
☽	28.7	10.9	23	5	16.9	28.8	10.6	22.5	4.4	16.4	28.6	11	23.7	6.9	20.5	4.6	19.2	4.1	19.4	4.7	19.9	4.9	19.5	3.6	17.2	0.4	13.2	25.7	8	20.1
☿	16.7	18.1	19.6	21.1	22.7	24.3	25.9	27.6	29.4	1.1	3	4.8	6.7	8.7	10.6	12.7	14.7	16.8	18.9	21	23.2	25.4	27.5	29.7	1.9	4.1	6.3	8.5	10.6	12.7
♀	23.3	24.4	25.5	26.6	27.6	28.7	29.8	0.8	1.9	2.9	4	5	6.1	7.1	8.1	9.1	10.1	11.2	12.2	13.2	14.1	15.1	16.1	17.1	18	19	19.9	20.9	21.8	22.7
♂	7.3	8	8.7	9.4	10.1	10.8	11.5	12.2	12.9	13.6	14.3	15	15.7	16.4	17	17.7	18.4	19.1	19.8	20.5	21.2	21.9	22.5	23.2	23.9	24.6	25.3	25.9	26.6	27.3

♃ (1 6 11 16 21 26): 8.1 9 9.7 10.5 11.2 11.8 — ♄: 25.5 25.6 25.7 25.8 26 26.2 — ♅ (1 11 21): 7.9 8.4 9 — ♆: 17.0R 16.8 16.8 — ♇: 17.6 17.8 18

VII

	1	2	3	4	5	6	7	8	9	10	11	12	13	14	15	16	17	18	19	20	21	22	23	24	25	26	27	28	29	30	31
☉	8.4	9.3	10.3	11.2	12.2	13.1	14.1	15	16	17	17.9	18.9	19.8	20.8	21.7	22.7	23.6	24.6	25.5	26.5	27.4	28.4	29.4	0.3	1.3	2.2	3.2	4.1	5.1	6	7
☽	2.1	14	25.8	7.7	19.6	1.5	13.5	25.6	7.9	20.4	3.2	16.3	29.8	13.8	28.1	12.9	28	13.1	28.3	13.3	27.9	12.1	25.9	9.2	22.1	4.6	16.9	28.9	10.9	22.7	4.6
☿	14.9	17	19	21.1	23.1	25.1	27	28.9	0.8	2.7	4.5	6.3	8	9.8	11.5	13.1	14.7	16.3	17.9	19.4	20.9	22.4	23.8	25.2	26.6	27.9	29.2	0.5	1.7	2.8	4
♀	23.7	24.6	25.5	26.4	27.2	28.1	29	29.8	0.7	1.5	2.3	3.1	3.9	4.7	5.4	6.2	6.9	7.6	8.3	9	9.7	10.3	11	11.6	12.2	12.7	13.3	13.8	14.3	14.8	15.2
♂	28	28.7	29.3	0	0.7	1.4	2	2.7	3.4	4.1	4.7	5.4	6.1	6.7	7.4	8.1	8.7	9.4	10.1	10.7	11.4	12.1	12.7	13.4	14	14.7	15.4	16	16.7	17.3	18

♃ (1 6 11 16 21 26 31): 12.3 12.8 13.2 13.6 13.8 14 14.1 — ♄: 26.4 26.7 27.1 27.4 27.8 28.2 28.7 — ♅ (1 11 21 31): 9.6 10.2 10.8 11.4 — ♆: 16.8 16.8 16.9 17 — ♇: 18.2 18.5 18.8 19.1

VIII

	1	2	3	4	5	6	7	8	9	10	11	12	13	14	15	16	17	18	19	20	21	22	23	24	25	26	27	28	29	30	31
☉	8	8.9	9.9	10.8	11.8	12.7	13.7	14.7	15.6	16.6	17.5	18.5	19.5	20.4	21.4	22.3	23.3	24.3	25.2	26.2	27.1	28.1	29.1	0	1	2	2.9	3.9	4.9	5.8	6.8
☽	16.5	28.4	10.5	22.7	5	17.5	0.2	13.2	26.4	10	23.8	8	22.5	7.2	22	6.9	21.6	6.1	20.2	4	17.3	0.3	12.9	25.2	7.3	19.2	1.1	13	24.9	7	19.2
☿	5.1	6.1	7.1	8.1	9	9.9	10.7	11.4	12.1	12.8	13.3	13.8	14.2	14.6	14.9	15	15.1	15.1R	15.1	14.9	14.6	14.2	13.8	13.2	12.6	11.8	11	10.2	9.3	8.4	7.4
♀	15.6	16	16.4	16.8	17.1	17.3	17.6	17.8	18	18.1	18.2	18.3	18.3	18.3R	18.3	18.2	18.1	17.9	17.7	17.4	17.2	16.8	16.5	16.1	15.7	15.2	14.7	14.2	13.6	13.1	12.5
♂	18.7	19.3	20	20.6	21.3	21.9	22.6	23.2	23.9	24.5	25.2	25.8	26.5	27.1	27.8	28.4	29.1	29.7	0.4	1	1.6	2.3	2.9	3.6	4.2	4.9	5.5	6.1	6.8	7.4	8.1

♃ (1 6 11 16 21 26 31): 14.2 14.2R 14.1 13.9 13.7 13.4 13 — ♄: 28.8 29.2 29.7 0.2 0.8 1.3 1.9 — ♅ (1 11 21 31): 11.4 12 12.5 12.9 — ♆: 17 17.2 17.5 17.8 — ♇: 19.1 19.4 19.7 20.1

IX

	1	2	3	4	5	6	7	8	9	10	11	12	13	14	15	16	17	18	19	20	21	22	23	24	25	26	27	28	29	30
☉	7.8	8.7	9.7	10.7	11.6	12.6	13.6	14.5	15.5	16.5	17.5	18.4	19.4	20.4	21.4	22.3	23.3	24.3	25.3	26.2	27.2	28.2	29.2	0.1	1.1	2.1	3.1	4.1	5	6
☽	1.6	14.2	27	10.1	23.4	6.9	20.6	4.5	18.7	2.9	17.3	1.7	16.1	0.4	14.5	28.4	12	25.3	8.2	20.8	3.2	15.3	27.2	9.1	21	2.9	14.7	26.7	9.9	22.8
☿	6.5R	5.6	4.8	4	3.3	2.7	2.2	1.9	1.7	1.6D	1.7	2	2.4	2.9	3.6	4.5	5.4	6.5	7.7	9	10.4	11.9	13.4	15	16.6	18.3	20	21.8	23.6	25.3
♀	11.9R	11.3	10.7	10.1	9.4	8.8	8.2	7.6	7.1	6.5	6	5.5	5	4.5	4.1	3.7	3.4	3.1	2.8	2.6	2.4	2.3	2.2	2.1	2.1	2.1D	2.2	2.3	2.4	2.6
♂	8.7	9.3	10	10.6	11.2	11.9	12.5	13.1	13.8	14.4	15	15.7	16.3	16.9	17.5	18.2	18.8	19.4	20.1	20.7	21.3	21.9	22.6	23.2	23.8	24.4	25	25.7	26.3	26.9

♃ (1 6 11 16 21 26): 12.9R 12.5 11.9 11.4 10.7 10.1 — ♄: 2 2.6 3.2 3.8 4.4 5.1 — ♅ (1 11 21): 12.9 13.3 13.6 — ♆: 17.8 18.1 18.5 — ♇: 20.1 20.4 20.6

X

	1	2	3	4	5	6	7	8	9	10	11	12	13	14	15	16	17	18	19	20	21	22	23	24	25	26	27	28	29	30	31
☉	7	8	9	10	10.9	11.9	12.9	13.9	14.9	15.9	16.9	17.9	18.9	19.8	20.8	21.8	22.8	23.8	24.8	25.8	26.8	27.8	28.8	29.8	0.8	1.8	2.8	3.8	4.8	5.8	6.8
☽	6	19.5	3.2	17.2	1.3	15.5	29.7	13.9	28	12.1	26.1	9.9	23.6	7.1	20.4	3.4	16.2	28.8	11.1	23.2	5.1	17	28.8	10.7	22.8	5.2	17.8	0.9	14.3	28.1	12.3
☿	27.1	28.9	0.7	2.5	4.3	6.1	7.9	9.7	11.4	13.2	14.9	16.7	18.4	20.1	21.8	23.5	25.2	26.9	28.5	0.2	1.8	3.4	5	6.6	8.2	9.8	11.4	13	14.5	16.1	17.6
♀	2.8	3	3.3	3.6	3.9	4.3	4.7	5.1	5.6	6.1	6.6	7.1	7.7	8.2	8.8	9.5	10.1	10.8	11.5	12.2	12.9	13.6	14.4	15.1	15.9	16.7	17.5	18.4	19.2	20.1	20.9
♂	27.5	28.1	28.8	29.4	30	0.6	1.2	1.8	2.5	3.1	3.7	4.3	4.9	5.5	6.1	6.7	7.3	8	8.6	9.2	9.8	10.4	11	11.6	12.2	12.8	13.4	14	14.6	15.2	15.8

♃ (1 6 11 16 21 26 31): 9.4R 8.8 8.1 7.5 6.8 6.3 5.8 — ♄: 5.7 6.3 6.9 7.5 8.1 8.7 9.3 — ♅ (1 11 21 31): 13.8 14 14.0R 13.9 — ♆: 18.8 19.2 19.6 19.9 — ♇: 20.9 21.1 21.3 21.4

XI

	1	2	3	4	5	6	7	8	9	10	11	12	13	14	15	16	17	18	19	20	21	22	23	24	25	26	27	28	29	30
☉	7.8	8.8	9.8	10.8	11.8	12.8	13.8	14.8	15.8	16.8	17.8	18.8	19.8	20.8	21.8	22.8	23.8	24.8	25.8	26.9	27.9	28.9	29.9	0.9	1.9	2.9	3.9	4.9	6	7
☽	26.8	11.3	26	10.5	24.8	9	22.9	6.6	20.1	3.4	16.5	29.4	12.1	24.7	7.1	19.2	1.3	13.2	25	6.8	18.7	0.7	13	25.6	8.7	22.2	6.2	20.6	5.4	20.4
☿	19.2	20.7	22.2	23.7	25.2	26.7	28.2	29.7	1.2	2.6	4.1	5.6	7	8.4	9.9	11.3	12.7	14	15.4	16.7	18.1	19.4	20.6	21.9	23.1	24.3	25.4	26.5	27.5	28.4
♀	21.8	22.7	23.6	24.5	25.5	26.4	27.3	28.3	29.2	0.2	1.2	2.2	3.2	4.2	5.2	6.2	7.2	8.3	9.3	10.3	11.4	12.4	13.5	14.6	15.6	16.7	17.8	18.9	20	21.1
♂	16.4	17	17.6	18.2	18.8	19.4	19.9	20.5	21.1	21.7	22.3	22.9	23.5	24.1	24.6	25.2	25.8	26.4	27	27.5	28.1	28.7	29.3	29.9	0.4	1	1.6	2.1	2.7	3.3

♃ (1 6 11 16 21 26): 5.7R 5.2 4.9 4.6 4.4 4.3 — ♄: 9.4 10 10.5 11 11.5 12 — ♅ (1 11 21): 13.9R 13.8 13.6 — ♆: 20 20.3 20.6 — ♇: 21.4 21.5 21.5

XII

	1	2	3	4	5	6	7	8	9	10	11	12	13	14	15	16	17	18	19	20	21	22	23	24	25	26	27	28	29	30	31
☉	8	9	10	11	12	13.1	14.1	15.1	16.1	17.1	18.1	19.2	20.2	21.2	22.2	23.2	24.2	25.3	26.3	27.3	28.3	29.3	0.3	1.4	2.4	3.4	4.4	5.4	6.5	7.5	8.5
☽	5.4	20.3	5	19.4	3.4	17	0.4	13.4	26.3	8.9	21.3	3.6	15.8	27.8	9.7	21.6	3.4	15.2	27.1	9.1	21.3	3.9	16.8	0.2	14.1	28.5	13.3	28.5	13.7	29	14
☿	29.3	0.1	0.8	1.4	1.8	2.1	2.3	2.3R	2.1	1.8	1.2	0.5	29.5	28.5	27.2	25.9	24.5	23.2	21.8	20.6	19.4	18.4	17.6	16.9	16.5	16.2	16	16.1D	16.2	16.6	17
♀	22.2	23.3	24.4	25.5	26.6	27.7	28.9	30	1.1	2.3	3.4	4.5	5.7	6.8	8	9.1	10.3	11.4	12.6	13.8	14.9	16.1	17.3	18.4	19.6	20.8	22	23.2	24.3	25.5	26.7
♂	3.8	4.4	5	5.5	6.1	6.7	7.2	7.8	8.3	8.9	9.4	10	10.5	11.1	11.6	12.2	12.7	13.3	13.8	14.3	14.9	15.4	15.9	16.5	17	17.5	18.1	18.6	19.1	19.6	20.1

♃ (1 6 11 16 21 26 31): 4.2D 4.3 4.4 4.7 5 5.4 5.8 — ♄: 12.5 12.9 13.3 13.6 13.9 14.2 14.4 — ♅ (1 11 21 31): 13.3R 12.9 12.5 12.1 — ♆: 20.9 21.2 21.4 21.6 — ♇: 21.5R 21.5 21.4 21.2

1952

I

	1	2	3	4	5	6	7	8	9	10	11	12	13	14	15	16	17	18	19	20	21	22	23	24	25	26	27	28	29	30	31
☉	9.5	10.5	11.6	12.6	13.6	14.6	15.6	16.7	17.7	18.7	19.7	20.7	21.7	22.8	23.8	24.8	25.8	26.8	27.9	28.9	29.9	0.9	1.9	2.9	4	5	6	7	8	9	10.1
☽	28.7	13	26.8	10.2	23.2	5.9	18.4	0.7	12.8	24.7	6.7	18.5	0.3	12.2	24	6	18.1	0.3	12.9	25.8	9	22.7	6.9	21.5	6.5	21.7	6.9	22	6.9	21.4	5.5
☿	17.6	18.2	19	19.8	20.7	21.7	22.7	23.7	24.8	26	27.2	28.4	29.7	0.9	2.2	3.5	4.9	6.2	7.6	9	10.4	11.8	13.3	14.7	16.2	17.7	19.2	20.7	22.2	23.7	25.2
♀	27.9	29.1	0.3	1.5	2.7	3.8	5	6.2	7.4	8.6	9.8	11	12.2	13.5	14.7	15.9	17.1	18.3	19.5	20.7	21.9	23.1	24.3	25.6	26.8	28	29.2	0.4	1.6	2.9	4.1
♂	20.7	21.2	21.7	22.2	22.7	23.2	23.7	24.2	24.7	25.2	25.7	26.2	26.6	27.1	27.6	28.1	28.6	29	29.5	30	0.4	0.9	1.3	1.8	2.2	2.7	3.1	3.6	4	4.4	4.8

♃ (1 6 11 16 21 26 31): 5.9 6.5 7.1 7.8 8.5 9.3 10.2 — ♄: 14.5 14.7 14.8 14.9 15 15.0R 14.9 — ♅ (1 11 21 31): 12.1R 11.6 11.2 10.8 — ♆: 21.6 21.7 21.7 21.7R — ♇: 21.2R 21 20.8 20.6

II

	1	2	3	4	5	6	7	8	9	10	11	12	13	14	15	16	17	18	19	20	21	22	23	24	25	26	27	28	29
☉	11.1	12.1	13.1	14.1	15.1	16.1	17.2	18.2	19.2	20.2	21.2	22.2	23.2	24.2	25.3	26.3	27.3	28.3	29.3	0.3	1.3	2.3	3.3	4.3	5.3	6.3	7.3	8.4	9.4
☽	19.1	2.2	15	27.5	9.7	21.7	3.6	15.4	27.2	9.1	21	3	15.1	27.4	9.9	22.6	5.6	18.8	2.5	16.4	0.7	15.3	0.1	15.1	30	14.8	29.3	13.4	27.2
☿	26.8	28.3	29.9	1.5	3.1	4.7	6.3	7.9	9.6	11.2	12.9	14.6	16.3	18	19.7	21.5	23.2	25	26.8	28.6	0.4	2.2	4.1	5.9	7.8	9.7	11.6	13.5	15.4
♀	5.3	6.5	7.7	8.9	10.2	11.4	12.6	13.8	15.1	16.3	17.5	18.7	20	21.2	22.4	23.6	24.9	26.1	27.3	28.5	29.8	1	2.2	3.5	4.7	5.9	7.1	8.4	9.6
♂	5.3	5.7	6.1	6.5	6.9	7.3	7.7	8.1	8.5	8.8	9.2	9.6	10	10.3	10.7	11	11.4	11.7	12	12.3	12.7	13	13.3	13.6	13.9	14.1	14.4	14.7	14.9

♃ (1 6 11 16 21 26): 10.4 11.3 12.2 13.2 14.2 15.3 — ♄: 14.9R 14.8 14.7 14.5 14.3 14.1 — ♅ (1 11 21): 10.8R 10.5 10.2 — ♆: 21.7R 21.6 21.5 — ♇: 20.6R 20.3 20.1

III

	1	2	3	4	5	6	7	8	9	10	11	12	13	14	15	16	17	18	19	20	21	22	23	24	25	26	27	28	29	30	31
☉	10.4	11.4	12.4	13.4	14.4	15.4	16.4	17.4	18.4	19.4	20.4	21.4	22.4	23.4	24.4	25.4	26.4	27.3	28.3	29.3	0.3	1.3	2.3	3.3	4.3	5.3	6.3	7.3	8.3	9.2	10.2
☽	10.5	23.4	5.9	18.1	0.2	12	23.8	5.7	17.6	29.6	11.7	24.1	6.7	19.5	2.5	15.8	29.3	13	26.9	11	25.3	9.7	24.2	8.7	23.1	7.4	21.4	5	18.3	1.3	13.9
☿	17.3	19.2	21.1	23	24.9	26.8	28.7	0.5	2.3	4.1	5.8	7.5	9	10.6	12	13.3	14.6	15.7	16.7	17.6	18.4	19.1	19.6	20	20.3	20.4	20.4R	20.3	20.1	19.7	19.3
♀	10.8	12.1	13.3	14.5	15.7	17	18.2	19.4	20.7	21.9	23.1	24.4	25.6	26.8	28	29.3	0.5	1.7	3	4.2	5.4	6.7	7.9	9.1	10.4	11.6	12.8	14	15.3	16.5	17.7
♂	15.2	15.4	15.7	15.9	16.1	16.3	16.5	16.7	16.9	17.1	17.2	17.4	17.5	17.7	17.8	17.9	18	18.1	18.2	18.3	18.3	18.4	18.4	18.4	18.4	18.4	18.4R	18.4	18.4	18.3	18.3

♃ (1 6 11 16 21 26 31): 16.2 17.3 18.4 19.5 20.7 21.9 23.1 — ♄: 13.9R 13.6 13.2 12.9 12.5 12.1 11.7 — ♅ (1 11 21 31): 10.0R 9.9 9.9D 10 — ♆: 21.3R 21.1 20.9 20.6 — ♇: 19.9R 19.6 19.5 19.3

IV

	1	2	3	4	5	6	7	8	9	10	11	12	13	14	15	16	17	18	19	20	21	22	23	24	25	26	27	28	29	30
☉	11.2	12.2	13.2	14.2	15.2	16.1	17.1	18.1	19.1	20.1	21	22	23	24	25	25.9	26.9	27.9	28.9	29.9	0.8	1.8	2.8	3.8	4.7	5.7	6.7	7.6	8.6	9.6
☽	26.1	8.2	20.1	1.9	13.7	25.7	7.8	20.1	2.7	15.6	28.8	12.2	25.9	9.8	23.7	7.8	21.9	6.1	20.2	4.3	18.4	2.4	16.2	29.9	13.3	26.4	9.2	21.8	4	16
☿	18.7R	18.1	17.4	16.7	15.9	15.1	14.3	13.6	12.8	12.1	11.4	10.8	10.2	9.8	9.4	9.1	8.9	8.7	8.7	8.7D	8.8	9	9.3	9.7	10.1	10.6	11.2	11.8	12.5	13.3
♀	19	20.2	21.4	22.7	23.9	25.1	26.4	27.6	28.8	0	1.3	2.5	3.7	5	6.2	7.4	8.7	9.9	11.1	12.3	13.6	14.8	16	17.3	18.5	19.7	21	22.2	23.4	24.6
♂	18.2R	18.1	18	17.9	17.8	17.6	17.5	17.3	17.1	16.9	16.7	16.5	16.3	16	15.8	15.5	15.3	15	14.7	14.4	14.1	13.8	13.4	13.1	12.8	12.4	12.1	11.7	11.3	11

♃ (1 6 11 16 21 26): 23.3 24.5 25.7 26.9 28.1 29.3 — ♄: 11.7R 11.3 10.9 10.5 10.2 9.8 — ♅ (1 11 21): 10 10.2 10.4 — ♆: 20.6R 20.3 20 — ♇: 19.3R 19.2 19.1

V

	1	2	3	4	5	6	7	8	9	10	11	12	13	14	15	16	17	18	19	20	21	22	23	24	25	26	27	28	29	30	31
☉	10.6	11.5	12.5	13.5	14.4	15.4	16.4	17.3	18.3	19.3	20.2	21.2	22.2	23.1	24.1	25.1	26	27	28	28.9	29.9	0.8	1.8	2.8	3.7	4.7	5.6	6.6	7.6	8.5	9.5
☽	27.9	9.7	21.6	3.5	15.7	28.1	10.8	24	7.5	21.3	5.4	19.7	4.1	18.5	2.8	17	1.1	15	28.8	12.4	25.8	9.1	22.2	5	17.6	29.9	12.2	24.1	5.9	17.7	29.5
☿	14.1	15	15.9	16.9	17.9	19	20.1	21.3	22.5	23.7	25	26.3	27.7	29.1	0.6	2.1	3.6	5.1	6.7	8.4	10	11.7	13.5	15.2	17.1	18.9	20.8	22.7	24.7	26.7	28.7
♀	25.9	27.1	28.3	29.6	0.8	2	3.2	4.5	5.7	6.9	8.2	9.4	10.6	11.8	13.1	14.3	15.5	16.7	18	19.2	20.4	21.7	22.9	24.1	25.3	26.6	27.8	29	0.2	1.5	2.7
♂	10.6R	10.2	9.9	9.5	9.1	8.8	8.4	8	7.7	7.3	7	6.6	6.3	5.9	5.6	5.3	5	4.7	4.4	4.1	3.9	3.6	3.3	3.1	2.9	2.7	2.5	2.3	2.1	2	1.8

♃ (1 6 11 16 21 26 31): 0.5 1.7 2.9 4 5.2 6.3 7.5 — ♄: 9.5R 9.2 8.9 8.7 8.5 8.4 8.3 — ♅ (1 11 21 31): 10.7 11.1 11.6 12.1 — ♆: 19.8R 19.5 19.3 19.2 — ♇: 19.1D 19.1 19.2 19.3

VI

	1	2	3	4	5	6	7	8	9	10	11	12	13	14	15	16	17	18	19	20	21	22	23	24	25	26	27	28	29	30
☉	10.4	11.4	12.4	13.3	14.3	15.2	16.2	17.1	18.1	19.1	20	21	21.9	22.9	23.8	24.8	25.7	26.7	27.6	28.6	29.6	0.5	1.5	2.4	3.4	4.3	5.3	6.2	7.2	8.1
☽	11.5	23.6	6	18.8	2	15.7	29.8	14.2	28.9	13.7	28.5	13.2	27.6	11.8	25.7	9.4	22.7	5.9	18.8	1.5	14.1	26.4	8.6	20.6	2.4	14.2	26	7.8	19.8	1.9
☿	0.7	2.8	4.9	7.1	9.2	11.4	13.6	15.8	18	20.2	22.4	24.6	26.8	28.9	1	3.2	5.2	7.3	9.3	11.3	13.2	15.2	17.1	19	20.8	22.6	24.3	26	27.7	29.3
♀	3.9	5.2	6.4	7.6	8.8	10.1	11.3	12.5	13.8	15	16.2	17.4	18.7	19.9	21.1	22.3	23.6	24.8	26	27.3	28.5	29.7	0.9	2.2	3.4	4.6	5.9	7.1	8.3	9.5
♂	1.7R	1.6	1.5	1.4	1.3	1.2	1.2	1.2	1.1	1.1	1.1D	1.2	1.2	1.2	1.3	1.4	1.4	1.5	1.6	1.8	1.9	2	2.2	2.4	2.5	2.7	2.9	3.1	3.4	3.6

♃ (1 6 11 16 21 26): 7.7 8.8 9.8 10.9 11.9 12.8 — ♄: 8.3R 8.2 8.2D 8.2 8.3 8.4 — ♅ (1 11 21): 12.2 12.7 13.3 — ♆: 19.1R 19 19 — ♇: 19.3 19.5 19.7

VII

	1	2	3	4	5	6	7	8	9	10	11	12	13	14	15	16	17	18	19	20	21	22	23	24	25	26	27	28	29	30	31
☉	9.1	10	11	12	12.9	13.9	14.8	15.8	16.7	17.7	18.6	19.6	20.5	21.5	22.4	23.4	24.4	25.3	26.3	27.2	28.2	29.1	0.1	1	2	2.9	3.9	4.9	5.8	6.8	7.7
☽	14.3	27.1	10.2	23.9	8	22.6	7.4	22.5	7.6	22.6	7.3	21.8	5.9	19.5	2.9	15.9	28.6	11.1	23.4	5.5	17.5	29.3	11.1	22.9	4.7	16.6	28.5	10.7	23.1	5.8	19
☿	0.9	2.5	4	5.5	6.9	8.3	9.7	11	12.3	13.5	14.7	15.9	17	18.1	19.1	20.1	21	21.8	22.6	23.4	24.1	24.7	25.3	25.8	26.2	26.6	26.8	27	27.1	27.2R	27.1
♀	10.8	12	13.2	14.5	15.7	16.9	18.2	19.4	20.6	21.8	23.1	24.3	25.5	26.8	28	29.2	0.5	1.7	2.9	4.1	5.4	6.6	7.8	9.1	10.3	11.5	12.8	14	15.2	16.5	17.7
♂	3.8	4.1	4.3	4.6	4.9	5.2	5.5	5.8	6.1	6.4	6.8	7.1	7.5	7.8	8.2	8.6	8.9	9.3	9.7	10.1	10.5	10.9	11.4	11.8	12.2	12.7	13.1	13.6	14	14.5	15

♃ (1 6 11 16 21 26 31): 13.8 14.6 15.5 16.3 17 17.7 18.4 — ♄: 8.5 8.7 9 9.2 9.5 9.9 10.2 — ♅ (1 11 21 31): 13.9 14.5 15.1 15.7 — ♆: 18.9D 19 19 19.2 — ♇: 19.9 20.2 20.5 20.8

VIII

	1	2	3	4	5	6	7	8	9	10	11	12	13	14	15	16	17	18	19	20	21	22	23	24	25	26	27	28	29	30	31
☉	8.7	9.6	10.6	11.6	12.5	13.5	14.4	15.4	16.3	17.3	18.3	19.2	20.2	21.1	22.1	23.1	24	25	25.9	26.9	27.9	28.8	29.8	0.8	1.7	2.7	3.7	4.6	5.6	6.6	7.5
☽	2.5	16.5	0.9	15.7	0.8	16	1.2	16.2	0.9	15.2	29	12.4	25.4	8.1	20.4	2.6	14.5	26.4	8.2	20	1.8	13.7	26.6	7.7	20	2.5	15.3	28.4	11.8	25.7	9.9
☿	27.0R	26.7	26.4	26	25.5	25	24.4	23.7	22.9	22.2	21.4	20.5	19.7	18.9	18.2	17.4	16.8	16.2	15.7	15.3	15.1	14.9	14.9D	15	15.2	15.6	16.1	16.7	17.5	18.4	19.4
♀	18.9	20.2	21.4	22.6	23.9	25.1	26.3	27.6	28.8	0	1.2	2.5	3.7	4.9	6.2	7.4	8.6	9.9	11.1	12.3	13.6	14.8	16	17.3	18.5	19.7	21	22.2	23.4	24.7	25.9
♂	15.4	15.9	16.4	16.9	17.4	17.9	18.4	18.9	19.4	20	20.5	21	21.6	22.1	22.7	23.2	23.8	24.3	24.9	25.4	26	26.6	27.2	27.7	28.3	28.9	29.5	0.1	0.7	1.3	1.9

♃ (1 6 11 16 21 26 31): 18.5 19.1 19.6 20 20.3 20.6 20.8 — ♄: 10.3 10.7 11.1 11.6 12.1 12.6 13.1 — ♅ (1 11 21 31): 15.7 16.3 16.8 17.3 — ♆: 19.2 19.4 19.6 19.9 — ♇: 20.8 21.1 21.4 21.7

IX

	1	2	3	4	5	6	7	8	9	10	11	12	13	14	15	16	17	18	19	20	21	22	23	24	25	26	27	28	29	30
☉	8.5	9.5	10.4	11.4	12.4	13.3	14.3	15.3	16.3	17.2	18.2	19.2	20.1	21.1	22.1	23.1	24	25	26	27	28	28.9	29.9	0.9	1.9	2.8	3.8	4.8	5.8	6.8
☽	24.4	9.3	24.3	9.4	24.4	9.2	23.6	7.6	21.2	4.3	16.9	29.3	11.4	23.3	5.1	16.9	28.7	10.6	22.6	4.7	17.1	29.6	12.4	25.3	8.5	22	5.7	19.7	3.9	18.5
☿	20.5	21.7	23	24.5	26	27.5	29.2	0.9	2.6	4.4	6.2	8	9.9	11.8	13.7	15.5	17.4	19.3	21.2	23.1	24.9	26.8	28.6	0.4	2.2	4	5.8	7.5	9.3	11
♀	27.1	28.4	29.6	0.8	2.1	3.3	4.5	5.7	7	8.2	9.4	10.7	11.9	13.1	14.4	15.6	16.8	18	19.3	20.5	21.7	23	24.2	25.4	26.7	27.9	29.1	0.3	1.6	2.8
♂	2.5	3.1	3.8	4.4	5	5.6	6.3	6.9	7.5	8.2	8.8	9.4	10.1	10.7	11.4	12	12.7	13.4	14	14.7	15.4	16	16.7	17.4	18	18.7	19.4	20.1	20.8	21.5

♃ (1 6 11 16 21 26): 20.9 21 21.0R 20.9 20.8 20.5 — ♄: 13.2 13.8 14.3 14.9 15.5 16.1 — ♅ (1 11 21): 17.3 17.7 18 — ♆: 19.9 20.2 20.6 — ♇: 21.8 22 22.3

X

	1	2	3	4	5	6	7	8	9	10	11	12	13	14	15	16	17	18	19	20	21	22	23	24	25	26	27	28	29	30	31
☉	7.8	8.7	9.7	10.7	11.7	12.7	13.7	14.7	15.6	16.6	17.6	18.6	19.6	20.6	21.6	22.6	23.6	24.6	25.6	26.5	27.5	28.5	29.5	0.5	1.5	2.5	3.5	4.5	5.5	6.5	7.5
☽	3.1	17.9	2.7	17.4	1.7	15.7	29.3	12.4	25.2	7.6	19.7	1.6	13.4	25.1	7	19	1.2	13.5	26.2	9	22.1	5.5	18.9	2.6	16.4	0.3	14.4	28.6	12.9	27.3	11.6
☿	12.7	14.4	16.1	17.8	19.5	21.1	22.7	24.4	26	27.6	29.2	0.7	2.3	3.8	5.4	6.9	8.4	9.9	11.4	12.9	14.4	15.8	17.3	18.7	20.1	21.5	22.9	24.3	25.7	27	28.4
♀	4	5.3	6.5	7.7	8.9	10.2	11.4	12.6	13.8	15.1	16.3	17.5	18.7	20	21.2	22.4	23.6	24.9	26.1	27.3	28.5	29.8	1	2.2	3.4	4.6	5.9	7.1	8.3	9.5	10.7
♂	22.1	22.8	23.5	24.2	24.9	25.6	26.3	27	27.7	28.4	29.1	29.9	0.6	1.3	2	2.7	3.4	4.1	4.9	5.6	6.3	7	7.8	8.5	9.2	10	10.7	11.4	12.2	12.9	13.6

♃ (1 6 11 16 21 26 31): 20.2R 19.9 19.4 18.9 18.3 17.7 17 — ♄: 16.7 17.3 17.9 18.5 19.1 19.7 20.3 — ♅ (1 11 21 31): 18.3 18.4 18.5 18.5R — ♆: 20.9 21.3 21.7 22 — ♇: 22.6 22.8 23 23.1

XI

	1	2	3	4	5	6	7	8	9	10	11	12	13	14	15	16	17	18	19	20	21	22	23	24	25	26	27	28	29	30
☉	8.5	9.5	10.5	11.5	12.5	13.5	14.5	15.5	16.5	17.5	18.6	19.6	20.6	21.6	22.6	23.6	24.6	25.6	26.6	27.6	28.6	29.6	0.7	1.7	2.7	3.7	4.7	5.7	6.7	7.7
☽	25.9	10	23.8	7.2	20.3	3	15.4	27.5	9.4	21.3	3.1	14.9	27	9.3	21.8	4.7	17.9	1.4	15.1	29	13.1	27.1	11.3	25.3	9.4	23.5	7.5	21.4	5.2	18.9
☿	29.7	1	2.3	3.5	4.8	6	7.1	8.2	9.3	10.4	11.4	12.3	13.1	13.9	14.6	15.2	15.7	16.1	16.4	16.5	16.5R	16.3	15.9	15.3	14.6	13.7	12.6	11.4	10.1	8.8
♀	12	13.2	14.4	15.6	16.8	18.1	19.3	20.5	21.7	22.9	24.1	25.4	26.6	27.8	29	0.2	1.4	2.6	3.8	5.1	6.3	7.5	8.7	9.9	11.1	12.3	13.5	14.7	15.9	17.1
♂	14.4	15.1	15.9	16.6	17.3	18.1	18.8	19.6	20.3	21.1	21.8	22.6	23.3	24.1	24.8	25.6	26.3	27.1	27.9	28.6	29.4	0.1	0.9	1.7	2.4	3.2	3.9	4.7	5.5	6.2

♃ (1 6 11 16 21 26): 16.9R 16.2 15.5 14.9 14.2 13.6 — ♄: 20.5 21 21.6 22.2 22.7 23.3 — ♅ (1 11 21): 18.5R 18.4 18.2 — ♆: 22.1 22.4 22.8 — ♇: 23.1 23.2 23.3

XII

	1	2	3	4	5	6	7	8	9	10	11	12	13	14	15	16	17	18	19	20	21	22	23	24	25	26	27	28	29	30	31
☉	8.8	9.8	10.8	11.8	12.8	13.8	14.8	15.9	16.9	17.9	18.9	19.9	20.9	22	23	24	25	26	27	28.1	29.1	0.1	1.1	2.1	3.2	4.2	5.2	6.2	7.2	8.3	9.3
☽	2.3	15.5	28.3	10.9	23.2	5.3	17.2	29	10.8	22.7	4.7	17	29.7	12.6	26	9.8	23.9	8.2	22.7	7.2	21.7	6.1	20.3	4.4	18.2	1.8	15.2	28.5	11.5	24.3	6.8
☿	7.4R	6.1	4.8	3.6	2.6	1.8	1.1	0.7	0.4	0.3	0.3D	0.6	1	1.5	2.1	2.8	3.7	4.6	5.5	6.6	7.7	8.8	10	11.2	12.5	13.8	15.1	16.4	17.8	19.2	20.6
♀	18.3	19.5	20.7	21.9	23.1	24.3	25.5	26.7	27.9	29.1	0.3	1.5	2.7	3.8	5	6.2	7.4	8.6	9.8	10.9	12.1	13.3	14.4	15.6	16.8	17.9	19.1	20.3	21.4	22.6	23.7
♂	7	7.8	8.5	9.3	10.1	10.8	11.6	12.4	13.1	13.9	14.7	15.4	16.2	17	17.7	18.5	19.3	20	20.8	21.6	22.3	23.1	23.9	24.7	25.5	26.2	27	27.8	28.5	29.3	0.1

♃ (1 6 11 16 21 26 31): 13.0R 12.5 12.1 11.7 11.4 11.2 11 — ♄: 23.8 24.2 24.7 25.1 25.5 25.9 26.2 — ♅ (1 11 21 31): 17.9R 17.6 17.2 16.8 — ♆: 23.1 23.3 23.5 23.7 — ♇: 23.3R 23.2 23.1 23

I

	1	2	3	4	5	6	7	8	9	10	11	12	13	14	15	16	17	18	19	20	21	22	23	24	25	26	27	28	29	30	31
☉	♑ 10.3	11.3	12.3	13.3	14.4	15.4	16.4	17.4	18.4	19.5	20.5	21.5	22.5	23.5	24.6	25.6	26.6	27.6	28.6	29.6	♒ 0.7	1.7	2.7	3.7	4.7	5.8	6.8	7.8	8.8	9.8	10.8
☽	♋ 19.2	♌ 1.4	13.4	25.2	♍ 7	18.8	♎ 0.7	12.7	24.9	♏ 7.5	20.4	♐ 3.8	17.6	♑ 1.8	16.4	♒ 1.3	16.2	♓ 1.2	16	♈ 0.5	14.8	28.7	♉ 12.2	25.5	♊ 8.4	21.1	♋ 3.6	15.8	27.9	♌ 9.9	21.8
☿	♐ 22	23.4	24.8	26.3	27.7	29.2	♑ 0.7	2.1	3.6	5.1	6.7	8.2	9.7	11.2	12.8	14.3	15.9	17.5	19	20.6	22.2	23.8	25.4	27.1	28.7	♒ 0.3	2	3.7	5.3	7	8.7
♀	♒ 24.9	26	27.2	28.3	29.5	♓ 0.6	1.7	2.9	4	5.1	6.2	7.4	8.5	9.6	10.7	11.8	12.9	14	15.1	16.2	17.2	18.3	19.4	20.4	21.5	22.6	23.6	24.6	25.7	26.7	27.7
♂	♓ 0.9	1.6	2.4	3.2	3.9	4.7	5.5	6.2	7	7.8	8.6	9.3	10.1	10.9	11.6	12.4	13.2	13.9	14.7	15.5	16.2	17	17.8	18.5	19.3	20.1	20.8	21.6	22.4	23.1	23.9

♃ (1, 6, 11, 16, 21, 26, 31): ♉ 11.0R 11.0D 11 11.2 11.4 11.7 12.1
♄ (1, 6, 11, 16, 21, 26, 31): ♎ 26.2 26.5 26.7 26.9 27.1 27.2 27.3
♅ (1, 11, 21, 31): ♋ 16.7R 16.3 15.9 15.5
♆ (1, 11, 21, 31): ♎ 23.7 23.8 23.9 23.9R
♇ (1, 11, 21, 31): ♌ 22.9R 22.8 22.5 22.3

II

	1	2	3	4	5	6	7	8	9	10	11	12	13	14	15	16	17	18	19	20	21	22	23	24	25	26	27	28	29	30	31
☉	♒ 11.8	12.9	13.9	14.9	15.9	16.9	17.9	18.9	20	21	22	23	24	25	26	27	28	29	♓ 0.1	1.1	2.1	3.1	4.1	5.1	6.1	7.1	8.1	9.1			
☽	♍ 3.6	15.4	27.3	♎ 9.2	21.2	♏ 3.4	15.9	28.7	♐ 11.9	25.6	♑ 9.7	24.3	♒ 9.2	24.3	♓ 9.5	24.7	♈ 9.6	24.1	♉ 8.3	22	♊ 5.2	18.1	♋ 0.6	12.9	25	♌ 6.9	18.7	♍ 0.6			
☿	♒ 10.4	12.2	13.9	15.7	17.4	19.2	21	22.8	24.6	26.4	28.2	♓ 0	1.8	3.7	5.5	7.3	9.2	11	12.8	14.5	16.3	18	19.6	21.2	22.8	24.3	25.7	26.9			
♀	♓ 28.7	29.8	♈ 0.8	1.7	2.7	3.7	4.7	5.6	6.6	7.5	8.5	9.4	10.3	11.2	12.1	13	13.8	14.7	15.5	16.3	17.1	17.9	18.7	19.5	20.2	21	21.7	22.4			
♂	♓ 24.7	25.4	26.2	26.9	27.7	28.5	29.2	30	♈ 0.7	1.5	2.2	3	3.8	4.5	5.3	6	6.8	7.5	8.3	9	9.8	10.5	11.3	12	12.8	13.5	14.3	15			

♃ (1, 6, 11, 16, 21, 26): ♉ 12.2 12.6 13.2 13.8 14.5 15.2
♄ (1, 6, 11, 16, 21, 26): ♎ 27.3 27.3R 27.3 27.2 27.1 26.9
♅ (1, 11, 21): ♋ 15.5R 15.1 14.8
♆ (1, 11, 21): ♎ 23.9R 23.8 23.7
♇ (1, 11, 21): ♌ 22.3R 22 21.8

III

	1	2	3	4	5	6	7	8	9	10	11	12	13	14	15	16	17	18	19	20	21	22	23	24	25	26	27	28	29	30	31
☉	♓ 10.1	11.1	12.1	13.1	14.1	15.1	16.1	17.1	18.1	19.1	20.1	21.1	22.1	23.1	24.1	25.1	26.1	27.1	28.1	29.1	♈ 0.1	1.1	2.1	3.1	4.1	5	6	7	8	9	10
☽	♍ 12.4	24.2	♎ 6.1	18.1	♏ 0.2	12.5	25.1	♐ 7.8	21	♑ 4.4	18.3	♒ 2.6	17.3	♓ 2.3	17.5	♈ 2.8	17.8	♉ 2.6	16.9	♊ 0.8	14.2	27.1	♋ 9.6	21.9	♌ 3.9	15.7	27.5	♍ 9.3	21.1	♎ 3.1	15.1
☿	♓ 28.1	29.2	♈ 0.2	1	1.7	2.2	2.6	2.9	3	2.9R	2.7	2.4	1.9	1.4	0.7	♓ 29.9	29.1	28.2	27.3	26.3	25.4	24.5	23.7	22.9	22.2	21.6	21.1	20.6	20.3	20	19.8
♀	♈ 23.1	23.7	24.4	25	25.6	26.1	26.7	27.2	27.7	28.2	28.6	29	29.4	29.7	♉ 0.1	0.4	0.6	0.8	1	1.1	1.2	1.3	1.3	1.3R	1.3	1.2	1	0.9	0.6	0.4	0.1
♂	♈ 15.8	16.5	17.3	18	18.7	19.5	20.2	21	21.7	22.4	23.2	23.9	24.7	25.4	26.1	26.9	27.6	28.3	29.1	29.8	♉ 0.5	1.3	2	2.7	3.4	4.2	4.9	5.6	6.4	7.1	7.8

♃ (1, 6, 11, 16, 21, 26, 31): ♉ 15.7 16.5 17.3 18.3 19.2 20.2 21.2
♄ (1, 6, 11, 16, 21, 26, 31): ♎ 26.8R 26.6 26.3 26 25.7 25.4 25
♅ (1, 11, 21, 31): ♋ 14.6R 14.5 14.4 14.5D
♆ (1, 11, 21, 31): ♎ 23.6R 23.4 23.1 22.9
♇ (1, 11, 21, 31): ♌ 21.6R 21.4 21.2 21

IV

	1	2	3	4	5	6	7	8	9	10	11	12	13	14	15	16	17	18	19	20	21	22	23	24	25	26	27	28	29	30	31
☉	♈ 11	12	12.9	13.9	14.9	15.9	16.9	17.9	18.9	19.8	20.8	21.8	22.8	23.8	24.7	25.7	26.7	27.7	28.6	29.6	♉ 0.6	1.6	2.5	3.5	4.5	5.5	6.4	7.4	8.4	9.4	
☽	♎ 27.3	♏ 9.6	22.1	♐ 4.8	17.7	♑ 0.8	14.3	28	♒ 12	26.4	♓ 11.1	26	♈ 11	26	♉ 10.7	25	♊ 9	22.4	♋ 5.4	18	♌ 0.3	12.3	24.2	♍ 6	17.8	29.7	♎ 11.7	23.9	♏ 6.3	18.9	
☿	♓ 19.8R	19.8D	19.9	20.2	20.4	20.8	21.3	21.8	22.4	23.1	23.8	24.6	25.4	26.3	27.2	28.2	29.3	♈ 0.3	1.5	2.6	3.8	5.1	6.3	7.7	9	10.4	11.8	13.3	14.8	16.3	
♀	♈ 29.7R	29.3	28.9	28.5	28	27.5	26.9	26.4	25.8	25.2	24.6	24	23.3	22.7	22.1	21.4	20.8	20.2	19.7	19.1	18.6	18.1	17.6	17.2	16.8	16.4	16.1	15.8	15.6	15.4	
♂	♉ 8.5	9.2	10	10.7	11.4	12.1	12.8	13.6	14.3	15	15.7	16.4	17.1	17.8	18.6	19.3	20	20.7	21.4	22.1	22.8	23.5	24.2	24.9	25.6	26.3	27	27.7	28.4	29.1	

♃ (1, 6, 11, 16, 21, 26): ♉ 21.4 22.4 23.5 24.6 25.7 26.9
♄ (1, 6, 11, 16, 21, 26): ♎ 25.0R 24.6 24.2 23.8 23.4 23.1
♅ (1, 11, 21): ♋ 14.5 14.6 14.8
♆ (1, 11, 21): ♎ 22.8R 22.6 22.3
♇ (1, 11, 21): ♌ 21.0R 20.9 20.8

V

	1	2	3	4	5	6	7	8	9	10	11	12	13	14	15	16	17	18	19	20	21	22	23	24	25	26	27	28	29	30	31
☉	♉ 10.3	11.3	12.3	13.2	14.2	15.2	16.1	17.1	18.1	19	20	21	21.9	22.9	23.9	24.8	25.8	26.8	27.7	28.7	29.6	♊ 0.6	1.6	2.5	3.5	4.5	5.4	6.4	7.3	8.3	9.2
☽	♐ 1.7	14.7	27.8	♑ 11.2	24.7	♒ 8.5	22.5	♓ 6.7	21	♈ 5.6	20.2	♉ 4.7	19.1	♊ 3.2	17	♋ 0.4	13.4	26	♌ 8.3	20.3	♍ 2.2	14	25.9	♎ 7.8	20	♏ 2.3	14.9	27.8	♐ 10.9	24.2	♑ 7.8
☿	♈ 17.8	19.4	21	22.6	24.3	26	27.8	29.5	♉ 1.3	3.2	5	6.9	8.9	10.8	12.8	14.8	16.9	18.9	21	23.2	25.3	27.5	29.7	♊ 1.8	4	6.2	8.4	10.6	12.8	15	17.1
♀	♈ 15.2R	15.1	15	15	15.0D	15	15.1	15.2	15.4	15.5	15.8	16	16.3	16.6	17	17.3	17.8	18.2	18.6	19.1	19.6	20.2	20.7	21.3	21.9	22.5	23.2	23.8	24.5	25.2	25.9
♂	♉ 29.8	♊ 0.5	1.2	1.9	2.6	3.3	4	4.7	5.4	6.1	6.8	7.5	8.2	8.9	9.5	10.2	10.9	11.6	12.3	13	13.7	14.3	15	15.7	16.4	17.1	17.8	18.4	19.1	19.8	20.5

♃ (1, 6, 11, 16, 21, 26, 31): ♉ 28 29.2 ♊ 0.3 1.5 2.7 3.8 5
♄ (1, 6, 11, 16, 21, 26, 31): ♎ 22.7R 22.4 22 21.7 21.5 21.2 21
♅ (1, 11, 21, 31): ♋ 15.1 15.5 15.9 16.4
♆ (1, 11, 21, 31): ♎ 22.0R 21.8 21.6 21.4
♇ (1, 11, 21, 31): ♌ 20.8R 20.8D 20.9 21

VI

	1	2	3	4	5	6	7	8	9	10	11	12	13	14	15	16	17	18	19	20	21	22	23	24	25	26	27	28	29	30	31
☉	♊ 10.2	11.2	12.1	13.1	14	15	16	16.9	17.9	18.8	19.8	20.7	21.7	22.6	23.6	24.6	25.5	26.5	27.4	28.4	29.3	♋ 0.3	1.2	2.2	3.1	4.1	5	6	7	7.9	
☽	♑ 21.5	♒ 5.3	19.3	♓ 3.4	17.6	♈ 1.8	16	♉ 0.2	14.3	28.2	♊ 12	25.4	♋ 8.6	21.4	♌ 3.9	16.2	28.2	♍ 10.1	22	♎ 3.8	15.8	28	♏ 10.4	23.1	♐ 6.1	19.5	♑ 3.2	17.1	♒ 1.3	15.6	
☿	♊ 19.2	21.3	23.4	25.4	27.4	29.3	♋ 1.3	3.1	5	6.8	8.5	10.2	11.9	13.5	15.1	16.6	18.1	19.6	21	22.4	23.7	24.9	26.2	27.3	28.5	29.5	♌ 0.5	1.5	2.4	3.3	
♀	♈ 26.6	27.4	28.1	28.9	29.7	♉ 0.5	1.3	2.1	2.9	3.8	4.6	5.5	6.3	7.2	8.1	9	9.9	10.8	11.8	12.7	13.6	14.6	15.5	16.5	17.5	18.5	19.4	20.4	21.4	22.4	
♂	♊ 21.2	21.8	22.5	23.2	23.9	24.5	25.2	25.9	26.5	27.2	27.9	28.6	29.2	29.9	♋ 0.6	1.2	1.9	2.6	3.2	3.9	4.6	5.2	5.9	6.6	7.2	7.9	8.6	9.2	9.9	10.5	

♃ (1, 6, 11, 16, 21, 26): ♊ 5.2 6.4 7.6 8.7 9.9 11
♄ (1, 6, 11, 16, 21, 26): ♎ 21.0R 20.8 20.7 20.6 20.6 20.5D
♅ (1, 11, 21): ♋ 16.4 17 17.5
♆ (1, 11, 21): ♎ 21.4R 21.2 21.1
♇ (1, 11, 21): ♌ 21 21.1 21.3

VII

	1	2	3	4	5	6	7	8	9	10	11	12	13	14	15	16	17	18	19	20	21	22	23	24	25	26	27	28	29	30	31
☉	♋ 8.9	9.8	10.8	11.7	12.7	13.6	14.6	15.5	16.5	17.4	18.4	19.4	20.3	21.3	22.2	23.2	24.1	25.1	26	27	27.9	28.9	29.8	♌ 0.8	1.8	2.7	3.7	4.6	5.6	6.5	7.5
☽	♒ 29.9	♓ 14.3	28.6	♈ 12.8	26.9	♉ 10.8	24.5	♊ 8	21.3	♋ 4.4	17.2	29.8	♌ 12.1	24.2	♍ 6.2	18.1	30	♎ 11.8	23.8	♏ 6	18.4	♐ 1.1	14.2	27.6	♑ 11.5	25.8	♒ 10.3	25	♓ 9.8	24.5	♈ 9.1
☿	♌ 4.1	4.8	5.5	6.1	6.6	7.1	7.5	7.8	8.1	8.3	8.4	8.4R	8.3	8.2	7.9	7.6	7.3	6.8	6.3	5.8	5.2	4.5	3.8	3.1	2.4	1.7	1	0.4	♋ 29.7	29.2	28.7
♀	♉ 23.4	24.4	25.4	26.5	27.5	28.5	29.6	♊ 0.6	1.6	2.7	3.7	4.8	5.8	6.9	8	9	10.1	11.2	12.3	13.4	14.4	15.5	16.6	17.7	18.8	19.9	21	22.1	23.2	24.4	25.5
♂	♋ 11.2	11.9	12.5	13.2	13.8	14.5	15.1	15.8	16.5	17.1	17.8	18.4	19.1	19.7	20.4	21	21.7	22.3	23	23.6	24.3	24.9	25.6	26.2	26.9	27.5	28.2	28.8	29.5	♌ 0.1	0.8

♃ (1, 6, 11, 16, 21, 26, 31): ♊ 12.1 13.2 14.3 15.3 16.3 17.3 18.3
♄ (1, 6, 11, 16, 21, 26, 31): ♎ 20.6 20.7 20.8 21 21.2 21.4 21.7
♅ (1, 11, 21, 31): ♋ 18.1 18.7 19.4 20
♆ (1, 11, 21, 31): ♎ 21.1R 21.1D 21.2 21.3
♇ (1, 11, 21, 31): ♌ 21.6 21.8 22.1 22.4

VIII

	1	2	3	4	5	6	7	8	9	10	11	12	13	14	15	16	17	18	19	20	21	22	23	24	25	26	27	28	29	30	31
☉	♌ 8.4	9.4	10.4	11.3	12.3	13.2	14.2	15.2	16.1	17.1	18	19	19.9	20.9	21.9	22.8	23.8	24.8	25.7	26.7	27.6	28.6	29.6	♍ 0.5	1.5	2.5	3.4	4.4	5.4	6.3	7.3
☽	♈ 23.5	♉ 7.6	21.4	♊ 4.9	18.1	♋ 1.1	13.8	26.3	♌ 8.6	20.7	♍ 2.7	14.6	26.5	♎ 8.3	20.2	♏ 2.1	14.3	26.6	♐ 9.3	22.3	♑ 5.7	19.6	♒ 3.9	18.6	♓ 3.6	18.8	♈ 3.9	18.9	♉ 3.5	17.8	♊ 1.6
☿	♋ 28.3R	27.9	27.7	27.5	27.5D	27.6	27.7	28	28.4	28.9	29.6	♌ 0.3	1.2	2.1	3.2	4.4	5.6	7	8.4	9.9	11.5	13.2	14.9	16.7	18.5	20.4	22.3	24.2	26.2	28.1	♍ 0.1
♀	♊ 26.6	27.7	28.8	30	♋ 1.1	2.2	3.3	4.5	5.6	6.7	7.9	9	10.2	11.3	12.5	13.6	14.8	15.9	17.1	18.2	19.4	20.6	21.7	22.9	24.1	25.2	26.4	27.6	28.8	29.9	♌ 1.1
♂	♌ 1.4	2.1	2.7	3.4	4	4.7	5.3	5.9	6.6	7.2	7.9	8.5	9.2	9.8	10.4	11.1	11.7	12.4	13	13.6	14.3	14.9	15.6	16.2	16.8	17.5	18.1	18.7	19.4	20	20.7

♃ (1, 6, 11, 16, 21, 26, 31): ♊ 18.5 19.4 20.3 21.1 21.9 22.6 23.3
♄ (1, 6, 11, 16, 21, 26, 31): ♎ 21.7 22 22.4 22.8 23.2 23.6 24.1
♅ (1, 11, 21, 31): ♋ 20 20.6 21.1 21.6
♆ (1, 11, 21, 31): ♎ 21.3 21.5 21.7 22
♇ (1, 11, 21, 31): ♌ 22.4 22.8 23.1 23.4

IX

	1	2	3	4	5	6	7	8	9	10	11	12	13	14	15	16	17	18	19	20	21	22	23	24	25	26	27	28	29	30	31
☉	♍ 8.3	9.2	10.2	11.2	12.1	13.1	14.1	15	16	17	18	18.9	19.9	20.9	21.9	22.8	23.8	24.8	25.8	26.7	27.7	28.7	29.7	♎ 0.6	1.6	2.6	3.6	4.6	5.6	6.5	
☽	♊ 15.1	28.1	♋ 10.8	23.3	♌ 5.5	17.6	29.6	♍ 11.5	23.4	♎ 5.2	17.1	29	♏ 10.9	23.1	♐ 5.4	18	♑ 0.9	14.2	28	♒ 12.2	26.8	♓ 11.9	27.1	♈ 12.4	27.6	♉ 12.5	27	♊ 11	24.5	♋ 7.6	
☿	♍ 2.1	4	6	7.9	9.9	11.8	13.7	15.6	17.5	19.4	21.2	23	24.8	26.6	28.4	♎ 0.2	1.9	3.6	5.3	7	8.7	10.3	12	13.6	15.2	16.8	18.4	19.9	21.5	23	
♀	♌ 2.3	3.5	4.7	5.8	7	8.2	9.4	10.6	11.8	13	14.2	15.4	16.6	17.8	19	20.2	21.4	22.6	23.8	25	26.2	27.4	28.6	29.8	♍ 1	2.2	3.5	4.7	5.9	7.1	
♂	♌ 21.3	21.9	22.6	23.2	23.8	24.5	25.1	25.7	26.4	27	27.6	28.3	28.9	29.5	♍ 0.2	0.8	1.4	2.1	2.7	3.3	4	4.6	5.2	5.8	6.5	7.1	7.7	8.4	9	9.6	

♃ (1, 6, 11, 16, 21, 26): ♊ 23.5 24.1 24.6 25.1 25.5 25.9
♄ (1, 6, 11, 16, 21, 26): ♎ 24.2 24.7 25.2 25.7 26.3 26.8
♅ (1, 11, 21): ♋ 21.7 22.1 22.5
♆ (1, 11, 21): ♎ 22 22.3 22.7
♇ (1, 11, 21): ♌ 23.4 23.7 24

X

	1	2	3	4	5	6	7	8	9	10	11	12	13	14	15	16	17	18	19	20	21	22	23	24	25	26	27	28	29	30	31
☉	♎ 7.5	8.5	9.5	10.5	11.5	12.4	13.4	14.4	15.4	16.4	17.4	18.4	19.4	20.4	21.3	22.3	23.3	24.3	25.3	26.3	27.3	28.3	29.3	♏ 0.3	1.3	2.3	3.3	4.3	5.3	6.3	7.3
☽	♋ 20.3	♌ 2.6	14.7	26.7	♍ 8.6	20.4	♎ 2.2	14.1	26	♏ 8	20.2	♐ 2.4	14.8	27.4	♑ 10.3	23.5	♒ 7.1	21.1	♓ 5.5	20.3	♈ 5.4	20.6	♉ 5.8	20.8	♊ 5.4	19.5	♋ 3.1	16.3	29	♌ 11.4	23.5
☿	♎ 24.5	26	27.5	29	♏ 0.4	1.9	3.3	4.7	6.1	7.5	8.9	10.2	11.5	12.8	14.1	15.4	16.6	17.8	19	20.2	21.3	22.4	23.4	24.4	25.4	26.3	27.1	27.9	28.6	29.2	29.7
♀	♍ 8.3	9.5	10.8	12	13.2	14.4	15.7	16.9	18.1	19.4	20.6	21.8	23	24.3	25.5	26.7	28	29.2	♎ 0.4	1.7	2.9	4.2	5.4	6.6	7.9	9.1	10.4	11.6	12.8	14.1	15.3
♂	♍ 10.3	10.9	11.5	12.1	12.8	13.4	14	14.7	15.3	15.9	16.5	17.2	17.8	18.4	19	19.7	20.3	20.9	21.5	22.2	22.8	23.4	24	24.7	25.3	25.9	26.5	27.2	27.8	28.4	29

♃ (1, 6, 11, 16, 21, 26, 31): ♊ 26.1 26.3 26.4 26.5R 26.4 26.3 26.1
♄ (1, 6, 11, 16, 21, 26, 31): ♎ 27.4 28 28.6 29.2 29.8 ♏ 0.4 1
♅ (1, 11, 21, 31): ♋ 22.7 22.9 23.1 23.1R
♆ (1, 11, 21, 31): ♎ 23 23.4 23.8 24.1
♇ (1, 11, 21, 31): ♌ 24.3 24.5 24.7 24.8

XI

	1	2	3	4	5	6	7	8	9	10	11	12	13	14	15	16	17	18	19	20	21	22	23	24	25	26	27	28	29	30	31
☉	♏ 8.3	9.3	10.3	11.3	12.3	13.3	14.3	15.3	16.3	17.3	18.3	19.3	20.3	21.3	22.3	23.3	24.3	25.4	26.4	27.4	28.4	29.4	♐ 0.4	1.4	2.4	3.4	4.5	5.5	6.5	7.5	
☽	♍ 5.4	17.3	29.1	♎ 10.9	22.9	♏ 4.9	17.1	29.4	♐ 11.9	24.5	♑ 7.3	20.3	♒ 3.6	17.1	♓ 1	15.2	29.6	♈ 14.4	29.2	♉ 14.1	28.8	♊ 13.3	27.4	♋ 11	24.3	♌ 7.1	19.5	♍ 1.7	13.6	25.5	
☿	♐ 0.1	0.4	0.6	0.7R	0.6	0.4	♏ 30	29.4	28.7	27.8	26.7	25.6	24.3	23	21.7	20.3	19.1	17.9	16.9	16.1	15.4	14.9	14.7	14.6D	14.7	15	15.4	15.9	16.6	17.4	
♀	♎ 16.6	17.8	19.1	20.3	21.6	22.8	24.1	25.3	26.6	27.8	29.1	♏ 0.3	1.6	2.8	4.1	5.3	6.6	7.8	9.1	10.3	11.6	12.8	14.1	15.3	16.6	17.8	19.1	20.4	21.6	22.9	
♂	♍ 29.6	♎ 0.3	0.9	1.5	2.1	2.7	3.4	4	4.6	5.2	5.8	6.5	7.1	7.7	8.3	8.9	9.6	10.2	10.8	11.4	12	12.6	13.2	13.9	14.5	15.1	15.7	16.3	16.9	17.5	

♃ (1, 6, 11, 16, 21, 26): ♊ 26.0R 25.7 25.3 24.8 24.3 23.7
♄ (1, 6, 11, 16, 21, 26): ♏ 1.1 1.7 2.3 2.9 3.5 4.1
♅ (1, 11, 21): ♋ 23.1R 23 22.9
♆ (1, 11, 21): ♎ 24.2 24.5 24.9
♇ (1, 11, 21): ♌ 24.9 25 25

XII

	1	2	3	4	5	6	7	8	9	10	11	12	13	14	15	16	17	18	19	20	21	22	23	24	25	26	27	28	29	30	31
☉	♐ 8.5	9.5	10.5	11.5	12.6	13.6	14.6	15.6	16.6	17.6	18.7	19.7	20.7	21.7	22.7	23.7	24.8	25.8	26.8	27.8	28.8	29.9	♑ 0.9	1.9	2.9	3.9	4.9	6	7	8	9
☽	♎ 7.4	19.2	♏ 1.3	13.4	25.8	♐ 8.3	21.1	♑ 4	17.2	♒ 0.6	14.1	27.8	♓ 11.7	25.8	♈ 10	24.4	♉ 8.8	23.2	♊ 7.4	21.5	♋ 5.3	18.8	♌ 2	14.7	27.2	♍ 9.4	21.5	♎ 3.4	15.2	27.1	♏ 9.2
☿	♏ 18.3	19.3	20.4	21.5	22.7	23.9	25.1	26.5	27.8	29.2	♐ 0.5	1.9	3.4	4.8	6.2	7.7	9.2	10.7	12.1	13.6	15.1	16.7	18.2	19.7	21.2	22.7	24.3	25.8	27.3	28.9	♑ 0.4
♀	♏ 24.1	25.4	26.6	27.9	29.1	♐ 0.4	1.7	2.9	4.2	5.4	6.7	7.9	9.2	10.5	11.7	13	14.2	15.5	16.8	18	19.3	20.5	21.8	23	24.3	25.6	26.8	28.1	29.3	♑ 0.6	1.8
♂	♎ 18.2	18.8	19.4	20	20.6	21.2	21.8	22.4	23	23.7	24.3	24.9	25.5	26.1	26.7	27.3	27.9	28.5	29.1	29.7	♏ 0.3	0.9	1.5	2.1	2.7	3.3	3.9	4.5	5.1	5.7	6.3

♃ (1, 6, 11, 16, 21, 26, 31): ♊ 23.1R 22.4 21.8 21.1 20.4 19.8 19.1
♄ (1, 6, 11, 16, 21, 26, 31): ♏ 4.6 5.1 5.6 6.1 6.6 7 7.4
♅ (1, 11, 21, 31): ♋ 22.6R 22.3 22 21.6
♆ (1, 11, 21, 31): ♎ 25.2 25.4 25.7 25.8
♇ (1, 11, 21, 31): ♌ 25.0R 25 24.9 24.7

I

	1	2	3	4	5	6	7	8	9	10	11	12	13	14	15	16	17	18	19	20	21	22	23	24	25	26	27	28	29	30	31
☉	♑ 10	11.1	12.1	13.1	14.1	15.1	16.2	17.2	18.2	19.2	20.2	21.3	22.3	23.3	24.3	25.3	26.3	27.4	28.4	29.4	♒ 0.4	1.4	2.5	3.5	4.5	5.5	6.5	7.5	8.6	9.6	10.6
☽	♏ 21.4	♐ 3.8	16.6	29.6	♑ 12.9	26.5	♒ 10.3	24.3	♓ 8.4	22.6	♈ 6.8	21	♉ 5.2	19.2	♊ 3.2	17	♋ 0.5	13.9	27.1	♌ 10	22.6	♍ 5	17.2	29.2	♎ 11.2	23	♏ 4.9	16.9	29.1	♐ 11.6	24.3
☿	♑ 2	3.6	5.1	6.7	8.3	9.9	11.5	13.1	14.7	16.3	17.9	19.5	21.2	22.8	24.5	26.1	27.8	29.5	♒ 1.2	2.8	4.5	6.3	8	9.7	11.4	13.2	14.9	16.7	18.4	20.1	21.9
♀	♑ 3.1	4.4	5.6	6.9	8.1	9.4	10.7	11.9	13.2	14.4	15.7	16.9	18.2	19.5	20.7	22	23.2	24.5	25.7	27	28.3	29.5	♒ 0.8	2	3.3	4.5	5.8	7.1	8.3	9.6	10.8
♂	♏ 6.9	7.5	8.1	8.7	9.3	9.9	10.5	11.1	11.7	12.3	12.9	13.5	14	14.6	15.2	15.8	16.4	17	17.6	18.1	18.7	19.3	19.9	20.5	21	21.6	22.2	22.8	23.3	23.9	24.5

♃ (1, 6, 11, 16, 21, 26, 31): ♊ 19.0R 18.4 17.9 17.5 17.1 16.8 16.6
♄ (1, 6, 11, 16, 21, 26, 31): ♏ 7.5 7.8 8.2 8.5 8.7 8.9 9.1
♅ (1, 11, 21, 31): ♋ 21.5R 21.1 20.7 20.2
♆ (1, 11, 21, 31): ♎ 25.9 26 26 26.1R
♇ (1, 11, 21, 31): ♌ 24.7R 24.5 24.3 24.1

II

	1	2	3	4	5	6	7	8	9	10	11	12	13	14	15	16	17	18	19	20	21	22	23	24	25	26	27	28	29	30	31
☉	♒ 11.6	12.6	13.6	14.6	15.7	16.7	17.7	18.7	19.7	20.7	21.7	22.7	23.8	24.8	25.8	26.8	27.8	28.8	29.8	♓ 0.8	1.8	2.8	3.8	4.8	5.9	6.9	7.9	8.9			
☽	♑ 7.5	21	♒ 4.9	19.1	♓ 3.6	18.2	♈ 2.9	17.5	♉ 1.9	16.1	♊ 0	13.7	27.1	♋ 10.3	23.3	♌ 6	18.6	♍ 1	13.3	25.4	♎ 7.4	19.3	♏ 1.1	13	25	♐ 7.1	19.5	♑ 2.2			
☿	♒ 23.6	25.4	27.1	28.8	♓ 0.4	2.1	3.6	5.2	6.7	8.1	9.4	10.7	11.9	12.9	13.8	14.6	15.2	15.7	16	16.1	16.1R	15.9	15.5	15	14.4	13.6	12.7	11.7			
♀	♒ 12.1	13.3	14.6	15.8	17.1	18.4	19.6	20.9	22.1	23.4	24.6	25.9	27.1	28.4	29.6	♓ 0.9	2.1	3.4	4.7	5.9	7.2	8.4	9.7	10.9	12.2	13.4	14.7	15.9			
♂	♏ 25	25.6	26.2	26.7	27.3	27.9	28.4	29	29.6	♐ 0.1	0.7	1.2	1.8	2.3	2.9	3.4	4	4.5	5.1	5.6	6.1	6.7	7.2	7.8	8.3	8.8	9.3	9.9			

♃ (1, 6, 11, 16, 21, 26): ♊ 16.6R 16.4 16.4D 16.5 16.6 16.8
♄ (1, 6, 11, 16, 21, 26): ♏ 9.1 9.2 9.3 9.3 9.3R 9.3
♅ (1, 11, 21): ♋ 20.2R 19.8 19.5
♆ (1, 11, 21): ♎ 26.1R 26 25.9
♇ (1, 11, 21): ♌ 24.1R 23.8 23.6

III

	1	2	3	4	5	6	7	8	9	10	11	12	13	14	15	16	17	18	19	20	21	22	23	24	25	26	27	28	29	30	31
☉	♓ 9.9	10.9	11.9	12.9	13.9	14.9	15.9	16.9	17.9	18.9	19.9	20.9	21.9	22.9	23.9	24.9	25.9	26.9	27.9	28.9	29.8	♈ 0.8	1.8	2.8	3.8	4.8	5.8	6.8	7.8	8.8	9.7
☽	♑ 15.2	28.8	♒ 12.8	27.2	♓ 12	27.1	♈ 12.2	27.2	♉ 11.9	26.4	♊ 10.4	24.1	♋ 7.4	20.3	♌ 3	15.5	27.8	♍ 9.9	22	♎ 4	15.9	27.8	♏ 9.7	21.6	♐ 3.5	15.6	28	♑ 10.6	23.5	♒ 7	20.9
☿	♓ 10.7R	9.7	8.6	7.6	6.6	5.7	4.8	4.1	3.4	2.8	2.4	2.1	1.8	1.7	1.7D	1.8	2	2.3	2.6	3.1	3.6	4.2	4.8	5.5	6.3	7.2	8.1	9	10	11	12.1
♀	♓ 17.2	18.4	19.7	20.9	22.2	23.4	24.6	25.9	27.1	28.4	29.6	♈ 0.9	2.1	3.4	4.6	5.9	7.1	8.3	9.6	10.8	12.1	13.3	14.5	15.8	17	18.3	19.5	20.7	22	23.2	24.5
♂	♐ 10.4	10.9	11.4	12	12.5	13	13.5	14	14.5	15	15.5	16	16.5	17	17.5	18	18.5	18.9	19.4	19.9	20.4	20.8	21.3	21.8	22.2	22.7	23.1	23.6	24	24.5	24.9

♃ (1, 6, 11, 16, 21, 26, 31): ♊ 17 17.3 17.7 18.2 18.8 19.4 20.1
♄ (1, 6, 11, 16, 21, 26, 31): ♏ 9.2R 9.1 8.9 8.7 8.5 8.2 7.9
♅ (1, 11, 21, 31): ♋ 19.3R 19.1 19 19.0D
♆ (1, 11, 21, 31): ♎ 25.8R 25.6 25.4 25.1
♇ (1, 11, 21, 31): ♌ 23.4R 23.2 23 22.8

IV

	1	2	3	4	5	6	7	8	9	10	11	12	13	14	15	16	17	18	19	20	21	22	23	24	25	26	27	28	29	30	31
☉	♈ 10.7	11.7	12.7	13.7	14.7	15.7	16.6	17.6	18.6	19.6	20.6	21.6	22.5	23.5	24.5	25.5	26.5	27.4	28.4	29.4	♉ 0.4	1.3	2.3	3.3	4.3	5.2	6.2	7.2	8.2	9.1	
☽	♓ 5.3	20.1	♈ 5.3	20.6	♉ 5.9	21	♊ 5.7	19.9	♋ 3.7	17	29.9	♌ 12.5	24.9	♍ 7	19.1	♎ 1	12.9	24.8	♏ 6.7	18.6	♐ 0.5	12.6	24.8	♑ 7.1	19.8	♒ 2.7	16	29.8	♓ 14	28.7	
☿	♓ 13.2	14.4	15.6	16.8	18.1	19.4	20.7	22	23.4	24.8	26.3	27.8	29.3	♈ 0.8	2.4	4	5.6	7.2	8.9	10.6	12.3	14.1	15.8	17.6	19.5	21.3	23.2	25.1	27.1	29.1	
♀	♈ 25.7	26.9	28.2	29.4	♉ 0.6	1.9	3.1	4.3	5.6	6.8	8	9.3	10.5	11.7	13	14.2	15.4	16.6	17.9	19.1	20.3	21.5	22.8	24	25.2	26.4	27.7	28.9	♊ 0.1	1.3	
♂	♐ 25.3	25.7	26.2	26.6	27	27.4	27.8	28.2	28.6	29	29.4	29.7	♑ 0.1	0.5	0.8	1.2	1.5	1.9	2.2	2.5	2.9	3.2	3.5	3.8	4.1	4.3	4.6	4.9	5.2	5.4	

♃ (1, 6, 11, 16, 21, 26): ♊ 20.2 20.9 21.7 22.5 23.4 24.3
♄ (1, 6, 11, 16, 21, 26): ♏ 7.9R 7.6 7.2 6.8 6.5 6.1
♅ (1, 11, 21): ♋ 19 19.1 19.3
♆ (1, 11, 21): ♎ 25.1R 24.8 24.5
♇ (1, 11, 21): ♌ 22.8R 22.7 22.6

V

	1	2	3	4	5	6	7	8	9	10	11	12	13	14	15	16	17	18	19	20	21	22	23	24	25	26	27	28	29	30	31
☉	♉ 10.1	11.1	12	13	14	14.9	15.9	16.9	17.8	18.8	19.8	20.7	21.7	22.7	23.6	24.6	25.6	26.5	27.5	28.5	29.4	♊ 0.4	1.3	2.3	3.3	4.2	5.2	6.1	7.1	8.1	9
☽	♈ 13.7	28.9	♉ 14.2	29.3	♊ 14.1	28.5	♋ 12.4	25.9	♌ 8.9	21.5	♍ 3.9	16	28	♎ 9.9	21.7	♏ 3.6	15.5	27.5	♐ 9.6	21.9	♑ 4.2	16.8	29.6	♒ 12.6	26	♓ 9.7	23.7	♈ 8.1	22.8	♉ 7.7	22.7
☿	♉ 1.1	3.1	5.1	7.2	9.3	11.4	13.6	15.7	17.9	20.1	22.3	24.4	26.6	28.8	♊ 0.9	3	5.1	7.2	9.3	11.3	13.3	15.2	17.1	18.9	20.7	22.5	24.2	25.8	27.4	29	♋ 0.5
♀	♊ 2.6	3.8	5	6.2	7.4	8.7	9.9	11.1	12.3	13.5	14.7	15.9	17.2	18.4	19.6	20.8	22	23.2	24.4	25.6	26.8	28	29.3	♋ 0.5	1.7	2.9	4.1	5.3	6.5	7.7	8.9
♂	♑ 5.6	5.9	6.1	6.3	6.5	6.7	6.9	7.1	7.3	7.4	7.6	7.7	7.8	8	8.1	8.2	8.2	8.3	8.4	8.4	8.5	8.5	8.5	8.5R	8.5	8.5	8.4	8.4	8.3	8.2	8.1

♃ (1, 6, 11, 16, 21, 26, 31): ♊ 25.3 26.2 27.2 28.3 29.3 ♋ 0.4 1.5
♄ (1, 6, 11, 16, 21, 26, 31): ♏ 5.7R 5.3 5 4.6 4.3 4 3.7
♅ (1, 11, 21, 31): ♋ 19.5 19.8 20.3 20.7
♆ (1, 11, 21, 31): ♎ 24.3R 24 23.8 23.6
♇ (1, 11, 21, 31): ♌ 22.5R 22.5D 22.6 22.7

VI

	1	2	3	4	5	6	7	8	9	10	11	12	13	14	15	16	17	18	19	20	21	22	23	24	25	26	27	28	29	30	31
☉	♊ 10	10.9	11.9	12.8	13.8	14.8	15.7	16.7	17.6	18.6	19.5	20.5	21.5	22.4	23.4	24.3	25.3	26.2	27.2	28.1	29.1	♋ 0	1	2	2.9	3.9	4.8	5.8	6.7	7.7	
☽	♊ 7.6	22.3	♋ 6.7	20.6	♌ 4.1	17.2	29.9	♍ 12.3	24.5	♎ 6.5	18.4	♏ 0.2	12.2	24.1	♐ 6.3	18.5	♑ 1	13.7	26.5	♒ 9.6	22.9	♓ 6.5	20.2	♈ 4.3	18.5	♉ 2.9	17.4	♊ 2	16.5	♋ 0.8	
☿	♋ 1.9	3.3	4.7	6	7.2	8.4	9.5	10.6	11.6	12.6	13.5	14.3	15	15.7	16.4	16.9	17.4	17.9	18.2	18.5	18.7	18.8	18.8	18.8R	18.7	18.5	18.3	18	17.6	17.1	
♀	♋ 10.1	11.3	12.5	13.7	14.9	16.1	17.3	18.5	19.7	20.8	22	23.2	24.4	25.6	26.8	28	29.2	♌ 0.3	1.5	2.7	3.9	5.1	6.3	7.4	8.6	9.8	11	12.1	13.3	14.5	
♂	♑ 8.0R	7.9	7.8	7.7	7.5	7.3	7.2	7	6.8	6.6	6.4	6.1	5.9	5.7	5.4	5.1	4.9	4.6	4.3	4	3.7	3.4	3.1	2.8	2.5	2.2	1.9	1.6	1.3	1	

♃ (1, 6, 11, 16, 21, 26): ♋ 1.7 2.8 3.9 5 6.2 7.3
♄ (1, 6, 11, 16, 21, 26): ♏ 3.6R 3.4 3.2 3 2.8 2.7
♅ (1, 11, 21): ♋ 20.8 21.3 21.8
♆ (1, 11, 21): ♎ 23.6R 23.4 23.3
♇ (1, 11, 21): ♌ 22.7 22.8 23

VII

	1	2	3	4	5	6	7	8	9	10	11	12	13	14	15	16	17	18	19	20	21	22	23	24	25	26	27	28	29	30	31
☉	♋ 8.6	9.6	10.5	11.5	12.4	13.4	14.4	15.3	16.3	17.2	18.2	19.1	20.1	21	22	22.9	23.9	24.8	25.8	26.8	27.7	28.7	29.6	♌ 0.6	1.5	2.5	3.4	4.4	5.3	6.3	7.3
☽	♋ 14.9	28.7	♌ 12.1	25.2	♍ 8	20.4	♎ 2.6	14.6	26.5	♏ 8.4	20.3	♐ 2.4	14.6	27	♑ 9.7	22.7	♒ 5.9	19.4	♓ 3.1	17	♈ 1.1	15.3	29.5	♉ 13.7	27.9	♊ 12.1	26.1	♋ 10	23.7	♌ 7.2	20.4
☿	♋ 16.6R	16.1	15.5	14.9	14.3	13.7	13.1	12.5	11.9	11.4	10.9	10.4	10.1	9.7	9.5	9.4	9.3	9.3D	9.4	9.6	9.9	10.3	10.8	11.4	12.1	12.9	13.7	14.7	15.7	16.9	18.1
♀	♌ 15.7	16.8	18	19.2	20.3	21.5	22.6	23.8	25	26.1	27.3	28.4	29.6	♍ 0.7	1.9	3	4.2	5.3	6.5	7.6	8.7	9.9	11	12.2	13.3	14.4	15.5	16.7	17.8	18.9	20
♂	♑ 0.6R	0.3	0	♐ 29.7	29.5	29.2	28.9	28.6	28.4	28.1	27.9	27.6	27.4	27.2	27	26.8	26.6	26.5	26.3	26.2	26.1	25.9	25.9	25.8	25.7	25.6	25.6	25.6	25.5	25.5D	25.6

♃ (1, 6, 11, 16, 21, 26, 31): ♋ 8.4 9.6 10.7 11.8 13 14.1 15.2
♄ (1, 6, 11, 16, 21, 26, 31): ♏ 2.7R 2.6 2.7D 2.7 2.8 2.9 3.1
♅ (1, 11, 21, 31): ♋ 22.4 23 23.6 24.2
♆ (1, 11, 21, 31): ♎ 23.3R 23.3D 23.3 23.5
♇ (1, 11, 21, 31): ♌ 23.3 23.5 23.8 24.1

VIII

	1	2	3	4	5	6	7	8	9	10	11	12	13	14	15	16	17	18	19	20	21	22	23	24	25	26	27	28	29	30	31
☉	♌ 8.2	9.2	10.1	11.1	12	13	14	14.9	15.9	16.8	17.8	18.8	19.7	20.7	21.6	22.6	23.6	24.5	25.5	26.4	27.4	28.4	29.3	♍ 0.3	1.3	2.2	3.2	4.2	5.1	6.1	7.1
☽	♍ 3.3	15.9	28.3	♎ 10.5	22.5	♏ 4.4	16.3	28.2	♐ 10.3	22.5	♑ 5.1	17.9	♒ 1.2	14.7	28.7	♓ 12.8	27.2	♈ 11.7	26.1	♉ 10.5	24.7	♊ 8.8	22.7	♋ 6.3	19.8	♌ 3.1	16.2	29.1	♍ 11.8	24.2	♎ 6.5
☿	♋ 19.4	20.8	22.3	23.8	25.5	27.2	28.9	♌ 0.7	2.6	4.5	6.4	8.4	10.4	12.4	14.4	16.4	18.5	20.5	22.5	24.5	26.6	28.6	♍ 0.5	2.5	4.4	6.4	8.3	10.1	12	13.8	15.7
♀	♍ 21.1	22.3	23.4	24.5	25.6	26.7	27.8	28.9	30	♎ 1.1	2.2	3.2	4.3	5.4	6.5	7.5	8.6	9.7	10.7	11.8	12.9	13.9	14.9	16	17	18.1	19.1	20.1	21.1	22.1	23.1
♂	♐ 25.6	25.6	25.7	25.8	25.8	25.9	26	26.2	26.3	26.4	26.6	26.8	27	27.2	27.4	27.6	27.8	28.1	28.3	28.6	28.9	29.2	29.5	29.8	♑ 0.1	0.4	0.8	1.1	1.5	1.9	2.2

♃ (1, 6, 11, 16, 21, 26, 31): ♋ 15.4 16.4 17.5 18.5 19.6 20.5 21.5
♄ (1, 6, 11, 16, 21, 26, 31): ♏ 3.2 3.4 3.6 3.9 4.3 4.6 5
♅ (1, 11, 21, 31): ♋ 24.3 24.9 25.4 26
♆ (1, 11, 21, 31): ♎ 23.5 23.6 23.9 24.1
♇ (1, 11, 21, 31): ♌ 24.1 24.4 24.8 25.1

IX

	1	2	3	4	5	6	7	8	9	10	11	12	13	14	15	16	17	18	19	20	21	22	23	24	25	26	27	28	29	30	31
☉	♍ 8	9	10	10.9	11.9	12.9	13.8	14.8	15.8	16.8	17.7	18.7	19.7	20.6	21.6	22.6	23.6	24.5	25.5	26.5	27.5	28.5	29.4	♎ 0.4	1.4	2.4	3.4	4.3	5.3	6.3	
☽	♎ 18.6	♏ 0.6	12.5	24.3	♐ 6.2	18.2	♑ 0.4	13	25.9	♒ 9.2	23	♓ 7.2	21.8	♈ 6.6	21.5	♉ 6.3	21	♊ 5.4	19.5	♋ 3.3	16.8	30	♌ 12.9	25.7	♍ 8.3	20.7	♎ 3	15.1	27.1	♏ 9	
☿	♍ 17.5	19.2	21	22.7	24.4	26.1	27.8	29.5	♎ 1.1	2.7	4.3	5.9	7.4	9	10.5	12	13.5	15	16.4	17.8	19.3	20.6	22	23.4	24.7	26	27.3	28.6	29.8	♏ 1	
♀	♎ 24.1	25.1	26.1	27.1	28.1	29.1	♏ 0	1	1.9	2.9	3.8	4.7	5.6	6.6	7.5	8.3	9.2	10.1	11	11.8	12.6	13.5	14.3	15.1	15.9	16.7	17.4	18.2	18.9	19.6	
♂	♑ 2.6	3	3.4	3.8	4.2	4.7	5.1	5.5	6	6.4	6.9	7.4	7.9	8.3	8.8	9.3	9.8	10.3	10.8	11.4	11.9	12.4	12.9	13.5	14	14.6	15.1	15.7	16.3	16.8	

♃ (1, 6, 11, 16, 21, 26): ♋ 21.7 22.6 23.5 24.3 25.1 25.9
♄ (1, 6, 11, 16, 21, 26): ♏ 5.1 5.5 6 6.5 7 7.5
♅ (1, 11, 21): ♋ 26 26.5 26.9
♆ (1, 11, 21): ♎ 24.1 24.4 24.8
♇ (1, 11, 21): ♌ 25.1 25.4 25.7

X

	1	2	3	4	5	6	7	8	9	10	11	12	13	14	15	16	17	18	19	20	21	22	23	24	25	26	27	28	29	30	31
☉	♎ 7.3	8.3	9.2	10.2	11.2	12.2	13.2	14.2	15.2	16.2	17.1	18.1	19.1	20.1	21.1	22.1	23.1	24.1	25.1	26.1	27.1	28.1	29.1	♏ 0	1	2	3	4	5	6	7
☽	♏ 20.8	♐ 2.6	14.5	26.4	♑ 8.6	21.1	♒ 3.9	17.2	♓ 1	15.3	♈ 0	15.1	♉ 0.3	15.5	♊ 0.5	15.2	29.5	♋ 13.4	26.9	♌ 10	22.8	♍ 5.3	17.7	29.9	♎ 12	24	♏ 5.9	17.7	29.5	♐ 11.3	23.2
☿	♏ 2.2	3.3	4.5	5.5	6.6	7.6	8.6	9.5	10.3	11.1	11.9	12.6	13.2	13.7	14.1	14.4	14.6	14.8	14.7R	14.6	14.3	13.8	13.3	12.5	11.6	10.6	9.5	8.3	7	5.8	4.5
♀	♏ 20.3	21	21.7	22.3	22.9	23.6	24.1	24.7	25.2	25.8	26.3	26.7	27.2	27.6	28	28.3	28.7	29	29.2	29.4	29.6	29.8	29.9	30	♐ 0	0.1R	0	♏ 29.9	29.8	29.7	29.5
♂	♑ 17.4	18	18.6	19.2	19.7	20.3	20.9	21.5	22.1	22.7	23.4	24	24.6	25.2	25.8	26.5	27.1	27.7	28.4	29	29.7	♒ 0.3	0.9	1.6	2.2	2.9	3.6	4.2	4.9	5.5	6.2

♃ (1, 6, 11, 16, 21, 26, 31): ♋ 26.6 27.2 27.8 28.3 28.8 29.2 29.5
♄ (1, 6, 11, 16, 21, 26, 31): ♏ 8 8.6 9.1 9.7 10.3 10.9 11.5
♅ (1, 11, 21, 31): ♋ 27.2 27.5 27.6 27.7
♆ (1, 11, 21, 31): ♎ 25.1 25.5 25.8 26.2
♇ (1, 11, 21, 31): ♌ 26 26.2 26.4 26.6

XI

	1	2	3	4	5	6	7	8	9	10	11	12	13	14	15	16	17	18	19	20	21	22	23	24	25	26	27	28	29	30	31
☉	♏ 8	9	10	11	12	13	14	15	16.1	17.1	18.1	19.1	20.1	21.1	22.1	23.1	24.1	25.1	26.1	27.1	28.1	29.2	♐ 0.2	1.2	2.2	3.2	4.2	5.2	6.2	7.2	
☽	♑ 5.2	17.4	29.8	♒ 12.6	25.7	♓ 9.4	23.5	♈ 8.1	23.1	♉ 8.4	23.7	♊ 8.9	23.9	♋ 8.4	22.5	♌ 6.2	19.4	♍ 2.2	14.7	26.9	♎ 9	21	♏ 2.9	14.7	26.5	♐ 8.4	20.3	♑ 2.3	14.4	26.7	
☿	♏ 3.3R	2.2	1.2	0.4	♎ 29.7	29.2	29	28.9D	29	29.3	29.8	♏ 0.4	1.1	1.9	2.9	4	5.1	6.3	7.5	8.8	10.2	11.6	13	14.4	15.9	17.4	18.9	20.4	21.9	23.4	
♀	♏ 29.2R	29	28.7	28.3	27.9	27.5	27	26.6	26	25.5	24.9	24.4	23.8	23.2	22.6	22	21.4	20.8	20.2	19.6	19	18.5	18	17.5	17.1	16.7	16.3	15.9	15.6	15.4	
♂	♒ 6.9	7.5	8.2	8.9	9.6	10.2	10.9	11.6	12.3	13	13.7	14.3	15	15.7	16.4	17.1	17.8	18.5	19.2	19.9	20.6	21.3	22	22.7	23.4	24.1	24.8	25.5	26.2	26.9	

♃ (1, 6, 11, 16, 21, 26): ♋ 29.5 29.7 29.9 29.9 29.9R 29.8
♄ (1, 6, 11, 16, 21, 26): ♏ 11.6 12.2 12.8 13.4 14 14.6
♅ (1, 11, 21): ♋ 27.7 27.7R 27.6
♆ (1, 11, 21): ♎ 26.3 26.6 27
♇ (1, 11, 21): ♌ 26.6 26.7 26.8

XII

	1	2	3	4	5	6	7	8	9	10	11	12	13	14	15	16	17	18	19	20	21	22	23	24	25	26	27	28	29	30	31
☉	♐ 8.3	9.3	10.3	11.3	12.3	13.3	14.3	15.4	16.4	17.4	18.4	19.4	20.4	21.5	22.5	23.5	24.5	25.5	26.5	27.6	28.6	29.6	♑ 0.6	1.6	2.7	3.7	4.7	5.7	6.7	7.8	8.8
☽	♒ 9.2	22	♓ 5.2	18.7	♈ 2.6	16.9	♉ 1.6	16.6	♊ 1.7	16.8	♋ 1.8	16.4	♌ 0.7	14.5	27.9	♍ 10.8	23.4	♎ 5.7	17.7	29.6	♏ 11.5	23.3	♐ 5.2	17.1	29.2	♑ 11.4	23.7	♒ 6.3	19.1	♓ 2.1	15.4
☿	♏ 24.9	26.5	28	29.6	♐ 1.1	2.6	4.2	5.7	7.3	8.9	10.4	12	13.5	15.1	16.6	18.2	19.8	21.3	22.9	24.5	26.1	27.6	29.2	♑ 0.8	2.4	4	5.6	7.2	8.8	10.4	12
♀	♏ 15.2R	15	14.8	14.7	14.7	14.7D	14.7	14.7	14.8	15	15.2	15.4	15.6	15.9	16.2	16.6	17	17.4	17.8	18.3	18.8	19.3	19.9	20.5	21.1	21.7	22.3	23	23.7	24.4	25.1
♂	♒ 27.6	28.3	29	29.8	♓ 0.5	1.2	1.9	2.6	3.3	4	4.7	5.5	6.2	6.9	7.6	8.3	9	9.7	10.5	11.2	11.9	12.6	13.3	14	14.8	15.5	16.2	16.9	17.6	18.4	19.1

♃ (1, 6, 11, 16, 21, 26, 31): ♋ 29.6R 29.3 29 28.6 28.1 27.6 27
♄ (1, 6, 11, 16, 21, 26, 31): ♏ 15.2 15.7 16.3 16.8 17.3 17.8 18.3
♅ (1, 11, 21, 31): ♋ 27.4R 27.1 26.8 26.4
♆ (1, 11, 21, 31): ♎ 27.3 27.6 27.8 28
♇ (1, 11, 21, 31): ♌ 26.8R 26.8 26.7 26.5

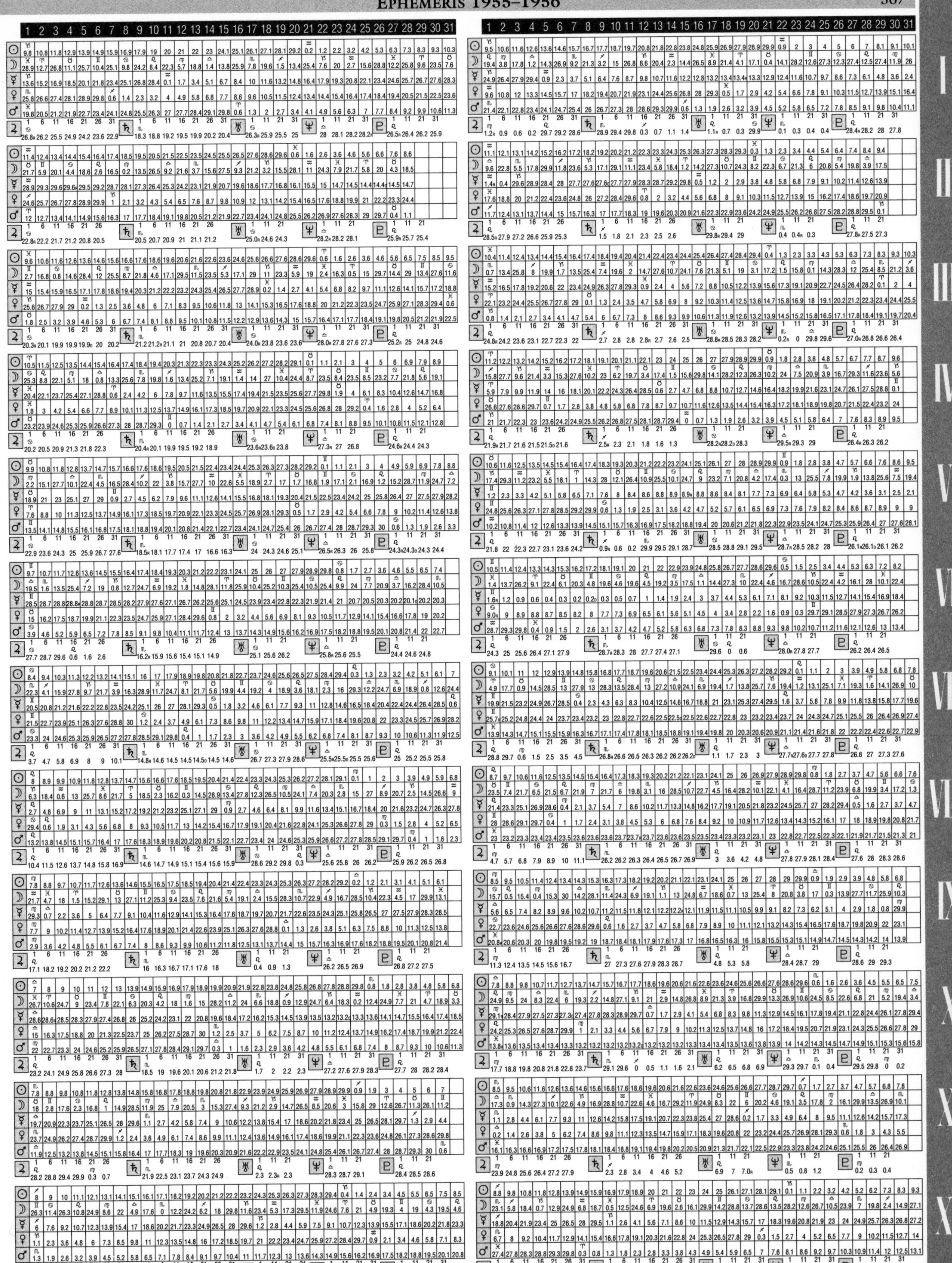

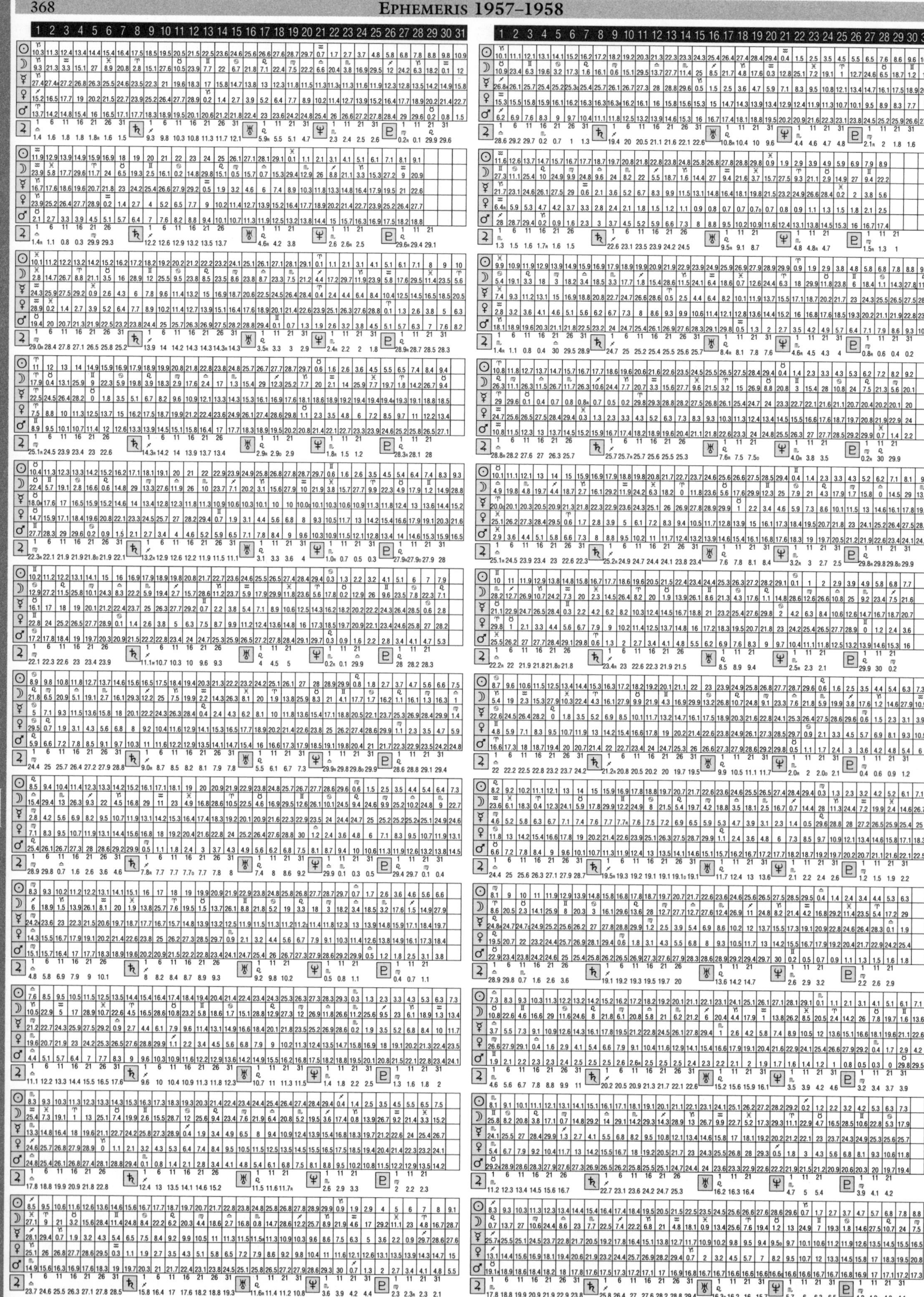

I

	1	2	3	4	5	6	7	8	9	10	11	12	13	14	15	16	17	18	19	20	21	22	23	24	25	26	27	28	29	30	31
☉	9.8	10.8	11.9	12.9	13.9	14.9	15.9	17	18	19	20	21	22.1	23.1	24.1	25.1	26.1	27.1	28.2	29.2	0.2	1.2	2.2	3.3	4.3	5.3	6.3	7.3	8.3	9.4	10.4
☽	21.2	5	19	3.1	17.4	1.8	16.3	0.7	14.9	28.9	12.6	25.8	8.7	21.2	3.4	15.4	27.3	9.1	20.9	2.9	15.1	27.5	10.2	23.2	6.6	20.1	3.9	17.8	1.8	15.9	29.9
☿	17.6	18.8	20	21.2	22.4	23.7	25	26.3	27.7	29	0.4	1.8	3.2	4.7	6.1	7.5	9	10.5	12	13.5	15	16.5	18	19.5	21.1	22.6	24.2	25.8	27.4	29	0.6
♀	22.1	23.3	24.6	25.8	27.1	28.3	29.6	0.8	2.1	3.3	4.6	5.9	7.1	8.4	9.6	10.9	12.1	13.4	14.6	15.9	17.1	18.4	19.6	20.9	22.1	23.4	24.6	25.9	27.1	28.4	29.6
♂	17.5	17.6	17.8	17.9	18.1	18.3	18.5	18.7	18.9	19.1	19.4	19.6	19.9	20.1	20.4	20.7	21	21.3	21.6	21.9	22.2	22.5	22.8	23.2	23.5	23.9	24.2	24.6	25	25.3	25.7

♃ 1 6 11 16 21 26 31: 24 24.9 25.7 26.6 27.3 28.1 28.8
♄ 1 6 11 16 21 26 31: 29.5 0.1 0.6 1.2 1.7 2.3 2.8
♅ 1 11 21 31: 15.7R 15.3 14.9 14.5
♆ 1 11 21 31: 6.6 6.7 6.9 6.9
♇ 1 11 21 31: 4.1R 3.9 3.7 3.5

II

	1	2	3	4	5	6	7	8	9	10	11	12	13	14	15	16	17	18	19	20	21	22	23	24	25	26	27	28	29	30	31
☉	11.4	12.4	13.4	14.4	15.4	16.5	17.5	18.5	19.5	20.5	21.5	22.5	23.5	24.6	25.6	26.6	27.6	28.6	29.6	0.6	1.6	2.6	3.6	4.6	5.6	6.6	7.7	8.7			
☽	14	28.1	12.2	26.2	10.1	23.9	7.5	20.8	3.9	16.6	29	11.2	23.2	5	16.8	28.7	10.7	22.8	5.3	18.1	1.3	14.9	28.8	12.9	27.3	11.8	26.2	10.6			
☿	2.2	3.8	5.5	7.1	8.8	10.5	12.2	13.9	15.6	17.3	19.1	20.8	22.6	24.4	26.2	28	29.8	1.7	3.5	5.4	7.3	9.1	11	12.9	14.8	16.6	18.5	20.4			
♀	0.9	2.1	3.4	4.6	5.9	7.1	8.4	9.6	10.8	12.1	13.3	14.6	15.8	17.1	18.3	19.5	20.8	22	23.3	24.5	25.7	27	28.2	29.5	0.7	1.9	3.2	4.4			
♂	26.1	26.5	26.9	27.3	27.7	28.1	28.5	28.9	29.3	29.8	0.2	0.6	1.1	1.5	2	2.4	2.9	3.3	3.8	4.2	4.7	5.2	5.6	6.1	6.6	7.1	7.6	8.1			

♃ 1 6 11 16 21 26: 28.9 29.5 0 0.5 1 1.3
♄ 1 6 11 16 21 26: 2.9 3.4 3.9 4.3 4.7 5.1
♅ 1 11 21: 14.4R 14 13.6
♆ 1 11 21: 6.9 7.0R 6.9
♇ 1 11 21: 3.5R 3.3 3

III

	1	2	3	4	5	6	7	8	9	10	11	12	13	14	15	16	17	18	19	20	21	22	23	24	25	26	27	28	29	30	31
☉	9.7	10.7	11.7	12.7	13.7	14.7	15.7	16.7	17.7	18.7	19.7	20.7	21.7	22.7	23.7	24.7	25.7	26.7	27.6	28.6	29.6	0.6	1.6	2.6	3.6	4.6	5.6	6.6	7.6	8.6	9.5
☽	24.9	9.1	23	6.8	20.4	3.7	16.9	29.8	12.5	24.9	7.2	19.3	1.2	13	24.8	6.7	18.6	0.8	13.2	26	9.2	22.8	6.8	21.2	5.9	20.7	5.6	20.5	5.1	19.5	3.6
☿	22.2	24	25.8	27.5	29.2	0.8	2.4	3.9	5.3	6.6	7.8	8.9	9.9	10.7	11.5	12	12.5	12.8	13	13.0R	12.9	12.7	12.3	11.9	11.3	10.7	9.9	9.2	8.3	7.5	6.6
♀	5.6	6.9	8.1	9.3	10.5	11.8	13	14.2	15.5	16.7	17.9	19.1	20.4	21.6	22.8	24	25.2	26.5	27.7	28.9	0.1	1.3	2.5	3.8	5	6.2	7.4	8.6	9.8	11	12.2
♂	8.5	9	9.5	10	10.5	11	11.5	12	12.6	13.1	13.6	14.1	14.6	15.1	15.7	16.2	16.7	17.2	17.8	18.3	18.8	19.4	19.9	20.4	21	21.5	22.1	22.6	23.1	23.7	24.2

♃ 1 6 11 16 21 26 31: 1.5 1.7 1.9 2 2.0R 1.9 1.8
♄ 1 6 11 16 21 26 31: 5.3 5.7 6 6.3 6.5 6.7 6.8
♅ 1 11 21 31: 13.3R 12.9 12.6 12.4
♆ 1 11 21 31: 6.8R 6.7 6.5 6.3
♇ 1 11 21 31: 2.8R 2.5 2.3 2.1

IV

	1	2	3	4	5	6	7	8	9	10	11	12	13	14	15	16	17	18	19	20	21	22	23	24	25	26	27	28	29	30	31
☉	10.5	11.5	12.5	13.5	14.5	15.5	16.4	17.4	18.4	19.4	20.4	21.4	22.3	23.3	24.3	25.3	26.2	27.2	28.2	29.2	0.2	1.1	2.1	3.1	4.1	5	6	7	7.9	8.9	
☽	17.3	0.7	13.8	26.6	9.2	21.6	3.8	15.8	27.8	9.6	21.4	3.2	15.1	27.1	9.2	21.6	4.3	17.4	0.9	14.8	29.2	14	29	14.2	29.4	14.4	29.1	13.3	27.2	10.6	
☿	5.8R	5	4.2	3.5	2.9	2.3	1.8	1.4	1.1	0.8	0.7	0.6	0.7D	0.8	1	1.3	1.7	2.1	2.6	3.2	3.8	4.6	5.3	6.2	7	8	9	10	11.1	12.2	
♀	13.4	14.6	15.8	17	18.2	19.4	20.6	21.8	23	24.2	25.4	26.6	27.8	29	0.1	1.3	2.5	3.7	4.9	6.1	7.2	8.4	9.6	10.8	11.9	13.1	14.3	15.4	16.6	17.8	
♂	24.8	25.3	25.9	26.4	27	27.5	28.1	28.7	29.2	29.8	0.3	0.9	1.5	2	2.6	3.2	3.7	4.3	4.9	5.4	6	6.6	7.1	7.7	8.3	8.9	9.4	10	10.6	11.2	

♃ 1 6 11 16 21 26: 1.7R 1.5 1.2 0.8 0.3 29.8
♄ 1 6 11 16 21 26: 6.9 7 7 7.1 7.0R 7
♅ 1 11 21: 12.4R 12.3 12.2D
♆ 1 11 21: 6.3R 6 5.7
♇ 1 11 21: 2.1R 1.9 1.8

V

	1	2	3	4	5	6	7	8	9	10	11	12	13	14	15	16	17	18	19	20	21	22	23	24	25	26	27	28	29	30	31
☉	9.9	10.9	11.8	12.8	13.8	14.7	15.7	16.7	17.6	18.6	19.6	20.5	21.5	22.5	23.4	24.4	25.4	26.3	27.3	28.3	29.2	0.2	1.1	2.1	3.1	4	5	5.9	6.9	7.9	8.8
☽	23.6	6.3	18.7	0.8	12.8	24.7	6.6	18.4	0.2	12.1	24	6.1	18.3	0.7	13.4	26.3	9.7	23.5	7.7	22.3	7.3	22.5	7.7	22.9	7.8	22.2	6.3	19.8	2.8	15.5	27.8
☿	13.3	14.6	15.8	17.1	18.4	19.8	21.2	22.6	24.1	25.6	27.1	28.7	0.3	1.9	3.6	5.3	7.1	8.8	10.7	12.5	14.4	16.3	18.2	20.2	22.2	24.3	26.4	28.5	0.6	2.7	4.9
♀	18.9	20.1	21.2	22.4	23.5	24.7	25.8	27	28.1	29.3	0.4	1.5	2.7	3.8	4.9	6.1	7.2	8.3	9.4	10.5	11.6	12.8	13.9	15	16.1	17.2	18.3	19.4	20.4	21.5	22.6
♂	11.7	12.3	12.9	13.5	14	14.6	15.2	15.8	16.4	17	17.5	18.1	18.7	19.3	19.9	20.5	21.1	21.6	22.2	22.8	23.4	24	24.6	25.2	25.8	26.4	27	27.6	28.2	28.8	29.3

♃ 1 6 11 16 21 26 31: 29.3R 28.7 28.1 27.5 26.8 26.2 25.6
♄ 1 6 11 16 21 26 31: 6.9R 6.8 6.6 6.4 6.1 5.9 5.6
♅ 1 11 21 31: 12.3 12.4 12.6 13
♆ 1 11 21 31: 5.5R 5.2 4.9 4.7
♇ 1 11 21 31: 1.7R 1.7 1.7D 1.7

VI

	1	2	3	4	5	6	7	8	9	10	11	12	13	14	15	16	17	18	19	20	21	22	23	24	25	26	27	28	29	30	31
☉	9.8	10.7	11.7	12.7	13.6	14.6	15.5	16.5	17.4	18.4	19.3	20.3	21.3	22.2	23.2	24.1	25.1	26	27	27.9	28.9	29.9	0.8	1.8	2.7	3.7	4.6	5.6	6.5	7.5	
☽	9.9	21.8	3.6	15.4	27.2	9.1	21.1	3.2	15.4	27.8	10.3	23.1	6.1	19.4	3	17	1.4	16.1	1.1	16.2	1.2	16.1	0.6	14.7	28.2	11.4	24.1	6.4	18.5	0.4	
☿	7.1	9.3	11.5	13.7	15.9	18.1	20.2	22.4	24.6	26.7	28.8	0.9	2.9	4.9	6.9	8.8	10.7	12.6	14.4	16.2	17.9	19.6	21.3	22.9	24.5	26	27.6	29	0.4	1.8	
♀	23.7	24.8	25.8	26.9	28	29	0.1	1.1	2.2	3.2	4.2	5.3	6.3	7.3	8.3	9.3	10.3	11.3	12.3	13.3	14.3	15.2	16.2	17.1	18.1	19	20	20.9	21.8	22.7	
♂	29.9	0.5	1.1	1.7	2.3	2.9	3.5	4.1	4.7	5.3	5.9	6.5	7.1	7.7	8.3	8.9	9.5	10.1	10.8	11.4	12	12.6	13.2	13.8	14.4	15	15.6	16.2	16.8	17.4	

♃ 1 6 11 16 21 26: 25.5R 24.9 24.3 23.8 23.4 23
♄ 1 6 11 16 21 26: 5.5R 5.2 4.9 4.5 4.1 3.8
♅ 1 11 21: 13 13.4 13.8
♆ 1 11 21: 4.7R 4.5 4.4
♇ 1 11 21: 1.7 1.9 2

VII

	1	2	3	4	5	6	7	8	9	10	11	12	13	14	15	16	17	18	19	20	21	22	23	24	25	26	27	28	29	30	31
☉	8.4	9.4	10.3	11.3	12.2	13.2	14.2	15.1	16.1	17	18	18.9	19.9	20.8	21.8	22.7	23.7	24.6	25.6	26.6	27.5	28.5	29.4	0.4	1.3	2.3	3.2	4.2	5.1	6.1	7.1
☽	12.2	24	5.9	17.9	30	12.2	24.7	7.3	20.1	3.1	16.3	29.7	13.4	27.3	11.5	25.9	10.6	25.3	10	24.5	8.8	22.8	6.3	19.4	2.1	14.5	26.6	8.6	20.4	2.3	14.2
☿	3.2	4.5	5.7	6.9	8.1	9.2	10.3	11.3	12.3	13.2	14.1	14.9	15.6	16.3	16.9	17.5	18	18.4	18.8	19	19.2	19.3	19.4R	19.3	19.2	19	18.7	18.3	17.8	17.3	16.7
♀	23.6	24.5	25.4	26.2	27.1	27.9	28.8	29.6	0.4	1.2	2	2.8	3.5	4.2	5	5.7	6.4	7.1	7.7	8.4	9	9.6	10.2	10.7	11.3	11.8	12.3	12.7	13.2	13.6	14
♂	18	18.7	19.3	19.9	20.5	21.1	21.7	22.3	22.9	23.6	24.2	24.8	25.4	26	26.6	27.2	27.9	28.5	29.1	29.7	0.3	1	1.6	2.2	2.8	3.4	4.1	4.7	5.3	5.9	6.6

♃ 1 6 11 16 21 26 31: 22.7R 22.4 22.3 22.2 22.1D 22.2 22.3
♄ 1 6 11 16 21 26 31: 3.4R 3 2.7 2.3 2 1.7 1.4
♅ 1 11 21 31: 14.3 14.9 15.5 16.1
♆ 1 11 21 31: 4.2R 4.2 4.2D 4.2
♇ 1 11 21 31: 2.2 2.5 2.7 3

VIII

	1	2	3	4	5	6	7	8	9	10	11	12	13	14	15	16	17	18	19	20	21	22	23	24	25	26	27	28	29	30	31
☉	8	9	9.9	10.9	11.8	12.8	13.8	14.7	15.7	16.6	17.6	18.6	19.5	20.5	21.4	22.4	23.4	24.3	25.3	26.2	27.2	28.2	29.1	0.1	1.1	2	3	4	4.9	5.9	6.9
☽	26.2	8.5	20.9	3.6	16.6	29.7	13.1	26.6	10.3	24.2	8.2	22.3	6.5	20.9	5.2	19.4	3.6	17.5	1.1	14.4	27.4	10.1	22.4	4.5	16.5	28.4	10.2	22.2	4.3	16.6	29.2
☿	16.1R	15.4	14.6	13.9	13.1	12.3	11.6	10.9	10.2	9.6	9	8.5	8.2	7.9	7.7	7.7D	7.7	7.9	8.3	8.7	9.3	10	10.8	11.7	12.7	13.9	15.1	16.5	17.9	19.4	21
♀	14.3	14.7	15	15.2	15.5	15.7	15.8	15.9	16	16.1	16.1R	16.1	16	15.9	15.8	15.6	15.4	15.1	14.8	14.5	14.1	13.7	13.3	12.8	12.3	11.8	11.2	10.7	10.1	9.5	8.8
♂	7.2	7.8	8.4	9.1	9.7	10.3	10.9	11.6	12.2	12.8	13.5	14.1	14.7	15.4	16	16.6	17.3	17.9	18.5	19.2	19.8	20.4	21.1	21.7	22.3	23	23.6	24.3	24.9	25.5	26.2

♃ 1 6 11 16 21 26 31: 22.3 22.5 22.8 23.2 23.6 24.1 24.6
♄ 1 6 11 16 21 26 31: 1.4R 1.2 0.9 0.8 0.6 0.5 0.5
♅ 1 11 21 31: 16.1 16.8 17.4 18
♆ 1 11 21 31: 4.2 4.4 4.5 4.7
♇ 1 11 21 31: 3.1 3.4 3.7 4

IX

	1	2	3	4	5	6	7	8	9	10	11	12	13	14	15	16	17	18	19	20	21	22	23	24	25	26	27	28	29	30	31
☉	7.8	8.8	9.8	10.7	11.7	12.7	13.6	14.6	15.6	16.6	17.5	18.5	19.5	20.4	21.4	22.4	23.4	24.3	25.3	26.3	27.3	28.2	29.2	0.2	1.2	2.2	3.1	4.1	5.1	6.1	
☽	12.1	25.2	8.7	22.5	6.5	20.6	4.8	19.1	3.4	17.6	1.7	15.7	29.6	13.3	26.7	10	22.9	5.7	18.1	0.4	12.5	24.4	6.3	18.2	0.1	12.2	24.5	7.1	20	3.3	
☿	22.7	24.4	26.2	28	29.8	1.7	3.6	5.5	7.4	9.3	11.2	13.2	15.1	17	18.9	20.7	22.6	24.5	26.3	28.1	29.9	1.7	3.5	5.2	7	8.7	10.4	12.1	13.8	15.4	
♀	8.2R	7.6	7	6.4	5.8	5.2	4.6	4.1	3.5	3.1	2.6	2.1	1.7	1.4	1.1	0.8	0.5	0.3	0.1	0	29.9	29.9	29.9D	29.9	30	0.1	0.2	0.4	0.6	0.9	
♂	26.8	27.5	28.1	28.7	29.4	0	0.7	1.3	2	2.6	3.3	3.9	4.6	5.2	5.9	6.5	7.2	7.8	8.5	9.1	9.8	10.4	11.1	11.8	12.4	13.1	13.7	14.4	15	15.7	

♃ 1 6 11 16 21 26: 24.7 25.4 26 26.7 27.5 28.3
♄ 1 6 11 16 21 26: 0.5R 0.4D 0.5 0.5 0.7 0.8
♅ 1 11 21: 18 18.6 19.2
♆ 1 11 21: 4.7 5 5.3
♇ 1 11 21: 4.1 4.4 4.7

X

	1	2	3	4	5	6	7	8	9	10	11	12	13	14	15	16	17	18	19	20	21	22	23	24	25	26	27	28	29	30	31
☉	7.1	8.1	9	10	11	12	13	14	15	15.9	16.9	17.9	18.9	19.9	20.9	21.9	22.9	23.9	24.9	25.9	26.8	27.8	28.8	29.8	0.8	1.8	2.8	3.8	4.8	5.8	6.8
☽	17	1.1	15.5	0.1	14.8	29.4	14	28.4	12.6	26.4	10	23.4	6.4	19.3	1.9	14.4	26.6	8.7	20.7	2.6	14.5	26.3	8.3	20.3	2.5	15.1	27.9	11.2	24.9	9.1	23.7
☿	17.1	18.7	20.3	21.9	23.5	25.1	26.7	28.2	29.8	1.3	2.8	4.3	5.8	7.3	8.7	10.2	11.6	13	14.4	15.8	17.2	18.6	19.9	21.3	22.6	23.9	25.1	26.4	27.6	28.8	29.9
♀	1.2	1.5	1.8	2.2	2.6	3	3.5	4	4.5	5	5.6	6.2	6.8	7.4	8.1	8.8	9.4	10.2	10.9	11.6	12.4	13.2	14	14.8	15.6	16.4	17.3	18.1	19	19.9	20.8
♂	16.4	17	17.7	18.4	19	19.7	20.3	21	21.7	22.3	23	23.7	24.4	25	25.7	26.4	27	27.7	28.4	29.1	29.7	0.4	1.1	1.8	2.4	3.1	3.8	4.5	5.2	5.8	6.5

♃ 1 6 11 16 21 26 31: 29.2 0.1 1 2 3 4 5
♄ 1 6 11 16 21 26 31: 1 1.2 1.5 1.8 2.1 2.5 2.9
♅ 1 11 21 31: 19.6 20.1 20.4 20.7
♆ 1 11 21 31: 5.6 6 6.3 6.7
♇ 1 11 21 31: 5 5.3 5.6 5.8

XI

	1	2	3	4	5	6	7	8	9	10	11	12	13	14	15	16	17	18	19	20	21	22	23	24	25	26	27	28	29	30	31
☉	7.8	8.8	9.8	10.8	11.8	12.8	13.8	14.8	15.8	16.8	17.8	18.9	19.9	20.9	21.9	22.9	23.9	24.9	25.9	26.9	27.9	28.9	29.9	1	2	3	4	5	6	7	
☽	8.6	23.7	8.8	23.8	8.5	22.8	6.8	20.3	3.5	16.3	28.9	11.2	23.4	5.5	17.5	29.4	11.2	23.1	5	16.9	29	11.2	23.6	6.3	19.5	3	17.1	1.6	16.6	1.8	
☿	1.1	2.2	3.2	4.2	5.1	6	6.8	7.6	8.2	8.8	9.3	9.6	9.8	9.9	9.8R	9.6	9.2	8.6	7.9	6.9	5.9	4.7	3.4	2	0.7	29.3	28.1	26.9	25.9	25.1	
♀	21.7	22.6	23.5	24.4	25.4	26.3	27.3	28.3	29.3	0.2	1.2	2.2	3.3	4.3	5.3	6.3	7.4	8.4	9.5	10.5	11.6	12.7	13.7	14.8	15.9	17	18.1	19.2	20.3	21.4	
♂	7.2	7.9	8.6	9.3	10	10.6	11.3	12	12.7	13.4	14.1	14.8	15.5	16.2	16.9	17.5	18.2	18.9	19.6	20.3	21	21.7	22.4	23.1	23.8	24.5	25.2	25.9	26.6	27.4	

♃ 1 6 11 16 21 26: 5.2 6.3 7.4 8.5 9.6 10.7
♄ 1 6 11 16 21 26: 3 3.4 3.9 4.3 4.8 5.4
♅ 1 11 21: 20.8 21 21.1
♆ 1 11 21: 6.7 7.1 7.5
♇ 1 11 21: 5.8 6 6.1

XII

	1	2	3	4	5	6	7	8	9	10	11	12	13	14	15	16	17	18	19	20	21	22	23	24	25	26	27	28	29	30	31
☉	8	9.1	10.1	11.1	12.1	13.1	14.1	15.1	16.2	17.2	18.2	19.2	20.2	21.2	22.3	23.3	24.3	25.3	26.3	27.4	28.4	29.4	0.4	1.4	2.4	3.5	4.5	5.5	6.5	7.5	8.6
☽	17.1	2.4	17.4	2.1	16.2	29.8	13	25.8	8.3	20.5	2.5	14.5	26.3	8.2	20.1	2	13.9	26	8.1	20.4	2.9	15.6	28.6	12	25.9	10.1	24.9	9.9	25.1	10.4	25.5
☿	24.5R	24	23.8	23.7D	23.8	24.1	24.5	25	25.7	26.5	27.3	28.3	29.3	0.4	1.5	2.7	3.9	5.2	6.5	7.8	9.2	10.5	11.9	13.3	14.7	16.2	17.6	19.1	20.5	22	23.5
♀	22.5	23.6	24.7	25.8	27	28.1	29.2	0.4	1.5	2.6	3.8	4.9	6.1	7.2	8.4	9.5	10.7	11.9	13	14.2	15.4	16.5	17.7	18.9	20.1	21.3	22.4	23.6	24.8	26	27.2
♂	28.1	28.8	29.5	0.2	0.9	1.6	2.3	3	3.7	4.4	5.2	5.9	6.6	7.3	8	8.7	9.5	10.2	10.9	11.6	12.3	13.1	13.8	14.5	15.2	15.9	16.7	17.4	18.1	18.9	19.6

♃ 1 6 11 16 21 26 31: 11.8 12.9 14.1 15.2 16.3 17.4 18.5
♄ 1 6 11 16 21 26 31: 5.9 6.4 7 7.6 8.2 8.7 9.3
♅ 1 11 21 31: 21.1R 21 20.8 20.6
♆ 1 11 21 31: 7.8 8.1 8.4 8.7
♇ 1 11 21 31: 6.1 6.2R 6.1 6

	1	2	3	4	5	6	7	8	9	10	11	12	13	14	15	16	17	18	19	20	21	22	23	24	25	26	27	28	29	30	31
☉	9.6	10.6	11.6	12.6	13.7	14.7	15.7	16.7	17.7	18.7	19.8	20.8	21.8	22.8	23.8	24.9	25.9	26.9	27.9	28.9	30	1	2	3	4	5	6.1	7.1	8.1	9.1	10.1
☽	10.3	24.6	8.4	21.7	4.6	17.1	29.3	11.3	23.2	5.1	16.9	28.8	10.8	22.9	5.1	17.5	30	12.6	25.5	8.6	22	5.8	19.8	4.2	18.9	3.7	18.7	3.5	18.1	2.4	16.2
☿	25	26.5	28	29.5	1	2.5	4.1	5.6	7.1	8.7	10.2	11.8	13.4	15	16.6	18.2	19.8	21.4	23	24.6	26.3	27.9	29.6	1.2	2.9	4.6	6.3	8	9.8	11.5	13.2
♀	28.4	29.6	0.8	2	3.2	4.4	5.6	6.8	8	9.2	10.4	11.6	12.8	14	15.2	16.4	17.6	18.8	20	21.3	22.5	23.7	24.9	26.1	27.3	28.5	29.8	1	2.2	3.4	4.6
♂	20.3	21	21.8	22.5	23.2	24	24.7	25.4	26.2	26.9	27.6	28.4	29.1	29.9	0.6	1.3	2.1	2.8	3.6	4.3	5	5.8	6.5	7.3	8	8.8	9.5	10.3	11	11.7	12.5

♃ 1 6 11 16 21 26 31: 18.7 19.8 20.9 21.9 23 24 24.9
♄ 1 6 11 16 21 26 31: 9.5 10 10.6 11.2 11.8 12.4 12.9
♅ 1 11 21 31: 20.5R 20.2 19.8 19.4
♆ 1 11 21 31: 8.7 8.9 9 9.1
♇ 1 11 21 31: 6.0R 5.9 5.7 5.5

	1	2	3	4	5	6	7	8	9	10	11	12	13	14	15	16	17	18	19	20	21	22	23	24	25	26	27	28	29	30	31
☉	11.1	12.2	13.2	14.2	15.2	16.2	17.2	18.2	19.2	20.3	21.3	22.3	23.3	24.3	25.3	26.3	27.3	28.3	29.4	0.4	1.4	2.4	3.4	4.4	5.4	6.4	7.4	8.4	9.4		
☽	29.6	12.6	25.2	7.5	19.6	1.5	13.4	25.2	7.2	19.2	1.5	13.9	26.5	9.3	22.3	5.6	19	2.6	16.5	0.5	14.7	29	13.4	27.9	12.2	26.4	10.4	24.1	7.4		
☿	15	16.7	18.5	20.3	22.1	23.9	25.7	27.4	29.2	1	2.8	4.6	6.3	8.1	9.8	11.5	13.1	14.7	16.2	17.6	19	20.3	21.4	22.5	23.4	24.2	24.8	25.3	25.7		
♀	5.9	7.1	8.3	9.5	10.8	12	13.2	14.4	15.7	16.9	18.1	19.3	20.6	21.8	23	24.2	25.5	26.7	27.9	29.1	0.4	1.6	2.8	4.1	5.3	6.5	7.8	9	10.2		
♂	13.2	14	14.7	15.5	16.3	17	17.8	18.5	19.3	20	20.8	21.5	22.3	23	23.8	24.6	25.3	26.1	26.8	27.6	28.4	29.1	29.9	0.6	1.4	2.2	2.9	3.7	4.4		

♃ 1 6 11 16 21 26: 25.1 26 26.9 27.8 28.6 29.4
♄ 1 6 11 16 21 26: 13 13.6 14.1 14.6 15.1 15.5
♅ 1 11 21: 19.4R 18.9 18.5
♆ 1 11 21: 9.1 9.1R 9.1
♇ 1 11 21: 5.5R 5.2 5

	1	2	3	4	5	6	7	8	9	10	11	12	13	14	15	16	17	18	19	20	21	22	23	24	25	26	27	28	29	30	31
☉	10.4	11.4	12.4	13.4	14.4	15.4	16.4	17.4	18.4	19.4	20.4	21.4	22.4	23.4	24.4	25.4	26.4	27.4	28.4	29.4	0.4	1.4	2.4	3.4	4.4	5.3	6.3	7.3	8.3	9.3	10.3
☽	20.3	3	15.3	27.4	9.4	21.3	3.2	15.1	27.2	9.6	22.1	5	18.1	1.5	15.2	29.1	13.1	27.3	11.5	25.7	9.9	24	8.1	22	5.7	19.2	2.5	15.5	28.3	10.8	23.2
☿	25.8	25.9R	25.7	25.4	25	24.4	23.7	23	22.1	21.2	20.2	19.2	18.2	17.3	16.4	15.6	14.8	14.1	13.5	13	12.6	12.4	12.2	12.1	12.1D	12.2	12.4	12.7	13.1	13.5	14.1
♀	11.4	12.7	13.9	15.1	16.4	17.6	18.8	20.1	21.3	22.5	23.8	25	26.2	27.4	28.7	29.9	1.1	2.4	3.6	4.8	6.1	7.3	8.5	9.8	11	12.2	13.5	14.7	15.9	17.2	18.4
♂	5.2	6	6.7	7.5	8.3	9	9.8	10.6	11.3	12.1	12.9	13.6	14.4	15.2	15.9	16.7	17.5	18.2	19	19.8	20.6	21.3	22.1	22.9	23.6	24.4	25.2	25.9	26.7	27.5	28.3

♃ 1 6 11 16 21 26 31: 29.9 0.6 1.2 1.7 2.2 2.6 3
♄ 1 6 11 16 21 26 31: 15.9 16.3 16.6 17 17.3 17.6 17.8
♅ 1 11 21 31: 18.1R 17.8 17.4 17.2
♆ 1 11 21 31: 9.0R 8.9 8.7 8.5
♇ 1 11 21 31: 4.8R 4.5 4.3 4.1

	1	2	3	4	5	6	7	8	9	10	11	12	13	14	15	16	17	18	19	20	21	22	23	24	25	26	27	28	29	30	31
☉	11.3	12.3	13.2	14.2	15.2	16.2	17.2	18.2	19.1	20.1	21.1	22.1	23.1	24.1	25	26	27	28	28.9	29.9	0.9	1.9	2.8	3.8	4.8	5.8	6.7	7.7	8.7	9.7	
☽	5.3	17.2	29.1	11	23	5.1	17.4	30	12.9	26.3	10	24	8.4	22.9	7.5	22.1	6.6	20.9	4.9	18.7	2.3	15.6	28.7	11.6	24.3	6.8	19.2	1.4	13.4	25.4	
☿	14.6	15.3	16	16.8	17.6	18.5	19.5	20.5	21.5	22.6	23.7	24.9	26.1	27.3	28.6	29.9	1.2	2.6	4	5.4	6.9	8.4	9.9	11.5	13.1	14.7	16.3	18	19.7	21.5	
♀	19.6	20.9	22.1	23.3	24.5	25.8	27	28.2	29.5	0.7	1.9	3.2	4.4	5.6	6.9	8.1	9.3	10.5	11.8	13	14.2	15.5	16.7	17.9	19.2	20.4	21.6	22.8	24.1	25.3	
♂	29	29.8	0.6	1.3	2.1	2.9	3.7	4.4	5.2	6	6.7	7.5	8.3	9.1	9.8	10.6	11.4	12.1	12.9	13.7	14.4	15.2	16	16.8	17.5	18.3	19.1	19.8	20.6	21.4	

♃ 1 6 11 16 21 26: 3 3.3 3.5 3.6 3.6R 3.6
♄ 1 6 11 16 21 26: 17.9 18 18.2 18.3 18.4 18.4
♅ 1 11 21: 17.2R 17 16.9
♆ 1 11 21: 8.5R 8.2 8
♇ 1 11 21: 4.0R 3.9 3.7

	1	2	3	4	5	6	7	8	9	10	11	12	13	14	15	16	17	18	19	20	21	22	23	24	25	26	27	28	29	30	31
☉	10.6	11.6	12.6	13.5	14.5	15.5	16.4	17.4	18.4	19.3	20.3	21.3	22.2	23.2	24.2	25.1	26.1	27.1	28	29	29.9	0.9	1.9	2.8	3.8	4.7	5.7	6.7	7.6	8.6	9.5
☽	7.2	19.1	1	13.1	25.3	7.9	20.8	4.2	18.1	2.3	17	1.9	17	2	16.8	1.3	15.4	29.2	12.6	25.7	8.6	21.2	3.6	15.9	28	10.1	22	3.9	15.7	27.6	9.5
☿	23.2	25	26.8	28.7	0.6	2.5	4.4	6.4	8.4	10.5	12.5	14.6	16.7	18.8	21	23.1	25.3	27.5	29.7	1.9	4.1	6.3	8.4	10.6	12.7	14.8	16.8	18.9	20.9	22.8	24.8
♀	26.5	27.8	29	0.2	1.4	2.7	3.9	5.1	6.4	7.6	8.8	10	11.3	12.5	13.7	15	16.2	17.4	18.6	19.9	21.1	22.3	23.6	24.8	26	27.2	28.5	29.7	0.9	2.2	3.4
♂	22.1	22.9	23.7	24.4	25.2	26	26.7	27.5	28.3	29	29.8	0.5	1.3	2.1	2.8	3.6	4.3	5.1	5.9	6.6	7.4	8.1	8.9	9.6	10.4	11.2	11.9	12.7	13.4	14.2	14.9

♃ 1 6 11 16 21 26 31: 3.4R 3.2 2.9 2.6 2.2 1.7 1.2
♄ 1 6 11 16 21 26 31: 18.4R 18.4 18.3 18.2 18 17.8 17.6
♅ 1 11 21 31: 17 17.1 17.3 17.5
♆ 1 11 21 31: 7.7R 7.4 7.2 6.9
♇ 1 11 21 31: 3.6R 3.6 3.6D 3.6

	1	2	3	4	5	6	7	8	9	10	11	12	13	14	15	16	17	18	19	20	21	22	23	24	25	26	27	28	29	30	31
☉	10.5	11.5	12.4	13.4	14.3	15.3	16.2	17.2	18.2	19.1	20.1	21	22	22.9	23.9	24.8	25.8	26.8	27.7	28.7	29.6	0.6	1.5	2.5	3.4	4.4	5.3	6.3	7.3	8.2	
☽	21.5	3.8	16.3	29.2	12.5	26.3	10.6	25.3	10.4	25.7	10.9	26	10.8	25.1	9	22.5	5.6	18.3	0.7	13	25.1	7.1	19	0.9	12.8	24.6	6.5	18.5	0.6	12.8	
☿	26.6	28.5	0.3	2	3.7	5.4	7	8.6	10.1	11.6	13	14.4	15.7	17	18.2	19.4	20.5	21.6	22.6	23.6	24.5	25.3	26.1	26.8	27.5	28.1	28.6	29.1	29.4	29.8	
♀	4.6	5.8	7.1	8.3	9.5	10.7	12	13.2	14.4	15.7	16.9	18.1	19.3	20.6	21.8	23	24.3	25.5	26.7	27.9	29.2	0.4	1.6	2.9	4.1	5.3	6.5	7.8	9	10.2	
♂	15.7	16.4	17.2	17.9	18.7	19.4	20.1	20.9	21.6	22.4	23.1	23.9	24.6	25.3	26.1	26.8	27.5	28.3	29	29.7	0.5	1.2	1.9	2.7	3.4	4.1	4.8	5.5	6.3	7	

♃ 1 6 11 16 21 26: 1.1R 0.5 29.9 29.3 28.6 28
♄ 1 6 11 16 21 26: 17.5R 17.2 16.9 16.6 16.3 15.9
♅ 1 11 21: 17.6 17.9 18.3
♆ 1 11 21: 6.9R 6.7 6.6
♇ 1 11 21: 3.7 3.8 3.9

	1	2	3	4	5	6	7	8	9	10	11	12	13	14	15	16	17	18	19	20	21	22	23	24	25	26	27	28	29	30	31
☉	9.2	10.1	11.1	12	13	13.9	14.9	15.8	16.8	17.7	18.7	19.6	20.6	21.6	22.5	23.5	24.4	25.4	26.3	27.3	28.2	29.2	0.1	1.1	2.1	3	4	4.9	5.9	6.8	7.8
☽	25.3	8.2	21.4	5.1	19.3	3.9	18.9	4.1	19.4	4.6	19.5	4	18	1.6	14.7	27.5	9.9	22.1	4.2	16.1	27.9	9.8	21.7	3.6	15.6	27.7	9.9	22.4	5	17.9	1.2
☿	30	0.1	0.2	0.2R	0.2	0	29.8	29.5	29.1	28.7	28.2	27.6	27.1	26.4	25.8	25.1	24.4	23.8	23.1	22.5	22	21.5	21	20.6	20.3	20.1	20	20.0D	20	20.2	20.5
♀	11.5	12.7	13.9	15.1	16.4	17.6	18.8	20.1	21.3	22.5	23.8	25	26.2	27.4	28.7	29.9	1.1	2.4	3.6	4.8	6.1	7.3	8.5	9.8	11	12.2	13.4	14.7	15.9	17.1	18.4
♂	7.7	8.4	9.1	9.9	10.6	11.3	12	12.7	13.4	14.1	14.8	15.5	16.2	16.9	17.6	18.3	19	19.7	20.4	21.1	21.8	22.5	23.1	23.8	24.5	25.2	25.9	26.5	27.2	27.9	28.6

♃ 1 6 11 16 21 26 31: 27.4R 26.8 26.2 25.7 25.2 24.8 24.4
♄ 1 6 11 16 21 26 31: 15.6R 15.2 14.8 14.5 14.1 13.8 13.4
♅ 1 11 21 31: 18.8 19.4 19.9 20.5
♆ 1 11 21 31: 6.4R 6.4 6.4D 6.4
♇ 1 11 21 31: 4.1 4.4 4.6 4.9

	1	2	3	4	5	6	7	8	9	10	11	12	13	14	15	16	17	18	19	20	21	22	23	24	25	26	27	28	29	30	31
☉	8.7	9.7	10.7	11.6	12.6	13.5	14.5	15.4	16.4	17.4	18.3	19.3	20.2	21.2	22.2	23.1	24.1	25	26	27	27.9	28.9	29.9	0.8	1.8	2.8	3.7	4.7	5.7	6.6	7.6
☽	14.8	28.8	13.2	27.9	12.8	27.9	12.9	27.7	12.2	26.3	10	23.2	6	18.5	0.8	12.8	24.7	6.6	18.4	0.3	12.4	24.5	6.8	19.3	2	15	28.1	11.5	25.2	9.1	23.3
☿	20.9	21.4	22	22.7	23.5	24.4	25.4	26.5	27.7	29	0.4	1.8	3.4	5	6.7	8.4	10.2	12.1	14	15.9	17.8	19.8	21.8	23.8	25.8	27.8	29.8	1.7	3.7	5.7	7.6
♀	19.6	20.8	22.1	23.3	24.5	25.8	27	28.2	29.5	0.7	1.9	3.2	4.4	5.6	6.8	8.1	9.3	10.5	11.8	13	14.2	15.5	16.7	17.9	19.2	20.4	21.6	22.9	24.1	25.3	26.6
♂	29.2	29.9	0.6	1.2	1.9	2.5	3.2	3.8	4.5	5.1	5.8	6.4	7.1	7.7	8.4	9	9.6	10.3	10.9	11.5	12.1	12.8	13.4	14	14.6	15.2	15.8	16.4	17	17.6	18.2

♃ 1 6 11 16 21 26 31: 24.4R 24.1 23.9 23.8 23.8D 23.8 23.9
♄ 1 6 11 16 21 26 31: 13.4R 13.1 12.8 12.6 12.3 12.2 12
♅ 1 11 21 31: 20.6 21.2 21.8 22.5
♆ 1 11 21 31: 6.4 6.5 6.7 6.9
♇ 1 11 21 31: 5 5.3 5.6 5.9

	1	2	3	4	5	6	7	8	9	10	11	12	13	14	15	16	17	18	19	20	21	22	23	24	25	26	27	28	29	30	31
☉	8.6	9.5	10.5	11.5	12.4	13.4	14.4	15.3	16.3	17.3	18.3	19.2	20.2	21.2	22.2	23.1	24.1	25.1	26.1	27	28	29	30	0.9	1.9	2.9	3.9	4.9	5.9	6.8	
☽	7.7	22.3	7	21.6	6.1	20.4	4.4	18	1.2	14.1	26.6	8.9	21	2.9	14.7	26.6	8.6	20.7	3	15.6	28.4	11.5	24.8	8.3	22.1	6	20	4.2	18.4	2.6	
☿	9.5	11.5	13.4	15.2	17.1	18.9	20.7	22.5	24.3	26.1	27.8	29.6	1.3	2.9	4.6	6.3	7.9	9.5	11.1	12.7	14.3	15.8	17.3	18.9	20.4	21.8	23.3	24.8	26.2	27.6	
♀	27.8	29	0.2	1.5	2.7	3.9	5.2	6.4	7.6	8.9	10.1	11.3	12.5	13.8	15	16.2	17.5	18.7	19.9	21.2	22.4	23.6	24.8	26.1	27.3	28.5	29.7	1	2.2	3.4	
♂	18.8	19.4	20	20.6	21.1	21.7	22.3	22.9	23.4	24	24.6	25.1	25.7	26.2	26.7	27.3	27.8	28.4	28.9	29.4	29.9	0.4	1	1.5	2	2.5	2.9	3.4	3.9	4.4	

♃ 1 6 11 16 21 26: 24 24.2 24.5 24.8 25.3 25.8
♄ 1 6 11 16 21 26: 12.0R 11.9 11.8 11.8D 11.8 11.9
♅ 1 11 21: 22.5 23.1 23.7
♆ 1 11 21: 6.9 7.1 7.4
♇ 1 11 21: 6 6.3 6.6

	1	2	3	4	5	6	7	8	9	10	11	12	13	14	15	16	17	18	19	20	21	22	23	24	25	26	27	28	29	30	31
☉	7.8	8.8	9.8	10.8	11.8	12.7	13.7	14.7	15.7	16.7	17.7	18.7	19.7	20.7	21.6	22.6	23.6	24.6	25.6	26.6	27.6	28.6	29.6	0.6	1.6	2.6	3.6	4.6	5.6	6.6	7.6
☽	16.9	1	15.1	29	12.7	26.1	9.2	22	4.5	16.8	28.8	10.8	22.6	4.5	16.5	28.6	11	23.8	6.8	20.2	4	18	2.2	16.6	0.9	15.2	29.4	13.5	27.4	11.2	24.8
☿	29	0.4	1.8	3.1	4.4	5.7	7	8.3	9.5	10.7	11.9	13.1	14.2	15.3	16.3	17.3	18.3	19.2	20	20.8	21.6	22.2	22.8	23.2	23.6	23.9	24	24.0R	23.9	23.6	23.2
♀	4.7	5.9	7.1	8.3	9.6	10.8	12	13.2	14.5	15.7	16.9	18.1	19.4	20.6	21.8	23	24.3	25.5	26.7	27.9	29.1	0.4	1.6	2.8	4	5.2	6.5	7.7	8.9	10.1	11.3
♂	4.9	5.3	5.8	6.2	6.7	7.1	7.6	8	8.4	8.8	9.3	9.7	10.1	10.5	10.8	11.2	11.6	12	12.3	12.7	13	13.3	13.7	14	14.3	14.6	14.9	15.2	15.4	15.7	16

♃ 1 6 11 16 21 26 31: 26.3 27 27.6 28.4 29.2 30 0.9
♄ 1 6 11 16 21 26 31: 12 12.1 12.3 12.6 12.8 13.1 13.4
♅ 1 11 21 31: 24.2 24.6 25 25.4
♆ 1 11 21 31: 7.8 8.1 8.5 8.8
♇ 1 11 21 31: 7 7.2 7.5 7.7

	1	2	3	4	5	6	7	8	9	10	11	12	13	14	15	16	17	18	19	20	21	22	23	24	25	26	27	28	29	30	31
☉	8.6	9.6	10.6	11.6	12.6	13.6	14.6	15.6	16.6	17.6	18.6	19.6	20.6	21.6	22.6	23.6	24.7	25.7	26.7	27.7	28.7	29.7	0.7	1.7	2.7	3.7	4.8	5.8	6.8	7.8	
☽	8.3	21.6	4.6	17.5	0.1	12.6	24.8	6.8	18.7	0.5	12.3	24.3	6.4	18.8	1.5	14.7	28.3	12.4	26.8	11.5	26.3	11.1	25.7	10.1	24.3	8.1	21.7	5	18.2	1.1	
☿	22.6R	21.8	20.9	19.9	18.8	17.5	16.2	14.9	13.6	12.3	11.2	10.2	9.4	8.8	8.3	8.1	8.0D	8.1	8.4	8.9	9.5	10.2	11	12	13	14.1	15.3	16.5	17.7	19.1	
♀	12.6	13.8	15	16.2	17.4	18.6	19.9	21.1	22.3	23.5	24.7	25.9	27.1	28.4	29.6	0.8	2	3.2	4.4	5.6	6.8	8	9.2	10.4	11.6	12.8	14	15.2	16.4	17.6	
♂	16.2	16.4	16.6	16.9	17.1	17.3	17.4	17.6	17.8	17.9	18	18.2	18.3	18.4	18.4	18.5	18.6	18.6	18.6	18.7	18.7R	18.7	18.6	18.6	18.5	18.5	18.4	18.3	18.2	18.1	

♃ 1 6 11 16 21 26: 1 2 2.9 3.9 4.9 6
♄ 1 6 11 16 21 26: 13.5 13.9 14.3 14.7 15.2 15.6
♅ 1 11 21: 25.4 25.6 25.8
♆ 1 11 21: 8.9 9.2 9.6
♇ 1 11 21: 7.7 7.9 8

	1	2	3	4	5	6	7	8	9	10	11	12	13	14	15	16	17	18	19	20	21	22	23	24	25	26	27	28	29	30	31
☉	8.8	9.8	10.8	11.9	12.9	13.9	14.9	15.9	16.9	17.9	19	20	21	22	23	24	25.1	26.1	27.1	28.1	29.1	0.2	1.2	2.2	3.2	4.2	5.3	6.3	7.3	8.3	9.3
☽	13.8	26.4	8.8	21	3.1	15	26.9	8.7	20.5	2.4	14.4	26.8	9.5	22.6	6.2	20.3	4.8	19.7	4.9	20.1	5.1	19.9	4.3	18.3	1.9	15.2	28.1	10.8	23.3	5.6	17.8
☿	20.4	21.8	23.2	24.6	26	27.5	28.9	0.4	1.9	3.4	4.9	6.4	7.9	9.4	11	12.5	14	15.6	17.1	18.6	20.2	21.7	23.3	24.8	26.4	28	29.5	1.1	2.7	4.3	5.8
♀	18.8	20	21.2	22.4	23.6	24.8	26	27.2	28.4	29.6	0.8	2	3.1	4.3	5.5	6.7	7.9	9	10.2	11.4	12.6	13.7	14.9	16.1	17.2	18.4	19.5	20.7	21.8	23	24.1
♂	17.9R	17.8	17.6	17.4	17.2	17	16.8	16.6	16.3	16.1	15.8	15.5	15.2	14.9	14.6	14.2	13.9	13.5	13.2	12.8	12.5	12.1	11.7	11.3	10.9	10.5	10.1	9.7	9.3	8.9	8.5

♃ 1 6 11 16 21 26 31: 7.1 8.2 9.3 10.4 11.6 12.7 13.9
♄ 1 6 11 16 21 26 31: 16.1 16.7 17.2 17.7 18.3 18.9 19.5
♅ 1 11 21 31: 25.8 25.8R 25.6 25.4
♆ 1 11 21 31: 10 10.3 10.6 10.8
♇ 1 11 21 31: 8.1 8.1R 8.1 8

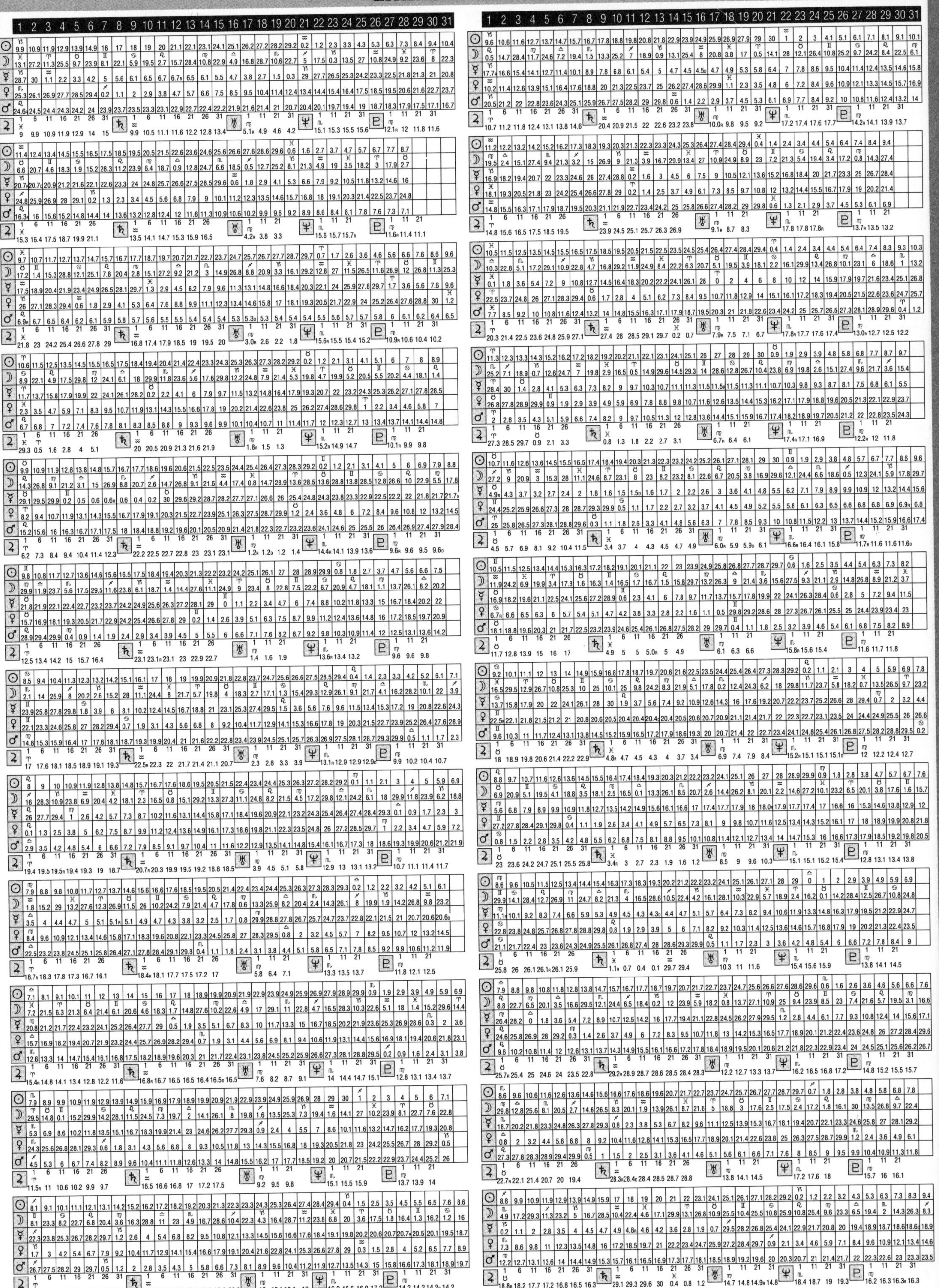

I

1965

	1	2	3	4	5	6	7	8	9	10	11	12	13	14	15	16	17	18	19	20	21	22	23	24	25	26	27	28	29	30	31
☉	♑ 10.4	11.4	12.4	13.4	14.5	15.5	16.5	17.5	18.5	19.6	20.6	21.6	22.6	23.6	24.6	25.7	26.7	27.7	28.7	29.7	♒ 0.8	1.8	2.8	3.8	4.8	5.8	6.9	7.9	8.9	9.9	10.9
☽	♐ 20.1	♑ 1.9	13.7	25.5	♒ 7.4	19.4	♓ 1.5	13.7	26.2	♈ 9	22.1	♉ 5.6	19.4	♊ 3.7	18.4	♋ 3.4	18.6	♌ 3.8	18.9	♍ 3.7	18.1	♎ 2	15.4	28.4	♏ 11	23.2	♐ 5.2	17.1	28.8	♑ 10.6	22.4
☿	♐ 19.2	19.6	20.2	20.9	21.6	22.5	23.4	24.3	25.3	26.4	27.5	28.7	29.8	♑ 1.1	2.3	3.6	4.9	6.2	7.5	8.9	10.3	11.7	13.1	14.5	15.9	17.4	18.8	20.3	21.8	23.3	24.8
♀	♐ 15.9	17.1	18.4	19.6	20.8	22.1	23.3	24.6	25.8	27.1	28.3	29.6	♑ 0.8	2.1	3.3	4.6	5.8	7.1	8.3	9.6	10.9	12.1	13.4	14.6	15.9	17.1	18.4	19.6	20.9	22.1	23.4
♂	♍ 23.8	24.1	24.4	24.6	24.9	25.1	25.4	25.6	25.8	26	26.2	26.4	26.6	26.8	26.9	27.1	27.2	27.3	27.5	27.6	27.7	27.8	27.8	27.9	28	28	28	28	28.1R	28	28

♃ (1, 6, 11, 16, 21, 26, 31): ♉ 16.3R 16.1 16.1D 16.2 16.3 16.5 16.8
♄ (1, 6, 11, 16, 21, 26, 31): ♓ 1.3 1.8 2.3 2.8 3.3 3.9 4.4
♅ (1, 11, 21, 31): ♍ 14.8R 14.6 14.4 14.1
♆ (1, 11, 21, 31): ♏ 19.3 19.6 19.8 19.9
♇ (1, 11, 21, 31): ♍ 16.3R 16.2 16 15.9

1966

	1	2	3	4	5	6	7	8	9	10	11	12	13	14	15	16	17	18	19	20	21	22	23	24	25	26	27	28	29	30	31
☉	♑ 10.1	11.1	12.2	13.2	14.2	15.2	16.2	17.3	18.3	19.3	20.3	21.3	22.4	23.4	24.4	25.4	26.4	27.5	28.5	29.5	♒ 0.5	1.5	2.5	3.6	4.6	5.6	6.6	7.6	8.6	9.7	10.7
☽	♈ 20.6	♉ 3.3	16.4	29.9	♊ 13.9	28.4	♋ 13.2	28.2	♌ 13.3	28.4	♍ 13.2	27.7	♎ 11.8	25.4	♏ 8.7	21.7	♐ 4.4	16.8	29.1	♑ 11.3	23.3	♒ 5.3	17.2	29	♓ 10.9	22.8	♈ 4.7	16.8	29.1	♉ 11.7	24.6
☿	♐ 20.5	21.8	23.2	24.6	26	27.5	28.9	♑ 0.4	1.8	3.3	4.8	6.3	7.8	9.3	10.8	12.3	13.9	15.4	17	18.5	20.1	21.7	23.3	24.9	26.5	28.1	29.7	♒ 1.4	3	4.7	6.4
♀	♒ 13.4	13.6	13.7	13.8	13.8	13.8R	13.8	13.7	13.6	13.4	13.2	13	12.7	12.4	12	11.6	11.2	10.7	10.2	9.7	9.2	8.6	8	7.4	6.8	6.2	5.5	4.9	4.3	3.7	3.2
♂	♒ 6.9	7.7	8.5	9.2	10	10.8	11.6	12.4	13.2	14	14.8	15.6	16.3	17.1	17.9	18.7	19.5	20.3	21.1	21.9	22.7	23.5	24.2	25	25.8	26.6	27.4	28.2	29	29.8	♓ 0.6

♃ (1, 6, 11, 16, 21, 26, 31): ♊ 24.4R 23.8 23.3 22.8 22.3 21.9 21.6
♄ (1, 6, 11, 16, 21, 26, 31): ♓ 12.4 12.8 13.3 13.7 14.2 14.7 15.3
♅ (1, 11, 21, 31): ♍ 19.6R 19.5 19.3 19
♆ (1, 11, 21, 31): ♏ 21.4 21.7 21.9 22
♇ (1, 11, 21, 31): ♍ 18.4R 18.4 18.2 18

II

1965

	1	2	3	4	5	6	7	8	9	10	11	12	13	14	15	16	17	18	19	20	21	22	23	24	25	26	27	28	29	30	31
☉	♒ 11.9	12.9	14	15	16	17	18	19	20	21.1	22.1	23.1	24.1	25.1	26.1	27.1	28.1	29.1	♓ 0.1	1.2	2.2	3.2	4.2	5.2	6.2	7.2	8.2	9.2			
☽	♒ 4.3	16.3	28.5	♓ 10.8	23.3	♈ 6	18.9	♉ 2	15.4	29.1	♊ 13.1	27.4	♋ 12.1	26.9	♌ 11.9	26.9	♍ 11.6	26	♎ 10	23.5	♏ 6.6	19.2	♐ 1.5	13.6	25.4	♑ 7.2	19	♒ 0.9			
☿	♑ 26.3	27.9	29.4	♒ 1	2.6	4.2	5.8	7.4	9	10.6	12.3	13.9	15.6	17.3	19	20.8	22.5	24.2	26	27.8	29.6	♓ 1.4	3.2	5.1	6.9	8.8	10.7	12.6			
♀	♑ 24.6	25.9	27.1	28.4	29.6	♒ 0.9	2.1	3.4	4.6	5.9	7.1	8.4	9.6	10.9	12.1	13.4	14.6	15.9	17.1	18.4	19.6	20.9	22.1	23.4	24.6	25.9	27.1	28.4			
♂	♍ 28.0R	27.9	27.9	27.8	27.7	27.6	27.5	27.4	27.3	27.1	27	26.8	26.6	26.4	26.2	25.9	25.7	25.5	25.2	24.9	24.6	24.3	24	23.7	23.4	23.1	22.7	22.4			

♃ (1, 6, 11, 16, 21, 26): ♉ 16.9 17.3 17.8 18.3 18.9 19.6
♄ (1, 6, 11, 16, 21, 26): ♓ 4.6 5.1 5.7 6.3 6.9 7.5
♅ (1, 11, 21): ♍ 14.1R 13.7 13.3
♆ (1, 11, 21): ♏ 19.9 20 20.0R
♇ (1, 11, 21): ♍ 15.8R 15.6 15.4

1966

	1	2	3	4	5	6	7	8	9	10	11	12	13	14	15	16	17	18	19	20	21	22	23	24	25	26	27	28	29	30	31
☉	♒ 11.7	12.7	13.7	14.7	15.7	16.8	17.8	18.8	19.8	20.8	21.8	22.8	23.8	24.9	25.9	26.9	27.9	28.9	29.9	♓ 0.9	1.9	2.9	3.9	4.9	5.9	7	8	9			
☽	♊ 8	21.9	♋ 6.2	21	♌ 6.2	21.5	♍ 6.9	22	♎ 6.8	21.1	♏ 5	18.4	♐ 1.3	13.9	26.2	♑ 8.4	20.3	♒ 2.3	14.1	26	♓ 7.9	19.8	♈ 1.7	13.8	26	♉ 8.3	20.9	♊ 3.8			
☿	♒ 8.1	9.8	11.5	13.2	14.9	16.7	18.4	20.2	22	23.8	25.6	27.4	29.2	♓ 1.1	2.9	4.8	6.6	8.4	10.3	12.1	13.9	15.7	17.5	19.2	21	22.6	24.2	25.7			
♀	♒ 2.6R	2.1	1.6	1.1	0.6	0.2	♑ 29.8	29.5	29.2	28.9	28.7	28.5	28.4	28.3	28.3	28.2D	28.3	28.3	28.4	28.6	28.8	29	29.2	29.5	29.8	♒ 0.2	0.6	1			
♂	♓ 1.4	2.1	2.9	3.7	4.5	5.3	6.1	6.9	7.7	8.4	9.2	10	10.8	11.6	12.4	13.2	14	14.7	15.5	16.3	17.1	17.9	18.7	19.4	20.2	21	21.8	22.6			

♃ (1, 6, 11, 16, 21, 26): ♊ 21.6R 21.4 21.3 21.3D 21.3 21.4
♄ (1, 6, 11, 16, 21, 26): ♓ 15.4 15.9 16.5 17.1 17.7 18.3
♅ (1, 11, 21): ♍ 19.0R 18.7 18.3
♆ (1, 11, 21): ♏ 22.1 22.1 22.2
♇ (1, 11, 21): ♍ 18.0R 17.8 17.6

III

1965

	1	2	3	4	5	6	7	8	9	10	11	12	13	14	15	16	17	18	19	20	21	22	23	24	25	26	27	28	29	30	31
☉	♓ 10.2	11.2	12.2	13.2	14.2	15.2	16.2	17.2	18.2	19.2	20.2	21.2	22.2	23.2	24.2	25.2	26.2	27.2	28.2	29.2	♈ 0.2	1.2	2.2	3.2	4.1	5.1	6.1	7.1	8.1	9.1	10.1
☽	♒ 12.9	25	♓ 7.4	20	♈ 2.8	15.8	29	♉ 12.3	25.9	♊ 9.6	23.5	♋ 7.6	21.9	♌ 6.4	20.9	♍ 5.5	19.9	♎ 4.1	17.9	♏ 1.4	14.4	27.1	♐ 9.4	21.5	♑ 3.4	15.2	27	♒ 9	21	♓ 3.3	15.9
☿	♓ 14.5	16.4	18.3	20.3	22.2	24.1	26	27.9	29.8	♈ 1.7	3.5	5.3	7.1	8.8	10.5	12	13.5	14.9	16.3	17.5	18.6	19.6	20.5	21.3	21.9	22.4	22.8	23.1	23.2	23.3R	23.2
♀	♒ 29.6	♓ 0.9	2.1	3.3	4.6	5.8	7.1	8.3	9.6	10.8	12.1	13.3	14.6	15.8	17.1	18.3	19.6	20.8	22	23.3	24.5	25.8	27	28.3	29.5	♈ 0.8	2	3.2	4.5	5.7	7
♂	♍ 22.0R	21.6	21.3	20.9	20.5	20.1	19.7	19.3	18.9	18.5	18.2	17.8	17.4	17	16.6	16.2	15.8	15.4	15.1	14.7	14.4	14	13.7	13.3	13	12.7	12.4	12.1	11.8	11.5	11.3

♃ (1, 6, 11, 16, 21, 26, 31): ♉ 20 20.8 21.6 22.4 23.3 24.3 25.3
♄ (1, 6, 11, 16, 21, 26, 31): ♓ 7.9 8.5 9.1 9.7 10.3 10.9 11.5
♅ (1, 11, 21, 31): ♍ 12.9R 12.5 12.1 11.7
♆ (1, 11, 21, 31): ♏ 20.0R 19.9 19.8 19.6
♇ (1, 11, 21, 31): ♍ 15.2R 14.9 14.6 14.4

1966

	1	2	3	4	5	6	7	8	9	10	11	12	13	14	15	16	17	18	19	20	21	22	23	24	25	26	27	28	29	30	31
☉	♓ 10	11	12	13	14	15	16	17	18	19	20	21	22	23	24	25	26	27	27.9	28.9	29.9	♈ 0.9	1.9	2.9	3.9	4.9	5.9	6.9	7.9	8.9	9.8
☽	♊ 17	♋ 0.7	14.8	29.4	♌ 14.4	29.6	♍ 14.9	♎ 0.1	15	29.5	♏ 13.5	27.1	♐ 10.1	22.8	♑ 5.1	17.3	29.2	♒ 11.1	22.9	♓ 4.8	16.7	28.7	♈ 10.8	23	♉ 5.4	17.9	♊ 0.7	13.7	27	♋ 10.6	24.5
☿	♓ 27.2	28.6	29.9	♈ 1	2.1	3	3.8	4.5	5	5.4	5.7	5.8	5.7R	5.5	5.2	4.7	4.1	3.5	2.7	1.9	1	0.1	♓ 29.2	28.3	27.4	26.6	25.9	25.2	24.5	24	23.6
♀	♒ 1.4	1.9	2.4	2.9	3.4	4	4.6	5.2	5.8	6.5	7.2	7.9	8.6	9.3	10	10.8	11.6	12.3	13.1	13.9	14.8	15.6	16.5	17.3	18.2	19.1	20	20.9	21.8	22.7	23.6
♂	♓ 23.4	24.1	24.9	25.7	26.5	27.3	28	28.8	29.6	♈ 0.4	1.1	1.9	2.7	3.5	4.2	5	5.8	6.6	7.3	8.1	8.9	9.6	10.4	11.2	11.9	12.7	13.5	14.2	15	15.8	16.5

♃ (1, 6, 11, 16, 21, 26, 31): ♊ 21.6 21.8 22.2 22.6 23.1 23.6 24.2
♄ (1, 6, 11, 16, 21, 26, 31): ♓ 18.7 19.3 19.9 20.5 21.1 21.7 22.3
♅ (1, 11, 21, 31): ♍ 17.9R 17.5 17.1 16.6
♆ (1, 11, 21, 31): ♏ 22.2R 22.1 22 21.8
♇ (1, 11, 21, 31): ♍ 17.3R 17.1 16.8 16.6

IV

1965

	1	2	3	4	5	6	7	8	9	10	11	12	13	14	15	16	17	18	19	20	21	22	23	24	25	26	27	28	29	30	31
☉	♈ 11.1	12.1	13	14	15	16	17	18	18.9	19.9	20.9	21.9	22.9	23.8	24.8	25.8	26.8	27.8	28.7	29.7	♉ 0.7	1.7	2.6	3.6	4.6	5.6	6.5	7.5	8.5	9.5	
☽	♓ 28.7	♈ 11.9	25.2	♉ 8.8	22.5	♊ 6.4	20.4	♋ 4.4	18.6	♌ 2.7	16.9	♍ 1	15.1	29	♎ 12.8	26.3	♏ 9.5	22.4	♐ 4.9	17.2	29.3	♑ 11.2	23.1	♒ 4.9	16.8	29	♓ 11.3	24	♈ 7	20.3	
☿	♈ 22.9R	22.6	22.2	21.7	21.1	20.4	19.7	18.9	18.2	17.4	16.6	15.9	15.2	14.5	13.9	13.4	12.9	12.5	12.2	12	11.8	11.8	11.8D	11.9	12.1	12.4	12.7	13.1	13.6	14.2	
♀	♈ 8.2	9.4	10.7	11.9	13.2	14.4	15.6	16.9	18.1	19.4	20.6	21.8	23.1	24.3	25.6	26.8	28	29.3	♉ 0.5	1.7	3	4.2	5.5	6.7	7.9	9.2	10.4	11.6	12.9	14.1	
♂	♍ 11.0R	10.8	10.6	10.4	10.2	10	9.8	9.6	9.5	9.4	9.2	9.1	9	8.9	8.9	8.8	8.8	8.7	8.7	8.7D	8.7	8.8	8.8	8.8	8.9	9	9	9.1	9.2	9.3	

♃ (1, 6, 11, 16, 21, 26): ♉ 25.5 26.5 27.5 28.6 29.7 ♊ 0.8
♄ (1, 6, 11, 16, 21, 26): ♓ 11.6 12.1 12.7 13.2 13.7 14.1
♅ (1, 11, 21): ♍ 11.6R 11.3 11
♆ (1, 11, 21): ♏ 19.6R 19.4 19.1
♇ (1, 11, 21): ♍ 14.4R 14.1 14

1966

	1	2	3	4	5	6	7	8	9	10	11	12	13	14	15	16	17	18	19	20	21	22	23	24	25	26	27	28	29	30	31
☉	♈ 10.8	11.8	12.8	13.8	14.8	15.8	16.7	17.7	18.7	19.7	20.7	21.6	22.6	23.6	24.6	25.6	26.5	27.5	28.5	29.5	♉ 0.5	1.4	2.4	3.4	4.4	5.3	6.3	7.3	8.2	9.2	
☽	♌ 8.9	23.5	♍ 8.4	23.3	♎ 8.3	23	♏ 7.5	21.5	♐ 5.1	18.3	♑ 1	13.5	25.6	♒ 7.6	19.5	♓ 1.4	13.3	25.2	♈ 7.4	19.6	♉ 2.1	14.7	27.6	♊ 10.7	23.9	♋ 7.5	21.2	♌ 5.2	19.3	♍ 3.7	
☿	♓ 23.2R	23	22.8	22.7	22.8D	22.9	23.1	23.4	23.8	24.2	24.7	25.3	26	26.7	27.5	28.3	29.2	♈ 0.1	1.1	2.1	3.2	4.3	5.5	6.7	7.9	9.2	10.5	11.9	13.3	14.7	
♀	♒ 24.6	25.5	26.5	27.4	28.4	29.4	♓ 0.3	1.3	2.3	3.3	4.3	5.3	6.4	7.4	8.4	9.4	10.5	11.5	12.6	13.6	14.7	15.7	16.8	17.9	18.9	20	21.1	22.2	23.2	24.3	
♂	♈ 17.3	18	18.8	19.6	20.3	21.1	21.8	22.6	23.4	24.1	24.9	25.6	26.4	27.1	27.9	28.6	29.4	♉ 0.1	0.9	1.6	2.4	3.1	3.8	4.6	5.3	6.1	6.8	7.6	8.3	9	

♃ (1, 6, 11, 16, 21, 26): ♊ 24.4 25 25.8 26.5 27.4 28.2
♄ (1, 6, 11, 16, 21, 26): ♓ 22.5 23 23.6 24.2 24.7 25.3
♅ (1, 11, 21): ♍ 16.6R 16.2 15.9
♆ (1, 11, 21): ♏ 21.8R 21.6 21.4
♇ (1, 11, 21): ♍ 16.5R 16.3 16.1

V

1965

	1	2	3	4	5	6	7	8	9	10	11	12	13	14	15	16	17	18	19	20	21	22	23	24	25	26	27	28	29	30	31
☉	♉ 10.4	11.4	12.4	13.3	14.3	15.3	16.2	17.2	18.2	19.1	20.1	21.1	22	23	24	24.9	25.9	26.9	27.8	28.8	29.7	♊ 0.7	1.7	2.6	3.6	4.5	5.5	6.5	7.4	8.4	9.3
☽	♉ 4	17.9	♊ 2.1	16.4	♋ 0.8	15.2	29.5	♌ 13.7	27.8	♍ 11.7	25.4	♎ 8.9	22.3	♏ 5.3	18.2	♐ 0.8	13.1	25.3	♑ 7.3	19.2	♒ 1.1	12.9	24.9	♓ 7	19.3	♈ 2	15	28.4	♉ 12.2	26.4	♊ 10.9
☿	♈ 14.8	15.5	16.3	17.1	17.9	18.9	19.8	20.9	21.9	23	24.2	25.4	26.6	27.9	29.3	♉ 0.6	2	3.5	5	6.5	8.1	9.7	11.3	13	14.7	16.4	18.2	20	21.9	23.8	25.7
♀	♉ 15.3	16.6	17.8	19	20.3	21.5	22.7	24	25.2	26.4	27.7	28.9	♊ 0.1	1.3	2.6	3.8	5	6.3	7.5	8.7	10	11.2	12.4	13.6	14.9	16.1	17.3	18.5	19.8	21	22.2
♂	♍ 9.5	9.6	9.7	9.9	10	10.2	10.4	10.6	10.8	11	11.2	11.5	11.7	11.9	12.2	12.5	12.7	13	13.3	13.6	13.9	14.2	14.5	14.8	15.1	15.5	15.8	16.2	16.5	16.9	17.2

♃ (1, 6, 11, 16, 21, 26, 31): ♊ 1.9 3 4.2 5.3 6.5 7.7 8.8
♄ (1, 6, 11, 16, 21, 26, 31): ♓ 14.6 15 15.4 15.7 16 16.3 16.6
♅ (1, 11, 21, 31): ♍ 10.8R 10.7 10.7D 10.8
♆ (1, 11, 21, 31): ♏ 18.9R 18.6 18.3 18.1
♇ (1, 11, 21, 31): ♍ 13.8R 13.7 13.7 13.7D

1966

	1	2	3	4	5	6	7	8	9	10	11	12	13	14	15	16	17	18	19	20	21	22	23	24	25	26	27	28	29	30	31
☉	♉ 10.2	11.2	12.1	13.1	14.1	15	16	17	17.9	18.9	19.9	20.8	21.8	22.8	23.7	24.7	25.7	26.6	27.6	28.5	29.5	♊ 0.5	1.4	2.4	3.4	4.3	5.3	6.2	7.2	8.2	9.1
☽	♍ 18.2	♎ 2.7	17.2	♏ 1.5	15.7	29.5	♐ 13	26.1	♑ 8.9	21.4	♒ 3.6	15.6	27.6	♓ 9.4	21.4	♈ 3.4	15.6	28	♉ 10.7	23.6	♊ 6.8	20.3	♋ 4	17.9	♌ 2	16.1	♍ 0.4	14.6	28.8	♎ 13	27
☿	♈ 16.1	17.6	19.1	20.7	22.3	23.9	25.6	27.2	28.9	♉ 0.7	2.5	4.3	6.1	8	9.9	11.8	13.8	15.8	17.8	19.9	22	24.1	26.2	28.4	♊ 0.6	2.8	4.9	7.1	9.3	11.5	13.7
♀	♓ 25.4	26.5	27.6	28.7	29.8	♈ 0.9	2	3.1	4.2	5.3	6.5	7.6	8.7	9.8	10.9	12.1	13.2	14.3	15.5	16.6	17.7	18.9	20	21.1	22.3	23.4	24.6	25.7	26.9	28	29.2
♂	♉ 9.8	10.5	11.2	12	12.7	13.4	14.2	14.9	15.6	16.4	17.1	17.8	18.6	19.3	20	20.7	21.5	22.2	22.9	23.6	24.3	25.1	25.8	26.5	27.2	27.9	28.6	29.4	♊ 0.1	0.8	1.5

♃ (1, 6, 11, 16, 21, 26, 31): ♊ 29.1 ♋ 0.1 1.1 2.1 3.1 4.1 5.2
♄ (1, 6, 11, 16, 21, 26, 31): ♓ 25.8 26.3 26.7 27.2 27.6 27.9 28.3
♅ (1, 11, 21, 31): ♍ 15.7R 15.6 15.5 15.5D
♆ (1, 11, 21, 31): ♏ 21.1R 20.8 20.6 20.3
♇ (1, 11, 21, 31): ♍ 16.0R 15.9 15.8 15.8D

VI

1965

	1	2	3	4	5	6	7	8	9	10	11	12	13	14	15	16	17	18	19	20	21	22	23	24	25	26	27	28	29	30	31
☉	♊ 10.3	11.3	12.2	13.2	14.1	15.1	16	17	18	18.9	19.9	20.8	21.8	22.7	23.7	24.6	25.6	26.6	27.5	28.5	29.4	♋ 0.4	1.3	2.3	3.2	4.2	5.1	6.1	7.1	8	
☽	♊ 25.6	♋ 10.4	25.2	♌ 9.9	24.3	♍ 8.5	22.3	♎ 5.9	19.1	♏ 2.1	14.8	27.3	♐ 9.6	21.8	♑ 3.8	15.7	27.6	♒ 9.4	21.3	♓ 3.3	15.4	27.7	♈ 10.3	23.2	♉ 6.6	20.4	♊ 4.6	19.2	♋ 4.2	19.3	
☿	♉ 27.7	29.7	♊ 1.7	3.8	5.9	8	10.2	12.3	14.5	16.7	18.9	21.1	23.3	25.5	27.7	29.8	♋ 2	4.1	6.2	8.3	10.3	12.3	14.3	16.3	18.2	20.1	21.9	23.7	25.5	27.2	
♀	♊ 23.5	24.7	25.9	27.1	28.4	29.6	♋ 0.8	2	3.3	4.5	5.7	6.9	8.1	9.4	10.6	11.8	13	14.3	15.5	16.7	17.9	19.1	20.4	21.6	22.8	24	25.2	26.5	27.7	28.9	
♂	♍ 17.6	18	18.4	18.8	19.2	19.6	20	20.4	20.8	21.2	21.6	22.1	22.5	22.9	23.4	23.8	24.3	24.7	25.2	25.6	26.1	26.6	27.1	27.5	28	28.5	29	29.5	30	♎ 0.5	

♃ (1, 6, 11, 16, 21, 26): ♊ 9.1 10.2 11.4 12.6 13.7 14.8
♄ (1, 6, 11, 16, 21, 26): ♓ 16.6 16.8 17 17.1 17.2 17.2
♅ (1, 11, 21): ♍ 10.8 10.9 11.2
♆ (1, 11, 21): ♏ 18.0R 17.8 17.6
♇ (1, 11, 21): ♍ 13.7 13.8 13.9

1966

	1	2	3	4	5	6	7	8	9	10	11	12	13	14	15	16	17	18	19	20	21	22	23	24	25	26	27	28	29	30	31
☉	♊ 10.1	11	12	12.9	13.9	14.9	15.8	16.8	17.7	18.7	19.6	20.6	21.6	22.5	23.5	24.4	25.4	26.3	27.3	28.2	29.2	♋ 0.1	1.1	2.1	3	4	4.9	5.9	6.8	7.8	
☽	♏ 10.9	24.6	♐ 8	21.2	♑ 4.2	16.9	29.3	♒ 11.5	23.6	♓ 5.5	17.4	29.3	♈ 11.3	23.5	♉ 6	18.8	♊ 2	15.5	29.4	♋ 13.5	27.9	♌ 12.4	26.9	♍ 11.3	25.6	♎ 9.7	23.7	♏ 7.4	20.8	♐ 4.1	
☿	♊ 15.9	18	20.2	22.3	24.4	26.4	28.4	♋ 0.4	2.4	4.3	6.1	8	9.7	11.5	13.2	14.8	16.5	18	19.6	21.1	22.5	23.9	25.3	26.6	27.8	29.1	♌ 0.2	1.4	2.4	3.5	
♀	♉ 0.3	1.5	2.6	3.8	4.9	6.1	7.2	8.4	9.6	10.7	11.9	13	14.2	15.4	16.5	17.7	18.9	20	21.2	22.4	23.6	24.7	25.9	27.1	28.3	29.4	♊ 0.6	1.8	3	4.2	
♂	♊ 2.2	2.9	3.6	4.3	5	5.7	6.4	7.2	7.9	8.6	9.3	10	10.7	11.4	12.1	12.8	13.5	14.1	14.8	15.5	16.2	16.9	17.6	18.3	19	19.7	20.4	21.1	21.7	22.4	

♃ (1, 6, 11, 16, 21, 26): ♋ 5.4 6.5 7.6 8.7 9.8 10.9
♄ (1, 6, 11, 16, 21, 26): ♓ 28.4 28.7 28.9 29.1 29.3 29.5
♅ (1, 11, 21): ♍ 15.5 15.6 15.8
♆ (1, 11, 21): ♏ 20.3R 20 19.8
♇ (1, 11, 21): ♍ 15.8 15.9 16

VII

1965

	1	2	3	4	5	6	7	8	9	10	11	12	13	14	15	16	17	18	19	20	21	22	23	24	25	26	27	28	29	30	31
☉	♋ 9	9.9	10.9	11.8	12.8	13.7	14.7	15.6	16.6	17.5	18.5	19.4	20.4	21.4	22.3	23.3	24.2	25.2	26.1	27.1	28	29	29.9	♌ 0.9	1.9	2.8	3.8	4.7	5.7	6.6	7.6
☽	♌ 4.4	19.4	♍ 4.1	18.5	♎ 2.5	16	29.1	♏ 11.9	24.4	♐ 6.7	18.8	♑ 0.7	12.6	24.5	♒ 6.3	18.2	♓ 0.1	12.1	24.3	♈ 6.6	19.2	♉ 2	15.3	28.9	♊ 13.1	27.6	♋ 12.5	27.7	♌ 13	28.2	♍ 13.1
☿	♋ 28.9	♌ 0.6	2.2	3.8	5.3	6.8	8.3	9.8	11.2	12.5	13.9	15.1	16.4	17.6	18.7	19.9	20.9	21.9	22.9	23.8	24.7	25.5	26.3	27	27.6	28.2	28.7	29.1	29.5	29.7	29.9
♀	♌ 0.1	1.3	2.6	3.8	5	6.2	7.4	8.6	9.9	11.1	12.3	13.5	14.7	15.9	17.2	18.4	19.6	20.8	22	23.2	24.4	25.6	26.8	28.1	29.3	♍ 0.5	1.7	2.9	4.1	5.3	6.5
♂	♎ 1	1.5	2	2.5	3	3.6	4.1	4.6	5.1	5.7	6.2	6.7	7.3	7.8	8.4	8.9	9.5	10	10.6	11.2	11.7	12.3	12.9	13.4	14	14.6	15.1	15.7	16.3	16.9	17.5

♃ (1, 6, 11, 16, 21, 26, 31): ♊ 16 17.1 18.2 19.2 20.3 21.3 22.3
♄ (1, 6, 11, 16, 21, 26, 31): ♓ 17.2R 17.2 17.1 17 16.8 16.6 16.4
♅ (1, 11, 21, 31): ♍ 11.5 11.9 12.4 12.9
♆ (1, 11, 21, 31): ♏ 17.4R 17.3 17.3 17.2D
♇ (1, 11, 21, 31): ♍ 14 14.2 14.5 14.8

1966

	1	2	3	4	5	6	7	8	9	10	11	12	13	14	15	16	17	18	19	20	21	22	23	24	25	26	27	28	29	30	31
☉	♋ 8.7	9.7	10.6	11.6	12.5	13.5	14.4	15.4	16.4	17.3	18.3	19.2	20.2	21.1	22.1	23	24	24.9	25.9	26.8	27.8	28.8	29.7	♌ 0.7	1.6	2.6	3.5	4.5	5.4	6.4	7.4
☽	♐ 17.2	♑ 0.1	12.8	25.2	♒ 7.5	19.7	♓ 1.7	13.6	25.4	♈ 7.3	19.3	♉ 1.5	14	26.8	♊ 10	23.7	♋ 7.9	22.4	♌ 7.1	22.1	♍ 7	21.7	♎ 6.2	20.4	♏ 4.3	17.8	♐ 1	14	26.8	♑ 9.4	21.8
☿	♌ 4.4	5.4	6.2	7	7.8	8.4	9.1	9.6	10.1	10.5	10.8	11.1	11.3	11.4	11.4R	11.4	11.2	11	10.7	10.4	9.9	9.4	8.9	8.2	7.6	6.9	6.2	5.4	4.7	4	3.3
♀	♊ 5.3	6.5	7.7	8.9	10.1	11.3	12.5	13.6	14.8	16	17.2	18.4	19.6	20.8	22	23.2	24.4	25.6	26.8	28	29.2	♋ 0.4	1.6	2.8	4	5.2	6.4	7.6	8.8	10	11.2
♂	♊ 23.1	23.8	24.5	25.2	25.8	26.5	27.2	27.9	28.6	29.2	29.9	♋ 0.6	1.3	1.9	2.6	3.3	4	4.6	5.3	6	6.6	7.3	8	8.7	9.3	10	10.6	11.3	12	12.6	13.3

♃ (1, 6, 11, 16, 21, 26, 31): ♋ 12.1 13.2 14.3 15.5 16.6 17.7 18.8
♄ (1, 6, 11, 16, 21, 26, 31): ♓ 29.6 29.7 29.7 29.7R 29.6 29.5 29.4
♅ (1, 11, 21, 31): ♍ 16.1 16.5 16.9 17.4
♆ (1, 11, 21, 31): ♏ 19.7R 19.5 19.4 19.4
♇ (1, 11, 21, 31): ♍ 16.1 16.3 16.5 16.8

VIII

1965

	1	2	3	4	5	6	7	8	9	10	11	12	13	14	15	16	17	18	19	20	21	22	23	24	25	26	27	28	29	30	31
☉	♌ 8.5	9.5	10.5	11.4	12.4	13.3	14.3	15.2	16.2	17.2	18.1	19.1	20	21	22	22.9	23.9	24.8	25.8	26.8	27.7	28.7	29.7	♍ 0.6	1.6	2.6	3.5	4.5	5.5	6.4	7.4
☽	♍ 27.7	♎ 11.8	25.4	♏ 8.5	21.3	♐ 3.7	15.8	27.8	♑ 9.7	21.5	♒ 3.4	15.2	27.2	♓ 9.2	21.3	♈ 3.6	16.1	28.7	♉ 11.6	24.8	♊ 8.3	22.2	♋ 6.6	21.3	♌ 6.3	21.4	♍ 6.5	21.5	♎ 6.1	20.3	♏ 4
☿	♍ 0.1	0.1R	0	♌ 29.9	29.7	29.4	29	28.5	27.9	27.3	26.6	25.8	25.1	24.2	23.4	22.6	21.7	21	20.2	19.6	19	18.5	18.1	17.8	17.7	17.6D	17.7	18	18.4	18.9	19.5
♀	♍ 7.7	8.9	10.1	11.3	12.6	13.8	15	16.2	17.4	18.6	19.8	21	22.2	23.4	24.6	25.8	27	28.2	29.4	♎ 0.6	1.8	3	4.1	5.3	6.5	7.7	8.9	10.1	11.3	12.5	13.7
♂	♎ 18.1	18.7	19.3	19.9	20.5	21.1	21.7	22.3	22.9	23.5	24.1	24.7	25.3	25.9	26.6	27.2	27.8	28.4	29.1	29.7	♏ 0.3	0.9	1.6	2.2	2.9	3.5	4.1	4.8	5.4	6.1	6.7

♃ (1, 6, 11, 16, 21, 26, 31): ♊ 22.5 23.4 24.3 25.2 26 26.8 27.5
♄ (1, 6, 11, 16, 21, 26, 31): ♓ 16.3R 16 15.7 15.4 15.1 14.7 14.3
♅ (1, 11, 21, 31): ♍ 13 13.5 14.1 14.7
♆ (1, 11, 21, 31): ♏ 17.2 17.3 17.4 17.5
♇ (1, 11, 21, 31): ♍ 14.8 15.1 15.4 15.8

1966

	1	2	3	4	5	6	7	8	9	10	11	12	13	14	15	16	17	18	19	20	21	22	23	24	25	26	27	28	29	30	31
☉	♌ 8.3	9.3	10.2	11.2	12.1	13.1	14.1	15	16	16.9	17.9	18.9	19.8	20.8	21.7	22.7	23.7	24.6	25.6	26.5	27.5	28.5	29.4	♍ 0.4	1.4	2.3	3.3	4.3	5.2	6.2	7.2
☽	♒ 4.1	16.2	28.2	♓ 10.1	22	♈ 3.8	15.7	27.7	♉ 9.8	22.3	♊ 5	18.2	♋ 1.9	16.1	♌ 0.7	15.7	♍ 0.9	16.1	♎ 1.2	16	♏ 0.4	14.3	27.9	♐ 11	23.9	♑ 6.5	18.8	♒ 1	13.1	25.1	♓ 7
☿	♌ 2.7R	2.1	1.6	1.2	0.8	0.6	0.4	0.3D	0.4	0.6	0.9	1.3	1.8	2.4	3.2	4	5	6.1	7.2	8.5	9.9	11.4	12.9	14.5	16.2	17.9	19.7	21.5	23.4	25.3	27.2
♀	♋ 12.4	13.6	14.8	16	17.2	18.4	19.6	20.9	22.1	23.3	24.5	25.7	26.9	28.1	29.4	♌ 0.6	1.8	3	4.2	5.5	6.7	7.9	9.1	10.4	11.6	12.8	14	15.3	16.5	17.7	18.9
♂	♋ 14	14.6	15.3	15.9	16.6	17.2	17.9	18.6	19.2	19.9	20.5	21.2	21.8	22.5	23.1	23.8	24.4	25.1	25.7	26.4	27	27.7	28.3	28.9	29.6	♌ 0.2	0.9	1.5	2.2	2.8	3.4

♃ (1, 6, 11, 16, 21, 26, 31): ♋ 19 20.1 21.2 22.2 23.2 24.3 25.2
♄ (1, 6, 11, 16, 21, 26, 31): ♓ 29.3R 29.2 28.9 28.7 28.4 28.1 27.7
♅ (1, 11, 21, 31): ♍ 17.5 18 18.6 19.2
♆ (1, 11, 21, 31): ♏ 19.4R 19.4D 19.5 19.6
♇ (1, 11, 21, 31): ♍ 16.9 17.2 17.5 17.8

IX

1965

	1	2	3	4	5	6	7	8	9	10	11	12	13	14	15	16	17	18	19	20	21	22	23	24	25	26	27	28	29	30	31
☉	♍ 8.4	9.3	10.3	11.3	12.2	13.2	14.2	15.1	16.1	17.1	18.1	19	20	21	22	22.9	23.9	24.9	25.9	26.8	27.8	28.8	29.8	♎ 0.7	1.7	2.7	3.7	4.7	5.6	6.6	
☽	♏ 17.2	30	♐ 12.4	24.6	♑ 6.5	18.4	♒ 0.2	12.1	24	♓ 6.1	18.3	♈ 0.6	13.1	25.8	♉ 8.6	21.7	♊ 4.9	18.5	♋ 2.3	16.4	♌ 0.9	15.5	♍ 0.3	15.1	29.8	♎ 14.3	28.4	♏ 12.1	25.3	♐ 8.1	
☿	♌ 20.3	21.2	22.2	23.4	24.6	25.9	27.4	28.9	♍ 0.5	2.1	3.8	5.6	7.3	9.2	11	12.8	14.7	16.6	18.5	20.3	22.2	24.1	25.9	27.7	29.6	♎ 1.4	3.2	5	6.8	8.5	
♀	♎ 14.9	16	17.2	18.4	19.6	20.8	22	23.1	24.3	25.5	26.7	27.9	29	♏ 0.2	1.4	2.6	3.7	4.9	6.1	7.2	8.4	9.6	10.8	11.9	13.1	14.2	15.4	16.6	17.7	18.9	
♂	♏ 7.4	8	8.7	9.3	10	10.7	11.3	12	12.7	13.3	14	14.7	15.3	16	16.7	17.4	18	18.7	19.4	20.1	20.8	21.5	22.1	22.8	23.5	24.2	24.9	25.6	26.3	27	

♃ (1, 6, 11, 16, 21, 26): ♊ 27.7 28.4 29 29.5 30 ♋ 0.4
♄ (1, 6, 11, 16, 21, 26): ♓ 14.2R 13.9 13.5 13.1 12.7 12.4
♅ (1, 11, 21): ♍ 14.8 15.4 16.1
♆ (1, 11, 21): ♏ 17.5 17.7 18
♇ (1, 11, 21): ♍ 15.8 16.2 16.5

1966

	1	2	3	4	5	6	7	8	9	10	11	12	13	14	15	16	17	18	19	20	21	22	23	24	25	26	27	28	29	30	31
☉	♍ 8.1	9.1	10.1	11	12	13	13.9	14.9	15.9	16.8	17.8	18.8	19.8	20.7	21.7	22.7	23.7	24.6	25.6	26.6	27.6	28.5	29.5	♎ 0.5	1.5	2.5	3.4	4.4	5.4	6.4	
☽	♓ 18.9	♈ 0.8	12.6	24.5	♉ 6.5	18.7	♊ 1.1	13.8	27	♋ 10.5	24.6	♌ 9.1	24	♍ 9.2	24.6	♎ 9.8	24.7	♏ 9.3	23.5	♐ 7.2	20.4	♑ 3.2	15.8	28.1	♒ 10.2	22.2	♓ 4.1	15.9	27.8	♈ 9.7	
☿	♌ 29.2	♍ 1.1	3.1	5	7	8.9	10.8	12.8	14.7	16.6	18.5	20.3	22.2	24	25.8	27.6	29.4	♎ 1.2	2.9	4.6	6.3	8	9.7	11.4	13	14.7	16.3	17.9	19.4	21	
♀	♌ 20.2	21.4	22.6	23.9	25.1	26.3	27.6	28.8	♍ 0	1.3	2.5	3.7	5	6.2	7.5	8.7	9.9	11.2	12.4	13.6	14.9	16.1	17.4	18.6	19.9	21.1	22.3	23.6	24.8	26.1	
♂	♌ 4.1	4.7	5.3	6	6.6	7.2	7.9	8.5	9.1	9.8	10.4	11	11.7	12.3	12.9	13.5	14.2	14.8	15.4	16	16.7	17.3	17.9	18.5	19.1	19.8	20.4	21	21.6	22.2	

♃ (1, 6, 11, 16, 21, 26): ♋ 25.4 26.4 27.3 28.2 29 29.8
♄ (1, 6, 11, 16, 21, 26): ♓ 27.7R 27.3 26.9 26.5 26.2 25.8
♅ (1, 11, 21): ♍ 19.3 19.9 20.5
♆ (1, 11, 21): ♏ 19.7 19.9 20.1
♇ (1, 11, 21): ♍ 17.9 18.2 18.6

X

1965

	1	2	3	4	5	6	7	8	9	10	11	12	13	14	15	16	17	18	19	20	21	22	23	24	25	26	27	28	29	30	31
☉	♎ 7.6	8.6	9.6	10.6	11.6	12.5	13.5	14.5	15.5	16.5	17.5	18.5	19.5	20.4	21.4	22.4	23.4	24.4	25.4	26.4	27.4	28.4	29.4	♏ 0.4	1.4	2.4	3.4	4.4	5.4	6.4	7.4
☽	♐ 20.6	♑ 2.8	14.8	26.6	♒ 8.5	20.4	♓ 2.4	14.6	26.9	♈ 9.5	22.3	♉ 5.3	18.5	♊ 1.9	15.4	29.2	♋ 13.1	27.1	♌ 11.3	25.7	♍ 10.1	24.4	♎ 8.7	22.8	♏ 6.6	20	♐ 3.2	15.9	28.4	♑ 10.6	22.6
☿	♎ 10.3	12	13.7	15.4	17.1	18.8	20.5	22.1	23.8	25.4	27	28.6	♏ 0.2	1.8	3.3	4.9	6.4	8	9.5	11	12.5	14	15.5	17	18.4	19.9	21.3	22.7	24.2	25.6	26.9
♀	♏ 20	21.2	22.3	23.5	24.6	25.8	26.9	28.1	29.2	♐ 0.4	1.5	2.6	3.8	4.9	6	7.2	8.3	9.4	10.5	11.6	12.8	13.9	15	16.1	17.2	18.3	19.4	20.5	21.6	22.7	23.8
♂	♏ 27.7	28.4	29.1	29.8	♐ 0.5	1.2	1.9	2.6	3.3	4.1	4.8	5.5	6.2	6.9	7.6	8.4	9.1	9.8	10.5	11.3	12	12.7	13.4	14.2	14.9	15.6	16.4	17.1	17.8	18.6	19.3

♃ (1, 6, 11, 16, 21, 26, 31): ♋ 0.7 1 1.2 1.3 1.3R 1.3 1.1
♄ (1, 6, 11, 16, 21, 26, 31): ♓ 12.0R 11.7 11.5 11.2 11 10.8 10.7
♅ (1, 11, 21, 31): ♍ 16.7 17.2 17.8 18.3
♆ (1, 11, 21, 31): ♏ 18.3 18.6 18.9 19.3
♇ (1, 11, 21, 31): ♍ 16.9 17.2 17.5 17.8

1966

	1	2	3	4	5	6	7	8	9	10	11	12	13	14	15	16	17	18	19	20	21	22	23	24	25	26	27	28	29	30	31
☉	♎ 7.4	8.4	9.3	10.3	11.3	12.3	13.3	14.3	15.3	16.2	17.2	18.2	19.2	20.2	21.2	22.2	23.2	24.2	25.2	26.2	27.2	28.1	29.1	♏ 0.1	1.1	2.1	3.1	4.1	5.1	6.1	7.1
☽	♈ 21.6	♉ 3.6	15.8	28.1	♊ 10.6	23.4	♋ 6.5	20	♌ 3.8	18.1	♍ 2.8	17.7	♎ 2.8	17.9	♏ 2.9	17.5	♐ 1.8	15.6	28.9	♑ 11.9	24.5	♒ 6.8	18.9	♓ 0.8	12.7	24.5	♈ 6.4	18.4	♉ 0.5	12.7	25.1
☿	♎ 22.6	24.1	25.6	27.2	28.7	♏ 0.1	1.6	3.1	4.5	5.9	7.3	8.7	10.1	11.5	12.8	14.2	15.5	16.7	18	19.3	20.5	21.7	22.8	23.9	25	26.1	27.1	28	28.9	29.8	♐ 0.5
♀	♍ 27.3	28.6	29.8	♎ 1.1	2.3	3.6	4.8	6.1	7.3	8.6	9.8	11.1	12.3	13.6	14.8	16.1	17.3	18.6	19.8	21.1	22.3	23.6	24.8	26.1	27.3	28.6	29.8	♏ 1.1	2.3	3.6	4.9
♂	♌ 22.8	23.5	24.1	24.7	25.3	25.9	26.5	27.1	27.7	28.3	28.9	29.5	♍ 0.1	0.7	1.4	2	2.6	3.2	3.8	4.3	4.9	5.5	6.1	6.7	7.3	7.9	8.5	9.1	9.7	10.3	10.9

♃ (1, 6, 11, 16, 21, 26, 31): ♌ 0.5 1.2 1.8 2.4 2.9 3.4 3.7
♄ (1, 6, 11, 16, 21, 26, 31): ♓ 25.4R 25 24.7 24.3 24 23.8 23.5
♅ (1, 11, 21, 31): ♍ 21.1 21.7 22.3 22.8
♆ (1, 11, 21, 31): ♏ 20.4 20.7 21 21.4
♇ (1, 11, 21, 31): ♍ 19 19.3 19.6 19.9

XI

1965

	1	2	3	4	5	6	7	8	9	10	11	12	13	14	15	16	17	18	19	20	21	22	23	24	25	26	27	28	29	30	31
☉	♏ 8.4	9.4	10.4	11.4	12.4	13.4	14.4	15.4	16.4	17.4	18.4	19.4	20.4	21.4	22.4	23.4	24.4	25.4	26.5	27.5	28.5	29.5	♐ 0.5	1.5	2.5	3.5	4.5	5.6	6.6	7.6	
☽	♒ 4.5	16.4	28.3	♓ 10.3	22.6	♈ 5	17.8	♉ 0.8	14.2	27.8	♊ 11.6	25.6	♋ 9.7	23.9	♌ 8.2	22.4	♍ 6.5	20.6	♎ 4.5	18.3	♏ 1.9	15.3	28.4	♐ 11.3	23.9	♑ 6.3	18.5	♒ 0.5	12.4	24.2	
☿	♏ 28.3	29.7	♐ 1	2.3	3.6	4.9	6.2	7.4	8.6	9.8	10.9	12	13	14	14.9	15.8	16.6	17.3	17.9	18.4	18.7	19	19.1	19.0R	18.8	18.4	17.8	17	16	14.9	
♀	♐ 24.8	25.9	27	28.1	29.1	♑ 0.2	1.3	2.3	3.4	4.4	5.4	6.5	7.5	8.5	9.5	10.6	11.6	12.6	13.5	14.5	15.5	16.5	17.4	18.4	19.3	20.3	21.2	22.1	23	23.9	
♂	♐ 20.1	20.8	21.5	22.3	23	23.8	24.5	25.3	26	26.8	27.5	28.3	29	29.8	♑ 0.5	1.3	2	2.8	3.6	4.3	5.1	5.8	6.6	7.4	8.1	8.9	9.7	10.4	11.2	12	

♃ (1, 6, 11, 16, 21, 26): ♋ 1.1R 0.8 0.5 0.1 ♊ 29.6 29.1
♄ (1, 6, 11, 16, 21, 26): ♓ 10.6R 10.5 10.5 10.5D 10.5 10.6
♅ (1, 11, 21): ♍ 18.3 18.7 19.1
♆ (1, 11, 21): ♏ 19.3 19.7 20.1
♇ (1, 11, 21): ♍ 17.8 18 18.2

1966

	1	2	3	4	5	6	7	8	9	10	11	12	13	14	15	16	17	18	19	20	21	22	23	24	25	26	27	28	29	30	31
☉	♏ 8.1	9.1	10.1	11.1	12.1	13.1	14.1	15.1	16.1	17.1	18.2	19.2	20.2	21.2	22.2	23.2	24.2	25.2	26.2	27.2	28.2	29.2	♐ 0.3	1.3	2.3	3.3	4.3	5.3	6.3	7.3	
☽	♊ 7.6	20.4	♋ 3.4	16.7	♌ 0.2	14	28.1	♍ 12.5	27	♎ 11.7	26.4	♏ 11	25.5	♐ 9.6	23.4	♑ 6.9	19.9	♒ 2.6	14.9	27.1	♓ 9	20.9	♈ 2.7	14.6	26.7	♉ 8.9	21.3	♊ 4	16.9	♋ 0.1	
☿	♐ 1.2	1.8	2.3	2.7	3	3.2	3.2R	3.1	2.9	2.4	1.8	1.1	0.1	♏ 29.1	27.9	26.6	25.3	23.9	22.6	21.4	20.2	19.3	18.4	17.8	17.4	17.2	17.1D	17.3	17.6	18	
♀	♏ 6.1	7.4	8.6	9.9	11.1	12.4	13.6	14.9	16.1	17.4	18.7	19.9	21.2	22.4	23.7	24.9	26.2	27.4	28.7	30	♐ 1.2	2.5	3.7	5	6.2	7.5	8.8	10	11.3	12.5	
♂	♍ 11.4	12	12.6	13.2	13.8	14.3	14.9	15.5	16.1	16.6	17.2	17.8	18.4	18.9	19.5	20.1	20.6	21.2	21.8	22.3	22.9	23.4	24	24.5	25.1	25.6	26.2	26.7	27.3	27.8	

♃ (1, 6, 11, 16, 21, 26): ♌ 3.8 4.1 4.3 4.4 4.5 4.5R
♄ (1, 6, 11, 16, 21, 26): ♓ 23.5R 23.3 23.1 23 22.9 22.9
♅ (1, 11, 21): ♍ 22.9 23.3 23.7
♆ (1, 11, 21): ♏ 21.4 21.8 22.1
♇ (1, 11, 21): ♍ 19.9 20.2 20.4

XII

1965

	1	2	3	4	5	6	7	8	9	10	11	12	13	14	15	16	17	18	19	20	21	22	23	24	25	26	27	28	29	30	31
☉	♐ 8.6	9.6	10.6	11.6	12.7	13.7	14.7	15.7	16.7	17.7	18.7	19.8	20.8	21.8	22.8	23.8	24.8	25.9	26.9	27.9	28.9	29.9	♑ 1	2	3	4	5	6.1	7.1	8.1	9.1
☽	♓ 6.1	18.1	♈ 0.3	12.8	25.6	♉ 8.7	22.2	♊ 6.1	20.4	♋ 4.9	19.5	♌ 4.2	18.8	♍ 3.2	17.4	♎ 1.4	15.1	28.5	♏ 11.7	24.7	♐ 7.4	20	♑ 2.3	14.6	26.6	♒ 8.6	20.5	♓ 2.3	14.2	26.1	♈ 8.3
☿	♐ 13.7R	12.4	11	9.6	8.3	7.1	5.9	5	4.2	3.5	3.1	2.9	2.8D	2.9	3.2	3.6	4.1	4.8	5.5	6.3	7.2	8.2	9.3	10.4	11.5	12.7	13.9	15.2	16.5	17.8	19.1
♀	♑ 24.8	25.7	26.5	27.4	28.2	29	29.8	♒ 0.6	1.4	2.2	2.9	3.7	4.4	5.1	5.7	6.4	7	7.6	8.2	8.8	9.3	9.9	10.4	10.8	11.2	11.7	12	12.4	12.7	12.9	13.2
♂	♑ 12.7	13.5	14.3	15	15.8	16.6	17.4	18.1	18.9	19.7	20.5	21.2	22	22.8	23.6	24.3	25.1	25.9	26.7	27.5	28.3	29	29.8	♒ 0.6	1.4	2.2	3	3.7	4.5	5.3	6.1

♃ (1, 6, 11, 16, 21, 26, 31): ♊ 28.5R 27.9 27.2 26.6 25.9 25.2 24.6
♄ (1, 6, 11, 16, 21, 26, 31): ♓ 10.7 10.9 11.1 11.4 11.7 12 12.4
♅ (1, 11, 21, 31): ♍ 19.4 19.5 19.6 19.6R
♆ (1, 11, 21, 31): ♏ 20.4 20.8 21.1 21.4
♇ (1, 11, 21, 31): ♍ 18.4 18.4 18.5R 18.4

1966

	1	2	3	4	5	6	7	8	9	10	11	12	13	14	15	16	17	18	19	20	21	22	23	24	25	26	27	28	29	30	31
☉	♐ 8.3	9.4	10.4	11.4	12.4	13.4	14.4	15.5	16.5	17.5	18.5	19.5	20.5	21.6	22.6	23.6	24.6	25.6	26.6	27.7	28.7	29.7	♑ 0.7	1.7	2.7	3.8	4.8	5.8	6.8	7.8	8.9
☽	♋ 13.5	27.1	♌ 10.9	24.9	♍ 8.9	23.1	♎ 7.3	21.5	♏ 5.7	19.9	♐ 3.9	17.8	♑ 1.4	14.7	27.7	♒ 10.4	22.7	♓ 4.9	16.8	28.7	♈ 10.5	22.4	♉ 4.5	16.8	29.3	♊ 12.3	25.5	♋ 9.1	23	♌ 7.1	21.3
☿	♏ 18.6	19.3	20.1	21	22	23.1	24.2	25.4	26.6	27.9	29.2	♐ 0.5	1.8	3.2	4.6	6	7.5	8.9	10.4	11.8	13.3	14.8	16.3	17.8	19.3	20.8	22.3	23.8	25.4	26.9	28.4
♀	♐ 13.8	15	16.3	17.6	18.8	20.1	21.3	22.6	23.8	25.1	26.3	27.6	28.9	♑ 0.1	1.4	2.6	3.9	5.1	6.4	7.7	8.9	10.2	11.4	12.7	13.9	15.2	16.4	17.7	19	20.2	21.5
♂	♍ 28.4	28.9	29.5	30	♎ 0.5	1.1	1.6	2.1	2.6	3.2	3.7	4.2	4.7	5.3	5.8	6.3	6.8	7.3	7.8	8.3	8.8	9.3	9.8	10.3	10.8	11.3	11.8	12.2	12.7	13.2	13.7

♃ (1, 6, 11, 16, 21, 26, 31): ♌ 4.3R 4.1 3.9 3.5 3.1 2.6 2
♄ (1, 6, 11, 16, 21, 26, 31): ♓ 22.9 23 23.1 23.3 23.4 23.7 24
♅ (1, 11, 21, 31): ♍ 24 24.3 24.4 24.4R
♆ (1, 11, 21, 31): ♏ 22.5 22.9 23.2 23.5
♇ (1, 11, 21, 31): ♍ 20.5 20.6 20.6 20.6R

I

II

III

IV

V

VI

VII

VIII

IX

X

XI

XII

I (1969)

	1	2	3	4	5	6	7	8	9	10	11	12	13	14	15	16	17	18	19	20	21	22	23	24	25	26	27	28	29	30	31
☉	♑ 10.4	11.4	12.4	13.5	14.5	15.5	16.5	17.5	18.6	19.6	20.6	21.6	22.6	23.7	24.7	25.7	26.7	27.7	28.7	29.8	♒ 0.8	1.8	2.8	3.8	4.9	5.9	6.9	7.9	8.9	9.9	10.9
☽	♊ 10.3	22.1	♋ 4	16	28	♌ 10.2	22.4	♍ 4.8	17.4	♎ 0.2	13.4	26.8	♏ 10.7	25	♐ 9.6	24.6	♑ 9.7	24.8	♒ 9.8	24.4	♓ 8.6	22.4	♈ 5.6	18.4	♉ 0.9	13.1	25.1	♊ 7	18.8	♋ 0.7	12.6
☿	♑ 24.6	26.1	27.7	29.2	♒ 0.8	2.3	3.7	5.2	6.6	7.9	9.2	10.4	11.5	12.6	13.5	14.3	15	15.5	15.8	16	16.0R	15.8	15.4	14.8	14.1	13.2	12.1	11	9.7	8.5	7.2
♀	♒ 25.7	26.8	27.9	29.1	♓ 0.2	1.3	2.4	3.5	4.7	5.8	6.9	8	9.1	10.2	11.2	12.3	13.4	14.5	15.5	16.6	17.6	18.7	19.7	20.8	21.8	22.8	23.9	24.9	25.9	26.9	27.9
♂	♏ 1.2	1.8	2.3	2.9	3.5	4	4.6	5.1	5.7	6.3	6.8	7.4	7.9	8.5	9	9.6	10.1	10.7	11.2	11.8	12.3	12.8	13.4	13.9	14.4	15	15.5	16	16.6	17.1	17.6

♃ 1: ♎ 5.5 · 6: 5.7 · 11: 5.9 · 16: 6 · 21: 6.1R · 26: 6 · 31: 5.9
♄ 1: ♈ 18.8 · 6: 18.9 · 11: 19.1 · 16: 19.3 · 21: 19.5 · 26: 19.8 · 31: 20.2
♅ 1: ♎ 4 · 11: 4.0R · 21: 3.9 · 31: 3.8
♆ 1: ♏ 27.8 · 11: 28.1 · 21: 28.3 · 31: 28.5
♇ 1: ♍ 25.1R · 11: 25 · 21: 24.9 · 31: 24.8

II (1969)

	1	2	3	4	5	6	7	8	9	10	11	12	13	14	15	16	17	18	19	20	21	22	23	24	25	26	27	28	29	30	31
☉	♒ 12	13	14	15	16	17	18	19.1	20.1	21.1	22.1	23.1	24.1	25.1	26.1	27.1	28.2	29.2	♓ 0.2	1.2	2.2	3.2	4.2	5.2	6.2	7.2	8.2	9.2			
☽	♋ 24.7	♌ 6.9	19.2	♍ 1.7	14.4	27.3	♎ 10.4	23.6	♏ 7.2	21	♐ 5.1	19.4	♑ 4	18.6	♒ 3.4	18	♓ 2.3	16.4	♈ 0.1	13.4	26.3	♉ 8.8	21.1	♊ 3.2	15.1	26.9	♋ 8.8	20.8			
☿	♒ 6.0R	4.9	3.9	3	2.2	1.5	1	0.6	0.4	0.3	0.3D	0.4	0.6	1	1.4	1.9	2.5	3.2	3.9	4.7	5.6	6.5	7.5	8.5	9.5	10.6	11.8	12.9			
♀	♓ 28.8	29.8	♈ 0.8	1.7	2.7	3.6	4.5	5.5	6.4	7.2	8.1	9	9.9	10.7	11.5	12.4	13.2	13.9	14.7	15.5	16.2	16.9	17.6	18.3	19	19.6	20.3	20.9			
♂	♏ 18.1	18.6	19.2	19.7	20.2	20.7	21.2	21.7	22.2	22.7	23.2	23.7	24.2	24.7	25.2	25.7	26.1	26.6	27.1	27.6	28	28.5	29	29.4	29.9	♐ 0.3	0.8	1.2			

♃ 1: ♎ 5.8R · 6: 5.6 · 11: 5.3 · 16: 5 · 21: 4.5 · 26: 4
♄ 1: ♈ 20.2 · 6: 20.6 · 11: 21 · 16: 21.5 · 21: 21.9 · 26: 22.4
♅ 1: ♎ 3.8R · 11: 3.5 · 21: 3.2
♆ 1: ♏ 28.5 · 11: 28.6 · 21: 28.7
♇ 1: ♍ 24.8R · 11: 24.6 · 21: 24.3

III (1969)

	1	2	3	4	5	6	7	8	9	10	11	12	13	14	15	16	17	18	19	20	21	22	23	24	25	26	27	28	29	30	31
☉	♓ 10.2	11.2	12.2	13.2	14.2	15.2	16.3	17.3	18.3	19.3	20.2	21.2	22.2	23.2	24.2	25.2	26.2	27.2	28.2	29.2	♈ 0.2	1.2	2.2	3.2	4.2	5.2	6.2	7.1	8.1	9.1	10.1
☽	♌ 2.9	15.3	27.8	♍ 10.6	23.6	♎ 6.9	20.4	♏ 4	17.9	♐ 1.9	16	♑ 0.2	14.4	28.7	♒ 12.9	27	♓ 11	24.7	♈ 8.1	21.2	♉ 4.1	16.6	28.9	♊ 11	22.9	♋ 4.8	16.7	28.7	♌ 10.8	23.2	♍ 5.9
☿	♒ 14.1	15.4	16.6	17.9	19.2	20.5	21.9	23.3	24.7	26.1	27.6	29.1	♓ 0.6	2.1	3.6	5.2	6.8	8.4	10	11.6	13.3	15	16.7	18.4	20.2	21.9	23.7	25.5	27.4	29.2	♈ 1.1
♀	♈ 21.4	22	22.5	23	23.5	24	24.4	24.8	25.1	25.5	25.8	26	26.2	26.4	26.6	26.7	26.8	26.8	26.8R	26.8	26.7	26.6	26.4	26.2	26	25.7	25.3	25	24.6	24.1	23.6
♂	♐ 1.7	2.1	2.5	3	3.4	3.8	4.2	4.6	5.1	5.5	5.9	6.3	6.6	7	7.4	7.8	8.1	8.5	8.9	9.2	9.6	9.9	10.2	10.6	10.9	11.2	11.5	11.8	12.1	12.4	12.7

♃ 1: ♎ 3.7R · 6: 3.1 · 11: 2.5 · 16: 1.9 · 21: 1.3 · 26: 0.6 · 31: ♍ 30
♄ 1: ♈ 22.7 · 6: 23.3 · 11: 23.8 · 16: 24.4 · 21: 25 · 26: 25.6 · 31: 26.2
♅ 1: ♎ 2.9R · 11: 2.5 · 21: 2 · 31: 1.6
♆ 1: ♏ 28.7R · 11: 28.7 · 21: 28.6 · 31: 28.5
♇ 1: ♍ 24.1R · 11: 23.9 · 21: 23.6 · 31: 23.3

IV (1969)

	1	2	3	4	5	6	7	8	9	10	11	12	13	14	15	16	17	18	19	20	21	22	23	24	25	26	27	28	29	30	31
☉	♈ 11.1	12.1	13.1	14.1	15	16	17	18	19	20	20.9	21.9	22.9	23.9	24.9	25.8	26.8	27.8	28.8	29.7	♉ 0.7	1.7	2.7	3.6	4.6	5.6	6.6	7.5	8.5	9.5	
☽	♍ 18.9	♎ 2.2	15.8	29.8	♏ 13.9	28.2	♐ 12.6	27	♑ 11.3	25.4	♒ 9.5	23.3	♓ 7	20.5	♈ 3.7	16.8	29.6	♉ 12.2	24.6	♊ 6.9	18.9	♋ 0.9	12.7	24.6	♌ 6.6	18.7	♍ 1.1	13.8	26.8	♎ 10.3	
☿	♈ 3	4.9	6.9	8.9	10.9	12.9	14.9	17	19	21.1	23.2	25.3	27.4	29.5	♉ 1.6	3.7	5.8	7.8	9.8	11.8	13.8	15.7	17.6	19.4	21.2	22.9	24.6	26.2	27.7	29.1	
♀	♈ 23.1R	22.6	22	21.5	20.9	20.3	19.6	19	18.4	17.7	17.1	16.5	15.9	15.3	14.8	14.2	13.7	13.3	12.8	12.4	12	11.7	11.4	11.2	11	10.8	10.6	10.6	10.5	10.5D	
♂	♐ 12.9	13.2	13.5	13.7	13.9	14.2	14.4	14.6	14.8	15	15.2	15.4	15.5	15.7	15.8	16	16.1	16.2	16.3	16.4	16.5	16.6	16.6	16.7	16.7	16.7	16.8	16.8R	16.7	16.7	

♃ 1: ♍ 29.9R · 6: 29.2 · 11: 28.7 · 16: 28.1 · 21: 27.6 · 26: 27.2
♄ 1: ♈ 26.3 · 6: 27 · 11: 27.6 · 16: 28.2 · 21: 28.9 · 26: 29.5
♅ 1: ♎ 1.6R · 11: 1.2 · 21: 0.8
♆ 1: ♏ 28.4R · 11: 28.3 · 21: 28
♇ 1: ♍ 23.3R · 11: 23.1 · 21: 22.8

V (1969)

	1	2	3	4	5	6	7	8	9	10	11	12	13	14	15	16	17	18	19	20	21	22	23	24	25	26	27	28	29	30	31
☉	♉ 10.5	11.4	12.4	13.4	14.3	15.3	16.3	17.2	18.2	19.2	20.1	21.1	22.1	23	24	25	25.9	26.9	27.8	28.8	29.8	♊ 0.7	1.7	2.7	3.6	4.6	5.5	6.5	7.5	8.4	9.4
☽	♎ 24.2	♏ 8.5	23	♐ 7.8	22.6	♑ 7.4	21.9	♒ 6.2	20.2	♓ 3.9	17.3	♈ 0.5	13.4	26.1	♉ 8.6	21	♊ 3.2	15.3	27.3	♋ 9.2	21	♌ 2.9	14.8	26.9	♍ 9.2	21.8	♎ 4.9	18.3	♏ 2.3	16.7	♐ 1.6
☿	♊ 0.5	1.8	3	4.2	5.3	6.3	7.2	8.1	8.8	9.5	10.1	10.6	11.1	11.4	11.7	11.9	12	12.0R	12	11.8	11.6	11.4	11	10.6	10.2	9.7	9.2	8.6	8.1	7.5	7
♀	♈ 10.5	10.6	10.7	10.8	11	11.2	11.5	11.8	12.1	12.4	12.8	13.2	13.6	14.1	14.5	15	15.6	16.1	16.7	17.3	17.9	18.5	19.2	19.9	20.6	21.3	22	22.7	23.5	24.2	25
♂	♐ 16.7R	16.6	16.6	16.5	16.4	16.3	16.2	16.1	15.9	15.8	15.6	15.4	15.2	15	14.8	14.6	14.4	14.1	13.9	13.6	13.3	13.1	12.8	12.5	12.2	11.9	11.5	11.2	10.9	10.6	10.2

♃ 1: ♍ 26.8R · 6: 26.6 · 11: 26.3 · 16: 26.2 · 21: 26.1 · 26: 26.1D · 31: 26.2
♄ 1: ♉ 0.1 · 6: 0.8 · 11: 1.4 · 16: 2 · 21: 2.6 · 26: 3.2 · 31: 3.7
♅ 1: ♎ 0.4R · 11: 0.2 · 21: ♍ 30 · 31: 29.9
♆ 1: ♏ 27.8R · 11: 27.5 · 21: 27.3 · 31: 27
♇ 1: ♍ 22.7R · 11: 22.5 · 21: 22.4 · 31: 22.4

VI (1969)

	1	2	3	4	5	6	7	8	9	10	11	12	13	14	15	16	17	18	19	20	21	22	23	24	25	26	27	28	29	30	31
☉	♊ 10.3	11.3	12.3	13.2	14.2	15.1	16.1	17	18	18.9	19.9	20.9	21.8	22.8	23.7	24.7	25.6	26.6	27.5	28.5	29.5	♋ 0.4	1.4	2.3	3.3	4.2	5.2	6.1	7.1	8	
☽	♐ 16.6	♑ 1.8	16.9	♒ 1.8	16.3	♓ 0.4	14.2	27.5	♈ 10.5	23.2	♉ 5.6	17.9	♊ 0.1	12.1	24.1	♋ 6	17.9	29.7	♌ 11.6	23.5	♍ 5.6	17.9	♎ 0.5	13.5	26.8	♏ 10.7	25.1	♐ 9.9	25.1	♑ 10.4	
☿	♊ 6.4R	5.9	5.4	5	4.6	4.2	3.9	3.7	3.5	3.4	3.4D	3.5	3.6	3.9	4.1	4.5	4.9	5.5	6	6.7	7.4	8.2	9.1	10	11	12.1	13.2	14.4	15.7	17	
♀	♈ 25.8	26.6	27.4	28.3	29.1	29.9	♉ 0.8	1.7	2.6	3.5	4.3	5.3	6.2	7.1	8	9	9.9	10.9	11.8	12.8	13.8	14.8	15.7	16.7	17.7	18.7	19.7	20.8	21.8	22.8	
♂	♐ 9.9R	9.5	9.2	8.9	8.5	8.2	7.8	7.5	7.2	6.8	6.5	6.2	5.9	5.6	5.3	5	4.7	4.5	4.2	4	3.7	3.5	3.3	3.1	2.9	2.7	2.6	2.4	2.3	2.2	

♃ 1: ♍ 26.2 · 6: 26.4 · 11: 26.6 · 16: 26.9 · 21: 27.3 · 26: 27.7
♄ 1: ♉ 3.9 · 6: 4.4 · 11: 4.9 · 16: 5.4 · 21: 5.9 · 26: 6.3
♅ 1: ♍ 29.9R · 11: 29.9D · 21: 30
♆ 1: ♏ 27.0R · 11: 26.7 · 21: 26.5
♇ 1: ♍ 22.4R · 11: 22.4D · 21: 22.5

VII (1969)

	1	2	3	4	5	6	7	8	9	10	11	12	13	14	15	16	17	18	19	20	21	22	23	24	25	26	27	28	29	30	31
☉	♋ 9	9.9	10.9	11.9	12.8	13.8	14.7	15.7	16.6	17.6	18.5	19.5	20.4	21.4	22.3	23.3	24.2	25.2	26.2	27.1	28.1	29	30	♌ 0.9	1.9	2.8	3.8	4.8	5.7	6.7	7.6
☽	♑ 25.7	♒ 10.8	25.5	♓ 9.8	23.7	♈ 7	20	♉ 2.7	15	27.2	♊ 9.3	21.2	♋ 3.1	14.9	26.8	♌ 8.7	20.6	♍ 2.7	14.8	27.2	♎ 9.8	22.8	♏ 6.1	19.9	♐ 4.1	18.7	♑ 3.7	18.8	♒ 4.1	19.2	♓ 4
☿	♊ 18.4	19.8	21.3	22.9	24.5	26.2	27.9	29.7	♋ 1.5	3.4	5.4	7.3	9.3	11.4	13.4	15.5	17.7	19.8	21.9	24.1	26.2	28.3	♌ 0.4	2.5	4.6	6.7	8.8	10.8	12.8	14.8	16.7
♀	♉ 23.8	24.9	25.9	26.9	28	29	♊ 0.1	1.2	2.2	3.3	4.4	5.4	6.5	7.6	8.7	9.7	10.8	11.9	13	14.1	15.2	16.3	17.4	18.5	19.6	20.8	21.9	23	24.1	25.2	26.4
♂	♐ 2.1R	2	1.9	1.8	1.8	1.7	1.7	1.7	1.7D	1.7	1.8	1.8	1.9	1.9	2	2.1	2.2	2.4	2.5	2.6	2.8	3	3.2	3.4	3.6	3.8	4	4.3	4.5	4.8	5.1

♃ 1: ♍ 28.2 · 6: 28.8 · 11: 29.4 · 16: ♎ 0.1 · 21: 0.8 · 26: 1.5 · 31: 2.3
♄ 1: ♉ 6.8 · 6: 7.2 · 11: 7.5 · 16: 7.8 · 21: 8.1 · 26: 8.4 · 31: 8.6
♅ 1: ♎ 0.1 · 11: 0.4 · 21: 0.7 · 31: 1.1
♆ 1: ♏ 26.3R · 11: 26.1 · 21: 26 · 31: 26
♇ 1: ♍ 22.6 · 11: 22.8 · 21: 23 · 31: 23.3

VIII (1969)

	1	2	3	4	5	6	7	8	9	10	11	12	13	14	15	16	17	18	19	20	21	22	23	24	25	26	27	28	29	30	31
☉	♌ 8.6	9.5	10.5	11.4	12.4	13.4	14.3	15.3	16.2	17.2	18.2	19.1	20.1	21	22	23	23.9	24.9	25.8	26.8	27.8	28.7	29.7	♍ 0.7	1.6	2.6	3.6	4.5	5.5	6.5	7.4
☽	♓ 18.4	♈ 2.3	15.8	28.9	♉ 11.6	24	♊ 6.1	18.1	♋ 0	11.9	23.7	♌ 5.6	17.6	29.7	♍ 11.9	24.3	♎ 6.9	19.7	♏ 2.8	16.2	29.9	♐ 13.9	28.3	♑ 12.9	27.8	♒ 12.7	27.5	♓ 12.1	26.5	♈ 10.5	24
☿	♌ 18.7	20.6	22.5	24.3	26.1	27.9	29.7	♍ 1.4	3.2	4.9	6.5	8.2	9.8	11.4	12.9	14.5	16	17.5	18.9	20.4	21.8	23.2	24.5	25.8	27.1	28.4	29.7	♎ 0.9	2	3.2	4.3
♀	♊ 27.5	28.6	29.8	♋ 0.9	2	3.2	4.3	5.4	6.6	7.7	8.9	10	11.2	12.3	13.5	14.7	15.8	17	18.1	19.3	20.5	21.6	22.8	24	25.2	26.3	27.5	28.7	29.9	♌ 1.1	2.2
♂	♐ 5.4	5.7	6	6.3	6.6	6.9	7.3	7.6	8	8.4	8.7	9.1	9.5	9.9	10.3	10.8	11.2	11.6	12.1	12.5	13	13.4	13.9	14.4	14.9	15.3	15.8	16.3	16.8	17.4	17.9

♃ 1: ♎ 2.5 · 6: 3.3 · 11: 4.2 · 16: 5.1 · 21: 6 · 26: 7 · 31: 8
♄ 1: ♉ 8.6 · 6: 8.7 · 11: 8.9 · 16: 8.9 · 21: 8.9 · 26: 8.9R · 31: 8.9
♅ 1: ♎ 1.1 · 11: 1.6 · 21: 2.1 · 31: 2.7
♆ 1: ♏ 25.9R · 11: 25.9D · 21: 26 · 31: 26.1
♇ 1: ♍ 23.3 · 11: 23.6 · 21: 23.9 · 31: 24.3

IX (1969)

	1	2	3	4	5	6	7	8	9	10	11	12	13	14	15	16	17	18	19	20	21	22	23	24	25	26	27	28	29	30	31
☉	♍ 8.4	9.4	10.3	11.3	12.3	13.2	14.2	15.2	16.1	17.1	18.1	19.1	20	21	22	23	23.9	24.9	25.9	26.9	27.8	28.8	29.8	♎ 0.8	1.8	2.7	3.7	4.7	5.7	6.7	
☽	♉ 7.2	19.9	♊ 2.4	14.5	26.5	♋ 8.4	20.3	♌ 2.2	14.2	26.3	♍ 8.5	21	♎ 3.7	16.6	29.8	♏ 13.1	26.7	♐ 10.5	24.6	♑ 8.7	23.1	♒ 7.5	22	♓ 6.4	20.6	♈ 4.7	18.5	♉ 1.9	15.1	27.8	
☿	♎ 5.4	6.4	7.4	8.3	9.2	10.1	10.8	11.6	12.3	12.9	13.4	13.9	14.2	14.5	14.7	14.8	14.8R	14.7	14.5	14.2	13.7	13.2	12.5	11.7	10.8	9.8	8.7	7.6	6.5	5.4	
♀	♌ 3.4	4.6	5.8	7	8.2	9.4	10.6	11.8	13	14.2	15.4	16.6	17.8	19	20.2	21.4	22.6	23.8	25	26.2	27.4	28.6	29.8	♍ 1.1	2.3	3.5	4.7	5.9	7.1	8.4	
♂	♐ 18.4	18.9	19.5	20	20.5	21.1	21.6	22.2	22.8	23.3	23.9	24.5	25.1	25.6	26.2	26.8	27.4	28	28.6	29.2	29.8	♑ 0.5	1.1	1.7	2.3	3	3.6	4.2	4.9	5.5	

♃ 1: ♎ 8.2 · 6: 9.2 · 11: 10.2 · 16: 11.3 · 21: 12.3 · 26: 13.4
♄ 1: ♉ 8.8R · 6: 8.7 · 11: 8.6 · 16: 8.4 · 21: 8.1 · 26: 7.9
♅ 1: ♎ 2.8 · 11: 3.4 · 21: 4
♆ 1: ♏ 26.1 · 11: 26.3 · 21: 26.5
♇ 1: ♍ 24.3 · 11: 24.7 · 21: 25

X (1969)

	1	2	3	4	5	6	7	8	9	10	11	12	13	14	15	16	17	18	19	20	21	22	23	24	25	26	27	28	29	30	31
☉	♎ 7.6	8.6	9.6	10.6	11.6	12.6	13.6	14.5	15.5	16.5	17.5	18.5	19.5	20.5	21.5	22.5	23.4	24.4	25.4	26.4	27.4	28.4	29.4	♏ 0.4	1.4	2.4	3.4	4.4	5.4	6.4	7.4
☽	♊ 10.3	22.5	♋ 4.6	16.4	28.3	♌ 10.2	22.2	♍ 4.4	16.8	29.6	♎ 12.6	25.9	♏ 9.5	23.3	♐ 7.3	21.4	♑ 5.6	19.7	♒ 3.9	18	♓ 2.1	16	29.8	♈ 13.5	26.9	♉ 10.1	23.1	♊ 5.8	18.2	♋ 0.4	12.4
☿	♎ 4.3R	3.3	2.4	1.5	0.9	0.4	0	♍ 29.9	29.9D	♎ 0.1	0.4	1	1.7	2.5	3.4	4.5	5.7	6.9	8.3	9.7	11.1	12.6	14.2	15.7	17.3	18.9	20.6	22.2	23.9	25.5	27.2
♀	♍ 9.6	10.8	12	13.3	14.5	15.7	16.9	18.2	19.4	20.6	21.9	23.1	24.3	25.6	26.8	28	29.3	♎ 0.5	1.7	3	4.2	5.5	6.7	7.9	9.2	10.4	11.7	12.9	14.2	15.4	16.7
♂	♑ 6.1	6.8	7.4	8.1	8.8	9.4	10.1	10.7	11.4	12.1	12.7	13.4	14.1	14.8	15.4	16.1	16.8	17.5	18.2	18.9	19.6	20.3	21	21.7	22.4	23.1	23.8	24.5	25.2	25.9	26.6

♃ 1: ♎ 14.5 · 6: 15.6 · 11: 16.7 · 16: 17.7 · 21: 18.8 · 26: 19.9 · 31: 21
♄ 1: ♉ 7.6R · 6: 7.2 · 11: 6.9 · 16: 6.5 · 21: 6.1 · 26: 5.7 · 31: 5.3
♅ 1: ♎ 4.6 · 11: 5.2 · 21: 5.9 · 31: 6.4
♆ 1: ♏ 26.7 · 11: 27 · 21: 27.3 · 31: 27.7
♇ 1: ♍ 25.4 · 11: 25.8 · 21: 26.1 · 31: 26.4

XI (1969)

	1	2	3	4	5	6	7	8	9	10	11	12	13	14	15	16	17	18	19	20	21	22	23	24	25	26	27	28	29	30	31
☉	♏ 8.4	9.4	10.4	11.4	12.4	13.4	14.4	15.4	16.4	17.4	18.4	19.4	20.4	21.4	22.5	23.5	24.5	25.5	26.5	27.5	28.5	29.5	♐ 0.5	1.5	2.5	3.6	4.6	5.6	6.6	7.6	
☽	♋ 24.3	♌ 6.1	18	30	♍ 12.2	24.7	♎ 7.5	20.8	♏ 4.4	18.4	♐ 2.7	17.2	♑ 1.7	16.3	♒ 0.7	14.9	28.9	♓ 12.7	26.3	♈ 9.7	23	♉ 6	18.9	♊ 1.6	14.1	26.4	♋ 8.5	20.4	♌ 2.3	14.1	
☿	♎ 28.8	♏ 0.5	2.2	3.8	5.5	7.1	8.7	10.4	12	13.6	15.3	16.9	18.5	20.1	21.7	23.3	24.9	26.5	28	29.6	♐ 1.2	2.8	4.3	5.9	7.5	9	10.6	12.1	13.7	15.2	
♀	♎ 17.9	19.1	20.4	21.6	22.9	24.1	25.4	26.6	27.9	29.1	♏ 0.4	1.6	2.9	4.1	5.4	6.7	7.9	9.2	10.4	11.7	12.9	14.2	15.4	16.7	17.9	19.2	20.4	21.7	23	24.2	
♂	♑ 27.3	28	28.7	29.4	♒ 0.2	0.9	1.6	2.3	3	3.8	4.5	5.2	5.9	6.7	7.4	8.1	8.9	9.6	10.3	11.1	11.8	12.5	13.3	14	14.7	15.5	16.2	16.9	17.7	18.4	

♃ 1: ♎ 21.2 · 6: 22.2 · 11: 23.3 · 16: 24.3 · 21: 25.3 · 26: 26.3
♄ 1: ♉ 5.2R · 6: 4.8 · 11: 4.4 · 16: 4.1 · 21: 3.7 · 26: 3.4
♅ 1: ♎ 6.5 · 11: 7 · 21: 7.5
♆ 1: ♏ 27.7 · 11: 28.1 · 21: 28.4
♇ 1: ♍ 26.4 · 11: 26.7 · 21: 27

XII (1969)

	1	2	3	4	5	6	7	8	9	10	11	12	13	14	15	16	17	18	19	20	21	22	23	24	25	26	27	28	29	30	31
☉	♐ 8.6	9.6	10.7	11.7	12.7	13.7	14.7	15.7	16.7	17.8	18.8	19.8	20.8	21.8	22.8	23.9	24.9	25.9	26.9	27.9	29	30	♑ 1	2	3	4	5.1	6.1	7.1	8.1	9.1
☽	♌ 25.9	♍ 7.9	20	♎ 2.5	15.3	28.6	♏ 12.3	26.5	♐ 11.2	26	♑ 11	26	♒ 10.8	25.3	♓ 9.4	23.3	♈ 6.7	19.9	♉ 2.9	15.6	28.2	♊ 10.6	22.8	♋ 5	16.9	28.8	♌ 10.7	22.4	♍ 4.3	16.2	28.3
☿	♐ 16.8	18.3	19.9	21.4	23	24.5	26.1	27.6	29.2	♑ 0.7	2.2	3.8	5.3	6.8	8.3	9.8	11.3	12.8	14.2	15.7	17.1	18.5	19.8	21.1	22.4	23.6	24.7	25.8	26.8	27.6	28.4
♀	♏ 25.5	26.7	28	29.2	♐ 0.5	1.8	3	4.3	5.5	6.8	8	9.3	10.6	11.8	13.1	14.3	15.6	16.8	18.1	19.4	20.6	21.9	23.1	24.4	25.7	26.9	28.2	29.4	♑ 0.7	1.9	3.2
♂	♒ 19.2	19.9	20.6	21.4	22.1	22.9	23.6	24.4	25.1	25.8	26.6	27.3	28.1	28.8	29.6	♓ 0.3	1.1	1.8	2.5	3.3	4	4.8	5.5	6.3	7	7.8	8.5	9.3	10	10.8	11.5

♃ 1: ♎ 27.2 · 6: 28.2 · 11: 29 · 16: 29.9 · 21: ♏ 0.7 · 26: 1.5 · 31: 2.2
♄ 1: ♉ 3.1R · 6: 2.8 · 11: 2.6 · 16: 2.4 · 21: 2.2 · 26: 2.1 · 31: 2.1
♅ 1: ♎ 7.9 · 11: 8.3 · 21: 8.5 · 31: 8.7
♆ 1: ♏ 28.8 · 11: 29.2 · 21: 29.5 · 31: 29.9
♇ 1: ♍ 27.1 · 11: 27.3 · 21: 27.4 · 31: 27.4R

I (1970)

	1	2	3	4	5	6	7	8	9	10	11	12	13	14	15	16	17	18	19	20	21	22	23	24	25	26	27	28	29	30	31
☉	♑ 10.2	11.2	12.2	13.2	14.2	15.3	16.3	17.3	18.3	19.3	20.4	21.4	22.4	23.4	24.4	25.4	26.5	27.5	28.5	29.5	♒ 0.5	1.6	2.6	3.6	4.6	5.6	6.6	7.7	8.7	9.7	10.7
☽	♎ 10.7	23.4	♏ 6.6	20.3	♐ 4.4	19.1	♑ 4.1	19.3	♒ 4.6	19.7	♓ 4.5	19	♈ 3	16.6	29.8	♉ 12.7	25.3	♊ 7.6	19.8	♋ 1.9	13.8	25.7	♌ 7.6	19.4	♍ 1.2	13.1	25.1	♎ 7.3	19.7	♏ 2.4	15.4
☿	♑ 29	29.5	29.8	30	30.0R	29.7	29.3	28.7	27.9	26.9	25.8	24.6	23.3	22	20.6	19.4	18.2	17.2	16.2	15.5	14.8	14.4	14.1	13.9	13.9D	14	14.2	14.5	15	15.5	16.1
♀	♑ 4.5	5.7	7	8.2	9.5	10.8	12	13.3	14.5	15.8	17	18.3	19.6	20.8	22.1	23.3	24.6	25.9	27.1	28.4	29.6	♒ 0.9	2.1	3.4	4.6	5.9	7.2	8.4	9.7	10.9	12.2
♂	♓ 12.2	13	13.7	14.5	15.2	16	16.7	17.5	18.2	19	19.7	20.4	21.2	21.9	22.7	23.4	24.2	24.9	25.6	26.4	27.1	27.9	28.6	29.3	♈ 0.1	0.8	1.6	2.3	3	3.8	4.5

♃ 1: ♏ 2.3 · 6: 3 · 11: 3.6 · 16: 4.1 · 21: 4.6 · 26: 5 · 31: 5.4
♄ 1: ♉ 2.1R · 6: 2.1D · 11: 2.1 · 16: 2.2 · 21: 2.3 · 26: 2.5 · 31: 2.7
♅ 1: ♎ 8.7 · 11: 8.8 · 21: 8.8R · 31: 8.6
♆ 1: ♏ 29.9 · 11: ♐ 0.2 · 21: 0.4 · 31: 0.6
♇ 1: ♍ 27.4R · 11: 27.3 · 21: 27.3 · 31: 27.1

II (1970)

	1	2	3	4	5	6	7	8	9	10	11	12	13	14	15	16	17	18	19	20	21	22	23	24	25	26	27	28	29	30	31
☉	♒ 11.7	12.7	13.7	14.8	15.8	16.8	17.8	18.8	19.8	20.8	21.9	22.9	23.9	24.9	25.9	26.9	27.9	28.9	29.9	♓ 0.9	1.9	3	4	5	6	7	8	9			
☽	♏ 28.9	♐ 12.9	27.3	♑ 12.1	27.3	♒ 12.5	27.7	♓ 12.7	27.4	♈ 11.7	25.5	♉ 8.9	21.8	♊ 4.4	16.8	28.9	♋ 10.8	22.7	♌ 4.5	16.3	28.2	♍ 10.1	22.1	♎ 4.3	16.7	29.3	♏ 12.1	25.2			
☿	♑ 16.8	17.6	18.4	19.3	20.3	21.3	22.3	23.4	24.5	25.7	26.9	28.1	29.3	♒ 0.6	1.9	3.2	4.5	5.9	7.3	8.7	10.1	11.6	13	14.5	16	17.5	19.1	20.6			
♀	♒ 13.4	14.7	16	17.2	18.5	19.7	21	22.2	23.5	24.7	26	27.2	28.5	29.7	♓ 1	2.3	3.5	4.8	6	7.3	8.5	9.8	11	12.3	13.5	14.8	16	17.3			
♂	♈ 5.2	6	6.7	7.5	8.2	8.9	9.7	10.4	11.1	11.9	12.6	13.3	14	14.8	15.5	16.2	17	17.7	18.4	19.1	19.9	20.6	21.3	22	22.8	23.5	24.2	24.9			

♃ 1: ♏ 5.4 · 6: 5.7 · 11: 5.8 · 16: 5.9 · 21: 6.0R · 26: 5.9
♄ 1: ♉ 2.8 · 6: 3.1 · 11: 3.4 · 16: 3.7 · 21: 4.1 · 26: 4.5
♅ 1: ♎ 8.6R · 11: 8.4 · 21: 8.1
♆ 1: ♐ 0.6 · 11: 0.8 · 21: 0.9
♇ 1: ♍ 27.1R · 11: 26.9 · 21: 26.7

III (1970)

	1	2	3	4	5	6	7	8	9	10	11	12	13	14	15	16	17	18	19	20	21	22	23	24	25	26	27	28	29	30	31
☉	♓ 10	11	12	13	14	15	16	17	18	19	20	21	22	23	24	25	26	27	28	29	30	♈ 1	2	2.9	3.9	4.9	5.9	6.9	7.9	8.9	9.9
☽	♐ 8.6	22.4	♑ 6.6	21.1	♒ 5.8	20.7	♓ 5.7	20.6	♈ 5.3	19.7	♉ 3.6	17.1	♊ 0.2	12.9	25.3	♋ 7.4	19.3	♌ 1.1	12.9	24.8	♍ 6.7	18.8	♎ 1.1	13.5	26.2	♏ 9.1	22.2	♐ 5.5	19.1	♑ 2.9	16.9
☿	♒ 22.2	23.8	25.4	27	28.6	♓ 0.3	2	3.6	5.4	7.1	8.8	10.6	12.4	14.2	16	17.9	19.7	21.6	23.5	25.5	27.4	29.4	♈ 1.3	3.3	5.3	7.4	9.4	11.4	13.5	15.5	17.6
♀	♓ 18.5	19.8	21	22.3	23.5	24.7	26	27.2	28.5	29.7	♈ 1	2.2	3.5	4.7	6	7.2	8.4	9.7	10.9	12.2	13.4	14.6	15.9	17.1	18.4	19.6	20.8	22.1	23.3	24.6	25.8
♂	♈ 25.7	26.4	27.1	27.8	28.5	29.2	30	♉ 0.7	1.4	2.1	2.8	3.5	4.2	5	5.7	6.4	7.1	7.8	8.5	9.2	9.9	10.6	11.3	12	12.7	13.5	14.2	14.9	15.6	16.3	17

♃ 1: ♏ 5.8R · 6: 5.7 · 11: 5.4 · 16: 5.1 · 21: 4.7 · 26: 4.2 · 31: 3.7
♄ 1: ♉ 4.8 · 6: 5.3 · 11: 5.8 · 16: 6.3 · 21: 6.9 · 26: 7.4 · 31: 8
♅ 1: ♎ 7.9R · 11: 7.5 · 21: 7 · 31: 6.6
♆ 1: ♐ 0.9 · 11: 0.9R · 21: 0.8 · 31: 0.7
♇ 1: ♍ 26.5R · 11: 26.2 · 21: 25.9 · 31: 25.7

IV (1970)

	1	2	3	4	5	6	7	8	9	10	11	12	13	14	15	16	17	18	19	20	21	22	23	24	25	26	27	28	29	30	31
☉	♈ 10.9	11.8	12.8	13.8	14.8	15.8	16.8	17.8	18.7	19.7	20.7	21.7	22.7	23.6	24.6	25.6	26.6	27.6	28.5	29.5	♉ 0.5	1.5	2.4	3.4	4.4	5.4	6.3	7.3	8.3	9.2	
☽	♒ 1.1	15.5	30	♓ 14.5	29.1	♈ 13.5	27.6	♉ 11.5	25	♊ 8.1	20.9	♋ 3.3	15.4	27.4	♌ 9.2	21	♍ 2.9	14.9	27.1	♎ 9.6	22.3	♏ 5.3	18.6	♐ 2.1	15.9	29.7	♑ 13.7	27.8	♒ 11.9	26.1	
☿	♈ 19.6	21.6	23.6	25.6	27.5	29.4	♉ 1.3	3.1	4.8	6.5	8.1	9.7	11.2	12.6	13.9	15.1	16.2	17.3	18.2	19.1	19.8	20.5	21.1	21.6	21.9	22.2	22.4	22.5	22.5R	22.4	
♀	♈ 27	28.3	29.5	♉ 0.7	2	3.2	4.4	5.7	6.9	8.1	9.4	10.6	11.8	13	14.3	15.5	16.7	18	19.2	20.4	21.6	22.9	24.1	25.3	26.5	27.7	29	♊ 0.2	1.4	2.6	
♂	♉ 17.7	18.4	19.1	19.8	20.5	21.2	21.8	22.5	23.2	23.9	24.6	25.3	26	26.7	27.4	28.1	28.8	29.5	♊ 0.1	0.8	1.5	2.2	2.9	3.6	4.3	4.9	5.6	6.3	7	7.7	

♃ 1: ♏ 3.6R · 6: 3 · 11: 2.4 · 16: 1.8 · 21: 1.2 · 26: 0.5
♄ 1: ♉ 8.1 · 6: 8.7 · 11: 9.3 · 16: 10 · 21: 10.6 · 26: 11.2
♅ 1: ♎ 6.6R · 11: 6.1 · 21: 5.7
♆ 1: ♐ 0.7R · 11: 0.5 · 21: 0.3
♇ 1: ♍ 25.6R · 11: 25.4 · 21: 25.2

V (1970)

	1	2	3	4	5	6	7	8	9	10	11	12	13	14	15	16	17	18	19	20	21	22	23	24	25	26	27	28	29	30	31
☉	♉ 10.2	11.2	12.2	13.1	14.1	15.1	16	17	18	18.9	19.9	20.9	21.8	22.8	23.8	24.7	25.7	26.7	27.6	28.6	29.5	♊ 0.5	1.5	2.4	3.4	4.3	5.3	6.3	7.2	8.2	9.1
☽	♓ 10.2	24.4	♈ 8.5	22.4	♉ 6.2	19.8	♊ 3.1	16.1	28.8	♋ 11.2	23.3	♌ 5.3	17.1	28.9	♍ 10.8	22.8	♎ 5.1	17.7	♏ 0.6	13.9	27.6	♐ 11.5	25.7	♑ 10	24.4	♒ 8.7	22.9	♓ 7.1	21.1	♈ 4.9	18.6
☿	♉ 22.2R	22	21.6	21.2	20.8	20.2	19.7	19.1	18.5	17.9	17.3	16.7	16.1	15.6	15.1	14.6	14.2	13.9	13.6	13.4	13.3	13.2	13.2D	13.3	13.5	13.7	14	14.4	14.9	15.4	16
♀	♊ 3.8	5.1	6.3	7.5	8.7	9.9	11.1	12.4	13.6	14.8	16	17.2	18.4	19.6	20.8	22.1	23.3	24.5	25.7	26.9	28.1	29.3	♋ 0.5	1.7	2.9	4.1	5.3	6.5	7.7	8.9	10.1
♂	♊ 8.4	9	9.7	10.4	11.1	11.7	12.4	13.1	13.8	14.4	15.1	15.8	16.5	17.1	17.8	18.5	19.2	19.8	20.5	21.2	21.8	22.5	23.2	23.8	24.5	25.2	25.8	26.5	27.2	27.8	28.5

♃ 1: ♎ 29.9R · 6: 29.3 · 11: 28.7 · 16: 28.2 · 21: 27.7 · 26: 27.2 · 31: 26.9
♄ 1: ♉ 11.9 · 6: 12.5 · 11: 13.2 · 16: 13.8 · 21: 14.4 · 26: 15.1 · 31: 15.7
♅ 1: ♎ 5.4R · 11: 5.1 · 21: 4.9 · 31: 4.7
♆ 1: ♐ 0.0R · 11: ♏ 29.8 · 21: 29.5 · 31: 29.2
♇ 1: ♍ 25.0R · 11: 24.8 · 21: 24.7 · 31: 24.7

VI (1970)

	1	2	3	4	5	6	7	8	9	10	11	12	13	14	15	16	17	18	19	20	21	22	23	24	25	26	27	28	29	30	31
☉	♊ 10.1	11.1	12	13	13.9	14.9	15.8	16.8	17.8	18.7	19.7	20.6	21.6	22.5	23.5	24.5	25.4	26.4	27.3	28.3	29.2	♋ 0.2	1.1	2.1	3	4	4.9	5.9	6.9	7.8	
☽	♉ 2.2	15.6	28.8	♊ 11.8	24.5	♋ 7	19.3	♌ 1.4	13.3	25.1	♍ 6.9	18.7	♎ 0.8	13.1	25.7	♏ 8.7	22.2	♐ 6	20.3	♑ 4.8	19.5	♒ 4.3	19	♓ 3.5	17.8	♈ 1.8	15.6	29.1	♉ 12.4	25.5	
☿	♉ 16.7	17.4	18.2	19.1	20	20.9	22	23.1	24.2	25.4	26.6	27.9	29.3	♊ 0.7	2.1	3.6	5.2	6.8	8.4	10.1	11.9	13.6	15.5	17.4	19.3	21.2	23.2	25.3	27.4	29.5	
♀	♋ 11.3	12.5	13.7	14.9	16.1	17.3	18.5	19.6	20.8	22	23.2	24.4	25.6	26.8	27.9	29.1	♌ 0.3	1.5	2.7	3.8	5	6.2	7.4	8.5	9.7	10.9	12.1	13.2	14.4	15.6	
♂	♊ 29.2	29.8	♋ 0.5	1.1	1.8	2.5	3.1	3.8	4.4	5.1	5.8	6.4	7.1	7.7	8.4	9	9.7	10.3	11	11.7	12.3	13	13.6	14.3	14.9	15.6	16.2	16.9	17.5	18.2	

♃ 1: ♎ 26.8R · 6: 26.5 · 11: 26.3 · 16: 26.1 · 21: 26.1 · 26: 26.1D
♄ 1: ♉ 15.8 · 6: 16.4 · 11: 17 · 16: 17.5 · 21: 18.1 · 26: 18.6
♅ 1: ♎ 4.7R · 11: 4.7 · 21: 4.7D
♆ 1: ♏ 29.2R · 11: 29 · 21: 28.7
♇ 1: ♍ 24.7R · 11: 24.7D · 21: 24.7

VII (1970)

	1	2	3	4	5	6	7	8	9	10	11	12	13	14	15	16	17	18	19	20	21	22	23	24	25	26	27	28	29	30	31
☉	♋ 8.8	9.7	10.7	11.6	12.6	13.5	14.5	15.4	16.4	17.3	18.3	19.2	20.2	21.2	22.1	23.1	24	25	25.9	26.9	27.8	28.8	29.7	♌ 0.7	1.7	2.6	3.6	4.5	5.5	6.4	7.4
☽	♊ 8.3	21	♋ 3.4	15.7	27.8	♌ 9.7	21.6	♍ 3.3	15.1	27	♎ 9	21.3	♏ 3.9	16.9	♐ 0.3	14.2	28.6	♑ 13.3	28.3	♒ 13.3	28.4	♓ 13.2	27.8	♈ 12	25.8	♉ 9.3	22.5	♊ 5.4	18	♋ 0.4	12.6
☿	♋ 1.6	3.7	5.9	8	10.2	12.4	14.6	16.7	18.9	21	23.1	25.2	27.3	29.3	♌ 1.3	3.3	5.3	7.2	9.1	11	12.9	14.7	16.5	18.2	19.9	21.6	23.3	24.9	26.5	28.1	29.7
♀	♌ 16.7	17.9	19	20.2	21.4	22.5	23.7	24.8	26	27.1	28.3	29.4	♍ 0.6	1.7	2.8	4	5.1	6.3	7.4	8.5	9.7	10.8	11.9	13	14.1	15.3	16.4	17.5	18.6	19.7	20.8
♂	♋ 18.8	19.5	20.1	20.8	21.4	22.1	22.7	23.4	24	24.7	25.3	26	26.6	27.2	27.9	28.5	29.2	29.8	♌ 0.5	1.1	1.8	2.4	3	3.7	4.3	5	5.6	6.3	6.9	7.5	8.2

♃ 1: ♎ 26.2 · 6: 26.3 · 11: 26.5 · 16: 26.8 · 21: 27.2 · 26: 27.6 · 31: 28.1
♄ 1: ♉ 19.1 · 6: 19.6 · 11: 20 · 16: 20.5 · 21: 20.8 · 26: 21.2 · 31: 21.5
♅ 1: ♎ 4.8 · 11: 5 · 21: 5.3 · 31: 5.7
♆ 1: ♏ 28.5R · 11: 28.3 · 21: 28.2 · 31: 28.1
♇ 1: ♍ 24.8 · 11: 25 · 21: 25.2 · 31: 25.5

VIII (1970)

	1	2	3	4	5	6	7	8	9	10	11	12	13	14	15	16	17	18	19	20	21	22	23	24	25	26	27	28	29	30	31
☉	♌ 8.3	9.3	10.3	11.2	12.2	13.1	14.1	15	16	17	17.9	18.9	19.8	20.8	21.8	22.7	23.7	24.6	25.6	26.6	27.5	28.5	29.5	♍ 0.4	1.4	2.4	3.3	4.3	5.3	6.2	7.2
☽	♋ 24.6	♌ 6.6	18.4	♍ 0.2	12	23.8	♎ 5.7	17.7	♏ 0	12.6	25.5	♐ 8.9	22.7	♑ 6.9	21.6	♒ 6.6	21.7	♓ 6.9	22	♈ 6.8	21.3	♉ 5.3	18.9	♊ 2.1	14.9	27.4	♋ 9.7	21.7	♌ 3.6	15.5	27.2
☿	♍ 1.2	2.7	4.1	5.6	7	8.3	9.7	11	12.2	13.5	14.7	15.8	17	18	19.1	20.1	21.1	22	22.8	23.6	24.4	25.1	25.7	26.3	26.7	27.2	27.5	27.8	27.9	28	28.0R
♀	♍ 21.9	23	24.1	25.2	26.3	27.4	28.5	29.6	♎ 0.6	1.7	2.8	3.8	4.9	6	7	8.1	9.1	10.2	11.2	12.2	13.3	14.3	15.3	16.3	17.3	18.4	19.4	20.3	21.3	22.3	23.3
♂	♌ 8.8	9.5	10.1	10.7	11.4	12	12.7	13.3	13.9	14.6	15.2	15.9	16.5	17.1	17.8	18.4	19	19.7	20.3	21	21.6	22.2	22.9	23.5	24.1	24.8	25.4	26.1	26.7	27.3	28

♃ 1: ♎ 28.2 · 6: 28.8 · 11: 29.4 · 16: ♏ 0 · 21: 0.7 · 26: 1.5 · 31: 2.3
♄ 1: ♉ 21.6 · 6: 21.9 · 11: 22.1 · 16: 22.3 · 21: 22.4 · 26: 22.5 · 31: 22.6
♅ 1: ♎ 5.7 · 11: 6.1 · 21: 6.6 · 31: 7.2
♆ 1: ♏ 28.1R · 11: 28.1D · 21: 28.1 · 31: 28.2
♇ 1: ♍ 25.5 · 11: 25.8 · 21: 26.1 · 31: 26.5

IX (1970)

	1	2	3	4	5	6	7	8	9	10	11	12	13	14	15	16	17	18	19	20	21	22	23	24	25	26	27	28	29	30	31
☉	♍ 8.2	9.1	10.1	11.1	12	13	14	14.9	15.9	16.9	17.9	18.8	19.8	20.8	21.7	22.7	23.7	24.7	25.6	26.6	27.6	28.6	29.6	♎ 0.5	1.5	2.5	3.5	4.5	5.4	6.4	
☽	♍ 9	20.9	♎ 2.8	14.8	27	♏ 9.3	22	♐ 4.9	18.2	♑ 1.8	15.8	♒ 0.3	15	♓ 0	15.2	♈ 0.3	15.2	29.8	♉ 14	27.7	♊ 11	23.9	♋ 6.4	18.6	♌ 0.5	12.4	24.2	♍ 5.9	17.8	29.7	
☿	♍ 27.9R	27.6	27.3	26.9	26.4	25.7	25	24.2	23.3	22.3	21.4	20.3	19.3	18.3	17.4	16.5	15.7	15	14.5	14.1	13.9	13.8	13.9D	14.1	14.5	15.1	15.8	16.6	17.6	18.7	
♀	♎ 24.3	25.2	26.2	27.1	28.1	29	29.9	♏ 0.8	1.8	2.6	3.5	4.4	5.3	6.1	7	7.8	8.7	9.5	10.3	11.1	11.8	12.6	13.3	14.1	14.8	15.5	16.2	16.8	17.5	18.1	
♂	♌ 28.6	29.2	29.9	♍ 0.5	1.1	1.8	2.4	3.1	3.7	4.3	5	5.6	6.2	6.9	7.5	8.1	8.8	9.4	10	10.7	11.3	11.9	12.6	13.2	13.8	14.5	15.1	15.8	16.4	17	

♃ 1: ♏ 2.5 · 6: 3.3 · 11: 4.2 · 16: 5.1 · 21: 6.1 · 26: 7.1
♄ 1: ♉ 22.6 · 6: 22.6R · 11: 22.6 · 16: 22.5 · 21: 22.4 · 26: 22.2
♅ 1: ♎ 7.2 · 11: 7.8 · 21: 8.4
♆ 1: ♏ 28.2 · 11: 28.4 · 21: 28.6
♇ 1: ♍ 26.5 · 11: 26.9 · 21: 27.2

X (1970)

	1	2	3	4	5	6	7	8	9	10	11	12	13	14	15	16	17	18	19	20	21	22	23	24	25	26	27	28	29	30	31
☉	♎ 7.4	8.4	9.4	10.4	11.3	12.3	13.3	14.3	15.3	16.3	17.3	18.3	19.2	20.2	21.2	22.2	23.2	24.2	25.2	26.2	27.2	28.2	29.2	♏ 0.2	1.2	2.2	3.2	4.2	5.2	6.2	7.2
☽	♎ 11.8	24	♏ 6.4	19	♐ 1.9	14.9	28.2	♑ 11.8	25.6	♒ 9.8	24.2	♓ 8.9	23.7	♈ 8.5	23.3	♉ 7.8	22.1	♊ 5.9	19.2	♋ 2.1	14.7	26.9	♌ 8.9	20.7	♍ 2.5	14.3	26.2	♎ 8.3	20.5	♏ 3	15.7
☿	♍ 19.9	21.2	22.6	24.1	25.6	27.2	28.8	♎ 0.4	2.1	3.8	5.5	7.2	9	10.7	12.5	14.2	15.9	17.7	19.4	21.1	22.8	24.5	26.2	27.9	29.6	♏ 1.2	2.9	4.6	6.2	7.8	9.5
♀	♏ 18.7	19.3	19.9	20.4	20.9	21.4	21.9	22.3	22.7	23.1	23.5	23.8	24.1	24.4	24.6	24.8	24.9	25.1	25.2	25.2	25.2R	25.2	25.1	25	24.8	24.6	24.4	24.1	23.8	23.5	23.1
♂	♍ 17.7	18.3	18.9	19.6	20.2	20.8	21.5	22.1	22.7	23.4	24	24.6	25.3	25.9	26.5	27.2	27.8	28.4	29.1	29.7	♎ 0.4	1	1.6	2.3	2.9	3.5	4.2	4.8	5.4	6.1	6.7

♃ 1: ♏ 8.1 · 6: 9.1 · 11: 10.1 · 16: 11.2 · 21: 12.3 · 26: 13.3 · 31: 14.4
♄ 1: ♉ 22.0R · 6: 21.8 · 11: 21.5 · 16: 21.2 · 21: 20.8 · 26: 20.5 · 31: 20.1
♅ 1: ♎ 9.1 · 11: 9.7 · 21: 10.3 · 31: 10.9
♆ 1: ♏ 28.8 · 11: 29.1 · 21: 29.4 · 31: 29.8
♇ 1: ♍ 27.6 · 11: 28 · 21: 28.3 · 31: 28.6

XI (1970)

	1	2	3	4	5	6	7	8	9	10	11	12	13	14	15	16	17	18	19	20	21	22	23	24	25	26	27	28	29	30	31
☉	♏ 8.2	9.2	10.2	11.2	12.2	13.2	14.2	15.2	16.2	17.2	18.2	19.2	20.2	21.2	22.2	23.2	24.2	25.2	26.2	27.3	28.3	29.3	♐ 0.3	1.3	2.3	3.3	4.3	5.3	6.4	7.4	
☽	♏ 28.7	♐ 11.8	25.2	♑ 8.7	22.4	♒ 6.2	20.2	♓ 4.4	18.7	♈ 3.1	17.5	♉ 1.9	16.1	♊ 0.1	13.8	27.1	♋ 10	22.5	♌ 4.8	16.8	28.6	♍ 10.4	22.2	♎ 4.2	16.3	28.7	♏ 11.4	24.5	♐ 7.8	21.4	
☿	♏ 11.1	12.7	14.3	15.9	17.5	19	20.6	22.2	23.7	25.3	26.8	28.4	29.9	♐ 1.5	3	4.5	6	7.6	9.1	10.6	12.1	13.6	15	16.5	18	19.5	20.9	22.4	23.8	25.2	
♀	♏ 22.7R	22.2	21.7	21.2	20.7	20.1	19.5	19	18.4	17.7	17.1	16.5	15.9	15.3	14.8	14.2	13.7	13.2	12.7	12.2	11.8	11.4	11.1	10.8	10.5	10.3	10.1	10	9.8	9.8	
♂	♎ 7.3	8	8.6	9.2	9.9	10.5	11.1	11.8	12.4	13	13.7	14.3	15	15.6	16.2	16.9	17.5	18.1	18.8	19.4	20	20.7	21.3	21.9	22.6	23.2	23.8	24.5	25.1	25.8	

♃ 1: ♏ 14.7 · 6: 15.8 · 11: 16.9 · 16: 18 · 21: 19.1 · 26: 20.1
♄ 1: ♉ 20.0R · 6: 19.6 · 11: 19.2 · 16: 18.8 · 21: 18.4 · 26: 18
♅ 1: ♎ 11 · 11: 11.5 · 21: 12.1
♆ 1: ♏ 29.8 · 11: ♐ 0.2 · 21: 0.5
♇ 1: ♍ 28.7 · 11: 29 · 21: 29.2

XII (1970)

	1	2	3	4	5	6	7	8	9	10	11	12	13	14	15	16	17	18	19	20	21	22	23	24	25	26	27	28	29	30	31
☉	♐ 8.4	9.4	10.4	11.4	12.4	13.5	14.5	15.5	16.5	17.5	18.5	19.5	20.6	21.6	22.6	23.6	24.6	25.6	26.7	27.7	28.7	29.7	♑ 0.7	1.8	2.8	3.8	4.8	5.8	6.9	7.9	8.9
☽	♑ 5.1	19.1	♒ 3.1	17.1	♓ 1.2	15.3	29.4	♈ 13.4	27.4	♉ 11.3	25.1	♊ 8.7	22.1	♋ 5.1	17.9	♌ 0.3	12.5	24.5	♍ 6.4	18.2	30	♎ 11.9	24.1	♏ 6.5	19.3	♐ 2.5	16.1	30	♑ 14.2	28.6	♒ 13
☿	♐ 26.7	28.1	29.4	♑ 0.8	2.1	3.4	4.7	5.9	7.1	8.2	9.2	10.2	11.1	11.9	12.6	13.2	13.7	14	14.1	14.0R	13.8	13.4	12.8	11.9	10.9	9.8	8.6	7.2	5.9	4.5	3.2
♀	♏ 9.8R	9.8D	9.8	9.9	10.1	10.3	10.5	10.7	11	11.3	11.7	12	12.5	12.9	13.4	13.9	14.4	14.9	15.5	16.1	16.7	17.4	18	18.7	19.4	20.1	20.9	21.6	22.4	23.2	24
♂	♎ 26.4	27	27.7	28.3	28.9	29.6	♏ 0.2	0.8	1.5	2.1	2.7	3.4	4	4.6	5.3	5.9	6.5	7.2	7.8	8.5	9.1	9.7	10.4	11	11.6	12.3	12.9	13.5	14.2	14.8	15.4

♃ 1: ♏ 21.2 · 6: 22.3 · 11: 23.4 · 16: 24.4 · 21: 25.4 · 26: 26.4 · 31: 27.4
♄ 1: ♉ 17.6R · 6: 17.3 · 11: 16.9 · 16: 16.6 · 21: 16.4 · 26: 16.2 · 31: 16
♅ 1: ♎ 12.5 · 11: 12.9 · 21: 13.2 · 31: 13.4
♆ 1: ♐ 0.9 · 11: 1.3 · 21: 1.6 · 31: 2
♇ 1: ♍ 29.4 · 11: 29.6 · 21: 29.7 · 31: 29.7

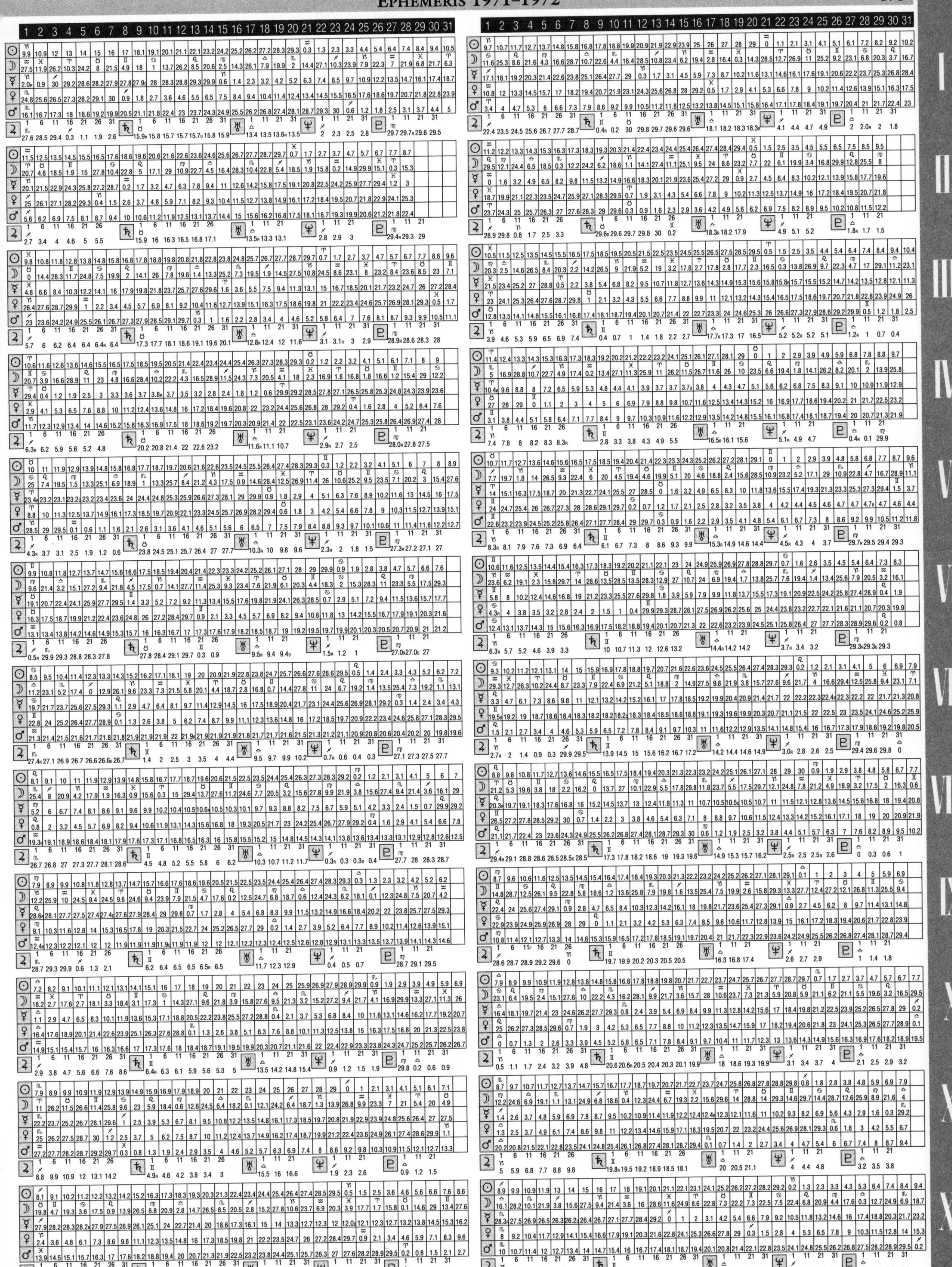

I

1973

	1	2	3	4	5	6	7	8	9	10	11	12	13	14	15	16	17	18	19	20	21	22	23	24	25	26	27	28	29	30	31
☉	10.4	11.5	12.5	13.5	14.5	15.5	16.6	17.6	18.6	19.6	20.6	21.6	22.7	23.7	24.7	25.7	26.7	27.8	28.8	29.8	0.8	1.8	2.8	3.9	4.9	5.9	6.9	7.9	8.9	10	11
☽	0.6	12.4	24.3	6.2	18.4	0.6	13.1	25.7	8.6	21.7	5.1	18.7	2.7	16.9	1.4	16.1	0.8	15.6	0.2	14.6	28.6	12.3	25.5	8.4	20.9	3.1	15.1	27	8.8	20.6	2.5
☿	24.6	26.1	27.6	29.1	0.6	2.1	3.6	5.1	6.7	8.2	9.8	11.3	12.9	14.4	16	17.6	19.2	20.8	22.4	24	25.7	27.3	28.9	0.6	2.3	4	5.6	7.3	9.1	10.8	12.5
♀	16.5	17.8	19	20.3	21.5	22.7	24	25.2	26.5	27.8	29	0.3	1.5	2.8	4	5.3	6.5	7.8	9	10.3	11.5	12.8	14	15.3	16.5	17.8	19	20.3	21.5	22.8	24
♂	0.9	1.6	2.3	3	3.6	4.3	5	5.7	6.4	7	7.7	8.4	9.1	9.8	10.5	11.2	11.8	12.5	13.2	13.9	14.6	15.3	16	16.7	17.4	18	18.7	19.4	20.1	20.8	21.5

♃ 1: 17.8, 6: 19, 11: 20.2, 16: 21.3, 21: 22.5, 26: 23.6, 31: 24.8 — ♄ 1: 15.3R, 6: 15, 11: 14.6, 16: 14.4, 21: 14.1, 26: 13.9, 31: 13.8 — ♅ 1: 22.7, 11: 22.9, 21: 23, 31: 23.0R — ♆ 1: 6.2, 11: 6.5, 21: 6.8, 31: 7 — ♇ 1: 4.4, 11: 4.4R, 21: 4.4, 31: 4.2

1974

	1	2	3	4	5	6	7	8	9	10	11	12	13	14	15	16	17	18	19	20	21	22	23	24	25	26	27	28	29	30	31
☉	10.2	11.2	12.2	13.2	14.3	15.3	16.3	17.3	18.3	19.4	20.4	21.4	22.4	23.4	24.5	25.5	26.5	27.5	28.5	29.5	0.6	1.6	2.6	3.6	4.6	5.7	6.7	7.7	8.7	9.7	10.7
☽	1.3	14.1	27.4	11.1	25.2	9.7	24.7	9.8	25.1	10.3	25.3	9.9	24	7.7	20.9	3.7	16.2	28.4	10.4	22.2	4	15.8	27.6	9.5	21.4	3.5	15.8	28.2	10.8	23.6	6.8
☿	5.3	6.9	8.5	10.1	11.7	13.3	14.9	16.5	18.1	19.8	21.4	23.1	24.7	26.4	28.1	29.7	1.4	3.1	4.8	6.5	8.2	10	11.7	13.4	15.1	16.8	18.6	20.3	22	23.6	25.3
♀	11.3	11.3	11.4	11.4R	11.3	11.2	11.1	10.9	10.7	10.4	10.1	9.8	9.4	9	8.5	8.1	7.5	7	6.4	5.9	5.3	4.7	4	3.4	2.8	2.2	1.6	1	0.4	29.9	29.4
♂	2.5	2.9	3.3	3.7	4	4.4	4.8	5.2	5.6	6	6.4	6.8	7.3	7.7	8.1	8.6	9	9.5	9.9	10.4	10.8	11.3	11.7	12.2	12.7	13.2	13.6	14.1	14.6	15.1	15.6

♃ 1: 14.4, 6: 15.5, 11: 16.6, 16: 17.8, 21: 18.9, 26: 20.1, 31: 21.3 — ♄ 1: 0.5R, 6: 0.1, 11: 29.8, 16: 29.4, 21: 29.1, 26: 28.8, 31: 28.5 — ♅ 1: 27.3, 11: 27.6, 21: 27.7, 31: 27.8 — ♆ 1: 8.3, 11: 8.7, 21: 8.9, 31: 9.2 — ♇ 1: 6.8, 11: 6.8R, 21: 6.8, 31: 6.7

II

1973

	1	2	3	4	5	6	7	8	9	10	11	12	13	14	15	16	17	18	19	20	21	22	23	24	25	26	27	28	29	30	31
☉	12	13	14	15	16.1	17.1	18.1	19.1	20.1	21.1	22.1	23.1	24.1	25.2	26.2	27.2	28.2	29.2	0.2	1.2	2.2	3.2	4.2	5.2	6.2	7.3	8.3	9.3			
☽	14.6	26.9	9.5	22.2	5.2	18.5	2	15.6	29.5	13.4	27.5	11.7	26	10.3	24.5	8.7	22.8	6.6	20.1	3.3	16.1	28.7	10.9	22.9	4.8	16.6	28.5	10.4			
☿	14.3	16	17.8	19.6	21.3	23.1	24.9	26.7	28.5	0.3	2.2	4	5.7	7.5	9.3	11	12.7	14.4	16	17.6	19.1	20.6	21.9	23.2	24.3	25.3	26.2	27			
♀	25.3	26.5	27.8	29	0.3	1.5	2.8	4	5.3	6.5	7.8	9	10.3	11.5	12.8	14	15.3	16.5	17.8	19	20.3	21.5	22.8	24	25.3	26.5	27.8	29			
♂	22.2	22.9	23.6	24.3	25	25.7	26.4	27.1	27.7	28.4	29.1	29.8	0.5	1.2	1.9	2.6	3.3	4	4.7	5.4	6.1	6.8	7.5	8.2	8.9	9.6	10.3	11			

♃ 1: 25, 6: 26.2, 11: 27.3, 16: 28.4, 21: 29.5, 26: 0.6 — ♄ 1: 13.8R, 6: 13.7, 11: 13.6, 16: 13.6D, 21: 13.7, 26: 13.8 — ♅ 1: 23.0R, 11: 22.9, 21: 22.8 — ♆ 1: 7.1, 11: 7.2, 21: 7.4 — ♇ 1: 4.2R, 11: 4.1, 21: 3.9

1974

	1	2	3	4	5	6	7	8	9	10	11	12	13	14	15	16	17	18	19	20	21	22	23	24	25	26	27	28	29	30	31
☉	11.7	12.8	13.8	14.8	15.8	16.8	17.8	18.8	19.9	20.9	21.9	22.9	23.9	24.9	25.9	26.9	27.9	29	30	1	2	3	4	5	6	7	8	9			
☽	20.3	4.1	18.4	3	17.9	3	18.2	3.2	17.9	2.3	16.1	29.5	12.4	24.9	7.1	19	0.8	12.6	24.4	6.3	18.2	0.4	12.7	25.2	7.8	20.7	3.7	17			
☿	26.9	28.5	0.1	1.6	3	4.4	5.7	6.9	8	9	9.9	10.6	11.2	11.6	11.8	11.8R	11.7	11.4	11	10.4	9.6	8.8	7.8	6.8	5.7	4.6	3.5	2.5			
♀	28.9R	28.4	28	27.6	27.2	26.9	26.6	26.4	26.2	26	25.9	25.8	25.8	25.8D	25.9	26	26.1	26.2	26.4	26.7	26.9	27.2	27.6	27.9	28.3	28.6	29.2	29.7			
♂	16.1	16.6	17.1	17.6	18.1	18.6	19.1	19.6	20.1	20.7	21.2	21.7	22.2	22.7	23.3	23.8	24.3	24.9	25.4	26	26.5	27	27.6	28.1	28.7	29.2	29.8	0.3			

♃ 1: 21.5, 6: 22.7, 11: 23.9, 16: 25.1, 21: 26.3, 26: 27.5 — ♄ 1: 28.4R, 6: 28.2, 11: 28, 16: 27.9, 21: 27.8, 26: 27.8 — ♅ 1: 27.8R, 11: 27.7, 21: 27.6 — ♆ 1: 9.2, 11: 9.4, 21: 9.5 — ♇ 1: 6.7R, 11: 6.5, 21: 6.3

III

1973

	1	2	3	4	5	6	7	8	9	10	11	12	13	14	15	16	17	18	19	20	21	22	23	24	25	26	27	28	29	30	31
☉	10.3	11.3	12.3	13.3	14.3	15.3	16.3	17.3	18.3	19.3	20.3	21.3	22.3	23.3	24.3	25.3	26.3	27.3	28.3	29.2	0.2	1.2	2.2	3.2	4.2	5.2	6.2	7.2	8.2	9.2	10.1
☽	22.6	5	17.7	0.8	14.2	27.9	11.8	25.9	10.1	24.4	8.5	22.7	6.7	20.7	4.5	18.3	1.9	15.3	28.5	11.4	24.1	6.6	18.8	0.8	12.6	24.4	6.3	18.2	0.4	12.9	25.7
☿	27.6	28.1	28.4	28.6	28.6R	28.4	28.1	27.7	27.1	26.4	25.7	24.8	23.9	23	22	21	20.1	19.2	18.4	17.7	17	16.4	15.9	15.6	15.3	15.1	15	15.0D	15.1	15.3	15.6
♀	0.3	1.5	2.8	4	5.3	6.5	7.8	9	10.3	11.5	12.8	14	15.2	16.5	17.7	19	20.2	21.5	22.7	24	25.2	26.5	27.7	28.9	0.2	1.4	2.7	3.9	5.2	6.4	7.6
♂	11.7	12.4	13.1	13.8	14.5	15.3	16	16.7	17.4	18.1	18.8	19.5	20.2	20.9	21.6	22.3	23	23.7	24.4	25.1	25.8	26.6	27.3	28	28.7	29.4	0.1	0.8	1.5	2.2	2.9

♃ 1: 1.2, 6: 2.2, 11: 3.2, 16: 4.1, 21: 5.1, 26: 5.9, 31: 6.8 — ♄ 1: 13.9, 6: 14, 11: 14.2, 16: 14.5, 21: 14.8, 26: 15.1, 31: 15.5 — ♅ 1: 22.6R, 11: 22.3, 21: 21.9, 31: 21.5 — ♆ 1: 7.4, 11: 7.4R, 21: 7.4, 31: 7.3 — ♇ 1: 3.7R, 11: 3.4, 21: 3.1, 31: 2.9

1974

	1	2	3	4	5	6	7	8	9	10	11	12	13	14	15	16	17	18	19	20	21	22	23	24	25	26	27	28	29	30	31
☉	10	11	12	13	14	15	16	17	18	19	20	21	22	23	24	25	26	27	28	29	30	1	2	3	4	5	5.9	6.9	7.9	8.9	9.9
☽	0.5	14.2	28.2	12.5	27	11.8	26.6	11.3	25.9	10.1	24	7.4	20.4	2.9	15.2	27.2	9	20.8	2.6	14.6	26.7	9	21.5	4.3	17.3	0.5	13.8	27.4	11.1	25	8.9
☿	1.5R	0.6	29.8	29.1	28.5	28	27.6	27.3	27.2	27.1D	27.2	27.4	27.6	28	28.4	28.9	29.5	0.1	0.8	1.6	2.4	3.3	4.2	5.2	6.2	7.3	8.4	9.6	10.8	12	13.2
♀	0.2	0.7	1.3	1.9	2.5	3.1	3.7	4.4	5.1	5.8	6.5	7.2	8	8.7	9.5	10.3	11.1	11.9	12.8	13.6	14.5	15.3	16.2	17.1	18	18.9	19.8	20.7	21.7	22.6	23.6
♂	0.9	1.4	2	2.5	3.1	3.7	4.2	4.8	5.4	5.9	6.5	7	7.6	8.2	8.8	9.3	9.9	10.5	11	11.6	12.2	12.8	13.4	13.9	14.5	15.1	15.7	16.3	16.8	17.4	18

♃ 1: 28.2, 6: 29.4, 11: 0.6, 16: 1.8, 21: 2.9, 26: 4, 31: 5.1 — ♄ 1: 27.8, 6: 27.8, 11: 27.9, 16: 28, 21: 28.2, 26: 28.4, 31: 28.7 — ♅ 1: 27.4R, 11: 27.1, 21: 26.8, 31: 26.4 — ♆ 1: 9.6, 11: 9.6, 21: 9.6R, 31: 9.5 — ♇ 1: 6.1R, 11: 5.9, 21: 5.6, 31: 5.3

IV

1973

	1	2	3	4	5	6	7	8	9	10	11	12	13	14	15	16	17	18	19	20	21	22	23	24	25	26	27	28	29	30	31
☉	11.1	12.1	13.1	14.1	15.1	16.1	17	18	19	20	21	21.9	22.9	23.9	24.9	25.9	26.8	27.8	28.8	29.8	0.8	1.7	2.7	3.7	4.7	5.6	6.6	7.6	8.5	9.5	
☽	8.9	22.6	6.6	20.9	5.5	20.1	4.7	19.2	3.5	17.6	1.4	15	28.5	11.7	24.7	7.6	20.2	2.7	14.9	27	8.9	20.8	2.5	14.4	26.3	8.4	20.9	3.7	16.9	0.6	
☿	16	16.4	16.9	17.5	18.2	18.9	19.7	20.5	21.4	22.3	23.3	24.4	25.4	26.5	27.7	28.9	0.1	1.4	2.7	4.1	5.4	6.8	8.3	9.8	11.3	12.8	14.3	15.9	17.6	19.2	
♀	8.9	10.1	11.4	12.6	13.8	15.1	16.3	17.6	18.8	20	21.3	22.5	23.8	25	26.2	27.5	28.7	30	1.2	2.4	3.7	4.9	6.1	7.4	8.6	9.8	11.1	12.3	13.5	14.8	
♂	3.6	4.4	5.1	5.8	6.5	7.2	7.9	8.6	9.3	10	10.7	11.5	12.2	12.9	13.6	14.3	15	15.7	16.4	17.1	17.8	18.6	19.3	20	20.7	21.4	22.1	22.8	23.5	24.2	

♃ 1: 6.9, 6: 7.7, 11: 8.4, 16: 9.1, 21: 9.7, 26: 10.3 — ♄ 1: 15.6, 6: 16, 11: 16.4, 16: 16.9, 21: 17.4, 26: 17.9 — ♅ 1: 21.5R, 11: 21, 21: 20.6 — ♆ 1: 7.3R, 11: 7.1, 21: 7 — ♇ 1: 2.8R, 11: 2.6, 21: 2.3

1974

	1	2	3	4	5	6	7	8	9	10	11	12	13	14	15	16	17	18	19	20	21	22	23	24	25	26	27	28	29	30	31
☉	10.9	11.9	12.9	13.8	14.8	15.8	16.8	17.8	18.8	19.7	20.7	21.7	22.7	23.7	24.7	25.6	26.6	27.6	28.6	29.5	0.5	1.5	2.5	3.4	4.4	5.4	6.4	7.3	8.3	9.3	
☽	23.1	7.3	21.6	6	20.3	4.5	18.4	2	15.3	28.2	10.7	23	5	16.9	28.7	10.6	22.6	4.7	17.1	29.8	12.8	26.1	9.7	23.5	7.5	21.6	5.7	19.9	4.1	18.2	
☿	14.5	15.8	17.2	18.6	20	21.4	22.9	24.4	25.9	27.4	29	0.6	2.2	3.9	5.5	7.2	9	10.7	12.5	14.3	16.1	18	19.9	21.8	23.8	25.7	27.7	29.7	1.8	3.9	
♀	24.5	25.5	26.5	27.4	28.4	29.4	0.4	1.4	2.4	3.4	4.5	5.5	6.5	7.6	8.6	9.6	10.7	11.7	12.8	13.9	14.9	16	17.1	18.1	19.2	20.3	21.4	22.5	23.6	24.7	
♂	18.6	19.2	19.8	20.3	20.9	21.5	22.1	22.7	23.3	23.9	24.5	25.1	25.6	26.2	26.8	27.4	28	28.6	29.2	29.8	0.4	1	1.6	2.2	2.8	3.4	4	4.6	5.2	5.8	

♃ 1: 5.3, 6: 6.4, 11: 7.5, 16: 8.5, 21: 9.4, 26: 10.4 — ♄ 1: 28.7, 6: 29, 11: 29.4, 16: 29.8, 21: 0.2, 26: 0.6 — ♅ 1: 26.4R, 11: 26, 21: 25.5 — ♆ 1: 9.5R, 11: 9.4, 21: 9.2 — ♇ 1: 5.3R, 11: 5, 21: 4.8

V

1973

	1	2	3	4	5	6	7	8	9	10	11	12	13	14	15	16	17	18	19	20	21	22	23	24	25	26	27	28	29	30	31
☉	10.5	11.5	12.4	13.4	14.4	15.3	16.3	17.3	18.2	19.2	20.2	21.1	22.1	23.1	24	25	26	26.9	27.9	28.9	29.8	0.8	1.7	2.7	3.7	4.6	5.6	6.5	7.5	8.4	9.4
☽	14.8	29.4	14.2	29.2	14.2	29	13.6	27.9	11.8	25.4	8.7	21.7	4.5	17	29.4	11.6	23.7	5.6	17.5	29.3	11.1	22.9	4.9	17	29.4	12.2	25.4	9	23.1	7.6	22.5
☿	20.9	22.6	24.4	26.1	27.9	29.8	1.6	3.5	5.5	7.4	9.4	11.4	13.5	15.6	17.6	19.8	21.9	24.1	26.2	28.4	0.6	2.8	5	7.2	9.4	11.5	13.7	15.8	17.9	19.9	21.9
♀	16	17.2	18.5	19.7	20.9	22.2	23.4	24.6	25.9	27.1	28.3	29.6	0.8	2	3.3	4.5	5.7	6.9	8.2	9.4	10.6	11.9	13.1	14.3	15.5	16.8	18	19.2	20.4	21.7	22.9
♂	24.9	25.6	26.3	27.1	27.8	28.5	29.2	29.9	0.6	1.3	2	2.7	3.4	4.1	4.8	5.5	6.2	6.9	7.6	8.3	9	9.7	10.4	11.1	11.8	12.5	13.2	13.9	14.6	15.2	15.9

♃ 1: 10.7, 6: 11.2, 11: 11.5, 16: 11.8, 21: 12, 26: 12.1, 31: 12.1R — ♄ 1: 18.5, 6: 19, 11: 19.6, 16: 20.2, 21: 20.9, 26: 21.5, 31: 22.1 — ♅ 1: 20.2R, 11: 19.8, 21: 19.5, 31: 19.2 — ♆ 1: 6.7R, 11: 6.5, 21: 6.2, 31: 6 — ♇ 1: 2.1R, 11: 1.9, 21: 1.8, 31: 1.7

1974

	1	2	3	4	5	6	7	8	9	10	11	12	13	14	15	16	17	18	19	20	21	22	23	24	25	26	27	28	29	30	31
☉	10.2	11.2	12.2	13.2	14.1	15.1	16.1	17	18	19	19.9	20.9	21.9	22.8	23.8	24.8	25.7	26.7	27.6	28.6	29.6	0.5	1.5	2.5	3.4	4.4	5.3	6.3	7.3	8.2	9.2
☽	2.3	16.3	0.2	13.9	27.4	10.6	23.6	6.3	18.7	0.9	12.9	24.8	6.6	18.5	0.5	12.6	25.1	7.8	21	4.4	18.3	2.4	16.8	1.3	15.9	0.5	14.9	29.2	13.2	27	10.6
☿	5.9	8.1	10.2	12.3	14.5	16.7	18.8	21	23.2	25.3	27.5	29.6	1.7	3.7	5.8	7.8	9.7	11.7	13.5	15.4	17.2	18.9	20.6	22.2	23.8	25.3	26.8	28.2	29.6	0.9	2.1
♀	25.8	26.9	28	29.1	0.2	1.3	2.4	3.5	4.6	5.7	6.9	8	9.1	10.2	11.4	12.5	13.6	14.8	15.9	17	18.2	19.3	20.5	21.6	22.8	23.9	25	26.2	27.3	28.5	29.7
♂	6.4	7	7.6	8.2	8.8	9.4	10	10.6	11.2	11.8	12.4	13	13.6	14.2	14.8	15.4	16	16.6	17.2	17.8	18.4	19	19.6	20.2	20.8	21.5	22.1	22.7	23.3	23.9	24.5

♃ 1: 11.3, 6: 12.1, 11: 13, 16: 13.7, 21: 14.4, 26: 15.1, 31: 15.7 — ♄ 1: 1.1, 6: 1.6, 11: 2.1, 16: 2.7, 21: 3.2, 26: 3.8, 31: 4.4 — ♅ 1: 25.1R, 11: 24.7, 21: 24.4, 31: 24.1 — ♆ 1: 9.0R, 11: 8.7, 21: 8.5, 31: 8.2 — ♇ 1: 4.6R, 11: 4.4, 21: 4.2, 31: 4.1

VI

1973

	1	2	3	4	5	6	7	8	9	10	11	12	13	14	15	16	17	18	19	20	21	22	23	24	25	26	27	28	29	30	31
☉	10.4	11.3	12.3	13.2	14.2	15.2	16.1	17.1	18	19	19.9	20.9	21.8	22.8	23.8	24.7	25.7	26.6	27.6	28.5	29.5	0.4	1.4	2.3	3.3	4.3	5.2	6.2	7.1	8.1	
☽	7.6	22.8	7.9	22.8	7.3	21.5	5.2	18.5	1.5	14.1	26.5	8.7	20.7	2.6	14.4	26.3	8.1	19.9	1.8	13.9	26.1	8.6	21.4	4.5	18	2	16.3	1	16	1.2	
☿	23.9	25.9	27.8	29.6	1.5	3.3	5	6.7	8.3	9.9	11.5	13	14.5	15.9	17.3	18.6	19.9	21.1	22.3	23.4	24.5	25.5	26.5	27.4	28.3	29.1	29.8	0.5	1.1	1.6	
♀	24.1	25.3	26.6	27.8	29	0.2	1.5	2.7	3.9	5.1	6.4	7.6	8.8	10	11.3	12.5	13.7	14.9	16.1	17.4	18.6	19.8	21	22.3	23.5	24.7	25.9	27.1	28.3	29.6	
♂	16.6	17.3	18	18.7	19.4	20	20.7	21.4	22.1	22.8	23.4	24.1	24.8	25.4	26.1	26.8	27.4	28.1	28.8	29.4	0.1	0.7	1.4	2	2.7	3.3	4	4.6	5.3	5.9	

♃ 1: 12.1R, 6: 12.1, 11: 11.9, 16: 11.7, 21: 11.4, 26: 11.1 — ♄ 1: 22.3, 6: 22.9, 11: 23.5, 16: 24.2, 21: 24.8, 26: 25.5 — ♅ 1: 19.2R, 11: 19, 21: 18.9 — ♆ 1: 5.9R, 11: 5.7, 21: 5.4 — ♇ 1: 1.7R, 11: 1.7, 21: 1.7D

1974

	1	2	3	4	5	6	7	8	9	10	11	12	13	14	15	16	17	18	19	20	21	22	23	24	25	26	27	28	29	30	31
☉	10.1	11.1	12.1	13	14	14.9	15.9	16.8	17.8	18.7	19.7	20.7	21.6	22.6	23.5	24.5	25.4	26.4	27.3	28.3	29.3	0.2	1.2	2.1	3.1	4	5	5.9	6.9	7.8	
☽	23.9	7	19.8	2.4	14.8	27.1	9.1	21.1	2.9	14.8	26.7	8.6	20.8	3.2	15.9	29	12.5	26.5	10.8	25.5	10.3	25.3	10.3	25	9.5	23.7	7.4	20.9	4	16.8	
☿	3.3	4.4	5.5	6.5	7.5	8.4	9.2	10	10.6	11.3	11.8	12.3	12.7	13.1	13.3	13.5	13.6	13.6R	13.6	13.5	13.3	13	12.7	12.3	11.9	11.4	10.9	10.3	9.7	9.1	
♀	0.8	2	3.1	4.3	5.4	6.6	7.8	8.9	10.1	11.2	12.4	13.6	14.7	15.9	17.1	18.3	19.4	20.6	21.8	22.9	24.1	25.3	26.5	27.7	28.8	0	1.2	2.4	3.6	4.7	
♂	25.1	25.7	26.3	26.9	27.6	28.2	28.8	29.4	30	0.6	1.2	1.8	2.4	3	3.7	4.3	4.9	5.5	6.1	6.7	7.3	7.9	8.6	9.2	9.8	10.4	11	11.6	12.3	12.9	

♃ 1: 15.8, 6: 16.3, 11: 16.7, 16: 17.1, 21: 17.4, 26: 17.6 — ♄ 1: 4.6, 6: 5.2, 11: 5.8, 16: 6.4, 21: 7.1, 26: 7.7 — ♅ 1: 24.1R, 11: 23.8, 21: 23.7 — ♆ 1: 8.2R, 11: 7.9, 21: 7.7 — ♇ 1: 4.1R, 11: 4.1, 21: 4.1D

VII

1973

	1	2	3	4	5	6	7	8	9	10	11	12	13	14	15	16	17	18	19	20	21	22	23	24	25	26	27	28	29	30	31
☉	9	10	10.9	11.9	12.8	13.8	14.7	15.7	16.7	17.6	18.6	19.5	20.5	21.4	22.4	23.3	24.3	25.2	26.2	27.1	28.1	29.1	0	1	1.9	2.9	3.8	4.8	5.7	6.7	7.7
☽	16.3	1.3	16	0.3	14.2	27.6	10.6	23.2	5.6	17.7	29.6	11.4	23.2	5	16.9	28.9	11	23.2	5.7	18.3	1.2	14.4	27.9	11.7	25.8	10.3	24.9	9.8	24.7	9.6	24.2
☿	2.1	2.5	2.8	3.1	3.2	3.3	3.3R	3.3	3.1	2.9	2.6	2.3	1.8	1.3	0.8	0.2	29.6	28.9	28.2	27.6	26.9	26.2	25.6	25	24.5	24	23.6	23.3	23	22.9	22.9D
♀	0.8	2	3.2	4.4	5.6	6.9	8.1	9.3	10.5	11.7	12.9	14.1	15.4	16.6	17.8	19	20.2	21.4	22.6	23.8	25.1	26.3	27.5	28.7	29.9	1.1	2.3	3.5	4.7	5.9	7.1
♂	6.5	7.2	7.8	8.4	9	9.7	10.3	10.9	11.5	12.1	12.7	13.3	13.9	14.5	15.1	15.7	16.3	16.9	17.4	18	18.6	19.1	19.7	20.2	20.8	21.3	21.9	22.4	22.9	23.5	24

♃ 1: 10.6R, 6: 10.2, 11: 9.6, 16: 9, 21: 8.4, 26: 7.8, 31: 7.1 — ♄ 1: 26.1, 6: 26.8, 11: 27.4, 16: 28, 21: 28.6, 26: 29.2, 31: 29.8 — ♅ 1: 18.9, 11: 19, 21: 19.2, 31: 19.4 — ♆ 1: 5.2R, 11: 5, 21: 4.8, 31: 4.7 — ♇ 1: 1.8, 11: 1.9, 21: 2.1, 31: 2.3

1974

	1	2	3	4	5	6	7	8	9	10	11	12	13	14	15	16	17	18	19	20	21	22	23	24	25	26	27	28	29	30	31
☉	8.8	9.7	10.7	11.7	12.6	13.6	14.5	15.5	16.4	17.4	18.3	19.3	20.2	21.2	22.1	23.1	24	25	26	26.9	27.9	28.8	29.8	0.7	1.7	2.6	3.6	4.6	5.5	6.5	7.4
☽	29.3	11.6	23.8	5.8	17.8	29.7	11.5	23.4	5.2	17.2	29.4	11.8	24.4	7.4	20.9	4.7	19	3.7	18.8	4	19.2	4.3	19	3.4	17.2	0.7	13.7	26.4	8.7	20.9	2.9
☿	8.5R	7.9	7.4	6.8	6.3	5.8	5.4	5.1	4.8	4.6	4.4	4.4	4.4D	4.5	4.8	5.1	5.5	6	6.5	7.2	8	8.8	9.7	10.8	11.9	13.1	14.4	15.7	17.1	18.7	20.2
♀	5.9	7.1	8.3	9.5	10.7	11.9	13	14.2	15.4	16.6	17.8	19	20.2	21.4	22.6	23.8	25	26.2	27.4	28.6	29.8	1	2.2	3.4	4.6	5.8	7	8.2	9.4	10.6	11.8
♂	13.5	14.1	14.7	15.3	16	16.6	17.2	17.8	18.4	19.1	19.7	20.3	20.9	21.5	22.2	22.8	23.4	24	24.6	25.3	25.9	26.5	27.1	27.8	28.4	29	29.6	0.3	0.9	1.5	2.1

♃ 1: 17.8, 6: 17.9, 11: 17.8R, 16: 17.7, 21: 17.6, 26: 17.3, 31: 17 — ♄ 1: 8.4, 6: 9, 11: 9.7, 16: 10.3, 21: 11, 26: 11.6, 31: 12.2 — ♅ 1: 23.7R, 11: 23.7D, 21: 23.8, 31: 24 — ♆ 1: 7.4R, 11: 7.2, 21: 7.1, 31: 6.9 — ♇ 1: 4.1, 11: 4.2, 21: 4.4, 31: 4.6

VIII

1973

	1	2	3	4	5	6	7	8	9	10	11	12	13	14	15	16	17	18	19	20	21	22	23	24	25	26	27	28	29	30	31
☉	8.6	9.6	10.5	11.5	12.4	13.4	14.4	15.3	16.3	17.2	18.2	19.1	20.1	21.1	22	23	24	24.9	25.9	26.8	27.8	28.8	29.7	0.7	1.7	2.6	3.6	4.6	5.5	6.5	7.5
☽	8.6	22.5	6	19.1	1.8	14.1	26.2	8.1	19.9	1.7	13.6	25.5	7.7	20	2.5	15.2	28.2	11.4	24.8	8.4	22.2	6.2	20.4	4.7	19.2	3.7	18.3	2.6	16.8	0.6	14.1
☿	22.9	23.1	23.4	23.7	24.2	24.8	25.5	26.3	27.3	28.3	29.4	0.6	1.9	3.3	4.8	6.3	8	9.7	11.4	13.2	15.1	17	18.9	20.8	22.8	24.8	26.8	28.7	0.7	2.7	4.7
♀	8.3	9.6	10.8	12	13.2	14.4	15.6	16.8	18	19.2	20.4	21.6	22.8	24	25.2	26.4	27.6	28.8	29.9	1.1	2.3	3.5	4.7	5.9	7.1	8.3	9.5	10.7	11.9	13	14.2
♂	24.5	25	25.5	26	26.5	27	27.4	27.9	28.4	28.9	29.3	29.7	0.2	0.6	1	1.4	1.8	2.2	2.6	3	3.4	3.7	4.1	4.4	4.7	5.1	5.4	5.7	6	6.2	6.5

♃ 1: 7.0R, 6: 6.4, 11: 5.7, 16: 5.1, 21: 4.6, 26: 4, 31: 3.6 — ♄ 1: 29.9, 6: 0.4, 11: 1, 16: 1.5, 21: 1.9, 26: 2.4, 31: 2.8 — ♅ 1: 19.5, 11: 19.8, 21: 20.2, 31: 20.7 — ♆ 1: 4.7R, 11: 4.7, 21: 4.7D, 31: 4.7 — ♇ 1: 2.3, 11: 2.6, 21: 2.9, 31: 3.3

1974

	1	2	3	4	5	6	7	8	9	10	11	12	13	14	15	16	17	18	19	20	21	22	23	24	25	26	27	28	29	30	31
☉	8.4	9.3	10.3	11.2	12.2	13.2	14.1	15.1	16	17	18	18.9	19.9	20.8	21.8	22.8	23.7	24.7	25.6	26.6	27.6	28.5	29.5	0.5	1.4	2.4	3.4	4.3	5.3	6.3	7.2
☽	14.8	26.7	8.5	20.4	2.3	14.2	26.3	8.5	21	3.6	16.6	29.9	13.6	27.7	12.3	27.2	12.4	27.6	12.8	27.7	12.2	26.2	9.7	22.8	5.5	17.8	29.9	11.8	23.7	5.5	17.3
☿	21.9	23.6	25.4	27.2	29.1	1	2.9	4.9	6.9	9	11	13.1	15.1	17.2	19.2	21.3	23.3	25.3	27.3	29.3	1.2	3.2	5.1	7	8.8	10.7	12.5	14.3	16.1	17.9	19.6
♀	13	14.2	15.4	16.7	17.9	19.1	20.3	21.5	22.7	23.9	25.1	26.4	27.6	28.8	0	1.2	2.5	3.7	4.9	6.1	7.3	8.6	9.8	11	12.2	13.5	14.7	15.9	17.1	18.4	19.6
♂	2.8	3.4	4	4.7	5.3	5.9	6.5	7.2	7.8	8.4	9.1	9.7	10.3	11	11.6	12.2	12.9	13.5	14.1	14.8	15.4	16	16.7	17.3	17.9	18.6	19.2	19.9	20.5	21.1	21.8

♃ 1: 16.9R, 6: 16.5, 11: 16, 16: 15.5, 21: 14.9, 26: 14.3, 31: 13.6 — ♄ 1: 12.3, 6: 12.9, 11: 13.5, 16: 14.1, 21: 14.6, 26: 15.2, 31: 15.7 — ♅ 1: 24, 11: 24.3, 21: 24.7, 31: 25.2 — ♆ 1: 6.9R, 11: 6.9, 21: 6.8D, 31: 6.9 — ♇ 1: 4.7, 11: 4.9, 21: 5.2, 31: 5.6

IX

1973

	1	2	3	4	5	6	7	8	9	10	11	12	13	14	15	16	17	18	19	20	21	22	23	24	25	26	27	28	29	30	31
☉	8.4	9.4	10.4	11.3	12.3	13.3	14.2	15.2	16.2	17.1	18.1	19.1	20.1	21	22	23	24	24.9	25.9	26.9	27.9	28.8	29.8	0.8	1.8	2.8	3.7	4.7	5.7	6.7	
☽	27.2	9.9	22.2	4.3	16.2	28	9.8	21.7	3.8	16	28.6	11.4	24.5	7.9	21.4	5.2	19.1	3	17.1	1.2	15.3	29.4	13.6	27.7	11.6	25.4	9	22.3	5.2	17.8	
☿	6.6	8.6	10.5	12.4	14.3	16.2	18.1	19.9	21.7	23.5	25.3	27.1	28.8	0.6	2.3	4	5.6	7.3	8.9	10.6	12.2	13.8	15.3	16.9	18.4	20	21.5	23	24.5	25.9	
♀	15.4	16.6	17.8	19	20.1	21.3	22.5	23.7	24.9	26	27.2	28.4	29.6	0.7	1.9	3.1	4.2	5.4	6.6	7.7	8.9	10.1	11.2	12.4	13.6	14.7	15.9	17	18.2	19.3	
♂	6.8	7	7.3	7.5	7.7	7.9	8.1	8.2	8.4	8.6	8.7	8.8	8.9	9	9.1	9.2	9.2	9.2	9.3	9.3R	9.3	9.2	9.2	9.1	9.1	9	8.9	8.8	8.7	8.5	

♃ 1: 3.5R, 6: 3.1, 11: 2.8, 16: 2.5, 21: 2.4, 26: 2.3 — ♄ 1: 2.9, 6: 3.2, 11: 3.6, 16: 3.9, 21: 4.1, 26: 4.3 — ♅ 1: 20.7, 11: 21.3, 21: 21.8 — ♆ 1: 4.7, 11: 4.8, 21: 5 — ♇ 1: 3.3, 11: 3.7, 21: 4

1974

	1	2	3	4	5	6	7	8	9	10	11	12	13	14	15	16	17	18	19	20	21	22	23	24	25	26	27	28	29	30	31
☉	8.2	9.2	10.1	11.1	12.1	13	14	15	15.9	16.9	17.9	18.9	19.8	20.8	21.8	22.8	23.7	24.7	25.7	26.7	27.6	28.6	29.6	0.6	1.5	2.5	3.5	4.5	5.5	6.5	
☽	29.3	11.3	23.4	5.6	18	0.6	13.4	26.4	9.6	23.3	7.2	21.5	6.2	21.1	6.1	21.1	6	20.4	4.5	18.1	1.2	13.9	26.3	8.4	20.3	2.1	14	25.9	7.9	20	
☿	21.3	23	24.7	26.4	28	29.6	1.2	2.8	4.3	5.9	7.4	8.9	10.4	11.8	13.3	14.7	16.1	17.5	18.9	20.2	21.5	22.8	24.1	25.3	26.5	27.7	28.9	30	1.1	2.1	
♀	20.8	22.1	23.3	24.5	25.8	27	28.2	29.5	0.7	1.9	3.2	4.4	5.6	6.9	8.1	9.4	10.6	11.8	13.1	14.3	15.6	16.8	18.1	19.3	20.5	21.8	23	24.3	25.5	26.8	
♂	22.4	23.1	23.7	24.3	25	25.6	26.3	26.9	27.6	28.2	28.8	29.5	0.1	0.8	1.4	2.1	2.7	3.4	4	4.7	5.3	6	6.6	7.3	7.9	8.6	9.2	9.9	10.5	11.2	

♃ 1: 13.5R, 6: 12.9, 11: 12.2, 16: 11.5, 21: 10.9, 26: 10.3 — ♄ 1: 15.7, 6: 16.2, 11: 16.6, 16: 17.1, 21: 17.4, 26: 17.8 — ♅ 1: 25.2, 11: 25.7, 21: 26.3 — ♆ 1: 6.9, 11: 7, 21: 7.1 — ♇ 1: 5.6, 11: 6, 21: 6.3

X

1973

	1	2	3	4	5	6	7	8	9	10	11	12	13	14	15	16	17	18	19	20	21	22	23	24	25	26	27	28	29	30	31
☉	7.7	8.7	9.6	10.6	11.6	12.6	13.6	14.6	15.6	16.5	17.5	18.5	19.5	20.5	21.5	22.5	23.5	24.5	25.5	26.5	27.5	28.4	29.4	0.4	1.4	2.4	3.4	4.4	5.4	6.4	7.4
☽	0.1	12.2	24.1	5.9	17.7	29.6	11.7	24	6.7	19.7	3.1	16.8	0.8	15	29.3	13.6	27.9	12.1	26.2	10.2	24.1	7.8	21.4	4.7	17.9	0.8	13.5	25.9	8.1	20.1	2
☿	27.4	28.8	0.2	1.6	3	4.4	5.7	7	8.4	9.6	10.9	12.1	13.4	14.5	15.7	16.8	17.9	19	20	20.9	21.8	22.7	23.5	24.2	24.8	25.4	25.9	26.2	26.5	26.6	26.6R
♀	20.5	21.6	22.8	23.9	25.1	26.2	27.3	28.5	29.6	0.8	1.9	3	4.1	5.3	6.4	7.5	8.6	9.7	10.9	12	13.1	14.2	15.3	16.4	17.5	18.6	19.7	20.8	21.8	22.9	24
♂	8.4R	8.2	8	7.8	7.6	7.4	7.2	6.9	6.7	6.4	6.1	5.8	5.5	5.2	4.9	4.6	4.3	4	3.6	3.3	3	2.6	2.3	2	1.6	1.3	1	0.6	0.3	30	29.7

♃ 1: 2.3, 6: 2.4, 11: 2.5, 16: 2.8, 21: 3.1, 26: 3.5, 31: 4 — ♄ 1: 4.5, 6: 4.6, 11: 4.7, 16: 4.7, 21: 4.7R, 26: 4.7, 31: 4.6 — ♅ 1: 22.4, 11: 23.1, 21: 23.7, 31: 24.3 — ♆ 1: 5.2, 11: 5.5, 21: 5.8, 31: 6.1 — ♇ 1: 4.4, 11: 4.8, 21: 5.2, 31: 5.5

1974

	1	2	3	4	5	6	7	8	9	10	11	12	13	14	15	16	17	18	19	20	21	22	23	24	25	26	27	28	29	30	31
☉	7.4	8.4	9.4	10.4	11.4	12.4	13.3	14.3	15.3	16.3	17.3	18.3	19.3	20.3	21.3	22.2	23.2	24.2	25.2	26.2	27.2	28.2	29.2	0.2	1.2	2.2	3.2	4.2	5.2	6.2	7.2
☽	2.4	14.8	27.5	10.4	23.4	6.6	20.1	3.7	17.6	1.7	16.1	0.6	15.3	29.9	14.4	28.6	12.5	26	9.1	21.8	4.2	16.4	28.3	10.2	22.1	4	16.1	28.3	10.8	23.5	6.5
☿	3.1	4.1	5	5.9	6.7	7.5	8.2	8.8	9.3	9.8	10.2	10.4	10.6	10.6R	10.5	10.3	10	9.5	8.8	8	7.1	6.1	4.9	3.7	2.5	1.2	30	28.8	27.7	26.8	26.1
♀	28	29.3	0.5	1.7	3	4.2	5.5	6.7	8	9.2	10.5	11.7	13	14.2	15.5	16.7	18	19.2	20.5	21.7	23	24.3	25.5	26.8	28	29.3	0.5	1.8	3	4.3	5.5
♂	11.9	12.5	13.2	13.8	14.5	15.2	15.8	16.5	17.1	17.8	18.5	19.1	19.8	20.4	21.1	21.8	22.4	23.1	23.8	24.4	25.1	25.8	26.4	27.1	27.8	28.5	29.1	29.8	0.5	1.2	1.8

♃ 1: 9.8R, 6: 9.3, 11: 8.9, 16: 8.6, 21: 8.3, 26: 8.1, 31: 8 — ♄ 1: 18, 6: 18.3, 11: 18.5, 16: 18.7, 21: 18.8, 26: 18.9, 31: 18.9 — ♅ 1: 26.8, 11: 27.5, 21: 28.1, 31: 28.7 — ♆ 1: 7.3, 11: 7.6, 21: 7.9, 31: 8.2 — ♇ 1: 6.7, 11: 7.1, 21: 7.5, 31: 7.8

XI

1973

	1	2	3	4	5	6	7	8	9	10	11	12	13	14	15	16	17	18	19	20	21	22	23	24	25	26	27	28	29	30	31
☉	8.4	9.4	10.4	11.4	12.4	13.4	14.4	15.4	16.4	17.5	18.5	19.5	20.5	21.5	22.5	23.5	24.5	25.5	26.5	27.5	28.5	29.5	0.6	1.6	2.6	3.6	4.6	5.6	6.6	7.6	
☽	13.8	25.6	7.5	19.5	1.8	14.5	27.6	11.1	25	9.3	23.9	8.6	23.4	8.1	22.6	6.9	21	4.7	18.2	1.5	14.5	27.3	9.9	22.3	4.5	16.5	28.4	10.2	22	3.8	
☿	26.4R	26.1	25.7	25	24.3	23.3	22.2	21.1	19.8	18.5	17.1	15.8	14.6	13.5	12.6	11.8	11.2	10.8	10.6	10.6D	10.7	11.1	11.5	12.2	12.9	13.8	14.7	15.7	16.8	18	
♀	25.1	26.1	27.2	28.3	29.3	0.4	1.4	2.5	3.5	4.5	5.5	6.6	7.6	8.6	9.6	10.6	11.6	12.5	13.5	14.5	15.4	16.4	17.3	18.2	19.2	20.1	21	21.9	22.7	23.6	
♂	29.4R	29.1	28.8	28.5	28.2	28	27.7	27.5	27.2	27	26.8	26.6	26.4	26.3	26.1	26	25.9	25.7	25.6	25.5	25.5	25.4	25.4	25.3	25.3	25.3D	25.3	25.3	25.4	25.4	

♃ 1: 4.1, 6: 4.6, 11: 5.2, 16: 5.9, 21: 6.7, 26: 7.4 — ♄ 1: 4.5R, 6: 4.4, 11: 4.2, 16: 3.9, 21: 3.7, 26: 3.3 — ♅ 1: 24.4, 11: 25, 21: 25.6 — ♆ 1: 6.1, 11: 6.5, 21: 6.8 — ♇ 1: 5.5, 11: 5.9, 21: 6.1

1974

	1	2	3	4	5	6	7	8	9	10	11	12	13	14	15	16	17	18	19	20	21	22	23	24	25	26	27	28	29	30	31
☉	8.2	9.2	10.2	11.2	12.2	13.2	14.2	15.2	16.2	17.2	18.2	19.2	20.2	21.2	22.2	23.2	24.3	25.3	26.3	27.3	28.3	29.3	0.3	1.3	2.3	3.3	4.4	5.4	6.4	7.4	
☽	19.7	3.2	16.8	0.6	14.5	28.5	12.7	26.8	11.1	25.3	9.4	23.4	7.2	20.8	4	17	29.6	12	24.2	6.1	18	29.9	11.8	23.9	6.2	18.7	1.6	14.8	28.3	12.1	
☿	25.5R	25.1	24.9	24.9D	25.1	25.4	25.9	26.6	27.4	28.3	29.3	0.4	1.5	2.8	4.1	5.4	6.8	8.2	9.7	11.1	12.6	14.1	15.7	17.2	18.7	20.3	21.8	23.4	24.9	26.5	
♀	6.8	8	9.3	10.6	11.8	13.1	14.3	15.6	16.8	18.1	19.3	20.6	21.8	23.1	24.4	25.6	26.9	28.1	29.4	0.6	1.9	3.2	4.4	5.7	6.9	8.2	9.4	10.7	11.9	13.2	
♂	2.5	3.2	3.9	4.5	5.2	5.9	6.6	7.2	7.9	8.6	9.3	10	10.7	11.3	12	12.7	13.4	14.1	14.8	15.5	16.1	16.8	17.5	18.2	18.9	19.6	20.3	21	21.7	22.4	

♃ 1: 8.0R, 6: 8.0D, 11: 8.1, 16: 8.3, 21: 8.5, 26: 8.8 — ♄ 1: 18.9R, 6: 18.9, 11: 18.8, 16: 18.7, 21: 18.5, 26: 18.3 — ♅ 1: 28.8, 11: 29.4, 21: 30 — ♆ 1: 8.2, 11: 8.6, 21: 8.9 — ♇ 1: 7.9, 11: 8.2, 21: 8.5

XII

1973

	1	2	3	4	5	6	7	8	9	10	11	12	13	14	15	16	17	18	19	20	21	22	23	24	25	26	27	28	29	30	31
☉	8.7	9.7	10.7	11.7	12.7	13.7	14.7	15.8	16.8	17.8	18.8	19.8	20.8	21.9	22.9	23.9	24.9	25.9	26.9	28	29	30	1	2	3.1	4.1	5.1	6.1	7.1	8.2	9.2
☽	15.7	27.7	10	22.6	5.5	19	2.8	17.2	1.9	16.8	2	17.1	2	16.7	1	14.9	28.4	11.5	24.4	6.9	19.2	1.3	13.3	25.2	7	18.8	0.6	12.5	24.4	6.5	18.7
☿	19.2	20.5	21.8	23.1	24.5	25.9	27.3	28.7	0.2	1.6	3.1	4.6	6.1	7.6	9.1	10.6	12.1	13.6	15.1	16.7	18.2	19.7	21.3	22.8	24.4	25.9	27.5	29	0.6	2.1	3.7
♀	24.5	25.3	26.1	27	27.8	28.5	29.3	0.1	0.8	1.5	2.2	2.9	3.6	4.2	4.9	5.5	6	6.6	7.1	7.6	8.1	8.6	9	9.4	9.7	10	10.3	10.6	10.8	11	11.2
♂	25.5	25.5	25.6	25.7	25.8	26	26.1	26.2	26.4	26.5	26.7	26.9	27.1	27.3	27.5	27.8	28	28.2	28.5	28.8	29	29.3	29.6	29.9	0.2	0.5	0.8	1.2	1.5	1.8	2.2

♃ 1: 8.3, 6: 9.2, 11: 10.1, 16: 11.1, 21: 12.1, 26: 13.1, 31: 14.2 — ♄ 1: 3.0R, 6: 2.6, 11: 2.2, 16: 1.8, 21: 1.4, 26: 1, 31: 0.6 — ♅ 1: 26.1, 11: 26.6, 21: 27, 31: 27.3 — ♆ 1: 7.2, 11: 7.6, 21: 8, 31: 8.3 — ♇ 1: 6.4, 11: 6.6, 21: 6.7, 31: 6.8

1974

	1	2	3	4	5	6	7	8	9	10	11	12	13	14	15	16	17	18	19	20	21	22	23	24	25	26	27	28	29	30	31
☉	8.4	9.4	10.4	11.5	12.5	13.5	14.5	15.5	16.5	17.5	18.6	19.6	20.6	21.6	22.6	23.6	24.7	25.7	26.7	27.7	28.7	29.8	0.8	1.8	2.8	3.8	4.8	5.9	6.9	7.9	8.9
☽	26.2	10.5	24.9	9.3	23.6	7.9	22	5.9	19.7	3.2	16.6	29.7	12.6	25.3	7.7	20	2.1	14.1	25.9	7.8	19.7	1.7	13.9	26.4	9.3	22.5	6.2	20.2	4.7	19.4	4.3
☿	28	29.6	1.2	2.7	4.3	5.8	7.4	9	10.5	12.1	13.7	15.2	16.8	18.4	19.9	21.5	23.1	24.7	26.2	27.8	29.4	1	2.6	4.2	5.8	7.4	9	10.6	12.2	13.8	15.4
♀	14.5	15.7	17	18.2	19.5	20.7	22	23.3	24.5	25.8	27	28.3	29.5	0.8	2	3.3	4.6	5.8	7.1	8.3	9.6	10.8	12.1	13.4	14.6	15.9	17.1	18.4	19.6	20.9	22.1
♂	23.1	23.8	24.5	25.2	25.9	26.6	27.3	28	28.7	29.4	0.1	0.8	1.5	2.2	2.9	3.6	4.3	5	5.7	6.4	7.1	7.8	8.5	9.3	10	10.7	11.4	12.1	12.8	13.5	14.3

♃ 1: 9.3, 6: 9.7, 11: 10.3, 16: 10.9, 21: 11.6, 26: 12.4, 31: 13.2 — ♄ 1: 18.1R, 6: 17.8, 11: 17.5, 16: 17.1, 21: 16.7, 26: 16.3, 31: 15.9 — ♅ 1: 0.5, 11: 1, 21: 1.5, 31: 1.8 — ♆ 1: 9.3, 11: 9.7, 21: 10, 31: 10.4 — ♇ 1: 8.8, 11: 9, 21: 9.1, 31: 9.2

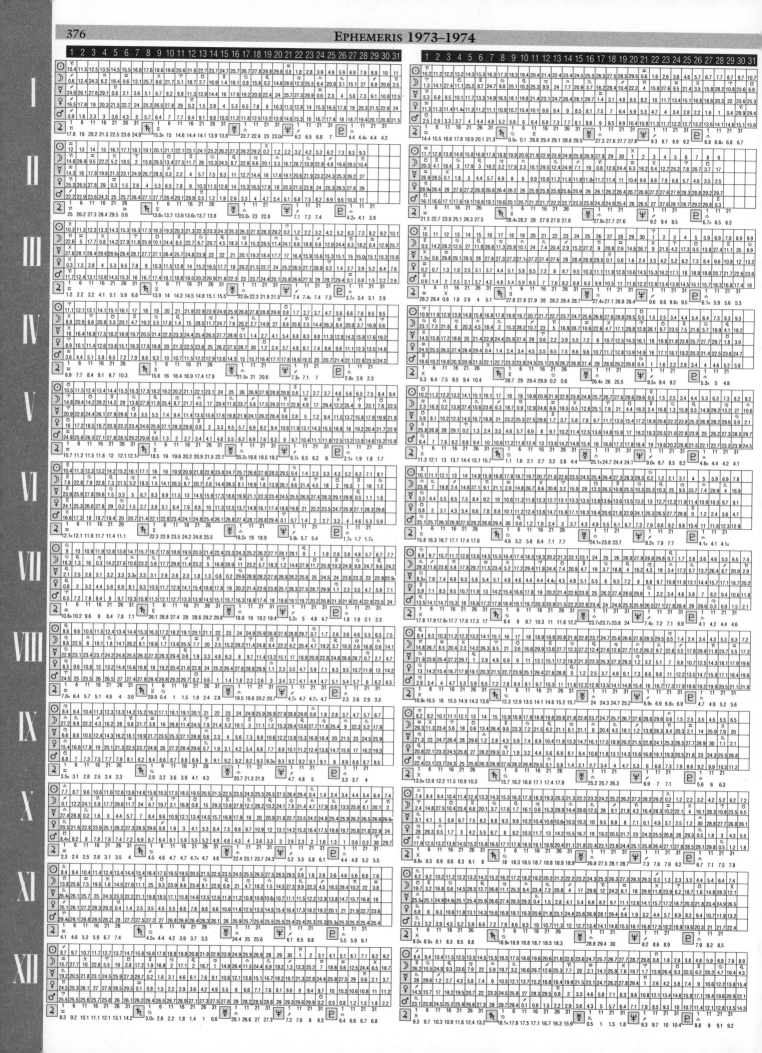

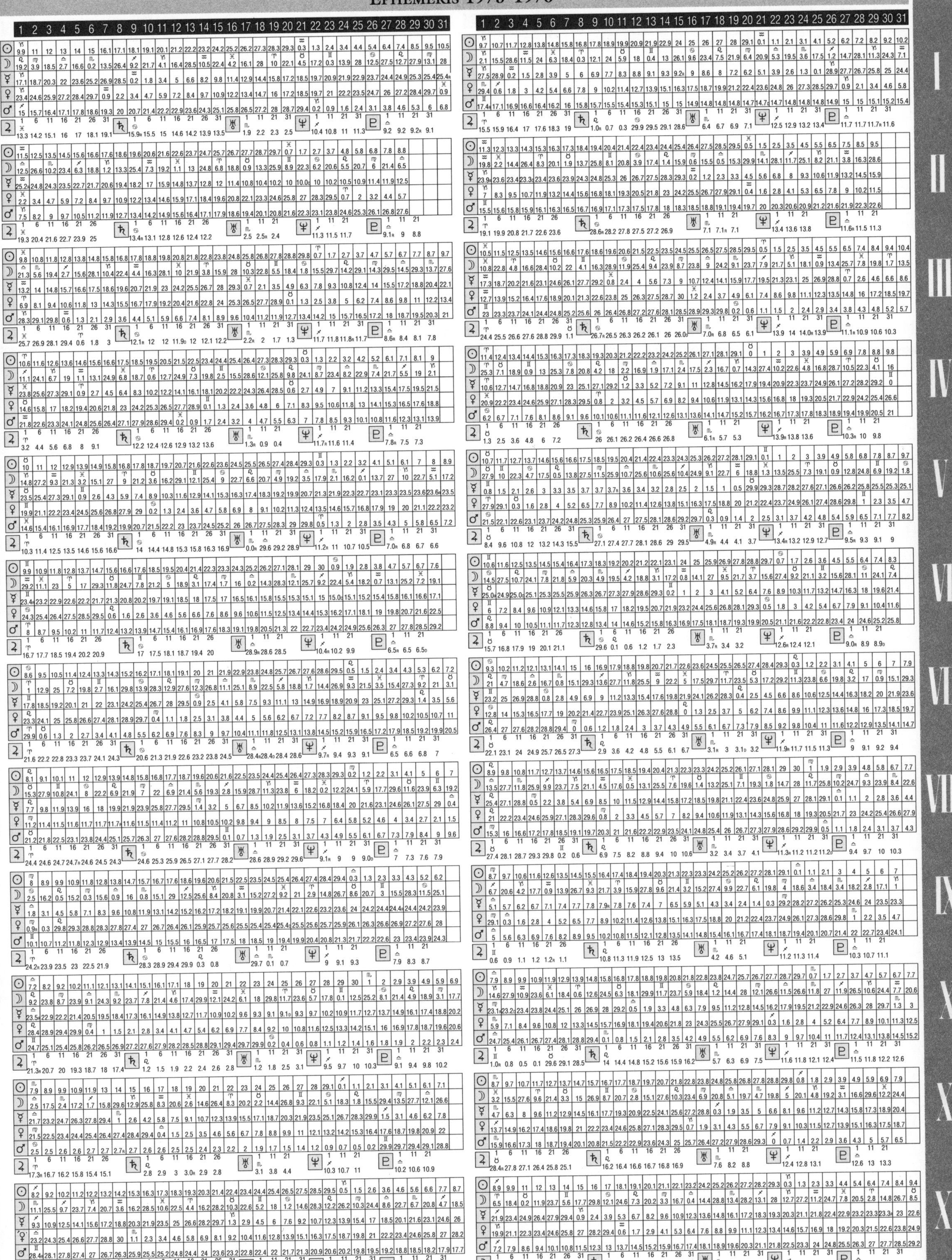

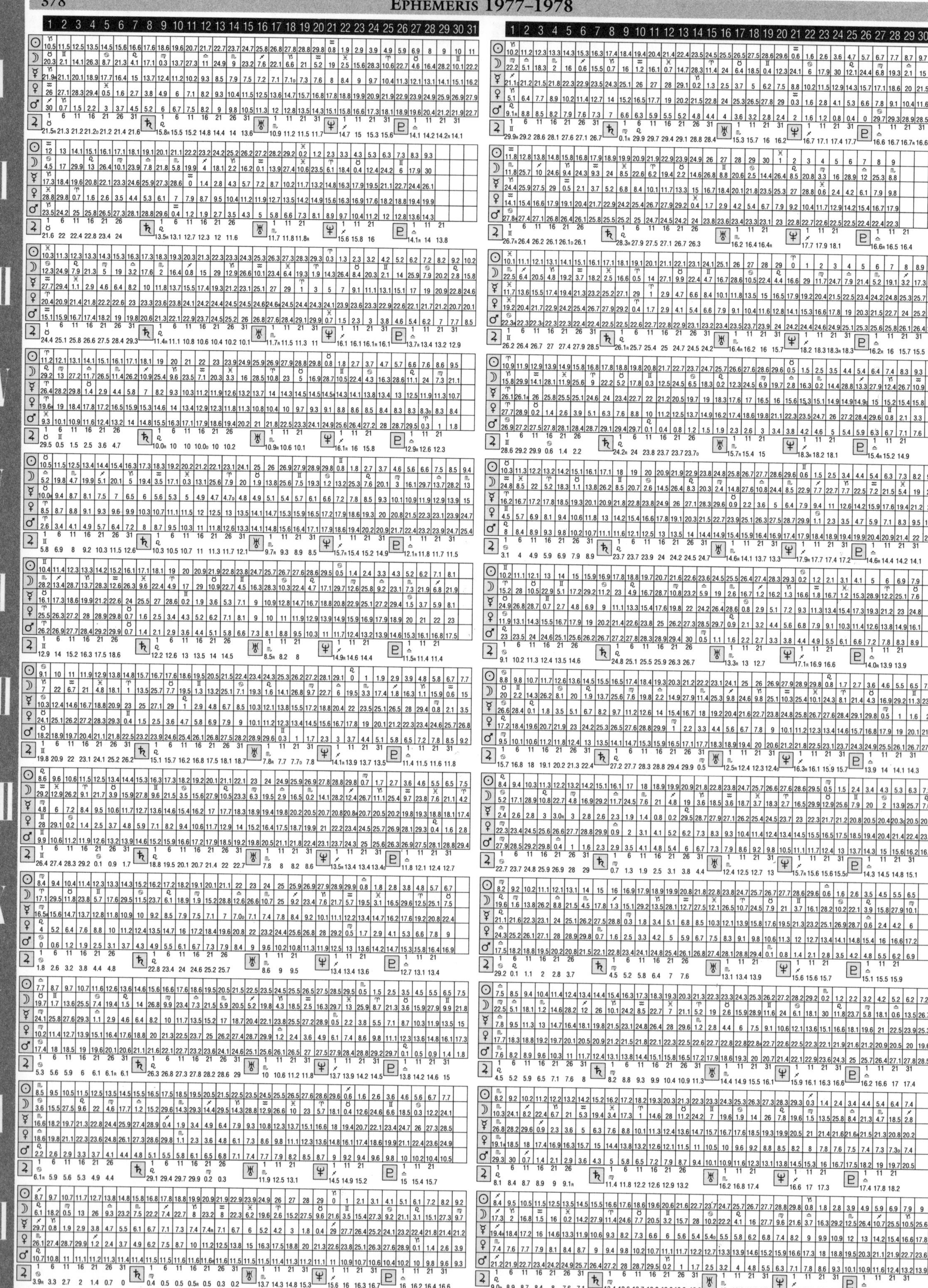

I

II

III

IV

V

VI

VII

VIII

IX

X

XI

XII

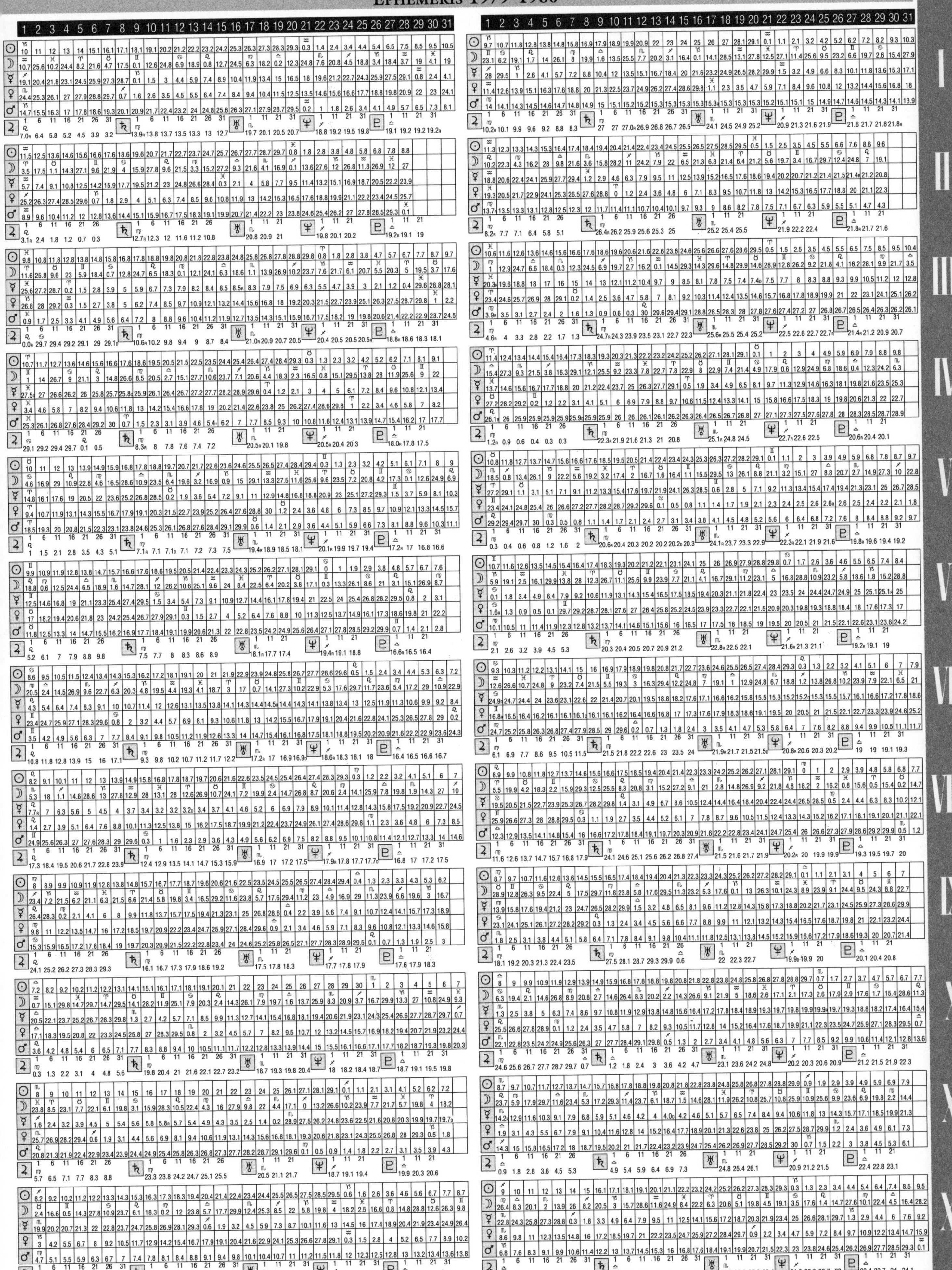

1981

I

	1	2	3	4	5	6	7	8	9	10	11	12	13	14	15	16	17	18	19	20	21	22	23	24	25	26	27	28	29	30	31
☉	10.5	11.5	12.5	13.6	14.6	15.6	16.6	17.6	18.6	19.7	20.7	21.7	22.7	23.7	24.8	25.8	26.8	27.8	28.8	29.9	0.9	1.9	2.9	3.9	4.9	6	7	8	9	10	11
☽	10.1	22.1	4.2	16.5	29.1	11.9	24.9	8.2	21.6	5.3	19.1	3.1	17.1	1.3	15.6	29.8	14	28.2	12.1	25.8	9.3	22.4	5.3	17.8	0.1	12.2	24.1	6	17.9	29.9	12
☿	10.8	12.5	14.1	15.7	17.3	19	20.6	22.3	23.9	25.6	27.2	28.9	0.6	2.3	4	5.6	7.3	9	10.7	12.4	14	15.7	17.3	19	20.6	22.1	23.6	25.1	26.5	27.9	29.1
♀	17.2	18.4	19.7	20.9	22.2	23.4	24.7	25.9	27.2	28.4	29.7	0.9	2.2	3.4	4.7	5.9	7.2	8.4	9.7	10.9	12.2	13.4	14.7	15.9	17.2	18.4	19.7	20.9	22.2	23.4	24.7
♂	0.9	1.6	2.4	3.2	4	4.8	5.6	6.4	7.1	7.9	8.7	9.5	10.3	11.1	11.9	12.7	13.5	14.2	15	15.8	16.6	17.4	18.2	19	19.8	20.6	21.4	22.2	22.9	23.7	24.5

♃ 1 6 11 16 21 26 31: 9.5 9.8 10.1 10.3 10.4 10.4R 10.3 — ♄ 1 6 11 16 21 26 31: 9.5 9.6 9.7 9.8 9.8R 9.7 9.6 — ♅ 1 11 21 31: 28.4 28.9 29.3 29.6 — ♆ 1 11 21 31: 23.1 23.4 23.7 24 — ♇ 1 11 21 31: 24.2 24.3 24.3 24.3R

II

	1	2	3	4	5	6	7	8	9	10	11	12	13	14	15	16	17	18	19	20	21	22	23	24	25	26	27	28
☉	12.1	13.1	14.1	15.1	16.1	17.1	18.1	19.1	20.2	21.2	22.2	23.2	24.2	25.2	26.2	27.2	28.2	29.3	0.3	1.3	2.3	3.3	4.3	5.3	6.3	7.3	8.3	9.3
☽	24.4	7.1	20.1	3.4	17	0.9	15.1	29.4	13.7	28.1	12.4	26.6	10.6	24.4	8.1	21.6	4.9	17.9	0.8	13.4	25.8	8	20.1	2	13.9	25.8	7.7	19.8
☿	0.3	1.4	2.3	3.2	3.8	4.4	4.7	4.9	4.9R	4.7	4.4	3.8	3.2	2.3	1.4	0.4	29.3	28.1	27	25.9	24.8	23.8	23	22.2	21.5	20.9	20.5	20.1
♀	25.9	27.2	28.4	29.7	0.9	2.2	3.4	4.7	6	7.2	8.5	9.7	11	12.2	13.5	14.7	16	17.2	18.5	19.7	21	22.2	23.5	24.7	26	27.2	28.5	29.7
♂	25.3	26.1	26.9	27.7	28.5	29.3	0.1	0.9	1.6	2.4	3.2	4	4.8	5.6	6.4	7.2	8	8.8	9.5	10.3	11.1	11.9	12.7	13.5	14.3	15.1	15.8	16.6

♃ 1 6 11 16 21 26: 10.3R 10.2 9.9 9.6 9.2 8.8 — ♄ 1 6 11 16 21 26: 9.6R 9.5 9.3 9.1 8.8 8.5 — ♅ 1 11 21: 29.7 29.9 0 — ♆ 1 11 21: 24.1 24.3 24.5 — ♇ 1 11 21: 24.3R 24.3 24.2

III

	1	2	3	4	5	6	7	8	9	10	11	12	13	14	15	16	17	18	19	20	21	22	23	24	25	26	27	28	29	30	31
☉	10.3	11.3	12.3	13.3	14.3	15.3	16.3	17.3	18.3	19.3	20.3	21.3	22.3	23.3	24.3	25.3	26.3	27.3	28.3	29.3	0.3	1.3	2.3	3.3	4.3	5.3	6.2	7.2	8.2	9.2	10.2
☽	2.2	14.8	27.9	11.3	25.2	9.4	24	8.7	23.6	8.4	23	7.3	21.3	5	18.5	1.6	14.5	27.2	9.7	22.1	4.3	16.4	28.4	10.3	22.2	4	16	28	10.3	22.9	5.8
☿	19.9	19.9	19.9R	20	20.2	20.6	21	21.4	22	22.6	23.4	24.1	24.9	25.8	26.7	27.7	28.7	29.8	0.9	2	3.2	4.4	5.7	7	8.3	9.6	11	12.4	13.8	15.2	16.7
♀	1	2.2	3.4	4.7	5.9	7.2	8.4	9.7	10.9	12.2	13.4	14.7	15.9	17.2	18.4	19.7	20.9	22.2	23.4	24.6	25.9	27.1	28.4	29.6	0.9	2.1	3.3	4.6	5.8	7.1	8.3
♂	17.4	18.2	19	19.8	20.6	21.3	22.1	22.9	23.7	24.5	25.3	26	26.8	27.6	28.4	29.2	29.9	0.7	1.5	2.3	3	3.8	4.6	5.4	6.1	6.9	7.7	8.5	9.2	10	10.8

♃ 1 6 11 16 21 26 31: 8.5R 8 7.4 6.8 6.2 5.5 4.9 — ♄ 1 6 11 16 21 26 31: 8.4R 8 7.7 7.3 6.9 6.5 6.1 — ♅ 1 11 21 31: 0.1 0.1R 0 29.8 — ♆ 1 11 21 31: 24.7 24.8 24.8 24.9R — ♇ 1 11 21 31: 24.0R 23.8 23.6 23.3

IV

	1	2	3	4	5	6	7	8	9	10	11	12	13	14	15	16	17	18	19	20	21	22	23	24	25	26	27	28	29	30
☉	11.2	12.2	13.2	14.1	15.1	16.1	17.1	18.1	19.1	20	21	22	23	24	24.9	25.9	26.9	27.9	28.9	29.8	0.8	1.8	2.8	3.7	4.7	5.7	6.7	7.6	8.6	9.6
☽	19.2	3.1	17.5	2.2	17.3	2.5	17.6	2.6	17.2	1.4	15.2	28.6	11.6	24.3	6.8	19	1.2	13.2	25.2	7.1	19	0.9	12.8	24.7	6.8	19.1	1.6	14.5	27.8	11.5
☿	18.2	19.7	21.3	22.8	24.4	26.1	27.7	29.4	1.1	2.8	4.5	6.3	8.1	9.9	11.8	13.6	15.5	17.5	19.4	21.4	23.4	25.4	27.5	29.5	1.6	3.7	5.9	8	10.2	12.3
♀	9.6	10.8	12	13.3	14.5	15.8	17	18.2	19.5	20.7	22	23.2	24.4	25.7	26.9	28.2	29.4	0.6	1.9	3.1	4.3	5.6	6.8	8	9.3	10.5	11.8	13	14.2	15.5
♂	11.5	12.3	13.1	13.8	14.6	15.4	16.1	16.9	17.7	18.4	19.2	20	20.7	21.5	22.2	23	23.8	24.5	25.3	26	26.8	27.5	28.3	29	29.8	0.5	1.3	2	2.8	3.5

♃ 1 6 11 16 21 26: 4.8R 4.1 3.5 2.9 2.4 1.9 — ♄ 1 6 11 16 21 26: 6.1R 5.7 5.3 4.9 4.6 4.3 — ♅ 1 11 21: 29.8R 29.5 29.2 — ♆ 1 11 21: 24.9R 24.8 24.7 — ♇ 1 11 21: 23.3R 23 22.7

V

	1	2	3	4	5	6	7	8	9	10	11	12	13	14	15	16	17	18	19	20	21	22	23	24	25	26	27	28	29	30	31
☉	10.5	11.5	12.5	13.5	14.4	15.4	16.4	17.3	18.3	19.3	20.2	21.2	22.2	23.1	24.1	25.1	26	27	27.9	28.9	29.9	0.8	1.8	2.8	3.7	4.7	5.6	6.6	7.6	8.5	9.5
☽	25.8	10.5	25.6	10.8	26.2	11.3	26.2	10.6	24.5	8	21	3.7	16.1	28.3	10.3	22.3	4.1	16	27.9	9.8	21.8	3.9	16.1	28.4	11	23.9	7.2	20.8	4.9	19.4	4.2
☿	14.5	16.6	18.8	20.9	23	25.1	27.2	29.2	1.2	3.2	5.1	7	8.8	10.6	12.3	13.9	15.6	17.1	18.6	20	21.4	22.7	24	25.2	26.4	27.4	28.4	29.4	0.3	1.1	1.8
♀	16.7	17.9	19.2	20.4	21.6	22.9	24.1	25.3	26.5	27.8	29	0.2	1.5	2.7	3.9	5.2	6.4	7.6	8.8	10.1	11.3	12.5	13.8	15	16.2	17.4	18.7	19.9	21.1	22.3	23.6
♂	4.3	5	5.8	6.5	7.3	8	8.7	9.5	10.2	11	11.7	12.4	13.2	13.9	14.6	15.4	16.1	16.8	17.6	18.3	19	19.8	20.5	21.2	21.9	22.7	23.4	24.1	24.8	25.5	26.3

♃ 1 6 11 16 21 26 31: 1.5R 1.2 0.9 0.7 0.5 0.5 0.5D — ♄ 1 6 11 16 21 26 31: 4.0R 3.7 3.5 3.3 3.2 3.1 3 — ♅ 1 11 21 31: 28.8R 28.4 28 27.6 — ♆ 1 11 21 31: 24.5R 24.3 24.1 23.9 — ♇ 1 11 21 31: 22.5R 22.2 22 21.8

VI

	1	2	3	4	5	6	7	8	9	10	11	12	13	14	15	16	17	18	19	20	21	22	23	24	25	26	27	28	29	30
☉	10.4	11.4	12.3	13.3	14.3	15.2	16.2	17.1	18.1	19.1	20	21	21.9	22.9	23.8	24.8	25.7	26.7	27.6	28.6	29.5	0.5	1.5	2.4	3.4	4.3	5.3	6.2	7.2	8.1
☽	19.3	4.5	19.6	4.5	19	3	16.6	29.8	12.5	24.9	7.1	19.1	1	12.9	24.8	6.7	18.7	0.8	13.1	25.5	8.1	20.9	4	17.3	1	14.9	29.2	13.8	28.5	13.4
☿	2.5	3.1	3.6	4.1	4.5	4.8	5	5.1	5.2	5.2R	5.1	5	4.8	4.5	4.1	3.7	3.3	2.8	2.3	1.7	1.1	0.6	0	29.4	28.9	28.4	27.9	27.5	27.1	26.8
♀	24.8	26	27.2	28.5	29.7	0.9	2.1	3.4	4.6	5.8	7	8.3	9.5	10.7	11.9	13.1	14.4	15.6	16.8	18	19.2	20.5	21.7	22.9	24.1	25.3	26.6	27.8	29	0.2
♂	27	27.7	28.4	29.1	29.8	0.6	1.3	2	2.7	3.4	4.1	4.8	5.5	6.2	7	7.7	8.4	9.1	9.8	10.5	11.2	11.9	12.6	13.3	14	14.7	15.4	16.1	16.7	17.4

♃ 1 6 11 16 21 26: 0.5 0.6 0.8 1 1.3 1.7 — ♄ 1 6 11 16 21 26: 3.0R 3.0D 3 3.1 3.2 3.4 — ♅ 1 11 21: 27.6R 27.2 26.8 — ♆ 1 11 21: 23.8R 23.6 23.3 — ♇ 1 11 21: 21.8R 21.7 21.6

VII

	1	2	3	4	5	6	7	8	9	10	11	12	13	14	15	16	17	18	19	20	21	22	23	24	25	26	27	28	29	30	31
☉	9.1	10	11	11.9	12.9	13.9	14.8	15.8	16.7	17.7	18.6	19.6	20.5	21.5	22.4	23.4	24.3	25.3	26.3	27.2	28.2	29.1	0.1	1	2	2.9	3.9	4.8	5.8	6.8	7.7
☽	28.2	12.8	27.2	11.2	24.8	7.9	20.8	3.2	15.5	27.5	9.4	21.3	3.2	15.2	27.3	9.6	22.1	4.8	17.7	0.9	14.2	27.9	11.7	25.7	9.9	24.2	8.6	23	7.3	21.6	5.6
☿	26.6R	26.4	26.4	26.4D	26.4	26.6	26.8	27.2	27.6	28.1	28.7	29.4	0.1	0.9	1.9	2.9	4	5.1	6.4	7.7	9.1	10.5	12	13.5	15.3	17	18.8	20.7	22.6	24.5	26.5
♀	1.4	2.6	3.9	5.1	6.3	7.5	8.7	9.9	11.1	12.4	13.6	14.8	16	17.2	18.4	19.6	20.8	22.1	23.2	24.5	25.7	26.9	28.1	29.3	0.5	1.7	2.9	4.1	5.3	6.5	7.8
♂	18.1	18.8	19.5	20.2	20.9	21.6	22.3	23	23.6	24.3	25	25.7	26.4	27	27.7	28.4	29.1	29.8	0.4	1.1	1.8	2.5	3.1	3.8	4.5	5.1	5.8	6.5	7.1	7.8	8.5

♃ 1 6 11 16 21 26 31: 2.1 2.7 3.2 3.8 4.5 5.2 6 — ♄ 1 6 11 16 21 26 31: 3.6 3.8 4.1 4.4 4.7 5.1 5.5 — ♅ 1 11 21 31: 26.5R 26.3 26.1 26.1 — ♆ 1 11 21 31: 23.0R 22.8 22.6 22.4 — ♇ 1 11 21 31: 21.5R 21.6D 21.6 21.8

VIII

	1	2	3	4	5	6	7	8	9	10	11	12	13	14	15	16	17	18	19	20	21	22	23	24	25	26	27	28	29	30	31
☉	8.7	9.6	10.6	11.5	12.5	13.5	14.4	15.4	16.3	17.3	18.3	19.2	20.2	21.1	22.1	23.1	24	25	25.9	26.9	27.9	28.8	29.8	0.8	1.7	2.7	3.6	4.6	5.6	6.5	7.5
☽	19.4	2.8	15.9	28.7	11.2	23.5	5.5	17.4	29.3	11.2	23.2	5.4	17.9	0.6	13.6	26.9	10.4	24.3	8.3	22.4	6.7	20.9	5.1	19.3	3.3	17.3	1	14.6	28	11.2	24.1
☿	28.5	0.5	2.5	4.6	6.7	8.8	10.8	12.9	15	17	19.1	21.1	23.1	25.1	27.1	29	0.9	2.8	4.7	6.5	8.4	10.2	12	13.7	15.5	17.2	18.9	20.5	22.2	23.8	25.4
♀	9	10.2	11.4	12.6	13.8	15	16.2	17.4	18.6	19.8	21	22.2	23.4	24.6	25.8	26.9	28.1	29.3	0.5	1.7	2.9	4.1	5.3	6.5	7.7	8.9	10	11.2	12.4	13.6	14.8
♂	9.1	9.8	10.5	11.1	11.8	12.5	13.1	13.8	14.4	15.1	15.7	16.4	17.1	17.7	18.4	19	19.7	20.3	21	21.6	22.3	22.9	23.5	24.2	24.8	25.5	26.1	26.8	27.4	28	28.7

♃ 1 6 11 16 21 26 31: 6.1 6.9 7.8 8.7 9.6 10.5 11.5 — ♄ 1 6 11 16 21 26 31: 5.6 6 6.5 7 7.5 8 8.5 — ♅ 1 11 21 31: 26.1R 26.1D 26.2 26.4 — ♆ 1 11 21 31: 22.4R 22.2 22.1 22.1 — ♇ 1 11 21 31: 21.8 22 22.2 22.5

IX

	1	2	3	4	5	6	7	8	9	10	11	12	13	14	15	16	17	18	19	20	21	22	23	24	25	26	27	28	29	30
☉	8.5	9.4	10.4	11.4	12.4	13.3	14.3	15.3	16.2	17.2	18.2	19.2	20.1	21.1	22.1	23.1	24	25	26	27	27.9	28.9	29.9	0.9	1.8	2.8	3.8	4.8	5.8	6.8
☽	6.8	19.2	1.4	13.4	25.4	7.2	19.1	1.1	13.3	25.8	8.6	21.8	5.4	19.3	3.6	18.1	2.7	17.3	1.8	16.1	0.2	14	27.7	11.1	24.3	7.3	20.1	2.8	15.2	27.5
☿	27	28.6	0.1	1.6	3.1	4.6	6.1	7.5	8.9	10.3	11.7	13	14.3	15.6	16.9	18.2	19.4	20.6	21.7	22.9	24	25	26	27	27.9	28.8	29.6	0.4	1.1	1.8
♀	16	17.1	18.3	19.5	20.7	21.9	23	24.2	25.4	26.6	27.7	28.9	0.1	1.2	2.4	3.6	4.7	5.9	7.1	8.2	9.4	10.5	11.7	12.9	14	15.2	16.3	17.5	18.6	19.8
♂	29.3	30	0.6	1.2	1.9	2.5	3.1	3.8	4.4	5	5.6	6.3	6.9	7.5	8.2	8.8	9.4	10	10.6	11.3	11.9	12.5	13.1	13.7	14.3	15	15.6	16.2	16.8	17.4

♃ 1 6 11 16 21 26: 11.7 12.7 13.7 14.7 15.8 16.8 — ♄ 1 6 11 16 21 26: 8.7 9.2 9.8 10.4 11 11.6 — ♅ 1 11 21: 26.4 26.7 27 — ♆ 1 11 21: 22.1R 22.1D 22.2 — ♇ 1 11 21: 22.6 22.9 23.2

X

	1	2	3	4	5	6	7	8	9	10	11	12	13	14	15	16	17	18	19	20	21	22	23	24	25	26	27	28	29	30	31
☉	7.7	8.7	9.7	10.7	11.7	12.7	13.6	14.6	15.6	16.6	17.6	18.6	19.6	20.6	21.6	22.5	23.5	24.5	25.5	26.5	27.5	28.5	29.5	0.5	1.5	2.5	3.5	4.5	5.5	6.5	7.5
☽	9.6	21.6	3.5	15.3	27.1	9.1	21.2	3.7	16.5	29.7	13.4	27.6	12.2	27	12.1	27.1	11.9	26.5	10.7	24.6	8.1	21.3	4.2	16.8	29.1	11.9	24	6	18.2	0.1	11.9
☿	2.3	2.8	3.2	3.5	3.8	3.9	3.8R	3.7	3.4	3	2.5	1.8	1	0.1	29.1	27.9	26.7	25.5	24.3	23.1	22	20.9	20.1	19.3	18.8	18.4	18.3	18.3D	18.5	18.9	19.4
♀	20.9	22.1	23.2	24.3	25.5	26.6	27.7	28.9	0	1.1	2.3	3.4	4.5	5.6	6.7	7.9	9	10.1	11.2	12.3	13.4	14.5	15.6	16.7	17.8	18.9	19.9	21	22.1	23.1	24.2
♂	18	18.6	19.2	19.8	20.4	21	21.6	22.2	22.8	23.4	24	24.6	25.2	25.8	26.4	27	27.6	28.2	28.8	29.4	0	0.5	1.1	1.7	2.3	2.9	3.4	4	4.6	5.2	5.7

♃ 1 6 11 16 21 26 31: 17.9 19 20.1 21.2 22.2 23.3 24.4 — ♄ 1 6 11 16 21 26 31: 12.2 12.8 13.4 14 14.7 15.3 15.8 — ♅ 1 11 21 31: 27.4 27.9 28.4 29 — ♆ 1 11 21 31: 22.3 22.5 22.7 23 — ♇ 1 11 21 31: 23.6 24 24.4 24.8

XI

	1	2	3	4	5	6	7	8	9	10	11	12	13	14	15	16	17	18	19	20	21	22	23	24	25	26	27	28	29	30
☉	8.5	9.5	10.5	11.5	12.5	13.5	14.5	15.5	16.5	17.5	18.5	19.5	20.5	21.5	22.5	23.6	24.6	25.6	26.6	27.6	28.6	29.6	0.6	1.6	2.6	3.7	4.7	5.7	6.7	7.7
☽	23.7	5.5	17.5	29.6	11.9	24.6	7.8	21.4	5.6	20.2	5.2	20.4	5.7	20.9	5.8	20.3	4.3	17.9	1.1	14	26.6	9	21.1	3.2	15.1	27.1	8.9	20.7	2.5	14.4
☿	20.1	20.9	21.9	22.9	24	25.2	26.5	27.9	29.2	0.7	2.1	3.6	5.1	6.6	8.2	9.7	11.3	12.9	14.4	16	17.6	19.2	20.7	22.3	23.9	25.5	27.1	28.6	0.2	1.8
♀	25.3	26.3	27.4	28.4	29.5	0.5	1.5	2.6	3.6	4.6	5.6	6.6	7.6	8.6	9.6	10.5	11.5	12.5	13.4	14.4	15.3	16.2	17.1	18	18.9	19.8	20.7	21.5	22.4	23.2
♂	6.3	6.9	7.4	8	8.6	9.1	9.7	10.3	10.8	11.4	11.9	12.5	13	13.6	14.1	14.7	15.2	15.8	16.3	16.8	17.4	17.9	18.4	19	19.5	20	20.5	21.1	21.6	22.1

♃ 1 6 11 16 21 26: 24.6 25.7 26.7 27.8 28.8 29.8 — ♄ 1 6 11 16 21 26: 16 16.5 17.1 17.6 18.2 18.7 — ♅ 1 11 21: 29.1 29.7 0.3 — ♆ 1 11 21: 23 23.3 23.6 — ♇ 1 11 21: 24.8 25.2 25.6

XII

	1	2	3	4	5	6	7	8	9	10	11	12	13	14	15	16	17	18	19	20	21	22	23	24	25	26	27	28	29	30	31
☉	8.7	9.7	10.7	11.8	12.8	13.8	14.8	15.8	16.8	17.8	18.9	19.9	20.9	21.9	22.9	24	25	26	27	28	29	0.1	1.1	2.1	3.1	4.1	5.2	6.2	7.2	8.2	9.2
☽	26.4	8.5	20.9	3.6	16.6	0.1	14	28.5	13.3	28.4	13.7	28.9	14	28.7	12.8	26.8	10.2	23.1	5.7	18.1	0	11.8	23.6	5.5	17.4	29.5	11.4	23.5	5.6	18	0.5
☿	3.4	4.9	6.5	8.1	9.7	11.2	12.8	14.4	15.9	17.5	19.1	20.7	22.2	23.8	25.4	27	28.5	0.1	1.7	3.3	4.9	6.5	8.1	9.6	11.2	12.8	14.4	16.1	17.7	19.3	20.9
♀	24.1	24.9	25.7	26.4	27.2	27.9	28.7	29.4	0.1	0.8	1.4	2.1	2.7	3.3	3.8	4.4	4.9	5.4	5.8	6.3	6.7	7.1	7.4	7.7	8	8.2	8.4	8.6	8.7	8.8	8.9
♂	22.6	23.1	23.6	24.1	24.6	25.1	25.6	26.1	26.6	27.1	27.6	28.1	28.6	29.1	29.5	30	0.5	0.9	1.4	1.9	2.3	2.8	3.2	3.6	4.1	4.5	5	5.4	5.8	6.2	6.6

♃ 1 6 11 16 21 26 31: 0.8 1.7 2.6 3.5 4.4 5.2 5.9 — ♄ 1 6 11 16 21 26 31: 19.2 19.6 20 20.4 20.8 21.2 21.4 — ♅ 1 11 21 31: 0.9 1.5 2.1 2.6 — ♆ 1 11 21 31: 24 24.4 24.7 25.1 — ♇ 1 11 21 31: 25.9 26.2 26.5 26.7

1982

I

	1	2	3	4	5	6	7	8	9	10	11	12	13	14	15	16	17	18	19	20	21	22	23	24	25	26	27	28	29	30	31
☉	10.2	11.3	12.3	13.3	14.3	15.3	16.4	17.4	18.4	19.4	20.4	21.5	22.5	23.5	24.5	25.5	26.6	27.6	28.6	29.6	0.6	1.6	2.7	3.7	4.7	5.7	6.7	7.7	8.8	9.8	10.8
☽	13.3	26.4	9.8	23.5	7.7	22.1	6.9	21.9	6.9	21.8	6.5	20.9	4.8	18.4	1.5	14.2	26.6	8.7	20.6	2.5	14.3	26.1	8	20.1	2.3	14.8	27.4	10.3	23.4	6.7	20.2
☿	22.5	24.1	25.7	27.3	28.9	0.5	2	3.6	5.1	6.6	8	9.4	10.7	12	13.2	14.3	15.4	16.3	17.1	17.7	18.2	18.5	18.6	18.6R	18.4	17.9	17.3	16.5	15.6	14.5	13.4
♀	8.9R	8.9	8.8	8.7	8.5	8.3	8.1	7.8	7.5	7.1	6.7	6.3	5.9	5.4	4.8	4.3	3.7	3.1	2.5	1.9	1.3	0.7	0.1	29.5	28.9	28.3	27.7	27.2	26.7	26.2	25.8
♂	7.1	7.5	7.9	8.3	8.7	9	9.4	9.8	10.2	10.5	10.9	11.2	11.6	12	12.3	12.6	13	13.3	13.6	13.9	14.2	14.5	14.8	15	15.3	15.6	15.8	16.1	16.3	16.5	16.8

♃ 1 6 11 16 21 26 31: 6.1 6.8 7.4 8 8.6 9 9.4 — ♄ 1 6 11 16 21 26 31: 21.5 21.7 21.9 22 22.2 22.2 22.2 — ♅ 1 11 21 31: 2.7 3.2 3.6 4 — ♆ 1 11 21 31: 25.2 25.5 25.9 26.2 — ♇ 1 11 21 31: 26.7 26.8 26.9 26.9R

II

	1	2	3	4	5	6	7	8	9	10	11	12	13	14	15	16	17	18	19	20	21	22	23	24	25	26	27	28
☉	11.8	12.8	13.8	14.8	15.9	16.9	17.9	18.9	19.9	20.9	21.9	23	24	25	26	27	28	29	0	1	2	3	4.1	5.1	6.1	7.1	8.1	9.1
☽	4	18	2.2	16.5	1	15.6	0.1	14.5	28.7	12.6	26.1	9.3	22	4.5	16.7	28.6	10.5	22.3	4.2	16.1	28.3	10.8	23.5	6.4	19.7	3.2	17	0.8
☿	12.2R	10.9	9.7	8.5	7.4	6.4	5.5	4.7	4.1	3.6	3.3	3	2.9	3.0D	3.1	3.3	3.7	4.1	4.6	5.2	5.9	6.7	7.5	8.3	9.2	10.2	11.2	12.3
♀	25.3R	25	24.6	24.3	24.1	23.8	23.7	23.5	23.4	23.4	23.4D	23.4	23.5	23.6	23.7	23.9	24.1	24.4	24.6	25	25.3	25.7	26.1	26.5	27	27.5	28	28.6
♂	17	17.2	17.4	17.6	17.7	17.9	18.1	18.2	18.4	18.5	18.6	18.7	18.8	18.9	19	19	19.1	19.1	19.2	19.2	19.2	19.2R	19.1	19.1	19.1	19	18.9	18.8

♃ 1 6 11 16 21: 9.5 9.8 10.1 10.2 10.3R — ♄ 1 6 11 16 21 26: 22.2R 22.2 22.1 22 21.9 21.7 — ♅ 1 11 21: 4 4.3 4.5 — ♆ 1 11 21: 26.2 26.5 26.7 — ♇ 1 11 21: 26.9R 26.9 26.8

III

	1	2	3	4	5	6	7	8	9	10	11	12	13	14	15	16	17	18	19	20	21	22	23	24	25	26	27	28	29	30	31
☉	10.1	11.1	12.1	13.1	14.1	15.1	16.1	17.1	18.1	19.1	20.1	21.1	22.1	23.1	24.1	25.1	26.1	27.1	28.1	29.1	0.1	1.1	2	3	4	5	6	7	8	9	10
☽	14.8	28.9	13	27.2	11.3	25.4	9.4	23.4	7.2	20.8	4.1	17.1	29.9	12.3	24.5	6.4	18.3	0.1	12	24	6.2	18.7	1.6	14.9	28.5	12.4	26.6	11	25.4	9.7	24
☿	13.3	14.5	15.6	16.8	18.1	19.3	20.6	21.9	23.3	24.6	26	27.4	28.9	0.3	1.8	3.3	4.8	6.4	7.9	9.5	11.1	12.8	14.4	16.1	17.8	19.5	21.2	23	24.8	26.6	28.4
♀	29.1	29.7	0.3	1	1.6	2.3	3	3.7	4.4	5.1	5.9	6.7	7.5	8.3	9.1	9.9	10.7	11.6	12.4	13.3	14.2	15.1	16	16.9	17.8	18.8	19.7	20.7	21.6	22.6	23.5
♂	18.7R	18.6	18.5	18.4	18.2	18.1	17.9	17.7	17.5	17.3	17.1	16.8	16.6	16.3	16	15.8	15.5	15.2	14.8	14.5	14.2	13.9	13.5	13.1	12.8	12.4	12	11.7	11.3	10.9	10.5

♃ 1 6 11 16 21 26 31: 10.3R 10.2 10 9.7 9.4 9 8.5 — ♄ 1 6 11 16 21 26 31: 21.5R 21.3 21 20.7 20.3 20 19.6 — ♅ 1 11 21 31: 4.6 4.6R 4.6 4.4 — ♆ 1 11 21 31: 26.8 27 27 27.0R — ♇ 1 11 21 31: 26.7R 26.5 26.2 26

IV

	1	2	3	4	5	6	7	8	9	10	11	12	13	14	15	16	17	18	19	20	21	22	23	24	25	26	27	28	29	30
☉	10.9	11.9	12.9	13.9	14.9	15.9	16.9	17.8	18.8	19.8	20.8	21.8	22.8	23.7	24.7	25.7	26.7	27.6	28.6	29.6	0.6	1.6	2.5	3.5	4.5	5.5	6.4	7.4	8.4	9.3
☽	8.1	22.1	6	19.7	3.2	16.6	29.7	12.7	25.5	8	20.3	2.4	14.4	26.2	8	19.9	1.9	14.1	26.6	9.6	22.9	6.7	20.9	5.5	20.2	5	19.8	4.4	18.7	2.8
☿	0.3	2.1	4	5.9	7.9	9.8	11.8	13.8	15.9	17.9	20	22.1	24.1	26.3	28.4	0.5	2.6	4.7	6.8	8.9	10.9	12.9	14.9	16.9	18.8	20.7	22.5	24.2	25.9	27.6
♀	24.5	25.5	26.5	27.5	28.5	29.5	0.5	1.5	2.5	3.6	4.6	5.7	6.7	7.7	8.8	9.8	10.9	12	13	14.1	15.2	16.3	17.3	18.4	19.5	20.6	21.7	22.8	23.9	25
♂	10.1R	9.8	9.4	9	8.6	8.2	7.8	7.4	7.1	6.7	6.3	6	5.6	5.3	5	4.6	4.3	4	3.7	3.5	3.2	2.9	2.7	2.4	2.2	2	1.8	1.6	1.4	1.3

♃ 1 6 11 16 21 26: 8.4R 7.9 7.3 6.7 6.1 5.5 — ♄ 1 6 11 16 21 26: 19.5R 19.2 18.8 18.4 18 17.6 — ♅ 1 11 21: 4.4R 4.2 3.9 — ♆ 1 11 21: 27.0R 27 26.9 — ♇ 1 11 21: 26.0R 25.7 25.4

V

	1	2	3	4	5	6	7	8	9	10	11	12	13	14	15	16	17	18	19	20	21	22	23	24	25	26	27	28	29	30	31
☉	10.3	11.3	12.3	13.2	14.2	15.2	16.1	17.1	18.1	19	20	21	21.9	22.9	23.9	24.8	25.8	26.7	27.7	28.7	29.6	0.6	1.6	2.5	3.5	4.4	5.4	6.4	7.3	8.3	9.2
☽	16.6	0.1	13.4	26.5	9.3	22	4.4	16.7	28.9	10.8	22.7	4.5	16.3	28.1	10.1	22.3	4.8	17.7	1.1	14.9	29.2	13.8	28.8	13.8	29	13.9	28.5	12.8	26.7	10.3	23.5
☿	29.2	0.7	2.1	3.5	4.8	6	7.2	8.3	9.3	10.2	11.1	11.8	12.5	13.2	13.7	14.1	14.5	14.8	15	15.1	15.2	15.2R	15	14.9	14.6	14.3	13.9	13.5	13	12.5	12
♀	26.1	27.2	28.3	29.4	0.6	1.7	2.8	3.9	5	6.2	7.3	8.4	9.5	10.7	11.8	12.9	14.1	15.2	16.4	17.5	18.6	19.8	20.9	22.1	23.2	24.4	25.5	26.7	27.8	29	0.2
♂	1.1R	1	0.9	0.8	0.7	0.6	0.5	0.5	0.4	0.4	0.4	0.4D	0.4	0.4	0.4	0.5	0.5	0.6	0.7	0.8	0.9	1	1.1	1.3	1.4	1.6	1.8	1.9	2.1	2.3	2.5

♃ 1 6 11 16 21 26 31: 4.8R 4.2 3.6 3 2.5 2 1.6 — ♄ 1 6 11 16 21 26 31: 17.3R 17 16.7 16.4 16.2 16 15.8 — ♅ 1 11 21 31: 3.5R 3.2 2.8 2.3 — ♆ 1 11 21 31: 26.8R 26.6 26.4 26.1 — ♇ 1 11 21 31: 25.1R 24.9 24.6 24.4

VI

	1	2	3	4	5	6	7	8	9	10	11	12	13	14	15	16	17	18	19	20	21	22	23	24	25	26	27	28	29	30
☉	10.2	11.2	12.1	13.1	14	15	15.9	16.9	17.9	18.8	19.8	20.7	21.7	22.6	23.6	24.5	25.5	26.5	27.4	28.4	29.3	0.3	1.2	2.2	3.1	4.1	5	6	7	7.9
☽	6.4	19	1.4	13.7	25.7	7.7	19.6	1.4	13.2	25	6.9	18.9	1.2	13.7	26.5	9.8	23.5	7.6	22.2	7.1	22.3	7.5	22.6	7.4	21.9	6.1	19.7	3	15.9	28.4
☿	11.4R	10.9	10.3	9.8	9.2	8.7	8.3	7.9	7.5	7.2	6.9	6.8	6.7	6.6D	6.7	6.8	7	7.2	7.6	8	8.5	9.1	9.7	10.4	11.2	12.1	13	14	15.1	16.2
♀	1.3	2.5	3.6	4.8	6	7.1	8.3	9.5	10.6	11.8	13	14.1	15.3	16.5	17.6	18.8	20	21.2	22.3	23.5	24.7	25.9	27.1	28.2	29.4	0.6	1.8	3	4.1	5.3
♂	2.8	3	3.2	3.5	3.7	4	4.3	4.5	4.8	5.1	5.4	5.8	6.1	6.4	6.7	7.1	7.4	7.8	8.1	8.5	8.9	9.3	9.7	10	10.4	10.9	11.3	11.7	12.1	12.5

♃ 1 6 11 16 21 26: 1.5R 1.1 0.9 0.7 0.5 0.4 — ♄ 1 6 11 16 21 26: 15.8R 15.6 15.6 15.5 15.5D 15.6 — ♅ 1 11 21: 2.3R 1.9 1.5 — ♆ 1 11 21: 26.1R 25.8 25.6 — ♇ 1 11 21: 24.4R 24.3 24.2

VII

	1	2	3	4	5	6	7	8	9	10	11	12	13	14	15	16	17	18	19	20	21	22	23	24	25	26	27	28	29	30	31
☉	8.9	9.8	10.8	11.7	12.7	13.6	14.6	15.5	16.5	17.4	18.4	19.3	20.3	21.3	22.2	23.2	24.1	25.1	26	27	27.9	28.9	29.8	0.8	1.8	2.7	3.7	4.6	5.6	6.5	7.5
☽	10.7	22.8	4.7	16.6	28.4	10.2	22	4	16	28.2	10.5	23.1	6	19.3	2.9	16.8	1.2	15.8	0.8	15.8	0.9	15.8	0.4	14.6	28.4	11.8	24.7	7.3	19.6	1.6	13.5
☿	17.4	18.6	20	21.4	22.8	24.3	25.9	27.5	29.2	0.9	2.7	4.6	6.5	8.4	10.4	12.4	14.4	16.5	18.6	20.7	22.9	25	27.1	29.2	1.4	3.5	5.6	7.6	9.7	11.7	13.8
♀	6.5	7.7	8.9	10.1	11.3	12.5	13.6	14.8	16	17.2	18.4	19.6	20.8	22	23.2	24.4	25.6	26.8	28	29.2	0.4	1.6	2.8	4	5.2	6.4	7.6	8.8	10	11.2	12.5
♂	13	13.4	13.8	14.3	14.8	15.2	15.7	16.1	16.6	17.1	17.6	18.1	18.5	19	19.5	20	20.5	21.1	21.6	22.1	22.6	23.1	23.7	24.2	24.7	25.3	25.8	26.4	26.9	27.5	28

♃ 1 6 11 16 21 26 31: 0.5 0.5 0.7 0.9 1.2 1.6 2 — ♄ 1 6 11 16 21 26 31: 15.6 15.8 15.9 16.1 16.4 16.7 17 — ♅ 1 11 21 31: 1.2R 0.9 0.7 0.6 — ♆ 1 11 21 31: 25.3R 25 24.8 24.6 — ♇ 1 11 21 31: 24.1R 24.1D 24.2 24.3

VIII

	1	2	3	4	5	6	7	8	9	10	11	12	13	14	15	16	17	18	19	20	21	22	23	24	25	26	27	28	29	30	31
☉	8.4	9.4	10.4	11.3	12.3	13.2	14.2	15.1	16.1	17.1	18	19	19.9	20.9	21.9	22.8	23.8	24.7	25.7	26.7	27.6	28.6	29.6	0.5	1.5	2.5	3.4	4.4	5.3	6.3	7.3
☽	25.3	7.1	18.9	0.9	12.9	25.2	7.6	20.2	3	16.1	29.4	13	26.9	11	25.3	9.9	24.7	9.4	24.1	8.6	22.8	6.6	20	3	15.6	27.9	9.9	21.8	3.6	15.4	27.3
☿	15.7	17.7	19.7	21.6	23.5	25.3	27.2	29	0.7	2.5	4.2	5.9	7.6	9.3	10.9	12.5	14.1	15.7	17.2	18.7	20.2	21.6	23.1	24.5	25.9	27.2	28.5	29.8	1.1	2.3	3.5
♀	13.7	14.9	16.1	17.3	18.5	19.7	20.9	22.1	23.4	24.6	25.8	27	28.2	29.4	0.7	1.9	3.1	4.3	5.6	6.8	8	9.2	10.4	11.7	12.9	14.1	15.4	16.6	17.8	19	20.3
♂	28.6	29.2	29.7	0.3	0.9	1.4	2	2.6	3.2	3.8	4.4	5	5.6	6.2	6.8	7.4	8	8.6	9.2	9.8	10.4	11	11.7	12.3	12.9	13.5	14.2	14.8	15.4	16.1	16.7

♃ 1 6 11 16 21 26 31: 2.1 2.6 3.2 3.8 4.5 5.2 6 — ♄ 1 6 11 16 21 26 31: 17 17.4 17.8 18.2 18.6 19.1 19.6 — ♅ 1 11 21 31: 0.6R 0.6D 0.6 0.8 — ♆ 1 11 21 31: 24.6R 24.5 24.3 24.3 — ♇ 1 11 21 31: 24.3 24.5 24.7 25

IX

	1	2	3	4	5	6	7	8	9	10	11	12	13	14	15	16	17	18	19	20	21	22	23	24	25	26	27	28	29	30
☉	8.2	9.2	10.2	11.2	12.1	13.1	14.1	15	16	17	17.9	18.9	19.9	20.9	21.8	22.8	23.8	24.8	25.7	26.7	27.7	28.7	29.7	0.6	1.6	2.6	3.6	4.6	5.5	6.5
☽	9.4	21.6	4.1	16.8	29.8	13	26.4	9.9	23.7	7.5	21.6	5.7	20	4.3	18.7	3	17.2	1.1	14.8	28.1	11	23.6	5.8	17.9	29.7	11.5	23.4	5.3	17.4	29.8
☿	4.7	5.9	7	8	9.1	10.1	11	11.9	12.7	13.5	14.3	14.9	15.5	16.1	16.5	16.9	17.2	17.4	17.5	17.5R	17.4	17.2	16.8	16.3	15.8	15	14.2	13.3	12.3	11.2
♀	21.5	22.7	24	25.2	26.4	27.7	28.9	0.1	1.4	2.6	3.8	5.1	6.3	7.6	8.8	10	11.3	12.5	13.8	15	16.2	17.5	18.7	20	21.2	22.5	23.7	25	26.2	27.4
♂	17.4	18	18.7	19.3	20	20.6	21.3	21.9	22.6	23.2	23.9	24.6	25.2	25.9	26.6	27.3	27.9	28.6	29.3	30	0.7	1.3	2	2.7	3.4	4.1	4.8	5.5	6.2	6.9

♃ 1 6 11 16 21 26: 6.1 7 7.8 8.7 9.6 10.6 — ♄ 1 6 11 16 21 26: 19.7 20.2 20.7 21.3 21.9 22.4 — ♅ 1 11 21: 0.8 1 1.3 — ♆ 1 11 21: 24.3R 24.3D 24.3 — ♇ 1 11 21: 25 25.4 25.7

X

	1	2	3	4	5	6	7	8	9	10	11	12	13	14	15	16	17	18	19	20	21	22	23	24	25	26	27	28	29	30	31
☉	7.5	8.5	9.5	10.5	11.4	12.4	13.4	14.4	15.4	16.4	17.4	18.3	19.3	20.3	21.3	22.3	23.3	24.3	25.3	26.3	27.3	28.3	29.3	0.3	1.3	2.3	3.3	4.2	5.2	6.2	7.2
☽	12.5	25.5	8.9	22.4	6.3	20.2	4.3	18.4	2.5	16.6	0.7	14.8	28.7	12.6	26.4	9.9	23.2	6.3	19.1	1.5	13.7	25.7	7.6	19.4	1.2	13.1	25.3	7.7	20.5	3.6	17.2
☿	10.1R	9	7.8	6.7	5.7	4.8	4	3.4	2.9	2.6	2.5	2.5D	2.7	3.1	3.7	4.4	5.2	6.2	7.3	8.5	9.8	11.2	12.6	14	15.4	17	18.6	20.1	21.4	23.4	25
♀	28.7	29.9	1.2	2.4	3.7	4.9	6.2	7.4	8.7	9.9	11.2	12.4	13.7	14.9	16.2	17.4	18.7	19.9	21.2	22.4	23.7	24.9	26.2	27.4	28.7	29.9	1.2	2.5	3.7	5	6.2
♂	7.6	8.3	9	9.7	10.4	11.1	11.8	12.5	13.2	14	14.7	15.4	16.1	16.8	17.6	18.3	19	19.7	20.5	21.2	21.9	22.7	23.4	24.1	24.9	25.6	26.3	27.1	27.8	28.6	29.3

♃ 1 6 11 16 21 26 31: 11.6 12.6 13.6 14.7 15.7 16.8 17.9 — ♄ 1 6 11 16 21 26 31: 23 23.6 24.2 24.8 25.4 26 26.6 — ♅ 1 11 21 31: 1.7 2.2 2.7 3.2 — ♆ 1 11 21 31: 24.5 24.6 24.8 25.1 — ♇ 1 11 21 31: 26.1 26.5 26.9 27.3

XI

	1	2	3	4	5	6	7	8	9	10	11	12	13	14	15	16	17	18	19	20	21	22	23	24	25	26	27	28	29	30
☉	8.2	9.2	10.2	11.2	12.2	13.3	14.3	15.3	16.3	17.3	18.3	19.3	20.3	21.3	22.3	23.3	24.3	25.3	26.3	27.3	28.4	29.4	0.4	1.4	2.4	3.4	4.4	5.4	6.4	7.5
☽	1.1	15.3	29.8	14.3	28.8	13.2	27.5	11.6	25.6	9.3	22.9	6.2	19.4	2.3	15	27.5	9.8	21.9	3.8	15.6	27.4	9.2	21.1	3.2	15.6	28.3	11.5	25.1	9.1	23.5
☿	26.6	28.3	29.9	1.6	3.2	4.9	6.5	8.2	9.8	11.4	13	14.7	16.3	17.9	19.5	21.1	22.7	24.3	25.9	27.5	29.1	0.6	2.2	3.8	5.4	6.9	8.5	10.1	11.6	13.2
♀	7.5	8.7	10	11.2	12.5	13.7	15	16.3	17.5	18.8	20	21.3	22.5	23.8	25	26.3	27.6	28.8	0.1	1.3	2.6	3.8	5.1	6.4	7.6	8.9	10.1	11.4	12.6	13.9
♂	0	0.8	1.5	2.3	3	3.8	4.5	5.3	6	6.8	7.5	8.3	9.1	9.8	10.6	11.3	12.1	12.9	13.6	14.4	15.1	15.9	16.7	17.4	18.2	19	19.8	20.5	21.3	22.1

♃ 1 6 11 16 21 26: 18.1 19.2 20.3 21.4 22.5 23.6 — ♄ 1 6 11 16 21 26: 26.8 27.4 28 28.5 29.1 29.6 — ♅ 1 11 21: 3.3 3.9 4.5 — ♆ 1 11 21: 25.1 25.4 25.7 — ♇ 1 11 21: 27.3 27.7 28.1

XII

	1	2	3	4	5	6	7	8	9	10	11	12	13	14	15	16	17	18	19	20	21	22	23	24	25	26	27	28	29	30	31
☉	8.5	9.5	10.5	11.5	12.5	13.5	14.6	15.6	16.6	17.6	18.6	19.6	20.7	21.7	22.7	23.7	24.7	25.7	26.8	27.8	28.8	29.8	0.8	1.8	2.9	3.9	4.9	5.9	6.9	8	9
☽	8.2	23.2	8.1	23	7.6	22	6.1	19.8	3.2	16.3	29.2	11.8	24.2	6.4	18.4	0.4	12.2	24	5.8	17.6	29.5	11.6	23.9	6.6	19.6	3.1	17	1.3	16.1	1.1	16.3
☿	14.7	16.3	17.8	19.4	21	22.5	24.1	25.6	27.2	28.7	0.3	1.8	3.4	4.9	6.4	8	9.5	11	12.5	14	15.5	17	18.4	19.8	21.2	22.6	23.9	25.2	26.4	27.5	28.5
♀	15.1	16.4	17.6	18.9	20.2	21.4	22.7	23.9	25.2	26.4	27.7	29	0.2	1.5	2.7	4	5.2	6.5	7.7	9	10.3	11.5	12.8	14	15.3	16.5	17.8	19	20.3	21.6	22.8
♂	22.8	23.6	24.4	25.2	25.9	26.7	27.5	28.3	29	29.8	0.6	1.4	2.1	2.9	3.7	4.5	5.3	6	6.8	7.6	8.4	9.2	10	10.7	11.5	12.3	13.1	13.9	14.7	15.5	16.2

♃ 1 6 11 16 21 26 31: 24.7 25.8 26.9 27.9 29 30 1 — ♄ 1 6 11 16 21 26 31: 0.2 0.7 1.2 1.6 2.1 2.5 2.8 — ♅ 1 11 21 31: 5.1 5.7 6.3 6.9 — ♆ 1 11 21 31: 26.1 26.5 26.8 27.2 — ♇ 1 11 21 31: 28.4 28.7 29 29.2

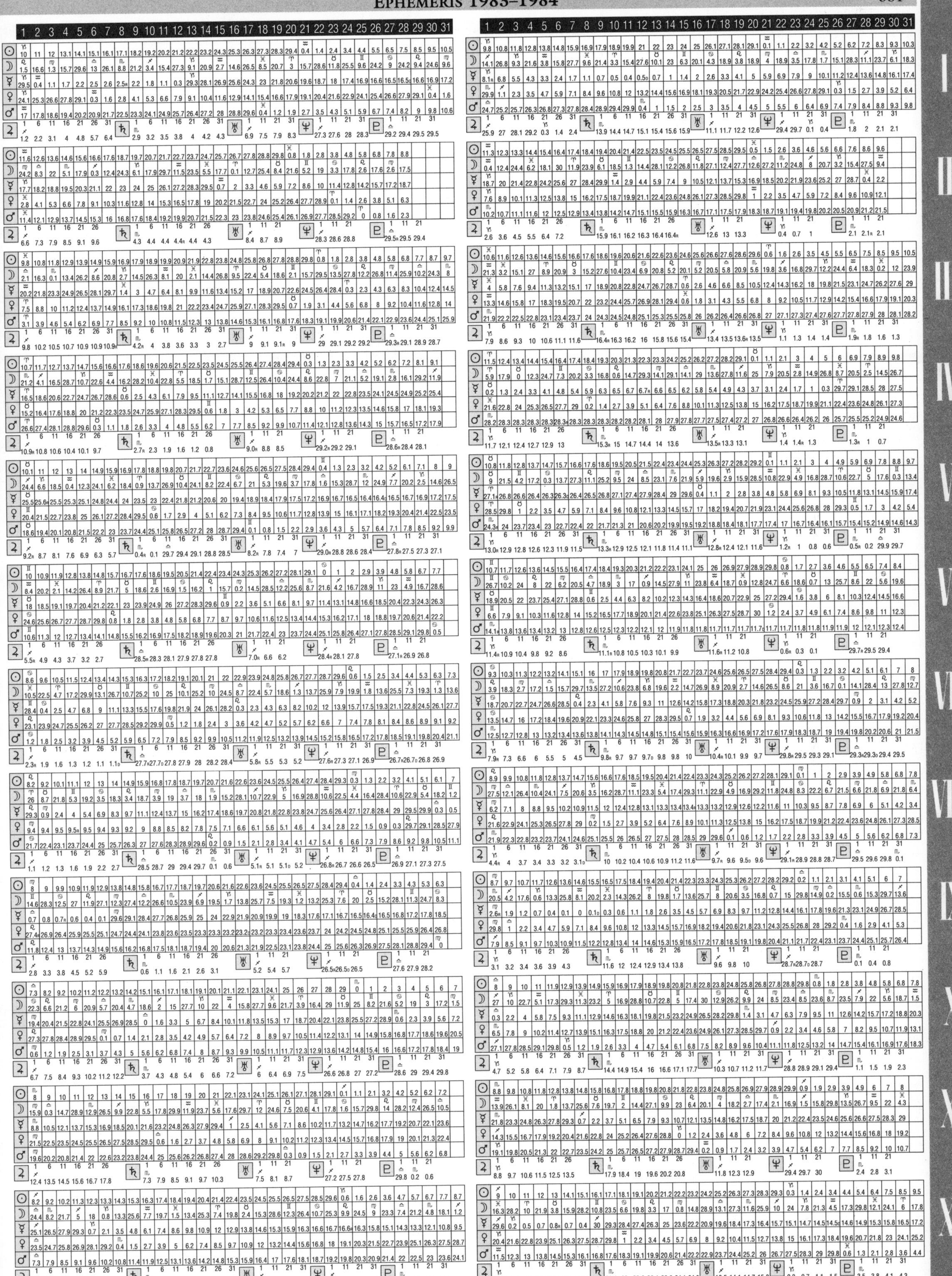

I

II

III

IV

V

VI

VII

VIII

IX

X

XI

XII

I

1985

	1	2	3	4	5	6	7	8	9	10	11	12	13	14	15	16	17	18	19	20	21	22	23	24	25	26	27	28	29	30	31
☉	♑ 10.5	11.5	12.6	13.6	14.6	15.6	16.6	17.7	18.7	19.7	20.7	21.7	22.8	23.8	24.8	25.8	26.8	27.8	28.9	29.9	♒ 0.9	1.9	2.9	4	5	6	7	8	9	10.1	11.1
☽	♈ 29.7	♉ 11.7	23.8	♊ 6.2	19	♋ 2	15.4	29.1	♌ 13.1	27.2	♍ 11.5	25.7	♎ 9.9	24.1	♏ 8.1	22	♐ 5.8	19.5	♑ 3.1	16.5	29.6	♒ 12.6	25.3	♓ 7.7	19.9	♈ 1.9	13.8	25.6	♉ 7.4	19.4	♊ 1.5
☿	♐ 18	18.9	19.8	20.8	21.9	23	24.1	25.3	26.5	27.8	29	♑ 0.3	1.6	3	4.3	5.7	7.1	8.5	9.9	11.4	12.8	14.3	15.7	17.2	18.7	20.2	21.7	23.3	24.8	26.4	27.9
♀	♒ 26.4	27.5	28.6	29.7	♓ 0.8	1.9	3	4.1	5.2	6.3	7.4	8.5	9.5	10.6	11.7	12.7	13.8	14.8	15.9	16.9	17.9	19	20	21	22	23	24	24.9	25.9	26.9	27.8
♂	♓ 5.1	5.9	6.7	7.4	8.2	9	9.7	10.5	11.2	12	12.8	13.5	14.3	15.1	15.8	16.6	17.3	18.1	18.9	19.6	20.4	21.1	21.9	22.7	23.4	24.2	24.9	25.7	26.4	27.2	28

♃ (1, 6, 11, 16, 21, 26, 31): ♑ 21.5, 22.6, 23.8, 25, 26.1, 27.3, 28.5
♄ (1, 6, 11, 16, 21, 26, 31): ♏ 24.7, 25.2, 25.6, 26, 26.4, 26.8, 27.1
♅ (1, 11, 21, 31): ♐ 15.4, 15.9, 16.4, 16.9
♆ (1, 11, 21, 31): ♑ 1.5, 1.9, 2.2, 2.5
♇ (1, 11, 21, 31): ♏ 4.4, 4.6, 4.7, 4.7

1986

	1	2	3	4	5	6	7	8	9	10	11	12	13	14	15	16	17	18	19	20	21	22	23	24	25	26	27	28	29	30	31
☉	♑ 10.3	11.3	12.3	13.3	14.4	15.4	16.4	17.4	18.4	19.5	20.5	21.5	22.5	23.5	24.5	25.6	26.6	27.6	28.6	29.6	♒ 0.7	1.7	2.7	3.7	4.7	5.7	6.8	7.8	8.8	9.8	10.8
☽	♍ 5.1	18.3	♎ 1.8	15.6	29.6	♏ 13.8	28.3	♐ 13	27.7	♑ 12.4	27	♒ 11.2	25.1	♓ 8.5	21.5	♈ 4.1	16.4	28.4	♉ 10.2	22	♊ 3.8	15.8	27.8	♋ 10.1	22.7	♌ 5.5	18.5	♍ 1.7	15.2	28.8	♎ 12.5
☿	♐ 22.9	24.3	25.8	27.3	28.7	♑ 0.2	1.7	3.2	4.7	6.2	7.8	9.3	10.8	12.4	13.9	15.5	17.1	18.7	20.2	21.8	23.5	25.1	26.7	28.3	30	♒ 1.6	3.3	5	6.7	8.4	10.1
♀	♑ 5.8	7.1	8.3	9.6	10.9	12.1	13.4	14.6	15.9	17.1	18.4	19.7	20.9	22.2	23.4	24.7	26	27.2	28.5	29.7	♒ 1	2.2	3.5	4.8	6	7.3	8.5	9.8	11	12.3	13.5
♂	♏ 10.6	11.2	11.8	12.4	13	13.6	14.2	14.8	15.5	16.1	16.7	17.3	17.9	18.5	19.1	19.7	20.3	20.9	21.5	22.1	22.7	23.3	23.9	24.5	25.1	25.7	26.3	26.9	27.5	28.1	28.7

♃ (1, 6, 11, 16, 21, 26, 31): ♒ 18.3, 19.3, 20.4, 21.6, 22.7, 23.9, 25.1
♄ (1, 6, 11, 16, 21, 26, 31): ♐ 5.2, 5.7, 6.2, 6.6, 7.1, 7.5, 7.9
♅ (1, 11, 21, 31): ♐ 19.5, 20.1, 20.6, 21.1
♆ (1, 11, 21, 31): ♑ 3.6, 4, 4.3, 4.7
♇ (1, 11, 21, 31): ♏ 6.9, 7.1, 7.3, 7.3

II

1985

	1	2	3	4	5	6	7	8	9	10	11	12	13	14	15	16	17	18	19	20	21	22	23	24	25	26	27	28	29	30	31
☉	♒ 12.1	13.1	14.1	15.1	16.1	17.2	18.2	19.2	20.2	21.2	22.2	23.2	24.2	25.2	26.3	27.3	28.3	29.3	♓ 0.3	1.3	2.3	3.3	4.3	5.3	6.3	7.3	8.3	9.4			
☽	♊ 14	26.7	♋ 9.9	23.6	♌ 7.6	22	♍ 6.6	21.3	♎ 6	20.5	♏ 4.8	18.9	♐ 2.8	16.4	29.7	♑ 12.9	25.9	♒ 8.7	21.4	♓ 3.8	16.1	28.1	♈ 10.1	21.9	♉ 3.7	15.5	27.4	♊ 9.5			
☿	♑ 29.5	♒ 1.1	2.7	4.3	5.9	7.6	9.2	10.9	12.5	14.2	15.9	17.6	19.4	21.1	22.9	24.6	26.4	28.2	♓ 0	1.9	3.7	5.6	7.4	9.3	11.2	13.1	15	16.9			
♀	♓ 28.7	29.7	♈ 0.6	1.5	2.4	3.3	4.2	5	5.9	6.7	7.5	8.3	9.1	9.9	10.7	11.4	12.2	12.9	13.6	14.2	14.9	15.5	16.1	16.7	17.3	17.8	18.3	18.8			
♂	♓ 28.7	29.5	♈ 0.2	1	1.7	2.5	3.2	4	4.7	5.5	6.2	7	7.7	8.5	9.2	10	10.7	11.5	12.2	12.9	13.7	14.4	15.2	15.9	16.6	17.4	18.1	18.9			

♃ (1, 6, 11, 16, 21, 26): ♑ 28.7, 29.9, ♒ 1, 2.1, 3.2, 4.3
♄ (1, 6, 11, 16, 21, 26): ♏ 27.1, 27.4, 27.6, 27.8, 27.9, 28
♅ (1, 11, 21): ♐ 16.9, 17.3, 17.6
♆ (1, 11, 21): ♑ 2.6, 2.9, 3.1
♇ (1, 11, 21): ♏ 4.7, 4.7R, 4.7

1986

	1	2	3	4	5	6	7	8	9	10	11	12	13	14	15	16	17	18	19	20	21	22	23	24	25	26	27	28	29	30	31
☉	♒ 11.8	12.9	13.9	14.9	15.9	16.9	17.9	18.9	19.9	21	22	23	24	25	26	27	28	29	♓ 0.1	1.1	2.1	3.1	4.1	5.1	6.1	7.1	8.1	9.1			
☽	♎ 26.3	♏ 10.3	24.4	♐ 8.6	22.8	♑ 7.1	21.4	♒ 5.5	19.4	♓ 3.1	16.4	29.3	♈ 11.9	24.1	♉ 6.2	18	29.9	♊ 11.7	23.6	♋ 5.8	18.1	♌ 0.8	13.9	27.2	♍ 10.8	24.7	♎ 8.7	22.8			
☿	♒ 11.8	13.5	15.3	17	18.8	20.6	22.4	24.2	26	27.8	29.6	♓ 1.4	3.3	5.1	6.9	8.7	10.5	12.2	14	15.7	17.4	19	20.6	22.1	23.5	24.8	26.1	27.2			
♀	♒ 14.8	16.1	17.3	18.6	19.8	21.1	22.3	23.6	24.8	26.1	27.3	28.6	29.9	♓ 1.1	2.4	3.6	4.9	6.1	7.4	8.6	9.9	11.1	12.4	13.6	14.9	16.1	17.4	18.6			
♂	♏ 29.3	29.8	♐ 0.4	1	1.6	2.2	2.8	3.4	4	4.5	5.1	5.7	6.3	6.9	7.5	8	8.6	9.2	9.8	10.3	10.9	11.5	12	12.6	13.2	13.7	14.3	14.9			

♃ (1, 6, 11, 16, 21, 26): ♒ 25.3, 26.5, 27.7, 28.9, ♓ 0.1, 1.3
♄ (1, 6, 11, 16, 21, 26): ♐ 8, 8.3, 8.6, 8.9, 9.1, 9.3
♅ (1, 11, 21): ♐ 21.1, 21.5, 21.9
♆ (1, 11, 21): ♑ 4.7, 5, 5.3
♇ (1, 11, 21): ♏ 7.4, 7.4R, 7.3

III

1985

	1	2	3	4	5	6	7	8	9	10	11	12	13	14	15	16	17	18	19	20	21	22	23	24	25	26	27	28	29	30	31
☉	♓ 10.4	11.4	12.4	13.4	14.4	15.4	16.4	17.4	18.4	19.4	20.4	21.4	22.4	23.4	24.4	25.4	26.4	27.3	28.3	29.3	♈ 0.3	1.3	2.3	3.3	4.3	5.3	6.3	7.3	8.3	9.2	10.2
☽	♊ 21.9	♋ 4.6	17.8	♌ 1.5	15.6	♍ 0.2	15.1	♎ 0.1	15.2	♏ 0.1	14.8	29.1	♐ 13.1	26.7	♑ 10	23	♒ 5.7	18.2	♓ 0.6	12.8	24.8	♈ 6.8	18.6	♉ 0.4	12.2	24	♊ 6	18.1	♋ 0.4	13.1	26.2
☿	♓ 18.8	20.7	22.6	24.5	26.4	28.2	♈ 0	1.8	3.5	5.2	6.8	8.3	9.8	11.2	12.4	13.6	14.7	15.6	16.5	17.1	17.7	18.2	18.5	18.6	18.7R	18.6	18.4	18	17.6	17.1	16.4
♀	♈ 19.3	19.7	20.1	20.5	20.8	21.1	21.4	21.6	21.8	22	22.1	22.2	22.3	22.3R	22.3	22.2	22.1	21.9	21.7	21.5	21.2	20.9	20.5	20.1	19.7	19.3	18.8	18.2	17.7	17.1	16.5
♂	♈ 19.6	20.3	21.1	21.8	22.5	23.3	24	24.7	25.5	26.2	26.9	27.7	28.4	29.1	29.9	♉ 0.6	1.3	2	2.8	3.5	4.2	4.9	5.7	6.4	7.1	7.8	8.5	9.3	10	10.7	11.4

♃ (1, 6, 11, 16, 21, 26, 31): ♒ 5, 6, 7, 8, 9, 9.9, 10.8
♄ (1, 6, 11, 16, 21, 26, 31): ♏ 28.1, 28.1, 28.1R, 28.1, 28, 27.8, 27.7
♅ (1, 11, 21, 31): ♐ 17.8, 17.9, 18, 18.0R
♆ (1, 11, 21, 31): ♑ 3.3, 3.4, 3.6, 3.6
♇ (1, 11, 21, 31): ♏ 4.6R, 4.4, 4.2, 4

1986

	1	2	3	4	5	6	7	8	9	10	11	12	13	14	15	16	17	18	19	20	21	22	23	24	25	26	27	28	29	30	31
☉	♓ 10.1	11.1	12.1	13.1	14.1	15.1	16.1	17.1	18.1	19.1	20.1	21.1	22.1	23.1	24.1	25.1	26.1	27.1	28.1	29.1	♈ 0.1	1.1	2.1	3.1	4.1	5	6	7	8	9	10
☽	♏ 7	21.2	♐ 5.4	19.5	♑ 3.5	17.5	♒ 1.3	15	28.4	♓ 11.7	24.6	♈ 7.3	19.8	♉ 2	14	25.9	♊ 7.7	19.5	♋ 1.5	13.6	26	♌ 8.7	21.8	♍ 5.3	19.1	♎ 3.3	17.8	♏ 2.4	17	♐ 1.6	16.1
☿	♓ 28.2	29.1	29.8	♈ 0.4	0.9	1.2	1.3	1.3R	1.1	0.8	0.4	♓ 29.8	29.2	28.4	27.6	26.7	25.7	24.8	23.9	23	22.1	21.3	20.6	19.9	19.3	18.9	18.5	18.2	18	17.9	18.0D
♀	♓ 19.9	21.1	22.4	23.6	24.9	26.1	27.3	28.6	29.8	♈ 1.1	2.3	3.6	4.8	6.1	7.3	8.5	9.8	11	12.3	13.5	14.7	16	17.2	18.5	19.7	20.9	22.2	23.4	24.7	25.9	27.1
♂	♐ 15.4	16	16.6	17.1	17.7	18.2	18.8	19.3	19.9	20.4	21	21.5	22.1	22.6	23.1	23.7	24.2	24.7	25.3	25.8	26.3	26.8	27.4	27.9	28.4	28.9	29.4	29.9	♑ 0.4	0.9	1.4

♃ (1, 6, 11, 16, 21, 26, 31): ♓ 2, 3.2, 4.4, 5.6, 6.7, 7.9, 9
♄ (1, 6, 11, 16, 21, 26, 31): ♐ 9.4, 9.6, 9.6, 9.7, 9.7R, 9.7, 9.6
♅ (1, 11, 21, 31): ♐ 22.1, 22.3, 22.4, 22.4R
♆ (1, 11, 21, 31): ♑ 5.4, 5.6, 5.7, 5.8
♇ (1, 11, 21, 31): ♏ 7.2R, 7.1, 6.9, 6.7

IV

1985

	1	2	3	4	5	6	7	8	9	10	11	12	13	14	15	16	17	18	19	20	21	22	23	24	25	26	27	28	29	30	31
☉	♈ 11.2	12.2	13.2	14.2	15.2	16.1	17.1	18.1	19.1	20.1	21.1	22	23	24	25	26	26.9	27.9	28.9	29.9	♉ 0.8	1.8	2.8	3.8	4.7	5.7	6.7	7.7	8.6	9.6	
☽	♌ 9.7	23.8	♍ 8.3	23.1	♎ 8.3	23.5	♏ 8.7	23.7	♐ 8.3	22.5	♑ 6.3	19.6	♒ 2.6	15.3	27.7	♓ 9.9	21.9	♈ 3.8	15.6	27.4	♉ 9.2	21.1	♊ 3	15	27.2	♋ 9.6	22.3	♌ 5.4	18.8	♍ 2.7	
☿	♈ 15.8R	15	14.2	13.4	12.6	11.8	11	10.3	9.6	9	8.4	7.9	7.5	7.2	6.9	6.8	6.7	6.8D	6.9	7.1	7.3	7.7	8.1	8.6	9.2	9.8	10.5	11.2	12	12.9	
♀	♈ 15.9R	15.3	14.7	14	13.4	12.8	12.2	11.6	11	10.4	9.9	9.4	8.9	8.4	8	7.6	7.3	7	6.7	6.5	6.3	6.2	6.1	6	6	6.0D	6.1	6.2	6.3	6.5	
♂	♉ 12.1	12.8	13.5	14.3	15	15.7	16.4	17.1	17.8	18.5	19.2	19.9	20.6	21.3	22	22.8	23.5	24.2	24.9	25.6	26.3	27	27.7	28.4	29.1	29.7	♊ 0.4	1.1	1.8	2.5	

♃ (1, 6, 11, 16, 21, 26): ♒ 11, 11.8, 12.6, 13.3, 13.9, 14.6
♄ (1, 6, 11, 16, 21, 26): ♏ 27.6R, 27.4, 27.2, 26.9, 26.6, 26.3
♅ (1, 11, 21): ♐ 18.0R, 17.8, 17.6
♆ (1, 11, 21): ♑ 3.6, 3.6R, 3.6
♇ (1, 11, 21): ♏ 4.0R, 3.7, 3.4

1986

	1	2	3	4	5	6	7	8	9	10	11	12	13	14	15	16	17	18	19	20	21	22	23	24	25	26	27	28	29	30	31
☉	♈ 11	12	13	13.9	14.9	15.9	16.9	17.9	18.9	19.8	20.8	21.8	22.8	23.8	24.7	25.7	26.7	27.7	28.7	29.6	♉ 0.6	1.6	2.6	3.5	4.5	5.5	6.5	7.4	8.4	9.4	
☽	♑ 0.3	14.4	28.2	♒ 11.7	25	♓ 8.1	20.9	♈ 3.5	16	28.2	♉ 10.2	22.2	♊ 4	15.8	27.7	♋ 9.6	21.7	♌ 4.1	16.7	29.8	♍ 13.2	27.1	♎ 11.5	26.1	♏ 11	26.1	♐ 11.1	25.9	♑ 10.5	24.7	
☿	♓ 18.1	18.3	18.5	18.9	19.3	19.8	20.4	21.1	21.8	22.6	23.4	24.3	25.2	26.2	27.2	28.3	29.4	♈ 0.6	1.8	3	4.3	5.6	6.9	8.3	9.7	11.1	12.6	14.1	15.7	17.2	
♀	♈ 28.4	29.6	♉ 0.8	2.1	3.3	4.5	5.8	7	8.2	9.4	10.7	11.9	13.1	14.4	15.6	16.8	18	19.3	20.5	21.7	22.9	24.2	25.4	26.6	27.8	29	♊ 0.3	1.5	2.7	3.9	
♂	♑ 1.9	2.4	2.9	3.4	3.9	4.4	4.8	5.3	5.8	6.3	6.7	7.2	7.6	8.1	8.5	9	9.4	9.9	10.3	10.7	11.1	11.6	12	12.4	12.8	13.2	13.6	14	14.3	14.7	

♃ (1, 6, 11, 16, 21, 26): ♓ 9.2, 10.3, 11.4, 12.4, 13.4, 14.4
♄ (1, 6, 11, 16, 21, 26): ♐ 9.6R, 9.4, 9.3, 9.1, 8.8, 8.6
♅ (1, 11, 21): ♐ 22.4R, 22.3, 22.1
♆ (1, 11, 21): ♑ 5.8, 5.8R, 5.8
♇ (1, 11, 21): ♏ 6.7R, 6.4, 6.1

V

1985

	1	2	3	4	5	6	7	8	9	10	11	12	13	14	15	16	17	18	19	20	21	22	23	24	25	26	27	28	29	30	31
☉	♉ 10.6	11.5	12.5	13.5	14.5	15.4	16.4	17.4	18.3	19.3	20.3	21.2	22.2	23.2	24.1	25.1	26	27	28	28.9	29.9	♊ 0.9	1.8	2.8	3.7	4.7	5.7	6.6	7.6	8.5	9.5
☽	♍ 17	♎ 1.6	16.6	♏ 1.7	16.9	♐ 1.9	16.7	♑ 1.1	15	28.5	♒ 11.6	24.3	♓ 6.7	18.8	♈ 0.8	12.6	24.4	♉ 6.2	18	30	♊ 12.1	24.3	♋ 6.7	19.3	♌ 2.2	15.4	28.8	♍ 12.5	26.6	♎ 11	25.6
☿	♈ 13.8	14.8	15.8	16.9	18	19.2	20.4	21.6	22.9	24.2	25.6	27	28.4	29.9	♉ 1.4	2.9	4.5	6.1	7.8	9.5	11.2	13	14.8	16.6	18.5	20.4	22.3	24.3	26.3	28.3	♊ 0.4
♀	♈ 6.7	6.9	7.2	7.5	7.8	8.2	8.6	9	9.5	9.9	10.4	11	11.5	12.1	12.7	13.3	13.9	14.6	15.2	15.9	16.6	17.3	18.1	18.8	19.6	20.4	21.1	21.9	22.8	23.6	24.4
♂	♊ 3.2	3.9	4.6	5.3	6	6.7	7.4	8	8.7	9.4	10.1	10.8	11.5	12.2	12.8	13.5	14.2	14.9	15.6	16.3	16.9	17.6	18.3	19	19.6	20.3	21	21.7	22.3	23	23.7

♃ (1, 6, 11, 16, 21, 26, 31): ♒ 15.1, 15.6, 16, 16.4, 16.6, 16.8, 16.9
♄ (1, 6, 11, 16, 21, 26, 31): ♏ 25.9R, 25.6, 25.2, 24.8, 24.4, 24.1, 23.7
♅ (1, 11, 21, 31): ♐ 17.4R, 17, 16.7, 16.3
♆ (1, 11, 21, 31): ♑ 3.4R, 3.3, 3.1, 2.9
♇ (1, 11, 21, 31): ♏ 3.2R, 2.9, 2.6, 2.4

1986

	1	2	3	4	5	6	7	8	9	10	11	12	13	14	15	16	17	18	19	20	21	22	23	24	25	26	27	28	29	30	31
☉	♉ 10.3	11.3	12.3	13.3	14.2	15.2	16.2	17.1	18.1	19.1	20	21	22	22.9	23.9	24.9	25.8	26.8	27.7	28.7	29.7	♊ 0.6	1.6	2.6	3.5	4.5	5.4	6.4	7.4	8.3	9.3
☽	♒ 8.5	22	♓ 5.1	18	♈ 0.5	12.8	25	♉ 7	18.9	♊ 0.8	12.6	24.4	♋ 6.3	18.3	♌ 0.4	12.7	25.3	♍ 8.3	21.6	♎ 5.4	19.6	♏ 4.3	19.3	♐ 4.5	19.7	♑ 4.8	19.7	♒ 4.2	18.2	♓ 1.7	14.8
☿	♈ 18.8	20.5	22.1	23.8	25.5	27.3	29.1	♉ 0.9	2.7	4.6	6.5	8.5	10.4	12.4	14.5	16.5	18.6	20.7	22.8	25	27.2	29.3	♊ 1.5	3.7	5.9	8.1	10.3	12.5	14.6	16.7	18.9
♀	♊ 5.1	6.3	7.6	8.8	10	11.2	12.4	13.6	14.8	16.1	17.3	18.5	19.7	20.9	22.1	23.3	24.5	25.7	26.9	28.1	29.3	♋ 0.5	1.7	2.9	4.1	5.3	6.5	7.7	8.9	10.1	11.3
♂	♑ 15.1	15.5	15.8	16.2	16.5	16.8	17.2	17.5	17.8	18.1	18.4	18.7	19	19.3	19.6	19.8	20.1	20.3	20.6	20.8	21	21.2	21.4	21.6	21.8	21.9	22.1	22.2	22.4	22.5	22.6

♃ (1, 6, 11, 16, 21, 26, 31): ♓ 15.4, 16.3, 17.1, 17.9, 18.7, 19.4, 20.1
♄ (1, 6, 11, 16, 21, 26, 31): ♐ 8.3R, 8, 7.6, 7.3, 6.9, 6.6, 6.2
♅ (1, 11, 21, 31): ♐ 21.9R, 21.6, 21.2, 20.8
♆ (1, 11, 21, 31): ♑ 5.7R, 5.5, 5.3, 5.1
♇ (1, 11, 21, 31): ♏ 5.8R, 5.6, 5.3, 5.1

VI

1985

	1	2	3	4	5	6	7	8	9	10	11	12	13	14	15	16	17	18	19	20	21	22	23	24	25	26	27	28	29	30	31
☉	♊ 10.5	11.4	12.4	13.3	14.3	15.2	16.2	17.2	18.1	19.1	20	21	21.9	22.9	23.9	24.8	25.8	26.7	27.7	28.6	29.6	♋ 0.5	1.5	2.4	3.4	4.4	5.3	6.3	7.2	8.2	
☽	♏ 10.4	25.3	♐ 10.1	24.8	♑ 9.2	23.2	♒ 6.8	20	♓ 2.7	15.2	27.3	♈ 9.2	21.1	♉ 2.8	14.7	26.6	♊ 8.7	21	♋ 3.5	16.2	29.2	♌ 12.3	25.7	♍ 9.3	23.1	♎ 7.1	21.3	♏ 5.6	20	♐ 4.5	
☿	♊ 2.5	4.6	6.7	8.9	11.1	13.3	15.5	17.7	19.9	22.1	24.3	26.4	28.6	♋ 0.7	2.8	4.9	6.9	8.9	10.9	12.9	14.8	16.7	18.5	20.3	22.1	23.8	25.5	27.1	28.7	♌ 0.3	
♀	♈ 25.3	26.1	27	27.9	28.8	29.7	♉ 0.6	1.5	2.4	3.4	4.3	5.2	6.2	7.2	8.1	9.1	10.1	11.1	12.1	13.1	14.1	15.1	16.1	17.1	18.1	19.1	20.2	21.2	22.3	23.3	
♂	♊ 24.4	25	25.7	26.4	27	27.7	28.4	29.1	29.7	♋ 0.4	1.1	1.7	2.4	3.1	3.7	4.4	5	5.7	6.4	7	7.7	8.4	9	9.7	10.3	11	11.6	12.3	13	13.6	

♃ (1, 6, 11, 16, 21, 26): ♒ 16.9, 17.0R, 16.9, 16.8, 16.6, 16.3
♄ (1, 6, 11, 16, 21, 26): ♏ 23.6R, 23.3, 23, 22.7, 22.4, 22.2
♅ (1, 11, 21): ♐ 16.2R, 15.8, 15.4
♆ (1, 11, 21): ♑ 2.8R, 2.6, 2.3
♇ (1, 11, 21): ♏ 2.4R, 2.2, 2.1

1986

	1	2	3	4	5	6	7	8	9	10	11	12	13	14	15	16	17	18	19	20	21	22	23	24	25	26	27	28	29	30	31
☉	♊ 10.2	11.2	12.1	13.1	14.1	15	16	16.9	17.9	18.8	19.8	20.8	21.7	22.7	23.6	24.6	25.5	26.5	27.4	28.4	29.4	♋ 0.3	1.3	2.2	3.2	4.1	5.1	6	7	7.9	
☽	♓ 27.5	♈ 9.9	22.1	♉ 4.1	16	27.8	♊ 9.6	21.5	♋ 3.3	15.3	27.4	♌ 9.6	22	♍ 4.6	17.5	♎ 0.8	14.4	28.4	♏ 12.9	27.7	♐ 12.8	28.1	♑ 13.3	28.2	♒ 12.8	27	♓ 10.6	23.8	♈ 6.5	18.9	
☿	♊ 20.9	23	25	27	28.9	♋ 0.8	2.6	4.5	6.2	8	9.7	11.3	12.9	14.4	16	17.4	18.8	20.2	21.5	22.8	24.1	25.2	26.4	27.5	28.5	29.5	♌ 0.4	1.2	2	2.8	
♀	♋ 12.5	13.7	14.9	16.1	17.3	18.4	19.6	20.8	22	23.2	24.4	25.5	26.7	27.9	29.1	♌ 0.3	1.4	2.6	3.8	5	6.1	7.3	8.5	9.6	10.8	12	13.1	14.3	15.4	16.6	
♂	♑ 22.7	22.8	22.9	23	23	23.1	23.1	23.1	23.1	23.1R	23.1	23.1	23	23	22.9	22.8	22.7	22.6	22.5	22.4	22.2	22.1	21.9	21.7	21.5	21.3	21.1	20.9	20.7	20.4	

♃ (1, 6, 11, 16, 21, 26): ♓ 20.2, 20.8, 21.3, 21.7, 22.1, 22.4
♄ (1, 6, 11, 16, 21, 26): ♐ 6.1R, 5.7, 5.4, 5, 4.7, 4.4
♅ (1, 11, 21): ♐ 20.8R, 20.4, 20
♆ (1, 11, 21): ♑ 5.1R, 4.8, 4.6
♇ (1, 11, 21): ♏ 5.1R, 4.9, 4.7

VII

1985

	1	2	3	4	5	6	7	8	9	10	11	12	13	14	15	16	17	18	19	20	21	22	23	24	25	26	27	28	29	30	31
☉	♋ 9.1	10.1	11	12	12.9	13.9	14.8	15.8	16.7	17.7	18.7	19.6	20.6	21.5	22.5	23.4	24.4	25.3	26.3	27.2	28.2	29.1	♌ 0.1	1.1	2	3	3.9	4.9	5.8	6.8	7.7
☽	♐ 19	♑ 3.3	17.5	♒ 1.4	14.9	28	♓ 10.8	23.2	♈ 5.4	17.3	29.1	♉ 10.9	22.8	♊ 4.8	17	29.5	♋ 12.3	25.3	♌ 8.7	22.3	♍ 6	20	♎ 4	18.1	♏ 2.2	16.3	♐ 0.5	14.6	28.6	♑ 12.6	26.3
☿	♌ 1.8	3.3	4.8	6.2	7.6	8.9	10.2	11.5	12.7	13.9	15	16.1	17.1	18.1	19	19.9	20.7	21.4	22.1	22.8	23.3	23.9	24.3	24.7	24.9	25.1	25.3	25.3	25.3R	25.2	24.9
♀	♉ 24.4	25.4	26.5	27.5	28.6	29.7	♊ 0.7	1.8	2.9	4	5	6.1	7.2	8.3	9.4	10.5	11.6	12.7	13.8	14.9	16	17.2	18.3	19.4	20.5	21.6	22.8	23.9	25	26.2	27.3
♂	♋ 14.3	14.9	15.6	16.2	16.9	17.6	18.2	18.9	19.5	20.2	20.8	21.5	22.1	22.8	23.4	24.1	24.7	25.4	26	26.7	27.3	28	28.6	29.3	29.9	♌ 0.6	1.2	1.8	2.5	3.1	3.8

♃ (1, 6, 11, 16, 21, 26, 31): ♒ 15.9R, 15.5, 15, 14.5, 13.9, 13.3, 12.6
♄ (1, 6, 11, 16, 21, 26, 31): ♏ 22.0R, 21.8, 21.6, 21.5, 21.5, 21.5D, 21.5
♅ (1, 11, 21, 31): ♐ 15.0R, 14.7, 14.4, 14.2
♆ (1, 11, 21, 31): ♑ 2.0R, 1.8, 1.5, 1.3
♇ (1, 11, 21, 31): ♏ 2.0R, 1.9, 2.0D, 2

1986

	1	2	3	4	5	6	7	8	9	10	11	12	13	14	15	16	17	18	19	20	21	22	23	24	25	26	27	28	29	30	31
☉	♋ 8.9	9.8	10.8	11.7	12.7	13.7	14.6	15.6	16.5	17.5	18.4	19.4	20.3	21.3	22.2	23.2	24.1	25.1	26.1	27	28	28.9	29.9	♌ 0.8	1.8	2.7	3.7	4.6	5.6	6.6	7.5
☽	♉ 1	13	24.8	♊ 6.6	18.4	♋ 0.3	12.3	24.4	♌ 6.7	19.1	♍ 1.7	14.4	27.4	♎ 10.7	24.3	♏ 8.2	22.4	♐ 7	21.8	♑ 6.8	21.7	♒ 6.6	21.1	♓ 5.3	18.9	♈ 2.1	14.9	27.3	♉ 9.5	21.4	♊ 3.3
☿	♌ 3.5	4.1	4.6	5.1	5.5	5.8	6.1	6.3	6.4	6.4R	6.4	6.2	6	5.7	5.4	5	4.5	3.9	3.3	2.7	2	1.3	0.6	♋ 29.9	29.3	28.6	28	27.4	27	26.5	26.2
♀	♌ 17.8	18.9	20.1	21.2	22.4	23.5	24.7	25.8	27	28.1	29.2	♍ 0.4	1.5	2.6	3.8	4.9	6	7.1	8.3	9.4	10.5	11.6	12.7	13.8	15	16.1	17.2	18.3	19.4	20.5	21.5
♂	♑ 20.2R	20	19.7	19.4	19.2	18.9	18.6	18.3	18	17.7	17.5	17.2	16.9	16.6	16.3	16	15.7	15.4	15.2	14.9	14.6	14.4	14.1	13.9	13.7	13.4	13.2	13	12.8	12.6	12.5

♃ (1, 6, 11, 16, 21, 26, 31): ♓ 22.6, 22.8, 22.9, 22.8R, 22.7, 22.6, 22.3
♄ (1, 6, 11, 16, 21, 26, 31): ♐ 4.1R, 3.9, 3.6, 3.5, 3.3, 3.2, 3.1
♅ (1, 11, 21, 31): ♐ 19.6R, 19.2, 18.9, 18.7
♆ (1, 11, 21, 31): ♑ 4.3R, 4, 3.8, 3.6
♇ (1, 11, 21, 31): ♏ 4.6R, 4.5, 4.6D, 4.6

VIII

1985

	1	2	3	4	5	6	7	8	9	10	11	12	13	14	15	16	17	18	19	20	21	22	23	24	25	26	27	28	29	30	31
☉	♌ 8.7	9.7	10.6	11.6	12.5	13.5	14.4	15.4	16.4	17.3	18.3	19.2	20.2	21.2	22.1	23.1	24	25	26	26.9	27.9	28.9	29.8	♍ 0.8	1.8	2.7	3.7	4.6	5.6	6.6	7.5
☽	♒ 9.9	23.2	♓ 6.1	18.8	♈ 1.2	13.3	25.2	♉ 7	18.8	♊ 0.7	12.8	25.1	♋ 7.7	20.6	♌ 3.9	17.6	♍ 1.6	15.8	♎ 0.2	14.5	28.9	♏ 13.1	27.3	♐ 11.3	25.2	♑ 8.9	22.4	♒ 5.8	19	♓ 1.9	14.6
☿	♌ 24.6R	24.3	23.8	23.3	22.7	22	21.3	20.5	19.8	18.9	18.1	17.4	16.6	15.9	15.2	14.6	14.1	13.7	13.4	13.3	13.2D	13.3	13.5	13.8	14.3	14.9	15.6	16.4	17.4	18.5	19.6
♀	♊ 28.4	29.6	♋ 0.7	1.9	3	4.2	5.3	6.5	7.6	8.8	9.9	11.1	12.2	13.4	14.6	15.7	16.9	18.1	19.2	20.4	21.6	22.8	23.9	25.1	26.3	27.5	28.6	29.8	♌ 1	2.2	3.4
♂	♌ 4.4	5.1	5.7	6.4	7	7.6	8.3	8.9	9.6	10.2	10.8	11.5	12.1	12.8	13.4	14.1	14.7	15.3	16	16.6	17.2	17.9	18.5	19.2	19.8	20.4	21.1	21.7	22.3	23	23.6

♃ (1, 6, 11, 16, 21, 26, 31): ♒ 12.5R, 11.8, 11.2, 10.6, 10, 9.4, 8.9
♄ (1, 6, 11, 16, 21, 26, 31): ♏ 21.5, 21.6, 21.7, 21.8, 22, 22.3, 22.5
♅ (1, 11, 21, 31): ♐ 14.2R, 14, 14, 14.0D
♆ (1, 11, 21, 31): ♑ 1.3R, 1.1, 1, 0.9
♇ (1, 11, 21, 31): ♏ 2, 2.2, 2.4, 2.6

1986

	1	2	3	4	5	6	7	8	9	10	11	12	13	14	15	16	17	18	19	20	21	22	23	24	25	26	27	28	29	30	31
☉	♌ 8.5	9.4	10.4	11.3	12.3	13.3	14.2	15.2	16.1	17.1	18.1	19	20	20.9	21.9	22.9	23.8	24.8	25.7	26.7	27.7	28.6	29.6	♍ 0.6	1.5	2.5	3.4	4.4	5.4	6.3	7.3
☽	♊ 15.1	27	♋ 9	21.1	♌ 3.4	15.9	28.5	♍ 11.4	24.4	♎ 7.7	21.1	♏ 4.8	18.7	♐ 2.8	17.1	♑ 1.6	16.2	♒ 0.8	15.2	29.5	♓ 13.4	27	♈ 10.1	22.9	♉ 5.3	17.5	29.5	♊ 11.4	23.2	♋ 5.1	17.2
☿	♋ 25.9R	25.8	25.7	25.8D	25.9	26.2	26.6	27.1	27.7	28.4	29.2	♌ 0.1	1.1	2.3	3.5	4.8	6.2	7.7	9.3	10.9	12.6	14.4	16.2	18.1	20	21.9	23.8	25.8	27.8	29.7	♍ 1.7
♀	♍ 22.6	23.7	24.8	25.9	26.9	28	29.1	♎ 0.1	1.2	2.3	3.3	4.4	5.4	6.4	7.5	8.5	9.5	10.6	11.6	12.6	13.6	14.6	15.6	16.6	17.5	18.5	19.5	20.4	21.4	22.3	23.3
♂	♑ 12.3R	12.2	12	11.9	11.8	11.7	11.6	11.6	11.5	11.5	11.4	11.4	11.4D	11.4	11.5	11.5	11.6	11.6	11.7	11.8	11.9	12.1	12.2	12.4	12.5	12.7	12.9	13.1	13.3	13.5	13.8

♃ (1, 6, 11, 16, 21, 26, 31): ♓ 22.3R, 21.9, 21.5, 21, 20.5, 19.9, 19.3
♄ (1, 6, 11, 16, 21, 26, 31): ♐ 3.1R, 3.1, 3.1D, 3.1, 3.2, 3.4, 3.5
♅ (1, 11, 21, 31): ♐ 18.6R, 18.5, 18.4, 18.4D
♆ (1, 11, 21, 31): ♑ 3.5R, 3.4, 3.2, 3.1
♇ (1, 11, 21, 31): ♏ 4.6, 4.7, 4.9, 5.2

IX

1985

	1	2	3	4	5	6	7	8	9	10	11	12	13	14	15	16	17	18	19	20	21	22	23	24	25	26	27	28	29	30	31
☉	♍ 8.5	9.5	10.4	11.4	12.4	13.4	14.3	15.3	16.3	17.2	18.2	19.2	20.2	21.1	22.1	23.1	24.1	25	26	27	28	28.9	29.9	♎ 0.9	1.9	2.9	3.8	4.8	5.8	6.8	
☽	♓ 27.1	♈ 9.3	21.3	♉ 3.2	15	26.8	♊ 8.7	20.7	♋ 3	15.6	28.6	♌ 12.1	25.9	♍ 10.2	24.7	♎ 9.5	24.3	♏ 9	23.6	♐ 7.9	22	♑ 5.8	19.3	♒ 2.6	15.7	28.5	♓ 11.1	23.5	♈ 5.7	17.8	
☿	♌ 20.9	22.3	23.8	25.3	26.9	28.6	♍ 0.3	2.1	3.9	5.8	7.6	9.5	11.4	13.3	15.2	17.1	19	20.8	22.7	24.6	26.4	28.3	♎ 0.1	1.9	3.7	5.4	7.2	9	10.7	12.4	
♀	♌ 4.6	5.8	7	8.2	9.4	10.6	11.8	12.9	14.1	15.4	16.6	17.8	19	20.2	21.4	22.6	23.8	25	26.2	27.4	28.7	29.9	♍ 1.1	2.3	3.5	4.7	6	7.2	8.4	9.6	
♂	♌ 24.3	24.9	25.5	26.2	26.8	27.4	28.1	28.7	29.3	30	♍ 0.6	1.2	1.9	2.5	3.1	3.8	4.4	5	5.7	6.3	6.9	7.6	8.2	8.8	9.5	10.1	10.7	11.4	12	12.6	

♃ (1, 6, 11, 16, 21, 26): ♒ 8.8R, 8.3, 7.9, 7.6, 7.4, 7.2
♄ (1, 6, 11, 16, 21, 26): ♏ 22.6, 22.9, 23.2, 23.6, 24, 24.4
♅ (1, 11, 21): ♐ 14, 14.1, 14.3
♆ (1, 11, 21): ♑ 0.9R, 0.9, 0.9D
♇ (1, 11, 21): ♏ 2.6, 2.9, 3.3

1986

	1	2	3	4	5	6	7	8	9	10	11	12	13	14	15	16	17	18	19	20	21	22	23	24	25	26	27	28	29	30	31
☉	♍ 8.3	9.2	10.2	11.2	12.2	13.1	14.1	15.1	16	17	18	19	19.9	20.9	21.9	22.8	23.8	24.8	25.8	26.7	27.7	28.7	29.7	♎ 0.7	1.6	2.6	3.6	4.6	5.6	6.5	
☽	♋ 29.4	♌ 11.9	24.6	♍ 7.5	20.7	♎ 4.2	17.8	♏ 1.6	15.5	29.6	♐ 13.7	27.9	♑ 12.2	26.4	♒ 10.5	24.5	♓ 8.3	21.9	♈ 5.2	18.1	♉ 0.8	13.2	25.4	♊ 7.4	19.2	♋ 1.1	13	25.1	♌ 7.3	19.9	
☿	♍ 3.7	5.6	7.6	9.5	11.5	13.4	15.3	17.2	19	20.9	22.7	24.5	26.3	28.1	29.8	♎ 1.6	3.3	5	6.7	8.3	10	11.6	13.2	14.8	16.4	18	19.5	21.1	22.6	24.1	
♀	♎ 24.2	25.1	26.1	27	27.9	28.8	29.6	♏ 0.5	1.4	2.2	3	3.9	4.7	5.5	6.3	7	7.8	8.5	9.3	10	10.7	11.4	12	12.7	13.3	13.9	14.5	15.1	15.6	16.1	
♂	♑ 14	14.3	14.5	14.8	15.1	15.4	15.7	16	16.4	16.7	17.1	17.4	17.8	18.2	18.6	19	19.4	19.8	20.2	20.6	21.1	21.5	21.9	22.4	22.9	23.3	23.8	24.3	24.8	25.3	

♃ (1, 6, 11, 16, 21, 26): ♓ 19.2R, 18.5, 17.8, 17.2, 16.5, 15.9
♄ (1, 6, 11, 16, 21, 26): ♐ 3.6, 3.8, 4, 4.3, 4.6, 5
♅ (1, 11, 21): ♐ 18.4, 18.4, 18.6
♆ (1, 11, 21): ♑ 3.1R, 3, 3.1D
♇ (1, 11, 21): ♏ 5.2, 5.5, 5.8

X

1985

	1	2	3	4	5	6	7	8	9	10	11	12	13	14	15	16	17	18	19	20	21	22	23	24	25	26	27	28	29	30	31
☉	♎ 7.8	8.8	9.7	10.7	11.7	12.7	13.7	14.7	15.7	16.6	17.6	18.6	19.6	20.6	21.6	22.6	23.6	24.6	25.6	26.6	27.5	28.5	29.5	♏ 0.5	1.5	2.5	3.5	4.5	5.5	6.5	7.5
☽	♈ 29.7	♉ 11.5	23.3	♊ 5.1	17	29	♋ 11.2	23.8	♌ 6.8	20.1	♍ 4	18.3	♎ 2.9	17.9	♏ 3	18.1	♐ 3	17.7	♑ 2	15.9	29.5	♒ 12.7	25.5	♓ 8.1	20.5	♈ 2.6	14.6	26.5	♉ 8.4	20.2	♊ 2
☿	♎ 14.1	15.8	17.5	19.1	20.8	22.4	24	25.6	27.2	28.8	♏ 0.4	1.9	3.4	5	6.5	8	9.5	11	12.5	13.9	15.4	16.8	18.2	19.7	21.1	22.4	23.8	25.2	26.5	27.8	29.1
♀	♍ 10.9	12.1	13.3	14.5	15.8	17	18.2	19.5	20.7	21.9	23.2	24.4	25.6	26.9	28.1	29.3	♎ 0.6	1.8	3.1	4.3	5.5	6.8	8	9.3	10.5	11.8	13	14.2	15.5	16.7	18
♂	♍ 13.3	13.9	14.5	15.1	15.8	16.4	17	17.7	18.3	18.9	19.6	20.2	20.8	21.4	22.1	22.7	23.3	24	24.6	25.2	25.8	26.5	27.1	27.7	28.4	29	29.6	♎ 0.2	0.9	1.5	2.1

♃ (1, 6, 11, 16, 21, 26, 31): ♒ 7.1R, 7.1D, 7.2, 7.4, 7.6, 8, 8.4
♄ (1, 6, 11, 16, 21, 26, 31): ♏ 24.9, 25.3, 25.8, 26.4, 26.9, 27.4, 28
♅ (1, 11, 21, 31): ♐ 14.6, 15, 15.4, 15.9
♆ (1, 11, 21, 31): ♑ 0.9, 1.1, 1.3, 1.5
♇ (1, 11, 21, 31): ♏ 3.6, 4, 4.4, 4.8

1986

	1	2	3	4	5	6	7	8	9	10	11	12	13	14	15	16	17	18	19	20	21	22	23	24	25	26	27	28	29	30	31
☉	♎ 7.5	8.5	9.5	10.5	11.5	12.5	13.4	14.4	15.4	16.4	17.4	18.4	19.4	20.4	21.3	22.3	23.3	24.3	25.3	26.3	27.3	28.3	29.3	♏ 0.3	1.3	2.3	3.3	4.3	5.3	6.3	7.3
☽	♍ 2.7	15.9	29.4	♎ 13.2	27.3	♏ 11.5	25.9	♐ 10.3	24.7	♑ 9	23.1	♒ 7.1	20.9	♓ 4.5	17.8	♈ 1	13.9	26.6	♉ 9	21.3	♊ 3.4	15.3	27.2	♋ 9.1	21	♌ 3	15.2	27.7	♍ 10.5	23.8	♎ 7.4
☿	♎ 25.6	27.1	28.5	30	♏ 1.4	2.8	4.2	5.6	7	8.3	9.7	11	12.3	13.5	14.8	16	17.2	18.3	19.5	20.5	21.6	22.6	23.6	24.5	25.3	26.1	26.8	27.5	28	28.5	28.8
♀	♏ 16.6	17.1	17.5	17.9	18.3	18.7	19	19.3	19.5	19.8	20	20.1	20.2	20.3	20.4	20.4R	20.4	20.3	20.2	20	19.8	19.6	19.3	19	18.7	18.3	17.9	17.4	16.9	16.4	15.9
♂	♑ 25.8	26.3	26.8	27.3	27.8	28.4	28.9	29.4	30	♒ 0.5	1.1	1.6	2.2	2.8	3.3	3.9	4.5	5.1	5.7	6.2	6.8	7.4	8	8.6	9.2	9.9	10.5	11.1	11.7	12.3	12.9

♃ (1, 6, 11, 16, 21, 26, 31): ♓ 15.3R, 14.8, 14.3, 13.9, 13.5, 13.3, 13.1
♄ (1, 6, 11, 16, 21, 26, 31): ♐ 5.4, 5.8, 6.2, 6.7, 7.2, 7.7, 8.2
♅ (1, 11, 21, 31): ♐ 18.9, 19.2, 19.6, 20
♆ (1, 11, 21, 31): ♑ 3.1, 3.2, 3.4, 3.6
♇ (1, 11, 21, 31): ♏ 6.1, 6.5, 6.9, 7.3

XI

1985

	1	2	3	4	5	6	7	8	9	10	11	12	13	14	15	16	17	18	19	20	21	22	23	24	25	26	27	28	29	30	31
☉	♏ 8.5	9.5	10.5	11.5	12.5	13.5	14.5	15.5	16.5	17.5	18.5	19.6	20.6	21.6	22.6	23.6	24.6	25.6	26.6	27.6	28.6	29.6	♐ 0.6	1.7	2.7	3.7	4.7	5.7	6.7	7.7	
☽	♊ 13.8	25.7	♋ 7.8	20.1	♌ 2.6	15.5	28.7	♍ 12.4	26.5	♎ 11	25.9	♏ 11	26.3	♐ 11.4	26.4	♑ 11	25.1	♒ 8.8	22.1	♓ 4.9	17.4	29.6	♈ 11.7	23.5	♉ 5.3	17.1	28.9	♊ 10.8	22.8	♋ 4.9	
☿	♐ 0.4	1.7	2.9	4.1	5.2	6.4	7.5	8.5	9.5	10.5	11.3	12.1	12.9	13.5	14.1	14.5	14.8	15	15.0R	14.9	14.6	14.1	13.4	12.6	11.6	10.5	9.2	7.9	6.5	5.1	
♀	♎ 19.2	20.5	21.7	23	24.2	25.5	26.7	28	29.2	♏ 0.5	1.7	3	4.2	5.5	6.7	8	9.2	10.5	11.8	13	14.3	15.5	16.8	18	19.3	20.5	21.8	23.1	24.3	25.6	
♂	♎ 2.7	3.4	4	4.6	5.3	5.9	6.5	7.1	7.8	8.4	9	9.6	10.3	10.9	11.5	12.1	12.8	13.4	14	14.6	15.2	15.9	16.5	17.1	17.7	18.4	19	19.6	20.2	20.8	

♃ (1, 6, 11, 16, 21, 26): ♒ 8.4, 8.9, 9.5, 10.1, 10.8, 11.5
♄ (1, 6, 11, 16, 21, 26): ♏ 28.1, 28.7, 29.3, 29.9, ♐ 0.5, 1.1
♅ (1, 11, 21): ♐ 15.9, 16.5, 17
♆ (1, 11, 21): ♑ 1.5, 1.8, 2.1
♇ (1, 11, 21): ♏ 4.8, 5.3, 5.6

1986

	1	2	3	4	5	6	7	8	9	10	11	12	13	14	15	16	17	18	19	20	21	22	23	24	25	26	27	28	29	30	31
☉	♏ 8.3	9.3	10.3	11.3	12.3	13.3	14.3	15.3	16.3	17.3	18.3	19.3	20.3	21.3	22.3	23.3	24.3	25.4	26.4	27.4	28.4	29.4	♐ 0.4	1.4	2.4	3.4	4.4	5.5	6.5	7.5	
☽	♎ 21.4	♏ 5.8	20.5	♐ 5.4	20.2	♑ 5	19.6	♒ 3.8	17.8	♓ 1.4	14.7	27.7	♈ 10.5	23.1	♉ 5.4	17.7	29.8	♊ 11.8	23.7	♋ 5.5	17.4	29.3	♌ 11.3	23.4	♍ 5.8	18.6	♎ 1.7	15.2	29.3	♏ 13.8	
☿	♏ 29.1	29.2	29.1R	29	28.6	28.1	27.5	26.6	25.7	24.6	23.4	22.1	20.7	19.4	18.1	16.9	15.8	14.9	14.2	13.6	13.3	13.1	13.1D	13.3	13.7	14.2	14.8	15.6	16.5	17.4	
♀	♏ 15.3R	14.8	14.2	13.6	13	12.3	11.7	11.1	10.5	10	9.4	8.9	8.4	7.9	7.4	7	6.6	6.3	5.9	5.7	5.4	5.2	5.1	5	4.9	4.9	4.9D	5	5.1	5.2	
♂	♒ 13.6	14.2	14.8	15.5	16.1	16.7	17.4	18	18.7	19.3	20	20.6	21.3	21.9	22.6	23.3	23.9	24.6	25.2	25.9	26.6	27.2	27.9	28.6	29.3	29.9	♓ 0.6	1.3	2	2.6	

♃ (1, 6, 11, 16, 21, 26): ♓ 13.1R, 13, 13.0D, 13.1, 13.2, 13.5
♄ (1, 6, 11, 16, 21, 26): ♐ 8.3, 8.9, 9.4, 10, 10.6, 11.2
♅ (1, 11, 21): ♐ 20.1, 20.6, 21.1
♆ (1, 11, 21): ♑ 3.6, 3.9, 4.2
♇ (1, 11, 21): ♏ 7.3, 7.7, 8.1

XII

1985

	1	2	3	4	5	6	7	8	9	10	11	12	13	14	15	16	17	18	19	20	21	22	23	24	25	26	27	28	29	30	31
☉	♐ 8.7	9.8	10.8	11.8	12.8	13.8	14.8	15.8	16.9	17.9	18.9	19.9	20.9	21.9	23	24	25	26	27	28.1	29.1	♑ 0.1	1.1	2.1	3.1	4.2	5.2	6.2	7.2	8.2	9.3
☽	♋ 17.1	29.5	♌ 12.1	25	♍ 8.1	21.6	♎ 5.5	19.7	♏ 4.3	19.2	♐ 4.3	19.4	♑ 4.3	19.1	♒ 3.4	17.2	♓ 0.6	13.6	26.1	♈ 8.3	20.3	♉ 2.1	13.9	25.7	♊ 7.5	19.5	♋ 1.7	14	26.5	♌ 9.1	22
☿	♐ 3.8R	2.6	1.5	0.6	♏ 29.9	29.3	29	28.8	28.8D	29	29.3	29.8	♐ 0.3	1	1.8	2.7	3.7	4.7	5.8	6.9	8.1	9.3	10.6	11.9	13.2	14.5	15.9	17.2	18.6	20	21.5
♀	♏ 26.8	28.1	29.3	♐ 0.6	1.8	3.1	4.4	5.6	6.9	8.1	9.4	10.7	11.9	13.2	14.4	15.7	16.9	18.2	19.5	20.7	22	23.2	24.5	25.8	27	28.3	29.5	♑ 0.8	2	3.3	4.6
♂	♎ 21.5	22.1	22.7	23.3	23.9	24.6	25.2	25.8	26.4	27	27.7	28.3	28.9	29.5	♏ 0.1	0.8	1.4	2	2.6	3.2	3.8	4.4	5.1	5.7	6.3	6.9	7.5	8.1	8.7	9.4	10

♃ (1, 6, 11, 16, 21, 26, 31): ♒ 12.3, 13.2, 14.1, 15, 16, 17, 18.1
♄ (1, 6, 11, 16, 21, 26, 31): ♐ 1.7, 2.3, 2.8, 3.4, 4, 4.5, 5.1
♅ (1, 11, 21, 31): ♐ 17.6, 18.2, 18.9, 19.4
♆ (1, 11, 21, 31): ♑ 2.4, 2.8, 3.2, 3.6
♇ (1, 11, 21, 31): ♏ 6, 6.3, 6.6, 6.9

1986

	1	2	3	4	5	6	7	8	9	10	11	12	13	14	15	16	17	18	19	20	21	22	23	24	25	26	27	28	29	30	31
☉	♐ 8.5	9.5	10.5	11.5	12.6	13.6	14.6	15.6	16.6	17.6	18.6	19.7	20.7	21.7	22.7	23.7	24.8	25.8	26.8	27.8	28.8	29.8	♑ 0.9	1.9	2.9	3.9	4.9	6	7	8	9
☽	♏ 28.6	♐ 13.8	29.1	♑ 14.2	29.1	♒ 13.7	27.8	♓ 11.5	24.7	♈ 7.6	20.1	♉ 2.5	14.6	26.7	♊ 8.6	20.5	♋ 2.4	14.3	26.2	♌ 8.1	20.1	♍ 2.3	14.6	27.3	♎ 10.2	23.6	♏ 7.5	21.8	♐ 6.6	21.8	♑ 7.1
☿	♏ 18.4	19.6	20.7	21.9	23.2	24.5	25.8	27.2	28.6	30	♐ 1.4	2.8	4.3	5.8	7.2	8.7	10.2	11.7	13.2	14.7	16.2	17.8	19.3	20.8	22.3	23.9	25.4	27	28.5	♑ 0.1	1.6
♀	♏ 5.4	5.6	5.8	6.1	6.4	6.8	7.1	7.5	8	8.4	8.9	9.5	10	10.6	11.2	11.8	12.4	13.1	13.7	14.4	15.2	15.9	16.7	17.4	18.2	19	19.8	20.6	21.5	22.3	23.2
♂	♓ 3.3	4	4.7	5.4	6	6.7	7.4	8.1	8.8	9.5	10.2	10.9	11.5	12.2	12.9	13.6	14.3	15	15.7	16.4	17.1	17.8	18.5	19.2	19.9	20.6	21.3	22	22.7	23.4	24.1

♃ (1, 6, 11, 16, 21, 26, 31): ♓ 13.8, 14.2, 14.7, 15.3, 15.9, 16.6, 17.4
♄ (1, 6, 11, 16, 21, 26, 31): ♐ 11.8, 12.4, 13, 13.6, 14.1, 14.7, 15.3
♅ (1, 11, 21, 31): ♐ 21.7, 22.3, 22.9, 23.5
♆ (1, 11, 21, 31): ♑ 4.6, 4.9, 5.3, 5.7
♇ (1, 11, 21, 31): ♏ 8.5, 8.9, 9.2, 9.4

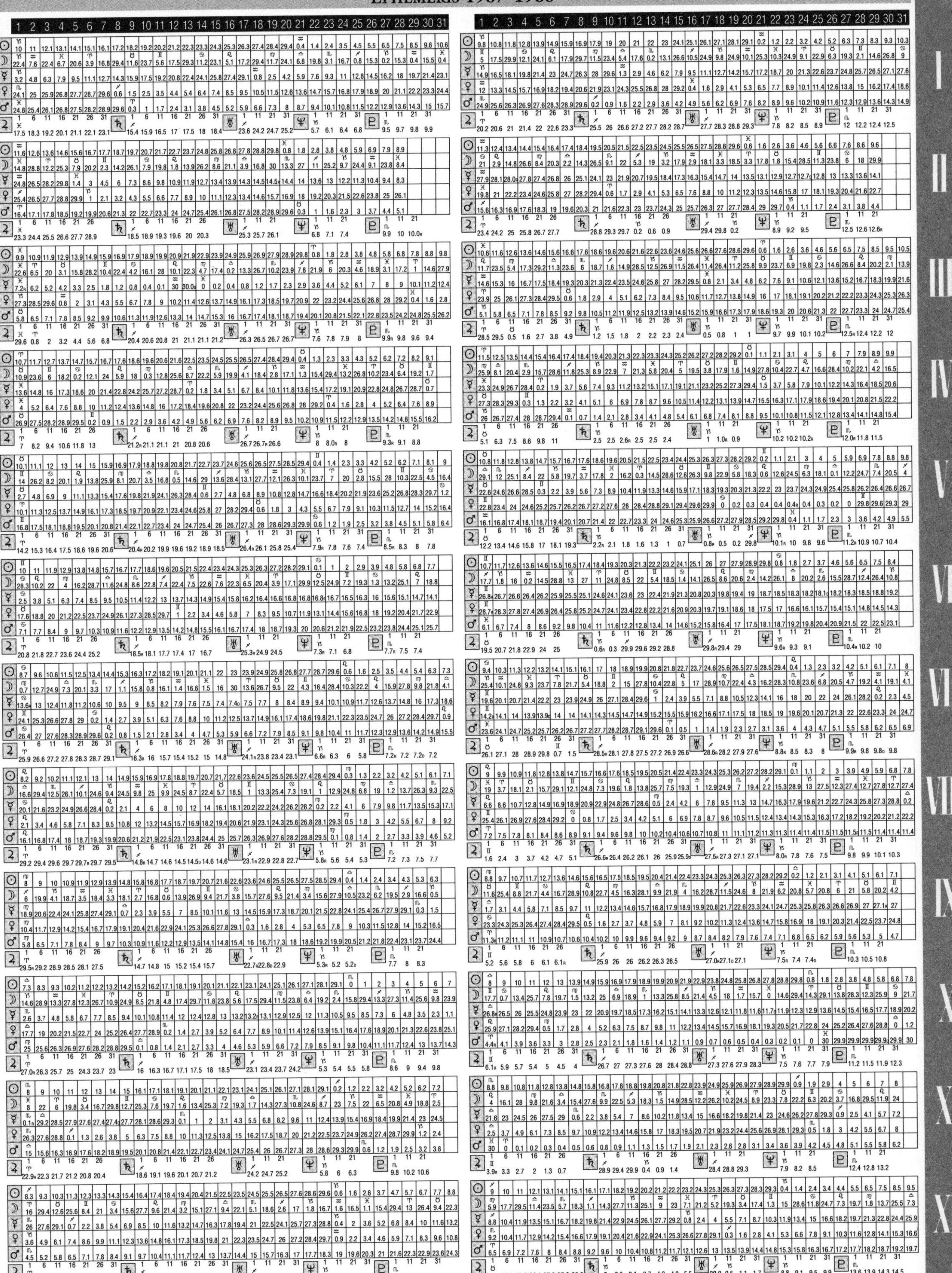

I

II

III

IV

V

VI

VII

VIII

IX

X

XI

XII

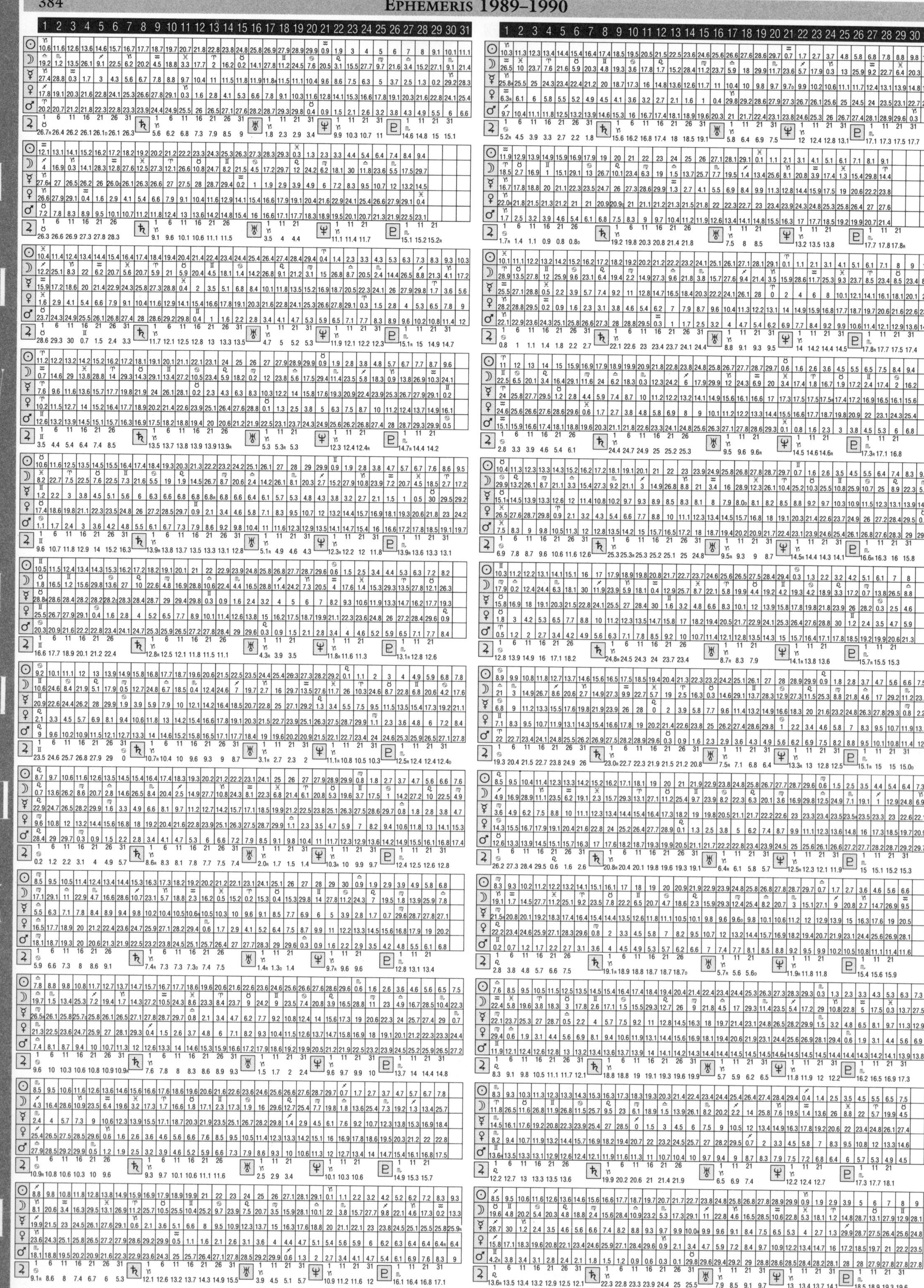

I

	1	2	3	4	5	6	7	8	9	10	11	12	13	14	15	16	17	18	19	20	21	22	23	24	25	26	27	28	29	30	31
☉	♑ 10.1	11.1	12.1	13.1	14.1	15.2	16.2	17.2	18.2	19.2	20.3	21.3	22.3	23.3	24.3	25.3	26.4	27.4	28.4	29.4	♒ 0.4	1.5	2.5	3.5	4.5	5.5	6.5	7.6	8.6	9.6	10.6
☽	♋ 13.2	28.2	♌ 12.9	27.1	♍ 10.9	24.3	♎ 7.2	19.8	♏ 2	14.1	26	♐ 7.8	19.6	♑ 1.5	13.4	25.4	♒ 7.6	19.9	♓ 2.4	15.1	28.1	♈ 11.3	24.8	♉ 8.6	22.8	♊ 7.1	21.8	♋ 6.5	21.3	♌ 6.1	20.6
☿	♐ 24.3R	23.9	23.7	23.7D	23.8	24.1	24.4	24.9	25.5	26.2	27	27.8	28.7	29.7	♑ 0.7	1.7	2.9	4	5.2	6.4	7.6	8.9	10.2	11.5	12.8	14.2	15.6	16.9	18.3	19.8	21.2
♀	♑ 24.7	26	27.2	28.5	29.7	♒ 1	2.3	3.5	4.8	6	7.3	8.5	9.8	11	12.3	13.5	14.8	16	17.3	18.5	19.8	21	22.3	23.5	24.8	26	27.3	28.5	29.8	♓ 1	2.3
♂	♉ 27.7R	27.7D	27.8	27.8	27.8	27.9	27.9	28	28.1	28.2	28.3	28.4	28.6	28.7	28.9	29	29.2	29.4	29.6	29.8	30	♊ 0.2	0.4	0.7	0.9	1.2	1.5	1.7	2	2.3	2.6

♃	1	6	11	16	21	26	31
	♌ 12.0R	11.5	10.9	10.3	9.6	9	8.3
♄	1	6	11	16	21	26	31
	♑ 25.7	26.2	26.8	27.4	28	28.6	29.2
♅	1	11	21	31			
	♑ 9.7	10.3	10.9	11.5			
♆	1	11	21	31			
	♑ 14.1	14.5	14.9	15.2			
♇	1	11	21	31			
	♏ 19.6	19.9	20.1	20.2			

	1	2	3	4	5	6	7	8	9	10	11	12	13	14	15	16	17	18	19	20	21	22	23	24	25	26	27	28	29	30	31
☉	♑ 9.8	10.8	11.9	12.9	13.9	14.9	15.9	16.9	18	19	20	21	22	23.1	24.1	25.1	26.1	27.1	28.2	29.2	♒ 0.2	1.2	2.2	3.2	4.3	5.3	6.3	7.3	8.3	9.3	10.4
☽	♏ 26.2	♐ 8.4	20.5	♑ 2.4	14.3	26.1	♒ 7.9	19.7	♓ 1.5	13.5	25.7	♈ 8.1	20.8	♉ 3.8	17.3	♊ 1.2	15.6	♋ 0.3	15.4	♌ 0.7	15.9	♍ 1	15.8	♎ 0.2	14.1	27.5	♏ 10.5	23.1	♐ 5.4	17.5	29.4
☿	♐ 18.1	19.3	20.5	21.8	23.1	24.4	25.8	27.1	28.5	29.9	♑ 1.3	2.7	4.2	5.6	7.1	8.5	10	11.5	13	14.5	16.1	17.6	19.1	20.7	22.2	23.8	25.4	27	28.6	♒ 0.2	1.8
♀	♐ 0.4	1.6	2.9	4.1	5.3	6.5	7.7	8.9	10.1	11.3	12.5	13.8	15	16.2	17.4	18.6	19.9	21.1	22.3	23.5	24.7	26	27.2	28.4	29.6	♑ 0.9	2.1	3.3	4.5	5.8	7
♂	♐ 23.8	24.5	25.3	26	26.8	27.5	28.2	29	29.7	♑ 0.5	1.2	1.9	2.7	3.4	4.2	4.9	5.7	6.4	7.2	7.9	8.7	9.4	10.2	10.9	11.7	12.4	13.2	13.9	14.7	15.4	16.2

♃	1	6	11	16	21	26	31
	♍ 14.6R	14.6	14.4	14.2	13.9	13.5	13.1
♄	1	6	11	16	21	26	31
	♒ 5.9	6.4	7	7.6	8.2	8.8	9.4
♅	1	11	21	31			
	♑ 13.7	14.3	14.9	15.4			
♆	1	11	21	31			
	♑ 16.2	16.6	17	17.3			
♇	1	11	21	31			
	♏ 22.1	22.4	22.6	22.8			

II

	1	2	3	4	5	6	7	8	9	10	11	12	13	14	15	16	17	18	19	20	21	22	23	24	25	26	27	28	29	30	31
☉	♒ 11.6	12.6	13.6	14.7	15.7	16.7	17.7	18.7	19.7	20.7	21.8	22.8	23.8	24.8	25.8	26.8	27.8	28.8	29.8	♓ 0.8	1.9	2.9	3.9	4.9	5.9	6.9	7.9	8.9			
☽	♍ 4.9	18.7	♎ 2.2	15.2	27.9	♏ 10.2	22.3	♐ 4.3	16.1	27.9	♑ 9.8	21.8	♒ 3.9	16.3	28.9	♓ 11.8	24.9	♈ 8.2	21.8	♉ 5.5	19.4	♊ 3.4	17.6	♋ 1.8	16.1	♌ 0.5	14.7	28.9			
☿	♑ 22.7	24.1	25.6	27.1	28.6	♒ 0.1	1.6	3.2	4.8	6.3	7.9	9.5	11.1	12.7	14.4	16	17.7	19.4	21.1	22.8	24.5	26.3	28	29.8	♓ 1.6	3.4	5.2	7.1			
♀	♓ 3.5	4.7	6	7.2	8.5	9.7	11	12.2	13.5	14.7	15.9	17.2	18.4	19.7	20.9	22.1	23.4	24.6	25.8	27.1	28.3	29.5	♈ 0.8	2	3.2	4.5	5.7	6.9			
♂	♊ 2.9	3.2	3.5	3.8	4.2	4.5	4.8	5.2	5.6	5.9	6.3	6.7	7	7.4	7.8	8.2	8.6	9	9.4	9.8	10.2	10.6	11.1	11.5	11.9	12.4	12.8	13.2			

♃	1	6	11	16	21	26
	♌ 8.2R	7.5	6.9	6.3	5.7	5.2
♄	1	6	11	16	21	26
	♑ 29.3	29.9	♒ 0.5	1	1.6	2.1
♅	1	11	21			
	♑ 11.5	12	12.5			
♆	1	11	21			
	♑ 15.3	15.6	15.9			
♇	1	11	21			
	♏ 20.3	20.3	20.4			

	1	2	3	4	5	6	7	8	9	10	11	12	13	14	15	16	17	18	19	20	21	22	23	24	25	26	27	28	29	30	31
☉	♒ 11.4	12.4	13.4	14.4	15.4	16.4	17.5	18.5	19.5	20.5	21.5	22.5	23.5	24.5	25.6	26.6	27.6	28.6	29.6	♓ 0.6	1.6	2.6	3.6	4.6	5.6	6.6	7.6	8.7	9.7		
☽	♑ 11.3	23	♒ 4.8	16.7	28.6	♓ 10.6	22.7	♈ 5	17.5	♉ 0.2	13.2	26.5	♊ 10.2	24.3	♋ 8.8	23.6	♌ 8.6	23.8	♍ 8.9	23.8	♎ 8.4	22.5	♏ 6.1	19.2	♐ 1.8	14.2	26.2	♑ 8.1	19.9		
☿	♒ 3.5	5.1	6.8	8.4	10.1	11.8	13.5	15.2	17	18.7	20.5	22.2	24	25.8	27.6	29.5	♓ 1.3	3.1	5	6.9	8.7	10.6	12.5	14.3	16.2	18	19.9	21.7	23.5		
♀	♑ 8.2	9.5	10.7	11.9	13.1	14.4	15.6	16.8	18.1	19.3	20.5	21.8	23	24.2	25.5	26.7	27.9	29.1	♒ 0.4	1.6	2.8	4.1	5.3	6.6	7.8	9	10.3	11.5	12.7		
♂	♑ 16.9	17.7	18.5	19.2	20	20.7	21.5	22.2	23	23.8	24.5	25.3	26	26.8	27.6	28.3	29.1	29.9	♒ 0.6	1.4	2.2	2.9	3.7	4.5	5.2	6	6.8	7.5	8.3		

♃	1	6	11	16	21	26
	♍ 13.0R	12.5	11.9	11.3	10.7	10.1
♄	1	6	11	16	21	26
	♒ 9.5	10.1	10.7	11.3	11.8	12.4
♅	1	11	21			
	♑ 15.5	16	16.5			
♆	1	11	21			
	♑ 17.4	17.7	18			
♇	1	11	21			
	♏ 22.8	22.9	23			

III

	1	2	3	4	5	6	7	8	9	10	11	12	13	14	15	16	17	18	19	20	21	22	23	24	25	26	27	28	29	30	31
☉	♓ 9.9	10.9	11.9	12.9	13.9	14.9	15.9	16.9	17.9	18.9	19.9	20.9	21.9	22.9	23.9	24.9	25.9	26.9	27.9	28.9	29.9	♈ 0.9	1.9	2.9	3.8	4.8	5.8	6.8	7.8	8.8	9.8
☽	♍ 12.9	26.6	♎ 10	23	♏ 5.7	18.1	♐ 0.2	12.1	24	♑ 5.8	17.7	29.7	♒ 12	24.6	♓ 7.4	20.7	♈ 4.2	18	♉ 1.9	16	♊ 0.2	14.4	28.5	♋ 12.6	26.7	♌ 10.6	24.4	♍ 8.2	21.7	♎ 5.1	18.2
☿	♓ 8.9	10.8	12.7	14.6	16.5	18.4	20.4	22.3	24.3	26.2	28.2	♈ 0.1	2.1	4	5.9	7.8	9.6	11.4	13.1	14.8	16.5	18	19.5	20.9	22.2	23.4	24.4	25.4	26.3	27	27.7
♀	♈ 8.2	9.4	10.6	11.8	13.1	14.3	15.5	16.7	18	19.2	20.4	21.6	22.8	24.1	25.3	26.5	27.7	28.9	♉ 0.1	1.3	2.5	3.7	5	6.2	7.4	8.6	9.8	11	12.2	13.4	14.6
♂	♊ 13.7	14.1	14.6	15	15.5	16	16.4	16.9	17.4	17.9	18.3	18.8	19.3	19.8	20.3	20.8	21.3	21.8	22.3	22.8	23.3	23.8	24.3	24.8	25.3	25.8	26.3	26.8	27.4	27.9	28.4

♃	1	6	11	16	21	26	31
	♌ 4.9R	4.5	4.2	3.9	3.7	3.6	3.5D
♄	1	6	11	16	21	26	31
	♒ 2.4	2.9	3.4	3.9	4.3	4.7	5.1
♅	1	11	21	31			
	♑ 12.8	13.2	13.5	13.7			
♆	1	11	21	31			
	♑ 16.1	16.4	16.5	16.7			
♇	1	11	21	31			
	♏ 20.4R	20.3	20.2	20			

	1	2	3	4	5	6	7	8	9	10	11	12	13	14	15	16	17	18	19	20	21	22	23	24	25	26	27	28	29	30	31
☉	♓ 10.7	11.7	12.7	13.7	14.7	15.7	16.7	17.7	18.7	19.7	20.7	21.7	22.7	23.7	24.7	25.7	26.7	27.6	28.6	29.6	♈ 0.6	1.6	2.6	3.6	4.6	5.6	6.6	7.6	8.6	9.5	10.5
☽	♒ 1.7	13.5	25.4	♓ 7.4	19.6	♈ 2	14.5	27.3	♉ 10.2	23.3	♊ 6.7	20.3	♋ 4.2	18.3	♌ 2.8	17.5	♍ 2.3	17.2	♎ 1.9	16.3	♏ 0.4	14	27.2	♐ 9.9	22.3	♑ 4.4	16.3	28.2	♒ 10	21.8	♓ 3.8
☿	♓ 25.2	26.9	28.6	♈ 0.2	1.7	3.1	4.4	5.7	6.8	7.9	8.8	9.5	10.2	10.7	11	11.2	11.3	11.2R	11	10.7	10.3	9.7	9.1	8.3	7.6	6.7	5.9	5	4.1	3.3	2.5
♀	♒ 14	15.2	16.4	17.7	18.9	20.1	21.4	22.6	23.8	25.1	26.3	27.5	28.8	♓ 0	1.2	2.5	3.7	4.9	6.2	7.4	8.7	9.9	11.1	12.4	13.6	14.8	16.1	17.3	18.5	19.8	21
♂	♒ 9.1	9.8	10.6	11.4	12.2	12.9	13.7	14.5	15.2	16	16.8	17.6	18.3	19.1	19.9	20.7	21.4	22.2	23	23.7	24.5	25.3	26.1	26.8	27.6	28.4	29.2	29.9	♓ 0.7	1.5	2.3

♃	1	6	11	16	21	26	31
	♍ 9.5R	8.9	8.3	7.6	7.1	6.5	6.1
♄	1	6	11	16	21	26	31
	♒ 12.9	13.4	13.9	14.4	14.9	15.4	15.8
♅	1	11	21	31			
	♑ 16.9	17.3	17.6	17.8			
♆	1	11	21	31			
	♑ 18.3	18.5	18.7	18.8			
♇	1	11	21	31			
	♏ 23.0R	22.9	22.8	22.6			

IV

	1	2	3	4	5	6	7	8	9	10	11	12	13	14	15	16	17	18	19	20	21	22	23	24	25	26	27	28	29	30	31
☉	♈ 10.8	11.8	12.7	13.7	14.7	15.7	16.7	17.7	18.7	19.6	20.6	21.6	22.6	23.6	24.5	25.5	26.5	27.5	28.4	29.4	♉ 0.4	1.4	2.4	3.3	4.3	5.3	6.3	7.2	8.2	9.2	
☽	♏ 1	13.6	26	♐ 8	20	♑ 1.8	13.6	25.5	♒ 7.6	19.9	♓ 2.5	15,5	29	♈ 12.8	26.9	♉ 11.4	25.9	♊ 10.5	25	♋ 9.4	23.5	♌ 7.5	21.2	♍ 4.8	18.1	♎ 1.3	14.3	27.1	♏ 9.6	22	
☿	♈ 28.2	28.6	28.8	29	29.0R	28.9	28.7	28.4	28.1	27.6	27	26.4	25.7	25	24.3	23.6	22.8	22.1	21.4	20.8	20.2	19.6	19.2	18.8	18.5	18.2	18.1	18	18.0D	18.1	
♀	♉ 15.8	17	18.2	19.3	20.5	21.7	22.9	24.1	25.3	26.5	27.6	28.8	30	♊ 1.2	2.3	3.5	4.7	5.9	7	8.2	9.4	10.5	11.7	12.8	14	15.1	16.3	17.4	18.6	19.7	
♂	♊ 28.9	29.5	30	♋ 0.5	1	1.6	2.1	2.6	3.2	3.7	4.3	4.8	5.4	5.9	6.4	7	7.5	8.1	8.6	9.2	9.7	10.3	10.9	11.4	12	12.5	13.1	13.6	14.2	14.8	

♃	1	6	11	16	21	26
	♌ 3.6	3.6	3.8	4	4.3	4.6
♄	1	6	11	16	21	26
	♒ 5.2	5.5	5.8	6.1	6.3	6.5
♅	1	11	21			
	♑ 13.7	13.8	13.8R			
♆	1	11	21			
	♑ 16.7	16.7	16.8R			
♇	1	11	21			
	♏ 20.0R	19.8	19.5			

	1	2	3	4	5	6	7	8	9	10	11	12	13	14	15	16	17	18	19	20	21	22	23	24	25	26	27	28	29	30	31
☉	♈ 11.5	12.5	13.5	14.5	15.5	16.4	17.4	18.4	19.4	20.4	21.4	22.3	23.3	24.3	25.3	26.3	27.2	28.2	29.2	♉ 0.2	1.1	2.1	3.1	4.1	5	6	7	8	8.9	9.9	
☽	♓ 16	28.4	♈ 11	23.9	♉ 6.9	20.2	♊ 3.6	17.2	♋ 1	14.9	28.9	♌ 13.2	27.5	♍ 11.9	26.3	♎ 10.6	24.7	♏ 8.5	22	♐ 5	17.8	♑ 0.2	12.3	24.2	♒ 6.1	17.9	29.8	♓ 11.9	24.2	♈ 6.7	
☿	♈ 1.8R	1.1	0.5	♓ 30	29.6	29.2	29	28.8	28.7	28.8D	28.9	29.1	29.3	29.7	♈ 0.1	0.6	1.2	1.8	2.5	3.3	4.1	5	5.9	6.9	7.9	9	10.1	11.3	12.5	13.7	
♀	♓ 22.2	23.5	24.7	25.9	27.2	28.4	29.6	♈ 0.9	2.1	3.3	4.6	5.8	7	8.3	9.5	10.7	12	13.2	14.4	15.7	16.9	18.1	19.4	20.6	21.8	23	24.3	25.5	26.7	28	
♂	♓ 3	3.8	4.6	5.4	6.1	6.9	7.7	8.5	9.2	10	10.8	11.6	12.3	13.1	13.9	14.7	15.4	16.2	17	17.8	18.5	19.3	20.1	20.8	21.6	22.4	23.2	23.9	24.7	25.5	

♃	1	6	11	16	21	26
	♍ 6.0R	5.6	5.2	5	4.8	4.7
♄	1	6	11	16	21	26
	♒ 15.9	16.3	16.7	17	17.4	17.6
♅	1	11	21			
	♑ 17.8	18	18			
♆	1	11	21			
	♑ 18.9	18.9	19.0R			
♇	1	11	21			
	♏ 22.6R	22.4	22.1			

V

	1	2	3	4	5	6	7	8	9	10	11	12	13	14	15	16	17	18	19	20	21	22	23	24	25	26	27	28	29	30	31
☉	♉ 10.1	11.1	12.1	13	14	15	16	16.9	17.9	18.9	19.8	20.8	21.8	22.7	23.7	24.7	25.6	26.6	27.5	28.5	29.5	♊ 0.4	1.4	2.4	3.3	4.3	5.2	6.2	7.2	8.1	9.1
☽	♐ 4.2	16.2	28.1	♑ 9.9	21.7	♒ 3.5	15.6	27.9	♓ 10.5	23.5	♈ 7	21	♉ 5.4	20	♊ 5	19.9	♋ 4.8	19.5	♌ 3.9	17.9	♍ 1.7	15.1	28.3	♎ 11.2	23.9	♏ 6.4	18.7	♐ 0.8	12.8	24.7	♑ 6.6
☿	♈ 18.3	18.5	18.8	19.2	19.7	20.2	20.8	21.5	22.2	23	23.9	24.8	25.7	26.8	27.8	28.9	♉ 0.1	1.3	2.5	3.8	5.1	6.5	7.9	9.3	10.8	12.4	13.9	15.5	17.2	18.9	20.6
♀	♊ 20.9	22	23.2	24.3	25.4	26.6	27.7	28.8	29.9	♋ 1.1	2.2	3.3	4.4	5.5	6.6	7.7	8.8	9.9	11	12.1	13.2	14.3	15.3	16.4	17.5	18.5	19.6	20.7	21.7	22.8	23.8
♂	♋ 15.3	15.9	16.5	17	17.6	18.2	18.7	19.3	19.9	20.4	21	21.6	22.2	22.7	23.3	23.9	24.5	25.1	25.6	26.2	26.8	27.4	28	28.5	29.1	29.7	♌ 0.3	0.9	1.5	2	2.6

♃	1	6	11	16	21	26	31
	♌ 5.1	5.5	6.1	6.7	7.4	8.1	8.8
♄	1	6	11	16	21	26	31
	♒ 6.6	6.7	6.8	6.8	6.8R	6.8	6.7
♅	1	11	21	31			
	♑ 13.7R	13.6	13.4	13.1			
♆	1	11	21	31			
	♑ 16.7R	16.6	16.5	16.3			
♇	1	11	21	31			
	♏ 19.2R	19	18.7	18.4			

	1	2	3	4	5	6	7	8	9	10	11	12	13	14	15	16	17	18	19	20	21	22	23	24	25	26	27	28	29	30	31
☉	♉ 10.9	11.8	12.8	13.8	14.8	15.7	16.7	17.7	18.6	19.6	20.6	21.5	22.5	23.5	24.4	25.4	26.3	27.3	28.3	29.2	♊ 0.2	1.2	2.1	3.1	4	5	6	6.9	7.9	8.8	9.8
☽	♈ 19.5	♉ 2.7	16.1	29.7	♊ 13.6	27.5	♋ 11.6	25.8	♌ 10	24.1	♍ 8.3	22.4	♎ 6.3	20.2	♏ 3.8	17.2	♐ 0.3	13.2	25.8	♑ 8.1	20.2	♒ 2.1	14	25.8	♓ 7.7	19.8	♈ 2.1	14.7	27.7	♉ 11	24.6
☿	♈ 15	16.3	17.6	19	20.5	21.9	23.4	24.9	26.5	28.1	29.7	♉ 1.4	3.1	4.8	6.6	8.4	10.2	12.1	14	15.9	17.9	19.8	21.9	23.9	26	28.1	♊ 0.3	2.4	4.6	6.8	9
♀	♈ 29.2	♉ 0.4	1.7	2.9	4.1	5.4	6.6	7.8	9	10.3	11.5	12.7	14	15.2	16.4	17.7	18.9	20.1	21.3	22.6	23.8	25	26.3	27.5	28.7	29.9	♊ 1.2	2.4	3.6	4.9	6.1
♂	♓ 26.2	27	27.8	28.5	29.3	♈ 0.1	0.9	1.6	2.4	3.1	3.9	4.7	5.4	6.2	7	7.7	8.5	9.3	10	10.8	11.5	12.3	13	13.8	14.6	15.3	16.1	16.8	17.6	18.3	19.1

♃	1	6	11	16	21	26	31
	♍ 4.6D	4.7	4.8	5	5.2	5.6	6
♄	1	6	11	16	21	26	31
	♒ 17.9	18.1	18.2	18.4	18.4	18.5	18.5R
♅	1	11	21	31			
	♑ 18.0R	17.9	17.7	17.4			
♆	1	11	21	31			
	♑ 18.9R	18.8	18.7	18.5			
♇	1	11	21	31			
	♏ 21.9R	21.6	21.3	21.1			

VI

	1	2	3	4	5	6	7	8	9	10	11	12	13	14	15	16	17	18	19	20	21	22	23	24	25	26	27	28	29	30	31
☉	♊ 10	11	11.9	12.9	13.9	14.8	15.8	16.7	17.7	18.6	19.6	20.6	21.5	22.5	23.4	24.4	25.3	26.3	27.2	28.2	29.2	♋ 0.1	1.1	2	3	3.9	4.9	5.8	6.8	7.7	
☽	♑ 18.3	♒ 0.1	12	24.1	♓ 6.4	19	♈ 2	15.4	29.3	♉ 13.6	28.4	♊ 13.4	28.5	♋ 13.7	28.6	♌ 13.3	27.6	♍ 11.5	25	♎ 8.1	20.9	♏ 3.5	15.7	27.9	♐ 9.8	21.7	♑ 3.5	15.3	27.1	♒ 9	
☿	♉ 22.4	24.2	26	27.9	29.8	♊ 1.8	3.8	5.8	7.8	9.9	12	14.2	16.3	18.5	20.7	22.9	25.1	27.3	29.5	♋ 1.7	3.8	6	8.1	10.2	12.3	14.3	16.4	18.3	20.3	22.2	
♀	♋ 24.8	25.9	26.9	27.9	28.9	29.9	♌ 1	2	2.9	3.9	4.9	5.9	6.9	7.8	8.8	9.7	10.7	11.6	12.5	13.4	14.3	15.2	16.1	17	17.8	18.7	19.5	20.4	21.2	22	
♂	♌ 3.2	3.8	4.4	5	5.6	6.2	6.8	7.4	7.9	8.5	9.1	9.7	10.3	10.9	11.5	12.1	12.7	13.3	13.9	14.5	15.1	15.7	16.3	16.9	17.5	18.1	18.7	19.3	19.9	20.5	

♃	1	6	11	16	21	26
	♌ 9	9.8	10.7	11.5	12.5	13.4
♄	1	6	11	16	21	26
	♒ 6.7R	6.5	6.3	6.1	5.9	5.6
♅	1	11	21			
	♑ 13.1R	12.7	12.4			
♆	1	11	21			
	♑ 16.3R	16.1	15.8			
♇	1	11	21			
	♏ 18.4R	18.2	18			

	1	2	3	4	5	6	7	8	9	10	11	12	13	14	15	16	17	18	19	20	21	22	23	24	25	26	27	28	29	30	31
☉	♊ 10.8	11.7	12.7	13.6	14.6	15.5	16.5	17.5	18.4	19.4	20.3	21.3	22.2	23.2	24.1	25.1	26.1	27	28	28.9	29.9	♋ 0.8	1.8	2.7	3.7	4.6	5.6	6.6	7.5	8.5	
☽	♊ 8.6	22.8	♋ 7.2	21.8	♌ 6.3	20.7	♍ 5.1	19.2	♎ 3.1	16.8	♏ 0.3	13.5	26.5	♐ 9.3	21.8	♑ 4.2	16.3	28.3	♒ 10.3	22.1	♓ 4	15.9	27.9	♈ 10.2	22.8	♉ 5.7	19	♊ 2.8	16.9	♋ 1.4	
☿	♊ 11.2	13.4	15.6	17.7	19.9	22.1	24.2	26.3	28.4	♋ 0.5	2.5	4.5	6.5	8.4	10.2	12.1	13.9	15.7	17.4	19.1	20.7	22.3	23.9	25.4	26.9	28.3	29.7	♌ 1.1	2.4	3.6	
♀	♊ 7.3	8.5	9.8	11	12.2	13.5	14.7	15.9	17.1	18.4	19.6	20.8	22.1	23.3	24.5	25.7	27	28.2	29.4	♋ 0.7	1.9	3.1	4.3	5.6	6.8	8	9.3	10.5	11.7	12.9	
♂	♈ 19.8	20.6	21.3	22.1	22.8	23.6	24.3	25.1	25.8	26.6	27.3	28	28.8	29.5	♉ 0.3	1	1.7	2.5	3.2	3.9	4.7	5.4	6.1	6.8	7.6	8.3	9	9.7	10.5	11.2	

♃	1	6	11	16	21	26
	♍ 6.1	6.5	7.1	7.7	8.3	9
♄	1	6	11	16	21	26
	♒ 18.5R	18.4	18.3	18.2	18	17.8
♅	1	11	21			
	♑ 17.4R	17.1	16.7			
♆	1	11	21			
	♑ 18.5R	18.3	18.1			
♇	1	11	21			
	♏ 21.0R	20.8	20.6			

VII

	1	2	3	4	5	6	7	8	9	10	11	12	13	14	15	16	17	18	19	20	21	22	23	24	25	26	27	28	29	30	31
☉	♋ 8.7	9.6	10.6	11.6	12.5	13.5	14.4	15.4	16.3	17.3	18.2	19.2	20.1	21.1	22	23	23.9	24.9	25.9	26.8	27.8	28.7	29.7	♌ 0.6	1.6	2.5	3.5	4.4	5.4	6.4	7.3
☽	♒ 21	♓ 3.1	15.5	28.1	♈ 11	24.4	♉ 8.1	22.3	♊ 6.9	21.8	♋ 6.9	22.1	♌ 7.1	22	♍ 6.5	20.5	♎ 4.2	17.4	♏ 0.2	12.6	24.8	♐ 6.8	18.7	♑ 0.5	12.3	24.1	♒ 6	18.1	♓ 0.2	12.5	25.1
☿	♋ 24.1	26	27.8	29.6	♌ 1.3	3	4.7	6.3	8	9.5	11.1	12.6	14	15.5	16.9	18.2	19.5	20.8	22	23.2	24.4	25.5	26.6	27.6	28.6	29.5	♍ 0.4	1.2	2	2.7	3.3
♀	♌ 22.8	23.5	24.3	25.1	25.8	26.5	27.2	27.9	28.6	29.2	29.9	♍ 0.5	1.1	1.6	2.2	2.7	3.2	3.7	4.2	4.6	5	5.4	5.7	6	6.3	6.5	6.8	6.9	7.1	7.2	7.3
♂	♌ 21.1	21.7	22.4	23	23.6	24.2	24.8	25.4	26	26.6	27.2	27.8	28.5	29.1	29.7	♍ 0.3	0.9	1.5	2.1	2.8	3.4	4	4.6	5.2	5.9	6.5	7.1	7.7	8.3	9	9.6

♃	1	6	11	16	21	26	31
	♌ 14.4	15.4	16.4	17.4	18.5	19.5	20.6
♄	1	6	11	16	21	26	31
	♒ 5.3R	5	4.7	4.3	3.9	3.6	3.2
♅	1	11	21	31			
	♑ 12.0R	11.5	11.2	10.8			
♆	1	11	21	31			
	♑ 15.6R	15.3	15	14.8			
♇	1	11	21	31			
	♏ 17.8R	17.7	17.6	17.6D			

	1	2	3	4	5	6	7	8	9	10	11	12	13	14	15	16	17	18	19	20	21	22	23	24	25	26	27	28	29	30	31
☉	♋ 9.4	10.4	11.3	12.3	13.2	14.2	15.1	16.1	17	18	18.9	19.9	20.9	21.8	22.8	23.7	24.7	25.6	26.6	27.5	28.5	29.4	♌ 0.4	1.4	2.3	3.3	4.2	5.2	6.1	7.1	8
☽	♋ 16.2	♌ 1.1	16	♍ 0.8	15.4	29.7	♎ 13.7	27.3	♏ 10.5	23.5	♐ 6.1	18.6	♑ 0.9	13	25	♒ 6.9	18.8	♓ 0.6	12.5	24.4	♈ 6.5	18.7	♉ 1.3	14.1	27.3	♊ 11	25.1	♋ 9.6	24.5	♌ 9.7	24.9
☿	♌ 4.9	6	7.2	8.3	9.3	10.3	11.2	12.1	12.9	13.6	14.3	15	15.5	16	16.5	16.8	17.1	17.3	17.4	17.5	17.4R	17.3	17.1	16.8	16.5	16	15.5	15	14.3	13.6	12.9
♀	♋ 14.2	15.4	16.6	17.9	19.1	20.3	21.6	22.8	24	25.2	26.5	27.7	28.9	♌ 0.2	1.4	2.6	3.8	5.1	6.3	7.5	8.8	10	11.2	12.5	13.7	14.9	16.1	17.4	18.6	19.8	21.1
♂	♉ 11.9	12.6	13.3	14.1	14.8	15.5	16.2	16.9	17.6	18.3	19	19.7	20.4	21.1	21.8	22.5	23.2	23.9	24.6	25.3	26	26.7	27.4	28.1	28.8	29.5	♊ 0.1	0.8	1.5	2.2	2.8

♃	1	6	11	16	21	26	31
	♍ 9.7	10.5	11.3	12.2	13.1	14	14.9
♄	1	6	11	16	21	26	31
	♒ 17.6R	17.3	17	16.7	16.4	16	15.7
♅	1	11	21	31			
	♑ 16.3R	15.9	15.5	15.1			
♆	1	11	21	31			
	♑ 17.8R	17.5	17.3	17			
♇	1	11	21	31			
	♏ 20.4R	20.3	20.2	20.2D			

VIII

	1	2	3	4	5	6	7	8	9	10	11	12	13	14	15	16	17	18	19	20	21	22	23	24	25	26	27	28	29	30	31
☉	♌ 8.3	9.2	10.2	11.1	12.1	13.1	14	15	15.9	16.9	17.9	18.8	19.8	20.7	21.7	22.7	23.6	24.6	25.5	26.5	27.5	28.4	29.4	♍ 0.4	1.3	2.3	3.2	4.2	5.2	6.1	7.1
☽	♈ 7.8	20.8	♉ 4.2	17.8	♊ 1.8	16.1	♋ 0.7	15.6	♌ 0.5	15.5	♍ 0.2	14.8	28.9	♎ 12.6	25.9	♏ 8.8	21.2	♐ 3.4	15.4	27.3	♑ 9	20.9	♒ 2.8	14.8	27	♓ 9.4	22	♈ 4.8	17.9	♉ 1.1	14.6
☿	♍ 3.9	4.4	4.9	5.2	5.5	5.7	5.9	5.9R	5.9	5.7	5.5	5.2	4.8	4.3	3.7	3.1	2.4	1.6	0.8	♌ 29.9	29	28.2	27.3	26.5	25.7	25	24.4	23.9	23.5	23.2	23.1
♀	♍ 7.3	7.3R	7.3	7.2	7.1	6.9	6.7	6.5	6.2	5.9	5.5	5.1	4.7	4.3	3.8	3.3	2.7	2.2	1.6	1	0.4	♌ 29.7	29.1	28.5	27.9	27.3	26.7	26.1	25.5	25	24.5
♂	♍ 10.2	10.8	11.5	12.1	12.7	13.3	14	14.6	15.2	15.8	16.5	17.1	17.7	18.4	19	19.6	20.3	20.9	21.5	22.2	22.8	23.4	24.1	24.7	25.3	26	26.6	27.3	27.9	28.5	29.2

♃	1	6	11	16	21	26	31
	♌ 20.8	21.9	23	24.1	25.2	26.3	27.4
♄	1	6	11	16	21	26	31
	♒ 3.1R	2.8	2.4	2.1	1.7	1.4	1.2
♅	1	11	21	31			
	♑ 10.8R	10.4	10.2	10			
♆	1	11	21	31			
	♑ 14.7R	14.5	14.3	14.2			
♇	1	11	21	31			
	♏ 17.6	17.6	17.7	17.9			

	1	2	3	4	5	6	7	8	9	10	11	12	13	14	15	16	17	18	19	20	21	22	23	24	25	26	27	28	29	30	31
☉	♌ 9	10	10.9	11.9	12.8	13.8	14.7	15.7	16.7	17.6	18.6	19.5	20.5	21.5	22.4	23.4	24.3	25.3	26.3	27.2	28.2	29.2	♍ 0.1	1.1	2	3	4	4.9	5.9	6.9	7.8
☽	♍ 10	24.9	♎ 9.5	23.5	♏ 7.2	20.4	♐ 3.2	15.7	28	♑ 10	22	♒ 3.9	15.7	27.6	♓ 9.5	21.4	♈ 3.4	15.5	27.8	♉ 10.4	23.1	♊ 6.3	19.8	♋ 3.8	18.1	♌ 2.9	18.1	♍ 3.3	18.6	♎ 3.6	18.3
☿	♌ 12.2R	11.4	10.7	9.9	9.2	8.5	7.9	7.4	6.9	6.5	6.2	6	6	6.0D	6.2	6.5	6.9	7.4	8.1	8.8	9.7	10.7	11.8	13	14.3	15.7	17.2	18.8	20.4	22.1	23.9
♀	♌ 22.3	23.5	24.8	26	27.2	28.5	29.7	♍ 0.9	2.1	3.4	4.6	5.8	7.1	8.3	9.5	10.7	12	13.2	14.4	15.7	16.9	18.1	19.4	20.6	21.8	23	24.3	25.5	26.7	28	29.2
♂	♊ 3.5	4.2	4.9	5.5	6.2	6.9	7.5	8.2	8.8	9.5	10.2	10.8	11.5	12.1	12.7	13.4	14	14.7	15.3	15.9	16.6	17.2	17.8	18.5	19.1	19.7	20.3	20.9	21.6	22.2	22.8

♃	1	6	11	16	21	26	31
	♍ 15.1	16.1	17.1	18.1	19.2	20.2	21.3
♄	1	6	11	16	21	26	31
	♒ 15.6R	15.2	14.9	14.5	14.1	13.8	13.4
♅	1	11	21	31			
	♑ 15.1R	14.8	14.5	14.3			
♆	1	11	21	31			
	♑ 17.0R	16.7	16.5	16.4			
♇	1	11	21	31			
	♏ 20.2	20.2	20.3	20.4			

IX

	1	2	3	4	5	6	7	8	9	10	11	12	13	14	15	16	17	18	19	20	21	22	23	24	25	26	27	28	29	30	31
☉	♍ 8.1	9	10	11	12	12.9	13.9	14.9	15.8	16.8	17.8	18.7	19.7	20.7	21.7	22.6	23.6	24.6	25.6	26.5	27.5	28.5	29.5	♎ 0.5	1.4	2.4	3.4	4.4	5.4	6.3	
☽	♉ 28.2	♊ 12.1	26.2	♋ 10.5	25	♌ 9.6	24.2	♍ 8.7	23	♎ 7	20.7	♏ 4	16.9	29.4	♐ 11.6	23.5	♑ 5.4	17.2	29	♒ 11	23.1	♓ 5.5	18.2	♈ 1.1	14.3	27.7	♉ 11.4	25.1	♊ 9	23	
☿	♌ 23.1D	23.2	23.5	23.9	24.4	25.1	25.9	26.9	27.9	29.1	♍ 0.4	1.7	3.2	4.7	6.3	8	9.7	11.5	13.2	15	16.9	18.7	20.5	22.4	24.2	26.1	27.9	29.7	♎ 1.6	3.4	
♀	♌ 24.0R	23.5	23.1	22.7	22.4	22.1	21.8	21.6	21.4	21.2	21.1	21	21	21.0D	21	21.1	21.2	21.4	21.6	21.8	22.1	22.4	22.7	23.1	23.4	23.9	24.3	24.8	25.3	25.8	
♂	♍ 29.8	♎ 0.5	1.1	1.8	2.4	3.1	3.7	4.3	5	5.6	6.3	6.9	7.6	8.2	8.9	9.6	10.2	10.9	11.5	12.2	12.8	13.5	14.1	14.8	15.5	16.1	16.8	17.4	18.1	18.8	

♃	1	6	11	16	21	26
	♌ 27.6	28.7	29.7	♍ 0.8	1.8	2.9
♄	1	6	11	16	21	26
	♒ 1.1R	0.9	0.7	0.5	0.4	0.3
♅	1	11	21			
	♑ 10.0R	9.9	9.8D			
♆	1	11	21			
	♑ 14.2R	14.1	14			
♇	1	11	21			
	♏ 17.9	18.1	18.4			

	1	2	3	4	5	6	7	8	9	10	11	12	13	14	15	16	17	18	19	20	21	22	23	24	25	26	27	28	29	30	31
☉	♍ 8.8	9.8	10.7	11.7	12.7	13.7	14.6	15.6	16.6	17.5	18.5	19.5	20.5	21.4	22.4	23.4	24.4	25.3	26.3	27.3	28.3	29.2	♎ 0.2	1.2	2.2	3.2	4.1	5.1	6.1	7.1	
☽	♏ 2.5	16.3	29.5	♐ 12.4	24.8	♑ 7	19	♒ 0.9	12.7	24.6	♓ 6.5	18.4	♈ 0.5	12.6	24.9	♉ 7.4	20	♊ 2.9	16	29.4	♋ 13.2	27.4	♌ 11.9	26.8	♍ 11.8	26.9	♎ 11.9	26.5	♏ 10.8	24.6	
☿	♌ 25.7	27.5	29.4	♍ 1.3	3.2	5.1	7	9	10.9	12.8	14.7	16.6	18.5	20.4	22.3	24.1	26	27.8	29.6	♎ 1.4	3.1	4.9	6.6	8.4	10.1	11.7	13.4	15.1	16.7	18.4	
♀	♎ 0.4	1.6	2.9	4.1	5.3	6.5	7.8	9	10.2	11.5	12.7	13.9	15.1	16.4	17.6	18.8	20	21.3	22.5	23.7	24.9	26.2	27.4	28.6	29.8	♏ 1.1	2.3	3.5	4.7	5.9	
♂	♊ 23.4	24	24.6	25.2	25.8	26.4	26.9	27.5	28.1	28.7	29.3	29.8	♋ 0.4	1	1.5	2.1	2.7	3.2	3.8	4.3	4.9	5.4	5.9	6.5	7	7.5	8	8.5	9.1	9.6	

♃	1	6	11	16	21	26
	♍ 21.5	22.6	23.6	24.7	25.8	26.9
♄	1	6	11	16	21	26
	♒ 13.4R	13.1	12.8	12.5	12.3	12.1
♅	1	11	21			
	♑ 14.2R	14.1	14			
♆	1	11	21			
	♑ 16.4R	16.3	16.2			
♇	1	11	21			
	♏ 20.5	20.7	20.9			

X

	1	2	3	4	5	6	7	8	9	10	11	12	13	14	15	16	17	18	19	20	21	22	23	24	25	26	27	28	29	30	31
☉	♎ 7.3	8.3	9.3	10.3	11.3	12.2	13.2	14.2	15.2	16.2	17.2	18.2	19.2	20.1	21.1	22.1	23.1	24.1	25.1	26.1	27.1	28.1	29.1	♏ 0.1	1.1	2.1	3.1	4.1	5.1	6.1	7.1
☽	♋ 7	21.2	♌ 5.3	19.5	♍ 3.7	17.8	♎ 1.7	15.4	28.9	♏ 12	24.8	♐ 7.2	19.4	♑ 1.4	13.2	25	♒ 6.9	18.9	♓ 1.1	13.6	26.4	♈ 9.6	23.2	♉ 7	21	♊ 5.2	19.5	♋ 3.8	18	♌ 2.1	16.2
☿	♎ 5.2	7	8.8	10.5	12.3	14	15.7	17.4	19.1	20.8	22.5	24.2	25.8	27.4	29.1	♏ 0.7	2.3	3.9	5.4	7	8.6	10.1	11.7	13.2	14.7	16.2	17.7	19.2	20.7	22.2	23.6
♀	♌ 26.3	26.9	27.5	28.1	28.7	29.4	♍ 0.1	0.8	1.5	2.2	2.9	3.7	4.5	5.3	6.1	6.9	7.7	8.6	9.4	10.3	11.2	12.1	13	13.9	14.8	15.8	16.7	17.7	18.6	19.6	20.6
♂	♎ 19.4	20.1	20.8	21.4	22.1	22.8	23.4	24.1	24.8	25.4	26.1	26.8	27.5	28.1	28.8	29.5	♏ 0.1	0.8	1.5	2.2	2.9	3.5	4.2	4.9	5.6	6.3	6.9	7.6	8.3	9	9.7

♃	1	6	11	16	21	26	31
	♍ 3.9	4.9	5.8	6.7	7.6	8.5	9.3
♄	1	6	11	16	21	26	31
	♒ 0.2R	0.2D	0.2	0.3	0.4	0.6	0.7
♅	1	11	21	31			
	♑ 9.9	10	10.3	10.6			
♆	1	11	21	31			
	♑ 14	14.1	14.2	14.3			
♇	1	11	21	31			
	♏ 18.7	19	19.4	19.8			

	1	2	3	4	5	6	7	8	9	10	11	12	13	14	15	16	17	18	19	20	21	22	23	24	25	26	27	28	29	30	31
☉	♎ 8.1	9.1	10	11	12	13	14	15	16	16.9	17.9	18.9	19.9	20.9	21.9	22.9	23.9	24.9	25.9	26.9	27.8	28.8	29.8	♏ 0.8	1.8	2.8	3.8	4.8	5.8	6.8	7.8
☽	♐ 8	20.8	♑ 3.4	15.6	27.6	♒ 9.5	21.3	♓ 3.2	15.1	27.2	♈ 9.4	21.7	♉ 4.3	17	29.9	♊ 13	26.3	♋ 9.8	23.6	♌ 7.6	21.9	♍ 6.4	21	♎ 5.7	20.3	♏ 4.7	18.8	♐ 2.5	15.9	28.8	♑ 11.3
☿	♎ 20	21.6	23.2	24.7	26.3	27.8	29.4	♏ 0.9	2.4	3.9	5.4	6.8	8.3	9.7	11.1	12.6	14	15.3	16.7	18	19.4	20.7	22	23.3	24.5	25.7	26.9	28.1	29.2	♐ 0.3	1.4
♀	♏ 7.2	8.4	9.6	10.8	12	13.3	14.5	15.7	16.9	18.1	19.4	20.6	21.8	23	24.2	25.5	26.7	27.9	29.1	♐ 0.3	1.5	2.8	4	5.2	6.4	7.6	8.8	10	11.2	12.5	13.7
♂	♋ 10.1	10.6	11.1	11.5	12	12.5	13	13.5	13.9	14.4	14.8	15.3	15.7	16.2	16.6	17	17.4	17.8	18.3	18.7	19.1	19.4	19.8	20.2	20.6	20.9	21.3	21.6	22	22.3	22.6

♃	1	6	11	16	21	26	31
	♍ 28	29	♎ 0.1	1.1	2.2	3.2	4.2
♄	1	6	11	16	21	26	31
	♒ 12.0R	11.9	11.8	11.8	11.8D	11.9	12
♅	1	11	21	31			
	♑ 14.1	14.2	14.4	14.7			
♆	1	11	21	31			
	♑ 16.2	16.2	16.3	16.5			
♇	1	11	21	31			
	♏ 21.2	21.5	21.9	22.3			

XI

	1	2	3	4	5	6	7	8	9	10	11	12	13	14	15	16	17	18	19	20	21	22	23	24	25	26	27	28	29	30	31
☉	♏ 8.1	9.1	10.1	11.1	12.1	13.1	14.1	15.1	16.1	17.1	18.1	19.1	20.1	21.1	22.1	23.1	24.1	25.1	26.1	27.2	28.2	29.2	♐ 0.2	1.2	2.2	3.2	4.2	5.2	6.3	7.3	
☽	♍ 0.1	13.9	27.6	♎ 11.1	24.4	♏ 7.5	20.4	♐ 2.9	15.3	27.4	♑ 9.3	21.1	♒ 2.9	14.7	26.7	♓ 8.9	21.4	♈ 4.3	17.5	♉ 1.3	15.3	29.8	♊ 14.4	29.1	♋ 13.8	28.4	♌ 12.8	27	♍ 10.9	24.5	
☿	♏ 25.1	26.5	28	29.4	♐ 0.8	2.2	3.6	4.9	6.3	7.6	8.9	10.2	11.5	12.7	13.9	15.1	16.2	17.3	18.4	19.4	20.3	21.1	21.9	22.6	23.2	23.6	24	24.1	24.2R	24	
♀	♍ 21.6	22.5	23.6	24.6	25.6	26.6	27.6	28.7	29.7	♎ 0.8	1.8	2.9	3.9	5	6.1	7.2	8.3	9.3	10.4	11.5	12.6	13.8	14.9	16	17.1	18.2	19.4	20.5	21.6	22.8	
♂	♏ 10.4	11.1	11.8	12.4	13.1	13.8	14.5	15.2	15.9	16.6	17.3	18	18.7	19.4	20.1	20.8	21.5	22.2	22.9	23.6	24.3	25	25.7	26.4	27.1	27.8	28.5	29.2	29.9	♐ 0.7	

♃	1	6	11	16	21	26
	♍ 9.5	10.2	10.9	11.6	12.2	12.7
♄	1	6	11	16	21	26
	♒ 0.8	1	1.3	1.6	2	2.4
♅	1	11	21			
	♑ 10.6	11	11.4			
♆	1	11	21			
	♑ 14.3	14.6	14.8			
♇	1	11	21			
	♏ 19.8	20.2	20.6			

	1	2	3	4	5	6	7	8	9	10	11	12	13	14	15	16	17	18	19	20	21	22	23	24	25	26	27	28	29	30	31
☉	♏ 8.8	9.8	10.8	11.8	12.8	13.8	14.8	15.8	16.8	17.8	18.9	19.9	20.9	21.9	22.9	23.9	24.9	25.9	26.9	27.9	28.9	29.9	♐ 1	2	3	4	5	6	7	8	
☽	♑ 23.6	♒ 5.6	17.5	29.4	♓ 11.3	23.3	♈ 5.4	17.8	♉ 0.4	13.2	26.2	♊ 9.5	23	♋ 6.7	20.5	♌ 4.4	18.5	♍ 2.7	16.9	♎ 1.1	15.4	29.5	♏ 13.4	27.2	♐ 10.6	23.7	♑ 6.6	19.1	♒ 1.4	13.4	
☿	♐ 2.4	3.3	4.2	5.1	5.8	6.5	7.1	7.6	8	8.2	8.4	8.4R	8.2	7.8	7.3	6.7	5.8	4.8	3.7	2.4	1.1	♏ 29.8	28.4	27.1	25.9	24.8	23.9	23.2	22.7	22.4	
♀	♐ 14.9	16.1	17.3	18.5	19.7	20.9	22.1	23.3	24.5	25.7	27	28.2	29.4	♑ 0.6	1.8	3	4.2	5.4	6.6	7.8	9	10.2	11.4	12.5	13.7	14.9	16.1	17.3	18.5	19.7	
♂	♋ 22.9	23.2	23.5	23.8	24.1	24.4	24.6	24.9	25.1	25.3	25.6	25.8	26	26.2	26.3	26.5	26.7	26.8	26.9	27.1	27.2	27.3	27.4	27.4	27.5	27.5	27.6	27.6	27.6R	27.6	

♃	1	6	11	16	21	26
	♎ 4.4	5.4	6.3	7.2	8.1	8.9
♄	1	6	11	16	21	26
	♒ 12	12.2	12.4	12.6	12.9	13.2
♅	1	11	21			
	♑ 14.7	15	15.5			
♆	1	11	21			
	♑ 16.5	16.7	17			
♇	1	11	21			
	♏ 22.3	22.7	23.1			

XII

	1	2	3	4	5	6	7	8	9	10	11	12	13	14	15	16	17	18	19	20	21	22	23	24	25	26	27	28	29	30	31
☉	♐ 8.3	9.3	10.3	11.3	12.3	13.4	14.4	15.4	16.4	17.4	18.4	19.4	20.5	21.5	22.5	23.5	24.5	25.6	26.6	27.6	28.6	29.6	♑ 0.6	1.7	2.7	3.7	4.7	5.7	6.8	7.8	8.8
☽	♎ 7.9	21.1	♏ 4	16.7	29.2	♐ 11.5	23.6	♑ 5.6	17.5	29.3	♒ 11.1	22.9	♓ 4.8	17	29.4	♈ 12.2	25.4	♉ 9.1	23.2	♊ 7.7	22.5	♋ 7.6	22.7	♌ 7.7	22.5	♍ 6.9	21	♎ 4.7	18.1	♏ 1	13.7
☿	♐ 23.7R	23.2	22.6	21.7	20.7	19.5	18.2	16.9	15.5	14.1	12.8	11.6	10.6	9.7	9	8.4	8.1	7.9	7.9D	8.1	8.4	8.8	9.4	10.1	10.8	11.7	12.6	13.6	14.6	15.7	16.9
♀	♎ 23.9	25	26.2	27.3	28.5	29.6	♏ 0.8	2	3.1	4.3	5.5	6.6	7.8	9	10.2	11.3	12.5	13.7	14.9	16.1	17.3	18.5	19.6	20.8	22	23.2	24.4	25.6	26.8	28	29.2
♂	♐ 1.4	2.1	2.8	3.5	4.2	4.9	5.7	6.4	7.1	7.8	8.5	9.2	10	10.7	11.4	12.1	12.9	13.6	14.3	15	15.8	16.5	17.2	17.9	18.7	19.4	20.1	20.9	21.6	22.3	23.1

♃	1	6	11	16	21	26	31
	♍ 13.2	13.6	14	14.3	14.5	14.6	14.6R
♄	1	6	11	16	21	26	31
	♒ 2.8	3.2	3.7	4.2	4.7	5.2	5.7
♅	1	11	21	31			
	♑ 11.9	12.5	13	13.6			
♆	1	11	21	31			
	♑ 15.1	15.5	15.8	16.2			
♇	1	11	21	31			
	♏ 21	21.4	21.8	22.1			

	1	2	3	4	5	6	7	8	9	10	11	12	13	14	15	16	17	18	19	20	21	22	23	24	25	26	27	28	29	30	31
☉	♐ 9	10.1	11.1	12.1	13.1	14.1	15.1	16.2	17.2	18.2	19.2	20.2	21.2	22.3	23.3	24.3	25.3	26.3	27.3	28.4	29.4	♑ 0.4	1.4	2.4	3.5	4.5	5.5	6.5	7.5	8.5	9.6
☽	♒ 25.3	♓ 7.2	19.1	♈ 1.1	13.3	25.7	♉ 8.3	21.4	♊ 4.7	18.3	♋ 2.3	16.4	♌ 0.7	15.1	29.4	♍ 13.7	27.9	♎ 11.9	25.8	♏ 9.5	22.9	♐ 6.2	19.3	♑ 2.1	14.7	27.1	♒ 9.3	21.3	♓ 3.2	15.1	27
☿	♏ 22.2R	22.2D	22.4	22.8	23.3	23.9	24.7	25.5	26.4	27.4	28.5	29.6	♐ 0.8	2	3.3	4.6	5.9	7.2	8.6	10	11.4	12.8	14.2	15.7	17.1	18.6	20.1	21.5	23	24.5	26
♀	♑ 20.9	22.1	23.2	24.4	25.6	26.8	28	29.1	♒ 0.3	1.5	2.6	3.8	5	6.1	7.3	8.5	9.6	10.8	11.9	13.1	14.2	15.4	16.5	17.7	18.8	19.9	21.1	22.2	23.3	24.4	25.6
♂	♋ 27.6R	27.5	27.5	27.4	27.4	27.3	27.2	27	26.9	26.8	26.6	26.4	26.2	26	25.8	25.6	25.3	25.1	24.8	24.5	24.2	23.9	23.6	23.3	23	22.6	22.3	21.9	21.5	21.2	20.8

♃	1	6	11	16	21	26	31
	♎ 9.7	10.5	11.2	11.8	12.4	12.9	13.4
♄	1	6	11	16	21	26	31
	♒ 13 6	13.9	14.3	14.8	15.2	15.7	16.2
♅	1	11	21	31			
	♑ 15.9	16.5	17	17.6			
♆	1	11	21	31			
	♑ 17.3	17.6	18	18.3			
♇	1	11	21	31			
	♏ 23.5	23.9	24.3	24.6			

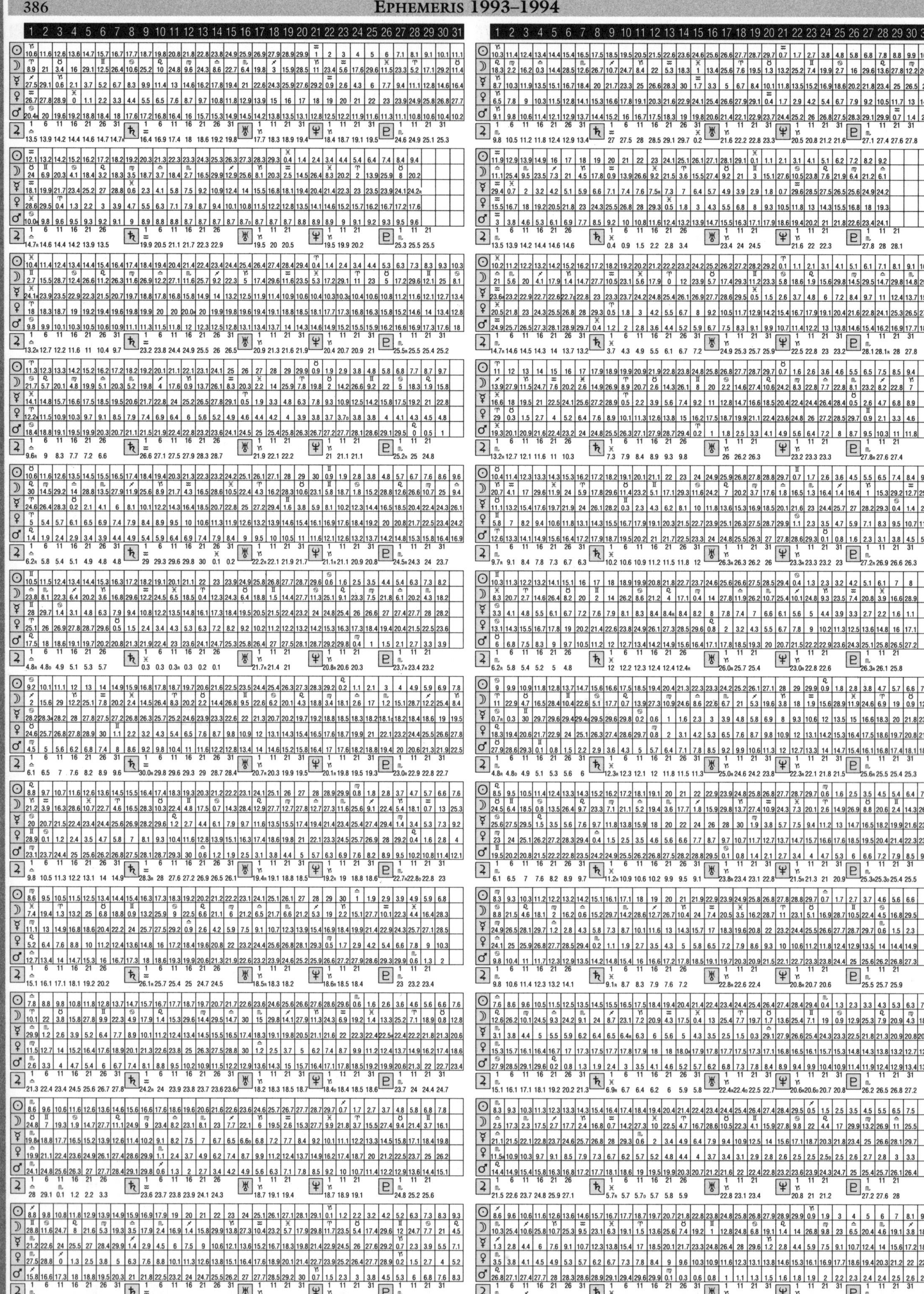

I

	1	2	3	4	5	6	7	8	9	10	11	12	13	14	15	16	17	18	19	20	21	22	23	24	25	26	27	28	29	30	31
☉	10.6	11.6	12.6	13.6	14.7	15.7	16.7	17.7	18.7	19.8	20.8	21.8	22.8	23.8	24.9	25.9	26.9	27.9	28.9	29.9	1	2	3	4	5	6	7.1	8.1	9.1	10.1	11.1
☽	8.9	21	3.4	16	29.1	12.5	26.4	10.6	25.2	10	24.8	9.6	24.3	8.6	22.7	6.4	19.8	3	15.9	28.5	11	23.4	5.6	17.6	29.6	11.5	23.3	5.2	17.1	29.2	11.4
☿	27.5	29.1	0.6	2.1	3.7	5.2	6.7	8.3	9.9	11.4	13	14.6	16.2	17.8	19.4	21	22.6	24.3	25.9	27.6	29.2	0.9	2.6	4.3	6	7.7	9.4	11.1	12.8	14.6	16.4
♀	26.7	27.8	28.9	0	1.1	2.2	3.3	4.4	5.5	6.5	7.6	8.7	9.7	10.8	11.8	12.9	13.9	15	16	17	18	19	20	21	22	23	23.9	24.9	25.8	26.8	27.7
♂	20.4R	20	19.6	19.2	18.8	18.4	18	17.6	17.2	16.8	16.4	16	15.7	15.3	14.9	14.5	14.2	13.8	13.5	13.1	12.8	12.5	12.2	11.9	11.6	11.3	11.1	10.8	10.6	10.4	10.2

♃ (1 6 11 16 21 26 31): 13.5 13.9 14.2 14.4 14.6 14.7 14.7R — ♄ (1 6 11 16 21 26 31): 16.4 16.9 17.4 18 18.6 19.2 19.8 — ♅ (1 11 21 31): 17.7 18.3 18.9 19.4 — ♆ (1 11 21 31): 18.4 18.7 19.1 19.5 — ♇ (1 11 21 31): 24.6 24.9 25.1 25.3

II

	1	2	3	4	5	6	7	8	9	10	11	12	13	14	15	16	17	18	19	20	21	22	23	24	25	26	27	28
☉	12.1	13.2	14.2	15.2	16.2	17.2	18.2	19.2	20.3	21.3	22.3	23.3	24.3	25.3	26.3	27.3	28.3	29.3	0.4	1.4	2.4	3.4	4.4	5.4	6.4	7.4	8.4	9.4
☽	24	6.9	20.3	4.1	18.4	3.2	18.3	3.5	18.7	3.7	18.4	2.7	16.5	29.9	12.9	25.6	8.1	20.3	2.5	14.5	26.4	8.3	20.2	2	13.9	25.9	8	20.2
☿	18.1	19.9	21.7	23.4	25.2	27	28.8	0.6	2.3	4.1	5.8	7.5	9.2	10.9	12.4	14	15.5	16.8	18.1	19.4	20.4	21.4	22.3	23	23.5	23.9	24.1	24.2R
♀	28.6	29.5	0.4	1.3	2.2	3	3.9	4.7	5.5	6.3	7.1	7.9	8.7	9.4	10.1	10.8	11.5	12.2	12.8	13.5	14.1	14.6	15.2	15.7	16.2	16.7	17.2	17.6
♂	10.0R	9.8	9.6	9.5	9.3	9.2	9.1	9	8.9	8.8	8.8	8.7	8.7	8.7	8.7	8.7D	8.7	8.7	8.7	8.8	8.9	8.9	9	9.1	9.2	9.3	9.5	9.6

♃ (1 6 11 16 21 26): 14.7R 14.6 14.4 14.2 13.9 13.5 — ♄ (1 6 11 16 21 26): 19.9 20.5 21.1 21.7 22.3 22.9 — ♅ (1 11 21): 19.5 20 20.5 — ♆ (1 11 21): 19.5 19.9 20.2 — ♇ (1 11 21): 25.3 25.5 25.5

III

	1	2	3	4	5	6	7	8	9	10	11	12	13	14	15	16	17	18	19	20	21	22	23	24	25	26	27	28	29	30	31
☉	10.4	11.4	12.4	13.4	14.4	15.4	16.4	17.4	18.4	19.4	20.4	21.4	22.4	23.4	24.4	25.4	26.4	27.4	28.4	29.4	0.4	1.4	2.4	3.4	4.4	5.3	6.3	7.3	8.3	9.3	10.3
☽	2.7	15.5	28.7	12.4	26.6	11.2	26.3	11.6	26.9	12.2	27.1	11.6	25.7	9.2	22.3	5	17.4	29.6	11.6	23.5	5.3	17.2	29.1	11	23	5	17.2	29.6	12.1	25	8.1
☿	24.1R	23.9	23.5	22.9	22.3	21.5	20.7	19.7	18.8	17.8	16.8	15.8	14.9	14	13.2	12.5	11.9	11.4	10.9	10.6	10.4	10.3	10.3D	10.4	10.6	10.8	11.2	11.6	12.1	12.7	13.4
♀	18	18.3	18.7	19	19.2	19.4	19.6	19.8	19.9	20	20	20.0R	20	19.9	19.8	19.6	19.4	19.1	18.8	18.5	18.1	17.7	17.3	16.8	16.3	15.8	15.2	14.6	14	13.4	12.8
♂	9.8	9.9	10.1	10.3	10.5	10.6	10.9	11.1	11.3	11.5	11.8	12	12.3	12.5	12.8	13.1	13.4	13.7	14	14.3	14.6	14.9	15.2	15.5	15.9	16.2	16.6	16.9	17.3	17.6	18

♃ (1 6 11 16 21 26 31): 13.2R 12.7 12.2 11.6 11 10.4 9.7 — ♄ (1 6 11 16 21 26 31): 23.2 23.8 24.4 24.9 25.5 26 26.5 — ♅ (1 11 21 31): 20.9 21.3 21.6 21.9 — ♆ (1 11 21 31): 20.4 20.7 20.9 21 — ♇ (1 11 21 31): 25.5R 25.5 25.4 25.2

IV

	1	2	3	4	5	6	7	8	9	10	11	12	13	14	15	16	17	18	19	20	21	22	23	24	25	26	27	28	29	30
☉	11.3	12.3	13.3	14.2	15.2	16.2	17.2	18.2	19.2	20.1	21.1	22.1	23.1	24.1	25	26	27	28	29	29.9	0.9	1.9	2.9	3.8	4.8	5.8	6.8	7.7	8.7	9.7
☽	21.7	5.7	20.1	4.8	19.9	5.1	20.3	5.2	19.8	4	17.6	0.9	13.7	26.1	8.3	20.3	2.2	14	25.9	7.8	19.8	2	14.2	26.6	9.2	22	5	18.3	1.9	15.8
☿	14.1	14.8	15.7	16.6	17.5	18.5	19.5	20.6	21.7	22.9	24	25.2	26.5	27.8	29.1	0.5	1.9	3.3	4.8	6.3	7.8	9.3	10.9	12.5	14.2	15.8	17.5	19.2	21	22.8
♀	12.2R	11.5	10.9	10.3	9.7	9.1	8.5	7.9	7.4	6.9	6.4	6	5.6	5.2	4.9	4.6	4.4	4.2	4	3.9	3.8	3.7	3.7D	3.8	3.9	4	4.1	4.3	4.5	4.8
♂	18.4	18.8	19.1	19.5	19.9	20.3	20.7	21.1	21.5	21.9	22.4	22.8	23.2	23.6	24.1	24.5	25	25.4	25.8	26.3	26.7	27.2	27.7	28.1	28.6	29.1	29.5	0	0.5	1

♃ (1 6 11 16 21 26): 9.6R 9 8.3 7.7 7.2 6.6 — ♄ (1 6 11 16 21 26): 26.6 27.1 27.5 27.9 28.3 28.7 — ♅ (1 11 21): 21.9 22.1 22.2 — ♆ (1 11 21): 21 21.1 21.1 — ♇ (1 11 21): 25.2R 25 24.8

V

	1	2	3	4	5	6	7	8	9	10	11	12	13	14	15	16	17	18	19	20	21	22	23	24	25	26	27	28	29	30	31
☉	10.6	11.6	12.6	13.5	14.5	15.5	16.5	17.4	18.4	19.4	20.3	21.3	22.3	23.2	24.2	25.1	26.1	27.1	28	29	30	0.9	1.9	2.8	3.8	4.8	5.7	6.7	7.6	8.6	9.6
☽	30	14.5	29.2	14	28.8	13.5	27.9	11.9	25.6	8.9	21.7	4.3	16.5	28.6	10.5	22.4	4.3	16.2	28.3	10.6	23.1	5.8	18.7	1.8	15.2	28.8	12.6	26.6	10.7	25	9.4
☿	24.6	26.4	28.3	0.2	2.1	4.1	6	8.1	10.1	12.2	14.3	16.4	18.5	20.7	22.8	25	27.2	29.4	1.6	3.8	5.9	8.1	10.2	12.3	14.4	16.5	18.5	20.4	22.4	24.3	26.1
♀	5	5.4	5.7	6.1	6.5	6.9	7.4	7.9	8.4	8.9	9.5	10	10.6	11.3	11.9	12.6	13.2	13.9	14.6	15.4	16.1	16.9	17.6	18.4	19.2	20	20.8	21.7	22.5	23.4	24.2
♂	1.4	1.9	2.4	2.9	3.4	3.9	4.4	4.9	5.4	5.9	6.4	6.9	7.4	7.9	8.4	9	9.5	10	10.5	11	11.6	12.1	12.6	13.2	13.7	14.2	14.8	15.3	15.8	16.4	16.9

♃ (1 6 11 16 21 26 31): 6.2R 5.8 5.4 5.1 4.9 4.8 4.8 — ♄ (1 6 11 16 21 26 31): 29 29.3 29.6 29.8 30 0.1 0.2 — ♅ (1 11 21 31): 22.2R 22.1 21.9 21.7 — ♆ (1 11 21 31): 21.1R 21.1 20.9 20.8 — ♇ (1 11 21 31): 24.5R 24.3 24 23.7

VI

	1	2	3	4	5	6	7	8	9	10	11	12	13	14	15	16	17	18	19	20	21	22	23	24	25	26	27	28	29	30
☉	10.5	11.5	12.4	13.4	14.4	15.3	16.3	17.2	18.2	19.1	20.1	21.1	22	23	23.9	24.9	25.8	26.8	27.7	28.7	29.6	0.6	1.6	2.5	3.5	4.4	5.4	6.3	7.3	8.2
☽	23.8	8.1	22.3	6.4	20.2	3.6	16.8	29.6	12.2	24.5	6.5	18.5	0.4	12.3	24.3	6.4	18.8	1.5	14.4	27.7	11.3	25.1	9.1	23.3	7.5	21.8	6.1	20.2	4.3	18.4
☿	28	29.7	1.4	3.1	4.8	6.3	7.9	9.4	10.8	12.2	13.5	14.8	16.1	17.3	18.4	19.5	20.5	21.5	22.4	23.2	24	24.8	25.4	26	26.6	27	27.4	27.7	28	28.2
♀	25.1	26	26.9	27.8	28.7	29.6	0.5	1.5	2.4	3.4	4.3	5.3	6.3	7.2	8.2	9.2	10.2	11.2	12.2	13.2	14.2	15.3	16.3	17.3	18.4	19.4	20.4	21.5	22.5	23.6
♂	17.5	18	18.6	19.1	19.7	20.2	20.8	21.3	21.9	22.4	23	23.6	24.1	24.7	25.3	25.8	26.4	27	27.5	28.1	28.7	29.2	29.8	0.4	1	1.5	2.1	2.7	3.3	3.9

♃ (1 6 11 16 21 26): 4.8R 4.8D 4.9 5.1 5.3 5.7 — ♄ (1 6 11 16 21 26): 0.3 0.3 0.3R 0.3 0.2 0.1 — ♅ (1 11 21): 21.7R 21.4 21 — ♆ (1 11 21): 20.8R 20.6 20.3 — ♇ (1 11 21): 23.7R 23.4 23.2

VII

	1	2	3	4	5	6	7	8	9	10	11	12	13	14	15	16	17	18	19	20	21	22	23	24	25	26	27	28	29	30	31
☉	9.2	10.1	11.1	12	13	14	14.9	15.9	16.8	17.8	18.7	19.7	20.6	21.6	22.5	23.5	24.4	25.4	26.3	27.3	28.3	29.2	0.2	1.1	2.1	3	4	4.9	5.9	6.9	7.8
☽	2	15.6	29	12.2	25.1	7.8	20.2	2.4	14.5	26.4	8.3	20.2	2.2	14.4	26.8	9.5	22.6	6.2	20.1	4.3	18.8	3.4	18.1	2.6	17	1.2	15.1	28.7	12.2	25.4	8.4
☿	28.2	28.3R	28.2	28	27.8	27.5	27.2	26.8	26.3	25.7	25.2	24.6	23.9	23.3	22.6	22	21.3	20.7	20.2	19.7	19.2	18.8	18.5	18.3	18.2	18.1D	18.2	18.4	18.6	19	19.5
♀	24.6	25.7	26.8	27.8	28.9	30	1.1	2.2	3.2	4.3	5.4	6.5	7.6	8.7	9.8	10.9	12	13.1	14.3	15.4	16.5	17.6	18.7	19.9	21	22.1	23.2	24.4	25.5	26.6	27.8
♂	4.5	5	5.6	6.2	6.8	7.4	8	8.6	9.2	9.8	10.4	11	11.6	12.2	12.8	13.4	14	14.6	15.2	15.8	16.4	17	17.6	18.2	18.8	19.4	20	20.6	21.3	21.9	22.5

♃ (1 6 11 16 21 26 31): 6.1 6.5 7 7.6 8.2 8.9 9.6 — ♄ (1 6 11 16 21 26 31): 30.0R 29.8 29.6 29.3 29 28.7 28.4 — ♅ (1 11 21 31): 20.7R 20.3 19.9 19.5 — ♆ (1 11 21 31): 20.1R 19.8 19.5 19.3 — ♇ (1 11 21 31): 23.0R 22.9 22.8 22.7

VIII

	1	2	3	4	5	6	7	8	9	10	11	12	13	14	15	16	17	18	19	20	21	22	23	24	25	26	27	28	29	30	31
☉	8.8	9.7	10.7	11.6	12.6	13.6	14.5	15.5	16.4	17.4	18.3	19.3	20.3	21.2	22.2	23.1	24.1	25.1	26	27	28	28.9	29.9	0.8	1.8	2.8	3.7	4.7	5.7	6.6	7.6
☽	21.2	3.9	16.3	28.6	10.7	22.7	4.6	16.5	28.3	10.3	22.4	4.8	17.5	0.7	14.3	28.4	12.9	27.7	12.7	27.3	12	26.1	11.6	25.6	9.1	22.4	5.4	18.1	0.7	13	25.3
☿	20	20.7	21.5	22.4	23.4	24.4	25.6	26.9	28.2	29.6	1.2	2.7	4.4	6.1	7.9	9.7	11.6	13.5	15.5	17.4	19.4	21.4	23.4	25.4	27.4	29.4	1.4	3.4	5.3	7.3	9.2
♀	28.9	0.1	1.2	2.4	3.5	4.7	5.8	7	8.1	9.3	10.4	11.6	12.8	13.9	15.1	16.3	17.4	18.6	19.8	21	22.1	23.3	24.5	25.7	26.9	28	29.2	0.4	1.6	2.8	4
♂	23.1	23.7	24.4	25	25.6	26.2	26.8	27.5	28.1	28.7	29.3	30	0.6	1.2	1.9	2.5	3.1	3.8	4.4	5	5.7	6.3	6.9	7.6	8.2	8.9	9.5	10.2	10.8	11.4	12.1

♃ (1 6 11 16 21 26 31): 9.8 10.5 11.3 12.2 13.1 14 14.9 — ♄ (1 6 11 16 21 26 31): 28.3R 28 27.6 27.2 26.9 26.5 26.1 — ♅ (1 11 21 31): 19.4R 19.1 18.8 18.5 — ♆ (1 11 21 31): 19.2R 19 18.8 18.6 — ♇ (1 11 21 31): 22.7R 22.8D 22.8 23

IX

	1	2	3	4	5	6	7	8	9	10	11	12	13	14	15	16	17	18	19	20	21	22	23	24	25	26	27	28	29	30
☉	8.6	9.5	10.5	11.5	12.5	13.4	14.4	15.4	16.3	17.3	18.3	19.3	20.2	21.2	22.2	23.1	24.1	25.1	26.1	27	28	29	30	1	1.9	2.9	3.9	4.9	5.9	6.8
☽	7.4	19.4	1.3	13.2	25	6.8	18.8	0.9	13.2	25.9	9	22.5	6.6	21.1	6	21.2	6.5	21.7	6.6	21.2	5.3	19	2.2	15.1	27.7	10.1	22.3	4.4	16.4	28.3
☿	11.1	13	14.9	16.8	18.6	20.4	22.2	24	25.7	27.5	29.2	0.9	2.6	4.2	5.9	7.5	9.1	10.7	12.2	13.8	15.4	16.8	18.4	19.9	21.4	22.9	24.3	25.8	27.1	28.5
♀	5.2	6.4	7.6	8.8	10	11.2	12.4	13.6	14.8	16	17.2	18.4	19.6	20.8	22	23.2	24.4	25.6	26.8	28.1	29.3	0.5	1.7	2.9	4.2	5.4	6.6	7.8	9	10.3
♂	12.7	13.4	14	14.7	15.3	16	16.7	17.3	18	18.6	19.3	19.9	20.6	21.3	21.9	22.6	23.2	23.9	24.6	25.2	25.9	26.6	27.2	27.9	28.6	29.3	29.9	0.6	1.3	2

♃ (1 6 11 16 21 26): 15.1 16.1 17.1 18.1 19.2 20.2 — ♄ (1 6 11 16 21 26): 26.1R 25.7 25.4 25 24.7 24.5 — ♅ (1 11 21): 18.5R 18.3 18.2 — ♆ (1 11 21): 18.6R 18.5 18.4 — ♇ (1 11 21): 23 23.2 23.4

X

	1	2	3	4	5	6	7	8	9	10	11	12	13	14	15	16	17	18	19	20	21	22	23	24	25	26	27	28	29	30	31
☉	7.8	8.8	9.8	10.8	11.8	12.8	13.7	14.7	15.7	16.7	17.7	18.7	19.7	20.7	21.7	22.6	23.6	24.6	25.6	26.6	27.6	28.6	29.6	0.6	1.6	2.6	3.6	4.6	5.6	6.6	7.6
☽	10.1	22	3.8	15.8	27.8	9.9	22.3	4.9	17.9	1.4	15.3	29.6	14.4	29.5	14.7	30	15	29.8	14.1	27.9	11.3	24.3	6.9	19.2	1.4	13.3	25.2	7.1	18.9	0.8	12.8
☿	29.9	1.2	2.6	3.9	5.2	6.4	7.7	8.9	10.1	11.2	12.4	13.4	14.5	15.5	16.5	17.4	18.3	19.1	19.8	20.5	21.1	21.6	22	22.3	22.5	22.5R	22.4	22.2	21.8	21.3	20.6
♀	11.5	12.7	14	15.2	16.4	17.6	18.9	20.1	21.3	22.6	23.8	25	26.3	27.5	28.8	30	1.2	2.5	3.7	5	6.2	7.4	8.7	9.9	11.2	12.4	13.7	14.9	16.2	17.4	18.6
♂	2.6	3.3	4	4.7	5.4	6	6.7	7.4	8.1	8.8	9.5	10.2	10.9	11.5	12.2	12.9	13.6	14.3	15	15.7	16.4	17.1	17.8	18.5	19.2	19.9	20.6	21.3	22	22.7	23.4

♃ (1 6 11 16 21 26 31): 21.3 22.4 23.4 24.5 25.6 26.7 27.8 — ♄ (1 6 11 16 21 26 31): 24.2R 24 23.9 23.8 23.7 23.6 23.6D — ♅ (1 11 21 31): 18.2 18.3 18.5 18.7 — ♆ (1 11 21 31): 18.4D 18.4 18.5 18.6 — ♇ (1 11 21 31): 23.7 24 24.4 24.7

XI

	1	2	3	4	5	6	7	8	9	10	11	12	13	14	15	16	17	18	19	20	21	22	23	24	25	26	27	28	29	30
☉	8.6	9.6	10.6	11.6	12.6	13.6	14.6	15.6	16.6	17.6	18.6	19.6	20.6	21.6	22.6	23.6	24.6	25.7	26.7	27.7	28.7	29.7	0.7	1.7	2.7	3.7	4.8	5.8	6.8	7.8
☽	24.8	7	19.3	1.9	14.7	27.7	11.1	24.9	9	23.4	8.2	23.1	8.1	23	7.7	22.1	6	19.5	2.6	15.3	27.7	9.9	21.8	3.7	15.5	27.4	9.7	21.8	4.1	16.1
☿	19.8R	18.8	17.7	16.5	15.3	13.9	12.6	11.4	10.2	9.1	8.2	7.5	7	6.7	6.6	6.6D	6.8	7.2	7.7	8.4	9.2	10.1	11.1	12.2	13.3	14.5	15.8	17.1	18.4	19.8
♀	19.9	21.1	22.4	23.6	24.9	26.1	27.4	28.6	29.9	1.1	2.4	3.7	4.9	6.2	7.4	8.7	9.9	11.2	12.4	13.7	14.9	16.2	17.4	18.7	20	21.2	22.5	23.7	25	26.2
♂	24.1	24.8	25.6	26.3	27	27.7	28.4	29.1	29.8	0.5	1.3	2	2.7	3.4	4.2	4.9	5.6	6.3	7.1	7.8	8.5	9.2	10	10.7	11.4	12.2	12.9	13.6	14.4	15.1

♃ (1 6 11 16 21 26): 28 29.1 0.1 1.2 2.2 3.3 — ♄ (1 6 11 16 21 26): 23.6 23.7 23.8 23.9 24.1 24.3 — ♅ (1 11 21): 18.7 19.1 19.4 — ♆ (1 11 21): 18.7 18.9 19.1 — ♇ (1 11 21): 24.8 25.2 25.6

XII

	1	2	3	4	5	6	7	8	9	10	11	12	13	14	15	16	17	18	19	20	21	22	23	24	25	26	27	28	29	30	31
☉	8.8	9.8	10.8	11.8	12.9	13.9	14.9	15.9	16.9	17.9	19	20	21	22	23	24	25.1	26.1	27.1	28.1	29.1	0.1	1.2	2.2	3.2	4.2	5.2	6.3	7.3	8.3	9.3
☽	28.8	11.6	24.7	8	21.6	5.3	19.3	3.5	17.9	2.4	16.9	1.4	15.8	29.9	13.8	27.3	10.4	23.2	5.7	17.9	29.8	11.7	23.5	5.4	17.4	29.6	12	24.7	7.7	21	4.5
☿	21.2	22.6	24	25.5	27	28.4	29.9	1.4	2.9	4.5	6	7.5	9	10.6	12.1	13.6	15.2	16.7	18.3	19.8	21.4	22.9	24.5	26	27.6	29.2	0.7	2.3	3.9	5.5	7.1
♀	27.5	28.8	0	1.3	2.5	3.8	5	6.3	7.6	8.8	10.1	11.3	12.6	13.8	15.1	16.4	17.6	18.9	20.1	21.4	22.7	23.9	25.2	26.4	27.7	28.9	0.2	1.5	2.7	4	5.2
♂	15.8	16.6	17.3	18	18.8	19.5	20.3	21	21.8	22.5	23.2	24	24.7	25.5	26.2	27	27.7	28.5	29.2	30	0.7	1.5	2.3	3	3.8	4.5	5.3	6	6.8	7.6	8.3

♃ (1 6 11 16 21 26 31): 4.3 5.2 6.2 7.1 8 8.8 9.6 — ♄ (1 6 11 16 21 26 31): 24.6 24.9 25.2 25.6 26 26.4 26.9 — ♅ (1 11 21 31): 19.9 20.4 21 21.5 — ♆ (1 11 21 31): 19.4 19.7 20.1 20.4 — ♇ (1 11 21 31): 26 26.4 26.7 27.1

I

	1	2	3	4	5	6	7	8	9	10	11	12	13	14	15	16	17	18	19	20	21	22	23	24	25	26	27	28	29	30	31
☉	10.3	11.4	12.4	13.4	14.4	15.4	16.5	17.5	18.5	19.5	20.5	21.5	22.6	23.6	24.6	25.6	26.6	27.7	28.7	29.7	0.7	1.7	2.7	3.8	4.8	5.8	6.8	7.8	8.8	9.9	10.9
☽	18.3	2.2	16.2	0.3	14.4	28.5	12.6	26.7	10.7	24.7	8.4	22	5.3	18.3	1	13.4	25.6	7.6	19.5	1.3	13.2	25.2	7.4	19.9	2.7	16	29.6	13.6	27.8	12.2	26.6
☿	8.7	10.3	11.9	13.5	15.1	16.7	18.4	20	21.7	23.3	25	26.6	28.3	30	1.7	3.3	5	6.7	8.4	10.1	11.8	13.5	15.2	16.9	18.6	20.2	21.8	23.4	25	26.5	28
♀	6.5	7.8	9	10.3	11.5	12.8	14.1	15.3	16.6	17.8	19.1	20.3	21.6	22.9	24.1	25.4	26.6	27.9	29.1	0.4	1.7	2.9	4.2	5.4	6.7	7.9	9.2	10.5	11.7	13	14.2
♂	9.1	9.8	10.6	11.4	12.1	12.9	13.7	14.4	15.2	16	16.7	17.5	18.3	19	19.8	20.6	21.4	22.1	22.9	23.7	24.4	25.2	26	26.8	27.5	28.3	29.1	29.9	0.7	1.4	2.2

♃ (1 6 11 16 21 26 31): 9.8 10.5 11.2 11.8 12.4 12.9 13.4 — ♄ (1 6 11 16 21 26 31): 27 27.5 28 28.5 29.1 29.7 0.2 — ♅ (1 11 21 31): 21.6 22.2 22.8 23.3 — ♆ (1 11 21 31): 20.5 20.8 21.2 21.6 — ♇ (1 11 21 31): 27.1 27.4 27.6 27.8

II

	1	2	3	4	5	6	7	8	9	10	11	12	13	14	15	16	17	18	19	20	21	22	23	24	25	26	27	28
☉	11.9	12.9	13.9	14.9	16	17	18	19	20	21	22	23	24.1	25.1	26.1	27.1	28.1	29.1	0.1	1.1	2.1	3.1	4.1	5.1	6.2	7.2	8.2	9.2
☽	11.1	25.4	9.5	23.5	7.3	21	4.5	17.8	0.9	13.9	26.6	9.2	21.5	3.6	15.5	27.4	9.2	21	3	15.1	27.6	10.5	23.8	7.6	21.9	6.4	21.2	6.1
☿	29.4	0.7	2	3.2	4.2	5.1	5.9	6.6	7.1	7.4	7.6	7.5R	7.3	7	6.4	5.7	4.9	3.9	2.9	1.8	0.7	29.6	28.5	27.5	26.5	25.6	24.9	24.2
♀	15.5	16.7	18	19.2	20.5	21.8	23	24.3	25.5	26.8	28	29.3	0.5	1.8	3	4.3	5.5	6.8	8	9.3	10.5	11.8	13	14.3	15.5	16.8	18	19.3
♂	3	3.8	4.6	5.3	6.1	6.9	7.7	8.5	9.2	10	10.8	11.6	12.4	13.2	13.9	14.7	15.5	16.3	17.1	17.9	18.6	19.4	20.2	21	21.8	22.6	23.4	24.1

♃ (1 6 11 16 21 26): 13.5 13.9 14.2 14.4 14.6 14.6 — ♄ (1 6 11 16 21 26): 0.4 0.9 1.5 2.2 2.8 3.4 — ♅ (1 11 21): 23.4 24 24.5 — ♆ (1 11 21): 21.6 22 22.3 — ♇ (1 11 21): 27.8 28 28.1

III

	1	2	3	4	5	6	7	8	9	10	11	12	13	14	15	16	17	18	19	20	21	22	23	24	25	26	27	28	29	30	31
☉	10.2	11.2	12.2	13.2	14.2	15.2	16.2	17.2	18.2	19.2	20.2	21.2	22.2	23.2	24.2	25.2	26.2	27.2	28.2	29.2	0.1	1.1	2.1	3.1	4.1	5.1	6.1	7.1	8.1	9.1	10.1
☽	21	5.6	20	4.1	17.9	1.4	14.7	27.7	10.5	23.1	5.6	17.9	0	12	23.9	5.7	17.4	29.3	11.2	23.3	5.8	18.6	1.6	15.6	29.8	14.5	29.5	14.7	29.8	14.8	29.6
☿	23.6R	23.2	22.9	22.7	22.6	22.7D	22.8	23	23.3	23.7	24.2	24.8	25.4	26.1	26.9	27.7	28.6	29.5	0.5	1.5	2.6	3.7	4.8	6	7.2	8.4	9.7	11	12.4	13.7	15.1
♀	20.5	21.8	23	24.3	25.5	26.8	28	29.3	0.5	1.8	3	4.2	5.5	6.7	8	9.2	10.5	11.7	12.9	14.2	15.4	16.7	17.9	19.1	20.4	21.6	22.8	24.1	25.3	26.5	27.8
♂	24.9	25.7	26.5	27.3	28.1	28.9	29.7	0.4	1.2	2	2.8	3.6	4.4	5.2	5.9	6.7	7.5	8.3	9.1	9.9	10.7	11.4	12.2	13	13.8	14.6	15.4	16.2	16.9	17.7	18.5

♃ (1 6 11 16 21 26 31): 14.7R 14.6 14.5 14.3 14 13.7 13.2 — ♄ (1 6 11 16 21 26 31): 3.7 4.3 4.9 5.5 6.1 6.7 7.2 — ♅ (1 11 21 31): 24.9 25.3 25.7 25.9 — ♆ (1 11 21 31): 22.5 22.8 23 23.2 — ♇ (1 11 21 31): 28.1 28.1R 28 27.8

IV

	1	2	3	4	5	6	7	8	9	10	11	12	13	14	15	16	17	18	19	20	21	22	23	24	25	26	27	28	29	30
☉	11	12	13	14	15	16	17	17.9	18.9	19.9	20.9	21.9	22.8	23.8	24.8	25.8	26.8	27.7	28.7	29.7	0.7	1.6	2.6	3.6	4.6	5.5	6.5	7.5	8.5	9.4
☽	13.9	27.9	11.5	24.7	7.6	20.2	2.6	14.9	26.9	8.9	20.7	2.6	14.3	26.1	8	20	2.2	14.6	27.4	10.6	24.2	8.3	22.8	7.7	22.8	8.1	23.2	8.2	22.8	7
☿	16.6	18	19.5	21	22.5	24.1	25.6	27.2	28.9	0.5	2.2	3.9	5.6	7.4	9.2	11	12.8	14.7	16.6	18.5	20.4	22.4	24.4	26.4	28.4	0.5	2.6	4.7	6.8	8.9
♀	29	0.3	1.5	2.7	4	5.2	6.4	7.6	8.9	10.1	11.3	12.6	13.8	15	16.2	17.5	18.7	19.9	21.1	22.4	23.6	24.8	26	27.2	28.5	29.7	0.9	2.1	3.3	4.6
♂	19.3	20.1	20.9	21.6	22.4	23.2	24	24.8	25.5	26.3	27.1	27.9	28.7	29.4	0.2	1	1.8	2.5	3.3	4.1	4.9	5.6	6.4	7.2	8	8.7	9.5	10.3	11	11.8

♃ (1 6 11 16 21 26): 13.2R 12.7 12.1 11.6 11 10.3 — ♄ (1 6 11 16 21 26): 7.3 7.9 8.4 8.9 9.3 9.8 — ♅ (1 11 21): 26 26.2 26.3 — ♆ (1 11 21): 23.2 23.3 23.3 — ♇ (1 11 21): 27.8R 27.6 27.4

V

	1	2	3	4	5	6	7	8	9	10	11	12	13	14	15	16	17	18	19	20	21	22	23	24	25	26	27	28	29	30	31
☉	10.4	11.4	12.3	13.3	14.3	15.3	16.2	17.2	18.2	19.1	20.1	21.1	22	23	24	24.9	25.9	26.8	27.8	28.8	29.7	0.7	1.7	2.6	3.6	4.5	5.5	6.5	7.4	8.4	9.3
☽	20.7	4.1	17	29.6	11.9	24	5.9	17.8	29.6	11.4	23.2	5.1	17.1	29.3	11.6	24.2	7	20.2	3.7	17.6	1.8	16.5	1.3	16.4	1.4	16.4	1	15.3	29.2	12.7	25.7
☿	11.1	13.2	15.4	17.6	19.7	21.9	24	26.1	28.2	0.3	2.3	4.3	6.2	8.1	10	11.8	13.6	15.3	16.9	18.5	20.1	21.6	23	24.4	25.7	27	28.2	29.3	0.4	1.4	2.4
♀	5.8	7	8.2	9.4	10.6	11.8	13.1	14.3	15.5	16.7	17.9	19.1	20.3	21.5	22.7	23.9	25.1	26.3	27.5	28.7	29.9	1.1	2.3	3.5	4.7	5.9	7.1	8.3	9.5	10.7	11.9
♂	12.6	13.3	14.1	14.9	15.6	16.4	17.2	17.9	18.7	19.5	20.2	21	21.7	22.5	23.3	24	24.8	25.5	26.3	27	27.8	28.6	29.3	0.1	0.8	1.6	2.3	3.1	3.8	4.5	5.3

♃ (1 6 11 16 21 26 31): 9.7R 9.1 8.4 7.8 7.3 6.7 6.3 — ♄ (1 6 11 16 21 26 31): 10.2 10.6 10.9 11.2 11.5 11.8 12 — ♅ (1 11 21 31): 26.3R 26.3 26.2 26 — ♆ (1 11 21 31): 23.3R 23.3 23.2 23 — ♇ (1 11 21 31): 27.2R 26.9 26.6 26.3

VI

	1	2	3	4	5	6	7	8	9	10	11	12	13	14	15	16	17	18	19	20	21	22	23	24	25	26	27	28	29	30
☉	10.3	11.3	12.2	13.2	14.1	15.1	16	17	18	18.9	19.9	20.8	21.8	22.7	23.7	24.6	25.6	26.6	27.5	28.5	29.4	0.4	1.3	2.3	3.2	4.2	5.1	6.1	7	8
☽	8.3	20.7	2.7	14.6	26.4	8.2	20	2	14	26.2	8.6	21.2	4	17.1	0.4	14	27.8	11.9	26.2	10.7	25.4	10.1	24.8	9.3	23.5	7.4	20.8	3.9	16.6	28.9
☿	3.3	4.1	4.8	5.5	6.1	6.7	7.2	7.6	7.9	8.1	8.3	8.4	8.4R	8.4	8.2	8	7.8	7.4	7	6.6	6.1	5.6	5	4.4	3.9	3.3	2.7	2.2	1.6	1.1
♀	13.1	14.3	15.5	16.7	17.8	19	20.2	21.4	22.6	23.8	24.9	26.1	27.3	28.5	29.6	0.8	2	3.2	4.3	5.5	6.7	7.8	9	10.2	11.3	12.5	13.6	14.8	16	17.1
♂	6	6.8	7.5	8.3	9	9.7	10.5	11.2	12	12.7	13.4	14.2	14.9	15.6	16.4	17.1	17.8	18.5	19.3	20	20.7	21.5	22.2	22.9	23.6	24.3	25.1	25.8	26.5	27.2

♃ (1 6 11 16 21 26): 6.2R 5.8 5.4 5.2 5 4.8 — ♄ (1 6 11 16 21 26): 12 12.2 12.3 12.4 12.4 12.4R — ♅ (1 11 21): 26.0R 25.7 25.4 — ♆ (1 11 21): 23.0R 22.8 22.6 — ♇ (1 11 21): 26.3R 26.1 25.8

VII

	1	2	3	4	5	6	7	8	9	10	11	12	13	14	15	16	17	18	19	20	21	22	23	24	25	26	27	28	29	30	31
☉	9	9.9	10.9	11.8	12.8	13.7	14.7	15.6	16.6	17.5	18.5	19.4	20.4	21.3	22.3	23.3	24.2	25.2	26.1	27.1	28	29	29.9	0.9	1.8	2.8	3.8	4.7	5.7	6.6	7.6
☽	11	22.9	4.7	16.5	28.4	10.4	22.6	5.1	17.7	0.7	13.9	27.3	10.9	24.6	8.6	22.6	6.7	21	5.3	19.6	3.8	18	1.9	15.6	28.9	11.9	24.6	6.9	19	0.9	12.7
☿	0.7R	0.3	30	29.7	29.6	29.4	29.4D	29.5	29.6	29.8	0.2	0.6	1	1.6	2.3	3	3.9	4.8	5.8	6.9	8	9.3	10.6	12	13.5	15	16.6	18.3	20	21.8	23.6
♀	18.3	19.4	20.6	21.7	22.9	24	25.1	26.3	27.4	28.6	29.7	0.8	2	3.1	4.2	5.3	6.5	7.6	8.7	9.8	10.9	12	13.1	14.2	15.3	16.4	17.5	18.6	19.7	20.8	21.9
♂	27.9	28.6	29.3	0.1	0.8	1.5	2.2	2.9	3.6	4.3	5	5.7	6.4	7.1	7.8	8.5	9.2	9.9	10.6	11.3	12	12.7	13.3	14	14.7	15.4	16.1	16.8	17.4	18.1	18.8

♃ (1 6 11 16 21 26 31): 4.8R 4.8D 4.9 5.1 5.3 5.6 6 — ♄ (1 6 11 16 21 26 31): 12.3R 12.3 12.1 12 11.8 11.5 11.3 — ♅ (1 11 21 31): 25.0R 24.6 24.2 23.8 — ♆ (1 11 21 31): 22.3R 22.1 21.8 21.5 — ♇ (1 11 21 31): 25.6R 25.5 25.4 25.3

VIII

	1	2	3	4	5	6	7	8	9	10	11	12	13	14	15	16	17	18	19	20	21	22	23	24	25	26	27	28	29	30	31
☉	8.5	9.5	10.5	11.4	12.4	13.3	14.3	15.2	16.2	17.2	18.1	19.1	20	21	22	22.9	23.9	24.8	25.8	26.8	27.7	28.7	29.7	0.6	1.6	2.5	3.5	4.5	5.4	6.4	7.4
☽	24.5	6.4	18.5	0.8	13.5	26.4	9.7	23.3	7.1	21.1	5.2	19.4	3.6	17.7	1.8	15.9	29.8	13.7	27.4	10.9	24.3	7.3	20.1	2.6	14.9	26.9	8.8	20.6	2.4	14.3	26.4
☿	25.6	27.5	29.5	1.5	3.5	5.6	7.6	9.7	11.8	13.8	15.9	18	20	22	24	26	28	30	1.9	3.8	5.7	7.5	9.4	11.2	13	14.7	16.5	18.2	19.9	21.6	23.3
♀	23	24	25.1	26.2	27.2	28.3	29.4	0.4	1.5	2.5	3.5	4.6	5.6	6.6	7.7	8.7	9.7	10.7	11.7	12.7	13.7	14.7	15.7	16.6	17.6	18.5	19.5	20.4	21.4	22.3	23.2
♂	19.5	20.2	20.8	21.5	22.2	22.8	23.5	24.2	24.9	25.5	26.2	26.8	27.5	28.2	28.8	29.5	0.1	0.8	1.4	2.1	2.7	3.4	4	4.7	5.3	6	6.6	7.2	7.9	8.5	9.2

♃ (1 6 11 16 21 26 31): 6.1 6.5 7 7.6 8.2 8.9 9.7 — ♄ (1 6 11 16 21 26 31): 11.2R 10.9 10.6 10.2 9.9 9.5 9.1 — ♅ (1 11 21 31): 23.8R 23.4 23.1 22.8 — ♆ (1 11 21 31): 21.5R 21.3 21 20.9 — ♇ (1 11 21 31): 25.3R 25.3D 25.4 25.5

IX

	1	2	3	4	5	6	7	8	9	10	11	12	13	14	15	16	17	18	19	20	21	22	23	24	25	26	27	28	29	30
☉	8.3	9.3	10.3	11.2	12.2	13.2	14.2	15.1	16.1	17.1	18	19	20	21	21.9	22.9	23.9	24.9	25.8	26.8	27.8	28.8	29.7	0.7	1.7	2.7	3.7	4.6	5.6	6.6
☽	8.8	21.5	4.6	18.1	2	16.2	0.6	15.2	29.7	14.2	28.6	12.7	26.7	10.4	24	7.4	20.5	3.5	16.2	28.7	11	23.1	5.1	16.9	28.7	10.5	22.4	4.5	16.8	29.5
☿	24.9	26.5	28.1	29.7	1.2	2.8	4.3	5.8	7.3	8.7	10.1	11.6	13	14.3	15.7	17	18.3	19.6	20.8	22	23.2	24.4	25.5	26.6	27.7	28.7	29.7	0.6	1.5	2.3
♀	24.1	25	25.9	26.8	27.7	28.5	29.4	0.2	1.1	1.9	2.7	3.5	4.3	5	5.8	6.5	7.2	7.9	8.6	9.3	10	10.6	11.2	11.8	12.4	12.9	13.5	14	14.4	14.9
♂	9.8	10.4	11	11.7	12.3	12.9	13.5	14.2	14.8	15.4	16	16.6	17.2	17.8	18.5	19.1	19.7	20.3	20.9	21.5	22.1	22.7	23.3	23.8	24.4	25	25.6	26.2	26.8	27.3

♃ (1 6 11 16 21 26): 9.8 10.6 11.4 12.3 13.2 14.1 — ♄ (1 6 11 16 21 26): 9.1R 8.7 8.3 7.9 7.6 7.2 — ♅ (1 11 21): 22.8R 22.6 22.4 — ♆ (1 11 21): 20.8R 20.7 20.6 — ♇ (1 11 21): 25.5 25.7 25.9

X

	1	2	3	4	5	6	7	8	9	10	11	12	13	14	15	16	17	18	19	20	21	22	23	24	25	26	27	28	29	30	31
☉	7.6	8.6	9.6	10.5	11.5	12.5	13.5	14.5	15.5	16.5	17.5	18.4	19.4	20.4	21.4	22.4	23.4	24.4	25.4	26.4	27.4	28.4	29.4	0.4	1.3	2.3	3.3	4.3	5.3	6.3	7.3
☽	12.6	26.2	10.1	24.5	9.3	24.2	9.1	24	8.7	23.1	7.2	20.9	4.3	17.5	0.4	13	25.4	7.7	19.7	1.7	13.6	25.4	7.1	19	0.9	12.9	25.3	7.9	20.9	4.3	18.2
☿	3.1	3.8	4.4	5	5.5	5.9	6.2	6.4	6.5	6.4R	6.3	6	5.6	5	4.3	3.5	2.5	1.5	0.3	29.1	27.9	26.6	25.4	24.3	23.3	22.5	21.8	21.3	20.9	20.8	20.9D
♀	15.3	15.7	16.1	16.4	16.7	17	17.3	17.5	17.7	17.8	17.9	18	18	18.0R	17.9	17.8	17.7	17.5	17.3	17.1	16.8	16.5	16.1	15.7	15.3	14.8	14.3	13.8	13.2	12.7	12.1
♂	27.9	28.5	29.1	29.6	0.2	0.8	1.3	1.9	2.4	3	3.5	4.1	4.6	5.2	5.7	6.2	6.8	7.3	7.8	8.4	8.9	9.4	9.9	10.4	10.9	11.4	11.9	12.4	12.9	13.4	13.9

♃ (1 6 11 16 21 26 31): 15.1 16.1 17.1 18.1 19.2 20.2 21.3 — ♄ (1 6 11 16 21 26 31): 6.9R 6.7 6.4 6.2 6 5.9 5.8 — ♅ (1 11 21 31): 22.4R 22.4D 22.5 22.7 — ♆ (1 11 21 31): 20.6R 20.6D 20.7 20.8 — ♇ (1 11 21 31): 26.2 26.5 26.8 27.2

XI

	1	2	3	4	5	6	7	8	9	10	11	12	13	14	15	16	17	18	19	20	21	22	23	24	25	26	27	28	29	30
☉	8.3	9.3	10.3	11.3	12.3	13.3	14.3	15.4	16.4	17.4	18.4	19.4	20.4	21.4	22.4	23.4	24.4	25.4	26.4	27.4	28.4	29.5	0.5	1.5	2.5	3.5	4.5	5.5	6.5	7.5
☽	2.5	17.3	2.3	17.5	2.7	17.7	2.4	16.8	0.7	14.2	27.3	10	22.5	4.7	16.7	28.6	10.5	22.3	4.1	15.9	27.8	9.8	22	4.4	17	29.9	13.2	26.9	11	25.5
☿	21.1	21.5	22.1	22.8	23.7	24.6	25.7	26.8	28	29.3	0.6	2	3.4	4.9	6.4	7.9	9.4	10.9	12.5	14	15.6	17.1	18.7	20.3	21.8	23.4	25	26.6	28.1	29.7
♀	11.5R	10.9	10.3	9.7	9.1	8.5	7.9	7.3	6.7	6.2	5.7	5.2	4.8	4.4	4	3.7	3.4	3.1	2.9	2.8	2.6	2.5	2.5	2.5D	2.5	2.6	2.7	2.8	3	3.3
♂	14.4	14.9	15.4	15.8	16.3	16.8	17.2	17.7	18.1	18.6	19	19.5	19.9	20.3	20.7	21.2	21.6	22	22.4	22.8	23.2	23.6	23.9	24.3	24.7	25	25.4	25.7	26.1	26.4

♃ (1 6 11 16 21 26): 21.5 22.6 23.7 24.8 25.9 27.1 — ♄ (1 6 11 16 21 26): 5.7R 5.7 5.7D 5.7 5.8 5.9 — ♅ (1 11 21): 22.8 23.1 23.4 — ♆ (1 11 21): 20.8 21 21.2 — ♇ (1 11 21): 27.2 27.6 28

XII

	1	2	3	4	5	6	7	8	9	10	11	12	13	14	15	16	17	18	19	20	21	22	23	24	25	26	27	28	29	30	31
☉	8.6	9.6	10.6	11.6	12.6	13.6	14.6	15.7	16.7	17.7	18.7	19.7	20.7	21.8	22.8	23.8	24.8	25.8	26.8	27.9	28.9	29.9	0.9	1.9	3	4	5	6	7	8.1	9.1
☽	10.3	25.4	10.6	25.8	10.7	25.3	9.5	23.1	6.3	19.1	1.5	13.6	25.6	7.4	19.2	1	12.8	24.8	6.8	19.1	1.4	14	26.8	9.8	23	6.5	20.4	4.6	19.1	3.8	18.8
☿	1.3	2.8	4.4	6	7.6	9.1	10.7	12.3	13.8	15.4	17	18.5	20.1	21.7	23.3	24.8	26.4	28	29.6	1.2	2.8	4.4	5.9	7.5	9.1	10.7	12.4	14	15.6	17.2	18.8
♀	3.5	3.8	4.1	4.5	4.9	5.3	5.7	6.2	6.7	7.3	7.8	8.4	9	9.6	10.3	10.9	11.6	12.3	13.1	13.8	14.6	15.3	16.1	16.9	17.7	18.6	19.4	20.3	21.2	22	22.9
♂	26.8	27.1	27.4	27.7	28	28.3	28.6	28.9	29.1	29.4	29.6	29.9	0.1	0.3	0.6	0.8	1	1.1	1.3	1.5	1.6	1.8	1.9	2	2.2	2.3	2.4	2.4	2.5	2.6	2.6

♃ (1 6 11 16 21 26 31): 28.2 29.3 0.3 1.4 2.5 3.5 4.5 — ♄ (1 6 11 16 21 26 31): 6.1 6.3 6.5 6.8 7.2 7.5 7.9 — ♅ (1 11 21 31): 23.8 24.3 24.9 25.4 — ♆ (1 11 21 31): 21.5 21.8 22.2 22.5 — ♇ (1 11 21 31): 28.4 28.8 29.2 29.5

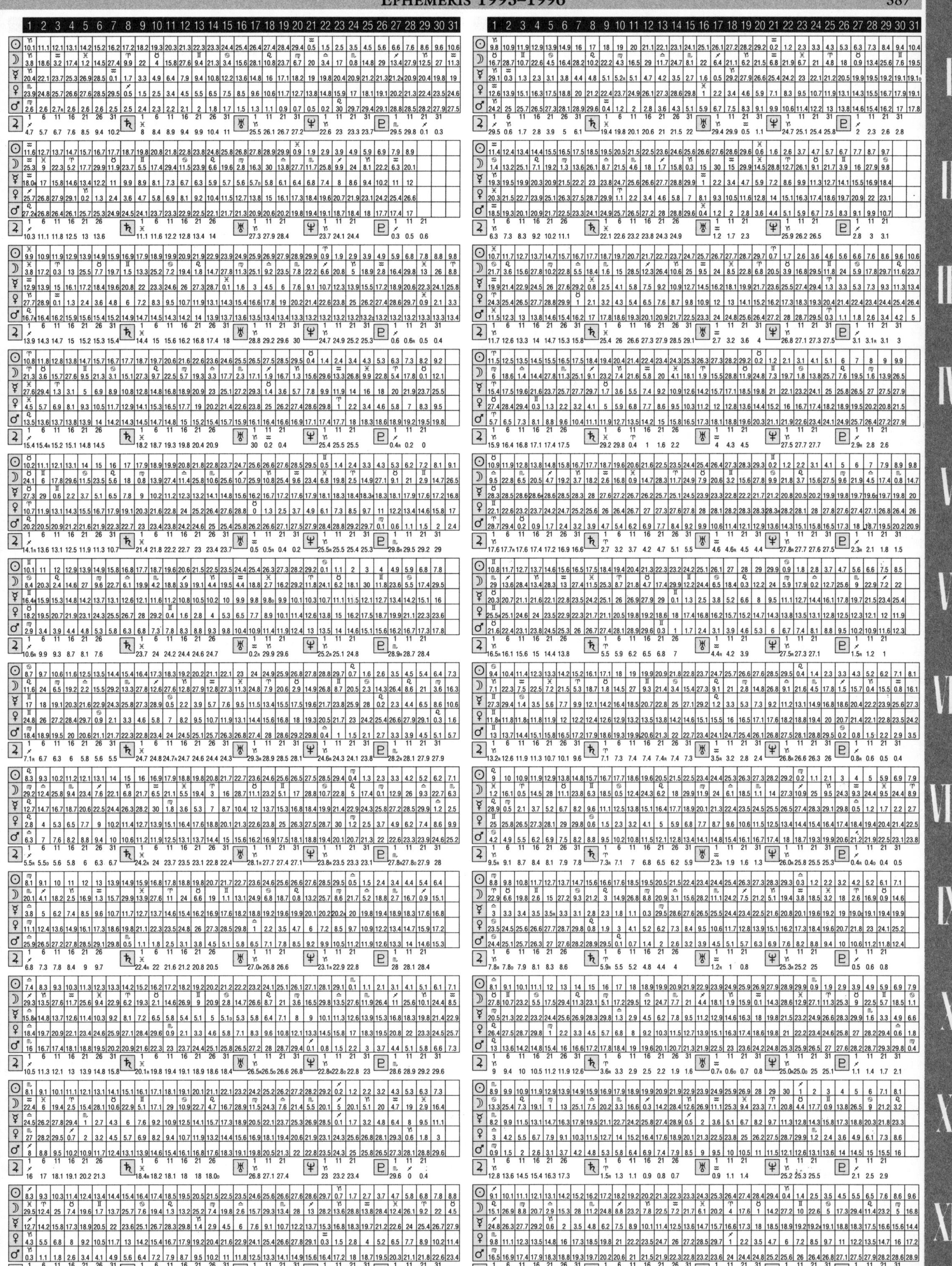

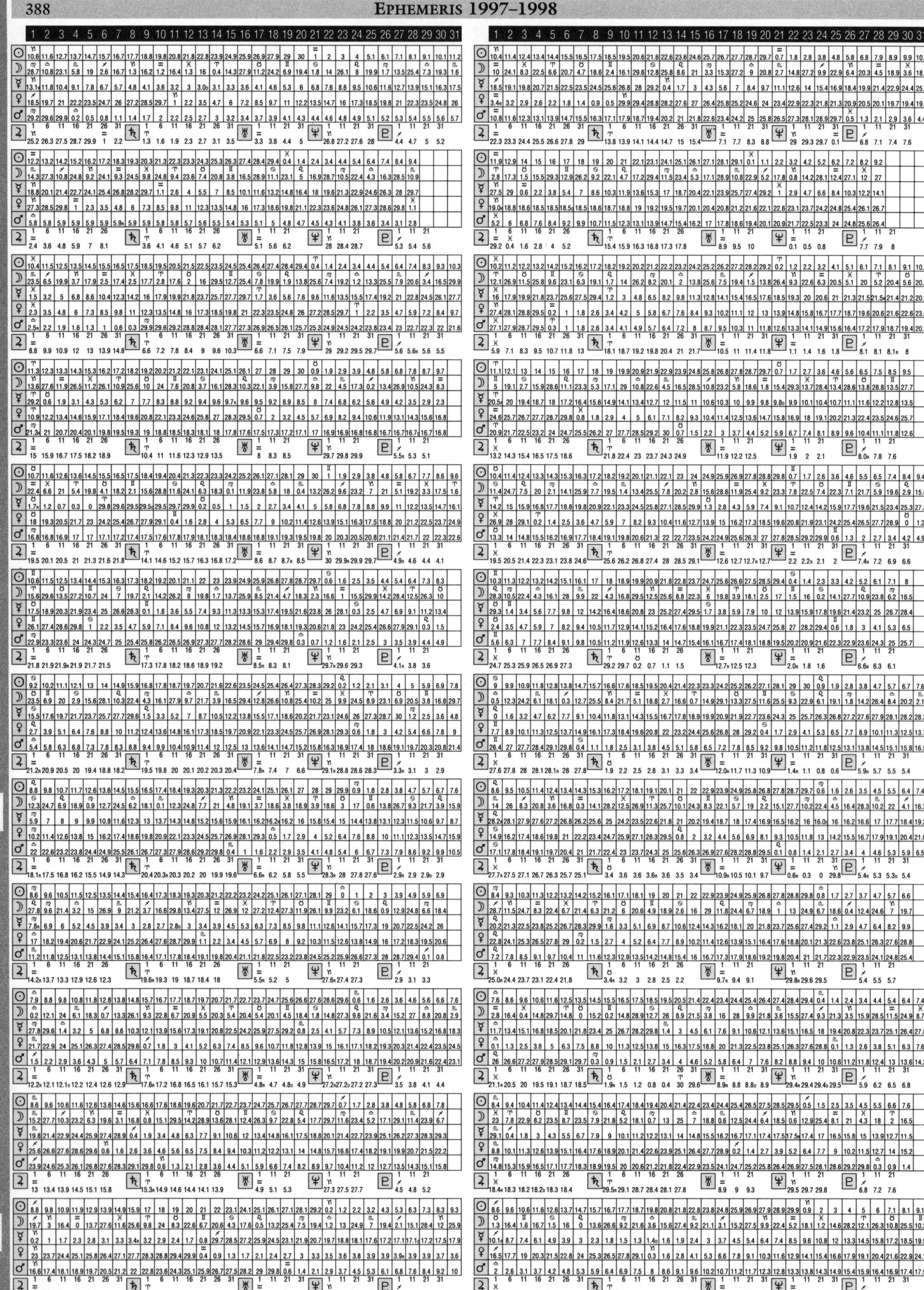

1997

I

	1	2	3	4	5	6	7	8	9	10	11	12	13	14	15	16	17	18	19	20	21	22	23	24	25	26	27	28	29	30	31
☉	♑ 10.6	11.6	12.7	13.7	14.7	15.7	16.7	17.7	18.8	19.8	20.8	21.8	22.8	23.9	24.9	25.9	26.9	27.9	29	30	♒ 1	2	3	4	5.1	6.1	7.1	8.1	9.1	10.1	11.2
☽	♍ 28.7	♎ 10.8	23.1	♏ 5.8	19	♐ 2.6	16.7	♑ 1.3	16.2	♒ 1.2	16.4	♓ 1.3	16	♈ 0.4	14.3	27.9	♉ 11.2	24.2	♊ 6.9	19.4	♋ 1.8	14	26.1	♌ 8	19.9	♍ 1.7	13.5	25.4	♎ 7.3	19.3	♏ 1.6
☿	♑ 13.1R	11.8	10.4	9.1	7.8	6.7	5.7	4.8	4.1	3.6	3.2	3	3.0D	3.1	3.3	3.6	4.1	4.6	5.3	6	6.8	7.6	8.6	9.5	10.6	11.6	12.7	13.9	15.1	16.3	17.5
♀	♐ 18.5	19.7	21	22.2	23.5	24.7	26	27.2	28.5	29.7	♑ 1	2.2	3.5	4.7	6	7.2	8.5	9.7	11	12.2	13.5	14.7	16	17.3	18.5	19.8	21	22.3	23.5	24.8	26
♂	♍ 29.2	29.6	29.9	♎ 0.2	0.5	0.8	1.1	1.4	1.7	2	2.2	2.5	2.7	3	3.2	3.4	3.7	3.9	4.1	4.3	4.4	4.6	4.8	4.9	5.1	5.2	5.3	5.4	5.5	5.6	5.7

♃ 1, 6, 11, 16, 21, 26, 31: ♑ 25.2, 26.3, 27.5, 28.7, 29.9, ♒ 1, 2.2 · ♄ 1, 6, 11, 16, 21, 26, 31: ♈ 1.3, 1.6, 1.9, 2.3, 2.7, 3.1, 3.5 · ♅ 1, 11, 21, 31: ♒ 3.3, 3.8, 4.4, 5 · ♆ 1, 11, 21, 31: ♑ 26.8, 27.2, 27.6, 28 · ♇ 1, 11, 21, 31: ♐ 4.4, 4.7, 5, 5.2

II

	1	2	3	4	5	6	7	8	9	10	11	12	13	14	15	16	17	18	19	20	21	22	23	24	25	26	27	28	29	30	31
☉	♒ 12.2	13.2	14.2	15.2	16.2	17.2	18.3	19.3	20.3	21.3	22.3	23.3	24.3	25.3	26.3	27.4	28.4	29.4	♓ 0.4	1.4	2.4	3.4	4.4	5.4	6.4	7.4	8.4	9.4			
☽	♏ 14.3	27.3	♐ 10.8	24.8	♑ 9.2	24.1	♒ 9.3	24.5	♓ 9.8	24.8	♈ 9.4	23.6	♉ 7.4	20.8	♊ 3.8	16.5	28.9	♋ 11.1	23.1	♌ 5	16.9	28.7	♍ 10.5	22.4	♎ 4.3	16.3	28.5	♏ 10.9			
☿	♑ 18.8	20.1	21.4	22.7	24.1	25.4	26.8	28.2	29.7	♒ 1.1	2.6	4	5.5	7	8.5	10.1	11.6	13.2	14.8	16.4	18	19.6	21.3	22.9	24.6	26.3	28	29.7			
♀	♑ 27.3	28.5	29.8	♒ 1	2.3	3.5	4.8	6	7.3	8.5	9.8	11	12.3	13.5	14.8	16	17.3	18.6	19.8	21.1	22.3	23.6	24.8	26.1	27.3	28.6	29.8	♓ 1.1			
♂	♎ 5.8	5.8	5.9	5.9	5.9	5.9	5.9R	5.9	5.9	5.8	5.8	5.7	5.6	5.5	5.4	5.3	5.1	5	4.8	4.7	4.5	4.3	4.1	3.8	3.6	3.4	3.1	2.8			

♃ 1, 6, 11, 16, 21, 26: ♒ 2.4, 3.6, 4.8, 5.9, 7, 8.1 · ♄ 1, 6, 11, 16, 21, 26: ♈ 3.6, 4.1, 4.6, 5.1, 5.7, 6.2 · ♅ 1, 11, 21: ♒ 5.1, 5.6, 6.2 · ♆ 1, 11, 21: ♑ 28, 28.4, 28.7 · ♇ 1, 11, 21: ♐ 5.3, 5.4, 5.6

III

	1	2	3	4	5	6	7	8	9	10	11	12	13	14	15	16	17	18	19	20	21	22	23	24	25	26	27	28	29	30	31
☉	♓ 10.4	11.5	12.5	13.5	14.5	15.5	16.5	17.5	18.5	19.5	20.5	21.5	22.5	23.5	24.5	25.4	26.4	27.4	28.4	29.4	♈ 0.4	1.4	2.4	3.4	4.4	5.4	6.4	7.4	8.3	9.3	10.3
☽	♏ 23.5	♐ 6.5	19.9	♑ 3.7	17.9	♒ 2.5	17.4	♓ 2.5	17.7	♈ 2.8	17.6	♉ 2	16	29.5	♊ 12.7	25.4	♋ 7.8	19.9	♌ 1.9	13.8	25.6	♍ 7.4	19.2	♎ 1.2	13.3	25.5	♏ 7.9	20.6	♐ 3.4	16.5	29.9
☿	♓ 1.5	3.2	5	6.8	8.6	10.4	12.3	14.2	16	17.9	19.9	21.8	23.7	25.7	27.7	29.7	♈ 1.7	3.6	5.6	7.6	9.6	11.6	13.5	15.5	17.4	19.2	21	22.8	24.5	26.1	27.7
♀	♓ 2.3	3.5	4.8	6	7.3	8.5	9.8	11	12.3	13.5	14.8	16	17.3	18.5	19.8	21	22.3	23.5	24.8	26	27.2	28.5	29.7	♈ 1	2.2	3.5	4.7	5.9	7.2	8.4	9.7
♂	♎ 2.5R	2.2	1.9	1.6	1.3	1	0.6	0.3	♍ 29.9	29.6	29.2	28.8	28.4	28.1	27.7	27.3	26.9	26.5	26.1	25.7	25.3	24.9	24.5	24.2	23.8	23.4	23	22.7	22.3	22	21.6

♃ 1, 6, 11, 16, 21, 26, 31: ♒ 8.8, 9.9, 10.9, 12, 13, 13.9, 14.8 · ♄ 1, 6, 11, 16, 21, 26, 31: ♈ 6.6, 7.2, 7.8, 8.4, 9, 9.6, 10.3 · ♅ 1, 11, 21, 31: ♒ 6.6, 7.1, 7.5, 7.9 · ♆ 1, 11, 21, 31: ♑ 29, 29.2, 29.5, 29.7 · ♇ 1, 11, 21, 31: ♐ 5.6, 5.6R, 5.6, 5.5

IV

	1	2	3	4	5	6	7	8	9	10	11	12	13	14	15	16	17	18	19	20	21	22	23	24	25	26	27	28	29	30	31
☉	♈ 11.3	12.3	13.3	14.3	15.3	16.2	17.2	18.2	19.2	20.2	21.2	22.1	23.1	24.1	25.1	26.1	27	28	29	30	♉ 0.9	1.9	2.9	3.9	4.8	5.8	6.8	7.8	8.7	9.7	
☽	♑ 13.6	27.6	♒ 11.9	26.5	♓ 11.2	26.1	♈ 10.9	25.6	♉ 10	24	♊ 7.6	20.8	♋ 3.7	16.1	28.3	♌ 10.3	22.1	♍ 3.9	15.8	27.7	♎ 9.8	22	♏ 4.5	17.3	♐ 0.2	13.4	26.9	♑ 10.5	24.3	♒ 8.3	
☿	♈ 29.2	♉ 0.6	1.9	3.1	4.3	5.3	6.2	7	7.7	8.3	8.8	9.2	9.4	9.6	9.7R	9.6	9.5	9.2	8.9	8.5	8	7.4	6.8	6.2	5.6	4.9	4.2	3.5	2.9	2.3	
♀	♈ 10.9	12.2	13.4	14.6	15.9	17.1	18.4	19.6	20.8	22.1	23.3	24.6	25.8	27	28.3	29.5	♉ 0.7	2	3.2	4.5	5.7	6.9	8.2	9.4	10.6	11.9	13.1	14.3	15.6	16.8	
♂	♍ 21.3R	21	20.7	20.4	20.1	19.8	19.5	19.3	19	18.8	18.5	18.3	18.1	18	17.8	17.6	17.5	17.3	17.2	17.1	17	16.9	16.9	16.8	16.8	16.7	16.7	16.7D	16.7	16.8	

♃ 1, 6, 11, 16, 21, 26: ♒ 15, 15.9, 16.7, 17.5, 18.2, 18.9 · ♄ 1, 6, 11, 16, 21, 26: ♈ 10.4, 11, 11.6, 12.3, 12.9, 13.5 · ♅ 1, 11, 21: ♒ 8, 8.3, 8.5 · ♆ 1, 11, 21: ♑ 29.7, 29.8, 29.9 · ♇ 1, 11, 21: ♐ 5.5R, 5.3, 5.1

V

	1	2	3	4	5	6	7	8	9	10	11	12	13	14	15	16	17	18	19	20	21	22	23	24	25	26	27	28	29	30	31
☉	♉ 10.7	11.6	12.6	13.6	14.5	15.5	16.5	17.5	18.4	19.4	20.4	21.3	22.3	23.3	24.2	25.2	26.1	27.1	28.1	29	30	♊ 1	1.9	2.9	3.8	4.8	5.8	6.7	7.7	8.6	9.6
☽	♒ 22.4	♓ 6.6	21	♈ 5.4	19.8	♉ 4.1	18.2	♊ 2.1	15.6	28.8	♋ 11.6	24.1	♌ 6.3	18.3	♍ 0.1	11.9	23.8	♎ 5.8	18	♏ 0.4	13.2	26.2	♐ 9.6	23.2	♑ 7	21	♒ 5.1	19.2	♓ 3.3	17.5	♈ 1.6
☿	♉ 1.7R	1.2	0.7	0.3	0	♈ 29.8	29.6	29.5	29.5D	29.5	29.7	29.9	♉ 0.2	0.5	1	1.5	2	2.7	3.4	4.1	5	5.8	6.8	7.8	8.8	9.9	11	12.2	13.5	14.7	16.1
♀	♉ 18	19.3	20.5	21.7	23	24.2	25.4	26.7	27.9	29.1	♊ 0.4	1.6	2.8	4	5.3	6.5	7.7	9	10.2	11.4	12.6	13.9	15.1	16.3	17.5	18.8	20	21.2	22.5	23.7	24.9
♂	♍ 16.8	16.8	16.9	17	17	17.1	17.2	17.4	17.5	17.6	17.8	17.9	18.1	18.3	18.4	18.6	18.8	19.1	19.3	19.5	19.8	20	20.3	20.5	20.8	21.1	21.4	21.7	22	22.3	22.6

♃ 1, 6, 11, 16, 21, 26, 31: ♒ 19.5, 20.1, 20.5, 21, 21.3, 21.6, 21.8 · ♄ 1, 6, 11, 16, 21, 26, 31: ♈ 14.1, 14.6, 15.2, 15.7, 16.3, 16.8, 17.2 · ♅ 1, 11, 21, 31: ♒ 8.6, 8.7, 8.7R, 8.5 · ♆ 1, 11, 21, 31: ♑ 30, 29.9R, 29.9, 29.7 · ♇ 1, 11, 21, 31: ♐ 4.9R, 4.6, 4.4, 4.1

VI

	1	2	3	4	5	6	7	8	9	10	11	12	13	14	15	16	17	18	19	20	21	22	23	24	25	26	27	28	29	30	31
☉	♊ 10.6	11.5	12.5	13.4	14.4	15.3	16.3	17.3	18.2	19.2	20.1	21.1	22	23	23.9	24.9	25.9	26.8	27.8	28.7	29.7	♋ 0.6	1.6	2.5	3.5	4.4	5.4	6.4	7.3	8.3	
☽	♈ 15.6	29.6	♉ 13.5	27.2	♊ 10.7	24	♋ 7	19.7	♌ 2.1	14.2	26.2	♍ 8	19.8	♎ 1.7	13.7	25.9	♏ 8.5	21.4	♐ 4.7	18.3	♑ 2.3	16.6	♒ 1	15.5	29.9	♓ 14.2	28.4	♈ 12.5	26.3	♉ 10	
☿	♉ 17.5	18.9	20.3	21.9	23.4	25	26.6	28.3	♊ 0.1	1.8	3.6	5.5	7.4	9.3	11.3	13.3	15.3	17.4	19.5	21.6	23.8	26	28.1	♋ 0.3	2.5	4.7	6.9	9.1	11.2	13.4	
♀	♊ 26.1	27.4	28.6	29.8	♋ 1	2.2	3.5	4.7	5.9	7.1	8.4	9.6	10.8	12	13.2	14.5	15.7	16.9	18.1	19.3	20.6	21.8	23	24.2	25.4	26.6	27.9	29.1	♌ 0.3	1.5	
♂	♍ 22.9	23.3	23.6	24	24.3	24.7	25	25.4	25.8	26.2	26.5	26.9	27.3	27.7	28.2	28.6	29	29.4	29.8	♎ 0.3	0.7	1.2	1.6	2.1	2.5	3	3.5	3.9	4.4	4.9	

♃ 1, 6, 11, 16, 21, 26: ♒ 21.8, 21.9, 21.9R, 21.9, 21.7, 21.5 · ♄ 1, 6, 11, 16, 21, 26: ♈ 17.3, 17.8, 18.2, 18.6, 18.9, 19.2 · ♅ 1, 11, 21: ♒ 8.5R, 8.3, 8.1 · ♆ 1, 11, 21: ♑ 29.7R, 29.6, 29.3 · ♇ 1, 11, 21: ♐ 4.1R, 3.8, 3.6

VII

	1	2	3	4	5	6	7	8	9	10	11	12	13	14	15	16	17	18	19	20	21	22	23	24	25	26	27	28	29	30	31
☉	♋ 9.2	10.2	11.1	12.1	13	14	14.9	15.9	16.8	17.8	18.7	19.7	20.7	21.6	22.6	23.5	24.5	25.4	26.4	27.3	28.3	29.2	♌ 0.2	1.2	2.1	3.1	4	5	5.9	6.9	7.8
☽	♉ 23.5	♊ 6.9	20	♋ 2.9	15.6	28.1	♌ 10.3	22.4	♍ 4.3	16.1	27.9	♎ 9.7	21.7	♏ 3.9	16.5	29.4	♐ 12.8	26.6	♑ 10.8	25.4	♒ 10.2	25	♓ 9.9	24.5	♈ 8.9	23.1	♉ 6.9	20.5	♊ 3.8	16.8	29.7
☿	♋ 15.5	17.6	19.7	21.7	23.7	25.7	27.7	29.6	♌ 1.5	3.3	5.2	7	8.7	10.5	12.2	13.8	15.5	17.1	18.6	20.2	21.7	23.1	24.6	26	27.3	28.7	30	♍ 1.2	2.5	3.6	4.8
♀	♌ 2.7	3.9	5.1	6.4	7.6	8.8	10	11.2	12.4	13.6	14.8	16.1	17.3	18.5	19.7	20.9	22.1	23.3	24.5	25.7	26.9	28.1	29.3	♍ 0.6	1.8	3	4.2	5.4	6.6	7.8	9
♂	♎ 5.4	5.8	6.3	6.8	7.3	7.8	8.3	8.8	9.4	9.9	10.4	10.9	11.4	12	12.5	13	13.6	14.1	14.7	15.2	15.8	16.3	16.9	17.4	18	18.6	19.1	19.7	20.3	20.8	21.4

♃ 1, 6, 11, 16, 21, 26, 31: ♒ 21.2R, 20.9, 20.5, 20, 19.4, 18.8, 18.2 · ♄ 1, 6, 11, 16, 21, 26, 31: ♈ 19.5, 19.8, 20, 20.1, 20.2, 20.3, 20.4 · ♅ 1, 11, 21, 31: ♒ 7.8R, 7.4, 7, 6.6 · ♆ 1, 11, 21, 31: ♑ 29.1R, 28.8, 28.6, 28.3 · ♇ 1, 11, 21, 31: ♐ 3.3R, 3.1, 3, 2.9

VIII

	1	2	3	4	5	6	7	8	9	10	11	12	13	14	15	16	17	18	19	20	21	22	23	24	25	26	27	28	29	30	31
☉	♌ 8.8	9.8	10.7	11.7	12.6	13.6	14.5	15.5	16.5	17.4	18.4	19.3	20.3	21.3	22.2	23.2	24.1	25.1	26.1	27	28	29	29.9	♍ 0.9	1.8	2.8	3.8	4.7	5.7	6.7	7.6
☽	♋ 12.3	24.7	♌ 6.9	18.9	♍ 0.9	12.7	24.5	♎ 6.2	18.1	♏ 0.1	12.3	24.8	♐ 7.7	21	♑ 4.8	19.1	♒ 3.7	18.6	♓ 3.8	18.9	♈ 3.9	18.6	♉ 3	17	♊ 0.6	13.8	26.7	♋ 9.3	21.7	♌ 3.9	15.9
☿	♍ 5.9	7	8	9	9.9	10.8	11.6	12.3	13	13.7	14.3	14.8	15.2	15.6	15.9	16.1	16.2	16.2R	16.2	16	15.8	15.4	15	14.4	13.8	13.1	12.3	11.5	10.6	9.7	8.7
♀	♍ 10.2	11.4	12.6	13.8	15	16.2	17.4	18.6	19.8	20.9	22.1	23.3	24.5	25.7	26.9	28.1	29.3	♎ 0.5	1.7	2.9	4	5.2	6.4	7.6	8.8	10	11.1	12.3	13.5	14.7	15.9
♂	♎ 22	22.6	23.2	23.8	24.4	24.9	25.5	26.1	26.7	27.3	27.9	28.6	29.2	29.8	♏ 0.4	1	1.6	2.2	2.9	3.5	4.1	4.8	5.4	6	6.7	7.3	7.9	8.6	9.2	9.9	10.5

♃ 1, 6, 11, 16, 21, 26, 31: ♒ 18.1R, 17.5, 16.8, 16.2, 15.5, 14.9, 14.3 · ♄ 1, 6, 11, 16, 21, 26, 31: ♈ 20.4, 20.3R, 20.3, 20.2, 20, 19.9, 19.6 · ♅ 1, 11, 21, 31: ♒ 6.6R, 6.2, 5.8, 5.5 · ♆ 1, 11, 21, 31: ♑ 28.3R, 28, 27.8, 27.6 · ♇ 1, 11, 21, 31: ♐ 2.9R, 2.9, 2.9D, 2.9

IX

	1	2	3	4	5	6	7	8	9	10	11	12	13	14	15	16	17	18	19	20	21	22	23	24	25	26	27	28	29	30	31
☉	♍ 8.6	9.6	10.5	11.5	12.5	13.5	14.4	15.4	16.4	17.3	18.3	19.3	20.3	21.2	22.2	23.2	24.2	25.1	26.1	27.1	28.1	29	♎ 0	1	2	3	3.9	4.9	5.9	6.9	
☽	♌ 27.8	♍ 9.6	21.4	♎ 3.2	15	26.9	♏ 9	21.2	♐ 3.7	16.6	29.8	♑ 13.4	27.5	♒ 12	26.9	♓ 12	27.2	♈ 12.4	27.3	♉ 11.9	26.1	♊ 9.9	23.2	♋ 6.1	18.6	♌ 0.9	12.9	24.8	♍ 6.6	18.4	
☿	♍ 7.8R	6.9	6	5.2	4.5	3.9	3.4	3	2.8	2.7	2.8D	3	3.4	3.9	4.5	5.3	6.3	7.3	8.5	9.8	11.1	12.6	14.1	15.7	17.3	19	20.7	22.5	24.2	26	
♀	♎ 17	18.2	19.4	20.6	21.7	22.9	24.1	25.2	26.4	27.6	28.7	29.9	♏ 1.1	2.2	3.4	4.5	5.7	6.9	8	9.2	10.3	11.5	12.6	13.8	14.9	16	17.2	18.3	19.5	20.6	
♂	♏ 11.2	11.8	12.5	13.1	13.8	14.4	15.1	15.8	16.4	17.1	17.8	18.4	19.1	19.8	20.4	21.1	21.8	22.5	23.2	23.8	24.5	25.2	25.9	26.6	27.3	28	28.7	29.4	♐ 0.1	0.8	

♃ 1, 6, 11, 16, 21, 26: ♒ 14.2R, 13.7, 13.3, 12.9, 12.6, 12.3 · ♄ 1, 6, 11, 16, 21, 26: ♈ 19.6R, 19.3, 19, 18.7, 18.4, 18 · ♅ 1, 11, 21: ♒ 5.5R, 5.2, 5 · ♆ 1, 11, 21: ♑ 27.6R, 27.4, 27.3 · ♇ 1, 11, 21: ♐ 2.9, 3.1, 3.3

X

	1	2	3	4	5	6	7	8	9	10	11	12	13	14	15	16	17	18	19	20	21	22	23	24	25	26	27	28	29	30	31
☉	♎ 7.9	8.8	9.8	10.8	11.8	12.8	13.8	14.8	15.7	16.7	17.7	18.7	19.7	20.7	21.7	22.7	23.7	24.7	25.6	26.6	27.6	28.6	29.6	♏ 0.6	1.6	2.6	3.6	4.6	5.6	6.6	7.6
☽	♎ 0.2	12.1	24	♏ 6.1	18.3	♐ 0.7	13.3	26.1	♑ 9.3	22.8	♒ 6.7	20.9	♓ 5.5	20.3	♈ 5.4	20.4	♉ 5.4	20.1	♊ 4.5	18.4	♋ 1.8	14.8	27.3	♌ 9.6	21.6	♍ 3.4	15.2	27	♎ 8.8	20.8	♏ 2.9
☿	♍ 27.8	29.6	♎ 1.4	3.2	5	6.8	8.6	10.3	12.1	13.9	15.6	17.3	19.1	20.8	22.5	24.2	25.9	27.5	29.2	♏ 0.8	2.5	4.1	5.7	7.3	8.9	10.5	12.1	13.6	15.2	16.8	18.3
♀	♏ 21.7	22.9	24	25.1	26.3	27.4	28.5	29.6	♐ 0.7	1.8	3	4.1	5.2	6.3	7.4	8.5	9.6	10.7	11.8	12.8	13.9	15	16.1	17.1	18.2	19.3	20.3	21.4	22.4	23.5	24.5
♂	♐ 1.5	2.2	2.9	3.6	4.3	5	5.7	6.4	7.1	7.8	8.5	9.3	10	10.7	11.4	12.1	12.9	13.6	14.3	15	15.8	16.5	17.2	18	18.7	19.4	20.2	20.9	21.6	22.4	23.1

♃ 1, 6, 11, 16, 21, 26, 31: ♒ 12.2R, 12.1, 12.1D, 12.2, 12.4, 12.6, 12.9 · ♄ 1, 6, 11, 16, 21, 26, 31: ♈ 17.6R, 17.2, 16.8, 16.5, 16.1, 15.7, 15.3 · ♅ 1, 11, 21, 31: ♒ 4.8R, 4.7, 4.8D, 4.9 · ♆ 1, 11, 21, 31: ♑ 27.2R, 27.2D, 27.2, 27.3 · ♇ 1, 11, 21, 31: ♐ 3.5, 3.8, 4.1, 4.4

XI

	1	2	3	4	5	6	7	8	9	10	11	12	13	14	15	16	17	18	19	20	21	22	23	24	25	26	27	28	29	30	31
☉	♏ 8.6	9.6	10.6	11.6	12.6	13.6	14.6	15.6	16.6	17.6	18.6	19.6	20.7	21.7	22.7	23.7	24.7	25.7	26.7	27.7	28.7	29.7	♐ 0.7	1.7	2.8	3.8	4.8	5.8	6.8	7.8	
☽	♏ 15.2	27.7	♐ 10.3	23.2	♑ 6.3	19.6	♒ 3.1	16.8	♓ 0.8	15.1	29.5	♈ 14.2	28.9	♉ 13.6	28.1	♊ 12.4	26.3	♋ 9.7	22.8	♌ 5.4	17.7	29.7	♍ 11.6	23.4	♎ 5.2	17.1	29.1	♏ 11.4	23.9	♐ 6.7	
☿	♏ 19.8	21.4	22.9	24.4	25.9	27.4	28.9	♐ 0.4	1.9	3.4	4.8	6.3	7.7	9.1	10.6	12	13.4	14.8	16.1	17.5	18.8	20.1	21.4	22.7	23.9	25.1	26.2	27.3	28.3	29.3	
♀	♐ 25.6	26.6	27.6	28.6	29.6	♑ 0.6	1.6	2.6	3.6	4.6	5.6	6.5	7.5	8.4	9.4	10.3	11.2	12.2	13.1	14	14.8	15.7	16.6	17.4	18.2	19.1	19.9	20.7	21.5	22.2	
♂	♐ 23.9	24.6	25.3	26.1	26.8	27.6	28.3	29.1	29.8	♑ 0.6	1.3	2.1	2.8	3.6	4.4	5.1	5.9	6.6	7.4	8.2	8.9	9.7	10.4	11.2	12	12.7	13.5	14.3	15.1	15.8	

♃ 1, 6, 11, 16, 21, 26: ♒ 13, 13.4, 13.9, 14.5, 15.1, 15.8 · ♄ 1, 6, 11, 16, 21, 26: ♈ 15.3R, 14.9, 14.6, 14.4, 14.1, 13.9 · ♅ 1, 11, 21: ♒ 4.9, 5.1, 5.3 · ♆ 1, 11, 21: ♑ 27.3, 27.5, 27.7 · ♇ 1, 11, 21: ♐ 4.5, 4.8, 5.2

XII

	1	2	3	4	5	6	7	8	9	10	11	12	13	14	15	16	17	18	19	20	21	22	23	24	25	26	27	28	29	30	31
☉	♐ 8.8	9.8	10.9	11.9	12.9	13.9	14.9	15.9	17	18	19	20	21	22	23.1	24.1	25.1	26.1	27.1	28.1	29.2	♑ 0.2	1.2	2.2	3.2	4.3	5.3	6.3	7.3	8.3	9.3
☽	♐ 19.7	♑ 3	16.4	♒ 0	13.7	27.6	♓ 11.6	25.6	♈ 9.8	24	♉ 8.3	22.6	♊ 6.7	20.6	♋ 4.3	17.6	♌ 0.5	13.2	25.4	♍ 7.5	19.4	♎ 1.2	13	24.9	♏ 7	19.4	♐ 2.1	15.1	28.4	♑ 12	25.9
☿	♑ 0.2	1	1.7	2.3	2.8	3.1	3.3	3.4R	3.2	2.9	2.4	1.7	0.8	♐ 29.7	28.5	27.2	25.9	24.5	23.1	21.9	20.7	19.7	18.8	18.1	17.6	17.2	17.1	17.1D	17.2	17.5	17.9
♀	♑ 23	23.7	24.4	25.1	25.8	26.4	27.1	27.7	28.3	28.8	29.4	29.9	♒ 0.4	0.9	1.3	1.7	2.1	2.4	2.7	3	3.3	3.5	3.6	3.8	3.9	3.9	3.9R	3.9	3.9	3.7	3.6
♂	♑ 16.6	17.4	18.1	18.9	19.7	20.5	21.2	22	22.8	23.6	24.3	25.1	25.9	26.7	27.5	28.2	29	29.8	♒ 0.6	1.4	2.1	2.9	3.7	4.5	5.3	6.1	6.8	7.6	8.4	9.2	10

♃ 1, 6, 11, 16, 21, 26, 31: ♒ 16.5, 17.4, 18.2, 19.1, 20, 21, 22 · ♄ 1, 6, 11, 16, 21, 26, 31: ♈ 13.8R, 13.6, 13.6, 13.5, 13.6D, 13.6, 13.7 · ♅ 1, 11, 21, 31: ♒ 5.7, 6.1, 6.6, 7.1 · ♆ 1, 11, 21, 31: ♑ 27.9, 28.2, 28.6, 28.9 · ♇ 1, 11, 21, 31: ♐ 5.6, 6, 6.4, 6.8

1998

I

	1	2	3	4	5	6	7	8	9	10	11	12	13	14	15	16	17	18	19	20	21	22	23	24	25	26	27	28	29	30	31
☉	♑ 10.4	11.4	12.4	13.4	14.4	15.5	16.5	17.5	18.5	19.5	20.6	21.6	22.6	23.6	24.6	25.7	26.7	27.7	28.7	29.7	♒ 0.7	1.8	2.8	3.8	4.8	5.8	6.8	7.9	8.9	9.9	10.9
☽	♒ 10	24.1	♓ 8.3	22.5	♈ 6.6	20.7	♉ 4.7	18.6	♊ 2.4	16.1	29.6	♋ 12.8	25.8	♌ 8.6	21	♍ 3.3	15.3	27.2	♎ 9	20.8	♏ 2.7	14.8	27.2	♐ 9.9	22.9	♑ 6.4	20.3	♒ 4.5	18.9	♓ 3.6	18.2
☿	♐ 18.5	19.1	19.8	20.7	21.5	22.5	23.5	24.5	25.6	26.8	28	29.2	♑ 0.4	1.7	3	4.3	5.6	7	8.4	9.7	11.1	12.6	14	15.4	16.9	18.4	19.9	21.4	22.9	24.4	25.9
♀	♒ 3.4R	3.2	2.9	2.6	2.2	1.8	1.4	0.9	0.5	♑ 29.9	29.4	28.8	28.2	27.6	27	26.4	25.8	25.2	24.6	24	23.4	22.9	22.3	21.8	21.3	20.9	20.5	20.1	19.7	19.4	19.2
♂	♒ 10.8	11.6	12.3	13.1	13.9	14.7	15.5	16.3	17.1	17.9	18.7	19.4	20.2	21	21.8	22.6	23.4	24.2	25	25.8	26.5	27.3	28.1	28.9	29.7	♓ 0.5	1.3	2.1	2.9	3.6	4.4

♃ 1, 6, 11, 16, 21, 26, 31: ♒ 22.3, 23.3, 24.4, 25.5, 26.6, 27.8, 29 · ♄ 1, 6, 11, 16, 21, 26, 31: ♈ 13.8, 13.9, 14.1, 14.4, 14.7, 15, 15.4 · ♅ 1, 11, 21, 31: ♒ 7.1, 7.7, 8.3, 8.8 · ♆ 1, 11, 21, 31: ♑ 29, 29.3, 29.7, ♒ 0.1 · ♇ 1, 11, 21, 31: ♐ 6.8, 7.1, 7.4, 7.6

II

	1	2	3	4	5	6	7	8	9	10	11	12	13	14	15	16	17	18	19	20	21	22	23	24	25	26	27	28	29	30	31
☉	♒ 11.9	12.9	14	15	16	17	18	19	20	21	22.1	23.1	24.1	25.1	26.1	27.1	28.1	29.1	♓ 0.1	1.1	2.2	3.2	4.2	5.2	6.2	7.2	8.2	9.2			
☽	♈ 2.8	17.3	♉ 1.5	15.5	29.3	♊ 12.9	26.2	♋ 9.2	22.1	♌ 4.7	17.2	29.4	♍ 11.5	23.4	♎ 5.3	17.1	28.9	♏ 10.8	22.9	♐ 5.2	17.8	♑ 0.8	14.2	28.1	♒ 12.4	27.1	♓ 12	27			
☿	♑ 27.5	29	♒ 0.6	2.2	3.8	5.4	7	8.6	10.3	11.9	13.6	15.3	17	18.7	20.4	22.1	23.9	25.7	27.4	29.2	♓ 1	2.9	4.7	6.6	8.4	10.3	12.2	14.1			
♀	♑ 19.0R	18.8	18.6	18.5	18.5	18.5D	18.5	18.6	18.7	18.8	19	19.2	19.5	19.7	20.1	20.4	20.8	21.2	21.6	22.1	22.6	23.1	23.7	24.2	24.8	25.4	26.1	26.7			
♂	♓ 5.2	6	6.8	7.6	8.4	9.2	9.9	10.7	11.5	12.3	13.1	13.9	14.7	15.4	16.2	17	17.8	18.6	19.4	20.1	20.9	21.7	22.5	23.3	24	24.8	25.6	26.4			

♃ 1, 6, 11, 16, 21, 26: ♒ 29.2, ♓ 0.4, 1.6, 2.8, 4, 5.2 · ♄ 1, 6, 11, 16, 21, 26: ♈ 15.4, 15.9, 16.3, 16.8, 17.3, 17.8 · ♅ 1, 11, 21: ♒ 8.9, 9.5, 10 · ♆ 1, 11, 21: ♒ 0.1, 0.5, 0.8 · ♇ 1, 11, 21: ♐ 7.7, 7.9, 8

III

	1	2	3	4	5	6	7	8	9	10	11	12	13	14	15	16	17	18	19	20	21	22	23	24	25	26	27	28	29	30	31
☉	♓ 10.2	11.2	12.2	13.2	14.2	15.2	16.2	17.2	18.2	19.2	20.2	21.2	22.2	23.2	24.2	25.2	26.2	27.2	28.2	29.2	♈ 0.2	1.2	2.2	3.2	4.1	5.1	6.1	7.1	8.1	9.1	10.1
☽	♈ 12.1	26.9	♉ 11.5	25.8	♊ 9.6	23.1	♋ 6.3	19.1	♌ 1.7	14	26.2	♍ 8.2	20.1	♎ 2	13.8	25.6	♏ 7.5	19.4	♐ 1.5	13.8	26.4	♑ 9.3	22.6	♒ 6.3	20.5	♓ 5.1	20	♈ 5.2	20.4	♉ 5.6	20.5
☿	♓ 16	17.9	19.9	21.8	23.7	25.6	27.5	29.4	♈ 1.2	3	4.8	6.5	8.2	9.8	11.3	12.8	14.1	15.4	16.5	17.6	18.5	19.3	20	20.6	21	21.3	21.5	21.5R	21.4	21.2	20.9
♀	♑ 27.4	28.1	28.8	29.5	♒ 0.2	1	1.8	2.6	3.4	4.2	5	5.8	6.7	7.6	8.4	9.3	10.2	11.1	12	13	13.9	14.8	15.8	16.7	17.7	18.7	19.6	20.6	21.6	22.6	23.6
♂	♓ 27.1	27.9	28.7	29.5	♈ 0.3	1	1.8	2.6	3.4	4.1	4.9	5.7	6.4	7.2	8	8.7	9.5	10.3	11	11.8	12.6	13.3	14.1	14.9	15.6	16.4	17.2	17.9	18.7	19.4	20.2

♃ 1, 6, 11, 16, 21, 26, 31: ♓ 5.9, 7.1, 8.3, 9.5, 10.7, 11.8, 13 · ♄ 1, 6, 11, 16, 21, 26, 31: ♈ 18.1, 18.7, 19.2, 19.8, 20.4, 21, 21.7 · ♅ 1, 11, 21, 31: ♒ 10.5, 11, 11.4, 11.8 · ♆ 1, 11, 21, 31: ♒ 1.1, 1.4, 1.6, 1.8 · ♇ 1, 11, 21, 31: ♐ 8.1, 8.1, 8.1R, 8

IV

	1	2	3	4	5	6	7	8	9	10	11	12	13	14	15	16	17	18	19	20	21	22	23	24	25	26	27	28	29	30	31
☉	♈ 11.1	12.1	13	14	15	16	17	18	19	19.9	20.9	21.9	22.9	23.9	24.8	25.8	26.8	27.8	28.7	29.7	♉ 0.7	1.7	2.7	3.6	4.6	5.6	6.5	7.5	8.5	9.5	
☽	♊ 5	19.1	♋ 2.7	15.9	28.6	♌ 11.1	23.3	♍ 5.3	17.1	29	♎ 10.8	22.6	♏ 4.5	16.5	28.5	♐ 10.8	23.2	♑ 5.8	18.6	♒ 1.8	15.4	29.3	♓ 13.7	28.4	♈ 13.4	28.6	♉ 13.8	28.8	♊ 13.5	27.7	
☿	♈ 20.5R	20	19.4	18.7	18	17.2	16.4	15.6	14.9	14.1	13.4	12.7	12	11.5	11	10.6	10.3	10	9.9	9.8	9.8D	9.9	10.1	10.4	10.7	11.1	11.6	12.2	12.8	13.5	
♀	♒ 24.6	25.7	26.7	27.7	28.7	29.8	♓ 0.8	1.8	2.9	4	5	6.1	7.1	8.2	9.3	10.4	11.4	12.5	13.6	14.7	15.8	16.9	18	19.1	20.2	21.3	22.4	23.5	24.6	25.7	
♂	♈ 20.9	21.7	22.5	23.2	24	24.7	25.5	26.2	27	27.7	28.5	29.2	30	♉ 0.7	1.5	2.2	3	3.7	4.4	5.2	5.9	6.7	7.4	8.1	8.9	9.6	10.4	11.1	11.8	12.6	

♃ 1, 6, 11, 16, 21, 26: ♓ 13.2, 14.3, 15.4, 16.5, 17.5, 18.6 · ♄ 1, 6, 11, 16, 21, 26: ♈ 21.8, 22.4, 23, 23.7, 24.3, 24.9 · ♅ 1, 11, 21: ♒ 11.9, 12.2, 12.5 · ♆ 1, 11, 21: ♒ 1.9, 2, 2.1 · ♇ 1, 11, 21: ♐ 8.0R, 7.8, 7.6

V

	1	2	3	4	5	6	7	8	9	10	11	12	13	14	15	16	17	18	19	20	21	22	23	24	25	26	27	28	29	30	31
☉	♉ 10.4	11.4	12.4	13.3	14.3	15.3	16.3	17.2	18.2	19.2	20.1	21.1	22.1	23	24	24.9	25.9	26.9	27.8	28.8	29.8	♊ 0.7	1.7	2.6	3.6	4.6	5.5	6.5	7.4	8.4	9.4
☽	♋ 11.4	24.7	♌ 7.5	20	♍ 2.1	14.1	25.9	♎ 7.7	19.5	♏ 1.4	13.4	25.5	♐ 7.8	20.2	♑ 2.8	15.6	28.6	♒ 11.9	25.4	♓ 9.2	23.3	♈ 7.8	22.5	♉ 7.4	22.3	♊ 7.1	21.7	♋ 5.9	19.6	♌ 2.9	15.8
☿	♈ 14.2	15	15.9	16.8	17.7	18.8	19.8	20.9	22.1	23.3	24.5	25.8	27.1	28.5	29.9	♉ 1.3	2.8	4.3	5.9	7.4	9.1	10.7	12.4	14.2	15.9	17.7	19.6	21.5	23.4	25.3	27.3
♀	♓ 26.9	28	29.1	♈ 0.2	1.4	2.5	3.6	4.7	5.9	7	8.2	9.3	10.4	11.6	12.7	13.9	15	16.2	17.3	18.5	19.6	20.8	21.9	23.1	24.2	25.4	26.5	27.7	28.9	♉ 0	1.2
♂	♉ 13.3	14	14.8	15.5	16.2	16.9	17.7	18.4	19.1	19.8	20.6	21.3	22	22.7	23.5	24.2	24.9	25.6	26.3	27	27.8	28.5	29.2	29.9	♊ 0.6	1.3	2	2.7	3.4	4.2	4.9

♃ 1, 6, 11, 16, 21, 26, 31: ♓ 19.5, 20.5, 21.4, 22.3, 23.1, 23.8, 24.6 · ♄ 1, 6, 11, 16, 21, 26, 31: ♈ 25.6, 26.2, 26.8, 27.4, 28, 28.5, 29.1 · ♅ 1, 11, 21, 31: ♒ 12.6, 12.7, 12.7R, 12.7 · ♆ 1, 11, 21, 31: ♒ 2.2, 2.2R, 2.1, 2 · ♇ 1, 11, 21, 31: ♐ 7.4R, 7.2, 6.9, 6.6

VI

	1	2	3	4	5	6	7	8	9	10	11	12	13	14	15	16	17	18	19	20	21	22	23	24	25	26	27	28	29	30	31
☉	♊ 10.3	11.3	12.2	13.2	14.2	15.1	16.1	17	18	18.9	19.9	20.9	21.8	22.8	23.7	24.7	25.6	26.6	27.5	28.5	29.4	♋ 0.4	1.4	2.3	3.3	4.2	5.2	6.1	7.1	8	
☽	♌ 28.3	♍ 10.5	22.4	♎ 4.3	16.1	28	♏ 9.9	22	♐ 4.3	16.8	29.5	♑ 12.5	25.6	♒ 8.8	22.3	♓ 6	19.8	♈ 3.9	18.1	♉ 2.5	17	♊ 1.5	16	♋ 0.2	14.1	27.7	♌ 10.9	23.8	♍ 6.2	18.5	
☿	♉ 29.3	♊ 1.4	3.4	5.6	7.7	9.8	12	14.2	16.4	18.6	20.8	23	25.2	27.4	29.5	♋ 1.7	3.8	5.9	7.9	10	12	13.9	15.9	17.8	19.6	21.4	23.2	25	26.7	28.4	
♀	♉ 2.4	3.5	4.7	5.9	7	8.2	9.4	10.5	11.7	12.9	14.1	15.2	16.4	17.6	18.8	19.9	21.1	22.3	23.5	24.7	25.8	27	28.2	29.4	♊ 0.6	1.8	3	4.1	5.3	6.5	
♂	♊ 5.6	6.3	7	7.7	8.4	9.1	9.8	10.5	11.2	11.9	12.6	13.3	14	14.7	15.4	16.1	16.7	17.4	18.1	18.8	19.5	20.2	20.9	21.6	22.3	22.9	23.6	24.3	25	25.7	

♃ 1, 6, 11, 16, 21, 26: ♓ 24.7, 25.3, 25.9, 26.5, 26.9, 27.3 · ♄ 1, 6, 11, 16, 21, 26: ♈ 29.2, 29.7, ♉ 0.2, 0.7, 1.1, 1.5 · ♅ 1, 11, 21: ♒ 12.7R, 12.5, 12.3 · ♆ 1, 11, 21: ♒ 2.0R, 1.8, 1.6 · ♇ 1, 11, 21: ♐ 6.6R, 6.3, 6.1

VII

	1	2	3	4	5	6	7	8	9	10	11	12	13	14	15	16	17	18	19	20	21	22	23	24	25	26	27	28	29	30	31
☉	♋ 9	9.9	10.9	11.8	12.8	13.8	14.7	15.7	16.6	17.6	18.5	19.5	20.4	21.4	22.3	23.3	24.2	25.2	26.2	27.1	28.1	29	30	♌ 0.9	1.9	2.8	3.8	4.7	5.7	6.7	7.6
☽	♎ 0.5	12.3	24.2	♏ 6.1	18.1	♐ 0.3	12.7	25.5	♑ 8.4	21.7	♒ 5.1	18.8	♓ 2.7	16.6	♈ 0.7	14.9	29.1	♉ 13.3	27.5	♊ 11.6	25.5	♋ 9.3	22.9	♌ 6.1	19.1	♍ 1.8	14.2	26.4	♎ 8.4	20.2	♏ 2.1
☿	♌ 0	1.6	3.2	4.7	6.2	7.7	9.1	10.4	11.8	13.1	14.3	15.5	16.7	17.8	18.9	19.9	20.9	21.9	22.7	23.6	24.3	25	25.7	26.3	26.8	27.2	27.6	27.9	28.1	28.2	28.3
♀	♊ 7.7	8.9	10.1	11.3	12.5	13.7	14.9	16.1	17.3	18.4	19.6	20.8	22	23.2	24.4	25.6	26.8	28	29.2	♋ 0.4	1.7	2.9	4.1	5.3	6.5	7.7	8.9	10.1	11.3	12.5	13.7
♂	♊ 26.4	27	27.7	28.4	29.1	29.8	♋ 0.4	1.1	1.8	2.5	3.1	3.8	4.5	5.1	5.8	6.5	7.2	7.8	8.5	9.2	9.8	10.5	11.2	11.8	12.5	13.1	13.8	14.5	15.1	15.8	16.5

♃ 1, 6, 11, 16, 21, 26, 31: ♓ 27.6, 27.8, 28, 28.1, 28.1R, 28, 27.8 · ♄ 1, 6, 11, 16, 21, 26, 31: ♉ 1.9, 2.2, 2.5, 2.8, 3.1, 3.3, 3.4 · ♅ 1, 11, 21, 31: ♒ 12.0R, 11.7, 11.3, 10.9 · ♆ 1, 11, 21, 31: ♒ 1.4R, 1.1, 0.8, 0.6 · ♇ 1, 11, 21, 31: ♐ 5.9R, 5.7, 5.5, 5.4

VIII

	1	2	3	4	5	6	7	8	9	10	11	12	13	14	15	16	17	18	19	20	21	22	23	24	25	26	27	28	29	30	31
☉	♌ 8.6	9.5	10.5	11.4	12.4	13.4	14.3	15.3	16.2	17.2	18.1	19.1	20.1	21	22	22.9	23.9	24.9	25.8	26.8	27.8	28.7	29.7	♍ 0.6	1.6	2.6	3.5	4.5	5.5	6.4	7.4
☽	♏ 14	26	♐ 8.3	20.8	♑ 3.6	16.8	♒ 0.3	14.1	28.2	♓ 12.5	26.9	♈ 11.3	25.7	♉ 10.1	24.3	♊ 8.3	22.1	♋ 5.7	19	♌ 2.2	15.1	27.7	♍ 10.2	22.4	♎ 4.5	16.4	28.3	♏ 10.2	22	♐ 4.1	16.3
☿	♌ 28.2R	28.1	27.9	27.6	27.2	26.8	26.2	25.6	25	24.2	23.5	22.6	21.8	21	20.2	19.4	18.7	18	17.4	16.9	16.5	16.2	16	16.0D	16	16.2	16.6	17	17.7	18.4	19.2
♀	♋ 14.9	16.2	17.4	18.6	19.8	21	22.2	23.4	24.7	25.9	27.1	28.3	29.5	♌ 0.8	2	3.2	4.4	5.6	6.9	8.1	9.3	10.5	11.8	13	14.2	15.5	16.7	17.9	19.1	20.4	21.6
♂	♋ 17.1	17.8	18.4	19.1	19.7	20.4	21	21.7	22.4	23	23.7	24.3	25	25.6	26.3	26.9	27.6	28.2	28.8	29.5	♌ 0.1	0.8	1.4	2.1	2.7	3.4	4	4.6	5.3	5.9	6.5

♃ 1, 6, 11, 16, 21, 26, 31: ♓ 27.7R, 27.5, 27.1, 26.7, 26.3, 25.7, 25.1 · ♄ 1, 6, 11, 16, 21, 26, 31: ♉ 3.4, 3.6, 3.6, 3.6R, 3.6, 3.5, 3.4 · ♅ 1, 11, 21, 31: ♒ 10.9R, 10.5, 10.1, 9.7 · ♆ 1, 11, 21, 31: ♒ 0.6R, 0.3, 0, ♑ 29.8 · ♇ 1, 11, 21, 31: ♐ 5.4R, 5.3, 5.3D, 5.4

IX

	1	2	3	4	5	6	7	8	9	10	11	12	13	14	15	16	17	18	19	20	21	22	23	24	25	26	27	28	29	30	31
☉	♍ 8.4	9.3	10.3	11.3	12.2	13.2	14.2	15.2	16.1	17.1	18.1	19	20	21	22	22.9	23.9	24.9	25.9	26.8	27.8	28.8	29.8	♎ 0.8	1.7	2.7	3.7	4.7	5.7	6.6	
☽	♐ 28.7	♑ 11.5	24.7	♒ 8.3	22.4	♓ 6.7	21.4	♈ 6.3	21.2	♉ 6	20.6	♊ 4.9	18.9	♋ 2.6	16	29	♌ 11.8	24.4	♍ 6.7	18.9	♎ 1	13	24.9	♏ 6.7	18.6	♐ 0.4	12.4	24.6	♑ 7	19.7	
☿	♌ 20.2	21.3	22.5	23.8	25.2	26.7	28.3	29.9	♍ 1.6	3.3	5.1	6.9	8.7	10.6	12.4	14.3	16.2	18.1	20	21.8	23.7	25.6	27.4	29.2	♎ 1.1	2.9	4.7	6.4	8.2	9.9	
♀	♌ 22.8	24.1	25.3	26.5	27.8	29	♍ 0.2	1.5	2.7	4	5.2	6.4	7.7	8.9	10.2	11.4	12.6	13.9	15.1	16.4	17.6	18.8	20.1	21.3	22.6	23.8	25.1	26.3	27.6	28.8	
♂	♌ 7.2	7.8	8.5	9.1	9.7	10.4	11	11.6	12.3	12.9	13.5	14.2	14.8	15.4	16	16.7	17.3	17.9	18.6	19.2	19.8	20.4	21	21.7	22.3	22.9	23.5	24.1	24.8	25.4	

♃ 1, 6, 11, 16, 21, 26: ♓ 25.0R, 24.4, 23.7, 23.1, 22.4, 21.8 · ♄ 1, 6, 11, 16, 21, 26: ♉ 3.4R, 3.2, 3, 2.8, 2.5, 2.2 · ♅ 1, 11, 21: ♒ 9.7R, 9.4, 9.1 · ♆ 1, 11, 21: ♑ 29.8R, 29.6, 29.5 · ♇ 1, 11, 21: ♐ 5.4, 5.5, 5.7

X

	1	2	3	4	5	6	7	8	9	10	11	12	13	14	15	16	17	18	19	20	21	22	23	24	25	26	27	28	29	30	31
☉	♎ 7.6	8.6	9.6	10.6	11.6	12.5	13.5	14.5	15.5	16.5	17.5	18.5	19.5	20.5	21.4	22.4	23.4	24.4	25.4	26.4	27.4	28.4	29.4	♏ 0.4	1.4	2.4	3.4	4.4	5.4	6.4	7.4
☽	♒ 2.8	16.4	♓ 0.4	14.8	29.7	♈ 14.8	♉ 0	15.2	♊ 0.2	14.8	28.9	♋ 12.7	26	♌ 8.9	21.5	♍ 3.8	16	28	♎ 9.9	21.8	♏ 3.6	15.5	27.4	♐ 9.3	21.3	♑ 3.5	15.9	28.5	♒ 11.5	24.9	♓ 8.7
☿	♎ 11.7	13.4	15.1	16.8	18.5	20.1	21.8	23.4	25	26.7	28.2	29.8	♏ 1.4	3	4.5	6.1	7.6	9.1	10.6	12.1	13.6	15.1	16.5	18	19.4	20.8	22.3	23.7	25.1	26.4	27.8
♀	♎ 0.1	1.3	2.5	3.8	5	6.3	7.5	8.8	10	11.3	12.5	13.8	15	16.3	17.5	18.8	20	21.3	22.5	23.8	25.1	26.3	27.6	28.8	♏ 0.1	1.3	2.6	3.8	5.1	6.3	7.6
♂	♌ 26	26.6	27.2	27.9	28.5	29.1	29.7	♍ 0.3	0.9	1.5	2.1	2.7	3.4	4	4.6	5.2	5.8	6.4	7	7.6	8.2	8.8	9.4	10	10.6	11.2	11.8	12.4	13	13.6	14.2

♃ 1, 6, 11, 16, 21, 26, 31: ♓ 21.1R, 20.5, 20, 19.5, 19.1, 18.7, 18.5 · ♄ 1, 6, 11, 16, 21, 26, 31: ♉ 1.9R, 1.5, 1.2, 0.8, 0.4, ♈ 30, 29.6 · ♅ 1, 11, 21, 31: ♒ 8.9R, 8.8, 8.8D, 8.9 · ♆ 1, 11, 21, 31: ♑ 29.4R, 29.4, 29.4D, 29.5 · ♇ 1, 11, 21, 31: ♐ 5.9, 6.2, 6.5, 6.8

XI

	1	2	3	4	5	6	7	8	9	10	11	12	13	14	15	16	17	18	19	20	21	22	23	24	25	26	27	28	29	30	31
☉	♏ 8.4	9.4	10.4	11.4	12.4	13.4	14.4	15.4	16.4	17.4	18.4	19.4	20.4	21.4	22.4	23.4	24.4	25.4	26.5	27.5	28.5	29.5	♐ 0.5	1.5	2.5	3.5	4.5	5.5	6.6	7.6	
☽	♓ 23	♈ 7.8	22.9	♉ 8.2	23.5	♊ 8.7	23.5	♋ 7.9	21.8	♌ 5.2	18.1	♍ 0.7	13	25	♎ 7	18.8	♏ 0.6	12.5	24.4	♐ 6.4	18.5	♑ 0.6	12.9	25.4	♒ 8.1	21	♓ 4.3	18	♈ 2	16.5	
☿	♏ 29.1	♐ 0.4	1.8	3	4.3	5.5	6.7	7.9	9	10.1	11.2	12.2	13.1	14	14.8	15.5	16.2	16.7	17.1	17.4	17.5	17.5R	17.4	17	16.5	15.8	15	13.9	12.7	11.5	
♀	♏ 8.8	10.1	11.3	12.6	13.9	15.1	16.4	17.6	18.9	20.1	21.4	22.6	23.9	25.1	26.4	27.7	28.9	♐ 0.2	1.4	2.7	3.9	5.2	6.4	7.7	9	10.2	11.5	12.7	14	15.2	
♂	♍ 14.8	15.3	15.9	16.5	17.1	17.7	18.3	18.9	19.5	20	20.6	21.2	21.8	22.4	22.9	23.5	24.1	24.7	25.2	25.8	26.4	26.9	27.5	28.1	28.6	29.2	29.8	♎ 0.3	0.9	1.4	

♃ 1, 6, 11, 16, 21, 26: ♓ 18.4R, 18.3, 18.2, 18.2D, 18.3, 18.4 · ♄ 1, 6, 11, 16, 21, 26: ♈ 29.5R, 29.1, 28.7, 28.4, 28.1, 27.8 · ♅ 1, 11, 21: ♒ 8.9, 9, 9.3 · ♆ 1, 11, 21: ♑ 29.5, 29.7, 29.8 · ♇ 1, 11, 21: ♐ 6.8, 7.2, 7.6

XII

	1	2	3	4	5	6	7	8	9	10	11	12	13	14	15	16	17	18	19	20	21	22	23	24	25	26	27	28	29	30	31
☉	♐ 8.6	9.6	10.6	11.6	12.6	13.7	14.7	15.7	16.7	17.7	18.7	19.8	20.8	21.8	22.8	23.8	24.8	25.9	26.9	27.9	28.9	29.9	♑ 0.9	2	3	4	5	6	7.1	8.1	9.1
☽	♉ 1.3	16.4	♊ 1.6	16.7	♋ 1.5	16	♌ 0	13.6	26.6	♍ 9.2	21.6	♎ 3.6	15.6	27.4	♏ 9.2	21.1	♐ 3.1	15.2	27.5	♑ 9.9	22.4	♒ 5.2	18.1	♓ 1.2	14.6	28.2	♈ 12.1	26.3	♉ 10.8	25.5	♊ 10.2
☿	♐ 10.1R	8.7	7.4	6.1	4.9	3.9	3	2.3	1.8	1.5	1.3	1.4D	1.6	1.9	2.4	3	3.7	4.5	5.4	6.4	7.4	8.5	9.6	10.8	12	13.3	14.5	15.8	17.2	18.5	19.9
♀	♐ 16.5	17.7	19	20.3	21.5	22.8	24	25.3	26.5	27.8	29.1	♑ 0.3	1.6	2.8	4.1	5.3	6.6	7.8	9.1	10.3	11.6	12.9	14.1	15.4	16.6	17.9	19.1	20.4	21.6	22.9	24.1
♂	♎ 2	2.6	3.1	3.7	4.2	4.8	5.3	5.9	6.4	6.9	7.5	8	8.6	9.1	9.6	10.2	10.7	11.2	11.7	12.3	12.8	13.3	13.8	14.3	14.9	15.4	15.9	16.4	16.9	17.4	17.9

♃ 1, 6, 11, 16, 21, 26, 31: ♓ 18.7, 19, 19.4, 19.9, 20.5, 21.1, 21.8 · ♄ 1, 6, 11, 16, 21, 26, 31: ♈ 27.5R, 27.3, 27.1, 26.9, 26.8, 26.8, 26.8D · ♅ 1, 11, 21, 31: ♒ 9.6, 10, 10.4, 10.9 · ♆ 1, 11, 21, 31: ♒ 0.1, 0.4, 0.7, 1 · ♇ 1, 11, 21, 31: ♐ 8, 8.4, 8.7, 9.1

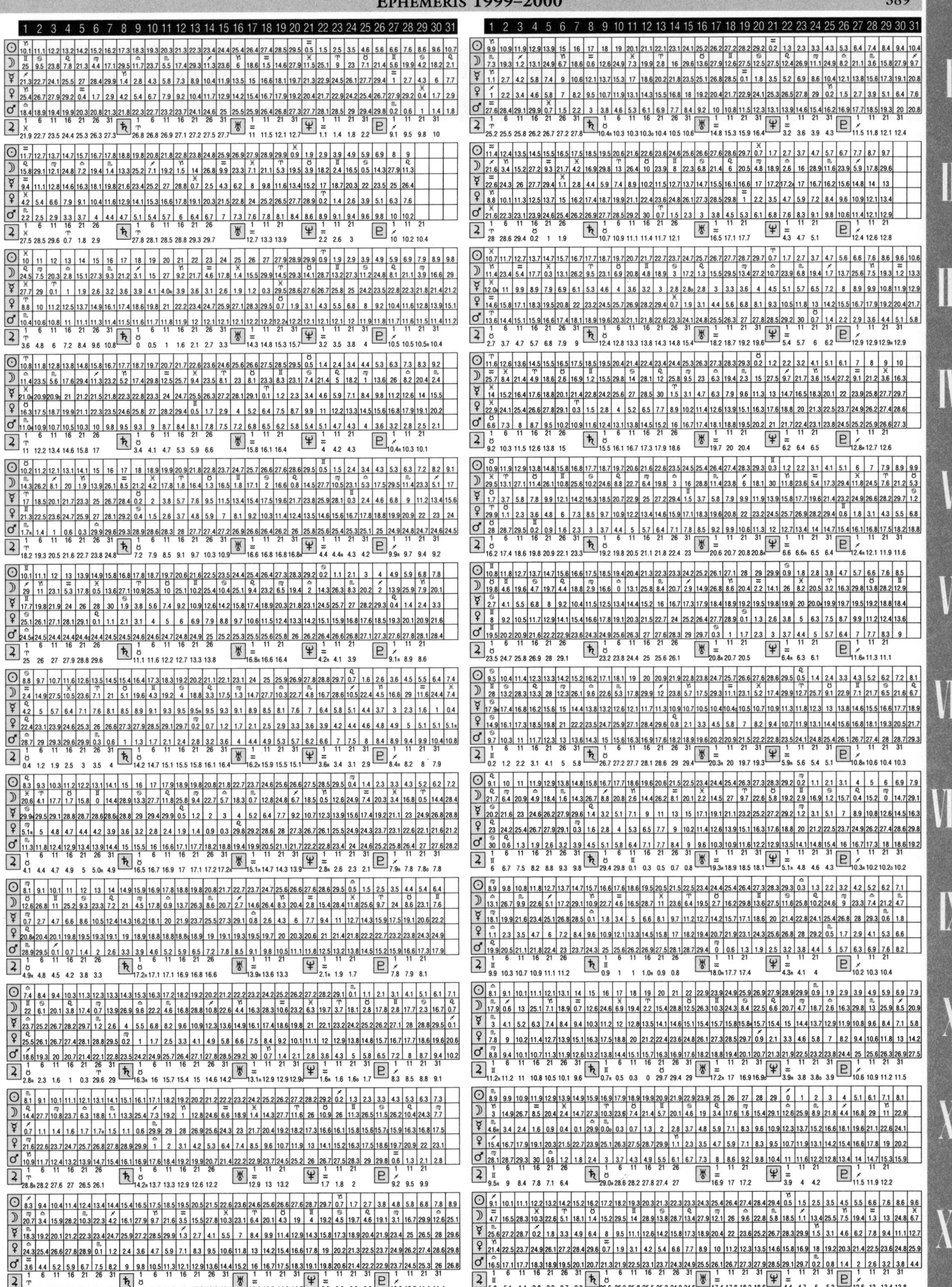

	I	II	III	IV	V	VI	VII	VIII	IX	X	XI	XII
1910	20 ♒ 21.59	19 ♓ 12.28	21 ♈ 12.03	20 ♉ 23.47	21 ♊ 23.31	22 ♋ 7.5	23 ♌ 18.44	24 ♍ 1.29	23 ♎ 22.32	24 ♏ 7.12	23 ♐ 4.12	22 ♑ 17.13
1911	21 ♒ 3.52	19 ♓ 18.21	21 ♈ 17.55	21 ♉ 5.37	22 ♊ 5.2	22 ♋ 13.37	24 ♌ 0.3	24 ♍ 7.14	24 ♎ 4.19	24 ♏ 12.59	23 ♐ 9.57	22 ♑ 22.54
1912	21 ♒ 9.3	19 ♓ 23.56	20 ♈ 23.3	20 ♉ 11.12	21 ♊ 10.58	21 ♋ 19.18	23 ♌ 6.15	23 ♍ 13.02	23 ♎ 10.09	23 ♏ 18.51	22 ♐ 15.49	22 ♑ 4.46
1913	20 ♒ 15.2	19 ♓ 5.45	21 ♈ 5.19	20 ♉ 17.04	21 ♊ 16.51	22 ♋ 1.11	23 ♌ 12.05	23 ♍ 18.49	23 ♎ 15.54	24 ♏ 0.36	22 ♐ 21.36	22 ♑ 10.36
1914	20 ♒ 21.13	19 ♓ 11.39	21 ♈ 11.12	20 ♉ 22.54	21 ♊ 22.38	22 ♋ 6.56	23 ♌ 17.48	24 ♍ 0.31	23 ♎ 21.35	24 ♏ 6.18	23 ♐ 3.21	22 ♑ 16.23
1915	21 ♒ 3	19 ♓ 17.24	21 ♈ 16.52	21 ♉ 4.3	22 ♊ 4.11	22 ♋ 12.3	23 ♌ 23.27	24 ♍ 6.16	24 ♎ 3.25	24 ♏ 12.1	23 ♐ 9.14	22 ♑ 22.16
1916	21 ♒ 8.54	19 ♓ 23.19	20 ♈ 22.48	20 ♉ 10.25	21 ♊ 10.07	21 ♋ 18.25	23 ♌ 5.22	23 ♍ 12.1	23 ♎ 9.16	23 ♏ 17.58	22 ♐ 14.58	22 ♑ 3.59
1917	20 ♒ 14.38	19 ♓ 5.06	21 ♈ 4.38	20 ♉ 16.18	21 ♊ 15.6	22 ♋ 0.15	23 ♌ 11.09	23 ♍ 17.55	23 ♎ 15.01	23 ♏ 23.44	22 ♐ 20.45	22 ♑ 9.46
1918	20 ♒ 20.25	19 ♓ 10.53	21 ♈ 10.27	20 ♉ 22.07	21 ♊ 21.47	22 ♋ 6.01	23 ♌ 16.52	23 ♍ 23.38	23 ♎ 20.46	24 ♏ 5.33	23 ♐ 2.39	22 ♑ 15.42
1919	21 ♒ 2.21	19 ♓ 16.48	21 ♈ 16.2	21 ♉ 3.6	22 ♊ 3.41	22 ♋ 11.55	23 ♌ 22.46	24 ♍ 5.3	24 ♎ 2.37	24 ♏ 11.23	23 ♐ 8.26	22 ♑ 21.28
1920	21 ♒ 8.05	19 ♓ 22.3	20 ♈ 22	20 ♉ 9.4	21 ♊ 9.23	21 ♋ 17.41	23 ♌ 4.36	23 ♍ 11.22	23 ♎ 8.29	23 ♏ 17.14	22 ♐ 14.16	22 ♑ 3.18
1921	20 ♒ 13.56	19 ♓ 4.21	21 ♈ 3.52	20 ♉ 15.33	21 ♊ 15.18	21 ♋ 23.37	23 ♌ 10.32	23 ♍ 17.16	23 ♎ 14.21	23 ♏ 23.03	22 ♐ 20.06	22 ♑ 9.09
1922	20 ♒ 19.49	19 ♓ 10.17	21 ♈ 9.5	20 ♉ 21.3	21 ♊ 21.11	22 ♋ 5.28	23 ♌ 16.21	23 ♍ 23.05	23 ♎ 20.1	24 ♏ 4.54	23 ♐ 1.56	22 ♑ 14.58
1923	21 ♒ 1.36	19 ♓ 16.01	21 ♈ 15.3	21 ♉ 3.06	22 ♊ 2.46	22 ♋ 11.04	23 ♌ 22.01	24 ♍ 4.52	24 ♎ 2.04	24 ♏ 10.51	23 ♐ 7.54	22 ♑ 20.54
1924	21 ♒ 7.3	19 ♓ 21.53	20 ♈ 21.22	20 ♉ 8.6	21 ♊ 8.42	21 ♋ 17.01	23 ♌ 3.58	23 ♍ 10.49	23 ♎ 7.59	23 ♏ 16.45	22 ♐ 13.47	22 ♑ 2.46
1925	20 ♒ 13.21	19 ♓ 3.44	21 ♈ 3.13	20 ♉ 14.52	21 ♊ 14.34	21 ♋ 22.51	23 ♌ 9.46	23 ♍ 16.34	23 ♎ 13.44	23 ♏ 22.32	22 ♐ 19.36	22 ♑ 8.38
1926	20 ♒ 19.14	19 ♓ 9.36	21 ♈ 9.03	20 ♉ 20.38	21 ♊ 20.16	22 ♋ 4.31	23 ♌ 15.26	23 ♍ 22.15	23 ♎ 19.27	24 ♏ 4.19	23 ♐ 1.28	22 ♑ 14.34
1927	21 ♒ 1.13	19 ♓ 15.35	21 ♈ 15	21 ♉ 2.33	22 ♊ 2.09	22 ♋ 10.23	23 ♌ 21.18	24 ♍ 4.07	24 ♎ 1.18	24 ♏ 10.08	23 ♐ 7.15	22 ♑ 20.19
1928	21 ♒ 6.57	19 ♓ 21.2	20 ♈ 20.45	20 ♉ 8.18	21 ♊ 7.54	21 ♋ 16.08	23 ♌ 3.04	23 ♍ 9.54	23 ♎ 7.06	23 ♏ 15.55	22 ♐ 13.01	22 ♑ 2.05
1929	20 ♒ 12.43	19 ♓ 3.08	21 ♈ 2.36	20 ♉ 14.12	21 ♊ 13.49	21 ♋ 22.02	23 ♌ 8.55	23 ♍ 15.42	23 ♎ 12.53	23 ♏ 21.42	22 ♐ 18.49	22 ♑ 7.54
1930	20 ♒ 18.34	19 ♓ 9.01	21 ♈ 8.31	20 ♉ 20.08	21 ♊ 19.44	22 ♋ 3.54	23 ♌ 14.43	23 ♍ 21.28	23 ♎ 18.37	24 ♏ 3.27	23 ♐ 0.35	22 ♑ 13.4
1931	21 ♒ 0.19	19 ♓ 14.41	21 ♈ 14.07	21 ♉ 1.41	22 ♊ 1.17	22 ♋ 9.29	23 ♌ 20.22	24 ♍ 3.11	24 ♎ 0.24	24 ♏ 9.16	23 ♐ 6.25	22 ♑ 19.3
1932	21 ♒ 6.08	19 ♓ 20.3	20 ♈ 19.55	20 ♉ 7.29	21 ♊ 7.08	21 ♋ 15.24	23 ♌ 2.19	23 ♍ 9.07	23 ♎ 6.17	23 ♏ 15.04	22 ♐ 12.11	22 ♑ 1.15
1933	20 ♒ 11.54	19 ♓ 2.17	21 ♈ 1.45	20 ♉ 13.2	21 ♊ 12.58	21 ♋ 21.13	23 ♌ 8.06	23 ♍ 14.53	23 ♎ 12.01	23 ♏ 20.48	22 ♐ 17.54	22 ♑ 6.58
1934	20 ♒ 17.38	19 ♓ 8.03	21 ♈ 7.29	20 ♉ 19.02	21 ♊ 18.37	22 ♋ 2.49	23 ♌ 13.43	23 ♍ 20.33	23 ♎ 17.46	24 ♏ 2.36	22 ♐ 23.45	22 ♑ 12.5
1935	20 ♒ 23.29	19 ♓ 13.53	21 ♈ 13.19	21 ♉ 0.52	22 ♊ 0.27	22 ♋ 8.4	23 ♌ 19.34	24 ♍ 2.25	23 ♎ 23.39	24 ♏ 8.3	23 ♐ 5.35	22 ♑ 18.37
1936	21 ♒ 5.13	19 ♓ 19.34	20 ♈ 18.59	20 ♉ 6.32	21 ♊ 6.09	21 ♋ 14.23	23 ♌ 1.2	23 ♍ 8.12	23 ♎ 5.27	23 ♏ 14.19	22 ♐ 11.26	22 ♑ 0.27
1937	20 ♒ 11.02	19 ♓ 1.22	21 ♈ 0.46	20 ♉ 12.21	21 ♊ 11.59	21 ♋ 20.14	23 ♌ 7.09	23 ♍ 13.59	23 ♎ 11.14	23 ♏ 20.07	22 ♐ 17.17	22 ♑ 6.22
1938	20 ♒ 16.59	19 ♓ 7.2	21 ♈ 6.44	20 ♉ 18.16	21 ♊ 17.52	22 ♋ 2.05	23 ♌ 12.58	23 ♍ 19.47	23 ♎ 17.01	24 ♏ 1.55	22 ♐ 23.07	22 ♑ 12.14
1939	20 ♒ 22.52	19 ♓ 13.1	21 ♈ 12.29	20 ♉ 23.56	21 ♊ 23.28	22 ♋ 7.41	23 ♌ 18.38	24 ♍ 1.32	23 ♎ 22.51	24 ♏ 7.47	23 ♐ 4.59	22 ♑ 18.06
1940	21 ♒ 4.45	19 ♓ 19.05	20 ♈ 18.25	20 ♉ 5.52	21 ♊ 5.24	21 ♋ 13.38	23 ♌ 0.36	23 ♍ 7.3	23 ♎ 4.46	23 ♏ 13.4	22 ♐ 10.5	21 ♑ 23.56
1941	20 ♒ 10.35	19 ♓ 0.57	21 ♈ 0.22	20 ♉ 11.52	21 ♊ 11.24	21 ♋ 19.35	23 ♌ 6.27	23 ♍ 13.18	23 ♎ 10.34	23 ♏ 19.28	22 ♐ 16.39	22 ♑ 5.45
1942	20 ♒ 16.25	19 ♓ 6.48	21 ♈ 6.11	20 ♉ 17.4	21 ♊ 17.1	22 ♋ 1.18	23 ♌ 12.08	23 ♍ 18.59	23 ♎ 16.17	24 ♏ 1.16	22 ♐ 22.31	22 ♑ 11.4
1943	20 ♒ 22.2	19 ♓ 12.41	21 ♈ 12.04	20 ♉ 23.33	21 ♊ 23.05	22 ♋ 7.14	23 ♌ 18.06	24 ♍ 0.56	23 ♎ 22.13	24 ♏ 7.09	23 ♐ 4.22	22 ♑ 17.29
1944	21 ♒ 4.07	19 ♓ 18.28	20 ♈ 17.49	20 ♉ 5.19	21 ♊ 4.52	21 ♋ 13.04	22 ♌ 23.57	23 ♍ 6.48	23 ♎ 4.02	23 ♏ 12.57	22 ♐ 10.08	21 ♑ 23.16
1945	20 ♒ 9.54	19 ♓ 0.16	20 ♈ 23.38	20 ♉ 11.08	21 ♊ 10.42	21 ♋ 18.54	23 ♌ 5.47	23 ♍ 12.37	23 ♎ 9.51	23 ♏ 18.44	22 ♐ 15.56	22 ♑ 5.04
1946	20 ♒ 15.45	19 ♓ 6.09	21 ♈ 5.33	20 ♉ 17.03	21 ♊ 16.36	22 ♋ 0.46	23 ♌ 11.39	23 ♍ 18.28	23 ♎ 15.42	24 ♏ 0.36	22 ♐ 21.47	22 ♑ 10.54
1947	20 ♒ 21.32	19 ♓ 11.53	21 ♈ 11.13	20 ♉ 22.4	21 ♊ 22.1	22 ♋ 6.21	23 ♌ 17.16	24 ♍ 0.11	23 ♎ 21.3	24 ♏ 6.27	23 ♐ 3.39	22 ♑ 16.44
1948	21 ♒ 3.19	19 ♓ 17.38	20 ♈ 16.58	20 ♉ 4.26	21 ♊ 3.59	21 ♋ 12.12	22 ♌ 23.09	23 ♍ 6.04	23 ♎ 3.23	23 ♏ 12.19	22 ♐ 9.3	21 ♑ 22.34
1949	20 ♒ 9.1	18 ♓ 23.28	20 ♈ 22.49	20 ♉ 10.19	21 ♊ 9.52	21 ♋ 18.04	23 ♌ 4.58	23 ♍ 11.5	23 ♎ 9.07	23 ♏ 18.04	22 ♐ 15.17	22 ♑ 4.24
1950	20 ♒ 15.01	19 ♓ 5.19	21 ♈ 4.36	20 ♉ 16	21 ♊ 15.28	21 ♋ 23.37	23 ♌ 10.31	23 ♍ 17.24	23 ♎ 14.45	23 ♏ 23.46	22 ♐ 21.03	22 ♑ 10.14
1951	20 ♒ 20.53	19 ♓ 11.11	21 ♈ 10.27	20 ♉ 21.49	21 ♊ 21.17	22 ♋ 5.26	23 ♌ 16.22	23 ♍ 23.17	23 ♎ 20.38	24 ♏ 5.38	23 ♐ 2.52	22 ♑ 16.01
1952	21 ♒ 2.39	19 ♓ 16.58	20 ♈ 16.15	20 ♉ 3.38	21 ♊ 3.05	21 ♋ 11.14	22 ♌ 22.09	23 ♍ 5.04	23 ♎ 2.25	23 ♏ 11.23	22 ♐ 8.37	21 ♑ 21.44
1953	20 ♒ 8.22	18 ♓ 22.42	20 ♈ 22.02	20 ♉ 9.27	21 ♊ 8.54	21 ♋ 17.01	23 ♌ 3.53	23 ♍ 10.47	23 ♎ 8.07	23 ♏ 17.07	22 ♐ 14.23	22 ♑ 3.32
1954	20 ♒ 14.12	19 ♓ 4.33	21 ♈ 3.54	20 ♉ 15.21	21 ♊ 14.49	21 ♋ 22.56	23 ♌ 9.46	23 ♍ 16.37	23 ♎ 13.57	23 ♏ 22.58	22 ♐ 20.15	22 ♑ 9.25
1955	20 ♒ 20.03	19 ♓ 10.2	21 ♈ 9.36	20 ♉ 20.59	21 ♊ 20.26	22 ♋ 4.33	23 ♌ 15.26	23 ♍ 22.2	23 ♎ 19.42	24 ♏ 4.44	23 ♐ 2.02	22 ♑ 15.12

	I	II	III	IV	V	VI	VII	VIII	IX	X	XI	XII
1956	21 ♒ 1.5	19 ♓ 16.06	20 ♈ 15.22	20 ♉ 2.45	21 ♊ 2.14	21 ♋ 10.25	22 ♌ 21.21	23 ♍ 4.16	23 ♎ 1.36	23 ♏ 10.36	22 ♐ 7.51	21 ♑ 21.01
1957	20 ♒ 7.4	18 ♓ 21.59	20 ♈ 21.18	20 ♉ 8.43	21 ♊ 8.12	21 ♋ 16.22	23 ♌ 3.16	23 ♍ 10.09	23 ♎ 7.27	23 ♏ 16.25	22 ♐ 13.4	22 ♑ 2.5
1958	20 ♒ 13.3	19 ♓ 3.5	21 ♈ 3.07	20 ♉ 14.28	21 ♊ 13.52	21 ♋ 21.58	23 ♌ 8.52	23 ♍ 15.47	23 ♎ 13.1	23 ♏ 22.12	22 ♐ 19.3	22 ♑ 8.41
1959	20 ♒ 19.21	19 ♓ 9.39	21 ♈ 8.56	20 ♉ 20.18	21 ♊ 19.43	22 ♋ 3.51	23 ♌ 14.47	23 ♍ 21.45	23 ♎ 19.09	24 ♏ 4.12	23 ♐ 1.28	22 ♑ 14.36
1960	21 ♒ 1.11	19 ♓ 15.28	20 ♈ 14.44	20 ♉ 2.07	21 ♊ 1.35	21 ♋ 9.44	22 ♌ 20.39	23 ♍ 3.36	23 ♎ 0.6	23 ♏ 10.03	22 ♐ 7.19	21 ♑ 20.27
1961	20 ♒ 7.03	18 ♓ 21.18	20 ♈ 20.34	20 ♉ 7.57	21 ♊ 7.24	21 ♋ 15.31	23 ♌ 2.25	23 ♍ 9.2	23 ♎ 6.43	23 ♏ 15.48	22 ♐ 13.08	22 ♑ 2.2
1962	20 ♒ 12.59	19 ♓ 3.16	21 ♈ 2.31	20 ♉ 13.52	21 ♊ 13.19	21 ♋ 21.26	23 ♌ 8.2	23 ♍ 15.14	23 ♎ 12.37	23 ♏ 21.41	22 ♐ 19.03	22 ♑ 8.16
1963	20 ♒ 18.55	19 ♓ 9.1	21 ♈ 8.21	20 ♉ 19.37	21 ♊ 18.59	22 ♋ 3.06	23 ♌ 14.01	23 ♍ 20.59	23 ♎ 18.25	24 ♏ 3.3	23 ♐ 0.5	22 ♑ 14.03
1964	21 ♒ 0.42	19 ♓ 14.59	20 ♈ 14.11	20 ♉ 1.29	21 ♊ 0.51	21 ♋ 8.58	22 ♌ 19.54	23 ♍ 2.53	23 ♎ 0.18	23 ♏ 9.22	22 ♐ 6.4	21 ♑ 19.51
1965	20 ♒ 6.3	18 ♓ 20.49	20 ♈ 20.06	20 ♉ 7.28	21 ♊ 6.52	21 ♋ 14.57	23 ♌ 1.49	23 ♍ 8.44	23 ♎ 6.07	23 ♏ 15.11	22 ♐ 12.3	22 ♑ 1.42
1966	20 ♒ 12.21	19 ♓ 2.39	21 ♈ 1.54	20 ♉ 13.13	21 ♊ 12.34	21 ♋ 20.35	23 ♌ 7.25	23 ♍ 14.19	23 ♎ 11.45	23 ♏ 20.52	22 ♐ 18.16	22 ♑ 7.3
1967	20 ♒ 18.09	19 ♓ 8.25	21 ♈ 7.39	20 ♉ 18.57	21 ♊ 18.2	22 ♋ 2.25	23 ♌ 13.18	23 ♍ 20.14	23 ♎ 17.39	24 ♏ 2.45	23 ♐ 0.06	22 ♑ 13.18
1968	20 ♒ 23.55	19 ♓ 14.11	20 ♈ 13.24	20 ♉ 0.43	21 ♊ 0.08	21 ♋ 8.15	22 ♌ 19.09	23 ♍ 2.04	22 ♎ 23.27	23 ♏ 8.31	22 ♐ 5.5	21 ♑ 19.02
1969	20 ♒ 5.4	18 ♓ 19.56	20 ♈ 19.1	20 ♉ 6.29	21 ♊ 5.52	21 ♋ 13.57	23 ♌ 0.5	23 ♍ 7.45	23 ♎ 5.08	23 ♏ 14.12	22 ♐ 11.32	22 ♑ 0.45
1970	20 ♒ 11.25	19 ♓ 1.43	21 ♈ 0.58	20 ♉ 12.17	21 ♊ 11.4	21 ♋ 19.45	23 ♌ 6.38	23 ♍ 13.35	23 ♎ 11	23 ♏ 20.05	22 ♐ 17.25	22 ♑ 6.37
1971	20 ♒ 17.14	19 ♓ 7.29	21 ♈ 6.4	20 ♉ 17.56	21 ♊ 17.17	22 ♋ 1.21	23 ♌ 12.17	23 ♍ 19.17	23 ♎ 16.46	24 ♏ 1.54	22 ♐ 23.15	22 ♑ 12.25
1972	20 ♒ 22.6	19 ♓ 13.12	20 ♈ 12.23	19 ♉ 23.39	20 ♊ 23.01	21 ♋ 7.08	22 ♌ 18.04	23 ♍ 1.05	22 ♎ 22.34	23 ♏ 7.42	22 ♐ 5.04	21 ♑ 18.14
1973	20 ♒ 4.5	18 ♓ 19.03	20 ♈ 18.14	20 ♉ 5.32	21 ♊ 4.56	21 ♋ 13.03	22 ♌ 23.57	23 ♍ 6.55	23 ♎ 4.23	23 ♏ 13.31	22 ♐ 10.55	22 ♑ 0.09
1974	20 ♒ 10.47	19 ♓ 1	21 ♈ 0.08	20 ♉ 11.2	21 ♊ 10.38	21 ♋ 18.39	23 ♌ 5.32	23 ♍ 12.3	23 ♎ 10	23 ♏ 19.12	22 ♐ 16.4	22 ♑ 5.57
1975	20 ♒ 16.38	19 ♓ 6.51	21 ♈ 5.59	20 ♉ 17.09	21 ♊ 16.26	22 ♋ 0.28	23 ♌ 11.24	23 ♍ 18.25	23 ♎ 15.57	24 ♏ 1.07	22 ♐ 22.32	22 ♑ 11.47
1976	20 ♒ 22.26	19 ♓ 12.41	20 ♈ 11.51	19 ♉ 23.05	20 ♊ 22.23	21 ♋ 6.26	22 ♌ 17.2	23 ♍ 0.2	22 ♎ 21.5	23 ♏ 6.59	22 ♐ 4.23	21 ♑ 17.37
1977	20 ♒ 4.16	18 ♓ 18.32	20 ♈ 17.44	20 ♉ 4.59	21 ♊ 4.17	21 ♋ 12.16	22 ♌ 23.06	23 ♍ 6.02	23 ♎ 3.31	23 ♏ 12.42	22 ♐ 10.08	21 ♑ 23.24
1978	20 ♒ 10.05	19 ♓ 0.22	20 ♈ 23.35	20 ♉ 10.52	21 ♊ 10.11	21 ♋ 18.12	23 ♌ 5.02	23 ♍ 11.58	23 ♎ 9.27	23 ♏ 18.39	22 ♐ 16.06	22 ♑ 5.22
1979	20 ♒ 16.01	19 ♓ 6.14	21 ♈ 5.23	20 ♉ 16.37	21 ♊ 15.56	21 ♋ 23.59	23 ♌ 10.51	23 ♍ 17.49	23 ♎ 15.18	24 ♏ 0.29	22 ♐ 21.55	22 ♑ 11.11
1980	20 ♒ 21.5	19 ♓ 12.03	20 ♈ 11.11	19 ♉ 22.25	20 ♊ 21.44	21 ♋ 5.49	22 ♌ 16.44	22 ♍ 23.42	22 ♎ 21.1	23 ♏ 6.19	22 ♐ 3.42	21 ♑ 16.57
1981	20 ♒ 3.37	18 ♓ 17.53	20 ♈ 17.04	20 ♉ 4.2	21 ♊ 3.42	21 ♋ 11.47	22 ♌ 22.42	23 ♍ 5.4	23 ♎ 3.07	23 ♏ 12.14	22 ♐ 9.37	21 ♑ 22.52
1982	20 ♒ 9.32	18 ♓ 23.48	20 ♈ 22.57	20 ♉ 10.09	21 ♊ 9.25	21 ♋ 17.25	23 ♌ 4.18	23 ♍ 11.17	23 ♎ 8.48	23 ♏ 17.59	22 ♐ 15.25	22 ♑ 4.39
1983	20 ♒ 15.18	19 ♓ 5.32	21 ♈ 4.4	20 ♉ 15.52	21 ♊ 15.08	21 ♋ 23.1	23 ♌ 10.06	23 ♍ 17.1	23 ♎ 14.44	23 ♏ 23.56	22 ♐ 21.2	22 ♑ 10.32
1984	20 ♒ 21.07	19 ♓ 11.18	20 ♈ 10.26	19 ♉ 21.4	20 ♊ 20.59	21 ♋ 5.04	22 ♌ 16	22 ♍ 23.02	22 ♎ 20.35	23 ♏ 5.47	22 ♐ 3.12	21 ♑ 16.25
1985	20 ♒ 2.59	18 ♓ 17.09	20 ♈ 16.16	20 ♉ 3.27	21 ♊ 2.45	21 ♋ 10.46	22 ♌ 21.38	23 ♍ 4.37	23 ♎ 2.09	23 ♏ 11.24	22 ♐ 8.52	21 ♑ 22.09
1986	20 ♒ 8.48	18 ♓ 22.6	20 ♈ 22.05	20 ♉ 9.14	21 ♊ 8.3	21 ♋ 16.32	23 ♌ 3.26	23 ♍ 10.27	23 ♎ 8	23 ♏ 17.16	22 ♐ 14.45	22 ♑ 4.03
1987	20 ♒ 14.42	19 ♓ 4.51	21 ♈ 3.54	20 ♉ 14.59	21 ♊ 14.12	21 ♋ 22.13	23 ♌ 9.08	23 ♍ 16.12	23 ♎ 13.47	23 ♏ 23.02	22 ♐ 20.31	22 ♑ 9.47
1988	20 ♒ 20.26	19 ♓ 10.37	20 ♈ 9.41	19 ♉ 20.47	20 ♊ 19.59	21 ♋ 3.58	22 ♌ 14.53	22 ♍ 21.56	22 ♎ 19.31	23 ♏ 4.46	22 ♐ 2.13	21 ♑ 15.29
1989	20 ♒ 2.09	18 ♓ 16.22	20 ♈ 15.3	20 ♉ 2.41	21 ♊ 1.56	21 ♋ 9.55	22 ♌ 20.47	23 ♍ 3.48	23 ♎ 1.22	23 ♏ 10.37	22 ♐ 8.06	21 ♑ 21.23
1990	20 ♒ 8.03	18 ♓ 22.15	20 ♈ 21.21	20 ♉ 8.28	21 ♊ 7.39	21 ♋ 15.35	23 ♌ 2.24	23 ♍ 9.23	23 ♎ 6.57	23 ♏ 16.16	22 ♐ 13.49	22 ♑ 3.08
1991	20 ♒ 13.48	19 ♓ 3.6	21 ♈ 3.03	20 ♉ 14.1	21 ♊ 13.22	21 ♋ 21.2	23 ♌ 8.13	23 ♍ 15.15	23 ♎ 12.5	23 ♏ 22.07	22 ♐ 19.38	22 ♑ 8.55
1992	20 ♒ 19.34	19 ♓ 9.45	20 ♈ 8.5	19 ♉ 19.59	20 ♊ 19.14	21 ♋ 3.16	22 ♌ 14.11	22 ♍ 21.12	22 ♎ 18.45	23 ♏ 3.59	22 ♐ 1.28	21 ♑ 14.45
1993	20 ♒ 1.25	18 ♓ 15.37	20 ♈ 14.43	20 ♉ 1.51	21 ♊ 1.04	21 ♋ 9.02	22 ♌ 19.53	23 ♍ 2.52	23 ♎ 0.24	23 ♏ 9.39	22 ♐ 7.09	21 ♑ 20.28
1994	20 ♒ 7.09	18 ♓ 21.24	20 ♈ 20.3	20 ♉ 7.38	21 ♊ 6.51	21 ♋ 14.5	23 ♌ 1.43	23 ♍ 8.46	23 ♎ 6.21	23 ♏ 15.38	22 ♐ 13.08	22 ♑ 2.25
1995	20 ♒ 13.03	19 ♓ 3.13	21 ♈ 2.16	20 ♉ 13.24	21 ♊ 12.36	21 ♋ 20.36	23 ♌ 7.31	23 ♍ 14.37	23 ♎ 12.15	23 ♏ 21.33	22 ♐ 19.03	22 ♑ 8.19
1996	20 ♒ 18.55	19 ♓ 9.03	20 ♈ 8.05	19 ♉ 19.12	20 ♊ 18.25	21 ♋ 2.26	22 ♌ 13.21	22 ♍ 20.25	22 ♎ 18.02	23 ♏ 3.2	22 ♐ 0.51	21 ♑ 14.08
1997	20 ♒ 0.45	18 ♓ 14.54	20 ♈ 13.57	20 ♉ 1.05	21 ♊ 0.2	21 ♋ 8.22	22 ♌ 19.17	23 ♍ 2.21	22 ♎ 23.57	23 ♏ 9.16	22 ♐ 6.49	21 ♑ 20.09
1998	20 ♒ 6.48	18 ♓ 20.57	20 ♈ 19.57	20 ♉ 6.59	21 ♊ 6.08	21 ♋ 14.05	23 ♌ 0.58	23 ♍ 8.01	23 ♎ 5.39	23 ♏ 15.01	22 ♐ 12.36	22 ♑ 1.58
1999	20 ♒ 12.39	19 ♓ 2.49	21 ♈ 1.48	20 ♉ 12.48	21 ♊ 11.55	21 ♋ 19.51	23 ♌ 6.46	23 ♍ 13.53	23 ♎ 11.33	23 ♏ 20.54	22 ♐ 18.27	22 ♑ 7.46
2000	20 ♒ 18.25	19 ♓ 8.35	20 ♈ 7.37	19 ♉ 18.41	20 ♊ 17.51	21 ♋ 1.5	22 ♌ 12.45	22 ♍ 19.5	22 ♎ 17.3	23 ♏ 2.49	22 ♐ 0.21	21 ♑ 13.4

Table 1

	I	II	III	IV	V	VI	VII	VIII	IX	X	XI	XII
1	6 37 24	8 39 38	10 33 58	12 36 11	14 34 28	16 36 41	18 34 57	20 37 11	22 39 24	0 37 41	2 39 54	4 38 10
2	6 41 21	8 43 34	10 37 54	12 40 7	14 38 24	16 40 37	18 38 54	20 41 7	22 43 20	0 41 37	2 43 50	4 42 7
3	6 45 17	8 47 31	10 41 51	12 44 4	14 42 21	16 44 34	18 42 51	20 45 4	22 47 17	0 45 34	2 47 47	4 46 4
4	6 49 14	8 51 27	10 45 47	12 48 1	14 46 17	16 48 30	18 46 47	20 49 0	22 51 14	0 49 30	2 51 43	4 50 0
5	6 53 11	8 55 24	10 49 44	12 51 57	14 50 14	16 52 27	18 50 44	20 52 57	22 55 10	0 53 27	2 55 40	4 53 57
6	6 57 7	8 59 20	10 53 40	12 55 54	14 54 10	16 56 24	18 54 40	20 56 53	22 59 7	0 57 23	2 59 37	4 57 53
7	7 1 4	9 3 17	10 57 37	12 59 50	14 58 7	17 0 20	18 58 37	21 0 50	23 3 3	1 1 20	3 3 33	5 1 50
8	7 5 0	9 7 13	11 1 34	13 3 47	15 2 3	17 4 17	19 2 33	21 4 47	23 6 60	1 5 16	3 7 30	5 5 46
9	7 8 57	9 11 10	11 5 30	13 7 43	15 5 60	17 8 13	19 6 30	21 8 43	23 10 56	1 9 13	3 11 26	5 9 43
10	7 12 53	9 15 7	11 9 27	13 11 40	15 9 57	17 12 10	19 10 26	21 12 40	23 14 53	1 13 10	3 15 23	5 13 39
11	7 16 50	9 19 3	11 13 23	13 15 36	15 13 53	17 16 6	19 14 23	21 16 36	23 18 49	1 17 6	3 19 19	5 17 36
12	7 20 46	9 22 60	11 17 20	13 19 33	15 17 50	17 20 3	19 18 20	21 20 33	23 22 46	1 21 3	3 23 16	5 21 33
13	7 24 43	9 26 56	11 21 16	13 23 30	15 21 46	17 23 59	19 22 16	21 24 29	23 26 43	1 24 59	3 27 12	5 25 29
14	7 28 40	9 30 53	11 25 13	13 27 26	15 25 43	17 27 56	19 26 13	21 28 26	23 30 39	1 28 56	3 31 9	5 29 26
15	7 32 36	9 34 49	11 29 9	13 31 23	15 29 39	17 31 53	19 30 9	21 32 22	23 34 36	1 32 52	3 35 6	5 33 22
16	7 36 33	9 38 46	11 33 6	13 35 19	15 33 36	17 35 49	19 34 6	21 36 19	23 38 32	1 36 49	3 39 2	5 37 19
17	7 40 29	9 42 42	11 37 3	13 39 16	15 37 32	17 39 46	19 38 2	21 40 16	23 42 29	1 40 45	3 42 59	5 41 15
18	7 44 26	9 46 39	11 40 59	13 43 12	15 41 29	17 43 42	19 41 59	21 44 12	23 46 25	1 44 42	3 46 55	5 45 12
19	7 48 22	9 50 36	11 44 56	13 47 9	15 45 26	17 47 39	19 45 55	21 48 9	23 50 22	1 48 39	3 50 52	5 49 8
20	7 52 19	9 54 32	11 48 52	13 51 5	15 49 22	17 51 35	19 49 52	21 52 5	23 54 18	1 52 35	3 54 48	5 53 5
21	7 56 15	9 58 29	11 52 49	13 55 2	15 53 19	17 55 32	19 53 49	21 56 2	23 58 15	1 56 32	3 58 45	5 57 1
22	8 0 12	10 2 25	11 56 45	13 58 59	15 57 15	17 59 28	19 57 45	21 59 58	0 2 12	2 0 28	4 2 41	6 0 58
23	8 4 9	10 6 22	12 0 42	14 2 55	16 1 12	18 3 25	20 1 42	22 3 55	0 6 8	2 4 25	4 6 38	6 4 55
24	8 8 5	10 10 18	12 4 38	14 6 52	16 5 8	18 7 22	20 5 38	22 7 51	0 10 5	2 8 21	4 10 35	6 8 51
25	8 12 2	10 14 15	12 8 35	14 10 48	16 9 5	18 11 18	20 9 35	22 11 48	0 14 1	2 12 18	4 14 31	6 12 48
26	8 15 58	10 18 11	12 12 32	14 14 45	16 13 1	18 15 15	20 13 31	22 15 45	0 17 58	2 16 14	4 18 28	6 16 44
27	8 19 55	10 22 8	12 16 28	14 18 41	16 16 58	18 19 11	20 17 28	22 19 41	0 21 54	2 20 11	4 22 24	6 20 41
28	8 23 51	10 26 5	12 20 25	14 22 38	16 20 55	18 23 8	20 21 24	22 23 38	0 25 51	2 24 8	4 26 21	6 24 37
29	8 27 48	10 30 1	12 24 21	14 26 34	16 24 51	18 27 4	20 25 21	22 27 34	0 29 47	2 28 4	4 30 17	6 28 34
30	8 31 44		12 28 18	14 30 31	16 28 48	18 31 1	20 29 18	22 31 31	0 33 44	2 32 1	4 34 14	6 32 30
31	8 35 41		12 32 14		16 32 44		20 33 14	22 35 27		2 35 57		6 36 27

Year Corrections

Table 1	+	Table 2	+	Table 3	+	Table 4	+
1920	0 0 0	1921	0 0 0	1922	0 0 0	1923	0 0 0
1924	0 0 7	1925	0 0 7	1926	0 0 7	1927	0 0 7
1928	0 0 15	1929	0 0 15	1930	0 0 15	1931	0 0 15
1932	0 0 22	1933	0 0 22	1934	0 0 22	1935	0 0 22
1936	0 0 30	1937	0 0 30	1938	0 0 30	1939	0 0 30
1940	0 0 37	1941	0 0 37	1942	0 0 37	1943	0 0 37
1944	0 0 44	1945	0 0 44	1946	0 0 44	1947	0 0 44
1948	0 0 52	1949	0 0 52	1950	0 0 52	1951	0 0 52
1952	0 0 59	1953	0 0 59	1954	0 0 59	1955	0 0 59
1956	0 1 6	1957	0 1 6	1958	0 1 6	1959	0 1 6
1960	0 1 14	1961	0 1 14	1962	0 1 14	1963	0 1 14
1964	0 1 21	1965	0 1 21	1966	0 1 21	1967	0 1 21
1968	0 1 29	1969	0 1 29	1970	0 1 29	1971	0 1 29
1972	0 1 36	1973	0 1 36	1974	0 1 36	1975	0 1 36
1976	0 1 43	1977	0 1 43	1978	0 1 43	1979	0 1 43
1980	0 1 51	1981	0 1 51	1982	0 1 51	1983	0 1 51
1984	0 1 58	1985	0 1 58	1986	0 1 58	1987	0 1 58
1988	0 2 6	1989	0 2 6	1990	0 2 6	1991	0 2 6
1992	0 2 13	1993	0 2 13	1994	0 2 13	1995	0 2 13
1996	0 2 20	1997	0 2 20	1998	0 2 20	1999	0 2 20
2000	0 2 28	2001	0 2 28	2002	0 2 28	2003	0 2 28
2004	0 2 35	2005	0 2 35	2006	0 2 35	2007	0 2 35
2008	0 2 42	2009	0 2 42	2010	0 2 42	2011	0 2 42
2012	0 2 50	2013	0 2 50	2014	0 2 50	2015	0 2 50
2016	0 2 57	2017	0 2 57	2018	0 2 57	2019	0 2 57

The large tables show basic sidereal times to which, in order to find the true ST for any given birth time, we must add a period of time shown in the smaller year correction table. That smaller table also shows to which of the larger tables we must refer.

For example, for a birth on 4 July 1981 we discover that 1981 is in the column marked Table 2 and that the amount to be added is 1 minute 51 seconds.Looking at Table 2, the second of the large sidereal time tables, we find that the sidereal time for 4 July 1981 is 18.45.50. Add 1.51 to this and we arrive at 18.47.41, which is the correct sidereal time for midnight on that date.

Table 2

	I	II	III	IV	V	VI	VII	VIII	IX	X	XI	XII
1	6 40 24	8 42 37	10 33 0	12 35 14	14 33 30	16 35 43	18 34 0	20 36 13	22 38 27	0 36 43	2 38 56	4 37 13
2	6 44 20	8 46 33	10 36 57	12 39 10	14 37 27	16 39 40	18 37 57	20 40 10	22 42 23	0 40 40	2 42 53	4 41 10
3	6 48 17	8 50 30	10 40 53	12 43 7	14 41 23	16 43 37	18 41 53	20 44 6	22 46 20	0 44 36	2 46 50	4 45 6
4	6 52 13	8 54 26	10 44 50	12 47 3	14 45 20	16 47 33	18 45 50	20 48 3	22 50 16	0 48 33	2 50 46	4 49 3
5	6 56 10	8 58 23	10 48 47	12 50 60	14 49 16	16 51 30	18 49 46	20 51 60	22 54 13	0 52 29	2 54 43	4 52 59
6	7 0 6	9 2 20	10 52 43	12 54 56	14 53 13	16 55 26	18 53 43	20 55 56	22 58 9	0 56 26	2 58 39	4 56 56
7	7 4 3	9 6 16	10 56 40	12 58 53	14 57 10	16 59 23	18 57 39	20 59 53	23 2 6	1 0 23	3 2 36	5 0 52
8	7 7 59	9 10 13	11 0 36	13 2 49	15 1 6	17 3 19	19 1 36	21 3 49	23 6 2	1 4 19	3 6 32	5 4 49
9	7 11 56	9 14 9	11 4 33	13 6 46	15 5 3	17 7 16	19 5 33	21 7 46	23 9 59	1 8 16	3 10 29	5 8 46
10	7 15 53	9 18 6	11 8 29	13 10 43	15 8 59	17 11 12	19 9 29	21 11 42	23 13 56	1 12 12	3 14 25	5 12 42
11	7 19 49	9 22 2	11 12 26	13 14 39	15 12 56	17 15 9	19 13 26	21 15 39	23 17 52	1 16 9	3 18 22	5 16 39
12	7 23 46	9 25 59	11 16 22	13 18 36	15 16 52	17 19 6	19 17 22	21 19 35	23 21 49	1 20 5	3 22 19	5 20 35
13	7 27 42	9 29 55	11 20 19	13 22 32	15 20 49	17 23 2	19 21 19	21 23 32	23 25 45	1 24 2	3 26 15	5 24 32
14	7 31 39	9 33 52	11 24 16	13 26 29	15 24 45	17 26 59	19 25 15	21 27 29	23 29 42	1 27 58	3 30 12	5 28 28
15	7 35 35	9 37 49	11 28 12	13 30 25	15 28 42	17 30 55	19 29 12	21 31 25	23 33 38	1 31 55	3 34 8	5 32 25
16	7 39 32	9 41 45	11 32 9	13 34 22	15 32 39	17 34 52	19 33 8	21 35 22	23 37 35	1 35 52	3 38 5	5 36 21
17	7 43 28	9 45 42	11 36 5	13 38 18	15 36 35	17 38 48	19 37 5	21 39 18	23 41 31	1 39 48	3 42 1	5 40 18
18	7 47 25	9 49 38	11 40 2	13 42 15	15 40 32	17 42 45	19 41 2	21 43 15	23 45 28	1 43 45	3 45 58	5 44 15
19	7 51 22	9 53 35	11 43 58	13 46 12	15 44 28	17 46 41	19 44 58	21 47 11	23 49 25	1 47 41	3 49 54	5 48 11
20	7 55 18	9 57 31	11 47 55	13 50 8	15 48 25	17 50 38	19 48 55	21 51 8	23 53 21	1 51 38	3 53 51	5 52 8
21	7 59 15	10 1 28	11 51 51	13 54 5	15 52 21	17 54 35	19 52 51	21 55 4	23 57 18	1 55 34	3 57 48	5 56 4
22	8 3 11	10 5 24	11 55 48	13 58 1	15 56 18	17 58 31	19 56 48	21 59 1	0 1 14	1 59 31	4 1 44	6 0 1
23	8 7 8	10 9 21	11 59 45	14 1 58	16 0 14	18 2 28	20 0 44	22 2 58	0 5 11	2 3 27	4 5 41	6 3 57
24	8 11 4	10 13 18	12 3 41	14 5 54	16 4 11	18 6 24	20 4 41	22 6 54	0 9 7	2 7 24	4 9 37	6 7 54
25	8 15 1	10 17 14	12 7 38	14 9 51	16 8 8	18 10 21	20 8 37	22 10 51	0 13 4	2 11 21	4 13 34	6 11 50
26	8 18 57	10 21 11	12 11 34	14 13 47	16 12 4	18 14 17	20 12 34	22 14 47	0 17 0	2 15 17	4 17 30	6 15 47
27	8 22 54	10 25 7	12 15 31	14 17 44	16 16 1	18 18 14	20 16 31	22 18 44	0 20 57	2 19 14	4 21 27	6 19 44
28	8 26 51	10 29 4	12 19 27	14 21 41	16 19 57	18 22 10	20 20 27	22 22 40	0 24 54	2 23 10	4 25 23	6 23 40
29	8 30 47		12 23 24	14 25 37	16 23 54	18 26 7	20 24 24	22 26 37	0 28 50	2 27 7	4 29 20	6 27 37
30	8 34 44		12 27 20	14 29 34	16 27 50	18 30 4	20 28 20	22 30 33	0 32 47	2 31 3	4 33 17	6 31 33
31	8 38 40		12 31 17		16 31 47		20 32 17	22 34 30		2 34 60		6 35 30

Year Corrections

Table 1	+	Table 2	+	Table 3	+	Table 4	+
1920	0 0 0	1921	0 0 0	1922	0 0 0	1923	0 0 0
1924	0 0 7	1925	0 0 7	1926	0 0 7	1927	0 0 7
1928	0 0 15	1929	0 0 15	1930	0 0 15	1931	0 0 15
1932	0 0 22	1933	0 0 22	1934	0 0 22	1935	0 0 22
1936	0 0 30	1937	0 0 30	1938	0 0 30	1939	0 0 30
1940	0 0 37	1941	0 0 37	1942	0 0 37	1943	0 0 37
1944	0 0 44	1945	0 0 44	1946	0 0 44	1947	0 0 44
1948	0 0 52	1949	0 0 52	1950	0 0 52	1951	0 0 52
1952	0 0 59	1953	0 0 59	1954	0 0 59	1955	0 0 59
1956	0 1 6	1957	0 1 6	1958	0 1 6	1959	0 1 6
1960	0 1 14	1961	0 1 14	1962	0 1 14	1963	0 1 14
1964	0 1 21	1965	0 1 21	1966	0 1 21	1967	0 1 21
1968	0 1 29	1969	0 1 29	1970	0 1 29	1971	0 1 29
1972	0 1 36	1973	0 1 36	1974	0 1 36	1975	0 1 36
1976	0 1 43	1977	0 1 43	1978	0 1 43	1979	0 1 43
1980	0 1 51	1981	0 1 51	1982	0 1 51	1983	0 1 51
1984	0 1 58	1985	0 1 58	1986	0 1 58	1987	0 1 58
1988	0 2 6	1989	0 2 6	1990	0 2 6	1991	0 2 6
1992	0 2 13	1993	0 2 13	1994	0 2 13	1995	0 2 13
1996	0 2 20	1997	0 2 20	1998	0 2 20	1999	0 2 20
2000	0 2 28	2001	0 2 28	2002	0 2 28	2003	0 2 28
2004	0 2 35	2005	0 2 35	2006	0 2 35	2007	0 2 35
2008	0 2 42	2009	0 2 42	2010	0 2 42	2011	0 2 42
2012	0 2 50	2013	0 2 50	2014	0 2 50	2015	0 2 50
2016	0 2 57	2017	0 2 57	2018	0 2 57	2019	0 2 57

Table 3

	I	II	III	IV	V	VI	VII	VIII	IX	X	XI	XII
1	6 39 26	8 41 40	10 32 3	12 34 16	14 32 33	16 34 46	18 33 3	20 35 16	22 37 29	0 35 46	2 37 59	4 36 16
2	6 43 23	8 45 36	10 35 60	12 38 13	14 36 30	16 38 43	18 36 59	20 39 13	22 41 26	0 39 42	2 41 56	4 40 12
3	6 47 19	8 49 33	10 39 56	12 42 9	14 40 26	16 42 39	18 40 56	20 43 9	22 45 22	0 43 39	2 45 52	4 44 9
4	6 51 16	8 53 29	10 43 53	12 46 6	14 44 23	16 46 36	18 44 52	20 47 6	22 49 19	0 47 36	2 49 49	4 48 5
5	6 55 13	8 57 26	10 47 49	12 50 3	14 48 19	16 50 32	18 48 49	20 51 2	22 53 15	0 51 32	2 53 45	4 52 2
6	6 59 9	9 1 22	10 51 46	12 53 59	14 52 16	16 54 29	18 52 46	20 54 59	22 57 12	0 55 29	2 57 42	4 55 59
7	7 3 6	9 5 19	10 55 42	12 57 56	14 56 12	16 58 25	18 56 42	20 58 55	23 1 9	0 59 25	3 1 38	4 59 55
8	7 7 2	9 9 15	10 59 39	13 1 52	15 0 9	17 2 22	19 0 39	21 2 52	23 5 5	1 3 22	3 5 35	5 3 52
9	7 10 59	9 13 12	11 3 36	13 5 49	15 4 5	17 6 19	19 4 35	21 6 48	23 9 2	1 7 18	3 9 32	5 7 48
10	7 14 55	9 17 9	11 7 32	13 9 45	15 8 2	17 10 15	19 8 32	21 10 45	23 12 58	1 11 15	3 13 28	5 11 45
11	7 18 52	9 21 5	11 11 29	13 13 42	15 11 59	17 14 12	19 12 28	21 14 42	23 16 55	1 15 11	3 17 25	5 15 41
12	7 22 48	9 25 2	11 15 25	13 17 38	15 15 55	17 18 8	19 16 25	21 18 38	23 20 51	1 19 8	3 21 21	5 19 38
13	7 26 45	9 28 58	11 19 22	13 21 35	15 19 52	17 22 5	19 20 21	21 22 35	23 24 48	1 23 5	3 25 18	5 23 34
14	7 30 42	9 32 55	11 23 18	13 25 32	15 23 48	17 26 1	19 24 18	21 26 31	23 28 44	1 27 1	3 29 14	5 27 31
15	7 34 38	9 36 51	11 27 15	13 29 28	15 27 45	17 29 58	19 28 15	21 30 28	23 32 41	1 30 58	3 33 11	5 31 28
16	7 38 35	9 40 48	11 31 11	13 33 25	15 31 41	17 33 54	19 32 11	21 34 24	23 36 38	1 34 54	3 37 7	5 35 24
17	7 42 31	9 44 44	11 35 8	13 37 21	15 35 38	17 37 51	19 36 8	21 38 21	23 40 34	1 38 51	3 41 4	5 39 21
18	7 46 28	9 48 41	11 39 5	13 41 18	15 39 34	17 41 48	19 40 4	21 42 17	23 44 31	1 42 47	3 45 1	5 43 17
19	7 50 24	9 52 38	11 43 1	13 45 14	15 43 31	17 45 44	19 44 1	21 46 14	23 48 27	1 46 44	3 48 57	5 47 14
20	7 54 21	9 56 34	11 46 58	13 49 11	15 47 28	17 49 41	19 47 57	21 50 11	23 52 24	1 50 40	3 52 54	5 51 10
21	7 58 17	10 0 31	11 50 54	13 53 7	15 51 24	17 53 37	19 51 54	21 54 7	23 56 20	1 54 37	3 56 50	5 55 7
22	8 2 14	10 4 27	11 54 51	13 57 4	15 55 21	17 57 34	19 55 50	21 58 4	0 0 17	1 58 34	4 0 47	5 59 3
23	8 6 11	10 8 24	11 58 47	14 1 1	15 59 17	18 1 30	19 59 47	22 2 0	0 4 13	2 2 30	4 4 43	6 3 0
24	8 10 7	10 12 20	12 2 44	14 4 57	16 3 14	18 5 27	20 3 44	22 5 57	0 8 10	2 6 27	4 8 40	6 6 57
25	8 14 4	10 16 17	12 6 40	14 8 54	16 7 10	18 9 23	20 7 40	22 9 53	0 12 7	2 10 23	4 12 36	6 10 53
26	8 18 0	10 20 13	12 10 37	14 12 50	16 11 7	18 13 20	20 11 37	22 13 50	0 16 3	2 14 20	4 16 33	6 14 50
27	8 21 57	10 24 10	12 14 34	14 16 47	16 15 3	18 17 17	20 15 33	22 17 46	0 19 60	2 18 16	4 20 30	6 18 46
28	8 25 53	10 28 7	12 18 30	14 20 43	16 18 60	18 21 13	20 19 30	22 21 43	0 23 56	2 22 13	4 24 26	6 22 43
29	8 29 50		12 22 27	14 24 40	16 22 57	18 25 10	20 23 26	22 25 40	0 27 53	2 26 9	4 28 23	6 26 39
30	8 33 46		12 26 23	14 28 36	16 26 53	18 29 6	20 27 23	22 29 36	0 31 49	2 30 6	4 32 19	6 30 36
31	8 37 43		12 30 20		16 30 50		20 31 19	22 33 33		2 34 3		6 34 32

Year Corrections

Table 1	+	Table 2	+	Table 3	+	Table 4	+
1920	0 0 0	**1921**	0 0 0	**1922**	0 0 0	**1923**	0 0 0
1924	0 0 7	**1925**	0 0 7	**1926**	0 0 7	**1927**	0 0 7
1928	0 0 15	**1929**	0 0 15	**1930**	0 0 15	**1931**	0 0 15
1932	0 0 22	**1933**	0 0 22	**1934**	0 0 22	**1935**	0 0 22
1936	0 0 30	**1937**	0 0 30	**1938**	0 0 30	**1939**	0 0 30
1940	0 0 37	**1941**	0 0 37	**1942**	0 0 37	**1943**	0 0 37
1944	0 0 44	**1945**	0 0 44	**1946**	0 0 44	**1947**	0 0 44
1948	0 0 52	**1949**	0 0 52	**1950**	0 0 52	**1951**	0 0 52
1952	0 0 59	**1953**	0 0 59	**1954**	0 0 59	**1955**	0 0 59
1956	0 1 6	**1957**	0 1 6	**1958**	0 1 6	**1959**	0 1 6
1960	0 1 14	**1961**	0 1 14	**1962**	0 1 14	**1963**	0 1 14
1964	0 1 21	**1965**	0 1 21	**1966**	0 1 21	**1967**	0 1 21
1968	0 1 29	**1969**	0 1 29	**1970**	0 1 29	**1971**	0 1 29
1972	0 1 36	**1973**	0 1 36	**1974**	0 1 36	**1975**	0 1 36
1976	0 1 43	**1977**	0 1 43	**1978**	0 1 43	**1979**	0 1 43
1980	0 1 51	**1981**	0 1 51	**1982**	0 1 51	**1983**	0 1 51
1984	0 1 58	**1985**	0 1 58	**1986**	0 1 58	**1987**	0 1 58
1988	0 2 6	**1989**	0 2 6	**1990**	0 2 6	**1991**	0 2 6
1992	0 2 13	**1993**	0 2 13	**1994**	0 2 13	**1995**	0 2 13
1996	0 2 20	**1997**	0 2 20	**1998**	0 2 20	**1999**	0 2 20
2000	0 2 28	**2001**	0 2 28	**2002**	0 2 28	**2003**	0 2 28
2004	0 2 35	**2005**	0 2 35	**2006**	0 2 35	**2007**	0 2 35
2008	0 2 42	**2009**	0 2 42	**2010**	0 2 42	**2011**	0 2 42
2012	0 2 50	**2013**	0 2 50	**2014**	0 2 50	**2015**	0 2 50
2016	0 2 57	**2017**	0 2 57	**2018**	0 2 57	**2019**	0 2 57

Table 4

	I	II	III	IV	V	VI	VII	VIII	IX	X	XI	XII
1	6 38 29	8 40 42	10 31 6	12 33 19	14 31 36	16 33 49	18 32 6	20 34 19	22 36 32	0 34 49	2 37 2	4 35 18
2	6 42 26	8 44 39	10 35 2	12 37 16	14 35 32	16 37 45	18 36 2	20 38 15	22 40 29	0 38 45	2 40 58	4 39 15
3	6 46 22	8 48 35	10 38 59	12 41 12	14 39 29	16 41 42	18 39 59	20 42 12	22 44 25	0 42 42	2 44 55	4 43 12
4	6 50 19	8 52 32	10 42 55	12 45 9	14 43 25	16 45 39	18 43 55	20 46 8	22 48 22	0 46 38	2 48 52	4 47 8
5	6 54 15	8 56 28	10 46 52	12 49 5	14 47 22	16 49 35	18 47 52	20 50 5	22 52 18	0 50 35	2 52 48	4 51 5
6	6 58 12	9 0 25	10 50 49	12 53 2	14 51 18	16 53 32	18 51 48	20 54 2	22 56 15	0 54 31	2 56 45	4 55 1
7	7 2 8	9 4 22	10 54 45	12 56 58	14 55 15	16 57 28	18 55 45	20 57 58	23 0 11	0 58 28	3 0 41	4 58 58
8	7 6 5	9 8 18	10 58 42	13 0 55	14 59 12	17 1 25	18 59 41	21 1 55	23 4 8	1 2 25	3 4 38	5 2 54
9	7 10 1	9 12 15	11 2 38	13 4 51	15 3 8	17 5 21	19 3 38	21 5 51	23 8 4	1 6 21	3 8 34	5 6 51
10	7 13 58	9 16 11	11 6 35	13 8 48	15 7 5	17 9 18	19 7 35	21 9 48	23 12 1	1 10 18	3 12 31	5 10 47
11	7 17 55	9 20 8	11 10 31	13 12 45	15 11 1	17 13 14	19 11 31	21 13 44	23 15 58	1 14 14	3 16 27	5 14 44
12	7 21 51	9 24 4	11 14 28	13 16 41	15 14 58	17 17 11	19 15 28	21 17 41	23 19 54	1 18 11	3 20 24	5 18 41
13	7 25 48	9 28 1	11 18 24	13 20 38	15 18 54	17 21 8	19 19 24	21 21 37	23 23 51	1 22 7	3 24 21	5 22 37
14	7 29 44	9 31 57	11 22 21	13 24 34	15 22 51	17 25 4	19 23 21	21 25 34	23 27 47	1 26 4	3 28 17	5 26 34
15	7 33 41	9 35 54	11 26 18	13 28 31	15 26 47	17 29 1	19 27 17	21 29 31	23 31 44	1 30 0	3 32 14	5 30 30
16	7 37 37	9 39 51	11 30 14	13 32 27	15 30 44	17 32 57	19 31 14	21 33 27	23 35 40	1 33 57	3 36 10	5 34 27
17	7 41 34	9 43 47	11 34 11	13 36 24	15 34 41	17 36 54	19 35 10	21 37 24	23 39 37	1 37 54	3 40 7	5 38 23
18	7 45 30	9 47 44	11 38 7	13 40 20	15 38 37	17 40 50	19 39 7	21 41 20	23 43 33	1 41 50	3 44 3	5 42 20
19	7 49 27	9 51 40	11 42 4	13 44 17	15 42 34	17 44 47	19 43 4	21 45 17	23 47 30	1 45 47	3 47 60	5 46 16
20	7 53 24	9 55 37	11 46 0	13 48 14	15 46 30	17 48 43	19 47 0	21 49 13	23 51 27	1 49 43	3 51 56	5 50 13
21	7 57 20	9 59 33	11 49 57	13 52 10	15 50 27	17 52 40	19 50 57	21 53 10	23 55 23	1 53 40	3 55 53	5 54 10
22	8 1 17	10 3 30	11 53 53	13 56 7	15 54 23	17 56 37	19 54 53	21 57 6	23 59 20	1 57 36	3 59 50	5 58 6
23	8 5 13	10 7 26	11 57 50	14 0 3	15 58 20	18 0 33	19 58 50	22 1 3	0 3 16	2 1 33	4 3 46	6 2 3
24	8 9 10	10 11 23	12 1 47	14 3 60	16 2 16	18 4 30	20 2 46	22 4 60	0 7 13	2 5 29	4 7 43	6 5 59
25	8 13 6	10 15 20	12 5 43	14 7 56	16 6 13	18 8 26	20 6 43	22 8 56	0 11 9	2 9 26	4 11 39	6 9 56
26	8 17 3	10 19 16	12 9 40	14 11 53	16 10 10	18 12 23	20 10 39	22 12 53	0 15 6	2 13 23	4 15 36	6 13 52
27	8 20 59	10 23 13	12 13 36	14 15 49	16 14 6	18 16 19	20 14 36	22 16 49	0 19 2	2 17 19	4 19 32	6 17 49
28	8 24 56	10 27 9	12 17 33	14 19 46	16 18 3	18 20 16	20 18 33	22 20 46	0 22 59	2 21 16	4 23 29	6 21 45
29	8 28 53		12 21 29	14 23 43	16 21 59	18 24 12	20 22 29	22 24 42	0 26 56	2 25 12	4 27 25	6 25 42
30	8 32 49		12 25 26	14 27 39	16 25 56	18 28 9	20 26 26	22 28 39	0 30 52	2 29 9	4 31 22	6 29 39
31	8 36 46		12 29 22		16 29 52		20 30 22	22 32 35		2 33 5		6 33 35

Year Corrections

Table 1	+	Table 2	+	Table 3	+	Table 4	+
1920	0 0 0	1921	0 0 0	1922	0 0 0	1923	0 0 0
1924	0 0 7	1925	0 0 7	1926	0 0 7	1927	0 0 7
1928	0 0 15	1929	0 0 15	1930	0 0 15	1931	0 0 15
1932	0 0 22	1933	0 0 22	1934	0 0 22	1935	0 0 22
1936	0 0 30	1937	0 0 30	1938	0 0 30	1939	0 0 30
1940	0 0 37	1941	0 0 37	1942	0 0 37	1943	0 0 37
1944	0 0 44	1945	0 0 44	1946	0 0 44	1947	0 0 44
1948	0 0 52	1949	0 0 52	1950	0 0 52	1951	0 0 52
1952	0 0 59	1953	0 0 59	1954	0 0 59	1955	0 0 59
1956	0 1 6	1957	0 1 6	1958	0 1 6	1959	0 1 6
1960	0 1 14	1961	0 1 14	1962	0 1 14	1963	0 1 14
1964	0 1 21	1965	0 1 21	1966	0 1 21	1967	0 1 21
1968	0 1 29	1969	0 1 29	1970	0 1 29	1971	0 1 29
1972	0 1 36	1973	0 1 36	1974	0 1 36	1975	0 1 36
1976	0 1 43	1977	0 1 43	1978	0 1 43	1979	0 1 43
1980	0 1 51	1981	0 1 51	1982	0 1 51	1983	0 1 51
1984	0 1 58	1985	0 1 58	1986	0 1 58	1987	0 1 58
1988	0 2 6	1989	0 2 6	1990	0 2 6	1991	0 2 6
1992	0 2 13	1993	0 2 13	1994	0 2 13	1995	0 2 13
1996	0 2 20	1997	0 2 20	1998	0 2 20	1999	0 2 20
2000	0 2 28	2001	0 2 28	2002	0 2 28	2003	0 2 28
2004	0 2 35	2005	0 2 35	2006	0 2 35	2007	0 2 35
2008	0 2 42	2009	0 2 42	2010	0 2 42	2011	0 2 42
2012	0 2 50	2013	0 2 50	2014	0 2 50	2015	0 2 50
2016	0 2 57	2017	0 2 57	2018	0 2 57	2019	0 2 57

ST	MC	2°0' ASC	4°0' ASC	7°0' ASC	11°0' ASC	14°0' ASC	18°0' ASC	21°59' ASC	25°19' ASC	28°40' ASC	30°2' ASC	31°46' ASC	33°20' ASC	35°39' ASC	37°58' ASC	40°43' ASC	41°54' ASC	45°30' ASC	48°50' ASC	50°22' ASC	51°32' ASC	52°57' ASC	54°34' ASC	56°28' ASC	57°29 ASC	59°0' ASC	59°56' ASC
	°	° '	° '	° '	° '	° '	° '	° '	° '	° '	° '	° '	° '	° '	° '	° '	° '	° '	° '	° '	° '	° '	° '	° '	° '	° '	° '
0 0 0	0 ♈	0 ♋ 48	1 ♋ 36	2 ♋ 48	4 ♋ 25	5 ♋ 40	7 ♋ 22	9 ♋ 8	10 ♋ 40	12 ♋ 16	12 ♋ 57	13 ♋ 50	14 ♋ 40	15 ♋ 56	17 ♋ 15	18 ♋ 54	19 ♋ 39	22 ♋ 3	24 ♋ 28	25 ♋ 40	26 ♋ 36	27 ♋ 48	29 ♋ 13	0 ♌ 59	1 ♌ 58	3 ♌ 31	4 ♌ 30
0 3 40	1	1 38	2 26	3 38	5 16	6 30	8 12	9 57	11 28	13 5	13 45	14 38	15 27	16 42	18 1	19 39	20 24	22 46	25 10	26 21	27 16	28 27	29 51	1 36	2 35	4 6	5 4
0 7 20	2	2 29	3 17	4 29	6 6	7 20	9 1	10 46	12 17	13 53	14 33	15 25	16 14	17 29	18 47	20 24	21 8	23 29	25 51	27 1	27 57	29 6	0 ♌ 30	2 13	3 11	4 41	5 39
0 11 1	3	3 19	4 7	5 19	6 56	8 10	9 51	11 35	13 5	14 41	15 21	16 13	17 1	18 15	19 33	21 9	21 53	24 12	26 33	27 42	28 37	29 46	1 8	2 50	3 47	5 16	6 13
0 14 41	4	4 10	4 57	6 9	7 46	9 0	10 40	12 24	13 54	15 28	16 8	17 0	17 48	19 2	20 18	21 54	22 37	24 55	27 14	28 23	29 17	0 ♌ 25	1 46	3 27	4 23	5 51	6 47
0 18 21	5	5 0	5 48	7 0	8 36	9 49	11 30	13 13	14 42	16 16	16 56	17 47	18 35	19 48	21 4	22 39	23 21	25 38	27 56	29 3	29 57	1 4	2 24	4 3	4 59	6 26	7 21
0 22 2	6	5 51	6 38	7 50	9 26	10 39	12 19	14 2	15 31	17 4	17 43	18 34	19 22	20 34	21 49	23 23	24 5	26 21	28 37	29 44	0 ♌ 37	1 43	3 2	4 40	5 35	7 0	7 55
0 25 42	7	6 42	7 29	8 40	10 16	11 29	13 8	14 50	16 19	17 52	18 31	19 21	20 8	21 20	22 35	24 8	24 50	27 3	29 18	0 ♌ 24	1 16	2 22	3 40	5 17	6 11	7 35	8 29
0 29 23	8	7 32	8 20	9 31	11 6	12 19	13 58	15 39	17 7	18 39	19 18	20 8	20 55	22 6	23 20	24 52	25 34	27 46	29 59	1 5	1 56	3 1	4 18	5 53	6 47	8 10	9 3
0 33 4	9	8 23	9 10	10 21	11 56	13 9	14 47	16 28	17 56	19 27	20 5	20 55	21 41	22 52	24 5	25 37	26 18	28 29	0 ♌ 40	1 45	2 36	3 40	4 56	6 30	7 23	8 45	9 37
0 36 45	10	9 14	10 1	11 12	12 47	13 59	15 37	17 17	18 44	20 15	20 53	21 42	22 28	23 38	24 50	26 21	27 1	29 11	1 21	2 25	3 15	4 18	5 34	7 7	7 59	9 20	10 11
0 40 27	11	10 5	10 52	12 2	13 37	14 49	16 26	18 6	19 32	21 2	21 40	22 29	23 14	24 24	25 36	27 5	27 45	29 54	2 2	3 5	3 55	4 57	6 11	7 43	8 35	9 54	10 45
0 44 8	12	10 56	11 43	12 53	14 27	15 38	17 15	18 55	20 20	21 50	22 27	23 16	24 1	25 9	26 21	27 49	28 29	0 ♌ 36	2 43	3 45	4 34	5 36	6 49	8 20	9 10	10 29	11 19
0 47 50	13	11 47	12 33	13 44	15 17	16 28	18 5	19 43	21 9	22 37	23 14	24 3	24 47	25 55	27 6	28 34	29 13	1 18	3 24	4 26	5 14	6 15	7 27	8 56	9 46	11 4	11 53
0 51 32	14	12 38	13 25	14 34	16 8	17 18	18 54	20 32	21 57	23 25	24 2	24 50	25 34	26 41	27 51	29 18	29 57	2 1	4 5	5 6	5 53	6 53	8 5	9 33	10 22	11 39	12 27
0 55 15	15	13 29	14 16	15 25	16 58	18 9	19 44	21 21	22 45	24 12	24 49	25 36	26 20	27 27	28 36	0 ♌ 2	0 ♌ 40	2 43	4 46	5 46	6 33	7 32	8 42	10 9	10 58	12 13	13 1
0 58 57	16	14 21	15 7	16 16	17 49	18 59	20 33	22 10	23 33	25 0	25 36	26 23	27 7	28 13	29 21	0 46	1 24	3 26	5 27	6 26	7 12	8 11	9 20	10 46	11 34	12 48	13 36
1 2 40	17	15 12	15 58	17 7	18 39	19 49	21 23	22 59	24 22	25 48	26 24	27 10	27 53	28 58	0 ♌ 6	1 30	2 8	4 8	6 8	7 6	7 52	8 49	9 58	11 23	12 10	13 23	14 10
1 6 24	18	16 4	16 50	17 59	19 30	20 39	22 13	23 48	25 10	26 35	27 11	27 57	28 40	29 44	0 51	2 15	2 52	4 50	6 48	7 46	8 31	9 28	10 36	11 59	12 46	13 58	14 44
1 10 7	19	16 56	17 42	18 50	20 21	21 30	23 3	24 37	25 59	27 23	27 58	28 44	29 26	0 ♌ 30	1 37	2 59	3 36	5 33	7 29	8 26	9 11	10 7	11 14	12 36	13 22	14 33	15 18
1 13 52	20	17 48	18 33	19 41	21 12	22 20	23 53	25 26	26 47	28 11	28 46	29 31	0 ♌ 13	1 16	2 22	3 43	4 19	6 15	8 10	9 6	9 50	10 46	11 51	13 12	13 58	15 8	15 52
1 17 36	21	18 40	19 25	20 33	22 3	23 11	24 43	26 16	27 36	28 58	29 33	0 ♌ 18	0 59	2 2	3 7	4 27	5 3	6 57	8 51	9 46	10 30	11 25	12 29	13 49	14 34	15 43	16 27
1 21 21	22	19 32	20 17	21 25	22 54	24 2	25 33	27 5	28 24	29 46	0 ♌ 21	1 5	1 46	2 48	3 52	5 12	5 47	7 40	9 32	10 27	11 10	12 3	13 7	14 26	15 10	16 18	17 1
1 25 7	23	20 25	21 10	22 17	23 46	24 53	26 23	27 54	29 13	0 ♌ 34	1 8	1 52	2 33	3 34	4 37	5 56	6 31	8 22	10 13	11 7	11 49	12 42	13 45	15 3	15 46	16 53	17 36
1 28 52	24	21 18	22 2	23 9	24 37	25 44	27 13	28 44	0 ♌ 2	1 22	1 56	2 39	3 19	4 20	5 23	6 40	7 15	9 5	10 54	11 47	12 29	13 21	14 23	15 40	16 22	17 28	18 10
1 32 39	25	22 11	22 55	24 1	25 29	26 35	28 4	29 34	0 51	2 10	2 44	3 27	4 6	5 6	6 8	7 25	7 59	9 47	11 35	12 28	13 9	14 0	15 1	16 16	16 58	18 3	18 45
1 36 26	26	23 4	23 48	24 54	26 21	27 26	28 54	0 ♌ 23	1 40	2 59	3 32	4 14	4 53	5 52	6 54	8 9	8 43	10 30	12 16	13 8	13 48	14 39	15 39	16 53	17 35	18 39	19 19
1 40 13	27	23 57	24 41	25 46	27 13	28 18	29 45	1 13	2 29	3 47	4 19	5 1	5 40	6 39	7 39	8 54	9 27	11 13	12 58	13 48	14 28	15 18	16 18	17 30	18 11	19 14	19 54
1 44 1	28	24 51	25 34	26 39	28 5	29 9	0 ♌ 36	2 3	3 18	4 35	5 8	5 49	6 27	7 25	8 25	9 39	10 11	11 55	13 39	14 29	15 8	15 57	16 56	18 8	18 48	19 49	20 29
1 47 49	29	25 44	26 28	27 32	28 57	0 ♌ 1	1 27	2 54	4 8	5 24	5 56	6 37	7 14	8 12	9 11	10 23	10 56	12 38	14 20	15 9	15 48	16 37	17 34	18 45	19 24	20 25	21 4
1 51 38	30	26 38	27 22	28 25	29 50	0 53	2 18	3 44	4 57	6 13	6 44	7 24	8 2	8 58	9 56	11 8	11 40	13 21	15 2	15 50	16 28	17 16	18 12	19 22	20 1	21 1	21 39
1 51 38	0 ♉	26 ♋ 38	27 ♋ 22	28 ♋ 25	29 ♋ 50	0 ♌ 53	2 ♌ 18	3 ♌ 44	4 ♌ 57	6 ♌ 13	6 ♌ 44	7 ♌ 24	8 ♌ 2	8 ♌ 58	9 ♌ 56	11 ♌ 8	11 ♌ 40	13 ♌ 21	15 ♌ 2	15 ♌ 50	16 ♌ 28	17 ♌ 16	18 ♌ 12	19 ♌ 22	20 ♌ 1	21 ♌ 1	21 ♌ 39
1 55 28	1	27 33	28 15	29 19	0 ♌ 43	1 45	3 10	4 34	5 47	7 1	7 32	8 12	8 49	9 45	10 42	11 53	12 24	14 4	15 43	16 31	17 8	17 55	18 51	19 59	20 37	21 36	22 14
1 59 18	2	28 27	29 10	0 ♌ 13	1 36	2 38	4 1	5 25	6 37	7 50	8 21	9 0	9 37	10 32	11 28	12 38	13 9	14 47	16 25	17 12	17 49	18 35	19 30	20 37	21 14	22 12	22 49
2 3 9	3	29 22	0 ♌ 4	1 7	2 29	3 30	4 53	6 16	7 26	8 39	9 9	9 48	10 24	11 19	12 14	13 23	13 54	15 31	17 6	17 53	18 29	19 14	20 8	21 14	21 51	22 48	23 24
2 7 0	4	0 ♌ 17	0 59	2 1	3 22	4 23	5 45	7 7	8 17	9 28	9 58	10 37	11 12	12 6	13 1	14 8	14 38	16 14	17 48	18 34	19 9	19 54	20 47	21 52	22 28	23 24	24 0
2 10 52	5	1 13	1 54	2 55	4 16	5 16	6 37	7 58	9 7	10 18	10 47	11 25	12 0	12 53	13 47	14 54	15 23	16 57	18 30	19 15	19 50	20 34	21 26	22 30	23 5	24 0	24 35
2 14 45	6	2 8	2 49	3 50	5 10	6 9	7 29	8 49	9 57	11 7	11 36	12 14	12 48	13 40	14 33	15 39	16 8	17 41	19 12	19 56	20 30	21 14	22 5	23 7	23 42	24 36	25 11
2 18 38	7	3 4	3 45	4 45	6 4	7 3	8 22	9 41	10 48	11 57	12 25	13 2	13 36	14 27	15 20	16 25	16 53	18 24	19 54	20 37	21 11	21 54	22 44	23 45	24 20	25 13	25 46
2 22 32	8	4 0	4 41	5 40	6 58	7 57	9 14	10 32	11 39	12 47	13 15	13 51	14 25	15 15	16 7	17 10	17 39	19 8	20 36	21 19	21 52	22 34	23 23	24 23	24 57	25 49	26 22
2 26 26	9	4 57	5 37	6 36	7 53	8 50	10 7	11 24	12 30	13 37	14 4	14 40	15 13	16 3	16 54	17 56	18 24	19 52	21 18	22 0	22 33	23 14	24 2	25 2	25 35	26 25	26 58
2 30 22	10	5 54	6 33	7 31	8 48	9 45	11 0	12 16	13 21	14 27	14 54	15 29	16 2	16 50	17 41	18 42	19 9	20 36	22 1	22 42	23 14	23 54	24 42	25 40	26 12	27 2	27 34
2 34 17	11	6 51	7 30	8 27	9 43	10 39	11 54	13 8	14 12	15 17	15 44	16 19	16 50	17 38	18 28	19 28	19 55	21 20	22 43	23 24	23 55	24 34	25 21	26 18	26 50	27 39	28 10
2 38 14	12	7 48	8 27	9 24	10 38	11 33	12 47	14 1	15 3	16 7	16 34	17 8	17 39	18 27	19 15	20 15	20 41	22 4	23 26	24 5	24 36	25 15	26 1	26 57	27 28	28 16	28 46
2 42 11	13	8 46	9 24	10 20	11 34	12 28	13 41	14 54	15 55	16 58	17 24	17 58	18 28	19 15	20 2	21 1	21 27	22 48	24 9	24 47	25 18	25 56	26 40	27 35	28 6	28 53	29 23
2 46 9	14	9 44	10 22	11 17	12 30	13 23	14 35	15 46	16 47	17 49	18 15	18 48	19 18	20 3	20 50	21 47	22 13	23 33	24 52	25 30	25 59	26 36	27 20	28 14	28 44	29 30	29 59
2 50 8	15	10 43	11 20	12 14	13 26	14 19	15 29	16 40	17 39	18 40	19 5	19 38	20 7	20 52	21 38	22 34	22 59	24 17	25 35	26 12	26 41	27 17	28 0	28 53	29 22	0 ♍ 7	0 ♍ 36
2 54 8	16	11 42	12 18	13 12	14 22	15 14	16 24	17 33	18 31	19 31	19 56	20 28	20 57	21 41	22 26	23 21	23 45	25 2	26 18	26 54	27 23	27 58	28 40	29 32	0 ♍ 0	0 44	1 13
2 58 8	17	12 41	13 17	14 10	15 19	16 10	17 18	18 26	19 24	20 23	20 47	21 18	21 47	22 30	23 14	24 8	24 32	25 47	27 1	27 37	28 5	28 39	29 21	0 ♍ 11	0 39	1 22	1 49
3 2 9	18	13 40	14 16	15 8	16 16	17 6	18 13	19 20	20 17	21 14	21 38	22 9	22 37	23 19	24 2	24 55	25 18	26 32	27 45	28 19	28 47	29 21	0 ♍ 1	0 50	1 17	2 0	2 26
3 6 10	19	14 40	15 15	16 6	17 13	18 3	19 9	20 14	21 10	22 6	22 29	22 59	23 27	24 8	24 50	25 42	26 5	27 17	28 28	29 2	29 29	0 ♍ 2	0 41	1 30	1 56	2 37	3 3
3 10 13	20	15 40	16 14	17 5	18 11	19 0	20 4	21 8	22 3	22 58	23 21	23 50	24 17	24 57	25 39	26 30	26 52	28 3	29 12	29 45	0 ♍ 11	0 44	1 22	2 9	2 35	3 15	3 41
3 14 16	21	16 41	17 14	18 4	19 9	19 57	21 0	22 3	22 56	23 50	24 13	24 41	25 8	25 47	26 28	27 17	27 39	28 48	29 56	0 ♍ 28	0 54	1 25	2 3	2 49	3 14	3 53	4 18
3 18 20	22	17 42	18 15	19 3	20 7	20 54	21 56	22 58	23 50	24 43	25 4	25 33	25 58	26 37	27 17	28 5	28 26	29 34	0 ♍ 40	1 11	1 36	2 7	2 44	3 28	3 53	4 31	4 56
3 22 24	23	18 43	19 15	20 3	21 5	21 51	22 52	23 52	24 43	25 35	25 57	26 24	26 49	27 27	28 6	28 53	29 14	0 ♍ 19	1 24	1 55	2 19	2 49	3 25	4 8	4 32	5 10	5 33
3 26 30	24	19 44	20 16	21 3	22 4	22 49	23 48	24 48	25 37	26 28	26 49	27 16	27 40	28 17	28 55	29 41	0 ♍ 1	1 5	2 8	2 38	3 2	3 31	4 6	4 48	5 12	5 48	6 11
3 30 36	25	20 46	21 18	22 3	23 3	23 47	24 45	25 43	26 32	27 21	27 41	28 8	28 31	29 7	29 44	0 ♍ 29	0 49	1 51	2 52	3 22	3 45	4 13	4 47	5 28	5 51	6 27	6 49
3 34 42	26	21 49	22 19	23 4	24 2	24 45	25 42	26 39	27 26	28 14	28 34	29 0	29 23	29 58	0 ♍ 34	1 18	1 37	2 38	3 37	4 6	4 28	4 56	5 29	6 9	6 31	7 5	7 27
3 38 50	27	22 51	23 21	24 5	25 2	25 44	26 39	27 34	28 21	29 8	29 27	29 52	0 ♍ 14	0 ♍ 49	1 23	2 6	2 25	3 24	4 22	4 50	5 11	5 38	6 10	6 49	7 11	7 44	8 5
3 42 58	28	23 54	24 24	25 6	26 2	26 43	27 37	28 30	29 15	0 ♍ 1	0 ♍ 20	0 ♍ 44	1 6	1 39	2 13	2 55	3 13	4 10	5 7	5 34	5 55	6 21	6 52	7 30	7 51	8 23	8 43
3 47 7	29	24 58	25 26	26 8	27 2	27 42	28 35	29 27	0 ♍ 11	0 55	1 13	1 37	1 58	2 31	3 3	3 44	4 1	4 57	5 52	6 18	6 38	7 4	7 34	8 10	8 31	9 2	9 22
3 51 16	30	26 1	26 29	27 10	28 3	28 41	29 33	0 ♍ 23	1 6	1 49	2 7	2 30	2 50	3 22	3 54	4 33	4 50	5 44	6 37	7 2	7 22	7 47	8 16	8 51	9 11	9 41	10 0
3 51 16	0 ♊	26 ♌ 1	26 ♌ 29	27 ♌ 10	28 ♌ 3	28 ♌ 41	29 ♌ 33	0 ♍ 23	1 ♍ 6	1 ♍ 49	2 ♍ 7	2 ♍ 30	2 ♍ 50	3 ♍ 22	3 ♍ 54	4 ♍ 33	4 ♍ 50	5 ♍ 44	6 ♍ 37	7 ♍ 2	7 ♍ 22	7 ♍ 47	8 ♍ 16	8 ♍ 51	9 ♍ 11	9 ♍ 41	10 ♍ 0
3 55 26	1	27 6	27 33	28 12	29 3	29 41	0 ♍ 31	1 20	2 1	2 43	3 0	3 23	3 43	4 13	4 44	5 22	5 39	6 31	7 22	7 47	8 6	8 30	8 58	9 32	9 51	10 20	10 39
3 59 37	2	28 10	28 36	29 15	0 ♍ 4	0 ♍ 41	1 29	2 17	2 57	3 38	3 54	4 16	4 35	5 5	5 35	6 11	6 27	7 18	8 7	8 31	8 50	9 13	9 40	10 13	10 31	11 0	11 18
4 3 49	3	29 15	29 40	0 ♍ 17	1 6	1 41	2 28	3 14	3 53	4 32	4 48	5 9	5 28	5 56	6 25	7 1	7 16	8 5	8 53	9 16	9 34	9 56	10 22	10 54	11 12	11 39	11 57
4 8 1	4	0 ♍ 20	0 ♍ 44	1 21	2 7	2 42	3 27	4 12	4 49	5 27	5 43	6 3	6 21	6 48	7 16	7 50	8 5	8 53	9 39	10 1	10 18	10 39	11 5	11 36	11 53	12 19	12 36
4 12 14	5	1 25	1 49	2 24	3 9	3 42	4 26	5 9	5 45	6 22	6 37	6 56	7 14	7 40	8 7	8 40	8 55	9 40	10 24	10 46	11 2	11 23	11 47	12 17	12 33	12 59	13 15
4 16 27	6	2 31	2 54	3 28	4 11	4 43	5 25	6 7	6 42	7 17	7 32	7 50	8 7	8 33	8 58	9 30	9 44	10 28	11 10	11 31	11 47	12 7	12 30	12 58	13 14	13 39	13 54
4 20 41	7	3 37	3 59	4 32	5 14	5 45	6 25	7 5	7 38	8 12	8 26	8 44	9 0	9 25	9 50	10 20	10 34	11 15	11 56	12 16	12 31	12 50	13 13	13 40	13 55	14 19	14 33
4 24 56	8	4 43	5 5	5 36	6 16	6 46	7 25	8 3	8 35	9 8	9 21	9 38	9 54	10 17	10 41	11 10	11 23	12 3	12 42	13 1	13 16	13 34	13 56	14 22	14 36	14 59	15 13
4 29 11	9	5 50	6 11	6 41	7 19	7 48	8 25	9 2	9 32	10 4	10 16	10 33	10 48	11 10	11 33	12 1	12 13	12 51	13 29	13 47	14 1	14 18	14 39	15 4	15 18	15 39	15 52
4 33 27	10	6 57	7 17	7 45	8 22	8 50	9 25	10 0	10 30	10 59	11 12	11 27	11 41	12 3	12 25	12 51	13 3	13 39	14 15	14 32	14 46	15 2	15 22	15 46	15 59	16 19	16 32
4 37 43	11	8 4	8 23	8 50	9 26	9 52	10 26	10 59	11 27	11 55	12 7	12 22	12 35	12 56	13 17	13 42	13 53	14 28	15 2	15 18	15 31	15 46	16 5	16 28	16 40	17 0	17 12
4 41 59	12	9 12	9 30	9 56	10 29	10 54	11 26	11 58	12 25	12 51	13 3	13 17	13 30	13 49	14 9	14 33	14 43	15 16	15 48	16 4	16 16	16 31	16 48	17 10	17 22	17 40	17 52
4 46 17	13	10 20	10 37	11 1	11 33	11 56	12 27	12 57	13 22	13 48	13 58	14 12	14 24	14 42	15 1	15 23	15 33	16 5	16 35	16 50	17 1	17 15	17 32	17 52	18 3	18 21	18 32
4 50 34	14	11 28	11 44	12 7	12 37	12 59	13 28	13 56	14 20	14 44	14 54	15 7	15 18	15 35	15 53	16 14	16 24	16 53	17 22	17 36	17 46	18 0	18 15	18 34	18 45	19 1	19 12
4 54 53	15	12 36	12 51	13 13	13 41	14 2	14 29	14 56	15 18	15 41	15 50	16 2	16 13	16 29	16 45	17 5	17 14	17 42	18 9	18 22	18 32	18 44	18 59	19 17	19 27	19 42	19 52
4 59 11	16	13 44	13 59	14 19	14 46	15 5	15 30	15 55	16 16	16 37	16 46	16 57	17 7	17 22	17 38	17 57	18 5	18 31	18 56	19 8	19 17	19 29	19 43	19 59	20 9	20 23	20 32
5 3 30	17	14 53	15 6	15 25	15 50	16 8	16 32	16 55	17 15	17 34	17 42	17 53	18 2	18 16	18 30	18 48	18 55	19 19	19 43	19 54	20 3	20 14	20 26	20 42	20 51	21 4	21 12
5 7 49	18	16 2	16 14	16 32	16 55	17 12	17 34	17 55	18 13	18 31	18 39	18 48	18 57	19 10	19 23	19 39	19 46	20 8	20 30	20 40	20 48	20 58	21 10	21 25	21 33	21 45	21 53
5 12 9	19	17 11	17 22	17 39	18 0	18 15	18 35	18 55	19 12	19 28	19 35	19 44	19 52	20 4	20 16	20 31	20 37	20 57	21 17	21 27	21 34	21 43	21 54	22 7	22 15	22 26	22 33
5 16 29	20	18 21	18 31	18 46	19 5	19 19	19 37	19 55	20 10	20 25	20 32	20 39	20 47	20 58	21 9	21 22	21 28	21 47	22 5	22 13	22 20	22 28	22 38	22 50	22 57	23 7	23 13
5 20 49	21	19 30	19 39	19 53	20 10	20 23	20 39	20 55	21 9	21 23	21 28	21 35	21 42	21 52	22 2	22 14	22 19	22 36	22 52	23 0	23 6	23 13	23 22	23 33	23 39	23 48	23 54
5 25 10	22	20 40	20 48	21 0	21 15	21 26	21 41	21 56	22 8	22 20	22 25	22 31	22 37	22 46	22 55	23 5	23 10	23 25	23 39	23 46	23 52	23 58	24 6	24 16	24 21	24 29	24 34
5 29 31	23	21 49	21 57	22 7	22 21	22 30	22 43	22 56	23 7	23 17	23 22	23 27	23 32	23 40	23 48	23 57	24 1	24 14	24 27	24 33	24 38	24 43	24 50	24 59	25 3	25 11	25 15
5 33 51	24	22 59	23 5	23 14	23 26	23 34	23 46	23 56	24 5	24 15	24 18	24 23	24 28	24 34	24 41	24 49	24 52	25 3	25 14	25 20	25 24	25 29	25 34	25 42	25 46	25 52	25 56
5 38 13	25	24 9	24 14	24 22	24 32	24 39	24 48	24 57	25 4	25 12	25 15	25 19	25 23	25 28	25 34	25 41	25 44	25 53	26 2	26 6	26 10	26 14	26 19	26 25	26 28	26 33	26 36
5 42 34	26	25 19	25 23	25 29	25 37	25 43	25 50	25 57	26 4	26 10	26 12	26 15	26 18	26 23	26 27	26 32	26 35	26 42	26 49	26 53	26 56	26 59	27 3	27 8	27 10	27 14	27 17
5 46 55	27	26 29	26 33	26 37	26 43	26 47	26 53	26 58	27 3	27 7	27 9	27 11	27 14	27 17	27 20	27 24	27 26	27 32	27 37	27 40	27 42	27 44	27 47	27 51	27 53	27 56	27 58
5 51 17	28	27 40	27 42	27 45	27 49	27 51	27 55	27 59	28 2	28 5	28 6	28 8	28 9	28 11	28 13	28 16	28 17	28 21	28 25	28 26	28 28	28 29	28 31	28 34	28 35	28 37	28 38
5 55 38	29	28 50	28 51	28 52	28 54	28 56	28 58	28 59	29 1	29 2	29 3	29 4	29 5	29 6	29 7	29 8	29 9	29 11	29 12	29 13	29 14	29 15	29 16	29 17	29 18	29 19	29 19
6 0 0	30	0 ♎ 0	0 ♎ 0	0 ♎ 0	0 ♎ 0	0 ♎ 0	0 ♎ 0	0 ♎ 0	0 ♎ 0	0 ♎ 0	0 ♎ 0	0 ♎ 0	0 ♎ 0	0 ♎ 0	0 ♎ 0	0 ♎ 0	0 ♎ 0	0 ♎ 0	0 ♎ 0	0 ♎ 0	0 ♎ 0	0 ♎ 0	0 ♎ 0	0 ♎ 0	0 ♎ 0	0 ♎ 0	0 ♎ 0

ST	MC °	2°0' ASC ° ′	4°0' ASC ° ′	7°0' ASC ° ′	11°0' ASC ° ′	14°0' ASC ° ′	18°0' ASC ° ′	21°59' ASC ° ′	25°19' ASC ° ′	28°40' ASC ° ′	30°2' ASC ° ′	31°46' ASC ° ′	33°20' ASC ° ′	35°39' ASC ° ′	37°58' ASC ° ′	40°43' ASC ° ′	41°54' ASC ° ′	45°30' ASC ° ′	48°50' ASC ° ′	50°22' ASC ° ′	51°32' ASC ° ′	52°57' ASC ° ′	54°34' ASC ° ′	56°28' ASC ° ′	57°29 ASC ° ′	59°0' ASC ° ′	59°56' ASC ° ′
6 0 0	0 ♋	0 ≏ 0	0 ≏ 0	0 ≏ 0	0 ≏ 0	0 ≏ 0	0 ≏ 0	0 ≏ 0	0 ≏ 0	0 ≏ 0	0 ≏ 0	0 ≏ 0	0 ≏ 0	0 ≏ 0	0 ≏ 0	0 ≏ 0	0 ≏ 0	0 ≏ 0	0 ≏ 0	0 ≏ 0	0 ≏ 0	0 ≏ 0	0 ≏ 0	0 ≏ 0	0 ≏ 0	0 ≏ 0	0 ≏ 0
6 4 22	1	1 10	1 9	1 8	1 6	1 4	1 2	1 1	0 59	0 58	0 57	0 56	0 55	0 54	0 53	0 52	0 51	0 49	0 48	0 47	0 46	0 45	0 44	0 43	0 42	0 41	0 41
6 8 43	2	2 20	2 18	2 15	2 11	2 9	2 5	2 1	1 58	1 55	1 54	1 52	1 51	1 49	1 47	1 44	1 43	1 39	1 35	1 34	1 32	1 31	1 29	1 26	1 25	1 23	1 22
6 13 5	3	3 31	3 27	3 23	3 17	3 13	3 7	3 2	2 57	2 53	2 51	2 49	2 46	2 43	2 40	2 36	2 34	2 28	2 23	2 20	2 18	2 16	2 13	2 9	2 7	2 4	2 2
6 17 26	4	4 41	4 37	4 31	4 23	4 17	4 10	4 3	3 56	3 50	3 48	3 45	3 42	3 37	3 33	3 28	3 25	3 18	3 11	3 7	3 4	3 1	2 57	2 52	2 50	2 46	2 43
6 21 47	5	5 51	5 46	5 38	5 28	5 21	5 12	5 3	4 56	4 48	4 45	4 41	4 37	4 32	4 26	4 19	4 16	4 7	3 58	3 54	3 50	3 46	3 41	3 35	3 32	3 27	3 24
6 26 9	6	7 1	6 55	6 46	6 34	6 26	6 14	6 4	5 55	5 45	5 42	5 37	5 32	5 26	5 19	5 11	5 8	4 57	4 46	4 40	4 36	4 31	4 26	4 18	4 14	4 8	4 4
6 30 29	7	8 11	8 3	7 53	7 39	7 30	7 17	7 4	6 53	6 43	6 38	6 33	6 28	6 20	6 12	6 3	5 59	5 46	5 33	5 27	5 22	5 17	5 10	5 1	4 57	4 49	4 45
6 34 50	8	9 20	9 12	9 0	8 45	8 34	8 19	8 4	7 52	7 40	7 35	7 29	7 23	7 14	7 5	6 55	6 50	6 35	6 21	6 14	6 8	6 2	5 54	5 44	5 39	5 31	5 26
6 39 11	9	10 30	10 21	10 7	9 50	9 37	9 21	9 5	8 51	8 37	8 32	8 25	8 18	8 8	7 58	7 46	7 41	7 24	7 8	7 0	6 54	6 47	6 38	6 27	6 21	6 12	6 6
6 43 31	10	11 39	11 29	11 14	10 55	10 41	10 23	10 5	9 50	9 35	9 28	9 21	9 13	9 2	8 51	8 38	8 32	8 13	7 55	7 47	7 40	7 32	7 22	7 10	7 3	6 53	6 47
6 47 51	11	12 49	12 38	12 21	12 0	11 45	11 25	11 5	10 48	10 32	10 25	10 16	10 8	9 56	9 44	9 29	9 23	9 3	8 43	8 33	8 26	8 17	8 6	7 53	7 45	7 34	7 27
6 52 11	12	13 58	13 46	13 28	13 5	12 48	12 26	12 5	11 47	11 29	11 21	11 12	11 3	10 50	10 37	10 21	10 14	9 52	9 30	9 20	9 12	9 2	8 50	8 35	8 27	8 15	8 7
6 56 30	13	15 7	14 54	14 35	14 10	13 52	13 28	13 5	12 45	12 26	12 18	12 7	11 58	11 44	11 30	11 12	11 5	10 41	10 17	10 6	9 57	9 46	9 34	9 18	9 9	8 56	8 48
7 0 49	14	16 16	16 1	15 41	15 14	14 55	14 30	14 5	13 44	13 23	13 14	13 3	12 53	12 38	12 22	12 3	11 55	11 29	11 4	10 52	10 43	10 31	10 17	10 1	9 51	9 37	9 28
7 5 7	15	17 24	17 9	16 47	16 19	15 58	15 31	15 4	14 42	14 19	14 10	13 58	13 47	13 31	13 15	12 55	12 46	12 18	11 51	11 38	11 28	11 16	11 1	10 43	10 33	10 18	10 8
7 9 26	16	18 32	18 16	17 53	17 23	17 1	16 32	16 4	15 40	15 16	15 6	14 53	14 42	14 25	14 7	13 46	13 36	13 7	12 38	12 24	12 14	12 0	11 45	11 26	11 15	10 59	10 48
7 13 43	17	19 40	19 23	18 59	18 27	18 4	17 33	17 3	16 38	16 12	16 2	15 48	15 36	15 18	14 59	14 37	14 27	13 55	13 25	13 10	12 59	12 45	12 28	12 8	11 57	11 39	11 28
7 18 1	18	20 48	20 30	20 4	19 31	19 6	18 34	18 2	17 35	17 9	16 57	16 43	16 30	16 11	15 51	15 27	15 17	14 44	14 12	13 56	13 44	13 29	13 12	12 50	12 38	12 20	12 8
7 22 17	19	21 56	21 37	21 10	20 34	20 8	19 34	19 1	18 33	18 5	17 53	17 38	17 25	17 4	16 43	16 18	16 7	15 32	14 58	14 42	14 29	14 14	13 55	13 32	13 20	13 0	12 48
7 26 33	20	23 3	22 43	22 15	21 38	21 10	20 35	20 0	19 30	19 1	18 48	18 33	18 19	17 57	17 35	17 9	16 57	16 21	15 45	15 28	15 14	14 58	14 38	14 14	14 1	13 41	13 28
7 30 49	21	24 10	23 49	23 19	22 41	22 12	21 35	20 58	20 28	19 56	19 44	19 27	19 12	18 50	18 27	17 59	17 47	17 9	16 31	16 13	15 59	15 42	15 21	14 56	14 42	14 21	14 8
7 35 4	22	25 17	24 55	24 24	23 44	23 14	22 35	21 57	21 25	20 52	20 39	20 22	20 6	19 43	19 19	18 50	18 37	17 57	17 18	16 59	16 44	16 26	16 4	15 38	15 24	15 1	14 47
7 39 19	23	26 23	26 1	25 28	24 46	24 15	23 35	22 55	22 22	21 48	21 34	21 16	21 0	20 35	20 10	19 40	19 26	18 45	18 4	17 44	17 29	17 10	16 47	16 20	16 5	15 41	15 27
7 43 33	24	27 29	27 6	26 32	25 49	25 17	24 35	23 53	23 18	22 43	22 28	22 10	21 53	21 27	21 2	20 30	20 16	19 32	18 50	18 29	18 13	17 53	17 30	17 2	16 46	16 21	16 6
7 47 46	25	28 35	28 11	27 36	26 51	26 18	25 34	24 51	24 15	23 38	23 23	23 4	22 46	22 20	21 53	21 20	21 5	20 20	19 36	19 14	18 58	18 37	18 13	17 43	17 27	17 1	16 45
7 51 59	26	29 40	29 16	28 39	27 53	27 18	26 33	25 48	25 11	24 33	24 17	23 57	23 39	23 12	22 44	22 10	21 55	21 7	20 21	19 59	19 42	19 21	18 55	18 24	18 7	17 41	17 24
7 56 11	27	0 ♏ 45	0 ♏ 20	29 43	28 54	28 19	27 32	26 46	26 7	25 28	25 12	24 51	24 32	24 4	23 35	22 59	22 44	21 55	21 7	20 44	20 26	20 4	19 38	19 6	18 48	18 21	18 3
8 0 23	28	1 50	1 24	0 ♏ 45	29 56	29 19	28 31	27 43	27 3	26 22	26 6	25 44	25 25	24 55	24 25	23 49	23 33	22 42	21 53	21 29	21 10	20 47	20 20	19 47	19 29	19 0	18 42
8 4 34	29	2 54	2 27	1 48	0 ♏ 57	0 ♏ 19	29 29	28 40	27 59	27 17	27 0	26 37	26 17	25 47	25 16	24 38	24 21	23 29	22 38	22 13	21 54	21 30	21 2	20 28	20 9	19 40	19 21
8 8 44	30	3 59	3 31	2 50	1 57	1 19	0 ♏ 27	29 37	28 54	28 11	27 53	27 30	27 10	26 38	26 6	25 27	25 10	24 16	23 23	22 58	22 38	22 13	21 44	21 9	20 49	20 19	20 0
8 8 44	0 ♌	3 ♏ 59	3 ♏ 31	2 ♏ 50	1 ♏ 57	1 ♏ 19	0 ♏ 27	29 ≏ 37	28 ≏ 54	28 ≏ 11	27 ≏ 53	27 ≏ 30	27 ≏ 10	26 ≏ 38	26 ≏ 6	25 ≏ 27	25 ≏ 10	24 ≏ 16	23 ≏ 23	22 ≏ 58	22 ≏ 38	22 ≏ 13	21 ≏ 44	21 ≏ 9	20 ≏ 49	20 ≏ 19	20 ≏ 0
8 12 53	1	5 2	4 34	3 52	2 58	2 18	1 25	0 ♏ 33	29 49	29 5	28 47	28 23	28 2	27 29	26 57	26 16	25 59	25 3	24 8	23 42	23 22	22 56	22 26	21 50	21 29	20 58	20 38
8 17 2	2	6 6	5 36	4 54	3 58	3 17	2 23	1 30	0 ♏ 45	29 59	29 40	29 16	28 54	28 21	27 47	27 5	26 47	25 50	24 53	24 26	24 5	23 39	23 8	22 30	22 9	21 37	21 17
8 21 10	3	7 9	6 39	5 55	4 58	4 16	3 21	2 26	1 39	0 ♏ 52	0 ♏ 33	0 ♏ 8	29 46	29 11	28 37	27 54	27 35	26 36	25 38	25 10	24 49	24 22	23 50	23 11	22 49	22 16	21 55
8 25 18	4	8 11	7 41	6 56	5 58	5 15	4 18	3 21	2 34	1 46	1 26	1 0	0 ♏ 37	0 ♏ 2	29 26	28 42	28 23	27 22	26 23	25 54	25 32	25 4	24 31	23 51	23 29	22 55	22 33
8 29 24	5	9 14	8 42	7 57	6 57	6 13	5 15	4 17	3 28	2 39	2 19	1 52	1 29	0 53	0 ♏ 16	29 31	29 11	28 9	27 8	26 38	26 15	25 47	25 13	24 32	24 9	23 33	23 11
8 33 30	6	10 16	9 44	8 57	7 56	7 11	6 12	5 12	4 23	3 32	3 11	2 44	2 20	1 43	1 5	0 ♏ 19	29 59	28 55	27 52	27 22	26 58	26 29	25 54	25 12	24 48	24 12	23 49
8 37 36	7	11 17	10 45	9 57	8 55	8 9	7 8	6 8	5 17	4 25	4 3	3 36	3 11	2 33	1 54	1 7	0 ♏ 46	29 41	28 36	28 5	27 41	27 11	26 35	25 52	25 28	24 50	24 27
8 41 40	8	12 18	11 45	10 57	9 53	9 6	8 4	7 2	6 10	5 17	4 56	4 27	4 2	3 23	2 43	1 55	1 34	0 ♏ 26	29 20	28 49	28 24	27 53	27 16	26 32	26 7	25 29	25 4
8 45 44	9	13 19	12 46	11 56	10 51	10 3	9 0	7 57	7 4	6 10	5 47	5 19	4 52	4 13	3 32	2 43	2 21	1 12	0 ♏ 4	29 32	29 6	28 35	27 57	27 11	26 46	26 7	25 42
8 49 47	10	14 20	13 46	12 55	11 49	11 0	9 56	8 52	7 57	7 2	6 39	6 10	5 43	5 3	4 21	3 30	3 8	1 57	0 48	0 ♏ 15	29 49	29 16	28 38	27 51	27 25	26 45	26 19
8 53 50	11	15 20	14 45	13 54	12 47	11 57	10 51	9 46	8 50	7 54	7 31	7 1	6 33	5 52	5 10	4 18	3 55	2 43	1 32	0 58	0 ♏ 31	29 58	29 19	28 30	28 4	27 23	26 57
8 57 51	12	16 20	15 44	14 52	13 44	12 54	11 47	10 40	9 43	8 46	8 22	7 51	7 23	6 41	5 58	5 5	4 42	3 28	2 15	1 41	1 13	0 ♏ 39	29 59	29 10	28 43	28 0	27 34
9 1 52	13	17 19	16 43	15 50	14 41	13 50	12 42	11 34	10 36	9 37	9 13	8 42	8 13	7 30	6 46	5 52	5 28	4 13	2 59	2 23	1 55	1 21	0 ♏ 39	29 49	29 21	28 38	28 11
9 5 52	14	18 18	17 42	16 48	15 38	14 46	13 36	12 27	11 29	10 29	10 4	9 32	9 3	8 19	7 34	6 39	6 15	4 58	3 42	3 6	2 37	2 2	1 20	0 ♏ 28	0 ♏ 0	29 16	28 47
9 9 52	15	19 17	18 40	17 46	16 34	15 41	14 31	13 20	12 21	11 20	10 55	10 22	9 53	9 8	8 22	7 26	7 1	5 43	4 25	3 48	3 19	2 43	2 0	1 7	0 38	29 53	29 24
9 13 51	16	20 16	19 38	18 43	17 30	16 37	15 25	14 14	13 13	12 11	11 45	11 12	10 42	9 57	9 10	8 13	7 47	6 27	5 8	4 30	4 1	3 24	2 40	1 46	1 16	0 ♏ 30	0 ♏ 1
9 17 49	17	21 14	20 36	19 40	18 26	17 32	16 19	15 6	14 5	13 2	12 36	12 2	11 32	10 45	9 58	8 59	8 33	7 12	5 51	5 13	4 42	4 4	3 20	2 25	1 54	1 7	0 37
9 21 46	18	22 12	21 33	20 36	19 22	18 27	17 13	15 59	14 57	13 53	13 26	12 52	12 21	11 33	10 45	9 45	9 19	7 56	6 34	5 55	5 24	4 45	3 59	3 3	2 32	1 44	1 14
9 25 43	19	23 9	22 30	21 33	20 17	19 21	18 6	16 52	15 48	14 43	14 16	13 41	13 10	12 22	11 32	10 32	10 5	8 40	7 17	6 36	6 5	5 26	4 39	3 42	3 10	2 21	1 50
9 29 38	20	24 6	23 27	22 29	21 12	20 15	19 0	17 44	16 39	15 33	15 6	14 31	13 58	13 10	12 19	11 18	10 51	9 24	7 59	7 18	6 46	6 6	5 18	4 20	3 48	2 58	2 26
9 33 34	21	25 3	24 23	23 24	22 7	21 10	19 53	18 36	17 30	16 23	15 56	15 20	14 47	13 57	13 6	12 4	11 36	10 8	8 42	8 0	7 27	6 46	5 58	4 58	4 25	3 35	3 2
9 37 28	22	26 0	25 19	24 20	23 2	22 3	20 46	19 28	18 21	17 13	16 45	16 9	15 35	14 45	13 53	12 50	12 21	10 52	9 24	8 41	8 8	7 26	6 37	5 37	5 3	4 11	3 38
9 41 22	23	26 56	26 15	25 15	23 56	22 57	21 38	20 19	19 12	18 3	17 35	16 58	16 24	15 33	14 40	13 35	13 7	11 36	10 6	9 23	8 49	8 6	7 16	6 15	5 40	4 47	4 14
9 45 15	24	27 52	27 11	26 10	24 50	23 51	22 31	21 11	20 3	18 53	18 24	17 46	17 12	16 20	15 27	14 21	13 52	12 19	10 48	10 4	9 30	8 46	7 55	6 53	6 18	5 24	4 49
9 49 8	25	28 47	28 6	27 5	25 44	24 44	23 23	22 2	20 53	19 42	19 13	18 35	18 0	17 7	16 13	15 6	14 37	13 3	11 30	10 45	10 10	9 26	8 34	7 30	6 55	6 0	5 25
9 53 0	26	29 43	29 1	27 59	26 38	25 37	24 15	22 53	21 43	20 32	20 2	19 23	18 48	17 54	16 59	15 52	15 22	13 46	12 12	11 26	10 51	10 6	9 13	8 8	7 32	6 36	6 0
9 56 51	27	0 ♐ 38	29 56	28 53	27 31	26 30	25 7	23 44	22 34	21 21	20 51	20 12	19 36	18 41	17 46	16 37	16 6	14 29	12 54	12 7	11 31	10 46	9 52	8 46	8 9	7 12	6 36
10 0 42	28	1 33	0 ♐ 50	29 47	28 24	27 22	25 59	24 35	23 23	22 10	21 39	21 0	20 23	19 28	18 32	17 22	16 51	15 13	13 35	12 48	12 11	11 25	10 30	9 23	8 46	7 48	7 11
10 4 32	29	2 27	1 45	0 ♐ 41	29 17	28 15	26 50	25 26	24 13	22 59	22 28	21 48	21 11	20 15	19 18	18 7	17 36	15 56	14 17	13 29	12 52	12 5	11 9	10 1	9 23	8 24	7 46
10 8 22	30	3 22	2 38	1 35	0 ♐ 10	29 7	27 42	26 16	25 3	23 47	23 16	22 36	21 58	21 2	20 4	18 52	18 20	16 39	14 58	14 10	13 32	12 44	11 48	10 38	9 59	8 59	8 21
10 8 22	0 ♍	3 ♐ 22	2 ♐ 38	1 ♐ 35	0 ♐ 10	29 ♏ 7	27 ♏ 42	26 ♏ 16	25 ♏ 3	23 ♏ 47	23 ♏ 16	22 ♏ 36	21 ♏ 58	21 ♏ 2	20 ♏ 4	18 ♏ 52	18 ♏ 20	16 ♏ 39	14 ♏ 58	14 ♏ 10	13 ♏ 32	12 ♏ 44	11 ♏ 48	10 ♏ 38	9 ♏ 59	8 ♏ 59	8 ♏ 21
10 12 11	1	4 16	3 32	2 28	1 3	29 59	28 33	27 6	25 52	24 36	24 4	23 23	22 46	21 48	20 49	19 37	19 4	17 22	15 40	14 51	14 12	13 23	12 26	11 15	10 36	9 35	8 56
10 15 59	2	5 9	4 26	3 21	1 55	0 ♐ 51	29 24	27 57	26 42	25 25	24 52	24 11	23 33	22 35	21 35	20 21	19 49	18 5	16 21	15 31	14 52	14 3	13 4	11 52	11 12	10 11	9 31
10 19 47	3	6 3	5 19	4 14	2 47	1 42	0 ♐ 15	28 47	27 31	26 13	25 41	24 59	24 20	23 21	22 21	21 6	20 33	18 47	17 2	16 12	15 32	14 42	13 42	12 30	11 49	10 46	10 6
10 23 34	4	6 56	6 12	5 6	3 39	2 34	1 6	29 37	28 20	27 1	26 28	25 46	25 7	24 8	23 6	21 51	21 17	19 30	17 44	16 52	16 12	15 21	14 21	13 7	12 25	11 21	10 41
10 27 21	5	7 49	7 5	5 59	4 31	3 25	1 56	0 ♐ 26	29 9	27 50	27 16	26 33	25 54	24 54	23 52	22 35	22 1	20 13	18 25	17 32	16 51	16 0	14 59	13 44	13 2	11 57	11 15
10 31 8	6	8 42	7 58	6 51	5 23	4 16	2 47	1 16	29 58	28 38	28 4	27 21	26 41	25 40	24 37	23 20	22 45	20 55	19 6	18 13	17 31	16 39	15 37	14 20	13 38	12 32	11 50
10 34 53	7	9 35	8 50	7 43	6 14	5 7	3 37	2 6	0 ♐ 47	29 26	28 52	28 8	27 27	26 26	25 23	24 4	23 29	21 38	19 47	18 53	18 11	17 18	16 15	14 57	14 14	13 7	12 24
10 38 39	8	10 28	9 43	8 35	7 6	5 58	4 27	2 55	1 36	0 ♐ 14	29 39	28 55	28 14	27 12	26 8	24 48	24 13	22 20	20 28	19 33	18 50	17 57	16 53	15 34	14 50	13 42	12 59
10 42 24	9	11 20	10 35	9 27	7 57	6 49	5 17	3 44	2 24	1 2	0 ♐ 27	29 42	29 1	27 58	26 53	25 33	24 57	23 3	21 9	20 14	19 30	18 35	17 31	16 11	15 26	14 17	13 33
10 46 8	10	12 12	11 27	10 19	8 48	7 40	6 7	4 34	3 13	1 49	1 14	0 ♐ 29	29 47	28 44	27 38	26 17	25 41	23 45	21 50	20 54	20 10	19 14	18 9	16 48	16 2	14 52	14 8
10 49 53	11	13 4	12 18	11 10	9 39	8 30	6 57	5 23	4 1	2 37	2 2	1 16	0 ♐ 34	29 30	28 23	27 1	26 24	24 27	22 31	21 34	20 49	19 53	18 46	17 24	16 38	15 27	14 42
10 53 36	12	13 56	13 10	12 1	10 30	9 21	7 47	6 12	4 50	3 25	2 49	2 3	1 20	0 ♐ 16	29 9	27 45	27 8	25 10	23 12	22 14	21 29	20 32	19 24	18 1	17 14	16 2	15 16
10 57 20	13	14 48	14 2	12 53	11 21	10 11	8 37	7 1	5 38	4 12	3 36	2 50	2 7	1 2	29 54	28 30	27 52	25 52	23 52	22 54	22 8	21 11	20 2	18 37	17 50	16 37	15 50
11 1 3	14	15 39	14 53	13 44	12 11	11 1	9 27	7 50	6 27	5 0	4 24	3 37	2 53	1 47	0 ♐ 39	29 14	28 36	26 34	24 33	23 34	22 48	21 49	20 40	19 14	18 26	17 12	16 24
11 4 45	15	16 31	15 44	14 35	13 2	11 51	10 16	8 39	7 15	5 48	5 11	4 24	3 40	2 33	1 24	29 58	29 20	27 17	25 14	24 14	23 27	22 28	21 18	19 51	19 2	17 47	16 59
11 8 28	16	17 22	16 35	15 26	13 52	12 42	11 6	9 28	8 3	6 35	5 58	5 10	4 26	3 19	2 9	0 ♐ 42	0 ♐ 3	27 59	25 55	24 54	24 7	23 7	21 55	20 27	19 38	18 21	17 33
11 12 10	17	18 13	17 27	16 16	14 43	13 32	11 55	10 17	8 51	7 23	6 46	5 57	5 13	4 5	2 54	1 26	0 47	28 42	26 36	25 34	24 46	23 45	22 33	21 4	20 14	18 56	18 7
11 15 52	18	19 4	18 17	17 7	15 33	14 22	12 45	11 5	9 40	8 10	7 33	6 44	5 59	4 51	3 39	2 11	1 31	29 24	27 17	26 15	25 26	24 24	23 11	21 40	20 50	19 31	18 41
11 19 33	19	19 55	19 8	17 58	16 23	15 11	13 34	11 54	10 28	8 58	8 20	7 31	6 46	5 36	4 24	2 55	2 15	0 ♐ 6	27 58	26 55	26 5	25 3	23 49	22 17	21 25	20 6	19 15
11 23 15	20	20 46	19 59	18 48	17 13	16 1	14 23	12 43	11 16	9 45	9 7	8 18	7 32	6 22	5 10	3 39	2 59	0 49	28 39	27 35	26 45	25 42	24 26	22 53	22 1	20 40	19 49
11 26 56	21	21 37	20 50	19 39	18 4	16 51	15 13	13 32	12 4	10 33	9 55	9 5	8 19	7 8	5 55	4 23	3 42	1 31	29 20	28 15	27 24	26 20	25 4	23 30	22 37	21 15	20 23
11 30 37	22	22 28	21 40	20 29	18 54	17 41	16 2	14 21	12 53	11 21	10 42	9 52	9 5	7 54	6 40	5 8	4 26	2 14	0 ♐ 1	28 55	28 4	26 59	25 42	24 7	23 13	21 50	20 57
11 34 18	23	23 18	22 31	21 20	19 44	18 31	16 52	15 10	13 41	12 8	11 29	10 39	9 52	8 40	7 25	5 52	5 10	2 57	0 42	29 36	28 44	27 38	26 20	24 43	23 49	22 25	21 31
11 37 58	24	24 9	23 22	22 10	20 34	19 21	17 41	15 58	14 29	12 56	12 17	11 26	10 38	9 26	8 11	6 37	5 55	3 39	1 23	0 ♐ 16	29 23	28 17	26 58	25 20	24 25	23 0	22 5
11 41 39	25	25 0	24 12	23 0	21 24	20 11	18 30	16 47	15 18	13 44	13 4	12 13	11 25	10 12	8 56	7 21	6 39	4 22	2 4	0 57	0 ♐ 3	28 56	27 36	25 57	25 1	23 34	22 39
11 45 19	26	25 50	25 3	23 51	22 14	21 0	19 20	17 36	16 6	14 32	13 52	13 0	12 12	10 58	9 42	8 6	7 23	5 5	2 46	1 37	0 43	29 35	28 14	26 33	25 37	24 9	23 13
11 48 59	27	26 41	25 53	24 41	23 4	21 50	20 9	18 25	16 55	15 19	14 39	13 47	12 59	11 45	10 27	8 51	8 7	5 48	3 27	2 18	1 23	0 ♐ 14	28 52	27 10	26 13	24 44	23 47
11 52 40	28	27 31	26 43	25 31	23 54	22 40	20 59	19 14	17 43	16 7	15 27	14 35	13 46	12 31	11 13	9 36	8 52	6 31	4 9	2 59	2 3	0 54	29 30	27 47	26 49	25 19	24 21
11 56 20	29	28 22	27 34	26 22	24 44	23 30	21 48	20 3	18 32	16 55	16 15	15 22	14 33	13 18	11 59	10 21	9 36	7 14	4 50	3 39	2 44	1 33	0 ♐ 9	28 24	27 25	25 54	24 56
12 0 0	30	29 12	28 24	27 12	25 35	24 20	22 38	20 52	19 20	17 44	17 3	16 10	15 20	14 4	12 45	11 6	10 21	7 57	5 32	4 20	3 24	2 12	0 47	29 1	28 2	26 29	25 30

		2°0'	4°0'	7°0'	11°0'	14°0'	18°0'	21°59'	25°19'	28°40'	30°2'	31°46'	33°20'	35°39'	37°58'	40°43'	41°54'	45°30'	48°50'	50°22'	51°32'	52°57'	54°34'	56°28'	57°29	59°0'	59°56'
ST	MC	ASC	ASC	ASC	ASC	ASC	ASC	ASC	ASC	ASC	ASC	ASC	ASC	ASC	ASC	ASC	ASC	ASC	ASC	ASC	ASC	ASC	ASC	ASC	ASC	ASC	ASC
	°	° '	° '	° '	° '	° '	° '	° '	° '	° '	° '	° '	° '	° '	° '	° '	° '	° '	° '	° '	° '	° '	° '	° '	° '	° '	° '
12 0 0	0 ♎	29 ♐ 12	28 ♐ 24	27 ♐ 12	25 ♐ 35	24 ♐ 20	22 ♐ 38	20 ♐ 52	19 ♐ 20	17 ♐ 44	17 ♐ 3	16 ♐ 10	15 ♐ 20	14 ♐ 4	12 ♐ 45	11 ♐ 6	10 ♐ 21	7 ♐ 57	5 ♐ 32	4 ♐ 20	3 ♐ 24	2 ♐ 12	0 ♐ 47	29 ♏ 1	28 ♏ 2	26 ♏ 29	25 ♏ 30
12 3 40	1	0 ♑ 3	29 15	28 3	26 25	25 10	23 28	21 42	20 9	18 32	17 51	16 57	16 7	14 51	13 31	11 51	11 6	8 41	6 14	5 2	4 4	2 52	1 26	29 38	28 38	27 4	26 4
12 7 20	2	0 53	0 ♑ 5	28 53	27 15	26 0	24 18	22 31	20 58	19 20	18 39	17 45	16 55	15 38	14 17	12 36	11 51	9 24	6 56	5 43	4 45	3 32	2 4	0 ♐ 16	29 15	27 40	26 39
12 11 1	3	1 44	0 56	29 43	28 5	26 50	25 7	23 21	21 47	20 9	19 27	18 33	17 42	16 25	15 4	13 22	12 36	10 8	7 38	6 24	5 26	4 12	2 43	0 53	29 51	28 15	27 13
12 14 41	4	2 34	1 46	0 ♑ 34	28 56	27 41	25 57	24 10	22 36	20 58	20 16	19 21	18 30	17 12	15 50	14 8	13 22	10 52	8 20	7 6	6 6	4 52	3 22	1 31	0 ♐ 28	28 50	27 48
12 18 21	5	3 25	2 37	1 25	29 46	28 31	26 47	25 0	23 26	21 46	21 4	20 9	19 18	18 0	16 37	14 54	14 7	11 36	9 3	7 47	6 47	5 32	4 1	2 8	1 5	29 26	28 22
12 22 2	6	4 16	3 28	2 15	0 ♑ 37	29 21	27 38	25 50	24 15	22 35	21 53	20 58	20 6	18 47	17 24	15 40	14 53	12 21	9 46	8 29	7 29	6 12	4 40	2 46	1 42	0 ♐ 1	28 57
12 25 42	7	5 6	4 19	3 6	1 28	0 ♑ 12	28 28	26 40	25 5	23 24	22 42	21 46	20 55	19 35	18 11	16 26	15 39	13 5	10 29	9 11	8 10	6 53	5 20	3 24	2 19	0 37	29 32
12 29 23	8	5 57	5 9	3 57	2 18	1 3	29 19	27 30	25 55	24 14	23 31	22 35	21 43	20 23	18 59	17 13	16 25	13 50	11 12	9 54	8 52	7 33	5 59	4 2	2 56	1 13	0 ♐ 7
12 33 4	9	6 48	6 0	4 48	3 9	1 54	0 ♑ 9	28 20	26 45	25 3	24 20	23 24	22 32	21 11	19 46	17 59	17 11	14 35	11 55	10 36	9 33	8 14	6 39	4 40	3 33	1 49	0 42
12 36 45	10	7 39	6 51	5 39	4 0	2 45	1 0	29 11	27 35	25 53	25 10	24 13	23 21	22 0	20 34	18 46	17 58	15 20	12 39	11 19	10 15	8 55	7 19	5 18	4 11	2 25	1 17
12 40 27	11	8 30	7 42	6 30	4 52	3 36	1 51	0 ♑ 2	28 25	26 43	26 0	25 3	24 10	22 48	21 22	19 34	18 45	16 5	13 22	12 2	10 58	9 36	7 59	5 57	4 48	3 1	1 52
12 44 8	12	9 21	8 34	7 21	5 43	4 27	2 42	0 52	29 16	27 33	26 50	25 53	24 59	23 37	22 10	20 21	19 32	16 51	14 6	12 45	11 40	10 18	8 39	6 36	5 26	3 38	2 28
12 47 50	13	10 13	9 25	8 13	6 34	5 18	3 33	1 44	0 ♑ 7	28 24	27 40	26 42	25 49	24 26	22 59	21 9	20 19	17 37	14 51	13 28	12 23	11 0	9 20	7 15	6 4	4 14	3 3
12 51 32	14	11 4	10 17	9 5	7 26	6 10	4 25	2 35	0 58	29 14	28 30	27 33	26 39	25 16	23 48	21 57	21 7	18 23	15 35	14 12	13 6	11 42	10 1	7 54	6 43	4 51	3 39
12 55 15	15	11 56	11 8	9 56	8 18	7 2	5 17	3 26	1 49	0 ♑ 5	29 21	28 23	27 29	26 5	24 37	22 45	21 55	19 10	16 20	14 56	13 49	12 24	10 42	8 34	7 21	5 28	4 15
12 58 57	16	12 47	12 0	10 48	9 10	7 54	6 9	4 18	2 40	0 56	0 ♑ 12	29 14	28 19	26 55	25 27	23 34	22 43	19 57	17 6	15 40	14 33	13 7	11 23	9 13	8 0	6 5	4 51
13 2 40	17	13 39	12 52	11 40	10 2	8 46	7 1	5 10	3 32	1 48	1 3	0 ♑ 5	29 10	27 46	26 16	24 23	23 32	20 44	17 51	16 25	15 16	13 49	12 5	9 53	8 39	6 43	5 28
13 6 24	18	14 31	13 44	12 33	10 55	9 39	7 53	6 3	4 24	2 40	1 55	0 56	0 ♑ 1	28 36	27 6	25 12	24 21	21 31	18 37	17 10	16 1	14 33	12 46	10 33	9 18	7 20	6 4
13 10 7	19	15 23	14 37	13 25	11 47	10 31	8 46	6 55	5 17	3 32	2 47	1 48	0 53	29 27	27 57	26 2	25 10	22 19	19 23	17 55	16 45	15 16	13 29	11 14	9 58	7 58	6 41
13 13 52	20	16 16	15 29	14 18	12 40	11 24	9 39	7 48	6 10	4 24	3 39	2 40	1 45	0 ♑ 19	28 48	26 52	26 0	23 8	20 10	18 41	17 30	16 0	14 11	11 55	10 37	8 36	7 18
13 17 36	21	17 8	16 22	15 11	13 33	12 18	10 32	8 41	7 3	5 17	4 32	3 32	2 37	1 11	29 39	27 43	26 50	23 56	20 57	19 27	18 15	16 44	14 54	12 36	11 17	9 15	7 55
13 21 21	22	18 1	17 15	16 4	14 27	13 11	11 26	9 35	7 56	6 10	5 25	4 25	3 29	2 3	0 ♑ 31	28 34	27 40	24 45	21 44	20 14	19 1	17 29	15 37	13 17	11 58	9 53	8 33
13 25 7	23	18 54	18 8	16 57	15 20	14 5	12 20	10 29	8 50	7 4	6 18	5 18	4 22	2 55	1 23	29 25	28 31	25 35	22 32	21 0	19 47	18 14	16 21	13 59	12 39	10 32	9 11
13 28 52	24	19 47	19 1	17 51	16 14	14 59	13 14	11 23	9 44	7 57	7 12	6 12	5 16	3 48	2 15	0 ♑ 17	29 23	26 25	23 20	21 48	20 34	18 59	17 5	14 41	13 20	11 12	9 49
13 32 39	25	20 41	19 55	18 45	17 8	15 53	14 8	12 17	10 38	8 52	8 6	7 6	6 9	4 42	3 8	1 9	0 ♑ 14	27 15	24 9	22 35	21 21	19 45	17 50	15 24	14 1	11 51	10 27
13 36 26	26	21 34	20 49	19 39	18 3	16 48	15 3	13 12	11 33	9 46	9 0	8 0	7 3	5 35	4 1	2 1	1 7	28 6	24 58	23 24	22 8	20 31	18 34	16 7	14 43	12 31	11 6
13 40 13	27	22 28	21 43	20 33	18 57	17 43	15 58	14 7	12 28	10 41	9 55	8 55	7 58	6 30	4 55	2 55	1 59	28 58	25 48	24 12	22 56	21 18	19 20	16 50	15 25	13 11	11 45
13 44 1	28	23 22	22 37	21 28	19 52	18 38	16 54	15 3	13 24	11 37	10 51	9 50	8 53	7 24	5 50	3 48	2 53	29 50	26 38	25 2	23 44	22 6	20 6	17 34	16 8	13 52	12 24
13 47 49	29	24 16	23 32	22 23	20 48	19 33	17 49	15 59	14 20	12 33	11 47	10 46	9 49	8 20	6 45	4 43	3 47	0 ♑ 42	27 29	25 52	24 33	22 53	20 52	18 18	16 51	14 33	13 4
13 51 38	30	25 11	24 26	23 18	21 43	20 29	18 46	16 55	15 16	13 29	12 43	11 42	10 45	9 15	7 40	5 37	4 41	1 35	28 20	26 42	25 23	23 42	21 39	19 3	17 34	15 15	13 44
13 51 38	0 ♏	25 ♑ 11	24 ♑ 26	23 ♑ 18	21 ♑ 43	20 ♑ 29	18 ♑ 46	16 ♑ 55	15 ♑ 16	13 ♑ 29	12 ♑ 43	11 ♑ 42	10 ♑ 45	9 ♑ 15	7 ♑ 40	5 ♑ 37	4 ♑ 41	1 ♑ 35	28 ♐ 20	26 ♐ 42	25 ♐ 23	23 ♐ 42	21 ♐ 39	19 ♐ 3	17 ♐ 34	15 ♐ 15	13 ♐ 44
13 55 28	1	26 6	25 22	24 14	22 39	21 26	19 42	17 52	16 13	14 26	13 40	12 39	11 41	10 12	8 36	6 33	5 36	2 29	29 12	27 33	26 13	24 31	22 26	19 48	18 18	15 56	14 24
13 59 18	2	27 1	26 17	25 9	23 36	22 22	20 39	18 49	17 10	15 23	14 37	13 36	12 39	11 9	9 32	7 29	6 32	3 23	0 ♑ 5	28 24	27 4	25 20	23 14	20 34	19 3	16 39	15 5
14 3 9	3	27 57	27 13	26 6	24 32	23 19	21 37	19 47	18 8	16 21	15 35	14 34	13 36	12 6	10 29	8 25	7 28	4 18	0 58	29 17	27 55	26 10	24 3	21 21	19 48	17 22	15 47
14 7 0	4	28 52	28 9	27 2	25 29	24 17	22 34	20 45	19 6	17 19	16 33	15 32	14 34	13 4	11 27	9 22	8 25	5 14	1 52	0 ♑ 10	28 47	27 1	24 52	22 7	20 34	18 5	16 28
14 10 52	5	29 48	29 5	27 59	26 27	25 14	23 33	21 43	20 5	18 18	17 32	16 31	15 33	14 3	12 25	10 20	9 22	6 10	2 47	1 3	29 40	27 53	25 42	22 55	21 20	18 49	17 11
14 14 45	6	0 ♒ 45	0 ♒ 2	28 56	27 25	26 13	24 31	22 43	21 4	19 18	18 31	17 30	16 33	15 2	13 24	11 19	10 20	7 7	3 42	1 57	0 ♑ 33	28 45	26 32	23 43	22 7	19 33	17 54
14 18 38	7	1 41	0 59	29 54	28 23	27 11	25 30	23 42	22 4	20 18	19 31	18 30	17 33	16 2	14 24	12 18	11 19	8 5	4 38	2 53	1 27	29 38	27 23	24 32	22 54	20 18	18 37
14 22 32	8	2 38	1 56	0 ♒ 51	29 21	28 10	26 30	24 42	23 4	21 18	20 32	19 31	18 33	17 2	15 24	13 18	12 19	9 4	5 35	3 48	2 22	0 ♑ 31	28 15	25 22	23 42	21 4	19 21
14 26 26	9	3 36	2 54	1 50	0 ♒ 20	29 10	27 30	25 43	24 5	22 19	21 33	20 32	19 34	18 4	16 25	14 18	13 19	10 3	6 33	4 45	3 18	1 26	29 8	26 12	24 31	21 50	20 6
14 30 22	10	4 33	3 52	2 48	1 20	0 ♒ 10	28 30	26 44	25 7	23 21	22 35	21 34	20 36	19 5	17 27	15 20	14 21	11 3	7 31	5 43	4 15	2 21	0 ♑ 2	27 3	25 21	22 37	20 51
14 34 17	11	5 31	4 50	3 47	2 19	1 10	29 31	27 45	26 9	24 23	23 38	22 37	21 39	20 8	18 30	16 22	15 23	12 4	8 31	6 41	5 12	3 18	0 56	27 55	26 11	23 25	21 37
14 38 14	12	6 30	5 49	4 47	3 20	2 11	0 ♒ 33	28 47	27 11	25 26	24 41	23 40	22 42	21 11	19 33	17 25	16 26	13 6	9 31	7 40	6 11	4 15	1 52	28 48	27 2	24 14	22 23
14 42 11	13	7 28	6 48	5 47	4 20	3 12	1 35	29 50	28 15	26 30	25 44	24 44	23 46	22 16	20 37	18 29	17 29	14 9	10 32	8 41	7 10	5 13	2 48	29 42	27 54	25 3	23 11
14 46 9	14	8 27	7 48	6 47	5 21	4 14	2 37	0 ♒ 53	29 18	27 34	26 49	25 49	24 51	23 20	21 42	19 34	18 34	15 13	11 35	9 42	8 11	6 12	3 46	0 ♑ 37	28 48	25 53	23 59
14 50 8	15	9 27	8 48	7 47	6 23	5 16	3 40	1 57	0 ♒ 23	28 39	27 54	26 54	25 57	24 26	22 48	20 39	19 39	16 17	12 38	10 45	9 12	7 12	4 44	1 32	29 42	26 44	24 48
14 54 8	16	10 27	9 48	8 48	7 25	6 18	4 44	3 2	1 28	29 45	29 0	28 0	27 3	25 33	23 55	21 46	20 46	17 23	13 43	11 48	10 15	8 14	5 44	2 29	0 ♑ 37	27 36	25 38
14 58 8	17	11 27	10 49	9 50	8 27	7 22	5 48	4 7	2 34	0 ♒ 51	0 ♒ 7	29 7	28 10	26 40	25 2	22 53	21 53	18 30	14 48	12 53	11 19	9 16	6 44	3 27	1 33	28 29	26 29
15 2 9	18	12 27	11 50	10 52	9 30	8 25	6 53	5 12	3 40	1 58	1 14	0 ♒ 15	29 18	27 48	26 10	24 2	23 2	19 38	15 55	13 59	12 24	10 20	7 46	4 26	2 30	29 24	27 20
15 6 10	19	13 28	12 51	11 54	10 33	9 29	7 58	6 18	4 47	3 6	2 22	1 23	0 ♒ 27	28 57	27 20	25 11	24 11	20 47	17 3	15 6	13 30	11 25	8 49	5 27	3 29	0 ♑ 19	28 13
15 10 13	20	14 30	13 53	12 57	11 37	10 34	9 4	7 25	5 55	4 15	3 31	2 32	1 36	0 ♒ 7	28 30	26 22	25 22	21 57	18 12	16 14	14 38	12 31	9 54	6 28	4 28	1 15	29 7
15 14 16	21	15 31	14 55	14 0	12 42	11 39	10 10	8 33	7 3	5 24	4 40	3 42	2 47	1 18	29 41	27 34	26 34	23 9	19 23	17 24	15 47	13 39	11 0	7 32	5 30	2 13	0 ♑ 3
15 18 20	22	16 33	15 58	15 3	13 46	12 45	11 17	9 41	8 12	6 34	5 51	4 53	3 58	2 30	0 ♒ 54	28 46	27 46	24 22	20 35	18 35	16 57	14 49	12 7	8 36	6 32	3 12	0 59
15 22 24	23	17 36	17 1	16 7	14 52	13 51	12 24	10 49	9 22	7 45	7 2	6 5	5 10	3 43	2 7	0 ♒ 0	29 0	25 36	21 48	19 48	18 9	15 59	13 17	9 42	7 36	4 13	1 57
15 26 30	24	18 39	18 5	17 12	15 57	14 58	13 32	11 59	10 32	8 56	8 14	7 18	6 23	4 57	3 22	1 15	0 ♒ 16	26 51	23 3	21 2	19 23	17 12	14 27	10 50	8 42	5 15	2 56
15 30 36	25	19 42	19 9	18 17	17 4	16 5	14 41	13 9	11 44	10 9	9 27	8 31	7 37	6 11	4 37	2 31	1 32	28 8	24 19	22 18	20 38	18 26	15 40	12 0	9 50	6 19	3 57
15 34 42	26	20 46	20 13	19 22	18 10	17 13	15 50	14 19	12 56	11 22	10 41	9 45	8 52	7 27	5 54	3 49	2 50	29 26	25 37	23 36	21 55	19 42	16 54	13 11	10 59	7 24	5 0
15 38 50	27	21 50	21 18	20 28	19 17	18 21	17 0	15 31	14 8	12 36	11 55	11 1	10 8	8 44	7 11	5 7	4 9	0 ♒ 46	26 57	24 55	23 14	21 0	18 10	14 24	12 11	8 32	6 5
15 42 58	28	22 54	22 23	21 34	20 25	19 30	18 10	16 43	15 22	13 51	13 11	12 17	11 25	10 2	8 30	6 27	5 29	2 7	28 19	26 16	24 35	22 20	19 28	15 40	13 24	9 41	7 11
15 47 7	29	23 59	23 28	22 41	21 33	20 39	19 21	17 55	16 36	15 6	14 27	13 34	12 43	11 21	9 50	7 48	6 50	3 30	29 42	27 39	25 57	23 42	20 49	16 58	14 40	10 53	8 19
15 51 16	30	25 4	24 34	23 48	22 42	21 49	20 33	19 9	17 50	16 23	15 44	14 52	14 1	12 41	11 11	9 11	8 13	4 54	1 ♒ 7	29 4	27 22	25 6	22 12	18 18	15 58	12 7	9 30
15 51 16	0 ♐	25 ♒ 4	24 ♒ 34	23 ♒ 48	22 ♒ 42	21 ♒ 49	20 ♒ 33	19 ♒ 9	17 ♒ 50	16 ♒ 23	15 ♒ 44	14 ♒ 52	14 ♒ 1	12 ♒ 41	11 ♒ 11	9 ♒ 11	8 ♒ 13	4 ♒ 54	1 ♒ 7	29 ♑ 4	27 ♑ 22	25 ♑ 6	22 ♑ 12	18 ♑ 18	15 ♑ 58	12 ♑ 7	9 ♑ 30
15 55 26	1	26 10	25 41	24 55	23 51	22 59	21 45	20 23	19 6	17 40	17 2	16 11	15 21	14 2	12 33	10 34	9 38	6 20	2 34	0 ♒ 31	28 49	26 32	23 37	19 40	17 18	13 23	10 43
15 59 37	2	27 16	26 47	26 3	25 1	24 10	22 58	21 37	20 22	18 58	18 21	17 30	16 42	15 24	13 57	11 59	11 3	7 48	4 2	2 0	0 ♒ 18	28 0	25 4	21 5	18 41	14 42	11 59
16 3 49	3	28 22	27 54	27 12	26 11	25 22	24 11	22 53	21 39	20 17	19 41	18 51	18 4	16 47	15 21	13 26	12 31	9 17	5 33	3 31	1 49	29 32	26 34	22 33	20 7	16 4	13 18
16 8 1	4	29 29	29 2	28 20	27 21	26 34	25 25	24 8	22 57	21 37	21 1	20 13	19 26	18 11	16 47	14 53	13 59	10 48	7 6	5 5	3 23	1 ♒ 5	28 7	24 4	21 36	17 29	14 39
16 12 14	5	0 ♓ 36	0 ♓ 10	29 30	28 32	27 46	26 39	25 25	24 16	22 57	22 22	21 35	20 50	19 36	18 14	16 23	15 29	12 21	8 41	6 41	4 59	2 41	29 43	25 38	23 9	18 58	16 4
16 16 27	6	1 43	1 18	0 ♓ 39	29 44	28 59	27 54	26 42	25 35	24 19	23 45	22 59	22 14	21 3	19 42	17 53	17 1	13 55	10 18	8 19	6 38	4 21	1 ♒ 22	27 16	24 45	20 30	17 33
16 20 41	7	2 51	2 27	1 49	0 ♓ 56	0 ♓ 12	29 10	28 0	26 55	25 41	25 8	24 23	23 40	22 30	21 12	19 25	18 34	15 32	11 58	9 59	8 19	6 3	3 4	28 57	26 24	22 5	19 5
16 24 56	8	3 59	3 36	3 0	2 8	1 26	0 ♓ 26	29 18	28 15	27 4	26 32	25 49	25 7	23 59	22 42	20 58	20 8	17 10	13 39	11 43	10 3	7 48	4 50	0 ♒ 42	28 8	23 46	20 42
16 29 11	9	5 7	4 45	4 10	3 21	2 41	1 42	0 ♓ 37	29 36	28 27	27 56	27 15	26 34	25 28	24 14	22 33	21 44	18 50	15 23	13 28	11 50	9 36	6 39	2 30	29 55	25 30	22 23
16 33 27	10	6 16	5 55	5 22	4 34	3 55	3 0	1 57	0 ♓ 58	29 52	29 22	28 42	28 2	26 59	25 47	24 9	23 21	20 32	17 10	15 17	13 40	11 27	8 31	4 23	1 ♒ 48	27 20	24 10
16 37 43	11	7 25	7 5	6 33	5 48	5 11	4 17	3 17	2 21	1 ♓ 17	0 ♓ 48	0 ♓ 10	29 32	28 30	27 21	25 46	25 0	22 16	18 59	17 8	15 33	13 22	10 28	6 21	3 45	29 15	26 2
16 41 59	12	8 35	8 15	7 45	7 2	6 26	5 35	4 38	3 44	2 43	2 16	1 38	1 ♓ 2	0 ♓ 3	28 56	27 25	26 41	24 1	20 50	19 2	17 28	15 20	12 28	8 23	5 47	1 ♒ 15	28 0
16 46 17	13	9 44	9 26	8 57	8 16	7 42	6 54	5 59	5 8	4 10	3 43	3 8	2 33	1 37	0 ♓ 33	29 5	28 22	25 49	22 43	20 58	19 27	17 22	14 33	10 30	7 55	3 22	0 ♒ 4
16 50 34	14	10 54	10 37	10 10	9 31	8 59	8 13	7 21	6 32	5 37	5 12	4 38	4 5	3 11	2 10	0 ♓ 46	0 ♓ 6	27 38	24 39	22 57	21 29	19 27	16 41	12 42	10 8	5 35	2 16
16 54 53	15	12 5	11 48	11 22	10 46	10 16	9 32	8 44	7 57	7 5	6 41	6 9	5 38	4 47	3 49	2 29	1 50	29 29	26 38	24 59	23 34	21 35	18 54	14 59	12 27	7 55	4 35
16 59 11	16	13 15	13 0	12 36	12 1	11 33	10 52	10 6	9 23	8 34	8 11	7 41	7 11	6 23	5 29	4 13	3 36	1 ♓ 22	28 38	27 4	25 42	23 48	21 12	17 22	14 53	10 23	7 3
17 3 30	17	14 26	14 11	13 49	13 17	12 51	12 12	11 30	10 49	10 3	9 42	9 14	8 46	8 1	7 9	5 58	5 23	3 17	0 ♓ 41	29 12	27 53	26 4	23 33	19 51	17 25	12 59	9 40
17 7 49	18	15 37	15 23	15 3	14 33	14 9	13 33	12 53	12 16	11 33	11 13	10 47	10 21	9 39	8 51	7 44	7 12	5 13	2 47	1 ♓ 22	0 ♓ 8	28 23	26 0	22 26	20 4	15 44	12 27
17 12 9	19	16 48	16 36	16 16	15 49	15 27	14 54	14 17	13 43	13 3	12 45	12 21	11 57	11 18	10 33	9 31	9 1	7 11	4 54	3 35	2 25	0 ♓ 46	28 30	25 6	22 50	18 37	15 24
17 16 29	20	17 59	17 48	17 31	17 6	16 45	16 15	15 42	15 10	14 34	14 17	13 55	13 33	12 57	12 16	11 20	10 52	9 10	7 3	5 50	4 45	3 13	1 ♓ 5	27 52	25 43	21 40	18 32
17 20 49	21	19 11	19 1	18 45	18 22	18 4	17 37	17 7	16 38	16 5	15 50	15 30	15 10	14 37	14 0	13 9	12 44	11 11	9 15	8 7	7 8	5 43	3 45	0 ♓ 45	28 43	24 53	21 52
17 25 10	22	20 23	20 14	19 59	19 39	19 23	18 59	18 32	18 6	17 37	17 23	17 5	16 47	16 18	15 45	14 59	14 36	13 13	11 28	10 27	9 33	8 16	6 28	3 42	1 ♓ 49	28 15	25 24
17 29 31	23	21 34	21 27	21 14	20 56	20 42	20 21	19 57	19 35	19 9	18 57	18 41	18 25	18 0	17 31	16 50	16 30	15 16	13 43	12 49	12 1	10 52	9 15	6 46	5 3	1 ♓ 46	29 8
17 33 51	24	22 46	22 40	22 29	22 14	22 1	21 43	21 23	21 3	20 41	20 31	20 17	20 4	19 42	19 17	18 41	18 24	17 20	16 0	15 13	14 31	13 30	12 6	9 54	8 23	5 27	3 ♓ 5
17 38 13	25	23 58	23 53	23 44	23 31	23 21	23 6	22 49	22 32	22 14	22 5	21 54	21 43	21 24	21 3	20 33	20 19	19 25	18 18	17 38	17 2	16 11	15 0	13 7	11 49	9 17	7 13
17 42 34	26	25 11	25 6	24 59	24 49	24 41	24 28	24 15	24 2	23 47	23 40	23 31	23 22	23 7	22 50	22 26	22 14	21 31	20 37	20 5	19 36	18 55	17 56	16 25	15 21	13 15	11 31
17 46 55	27	26 23	26 20	26 14	26 7	26 0	25 51	25 41	25 31	25 20	25 15	25 8	25 1	24 50	24 37	24 19	24 10	23 38	22 57	22 32	22 11	21 39	20 55	19 45	18 56	17 20	16 0
17 51 17	28	27 35	27 33	27 29	27 24	27 20	27 14	27 7	27 1	26 53	26 50	26 45	26 41	26 33	26 25	26 13	26 7	25 45	25 17	25 1	24 47	24 26	23 56	23 9	22 36	21 30	20 35
17 55 38	29	28 48	28 46	28 45	28 42	28 40	28 37	28 34	28 30	28 27	28 25	28 23	28 20	28 17	28 12	28 6	28 3	27 52	27 39	27 30	27 23	27 13	26 58	26 34	26 17	25 44	25 16
18 0 0	30	0 ♈ 0	0 ♈ 0	0 ♈ 0	0 ♈ 0	0 ♈ 0	0 ♈ 0	0 ♈ 0	0 ♈ 0	0 ♈ 0	0 ♈ 0	0 ♈ 0	0 ♈ 0	0 ♈ 0	0 ♈ 0	0 ♈ 0	0 ♈ 0	0 ♈ 0	0 ♈ 0	0 ♈ 0	0 ♈ 0	0 ♈ 0	0 ♈ 0	0 ♈ 0	0 ♈ 0	0 ♈ 0	0 ♈ 0

ST	MC	2°0' ASC	4°0' ASC	7°0' ASC	11°0' ASC	14°0' ASC	18°0' ASC	21°59' ASC	25°19' ASC	28°40' ASC	30°2' ASC	31°46' ASC	33°20' ASC	35°39' ASC	37°58' ASC	40°43' ASC	41°54' ASC	45°30' ASC	48°50' ASC	50°22' ASC	51°32' ASC	52°57' ASC	54°34' ASC	56°28' ASC	57°29 ASC	59°0' ASC	59°56' ASC
	°	° ′	° ′	° ′	° ′	° ′	° ′	° ′	° ′	° ′	° ′	° ′	° ′	° ′	° ′	° ′	° ′	° ′	° ′	° ′	° ′	° ′	° ′	° ′	° ′	° ′	° ′
18 0 0	0 ♑	0 0	0 0	0 0	0 0	0 0	0 0	0 0	0 0	0 0	0 0	0 0	0 0	0 0	0 0	0 0	0 0	0 0	0 0	0 0	0 0	0 0	0 0	0 0	0 0	0 0	0 0
18 4 22	1	1 12	1 14	1 15	1 18	1 20	1 23	1 26	1 30	1 33	1 35	1 37	1 40	1 43	1 48	1 54	1 57	2 8	2 21	2 30	2 37	2 47	3 2	3 26	3 43	4 16	4 44
18 8 43	2	2 25	2 27	2 31	2 36	2 40	2 46	2 53	2 59	3 7	3 10	3 15	3 19	3 27	3 35	3 47	3 53	4 15	4 43	4 59	5 13	5 34	6 4	6 51	7 24	8 30	9 25
18 13 5	3	3 37	3 40	3 46	3 53	4 0	4 9	4 19	4 29	4 40	4 45	4 52	4 59	5 10	5 23	5 41	5 50	6 22	7 3	7 28	7 49	8 21	9 5	10 15	11 4	12 40	14 0
18 17 26	4	4 49	4 54	5 1	5 11	5 19	5 32	5 45	5 58	6 13	6 20	6 29	6 38	6 53	7 10	7 34	7 46	8 29	9 23	9 55	10 24	11 5	12 4	13 35	14 39	16 45	18 29
18 21 47	5	6 2	6 7	6 16	6 29	6 39	6 54	7 11	7 28	7 46	7 55	8 6	8 17	8 36	8 57	9 27	9 41	10 35	11 42	12 22	12 58	13 49	15 0	16 53	18 11	20 43	22 47
18 26 9	6	7 14	7 20	7 31	7 46	7 59	8 17	8 37	8 57	9 19	9 29	9 43	9 56	10 18	10 43	11 19	11 36	12 40	14 0	14 47	15 29	16 30	17 54	20 6	21 37	24 33	26 55
18 30 29	7	8 26	8 33	8 46	9 4	9 18	9 39	10 3	10 25	10 51	11 3	11 19	11 35	12 0	12 29	13 10	13 30	14 44	16 17	17 11	17 59	19 8	20 45	23 14	24 57	28 14	0 ♉ 52
18 34 50	8	9 37	9 46	10 1	10 21	10 37	11 1	11 28	11 54	12 23	12 37	12 55	13 13	13 42	14 15	15 1	15 24	16 47	18 32	19 33	20 27	21 44	23 32	26 18	28 11	1 ♉ 45	4 36
18 39 11	9	10 49	10 59	11 15	11 38	11 56	12 23	12 53	13 22	13 55	14 10	14 30	14 50	15 23	16 0	16 51	17 16	18 49	20 45	21 53	22 52	24 17	26 15	29 15	1 ♉ 17	5 7	8 8
18 43 31	10	12 1	12 12	12 29	12 54	13 15	13 45	14 18	14 50	15 26	15 43	16 5	16 27	17 3	17 44	18 40	19 8	20 50	22 57	24 10	25 15	26 47	28 55	2 ♉ 8	4 17	8 20	11 28
18 47 51	11	13 12	13 24	13 44	14 11	14 33	15 6	15 43	16 17	16 57	17 15	17 39	18 3	18 42	19 27	20 29	20 59	22 49	25 6	26 25	27 35	29 14	1 ♉ 30	4 54	7 10	11 23	14 36
18 52 11	12	14 23	14 37	14 57	15 27	15 51	16 27	17 7	17 44	18 27	18 47	19 13	19 39	20 21	21 9	22 16	22 48	24 47	27 13	28 38	29 52	1 ♉ 37	4 0	7 34	9 56	14 16	17 33
18 56 30	13	15 34	15 49	16 11	16 43	17 9	17 48	18 30	19 11	19 57	20 18	20 46	21 14	21 59	22 51	24 2	24 37	26 43	29 19	0 ♉ 48	2 ♉ 7	3 56	6 27	10 9	12 35	17 1	20 20
19 0 49	14	16 45	17 0	17 24	17 59	18 27	19 8	19 54	20 37	21 26	21 49	22 19	22 49	23 37	24 31	25 47	26 24	28 38	1 ♉ 22	2 56	4 18	6 12	8 48	12 38	15 7	19 37	22 57
19 5 7	15	17 55	18 12	18 38	19 14	19 44	20 28	21 16	22 3	22 55	23 19	23 51	24 22	25 13	26 11	27 31	28 10	0 ♉ 31	3 22	5 1	6 26	8 25	11 6	15 1	17 33	22 5	25 25
19 9 26	16	19 6	19 23	19 50	20 29	21 1	21 47	22 39	23 28	24 23	24 48	25 22	25 55	26 49	27 50	29 14	29 54	2 22	5 21	7 3	8 31	10 33	13 19	17 18	19 52	24 25	27 44
19 13 43	17	20 16	20 34	21 3	21 44	22 18	23 6	24 1	24 52	25 50	26 17	26 52	27 27	28 23	29 27	0 ♉ 55	1 ♉ 38	4 11	7 17	9 2	10 33	12 38	15 27	19 30	22 5	26 38	29 56
19 18 1	18	21 25	21 45	22 15	22 58	23 34	24 25	25 22	26 16	27 17	27 44	28 22	28 58	29 57	1 ♉ 4	2 35	3 19	5 59	9 10	10 58	12 32	14 40	17 32	21 37	24 13	28 45	2 ♊ 0
19 22 17	19	22 35	22 55	23 27	24 12	24 49	25 43	26 43	27 39	28 43	29 12	29 50	0 ♉ 28	1 ♉ 30	2 39	4 14	5 0	7 44	11 1	12 52	14 27	16 38	19 32	23 39	26 15	0 ♊ 45	3 58
19 26 33	20	23 44	24 5	24 38	25 26	26 5	27 0	28 3	29 2	0 ♉ 8	0 ♉ 38	1 ♉ 18	1 58	3 1	4 13	5 51	6 39	9 28	12 50	14 43	16 20	18 33	21 29	25 37	28 12	2 40	5 50
19 30 49	21	24 53	25 15	25 50	26 39	27 19	28 18	29 23	0 ♉ 24	1 33	2 4	2 45	3 26	4 32	5 46	7 27	8 16	11 10	14 37	16 32	18 10	20 24	23 21	27 30	0 ♊ 5	4 30	7 37
19 35 4	22	26 1	26 24	27 0	27 52	28 34	29 34	0 ♉ 42	1 45	2 56	3 28	4 11	4 53	6 1	7 18	9 2	9 52	12 50	16 21	18 17	19 57	22 12	25 10	29 18	1 52	6 14	9 18
19 39 19	23	27 9	27 33	28 11	29 4	29 48	0 ♉ 50	2 0	3 5	4 19	4 52	5 37	6 20	7 30	8 48	10 35	11 26	14 28	18 2	20 1	21 41	23 57	26 56	1 ♊ 3	3 36	7 55	10 55
19 43 33	24	28 17	28 42	29 21	0 ♉ 16	1 ♉ 1	2 6	3 18	4 25	5 41	6 15	7 1	7 46	8 57	10 18	12 7	12 59	16 5	19 42	21 41	23 22	25 39	28 38	2 44	5 15	9 30	12 27
19 47 46	25	29 24	29 50	0 ♉ 30	1 28	2 14	3 21	4 35	5 44	7 3	7 38	8 25	9 10	10 24	11 46	13 37	14 31	17 39	21 19	23 19	25 1	27 19	0 ♊ 17	4 22	6 51	11 2	13 56
19 51 59	26	0 ♉ 31	0 ♉ 58	1 40	2 39	3 26	4 35	5 52	7 3	8 23	8 59	9 47	10 34	11 49	13 13	15 7	16 1	19 12	22 54	24 55	26 37	28 55	1 53	5 56	8 24	12 31	15 21
19 56 11	27	1 38	2 6	2 48	3 49	4 38	5 49	7 7	8 21	9 43	10 19	11 9	11 56	13 13	14 39	16 34	17 29	20 43	24 27	26 29	28 11	0 ♊ 28	3 26	7 27	9 53	13 56	16 42
20 0 23	28	2 44	3 13	3 57	4 59	5 50	7 2	8 23	9 38	11 2	11 39	12 30	13 18	14 36	16 3	18 1	18 57	22 12	25 58	28 0	29 42	2 0	4 56	8 55	11 19	15 18	18 1
20 4 34	29	3 50	4 19	5 5	6 9	7 1	8 15	9 37	10 54	12 20	12 58	13 49	14 39	15 58	17 27	19 26	20 22	23 40	27 26	29 29	1 ♊ 11	3 28	6 23	10 20	12 42	16 37	19 17
20 8 44	30	4 56	5 26	6 12	7 18	8 11	9 27	10 51	12 10	13 37	14 16	15 8	15 59	17 19	18 49	20 49	21 47	25 6	28 53	0 ♊ 56	2 38	4 54	7 48	11 42	14 2	17 53	20 30
20 8 44	0 ♒	4 ♉ 56	5 ♉ 26	6 ♉ 12	7 ♉ 18	8 ♉ 11	9 ♉ 27	10 ♉ 51	12 ♉ 10	13 ♉ 37	14 ♉ 16	15 ♉ 8	15 ♉ 59	17 ♉ 19	18 ♉ 49	20 ♉ 49	21 ♉ 47	25 ♉ 6	28 ♉ 53	0 ♊ 56	2 ♊ 38	4 ♊ 54	7 ♊ 48	11 ♊ 42	14 ♊ 2	17 ♊ 53	20 ♊ 30
20 12 53	1	6 1	6 32	7 19	8 27	9 21	10 39	12 5	13 24	14 54	15 33	16 26	17 17	18 39	20 10	22 12	23 10	26 30	0 ♊ 18	2 21	4 3	6 18	9 11	13 2	15 20	19 7	21 41
20 17 2	2	7 6	7 37	8 26	9 35	10 30	11 50	13 17	14 38	16 9	16 49	17 43	18 35	19 58	21 30	23 33	24 31	27 53	1 41	3 44	5 25	7 40	10 32	14 20	16 36	20 19	22 49
20 21 10	3	8 10	8 42	9 32	10 43	11 39	13 0	14 29	15 52	17 24	18 5	18 59	19 52	21 16	22 49	24 53	25 51	29 14	3 3	5 5	6 46	9 0	11 50	15 36	17 49	21 28	23 55
20 25 18	4	9 14	9 47	10 38	11 50	12 47	14 10	15 41	17 4	18 38	19 19	20 15	21 8	22 33	24 6	26 11	27 10	0 ♊ 34	4 23	6 24	8 5	10 18	13 6	16 49	19 1	22 36	25 0
20 29 24	5	10 18	10 51	11 43	12 56	13 55	15 19	16 51	18 16	19 51	20 33	21 29	22 23	23 49	25 23	27 29	28 28	1 52	5 41	7 42	9 22	11 34	14 20	18 0	20 10	23 41	26 3
20 33 30	6	11 21	11 55	12 48	14 3	15 2	16 28	18 1	19 28	21 4	21 46	22 42	23 37	25 3	26 38	28 45	29 44	3 9	6 57	8 58	10 37	12 48	15 33	19 10	21 18	24 45	27 4
20 37 36	7	12 24	12 59	13 53	15 8	16 9	17 36	19 11	20 38	22 15	22 58	23 55	24 50	26 17	27 53	0 ♊ 0	1 ♊ 0	4 24	8 12	10 12	11 51	14 1	16 43	20 18	22 24	25 47	28 3
20 41 40	8	13 27	14 2	14 57	16 14	17 15	18 43	20 19	21 48	23 26	24 9	25 7	26 2	27 30	29 6	1 14	2 14	5 38	9 25	11 25	13 3	15 11	17 53	21 24	23 28	26 48	29 1
20 45 44	9	14 29	15 5	16 0	17 18	18 21	19 50	21 27	22 57	24 36	25 20	26 18	27 13	28 42	0 ♊ 19	2 26	3 26	6 51	10 37	12 36	14 13	16 21	19 0	22 28	24 30	27 47	29 57
20 49 47	10	15 30	16 7	17 3	18 23	19 26	20 56	22 35	24 5	25 45	26 29	27 28	28 24	29 53	1 30	3 38	4 38	8 3	11 48	13 46	15 22	17 29	20 6	23 32	25 32	28 45	0 ♋ 53
20 53 50	11	16 32	17 9	18 6	19 27	20 31	22 2	23 42	25 13	26 54	27 38	28 37	29 33	1 ♊ 3	2 40	4 49	5 49	9 13	12 57	14 54	16 30	18 35	21 11	24 33	26 31	29 41	1 47
20 57 51	12	17 33	18 10	19 8	20 30	21 35	23 7	24 48	26 20	28 2	28 46	29 45	0 ♊ 42	2 12	3 50	5 58	6 58	10 22	14 5	16 1	17 36	19 40	22 14	25 34	27 30	0 ♋ 36	2 40
21 1 52	13	18 33	19 11	20 10	21 33	22 38	24 12	25 53	27 26	29 9	29 53	0 ♊ 53	1 50	3 20	4 58	7 7	8 7	11 30	15 12	17 7	18 41	20 44	23 16	26 33	28 27	1 31	3 31
21 5 52	14	19 33	20 12	21 12	22 35	23 42	25 16	26 58	28 32	0 ♊ 15	1 ♊ 0	2 0	2 57	4 27	6 5	8 14	9 14	12 37	16 17	18 12	19 45	21 46	24 16	27 31	29 23	2 24	4 22
21 9 52	15	20 33	21 12	22 13	23 37	24 44	26 20	28 3	29 37	1 21	2 6	3 6	4 3	5 34	7 12	9 21	10 21	13 43	17 22	19 15	20 48	22 48	25 16	28 28	0 ♋ 18	3 16	5 12
21 13 51	16	21 33	22 12	23 13	24 39	25 46	27 23	29 7	0 ♊ 42	2 26	3 11	4 11	5 9	6 40	8 18	10 26	11 26	14 47	18 25	20 18	21 49	23 48	26 14	29 23	1 12	4 7	6 1
21 17 49	17	22 32	23 12	24 13	25 40	26 48	28 25	0 ♊ 10	1 45	3 30	4 16	5 16	6 14	7 44	9 23	11 31	12 31	15 51	19 28	21 19	22 50	24 47	27 12	0 ♋ 18	2 6	4 57	6 49
21 21 46	18	23 30	24 11	25 13	26 40	27 49	29 27	1 13	2 49	4 34	5 19	6 20	7 18	8 49	10 27	12 35	13 34	16 54	20 29	22 20	23 49	25 45	28 8	1 12	2 58	5 46	7 37
21 25 43	19	24 29	25 10	26 13	27 41	28 50	0 ♊ 29	2 15	3 51	5 37	6 22	7 23	8 21	9 52	11 30	13 38	14 37	17 56	21 29	23 19	24 48	26 42	29 4	2 5	3 49	6 35	8 23
21 29 38	20	25 27	26 8	27 12	28 40	29 50	1 30	3 16	4 53	6 39	7 25	8 26	9 24	10 55	12 33	14 40	15 39	18 57	22 29	24 17	25 45	27 39	29 58	2 57	4 39	7 23	9 9
21 33 34	21	26 24	27 6	28 10	29 40	0 ♊ 50	2 30	4 17	5 55	7 41	8 27	9 28	10 26	11 56	13 35	15 42	16 41	19 57	23 27	25 15	26 42	28 34	0 ♋ 52	3 48	5 29	8 10	9 54
21 37 28	22	27 22	28 4	29 9	0 ♊ 39	1 50	3 30	5 18	6 56	8 42	9 28	10 29	11 27	12 58	14 36	16 42	17 41	20 56	24 25	26 12	27 38	29 29	1 45	4 38	6 18	8 56	10 39
21 41 22	23	28 19	29 1	0 ♊ 6	1 37	2 49	4 30	6 18	7 56	9 42	10 29	11 30	12 27	13 58	15 36	17 42	18 41	21 55	25 22	27 7	28 33	0 ♋ 22	2 37	5 28	7 6	9 42	11 23
21 45 15	24	29 15	29 58	1 4	2 35	3 47	5 29	7 17	8 56	10 42	11 29	12 30	13 27	14 58	16 36	18 41	19 40	22 53	26 18	28 3	29 27	1 15	3 28	6 17	7 53	10 27	12 6
21 49 8	25	0 ♊ 12	0 ♊ 55	2 1	3 33	4 46	6 27	8 17	9 55	11 42	12 28	13 29	14 27	15 57	17 35	19 40	20 38	23 50	27 13	28 57	0 ♋ 20	2 7	4 18	7 5	8 40	11 11	12 49
21 53 0	26	1 8	1 51	2 58	4 31	5 43	7 26	9 15	10 54	12 41	13 27	14 28	15 26	16 56	18 33	20 38	21 35	24 46	28 8	29 50	1 13	2 59	5 8	7 53	9 26	11 55	13 32
21 56 51	27	2 3	2 47	3 54	5 28	6 41	8 23	10 13	11 52	13 39	14 25	15 26	16 24	17 54	19 31	21 35	22 32	25 42	29 2	0 ♋ 43	2 5	3 50	5 57	8 39	10 12	12 38	14 13
22 0 42	28	2 59	3 43	4 51	6 24	7 38	9 21	11 11	12 50	14 37	15 23	16 24	17 21	18 51	20 28	22 31	23 28	26 37	29 55	1 36	2 56	4 40	6 46	9 26	10 57	13 21	14 55
22 4 32	29	3 54	4 38	5 46	7 21	8 34	10 18	12 8	13 47	15 34	16 20	17 21	18 19	19 48	21 24	23 27	24 24	27 31	0 ♋ 48	2 27	3 47	5 29	7 34	10 12	11 42	14 4	15 36
22 8 22	30	4 49	5 34	6 42	8 17	9 31	11 14	13 5	14 44	16 31	17 17	18 18	19 15	20 45	22 20	24 23	25 19	28 25	1 40	3 18	4 37	6 18	8 21	10 57	12 26	14 45	16 16
22 8 22	0 ♓	4 ♊ 49	5 ♊ 34	6 ♊ 42	8 ♊ 17	9 ♊ 31	11 ♊ 14	13 ♊ 5	14 ♊ 44	16 ♊ 31	17 ♊ 17	18 ♊ 18	19 ♊ 15	20 ♊ 45	22 ♊ 20	24 ♊ 23	25 ♊ 19	28 ♊ 25	1 ♋ 40	3 ♋ 18	4 ♋ 37	6 ♋ 18	8 ♋ 21	10 ♋ 57	12 ♋ 26	14 ♋ 45	16 ♋ 16
22 12 11	1	5 44	6 28	7 37	9 12	10 27	12 11	14 1	15 40	17 27	18 13	19 14	20 11	21 40	23 15	25 17	26 13	29 18	2 31	4 8	5 27	7 7	9 8	11 42	13 9	15 27	16 56
22 15 59	2	6 38	7 23	8 32	10 8	11 22	13 6	14 57	16 36	18 23	19 9	20 10	21 7	22 36	24 10	26 12	27 7	0 ♋ 10	3 22	4 58	6 16	7 54	9 54	12 26	13 52	16 8	17 36
22 19 47	3	7 32	8 17	9 27	11 3	12 17	14 2	15 53	17 32	19 19	20 5	21 5	22 2	23 30	25 5	27 5	28 1	1 2	4 12	5 48	7 4	8 42	10 40	13 10	14 35	16 49	18 15
22 23 34	4	8 26	9 11	10 21	11 57	13 12	14 57	16 48	18 27	20 14	21 0	22 0	22 57	24 25	25 59	27 59	28 53	1 54	5 2	6 36	7 52	9 29	11 26	13 53	15 17	17 29	18 54
22 27 21	5	9 19	10 5	11 15	12 52	14 7	15 52	17 43	19 22	21 8	21 54	22 54	23 51	25 18	26 52	28 51	29 46	2 45	5 51	7 25	8 39	10 15	12 10	14 36	15 59	18 9	19 33
22 31 8	6	10 13	10 59	12 9	13 46	15 1	16 46	18 37	20 16	22 3	22 48	23 48	24 44	26 12	27 45	29 43	0 ♋ 37	3 35	6 40	8 12	9 26	11 1	12 55	15 19	16 40	18 48	20 11
22 34 53	7	11 6	11 52	13 3	14 40	15 55	17 40	19 31	21 10	22 56	23 42	24 42	25 38	27 5	28 37	0 ♋ 35	1 29	4 25	7 28	9 0	10 13	11 46	13 39	16 1	17 21	19 28	20 49
22 38 39	8	11 59	12 45	13 56	15 33	16 49	18 34	20 25	22 4	23 50	24 35	25 35	26 31	27 57	29 29	1 26	2 20	5 15	8 16	9 46	10 59	12 31	14 23	16 43	18 2	20 7	21 27
22 42 24	9	12 52	13 38	14 49	16 27	17 42	19 28	21 19	22 57	24 43	25 28	26 28	27 23	28 49	0 ♋ 21	2 17	3 10	6 4	9 3	10 33	11 45	13 16	15 6	17 24	18 43	20 45	22 5
22 46 8	10	13 44	14 31	15 42	17 20	18 36	20 21	22 12	23 50	25 36	26 21	27 20	28 15	29 41	1 12	3 8	4 0	6 52	9 50	11 19	12 30	14 0	15 49	18 5	19 23	21 24	22 42
22 49 53	11	14 37	15 23	16 35	18 13	19 29	21 14	23 5	24 43	26 28	27 13	28 12	29 7	0 ♋ 33	2 3	3 58	4 50	7 41	10 37	12 5	13 15	14 44	16 31	18 46	20 2	22 2	23 19
22 53 36	12	15 29	16 16	17 27	19 5	20 21	22 7	23 57	25 36	27 20	28 5	29 4	29 59	1 24	2 54	4 48	5 39	8 29	11 23	12 50	13 59	15 27	17 14	19 27	20 42	22 40	23 56
22 57 20	13	16 21	17 8	18 20	19 58	21 14	22 59	24 50	26 28	28 12	28 57	29 55	0 ♋ 50	2 14	3 44	5 37	6 28	9 16	12 9	13 35	14 44	16 11	17 55	20 7	21 21	23 17	24 32
23 1 3	14	17 13	18 0	19 12	20 50	22 6	23 51	25 42	27 20	29 4	29 48	0 ♋ 46	1 41	3 5	4 33	6 26	7 17	10 3	12 54	14 20	15 27	16 53	18 37	20 47	22 0	23 55	25 9
23 4 45	15	18 4	18 52	20 4	21 42	22 58	24 43	26 34	28 11	29 55	0 ♋ 39	1 37	2 31	3 55	5 23	7 15	8 5	10 50	13 40	15 4	16 11	17 36	19 18	21 26	22 39	24 32	25 45
23 8 28	16	18 56	19 43	20 55	22 34	23 50	25 35	27 25	29 2	0 ♋ 46	1 30	2 27	3 21	4 44	6 12	8 3	8 53	11 37	14 25	15 48	16 54	18 18	19 59	22 6	23 17	25 9	26 21
23 12 10	17	19 47	20 35	21 47	23 26	24 42	26 27	28 16	29 53	1 36	2 20	3 18	4 11	5 34	7 1	8 51	9 41	12 23	15 9	16 32	17 37	19 0	20 40	22 45	23 56	25 46	26 57
23 15 52	18	20 39	21 26	22 39	24 17	25 33	27 18	29 8	0 ♋ 44	2 27	3 10	4 7	5 1	6 23	7 50	9 39	10 28	13 9	15 54	17 15	18 20	19 42	21 21	23 24	24 34	26 22	27 32
23 19 33	19	21 30	22 18	23 30	25 8	26 24	28 9	29 58	1 35	3 17	4 0	4 57	5 50	7 12	8 38	10 26	11 15	13 55	16 38	17 58	19 2	20 24	22 1	24 3	25 12	26 59	28 8
23 23 15	20	22 21	23 9	24 21	26 0	27 15	29 0	0 ♋ 49	2 25	4 7	4 50	5 47	6 39	8 0	9 26	11 14	12 2	14 40	17 21	18 41	19 45	21 5	22 41	24 42	25 49	27 35	28 43
23 26 56	21	23 12	24 0	25 12	26 51	28 6	29 51	1 40	3 15	4 57	5 40	6 36	7 28	8 49	10 14	12 1	12 49	15 25	18 5	19 24	20 27	21 46	23 21	25 20	26 27	28 11	29 18
23 30 37	22	24 3	24 51	26 3	27 42	28 57	0 ♋ 41	2 30	4 5	5 46	6 29	7 25	8 17	9 37	11 1	12 47	13 35	16 10	18 48	20 6	21 8	22 27	24 1	25 58	27 4	28 47	29 53
23 34 18	23	24 54	25 41	26 54	28 32	29 48	1 32	3 20	4 55	6 36	7 18	8 14	9 5	10 25	11 49	13 34	14 21	16 55	19 31	20 49	21 50	23 7	24 40	26 36	27 41	29 23	0 ♌ 28
23 37 58	24	25 44	26 32	27 45	29 23	0 ♋ 39	2 22	4 10	5 45	7 25	8 7	9 2	9 54	11 13	12 36	14 20	15 7	17 39	20 14	21 31	22 31	23 48	25 20	27 14	28 18	29 59	1 3
23 41 39	25	26 35	27 23	28 35	0 ♋ 14	1 29	3 13	5 0	6 34	8 14	8 56	9 51	10 42	12 0	13 23	15 6	15 53	18 24	20 57	22 13	23 13	24 28	25 59	27 52	28 55	0 ♌ 34	1 38
23 45 19	26	27 26	28 14	29 26	1 4	2 19	4 3	5 50	7 24	9 2	9 44	10 39	11 30	12 48	14 10	15 52	16 38	19 8	21 40	22 54	23 54	25 8	26 38	28 29	29 32	1 10	2 12
23 48 59	27	28 16	29 4	0 ♋ 17	1 55	3 10	4 53	6 39	8 13	9 51	10 33	11 27	12 18	13 35	14 56	16 38	17 24	19 52	22 22	23 36	24 34	25 48	27 17	29 7	0 ♌ 9	1 45	2 47
23 52 40	28	29 7	29 55	1 7	2 45	4 0	5 42	7 29	9 2	10 40	11 21	12 15	13 5	14 22	15 43	17 24	18 9	20 36	23 4	24 17	25 15	26 28	27 56	29 44	0 45	2 20	3 21
23 56 20	29	29 57	0 ♋ 45	1 57	3 35	4 50	6 32	8 18	9 51	11 28	12 9	13 3	13 53	15 9	16 29	18 9	18 54	21 19	23 46	24 58	25 56	27 8	28 34	0 ♌ 22	1 22	2 56	3 56
0 0 0	30	0 ♋ 48	1 36	2 48	4 25	5 40	7 22	9 8	10 40	12 16	12 57	13 50	14 40	15 56	17 15	18 54	19 39	22 3	24 28	25 40	26 36	27 48	29 13	0 59	1 58	3 31	4 30

2000

	I	II	III	IV	V	VI	VII	VIII	IX	X	XI	XII
♂	28♒	22♓	14♈	7♉	28	20♊	10♋	30	20♌	9♍	28	16♎
♃	25♈D	28	3♉	9	16	24	0♊	6	10	11R	10	6
♄	10♉R	11D	12	16	19	23	27	29	1♊	1R	29♉	27
♅	15♒	17	18	20	21	21R	20	19	18	17	17D	17
♆	3♒	4	5	6	7	6R	6	5	4	4	4D	4
♇	11♐	12	13	13R	12	12	11	10	10D	11	12	13

2001

	I	II	III	IV	V	VI	VII	VIII	IX	X	XI	XII
♂	5♏	23	7♐	21	28	26R	17	16D	26	13♑	3♒	24
♃	2♊R	1D	3	8	14	20	27	4♋	10	14	16	14R
♄	25♉R	24D	25	28	1♊	5	9	12	14	15R	14	12
♅	19♒	20	22	24	25	25R	24	23	22	21	21D	21
♆	5♒	6	8	8	9	9R	8	7	7	6	6D	7
♇	14♐	15	15	15R	15	14	13	13	13D	13	14	15

2002

	I	II	III	IV	V	VI	VII	VIII	IX	X	XI	XII
♂	17♓	9♈	30	21♉	12♊	2♋	22	12♌	2♍	21	10♎	30
♃	11♋R	7	6	7D	11	17	23	30	7♌	12	16	18
♄	9♊R	8	8D	10	14	17	21	25	28	29	29R	27
♅	22♒	24	26	27	28	29	29R	28	26	25	25	25D
♆	7♒	9	10	11	11	11R	10	10	9	8	8D	9
♇	16♐	17	18	18R	17	16	16	15	15D	15	16	17

2003

	I	II	III	IV	V	VI	VII	VIII	IX	X	XI	XII
♂	20♏	10♐	28	17♑	5♒	22	5♓	10R	4	0D	7	21
♃	17♌R	13	10	8	9D	13	18	24	1♍	7	13	17
♄	24♊R	23	22D	23	26	30	3♋	7	11	13	13R	12
♅	26♒	28	29	1♓	2	3	3R	2	1	29♒	29	29D
♆	10♒	11	12	13	13	13R	13	12	11	11	10D	11
♇	18♐	19	20	20R	20	19	18	17	17D	18	18	19

2004

	I	II	III	IV	V	VI	VII	VIII	IX	X	XI	XII
♂	9♈	28	17♉	7♊	26	16♋	5♌	24	14♍	3♎	23	13♏
♃	19♍	18R	14	11	9	10D	13	19	25	1♎	8	13
♄	10♋R	7	6	7D	9	12	16	20	23	26	27	27R
♅	0♓	2	3	5	6	7	7R	6	5	4	3	3D
♆	12♒	13	14	15	15	15R	15	14	13	13	13D	13
♇	21♐	22	22	22R	22	21	20	20	20D	20	21	22

2005

	I	II	III	IV	V	VI	VII	VIII	IX	X	XI	XII
♂	4♐	26	16♑	8♒	30	22♓	13♈	2♉	17	23	17R	9
♃	17♎	19	18R	14	11	9	10D	13	19	25	1♏	8
♄	25♋R	22	21	20D	22	25	28	2♌	6	9	11	11R
♅	4♓	5	7	9	10	11	11R	10	9	8	7	7D
♆	14♒	15	16	17	18	18R	17	16	16	15	15D	15
♇	23♐	24	24	25R	24	24	23	22	22	22D	23	24

2006

	I	II	III	IV	V	VI	VII	VIII	IX	X	XI	XII
♂	11♉D	22	6♊	23	10♋	28	17♌	6♍	25	15♎	6♏	26
♃	13♏	17	19	18R	14	11	9	10D	13	19	25	2♐
♄	10♌R	8	5	4	5D	7	10	14	18	21	24	25
♅	8♓	9	11	12	14	15	15R	14	13	12	11	11D
♆	16♒	17	18	19	20	20R	19	19	18	17	17D	17
♇	25♐	26	27	27R	27	26	25	24	24	24D	25	26

2007

	I	II	III	IV	V	VI	VII	VIII	IX	X	XI	XII
♂	18♐	11♑	2♒	26	19♓	12♈	4♉	26	15♊	1♋	11	11R
♃	8♐	14	18	20	19R	16	12	10	11D	14	20	26
♄	24♌R	22	20	18	18D	20	22	26	30	3♍	6	8
♅	12♓	13	14	16	18	18	19R	18	17	16	15	15D
♆	18♒	19	20	21	22	22R	22	21	20	20	19D	20
♇	27♐	28	29	29R	29	28	27	27	26	26D	27	28

2008

	I	II	III	IV	V	VI	VII	VIII	IX	X	XI	XII
♂	30♊R	24D	29	11♋	25	12♌	30	18♍	8♎	28	19♏	11♐
♃	3♑	10	16	20	22	22R	19	15	13	13D	17	22
♄	8♍R	7	5	3	2	2D	5	8	12	15	19	21
♅	15♓	17	18	20	21	22	23R	22	21	20	19	19D
♆	20♒	21	22	23	24	24R	24	23	22	22	21	22D
♇	29♐	0♑	1	1	1R	0	30♐	29	29	29D	29	0♑

2009

	I	II	III	IV	V	VI	VII	VIII	IX	X	XI	XII
♂	4♑	27	19♒	13♓	7♈	0♉	22	14♊	4♋	22	7♌	17
♃	29♑	6♒	13	19	24	27	27R	24	20	17	18D	21
♄	22♍R	21	19	17	15	15D	17	19	23	27	0♎	3
♅	19♓	20	22	24	25	26	27	26R	25	24	23	23
♆	22♒	24	25	26	26	26R	26	26	25	24	24	24D
♇	1♑	2	3	3	3R	3	2	1	1	1D	1	2

2010

	I	II	III	IV	V	VI	VII	VIII	IX	X	XI	XII
♂	19♌R	9	1	3D	13	27	13♍	1♎	21	11♏	3♐	25
♃	26♒	3♓	10	17	24	29	3♈	3R	1	27♓	24	24D
♄	5♎	4R	3	0	29♍	28D	29	1♎	4	8	11	15
♅	23♓D	24	26	27	29	0♈	1	0R	29♓	28	27	27
♆	25♒	26	27	28	28	29R	28	28	27	26	26	26D
♇	3♑	4	5	5	5R	5	4	3	3	3D	3	4

2011

	I	II	III	IV	V	VI	VII	VIII	IX	X	XI	XII
♂	18♑	13♒	5♓	29	22♈	15♉	7♊	28	19♋	7♌	25	9♍
♃	27♓	2♈	8	15	22	29	5♉	9	10R	9	5	1
♄	17♎	17R	16	14	12	11	11D	12	15	19	22	26
♅	27♓D	28	29	1♈	3	4	5	4R	4	2	1	1
♆	27♒	28	29	30	1♓	1	1R	0	29♒	29	28	28D
♇	5♑	6	7	8	7R	7	6	5	5	5D	5	6

2012

	I	II	III	IV	V	VI	VII	VIII	IX	X	XI	XII
♂	20♍	23R	15	5	5D	15	29	16♎	5♏	26	18♐	11♑
♃	0♉D	3	7	13	20	28	4♊	10	15	16	15R	12
♄	28♎	29	29R	27	25	23	23D	24	26	29	3♏	7
♅	1♈D	2	3	5	7	8	8	8R	8	6	5	5
♆	29♒	30	1♓	2	3	3	3R	2	2	1	0	0D
♇	7♑	8	9	10	9R	9	8	8	7	7D	7	8

2013

	I	II	III	IV	V	VI	VII	VIII	IX	X	XI	XII
♂	5♒	29	21♓	15♈	8♉	0♊	21	12♋	3♌	21	10♍	26
♃	8♊R	6D	8	12	17	24	1♋	8	14	18	20	20R
♄	10♏	11	11R	10	8	6	5	5D	7	10	14	17
♅	5♈D	6	7	9	10	12	12	12R	12	11	9	9
♆	1♓	2	3	4	5	5	5R	5	4	3	3	3D
♇	9♑	10	11	12	12R	11	10	10	9	9D	9	10

2014

	I	II	III	IV	V	VI	VII	VIII	IX	X	XI	XII
♂	12♎	23	28	22R	11	10D	18	3♏	22	12♐	4♑	27
♃	16♋R	12	10	11D	15	20	27	3♌	10	16	20	23
♄	20♏	23	23	23R	21	18	17	17D	18	21	24	27
♅	9♈D	9	11	12	14	15	16	16R	16	15	14	13
♆	3♓	4	5	6	7	8	7R	7	6	5	5	5D
♇	11♑	12	13	14	14R	13	12	12	11	11D	11	12

2015

	I	II	III	IV	V	VI	VII	VIII	IX	X	XI	XII
♂	21♒	15♓	7♈	0♉	22	14♊	4♋	25	15♌	4♍	23	11♎
♃	22♌R	18	15	13	13D	17	22	28	4♍	11	17	21
♄	1♐	4	5	5R	3	1	29♏	28	29D	1♐	4	8
♅	13♈D	13	14	16	18	19	20	20R	20	19	18	17
♆	5♓	6	7	9	9	10	10R	9	8	8	7	7D
♇	13♑	14	15	16	16R	15	14	14	13	13D	13	14

2016

	I	II	III	IV	V	VI	VII	VIII	IX	X	XI	XII
♂	29♎	15♏	28	7♐	8R	28♏	23D	29	14♐	2♑	24	16♒
♃	23♍	22R	19	15	13	14D	17	22	28	5♎	11	17
♄	11♐	14	16	16R	15	13	11	10	10D	12	14	18
♅	17♈D	17	18	20	22	23	24	25R	24	23	22	21
♆	8♓	8	10	11	12	12	12R	11	11	10	9	9D
♇	15♑	16	17	17	17R	17	16	16	15	15D	15	16

2017

	I	II	III	IV	V	VI	VII	VIII	IX	X	XI	XII
♂	10♓	3♈	23	16♉	7♊	28	17♋	7♌	27	16♍	6♎	25
♃	21♎	23	22R	19	15	13	14D	17	22	28	5♏	11
♄	21♐	25	27	28	27R	26	23	22	21D	22	25	28
♅	21♈D	21	22	24	25	27	28	29	28R	27	26	25
♆	10♓	11	12	13	14	14	14R	14	13	12	12	11D
♇	17♑	18	19	19	19R	19	18	18	17	17D	17	18

2018

	I	II	III	IV	V	VI	VII	VIII	IX	X	XI	XII
♂	14♏	3♐	20	8♑	23	5♒	9R	3	29♑D	6♒	21	9♓
♃	17♏	21	23	22R	19	16	13	14D	17	22	28	5♐
♄	1♑	5	7	9	9R	8	6	4	3	3D	5	8
♅	25♈R	25D	26	28	29	1♉	2	3	2R	1	0	29♈
♆	12♓	13	14	15	16	16	16R	16	15	14	14	14D
♇	19♑	20	21	21	21R	21	20	20	19	19	19D	20

2019

	I	II	III	IV	V	VI	VII	VIII	IX	X	XI	XII
♂	30♓	21♈	10♉	1♊	20	10♋	29	19♌	9♍	28	18♎	8♏
♃	12♐	18	22	24	24R	21	17	15	15D	18	23	30
♄	11♑	15	18	20	21R	20	18	16	14	14D	15	18
♅	29♈R	29D	30	1♉	3	5	6	7	6R	6	4	3
♆	14♓	15	16	17	18	19	19R	18	18	17	16	16D
♇	21♑	22	22	23	23R	23	22	22	21	21	21D	22

2020

	I	II	III	IV	V	VI	VII	VIII	IX	X	XI	XII
♂	28♏	19♐	9♑	1♒	22	13♓	2♈	18	28	25R	16	17D
♃	7♑	14	20	24	27	27R	24	20	18	18D	21	26
♄	21♑	25	28	1♒	2	2R	0	28♑	26	25D	26	28
♅	3♉R	3D	4	5	7	9	10	11	11R	10	9	8
♆	16♓	17	18	19	20	21	21R	21	20	19	18	18D
♇	22♑	23	24	25	25R	25	24	23	23	23	23D	23

	GMT/+/-	H	M
Afghanistan	+	04	30
Albania[1]	+	01	
Algeria	+	01	
Andorra	+	01	
Angola	+	01	
Anguilla	–	04	
Antigua and Barbuda	–	04	
Antilles	–	04	
Argentina	–	03	
Aruba	–	04	
Ascension Island	GMT	00	
Australia			
Capital Territory	+	10	
New South Wales[7]	+	10	
Northern Territory	+	09	30
Queensland	+	10	
South Australia	+	09	30
Tasmania[1]	+		10
Victoria	+	10	
Western Australia	+	08	
Austria	+	01	
Azores	–	01	
Bahamas[1]	–	05	
Bahrain	+	03	
Bangladesh	+	06	
Barbados	–	04	
Belgium	+	01	
Belize	–	06	
Benin	+	01	
Bermuda	–	04	
Bhutan	+	06	
Bolivia	–	04	
Botswana	+	02	
Brazil[1]			
eastern[10]	–	03	
Territory of Acre	–	05	
western	–	04	
Brunei Darussalam	+	08	
Bulgaria	+	02	
Burkina Fasso	GMT	00	
Burma	+	06	30
Burundi	+	02	
Cambodia	+	07	
Cameroon	+	01	
Canada			
Alberta	–	07	
British Columbia[1]	–	08	
Manitoba[1]	–	06	
New Brunswick[1]	–	04	
Newfoundland[1]	–	03	30
Northwest Territories[1]			
E. of long. W.68°	–	04	
long. W.68° to W.85°	–	05	
long. W.85° to W.102°	–	06	
long. W.102° to W.120°	–	07	
W. of long. W.120°	–	08	
Nova Scotia[1]	–	04	
Ontario[1]			
E. of long. W.90°	–	05	
W. of long. W.90°	–	06	
Prince Edward Island[1]	–	04	
Quebec[1]			
E. of long. W.68°	–	04	
W. of long. W.68°	–	05	
Saskatchewan[1]	–	07	
Yukon[1]	–	09	
Canary Islands[3]	GMT	00	
Cape Verde Islands	–	01	
Cayman Islands	–	05	
Central African Republic[4]	+	01	
Chad	+	01	
Channel Islands	GMT	00	
Chatham Islands[4]	+	12	
Chile[1]	–	04	
China[8]	+	08	
Christmas Island, Indian Ocean	+	07	
Cocos (Keeling Island)	+	06	
Colombia	–	05	
Comoros	+	03	
Congo	+	01	
Cook Islands	–	10	30
Costa Rica	–	06	
Crete	+	02	
Cuba[1]	–	05	
Cyprus	+	02	
Czechoslovakia	+	01	
Denmark	+	01	
Djibouti	+	03	
Dominica	–	04	
Dominican Republic[2]	–	04	
Ecuador	–	05	
Egypt[1]	+	02	
El Salvador	–	06	
Equatorial Guinea	+	01	
Ethiopia	+	03	
Faëroe Islands	GMT	00	
Falkland Islands[11]	–	04	
Fiji	+	12	
Finland	+	02	
France[4]	+	01	
French Guiana	–	03	
French Polynesia	–	10	
Gabon	+	01	
Gambia	GMT	00	
Germany	+	01	
Ghana	GMT	00	
Gibraltar[4]	+	01	
Great Britain	GMT	00	
Greece	+	02	
Greenland	–	03	
Grenada[1]	–	04	
Guadeloupe	–	04	
Guam	+	10	
Guatemala	–	06	
Guinea-Bissau	GMT	00	

	GMT/+/-	H	M
Guinea Conakry	GMT	00	
Guinea Republic	GMT	00	
Guyana	–	03	
Haiti	–	05	
Honduras	–	06	
Hong Kong[1]	+	08	
Hungary	+	01	
Iceland	GMT	00	
India	+	05	30
Indonesia, Republic of			
Bali, Bangka, Billiton, Java, Madura, Sumatra	+	07	
Borneo, Celebes, Flores, Lombok, Sumba, Sumbawa, Timor	+	08	
Aru, Moluccas, Tanimbar, West Irian	+	09	
Iran	+	03	30
Iraq	+	03	
Ireland, Northern	GMT	00	
Irish Republic	+	01	
Israel	+	02	
Italy[1]	+	01	
Ivory Coast	GMT	00	
Jamaica	–	05	
Japan	+	09	
Jordan	+	02	
Kampuchea	+	07	
Kenya	+	03	
Kiribati	+	12	
Korea	+	09	
Kuwait	+	03	
Laos	+	07	
Latvia	+	03	
Lebanon[1]	+	02	
Lesotho	+	02	
Liberia	GMT	00	
Libya	+	01	
Liechtenstein	+	01	
Lithuania	+	03	
Luxembourg[4]	+	01	
Macao[1]	+	08	
Madagascar	+	03	
Madeira	GMT	00	
Malawi	+	02	
Malaysia	+	08	
Maldives	+	05	
Mali	GMT	00	
Malta	+	01	
Marshall Islands	+	12	
Martinique	–	04	
Mauritania	GMT	00	
Mauritius	+	04	
Mexico[12]	–	06	
Micronesia	+	09	
Midway Island	–	11	
Monaco[4]	+	01	
Mongolia	+	07	
Montserrat	–	04	
Morocco[1]	GMT	00	
Mozambique	+	02	
Namibia	+	02	
Nauru	+	12	
Nepal	+	05	45
Netherlands, the	+	01	
Nevis	–	04	
New Caledonia	+	11	
New Zealand	+	12	
Nicaragua	–	06	
Niger	+	01	
Nigeria	+	01	
Nive Island	–	11	
Norfolk Island	+	11	30
North Mariana Islands	+	10	
Norway[1]	+	01	
Oman	+	04	
Pakistan	+	05	
Palau	+	10	
Panama	–	05	
Papua New Guinea	+	10	
Paraguay	–	03	
Peru	–	05	
Philippines, the	+	08	
Pitcairn Island	–	08	30
Poland[1]	+	01	
Portugal	GMT	00	
Puerto Rico	–	04	
Quatar	+	03	
Réunion	+	04	
Rodriguez Island	+	04	
Romania	+	02	
Rwanda	+	02	
São Tomé and Principe	GMT	00	
St. Christopher	–	04	
St. Helena	GMT	00	
St. Lucia	–	04	
St. Pierre and Miquelon	–	04	
St. Vincent and the Grenadines	–	04	
Samoa	–	11	
San Marino	+	01	
Saudi Arabia	+	03	
Senegal	GMT	00	
Seychelles	+	04	
Sierra Leone	GMT	00	
Singapore	+	08	
Soloman Islands	+	11	
Somalia	+	03	
South Africa	+	02	
Spain[4]	+	01	
Sri Lanka	+	05	30
Sudan	+	02	
Surinam	–	03	
Swaziland	+	02	
Sweden	+	01	
Switzerland	+	01	
Syria[1]	+	02	

	GMT/+/-	H	M
Taiwan[1]	+	08	
Tanzania	+	03	
Thailand	+	07	
Tonga	+	13	
Trinidad and Tobago	–	04	
Tristan da Cunha	GMT	00	
Tunisia	+	01	
Turkey[1]	+	03	
Turks and Caicos Islands	–	05	
Tuvalu	+	12	
Uganda	+	03	
Union of Soviet Socialist Republics[9]			
W. of long. E.40°	+	03	
long. E.40° to E.52°30	+	04	
long. E.52°30′ to E.67°30′	+	05	
long. E.67°30′ to E.82°30′	+	06	
long. E.82°30′ to E.97°30′	+	07	
long. E.97°30′ to E.112°30′	+	08	
long. E.112°30′ to E.127°30′	+	09	
long. E.127°30′ to E.142°30′	+	10	
long. E.142°30′ to E.157°30′	+	11	
long. E.157°30′ to E.172°30′	+	12	
E. of long. E.172°30′	+	13	
United Arab Emirates	+	04	
United States of America			
Alabama[5]	–	06	
Alaska[5]			
E. of long. W.137°	–	08	
long. W.137° to W.141°	–	09	
long. W.141° to W.161°	–	10	
long. W.161° to W. 172°30′	–	11	
Arizona	–	07	
Arkansas[5]	–	06	
California[5]	–	08	
Colorado[5]	–	07	
Connecticut[5]	–	05	
Delaware[5]	–	05	
Florida[5,6]	–	05	
Georgia[5]	–	05	
Hawaii	–	10	
Idaho[5,6]	–	07	
Illinois[5]	–	06	
Indiana[5]	–	06	
Iowa[5]	–	06	
Kansas[5,6]	–	06	
Kentucky[5,6]	–	05	
Louisiana[5]	–	06	
Maine[5]	–	05	
Maryland[5]	–	05	
Massachusetts[5]	–	05	
Michigan[5,6]	–	05	
Minnesota[5]	–	06	
Mississippi[5]	–	06	
Missouri[5]	–	06	
Montana[5]	–	07	
Nebraska[5,6]	–	06	
Nevada[5]	–	08	
New Hampshire[5]	–	05	
New Jersey[5]	–	05	
New Mexico[5]	–	07	
New York[5]	–	05	
North Carolina[5]	–	05	
North Dakota[5,6]	–	06	
Ohio[5]	–	05	
Oklahoma[5]	–	06	
Oregon[5,6]	–	08	
Pennsylvania[5]	–	05	
Rhode Island[5]	–	05	
South Carolina[5]	–	05	
South Dakota[5]			
eastern	–	06	
western	–	07	
Tennessee[5,6]	–	06	
Texas[5]	–	06	
Utah[5,6]	–	07	
Vermont[5]	–	05	
Virginia[5]	–	05	
Washington D.C.[5]	–	05	
Washington[5]	–	08	
West Virginia[5]	–	05	
Wisconsin[5]	–	06	
Wyoming[5]	–	07	
Uruguay[1]	–	03	
Vanuatu	+	11	
Venezuela	–	04	
Vietnam	+	07	
Virgin Islands	–	04	
Wake Island	+	12	
Yemen	+	03	
Yemen Arab Republic	+	03	
Yugoslavia	+	01	
Zambia	+	02	
Zaire	+	01	
Zimbabwe	+	02	

[1]Summer time may be kept in these countries.
[2]Winter time may be kept in these countries.
[3]GMT is in general use throughout the year, but the legal standard time differs from GMT.
[4]This time is used throughout the year, but may differ from legal time.
[5]Summer (daylight saving) time, one hour fast on the time given, is kept in these states from the last Sunday in April to the last Sunday in October, changing at 02h 00m local clock time.
[6]This applies to the greater portion of the state.
[7]Except Broken Hill Area, which keeps 09h 30m.
[8]All the coast, but some areas may keep summer time.
[9]The boundaries between the zones are irregular; the longitudes given are approximate only.
[10]Including all the coast.
[11]Port Stanley keeps summer time September to March.
[12]Except the states of Sonora, Sinaloa, Nayarit, and the Southern District of Lower California, which keep 07h, and the Northern District of Lower California which keeps 08h.

Glossary

Terms in italics are defined elsewhere in the glossary.

Affliction A *planet* is afflicted when it is unfavorably *aspected.*

Air signs See *triplicities.*

Almanac A book containing astrological and astronomical data, and usually predictions and analyses of people or politics.

Angle The word refers to the four angles of a chart which form a cross within it: the points being the *Ascendant, Descendant, Midheaven* and *Imum Coeli.*

Apparent motion The Sun does not rise above the horizon: the Earth turns so that it appears to do so. Similarly, the Sun does not really travel through the signs, but it stands still; it is the Earth as it travels round the Sun that causes the phenomenon. The Sun's motion is apparent, not real.

Arc Any part of a circle, measured around its circumference.

Ascendant The degree of the *zodiac* rising over the eastern horizon at the moment of birth. Each degree takes some four minutes to rise.

Ascension, long and short Because the *ecliptic* and the equator are not parallel, some signs rise more quickly than others. Those that rise slowly (Capricorn, Aquarius, Pisces, Aries, Taurus and Gemini) are known as signs of short ascension, the others as signs of long ascension. (In southern latitudes these are reversed.)

Aspects One *planet* is in aspect to another when there is a specific number of degrees between them, measured around the circumference of the *birth chart.* When they are 90° apart, for instance, they are said to be in square aspect. Other aspects include the trine (120°), the sextile (60°), the opposition (180°), the semi-square (45°), the sesquare or sesquiquadrate, (135°), the semi-sextile (30°), the quincunx (150°). Planets are in conjunction when they occupy the same, or almost the same, degree.

Astrology The study of the influence on life on Earth of the other bodies in the solar system.

Astrological twins (time twins) Two people who share strong astrological factors, having been born at the same time, and in the same place.

Astronomy The science of measuring the movements of *planets* and *stars,* and investigating their physical nature.

Benefic An archaic expression meaning "favourable": ancient astrologers would have said, for instance, that Jupiter was the "greater benefic" and Venus the "lesser benefic". The word "malefic" was used to describe "unfavourable" *planets.*

Birth chart A diagram showing the precise position of all the *planets* at the time of birth. The mother of the new child, looking up at the sky at such a moment, could use the birth chart as a map to show where each planet is – apart, of course, from those below the horizon, which are also shown. The traditional word for the birth chart is the horoscope.

Birth time The precise time of birth, accurate to the minute.

Cardinal signs See *quadruplicities.*

Combust A *planet* is said to be "combust" when it is very near the Sun in the *birth chart*: the ancient theory was that the planet then lost some of its force.

Conception There have been attempts to draw up *birth charts* for the moment of conception. It is in the first few hours after conception that, medically, many physical characteristics are formed, and so it may be at that time that a physical astrological influence will be at work. However, it is impossible except under microscopic medical scrutiny to discover the precise time of conception – which is often considerably after coitus. Conception charts are, therefore, impracticable.

Constellations Those clusters of *stars* which inhabit the universe, 12 of which have become important in *astrology* as marking the 12 segments of the sky which form the *zodiac.*

Cusp The cusp of an astrological *sign* or *house* is the line dividing it from its neighbour. The cusp of the first house is marked by the *Ascendant*; the others follow around the circle of the *birth chart*, reading counter-clockwise. Similarly, the cusp of Aries is marked by the first degree of that sign.

Decan/Decanate Each sign is a 30° segment of the zodiacal circle, and is itself divided into three decans which measure 10° each.

Declination The distance of a *planet* north or south of the celestial *equator.*

Descendant The opposite point of the *birth chart* to the *Ascendant* – and the *cusp* of the seventh house.

Earth signs See *triplicities.*

Ecliptic The imaginary or *apparent motion* of the Sun around the Earth.

Elements See *triplicities.*

Elevation The *planet* nearest the *Midheaven* is said to be elevated; astronomically, the elevation marks the distance of a planet above the horizon – its altitude.

Ephemeris An ephemeris shows the precise daily position of the Sun and *planets.* Annual ephemerides are published; some books include listings for every day of a half-century. Ephemerides are now available on computers. No astrologer can work without them.

Equator The imaginary line drawn around the Earth, dividing it into northern and southern hemispheres. When this line is extended into space, it is called the celestial equator.

Esoteric astrology The study of the secret, symbolic meaning of *planets* and signs.

Feminine signs Traditionally, Taurus, Cancer, Virgo, Scorpio, Capricorn and Pisces are known as feminine signs; the other signs being masculine.

Similarly, feminine signs are referred to as negative, and the masculine signs as positive.

Fire signs See *triplicities.*

Fixed stars A very few astrologers consider fixed stars a part of the system; most however do not. See also *stars.*

Forecast Some astrologers use the word "forecast" to define their suggestions about coming trends in clients' lives. The definition is accurate: events are not predicted, possibilities are forecast – as in weather forecasting.

Free will Free will remains paramount to astrologers, as it does to most other people. Those people who claim that the astrological theory contests the doctrine of free will are ignorant of the present state of the science and its modern practitioners.

Geocentric The convention that the Earth, rather than the Sun, is at the centre of the solar system. This is a convenience only: no astrologer believes it to be true, but it is necessary to the astrological theory – just as, for a baby born on Mars, a *birth chart* would have to show that *planet* as the center of the system. The true picture of the solar system, with the Sun at the center, is heliocentric.

Grand trine A triangle formed in a *birth chart* by three *planets* set at 120° from each other.

Great Year The Earth's motion involves a slow "wobble" which results in its pole moving backwards through the *zodiac*, passing from one sign to another every 2,500 years or so. These periods are known as the Great Ages or, more precisely, the Great Months. The period during which the pole makes a complete circle is known as the Great Year.

Heliocentric See *Geocentric.*

Horary astrology The proposition that an astrologer can suggest an answer to a question by drawing up a chart for the moment when the question is put.

Horoscope See *birth chart.*

Houses The *birth chart* is divided into 12 houses (although these do not correspond to the segments of the chart occupied by the *zodiac* signs). See *house division.*

House division There are various different ways of dividing the chart into 12 *houses.* In this book we use the Equal House system. Other systems include Placidus, Regiomontanus, Campanus, Porphyry and Morinus.

IC/Imum Coeli The *meridian* point opposite the *MC.*

Inferior planets Mercury and Venus – the planets placed between the Earth and the Sun – are known as inferior. Those planets further from the Sun than Earth: i.e., Mars, Jupiter, Saturn, Uranus, Neptune and Pluto, are referred to as superior.

Lights, the The traditional term for the Sun and Moon.

Malefic See *benefic.*

Masculine signs See *feminine signs.*

Medical astrology There is an almost ageless association between astrology and medicine, based on the study of natal and progressed charts and what they reveal about the physique of the subject, and the treatment of possible illnesses.

MC/ Medium Coeli The *meridian* of the birth place. See also *IC.*

Meridian The meridian at Greenwich – the point from which time and space is measured – divides longitude into east and west; the meridian of the place of birth is used more personally by the astrologer.

Midheaven See *MC.*

Midpoint As the term suggests, the midpoint between two *planets* or *angles*, sometimes house *cusps.*

Mundane astrology The area of astrology which is concerned with politics and world events.

Mutable signs See *quadruplicities.*

Mutual reception *Planets* are in mutual reception when each is in the sign ruled by the other.

Negative signs See *feminine signs.*

Nodes The north and south nodes of the Moon are those points on the *ecliptic* where the Moon crosses it going either north or south.

Opposition See *aspects.*

Orb Astrologers allow an "orb" of influence for a planetary *aspect* – depending on the nature of the aspect. An aspect is considered, even if it is not exact to the precise degree.

Planets For convenience, astrologers call the Sun and Moon planets, though of course the Sun is a *star* (the only star used in *astrology*) and the Moon merely Earth's satellite. The other planets are Mercury, Venus, Mars, Jupiter, Saturn, Uranus, Neptune and Pluto. It is increasingly supposed by astronomers that another planet exists, beyond the orbit of Pluto.

Polarity Opposite or polar signs affect each other: each sign has a relationship with its partner across the *zodiac*: Aries/Libra, Taurus/Scorpio, Gemini/Sagittarius, Cancer/Capricorn, Leo/Aquarius, Virgo/Pisces. The term *polarity* expresses this fact.

Positive signs See *feminine signs.*

Precession of the Equinoxes The phenomenon concerns the shift which has resulted in the *zodiac* signs no longer occupying precisely the position vis-à-vis Earth that they occupied several thousand years ago. But astrologers use the *constellations'* names to denote areas of the *ecliptic* rather than the constellations themselves; the astrological theory is not (as astronomers tend to argue) devalued by the phenomenon.

Prediction Though the public in particular speaks of astrologers as "predicting", it cannot too often be emphasized that *astrology* cannot be relied upon to predict specific events.

Progressed horoscope The natal *birth chart* can, by various means (but usually by a system known as "a day for a year") be "progressed" to represent future periods. A horoscope drawn up for a future date is known as "progressed", and rather than "predictions" made from it, an astrologer will refer to "progressions".

Quadruplicities, the The *zodiac* signs have over millennia been divided into three groups of four – known as the quadruplicities: cardinal, fixed and mutable. The cardinal signs are Aries, Cancer, Libra and Capricorn; the fixed signs Taurus, Leo, Scorpio and Aquarius; and the mutable signs Gemini, Virgo, Sagittarius and Pisces. The signs in a particular group are said to share certain qualities.

Radix The basic *birth chart*, from which all astrological work begins.

Rectification An attempt to correct a perhaps uncertain *birth time* by studying the subject's characteristics and the events in his or her life.

Retrograde A *planet* sometimes looks, when seen from the Earth, as though it is travelling backwards through the *zodiac*. It is then said to be retrograde.

Rulership Different signs are "ruled" by different *planets*, and their influences can be affected by this fact. Recently discovered planets have been attributed to signs, displacing traditional sign rulers. There has been much discussion of sign rulerships, and some astrologers pay little attention to the theory. In another sense, countries and cities are said to be ruled by certain signs – England by Aries, North America by Gemini, and so on.

Sidereal time Time reckoned by the stars rather than by the Sun.

Signs See *Sun sign astrology.*

Solar chart An astrological chart drawn up with the Sun on the first *house cusp* – usually set up for a subject with an unknown *birth time*; also used by journalist astrologers writing *Sun sign* columns.

Southern latitudes The astrological theory is of course the same for people born in southern latitudes as in northern; the adjustment is easily made.

Stars, the For some inexplicable reason, popular journalists have come to believe that the stars have something to do with *astrology*, and continually write about what "the stars" say about their readers. A tiny minority of astrologers use the fixed stars which fall within the *zodiac*; for the majority, the stars quite simply have nothing to do with interpretation.

Stellium A group of *planets* gathered in one area of the *zodiac*: sometimes, a multiple conjunction.

Sun-sign astrology In newspaper Sun-sign columns, journalists make predictions for the day, month or year ahead on the basis of *solar charts* set up for those with specific Sun signs.

Superior planets See *inferior planets.*

Transit A *planet's* movement through a sign or *house*.

Triplicity Signs have over the millennia been assigned to the four elements: so fire signs are Aries, Leo and Sagittarius; earth signs are Taurus, Virgo and Capricorn; air signs are Gemini, Libra and Aquarius; and water signs Cancer, Scorpio and Pisces.

Zenith The point of the sky immediately overhead.

Zodiac The great circle made by the Sun as it seems to revolve around the Earth has from time immemorial been divided into sections (although it has not always been divided into 12 sections). The zodiac we know, with its mythological creatures and stories, dates from perhaps 5,000 years ago. Its history is fascinating and obscure.

Zodiacal Man During the evolution of *medical astrology* the 12 signs of the *zodiac* have become associated with various parts of the body – starting with Aries and the head and ending with Pisces and the feet. This useful form of shorthand is still used in modern medical astrology.

Teaching Bodies

The longest established and most reputable astrological teaching body in the world is the Faculty of Astrological Studies, which holds classes in central London, UK, but does most of its teaching by correspondence with almost every country in the world. The Faculty can be contacted at BM Box 7470, London WC1N 3XX, UK.

There are many reliable schools in other parts of the world. The editors of any of the journals listed on the next page should be able to provide the relevant information.

For information about astrology, contact the Urania Trust, The Astrological Centre, 396 Caledonian Road, London N1 1DN (telephone 071 700 0639; fax 071 700 6479). Please enclose a stamped, addressed envelope or International Reply Coupon.

Bibliography

Appleby, Derek, *Horary Astrology*, Northamptonshire, 1985

Burmyn, Lynne, *Planets in Combination*, California, 1985

Carter, Charles E.O., *An Encyclopedia of Psychological Astrology*, London, 1924

Dean, Geoffrey, *Recent Advances in Natal Astrology*, London, 1977

Ehresman, Nancy, and Albaugh, Stephen, *The Saturn Return*, Arizona, 1984

Eysenck, H.J., and Nias, D.K.B., *Astrology: Science or Superstition*, London, 1982

Filbey, John, *Natal Charting*, Northamptonshire, 1981; and Peter, *Astronomy for Astrologers*, London, 1984

Gauquelin, Michel, *The Scientific Basis of Astrology*, London, 1969; *The Truth about Astrology*, London, 1983; *Zodiac and Personality: an Empirical Study*, Skeptical Enquirer, Spring 1982

Gleadow, Rupert, *The Origin of the Zodiac*, London, 1969

Hamblin, David, *Harmonic Charts*, Northamptonshire, 1983

Herbst, Bill, *The Houses of the Horoscope*, California, 1988

Jansky, Robert C., *Modern Medical Astrology*, California, 1978; *Astrology, Nutrition and Health*, Massachusetts, 1977

Jung, C.G., *Synchronicity: An Acausal Connecting Principle*, London, 1960

Lindsay, Jack, *Origins of Astrology*, London, 1971

Nauman, Eileen, *The American Book of Nutrition and Medical Astrology*, California, 1982

Parker, Julia, *The Zodiac Family*, Northamptonshire, 1988; *The Astrologer's Handbook*, London 1985; Derek and Julia, *A History of Astrology*, London 1983; *The New Compleat Astrologer*, London, 1985; *Life Signs*, London, 1986

Rose, Christina, *Astrological Counselling*, Northamptonshire, 1982

Russell, Eric, *Astrology and Prediction*, New Jersey, 1972

Sawtell, Vanda, *Astrology and Biochemistry*, Northamptonshire, 1983

Shanks, Thomas G., *The American Atlas* (US latitudes and longitudes, time changes and time zones), California/Massachusetts, 1978; *The International Atlas* (world latitudes, longitudes and time changes), California, 1985

Thornton, Penny, *Synastry*, Northamptonshire, 1983

ASTROLOGICAL JOURNALS

United Kingdom

The Astrological Journal, 90, High Street, Langton Maltravers, Dorset BH19 3HD

Correlation, West Court, Bramshott Court, Bramshott, Liphook, Hants, GU30 7RG

Astrology (The Astrologer's Quarterly), 180, Wymering Mansions, Wymering Road, London W9 2NQ

Polarity, 9, Smallwood Road, London SW17 0TN

ISCWA Bulletin, 51, Bellevue Crescent, Clifton, Bristol BS8 1XX

Pulsar (Journal of the Scottish Astrological Association), 6, Bedford Mews, Dean Village, Edinburgh, EH4 3BT

Prediction, Link House, Dingwall Avenue, Croydon, Surrey CR9 2TA

Astrology and Medicine Newsletter, 41, Balcastle Gardens, Kilsyth, Glasgow G65 9PE

United States of America

The American Astrology Magazine, 475 Park Avenue, New York, NY 10016

Dell Horoscope Magazine, P.O. Box 53352, Boulder, CO 80521-1511

AFA Bulletin, Association for Astrological Networking, 8306 Wiltshire Boulevard, Suite 537, Beverley Hills, CA 90211

The ASCendant, P.O. Box 9346, Wetherfield, CT 06109

Aspects, P.O. Box 556, Encinco, CA 91426

Astro-Analytics, 16440 Haynes Street, Van Nuys, CA 91406-5717

Astro-Talk Bulletin, 315 Marion Avenue, Big Rapids, MI 49307

Cosmobiology International, P.O. Box 10631, Denver, CO 80210

Geocosmic News, 78 Hubbard Avenue, Stamford, CT 06906

The Horary Practitioner, 1420 N.W. Gillman, Suite 2154, Issaquah, WA 98027-5327

Kosmos, P.O. Box 38613, Los Angeles, CA 90038

Mutable Dilemma, 5953 W. 86th Street, Los Angeles, CA 90045

NCGR Journal, P.O. Box 34487, San Diego, CA 92103-0802

Urania, 330 E. 46th Street, New York, NY 10017

Welcome to Planet Earth, The Great Bear, P.O. Box 5164, Eugene, OR 97405

Austria

Qualitat der Zeit, Schrubertring 8, Stg. 2/7, 1010-Wien

Belgium

Quintile, Federation Astrologique Belge, Ave Marechal Joffre, 69, B-1190, Bruxelles

INFOsophia, 19 Avenue P.-H. Spaak, B-1070, Bruxelles

Canada

The Fraternity News, 13155 24th Avenue, Surrey, BC V4A 2G2

Eire

The Irish A.A. Journal, Henley Cottage, Upper Churchtown Road, Dublin 14

France

L'Astrologue, 44 rue Genéral Brunet, 75019 Paris

Trigone, 'Les Cabriolles', 36, Ave du Littoral, St Marguerite, 44380 Pornichet

Germany

Kosmischer Beobachter, Haus Walderug, Panoramastrasse 15, D-7547 Wildbad

Meridian, Brunnleacker 3, D-7801 Umkirch

Holland

Spica, Postbus 1310, 8001 BH Zwolle

Stichting Astro-Kring, Leyweg 362, 2545 EE's Gravenhag

India

The Astrological Magazine, Sri Rajeswari, 115/1, New Extension, Seshadripuram, Bangalore 560 020

Italy

Linguaggio Astrale, Via Giacinto Collegno. 12 bis, 10143 Torino

Spain

Mercurio-3, Ronda San Antonio 30, 2m, 08001 Barcelona

Switzerland

Astrologie Heute, Aemtlerstr 201, Postfach, CH-8040, Zurich

Astrological Sources of Characteristics

This reference list will help you get to know the astrological sources of many characteristics and personality traits. It is of necessity only a rough guide, and the astrological significators listed will often be modified by other astrological indications. As you become more experienced, you may well be able to extend the list for yourself.

Key

- Where a sign is mentioned, this refers to the Sun, Moon or Ascendant sign
- Where a planet is mentioned, this refers to the Sun, Moon or Ascendant ruler
- p.a. = positively aspected
- n.a. = negatively aspected
- p.a.b. = positive aspects between
- n.a.b. = negative aspects between
- Planet glyph followed by oblique and number 1-12 = planet in a house; e.g. ☽/12 = Moon in 12th house
- Planet glyph followed by oblique and sign glyph= planet in a sign; e.g. ☿/♏ = Mercury in Scorpio
- o. = often
- s. = sometimes
- f.s. = fire signs
- e.s. = earth signs
- a.s. = air signs
- w.s. = water signs

A

Absentmindedness = ☿/♓; n.a.b. ☿, ♆
Abstinence = ♍, ♑
Accident proneness = ♈; n.a. ♂, ♃
Acting ability = ♌, ♓, ♋
Adaptability = a.s.; ☿, ♊
Adventurousness = ♈, ♐; p.a.b. ♂, ♃
Agitation = ♊, ♍, ☿; n.a. ♂
Allergies = ♍
Aloofness = ♑; s. ♌, ♒
Ambition = p.a. ♄, ♑
Amorousness = p.a.b. ♀, ♂, ♉, ♏, ♎
Analytical = ♊, ♍; s. ♒
Anger = n.a.b. ☉, ♂; ♂/♈, ♏
Angst = ♑; s. ♒
Arrogance = ♑, s. ♌
Authoritarianism = ☽/♑; ♑, ♄; s. ♌

B

Baldness = f.s.; ♂/♈; o. ☉/♈
Beards = ♃, ♆, ♐, ♓
Beauty = ♉, ♎, ♀
Belligerence = n.a.b. ☉, ♂
Brazenness = n.a.b. ☉, ♂; s.n.a.b. ♂; ♂
Broad mindedness = ♃, ♐, ☿; p.a. ♃
Bullying = ♉; s. ♈
Bumptiousness = n.a.b. ☉, ♃

C

Catty = n.a.b. ☿, ♂
Changeability = ♋, ☽, ☿, ♊; n.a.b. ☽, ☿
Charm = ♉, ♎; ☉☌♀; p.a. ♀, ☽, s. ♃
Chastity = ♀/♍; ☿/♎; n.a.b. ☽, ♀
Cheerfulness = p.a.b. ☉, ♃; o.f.s.
Choleric = ♂, ♈; ♂/♈; n.a.b. ☿, ♂
Churlishness = ♄, ☽; n.a.b. ☿, ♄
Comfort loving = ♉, ♎, ♀; o. ♌
Communicative = ♊, ♍, ☿; ☉☌☿; p.a.b. ☽, ☿
Conceited = ♌; n.a. ☉, s.n.a. ☽, ♃
Condescension = ☽/♌; ♑
Coolness = ♒, ♑; ♀/♒; ☿☌♀/♒; n.a.b. ♀, ♅
Cowardice = ♆; n.a.b. ☿/♆; n.a. ☽; s.n.a.b. ♂, ♆
Crankiness = ♂/♒; n.a.b. ☉, ♅; s.n.a.b. ☽, ♅
Cynicism = n.a.b. ☿, ♂; o.n.a.b. ♂, ♅

D

Daring = ♈, ♉; p.a.b. ♂, ♃
Deceitfulness = ♓; n.a.b. ☉ or ☽/♆
Depression = n.a.b. ☉ or ☽, ♄; ♑, ♍, ♋
Detachment = ♊, ♒
Dictatorial = ♌
Diplomatic = ♎; p.a.b. ☽, ♀
Disciplinarian = ♑; n.a.b. ☉, ♄; ♄/10
Discretion = ♍, ♏
Discrimination = ♍; ☿/♍
Dramatic = ♌; ♃ / 10; p. & n.a.b. ☉ & ☽, ♃

E

Eccentricity = ♒, ♅, ♂/♒, n.a.b. ☉ & ☽, ♃, ♅
Economy = ♍, ♑
Egotism = ☉, ♃, ♄/10
Enthusiasm = f.s.♃, p.a.b. ☉, ♃, ♂/f.s.
Envy = ♉, ♎, n.a.b. ♀, ♄
Eroticism = ♀☌♂, ♉ ♏, s.p.a.b. ♀, ♇
Exaggeration = ♐, O. ♈, ♌; n.a. ♃

F·G

Faithfulness = ♀/♑, ♌, ♒; p.a.b. ☉, ♀, ♄
Fame = ☽/♌/10
Fearfulness= ♋
Fidget = ☿, ♊, ♍
Flamboyance = ♌, ♃, p.a.b. ☉, ♀, ♃
Flirtatiousness = ♀/♊, ♊
Forcefulness = ♇, ♅, p.a.b. ♂, ♇
Formality = ♌, ♑, p.a.b. ☉, ♄
Fortune hunter = ♉, s. ♑, ♍
Friendliness = ♊, ♍, ♒; p.a. ☽, ☿, ♀

Gambling = ♐, n.a.b. ☉, ♃; s. ♂, ♃, ♂/5
Glamor = ♀/♒, ♌, ♎
Gossip = ♍; n.a.b. ☿, ♂

H

Hastiness = ♊, ♈, ☿/♈, ♂/♈
Helpfulness = ♍, ♓, ♒ o. 12
Highmindedness = ☉, ☿/♌; ♃/♌; s. ♃/10
Homeliness = ♋, ♍, ☽
Humanitarianism = ♒, ♓, 11, o. 12

I

Idealism = p.a. ♆; o.p.a. ☽
Idleness = ♎, n.a. ♀
Illogicality = ♓, n.a. ♊. s.n.a. ☽, ☿
Imagination = w.s.; p.a. ☽, p.a. ♆
Immoderation= ♉, ♏, ♃, ♇
Impatience = ♈, ♊, o. ♍; s. ♋, ☽
Impertinence = ♊; ☿/♈; ♂/♊
Inadaptability = e.s.; n.a. ♅; o. ♒

Inconsistency = ♊, ♋; ☽/♊; ☿/♋, o. ♓
Indecision = ♎; n.a. ♀; n.a.b. ☽, ♀
Indigestion = ♍, s. ♉, ♏; n.a. ☽
Independence = ♒, ♈, ♐; p.a. ♂; p.a. ♅
Indifference = ☽/♐
Individuality = ♒
Indulgence = ♉, ♎, ♍
Infidelity = a.s.; ♊, ♀ ♊, o. ♐
Informality = ♐, ♈
Inhibition = ♄/1; n.a.b. ☉, ☽-♄
Inquisitiveness = ♊, ♏
Inscrutable = ☽, ☉/12; ♏, ♒
Insincerity = n.a.b. ☉, ☽, ☿-♆; s. ♎; ♍
Irony = n.a.b. ☿, ♂

J·K

Jealousy = ♏, ♉; s. ♎
Joyfulness = ☉/♌; ♐ p.a. ☉, ☽ or ♀
Joylessness = n.a. ♄; n.a.b. ☉, ☽, ♄, ♑
Justice = ♎, p.a.b. ☉, ♄; ☉ p.a. ♃

Kittenlike = ♀/♊, s.p.a.b. ☿, ♀

L

Laziness = ♎, s. ♉, n.a. ♀
Leadership = ♈, ♌, ☉/10
Leanness = ♊, ♑, s. ♈, ♏
Lecherousness = ♃, ♂, n.a.b. ♀, ♃, ♏
Lethargy = n.a.b. ☽, ♀-♎
Loneliness = ☉, ☽, or ♄/12; s. ♄/10
Logicality = p.a.b. ☿, ♄, ♅
Longevity = p.a.b. ☉, ☽, ♄
Loyalty = ♌, ♑, o. ♒
Luck = ♃/2; ♀, ♃/5
Luxury loving = ♉, ♌, ♎

M·N

Macabre = ♏, ♇/12, ☽/8
Malice = n.a.b. ☿/♄
Matchmaker = ♎, ♀
Materialism = ♉, ♑
Meanness = ♍, ♑, o. ♋
Melancholic = n.a. ♄; o. ♄/1
Memory = ♋, ☽
Mercurial = ♊, ☿, ☽/♊
Migraine = ♍, s. ♈, s. ♒
Mimicry = ♆, ☿, ♓, s. ♋
Money grubber = ♉, ♏
Musicality = ♉, ♑, p.a.b. ♀, ♄, s. ♎

Narcissism = ♌, ♎
Nosiness = ☿, ♍

O

Observation = p.a.b. ☿, ♅
Obsessiveness = ♉, ♍, ♏
Obstinacy = f.s. ♅
Optimism = f.s. ♃; p.a.b. ☉-♃
Oratory = ☿, ♊, ♍; ☉ or ☿/10

P·Q

Passivity = ♀, ♆
Patience = e.s. ☉; p.a.b. ☉, ☽, ♀-♄
Pennywise = ♍, ♑
Perception = ☿, p.a.b. ♀, ♄-♅; p.a. ♅
Perseverance = p.a.b. ☉, ♄, ♉, ♂/♉
Pessimism = ♄/♑; n.a.b. ☉, ☽, ☿-♄
Philosophical = ♐, ♃
Phlegmatic = p.a.b. ☉, ☽-♄; ♉
Pioneering = ♈, ♂, ♂/♈; p.a.b. ☉, ♂-♃; s. ♐
Placidity = ♀, ♆
Possessiveness = ♉, ♏, ♀
Potency = ♂, ♂/♈, ♏
Power complex = ♅/10, ♄/10; ♇/10; s. ☉/10
Practicality = e.s. ♄
Prejudice = ♋, f.s.
Psychic = w.s.; s.e.s.

Quality = ♌, ♑, ♉
Quickness = ☿, ♂
Quick-witted = ♊, ☿

R

Research = ♍, ♏, ☿, ♇
Reserved = ♋, ☽, ♆, ♓
Responsiveness = ☽/♎, ♋
Rheumatism = f.s.; n.a.b. ♂-♄
Rhythmical = ♋, ♎, o. ♓
Romantic = ☽, ♀/♉; ♎, ♋, ♓, ♆, ♒
Royalist = ♑, ♌
Ruthlessness = ♅☌♇, ♇; n.a.b. ♂, ♇

S

Sacrificial ♆, ♓, ♍, s. ☽, ♋
Sanguine = ♂, ♈, o. ♃, ♐
Salesmanship = ♊-☿/♊; s. ♍
Satirical = ♐, ♊, p. & n.a.b. ☿, ♂, ♅
Scepticism = ♊-☿
Scruffiness = ♐, ♓, ♋
Secretiveness = ♏, ♓♋, n.a.b. ☉, ☽ ☿/♆
Seductiveness = ♉, ♏, s. ♎
Self-indulgence = ♉, ♐, n.a.b. ☽, ♀, ♃-♇
Selfishness = ♈, ♂/1, o. ☉/1
Sentimentality = ☽, ♋, ♎; o. ♓ ♆

Showiness = n.a.b. ☉, ☽, ♀-♃, ♌
Snobbishness = ☿ or ♄/♌; ♊, ♑
Solitude = ♄, ♆, 12
Stability = ♉, ♑, p.a.b. ☉, ♄
Stubbornness = e.s. ♒; n.a.b. ☉, ♅

T

Tactfulness = ♀, ♎
Talkativeness = ☿, ♊, ♍
Temperamental = ♋, n.a.b. ☽-♄
Tenacity = ☽, ♋, p.a.b. ♂, ♄
Traditional = ♑, ♉

U·V

Untidiness = ♋, ♓

Vanity = ♌, ♃, ♀/♎, ♉
Vegetarianism = ♍, ♑
Vengefulness = ♏, ♇
Vigorousness = ☉/f.s.; ♂/♈; p.a. ♂
Virtuous = ☉/f.s.; ♂/♈; p.a. ♂
Voluptuous = ♉, ♎, ♏, p.a.b. ♀, ♂

W·Y

Well-meaning = ♋, ☽, ♍
Whole-hogger = ♉, ♏, ♐
Wickedness = n.a.b. ☿, ♆, ♇
Wistfulness = ♓, p. or n.a.b. ♀, ♆
Worrying = ♋, ♍

Youthfulness = ♊, ☿/♊

The Birth Chart

Equal House System

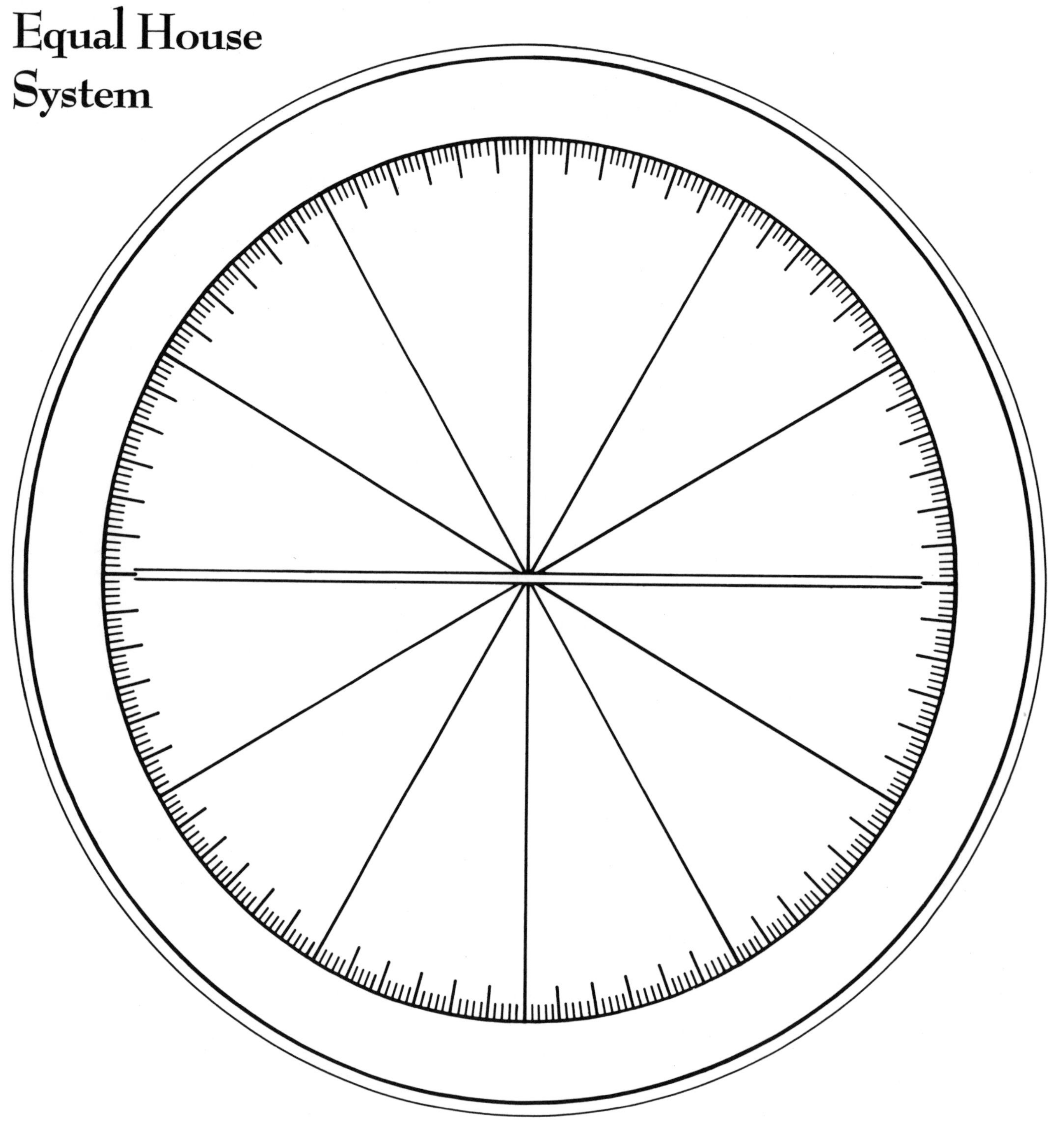

NAME ______________________

____

REFERENCE NO. ______________________

HOUSE SYSTEM ______________________

	Day	Month	Year
BIRTH DATE			
BIRTH PLACE			
LATITUDE			
LONGITUDE			

	Hours	Minutes
BIRTH TIME		
ZONE STANDARD (If East of Greenwich subtract, if West of Greenwich add)		
SUMMER/DAYLIGHT SAVING TIME (If in operation subtract)		
GREENWICH MEAN TIME		
SOUTHERN LATITUDES (Add 12 hours and reverse signs)		

TRADITIONAL FACTORS

RULING PLANET

RULER'S HOUSE

RISING PLANET

POSITIVE | NEGATIVE

ANGULAR

MUTUAL RECEPTION

TRIPLICITIES | QUADRUPLICITIES

Fire | Cardinal

Earth | Fixed

Air | Mutable

Water

PLANET ASPECTS

		☉	☽	☿	♀	♂	♃	♄	♅	♆	♇
SUN	☉										
MOON	☽										
MERCURY	☿										
VENUS	♀										
MARS	♂										
JUPITER	♃										
SATURN	♄										
URANUS	♅										
NEPTUNE	♆										
PLUTO	♇										
ASC	Asc										
MC	MC										

The Progressed Chart
Equal House System

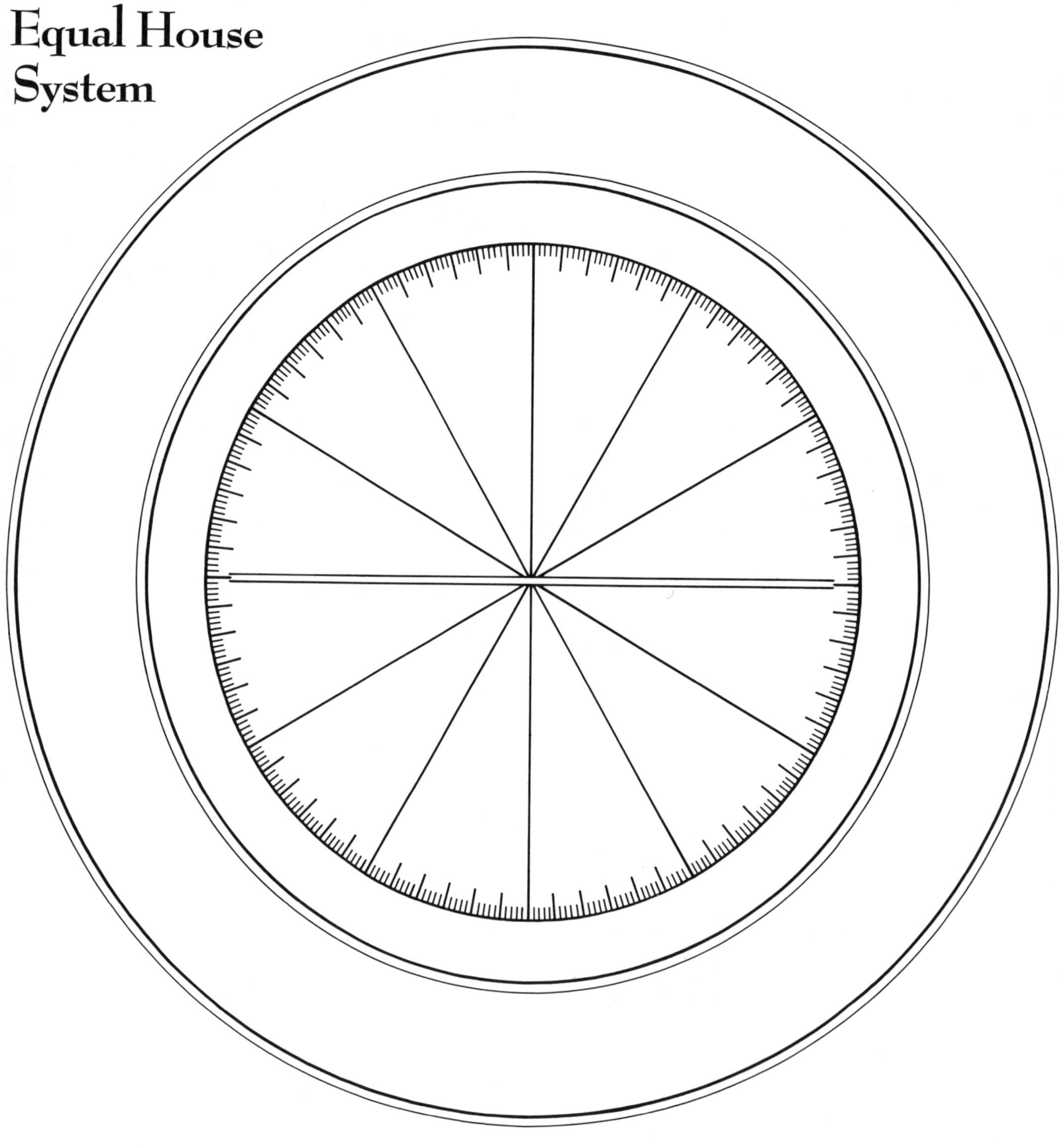

NAME

REFERENCE NO.

YEAR

MIDNIGHT POSITIONS ON

CORRESPONDING TO

INSTALLMENT

THE PROGRESSED ASPECTS

NATAL PLANETS NUMERICAL ORDER	SOLAR	MUTUAL		ASC MC

	LUNAR		ASPECTS		TRANSITS									
YEAR	MONTH	MOON'S LONG.	TO NATAL	TO PROG.	♇	♆	♅	♄	♃	♂	♀	☿	☉	NEW ☽ MOONS

Index

Apart from the technical terms to be found in the index, we have included certain characteristics, where these are typical of a particular sign or planet, or a set of astrological circumstances. More references to these characteristics will, however, inevitably be found elsewhere in the book.

A

B

C

D

E

S

T

U

V

W

Z

…dgments

…ments
… grateful to Chester … help in devising the … calculation presented in this …, and to Charles Harvey …F.Astrol.S. for his advice and his moral support.

We thank those of Julia's clients – especially Kenneth Morris and Laura Campbell – who have permitted the use of their birthcharts, and in some cases quotations from reports written for them.

Every writer on this subject must acknowledge a debt to those earlier writers – from Ptolemy to John Addey, from William Lilly to the Gauquelins – whose books have enlarged knowledge and extended boundaries. We list some of these in the Bibliography.

Astrological tables
Computer generated astrological calculations and data by Ananda Bagley of Electric Ephemeris Astrological Software House (396 Caledonian Road, London N1 1DN/ Stubberupvej 14, DK 4880 Nysted, Denmark); table layout by Paul Sally of Informac (London).

Dorling Kindersley would like to thank the following people for their help during the preparation of this book: Roger Daniels for design work; Stephanie Jackson, Jane Mason and Roger Smoothy for editorial assistance; Vanessa Luff and Mustafa Sami for design assistance; The Cooling Brown Partnership for DTP assistance.

Illustrators
Angus Hyland: illustrations on pages 130, 141, 148, 150, 168, 186, 194, 204.
Barry Jones: illustrations on pages 16-17, 19, 21, 22-3.
Peter Lawman, courtesy of Portal Gallery Ltd, London, UK: paintings on pages 1, 2, 4, 6, 8, 9, 78, 81, 85, 89, 93, 97, 101, 105, 109, 113, 117, 121, 125.
Vanessa Luff: decorative borders on pages 26-7, 28-9, 30-1, 33, 38-9, 40-1; medallion borders on pages 80-127; birth charts on pages 48-9, 58-9, 70-1.
Mustafa Sami: birth chart artworks throughout the book.
Anthony Sidwell: the planets on pages 30-1.
Alastair Taylor: case study illustrations on pages 158, 161, 162, 164, 167, 176, 185, 203, 207.
Jane Thompson: colour zodiac and planets artworks used throughout the book – the counters were engraved from her drawings; decorative borders on pages 80-127.

Photography
Studio photography: Geoff Dann.
Stylists: Barbara Stewart and Geoff Dann.
Picture research: Suzanne Williams.
Cell salts were supplied by Seven Seas Ltd, Marfleet, Hull.

Photographic acknowledgments
When pictures are used several times, they are credited only once.
The following abbreviations have been used:
BL The British Library, London
BM The British Museum, London
SM The Science Museum, London

The Bodleian Library, Oxford: 13, 14 (below left), 26 (top left), 36, 60, 73, 79, 129, 349.
The Bridgeman Art Library: 15 (below right)/BM, 16/BL, 18 (top)/BL, 23/BL, 26 (below right)/BL, 27 (left, centre top & below)/BL, 28 (left, top & right)/BL, 28 (below)/Musée Condé, Chantilly, 29 (left, top, right & below)/BL, 32/Biblioteca Estense, Modena, 99/Royal Geographical Society, London.
The British Library Board: 26 (top right), 27 (top right).
Michael Holford: 3/SM, 15 (left)/ SM, 20 (top)/SM, 22/SM, 24 (top left)/BM, 24 (below left), 24 (centre)/Ankara Museum, 24 (right)/ BM, 25 (left)/BM, 25 (top right).
Science Photo Library: 14 (centre), 20 (centre), 25 (below right).
Mary Evans Picture Library: 14 (right), 15 (top), 30 (top), 40, 42, 48, 56, 57, 80, 87, 91, 95, 111, 119, 218, 157, 172, 174, 178, 180, 182, 188, 192, 196, 199, 200, 348.
Museo Vaticano, Rome: 14 (top left).